Teacher Preparation Classroom

Your Class. Their Careers. Our Future. Will your students be prepared?

We invite you to explore our new, innovative and engaging website and all that it has to offer you, your course, and tomorrow's educators! Preview this site today at www.prenhall.com/teacherprep/demo. Just click on "go" on the login page to begin your exploration.

Organized around the major courses pre-service teachers take, the Teacher Preparation site provides media, student/teacher artifacts, strategies, research articles, and other resources to equip your students with the quality tools needed to excel in their courses and prepare them for their first classroom.

This ultimate on-line education resource will provide you and your students access to:

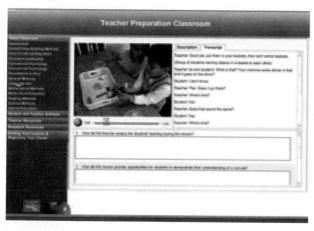

Online Video Library. More than 250 video clips—each tied to a course topic and framed by learning goals and Praxis-type questions—capture real teachers and students working in real classrooms.

Student and Teacher Artifacts. More than 200 student and teacher classroom artifacts—each tied to a course topic and framed by learning goals and application questions—provide a wealth of materials and experiences to help make your students observe children's developmental learning.

Lesson Plan Builder. Offers step-by-step guidelines and lesson plan examples to support students as they learn to build high quality lesson plans.

Research Articles. Over 500 articles from ASCD's renowned journal *Educational Leadership*. The site also includes *Research Navigator*, a searchable database of additional educational journals.

Teaching Strategies. Over 500 research-supported instructional strategies appropriate for a wide range of grade levels and content areas.

Licensure and Career Tools. Resources devoted to helping your students pass their licensure exam, learn standards, law, and public policies, plan a teaching portfolio, and succeed in their first year of teaching.

How to ORDER *Teacher Prep* for you and your students:
- For students to receive a *Teacher Prep* Access Code with this text, please provide your bookstore with ISBN 0-13-235072-6 when you **place** your textbook order. The bookstore **must** order the text with this ISBN to be eligible for this offer.

Upon ordering *Teacher Prep* for their students, instructors will be given a lifetime *Teacher Prep* Access Code. To receive your access code, please email: **Merrill.marketing@pearsoned.com** and provide the following information:
- Name and Affiliation
- Author/Title/Edition of Merrill text

HUMAN LEARNING

FIFTH EDITION

Jeanne Ellis Ormrod
University of Northern Colorado (Emerita)
University of New Hampshire

PEARSON

Merrill
Prentice Hall

Upper Saddle River, New Jersey
Columbus, Ohio

Library of Congress Cataloging-in-Publication Data

Ormrod, Jeanne Ellis.
    Human learning / Jeanne Ellis Ormrod. — 5th ed.
        p.   cm.
    Includes bibliographical references and index.
    ISBN-13: 978-0-13-232749-7 (hardcover)
    ISBN-10: 0-13-232749-X (hardcover)
    1. Learning, Psychology of.   2. Behaviorism (Psychology)   I. Title.
    BF318.O76 2008
    153.1'5—dc22

                                                    2007001269

Vice President and Executive Publisher: Jeffery W. Johnston
Publisher: Kevin M. Davis
Editorial Assistant: Sarah N. Kenoyer
Production Editor: Mary Harlan
Production Coordination: Thistle Hill Publishing Services, LLC
Design Coordinator: Diane C. Lorenzo
Cover Design: Diane C. Lorenzo
Cover Image: SuperStock
Production Manager: Laura Messerly
Director of Marketing: David Gesell
Marketing Manager: Autumn Purdy
Marketing Coordinator: Brian Mounts

This book was set in Berkeley by Integra Software Services. It was printed and bound by Courier/Westford. The cover was printed by Phoenix Color Corp.

Pearson Education Ltd.
Pearson Education Singapore Pte. Ltd.
Pearson Education Canada, Ltd.
Pearson Education–Japan

Pearson Education Australia Pty. Limited
Pearson Education North Asia Ltd.
Pearson Educación de Mexico, S.A. de C.V.
Pearson Education Malaysia Pte. Ltd.

PEARSON
Merrill
Prentice Hall

10 9 8 7 6 5 4 3
ISBN-13: 978-0-13-232749-7
ISBN-10:   0-13-232749-X

Preface

This fifth edition of *Human Learning* has truly been a joy to write. Each passing year brings new research findings about how human beings think and learn. As a result, each year also brings new strategies for helping learners of all ages acquire information and skills—and also beliefs, motives, and attitudes—that will be useful and productive both in and outside of the classroom. As my readers explore the nature of human learning in the pages ahead, I hope my fascination with the topic will be contagious.

I have written this textbook with particular students in mind: students who would like to learn about learning but often do not have much background in psychology. Such students may benefit from studying the historical roots of learning theories but prefer to focus their energies on studying contemporary perspectives and ideas. These students might find learning theories fascinating but lose patience when they cannot see the relevance of those theories to everyday practice. These students are capable of reading a dry, terse textbook but probably learn more effectively from a book that shows how different concepts relate to one another, provides numerous examples, and, especially, emphasizes meaningful learning—true *understanding*—of the material it presents.

In This Edition

Users of the fourth edition will notice a number of changes in this fifth edition. So that the book can more comfortably fit within the confines of a typical college semester, I have reduced the book from 18 to 16 chapters, in part by condensing the coverage of behaviorism from four chapters to three (I changed the title of chapter 4 from "Operant Conditioning" to "Instrumental Conditioning," so that it could include punishment as well as reinforcement) and by consolidating the three chapters on motivation into two chapters. I have also rearranged the chapters on cognitivist perspectives a bit—for instance, by (a) moving Piaget's and Vygotsky's developmental theories to their own chapter and (b) combining other early cognitive perspectives with an introduction to contemporary information processing theory.

As I do with every revision, I have updated each chapter with new research findings and citations. And consistent with our ever-evolving understanding of human learning, I have added many new topics and revised discussions of numerous others. Examples include a more in-depth discussion of how human learning differs from nonhuman animal learning (chapter 1); a single (rather than double) definition of learning (chapter 1); mirror neurons (chapter 2); use of high-stakes tests to assess achievement of instructional objectives (chapter 5); self-efficacy for learning versus self-efficacy for performance (chapter 6); a more in-depth critique of the dual-store model of memory (chapter 7); consolidation as a factor in long-term memory storage (chapter 8); worldviews (chapter 9); self-monitoring of retrieval (chapter 10); cautions in soliciting eyewitness testimony (chapter 10); more in-depth discussions of Piaget's and Vygotsky's theories of cognitive development (chapter 11); neo-Piagetian theories (chapter 11); discovery learning (chapter 11); blending information processing theory and sociocultural theory through such concepts as intersubjectivity, social construction of memory, and collaborative use of cognitive strategies (chapter 11); cultural differences in epistemological beliefs (chapter 12); a broadened view of transfer that includes emotional reactions and motivation (chapter 13); problem-based learning (chapter 13); group knowledge building and conceptual artifacts (chapter 14); contingent self-worth (chapter 15); secondary control (chapter 15); stereotype threat (chapter 15); and proximal goals (chapter 16). To make room for such things, I've deleted a few topics (e.g., the early behaviorist theories of Watson, Guthrie, and Hull; a detailed discussion of interpersonal attributions). These topics have not entirely disappeared, however, as they can still be found in readings on the book's Companion Website at **www.prenhall.com/ormrod**.

As has been the case in previous editions of this book, I've written many multiple-choice and essay questions for the *Test Bank* (ISBN: 0-13-232750-3) to focus on higher-level thinking skills. The *TestGen* (ISBN: 0-13-232751-1) provides the test questions in electronic format and enables instructors to create and customize exams.

Acknowledgments

Although I am listed as the sole author, I have certainly not written this book alone. Many people have helped me along the way:

- Frank Di Vesta, my adviser and mentor at Penn State, who taught me a great deal about learning and who absolutely refused to let me graduate until I also learned a great deal about writing.
- Kevin Davis, my editor at Merrill/Prentice Hall, who continues to guide, support, and inspire me in my efforts to shed light on the many ways in which psychology can inform practice in educational and therapeutic settings.
- The production staffs at Merrill/Prentice Hall and Thistle Hill Publishing Services—especially Mary Harlan, who handled the preliminaries and (as always) solicited my input before making important decisions, and Angela Urquhart, who skillfully transformed my rough manuscript into a polished publication.
- My colleagues across the nation who read early drafts or editions most thoroughly and conscientiously and whose suggestions have greatly improved the final product: Livingston Alexander, Western Kentucky University; Martha B. Bronson, Boston College; Margaret W. Cohen, University of Missouri at St. Louis; Ralph F. Darr Jr., The University of Akron; Jean C. Faieta, Edinboro University of Pennsylvania; Sarah Huyvaert, Eastern Michigan University; Janina Jolley, Clarion University of Pennsylvania; Joseph Kersting, Western Illinois University; Mary Lou Koran, University of Florida; Gerald Larson, Kent

State University; Mark Lewis, University of Texas at Tyler; Michael S. Meloth, University of Colorado; Karen Murphy, The Pennsylvania State University; John Newell, University of Florida at Gainesville; Jim O'Connor, California State University at Bakersfield; Sarah Peterson, Northern Illinois University; Jonathan Plucker, Indiana University; Steven Pulos, University of Northern Colorado; Daniel Robinson, University of Texas at Austin; Jack Snowman, Southern Illinois University; and Karen Zabrucky, Georgia State University.

- Colleagues who recently reviewed the fourth edition and offered many helpful suggestions for adding to and in other ways enhancing my discussions in the fifth edition: Joyce Alexander, Indiana University; Kay W. Allen, University of Central Florida; Nimisha Patel, Arizona State University; and Sarah Peterson, Duquesne University.
- My husband, Richard, and my children, Christina, Alex, and Jeffrey, who have been eternally supportive of my writing endeavors and who have provided me with numerous examples of human learning in action.
- My parents, James and Nancy Ellis, who long ago taught me the value of higher education.
- My students, who urged me to write the book in the first place.
- Other students around the globe, who continue to give me feedback about how I can make the book better. (An easy way to reach me is at jormrod@alumni.brown.edu.)

Jeanne Ellis Ormrod

Discover the Companion Website Accompanying This Book

THE PRENTICE HALL COMPANION WEBSITE:
A VIRTUAL LEARNING ENVIRONMENT

Technology is a constantly growing and changing aspect of our field that is creating a need for content and resources. To address this emerging need, Prentice Hall has developed an online learning environment for students and professors alike—Companion Websites—to support our textbooks.

In creating a Companion Website, our goal is to build on and enhance what the textbook already offers. For this reason, the content for each user-friendly website is organized by chapter and provides the professor and student with a variety of meaningful resources.

Common Companion Website features for students include:

- **Chapter Objectives**—outline key concepts from the text.
- **Interactive Self-quizzes**—complete with hints and automatic grading, provide immediate feedback for students. After students submit their answers for the interactive self-quizzes, the Companion Website **Results Reporter** computes a percentage grade, provides a graphic representation of how many questions were answered correctly and incorrectly, and gives a question-by-question analysis of the quiz. Students are given the option to send their quiz to up to four email addresses (professor, teaching assistant, study partner, etc.).
- **Essay Questions**—allow students to respond to themes and objectives of each chapter by applying what they have learned to real classroom situations.
- **Web Destinations**—link to www sites that relate to chapter content.

To take advantage of the many available resources, please visit the *Human Learning,* Fifth Edition, Companion Website at

www.prenhall.com/ormrod

Brief Contents

Contents

Cognitive Factors in Motivation   491

Note: Every effort has been made to provide accurate and current Internet information in this book. However, the Internet and information on it are constantly changing, so it is inevitable that some of the Internet addresses listed in this textbook will change.

CHAPTER 1

Perspectives on Learning

When my son Alex was in kindergarten, his teacher asked me *please* to do something about his shoes. I had been sending Alex off to school every morning with his shoelaces carefully and lovingly tied, yet by the time he arrived at his classroom door, the laces were untied and flopping every which way—a state to which they invariably returned within 10 minutes of his teacher's retying them. Alex and I tried a series of shoe-tying lessons, but with little success. As an alternative, I proposed that we double-knot the laces when we tied them each morning, but Alex rejected my suggestion as being too babyish. I purchased a couple of pairs of shoes that had Velcro straps instead of laces, but Alex gave the shoes such a workout that the Velcro quickly separated itself from the leather. By March, the teacher, justifiably irritated that she had to retie my son's shoes so many times each day, insisted that Alex learn to tie them himself. So I sat down with him and demonstrated, for the umpteenth time, how to put two laces together to make a presentable bow. This time, however, I accompanied my explanation with a magical statement: "Alex, when you learn to tie your shoes, I will give you a quarter." Alex had shoe-tying perfected in five minutes, and after that we didn't have a single complaint from school—well, not about his shoes anyway.

When my daughter Tina was in fourth grade, she experienced considerable difficulty with a series of homework assignments in subtraction. She had never learned the basic subtraction facts, despite my continually nagging her to practice them, the result being that she could not solve many two- and three-digit subtraction problems. One night, after her typical half-hour tantrum about "these stupid problems," my husband explained to Tina that subtraction was nothing more than reversed addition and that her knowledge of addition facts could help her with subtraction. Something must have clicked in Tina's head, because we weren't subjected to any more tantrums about subtraction. Multiplication, yes, but not subtraction.

Human learning takes many forms. Some instances of learning are readily observable, such as when a child learns to tie shoes. Other instances of learning are fairly subtle, such as when a child gains a better understanding of mathematical principles. And people learn for many reasons. Some learn for the external rewards their achievements bring—for example, for good grades, recognition, or money (consider my mercenary son). But others learn for less obvious, more internal reasons—perhaps to gain a sense of accomplishment, or perhaps simply to make life easier.

THE IMPORTANCE OF LEARNING

Many species have things easy compared to human beings, or at least so it would seem. Birds, for instance, are born with a wealth of knowledge that we humans must learn. Birds seem to be biologically hardwired with home-building skills; we either have to be taught something about framing, roofing, and dry walling or have to hire someone else to do these things for us. Birds know, without being taught, exactly when to fly south and how to get there; we have to look at our calendars and road maps. Birds instinctively know how to care for their young; meanwhile, we attend prenatal classes, read child-care books, and watch other people demonstrate how to change diapers.

However, it is human beings, not birds, who are getting ahead in this world. Humans have learned to make increasingly stronger and more comfortable homes for themselves, while birds are still making the same flimsy, drafty nests in which they have been living for thousands of years. Humans have developed fast, dependable modes of transportation for themselves and their possessions, while birds are still winging it. And humans are learning how better to feed and care for themselves and their offspring, so that each generation grows taller, stronger, and healthier than the previous one. Birds, meanwhile, are still eating worms and insects.

The ability to acquire a large body of knowledge and a wide variety of behaviors allows the human race a greater degree of flexibility and adaptability than is true for any other species on the planet. Because so little of our behavior is instinctive and so much of it is learned, we are able to benefit from our experiences. We discover which actions are likely to lead to successful outcomes and which are not, and we modify our behaviors accordingly. And as adults pass on to children the wisdom gleaned from their ancestors and from their own experiences, each generation is just that much more capable of behaving intelligently. Let's face it: We can get from New York to Miami in four hours, but how long does it take the birds?

To be sure, many nonhuman species learn a great deal over the course of their lifetimes. My dog Tobey has learned that his dinner is usually served around 4 o'clock and that having a leash attached to his collar means a walk is imminent. My cat Geisha has learned that her litter box is in the laundry room and that a loud hiss can effectively dissuade a human from picking her up when she isn't in the mood for cuddling. When I planted blueberry bushes outside my office window one summer, the neighborhood birds quickly discovered that the bushes were an abundant source of food and that the aluminum pie plates I hung to scare them away weren't actually going to harm them.

There are limits to what nonhuman species can learn, however. As an example, look at the painting in Figure 1.1. I watched 15-year-old Somjai paint it when I visited the Maetaman Elephant Camp in Thailand in 2006. Somjai clearly knows how to paint an elephant. What is

Figure 1.1
Fifteen-year-old Somjai's painting
of an elephant.

most remarkable about this fact is that Somjai *is* an elephant. Yet I have a photograph of Somjai painting an elephant on a different occasion, and the elephant he painted then looks remarkably similar to the one shown here. Furthermore, as Somjai paints, his trainer stands beside him, continually applying paint to his brush and using various commands to guide his sequence of strokes. And from what I could gather on my visit to the elephant camp, Somjai and one of his comrades paint *only* elephants (sometimes with a simple background, such as an outline of mountains or a tree), and they consistently depict the same side view of an elephant. Several other elephants at the camp paint daisylike flowers, but they can paint *only* daisylike flowers. A Google search for "elephant painting" on the Internet suggests to me that Somjai has a talent that's unusual in the elephant world. Many elephants apparently have little inclination for painting at all, and most of those that do paint only random strokes on the canvas.

In contrast to Somjai and his peers at Maetaman, most human beings can paint not only elephants and flowers but an infinite number of other things as well, and by Somjai's age they can do so without anyone else's assistance. Painting is, for humans, not simply executing a specific sequence of brush strokes. Instead, people seem to be guided by internal "somethings"—perhaps a mental image of an elephant or flower, and probably some general strategies for representing physical entities on paper—and they can adapt those "somethings" at will to the task at hand.

Instead of inheriting instincts that direct their day-to-day behaviors, then, human beings seem to inherit an ability to think and learn in ways that nonhumans cannot. The particular environment in which they live has a huge impact on the knowledge and skills they do and don't acquire. For instance, in order to learn to paint, they (like Somjai) must grow up in an environment that provides painting tools and encourages painting. And explicit instruction in various painting techniques can help them paint more elaborate and true-to-life pictures (Alland, 1983; Case & Okamoto, 1996).

DEFINING LEARNING

My son Alex's learning to tie his shoes and my daughter Tina's learning how subtraction relates to addition are both examples of human learning. Consider these additional examples:

- The mother of an 8-year-old boy insists that her son take on some household chores, for which he earns a small weekly allowance. The allowance, when saved for two or three weeks, enables the boy to purchase small toys of his own choosing. As a result, he develops an appreciation for the value of money.
- A college student from a small town is, for the first time, exposed to political viewpoints different from her own. After engaging in heated debates with classmates, she reflects on and gradually modifies her own political philosophy.
- A toddler is overly affectionate with a neighborhood dog, and the dog responds by biting the toddler's hand. After this incident, the child cries and runs quickly to his mother every time he sees a dog.

As you can see, learning is the means through which we acquire not only skills and knowledge, but values, attitudes, and emotional reactions as well.

For purposes of our discussion, we will define **learning** as a long-term change in mental representations or associations as a result of experience. Let's divide this definition into its three parts. First, learning is a *long-term change*: It isn't just a brief, transitory use of information—such as remembering a phone number long enough to dial it and then forgetting it—but it doesn't necessarily last forever. Second, learning involves *mental representations or associations* and so presumably has its basis in the brain. Third, learning is a change *as a result of experience,* rather than the result of physiological maturation, fatigue, use of alcohol or drugs, or onset of mental illness or dementia.

DETERMINING WHEN LEARNING HAS OCCURRED

Many psychologists would agree with the definition of learning I've just presented. However, some would prefer that the focus be on changes in *behavior* rather than on changes in mental representations or associations (more on this point shortly). In fact, regardless of how we define learning, we know that it has occurred only when we actually see it reflected in a person's behavior. For example, we might see a learner:

- Performing a completely new behavior—perhaps tying shoes correctly for the first time
- Changing the frequency of an existing behavior—perhaps more regularly cooperating with (rather than being aggressive toward or in some other way alienating) classmates
- Changing the speed of an existing behavior—perhaps recalling various subtraction facts more quickly than before

- Changing the intensity of an existing behavior—perhaps throwing increasingly outrageous temper tantrums as a way of obtaining desired objects
- Changing the complexity of an existing behavior—perhaps discussing a particular topic in greater depth and detail after receiving instruction about the topic
- Responding differently to a particular stimulus—perhaps crying and withdrawing at the sight of a dog after having previously been eager to interact with dogs

Throughout the book, we will continue to see these and other approaches to assessing learning.

RESEARCH, PRINCIPLES, AND THEORIES

Although psychologists may differ in their views of how best to define learning and determine when it has occurred, virtually all of them agree on one point: They can best understand the nature of learning by studying it objectively and systematically through *research*. The systematic study of behavior, including human and animal learning processes, has emerged only within the past 100 years or so, making psychology a relative newcomer to scientific inquiry. But in a century's time, tens of thousands of research studies have investigated how people and many other species learn.

Consistent patterns in research findings have led psychologists to make generalizations about learning processes through the formulation of both principles and theories of learning. **Principles** of learning identify certain factors that influence learning and describe the specific effects that these factors have. For example, consider this principle:

A behavior that is followed by a satisfying state of affairs (a reward) is more likely to increase in frequency than a behavior not followed by such a reward.

In this principle, a particular factor (a reward that follows a behavior) is identified as having a particular effect (an increase in the behavior's frequency). The principle can be observed in many situations, including the following:

- A pigeon is given a small pellet of food every time it turns its body in a complete circle. It begins turning more and more frequently.
- Dolphins who are given fish for "speaking" in dolphinese quickly become quite chatty.
- A boy who completes a perfect spelling paper and is praised for it by a favorite teacher works diligently for future success in spelling assignments.
- A textbook author who receives compliments when she wears her hair in a French braid styles her hair that way more and more often, especially when going to parties or other social events.

Principles are most useful when they can be applied to a wide variety of situations. The "reward" principle—many psychologists instead use the term *reinforcement*—is an example of such broad applicability: It applies to both human and nonhuman animals and holds true for different types of learning and for different rewards. When a principle such as this one is observed over and over again—when it stands the test of time—it is sometimes called a **law.**

Theories of learning provide explanations about the underlying mechanisms involved in learning. Whereas principles tell us *what* factors are important for learning, theories tell us *why* these factors are important. For example, consider one aspect of social cognitive theory (described in chapter 6):

> People learn what they pay attention to. A reward increases learning when it makes people pay attention to the information to be learned.

Here we have one possible explanation of why a reward affects learning: It increases attention, which in turn brings about learning.

In this book we'll consider a number of theories that can help us understand various aspects of learning. Some theories, collectively known as **behaviorism,** focus on the learning of tangible, observable behaviors or *responses,* such as tying shoes, solving a subtraction problem, or complaining about a stomachache in order to stay home from school. (Some behaviorists prefer to define learning as a change in behavior rather than a mental change.) Other theories, which fall within a general approach known as **cognitivism,** focus on the *thought processes* involved in human learning. Examples of such processes include finding relationships between addition and subtraction facts, using memory gimmicks to remember French vocabulary words, or constructing idiosyncratic and highly personalized interpretations of classic works of literature.

In upcoming chapters, I'll describe both behaviorist and cognitive views of learning; I'll also describe perspectives that lie somewhere between the two extremes. Most psychologists tend to align themselves with one perspective or another, and I, whose graduate training and research program have been rooted in cognitive traditions, am no exception. Yet I firmly believe that diverse theoretical perspectives all have important things to say about human learning and that all provide useful suggestions for helping people learn more effectively.

Advantages of Theories

Principles of learning tend to be fairly stable over time: Researchers observe many of the same factors affecting learning time and time again. In contrast, theories of learning continue to evolve, to the point where I must revise this book in significant ways every four or five years. Certainly, the changeable nature of theories can be frustrating, in that we can never be confident that we have the "real scoop" on how people learn. Yet it is precisely the dynamic nature of learning theories that enables us to gain an increasingly accurate understanding of what is, in fact, a very complex, multifaceted process.

Theories have several advantages over principles. First, they allow us to summarize the results of many research studies and integrate numerous principles of learning. In that sense, theories are often quite concise (psychologists use the term *parsimonious*).

Second, theories provide starting points for conducting new research; they suggest research questions worthy of study. For example, the theory that attention is more important than reward leads to the following prediction:

> When a particular situation or task draws an individual's attention to the information to be learned, learning occurs even in the absence of a reward.

In fact, this prediction has frequently been supported by research (e.g., Cermak & Craik, 1979; Faust & Anderson, 1967; Hyde & Jenkins, 1969).

Third, theories help us make sense of and explain research findings. Research conducted outside the context of a particular theoretical perspective can yield results that are trivial and nongeneralizable. Interpreted from a theoretical perspective, however, those same results can be quite meaningful. For example, consider an experiment by Seligman and Maier (1967). In this classic study, dogs were placed in individual cages and given a number of painful and unpredictable shocks. Some dogs were able to escape the shocks by pressing a panel in the cage, whereas others were unable to escape. The following day, the dogs were placed in different cages, and again shocks were administered. This time, however, each shock was preceded by a signal (a tone) that the shock was coming, and the dogs could avoid the shocks by jumping over a barrier as soon as they heard the tone. The dogs that had been able to escape the shocks on the preceding day learned to avoid the shocks altogether in this new situation, but the dogs that had been unable to escape previously did *not* learn to avoid the shocks. On the surface, this experiment, although interesting, might not seem especially relevant to human learning. Yet Seligman and his colleagues used this and other experiments to develop their theory of *learned helplessness:* People who learn that they have no control over unpleasant or painful events in one situation are unlikely, in later situations, to try to escape or avoid aversive events even when it is possible for them to do so. In chapter 16, we will look at learned helplessness more closely and incorporate it into a more general theoretical framework known as *attribution theory.*

Theories have a fourth advantage as well: By giving us ideas about the mechanisms that underlie human learning and performance, they can ultimately help us design learning environments and instructional strategies that facilitate human learning to the greatest possible degree. For example, consider the teacher who is familiar with the theory that attention is an essential ingredient in the learning process. That teacher may identify and use a variety of approaches—perhaps providing interesting reading materials, presenting intriguing problems, and praising good performance—that are likely to increase students' attention to academic subject matter. In contrast, consider the teacher who is familiar only with the principle that rewarded behaviors are learned. That teacher may use certain rewards—perhaps small toys or trinkets—that are counterproductive because they draw students' attention to items that are irrelevant to classroom learning tasks.

Potential Drawbacks of Theories

Despite their advantages, theories also have potential drawbacks. First, no single theory explains everything that researchers have discovered about learning. Current theories of learning tend to focus on specific aspects of learning. Behaviorist theories, for example, limit themselves to situations in which learning involves specific, overt responses. Cognitive theories tend to focus instead on how people interpret, integrate, and remember information. Observed phenomena that do not fit comfortably within a particular theoretical perspective are usually excluded from that perspective.

Second, theories affect what new information is published, thereby biasing the knowledge we have about learning. For example, imagine that several researchers propose a particular theory of learning and conduct a research study to support their idea. They obtain results that are opposite to what they expected and so cast doubt on their theory. If these researchers are fully committed to demonstrating that their theory is correct, they are unlikely to publish results that will indicate otherwise! In this way, theories may occasionally impede progress toward a truly accurate understanding of the learning process.

A Perspective on Theories and Principles

You should ultimately think of the learning theories I describe in this book as dynamic, changing models of how learning occurs. Each theory is based on several decades of research results, and each has some validity. However, as research continues in the decades ahead, theories of learning will inevitably be revised to account for the new evidence that emerges. In this sense, no single theory can be considered "fact."

At the same time, you might think of learning principles as relatively enduring conclusions about cause–effect relationships in the learning process. The "reward" principle was introduced by Edward Thorndike in 1898 and has remained with us in one form or another ever since. Thorndike's original theory of *why* reward affects learning, however, has largely been replaced by other explanations.

Both principles and theories help us predict the conditions under which successful learning is most likely to occur. To the extent that they are useful in this way, we are better off with them—imperfect and tentative as some of them may be—than without them.

APPLYING KNOWLEDGE ABOUT LEARNING TO INSTRUCTIONAL PRACTICE

A great deal of learning takes place in a classroom context, and most of it is beneficial. For example, it is in the classroom that most students learn how to read and how to subtract one number from another. Unfortunately, students may also learn things at school that are *not* in their best interests over the long run. For example, although students may learn to read, they may also learn that the "best" way to remember what they read is to memorize it, word for word, without necessarily trying to understand it.[1] And although students may learn their subtraction facts, they may also learn that mathematics is a boring or frustrating endeavor.

With human beings so dependent on their environment to acquire the knowledge and skills they will need in order to become productive members of society, the learning that takes place in their educational institutions—elementary schools, high schools, universities, and so on—cannot be left to chance. To maximize the "right" kinds of student learning, teachers must understand the factors that influence learning (principles) and the processes that underlie it (theories). They must also draw on research findings regarding the effectiveness of various instructional practices.

The principles, theories, and research I have included in the chapters ahead approach human learning from different, and occasionally seemingly contradictory, perspectives. Yet I hope you will take an eclectic attitude as you read the book, resisting the temptation to choose one approach over others as being the "right" one. Different perspectives are applicable in different situations, depending on the environmental factors under consideration, the specific subject matter being learned, and the objectives of instruction. Furthermore, each perspective offers unique insights into how and why human beings learn and how instruction might be designed to enhance their learning (e.g., see Catania, 1985; Epstein, 1991; Reynolds, Sinatra, & Jetton,

---

[1]We'll look at effective and ineffective learning and study strategies in chapters 8 and 12. In the meantime, you can find suggestions for effective studying on the Companion Website that accompanies this book. Go to www.prenhall.com/ormrod, click on the picture of this book, and look for the reading called "Study Tips."

1996). It is probably more helpful to think of theoretical perspectives in terms of their *usefulness* than in terms of their correctness.

As theories of learning continue to be revised and refined in the years to come, so, too, will instructional practices be revised and refined. In the meantime, we can use current theories to help people of all ages learn in increasingly effective and efficient ways.

OVERVIEW OF THE BOOK

In chapter 2, we will examine the physiological underpinnings of thinking and learning. There we will look at components of the human nervous system and consider where and how learning probably occurs in the brain. We will also consider what brain research tells us—as well as what it does *not* tell us—about thinking, learning, and instruction in classroom settings.

In part II of the book, we will explore principles and theories of learning from the behaviorist perspective, focusing on relationships between environmental events (stimuli) and the behaviors (responses) that people acquire as a result of those events. We will begin by examining the general assumptions of behaviorist theories (chapter 3) and then explore in depth the two most commonly used models of learning within the behaviorist perspective: classical conditioning (chapter 3) and instrumental conditioning (chapters 4 and 5).

In part III (chapter 6), we will make the transition from behaviorism to cognitivism as we examine social cognitive theory, a theory that has evolved over the years from its behaviorist roots into a blend of behaviorist and cognitive ideas regarding how and what people learn by observing those around them.

In part IV, we will turn to theories of learning that are almost entirely cognitive in nature. We will look at several cognitive perspectives, both old and new, that have contributed to our understanding of how people think and learn (chapter 7). We will then examine in detail some of the mental processes involved in learning and memory (chapters 8 and 10) and the nature of the "knowledge" that such processes yield (chapter 9).

Part V (chapter 11) will enable us to look at learning and cognition from a developmental perspective. Our focus will be on two early developmental theories—those of Swiss researcher Jean Piaget and Russian psychologist Lev Vygotsky—that continue to influence our understanding of how children learn and think even today.

As we proceed to part VI, we will continue our exploration of cognitive theories by examining more complex aspects of human learning and cognition. Specifically, we will look at how well people understand and regulate their own thinking processes—a phenomenon known as *metacognition*—and how effectively they can apply what they've learned in one situation to new tasks and problems (chapters 12 and 13). We will then consider how learning and cognition are sometimes a very social enterprise: People can often make better sense of situations and respond in more adaptive ways when they work together than any one of them might be able to do individually (chapter 14).

Finally, in part VII, we will consider the role that motivation plays in learning. We will look at motivation's effects on learning and behavior, consider some of the basic needs that human beings have, and consider how emotion (*affect*) is closely intertwined with both motivation and learning (chapter 15). We will also identify many cognitive factors that enter into and shape motivational processes (chapter 16).

Throughout the book, we will frequently identify educational implications of the principles and theories we are studying. I hope that once you have finished the final chapter, you will be convinced, as I am, that psychology has a great deal to offer about how we can enhance teaching and learning both inside and outside of the classroom.

SUMMARY

Learning allows human beings a greater degree of flexibility and adaptability than is true for any other species. A definition that incorporates many psychologists' ideas about the nature of *learning* is "a long-term change in mental representations or associations as a result of experience." However, some psychologists prefer that we define learning as a change in behavior rather than a mental change, and, in fact, we can be confident that learning has occurred only when we *do* see a behavior change of some kind.

An accurate, dependable understanding of the nature of human learning can emerge only by studying learning through objective, systematic research. Consistent patterns in research findings have led psychologists to formulate both *principles* (descriptions of what factors affect learning) and *theories* (explanations of why those factors have the effects they do) about learning. Principles tend to be fairly stable over time, whereas theories continue to evolve as new research findings are reported. Effective teachers draw on a wide variety of research findings, principles, and theoretical perspectives as they design and implement instruction.

CHAPTER 2

Learning and the Brain

Someone in my family has a broken brain; to protect his privacy, I will simply call him Loved One. As a child, Loved One was in most respects quite normal: He did well in school, spent after-school hours playing typical "boy" games with his friends, and often traveled to places near and far with his parents and siblings. People who knew him described him as smart, sweet, and sensitive. But even then, there were, perhaps, little cracks in his brain. For one thing, he had trouble delaying gratification: He always wanted things now, now, now. And he made many poor choices in his daily decision making—for example, leaving a pet turtle unattended on his bed (the turtle fell off the bed, broke its shell in two, and died the following day) and smashing unwanted toys on the back patio using a hammer that left huge "smash" marks on the patio itself.

When Loved One was 17, something went seriously wrong. Despite curfews and significant consequences for ignoring them, he would stay out until the wee hours of the morning; sometimes he didn't return home until the middle of the next day. He became increasingly hostile and defiant, and his parents found it impossible to reason with him. He often refused to get out of bed to go to school. His grades plummeted, and by December of his senior year, it was clear that he wouldn't have enough credits to graduate with his high school class. In January, his out-of-control behavior landed him in a juvenile detention center. While awaiting trial, he became increasingly lethargic until eventually he could barely move: He wouldn't eat and didn't seem able to walk or talk. When, on the day of his trial, he was brought into the courtroom in a wheelchair—awake but unresponsive—the judge remanded him to the state mental hospital.

Loved One has been officially diagnosed as having *bipolar disorder,* a condition characterized by periods of elation and intense activity (mania) followed by periods of deep sadness and lethargy (depression). Particularly during the manic periods, Loved One has **psychosis:** His thinking is impaired to the point where he cannot function normally. He seems unable to reason, make appropriate decisions, or control his impulses. Furthermore, he often has auditory hallucinations, hearing voices that aren't there. Such psychotic symptoms are often seen in another serious mental illness, *schizophrenia,* as well.

Medication does wonders for Loved One: It calms him down, clears his thoughts, gives him back his impulse control, and helps him appropriately interpret and respond to events in his daily life. Medication has enabled him to acquire his graduate equivalency diploma (GED) and earn Bs in occasional classes at a local community college. But like many people with mental illness, Loved One doesn't always stay on his medication. When he doesn't, his brain goes haywire and his behaviors land him in jail and, if he is lucky, back in the hospital. Loved One typically remembers very little of what he does or what happens to him when he is psychotic. That is probably just as well.

The human brain is an incredibly complex mechanism, and researchers have a long way to go in understanding how it works and why it doesn't always work as well as it should. Yet they have made considerable progress in the past two decades, and their knowledge about brain anatomy and physiology grows by leaps and bounds every year.

In this chapter we will look at the biological underpinnings of thinking and learning. We will begin by putting the basic building blocks of the human nervous system under the microscope. We will then examine various parts of the brain and the functions that each appears to have. Later, we will trace the brain's development over time (at that point we will speculate about why Loved One's brain broke down when it did) and look at theorists' beliefs about the physiological basis of learning. Finally, we will consider what educational implications we can draw—as well as what implications we *cannot* draw—from current knowledge and research about the brain. As we address these topics, we will discredit some common myths about the brain that currently run rampant in educational literature.

BASIC BUILDING BLOCKS OF THE HUMAN NERVOUS SYSTEM

The human nervous system has two main components. The **central nervous system,** comprising the brain and spinal cord, is the coordination center: It connects what we sense (e.g., what we see, hear, smell, taste, and feel) with what we do (e.g., how we move our arms and legs). The **peripheral nervous system** is the messenger system: It carries information from *receptor cells*—cells specialized to detect particular kinds of stimulation from the environment (e.g., light, sound, chemicals, heat, pressure)—to the central nervous system, and it carries directions back to various body parts (muscles, organs, etc.) about how to respond to that stimulation.

Nerve cells, or **neurons,** provide the means through which the nervous system transmits and coordinates information. Curiously, however, neurons don't directly touch one another; they send chemical messages to their neighbors across tiny spaces known as **synapses.** And neurons rely on other cells, known as **glial cells,** to give them structure and support. Let's briefly look at the nature of each of these key elements of the nervous system.

Neurons

Each neuron in the human body plays one of three roles. **Sensory neurons** carry incoming information from receptor cells. They convey this information to **interneurons,** which integrate and interpret input from multiple locations. The resulting "decisions" are transmitted to **motor neurons,** which send messages about how to behave and respond to appropriate parts of the body.[1] As you might guess, sensory neurons and motor neurons are located in the peripheral nervous system. The vast majority of interneurons are found in the central nervous system, especially in the brain.

Although neurons vary somewhat in shape and size, all of them have several features in common (see Figure 2.1). First, like all cells, they have a cell body, or **soma,** that contains the cell's nucleus and is responsible for the cell's health and well-being. In addition, they have a number of branchlike structures, known as **dendrites,** that receive messages from other neurons. They also have an **axon,** a long, armlike structure that transmits information on to additional neurons (occasionally, a neuron has more than one axon). The end of the axon may branch out numerous times, and the ends of its tiny branches have **terminal buttons,** which contain certain chemical substances (more about these substances shortly). For some (but not all) neurons, much of the axon is covered with a white, fatty substance known as a **myelin sheath.**

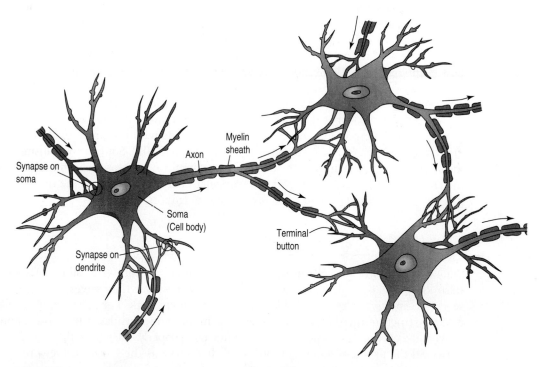

Figure 2.1
The nature of neurons and their interconnections.

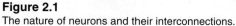

[1]You may sometimes see the terms *receptor neurons, adjuster neurons,* and *effector neurons* used for sensory neurons, interneurons, and motor neurons, respectively.

When a neuron's dendrites are stimulated by other cells (either receptor cells or other neurons), the dendrites become electrically charged. In some instances, the charges are so small that the neuron "ignores" them. But when the charges reach a certain level (known as the **threshold of excitation**), the neuron "fires," sending an electrical impulse along its axon to the terminal buttons. If the axon has a myelin sheath, the impulse travels quite rapidly: The "electrical message" leaps from one gap in the myelin to the next, almost as if it were playing leapfrog. If the axon does not have a myelin sheath, the impulse travels more slowly.

Synapses

The branching ends of a neuron's axon reach out to, but do not quite touch, the dendrites (in some cases, the somas) of other neurons. Whereas transmission of information within a neuron is electrical, transmission of information from one neuron to another is chemical. When an electrical impulse moves down a neuron's axon, it signals the terminal buttons to release chemicals known as **neurotransmitters.** These chemicals travel across the synapses and stimulate the dendrites or somas of neighboring neurons.

Different neurons specialize in different kinds of neurotransmitters. Perhaps in your readings about health, fitness, or related topics, you have seen references to dopamine, epinephrine, norepinephrine, serotonin, amino acids, or peptides. All of these are neurotransmitters, and each of them may play a unique role in the nervous system. For instance, dopamine is a key neurotransmitter in the frontal cortex, which, as you will discover shortly, is actively involved in consciousness, planning, and the inhibition of irrelevant behaviors and ideas (Goldman-Rakic, 1992). Some theorists suspect that schizophrenia and other serious psychiatric disorders may sometimes be the result of abnormal levels of dopamine (Barch, 2003; Clarke, Dalley, Crofts, Robbins, & Roberts, 2004). (Recall Loved One's difficulties with decision making and impulse control.)

Any single neuron may have synaptic connections with hundreds or thousands of other neurons (Goodman & Tessier-Lavigne, 1997; Lichtman, 2001). Some neurotransmitters increase the level of electrical activity in the neurons they stimulate, whereas others inhibit (i.e., decrease) the level of electrical activity. Whether a particular neuron fires, then, is the result of how much it is "encouraged" and "discouraged" by its many neighbors.

Glial Cells

Only about 10% of the cells in the nervous system are neurons. The other 90% are glial cells (also known as *neuroglia*). Glial cells do not carry messages themselves; rather, they serve in several supportive roles that enable neurons to do their work. For instance, glial cells provide a stable structure that helps to keep neurons in place and insulated from one another. They provide the chemicals that neurons need to function properly. They form the myelin sheaths that surround the axons of many neurons. And they serve as the clean-up crew, removing dead neurons and excess neurotransmitter substances.

In the human brain, these basic building blocks—neurons, synapses, and glial cells—make it possible for us to survive (e.g., by breathing and sleeping), to identify the stimuli we encounter (e.g., recognizing a friend or the family pet), to feel emotion (e.g., becoming afraid when we encounter danger), and to engage in the many conscious thought processes (e.g., planning, reading, solving mathematical problems) that are distinctly human.

BRAIN STRUCTURES AND FUNCTIONS

In some instances, sensory neurons connect directly with motor neurons in the spinal cord. For instance, if you touch something very hot, the sensory neurons traveling from your fingertips up your arm and into your spinal cord tell the motor neurons traveling back to your arm and hand muscles to quickly pull your fingers away. You make this automatic response, or **reflex,** without any thought whatsoever. Although your brain certainly perceives the heat you have encountered, your spinal cord enables you to remove yourself from danger before your brain deliberates on the situation at all.

For the most part, however, information from the outside world travels to the brain, which then decides whether and how to respond. The human brain is an incredibly complicated mechanism that involves somewhere in the neighborhood of *one hundred billion* neurons (Goodman & Tessier-Lavigne, 1997; Siegel, 1999). These neurons are, of course, microscopic, and they are interconnected in myriad ways. Thus, researchers have faced quite a challenge in figuring out how the brain works and what parts serve what functions, but they have made considerable progress nevertheless.

In this section, we will look at the methods that researchers use to study the nature and functions of various parts of the brain. We will then examine researchers' findings, identifying particular functions that different structures appear to serve and learning how the two hemispheres of the brain may play somewhat different roles in thinking and learning. Later, as we consider the interconnected nature of the brain, we will find that thinking—and in fact even a single "piece" of knowledge—is rarely, if ever, located in a single spot.

Methods in Brain Research

In their work, researchers have had several methodologies at their disposal:

- *Studies with animals.* Some researchers take liberties with animals (e.g., laboratory rats) that they would never take with human beings. For instance, they may remove a certain part of an animal's brain, insert a tiny needle into a certain location and electrically stimulate it, increase the levels of certain hormones, or inject chemicals that block certain neurotransmitters. They then observe changes in the animal's behavior and assume that these changes reflect the functions that particular brain structures, hormones, or neurotransmitters serve.
- *Postmortem studies.* Some individuals may, while living, agree to donate their brains for scientific study upon their deaths. Others may donate the brains of recently deceased family members for whom they are the legal next of kin. By examining the brains of children and adults of varying ages, researchers can determine typical human brain structures and how brain anatomy may change with development.
- *Case studies of people with brain injuries and other pathological conditions.* Researchers take detailed notes about what people with brain injuries or certain pathologies (e.g., schizophrenia, dyslexia) can and cannot do. After death, they examine the individuals' brains to identify areas of abnormality (e.g., specific sites of an injury, abnormal brain structures). If the absence of certain abilities is consistently associated with certain brain abnormalities, researchers reasonably conclude that the affected brain areas play a key role in those missing abilities.

- *Electrical recording.* Researchers place electrodes at strategic locations on a person's scalp and record patterns of electrical activity in the brain. The resulting record, known as an *electroencephalograph* (EEG), tends to show different patterns of brain waves for different activities (e.g., for sleep versus wakefulness). Often, researchers will collect EEG data as people perform specific tasks, yielding *event-related potentials* (ERPs) that provide some indication of the nature of the brain activity occurring during those tasks. In one recent study (Farwell & Smith, 2001), researchers using an EEG-based procedure called *memory and encoding related multifaceted electroencephalographic responses* (MERMER) could determine, with an accuracy rate of 90% or higher, which individuals had and had not experienced certain events.
- *Neuroimaging.* Using a variety of recent technological advances, researchers take pictures of blood flow or metabolism rates in various parts of the brain as people perform a particular task. Common techniques are positron emission tomography (PET), single-photo emission computerized tomography (SPECT), computerized axial tomography (CAT), magnetic resonance imaging (MRI), and functional magnetic resonance imaging (fMRI). Presumably, areas of greater blood flow or metabolic rate reflect areas of the brain that contribute in significant ways to the task in question.

None of these methods is perfect (Bruer & Greenough, 2001; Byrnes, 2001). Laboratory rats don't have many of the sophisticated cognitive abilities that humans do. Postmortem studies of normal human brains reveal an overall decline in the number of synapses in middle childhood and adolescence (more about this point later), but they don't tell us to what degree children also form *new* synapses as they grow. Brain injuries may simultaneously affect multiple regions of the brain. EEGs don't tell us precisely where particular thought processes are occurring. And neuroimaging involves expensive diagnostic equipment with only limited availability for basic research. Nevertheless, taken together, research using these techniques is helping scientists identify and begin to put together some of the pieces of the puzzle about how the human brain works and develops.

Parts of the Brain

The human brain includes a number of distinct structures that have somewhat different functions; structures especially pertinent to our discussion in this chapter are shown in Figure 2.2. Together these structures comprise three major components of the brain, which have emerged at different points along our evolutionary journey. The **hindbrain,** located in the lower part of the brain where the spinal cord enters the skull, appeared first in evolution and appears first in prenatal development. Made up of several smaller structures (e.g., the medulla, pons, and cerebellum), the hindbrain is involved in many basic physiological processes that keep us alive (breathing, swallowing, sleeping, heart rate, etc.). The cerebellum, at the lower rear of the brain, is actively involved in balance and complex motor behaviors (e.g., walking, riding a bicycle, playing racquetball).

Next in both evolutionary and prenatal development is the **midbrain,** which plays supporting roles in vision and hearing (e.g., helping to control and coordinate eye movements). Probably the most essential part of the midbrain is the **reticular formation** (also called the *reticular activating system,* or RAS), which extends into the hindbrain as well. The reticular formation is a key player in attention and consciousness; for example, it alerts us to potentially important stimuli that the body's receptors are encountering.

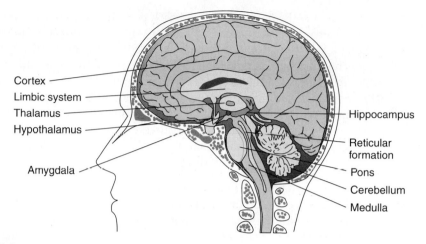

Figure 2.2
Key parts of the brain. The figure shows the middle of the brain; hence, the right and left sides of the cortex are missing.

Last to come along is the **forebrain,** located in the front and upper portions of the brain. The forebrain is where most of the mental "action" is in primates, especially human beings. Resting on top, like a thick, poorly combed toupee, is the **cerebral cortex**—often simply called the **cortex**—which is divided into two halves (**hemispheres**) that, on the surface, appear to be mirror images of each other. Neurologists conceptualize the hemispheres of the cortex as having four major parts, or *lobes,* named after the parts of the skull that cover them (see Figure 2.3):

- *Frontal lobes.* Located at the front and top of the cortex, the frontal lobes are where much of our conscious thinking seems to occur. The frontal lobes are largely responsible for a wide variety of very "human" activities, including language, attention, reasoning, decision making, planning, self-regulation, learning strategies, problem solving, consciously controlled movements, and interpretation of others' behaviors. In addition, the frontal lobes are instrumental in inhibiting irrelevant and inappropriate thoughts and actions. (I suspect that much of Loved One's illness involves malfunctioning of his frontal lobes.)

Figure 2.3
Side view of the cortex.

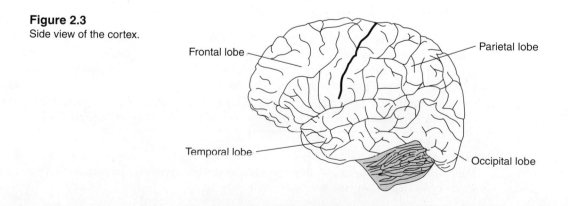

- *Parietal lobes.* Located in the upper back portion of the cortex, the parietal lobes receive and interpret somatosensory information—that is, information about temperature, pressure, texture, and pain. These lobes are also actively involved in paying attention, processing word sounds, and thinking about the spatial characteristics of objects and events.
- *Occipital lobes.* Located at the very back of the brain, the occipital lobes have major responsibility for interpreting and remembering visual information.
- *Temporal lobes.* At the sides, behind the ears, are the temporal lobes, which interpret and remember complex auditory information (e.g., speech, music). The temporal lobes also appear to be important in memory for information over the long run (something we will later call *long-term memory*), especially for concepts and general world knowledge.

In some cases, researchers have pinned down fairly specific regions of the cortex in which certain kinds of processing seem to occur. But many areas of the cortex are not so clearly specialized. These areas, known as *association areas,* appear to integrate information from various parts of the cortex, as well as from other parts of the brain, and so are essential for complex thinking and behavior.

Inside and below the cortex are several other parts of the forebrain. Following are some especially noteworthy ones:

- *Limbic system.* Closely connected with the cortex is a cluster of structures, collectively known as the limbic system, that are essential to learning, memory, emotion, and motivation. A small, seahorse-shaped structure known as the *hippocampus* (Greek for "seahorse") is intimately involved in attention and learning, especially for things that we consciously (rather than unconsciously) learn. Another structure, the *amygdala,* figures prominently in emotions (especially "negative" ones such as fear, stress, anger, and depression) and in automatic emotional reactions (e.g., aggression). Furthermore, the amygdala enables us to associate particular emotions with particular stimuli or memories (Adolphs & Damasio, 2001; Byrnes, 2001; Cahill et al., 1996).[2]
- *Thalamus.* The thalamus, located in the very middle of the brain, serves as a "switchboard operator" that receives incoming information from various sensory neurons and sends it on to appropriate areas of the cortex. It also plays a role in arousal, attention, and fear.
- *Hypothalamus.* Located beneath the thalamus, the hypothalamus regulates many activities related to survival, such as breathing, body temperature, hunger and thirst, mating, fighting, and fleeing from harm.

The Left and Right Hemispheres

To some degree, the left and right hemispheres have different specialties. Curiously, the left hemisphere is largely responsible for controlling the right side of the body, and vice versa. For most people, the left hemisphere seems to be in charge of language, with particular areas of the left frontal lobe, known as Broca's area and Wernicke's area, being involved in speech production and language comprehension, respectively. Reading and mathematical calculation skills also seem to be heavily dependent on the left hemisphere (Byrnes, 2001; Roberts & Kraft, 1987). In contrast,

---

[2]Although Figure 2.2 shows only one hippocampus and one amygdala, the human brain has two of each, which are located on opposite sides of the brain.

the right hemisphere is more dominant in visual and spatial processing, such as locating objects in space, perceiving shapes, comparing quantities, drawing and painting, mentally manipulating visual images, recognizing faces and facial expressions, and interpreting gestures (Byrnes, 2001; Ornstein, 1997). In general, the left side is more apt to handle details, whereas the right side is better suited for looking at and synthesizing an overall whole (Ornstein, 1997; Siegel, 1999).

Yet contrary to a popular myth, people rarely if ever think exclusively in one hemisphere; there is no such thing as "left-brain" or "right-brain" thinking. The two hemispheres are joined together by a collection of neurons (*the corpus callosum*) that enables constant communication back and forth, and so the hemispheres typically collaborate in day-to-day tasks. Let's take language comprehension as an example. The left hemisphere handles such basics as syntax and word meanings, but it seems to interpret what it hears and reads quite literally. The right hemisphere is better able to consider multiple meanings and take context into account; hence, it is more likely to detect sarcasm, irony, metaphors, and puns (Beeman & Chiarello, 1998; Ornstein, 1997). Without your right hemisphere, you would find no humor in the following joke:

> A woman went to a butcher to buy rabbit for a stew but the hares hanging at the butcher's are quite large. So, she says to the butcher, "I'd like to make some rabbit stew but these things are too big. Could you cut one in two for me?" . . . "Sorry ma'am [the butcher replies], we don't split hares here." (Ornstein, 1997, p. 109)

About 80% of human beings have left and right hemispheres that are specialized in the ways I've just described. For instance, the left hemisphere is the primary language hemisphere for more than 90% of right-handed individuals but for only about 60% of left-handed folks. People differ, too, in how "lopsided" their thinking is: Whereas some often rely predominantly on one hemisphere or the other (depending on the circumstances), others regularly think in a fairly balanced, two-sided manner (Ornstein, 1997; Siegel, 1999).

As you can see, then, functions of some areas of the brain (especially in the cortex) are hardly set in stone. Occasionally, one area may take over a function that another area typically serves. For example, if, before age 1, children sustain damage to the left hemisphere or have part of their left hemisphere surgically removed (perhaps to address severe epileptic seizures), the right hemisphere steps in and enables the children to acquire normal language capabilities (Beeman & Chiarello, 1998; Stiles & Thal, 1993). To some extent, which parts of the cortex handle which kinds of information depends on which messages from various sensory neurons end up at which locations; if surgical interventions rearrange where the messages go, the cortex accommodates the change (Byrnes, 2001). Furthermore, different areas of the cortex may take on different roles as a result of what specific stimuli and tasks present themselves while a particular part of the cortex is actively changing and maturing (Ornstein, 1997).

Interconnectedness of Brain Structures

As you may have noticed in our earlier discussion of various brain structures, many aspects of daily functioning—for instance, attention, learning, memory, and motor skills—are handled in multiple places. And as you just discovered, the two hemispheres usually work together to understand and respond to the world. Remember, too, that any single neuron is apt to have hundreds of synapses (or more) with other neurons. As information travels through the brain, messages go every which way—not only from "lower down" in the processing system (i.e., at points where sensory information first reaches the brain) to "higher up" (i.e., at points where information is synthesized and interpreted or where behaviors are chosen and controlled), but also in the opposite direction and across areas that handle very different sensory modalities and motor functions. In essence, learning or thinking about virtually anything tends to be *distributed* across many parts of the brain (Bressler, 2002; Thelen & Smith, 1998). A task as seemingly simple as identifying a particular word while reading a book or listening to speech will activate multiple areas of the cortex (Byrnes, 2001; Rayner, Foorman, Perfetti, Pesetsky, & Seidenberg, 2001).

In fact, probably even a single piece of information—for example, your address, telephone number, or birthday—is probably stashed away in your head in a distributed manner. In the 1920s, Karl Lashley (1929) worked extensively with rats in his efforts to determine where particular memories might be located. Lashley gave his rats a chance to learn their way around a particular maze and then removed certain sections of their brains to see whether they still remembered the maze. Regardless of which sections Lashley removed, the rats did not totally forget the maze; instead, they gradually remembered less and less as more and more of their brains were removed. It appeared that the rats remembered the maze in multiple places simultaneously, with each place contributing to the overall memory.

How does such a complex, interconnected mechanism—the human brain—come into being? Mother Nature's handiwork is quite a marvel. We look now at how the brain emerges and changes over the course of development.

DEVELOPMENT OF THE BRAIN

A second widespread myth about the brain is that it does all of its "maturing" within the first few years of life and that its development can best be nurtured by bombarding it with as much stimulation as possible—reading instruction, violin lessons, art classes, and so on—before its owner ever reaches kindergarten. Nothing could be further from the truth. Although much of the brain's development occurs before birth and the first few years after birth, the brain continues to develop throughout childhood, adolescence, and early adulthood. The early years are important, to be sure, but the kinds of experiences that nurture the brain's early development are fairly normal ones. In this section, we will trace brain development during the prenatal months and postnatal years and look at factors that influence its development. We will then address two questions with which researchers have wrestled: To what extent are there critical periods in brain development? and To what extent is the brain "prewired" to know or learn certain things? As you will discover, theorists have tentatively answered the first question but are still struggling with the second.

Prenatal Development

About 25 days after conception, the brain first emerges as a tiny tube. The tube grows longer and begins to fold inward to make pockets (Rayport, 1992). Three chambers appear, and these eventually become the forebrain, midbrain, and hindbrain. Neurons quickly form and reproduce in the inner part of the tube; between the 5th and 20th weeks of prenatal development, they do so at the astonishing rate of 50,000 to 100,000 new cells per second (Diamond & Hopson, 1998). The vast majority (but apparently not all) of the neurons a person will ever have are formed at this time (Bruer, 1999; R. A. Thompson & Nelson, 2001).

In the second trimester of prenatal development, the neurons migrate to various locations, drawn by a variety of chemicals and supported by glial cells. On their arrival, they send out dendrites and axons in an effort to connect with one another. Those that make contact survive and begin to take on particular functions, whereas those that do not (about half of them) tend to die off (Diamond & Hopson, 1998; Goldman-Rakic, 1986; Huttenlocher, 1993). Such deaths are not to be mourned, however. Programming human beings to overproduce neurons is apparently Mother Nature's way of ensuring that the brain would have a sufficient number with which to work. The excess ones are unnecessary and can quite reasonably be cast aside.

Development in Infancy and Early Childhood

At birth, the human brain is about one-fourth the size it will be in adulthood, but by age 3 it has reached three-fourths of its adult size (M. H. Johnson & de Haan, 2001; Kolb & Whishaw, 1990). The cerebral cortex is the least mature part of the brain at birth, and cortical changes that occur in infancy and early childhood probably account for many of the advancements we see in children's thinking and reasoning (e.g., Quartz & Sejnowski, 1997; Siegler & Alibali, 2005).

Several significant processes characterize brain development in the early years: synaptogenesis, differentiation, synaptic pruning, and myelination.

Synaptogenesis

Neurons begin to form synapses well before birth. But shortly after birth, the rate of synapse formation increases dramatically. Neurons sprout new dendrites going every which way, and so they come into contact with a great many of their neighbors. Thanks to this process of **synaptogenesis,** young children have many more synapses than adults do (Bruer, 1999; Byrnes, 2001). Eventually, the rapid proliferation of synapses comes to a halt. Exactly when it does varies for different parts of the brain; for instance, synapses reach their peak in the auditory cortex (temporal lobes) at about 3 months, in the visual cortex (occipital lobes) at about 12 months, and in the frontal lobes at age 2 or 3 (Bruer, 1999; Huttenlocher, 1979, 1990).

Differentiation

As neurons form synapses with one another, they also begin to take on particular functions (McCall & Plemons, 2001; Neville & Bruer, 2001). Through this process, known as **differentiation,** neurons become specialists, assuming some duties and steering clear of others.

Synaptic Pruning

As children encounter a wide variety of stimuli and experiences in their daily lives, some synapses come in quite handy and are used repeatedly. Other synapses are largely irrelevant and useless, and these gradually fade away. In fact, the system seems to be set up to *guarantee* that this cutting back, or **synaptic pruning,** occurs. Neurons require chemical substances known as *trophic factors* for their survival and well-being, and by transmitting messages to other neurons, they cause the recipients to secrete such chemicals. If neurons regularly receive trophic factors from the same sources, they form stable synapses with those sources. If they receive trophic factors from some neurons but not others, they pull their axons away from the "unsupportive" ones. And if they are so "unstimulating" that they rarely excite any of their neighbors, they wither and die (Byrnes, 2001). In some areas of the brain, the period of intensive synaptic pruning occurs fairly early (e.g., in the preschool or early elementary years); in other areas, it begins later and continues until well into adolescence (Bruer, 1999; Huttenlocher & Dabholkar, 1997; M. H. Johnson & de Haan, 2001).

Why do our brains create a great many synapses, only to eliminate a sizeable proportion of them later on? In the case of synapses, more is not necessarily better (Byrnes, 2001). Theorists speculate that by generating more synapses than we will ever need, we have the potential to adapt to a wide variety of conditions and circumstances. As we encounter certain regularities in our environment, we find that some synaptic connections make no sense, because they aren't consistent with what we typically encounter in the world or with how we typically need to respond to it. In fact, effective learning and behaving require not only that we think and do certain things but also that we *not* think or do *other* things—in other words, that we inhibit certain thoughts and actions (Dempster, 1992; Haier, 2001). Synaptic pruning, then, may be Mother Nature's way of making our brains more efficient.

Myelination

As noted earlier, a neuron's axon is in some cases covered with a myelin sheath, which greatly speeds up the rate with which an electrical charge travels along the axon. When neurons first form, they have no myelin; this substance arrives a bit later, courtesy of glial cells. The process of coating neural axons, known as **myelination**, occurs gradually over time. Some myelination begins near the end of the prenatal period (e.g., this is true in certain areas necessary for basic survival), but much of it occurs in the first few years after birth, with different areas becoming myelinated in a predictable sequence (Diamond & Hopson, 1998). Myelination accounts for a sizable proportion of the brain's postnatal increase in size (Byrnes, 2001). Without doubt, it also enhances the brain's capacity to respond to the world quickly and efficiently.[3]

Development in Middle Childhood, Adolescence, and Adulthood

Especially in the cortex, synaptic pruning continues into the middle childhood and adolescent years, and myelination continues into the twenties or beyond (M. H. Johnson & de Haan, 2001; Merzenich, 2001; C. A. Nelson, 2005; Paus et al., 1999). Several parts of the brain—notably the frontal and temporal lobes, hippocampus, amygdala, and corpus callosum, all of which play key roles in thinking and learning—increase significantly in size from middle childhood until late adolescence or adulthood (Giedd et al., 1999a; Sowell & Jernigan, 1998; Walker, 2002). The frontal lobes show evidence of considerable maturation during late adolescence and early adulthood, possibly enabling increasing facility in such areas as attention, planning, and impulse control (Luna & Sweeney, 2004; Pribram, 1997; Sowell, Thompson, Holmes, Jernigan, & Toga, 1999).

With puberty come changes in young people's hormone levels (e.g., estrogen, testosterone), and these hormones affect the continuing maturation of brain structures and possibly the

---

[3]Brain researchers sometimes use the terms *white matter* and *gray matter* in their discussions of the brain. White matter consists largely of axons that have myelin coatings (myelin has a whitish color). Gray matter, which is actually more brown than gray, consists largely of parts of neurons that have no myelin. As axons increasingly become myelinated with development, the proportion of white matter relative to gray matter increases (Bortfeld & Whitehurst, 2001; Gogtay et al., 2004).

production and effectiveness of neurotransmitters as well (Eisenberg, Martin, & Fabes, 1996; Kolb, Gibb, & Robinson, 2003; Walker, 2002). In any case, it appears that the levels of some neurotransmitters change at puberty; for instance, serotonin decreases, and dopamine increases in some areas of the cortex (Walker, 2002). If a particular hormone or neurotransmitter is abnormally high or low at this point, something can go seriously awry in brain functioning.

Recall how Loved One's symptoms, minor in the early years, intensified in high school. In most cases, bipolar disorder and schizophrenia don't appear until adolescence or early adulthood. Such disorders seem to be caused, at least in part, by abnormal brain structures or neurotransmitter levels—abnormalities that don't emerge, or at least don't have much effect, until after puberty (Carlson, 1999; Giedd et al., 1999b; Jacobsen et al., 1997a, 1997b).

Factors Influencing Brain Development

Heredity certainly plays a role in brain development. For example, genetic instructions guide such processes as cell migration, synaptogenesis, and myelination (Bruer, 1999). For the most part, heredity ensures that things go right as the brain continues to grow and restructure itself. Occasionally, however, flawed instructions can cause things to go wrong. For instance, identical twins (twins who began as a single fertilized egg that split in two and so have the same DNA) have a higher-than-average probability of sharing disabilities such as schizophrenia and dyslexia (Byrnes, 2001; Conklin & Iacono, 2002). Children with Down syndrome, who have an extra 21st chromosome, have fewer cortical neurons, fewer synapses, and less myelin (Byrnes, 2001).

Environmental factors have effects on brain development as well. One important factor is the amount and quality of the food one eats. Severe malnutrition is most problematic during prenatal development, when it results in reduced production of neurons and glial cells (Byrnes, 2001). After birth, malnutrition hampers cell growth, myelination, and performance on psychological measures of cognitive development (e.g., intelligence tests); fortunately, the effects of *short-term* impoverishment can often be reversed by better diets later on (Byrnes 2001; Sigman & Whaley, 1998). Good nutrition only goes so far, however: Providing vitamins, minerals, and other food supplements has little effect if children otherwise have reasonably adequate diets (Zigler & Hodapp, 1986).[4]

Environmental toxins, too, have an impact. When future mothers consume significant amounts of alcohol during pregnancy, their children often have *fetal alcohol syndrome,* a condition characterized by distinctive facial features, poor motor coordination, delayed language, and mental retardation (e.g., Dorris, 1989). Ingestion of excessive amounts of lead, mercury, cadmium, or pesticides can result in deficits in learning and cognitive abilities (Hubbs-Tait, Nation, Krebs, & Bellinger, 2005; Koger, Schettler, & Weiss, 2005). Exposure to radiation during the period of rapid neuron production in the first few months of prenatal development leads to mental retardation but has little effect at later points in development (Goldman-Rakic, 1986).

Opportunities to learn also influence brain growth. When rats learn how to navigate a complex maze or difficult obstacle course, researchers later find more and stronger synapses in relevant parts of their cortexes (Black, Isaacs, Anderson, Alcantara, & Greenough, 1990; Greenough, Juraska, & Volkmar, 1979; Kleim et al., 1998). People who have learned to read and write have, in their

---

[4]For a review of research on the possible effects of food supplements on learning and memory in adults, see McDaniel, Maier, and Einstein (2002).

corpus callosums, a thicker band of fibers connecting their parietal lobes (Castro-Caldas et al., 1999). People who learn to play a musical instrument show detectably different organizational patterns in the brain than nonmusicians (Elbert, Pantev, & Taub, 1995). Intensive interventions for congenital or acquired disabilities (e.g., blindness, dyslexia, brain damage from strokes, removal of certain parts of the brain) lead to reorganizations of brain structure or changes in patterns of brain activation (Amedi, Merabet, Bermpohl, & Pascual-Leone, 2005; Bach-y-Rita, 1981; Crill & Raichle, 1982; Small, Flores, & Noll, 1998). To the extent that the brain adapts itself in such ways to different circumstances and experiences, we say that it has **plasticity.**

To What Extent Are There Critical Periods in Brain Development?

Although the human brain is fairly adaptable to changing circumstances, it can't always bounce back when the environment offers too little stimulation or consistently presents the wrong kind of stimulation. In some cases, the *timing* of environmental stimulation (or lack thereof) makes a considerable difference. In other words, there are **critical periods**[5]—limited age ranges in which particular kinds of environmental stimulation have their greatest, and perhaps only, impact—in certain aspects of brain development. For example, let's revisit a point I made in the preceding section: Radiation has a substantial impact on brain development *only* in the early months of the prenatal period. And consider this intriguing finding: When accomplished musicians play their musical instruments, those who began their musical training before age 10 show greater activation in a certain part of their brains than those who began their training at an older age (Elbert et al., 1995). One group doesn't necessarily play better than the other, but the later-trained musicians appear to have missed a window of opportunity for fully developing the brain area that the earlier-trained musicians are using.

Researchers have consistently found evidence for critical periods in the development of visual perception. If kittens have one eye sewn shut for the first three months of life, they remain functionally blind in that eye throughout life: The eye itself begins to work once the stitches are removed (e.g., receptors in the retina respond to light), but the part of the cortex that receives signals from the previously nonseeing eye isn't able to interpret the information it gets (Hubel & Wiesel, 1970). A similar thing happens when monkeys have one eye sewn shut for the first six months of life, yet monkeys suffer no permanent loss of vision if the eye is sewn shut for six months during adulthood rather than infancy (Bruer, 1999; Hubel, Wiesel, & Levay, 1977; Levay, Wiesel, & Hubel, 1980). And when human beings are born with cataracts that prevent normal vision, early surgery is essential. If the cataracts are removed before age 2, children develop relatively normal vision, but if surgery is postponed until age 5 or older, children remain functionally blind in whichever eye was affected (Bruer, 1999). Curiously, it seems to be the *pattern* of light deprivation, rather than light deprivation per se, that affects development in visual areas of the cortex; when monkeys have *both* eyes sewn shut for the first six months, they develop normal vision (Bruer, 1999; Hubel et al., 1977; Levay et al., 1980). It appears that if, in the early months, one eye is stimulated more than the other, the cortex restructures itself to take

---

[5]Many developmentalists prefer the term *sensitive period,* which connotes a more open-ended, flexible window of opportunity. However, I have seen the term *critical period* more frequently in recent literature about brain development, hence my use of this term here.

advantage of the information it gets from the seeing eye and compensate for what it's not getting from the other eye.

In human beings, we find persuasive evidence that there may be critical periods in learning language as well. Children who have little or no exposure to language in the early years often have trouble acquiring language later on, even with intensive language instruction (Curtiss, 1977; Newport, 1990). Furthermore, in the first few days and weeks of life, infants can discriminate among speech sounds used in a wide variety of languages, but by the time they are 6 months old, they "hear" only those differences important in the language(s) spoken around them (Kuhl, Tsao, & Liu, 2003; Kuhl, Williams, & Lacerda, 1992). As an example, the English language treats "L" and "R" as two separate sounds, whereas Japanese clumps them together into a single sound; thus, children in English-speaking countries continue to hear the difference between them, whereas Japanese children quickly lose the ability to tell them apart. I think back with fondness to Kikuko, one of my apartment mates in graduate school. As a native Japanese speaker who didn't learn English until grade school, Kikuko often talked about taking her *umblella* with her on rainy days, and she thought that people counted *raps* as they ran the track at the gym.

Additional evidence for critical periods in language development comes from people who learn a second language. Typically, people learn how to pronounce a second language flawlessly only if they study it before midadolescence or, even better, in the preschool or early elementary years (Bialystok, 1994a; Collier, 1989; Flege, Munro, & MacKay, 1995). Children may also have an easier time mastering complex aspects of a second language's syntax when they are immersed in the language within the first 5 to 10 years of life (Bialystok, 1994a, 1994b; Bortfeld & Whitehurst, 2001; J. S. Johnson & Newport, 1989). The effects of age on language learning are especially noticeable when the second language is phonetically and syntactically very different from the first (Bialystok, 1994a; Doupe & Kuhl, 1999; Strozer, 1994).

However, most theorists doubt very much that there are critical periods for *all* skills and knowledge domains. Oftentimes people become quite proficient in topics or skills that they don't begin to tackle until they are teenagers or adults. For example, I didn't learn to drive until I was 16, didn't begin to study psychology until I reached college, and didn't begin to play racquetball until I was in graduate school, but with time and practice, I have acquired considerable mastery in those domains.

Experience-Expectant Versus Experience-Dependent Plasticity

So when is early experience important, and when is it *not* important? Greenough, Black, and Wallace (1987) have made a distinction that can help us make sense of what appear to be conflicting data. Mother Nature, it seems, has helped our brains evolve in such a way that we can adapt to the specific physical and cultural environments in which we find ourselves, but she assumes that we will have *some* stimulation early on to shape brain development. For skills that human beings have possessed for many millennia—visual perception, language, and so on—the brain is **experience-expectant:** It uses the experiences that human beings encounter in virtually any environment to fine-tune its powers. For instance, although the brain is initially capable of interpreting visual signals from both eyes, it will restructure itself to compensate for a nonseeing one. And although it comes equipped with what it needs to discriminate among many different speech sounds, it quickly learns to ignore subtle differences that are irrelevant for making sense of its native language, paving the way for more efficient discriminations among sounds that *are* important for language comprehension. Quite possibly, the phenomena of synaptogenesis, differentiation, and synaptic pruning provide the mechanisms by which the brain initially sets itself up to accommodate a wide variety of environments and then begins to zero in on the particular environment in which it actually finds itself (Bruer, 1999; Bruer & Greenough, 2001; Kuhl, Conboy, Padden, Nelson, & Pruit, 2005). Although such zeroing-in obviously enhances the brain's ability to deal efficiently with common, everyday situations (e.g., understanding and speaking in one's nature language), it may make it more difficult to "overrule" its usual ways of thinking in order to do something very different later on (e.g., learning a second language).

Many other content domains and skill areas—for instance, reading, music, driving a car, psychology, racquetball—are such recent additions to human culture (and none of these appears in *all* cultures) that Mother Nature has had neither the time nor inclination to make them part of our evolutionary heritage (Bruer, 1997, 1999; Byrnes, 2001). Domains and skills that are unique to particular cultures and social groups are **experience-dependent:** They emerge only when environmental conditions nurture them, and they can presumably emerge at almost any age. In fact, by strengthening weak synapses and forming new ones, human beings and other animals retain considerable experience-dependent plasticity throughout the lifespan (Bruer, 1999; Greenough et al., 1987; Merzenich, 2001). For example, at age 85, my mother-in-law moved from Arizona to be near us in our present home in New Hampshire. She easily learned the knowledge and skills she needed to survive and thrive in her new community: how to get to the bank, hardware store, hairdresser, and grocery store; which neighbors have talents and interests similar to her own; what political issues are simmering in town and across the state; and so on.

So let's return to our initial question: To what extent are there critical periods in brain development? It appears that critical periods exist for certain basic abilities such as visual perception and language. Even in these domains, however, the windows of opportunity remain open for different periods of time for different aspects of those abilities. For instance, there are different time frames for the development of color vision, motion perception, and depth perception, and different time frames for sound discrimination, pronunciation, and acquisition of syntactic structures (Bruer, 1999; Locke, 1993; Neville & Bruer, 2001). Furthermore, the windows of opportunity don't necessarily slam shut at particular ages. Rather, they close gradually over a prolonged period and in some cases stay open at least a crack for a very long time, particularly if the right kinds of experiences are provided. And for complex, culture-specific acquisitions— including most of the topics and skills that we teach in schools and universities—the windows sometimes remain wide open throughout childhood and much of adulthood (Bruer, 1999; McCall & Plemons, 2001; R. A. Thompson & Nelson, 2001).

To What Extent Is the Brain "Prewired" to Know or Learn Things?

Let's look once again at language. Speaking and understanding language is a miraculous accomplishment indeed; children must master not only the subtle motor movements involved in producing various consonants and vowels but also tens of thousands of word meanings plus syntactical structures so numerous and multifaceted that even linguists have been hard-pressed to identify and catalog them all. How children master language as quickly as they do remains one of the big mysteries of child development. Many theorists believe that, although children are obviously not born knowing a particular language, they *are* born with some predispositions that assist them in acquiring whichever language they hear spoken around them (e.g., Cairns, 1996; Gopnik, 1997; Hirsh-Pasek & Golinkoff, 1996; Lenneberg, 1967; Lightfoot, 1999). This perspective of language learning, known as **nativism,** is supported by three widely observed phenomena. First, everyday speech seems to be inadequate to enable children to acquire the complex, adultlike language that they eventually do acquire. In typical day-to-day conversations, adults often use incomplete sentences, are lax in their adherence to grammatical rules and, when talking to very young children, may use artificially short and simple language. In other words, there is a *poverty of the stimulus* in the language that children hear (Cook & Newson, 1996; Harris, 1992; Lightfoot, 1999). Second, to communicate effectively, children must derive innumerable unspoken, underlying rules that govern how words are put together and then use these rules to generate sentences they have never heard before (Chomsky, 1959, 1972; Littlewood, 1984; Pinker, 1993). Third, all children in a particular language community learn essentially the *same* language despite widely differing early childhood experiences and a general lack of systematic instruction in appropriate language use (Cromer, 1993; Lightfoot, 1999; Littlewood, 1984).

Some theorists have suggested that human beings may be prewired with respect to other domains as well. Consider these findings from research with infants:

- By 24 hours of age, infants have some ability to discriminate between objects that are close to them versus objects that are farther away (Slater, Mattock, & Brown, 1990). It's as if they can judge distance long before they have much opportunity to *learn* about distance.
- Infants as young as 1 or 2 days old may imitate an adult's facial expressions—perhaps pursing their lips, opening their mouths, or sticking out their tongues (Field, Woodson, Greenberg, & Cohen, 1982; Meltzoff & Moore, 1977; Reissland, 1988). It's as if they already connect certain things they see others do with certain things that they themselves can do. In fact, evidence is emerging that some primate species (possibly including human beings) have certain neurons that fire either when they perform a particular action themselves *or* when they watch *someone else* perform it (Iacoboni & Woods, 1999; Murata et al., 1997; Wicker et al., 2003). Such neurons, known as **mirror neurons,** might explain why infants can imitate others so early in life: Some of the same neurons are involved when they watch another person's behavior and when they engage in the behavior themselves.
- By 3 or 4 months, infants show signs of surprise when one solid object passes directly through another one, when an object seems to be suspended in midair, or when an object appears to move immediately from one place to another without traveling across the intervening space to get there (Baillargeon, 1994; Spelke, 1994; Spelke, Breinlinger, Macomber, & Jacobson, 1992). It appears, then, that young infants know that objects are substantive entities with definite boundaries, that objects will fall unless something holds them up, and that movements of objects across space are continuous and somewhat predictable.

Such findings suggest to some theorists (e.g., Baillargeon, 2004; M. Cole, 2006; Flavell, Miller, & Miller, 2002; Spelke, 2000) that infants have some biologically built-in **core knowledge** about the physical world. Knowledge of this kind would have an evolutionary advantage, of course—it would give infants a head start in learning about their environment—and evidence for it has been observed in other species as well (Spelke, 2000).

Nevertheless, the extent to which the human brain is hardwired with certain knowledge, or perhaps with predispositions to acquire that knowledge, is an unresolved issue, and it will likely remain so for quite some time. Unless researchers can assess infants' knowledge at the very moment of birth, they cannot rule out the possibility that experience and practice, rather than built-in knowledge, account for infants' early capabilities. Just imagine a couple of scientists in lab coats appearing in the hospital delivery room to ask if they can whisk the new baby away for a "research project." I doubt that they'd find many new parents willing to sign the necessary permission forms.

THE PHYSIOLOGICAL BASIS OF LEARNING

So how and where, from a physiological standpoint, does learning occur? Many theorists believe that the basis for learning lies in changes in interconnections among neurons—in particular, in the strengthening or weakening of existing synapses or the formation of new ones through changes in the number and complexity of dendrites at the "receiving" ends of neurons (Bruer & Greenough, 2001; Lichtman, 2001; Merzenich, 2001; Trachtenberg et al., 2002). But a second phenomenon may be involved as well. Until recently, it was common "knowledge" that all the neurons a person would ever own are produced in the first few weeks of the prenatal period. Some researchers have found, however, that **neurogenesis**—the formation of new neurons— continues throughout the lifespan in a particular part of the hippocampus and possibly also in certain regions of the frontal and parietal lobes (Gould, Beylin, Tanapat, Reeves, & Shors, 1999; Sapolsky, 1999; R. A. Thompson & Nelson, 2001). New learning experiences appear to enhance the survival rate and maturation of the young neurons; without such experiences, these neurons slowly die away (Gould et al., 1999; Leuner et al., 2004).

Most newly acquired information and skills seem to need some time to "firm up" in the cortex—a process called **consolidation** (Byrnes, 2001; Lee, Everitt, & Thomas, 2004; Siegel, 1999). For instance, a person who incurs a serious head injury (perhaps in an automobile accident) often cannot recall things that happened several seconds, minutes, days, or months prior to the injury, whereas memories of long-past events remain largely intact (Siegel, 1999; Squire, 1987). Such amnesia is especially common when the person is unconscious for a short time following the injury, presumably because the individual is no longer able to think about events that have recently occurred.

As for *where* learning occurs, the answer is: many places. The frontal lobes are active when we must pay attention and think about new information and events, and all of the lobes of the cortex may be active to a greater or lesser extent in interpreting new input in light of previously acquired knowledge (Byrnes, 2001). The small, seahorse-shaped hippocampus seems to be a central figure in the learning process, binding together the information it simultaneously receives from various parts of the brain (Bauer, 2002; Squire & Alvarez, 1998). The hippocampus also appears to be a key player in consolidating newly formed memories and making them accessible to later recall (Bauer, Wiebe, Carver, Waters, & Nelson, 2003). And its neighbor in the limbic system, the amygdala, is probably instrumental in the preverbal, emotional memories that very young children form (LeDoux, 1998; Nadel, 2005).

Even as researchers pin down how and where learning occurs, we must remember that knowledge of brain anatomy and physiology doesn't begin to tell us everything we need to know about learning, let alone about how we can best foster and enhance it in educational settings. Let's look now at what research about the brain does and does not tell us about appropriate and effective educational practice.

EDUCATIONAL IMPLICATIONS OF BRAIN RESEARCH

Extolling recent advances in brain research, some well-meaning but ill-informed individuals have drawn unwarranted inferences about its educational implications. For instance, you might hear people speaking of "building better brains," designing a "brain-based curriculum," or "teaching to the right brain." Such statements often reflect misconceptions about how the brain works. Brain research is only in its infancy, and much of what researchers have learned about brain functioning is still somewhat tentative and controversial (Byrnes, 2001). Following are several conclusions we can draw with some confidence.

◆ *Some loss of synapses is both inevitable and desirable.* Apparently in an effort to preserve as many of those early synapses as possible, some writers have suggested that infants and young children be immersed in stimulation-rich environments that get them off to a strong start in academics, athletics, and the arts. But as we have seen, synaptic pruning is inevitable, because synapses must compete for a limited supply of the trophic factors that ensure their survival. Furthermore, pruning is beneficial, not detrimental, because it eliminates useless synapses and thereby enhances the brain's efficiency. The sequence of synaptogenesis and synaptic pruning is a primary means by which Mother Nature ensures plasticity and adaptability in human functioning (Bruer, 1999; Byrnes & Fox, 1998). In fact, much learning and many advances in cognitive abilities (e.g., abstract reasoning) occur after most synaptic pruning has already taken place (Bruer, 1999).

◆ *Many environments nurture normal neurological development.* In domains where development depends on particular kinds of stimulation at particular ages (i.e., in domains characterized by critical periods), the necessary stimulation is found in experiences that children encounter in virtually any culture. For instance, to acquire normal binocular vision, children need regular and balanced visual input to both eyes. To acquire normal facility with language, children need ongoing exposure to a language, either spoken or manually signed (McCall & Plemons, 2001; Newport, 1990). Such experiences can be found not only in "enriching" child care and preschool environments but also in lower-income, inner-city neighborhoods and even in remote tribal groups in developing countries. We do not know to what extent, or even *if,* intensive, structured educational experiences promote greater brain growth in the early years than might otherwise be expected (Bruer, 1999; R. A. Thompson & Nelson, 2001).

One important caveat must be mentioned here, however: A *very* critical period is the prenatal period, especially the first few months after conception, when adequate nutrition and protection from environmental hazards (lead dust, mercury, radiation, etc.) are essential if the brain is to get off to a good start. The adverse effects of poor nutrition and environmental insults during this time period appear to be irreversible.

◆ *The early years are important for learning, but so are the later years.* Although complex environments appear not to be essential for *neurological* development, children often make greater *cognitive* gains—for instance, they have more knowledge and skills, and they earn higher scores on intelligence tests—in enriching preschool programs than they make without such programs (Bronfenbrenner, 1999; Ramey, 1992; Seitz, Rosenbaum, & Apfel, 1985; Zigler & Finn-Stevenson, 1987). Yet the gains made in the early years tend to diminish over time, and may disappear altogether, unless children continue to have stimulating experiences during the school years (Bronfenbrenner, 1999; Campbell & Ramey, 1995; Gustafsson & Undheim, 1996). Educators and policy makers should not put all of their eggs in one age-specific basket; nurturance of learning and cognitive growth must be a long-term enterprise (Brown & Bjorklund, 1998; McCall & Plemons, 2001).

♦ *There is no such thing as teaching to the "left brain" or to the "right brain."* Some writers have suggested that many adults and children specialize in one hemisphere or the other, to the point of being largely "left-brain" or "right-brain" thinkers and learners, and so they urge educators to accommodate the hemispheric preferences of every student. This *dichotomania* is "pseudo-science" that is sometimes used to justify letting students avoid disciplined, rational thinking (Ornstein, 1997; Stanovich, 1998). As we have seen, both hemispheres work in close collaboration in virtually all thinking and learning tasks. In the absence of performing surgical lobotomies (which I obviously don't recommend), attempts to train one side exclusively will be in vain.

♦ *In developmental domains characterized by critical periods, the windows of opportunity often remain at least a crack open.* The concept of *critical period* tells us the best time for a particular ability to be nurtured, but it doesn't necessarily tell us the *only* time. Sometimes, for a variety of reasons, children have little or no exposure to appropriate stimulation during the optimal time frame; for instance, children may not get needed cataract surgery until their families can afford it, and children who are congenitally deaf may not encounter a language they can actually perceive (e.g., American Sign Language) until they reach school age. Rather than fret over what should have happened but didn't, researchers and educators can better serve young people who have missed critical experiences by devising and implementing interventions that enable those individuals to make up some of the lost ground (Bruer, 1999).

♦ *Brain research can help us refine our theories of learning and cognition, but it can tell us little if anything about what to teach or how best to teach it.* As researchers continue to learn more about the architecture and functioning of the brain, they may find evidence that either supports or refutes various psychological explanations of how people learn and think. And as psychologists refine their theories of learning and cognition, they can gradually get a better handle on the kinds of instructional methods and therapeutic interventions that are most likely to foster effective learning and behavior.

Nevertheless, we can probably never boil down specific psychological phenomena—thoughts, knowledge, interpretations, and so on—into strictly physiological entities. For instance, brain research is unlikely to tell us what information and skills are most important for people to have; such things are often culture specific, and decisions about how to prioritize them are value-laden (Bloom & Tinker, 2001; Chalmers, 1996; Gardner, 2000). Nor does brain research give us many clues about how we can best help learners acquire important information and skills (Bandura, 2006; Kuhn & Franklin, 2006; Mayer, 1998). Fortunately, as you will discover in the chapters that follow, psychological theories of learning—theories derived from studies of human behavior rather than from brain anatomy and physiology—have a great deal to offer as we work to identify effective instructional and therapeutic techniques.

SUMMARY

Messages travel through the human nervous system (including the brain and spinal cord) by way of both (a) electrical transmissions that run through individual neurons and (b) chemical transmissions that traverse synapses between neurons. Synapses in the spinal cord are responsible for a few basic reflexes, but by and large the brain is the coordination and decision-making center for the body.

Using a growing arsenal of research methods (animal research, portmortem studies of human brains, case studies of people with pathological conditions, electrical recordings on the scalp, and neuroimaging technology), scientists have learned a great deal about how the brain works. In human beings, the largest and most recently evolved part of the brain—the *forebrain*—predominates in consciousness, thinking, learning, and the many distinctly "human" activities in which people engage. Even small, seemingly simple tasks (e.g., recognizing and understanding a particular word, remembering a specific bit of information) typically involve many parts of the brain (including both the left and right hemispheres) working in concert.

The beginnings of the brain emerge late in the first month of prenatal development; by the second trimester, the great majority of neurons a person will ever possess have formed and are migrating to their final locations. Synapses among neurons begin to form before birth; shortly after birth, the rate of synapse formation increases dramatically, to the point where children have many more synapses than adults do. Over the course of childhood and adolescence, the brain cuts back (i.e., *prunes*) little-used synapses, apparently as a means of adapting to its environment and increasing its efficiency. Although most brain development occurs during the prenatal period and early childhood years, some changes in brain structures and neurotransmitters continue into adolescence and adulthood. Genetic instructions are largely responsible for the course of neurological development, but nutrition, environmental toxins, and learning experiences have effects as well.

Researchers have found evidence for *critical periods* in the development of some basic, long-standing human abilities (e.g., visual perception and language). But many recent human achievements (e.g., literacy, mathematics) can probably be acquired at any age, and certainly the ability to form new synapses (i.e., to *learn*) remains throughout life. Some theorists hypothesize that certain knowledge and skills essential for people's basic survival (e.g., certain elements of language, basic knowledge about the physical world), or at least a predisposition to acquire these things quickly and easily, may be biologically built in.

Occasionally educators have drawn unwarranted implications from brain research. The early years are important, but providing intensive, structured programs for infants and preschoolers is unlikely to prevent synaptic pruning, and any other potential benefits of such programs for neurological development have yet to be demonstrated. Furthermore, efforts to teach to the "left brain" or "right brain" are ultimately in vain because the two hemispheres collaborate in virtually every task and activity. Educators and other practitioners must remember that learning and mastery of complex tasks can continue throughout the lifespan, and in fact many cognitive advancements (e.g., abstract thinking) don't emerge until late childhood, adolescence, or adulthood.

Part Two

Behaviorist Views of Learning

CHAPTER 3

Behaviorism and Classical Conditioning

You might say I have a "thing" about bees. Whenever a bee flies near me, I scream, wave my arms frantically, and run around like a wild woman. Yes, yes, I know, I would be better off if I remained perfectly still, but somehow I just can't control myself. My overreaction to bees is probably a result of several painful bee stings I received as a small child.

One way to explain how people develop involuntary responses to particular stimuli, such as my fearful reaction to bees, is a theory of learning known as *classical conditioning*. Classical conditioning is an example of *behaviorism,* a perspective I introduced in chapter 1. The first major theoretical perspective of learning to emerge in the twentieth century, behaviorism is the topic of chapters 3 through 5. In this chapter, we will identify basic assumptions of the behaviorist approach. We will then examine the nature of classical conditioning, looking at Ivan Pavlov's classic research with dogs and extending his ideas to human learning. Finally, we will derive several educational implications of behaviorist theories. In the following two chapters, we will continue our discussion of behaviorism by examining principles and applications of *instrumental conditioning.*[1]

---

[1]Three additional behaviorist perspectives—those of John Watson, Edwin Guthrie, and Clark Hull—were described in earlier editions of this book but have been omitted from this edition to make room for advancements in contemporary theories and research. You can learn more about these perspectives in the reading "Beyond Pavlov, Thorndike, and Skinner: Other Early Behaviorist Theories" on the book's Companion Website at www.prenhall.com/ormrod.

BASIC ASSUMPTIONS OF BEHAVIORISM

Prior to the twentieth century, the two dominant perspectives in psychology were *structuralism* (e.g., Wilhelm Wundt's work) and *functionalism* (e.g., John Dewey's writings). Although these two perspectives differed considerably in their underlying assumptions and topics of study, they shared a common weakness: They lacked a precise, carefully defined research methodology. The primary means of investigating learning and other psychological phenomena, especially for structuralists, was a method called **introspection**. People were asked to "look" inside their minds and describe what they were thinking. But in the early 1900s, some psychologists began to criticize the introspective approach for its subjectivity and lack of scientific rigor.[2] They worried that without more objective research methods, psychology as a discipline would never be considered a true "science."

Beginning with the efforts of the Russian physiologist Ivan Pavlov (to be described shortly) and the work of American psychologist Edward Thorndike (to be described in chapter 4), a more objective approach to the study of learning—one that focused on observable phenomena rather than on nonobservable mental events—emerged. These researchers looked primarily at *behavior*—something they could easily see and objectively describe—and so the behaviorist movement was born.

Behaviorists have not always agreed on the specific processes that account for learning. Yet many of them have historically shared certain basic assumptions:

- *Principles of learning should apply equally to different behaviors and to different species of animals.* Behaviorists typically assume that human beings and other animals learn in similar ways—an assumption known as **equipotentiality**. As a result of this assumption, behaviorists often apply to human learning the principles that they have derived primarily from research with such animals as rats and pigeons. In their discussions of learning, they often use the term **organism** to refer generically to a member of any species, human and nonhuman alike.

- *Learning processes can be studied most objectively when the focus of study is on stimuli and responses.* Behaviorists believe that psychologists must study learning through objective scientific inquiry, in much the same way that chemists and physicists study phenomena in the physical world. By focusing on two things they can observe and measure—more specifically, by focusing on **stimuli** in the environment and **responses** that organisms make to those stimuli—psychologists can maintain such objectivity. Behaviorist principles of learning often describe a relationship between a stimulus (**S**) and a response (**R**); hence, behaviorism is sometimes called **S–R psychology**.

- *Internal processes are largely excluded from scientific study.* Many behaviorists believe that because we cannot directly observe and measure internal processes (e.g., thoughts, motives, emotions), we should exclude these processes from research investigations, as well as from

---

[2]Later researchers confirmed early behaviorists' suspicion that people cannot always describe their own cognitive processes accurately (e.g., Nisbett & Wilson, 1977; Zuriff, 1985).

explanations of how learning occurs (e.g., Kimble, 2000; Watson, 1925). These behaviorists describe an organism as a "black box," with stimuli impinging on the box and responses emerging from it, but with the things going on inside of it remaining a mystery.[3]

. Not all behaviorists take a strict black-box perspective, however. Some insist that factors within the organism (O), such as motivation and the strength of stimulus–response associations—are also important in understanding learning and behavior (e.g., Hull, 1943, 1952). These **neobehaviorist** theorists are sometimes called S–O–R (stimulus–organism–response) theorists rather than S–R theorists. Especially in recent years, some behaviorists have asserted that they can effectively understand both human and animal behavior only when they consider cognitive processes as well as environmental events (e.g., Church, 1993; DeGrandpre, 2000; Rachlin, 1991; Wasserman, 1993).

◆ *Learning involves a behavior change.* In contrast to the definition of learning I presented in the first chapter, behaviorists have traditionally defined learning as a change in behavior. After all, as we noted in chapter 1, we can determine that learning has occurred only when we see it reflected in someone's actions. Some behaviorists propose that if no behavior change occurs, then learning cannot possibly be taking place at all.

But as behaviorists have increasingly brought cognitive factors into the picture, many have backed off from this behavior-based definition of learning. Instead, they treat learning and behavior as separate, albeit related, entities. A number of psychologists (e.g., Brown & Herrnstein, 1975; Estes, 1969; Herrnstein, 1977; Schwartz & Reisberg, 1991) have suggested that many behaviorist laws are more appropriately applied to an understanding of what influences the *performance* of learned behaviors, rather than what influences learning itself.

◆ *Organisms are born as blank slates.* Aside from certain species-specific instincts (such as the nest-building and migratory behaviors of birds) and biologically based disabilities (e.g., mental retardation and mental illness in human beings), organisms are not born with predispositions to behave in particular ways. Instead, organisms enter the world as "blank slates" (an idea often referred to by the Latin equivalent, *tabula rasa*) on which environmental experiences gradually "write." Because each organism has a unique set of environmental experiences, so, too, will it acquire its own unique set of behaviors.

◆ *Learning is largely the result of environmental events.* Rather than use the term *learning,* behaviorists often speak of **conditioning.** An organism *is conditioned* by environmental events. The passive form of this verb connotes many behaviorists' belief that because learning is the result of one's experiences, learning happens *to* an organism in a way that is often beyond the organism's control.

Some early behaviorists, such as B. F. Skinner, were **determinists:** They proposed that if we were to have complete knowledge of an organism's past experiences and present environmental circumstances, as well as knowledge of any genetic predispositions that the organism might have to behave in certain ways, we would be able to predict the organism's next response with total accuracy. Many contemporary behaviorists do not think so deterministically: In their view, any organism's behavior reflects a certain degree of variability that stimulus–response associations and genetics alone cannot explain (Epstein, 1991; Rachlin, 1991). Looking at how organisms have learned to respond to different stimuli can certainly help us understand why people and other animals behave as they do, but we will never be able to predict their actions with 100% certainty.

---

[3]This idea that the study of human behavior and learning should focus exclusively on stimuli and responses is sometimes called *radical behaviorism.*

♦ *The most useful theories tend to be parsimonious ones.* According to behaviorists, we should explain the learning of all behaviors, from the most simple to the most complex, by as few learning principles as possible; this assumption reflects a preference for **parsimony** (conciseness) in explaining learning and behavior. We will see an example of such parsimony in the first behaviorist theory we explore: classical conditioning.

CLASSICAL CONDITIONING

In the early 1900s, Ivan Pavlov, a Russian physiologist whose work on digestion earned him a Nobel Prize in 1904, was conducting a series of experiments related to salivation in dogs. To study a dog's salivation responses, he would make a surgical incision in the dog's mouth, enabling him to collect and measure its saliva. After strapping the dog into an immobile position, he would give it some powdered meat and observe its resulting salivation. Pavlov noticed that after a few of these experiences, the dog began to salivate before it saw or smelled the meat—in fact, it salivated as soon as the lab assistant entered the room with the meat. Apparently, the dog had learned that the lab assistant meant that food was on the way and responded accordingly. Pavlov devoted a good part of his later years to a systematic study of this learning process on which he had so inadvertently stumbled, and he eventually summarized his research in his book *Conditioned Reflexes* (Pavlov, 1927).

Pavlov's early studies went something like this:

1. He first observed whether the dog salivated in response to a particular stimulus—perhaps to a flash of light, the sound of a tuning fork, or the ringing of a bell. For simplicity's sake, we'll continue with our discussion using a bell as the stimulus in question. As you might imagine, the dog did not find the ringing of a bell especially appetizing and so did not salivate.
2. Pavlov rang the bell again, and this time followed it immediately with the presentation of some powdered meat. The dog, of course, salivated. Pavlov rang the bell several more times, always presenting meat immediately afterward. The dog salivated on each occasion.
3. Pavlov then rang the bell *without* presenting any meat. Nevertheless, the dog salivated. The bell, to which the dog had previously been unresponsive (in step 1), now led to a salivation response. There had been a change in behavior as a result of experience; from the behaviorist perspective, then, *learning* had taken place.

The learning phenomenon that Pavlov observed is now commonly known as **classical conditioning.**[4] Let's analyze the three steps in Pavlov's experiment in much the same way that Pavlov did:

1. A **neutral stimulus (NS)**—a stimulus to which the organism does not respond in any noticeable way—is identified. In the case of Pavlov's dog, the bell was originally a neutral stimulus that did not elicit a salivation response.

---

[4]Some psychologists instead use the term *respondent conditioning,* a label coined by B. F. Skinner to reflect its involuntary-response-to-a-stimulus nature.

Figure 3.1
A classical conditioning analysis
of how Pavlov's dog learned.

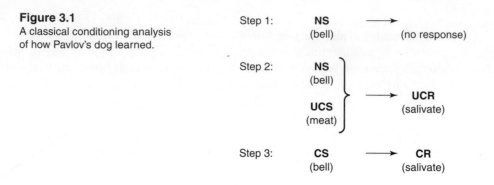

2. The neutral stimulus is presented just before another stimulus, one that *does* lead to a response. This second stimulus is called an **unconditioned stimulus (UCS)**, and the response to it is called an **unconditioned response (UCR)**, because the organism responds to the stimulus unconditionally, without having had to learn to do so. For Pavlov's dog, meat powder was an unconditioned stimulus to which the dog responded with the unconditioned response of salivation.

3. After being paired with an unconditioned stimulus, the previously neutral stimulus now elicits a response, so it is no longer "neutral." The NS has become a **conditioned stimulus (CS)** to which the organism has learned a **conditioned response (CR)**.[5] In Pavlov's experiment, the bell, after being paired with the meat (the unconditioned stimulus) became a conditioned stimulus that led to the conditioned response of salivation. The diagram in Figure 3.1 shows graphically what happened from a classical conditioning perspective.

Pavlov's studies of classical conditioning continued long after these initial experiments, and many of his findings have been replicated with other responses and in other species, including humans. Let's take a closer look at the process of classical conditioning and at some examples of how it might occur in human learning.

The Classical Conditioning Model

Classical conditioning has been demonstrated in many species, not only in dogs and laboratory rats but also in newborn human infants (Lipsitt & Kaye, 1964; Reese & Lipsitt, 1970), human fetuses still in the womb (Macfarlane, 1978), and even organisms as simple as flatworms (R. Thompson & McConnell, 1955). The applicability of classical conditioning clearly extends widely across the animal kingdom.

As Pavlov's experiments illustrated, classical conditioning typically occurs when two stimuli are presented at approximately the same time. One of these stimuli is an unconditioned stimulus: It has previously been shown to elicit an unconditioned response. The second stimulus,

---

[5]Pavlov's original terms were actually unconditio*nal* stimulus, unconditio*nal* response, conditio*nal* stimulus, and conditio*nal* response, but the mistranslations to "uncondition*ed*" remain in most classical conditioning literature.

The conditioned stimulus may
serve as a signal that the
unconditioned stimulus is coming.

through its association with the unconditioned stimulus, begins to elicit a response as well: It becomes a conditioned stimulus that brings about a conditioned response. In many cases, conditioning occurs relatively quickly; it is not unusual for an organism to show a conditioned response after the two stimuli have been presented together only five or six times, and sometimes after only one pairing (Rescorla, 1988).

Classical conditioning is most likely to occur when the conditioned stimulus is presented just *before* (perhaps by half a second) the unconditioned stimulus. For this reason, some psychologists describe classical conditioning as a form of **signal learning.** By being presented first, the conditioned stimulus serves as a signal that the unconditioned stimulus is coming, much as Pavlov's dog might have learned that the sound of a bell indicated that yummy meat powder was on its way.

Classical conditioning usually involves the learning of *involuntary* responses—responses over which the learner has no control. When we say that a stimulus **elicits** a response, we mean that the stimulus brings about a response automatically, without the individual having much control over the occurrence of that response. In most cases, the conditioned response is similar to the unconditioned response, with the two responses differing primarily in terms of which stimulus elicits the response and sometimes in terms of the strength of the response. Occasionally, however, the CR is quite different, perhaps even opposite to, the UCR (I'll give you an example in our discussion of drug addiction a bit later). But in one way or another, the conditioned response allows the organism to anticipate and prepare for the unconditioned stimulus that will soon follow (Rachlin, 1991; Schwartz & Reisberg, 1991).

Classical Conditioning in Human Learning

We can use classical conditioning theory to help us understand how people learn a variety of involuntary responses, especially responses associated with physiological functioning or emotion. For example, people can develop aversions to particular foods as a result of associating those foods with an upset stomach (Garb & Stunkard, 1974; Logue, 1979). To illustrate, after associating the taste of creamy cucumber salad dressing (CS) with the nausea I experienced during pregnancy (UCS), I developed an aversion (CR) to cucumber dressing that lasted for several years.

For many people, darkness is a conditioned stimulus for going to sleep, perhaps in part because it has frequently been associated with fatigue. I once became uncomfortably aware of how conditioned I was when I attended my daughter Tina's "astronomy night" at school. We parents were ushered into a classroom and invited to sit down. Then the lights were turned off, and we watched a half-hour filmstrip describing a NASA space museum. Although I am usually quite alert during the early evening hours, I found myself growing increasingly drowsy, and probably only my upright position in an uncomfortable metal chair kept me from losing consciousness altogether. In that situation, the darkness elicited a go-to-sleep response, and there were no stimuli (certainly not the filmstrip) to elicit a stay-awake response.

Attitudes, too, may be partly the result of classical conditioning. In one study (Olson & Fazio, 2001), college students sat at a computer while various cartoon characters (Pokemon characters with which they were unfamiliar) were presented on the screen. One character was consistently presented in conjunction with words and images that evoked positive feelings (e.g., "excellent," "awesome," pictures of puppies and a hot fudge sundae). A second character was consistently presented along with words and images that evoked negative feelings (e.g., "terrible," "awful," pictures of a cockroach and a man with a knife). Other characters were paired with more neutral words and images. Afterward, when the students were asked to rate some of the cartoon characters and other images they had seen on a scale of −4 (unpleasant) to +4 (pleasant), they rated the character associated with pleasant stimuli far more favorably than the character associated with unpleasant stimuli. Curiously, a positive attitude toward an initially neutral stimulus doesn't necessarily emerge only when people experience it in the company of other pleasant things. Simply experiencing it repeatedly in the *absence* of *un*pleasant things may be enough to engender a preference for it (Zajonc, 2001).

Classical conditioning is also a useful model for explaining some of the fears and phobias that people develop (Mineka & Zinbarg, 2006). For example, my bee phobia can probably be explained by the fact that bees (CS) were previously associated with a painful sting (UCS), such that I became increasingly fearful (CR) of the nasty insects. In a similar way, people who are bitten by a particular breed of dog sometimes become afraid of that breed, or even all dogs.

Probably the best-known example of a classically conditioned fear of an animal is the case of "Little Albert," an infant who learned to fear white rats through a procedure used by John Watson and Rosalie Rayner (1920). Albert was an even-tempered, 11-month-old child who rarely cried or displayed fearful reactions. One day, Albert was shown a white rat. As he reached out and touched the rat, a large steel bar behind him was struck, producing a loud, unpleasant noise. Albert jumped, obviously very upset by the startling noise. Nevertheless, he reached forward to touch the rat with his other hand, and the steel bar was struck once again. After five more pairings of the rat (CS) and the loud noise (UCS), Albert was truly rat-phobic: Whenever he saw the rat he cried hysterically and crawled away as quickly as his hands and knees could move him. Watson and Rayner reported that Albert responded in a similarly fearful manner to a rabbit, a dog, a sealskin coat, cotton wool, and a Santa Claus mask with a fuzzy beard, although none of these had ever been paired with the startling noise. (Watson and Rayner never "undid" their conditioning of poor Albert. Fortunately, the ethical standards of the American Psychological Association now prohibit such negligence.)

Fear of failure is yet another example of a response that may be classically conditioned. In some cases, people who are unusually afraid of failing may have previously associated failure with unpleasant circumstances; perhaps they've associated it with painful punishment from an angry parent or ridicule by insensitive classmates. Yet occasional failure is a natural consequence of attempting new tasks, whether in school, at home, or elsewhere. Teachers and parents must be careful that failure does not become such a strong conditioned stimulus that children resist new activities and challenging but potentially risky tasks.

These examples of classical conditioning in action will, I hope, help you recognize a classically conditioned response when you see one. We now turn to several general phenomena associated with classical conditioning.

Common Phenomena in Classical Conditioning

Pavlov and other behaviorists have described a number of phenomena related to classical conditioning. Here we will examine several of them: associative bias, importance of contingency, extinction, spontaneous recovery, generalization, stimulus discrimination, higher-order conditioning, and sensory preconditioning.

Associative Bias

Characteristics of the would-be conditioned stimulus affect the degree to which conditioning occurs. The more noticeable (*salient*) a neutral stimulus—the extent to which it is bright, loud, or otherwise intense—the more likely it is to become a conditioned stimulus when presented in conjunction with an unconditioned stimulus (Rachlin, 1991; Schwartz & Reisberg, 1991). Furthermore, some stimuli are especially likely to become associated with certain unconditioned stimuli; for example, food is more likely to become a conditioned stimulus associated with nausea (a UCS) than, say, a flash of light or the sound of a tuning fork. In other words, associations between certain stimuli are more likely to be made than are associations between others—a phenomenon known as **associative bias** (Garcia & Koelling, 1966; Hollis, 1997; Schwartz & Reisberg, 1991). Quite possibly, evolution has been at work here: Our ancestors could better adapt to their environments when they were predisposed to make associations that reflected true cause–effect relationships, such as associating nausea with the new food that instigated it (Öhman & Mineka, 2003; Timberlake & Lucas, 1989).

Importance of Contingency

Pavlov proposed that classical conditioning occurs when the unconditioned stimulus and the would-be conditioned stimulus are presented at approximately the same time; that is, there must be **contiguity** between the two stimuli. But contiguity alone seems to be insufficient. As noted earlier, classical conditioning is most likely to occur when the conditioned stimulus is presented just *before* the unconditioned stimulus. It is less likely to occur when the CS and UCS are presented at *exactly* the same time, and it rarely occurs when the CS is presented *after* the UCS (e.g., R. R. Miller & Barnet, 1993). And in some cases, people develop an aversion to certain foods (recall my aversion to creamy cucumber dressing) when the delay between the conditioned stimulus (food) and the unconditioned stimulus (nausea) is as much as 24 hours (Logue, 1979).

More recent theorists (e.g., Gallistel & Gibbon, 2001; Granger & Schlimmer, 1986; Rachlin, 1991; Rescorla, 1988) have suggested that **contingency** is the essential condition: The potential conditioned stimulus must occur when the unconditioned stimulus is likely to follow—in other words, when the CS serves as a signal that the UCS is probably on its way (recall my earlier reference to "signal learning"). When two stimuli that are usually presented separately occur together a few times by coincidence, classical conditioning is unlikely to occur.

Extinction

Let's return for a moment to Pavlov's dog. Remember that the dog learned to salivate at the sound of a bell alone after the bell had rung in conjunction with meat powder on several occasions. But what would happen if the bell continued to ring over and over without the meat powder's ever again being presented along with it? Pavlov discovered that repeated presentations of the conditioned stimulus *without* the unconditioned stimulus led to successively weaker and weaker conditioned responses. Eventually, the dog no longer salivated at the sound of the bell; in other words, the conditioned response disappeared. Pavlov called this phenomenon **extinction.**

Sometimes conditioned responses will extinguish, and sometimes they will not. The unpredictability of extinction is a source of frustration to anyone working with people who have acquired undesirable, yet involuntary, conditioned responses. Later in the chapter, we will identify some reasons why extinction doesn't always occur.

Spontaneous Recovery

Even though Pavlov quickly extinguished his dog's conditioned salivation response by repeatedly presenting the bell in the absence of meat powder, when he entered his laboratory the following day he discovered that the bell once again elicited salivation in the dog, almost as if extinction had never taken place. This reappearance of the salivation response after it had previously been extinguished is something Pavlov called **spontaneous recovery.**

In more general terms, spontaneous recovery is a recurrence of a conditioned response when a period of extinction is followed by a rest period. For example, if I am near lots of bees for a period of time, I eventually settle down and regain my composure. However, my first response on a later encounter with a bee is to fly off the handle once again.

Pavlov found that when a conditioned response appears in spontaneous recovery, it is typically weaker than the original conditioned response and extinguishes more quickly. In situations in which several spontaneous recoveries are observed (each one occurring after a period of rest), the reappearing CR becomes progressively weaker and disappears increasingly rapidly.

Generalization

You may recall that Little Albert, after being conditioned to fear a white rat, also became afraid of a rabbit, a dog, a white fur coat, cotton wool, and a fuzzy-bearded Santa Claus mask. When learners respond to other stimuli in the same way that they respond to conditioned stimuli, **generalization** is occurring. The more similar a stimulus is to the conditioned stimulus, the greater the probability of generalization. Albert exhibited fear of all objects that were white and fuzzy like the rat, but he was not afraid of his nonwhite, nonfuzzy toy blocks. In a similar way, a child who fears an abusive father may generalize that fear to other men, but not to women.

Generalization of conditioned responses to new stimuli is a common phenomenon (Bouton, 1994). In some cases, generalization of conditioned fear responses may actually increase over time; that is, as time goes on, an individual may become fearful of an increasing number of objects (McAllister & McAllister, 1965). Thus, dysfunctional conditioned responses that do not quickly extinguish may actually become more troublesome as the years go by.

Stimulus Discrimination

Pavlov observed that when he conditioned a dog to salivate in response to a high-pitched tone, the dog would generalize that conditioned response to a low-pitched tone. To teach the dog the difference between the two tones, Pavlov repeatedly presented the high tone in conjunction with meat powder and presented the low tone without meat. After several such presentations of the two tones, the dog eventually learned to salivate only at the high tone. In Pavlov's terminology, *differentiation* between the two tones had taken place. Psychologists today more frequently use the term **stimulus discrimination** for this phenomenon.

Stimulus discrimination occurs when one stimulus (the CS+) is presented in conjunction with an unconditioned stimulus, and another stimulus (the CS−) is presented in the absence of the UCS. The individual acquires a conditioned response to the CS+ but does not generalize the response to the CS−. For example, if a child who is abused by her father simultaneously has positive interactions with other adult men, she is not as likely to generalize her fear of her father to those other individuals.

Higher-Order Conditioning

Pavlov also observed a phenomenon known as **second-order conditioning,** or more generally **higher-order conditioning.** When a dog had been conditioned to salivate at the sound of a bell, and the bell was later presented in conjunction with a neutral stimulus such as a flash of light, that neutral stimulus would also begin to elicit a salivation response, even though it had never been directly associated with meat. In other words, the light flash became a conditioned stimulus through its pairing, not with the unconditioned stimulus but with another conditioned stimulus.

Higher-order conditioning works like this: First, a neutral stimulus (NS_1) becomes a conditioned stimulus (CS_1) by being paired with an unconditioned stimulus (UCS), so that it soon elicits a conditioned response (CR). Next, a second neutral stimulus (NS_2) is paired with CS_1, and it, too, begins to elicit a conditioned response; that second stimulus has also become a conditioned stimulus (CS_2).

A diagram of higher-order conditioning appears in Figure 3.2. Steps 1 and 2 depict the original conditioning; steps 3 and 4 depict higher-order conditioning, in which a second neutral stimulus becomes a CS_2 by virtue of its being paired with the CS_1.

Higher-order conditioning is a possible explanation for some of the fears that students exhibit in the classroom (e.g., Klein, 1987). Let's say, first of all, that failure has previously been associated with painful physical punishment. Then another situation—perhaps a test, an oral

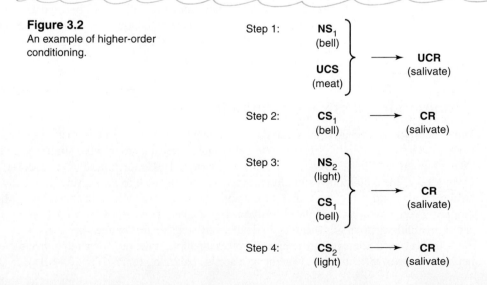

Figure 3.2
An example of higher-order conditioning.

presentation in front of classmates, or even school itself—becomes associated with failure. The painful punishment is the UCS. Failure, originally a neutral stimulus (NS_1), becomes a CS_1 after its association with the UCS. Some other aspect of school (e.g., a test), while first a neutral stimulus (NS_2), becomes an additional conditioned stimulus (CS_2) through its association with CS_1. In this way, a student may develop test anxiety, fear of public speaking, or even school phobia—fear of school itself.

Higher-order conditioning probably also explains the attitudes that college students developed in the Pokemon study (Olson & Fazio, 2001) described earlier. People aren't born with particular feelings about the words *awesome* or *awful,* nor do they necessarily have built-in reactions to pictures of hot fudge sundaes or cockroaches. Rather, people probably acquire particular feelings about the words and images through their experiences over time, to the point where these stimuli can provide a starting point for further classical conditioning.

Sensory Preconditioning

Higher-order conditioning is one way an individual can develop a conditioned response to a stimulus that has never been directly paired with an unconditioned stimulus. **Sensory preconditioning** is very similar to higher-order conditioning, except that the steps occur in a different order. Let me first illustrate the process by once again conditioning Pavlov's poor, overexploited dog. Suppose that we first present the sound of a bell and a flash of light simultaneously. Then we pair the bell with meat powder. Not only does the dog salivate in response to the sound of a bell, but we discover that it also salivates in response to the flash of light!

In more general terms, sensory preconditioning occurs like this: First, two neutral stimuli (NS_1 and NS_2) are presented simultaneously. Then one of these neutral stimuli (NS_1) is associated with an unconditioned stimulus (UCS), thus becoming a conditioned stimulus (CS_1) and eliciting a conditioned response (CR). In cases of sensory preconditioning, the second neutral stimulus (NS_2) *also* elicits the conditioned response (i.e., NS_2 has become CS_2) by virtue of its prior association with CS_1.

Klein (1987) has suggested that sensory preconditioning may be an alternative explanation for some cases of test anxiety. School (NS_1) is first associated with tests (NS_2). If school is later associated with some traumatic event (UCS), then not only will school become a conditioned stimulus (CS_1) eliciting anxiety (CR) but tests may become a conditioned stimulus (CS_2) as well. A diagram of how test anxiety might develop through sensory preconditioning is presented in Figure 3.3.

conhecimento

Cognition in Classical Conditioning

Many theorists now believe that classical conditioning often involves the formation of associations not between two stimuli but between internal *mental representations* of those stimuli (e.g., Bouton, 1994; Forsyth & Eifert, 1998; R. R. Miller & Barnet, 1993; Rachlin, 1991; Rescorla, 1988). Furthermore, the conditioned stimulus may enable an organism to *predict* (in a decidedly mental fashion) that the unconditioned stimulus is coming (Hollis, 1997; Martin & Levey, 1987; Mineka & Zinbarg, 2006; Rescorla, 1967, 1988). As you can see, then, behaviorists are now beginning to talk about the thinking processes that they so deliberately steered clear of in earlier years.

Classical conditioning doesn't *always* involve cognition, however. To be more precise, it doesn't necessarily involve conscious awareness (Baccus, Baldwin, & Packer, 2004; Papka, Ivry, &

Figure 3.3
An example of sensory preconditioning.

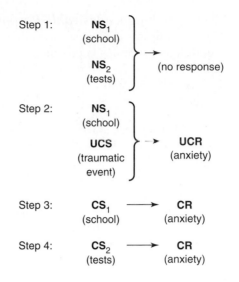

Woodruff-Pak, 1997; Schwartz & Reisberg, 1991).[6] For instance, when organisms receive certain drugs (e.g., morphine or insulin), the drugs, as unconditioned stimuli, naturally lead to certain physiological responses (e.g., reduced pain sensitivity or hypoglycemia). Curiously, stimuli presented prior to these drugs—perhaps a light, a tone, or the environmental context more generally—begin to elicit an *opposite* response (e.g., increased pain sensitivity or hyperglycemia), presumably to prepare for—in this case, to counteract—the pharmaceutical stimuli that will soon follow (e.g., Flaherty et al., 1980; Siegel, 1975, 1979).

Such physiological responses, which are almost certainly not consciously controlled by the recipients of the drugs, are one likely explanation for people's addictions to nicotine, alcohol, and street drugs. When habitual smokers and other substance abusers return to environments in which they have previously used an addictive substance, their bodies respond in counteractive ways that make the substance even more desirable or seemingly necessary. Meanwhile, they develop greater tolerance to their substance of choice and need increasing quantities to gain the same "high" or other sought-after physiological state (Conklin, 2006; McDonald & Siegel, 2004; Siegel, 2005; Siegel, Baptista, Kim, McDonald, & Weise-Kelly, 2000; Siegel, Hinson, Krank, & McCully, 1982).

Changing Undesirable Conditioned Responses

Conditioned responses are often difficult to eliminate because they are involuntary: People have little or no control over them. Yet some classically conditioned responses (e.g., some irrational fears) may be detrimental to an individual's functioning. How can we get rid of counterproductive conditioned responses? Extinction and counterconditioning are two possible methods.

---

[6]Some theorists have suggested that the amygdala plays a key role in "unthinking" forms of classical conditioning (Byrnes, 2001; LeDoux, 2003). As you may recall from chapter 2, this structure within the limbic system is actively involved in connecting particular emotional reactions to particular stimuli.

Extinguishing Undesirable Responses

One obvious way to eliminate a conditioned response is through the process of extinction. If the conditioned stimulus is presented in the absence of the unconditioned stimulus frequently enough, the conditioned response should disappear. Often this is exactly what happens.

Unfortunately, however, extinction is notoriously undependable as a means of eliminating conditioned responses: It simply doesn't always work. There are at least three reasons why:

1. The speed at which extinction occurs is unpredictable. If, during the conditioning process, the conditioned stimulus was sometimes presented in conjunction with the unconditioned stimulus but sometimes alone (i.e., the stimulus pairings were inconsistent), extinction is apt to be especially slow (Humphreys, 1939).
2. People (and many other species as well) tend to avoid a stimulus they have learned to fear, thus reducing the chances that they might eventually encounter the conditioned stimulus in the absence of the unconditioned stimulus. (We'll look more closely at avoidance learning in chapter 4.)
3. Even when a response has been extinguished, it may reappear through spontaneous recovery. We can never be totally sure when a response will spontaneously recover and when it will not. Spontaneous recovery is especially likely to occur if extinction has occurred in only one context; the conditioned response is apt to reappear in contexts in which extinction has not taken place (Bouton, 1994).

Counterconditioning More Desirable Responses

In an alternative procedure to extinction, called **counterconditioning**, one conditioned response is replaced with a new, more productive one. Counterconditioning tends to be more effective than extinction in eliminating undesirable conditioned responses. It also decreases the chances that those responses will recur through spontaneous recovery.

Mary Cover Jones's (1924) classic work with "Little Peter" provides an excellent example of counterconditioning. Peter was a 2-year-old boy who had somehow acquired a fear of rabbits. To rid Peter of his fear, Jones placed him in a high chair and gave him some candy. As he ate, she brought a rabbit into the far side of the same room. Under different circumstances the rabbit might have elicited anxiety; however, the pleasure Peter felt as he ate the candy was a stronger response and essentially overpowered any anxiety he might have felt about the rabbit's presence. Jones repeated the same procedure every day over a 2-month period, each time putting Peter in a high chair with candy and bringing the rabbit slightly closer than she had the time before, and Peter's anxiety about rabbits eventually disappeared.

In general, counterconditioning involves the following steps:

1. A new response that is **incompatible** with the existing conditioned response is chosen. Two responses are incompatible with each other when they cannot be performed at the same time. Because classically conditioned responses are often emotional in nature, an incompatible response is often some sort of opposite emotional reaction. For example, in the case of Little Peter, happiness was used as an incompatible response for fear. An alternative would be any response involving relaxation, because fear and anxiety create bodily tension.
2. A stimulus that elicits the incompatible response must be identified; for example, candy elicited a "happy" response for Peter. If we want to help someone develop

a happy response to a stimulus that has previously elicited displeasure, we need to find a stimulus that already elicits pleasure—perhaps a friend, a party, or a favorite food. If we want someone instead to acquire a relaxation response, we might ask that person to imagine lying in a cool, fragrant meadow or on a lawn chair by a swimming pool.

3. The stimulus that elicits the new response is presented to the individual, and the conditioned stimulus eliciting the undesirable conditioned response is *gradually* introduced into the situation. In treating Peter's fear of rabbits, Jones first gave Peter some candy; she then presented the rabbit at some distance from Peter, only gradually bringing it closer and closer in successive sessions. The trick in counterconditioning is to ensure that the stimulus eliciting the desirable response always has a *stronger* effect than the stimulus eliciting the undesirable response; otherwise, the latter response might prevail.

Counterconditioning provides a means for decreasing or eliminating many conditioned anxiety responses. For instance, in **systematic desensitization**, people who are excessively anxious in the presence of certain stimuli are asked to relax while imagining themselves in increasingly stressful situations involving those stimuli; in doing so, they gradually replace anxiety with a relaxation response (Wolpe, 1958, 1969; Wolpe & Plaud, 1997). Alternatively, people might virtually "experience" a series of stressful situations through the use of goggles and computer-generated images, all the while making a concerted effort to relax (P. Anderson, Rothbaum, & Hodges, 2003; Garcia-Palacios, Hoffman, Carlin, Furness, & Botella, 2002).

Systematic desensitization has been widely used as a means of treating such problems as test anxiety and fear of public speaking (Hughes, 1988; Garcia-Palacios et al., 2002; Morris, Kratochwill, & Aldridge, 1988; Silverman & Kearney, 1991). I should point out, however, that treating test anxiety alone, without remediating possible academic sources of a student's poor test performance as well, may reduce test anxiety without any concurrent improvement in test scores (Covington, 1992; Naveh-Benjamin, 1991; Tryon, 1980).

A technique I recommend to many graduate students who dread their required statistics courses because of mathematics anxiety is to find a math textbook that begins well below their own skill level—at the level of basic number facts, if necessary—so that the problems are not anxiety arousing. As they work through the text, the students begin to associate mathematics with success rather than failure. Programmed instruction (described in chapter 5) is another technique that can be useful in reducing anxiety about a given subject matter, because it allows a student to progress through potentially difficult material in small, easy steps.

EDUCATIONAL IMPLICATIONS OF BEHAVIORIST ASSUMPTIONS AND CLASSICAL CONDITIONING

From what we have learned about behaviorist ideas so far, we can derive several implications for instructional practice.

◆ *Practice is important.* From a behaviorist perspective, people are more likely to learn when they have a chance to *behave*—for instance, when they can talk, write, experiment, or demonstrate (e.g., see Drevno et al., 1994). Ideally, then, students should be active respondents throughout the learning process, rather than simply passive recipients of whatever information or skill is being taught.

Many behaviorists have stressed the idea that repetition of stimulus–response associations strengthens those associations. If people need to learn responses to particular stimuli thoroughly, then practice is essential. For example, students will learn basic addition and subtraction facts better and recall them more quickly if they repeat those facts numerous times (perhaps through the use of flash cards, or perhaps by applying those facts frequently in mathematical problem-solving tasks). In a similar way, many reading teachers believe that the best way for students to improve their reading level is simply to read, read, read.

◆ *Students should encounter academic subject matter in a positive climate and associate it with positive emotions.* The durability and generalizability of some classically conditioned responses point to the need for a positive classroom climate for students beginning on Day 1. Students should experience academic tasks in contexts that elicit pleasant emotions—feelings such as enjoyment, enthusiasm, and excitement—rather than in contexts that elicit anxiety, disappointment, or anger. When students associate academic subject matter with positive feelings, they are more likely to pursue it of their own accord. For instance, when children's early experiences with books are enjoyable ones, they are more likely to read frequently and widely in later years (Baker, Scher, & Mackler, 1997).

In contrast, when schoolwork or a teacher is associated with punishment, humiliation, failure, or frustration, school and its curriculum can become sources of excessive anxiety. Some classroom activities—including tests, oral presentations, and difficult subject matter—are especially likely to be associated with unpleasant circumstances such as failure or embarrassment, and students may soon become anxious when involved in them. Consider mathematics as an example. Young children typically enjoy counting activities, but as they move through the grade levels and encounter increasing challenging mathematical tasks, many begin to get frustrated and acquire feelings of anxiety and dislike for the discipline (Stodolsky, Salk, & Glaessner, 1991). Part of the problem may lie in the tendency for schools to teach some mathematical concepts before children are cognitively ready to deal with them. For instance, many developmental researchers have found that the ability to understand the concept of *proportion,* which underlies fractions and decimals, tends not to appear until age 11 or 12 at the earliest (Schliemann & Carraher, 1993; Tourniaire & Pulos, 1985; also see the discussion of Piaget's theory in chapter 11). Yet schools typically introduce fractions and decimals sometime around third or fourth grade, when students are only 8 to 10 years old.

Educators have often argued that school should be a place where a student encounters more success than failure, and classical conditioning provides a justification for their argument. To maximize such success, teachers should have students' existing knowledge, skills, and cognitive maturity in mind when they plan their curriculum, and they should provide the resources and assistance that students need to accomplish classroom tasks successfully. They should also take special precautions when asking students to engage in any potentially "risky" activities. For instance, when students must give oral presentations in class, their teacher might offer specific suggestions about what material to present and how to present it in such a way that classmates will react positively.

This is not to say, however, that students should *never* experience failure; as we will discover in chapter 11, challenging activities are more likely to promote cognitive growth than easy ones, and errors are inevitable when students must wrestle with difficult problems and tasks. But when students experience failure *too* frequently, either in their schoolwork or in their social relationships, school may quickly become a conditioned stimulus that leads to such counterproductive conditioned responses as fear and anxiety. These responses, once conditioned, may be very resistant to extinction and may interfere with a student's ability to learn effectively for years to come.

◆ *To break a bad habit, a learner must replace one S–R connection with another one.* You might think of a *bad habit* as an undesirable stimulus–response association. One early behaviorist (E. R. Guthrie, 1935) proposed three ingenious techniques specifically designed to break habits; the second and third reflect aspects of the *counterconditioning* approach described earlier:

- *Exhaustion method:* One way to break a stimulus–response habit is to continue to present the stimulus until the individual is too tired to respond in the habitual way. At that point, a new response will occur and a new S–R habit will form. For example, when breaking a bucking bronco, the persistent rider (the stimulus) stays on the horse's back until the horse is too exhausted to continue bucking; a new response (behavior reflecting acceptance of the rider, such as standing still) then becomes associated with the "rider" stimulus. Similarly, a teacher might eliminate a child's spitball-throwing behavior by having that child stay after school to make and throw spitballs until the child is too tired to continue.
- *Threshold method:* Another way of breaking a habit is to begin by presenting the stimulus very faintly, so that the individual does not respond to it in the habitual manner. The intensity of the stimulus is then increased so gradually that the individual continues not to respond to it. For example, when a child has test anxiety (in other words, when a test stimulus leads to an anxiety response), a teacher might eliminate the child's anxiety by first presenting tasks that are enjoyable for the child and that only remotely resemble a test. Over time, the teacher can present a series of tasks that increasingly (but gradually) begin to take on testlike qualities.
- *Incompatibility method:* A third method for breaking an S–R connection is to present the stimulus when the habitual response cannot occur and when an opposite, or *incompatible,* response will occur. For example, imagine a classroom of highly achievement-motivated students who are overly competitive with one another. To reduce such a competitive spirit, the teacher might divide the class into small groups and assign each group an academic task that requires cooperation rather than competition (e.g., developing an argument for one side of an issue in a class debate). Assigning grades on the basis of group performance rather than individual performance should further increase the likelihood that students will cooperate rather than compete. Under such conditions, cooperative behavior should replace competitive behavior.

◆ *Assessing learning involves looking for behavior changes.* Regardless of how effective a certain activity, lecture, or set of curriculum materials might potentially be, teachers should never assume that students are learning anything unless they actually observe students' behaviors changing as a result of instruction. Only behavior changes—for example, higher test scores, improved athletic performance, more appropriate social interaction skills, or better study habits—can ultimately confirm that learning has taken place.

SUMMARY

Behaviorism encompasses a group of theories that share several common assumptions, including the generalizability of learning principles across species, the importance of focusing on observable events, and the "blank slate" nature of organisms.

Early behaviorists insisted that psychology could be a true science only if it defined learning as a behavior change, and they focused solely on stimulus–response relationships. Today, however, some behaviorists make a distinction between learning and behavior, and some believe that relationships between stimuli and responses can be better understood when cognitive factors are also considered.

One groundbreaking researcher in the behaviorist tradition was Ivan Pavlov, who proposed that many involuntary responses are acquired through a process of *classical conditioning*. Such conditioning occurs when two stimuli are presented close together in time. One is an *unconditioned stimulus* that already elicits an *unconditioned response*. The second stimulus, through its association with the unconditioned stimulus, begins to elicit a response as well: It becomes a *conditioned stimulus* that brings about a *conditioned response*. But if the conditioned stimulus is later presented numerous times in the absence of the unconditioned stimulus, the conditioned response decreases and may eventually disappear (*extinction*). Nevertheless, it may reappear after a period of rest (*spontaneous recovery*).

Once an organism has learned to make a conditioned response in the presence of one conditioned stimulus, it may respond in the same way to a similar stimulus (*generalization*) unless the latter stimulus has repeatedly been experienced in the absence of the unconditioned stimulus (*stimulus discrimination*). Classically conditioned associations can build on one another through the processes of *higher-order condition-*

ing and *sensory preconditioning;* in both cases, a neutral stimulus may become a conditioned stimulus (eliciting a conditioned response), not directly by its association with the unconditioned stimulus but indirectly by its association with a stimulus that either has been or will be experienced in conjunction with the UCS.

Classical conditioning provides one possible explanation of how human beings acquire physiological responses (e.g., increased sensitivity to pain), emotional responses (e.g., anxiety), and attitudes (e.g., like or dislike) toward particular stimuli. It also offers two strategies for eliminating such responses: extinction and *counterconditioning* (i.e., replacing unproductive S–R relationships with more productive ones).

Our discussion of behaviorism thus far has yielded several educational implications. First, active responding and practice are important ingredients in effective learning. Second, the classical conditioning paradigm underscores the importance of helping learners experience academic subject matter in contexts that elicit pleasant rather than unpleasant emotions. Third, eliminating undesirable behaviors (e.g., breaking a "bad habit" or avoiding growth-producing situations) must in one way or another involve replacing existing S–R connections with more productive ones. Finally, teachers can ultimately determine that learning has occurred *only* when they observe changes in students' behaviors.

CHAPTER 4

Instrumental Conditioning

When my children were small, they often behaved in ways that they had learned would improve their circumstances. For example, when Alex needed money to buy something he desperately wanted, he engaged in behaviors he never did otherwise—for example, mowing the lawn or scrubbing the bathtub. Jeff had less interest in money than his older brother, but he would readily clean up the disaster area he called his bedroom if doing so enabled him to have a friend spend the night.

My children also learned *not* to engage in behaviors that led to unpleasant consequences. For instance, soon after Tina reached adolescence, she discovered the thrill of sneaking out late at night to join her friends at a local park or convenience store. Somehow Tina thought she would never be missed if she placed a doll's head on her pillow and stuffed a blanket under her bedspread to form the shape of a body. I can't say for sure how many times Tina tried this, but on two occasions I found the pseudo-Tina in bed and promptly locked the bedroom window that Tina had intended to use on her return; given the chilly night air, Tina had no choice but to ring the doorbell to gain admittance to the house. After being grounded for two weeks for each infraction, Tina started taking her curfew more seriously.

The idea that consequences affect behavior has influenced psychologists' thinking for more than 100 years and has been especially prominent in behaviorist learning theories. In particular, behaviorists talk about **instrumental conditioning:** Humans and nonhuman animals alike tend to behave in ways that bring them desirable consequences or enable them to avoid unpleasant ones.

In this chapter we will examine the work of two early American behaviorists—Edward Thorndike and B. F. Skinner—who emphasized the importance of consequences in learning. We will also look at research findings regarding the particular effects that rewards (more often called *reinforcers*) and punishments are likely to have on human behavior. At numerous points in the chapter we'll derive strategies for classroom practice, but we will save more systematic applications of instrumental conditioning for chapter 5, where we can give them our full attention.

THORNDIKE'S EARLY RESEARCH

In 1898, Edward Thorndike introduced a theory of learning that emphasized the role of experience in the strengthening and weakening of stimulus-response connections; this perspective is sometimes referred to as **connectionism**[1] (Thorndike, 1898, 1911, 1913). In his classic first experiment (his doctoral dissertation), Thorndike placed a cat in a "puzzle box" with a door that opened when a certain device (e.g., a wire loop) was appropriately manipulated. Thorndike observed the cat initiating numerous, apparently random movements in its attempts to get out of the box; eventually, by chance, the cat triggered the mechanism that opened the door and allowed escape. When returned to the box a second time, the cat again engaged in trial-and-error movements but managed to escape in less time than it had previously. With successive trials in the box, the cat, although continuing to demonstrate trial-and-error behavior, managed to escape within shorter and shorter time periods.

From his observations of cats in the puzzle box, Thorndike concluded that the learning of a response to a stimulus (e.g., making a particular response to a puzzle box's release mechanism) is affected by the consequence of that behavior (e.g., escape from a confining situation). We can sum up Thorndike's *law of effect* as follows:

> Responses to a situation that are followed by satisfaction are strengthened; responses that are followed by discomfort are weakened.

According to Thorndike, learning consists of trial-and-error behavior and a gradual "stamping in" of some behaviors and "stamping out" of others. More specifically, rewarded responses increase, and punished responses diminish and disappear.

Thorndike's original law of effect implied that reward and punishment have opposite but equal effects on behavior: One strengthens and the other weakens. But Thorndike's later research (1932a, 1932b) indicated that punishment may not be terribly effective in weakening responses. In one experiment (Thorndike, 1932a), college students completed a multiple-choice Spanish vocabulary test in which they were to choose the English translation for each of a long list of Spanish words. Every time a student chose the correct English word out of five alternatives, the experimenter said "Right!" (presumably rewarding the response); every time a student chose an incorrect alternative, the experimenter said "Wrong!" (presumably punishing the response). In

---

[1]Thorndike's connectionism should not be confused with a more contemporary perspective, known as either connectionism or parallel distributed processing, which we will discuss in chapter 9.

responding to the same multiple-choice questions over a series of trials, the students increased the responses for which they had been rewarded but did not necessarily decrease those for which they had been punished. In his *revised law of effect,* Thorndike (1935) continued to maintain that rewards strengthen the behaviors they follow, but he deemphasized the role of punishment. Instead, he proposed that punishment has an *indirect* effect on learning: As a result of experiencing an annoying state of affairs, an organism may engage in certain other behaviors (e.g., crying or running away) that interfere with performance of the punished response.

Not all of Thorndike's ideas have stood the test of time. His belief that satisfying consequences bring about changes in behavior—in other words, that rewards promote learning—continues to be a key component of behaviorist perspectives today. His views on punishment have been more controversial. As you'll see later in the chapter, many psychologists believe that under the right conditions, punishment can be quite effective in reducing behavior.

REWARDS AND REINFORCEMENT

Partly as a result of Thorndike's early findings, research has focused more heavily on the effects of pleasant consequences than on the effects of unpleasant ones. In the upcoming pages, we will look at Skinner's version of the "reward" part of Thorndike's law of effect; we will then consider a variety of consequences that people might find rewarding (reinforcing).

Skinner's Operant Conditioning

B. F. Skinner (1938, 1953, 1958, 1966b, 1971, 1989; Skinner & Epstein, 1982) is unquestionably the best-known learning theorist in the behaviorist tradition. Like Thorndike, Skinner proposed that organisms acquire those behaviors that are followed by certain consequences. To study the effects of consequences using precise measurement of responses in a carefully controlled environment, Skinner developed a piece of equipment, now known as a *Skinner box,* that has gained widespread popularity in animal learning research. As shown in Figure 4.1, the Skinner box used in studying rat behavior includes a metal bar that, when pushed down, causes a food tray to swing into reach long enough for the rat to grab a food pellet. In the pigeon version of the box, instead of a metal bar, a lighted plastic disk (a "key") is located on one wall; when the pigeon pecks the key, the food tray swings into reach for a short time.

Skinner found that rats will learn to press metal bars, and pigeons will learn to peck at round plastic disks, to get pellets of food. From his observations of rats and pigeons in their respective Skinner boxes under varying conditions, Skinner (1938) formulated a basic principle of **operant conditioning,** which can be paraphrased as follows:

> A response that is followed by a reinforcer is strengthened and is therefore more likely to occur again.

In other words, responses that are reinforced tend to increase in frequency. Because a response increase is a change in behavior, then, from a behaviorist viewpoint, reinforcement brings about learning.

Figure 4.1
A prototypic Skinner box: The food tray swings into reach to provide reinforcement.

Metal Bar

Skinner intentionally used the term *reinforcer* instead of *reward* to describe a consequence that increases the frequency of a behavior. The word *reward* implies that the stimulus or event following a behavior is somehow both pleasant and desirable, an implication that Skinner tried to avoid for two reasons. First, some individuals will work for what others believe to be unpleasant consequences; for example, as a child, my daughter Tina occasionally did something she knew would irritate me because she enjoyed watching me blow my stack. Second, like many behaviorists, Skinner preferred that psychological principles be restricted to the domain of objectively observable events. A reinforcer is defined not by allusion to "pleasantness" or "desirability"—both of which involve subjective judgments—but instead by its effect on behavior:

> A **reinforcer** is a stimulus or event that increases the frequency of a response it follows. (The act of following a response with a reinforcer is called **reinforcement.**)

Notice how I have just defined a reinforcer totally in terms of observable phenomena, without reliance on any subjective judgment.

Now that I have given you definitions of both operant conditioning and a reinforcer, I need to point out a major problem with my definitions: Taken together, they constitute circular reasoning. I have said that operant conditioning is an increase in a behavior when it is followed by a reinforcer, but I cannot seem to define a reinforcer in any other way except to say that it increases behavior. I am therefore using reinforcement to explain a behavior increase, and a behavior increase to explain reinforcement! Fortunately, an article by Meehl (1950) has enabled learning theorists to get out of this circular mess by pointing out the **transituational generality** of a reinforcer: Any single reinforcer—whether it be food, money, an opportunity to see a good friend, or something else altogether—is likely to increase many different behaviors in many different situations.

Operant conditioning has proven to be a very useful and powerful explanation of why human beings often act as they do, and its applications to instructional situations are almost limitless. Virtually any behavior—academic, social, psychomotor—can be learned or modified through operant conditioning. As a teacher, I keep reminding myself of what student behaviors I want to increase and try to follow those behaviors with positive consequences. For example, when typically quiet students raise their hands to answer a question or make a comment, I call on them and give them whatever positive feedback I can. I also try to make my classes lively, interesting, and humorous, as well as informative, so that students are reinforced for coming to class in the first place.

Unfortunately, undesirable behaviors can be reinforced just as easily as desirable ones. Aggression and criminal activity often lead to successful outcomes: Crime usually *does* pay. In school settings, disruptive behaviors may often get teachers' and classmates' attention when more productive behaviors do not (e.g., Craft, Alberg, & Heward, 1998; Flood, Wilder, Flood, & Masuda, 2002; Taylor & Romanczyk, 1994). Getting "sick" allows the school-phobic child to stay home from school. Students occasionally come to me at the end of the semester pleading for a higher grade than their class performance has warranted or else for the opportunity to complete an extra-credit project. I almost invariably turn them down, for a simple reason: I want good grades to result from good study habits and high achievement throughout the semester, not from begging behavior at my office door. Teachers must be extremely careful about what they reinforce and what they do not.

Important Conditions for Operant Conditioning

Three important conditions are necessary for operant conditioning to occur:

♦ *The reinforcer must follow the response.* "Reinforcers" that precede a response rarely have an effect on the response. For example, many years ago, a couple of instructors at my university were concerned that the practice of assigning course grades made students overly anxious and so interfered with learning. Thus, the instructors announced on the first day of class that everyone would receive a final course grade of A. Many students never attended class after that first day, so there was little learning with which any grade would interfere. Reinforcers must always, always *follow* the desired behavior.

♦ *The reinforcer must follow immediately.* A reinforcer tends to reinforce the response that immediately preceded it. Thus, reinforcement is less effective when its presentation is delayed: In the meantime, an organism may make one or more responses that are reinforced instead. Once, when I was teaching a pigeon named Ethel to peck a lighted plastic disk, I made a serious mistake: I waited too long after she had pecked the disk before reinforcing her, and in the meantime she had begun to turn around. After eating her food pellet, Ethel began to spin frantically in counterclockwise circles, and it was several minutes before I could get her back to the pecking response I had in mind for her.

Our schools are notorious for delayed reinforcement. How many times have you completed an exam or turned in a written assignment only to receive your grade days or even weeks later? Immediate reinforcers are typically more effective than delayed reinforcers in classroom situations (Kulik & Kulik, 1988). Immediate reinforcement is especially important for young children and animals (e.g., Critchfield & Kollins, 2001; Green, Fry, & Myerson, 1994).

♦ *The reinforcer must be contingent on the response.* Ideally, the reinforcer should be presented *only* when the desired response has occurred—that is, when the reinforcer is *contingent* on the response.[2] For example, teachers often specify certain conditions that children must meet before going on a field trip: They must bring their permission slips, they must complete previous assignments, and so on. When these teachers feel badly for children who have not met the stated conditions and allow them

---

[2]Conditioning can occur (albeit more slowly) without one-to-one contingency—that is, when some responses go unreinforced (more about this point in the section on schedules of reinforcement) and when reinforcement is occasionally presented in the absence of the desired response. What is essential is *conditional probability*: Reinforcement must be *more likely* to occur when the response is made than when it is not (Vollmer & Hackenberg, 2001).

	Classical Conditioning	**Operant Conditioning**
Occurs when	Two stimuli (UCS and CS) are paired	A response (R) is followed by a reinforcing stimulus (S_{Rf})
Association acquired	CS $\longrightarrow$ CR	R $\longrightarrow$ S_{Rf}
Nature of response	Involuntary: elicited by a stimulus	Voluntary: emitted by the organism

Figure 4.2
Differences between classical and operant conditioning.

to go on the field trip anyway, the reinforcement is not contingent on the response, and the children are not learning acceptable behavior. If anything, they are learning that rules can be broken!

Contrasting Operant Conditioning with Classical Conditioning

In both classical conditioning and operant conditioning, an organism shows an increase in a particular response. But operant conditioning differs from classical conditioning in three important ways (see Figure 4.2). As you learned in chapter 3, classical conditioning results from the pairing of two stimuli: an unconditioned stimulus (UCS) and an initially neutral stimulus that becomes a conditioned stimulus (CS). The organism learns to make a new, conditioned response (CR) to the CS, thus acquiring a CS→CR association. The CR is automatic and involuntary, such that the organism has virtually no control over what it is doing. Behaviorists typically say that the CS *elicits* the CR.

In contrast, operant conditioning results when a response is followed by a reinforcing stimulus (we'll use the symbol S_{Rf}). Rather than acquiring an S→R association (as in classical conditioning), the organism comes to associate a response with a particular consequence, thus acquiring an R→S_{Rf} association. The learned response is a voluntary one *emitted* by the organism, with the organism having complete control over whether the response occurs. Skinner coined the term *operant* to reflect the fact that the organism voluntarily *operates* on, and thereby has some effect on, the environment.

Some theorists have suggested that both classical and operant conditioning are based on the same underlying learning processes (Bower & Hilgard, 1981; Donahoe & Vegas, 2004). In most situations, however, the classical and operant conditioning models are differentially useful in explaining different learning phenomena, so many psychologists continue to treat them as two distinct forms of learning.

The Various Forms That Reinforcement Can Take

Behaviorists have identified a wide variety of stimuli and events that can reinforce and so increase learners' behaviors. They distinguish between two general categories of reinforcers: primary versus secondary. They also suggest that reinforcement can take either of two forms: positive or negative.

Primary Versus Secondary Reinforcers

A **primary reinforcer** is one that satisfies a built-in, perhaps biology-based, need or desire. Some primary reinforcers, such as food, water, oxygen, and warmth, are essential for physiological well-being. Others, such as a chocolate bar or a glass of wine, aren't essential, but they can enhance a *sense* of well-being. Still other primary reinforcers, such as physical affection, cuddling, and a smile, are more social in nature, and human beings have probably evolved to appreciate them as a way of enhancing social cohesiveness and so, indirectly, enhancing their chances of survival (Harlow & Zimmerman, 1959; Vollmer & Hackenberg, 2001). There may be individual differences regarding the consequences that serve as primary reinforcers; for example, sex is reinforcing to some individuals but not to others, and a particular drug may be a primary reinforcer for a drug addict but not necessarily for a nonaddicted individual (e.g., Lejuez, Schaal, & O'Donnell, 1998).

A **secondary reinforcer,** also known as a *conditioned reinforcer,* is a previously neutral stimulus that has become reinforcing to an organism through repeated association with another reinforcer (e.g., Wolfe, 1936). Examples of secondary reinforcers, which do not satisfy any built-in biological or social needs, are praise, good grades, money, and feelings of success.[3]

How do secondary reinforcers become reinforcing? An early explanation was that some stimuli become secondary reinforcers through the process of classical conditioning. A neutral stimulus is paired with an existing reinforcer (UCS) that elicits some feeling of satisfaction (UCR). That neutral stimulus becomes a CS (i.e., it becomes a secondary reinforcer) that elicits the same satisfaction (CR). For example, my daughter Tina learned very early that she could use money (CS) to buy candy (UCS) to satisfy her sweet tooth. The more often a secondary reinforcer has been associated with another reinforcer, and the stronger that other reinforcer is, the more powerful the secondary reinforcer will be (Bersh, 1951; D'Amato, 1955).

Some theorists have proposed that secondary reinforcers are effective to the extent that they give an organism information that a primary reinforcer is coming (Bower, McLean, & Meachem, 1966; Green & Rachlin, 1977; Mazur, 1993; Perone & Baron, 1980). This explanation has a decidedly cognitive flavor to it: An organism is *seeking information* about the environment rather than simply responding to that environment in a "thoughtless" manner.

The relative influences of primary and secondary reinforcers in our lives probably depend a great deal on economic circumstances. When such biological necessities as food and warmth are scarce, these primary reinforcers, as well as the secondary reinforcers closely associated with them (e.g., money), may be major factors in reinforcing behavior. But in times of economic well-being, when cupboards are full and houses are warm, such secondary reinforcers as praise, grades, and feelings of success are more likely to play a major role in the learning process.

---

[3]One could argue that praise enhances social relationships and so might be a primary reinforcer. However, praise involves language—a learned behavior—and not all individuals find it reinforcing, hence its categorization as a secondary reinforcer (e.g., see Vollmer & Hackenberg, 2001).

Positive Reinforcement

When people think about stimuli and events that are reinforcing for them, they typically think about positive reinforcement. In particular, **positive reinforcement** involves the *presentation* of a stimulus after the response. Positive reinforcement can take a variety of forms: Some are **extrinsic reinforcers,** in that they are provided by the outside environment, whereas others come from within the learner.

Material reinforcers.   A **material reinforcer,** or tangible reinforcer, is an actual object; food and toys are examples. Material reinforcers can be highly effective in changing behavior, especially for animals and young children. However, most psychologists recommend that at school, teachers use material reinforcers only as a last resort, when absolutely no other reinforcer works. Food, toys, trinkets, and similar items have a tendency to distract students' attention from the things they should be doing in class and so may be counterproductive over the long run.

Social reinforcers.   A **social reinforcer** is a gesture or sign (e.g., a smile, attention, praise, or "thank you") that one person gives another, usually to communicate positive regard. Social reinforcement is a common occurrence in the classroom and can be quite effective. Teacher attention, approval, praise, and appreciation are powerful classroom reinforcers (Burnett, 2001; Craft et al., 1998; Drabman, 1976; McKerchar & Thompson, 2004).[4] The attention and approval of peers can be effective as well (Bowers, Woods, Carlyon, & Friman, 2000; Evans & Oswalt, 1968; Flood et al., 2002).

Activity reinforcers.   Speaking nonbehavioristically, an **activity reinforcer** is an opportunity to engage in a favorite activity. (Quick quiz: Which word is the nonbehaviorist part of my definition, and why?) David Premack (1959, 1963) discovered that people will often perform one activity if doing so enables them to perform another. His **Premack principle** for activity reinforcers is as follows:

> A normally high-frequency response, when it follows a normally low-frequency response, will increase the frequency of the low-frequency response.

A high-frequency response is, in essence, a response that an organism enjoys doing, whereas a low-frequency response is one that the organism does not enjoy. Another way of stating the Premack principle, then, is that organisms will perform less-preferred tasks so that they can subsequently engage in more-preferred tasks.

To illustrate, I rarely do housework; I much prefer retreating to my home office to either read or write about human learning and behavior. I have found that I am more likely to do household chores if I make a higher-frequency behavior, such as reading a mystery novel or hosting a party, contingent on doing the housework. In a similar way, appropriate classroom behavior can be improved through the Premack principle. For instance, young children can quickly be taught to sit quietly and pay attention if they are allowed to engage in high-frequency, high-activity behaviors (e.g., interacting with classmates) only after they have been quiet and attentive for a certain period of time (Homme, deBaca, Devine, Steinhorst, & Rickert, 1963).

---

[4]We should note here that praise has potential downsides, depending on the specific message it conveys and the context in which it is given. We will consider possible negative effects of praise in chapters 15 and 16.

Positive feedback.   In some instances, material and social reinforcers may improve classroom behavior and lead to better learning of academic skills because they communicate a message that learners are performing well or making significant progress. Such **positive feedback** is clearly effective in bringing about desired behavior changes (Kladopoulos & McComas, 2001; Lhyle & Kulhavy, 1987; Ryan, Ormond, Imwold, & Rotunda, 2002; R. E. Smith & Smoll, 1997).

I once spent a half hour each day for several weeks working with Michael, a 9-year-old boy with a learning disability who was having difficulty learning cursive letters. In our first few sessions together, neither Michael nor I could see any improvement, and we were both becoming increasingly frustrated. To give ourselves more concrete feedback, I constructed a chart on a sheet of graph paper and explained to Michael how we would track his progress by marking off the number of cursive letters he could remember each day. I also told him that as soon as he had reached a dotted line near the top of the page (a line indicating that he had written all 26 letters correctly) for three days in a row, he could have a special treat (his choice was a purple felt-tip pen). Michael's daily performance began to improve dramatically. Not only was he making noticeable progress, but he also looked forward to charting his performance and seeing a higher mark each day. Within two weeks, Michael had met the criterion for his felt-tip pen: He had written all 26 cursive letters for three days in succession. As it turns out, the pen was probably not the key ingredient in our success: Michael didn't seem bothered by the fact that he lost it within 24 hours of earning it. Instead, I suspect that the concrete positive feedback about his own improvement was the true reinforcer that helped Michael to learn.

Feedback is especially likely to be effective when it communicates what students have and have not learned and when it gives them guidance about how they might improve their performance (Barbetta, Heward, Bradley, & Miller, 1994; Butler & Winne, 1995; Lhyle & Kulhavy, 1987; Tunstall & Gipps, 1996). Under such circumstances, even *negative* feedback can lead to enhanced performance. It is difficult to interpret this fact within a strictly behaviorist framework; it appears that students must be *thinking* about the information they receive and using it to modify their behavior and gain more favorable feedback later on.

Intrinsic reinforcers.   Oftentimes learners engage in certain behaviors not because of any external consequences but because of the internal good feelings—the **intrinsic reinforcers**—that such responses bring. Feeling successful after solving a difficult puzzle, feeling proud after returning a valuable item to its rightful owner, and feeling relieved after completing a difficult assignment are all examples of intrinsic reinforcers. People who continue to engage in responses for a long time without any obvious external reinforcers for their efforts are probably working for intrinsic sources of satisfaction.

For many students, the true reinforcers for learning are probably the internal reinforcers—the feelings of success, competence, mastery, and pride—that their accomplishments bring. For such students, other reinforcers are more helpful if they provide feedback that academic tasks have been performed well. Grades may be reinforcing for the same reason: Good grades reflect high achievement—a reason to feel proud.

Positive feedback and the intrinsic reinforcement that such feedback brings are probably the most productive forms of reinforcement in the classroom. Yet teachers must remember that what is reinforcing for one student may not be reinforcing for another; reinforcement, like beauty, is in the eyes of the beholder. In fact, consistent positive feedback and resulting feelings of success and mastery can occur only when instruction has been carefully tailored to individual skill levels and abilities, and only when students have learned to value academic achievement. When, for whatever reasons, students are not interested in achieving academic success, then other reinforcers, such as social and activity reinforcers—even material ones if necessary—can be useful in helping students acquire the knowledge and skills that will serve them well in the outside world.

Negative Reinforcement

In contrast to positive reinforcement, **negative reinforcement** increases a response through the *removal* of a stimulus, usually an aversive or unpleasant one. Don't let the word *negative* lead you astray here. It is not a value judgment, nor does it mean that an undesirable behavior is involved; it simply refers to the fact that something is being *taken away* from the situation. For example, imagine a rat in a Skinner box that often gives the rat an unpleasant electric shock. When the rat discovers that pressing a bar terminates the shock, its bar-pressing behavior increases considerably. Similarly, some cars emit an annoying sound if the keys are still in the ignition when the driver's door is opened; removal of the keys from the ignition is negatively reinforced (and so will presumably increase in frequency) because the sound stops.

Removal of guilt or anxiety can be an extremely powerful negative reinforcer for human beings. A child may confess to a crime committed days or even weeks earlier because she feels guilty about the transgression and wants to get it off her chest. Anxiety may drive one student to complete a term paper early, thereby removing an item from his things-to-do list. Another student confronted with the same term paper might procrastinate until the last minute, thereby removing anxiety—if only temporarily—about the more difficult aspects of researching for and writing the paper.

Negative reinforcement probably explains many of the *escape* behaviors that organisms learn. For instance, rats who are given a series of electric shocks will quickly learn to turn a wheel that enables them to escape to a different, shock-free environment (N. E. Miller, 1948). Likewise, children and adolescents acquire various ways of escaping unpleasant tasks and situations in the classroom and elsewhere. Making excuses ("My dog ate my homework!") and engaging in inappropriate classroom behaviors provide means of escaping tedious or frustrating academic assignments (Magee & Ellis, 2000; McKerchar & Thompson, 2004; Mueller, Edwards, & Trahant, 2003; Romaniuk et al., 2002). Lying about one's own behaviors ("I didn't do it—*he* did!") is potentially a way of escaping the playground supervisor's evil eye. Complaints about "stomachaches," chronic truancy, and dropping out of school are ways of escaping the school environment altogether. Some escape responses are productive ones, of course; for instance, many teenagers acquire tactful ways of rebuffing unwanted sexual advances or leaving a party where alcohol or drugs are in abundance.

The more aversive a situation is, the more likely people are to learn to escape it (e.g., Piliavin, Dovidio, Gaertner, & Clark, 1981; Piliavin, Piliavin, & Rodin, 1975). For example, children who

Common escape responses.

have particular difficulty with assignments are more likely to have dogs who allegedly eat their homework. And students who drop out before earning their high school diplomas are often those who have encountered repeated academic and social failure at school (Garnier, Stein, & Jacobs, 1997; Kumar, Gheen, & Kaplan, 2002; Rumberger, 1995).

Keep in mind that negative reinforcement can affect the behavior of teachers as well as the behavior of students. Teachers often behave in ways that get rid of aversive stimuli; for example, they may use classroom discipline strategies (responses such as yelling at students or promising less homework) that eliminate unpleasant stimuli (disorderly conduct) over the short run but are ineffective over the long run. As an illustration, if Ms. Jones yells at Marvin for talking too much, Marvin may temporarily stop talking, which negatively reinforces Ms. Jones's yelling behavior.[5] But if Marvin likes getting Ms. Jones's attention (a positive reinforcer for him), he will be chattering again before very long.

Both positive reinforcement and negative reinforcement *increase* the responses that they follow. In contrast, punishment *decreases* those responses. We turn to punishment now.

PUNISHMENT

Most behaviorists define **punishment** in terms of its effect: It decreases the frequency of the response it follows. Punishment can take either of two forms. **Punishment I** involves the *presentation* of a stimulus, typically an aversive one—for instance, a scolding or a failing grade. **Punishment II** involves the *removal* of a stimulus, usually a pleasant one; examples are fines for misbehaviors (because money is being taken away) and loss of privileges. Figure 4.3 illustrates the differences among positive reinforcement, negative reinforcement, Punishment I, and Punishment II.

Many people mistakenly use the term *negative reinforcement* when they are really talking about punishment. Although both phenomena may involve aversive stimuli, they differ in two critical respects. First, as you have seen, they have opposite effects: Negative reinforcement *increases* the frequency of a response, whereas punishment *decreases* the frequency of a response. A second crucial difference concerns the order of events. With negative reinforcement, the aversive stimulus *stops* when the response is emitted. With Punishment I, however, the aversive stimulus *begins* when the

Stimulus is	Nature of Stimulus	
	Pleasant	Aversive
Presented after the response	Positive Reinforcement (response increases)	Punishment I (response decreases)
Removed after the response	Punishment II (response decreases)	Negative Reinforcement (response increases)

Figure 4.3
Contrasting positive reinforcement, negative reinforcement, and punishment.

---

[5]Although behaving in a disruptive fashion is a response that Marvin makes, in this situation it serves as a *stimulus* that Ms. Jones wants to eliminate.

Figure 4.4

Negative reinforcement and Punishment I differ in terms of which occurs first—the aversive stimulus or the response.

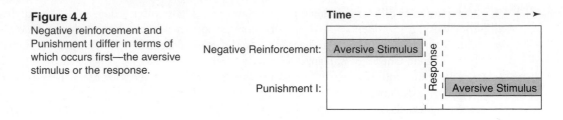

response is emitted. Figure 4.4 illustrates this difference graphically. The termination of an aversive stimulus negatively reinforces a response; the initiation of an aversive stimulus punishes a response.

Early research by both Thorndike (1932a, 1932b) and Skinner (1938) indicated that punishment was unlikely to reduce the behavior it followed. For instance, Skinner (1938) found that when rats were punished for a response that had previously been reinforced, the response was temporarily suppressed but soon returned to its prepunishment frequency. But later research revealed that punishment *can* be effective in many situations. As a result, many behaviorists have revived the "punishment" part of Thorndike's original law of effect, asserting that responses followed by an unpleasant state of affairs are in fact weakened (e.g., Aronfreed, 1968; Azrin & Holz, 1966; Conyers et al., 2004; Lerman & Vorndran, 2002; Parke, 1972, 1977; Walters & Grusec, 1977).

Oftentimes punishment decreases behaviors very quickly. For example, in one study (R. V. Hall et al., 1971, Experiment 1), punishment virtually eliminated the aggressive behavior of a 7-year-old deaf girl named Andrea. Initially, this girl often pinched and bit both herself and anybody else with whom she came in contact; the frequency of such responses (an average of 72 per school day) was so high that normal academic instruction was impossible. Following a period of data collection without any intervention (a *baseline* period), punishment for each aggressive act began: Whenever Andrea pinched or bit, her teacher pointed at her sternly and shouted "No!" Figure 4.5 shows the changes in Andrea's behavior. (The brief *reversal* to a nonreinforcement baseline period on day 25 was used to minimize the likelihood that other factors were responsible for the behavior change.) Even though Andrea was deaf, the shouting and pointing virtually eliminated her aggressiveness.

Figure 4.5

Number of bites and pinches by Andrea during the school day.

Reprinted with permission from "The Effective Use of Punishment to Modify Behavior in the Classroom" by R. V. Hall, S. Axelrod, M. Foundopoulos, J. Shellman, R. A. Campbell, & S. S. Cranston, 1972, in K. D. O'Leary & S. O'Leary (Eds.), *Classroom Management: The Successful Use of Behavior Modification*, p. 175. Copyright 1972 by Pergamon Press, Ltd.

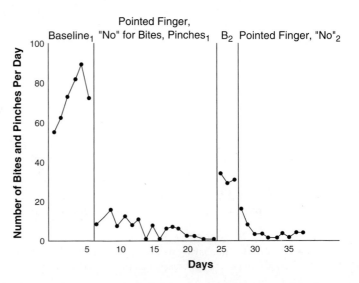

Effective Forms of Punishment

Several forms of punishment have been shown to be effective in reducing inappropriate behaviors in children and adolescents. Three of them—verbal reprimands, restitution, and overcorrection—involve imposing presumably unpleasant consequences and so are examples of Punishment I. Three others—time-out, in-house suspension, and response cost—involve the withdrawal of reinforcers and so are examples of Punishment II.

Verbal reprimands. Although some students find teacher attention of any kind to be reinforcing, most students (like Andrea) regard a **verbal reprimand**—a scolding or admonishment—as punishment (O'Leary, Kaufman, Kass, & Drabman, 1970; Van Houten, Nau, MacKenzie-Keating, Sameoto, & Colavecchia, 1982). In addition to suppressing undesirable behavior, occasional reprimands also appear to enhance the positive reinforcement value of praise (Pfiffner & O'Leary, 1987).

Reprimands are often more effective when they are immediate, brief, and accompanied by eye contact or a firm grip (Pfiffner & O'Leary, 1993; Van Houten et al., 1982). They may also be more effective when spoken quietly and in close proximity to the child being punished (Landrum & Kauffman, 2006; O'Leary et al., 1970; Van Houten et al., 1982); such unobtrusive reprimands are less likely to attract the (potentially reinforcing) attention of peers who are close by. Ideally, too, a reprimand should communicate that the individual is capable of better behavior (Parsons, Kaczala, & Meece, 1982; Pintrich & Schunk, 2002).

Restitution and overcorrection. Restitution and overcorrection involve requiring people to take actions that correct the results of their misdeeds. In **restitution,** a misbehaving individual must return the environment to the same state of affairs that it was in before the misbehavior. As examples, a child who breaks a window must pay for a new one, and a child who makes a mess must clean it up. Restitution is a good example of a *logical consequence,* whereby the punishment fits the crime (Dreikurs, 1998; Landrum & Kauffman, 2006; Nucci, 2001).

In the case of **restitutional overcorrection,** the punished individual must make things *better* than they were before the inappropriate behavior (Foxx & Azrin, 1973; Foxx & Bechtel, 1983; Rusch & Close, 1976). For example, a student who throws food in the lunchroom might be asked to mop the entire lunchroom floor, or the student who offends a classmate might be asked to apologize to the entire class.

Positive-practice overcorrection involves having an individual repeat an action, but this time doing it correctly, perhaps in an exaggerated fashion. For example, a student who runs dangerously down the school corridor might be asked to back up and then *walk* (perhaps at a normal pace, or perhaps very slowly) down the hall. Similarly, a student in a drivers' education class who neglects to stop at a stop sign might be asked to drive around the block, return to the same intersection, and come to a complete stop (perhaps counting aloud to five) before proceeding.

Teachers have given mixed views regarding the value of restitutional overcorrection and positive-practice overcorrection as methods of bringing about behavior improvement in school settings. In some cases, these techniques may be overly time consuming and draw unnecessary attention to the punished behavior (Schloss & Smith, 1994; Zirpoli & Melloy, 2001). When such approaches *are* used, they tend to be more effective when teachers portray them more as means for helping students acquire appropriate behavior than as punishment per se (Alberto & Troutman, 2003; Carey & Bucher, 1986; Zirpoli & Melloy, 2001).

Time-out.   A **time-out** involves placing a misbehaving individual in an environment with no reinforcers—in other words, in a dull, boring situation. Often, this time-out environment is a separate room, furnished sparsely or not at all, in which the individual cannot interact with others. At other times, it may be a corner of the classroom screened from the rest of the room by partitions or tall furniture. In any event, the time-out environment should be neither reinforcing, as the school corridor or principal's office is likely to be, nor frightening, as a dark closet might be (J. E. Walker & Shea, 1995; Wielkiewicz, 1986). Foxx and Shapiro (1978) have developed a procedure that easily incorporates time-out into a classroom context without requiring any special facilities. Students wear ribbons that make them eligible to participate in rewarding classroom activities. Students who misbehave remain in the classroom, but their ribbons are removed, making them ineligible to receive the reinforcers available to their classmates.

Time-out effectively reduces a variety of disruptive, aggressive, and dangerous behaviors (Frankel & Simmons, 1985; Lentz, 1988; Mace, Page, Ivancic, & O'Brien, 1986; MacPherson, Candee, & Hohman, 1974; Mathews, Friman, Barone, Ross, & Christophersen, 1987; Pfiffner & Barkley, 1998; Rortvedt & Miltenberger, 1994). Short time-outs that do not allow students to escape classroom tasks and so do not interfere with students' academic learning are often quite effective (Skiba & Raison, 1990); many psychologists argue that durations of 10 minutes (even as few as 2 minutes for preschool children) are sufficient. A key to using time-out effectively is that the inappropriate behavior must *stop* before the child is released from the time-out situation; *release from time-out* (a negative reinforcer) is therefore contingent on appropriate behavior.

In-house suspension.   At school, an **in-house suspension** is similar to a time-out in that punished students are placed in a quiet, boring room within the school building. However, it typically lasts one or more days rather than only a few minutes, with students being continually monitored by a member of the school staff. Students bring their schoolwork to the suspension room and must work quietly on classroom assignments. Thus, students have little opportunity to engage in the peer interactions that so many of them find reinforcing, and they cannot escape from (or fall behind in) any academic subject matter they might find unpleasant.

Although in-house suspension has not been systematically investigated through controlled research studies, teachers and school administrators report that these programs are often effective in reducing chronic misbehaviors, especially when part of the suspension session is devoted to teaching appropriate behaviors and tutoring academic skills and when the supervising teacher acts as a supportive resource rather than as a punisher (Gootman, 1998; Huff, 1988; Nichols et al., 1999; Pfiffner & Barkley, 1998; Sullivan, 1989).

Response cost.   **Response cost** involves the withdrawal of a previously earned reinforcer. A ticket for speeding (resulting in the payment of a fine) and the loss of previously earned privileges are examples. Response cost has been shown to reduce such misbehaviors as aggression, inappropriate speech, disruptiveness, hyperactivity, and tardiness (Conyers et al., 2004; Iwata & Bailey, 1974; Kazdin, 1972; Rapport, Murphy, & Bailey, 1982). It is especially effective when it's combined with reinforcement for appropriate behavior and when learners don't lose *everything* they've earned by making a few missteps within an overall desirable pattern of behavior (Landrum & Kauffman, 2006; Phillips, Phillips, Fixsen, & Wolf, 1971).

Earlier in the chapter I discussed the importance of reinforcement as a means of providing feedback about what constitutes appropriate behavior. In much the same way, punishment is probably effective to the extent that it gives feedback about inappropriate behavior. Sometimes students are truly unaware of how frequently they misbehave (e.g., Krumboltz & Krumboltz, 1972).

The forms of punishment just described are most likely to be effective when the punisher communicates the message that "I care about you and am trying to help you acquire behaviors that will help you be happy and productive over the long run." The punisher should also monitor the effects of the specific consequence being administered. For example, some children—for instance, those who want to escape an unpleasant task or occasionally enjoy a little time to themselves—are apt to find time-outs to be reinforcing rather than punishing (Alberto & Troutman, 2003; McClowry, 1998; Solnick, Rincover, & Peterson, 1977), and so their "punished" behaviors will increase rather than diminish.

Ineffective Forms of Punishment

Several forms of punishment are typically not recommended: physical punishment, psychological punishment, extra classwork, and out-of-school suspension. A fifth—missing recess—gets mixed reviews.

Physical punishment. Physical punishment may be the only means of keeping very young children from engaging in potentially harmful behaviors. For example, the toddler who takes delight in sticking metal objects into electrical outlets must be quickly informed in no uncertain terms that such behavior cannot continue. However, most experts advise against physical punishment for school-age children (Doyle, 1990; Landrum & Kauffman, 2006; Zirpoli & Melloy, 2001); furthermore, its use in the classroom is *illegal* in many places. The use of physical punishment with older children can lead to such undesirable behaviors as resentment of the teacher, inattention to school tasks, lying, aggression, vandalism, avoidance of school tasks, and truancy. It also provides a model of aggression, thus communicating the message that aggression is acceptable (Landrum & Kauffman, 2006). Occasional *mild* physical punishment (e.g., when a parent gives a child a gentle spanking) does not appear to be correlated with behavior problems later on, although in some cases it can intensify into physical abuse (Baumrind, Larzelere, & Cowan, 2002; Gunnoe & Mariner, 1997; Kazdin & Benjet, 2003).

Psychological punishment. Any consequence that seriously threatens a student's self-esteem or emotional well-being is **psychological punishment** and is not recommended (G. A. Davis &

Physical punishment models aggression.

How many times have I told you: Don't hit other people!

Thomas, 1989; J. E. Walker & Shea, 1995). Embarrassing remarks and public humiliation can lead to some of the same side effects as physical punishment (e.g., resentment of the teacher, inattention to school tasks, truancy from school) and have the potential to inflict long-term psychological harm. By deflating students' self-perceptions, psychological punishment can also lower their expectations for future performance and their motivation to learn and achieve (see the discussions of *self-efficacy* in chapters 6 and 15).

Extra classwork.   Asking a student to complete makeup work for time missed at school is a reasonable and justifiable request. But assigning extra classwork or homework beyond that required for other students is inappropriate if it is assigned simply to punish a student's wrongdoing (H. Cooper, 1989; Corno, 1996). In this case there is a very different side effect: A teacher inadvertently communicates the message that "schoolwork is unpleasant."

Out-of-school suspension.   Out-of-school suspension—in its most severe form this becomes permanent expulsion from school—is usually *not* an effective means of changing a student's behavior (Fenning & Bohanon, 2006; Nichols, Ludwin, & Iadicola, 1999; Skiba & Rausch, 2006). Many chronically misbehaving students are those who have difficulty with their academic work; many high school troublemakers, for example, are students with poor reading skills. Suspending such students from school puts these students at an even greater disadvantage and decreases still further their chances for academic success. Additionally, when students find school to be an aversive situation, removal from that environment is negatively reinforcing rather than punishing. (It is also negatively reinforcing to the school administrators who have gotten rid of their troublemakers!)

Missing recess.   In some situations missing recess may be a logical consequence for students who fail to complete their schoolwork during regular class time due to off-task behavior. Yet research indicates that, especially at the elementary level, students can more effectively concentrate on school tasks when they have occasional breaks from academic activities (Maxmell, Jarrett, & Dickerson, 1998; Pellegrini, Huberty, & Jones, 1995). Perhaps the best piece of advice is to withdraw recess privileges infrequently, if at all, and to monitor the effectiveness of such a consequence on students' classroom behavior over the long run.

Out-of-school suspension is not an effective punishment.

COMMON PHENOMENA IN INSTRUMENTAL CONDITIONING

Several phenomena are commonly observed in instrumental conditioning, especially with the use of reinforcement: superstitious behavior, shaping, chaining, extinction, effects of reinforcement schedules, and avoidance learning.

Superstitious Behavior   (*exemplo: moeda da sorte*)

What happens when reinforcement is random and not contingent on any particular behavior? Skinner once left eight pigeons in their cages overnight with the food tray mechanism adjusted to present reinforcement at regular intervals, regardless of what responses the pigeons were making at the time. By morning, six of the pigeons were acting bizarrely. One repeatedly thrust its head into an upper corner of the cage, and two others were swinging their heads and bodies in rhythmic pendulum movements (Skinner, 1948).

Randomly administered reinforcement tends to reinforce whatever response has occurred immediately beforehand, and an organism will increase that response, thus displaying what Skinner called **superstitious behavior.** A nonbehaviorist way of describing the learning of a superstitious behavior is that the organism thinks that the response and reinforcement are related when in fact they are not. For example, a student may have a "lucky sweater" to wear on exam days, or a football player may, before every game, perform a ritual totally unrelated to successful football.

Superstitious behavior in the classroom can occur either when reinforcement is not contingent on behavior or when students do not know which of their many responses are responsible for bringing about reinforcement. It behooves teachers to ensure that classroom reinforcers such as praise, attention, and grades are contingent on desired behaviors and that response–reinforcement contingencies are clearly specified.

Shaping

In order to be reinforced for a response, an organism must, of course, *make* the response. Sometimes, however, an organism lacks either the skill or the inclination to make a particular response. To handle such a situation, Skinner introduced a method called **shaping.**

To shape a particular behavior, we begin by reinforcing the first response that in any way approximates the desired behavior and then continue to reinforce it until the organism is emitting it fairly frequently. At that point, we reinforce only those responses that more closely resemble the desired behavior, then those that resemble it more closely still, until eventually only the desired behavior itself is being reinforced. In other words, shaping is a process of reinforcing successively closer and closer approximations to the desired behavior until that behavior is exhibited. (Hence this procedure is sometimes called *successive approximations*.)

To illustrate, when I taught my pigeon Ethel to peck a lighted disk in her Skinner box, I began by reinforcing her every time she faced the wall on which the disk was located. Once this response was occurring frequently, I began to reinforce her only when she moved her beak near the wall, then only when she touched the wall with her beak, then only when she pecked within a 2-inch radius of the disk, and so on. Within an hour, I had Ethel happily pecking the disk and eating the food pellets that followed each correct peck.

Legend has it that a group of students once shaped a professor of mine a few days after he had given a lecture on shaping. Every time the professor stood on the side of the classroom near the door, the students appeared interested in what he was saying, sitting forward in their seats and taking notes feverishly. Every time he walked away from the door, they acted bored, slouching back in their seats and looking anxiously at their watches. As the class went on, they reinforced the professor only as he moved closer and closer to the door until, by the end of class, he was lecturing from the hallway.[6]

In much the same way, teachers gradually shape a variety of academic skills and classroom behaviors as children move through the grade levels. For example, kindergarten children are taught to print their letters on wide-lined paper; they are praised for well-formed letters and for letters whose bottoms rest on one line and whose tops touch the line above. As children progress through the primary grades, the spaces between the lines become smaller, and teachers are more particular about how well the letters are written. Eventually, many children begin to write consistently sized and carefully shaped letters with the benefit of only a lower line, and eventually with no line at all. Teachers also shape the sedentary behavior of their students: As students grow older, teachers expect them to sit quietly in their seats for longer and longer periods. To some degree, we can think of mathematics as a shaped set of skills as well: Teachers introduce complex problem solving only after students have mastered more basic skills, such as counting, number recognition, and addition.

In a similar manner, teachers may inadvertently shape undesirable behavior. Let's say that a student named Molly frequently exhibits such disruptive responses as talking out of turn and physically annoying other students. Molly's teacher, Mr. Smith, realizes that because he has been reprimanding her for these responses, he has actually been giving her the attention that he knows she craves and so in essence has been reinforcing her for her disruptiveness. Mr. Smith decides not to reinforce Molly's disruptive behavior anymore. Unfortunately, although Mr. Smith can easily ignore minor infractions, he finds himself unable to ignore more extreme disruptions and so reprimands Molly for them. Rather than discouraging Molly's disruptive behavior, then, Mr. Smith is actually shaping it: He is unintentionally insisting that Molly be *very* disruptive, rather than just a little disruptive, in order to get reinforcement.

Chaining (Sequence)

Organisms can also learn a sequence, or *chain,* of responses through shaping. For example, when visiting a tourist trap in South Dakota many years ago, I watched a chicken play a solitary version of "baseball": As soon as the chicken heard the appropriate signal (triggered by the quarter I deposited in the side of its cage), it hit a ball with a horizontal bar (a bat of sorts) that it could swivel at home plate, then ran counterclockwise around a 3-foot-square baseball diamond back to home plate again (at which point it found some food in its feeding tray). The chicken's trainer had probably taught the chicken this complex chain of responses by first reinforcing only the last response in the sequence (running to home plate), then reinforcing the last two responses (running to third base and then to home plate), then reinforcing the last three

---

[6]Other students have reported the same rumor about their own professors. I suspect that the story may be one of those "urban legends" that has little or no basis in fact. It does provide a vivid example, however, and so I have included it here.

(running to second base, third base, and home plate), and so on, eventually reinforcing only the entire sequence.

This process of teaching a chain of responses by first reinforcing just one response, then reinforcing two responses in a row, then reinforcing a sequence of three, and so on is known as **chaining.** Just as a chicken can learn to play baseball, so, too, can people learn lengthy, fairly complex behaviors through chaining. For example, students in a tennis class might learn to hold their rackets a certain way, then stand with their feet apart facing the net as they watch for the ball, then move toward an approaching ball and adjust their position appropriately, and then swing their rackets to meet the ball. Similarly, students in a first-grade classroom might learn to put their work materials away, sit quietly at their desks, and then line up single file at the classroom door before going to lunch. Such complex actions are often acquired more easily one step at a time—in other words, through chaining.

Let's return to Somjai, the elephant whose painting of an elephant appears in chapter 1. Although the specific techniques that trainers use to teach elephants to create such paintings is a closely guarded secret, I suspect that their approach involves a combination of shaping and chaining. First, of course, Somjai's trainer would have needed to shape general painting behavior: Somjai had to learn to hold the brush with his trunk, point the brush toward the easel, apply an appropriate amount of pressure on the brush as it touched the canvas, move the brush across the canvas, and so on. Once Somjai had acquired a knack for painting, the trainer may have reinforced him for painting a horizontal-but-slightly-curved line (an elephant's "back") across the middle of the canvas, then for painting a back plus the top of a head, then for painting a back, head, and front-of-trunk, and so on. With time, practice, and patience, Somjai learned a very lengthy chain of responses indeed.[7]

Extinction

In classical conditioning, a CR decreases and may eventually disappear—that is, the response is extinguished—when the CS is repeatedly presented in the absence of the UCS. In instrumental conditioning, **extinction** occurs when a response decreases in frequency because it no longer leads to reinforcement. For example, class clowns who find that people no longer laugh at their jokes are likely to decrease their joke telling. Students who are never called on when they raise their hands may stop trying to participate in class discussions. Students who continue to fail exams despite hours of studying may eventually stop studying.

In the initial stages of the extinction process, we may sometimes see a brief *increase* in the behavior being extinguished—a phenomenon known as an **extinction burst** (Lerman & Iwata, 1995; Lerman, Iwata, & Wallace, 1999; McGill, 1999). We may also see increased variability in the kinds of responses that are exhibited (Rachlin, 1991). For example, students who find themselves doing poorly on exams may try studying more or studying differently; if such efforts

---

[7]The procedure I describe for teaching a chicken to play baseball illustrates *backward chaining,* which begins with the final response in the sequence and then adds, one by one, the responses that needed to precede it. The procedure I describe for teaching Somjai to paint an elephant illustrates *forward chaining,* reinforcing the first response in the sequence and then adding subsequent responses to the sequence that is reinforced. Research yields mixed results regarding the relative effectiveness of these two approaches with human beings (Zirpoli & Melloy, 2001).

continue to meet with failure, however, their studying behavior will eventually decrease and perhaps disappear altogether.

Although teachers certainly want to extinguish undesirable behaviors, such as disruptive joke telling, they need to take precautions that *desirable* behaviors are reinforced frequently enough that they *don't* extinguish. For example, if a teacher sees one or more students failing at classroom assignments time after time despite their best efforts, the teacher should look for the root of the problem. If only one student is failing, perhaps that student needs help in developing more appropriate study techniques, more individualized instruction, or placement in a situation better matched to his or her current knowledge and skills. But if many students find the same assignments too difficult to accomplish, something may be wrong with those assignments or with classroom instruction.

Effects of Reinforcement Schedules

One of the most critical factors affecting both the rate at which responses are learned and the rate at which they can be extinguished is the consistency of reinforcement (e.g., Staddon & Higa, 1991). To illustrate how consistency plays a role, consider this fantasy I have for the handful of students in my classes each semester who don't read the assigned textbook:

> The student is locked in a small room. The textbook lies on a nearby table. Every time the student opens the book to one of the assigned pages and looks at the page, a small piece of delicious junk food falls from a hole in the ceiling.

Essentially, I would like to put unmotivated students into my own version of a Skinner box—the Ormrod box!

Now imagine 20 students in 20 Ormrod boxes. Ten of these students, randomly selected, are in Group A: They receive a piece of junk food every time they open the textbook and look at it. The other 10 are in Group B: They get junk food for some of their book-reading responses (perhaps one response out of every four) but receive nothing for their efforts the rest of the time. Group A is receiving **continuous reinforcement:** Every response is reinforced. Group B is receiving **intermittent reinforcement:** Some of the responses are reinforced and some are not. Which group is going to increase its textbook-reading behavior faster? The answer, of course, is Group A, the group with continuous reinforcement. Continuously reinforced responses are acquired faster than intermittently reinforced responses.

Now suppose that, after a few hours in their respective Ormrod boxes, all 20 students have begun to show a high frequency of textbook-reading responses, so I turn off the junk-food-dropping mechanisms. Which students are first going to notice that they are no longer being reinforced? The answer again is Group A. Students who have been reinforced for every single response will notice rather quickly that reinforcement has stopped, and their textbook reading should extinguish rapidly (unless, of course, they find such behavior intrinsically reinforcing). In contrast, Group B students have been receiving reinforcement for only 25% of their responses, so they are accustomed to nonreinforcement; these students will probably continue to read their textbooks for some time before they realize that reinforcement has ceased. Intermittently reinforced responses are extinguished more slowly than continuously reinforced responses.

Behaviorists usually recommend reinforcing a response continuously until it occurs in the desired form and at the desired frequency. After that, it should be maintained through intermittent reinforcement so that it does not extinguish. Intermittent reinforcement can follow a variety of **reinforcement schedules,** each of which has different effects on resistance to extinction and on the frequency and pattern of the response being reinforced. We now look at several schedules and the behavior patterns that result from each one.

Ratio Schedules: Reinforcing a Certain Number of Responses

A **ratio schedule** is one in which reinforcement occurs after a certain number of responses have been emitted. That particular number can either be constant (a fixed-ratio schedule) or vary from one reinforcement to the next (a variable-ratio schedule).

Fixed ratio (FR).   In a fixed-ratio schedule, a reinforcer is presented after a certain constant number of responses have occurred. For example, reinforcement might occur after every third response (a 1:3 ratio schedule) or after every 50th response (a 1:50 schedule). Such a reinforcement schedule can lead to a high and consistent response rate over an indefinite period of time; for example, pigeons whose pecking is maintained on a high-ratio schedule may peck as often as 10 times per second (Ferster & Skinner, 1957).

Whitlock (1966) has described the use of a series of ratio schedules with a 6-year-old boy who had been unable to acquire basic reading skills. At first, the boy was asked to read words presented to him on flash cards. Every time he read a word correctly, he received a plastic poker chip as a reinforcer, reflecting a continuous reinforcement schedule. He could trade jars of 36 poker chips for a variety of activities; for example, with two jars he could play a game, and with seven jars he could watch a cartoon. Once the boy was able to read from beginning reader storybooks, he was reinforced on a 1:2 fixed-ratio schedule; that is, he received one chip for every two words he read correctly. Eventually he was reinforced for every four words (a 1:4 schedule), then for every page (one reinforcer for every 10 to 25 words), then for every story (one reinforcer for every 50 to 70 words), and finally for every four stories. After 15 sessions of such individualized instruction, reinforcement was phased out altogether, and the boy was placed in his classroom's regular reading program; three months later, he was still reading at grade level. (One thing has always struck me about this study: Because so many poker chips were required to make a "purchase," the boy must actually have bought very few activities. I suspect that his increasing success in reading was the true reinforcer in this case.)

Ratio schedules even as high as 1:1000, when introduced through a series of successively higher ratios (as was done in the Whitlock study), have been found to maintain a response (Ferster & Skinner, 1957). In fact, high ratios typically lead to higher rates of responding than low ratios (Collier, Hirsh, & Hamlin, 1972; Stephens, Pear, Wray, & Jackson, 1975), although organisms operating under high-ratio schedules tend to exhibit a **postreinforcement pause** (a temporary decrease in responding—a "coffee break" of sorts) after each reinforced response (Ferster & Skinner, 1957).

Variable ratio (VR).   A variable-ratio schedule is one in which reinforcement is presented after a particular, yet *changing*, number of responses have been emitted. This kind of schedule is described by the average number of responses needed to obtain reinforcement. For example, in a 1:5 VR schedule, reinforcement might first take place after four responses, then after seven more, then after three, and so on, with five responses being the average. As you can see, the occurrence of reinforcement in a VR schedule is somewhat unpredictable.

Playing a Las Vegas slot machine is an example of a response that is reinforced on a variable-ratio schedule. The more times you insert a quarter into the machine, the more times you will be

Telemarketing is reinforced on a variable-ratio schedule.

reinforced by having quarters come back out again, but those quarters do not come out after any predictable number of quarters have been inserted. In a similar way, telemarketing is reinforced on a VR schedule. The greater the number of calls made, the greater the number of sales, but the caller never knows just which call will lead to reinforcement.

Margaret, a friend of my daughter Tina during their elementary school years, was always very persistent when she wanted something; she seldom took "no" for an answer. A possible source of her persistence became clear to me one evening when Tina and I had dinner at a restaurant with Margaret and her mother. The girls gobbled their food quickly and went off to explore the restaurant while we mothers nursed our coffee. Margaret quickly returned to the table with a request:

> "Mom, can I have a quarter for a video game?"
> "No."
> "Please, Mom?"
> "I said no, Margaret."
> "But Tina has one." (I look innocently into space.)
> "No."
> "I'll pay you back as soon as we get home."
> "*No,* Margaret."
> "*Pretty please?!*" (Margaret puts on a desperate face.)
> "Oh, all right, here's a quarter."

Margaret's asking behaviors were probably on a variable-ratio reinforcement schedule: She had learned that persistence usually paid off.

Variable-ratio schedules result in higher response rates than fixed-ratio schedules. Furthermore, responses reinforced on a VR schedule are highly resistant to extinction. In fact, pigeons working on very high VR schedules may expend more energy responding than they gain in food reinforcement, thus eventually working themselves to death (Swenson, 1980).

Interval Schedules: Reinforcing the First Response After a Time Period

An **interval schedule** is one in which reinforcement is contingent on the first response emitted after a certain time interval has elapsed. This interval can either be constant (a fixed-interval schedule) or vary from one reinforcement to the next (a variable-interval schedule).

Fixed interval (FI).   With a fixed-interval schedule, reinforcement is contingent on the first response emitted after a particular, constant amount of time has gone by. For example, the organism may be reinforced for the first response emitted after five minutes, regardless of how many responses may or may not have been made during those five minutes. Following reinforcement, an additional five minutes must elapse before a response is reinforced.

We do not see the high rate of responding with a FI schedule that is observed for fixed- and variable-ratio schedules, nor do we see as much resistance to extinction. Furthermore, a fixed-interval schedule produces a unique response pattern: Following reinforcement, the response rate tapers way off in a postreinforcement pause until the end of the time interval approaches, at which point responding picks up again (e.g., Ferster & Skinner, 1957; Shimoff, Catania, & Matthews, 1981). To illustrate, when my daughter Tina was in fifth grade, she had a spelling test every Friday. She got the week's list of spelling words each Monday and so had four evenings in which to study the list. Occasionally she began on Wednesday, but she more often waited until Thursday night to study her spelling. If we were to graph Tina's studying behavior, it might look something like the graph in Figure 4.6. This "scallop" pattern is typical of behaviors reinforced on a fixed-interval schedule. For instance, in the U.S. Congress, bill-passing behavior increases considerably within the months preceding an election—when senators and congressmen are seeking votes and campaign contributions—and drops off considerably after the election (Critchfield, Haley, Sabo, Colbert, & Macropolis, 2003).

Variable interval (VI).   In a variable-interval schedule, reinforcement is contingent on the first response emitted after a certain time interval has elapsed, but the length of the interval changes from one occasion to the next. For example, the organism may be reinforced for the first response after five minutes, then the first response after eight minutes, then the first response after two minutes, and so on, with the VI schedule being identified by the average time interval.

Figure 4.6

Responses reinforced on a fixed-interval schedule show a "scallop" pattern.

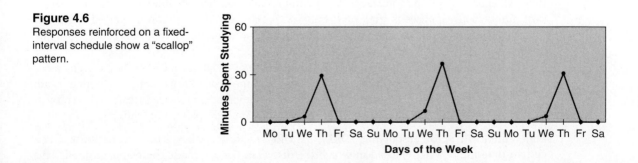

As an illustration, you may have a friend who really enjoys talking on the telephone, so that when you try to call this individual, you often hear a busy signal. If you have an urgent need to get in touch with your friend, you may continue to dial the phone number once every few minutes until eventually your call goes through. In a similar way, students who have been told that there is always the possibility of an unannounced ("pop") quiz in class are likely to study a little bit every night. They never know on exactly which day their studying will pay off. Your pattern of dialing your gabby friend and students' patterns of studying for pop quizzes are typical of the response pattern observed for variable-interval schedules: a slow, steady rate of responding. The longer the average time interval until reinforcement, the slower the response rate will be (e.g., Catania & Reynolds, 1968). (Please note that for other reasons, pop quizzes are generally not recommended. They may increase students' anxiety levels in the classroom, and, as you will discover in chapter 15, high levels of anxiety interfere with learning. Furthermore, pop quizzes don't allow for the fact that students' extracurricular activities and family obligations sometimes prevent completion of schoolwork the same day it is assigned.)

For both ratio and interval schedules, variable schedules lead to steadier response rates and greater resistance to extinction than fixed schedules do, probably because of the unpredictability of reinforcement: There is always the possibility that the next response will pay off. In most cases, a variable ratio is recommended for a high rate of responding, with a variable-interval schedule being better for a slow yet steady pace. Ideally, when continuous reinforcement is first replaced by intermittent reinforcement, the ratio should be small (e.g., 1:2 or 1:3) or the time interval short. The ratio or interval can then gradually be increased until the responses continue with very little reinforcement at all.

Differential Schedules: Reinforcing Rates of Responding

When a particular *rate* of responding is required, a **differential schedule of reinforcement** is appropriate: A specific number of responses occurring within a specific length of time leads to reinforcement. Researchers have investigated the effects of reinforcing both high and low rates of responding.

Differential rate of high responding (DRH).   A DRH schedule provides reinforcement only when a specific, *large* number of responses (or even more responses than that) have occurred within a particular period of time. For example, consider Tina's friend Margaret, the girl who persistently asked her mother for money to play a video game. Margaret may actually have been on a DRH schedule rather than a variable-ratio schedule, in that she had to ask for a quarter several times *all at once* to get reinforcement. With a ratio schedule, the time it takes to emit the necessary number of responses is irrelevant, but with a DRH schedule, this time period is critical. Because a DRH schedule requires many responses in a short amount of time, a high response rate is typical.

Theoretically, studying for regularly scheduled exams is really on a DRH schedule: The more studying that occurs in a short time period, the greater the probability of reinforcement at exam time. However, as Klein (1987) has pointed out, too many students instead treat exams as fixed-interval schedules and so exhibit a goof-off-now-and-cram-later pattern of studying.

Differential rate of low responding (DRL).   A DRL schedule reinforces the first response after a certain time interval has elapsed in which the organism has *not* made the response at all. This might sound like a fixed-interval schedule, but remember that in an FI schedule, responses during the time interval, although not reinforced, are otherwise acceptable. One example of a response on a DRL schedule is trying to start a car with a flooded engine. Repeated attempts at starting it will fail; you must wait for a few minutes, then try again, before you are likely to succeed.

Students' requests for their teacher's assistance are an example of responses that might be most appropriately reinforced on a DRL schedule. Reinforcing students continuously when they ask for the teacher's help might lead to a high rate of such requests, resulting in overdependence on the teacher. In contrast, reinforcing students who ask for help only after they have been working independently for a period of time will teach them that independence with occasional questions is quite acceptable. It is important to note, however, that learning the appropriate response pattern for a DRL schedule often takes time, because it requires one *not* to perform a previously reinforced behavior (Reynolds, 1975).

Avoidance Learning

Like most colleges and universities, my former university in Colorado had many faculty committees. When I first joined the faculty as an assistant professor, I eagerly agreed to serve on committees whenever I could, perceiving them to be a means of meeting other faculty members and having input into university decision making. But before long, I discovered that many faculty committees spent years chewing on the same issues without ever arriving at consensus or otherwise accomplishing very much. Having many other responsibilities on my plate (preparing for classes, grading students' papers, conducting research, etc.), I was frustrated by the amount of time I was wasting in such unproductive activities. The unpleasant feelings I experienced during meetings were aversive stimuli—they were punishing my go-to-a-meeting behavior. I soon found myself inventing excuses to leave meetings early ("I'm *so* sorry, but I have to take my son to the dentist"). In other words, I was acquiring escape behaviors that led to negative reinforcement. Eventually, I stopped volunteering to join committees in the first place, enabling me to avoid these aversive events altogether.

In general, **avoidance learning** is the process of learning to stay away from an aversive stimulus—perhaps one that causes pain, anxiety, or frustration. For avoidance learning to occur, an organism must have some sort of **pre-aversive stimulus,** a cue signaling the advent of the aversive stimulus. For example, rats who hear a buzzer and are then given an electric shock (making the buzzer a pre-aversive stimulus) easily learn to jump a hurdle as soon as the buzzer sounds, thereby avoiding the painful shock (Mowrer, 1938, 1939). Similarly, children quickly learn to pull a brass handle as soon as a light flashes so that they can avoid an unpleasantly loud noise (Robinson & Robinson, 1961). In my case, announcements of committee meetings and requests for new members were pre-aversive stimuli telling me that committee-avoiding behaviors were in order.

Avoidance learning can take either of two forms. In **active avoidance learning,** the organism must actively make a particular response to avoid an aversive event. Unfortunately, studying behavior is, in many cases, an instance of active avoidance learning. Ideally, studying should be an enjoyable activity in its own right (thereby providing intrinsic reinforcement), but many people do not enjoy it in the least (I, for one, would much rather read a mystery novel or watch a television game show). By studying fairly regularly, most students are able to avoid an aversive stimulus—a failing grade. Consider how rarely studying behavior occurs when there is no signal of possible impending doom (no pre-aversive stimulus), such as an assigned research report or an upcoming exam.

In **passive avoidance learning,** organisms learn that *not* making a particular response allows them to avoid an aversive event (e.g., Lewis & Maher, 1965; Seligman & Campbell, 1965). For example, people who feel awkward and uncomfortable in social situations tend not to go to parties or other social events. Likewise, students who have difficulty with mathematics rarely sign up for advanced math classes if they can help it.

From a behaviorist perspective, avoidance learning may often be a two-step process that involves both classical conditioning and instrumental conditioning (D'Amato, 1970; Mowrer, 1956; Mowrer & Lamoreaux, 1942). In the first step, because the pre-aversive stimulus and the aversive stimulus are presented close together in time, the organism learns to fear the pre-aversive stimulus through a process of classical conditioning, as alluded to in chapter 3 and illustrated in Figure 4.7. In the second step, an avoidance response leads to negative reinforcement (escape from the fear-inducing pre-aversive stimulus) and possibly also intrinsic positive reinforcement (feelings of relief about the escape).[8]

Avoidance behaviors are difficult to extinguish: Even when a previously aversive situation has lost all sources of unpleasantness, people continue to avoid it and so have no opportunity to learn that the situation is now a fairly comfortable one. For example, students who, through classical conditioning, have acquired math anxiety may avoid math classes indefinitely, even after they've developed the cognitive maturity necessary for comprehending previously troublesome concepts. If students never again enroll in a math class, they will never learn that they have nothing to fear!

Undoubtedly the best way to deal with avoidance behaviors in the classroom is to *prevent* such behaviors from being learned in the first place—something that can best be accomplished by minimizing aversive classroom events (see chapter 3). Another alternative is to extinguish any classically conditioned fear responses to pre-aversive stimuli through systematic desensitization (again see chapter 3). A third approach is less "warm and fuzzy" (i.e., it may initially engender some hard feelings) but can sometimes work quite well. In particular, we simply prevent learners from *making* unproductive avoidance responses, thereby enabling them to discover that they have nothing to fear about a situation. Imagine a math-anxious student who clearly has the

Figure 4.7
Learning to fear a pre-aversive stimulus through classical conditioning.

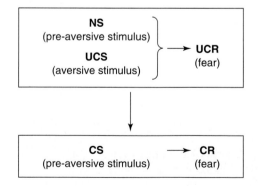

---

[8]Some exceptions to this two-step process have been observed (e.g., see Herrnstein, 1969; Kamin, 1956; Kamin, Brimer, & Black, 1963).

knowledge and skills necessary to succeed in a particular math class. A school advisor or coun-selor might insist that the student enroll in the class; once in class, the student can discover that mathematics is a rewarding experience rather than a frustrating one. In some circumstances, stu-dents don't necessarily know what is best for them.

EFFECTS OF ANTECEDENT STIMULI AND RESPONSES IN INSTRUMENTAL CONDITIONING

Up to this point I've portrayed instrumental conditioning as involving associations between responses and the consequences (reinforcements or punishments) that come immediately after. Yet humans and nonhumans alike learn to make different responses in different contexts. For instance, in our discussion of avoidance learning, we discovered that avoidance behaviors occur only when there is a pre-aversive stimulus of some kind to signal an upcoming aversive situation. More generally, some stimuli and responses, known as **antecedent stimuli** and **antecedent responses,** set the stage for certain behaviors to follow and, perhaps, for other behaviors *not* to follow. Here we will look at several concepts—cueing, setting events, generalization, and dis-crimination—that involve antecedent stimuli, as well as one concept—behavioral momentum—that involves antecedent responses.

Cueing

In his theory of operant conditioning, Skinner acknowledged that organisms often learn that a particular response leads to reinforcement only when a certain stimulus—something he called a **discriminative stimulus**—is present. This antecedent stimulus does not directly elicit the response as it does in classical conditioning. Rather, it increases the probability that the response will be followed by reinforcement; in Skinner's words, it "sets the occasion" for the response to be reinforced. We might diagram the relationship this way (we'll use the symbol S+ to represent the discriminative stimulus):

$$(S+) \quad R \rightarrow S_{Rf}$$

When an organism is more likely to make certain responses in the presence of certain stimuli, behaviorists say that the organism is under **stimulus control.**

In the classroom, the discriminative stimuli that set the occasions for certain desired behav-iors are not always obvious ones; for example, the only naturally occurring stimulus that sets the occasion for cleaning up work materials and getting ready to go to lunch might be a clock on the wall that says 11:55. Under such circumstances, teachers can provide additional discriminative stimuli that let students know how to behave—a strategy often called **cueing** or **prompting** (e.g., Northup et al., 1995; Shabani et al., 2002; Taylor & Levin, 1998).

Cueing sometimes involves nonverbal signals that remind students about desired responses. For example, during a cooperative learning activity, a teacher might quickly flash the overhead light on and off a few times to remind students to talk quietly rather than loudly. In other situa-tions, verbal cues are more helpful. For example, an elementary teacher whose class is preparing to go to the lunchroom might cue students by saying "Walk quietly and in single file" and then allowing them to proceed only if they behave as instructed. A middle school science teacher who wants to give students a subtle reminder about the importance of completing a reading assignment might say, "After you have all finished reading the section about great apes on pages 69 through 72, I will tell you about tomorrow's field trip to the zoo."[9]

Teachers can also use cueing to remind students about what responses are apt to lead to punishment. For example, a teacher might use body language (a scowl or furrowed brow), physical proximity (moving close to a student), or a brief verbal comment ("Lucy, put the magazine away") to discourage disruptive or off-task behaviors (Emmer, 1987; Northup et al., 1995; Woolfolk & Brooks, 1985).

Setting Events

Some behaviorists talk not about specific stimuli but instead about complex environmental conditions—**setting events**—under which certain behaviors are most likely to occur (Brown, Bryson-Brockmann, & Fox, 1986; Hoch, McComas, Johnson, Faranda, & Guenther, 2002; Morris, 1982; Wahler & Fox, 1981). For example, preschoolers are more likely to interact with their classmates during free play time if they have a relatively small area in which to play and if available toys (balls, puppets, toy housekeeping materials) encourage group activity (Brown, Fox, & Brady, 1987; Frost, Shin, & Jacobs, 1998; Martin, Brady, & Williams, 1991). Similarly, the nature of the games that children are asked to play influences the behaviors they exhibit: Cooperative games promote increases in cooperative behavior, whereas competitive games promote increases in aggressive behavior (Bay-Hinitz, Peterson, & Quilitch, 1994).

Generalization

When an organism has learned to respond in a certain way in the presence of one stimulus (the S+), it may respond in the same way in the presence of other stimuli; this phenomenon is known as **generalization.**[10] Just as is true in classical conditioning, generalization in instrumental conditioning is most likely to occur when a new stimulus is similar to a previously learned antecedent stimulus. For example, students in a kindergarten classroom (the classroom being the S+) may learn such appropriate classroom behaviors as raising their hands and waiting to be called on before speaking. Such behaviors are more likely to generalize to a similar situation (such as a first-grade classroom) than to a dissimilar situation (such as the family dinner table). This tendency of organisms to generalize more readily as stimuli become more similar to the original discriminative stimulus is known as a **generalization gradient.**

---

[9]Simple cues are often effective in nonclassroom settings as well. For instance, when people leave grocery stores, restaurants, or community centers, employees or signs that tell them to "buckle up" increase the likelihood that they will fasten their seat belts when they get into their cars (Austin, Alvero, & Olson, 1998; Cox, Cox, & Cox, 2005; Engerman, Austin, & Bailey, 1997).

[10]Behaviorists sometimes distinguish between *stimulus generalization*—that is, responding in the same, previously learned way to a similar stimulus—and *response generalization*—that is, making a response similar to one that has previously been acquired and reinforced. Our focus here is on stimulus generalization.

Stimulus Discrimination

In classical conditioning, stimulus discrimination occurs when one stimulus (the CS+) is presented in conjunction with an unconditioned stimulus, and another stimulus (the CS−) is presented in the absence of the UCS. A similar phenomenon happens in instrumental conditioning: A response may be reinforced in the presence of one stimulus (S+) but not in the presence of another stimulus (which we'll symbolize as S−):[11]

$$(S+) \quad R \to S_{Rf}$$
$$(S-) \quad R \to \varnothing \text{ (no response)}$$

Learning under what circumstances a response will and will not be reinforced is instrumental conditioning's form of **stimulus discrimination.** Stimulus discrimination is essentially a process of learning that a conditioned response made in the presence of S+ should not be generalized to S−.

Consider the preschooler who has learned to say "bee" whenever she sees this symbol:

b

She then sees a similar stimulus:

d

and responds "bee" once again—that is, she generalizes. (Anyone who has worked with young children who are learning their alphabet letters has probably observed that, consistent with the generalization gradient, children are much more likely to generalize the "bee" response to the letter *d* than to less similar letters, such as *s* or *y*.) If the teacher does not reinforce the child for the "bee" response to the symbol *d,* the student should eventually learn to discriminate between the letters *b* and *d.*

Behavioral Momentum

In many cases organisms are more likely to make desired responses if they are already making similar responses—a phenomenon known as **behavioral momentum** (Ardoin, Martens, & Wolfe, 1999; Lane, Falk, & Wehby, 2006; Mace et al., 1988; Nevin, Mandell, & Atak, 1983). A study with low-achieving adolescents (Belfiore, Lee, Vargas, & Skinner, 1997) illustrates this phenomenon nicely. Two girls (Allison, who was 14, and Roberta, who was 15) had a history of refusing to do the academic tasks that their teachers assigned. The researchers found that they could encourage the two students to work on difficult three-digit multiplication problems if they first gave the girls some simple one-digit problems. More generally, teachers can promote behavioral momentum by assigning easy or enjoyable tasks that lead naturally into more complex and potentially frustrating ones.

---

[11]Skinner instead used the symbols S^D (for discriminative stimulus) and S^Δ ("S-delta"). In my discussion here, I have used S+ and S− to make the parallel to stimulus discrimination in classical conditioning more obvious.

COGNITION AND MOTIVATION IN INSTRUMENTAL CONDITIONING

Many behaviorists now propose that instrumental conditioning can best be understood when we consider nonobservable mental processes as well as observable stimuli and responses. For example, they talk about an organism forming *expectations* as to what reinforcer or punishment is likely to follow a particular response (Colwill, 1993; Rachlin, 1991; Schwartz & Reisberg, 1991). They find that humans and nonhumans alike form mental *categories* of stimuli to which they respond; to illustrate, pigeons can be trained to discriminate (by making different responses) between members of different categories, including cats versus flowers, cars versus trucks, pictures of Charlie Brown versus pictures of other characters in *Peanuts* cartoons, and even different lengths of time (Killeen, 1991; Rachlin, 1991; Vaughan, 1988; Wasserman, 1993). And behaviorists are beginning to use such phrases as *paying attention* to discriminative stimuli, mentally *encoding* and finding *meaning* in response-reinforcement relationships, and *seeking information* about the environment—words and phrases with definite cognitive overtones (Colwill, 1993; Colwill & Rescorla, 1986; DeGrandpre, 2000; Rachlin, 1991; Rescorla, 1987; Schwartz & Reisberg, 1991).

Motivation, too, has increasingly come into the picture. In general, the larger and more appealing a reinforcer, the faster a response will be learned and the more frequently it will be exhibited (Atkinson, 1958; Siegel & Andrews, 1962). Even so, as noted at earlier points in the chapter, different learners are apt to find different consequences reinforcing and punishing. And in fact, a consequence that is reinforcing or punishing for a learner on one occasion may *not* be reinforcing or punishing on another. Learners' present circumstances and motivational states—whether they feel hungry or full, whether they crave attention or would rather be alone, and so on—are apt to affect their preferences for consequences at any particular time. For instance, a child is less likely to misbehave in order to gain an adult's attention if he is surrounded by enjoyable playthings than if he has little of interest to occupy his time (Ringdahl, Winborn, Andelman, & Kitsukawa, 2002). Attention-getting behavior is also less likely when a child is *already* receiving considerable adult attention regardless of what she does or doesn't do—that is, if attention isn't contingent on behaving in a particular way (Laraway, Snycerski, Michael, & Poling, 2003).[12]

Motivation and cognition may both come into play in two phenomena collectively known as **contrast effects** (Mast, Fagen, Rovee-Collier, & Sullivan, 1984; McHale, Brooks, & Wolach, 1982). One contrast effect—an **elation effect**—occurs when the amount of reinforcement is increased: An organism's response rate becomes *faster* than it would be if the reinforcement had always been at that higher level. An opposite contrast effect—a **depression effect**—occurs when the amount of reinforcement is decreased: The result is that the response rate becomes *slower* than it would be if reinforcement had always been that low. For example, in a classic early study by Crespi (1942), rats ran a runway to reach a food reinforcer at the far end. When rats accustomed to a small quantity of food were suddenly reinforced with a greater amount, they ran faster than rats who had always received the larger amount. Meanwhile, rats accustomed to a large amount of reinforcement who then began receiving less food ran more slowly than rats who had always had the smaller amount.

---

[12]In recent years, behaviorists have used the terms *establishing operation* and *motivating operation* to refer to events that alter the reinforcing or punishing value of a particular stimulus.

Human beings show contrast effects as well. For instance, in a study by Mast and colleagues (1984), 2- to 4-month-old infants were placed in cribs over which hung mobiles with 6 to 10 colorful objects. One end of a string was tied to each infant's ankle, and the other end was fastened to a mechanism that, when pulled, turned the infant's mobile. The infants quickly discovered that by kicking the appropriate leg, they could move the mobile and create a reinforcing visual display. Later on—for some babies as much as 24 hours later—the infants were placed in a similar arrangement, but this time with only a two-object mobile to move. They showed obvious displeasure with the reduction in reinforcement, perhaps crying or perhaps looking elsewhere for other sources of amusement. Such findings suggest that the depression effect may be at least partly due to negative emotional reactions to the reduction in reinforcement (Flaherty, 1985). Yet memory for the higher-quality earlier reinforcement must also have been involved, leading the infants to form expectations that they would enjoy similar benefits on future occasions (Mast et al., 1984). It's almost as if the babies (and Crespi's rats as well) were thinking, "Hey, what happened to the good stuff?!"

As we turn our attention to other theoretical perspectives beginning in chapter 6, we will increasingly see the many ways in which cognition and motivation influence learning and performance. Yet even relatively "thoughtless" and "unmotivated" views of instrumental conditioning have many implications for classroom practice and therapeutic intervention, as you will discover in the next chapter.

SUMMARY

While observing cats in a puzzle box, Edward Thorndike concluded that responses leading to satisfying consequences (rewards) are strengthened and that responses leading to unpleasant consequences (punishment) are weakened. In later years, Thorndike revised this *law of effect,* suggesting that a reward strengthens a response but punishment does not necessarily weaken it. B. F. Skinner echoed Thorndike's view and in his studies of *operant conditioning* focused on the ways in which satisfying consequences increase the frequency of voluntary behaviors. Rather than use the term *reward,* however, Skinner introduced the term *reinforcement*—a term that avoids the implication that a behavior-increasing consequence necessarily involves a pleasant, desirable stimulus. For example, in the case of *negative reinforcement,* rather than gaining a pleasant stimulus, an organism *gets rid* of an *unpleasant* stimulus.

In the past few decades, many behaviorists have returned to Thorndike's original law of effect, acknowledging that both reinforcements and punishments can alter the frequency of the responses they follow. The term *instrumental conditioning* includes both the "encouraging" effects of reinforcement and the "discouraging" effects of punishment. Not all forms of reinforcement and punishment are equally effective, however. For example, some learners often work for the intrinsic satisfaction that their accomplishments bring, whereas others are primarily interested in more external consequences, such as concrete objects, special privileges, or the attention of teachers and peers. And whereas some learners dislike being placed in a quiet, boring context when they misbehave—that is, when they're given a *time-out*—others seem to appreciate the peace and quiet that a brief time-out provides.

Behaviorists have identified a variety of phenomena in which reinforcement plays a key role. For instance, complex behaviors can be taught by reinforcing successive approximations to the desired behavior (*shaping*) or by reinforcing an increasingly long sequence of responses (*chaining*). A response that has previously been reinforced but is no longer being reinforced at all decreases (*extinction*); however, reinforcing a response *intermittently* can maintain it indefinitely, with the particular pattern of responding depending on the *schedule of reinforcement* that is used.

Antecedent stimuli and responses also affect the occurrence of a response. Certain kinds of antecedent events increase the frequency of particular behaviors; depending on the circumstances, these antecedents reflect phenomena known as *cueing, setting events,* or *behavioral momentum.* In general, organisms tend to *generalize* newly acquired responses to similar situations, but they can also learn to *discriminate* between situations in which particular responses are and are not likely to be reinforced.

In recent decades, behaviorists have begun to incorporate elements of cognition and motivation into their views of human behavior. As a result, the distinction between behaviorism and cognitivism has become increasingly blurry.

CHAPTER 5

Applications of Instrumental Conditioning

In recent decades, the psychological study of human learning has increasingly taken on a cognitivist bent. For example, if you were to browse through some of the psychology journals in the periodicals section of your university library, you would undoubtedly find "mental" terms (e.g., *cognitive process, memory*) far more common than behaviorist terms (e.g., *negative reinforcement, extinction*). Yet behaviorist ideas have hardly been left in the dust, because they have stamped an indelible imprint on the nature of psychological inquiry and theory building (Roediger, 2004). Even the most cognitivist theorists recognize that if they want to focus on the nature of human thinking, they must ultimately tie thought processes to behaviors they can objectively measure. And they acknowledge that a learner's immediate context—the stimuli that precede behavior and the consequences that follow it—can have profound influences on what the learner does and does not learn. But perhaps most importantly, behaviorism remains with us today because, when properly applied, behaviorist principles *work* (Roediger, 2004).

In this chapter we'll consider how both reinforcement and punishment can be effectively used in general classroom management and in a systematic approach to behavior change known as *applied behavior analysis*. We'll also look at the influence of behaviorist principles in several widely used instructional innovations: instructional goals and objectives, programmed instruction, computer-assisted instruction, and mastery learning.

APPLYING BEHAVIORIST PRINCIPLES TO CLASSROOM MANAGEMENT

On average, beginning teachers mention classroom management as their number one concern (Evertson & Weinstein, 2006; V. Jones, 1996; Veenman, 1984). Many of their students are easily distracted from academic tasks, and some consistently engage in disruptive behaviors that interfere with their own and classmates' learning.

B. F. Skinner wrote prolifically on why, from a behaviorist perspective, so many children and adolescents engage in nonproductive behaviors at school (e.g., Skinner, 1953, 1954, 1958, 1968, 1973). Skinner contended that reinforcement in the classroom usually occurs inconsistently and too long after a desired response has occurred. Although "natural" reinforcers (e.g., the opportunity to control one's environment or the intrinsically rewarding value of classroom subject matter) can sometimes reinforce (and therefore increase) appropriate academic behaviors, in fact most classroom reinforcers are artificially imposed. A problem inherent in traditional Western education, Skinner suggested, is that teachers must teach behaviors that will be useful to students in the *future* rather than in the present, so these behaviors are not likely to lead to the naturally positive consequences now that they might later on. (For example, although an adolescent might find algebra valuable when she becomes a mechanical engineer, she does not find it particularly useful in her current life.) As a result, teachers resort to artificial reinforcers such as teacher approval, grades, stickers, or free time to foster on-task behavior and academic achievement. Such reinforcers tend to be relatively ineffective, however, in part because their relationships to specific student responses are often unclear.

In desperation, teachers often find themselves punishing *mis*behaviors through such aversive consequences as displeasure, ridicule, and failing grades, rather than reinforcing appropriate responses (e.g., Landrum & Kauffman, 2006). As Skinner put it, teachers "induce students to learn by threatening them for not learning" (Skinner, 1968, p. 57). Not only are such aversive techniques ineffective, but they may also encourage students to engage in behaviors that allow them to escape or avoid classroom tasks.

Behaviorists have offered a variety of recommendations for using both reinforcement and punishment effectively, and we will look at their suggestions shortly. Before we do so, however, we need to be aware of and address potential drawbacks of reinforcement and punishment in classroom contexts.

Concerns About Using Reinforcement and Punishment in the Classroom

Over the years many criticisms have been voiced about the use of reinforcement and punishment with school-age children. Some are ill founded, whereas others should be taken more seriously. We will first examine common "bogus" complaints and then turn to more genuine concerns.

Bogus Complaints

Some criticisms directed toward the use of reinforcement and punishment in the classroom reflect either a misunderstanding of behaviorist principles or lack of awareness of empirical findings:

◆ *Reinforcement is bribery.* The bribery argument is probably the most frequent complaint leveled against the use of reinforcement in the classroom. However, the word *bribery* implies that the behavior being reinforced is somehow illegal or unethical. On the contrary, the appropriate use of reinforcement in the classroom can facilitate the attainment of educational objectives, all of which involve academically and socially desirable behaviors.

◆ *Reinforcement leads to dependence on concrete, external rewards for appropriate behavior.* Some critics propose that students should engage in learning simply for learning's sake; by reinforcing learning, they argue, teachers foster the expectation that students will always receive rewards for their accomplishments. This argument can be countered in two ways. First, as you learned in chapter 4, reinforcement does not necessarily involve material reinforcers. Social reinforcers, activities, feedback, and intrinsic reinforcers (e.g., feelings of success or accomplishment) are also effective in changing behavior, and the sensible teacher will use them instead of material reinforcers whenever possible.

Second, even when a teacher must use material reinforcers to change behavior, these reinforcers bring about desired changes that apparently *will not occur any other way.* Reinforcement is often useful when more traditional methods of changing behavior have failed to increase important academic and social skills or to decrease counterproductive behaviors. If the choice comes down to teaching Mary to read by reinforcing her for reading or else not teaching her to read at all, obviously Mary must learn to read using whatever means possible. We must remember, too, that when material reinforcers are used, social events (e.g., praise) that are paired with them should eventually become secondary reinforcers and so can be used instead.

◆ *Reinforcing one student for being good teaches other students to be bad.* "Hmmm," Leslie thinks. "Linda has been such a loudmouth the past few weeks that the teacher is now giving her raisins so she'll keep quiet. Maybe if I start shooting my mouth off, I'll start getting some raisins, too."

Reinforcement as bribery.

If students are thinking along these lines, something is clearly wrong with how reinforcement is being administered. All students should be reinforced for their appropriate behaviors. Praise and positive feedback should not be limited to a handful of chronic misbehavers but should be regularly given to all students. If the behavior of a particular student can be modified *only* with material reinforcers such as raisins, such reinforcement should be administered discretely and in private.

◆ *Punishment reduces self-esteem.* Certain forms of punishment, especially psychological punishment (e.g., public humiliation or ridicule), can indeed reduce self-esteem. But mild forms of punishment, such as brief time-outs or gentle reprimands, typically have little negative impact on students' long-term emotional well-being. In fact, when punishment can help students gain more productive and socially productive behaviors, it can indirectly *enhance* their self-confidence over the long run.

◆ *Eliminating a problem behavior does not eliminate the underlying cause of that behavior, and so other behavioral manifestations of that underlying cause may appear.* Reflected in this criticism is Sigmund Freud's notion of *symptom substitution:* Problem behaviors are a function of deep-rooted psychological conflicts, Freud suggested, so that when a behavior is eliminated without treatment of its underlying cause, another problem behavior will emerge in its place. The best rebuttal to the symptom substitution criticism is an empirical one: When problem behaviors are reduced through a systematic application of behaviorist techniques, symptom substitution rarely occurs (e.g., Rimm & Masters, 1974).

One likely reason for this finding is that changing an individual's behavior may indirectly address its underlying cause as well. For example, consider the girl who is inappropriately aggressive on the playground. This girl might truly want to interact effectively with her peers, but aggression is the only way she knows of initiating social interaction. Teaching and reinforcing the girl for good social skills, combined with punishing aggressive behaviors, not only help her develop friendships but also address the underlying cause of her aggression: her desire for companionship.

Genuine Concerns

The bogus complaints just listed can be easily rebutted. A few major criticisms of using reinforcement and punishment in instructional contexts should be taken more seriously, however:

◆ *Encouraging productive behaviors through reinforcement alone ignores cognitive factors that may be interfering with learning.* When students are capable of learning a new skill but are not motivated to do so, the use of reinforcement may be all that is needed to bring about the desired behavior change. But when cognitive deficiencies (e.g., insufficient background knowledge or specific learning disabilities) interfere with the acquisition of a new skill, reinforcement alone may be insufficient. In the latter situation, teachers may need to employ teaching techniques based more on cognitive learning theories—theories that we will explore in later chapters.

◆ *Reinforcement of some behaviors may interfere with maximal learning and performance over the long run.* Reinforcement for accomplishing a certain task can focus students' attention and effort more on getting the task done quickly, perhaps at a minimally acceptable level or perhaps by cheating, rather than on *learning* from the task. Especially when teachers want their students to engage in complex, higher-level thinking—for example, to think flexibly and creatively about academic subject matter—then extrinsic reinforcement simply for task accomplishment can be counterproductive (Brophy, 2004; Hennessey & Amabile, 1987; Lepper & Hodell, 1989; McCaslin & Good, 1996).

♦ *Extrinsic reinforcement of a personally enjoyable behavior may undermine the intrinsically reinforcing value of the behavior.* Individuals often engage in activities because of the intrinsic rewards (e.g., feelings of pleasure or accomplishment) that the activities bring. A number of research studies indicate that enjoyable behaviors can be increased by extrinsic reinforcers but will then decrease considerably once the reinforcers are removed. For example, in one early study, preschool children who were promised a fancy "good player award" for drawing pictures were, later on, *less* likely to draw pictures in a free-play situation than either (a) children who were given a similar award but not told about it in advance or (b) children who were not reinforced for drawing pictures (Lepper, Greene, & Nisbett, 1973). Similar results have been obtained in a study with college students: When students worked on a series of puzzles, those who were given money for correct solutions (but *not* those who were simply given positive feedback) were less likely to continue working on puzzles once reinforcement stopped (Deci, 1971).

Particularly when initial interest in an activity is high, when newly offered reinforcers are tangible (e.g., toys or money), when people know in advance that such reinforcers will be coming, and when simply doing the activity (rather than doing it *well*) is reinforced, intrinsic motivation to perform the activity is likely to be undermined (Cameron, 2001; Deci, Koestner, & Ryan, 2001). Possibly the *depression effect* is at work to some extent: As you discovered in chapter 4, human beings and nonhumans alike don't like having the quality or quantity of reinforcement reduced unexpectedly. We will consider a second possible explanation of this extrinsic-undermining-intrinsic effect in our discussion of self-determination in chapter 15.

♦ *A punished behavior is not "unlearned" and may return.* Punishment suppresses a response: It makes the response less likely to occur. However, this suppression effect is often only temporary: The punished behavior may eventually reappear, perhaps when the punishment stops or when the punisher is absent (Appel & Peterson, 1965; Lerman & Vorndran, 2002; Pfiffner & O'Leary, 1987; Skinner, 1938).

♦ *Punishment can have a variety of negative side effects.* Obviously, severe physical punishment can lead to bodily injury, and harsh psychological punishment is apt to have a long-term negative impact on emotional well-being. Even less severe punishments involving aversive stimuli (i.e., those that constitute Punishment I rather than Punishment II) can lead to a variety of counterproductive emotional responses—anger, fear, anxiety, and so on. Anger may, in turn, lead to aggression, especially in people already predisposed to making aggressive responses (Berkowitz & LePage, 1967; Landrum & Kauffman, 2006; Walters & Grusec, 1977). The fear and anxiety that punishment elicits can, through classical conditioning, become associated with other stimuli present at the time (Lerman & Vorndran, 2002; Skinner, 1938). For example, when a teacher punishes a student at school, that punishment (the UCS) may be associated with the teacher, the task, or the classroom, any of which may then become conditioned stimuli (CSs) that elicit fear and anxiety (CRs). In a similar manner, when an athletic coach continually yells at children for their poor performance during a game, negative attitudes toward the sport may result (Feltz, Chaase, Moritz, & Sullivan, 1999; R. E. Smith & Smoll, 1997).

Teachers must remember, too, that any stimulus that has become fear- and anxiety-inducing because of its association with punishment may lead to escape or avoidance behavior (see chapters 3 and 4). Escape and avoidance responses at school take many forms, including inattention, cheating, lying, refusal to participate in classroom activities, and truancy (e.g., Becker, 1971; Magee & Ellis, 2000; Skinner, 1938; Taylor & Romanczyk, 1994).

♦ *Improving behavior in one context may lead to more frequent behavior problems in another.* When reinforcement or punishment is consistently used in one situation, overall behavior may improve in that situation but decline in others—a phenomenon known as **behavioral contrast** (e.g., Simon, Ayllon, & Milan, 1982; Wahler, Vigilante, & Strand, 2004). For example, some children who behave badly at school may be described by their parents as being "little angels" at home. Such children are possibly being held to strict behavioral rules on the home front, with severe punishment following any infractions. If so, they may engage in the forbidden behaviors at school, where they can do so with milder consequences.

Despite such concerns, reinforcement and punishment can be highly effective means of bringing about desired behavior changes, as we shall see in the next two sections.

Using Reinforcement to Increase Desirable Behaviors

Behaviorists have offered a number of suggestions for using reinforcement effectively in classrooms and therapeutic contexts:

♦ *Specify desired behavior(s) up front.* Behaviorists recommend that the form and frequency of a desired behavior—the desired end result, or **terminal behavior**—be described at the very beginning in specific, concrete, observable terms. For instance, rather than talk about the need for students to "learn responsibility," teachers might instead talk about the importance of following instructions, bringing needed books and supplies to class every day, and turning in all assignments by their due dates. By specifying terminal behaviors up front, teachers give both themselves and their students targets to shoot for, and they can better determine whether they are, in fact, making progress toward those targets.

In identifying and reinforcing desired behaviors, it is often important to specify quality as well as quantity. For instance, rather than reinforcing students simply for sitting quietly at their desks, teachers should also reinforce them for working productively during that time. And rather than reinforcing students simply for the number of books they read (which may encourage students to read many short, simple books), teachers should reinforce them for completing challenging reading material appropriate for their level (McCaslin & Good, 1996).

♦ *Use extrinsic reinforcers only when desired behaviors are not already occurring on their own.* It's neither possible nor necessary to reinforce *every* good deed. Learners of all ages often find appropriate, productive behaviors intrinsically reinforcing. Furthermore, many extrinsic reinforcements lose their effectiveness when used repeatedly (Michael, 2000; Murphy, McSweeney, Smith, & McComas, 2003).

♦ *Identify consequences that are truly reinforcing for each learner.* In school settings, social reinforcers (such as praise) or activity reinforcers (such as special privileges, free time to pursue personal interests, or the opportunity to spend time with a favorite classmate) are often effective (Bates, 1979; Cipani, 2002; Northup et al., 1995; Piersel, 1987). In some cases, immediate feedback that a student has done something correctly is all the reinforcement a student needs, especially when it is not otherwise clear that the student has been successful (Bangert-Drowns, Kulik, Kulik, & Morgan, 1991; Harris & Rosenthal, 1985; Kulik & Kulik, 1988).

One of the most common mistakes that teachers make in applying behaviorist principles is to assume that certain consequences will be reinforcing for *all* students. A first-grade teacher once consulted me about one of her students, a boy so disruptive that he was able to spend only a half day in the classroom. In an effort to modify the disruptive behavior, the teacher had attached to the boy's desk a large sheet of heavy cardboard that was cut and painted to look like a clown, with a small red light bulb for a nose. When the boy exhibited appropriate classroom behaviors, such as sitting quietly or attending to an assigned task, the teacher would push a button on a remote control that lit up the red nose. "I don't understand why his behavior isn't changing," she told me. "Maybe this clown isn't reinforcing for the boy," I suggested. "Nonsense!" exclaimed the teacher. "The clown has always worked with *other* children!"

Not everyone will work for the same reinforcers; a consequence that increases desired behaviors for one child may not increase such behaviors for another. For example, although most students find their teacher's praise reinforcing, some students do not (e.g., Pfiffner, Rosén, & O'Leary, 1985). Some students may be afraid of being labeled "teacher's pet," especially if they value the friendship of peers who shun high achievers. Many Native American students, although they appreciate praise for group achievements, may feel uncomfortable when their individual efforts are singled out as being noteworthy (Fuller, 2001). And for some students, only material reinforcers will do. In such a situation, having parents provide the reinforcers at home for behaviors exhibited at school often works quite well (Barth, 1979; Kelley & Carper, 1988; Miller & Kelley, 1994; Wielkiewicz, 1986).

How can teachers determine what events will be reinforcing for different students? One way is to ask the students' parents, or even the students themselves. Children don't always have a good sense of what consequences they are truly likely to work for, however (Atance & Meltzoff, 2006; Northup, 2000), so perhaps a better approach is to observe them over a period of time to see what kinds of consequences seem to affect their behavior.

Teachers should keep in mind, too, that any single reinforcer won't necessarily maintain its reinforcing value indefinitely, especially if it is presented quite frequently (Bowman, Piazza, Fisher, Hagopian, & Kogan, 1997; Viken & McFall, 1994). For example, as much as you probably enjoy good food, you can eat only so much, and as much as you enjoy the praise of people you respect, constant praise gets tiresome after a while. It's certainly possible to get too much of a good thing.

The "reinforcer" must be reinforcing for the learner.

◆ *Make sure that learners will gain more than they lose by changing their behavior.* Consciously or otherwise, children and adults alike sometimes engage in a cost–benefit analysis when considering the consequences of different behaviors (Eccles & Wigfield, 1985; Feather, 1982; Friman & Poling, 1995; Perry & Fisher, 2001). Although they may have learned that a certain response will be reinforced, they will nevertheless not make that response if they have too much to lose, or too little to gain, by doing so. For people to change their behavior in order to earn reinforcement, it must be worth their while.

For example, people often recycle paper and aluminum cans if recycling containers are placed close at hand; they are much less likely to do so if they have to walk across the room or down the hall (Brothers, Krantz, & McClannahan, 1994; Ludwig, Gray, & Rowell, 1998). And consider the college student who estimates that she will have to study at least 20 hours a week to get an A in a history class. Although the A may be an effective reinforcer, it may not be worth the amount of time she will have to spend to earn it. Consider, too, the teenager who shies away from teacher praise because his peer group doesn't approve of academic achievement. It may be that teacher praise *is* a reinforcer to this student, but he risks losing his status in the group if he is praised too frequently or profusely. In this situation, praise given privately, out of the earshot of peers, will probably be much more reinforcing than public praise.

◆ *Make response–consequence contingencies explicit.* Reinforcement is typically more effective when learners know exactly what consequences will follow various behaviors. For example, kindergarten students are more likely to behave appropriately when they are told, "The quietest group will be first to get in line for recess." High school students are more likely to complete their Spanish assignments if they know that by doing so they will be able to take a field trip to a local Cinco de Mayo festival.

One explicit way of communicating contingencies is through a **contingency contract,** an agreement that specifies certain expectations for the student (the terminal behavior) and the consequences of the student's meeting those expectations (the reinforcer). For example, a student and teacher may agree that the student should turn in all homework assignments, on time and with at least 80% accuracy, every day for a week. If the student accomplishes this task, the contract might specify that the student will be given some time to engage in a favorite activity, or that the teacher and student will spend time after school studying a topic of mutual interest. Although a contingency contract can be as simple as a verbal agreement, more often it is an actual written contract. The student and teacher negotiate the conditions of the contract in one or more meetings, and then both of them sign and date the contract. Ideally, initial contracts require small tasks that a student can accomplish within a short time period, and both the desired behavior and the reinforcer are specified in precise, concrete terms (Homme, Csanyi, Gonzales, & Rechs, 1970; J. E. Walker & Shea, 1995).

A contingency contract can be used to encourage academic achievement; it can also be used to modify classroom behavior. For example, when a teacher and student develop a contract specifying that certain behaviors will lead to desired consequences, the contract might help the student to spend more class time attending to assigned work or to engage in more appropriate social behaviors on the playground. In fact, contingency contracting has been shown to be effective for addressing a wide variety of problems, including poor study habits (Brooke & Ruthren, 1984; Miller & Kelley, 1994), juvenile delinquency (Rueger & Liberman, 1984; Welch, 1985), and drug addiction (Anker & Crowley, 1982; Crowley, 1984; Rueger & Liberman, 1984).

◆ *Administer reinforcement consistently.* As you learned in chapter 4, responses increase more quickly when they are reinforced every time they occur—that is, when they lead to continuous reinforcement. In group situations (e.g., in classrooms), it is sometimes inconvenient to reinforce a behavior every time it occurs. But remember, continuous reinforcement brings about more rapid behavior change than intermittent reinforcement. If a student's behavior has been particularly disruptive and time consuming, a little extra time devoted *now* to the continuous reinforcement of appropriate behaviors (inconvenient as that may occasionally be) will probably save time over the long run.

◆ *Gradually shape complex behaviors.* In many situations, encouraging a desirable behavior requires a process of gradually *shaping* the behavior. Each response should be well learned before reinforcement proceeds to a closer approximation. If an attempt at shaping moves too quickly, such that each response is not well established before a more sophisticated one is expected, reinforcement may not bring about any lasting behavior change.

To illustrate, let's say that Ms. Garcia, a third-grade teacher, wants to reinforce Jack, an especially hyperactive student, for sitting quietly in his seat; her goal (the terminal behavior) is for him to sit quietly for 20 minutes. On the first morning of the intervention program, Jack sits quietly for 1 minute, and so Ms. Garcia reinforces him. She probably does not want to move on to a 2-minute criterion after he has met the 1-minute criterion only once. Instead, she should continue reinforcing Jack for 1-minute "sits" until it is clear, from the frequency of his sitting behavior, that she can begin to expect that behavior for a longer period.

◆ *When giving reinforcement publicly, make sure that all students have an opportunity to earn it.* In their attempts to improve the behavior of some students, teachers may unintentionally slight other, equally deserving students. Furthermore, some students may be unable to exhibit particular behaviors through little fault of their own. Consider the case of a young immigrant girl who had to adjust very quickly from a 10:00–5:00 school day in Vietnam to a 7:45–3:45 school day in the United States:

> [E]very week on Friday after school, the teacher would give little presents to kids that were good during the week. And if you were tardy, you wouldn't get a present. . . . I would never get one because I would always come to school late, and that hurt at first. I had a terrible time. I didn't look forward to going to school. (Igoa, 1995, p. 95)

Ultimately, school should be a place where *all* students can, in one way or another, earn reinforcement and in other ways be successful. Classrooms are busy places, however, and it may be all too easy to overlook a few students who desperately want and need a teacher's attention. In such cases the teacher can explicitly *teach* children appropriate ways of seeking out and getting reinforcement—for instance, by raising their hands or quietly approaching the teacher at an appropriate time, asking questions (e.g., "How am I doing?" "What do I do next?"), and keeping the teacher informed of their progress ("Look, I'm all finished!") (Craft, Alberg, & Heward, 1998, p. 402; K. A. Meyer, 1999).

◆ *Use objective criteria to monitor progress.* Regardless of whether we define learning as a mental change or a behavioral one, we know that learning has occurred only when we can see an actual change in behavior. Behaviorists urge us to assess that change in concrete, objective terms. More specifically, they suggest that we assess the frequency of a desired behavior both before and during any attempts to increase it through the use of reinforcement. The frequency of a behavior before reinforcement begins is called the **baseline** level of the behavior. Some behaviors occur frequently even when they are not being explicitly reinforced, whereas other behaviors occur rarely or not at all. Only by comparing the baseline frequency of a response with its frequency after reinforcement begins can teachers and other practitioners determine whether their use of reinforcement is actually bringing about a behavior change.

◆ *Foster the ability to delay gratification.* In the preceding chapter, I stressed the importance of *immediate* reinforcement in operant conditioning, especially for young children and animals. Fortunately, in situations when immediate reinforcement is impossible, environmental cues indicating that reinforcement will come later can be helpful (Fowler & Baer, 1981; Perin, 1943). For example, a teacher who wants to reinforce students' persistence through a difficult lesson might say, "Because we are working so hard this morning, after lunch we will rehearse the class play you all have been enjoying so much." Furthermore, older children and adults often respond more favorably to large, delayed reinforcers over small, immediate ones if that they know the larger ones will eventually appear (Green, Fry, & Myerson, 1994; Neef et al., 2005; Rotenberg & Mayer, 1990).

In general, learners become better able to work for delayed reinforcers—that is, to **delay gratification**—when the waiting period is increased gradually and when they learn strategies for coping with the wait—for instance, by engaging in an activity in the interim or by telling themselves "If I wait a little longer, I will get a bigger cookie" (Binder, Dixon, & Ghezzi, 2000; Dixon & Cummings, 2001; Dixon, Rehfeldt, & Randich, 2003; Freeland & Noell, 1999).

◆ *Once the terminal behavior has been acquired and is occurring regularly, gradually wean learners off of extrinsic reinforcers.* When a previously learned response is no longer reinforced *at all,* it may quickly disappear. From a behaviorist perspective, either of two conditions can prevent such extinction. In some cases, improvements in behavior begin to lead to intrinsic reinforcement—to internal feelings of accomplishment, pride, and so on—and so continue of their own accord. But not all important behaviors are, in and of themselves, intrinsically satisfying. When desired behavior involves a tedious but necessary activity—for instance, practicing basic math facts or cleaning up after messy art projects—an intermittent reinforcement schedule can help to maintain it indefinitely.

Strategies for Decreasing Undesirable Behaviors

In this and the preceding chapter, we have talked at length about how new responses can be learned, modified, and maintained through the use of reinforcement. But sometimes the goal may be to *decrease* and ideally eliminate, rather than increase, a behavior. Four possible methods of reducing and eliminating misbehavior are extinction, noncontingent reinforcement, reinforcement of other behaviors, and punishment.

Extinguishing Responses

A psychologist was once consulted about Jimmy, a child who had been hospitalized for an extended period. Nurses in the children's ward were very concerned because Jimmy kept banging his head on the side of his crib. Whenever they heard him doing so, they rushed to his room and restrained him, inadvertently reinforcing and maintaining the head-banging behavior with their attention. The psychologist successfully eliminated Jimmy's head banging through a process of extinction: A protective helmet was strapped on Jimmy's head to prevent injury, and the nurses were instructed to ignore Jimmy during his head-banging episodes. At the same time, because Jimmy clearly craved attention, the nurses *did* spend time with him on other occasions.

Extinction—making sure that a particular response no longer leads to reinforcement—is sometimes an effective means of eliminating inappropriate behavior in the classroom. Students who engage in disruptive behavior in class may stop if such behavior no longer results in the attention they seek (i.e., if their teacher and peers ignore them). Cheating on classroom assignments may soon disappear if students never receive credit for the scores they obtain on those assignments. We don't necessarily want to eliminate the particular reinforcers (e.g., attention, class credit) that have been operating in such circumstances; we simply need to make sure that those reinforcers are *not* contingent on inappropriate responses (e.g., Fischer, Iwata, & Mazaleski, 1997).

Unfortunately, extinction is often not a very dependable method of eliminating unwanted behavior, for several reasons. First, it is not always possible to identify the specific consequence that is actually reinforcing a response; for example, children who, like Jimmy, engage in head-banging behavior do so for different reasons—perhaps to gain adult attention, escape from unpleasant tasks (a form of negative reinforcement), or provide self-stimulation (Iwata, Pace, Cowdery, & Miltenberger, 1994). Second, there may be several reinforcers involved in maintaining a response, including some that are difficult to remove; for example, although a teacher may be able to ignore the jokes of a disruptive class clown, classmates may continue to reinforce the jokes (Landrum & Kauffman, 2006). Third, even if all sources of reinforcement can be removed, the behavior may show an extinction burst, increasing in frequency before it begins to decline (see chapter 4). Fourth, extinguished behaviors sometimes show spontaneous recovery: A response that has been extinguished one day may pop up again at a later date, perhaps in a different context (Alberto & Troutman, 2003; Skinner, 1953). Finally, some responses may be particularly resistant to extinction because they have previously been reinforced on an intermittent schedule. When responses cannot be extinguished for any of these reasons, other approaches are usually necessary.

Presenting Noncontingent Reinforcement

In recent years, some researchers have found that presenting desired consequences noncontingently—for instance, giving attention at unpredictable times or providing regular breaks from difficult tasks—can lead to a decrease in inappropriate behavior (Coleman & Holmes, 1998; Ecott & Critchfield, 2004; Hagopian, Crockett, van Stone, DeLeon, & Bowman, 2000; Ringdahl, Vollmer, Borrero, & Connell, 2001).[1] In this way, children gain the consequences they seek *without* having to act out to do so. The primary disadvantage of this approach, of course, is that children don't necessarily learn more appropriate behaviors to replace the counterproductive ones. Occasionally, too, it might lead to superstitious behavior (see chapter 4).

Reinforcing Other Behaviors

Rather than using noncontingent reinforcement, a teacher or therapist may identify specific behaviors that *will* be reinforced while also making sure that the inappropriate behavior is *not* reinforced. Sometimes a learner is reinforced for doing anything *except* for making a certain response during a certain time period; in this situation, the learner must never make that particular response at all.[2] As an example, consider the teacher who says, "I am going to write on

_____

[1]Some behaviorists call this approach a *time-based schedule*.

[2]This approach is known as *differential reinforcement of other behaviors* (a DRO schedule).

the chalkboard the name of every student who speaks out of turn today. If your name is not on the board by 3 o'clock, you can have a half hour of free time." A major drawback with this approach is that the teacher is not being fussy about *which* other behaviors the students exhibit, and some of them may be inappropriate.

In other instances, a teacher or therapist reinforces only certain other behaviors (e.g., Lerman, Kelley, Vorndran, Kuhn, & LaRue, 2002; Ringdahl et al., 2002; Vollmer, Roane, Ringdahl, & Marcus, 1999).[3] Ideally the other behaviors are *incompatible* with the behavior to be eliminated. (Recall our use of incompatible behaviors in counterconditioning and breaking habits in chapter 3.) The first step is to identify a response that is incompatible with the response to be eliminated—a response that cannot be performed at the same time as the undesirable response. That incompatible behavior is then reinforced whenever it occurs. For example, a child's inappropriate out-of-seat behavior may be reduced by reinforcing the child whenever he is sitting down. An aggressive student can be reinforced whenever she is interacting in a socially appropriate manner with her classmates. A tennis player who displays inappropriate emotional outbursts every time he misses a shot can be reinforced for keeping his frustration under control by standing still, taking several deep breaths, and then continuing to play (Allen, 1998). A chronic litterbug might be put in charge of his school's antilitter campaign and given considerable recognition and praise for his efforts (Krumboltz & Krumboltz, 1972).

Reinforcing other (possibly incompatible) behaviors has been shown to be effective in reducing a variety of inappropriate classroom behaviors (Parrish, Cataldo, Kolko, Neef, & Egel, 1986; Pinkston, Reese, LeBlanc, & Baer, 1973; Repp & Deitz, 1974; Repp, Barton, & Brulle, 1983). Typically its effectiveness far surpasses that of extinction alone (Allen, 1998; Lentz, 1988; Woods & Miltenberger, 1995; Zirpoli & Melloy, 2001).

Using Punishment

The use of punishment as a means of behavior control is widespread in both child-rearing and educational practice (Landrum & Kauffman, 2006; Straus, 2000a, 2000b). One likely reason for the prevalence of punishment as a disciplinary measure is that, because it tends to decrease or eliminate an undesirable behavior fairly quickly, the punisher is *negatively reinforced:* By using punishment, he or she gets rid of an unwanted state of affairs, at least temporarily.

Punishment is often used when methods such as extinction or reinforcement of incompatible behaviors are ineffective or impractical; furthermore, it appears that punishment may sometimes be more effective than other behaviorist techniques (Conyers et al., 2004; Corte, Wolf, & Locke, 1971; Frankel & Simmons, 1985; Lerman & Vorndran, 2002; Pfiffner & O'Leary, 1987). Punishment is especially advised when a behavior might harm either oneself or others; in such cases, using punishment to eliminate such behavior rapidly may actually be the most humane course of action.

Psychologists and educators have offered numerous suggestions for using punishment effectively, many of which decrease the chances of negative side effects. The guidelines that follow are among those most commonly cited:

◆ *Choose a "punishment" that is truly punishing without being overly severe.* Punishment, like reinforcement, is defined by its effect on behavior: True punishment decreases the response it follows, and typically it does so quite rapidly. (For example, return to Figure 4.5 and notice how

---

[3]This approach is known as either *differential reinforcement of alternative behavior* (a DRA schedule) or *differential reinforcement of incompatible behavior* (a DRI schedule).

quickly Andrea's biting and pinching decreased.) If a given consequence does not decrease the response it is meant to punish, the consequence may not be aversive to the individual being "punished"; in fact, it may even be reinforcing. For example, when my children were growing up, a common "punishment" around our house was to be sent to one's room. For my two sons, such a consequence was truly aversive because they would much rather socialize with other family members than be isolated in their rooms for any length of time. But when my daughter Tina was banished to her bedroom, she was probably being reinforced: She rearranged her furniture, listened to her radio, or settled under the covers with a good book. And the behaviors for which she was most often punished in this way—behaviors related in one way or another to annoying and teasing her brothers—seemed to increase rather than decrease.

As noted in chapter 4, certain forms of punishment, such as physical punishment and psychological punishment (e.g., public humiliation) tend not to be effective and should be avoided at all costs. Whatever consequence is used should be strong enough to be effective but not overly severe (Landrum & Kauffman, 2006; Lerman & Vorndran, 2002). Harsh punishments—those that far surpass the severity of the "crime"—are those most apt to lead to such undesirable side effects as resentment, hostility, aggression, or escape behavior. Furthermore, although severe punishment may quickly suppress a response, the response may reappear at its original level once the punisher has left the scene (Appel & Peterson, 1965; Azrin, 1960; Landrum & Kauffman, 2006). The ultimate purpose of administering punishment is to communicate that the limits of acceptable behavior have been exceeded; it should not be so excessive that it undermines the personal relationship between the punisher and the person being punished (Spaulding, 1992).

• *Inform learners ahead of time about what behaviors will be punished.* Punishment is most likely to deter behavior when an individual knows that the behavior will lead to punishment and what the punishment will be (Aronfreed, 1968; Landrum & Kauffman, 2006; also see chapter 6). I remember an incident when, as a 4-year-old, I was punished without warning. Sitting at lunch one day, apparently considering the adage "Waste not, want not," I licked a large quantity of peanut butter off my butter knife. An adult scolded me sternly for my behavior, and I was devastated. Being the Miss Goody-Two-Shoes I was at the time, I would never have engaged in knife-licking behavior if I had known it was unacceptable.

Often the knowledge that certain responses will be punished is, in and of itself, sufficient for improving behavior. For example, in a study by R. V. Hall and his colleagues (1971, Experiment 4),

Tina is "punished."

three high school students enrolled in a French class earned higher grades when after-school tutoring was the "punishment" for low grades. These students—Dave, Roy, and Debbie—had been consistently earning Ds and Fs on daily quizzes. Their teacher informed them that because they were obviously having difficulty with their French, they would have to come in for a half hour of tutoring after school whenever they received a grade lower than C. Quiz grades during baseline periods and during times when poor quiz performance would be punished are shown in Figure 5.1. (The *multiple baseline* approach, in which the intervention started at different times for different students, was used to demonstrate that the imposed consequence, rather than some other factor occurring at school or elsewhere, was the reason for the behavior change.) As you can see, none of the students ever needed to report for after-school tutoring. Apparently, the threat of punishment alone was sufficient to bring about desired study behaviors. Perhaps temporary removal of the threat—earned by studying for each quiz—was sufficient negative reinforcement to increase regular study habits.

One common mistake many teachers and parents make, however, is to continue to threaten punishment without ever following through. One warning is advisable, but repeated threats are not. The mother who continually says to her son, "If you hit your sister again, Tommy, I'll send you to your room for the rest of the week," but never actually sends Tommy to his room, is giving her son the message that no response–punishment contingency really exists.

One of the reasons that teachers and parents often fail to follow through with threatened punishment is that they too often bluff, proposing punishment that is impractical or unrealistically extreme. Tommy's mother does not punish her son because forcing Tommy to spend "the rest of

Figure 5.1

Quiz grades for three high school French class students.

Reprinted with permission from "The Effective Use of Punishment to Modify Behavior in the Classroom" by R. V. Hall, S. Axelrod, M. Foundopoulos, J. Shellman, R. A. Campbell, & S. S. Cranston, 1972, in K. D. O'Leary & S. O'Leary (Eds.), *Classroom Management: The Successful Use of Behavior Modification*, p. 180. Copyright © 1972 by Pergamon Press, Ltd.

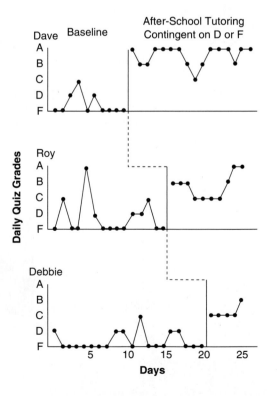

the week" in his room would be a major inconvenience for both of them. A teacher who threatens that certain behaviors will result in students not going on a promised field trip should do so only if he or she knows that leaving some students behind at school is logistically possible.

♦ *Describe unacceptable behaviors in clear, concrete terms.* Learners should understand exactly which responses will result in punishment. A student who is told, "If you disrupt the class again this morning, you will lose your free time," may not understand exactly what the teacher means by "disrupt" and so may continue to engage in inappropriate classroom behavior. The teacher should instead take the student aside and say something such as, "Sharon, there are two behaviors that are unacceptable in this classroom. When you talk without permission and when you get out of your seat during quiet reading time, you keep other children from getting their work done. This morning I expect you to talk and get out of your seat only when I give you permission to do so. Otherwise, you will have to sit quietly at your desk this afternoon when the other children have their free time."

♦ *Whenever possible, administer punishment immediately after the inappropriate behavior.* As is true for reinforcement, the effectiveness of punishment decreases dramatically when it is delayed (Landrum & Kauffman, 2006; Lerman & Vorndran, 2002; Trenholme & Baron, 1975; Walters & Grusec, 1977). The more closely punishment follows a misbehavior, the more effective it will be. When, for whatever reason, punishment cannot be administered immediately, the contingency between the behavior and the consequence must be made crystal clear (Aronfreed & Reber, 1965).

♦ *Administer punishment within the context of a generally warm, supportive environment.* Punishment is more effective when the person administering it has previously established a good working relationship with the learner (Landrum & Kauffman, 2006; Nucci, 2001). The message should ultimately be: "I care for you and want you to succeed, and your current behavior is interfering with your success."

♦ *Explain why the behavior is unacceptable.* Although behaviorists tend to focus attention on responses and their consequences, a significant body of research indicates that punishment is more effective when *reasons* are given for why certain behaviors cannot be tolerated (Baumrind, 1983; Hess & McDevitt, 1984; Hoffman, 1975; Parke, 1977; Perry & Perry, 1983). For example, in an example presented earlier, Sharon's teacher incorporated reasoning into her description of Sharon's inappropriate behaviors: "When you talk without permission and when you get out of your seat during quiet reading time, *you keep other children from getting their work done.*"

Providing reasons as to why behaviors are unacceptable has at least four advantages (Cheyne & Walters, 1970; Walters & Grusec, 1977):

1. When punishment is accompanied by reasoning, it appears to make the immediacy of punishment a less critical factor in its effectiveness.
2. Reasoning increases the likelihood that when one behavior is punished, similar misbehaviors are also suppressed; that is, the effect of the punishment generalizes to other misbehaviors.
3. If reasons are given, misbehaviors are likely to be suppressed even when the punisher is absent.
4. Older children apparently *expect* to be told why they cannot engage in certain behaviors and are likely to be defiant when reasons are not provided.

◆ *Be consistent in imposing punishment for inappropriate behavior.* Just as is true for reinforcement, punishment is far more effective when it *always* follows a particular response (Leff, 1969; Lerman & Vorndran, 2002; Parke & Deur, 1972). When a response is punished only occasionally, with other occurrences of that response being either ignored or reinforced, the response disappears slowly, if at all.

Consistency is important not only across time but also across contexts. When a student with chronic behavior problems has two or more teachers (a common situation for most middle school and high school students), then all teachers should coordinate their efforts. And ideally, teachers and parents should agree on the behaviors they will reinforce and punish. In this way, they minimize the likelihood of behavioral contrast between school and home.

Unfortunately, people can be punished only when they are caught in the act. Thieves are rarely apprehended, and speeders are ticketed only when they drive on roadways that are patrolled. Many undesirable classroom behaviors, such as talking out, getting out of one's seat, being aggressive, and cheating, may be reinforced as frequently as they are punished. To deal with the difficulty of detecting some undesirable student behaviors, the next two guidelines—modifying the situation so the misbehavior is less likely to occur and simultaneously reinforcing alternative behaviors—are especially critical.

◆ *Modify the environment so that misbehavior is less likely to occur.* The temptation to engage in a misbehavior should be reduced or, if possible, eliminated. For instance, troublemaking friends might be placed on opposite sides of the classroom or in different classes. Cheating on an exam can be reduced by having students sit apart from one another or administering two different forms of the exam to different students (Cizek, 2003).

◆ *Teach and reinforce more appropriate behaviors.* In and of itself, punishment tells an individual what *not* to do but not what should be done instead (Skinner, 1938). Punishment of misbehavior is typically more effective over the long run when it is combined with support for, as well as reinforcement of, more productive behaviors (Carey & Bucher, 1986; Landrum & Kauffman, 2006; Lerman & Vorndran, 2002; Ruef, Higgins, Glaeser, & Patnode, 1998). For example, when punishing aggression on the playground, teachers should remember also to teach and reinforce effective social skills. Teachers can punish a student for cheating, but they should also teach the student good study habits and reinforce the student for working well independently.

APPLIED BEHAVIOR ANALYSIS

Sometimes people's problem behaviors are so entrenched and counterproductive that they require intensive, systematic intervention. One effective approach in dealing with such behaviors is **applied behavior analysis (ABA),** also known as *behavior modification, behavior therapy,* or *contingency management.* ABA is based on the assumption that serious problem behaviors are, like most human behaviors, the result of past and present response–consequence contingencies. It involves the application of a variety of behaviorist concepts—reinforcement, shaping, cueing, extinction, punishment, and so on—to create an environment more conducive to productive behaviors.

Components of Applied Behavior Analysis

Although ABA interventions tend to be tailored to individual circumstances, several strategies are common to many of them:

◆ *Behaviors that are the focus of intervention are identified in observable, measurable terms.* Consistent with behaviorist tradition, teachers and therapists who use ABA focus their attention on specific, concrete responses, which they call **target behaviors.** In some cases an intervention might be aimed at increasing a target behavior to the point where it becomes a desired terminal behavior. In other instances an intervention is aimed at *decreasing* target behaviors. For example, in a program designed to address a child's aggressiveness, such target behaviors as screaming, hitting other people, and throwing objects might be the focus (Morris, 1985).

◆ *Behavior is measured both before and during the intervention.* Only through objective measurement of the target behavior during both baseline and intervention can we determine whether a particular intervention is effectively changing a target behavior. One way of measuring the target behavior is simply to count the overall number of times a given response occurs; for example, if we have designed a program to modify Johnny's hitting-others behavior, we would count each instance of hitting. A second method of behavior measurement is to examine the *rate* of responding by counting the number of responses occurring within a specified time interval; for example, we might count the number of times Johnny hits someone else during each hour of the day. Still a third method, called **time-sampling,** involves dividing the time period during which the individual is being observed into equal intervals and then seeing whether the target behavior occurred in each interval. For example, we might measure Johnny's hitting behavior by dividing his school day into 5-minute intervals and then counting the intervals in which hitting was observed.

In applied behavior analysis, target behaviors are observed and recorded as objectively as possible. Ideally, behaviorists recommend that one person (e.g., a teacher or therapist) administer the ABA intervention and at least two other individuals trained in observation techniques observe and record occurrences of the target behavior. If the method of behavior measurement is such that the behavior is being objectively and accurately recorded, the agreement between the recordings of the two observers (the **interrater reliability**) should be very high.

◆ *Environmental conditions that may be encouraging problem behaviors are identified.* It is often helpful to collect information not only about target behaviors but also about events that immediately precede and follow the behaviors. A teacher or therapist typically takes an *ABC* approach, observing the individual in his or her daily environment and collecting ongoing information about the following:

- **A**ntecedents: stimuli and events that the individual encounters
- **B**ehaviors: responses that the individual subsequently makes
- **C**onsequences: stimuli and events that immediately follow the behaviors

Figure 5.2 illustrates a short time sample of Johnny's hitting responses, with events antecedent and consequent to those responses also recorded.

Once such information is collected, the teacher or therapist looks for patterns in the data and identifies specific events that may be triggering or reinforcing a target behavior—an approach

Antecedent		Peer teased him			None observed	Peer hit him	
Target behavior (hitting)	no	yes	no	no	yes	yes	no
Consequence		scolded			scolded	none	
	9:00	9:02	9:04	9:06	9:08	9:10	9:15

(Times indicate start of each 2-minute interval)

Figure 5.2
A time sample of target behaviors in conjunction with antecedent and consequent events.

known as **functional analysis** or *functional behavioral assessment*.[4] As an example, consider Jeb, a 5-year-old boy with autism. Jeb's teachers reported that he spent a great deal of each school day covering his ears. Researchers Tang, Kennedy, Koppekin, and Caruso (2002) set out to determine why ear-covering behavior was so frequent. At 30-second intervals, they recorded (1) each occurrence of ear covering, (2) specific events occurring at the time (i.e., whether the response occurred during playtime, snack or lunch, instruction, and transition between activities, and whether another child was screaming), and (3) teacher behavior following each response (i.e., whether a teacher began, stopped, or continued interacting with Jeb). Figure 5.3 shows the frequency with which the ear-covering behavior occurred under various antecedent and consequent conditions. As you can see, the teachers typically did not change their behavior toward Jeb when he covered his ears, and so they were apparently not reinforcing the target behavior. A look at the antecedent stimuli is more enlightening: 80% of the ear-covering incidents occurred immediately after a classmate screamed. Quite possibly, Jeb had heightened sensitivity to loud noises, a characteristic seen in many children with autism (Sullivan, 1994; Williams, 1996).

◆ *A specific intervention or treatment plan is developed and implemented.* Developing a treatment plan involves determining the method by which a target behavior is to be modified. Sometimes a behavior's frequency can be increased simply by reinforcing the behavior every time it occurs. When the existing frequency (baseline) of a desired response is very low, however, the response may have to be shaped through the reinforcement of successively closer and closer approximations. An undesirable behavior can be eliminated through such methods as extinction, reinforcement of incompatible behaviors, or punishment. In many cases, explicit instruction is part of the intervention as well (e.g., Craft et al., 1998; Heck, Collins, & Peterson, 2001).

---

[4]In some functional analyses, the teacher or therapist systematically *manipulates* the environment as a way of testing various hypotheses about influential antecedent stimuli and consequences (Iwata, Dorsey, Slifer, Bauman, & Richman, 1982/1994; Van Camp et al., 2000). For examples of this approach, see K. M. Jones, Drew, and Weber (2000); Ellingson et al. (2000); Magee and Ellis (2000); K. A. Meyer (1999); Mueller, Sterling-Turner, and Scattone (2001); and Piazza et al. (1999).

Figure 5.3

Frequency of Jeb's ear-covering responses under various antecedent and consequent conditions.

Reprinted with permission from "Functional Analysis of Stereotypical Ear Covering in a Child with Autism" by J.-C. Tang, C. H. Kennedy, A. Koppekin, & Mary Caruso, 2002, *Journal of Applied Behavior Analysis, 35,* p. 96. Copyright © 2002 by the Society for the Experimental Analysis of Behavior, Inc.

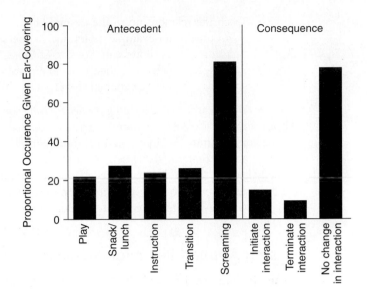

◆ *The treatment is monitored for effectiveness as it progresses, and it is modified if necessary.* When a desired behavior increases or an unwanted behavior decreases during the intervention program (compared with the baseline rate), the logical conclusion is that the ABA program is effective. When little change is observed from baseline to treatment, however, a modification of the program is warranted. Perhaps the teacher or therapist is trying to shape behavior too quickly. Perhaps the "reinforcer" is not really reinforcing, and a different reinforcer should be substituted. Perhaps an undesired behavior that the teacher or therapist is attempting to eliminate through extinction is being maintained by reinforcers beyond his or her control. An unsuccessful intervention program should be carefully examined for these and other possible explanations for its ineffectiveness and then modified accordingly.

◆ *Measures are taken to promote generalization of newly acquired behaviors.* Although people often generalize the responses they learn in one situation to other situations (e.g., R. V. Hall, Cristler, Cranston, & Tucker, 1970; H. M. Walker, Mattsen, & Buckley, 1971), there is no guarantee that they will do so. In fact, many ABA programs have limited success precisely because responses that are learned under some stimulus conditions do not generalize to others (Alberto & Troutman, 2003; Landrum & Kauffman, 2006; Schloss & Smith, 1994). Psychologists have suggested several strategies for promoting generalization during an ABA program:

- Teach the target behavior in a wide variety of contexts, including many realistic ones; if possible, teach the behavior in the actual situations in which it is ultimately desired (Emshoff, Redd, & Davidson, 1976; Haring & Liberty, 1990; B. M. Johnson et al., 2006; Stokes & Baer, 1977).
- Teach many different versions of the behavior; for example, when teaching interpersonal skills, teach a variety of ways to interact appropriately with others (Stokes & Baer, 1977).

- Teach the relationship of the desired behavior to reinforcers that occur naturally in the environment; for example, point out that better personal hygiene leads to positive attention from others (Bourbeau, Sowers, & Close, 1986; Stokes & Baer, 1977).
- Reinforce the behavior when it spontaneously occurs in new situations; in other words, specifically reinforce generalization (Stokes & Baer, 1977).

♦ *Treatment is phased out after the desired behavior is acquired.* Once the terminal behavior has been reached, the ABA program is gradually phased out. In many instances, the newly learned behaviors begin to be reinforcing in and of themselves; for example, the aggressive student who learns more acceptable social behaviors begins to acquire new friends, and the student who has finally learned to read begins to feel successful and enjoy reading. In other situations, maintaining the target behavior may require intermittent reinforcement, such as a series of successively higher variable-ratio reinforcement schedules.

Using Applied Behavior Analysis with Large Groups

Our emphasis until now has been on the use of applied behavior analysis with individuals. But ABA techniques can also be used to change the behavior of *groups* of people—for example, the behavior of an entire class of students. Two methods appear to be especially effective in working with groups: a group contingency and a token economy.

Group Contingency

In a **group contingency,** an entire group must perform a desired behavior in order for reinforcement to occur. For example, in one study (Lovitt, Guppy, & Blattner, 1969), the performance of a class of 32 fourth graders on their weekly spelling tests improved with a group contingency. In phase 1 of the study, baseline data indicated that about 12 students (38%) had perfect spelling tests in any given week. In phase 2, spelling tests were administered each of four days during the week; any student who obtained a perfect test score one day was given free time on any successive days that the same test was repeated. During this individually based contingency period, the average number of perfect spelling tests a week more than doubled to 25.5 (80%). In phase 3, the individual contingencies of phase 2 continued to apply; in addition, when the entire class achieved perfect spelling tests by Friday, the class was permitted to listen to the radio for 15 minutes. The group contingency of phase 3 led to 30 perfect spelling tests (94% of the class) a week!

The "good behavior game" is an example of how a group contingency can reduce classroom misbehaviors (Barrish, Saunders, & Wolf, 1969; Kellam, Rebok, Ialongo, & Mayer, 1994). In a study conducted by Barrish and her colleagues (1969), a class of particularly unruly fourth graders (seven of the students had repeatedly been referred to the principal for problem behaviors) was divided into two teams whose behaviors were carefully observed during reading and mathematics lessons. Every time a team member engaged in out-of-seat or talking-out behavior, that team received a mark on its designated part of the chalkboard. The team that had fewer marks during the lesson received special privileges (e.g., first in the lunch line or free time at the end of the day); if both teams had five marks or fewer, both won privileges.

Figure 5.4 shows the results of Barrish and colleagues' study. Notice how baseline data were first collected for both math and reading periods. The good behavior game was instituted in the mathematics period on Day 23; out-of-seat and talking-out behaviors decreased sharply during

Figure 5.4

Percentage of 1-minute intervals in which talking-out and out-of-seat behaviors occurred during math and reading periods.

From "Good Behavior Game: Effects of Individual Contingencies for Group Consequences on Disruptive Behavior in a Classroom" by H. H. Barrish, M. Saunders, & M. M. Wolf, 1969, *Journal of Applied Behavior Analysis, 2,* p. 122. Copyright © 1969 by *Journal of Applied Behavior Analysis.* Reprinted by permission.

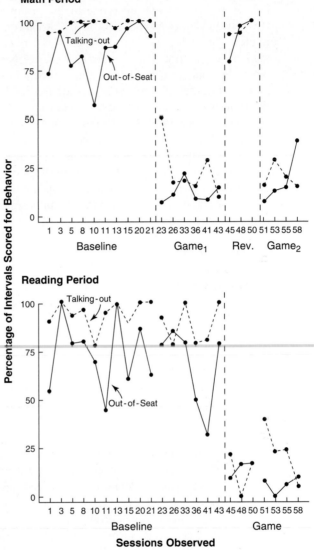

math instruction while continuing at a high frequency during reading. On Day 45, the game was initiated during reading instruction and stopped during math instruction; notice how the frequencies of misbehaviors changed accordingly. On Day 51, the game was reinstated in the math period, and again the misbehavior decreased to a low level in that class. (In this situation, two techniques were used to minimize the likelihood that other, unknown factors were responsible for the behavior changes: starting the game on different days for math versus reading—a multiple baseline approach—and switching from reinforcement to nonreinforcement and then back again—a technique called *reversal.*)

Group contingencies are clearly effective in improving academic achievement and classroom behavior, *provided that* everyone in the group is capable of making the desired responses (Barbetta, 1990; Heck et al., 2001; S. L. Robinson & Griesemer, 2006). Peer pressure and social reinforcement seem to play a role here (O'Leary & O'Leary, 1972; Swenson, 1980). Misbehaving students are encouraged by other students to change their behaviors and are frequently praised when the changes occur (D. W. Johnson & Johnson, 1987; Slavin, 1983b). In addition, when increased academic achievement is the desired behavior, high-achieving students often assist their lower-achieving classmates by tutoring and providing extra practice in the subject matter (Bronfenbrenner, 1970; D. W. Johnson & Johnson, 1987; Pigott, Fantuzzo, & Clement, 1986).

One challenge in using group contingencies is to identify a consequence that all students find reinforcing. A possible strategy here is use of a "mystery reinforcer" that varies from day to day. For instance, a teacher might have an envelope or jar containing slips of paper that describe various possibilities—free time, a pizza party, scratch-and-sniff stickers, and so on. Once students have, as a group, met the criterion for reinforcement, the teacher or a student pulls out a slip of paper identifying the surprise consequence for the day (S. L. Robinson & Griesemer, 2006).

Token Economy

A **token economy** involves a situation in which individuals who behave appropriately are reinforced with **tokens**—items that can later be traded for **backup reinforcers,** which are objects or privileges of each individual's choice. For example, a teacher using a token economy in the classroom might reinforce students with one poker chip for each completed assignment. Just before lunch, students can use their poker chips to "buy" small treats, free time in the reading center, or a prime position in the lunch line. A token economy typically includes the following elements:

1. *A set of rules* describing the responses that will be reinforced. The rules should be relatively few in number so that they can easily be remembered.
2. *Token reinforcers* that can be awarded immediately when appropriate behaviors are exhibited. Such items as poker chips, checkmarks on a grid sheet, play money, or points can be used. Even class grades have been successfully used as tokens (McKenzie, Clark, Wolf, Kothera, & Benson, 1968).
3. *A variety of backup reinforcers* (objects, activities, and privileges) for which tokens can be exchanged. Examples of backup reinforcers that have been shown to be effective in classroom token economies include free time (Osborne, 1969), participation in special events (Bushell, Wrobel, & Michaelis, 1968), and parent-awarded allowances (McKenzie et al., 1968).
4. *A "store" at which the backup reinforcers can be "purchased."* Young children should be allowed at least one purchase opportunity a day; for older children, one or two opportunities a week may be sufficient.

Token reinforcers are advantageous because teachers can use them to reward individual behaviors immediately and conveniently within a group setting. The fact that students can trade tokens for many different backup reinforcers is another advantage: Every individual can probably find at least one desirable item. In fact, children and adults alike seem to prefer having some choice in the reinforcers for which they work (Bowman et al., 1997; Fisher & Mazur, 1997; Geckeler, Libby, Graff, & Ahearn, 2000; Tiger, Hanley, & Hernandez, 2006). The tokens themselves often become effective reinforcers as well (Hundert, 1976). Perhaps they become secondary reinforcers through repeated association with other reinforcing objects and events, or perhaps they are effective simply because they provide feedback that learners are doing something right.

Adding a Cognitive Component to ABA

In recent years, many practitioners have added a cognitive element to ABA techniques, using such terms as *cognitive behavior modification, cognitive behavior therapy,* or *cognitive-behavioral intervention* to describe their approaches (Elliott & Busse, 1991; Hughes, 1988; T. R. Robinson, Smith, Miller, & Brownell, 1999; Yell, Robinson, & Drasgow, 2001). In such approaches, the teacher or therapist frequently models the desired behavior, the assumption being that such modeling helps the student understand the particular behavior that is desired and thereby facilitates the learning process. Another common strategy is **coaching,** whereby the teacher or therapist verbally instructs and guides the student as the latter practices appropriate behaviors. Cognitive approaches also focus on problem solving; for example, the teacher or therapist might ask the student to think carefully about the effects that various behaviors may have in problem situations and to choose those behaviors that are likely to bring about desired consequences.

Effectiveness of ABA

Applied behavior analysis has often been shown to bring about behavior change, and it frequently works where other techniques fail (e.g., O'Leary & O'Leary, 1972). Numerous studies point to its effectiveness in improving academic performance and study habits (Braukmann, Ramp, & Wolf, 1981; Glover & Gary, 1976; Harris & Sherman, 1973; Iwata, 1987; Lovitt et al., 1969; McLaughlin & Malaby, 1972; McLaughlin & Williams, 1988; McNamara, 1987; Piersel, 1987; Rapport & Bostow, 1976). It can also promote improvements in classroom attention, social skills, and personal hygiene (Braukmann et al., 1981; Iwata, 1987; McLaughlin & Williams, 1988; Packard, 1970; Schloss & Smith, 1994; Taylor & Kratochwill, 1978). Furthermore, it can effectively reduce such undesirable behaviors as hyperactivity, impulsivity, aggression, and violence (Ayllon, Layman, & Kandel, 1975; Braukmann et al., 1981; Frankel & Simmons, 1985; Mayer & Butterworth, 1979; Northup et al., 1995; Plummer, Baer, & LeBlanc, 1977; T. R. Robinson et al., 1999; Shafto & Sulzbacher, 1977; Wulbert & Dries, 1977).

Applied behavior analysis is especially beneficial for learners who must be continually motivated to engage in appropriate academic and social behaviors. It is therefore used frequently in the education and therapy of students with special needs, especially those with either significant learning difficulties or behavioral problems.

Although we know that ABA techniques work, we don't always know just *why* they work. One likely factor underlying their effectiveness is the use of clearly specified response–reinforcement contingencies. Because desired behaviors are described in specific, concrete terms, learners know exactly what is expected of them. And the immediate feedback that learners receive through reinforcement provides them with clear guidance as to when their behaviors are on target and when they are not.

Behaviorist principles have had a significant impact not only on classroom management and therapeutic intervention, but also on instructional practice, as we shall see now.

INSTRUCTIONAL OBJECTIVES

In its 1947 report, the President's Commission on Higher Education described the primary goal of the U.S. educational system as "the full, rounded, and continuing development of the person" (cited in Dyer, 1967, p. 14). At first glance, this might seem to be a worthwhile and appropriate goal for education, but on closer inspection, the statement provides very little specific information regarding what an educated person should be like. The President's Commission report is a good example of "word magic": It sounds nice, but we eventually realize that we don't have a clue as to what the words really mean (Dyer, 1967). When we don't know exactly what our educational objectives are, we don't know what or how to teach, nor do we know whether instruction is effectively accomplishing its goals.

As we've seen, a standard practice in behaviorist techniques is to specify the terminal behavior in precise, observable terms before conditioning begins, thereby helping us develop appropriate methods of shaping the desired behavior and of determining when that behavior has been acquired. This principle of *a priori* specification of the terminal behavior in observable, measurable terms has been applied to classroom instruction in the form of **instructional objectives,** descriptions of what students should know and be able to do at the end of instruction.

Behavioral Objectives

Initially, instructional objectives had a very behaviorist flavor and were known as **behavioral objectives.** Ideally, a behavioral objective has three components (Mager, 1962, 1984; Schloss & Smith, 1994). First, the outcome is stated in terms of an observable and measurable behavior. Consider this objective:

> The student will be aware of current events.

A student's "awareness" is not easily observable. The same objective can be stated in terms of one or more specific behaviors that a student should exhibit; consider this one as an example:

> The student will describe the major points of dissension between the Israelis and the Palestinians.

Some verbs (e.g., *be aware of, understand, appreciate, know, remember*) tell us little, if anything, about what students should actually be able to do, but others (e.g., *describe, write, compute, list, select*) clearly communicate observable responses. We can probably conceptualize almost any objective in behavioral terms if we think about the specific things people would have to do to convince someone that they had met the objective (Mager, 1972).

Second, a behavioral objective specifies the conditions under which the behavior should be exhibited. Sometimes we expect desired behaviors to occur in specific situations (i.e., under certain stimulus conditions). For example, when I taught a graduate course in educational assessment, one of my objectives was as follows:

> The student will correctly compute test–retest reliability.

I did not expect students to memorize the formula for calculating test–retest reliability, however. Rather, there was a condition under which I expected the behavior to occur:

Given the formula for a correlation coefficient, the student will correctly compute test–retest reliability.

Finally, a behavioral objective includes a criterion for judging the acceptable performance of the behavior. Many behaviors are not strictly right or wrong; instead, they vary on a continuum of relative "rightness" and "wrongness." In cases where right and wrong behaviors are not obvious, a behavioral objective should specify the criterion for acceptable performance, perhaps in terms of a certain percentage of correct answers, a certain time limit, or the degree of acceptable deviation from the correct response (Mager, 1962, 1984). Following are some examples to illustrate this point:

On weekly written spelling tests, the student will correctly spell at least 85% of the year's 500 spelling words.

Given a sheet of 100 addition problems involving the addition of two single-digit numbers, including all possible combinations of the digits 0 through 9, the student will correctly write the answers to these problems within 5 minutes.

Given the formula for a correlation coefficient, the student will correctly compute test–retest reliability, with differences from a computer-calculated coefficient being attributable to rounding-off errors.

Current Perspectives on Instructional Objectives

Traditional behavioral objectives have frequently been criticized for focusing on picayune, concrete details rather than on more central, but probably more abstract, educational goals. Many lists of behavioral objectives emphasize behaviors that depend on knowledge of facts rather than on behaviors that reflect more complex and sophisticated learning (e.g., Trachtenberg, 1974). In other words, they focus on **lower-level skills** rather than **higher-level skills.** Such lower-level objectives may be prevalent simply because they are the easiest ones to conceptualize and write.

In any given school year, students must accomplish a wide variety of tasks, including many that involve lower-level skills and many others that involve higher-level skills. Writing behavioral objectives that cover each and every one of them can become a burdensome, if not impossible, task. As a result, many educators have proposed that a smaller number of general, nonbehavioral objectives provide a reasonable alternative (e.g., Gronlund, 2000; Popham, 1995; Posner & Rudnitsky, 1986). But in such situations, it is helpful to list examples of behaviors that reflect each abstract objective. To illustrate, imagine that we want high school students to understand, evaluate, and critique the things that they read—an objective that certainly involves higher-level thinking skills. We might list behavioral manifestations of critical reading such as the following:

1. Distinguishes between main ideas and supporting details
2. Distinguishes between facts and opinions
3. Distinguishes between facts and inferences
4. Identifies cause-effect relations
5. Identifies errors in reasoning
6. Distinguishes between valid and invalid conclusions
7. Identifies assumptions underlying conclusions (Gronlund, 2000, p. 52; format adapted)

This is hardly an exhaustive list of what critical reading entails, but it does give us an idea of the terminal behaviors we want to see.

Usefulness and Effectiveness of Objectives

Although educators have largely drifted away from identifying specific behavioral objectives, more general instructional objectives—perhaps labeled as *goals, outcomes, standards, proficiencies, targets,* or *benchmarks*—continue to play a key role in curriculum design and assessment practices. From a teacher's perspective, instructional objectives serve several useful functions (Gronlund, 2000; Mager, 1962, 1984; Stiggins, 2001). First, specification of a lesson's objectives in precise terms helps a teacher choose the most effective method of teaching the lesson. For example, when teaching a unit on basic addition, a teacher might use flash cards if the objective is *rapid recall* of number facts but should probably use word problems or real-life problem-solving activities if the objective is the *application* of those number facts. A second advantage is that objectives, especially when described in behavioral terms, are easily communicated from one teacher to another. For example, although teachers may differ in their conception of what "application of addition principles" means, they will be likely to interpret "correct solution of addition word problems" similarly. Finally, objectives facilitate the evaluation of both students and instructional programs: Student accomplishment and program effectiveness can be evaluated on the basis of whether manifestations of the desired outcomes are observed.

From a student's perspective, instructional objectives have additional advantages. Students who are told what they should be able to do at the conclusion of an instructional unit know what they must focus on, have tangible goals to strive for, and are better able to judge how successfully they have learned (Gronlund, 2000; McAshan, 1979; Stiggins, 2001).

Despite such potential benefits, research studies investigating the effectiveness of objectives for improving academic performance have yielded mixed results. Objectives tend to focus teachers' and students' attention toward certain information and skills (those things that are included in the objectives) and away from other subject matter (Linn, 2003; McCrudden, Schraw, & Kambe, 2005; Slavin, 1990b). If the stated objectives encompass *everything* that students should learn, the use of objectives in the classroom will enhance learning. But if the objectives include only a portion of what the teacher deems to be important, while excluding other, equally important, material, some critical information and skills are not as likely to be learned as completely as they might otherwise be.

Basing major decisions on whether students achieve predetermined objectives—that is, making decisions about promotion, graduation, teacher salaries, school funding, etc., based on students' scores on a single **high-stakes test**—exacerbates the problem. When teachers are held accountable for their students' performance on a particular test, many of them will understandably devote many class hours to the knowledge and skills that the test assesses, and students may focus their studying efforts on that same material (Amrein & Berliner, 2002a; Darling-Hammond, 1991; Linn, 2003; Resnick & Resnick, 1996). The result is often that students perform at higher levels on the test *without* improving their achievement and abilities more generally (Amrein & Berliner, 2002b, 2002c; Jacob, 2003; Levin, 1998; Wolf, 1998).

In the United States, such concerns have recently come to a head with the passage of the No Child Left Behind Act of 2001—often known simply as NCLB. This legislation mandates that all states establish

> challenging academic content standards in academic subjects that—
>   (I) specify what children are expected to know and be able to do;
>   (II) contain coherent and rigorous content; and
> (III) encourage the teaching of advanced skills (P.L. 107–110, Sec. 1111).

School districts must annually assess students in grades 3–8 to determine whether students are making "adequate yearly progress" in meeting state-determined standards in reading and mathematics (as I write this fifth edition of the book, districts are also developing standards for science). The nature of this "progress" is defined by the state (and so differs from state to state), but assessment results must clearly show that all students, including those from diverse racial and socioeconomic groups, are moving forward. (Students with significant cognitive disabilities may be given alternative assessments, but they must show improvement commensurate with their ability levels.) Schools that demonstrate progress receive rewards, such as teacher bonuses or increased budgets. Schools that do not are subject to sanctions and corrective actions (e.g., administrative restructuring), and students have the option of attending a better public school at the school district's expense.

The intent behind NCLB—to boost children's academic achievement, especially that of children from minority groups and low-income backgrounds—is certainly laudable. However, many experts fear that its focus on increasing test scores and accountability, rather than on supporting and rewarding effective instructional practice, is misplaced. High standards for performance may be unrealistic for students who may have had poor nutrition and little preparation for academic work prior to the school years (Berliner, 2005; Kim & Sunderman, 2005; Linn, 2003). And many students may have little motivation to put forth their best effort on statewide exams, hence providing significant underestimates of what they have truly learned (Chabrán, 2003; K. E. Ryan, Ryan, Arbuthnot, & Samuels, 2005; Siskin, 2003). Whether such problems can be adequately addressed by revisions to the legislation or its implementation remains to be seen.

Formulating Different Levels of Objectives

In one form or another, objectives, standards, benchmarks—call them what you will—are here to stay, at least for the foreseeable future. The trick is to make sure that they truly reflect the knowledge and skills that are most important for learners to acquire. Part of the challenge is that teachers, parents, taxpayers, and even experts often disagree on the specific objectives that students at various grade levels should achieve. For example, some constituencies ask us to increase students' factual knowledge—a perspective sometimes referred to as "back to the basics" or "cultural literacy" (e.g., Hirsch, 1996). Others, meanwhile, encourage us to foster higher-level thinking skills such as problem solving and critical thinking and to help students develop the "habits of mind" (e.g., scientific reasoning, drawing inferences from historical documents) central to various academic disciplines (P. A. Alexander, 1997; Berliner, 1997; L. S. Shulman & Quinlan, 1996). In my own view, objectives that reflect fairly simplistic acquisitions—knowledge of basic math facts, locations of different continents and countries on the globe, and so on—are sometimes quite appropriate. But in many circumstances, objectives reflecting relatively sophisticated levels of learning are desirable, especially as students get older (e.g., see N. S. Cole, 1990).

Fortunately, educators have several resources from which they can draw as they formulate objectives for their students and school districts. Some resources take the form of **taxonomies** of objectives—descriptions of various behaviors we might want to see students demonstrate, often listed in order of increasing complexity (e.g., see Bloom, Englehart, Furst, Hill, & Krathwohl, 1956; Harrow, 1972; Krathwohl, Bloom, & Masia, 1964; Stiggins, 2001). One early and widely used example, Bloom's Taxonomy of Educational Objectives (Bloom et al., 1956), describes six general levels of knowing and using information, shown in Figure 5.5.

1. **Knowledge:** rote memorizing of information in a basically word-for-word fashion; for example, reciting definitions of terms or remembering lists of items.

2. **Comprehension:** translating information into one's own words; for example, rewording a definition or paraphrasing a rule.

3. **Application:** using information in a new situation; for example, applying mathematical principles to the solution of word problems or applying psychological theories of learning to educational practice.

4. **Analysis:** breaking information down into its constituent parts; for example, discovering the assumptions underlying a philosophical essay or identifying fallacies in a logical argument.

5. **Synthesis:** constructing something new by integrating several pieces of information; for example, developing a theory or presenting a logical defense for a particular point of view.

6. **Evaluation:** placing a value judgment on data; for example, critiquing a theory or determining the appropriateness of conclusions drawn from a research study.

Figure 5.5
Bloom's Taxonomy of Educational Objectives
(Adapted from Bloom, Englehart, Furst, Hill, & Krathwohl, 1956.)

Bloom and his colleagues originally presented the six levels as a hierarchy, with each one depending on those preceding it in the list. Although the hierarchical nature of Bloom's taxonomy is in doubt (L. W. Anderson et al., 2001; Furst, 1981; Krathwohl, 1994), it nevertheless provides a useful reminder that instructional objectives should often encompass higher-level cognitive skills as well as the knowledge of simple, discrete facts. In chapter 10, we'll look at a recent revision of Bloom's taxonomy that incorporates contemporary theoretical perspectives of learning and cognition.

An additional source of guidance comes from national (and in some cases international) standards created by professional organizations that represent various academic disciplines. Many discipline-specific professional groups have established standards for their discipline. Such standards typically reflect the combined thinking of many experts in a discipline and so almost certainly reflect much of the best of what the discipline has to offer. Examples are presented in Table 5.1.

Existing taxonomies and standards are certainly useful in helping teachers focus instruction on important educational objectives—including problem solving, critical thinking, and other higher-level processes—in various content domains. If teachers rely on content area standards exclusively, however, they are apt to neglect other, equally important objectives, such as helping students acquire effective work habits, study skills, and interpersonal behaviors. In addition to any existing standards teachers may draw on, then, they will also want to formulate some of their *own* objectives for their students' learning.

PROGRAMMED INSTRUCTION AND COMPUTER–ASSISTED INSTRUCTION

Recall B. F. Skinner's concern that reinforcement in the classroom is inconsistent and often presented long after desired responses have been made. To remedy the situation, Skinner (1954) developed a technique most frequently known as **programmed instruction,** or **PI.** Initially,

Table 5.1
Web sites with standards for various academic disciplines.

Content Domain	Organization	Internet Address	Once you get there . . .[a]
Civics and government	Center for Civic Education	www.civiced.org	Go to *Publications* and then to *Resource Materials.*
English and language arts	National Council of Teachers of English	www.ncte.org	Select *Standards* from the *Quick Links* menu.
Foreign language	American Council on the Teaching of Foreign Language	www.actfl.org	Go to *Publications.*
Geography	National Council for Geographic Education	www.ncge.org	Select *Geography Standards* from the *Geography* menu.
Health, physical education, and dance	National Association for Sport and Physical Education	www.aahperd.org/ NASPE	Click on *Standards & Guidelines* in the Quick Links box.
History	National Center for History in the Schools	www.sscnet.ucla. edu/nchs	Click on *Standards (Online).*
Information literacy	American Association of School Librarians	www.ala.org/aasl	Click on *Issues & Advocacy* and then on *Information Literacy.*
Mathematics	National Council of Teachers of Mathematics	www.nctm.org	Click on *NCTM Standards.*
Music	National Association for Music Education	www.menc.org	Click on *National Standards.*
Science	National Academy of Sciences	www.nap.edu	Type "National Science Education Standards" in the Find box.
Visual arts	National Art Education Association	naea-reston.org	Click on *Publications* and then on *Publications List.*

[a]These steps work for me as I finish the final draft of this book in September, 2006. Given the dynamic nature of many Web sites, you may find that you have to do something different when you get to the site in question.

programmed instruction involved a "teaching machine," a box enclosing a long roll of printed material that a student could advance past a display window, exposing small portions of information successively and systematically. In the 1960s and 1970s, PI increasingly took the form of programmed textbooks and, eventually, computer software.

Regardless of its medium, programmed instruction consists of several standard features. First, the material to be learned is presented through a series of discrete segments, or **frames.**

The first frame presents a new piece of information and poses a question about it. The student responds to the question and then moves to the next frame; that frame provides the correct answer to the question, presents more information, and asks another question. The student continues through the frames, encountering new information, responding to questions, and checking answers.

Intrinsic to programmed instruction are several behaviorist concepts and principles, including the following:

1. *Active responding.* The student must make a response in each frame.
2. *Shaping.* Instruction begins with information that the student already knows. New information to be learned is broken into tiny pieces, and instruction proceeds through a gradual presentation of increasingly more difficult pieces. As the successive pieces are presented and questions of increasing difficulty are answered, the terminal behavior is gradually shaped.
3. *Immediate reinforcement.* Shaping proceeds so slowly that students virtually always make a correct response; in this way, they practice appropriate rather than inappropriate responses, and so the probability of reinforcement is quite high. Each correct answer is reinforced immediately in the form of feedback that it is correct.[5]
4. *Individual differences in learning rate.* Programmed instruction is self-paced, allowing students to progress through an instructional unit at their own rate of speed.

Early programmed instruction involved a **linear program:** All students proceeded through exactly the same sequence of frames in exactly the same order. In 1961, Crowder and Martin introduced the **branching program,** which typically progresses in larger steps than a linear program (each frame presents more information), so that error rates in responding are somewhat higher. A student who responds incorrectly is directed to one or more "remedial" frames for further practice on that part of the lesson before being allowed to continue with new material.

The major advantage of a branching program is that it provides remedial instructional frames only for students who have difficulty with a particular concept; other students can move on to new information without having to spend time on practice they don't need. Unfortunately, however, a branching program can be cumbersome, at least in its textbook form. Students are referred to different frames, and often to different pages, for different responses, so progression through the program is rarely smooth. Fortunately, this drawback of the branching program was virtually eliminated by the advent of computer technology as an instructional medium.

Computer-assisted instruction, or **CAI,** is programmed instruction presented by means of a computer. It has several advantages not characteristic of paper-and-pencil forms of programmed instruction. First, branching programs can be used without having to instruct students to proceed to one frame or another; the computer automatically presents the

---

[5]Skinner believed that making errors interferes with learning, in large part because students practice incorrect responses. In contrast, many cognitive theorists believe that errors can sometimes be helpful, in that they encourage students to examine and reevaluate their reasoning and problem-solving strategies (e.g., see the discussion of conceptual change in chapter 9).

appropriate frame for any response the student gives. Second, because of the graphics capabilities of computers (e.g., complex moving visual displays can be included in lessons), CAI can present information in a way that traditional programmed instruction cannot. Third, the computer can record and maintain ongoing data for each student, including information such as how far a student has progressed in the program, how often he or she is right and wrong, how quickly he or she responds, and so on. With such data, a teacher can monitor each student's progress through the program and identify students who are having unusual difficulty with the material. And, finally, a computer can be used to provide instruction when flesh-and-blood teachers are not available; for example, CAI has been used to deliver college instruction in rural areas far removed from university settings.

Effectiveness of PI and CAI

Most research indicates that traditional (i.e., noncomputer-based) programmed instruction provides little if any advantage over traditional instructional methods (Kulik, Cohen, & Ebeling, 1980; Kulik, Schwalb, & Kulik, 1982). In contrast, CAI can sometimes lead to greater academic achievement and improved student attitudes toward schoolwork, at least in comparison with traditional instructional methods (Blok, Oostdam, Otter, & Overmaat, 2002; Christmann, Badgett, & Lucking, 1997; Fletcher-Flinn & Gravatt, 1995; Kulik, Kulik, & Cohen, 1980; Liao, 1992; Luyben, Hipworth, & Pappas, 2003). However, the differences in achievement for CAI versus traditional methods are typically small or moderate, rather than large.

Generally speaking, PI and CAI are more likely to be effective when behaviorist principles—opportunities for making active responses, immediate reinforcement of responses, gradual shaping of the terminal behavior, and so on—are adhered to (e.g., Kritch & Bostrow, 1998; Tudor, 1995). Exceptions have been noted, however. In one study of programmed instruction at the college level, occasional 10-second delays in feedback actually *enhanced* students' learning, apparently because the delays gave students more time to study the material in front of them (Crosbie & Kelly, 1994).

As cognitivism increasingly dominates theories of human learning, computer instruction is no longer restricted to the traditional, behaviorism-based CAI approach; hence, you may sometimes see reference to such terms as *computer-based instruction (CBI)* or *computer-assisted learning (CAL)* rather than CAI. Today's computer-based instruction encompasses a wide variety of innovations, including simulations that engage students in realistic activities (e.g., dissecting an animal, flying an airplane), "intelligent tutors" that diagnose and address specific problem areas, computer tools (e.g., word processing programs, spreadsheets, graphing programs, music composition software), and challenging problems and games. Later in the book, we'll consider how computer technology has been used to promote complex problem-solving skills (chapter 13) and enhance group learning and meaning-making (chapter 14).

MASTERY LEARNING

Inherent in the behaviorist perspective is the belief that, given appropriate environmental conditions, people are capable of acquiring many complex behaviors. Such optimism is reflected in **mastery learning**—an approach to instruction in which students must learn one lesson well (they must *master* the content) before proceeding to the next lesson. Underlying this approach is the assumption that most students *can* learn school subject matter if they are given sufficient time and instruction to do so.

Mastery learning is based, in part, on the concept of *shaping*. At first, a relatively simple response is reinforced until it is emitted frequently (i.e., until it is mastered), then a slightly more difficult response is reinforced, and so on until eventually the desired terminal behavior is acquired. Consistent with shaping, mastery learning usually includes the following components:

1. *Small, discrete units.* Course content is broken up into a number of separate units or lessons, with each unit covering a small amount of material.
2. *A logical sequence.* Units are sequenced such that basic concepts and procedures—those that provide the foundation for later units—are learned first. More complex concepts and procedures, including those that build on basic units, are learned later. For example, a unit in which students learn what a fraction *is* would obviously come before a unit in which they learn how to add two fractions together. The process through which the component parts of course content are identified and sequenced, going from simpler to more complex, is called **task analysis** (e.g., see Jonassen, Hannum, & Tessmer, 1989).
3. *Demonstration of mastery at the completion of each unit.* Before "graduating" from one unit to the next, students must show that they have mastered the current unit—for example, by taking a test on the unit's content.
4. *A concrete, observable criterion for mastery of each unit.* Mastery of a topic is defined in specific, concrete terms. For example, to pass a unit on adding fractions with the same denominator, students might have to answer at least 90% of test items correctly.
5. *Additional, remedial activities for students needing extra help or practice.* Students do not always demonstrate mastery on the first try. Additional support and resources— perhaps alternative approaches to instruction, different materials, workbooks, study groups, and individual tutoring—are provided for students who need them.

Students engaged in mastery learning often proceed through the various units at their own speed; hence, different students may be studying different units at any given time. But it is also possible for an entire class to proceed through a sequence at the same time: Students who master a unit earlier than their classmates can pursue various enrichment activities, or they can serve as tutors for those still working on the unit (Block, 1980; Guskey, 1985).

Mastery learning gained prominence during the 1960s, and many educators have advocated it in one form or another (e.g., Bloom, 1968, 1981; Carroll, 1963, 1989; Gentile & Lalley, 2003; Knutson, Simmons, Good, & McDonagh, 2004; Piotrowski & Reason, 2000). A particular form of mastery learning—Fred Keller's personalized system of instruction—has been used extensively at the college level. Let's take a closer look at what this approach entails.

Keller's Personalized System of Instruction (PSI)

As Michael (1974) has pointed out, traditional college instruction has definite weaknesses when viewed from the perspective of behaviorist principles. For example, students may not learn what grades they've earned for their work until days or weeks after they've submitted the work; hence, achievement is not immediately reinforced. Furthermore, students must frequently proceed to advanced material before they have mastered the more basic information necessary to understand it.

To remedy such weaknesses, Keller (1968, 1974) developed the **personalized system of instruction** (also known as **PSI** or the **Keller Plan**) as an alternative approach to teaching college students (also see Fox, 2004). In addition to the discrete units, logical sequence, self-pacing, and frequent measures of mastery characteristic of other mastery learning approaches, PSI encompasses the following features:

1. *Emphasis on individual study.* Most learning occurs through students' independent study of such written materials as textbooks and study guides. One-on-one tutoring provides additional assistance when necessary.
2. *Unit exams.* An examination on each unit assesses students' mastery of the material. Students receive immediate feedback about how well they have performed on unit exams.
3. *Supplementary instructional techniques.* Traditional group instructional methods (e.g., lectures, demonstrations, and discussions) are occasionally provided to supplement the material that appears in the textbook or other assigned readings. These group classes are optional but serve to motivate and stimulate students.
4. *Use of proctors.* Proctors, usually more advanced students, administer and score exams and tutor students on topics with which they are having difficulty.

The teacher of a PSI course plays a different role from that of someone using a more conventional approach to instruction. The PSI teacher is less of a lecturer and more of a curriculum developer, exam writer, proctor coordinator, and record keeper. Rather than leading students through course content, the PSI teacher instead provides an elaborate system whereby students, with the assistance of study guides and tutors, find their own way through the content.

Effectiveness of Mastery Learning and PSI

By and large, research findings indicate that mastery learning (including PSI) facilitates student learning and often leads to higher achievement than more traditional approaches (Arlin, 1984; Austin, 2000; Fox, 2004; Kulik, Kulik, & Bangert-Drowns, 1990). Furthermore, students in mastery learning programs often retain the things they have learned for longer periods of time (DuNann & Weber, 1976; Kulik, Kulik, & Cohen, 1979); to illustrate, in one study, college students in mastery-based psychology classes remembered 75 to 85% of the material after 4 months and 70 to 80% after 11 months (Semb, Ellis, & Araujo, 1993). And PSI, at least, facilitates better study habits: Although PSI students don't appear to study more than other students, they study regularly rather than procrastinating and cramming the way students in traditional courses often do (Born & Davis, 1974; Kulik et al., 1979). Low-achieving students in particular seem to benefit from a mastery learning approach (DuNann & Weber, 1976; Knutson et al., 2004; Kulik et al., 1990).

Mastery learning and PSI are not without their problems, however. In many cases, students who learn quickly receive less instruction than their classmates, raising a concern about possibly inequitable treatment of these students (Arlin, 1984). Furthermore, when, for logistical reasons, fast-learning students must wait until their slower classmates have also mastered the material, they learn less than they might otherwise (Arlin, 1984). Yet when all students are allowed to work at their own pace, teachers must assist and keep track of perhaps 25 or 30 students working on different tasks and succeeding at different rates; hence, they may do more "managing" (e.g., distributing materials, grading tests) than actual teaching (Berliner, 1989; Prawat, 1992).

Additional weaknesses have been noted for PSI in particular. One difficulty lies in the required mastery of material; some students are unable to meet the criterion for passing exams despite repeated assessments (Sussman, 1981). A second weakness is the lack of interaction among students—interaction that many students see as beneficial to their learning (Gasper, 1980). A third problem is related to the self-paced nature of a PSI course, which is sometimes compromised if university policy requires that students complete a course within a single quarter or semester (Sussman, 1981). Poorly motivated students are likely to procrastinate until finally they must withdraw from the course (Sussman, 1981; Swenson, 1980). Although, in general, withdrawal rates for PSI courses are not appreciably higher than those for traditional courses, they can be quite high if students take the course entirely on-line, without ever seeing a classroom or fellow classmates (Kulik et al., 1979, 1990; Pear & Crone-Todd, 1999). Several techniques have been shown to reduce procrastination and withdrawal from PSI, among them setting target dates for the completion of different units, giving bonus points for early completion of units, and eliminating the necessity for completing the course within a single college term (Bufford, 1976; Reiser & Sullivan, 1977; Sussman, 1981).

Mastery learning is probably most appropriately used when a teacher's main objective is for students to learn specific skills or a specific body of information prerequisite to later topics. In such situations, the immediate feedback and emphasis on mastery of course material may well be reasons why mastery learning increases student achievement, especially for low-achieving students. When the objective is something other than acquiring information or skills, however—for example, when the objective is for students to gain a better understanding of controversial issues or to work cooperatively with classmates to solve complex problems—a mastery approach may not be the method of choice.

WHEN BEHAVIORIST TECHNIQUES ARE MOST APPROPRIATE

Instructional methods based on concepts and principles of instrumental conditioning can be beneficial for most learners at one time or another, especially when important behaviors and skills require a lot of repetition and practice to master (Brophy, 2004). As you undoubtedly know from your own experience, tedious drill-and-practice activities often have little intrinsic appeal, and so some external consequence—perhaps a few M&Ms once in a while, or perhaps an occasional break to check and respond to incoming e-mail messages (an activity reinforcer)—can help keep you going.

Overall, however, behaviorist approaches are probably more appropriate for certain groups of students than for others. Frequent success experiences and reinforcements, such as those provided by mastery learning or programmed instruction, are especially beneficial to students who have previously had little success in their academic careers (Gentile & Lalley, 2003; Gustafsson & Undheim, 1996; Snow, 1989). Children officially identified as having a "developmental delay" or "learning disability" fall into this category, as do many students with chronic behavior problems. A regular pattern of academic success is exactly what such students need to bolster the low self-confidence resulting from a long string of academic failures.

Students with little motivation to engage in academic tasks can also profit from behaviorist techniques. The introduction of extrinsic reinforcers (material, social, or activity reinforcers) contingent on academic accomplishments can be helpful in motivating seemingly "uninterested" students to master essential skills (Cameron, 2001; Covington, 1992; Lepper, 1981).

Students with chronically high levels of anxiety are another group who stand to benefit. Such students often need considerable structure to feel comfortable in the classroom and perform well on academic tasks (Corno et al., 2002; Dowaliby & Schumer, 1973; Helmke, 1989). For instance, they need a classroom environment that specifies expectations for behavior and clearly lays out response–reinforcement contingencies. They also seem to require frequent success experiences and positive feedback. Many of the methods derived from behaviorist principles address the needs of anxious children especially well: Instructional objectives spell out desired behaviors in concrete terms, programmed instruction and mastery learning provide success and positive feedback, and applied behavior analysis techniques clearly communicate which behaviors will yield the reinforcers the students seek.

Finally, there are some students for whom little else works. Techniques based on behaviorist principles have been shown to be effective methods of changing even the most resilient of problem behaviors (Greer, 1983; Rimm & Masters, 1974). Such stubborn conditions as severe childhood autism and serious behavior disorders have been dealt with more successfully by applied behavior analysis than by any other method currently available.

Yet behaviorist approaches are probably not well suited for everyone. Bright students may find the gradual, inch-by-inch approach of programmed instruction slow and tedious. A token economy in a classroom of highly motivated college-bound adolescents may undermine the intrinsic desire of these students to achieve at a high level. Other learning theories, notably cognitive theories, are probably more useful in designing and implementing instruction for these students.

SUMMARY

If we look at typical classrooms from a behaviorist perspective, we realize that reinforcement comes far less frequently than it should (and often only after a considerable delay), and punishment comes all too often. The use of both reinforcement and punishment in classrooms has been subject to other criticisms as well; some reflect a misunderstanding of common behaviorist practices, but others are legitimate.

Nevertheless, the well-planned, systematic use of reinforcement can be highly effective in improving students' classroom learning and behavior when certain guidelines are followed. Among other things, desired behaviors should be specified up front, reinforcers should be tailored to individual students, and response–reinforcement contingencies should be explicitly communicated. Inappropriate behaviors can often be reduced through extinction, noncontingent reinforcement, reinforcement of other behaviors, or punishment. A number of strategies enhance punishment's effectiveness; for instance, punishment is more effective when students know in advance what behaviors will be punished and how, when it is administered within the context of a generally warm and supportive environment, and when it is accompanied by reasons why certain behaviors are unacceptable.

Applied behavior analysis (ABA) involves the application of behaviorist principles to address chronic, serious behavior problems. Typically it involves precise measurement of target behaviors, manipulation of antecedent events and consequences to change the frequency of various responses, ongoing monitoring of an intervention to ensure its effectiveness, and specific plans for generalization and phase-out. Such mechanisms as group contingencies and token economies allow teachers and therapists to use reinforcement effectively even in large-group settings. ABA techniques have been shown to improve a wide variety of academic and social behaviors, often in situations where other approaches have been unsuccessful.

Instructional objectives, and especially behavioral objectives (which describe educational outcomes in terms of precise, observable responses), are a direct outgrowth of the behaviorist concept of terminal behavior. Objectives facilitate communication among students and teachers; they also help in the selection of appropriate instructional strategies and evaluation techniques. Objectives tend to focus teachers' and students' attention on the information and skills they identify (an advantage) and away from other information and skills (a decided disadvantage if *all* important objectives have not been identified or are not being assessed).

Programmed instruction, computer-assisted instruction, and *mastery learning* incorporate such behaviorist principles as active responding, shaping, and immediate reinforcement. In general, noncomputer-based programmed instruction appears to be no more effective than traditional instructional methods, whereas computer-assisted instruction and mastery learning often lead to better learning. Behaviorist approaches to instruction are probably best used with certain kinds of students (e.g., those with a history of academic failure, low motivation, or high anxiety) rather than as a matter of course with all students.

Part Three

Social Cognitive Theory

CHAPTER 6

Social Cognitive Theory

One summer, my sons Alex and Jeff spent quite a bit of time with their Uncle Pete, a large man who could pick them both up at the same time and carry them around on his shoulders. Uncle Pete's feats of strength were quite a contrast to Mom's and Dad's difficulties in lifting either boy alone, or even in opening pickle jars. For several years after that summer, Alex and Jeff spoke often of wanting to be like Uncle Pete, and I found that I could talk them into eating many foods they had previously shunned simply by saying, "This is what helps Uncle Pete get big and strong." The ploy never did work for broccoli, however.

When my daughter Tina was in junior high school, some of her friends got in the habit of calling her every morning to find out what she would be wearing to school that day. Tina was apparently somewhat of a fashion trendsetter at school, and several other girls were mimicking her attire. Given the apparel in which Tina left for school most mornings, I shudder at the thought of what her cronies must have looked like.

Almost daily, we see instances of people watching others and learning from them. Young boys often emulate hero figures such as Superman, Batman, and Uncle Pete. Through watching and copying one another, preadolescent girls often begin to behave in similar ways, dressing alike, wearing their hair in faddish styles, and lusting after the same boys. Children imitate their

My daughter the trendsetter.

parents by developing similar hobbies and interests, by expressing similar political and religious beliefs, and by eventually raising their own children using the same disciplinary techniques with which they were raised. Students in the classroom learn many academic skills, including reading, writing, adding, and subtracting, at least partly through watching and imitating what their teachers and classmates do.

Such learning by observation and modeling is the focus of **social cognitive theory** (e.g., Bandura, 1977, 1986; Rosenthal & Zimmerman, 1978; Schunk, 1989c). Initially known as *social learning theory,* it evolved from behaviorism but now includes many of the ideas that cognitivists also hold, hence the gradual shift in label to social *cognitive* theory. In this chapter, we will consider social cognitive theory's perspective on how both environmental and cognitive factors interact to influence human learning and behavior. We will explore the phenomenon of *modeling,* examining the mental processes involved, the effects of modeling on behavior, and the characteristics of effective models. We will find that people's beliefs about their own ability to execute various behaviors successfully (that is, their *self-efficacy*) play a role in the responses they choose to make and the effort they exert in making those responses. And we will discover how, through the process of *self-regulation,* people become less and less influenced by environmental conditions as time goes on. At the end of the chapter, we will examine a number of implications of social cognitive theory for educational practice.

THE SOCIAL COGNITIVE APPROACH

Social cognitive theory focuses on what and how people learn from one another, encompassing such concepts as observational learning, imitation, and modeling. Although many species of animals can learn by imitation (Hayes & Hayes, 1952; Herbert & Harsh, 1944; Zentall, 2003), social cognitive theory deals primarily with human learning, and so we will be putting research involving laboratory animals aside for the time being.

The study of learning through imitation was launched in a 1941 book by behaviorists Neal Miller and John Dollard. But it was not until the early 1960s that a theory of imitation and modeling separate from its behaviorist roots began to take shape. Development of this theory was due in large part to the research and writings of Albert Bandura of Stanford University (e.g., Bandura, 1969, 1973, 1977, 1986, 1989; Bandura & Walters, 1963). Bandura's perspective has evolved considerably over the years and continues to be a driving force in studies of imitation and modeling. You will find numerous references to Bandura and others who build on his ideas (e.g., Dale Schunk, Barry Zimmerman) throughout the chapter.

General Principles of Social Cognitive Theory

Several general principles underlie social cognitive theory, including the following:

♦ *People can learn by observing the behaviors of others, as well as by observing the outcomes of those behaviors.* Many early behaviorists viewed learning largely as a matter of trial and error: People learn by making a variety of responses and then modifying their behavior based on the consequences (e.g., the reinforcement) that their responses bring. In contrast, social cognitive theorists propose that most learning takes place not through trial and error but instead through watching the behavior of other individuals (**models**).

♦ *Learning can occur without a change in behavior.* As we noted in chapter 3, behaviorists have traditionally defined learning as a change in behavior; thus, no learning can occur unless behavior *does* change. In contrast, social cognitive theorists argue that because people can learn through observation alone, their learning will not necessarily be reflected in their actions. Something learned at one time may be reflected in behavior exhibited at the same time, at a later time, or never.

♦ *The consequences of behavior play a role in learning.* The role of consequences in social cognitive theory has evolved as the theory itself has evolved. In Miller and Dollard's (1941) early theoretical analysis of learning new behaviors through imitation, reinforcement of the behaviors was also a critical factor. Instrumental conditioning continued to be a major component of Albert Bandura's early work as well (e.g., Bandura & Walters, 1963). In later years, however, the role of consequences was reconceptualized (Bandura, 1977, 1986; Rosenthal & Zimmerman, 1978). Contemporary social cognitive theorists propose that both reinforcement and punishment have less critical, *indirect* effects on learning—effects that we'll examine shortly.

♦ *Cognition also plays a role in learning.* Over the past 30 years, social cognitive theory has become increasingly "cognitive" in its analysis of human learning. For example, contemporary social cognitive theorists maintain that *awareness* of response–reinforcement and response–punishment contingencies is an essential component of the learning process. They also assert that *expectations* of future reinforcements and punishments can have a major impact on the behaviors that people exhibit. Finally, as you will soon see, social cognitive theorists incorporate such cognitive processes as *attention* and *retention* (memory) into their explanations of how learning occurs.

♦ *People can have considerable control over their actions and environments.* In behaviorist views of learning, people are largely at the mercy of environmental circumstances—what stimuli are encountered simultaneously (which can lead to classical conditioning), what consequences follow certain responses (which can lead to instrumental conditioning), and so on. In contemporary social cognitive theory, however, people can take active steps to create or modify their environments—perhaps by making changes themselves, or perhaps by convincing others to offer assistance and support—and they often do so consciously and intentionally. As social cognitive theorists put it, human beings have **personal agency** (Bandura, 2006).

We turn now to the ways in which environmental factors—reinforcement and punishment in particular—play a role in learning by observation. We will then look at how cognition is also involved.

ENVIRONMENTAL FACTORS IN SOCIAL LEARNING: REVISITING REINFORCEMENT AND PUNISHMENT

If we were to explain imitation from an instrumental conditioning perspective, we might propose that people imitate others because they are reinforced for doing so. In fact, this is exactly what Miller and Dollard proposed back in 1941. According to these theorists, an individual uses another person's behavior as a discriminative stimulus for an imitative response. The observer is then reinforced in some way for displaying imitation. For example, let's say that a French teacher carefully enunciates:

Comment allez vous? (Discriminative stimulus)

Students repeat the phrase in more or less the same way:

Comma tally voo?   (Response)

The teacher then praises them for their efforts:

Trés bien! Very good! (Reinforcement)

From a behaviorist perspective, imitation of other people's behavior is maintained by an intermittent reinforcement schedule: Individuals are not *always* reinforced for mimicking the responses of others, but they are reinforced often enough that they continue to copy those around them. Eventually imitation itself becomes a habit, a phenomenon Miller and Dollard called **generalized imitation.**

How the Environment Reinforces and Punishes Modeling

People are often reinforced for modeling the behaviors of others. Bandura has suggested that the environment reinforces modeling, but may also occasionally punish modeling, in several possible ways:

♦ *The observer is reinforced by the model.* In the French lesson dialogue presented above, the model—the teacher—reinforces students for imitative behavior. People often reinforce others who copy what they themselves do. For example, a group of teenage girls is more likely to welcome another girl into the group if she dresses as they do. A gang of antisocial boys will probably accept a new member only if he acts "tough."

Adults, such as parents and teachers, most often reinforce children for copying those behaviors that their culture deems to be appropriate. For example, when my children were young, I would occasionally hear one of them use polite, "adult" language on the telephone, perhaps along this line: "I'm sorry, but my mother is busy right now. If you will give me your name and number, I'll have her call you back in a few minutes." Such a statement was similar to what I myself would tell callers, and I was likely to praise the child profusely. However, a statement such as, "Ma! Telephone! Hurry up and get off the potty!" was definitely *not* learned through observation of the adults in the house, and I certainly never reinforced it.

♦ *The observer is reinforced by a third person.* On some occasions an individual is reinforced by a third person rather than by the model. For example, children are often reinforced by parents and teachers when they imitate other children. Something I used to tell my youngest child, Jeff, was this: "Oh, you're such a big boy now! You're getting dressed all by yourself, just like Alex does!"

During the Beatlemania of the 1960s, many teenage boys began sporting "moppet" haircuts like those of the Beatles. Such haircuts were "in," at least at my high school, and none of us girls would have ever been caught dead with a boy who had hair shorter than John Lennon's. My friends and I were, in essence, reinforcing boys who modeled themselves after the Beatles. In earlier days, we would have reinforced anyone who could play the guitar and bat his eyelashes in a come-hither fashion, just as Ricky Nelson used to do in the television show *Ozzie and Harriet.*

♦ *The imitated behavior itself leads to reinforcing consequences.* Many behaviors that we learn through observing others produce satisfying (reinforcing) results. For example, a French student who pronounces his *Comment allez vous?* correctly will have greater success communicating with a Parisian. An individual who can closely model a tennis instructor's body positions and arm movements is more likely to get the ball over the net and into the opponent's court.

♦ *Consequences of the model's behavior affect the observer's behavior vicariously.* When people observe a model making a particular response, they may also observe the consequence of the response. If a model is reinforced for a response, then the *observer* may show an increase in that response; this phenomenon is known as **vicarious reinforcement.** For example, if Andy sees Adam gain popularity among the girls because he can play the guitar and bat his eyelashes in a come-hither fashion, Andy may very well buy a guitar and take a few guitar lessons; he may also stand in front of the mirror practicing eyelash batting.

Reinforcement of the model affects the observer's behavior as well.

The power of vicarious reinforcement (and of **vicarious punishment** as well) was dramatically illustrated in an early study by Bandura (1965b). Children watched a film of a model hitting and kicking an inflated punching doll. One group of children saw the model reinforced for such aggressive behavior, a second group saw the model punished, and a third group saw the model receive no consequences for the aggression. When the children were then placed in a room with the doll, those who had seen the model being reinforced for aggression displayed the most aggressive behavior toward the doll: They had been vicariously reinforced for aggression. Conversely, those children who had seen the model punished for aggression were the least aggressive of the three groups: They had been vicariously punished for such behavior.

Problems with a Strict Behaviorist Analysis of Social Learning

Although early social learning theorists tried to explain imitative behavior from the perspective of instrumental conditioning, they encountered several difficulties in doing so. One problem is that completely new behaviors can be acquired simply by watching others perform them (Bandura, 1977, 1986; Rosenthal, Alford, & Rasp, 1972). In instrumental conditioning, however, new behaviors typically start from *existing* behaviors that are gradually shaped and modified over time.

A second difficulty is the phenomenon of **delayed imitation:** Some behaviors that are learned through observing others do not appear until a later time. In chapter 4, we diagrammed the relationship of antecedent stimulus, response, and reinforcement like this:

$$(S+) \quad R \rightarrow S_{Rf}$$

These three things follow one right after the other, with the response occurring in the presence of the discriminative stimulus. Yet as Bandura (1977) has pointed out, the response and resulting reinforcement do not always appear immediately after the discriminative stimulus but may instead occur days or even weeks later. For such delayed imitation to be exhibited, learning must actually take place when the discriminative stimulus is presented, despite the absence of reinforcement at that time.

Still a third problem lies in the powerful effect of vicarious reinforcement: Individuals sometimes exhibit behaviors for which they themselves are *never* reinforced.

To address the shortcomings of a behaviorist analysis, social cognitive theorists have suggested that consequences often have indirect rather than direct effects on learning (e.g., Bandura, 1977, 1986; Rosenthal & Zimmerman, 1978). Such effects require that cognitive factors be added to the picture, as you shall see now.

COGNITIVE FACTORS IN SOCIAL LEARNING

The cognitive side of social cognitive theory is evident in several of its central ideas:

   ◆ *Learning is, first and foremost, a mental (rather than behavioral) acquisition.* Social cognitive theorists make a distinction between *learning* through observation (something called **vicarious acquisition**) and the actual *performance* of what has been learned (Bandura, 1977, 1986; Rosenthal & Zimmerman, 1978). At least two sources of evidence indicate that learning results in some sort of mental representation of a behavior. For one thing, people can verbally describe a behavior they have observed but don't ever imitate (Bandura, 1965a). Second, people who observe a model perform a behavior may not demonstrate that behavior until some later time when they have a reason for doing so. For example, I previously described a study by Bandura (1965b) in which children watched a film of a model acting aggressively toward an inflated punching doll. As you may recall, the consequences of the aggression to the model (reinforcement, punishment, or no consequence) influenced the extent to which children themselves engaged in aggressive acts toward the doll. Later in the study, however, all of the children were promised rewards (stickers and fruit juice) if they could imitate the model's behavior. At that point, differences among the three groups of children disappeared! Clearly they had all *learned* the model's behavior equally well; the consequences to the model apparently affected their earlier performance but not their learning.

♦ *Certain cognitive processes are essential for learning to occur.* Social cognitive theorists describe specific cognitive processes (i.e., thinking) that occur when people are learning from a model. Among these are *paying attention* to what the model is doing, mentally *rehearsing* aspects of the model's performance, and forming mental representations (*memory codes*) of what the model has done. I will illustrate each of these ideas later in the chapter when I describe the conditions that Bandura suggests are necessary for successful modeling.

♦ *Learners must be aware of existing response–consequence contingencies.* According to social cognitive theorists, reinforcement and punishment have little effect on learning and behavior unless people have mental *awareness* of the response–reinforcement and response–punishment contingencies (Bandura, 1977, 1986; Spielberger & DeNike, 1966). Reinforcement increases the likelihood of a response only when an individual realizes which particular response has led to the reinforcement. Similarly, an individual must recognize what particular behavior is being punished before that behavior is likely to decrease. Consider a situation in which a student receives an F on a writing assignment, with comments such as "Poorly written" and "Disorganized" noted in the margins. For many students, such feedback is insufficient to bring about an improvement in writing because, among other things, it does not identify the specific parts of the assignment that are poorly written and disorganized.

♦ *Learners form expectations for future response–consequence contingencies.* Social cognitive theorists suggest that people will most likely perform the behaviors they've learned when they expect a payoff (i.e., reinforcement) for doing so. For example, I learned many years ago that the capital of Alaska is Juneau. Yet I have never had a reason to demonstrate this knowledge because I have never been tested on the capital of Alaska, nor have I ever been in Alaska desperately seeking the state capital. Now, of course, I do have a reason: I am hoping you'll be impressed by the fact that I know the capital of at least one of the 50 states.

More generally, when people are reinforced or punished for certain behaviors, they are likely to form **outcome expectations**—hypotheses about the results that future actions are likely to bring—and behave in ways that will maximize desirable consequences (Bandura, 1977, 1986, 1989, 1997; Rosenthal & Zimmerman, 1978). People may also form outcome expectations by seeing *others* reinforced or punished for certain behaviors, and they behave accordingly—a fact that explains the effectiveness of vicarious reinforcement and punishment.

The concept of **incentive**—anticipating that a particular reinforcement will occur if a particular behavior is performed—reflects this idea of expectation. You should notice a critical difference here between the role of reinforcement in instrumental conditioning and in social cognitive theory. In instrumental conditioning, reinforcement influences learning of the behavior it *follows*. In social cognitive theory, however, an *expectation* of reinforcement—an incentive—influences the learning of a behavior it *precedes* (Bandura, 1977, 1986).

◆ *Learners also form beliefs about their own ability to perform various behaviors.* Not only do people form expectations about the likely outcomes of various behaviors, but they also form **efficacy expectations,** beliefs about whether *they themselves* can execute particular behaviors successfully (Bandura, 1997; Schunk & Pajares, 2004). For example, imagine that you are in a class in which the instructor has clearly described the criteria for an A. But imagine, too, that you don't believe you have the knowledge and skills to meet the criteria. Even though you know what it takes for a high grade, you don't *have* what it takes (not in your own eyes, at least), and so you cannot achieve an A no matter what you do. We will examine the nature and effects of efficacy expectations, commonly known as *self-efficacy,* later in the chapter.

◆ *Outcome and efficacy expectations influence cognitive processes that promote learning.* The extent to which learners actively engage in cognitive processes essential for learning (paying attention, forming memory codes, etc.) depends on their beliefs about the likelihood that learning something will lead to reinforcement. For example, I have learned the hard way that when I tell my students they will not be held responsible for certain information, I am making a BIG MISTAKE. All I have to do is say something like, "Now I want you to listen carefully to what I have to say for the next five minutes, but *it won't be on the next test,*" and students put their pens down and settle back in their seats; if I'm teaching an early morning class, a few in the back row may start to nod off. People are less likely to pay attention to something when they do not anticipate a payoff for learning it.

◆ *The nonoccurrence of expected consequences is an influential consequence in and of itself.* In the social cognitive view, the nonoccurrence of expected reinforcement is often a form of punishment, and the nonoccurrence of expected punishment can be reinforcing (Bandura, 1977, 1986). Both of these principles involve situations in which outcome expectations are not being met. For example, once again imagine yourself as a student in a class in which the teacher has clearly described the criteria necessary to earn an A. But this time imagine that you think you *do* have the ability to meet those criteria. You work hard, and your performance meets the specified criteria, so you are naturally expecting an A. But at the last minute, your teacher adds an additional requirement: To earn an A, students must write a 20-page term paper. You are probably angry and frustrated (in a sense, you feel punished), because you had expected reinforcement based on the work you had already completed, and that reinforcement is now being withheld. Unexpected outcomes and *non*outcomes often evoke stronger emotional responses than expected ones do (e.g., Mellers, Schwartz, Ho, & Ritov, 1997).

The nonoccurrence of expected consequences can be just as influential when observed for a model rather than for oneself (Bandura, 1973, 1977, 1986; Walters & Parke, 1964; Walters, Parke, & Cane, 1965). For example, in a study by Walters and Parke (1964), children in three experimental groups watched a film in which a boy (the model) was told by a female experimenter not to play with a number of toys that lay on the table in front of him but instead to read a book that she had given him. Yet as soon as the woman left the room, the boy began to play with the toys. At this point, the film was different for the three experimental groups, as follows:

1. *Reward.* The woman returned, handed the boy some toys, and played with him affectionately.
2. *Punishment.* The woman returned, snatched away the toys the boy was playing with, shook him vigorously, and sat him back down with the book.
3. *No consequence.* The woman did not return to the room.

Children in these three groups, and children in a control group who did not view a film, were then taken to a room full of toys, told not to touch them, given a book to read, and left alone for 15 minutes. Children in the no-consequence group played with the toys (thus disobeying the experimenter's instructions) just as much as the reward group did. Children in the punishment group were more obedient, but the most obedient children were those in a fourth (control) group, who had not watched the disobedient model at all.

When people see others misbehave without negative consequences, they are more likely to misbehave themselves. For example, when my daughter was in elementary school, she came home almost daily with complaints about who had gotten away with what on the playground that day. When playground supervisors ignore transgressions day after day, their inaction not only perpetuates those misbehaviors but may cause them to increase. In the same way, I often wonder whether individuals who see others quite literally get away with murder aren't more likely to engage in criminal activities themselves.

It should be clear by now that social cognitive theory incorporates elements of both behaviorism and cognitivism. We have examined some of the environmental and cognitive factors that, from a social cognitive perspective, are involved in the learning process. We must also consider how environment and cognition *interact* with one another. We turn next to this topic—in particular, to Bandura's concept of reciprocal causation.

RECIPROCAL CAUSATION

We have already seen how the environment influences behavior and how mental processes occurring within a person (e.g., attention, expectations) influence behavior. Social cognitive theorists propose that, in a reciprocal fashion, behavior can also influence both the environment and the person. In fact, each of these three variables—environment, person, and behavior—influences the other two in an interaction known as **reciprocal causation** (Bandura, 1989, 2006; Schunk & Pajares, 2004; Zimmerman & Schunk, 2003).[1] The interaction of environment (E), person (P), and behavior (B) can be depicted like this:

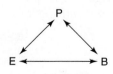

---

[1]Prior to 1989, Bandura used the term *reciprocal determinism.*

Certainly the environment influences a person's behavior. For example, the occurrence of a desirable or undesirable consequence as a result of a particular response influences the probability that an individual will make the response again. But an individual's *perception* of the environment (a "person" variable) can be equally influential on behavior. For example, I mentioned earlier that awareness of response–reinforcement contingencies influences the extent to which those contingencies affect behavior. Consider an experiment by Kaufman, Baron, and Kopp (1966) as a case in point. Participants in the experiment were all placed on a variable-interval reinforcement schedule, with the average interval before reinforcement being 1 minute, and told one of three things about the schedule they were on. People in Group 1 were told that they were on a 1-minute variable-interval schedule (i.e., they were told the truth). People in Group 2 were told that they were on a 1-minute *fixed*-interval schedule. People in Group 3 were told that they were on a variable-ratio (1:150) schedule. People's response patterns corresponded to the reinforcement schedules they *believed* they were on: Group 3 showed the fastest response rate, and Group 2 showed the slowest response rate, consistent with the response patterns that are actually observed for these different reinforcement schedules. Baron, Kaufman, and Stauber (1969) have reported similar results.

But reverse effects exist as well; that is, behavior affects both the environment and personal cognition. The responses people make (e.g., the academic courses they choose, the extracurricular activities they pursue, the company they keep) determine the learning opportunities they have and the consequences they experience (environmental variables). For example, individuals typically behave in ways that increase reinforcement and decrease punishment, and their actions may put them in situations that present new response–reinforcement contingencies.[2] Furthermore, the pattern of one's responses over time affects one's self-confidence and expectations for future success (person variables). A boy who stumbles and falls frequently may begin to think of himself as a klutz. By consistently performing well on mathematics assignments, a girl may begin to believe she is a math whiz.

Finally, person variables and environmental variables affect each other. For example, by directing attention (a person variable) to one stimulus and not to another, certain aspects of the environment will be experienced and others will not. And we have already seen how the consequences of past behaviors (an environmental variable) affect the expectations that people have (a person variable) regarding the outcomes of future behaviors.

One prime example of the interplay among environment, person, and behavior variables is modeling. We now look more closely at the modeling process.

MODELING

As we noted in chapter 2, children begin to imitate others' facial expressions within a day or two after birth and possibly are genetically prewired with an ability to imitate (recall our discussion of *mirror neurons*). By 6 to 9 months, infants can learn new ways of manipulating objects (e.g.,

---

[2]In recent years, I have seen a similar idea in behaviorist literature. Rosales-Ruiz and Baer (1997) define the term *behavioral cusp* as "any behavior change that brings the organism's behavior into contact with new contingencies that have even more far-reaching consequences" (p. 533). For example, when infants begin to crawl, they gain greater access to toys, other family members, and potentially hazardous objects. When students begin to read fluently, they open up many new opportunities for learning and instruction.

pushing a button on a box, shaking an egg-shaped rattle) by watching a model display those behaviors, and the infants will often remember the behaviors a day later (Collie & Hayne, 1999; Meltzoff, 1988a, 1988b). By 18 months, they may remember and imitate an action they have observed as much as a month earlier (Collie & Hayne, 1999).

According to Bandura (1977, 1986), many of the behaviors people exhibit have been acquired through observing and modeling what others do. In this section, we will consider the various ways in which modeling can affect behavior, the types of models that are most likely to influence learning, and the kinds of behaviors that can be modeled. We will also look at four processes essential for learning to occur through modeling. Before we proceed, however, I should point out that social cognitive theorists sometimes use the term *modeling* to describe what a model does (i.e., demonstrate a behavior) and at other times to describe what the observer does (i.e., mimic that behavior). I have tried to write this section in such a way that the term's meaning is always readily discernible from the context in which it is used.

How Modeling Affects Behavior

Social cognitive theorists (e.g., Bandura, 1977, 1986; Bandura & Walters, 1963; Rosenthal & Zimmerman, 1978) have proposed that modeling has several effects:

◆ *Modeling teaches new behaviors.* People can learn entirely new behaviors by observing others perform those behaviors. For example, by listening to and imitating the sounds made by others, a person learns to pronounce previously unknown words. And by watching how a parent swings a bat and following the parent's verbal instructions ("Keep your eye on the ball!"), a child learns to hit a baseball.

◆ *Modeling influences the frequency of previously learned behaviors.* As noted earlier, people are more likely to exhibit behaviors they have previously learned when they see others being reinforced for such behaviors; in other words, vicarious reinforcement has a **facilitation** effect. And people are less likely to perform behaviors for which they have seen others being punished; in other words, vicarious punishment has an **inhibition** effect.

◆ *Modeling may encourage previously forbidden behaviors.* In some situations, when people observe a model engaging in behavior that has previously been described as forbidden or "wrong," and especially when the model is reinforced for engaging in that behavior, they themselves are more likely to display the behavior. On these occasions, vicarious reinforcement has a **disinhibition** effect (because previously inhibited behavior is now reoccurring). For example, in studies by Walters and his colleagues (Walters & Thomas, 1963; Walters, Thomas, & Acker, 1962), adults viewed either a film depicting aggression and violence (*Rebel Without a Cause*) or a neutral film (*Picture Making by Teenagers*) and then were asked to administer "shocks" to other individuals. (These other individuals were confederates of the experimenter who did not really receive any shocks but behaved as if they did.) People who had watched the violent, aggressive film administered more frequent and more intense "shocks" to the confederates. The film had apparently disinhibited previously learned aggressive behavior.

◆ *Modeling increases the frequency of similar behaviors.* When a person observes a model performing a particular behavior, that person may display similar rather than identical behavior. For instance, a boy who sees his older brother excel at basketball but lacks his brother's height advantage may instead strive to become a successful soccer player. As a high school student,

I would have given my eyeteeth to become a "cool" cheerleader but did not have the gymnastic skills necessary for cheerleading. Instead, I became a majorette in the marching band, a position that was almost as cool.

Characteristics of Effective Models

Bandura has identified three general types of models. When we think of modeling, we most frequently think of a **live model**—an actual person demonstrating a particular behavior. But we can also learn from a **symbolic model**—a person or character portrayed in a book, film, television show, videogame, or other medium. For example, many children model their behavior after football players, rock singers, or such fictional characters as Harry Potter or Pippi Longstocking. Finally, we can learn from **verbal instructions**—descriptions of how to behave—without another human being, either live or symbolic, being present at all.

Individuals who are most likely to serve as live or symbolic models for others tend to have one or more characteristics:

- *The model is competent.* People demonstrating a particular behavior are more likely to be imitated by others if they are viewed as being competent, capable individuals (Bandura, 1986; Schunk, 1987). For example, a person trying to learn tennis is more likely to model the techniques of a successful tennis player than those of a friend who seldom gets the ball over the net. And a student trying to learn how to write a good term paper is more likely to look at the work of someone who has consistently received high grades on term papers than at the work of a student who tends to do poorly on such assignments. Even 3-year-olds have some ability to discriminate between the effective and ineffective behaviors they see modeled, and they are more likely to imitate those that produce desired results (Want & Harris, 2001).

- *The model has prestige and power.* Individuals who have high status, respect, and power, either within a small group or within society as a whole, are more likely to serve as models for others (Bandura, 1986). A child is more likely to imitate the behaviors of a student leader or a famous rock star than the behaviors of a class dunce or a rock-and-roll has-been. For instance, in

Models are often competent, prestigious, and powerful.

one study (Sasso & Rude, 1987), researchers identified several children who were popular with their peer group and several others who were less popular. They then taught these children methods of initiating appropriate ways of socially interacting with children who had physical disabilities. When other children later saw their popular classmates approaching and interacting with children with disabilities, they were likely to do so as well. If they instead observed relatively unpopular classmates behave in such a manner, they were less likely to follow suit.

◆ *The model behaves in stereotypical "gender-appropriate" ways.* Males are more likely to model behavior that is consistent with male stereotypes; similarly, females are more likely to model behaviors that follow traditional female patterns (Schunk, 1987). For example, in studies in which children watched adult models of both genders being aggressive (Bandura, Ross, & Ross, 1961, 1963), boys were more likely than girls to imitate the aggressive behaviors, presumably because aggression is a trait more frequently associated with males than with females.

This is *not* to say that youngsters shouldn't see models of both genders, however. Ideally, children and adolescents should see males and females alike modeling a wide variety of behaviors, including counterstereotypical ones. In doing so, they may begin to realize that most behaviors are truly appropriate for both genders (Bem, 1987; Bussey & Bandura, 1992; Huston, 1983; Weinraub et al., 1984).

◆ *The model's behavior is relevant to the observer's situation.* Individuals are more likely to model the behaviors of people they view as similar to themselves in some important way (Zimmerman, 2004). They are also more likely to model behaviors that have functional value in their own circumstances (Rosenthal & Bandura, 1978; Schunk, 1987). For example, as a child my daughter Tina modeled many of my behaviors, but she definitely did not model the way I dressed. She told me, in so many words, that she would be laughed out of school if she dressed the way I did.

Behaviors That Can Be Learned Through Modeling

Many behaviors are acquired, at least in part, through modeling. For example, a variety of studies with children and adults indicate that people:

- Become better readers when their parents read frequently at home (Hess & McDevitt, 1989)
- Acquire new social skills when they watch videos of people effectively using those skills (LeBlanc et al., 2003; Nikopoulos & Keenan, 2004)
- Master athletic skills more easily when shown specific techniques for improving their performance (Kitsantas, Zimmerman, & Cleary, 2000; Zimmerman & Kitsantas, 1997)
- Are more likely to resist the enticements of a stranger when a peer has modeled techniques for resisting such enticements (Poche, Yoder, & Miltenberger, 1988)
- May begin to respond emotionally to certain stimuli in the same ways that they see others (e.g., parents) react to those stimuli (Klinnert, 1984; Mineka & Zinbarg, 2006; Mumme & Fernald, 2003)
- May begin to deal with a fear-inducing situation with little or no fear after seeing a model behave fearlessly in that situation (Bandura, Grusec, & Menlove, 1967; Bandura & Menlove, 1968; Silverman & Kearney, 1991)
- Are more likely to show intolerance of racist statements when people around them refuse to tolerate such statements (Blanchard, Lilly, & Vaughn, 1991)

Considerable research has been conducted concerning the impact of modeling on three kinds of behavior in particular: academic skills, aggression, and morality.

Academic Skills

Students learn many academic skills by seeing others demonstrate those skills. For instance, they may learn how to solve long-division problems or write a cohesive paragraph or story partly by observing how their teachers and peers do these things (Braaksma, Rijlaarsdam, & van den Bergh, 2002; Sawyer, Graham, & Harris, 1992; Schunk, 1981; Schunk & Hanson, 1985; Schunk & Swartz, 1993). In small groups with classmates, they may adopt one another's strategies for conducting discussions about literature, for instance soliciting one another's opinions ("What do you think, Jalisha?"), voicing agreement or disagreement ("I agree with Kordell because . . . ," "I disagree with Janelle . . . "), and justifying points of view ("I think it shouldn't be allowed, because if he got to be king, who knows what he would do to the kingdom") (R. Anderson et al., 2001, pp. 14, 16–17, 25). And students' general attitudes toward school and academic achievement are influenced by the peers with whom they regularly associate (J. R. Harris, 1998).

Often, students learn academic skills more effectively when models demonstrate not only how to do something but also how to *think about* something—in other words, when models engage in **cognitive modeling** (Sawyer et al., 1992; Schunk, 1998; Schunk & Swartz, 1993; Zimmerman, 2004). As an example, consider how a teacher might model the thinking processes involved in long division:

> First I have to decide what number to divide 4 into. I take 276, start on the left and move toward the right until I have a number the same as or larger than 4. Is 2 larger than 4? No. Is 27 larger than 4? Yes. So my first division will be 4 into 27. Now I need to multiply 4 by a number that will give an answer the same as or slightly smaller than 27. How about 5? $5 \times 4 = 20$. No, too small. Let's try 6. $6 \times 4 = 24$. Maybe. Let's try 7. $7 \times 4 = 28$. No, too large. So 6 is correct. (Schunk, 1998, p. 146)

Aggression

Numerous research studies indicate that children become more aggressive when they observe aggressive or violent models (e.g., C. A. Anderson et al., 2003; Bandura, 1965b; Goldstein, Arnold, Rosenberg, Stowe, & Ortiz, 2001). In the classic study in this area (Bandura et al., 1961), preschoolers were taken one at a time to a playroom containing a variety of toys and were seated at a table where they could draw pictures. Some of these children then observed an aggressive model: An adult entered the room and engaged in numerous aggressive behaviors toward an inflatable punching doll, including kicking the doll in the air, straddling it and hitting it over the head with a wooden mallet, and making statements like "Pow!" "Kick him," and "Punch him in the nose." Other children instead observed a nonaggressive model: An adult came in and played in a constructive way with building blocks. Still other children saw no model while they were in the playroom. The children were then led to another room where they were mildly frustrated: Just as they began to play with some very attractive, entertaining toys, the toys were taken away from them. Finally, the children were taken to a third room in which both nonaggressive and aggressive toys (including the inflatable punching doll and wooden mallet) were present; their behaviors were recorded and coded for aggressive content by observers on the other side of a one-way mirror. Children who had seen the aggressive model were clearly the most aggressive of the three groups, and in fact they mimicked many of the same behaviors that they had seen the aggressive model display (e.g., straddling the doll and hitting it with the mallet). Children who had seen a nonaggressive model were even less aggressive than the no-model group. With regard to aggression, then, models can have an impact either way: Aggressive models will lead to increased aggression in children, and nonaggressive models will lead to decreased aggression.

Children can also learn aggression from observing it in films, television shows, or video games (C. A. Anderson et al., 2003; C. A. Anderson & Bushman, 2001; Steuer, Applefield, & Smith, 1971; Wartella, Caplovitz, & Lee, 2004).[3] In another study by Bandura and his colleagues (Bandura et al., 1963), preschool children who had seen a film of either an adult or a cartoon character being aggressive exhibited just as much aggression toward an inflatable doll as did children who had seen a live adult model; all of these children were significantly more aggressive than children who had not observed a model at all.

Morality

Children appear to acquire moral behaviors partly through observation and modeling. For instance, research has demonstrated the importance of modeling for generosity and other forms of altruism (Elliott & Vasta, 1970; Jordan, 2003; Radke-Yarrow, Zahn-Waxler, & Chapman, 1983; Rushton, 1980, 1982). Consider a study by Rushton (1975) as an example: Children first observed a model playing a bowling game and reinforcing himself with tokens for high performance. Some children saw the model donate half of the earned tokens to a poor boy named Bobby pictured on a poster in the room; other children observed the model keep all of his winnings for himself despite the poster. The children then had the opportunity to play the game and reward themselves with tokens. The more tokens they earned, the better prize they could purchase (therefore, donating to Bobby meant that they would have to purchase a lesser prize for themselves). Children who had watched generous models were more likely to donate some of their own tokens to Bobby than were children who had watched selfish models. This difference was true not only in the initial experimental session but also in a follow-up session two months later.

Models in the media can have an impact as well. Rather than encouraging aggression, some characters in popular media promote *prosocial* behaviors—those aimed at helping others rather than at enhancing one's own well-being (D. R. Anderson, 2003; Huston, Watkins, & Kunkel, 1989; Jordan, 2003; Rushton, 1980). For example, in a study by Friedrich and Stein (1973), a group of preschool children watched *Mister Rogers' Neighborhood*—a television show that stresses such prosocial behaviors as cooperation, sympathy, and sharing—for 30 minutes each day over a 4-week period. These children displayed more socially appropriate behavior and less aggression than children who instead watched shows with aggressive content (e.g., *Batman* and *Superman*) during the same period.

Moral judgments regarding right and wrong may also develop, at least in part, through modeling (Bandura & McDonald, 1963; Prentice, 1972; Schliefer & Douglas, 1973). For example, in a study by Bandura and McDonald (1963), experimenters presented children with pairs of stories such as the following:

---

[3]Some preliminary evidence suggests that aggressive lyrics in popular music may also increase aggression (C. A. Anderson et al., 2003).

1. John was in his room when his mother called him to dinner. John goes down, and opens the door to the dining room. But behind the door was a chair, and on the chair was a tray with fifteen cups on it. John did not know the cups were behind the door. He opens the door, the door hits the tray, bang go the fifteen cups, and they all get broken.

2. One day when Henry's mother was out, Henry tried to get some cookies out of the cupboard. He climbed up on a chair, but the cookie jar was still too high, and he couldn't reach it. But while he was trying to get the cookie jar, he knocked over a cup. The cup fell and broke. (Bandura & McDonald, 1963, p. 276)

In each pair, stories portrayed one well-intended child (such as John) who caused major damage and another child with less appropriate intentions (such as Henry) who did minor damage. For each pair of stories, the children were asked which child was naughtier. Some children consistently picked the child with the bad intentions as being naughtier; these children were then exposed to a model who used amount of damage as the criterion for naughtiness. Other children had a pattern of judging the well-meaning but more destructive child as being naughtier; they were exposed to a model who used bad intentions as the criterion for naughtiness. Observing the model had a profound effect on the children's later moral judgments: Children began to make moral decisions similar to those the model had made and opposite to their own previous judgments.

What about situations in which a model preaches one set of moral values and practices another? A review of research by Bryan (1975) leads to a clear conclusion: When children hear a model say one thing and do something else, they are more likely to imitate what the model *does* than what the model *says*. In other words, to be effective, models must practice what they preach.

Conditions Necessary for Effective Modeling to Occur

Bandura (1977, 1986) has suggested that four conditions are necessary before an individual can successfully model the behavior of someone else: attention, retention, motor reproduction, and motivation.

Attention

To imitate a behavior accurately, a person must first pay attention to the model and especially to the significant aspects of the modeled behavior. For example, if Martha wishes to learn how to swing a golf club, she should watch how the golf pro stands, how her legs are placed, how she holds the club, and so on. Paying attention to the irrelevant parts of the model or her behavior—how the pro clears her throat or how her socks don't quite match—will, of course, not be helpful.

I still remember my first French teacher, a woman who came to my fifth-grade class for an hour one day each week. This woman always wore the same dark green wool dress, which, unfortunately, turned to a turquoise color in places where she perspired. I remember focusing on those turquoise spots, fascinated that a wool dress could actually change color so dramatically just because of a little human sweat. Yes, I was paying attention to my model, but, no, I did not learn much French, because I did not pay attention to the important aspect of the model's behavior—her voice.

Retention

After paying attention, the learner must also remember the behavior that has been observed. One simple way to remember what one has seen, at least for the short run, is **rehearsal**—repeating whatever needs to be remembered over and over again (Vintere, Hemmes, Brown, & Poulson, 2004; Weiss & Klint, 1987). For instance, in a study by Vintere and colleagues (2004), an adult modeled a variety of multistep dance moves for 3- to 5-year-old preschoolers. The children learned the moves more quickly when they were instructed to repeat, or *rehearse,* the various steps to themselves while performing them. In executing a "butterfly dance," for example, they would say to themselves, "Slide, jump, slide, jump, run, and stop." Meanwhile, a "cupcake dance" was easier when they told themselves, "Step, step, jump, one, two, three" (p. 309).

According to Bandura, people store both verbal representations (such as step-by-step instructions or labels that describe the actions to be performed) and visual images of the behaviors they have seen. These verbal and visual **memory codes** serve as guides when people perform the observed behavior, whether they perform it immediately after the model has demonstrated it or at some time in the future. As an illustration of such memory codes, my son Jeff's swimming teacher used the words *chicken, airplane,* and *soldier* to describe the three arm movements of the elementary backstroke (see Figure 6.1). The words provided Jeff with verbal codes for these actions; the teacher's demonstration of them facilitated the formation of visual images.

Considerable evidence indicates that learning from a model is easier if learners have assistance in forming memory codes for the behaviors they observe (Alford & Rosenthal, 1973; Bandura, Jeffery, & Bachicha, 1974; Coates & Hartup, 1969; Cohen, 1989; Gerst, 1971; Rosenthal et al., 1972). For example, in a study by Gerst (1971), college students studied a number of words (hand signs) in sign language for the deaf. Students who were instructed

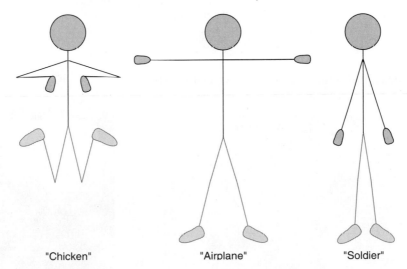

Arm Movements for the Elementary Backstroke

"Chicken"   "Airplane"   "Soldier"

Figure 6.1
Students often remember a model's behaviors more easily when those behaviors have verbal labels.

either to describe the signs verbally or to form mental images of them remembered the signs more successfully than an uninstructed control group; students who were instructed to develop verbal labels descriptive of the hand movements remembered the signs most accurately.

The storage of information in memory and the different forms that such stored information can take are topics that have been studied more extensively by cognitive theorists than by social cognitive theorists. So we will return to this topic of memory storage again, and in much greater detail, in chapters 8 and 9.

Motor Reproduction

A third condition necessary for successful modeling is, of course, actual replication of the behavior that a model has demonstrated. When an individual cannot reproduce an observed behavior, perhaps because of physical immaturity, lack of strength, or disability, this third process obviously does not occur. For example, a child with articulation difficulties may never be able to pronounce *sassafras* correctly, no matter how many times she hears the word spoken. And a toddler who watches his teenage brother throw a football does not possess the muscular coordination to mimic that throw.

In my never-ending battle with the bulge, I used to turn on Jane Fonda's physical workout videotape religiously every night (well, at least twice a month). Jane performed exercises in various pretzel-like contortions that I, even in my wildest dreams, would never be able to do. My body wasn't built to be folded in that many ways. Motor reproduction of everything I watched Model Jane do was simply not possible.

Not only must learners have the *ability* to perform an observed behavior, but ideally they should have an *opportunity* to perform it at the same time they observe it (e.g., Hayne, Barr, & Herbert, 2003). Reproduction of an observed behavior as it's being observed facilitates learning for at least two reasons. For one thing, it enables learners to encode the behavior not only in verbal and visual forms but perhaps in a *motoric* form as well—that is, in terms of the specific actions it encompasses (Cohen, 1989). Furthermore, by modeling a behavior in the presence of the model, learners can get feedback about how to improve their performance (Bandura, 1977;

Modeling cannot occur without the physical capability.

Schunk, 1981).[4] For instance, when children who have historically struggled with math are learning division, instruction that includes an opportunity for practice and immediate feedback about the quality of performance is clearly superior to instruction that provides no opportunity for such practice and feedback (Schunk, 1981).

Motivation

The final necessary factor in modeling is motivation: Learners must want to demonstrate what they have learned. For instance, many people who have grown up in our society have seen models on television point a gun in someone's ribs and say "Reach for the sky" (or something to that effect). Fortunately, very few people are motivated to model that behavior, at least with a real gun.

Although parents and teachers are often models for children, children do not model *all* of the behaviors they observe their parents and teachers performing. For example, although my children modeled my ways of speaking to people on the telephone and my cookie-baking techniques, for some reason they never seemed to copy my broccoli-cooking or floor-scrubbing behaviors. Children model behaviors only when they are motivated to do so.

To review, Bandura's four essential conditions for successful modeling are attention, retention, motor reproduction, and motivation. Because these conditions vary from person to person, different people will model the same behavior differently. For example, Martha and Mary might pay attention to different aspects of their tennis instructor's tennis swing: Martha may focus on how the instructor is standing, whereas Mary may attend more to the way the instructor grips her racket. Or the two girls might store different visual images of the swing, Martha remembering that the instructor was facing the net and Mary remembering her standing with the left shoulder toward the net. Martha may be stronger, but Mary may be more motivated to play tennis well. The end result is that Martha and Mary will model the same tennis swing differently. Not only will the four essential conditions for modeling lead to individual differences in modeled behaviors, but also the absence of any one of them will make modeling unlikely to occur at all.

One important ingredient in the fourth process—motivation—is self-efficacy, and in this respect learners are often *very* different from one another. We now zoom in on this concept.

SELF-EFFICACY

People are more likely to engage in certain behaviors when they believe they are capable of executing the behaviors successfully—that is, when they have high **self-efficacy** (Bandura, 1982, 1989, 2006; Schunk & Pajares, 2004). For example, I hope you believe that you are capable of understanding and remembering the ideas I present in this book; in other words, I hope you have high self-efficacy for learning about learning. You may or may not believe that with instruction and practice you will eventually be able to perform a passable swan dive; in other words, you may have high or low self-efficacy about learning to dive. You are probably quite skeptical that you could ever walk barefoot over hot coals, resulting in low self-efficacy regarding this activity.

---

[4]Note, however, that some children may prefer to practice newly learned behaviors in private before showing an adult what they have learned. For example, this may be the case for many Native American children (Fuller, 2001; Suina & Smolkin, 1994).

At first glance, the concept of self-efficacy may seem similar to such ideas as self-concept and self-esteem, but there's an important difference. In general, one's *self-concept* addresses the question "*Who* am I?" and *self-esteem* addresses the question "*How good* am I as a person?"[5] Both are typically characterized as pervading a wide variety of activities; thus, people are described as having generally high or low self-concepts and self-esteem. In contrast, *self-efficacy* addresses the question "*How well* can I do such-and-such?" In other words, it refers to learners' beliefs about their competence in a specific activity or domain. For instance, people may have high self-efficacy about learning to perform a swan dive but low self-efficacy about swimming the entire length of a swimming pool underwater. They may have higher self-efficacy about learning in social studies than in mathematics (Stodolsky, Salk, & Glaessner, 1991). In recent years, self-efficacy has been more prevalent than self-concept and self-esteem in theoretical explanations of research results, in part because researchers have defined it more consistently and in part because it is often more predictive of learners' performance (Bong & Clark, 1999; Bong & Skaalvik, 2003).

How Self–Efficacy Affects Behavior

According to social cognitive theorists (e.g., Bandura, 1997, 2000; Schunk & Pajares, 2004; Zimmerman, 1998; Zimmerman, Bandura, & Martinez-Pons, 1992), people's feelings of self-efficacy affect several aspects of their behavior, including their choice of activities, their goals, their effort and persistence, and ultimately their learning and achievement.

Choice of activities   People tend to choose tasks and activities at which they believe they can succeed; they tend to avoid those at which they think they will fail. For example, students who believe they can succeed at mathematics are more likely to take math courses than students who believe they are mathematically incompetent (Eccles, Wigfield, & Schiefele, 1998). Those who believe they can win a role in the school play are more likely to try out for the play than students with little faith in their acting or singing abilities.

Goals   People set higher goals for themselves when they have high self-efficacy in a particular domain. For instance, adolescents' choices of careers and occupational levels reflect subject areas in which they have high rather than low self-efficacy (Bandura, Barbaranelli, Caprara, & Pastorelli, 2001). Their choices are often consistent with traditional gender stereotypes: Boys are more likely to have high self-efficacy for, and so aspire to careers in, science and technology, whereas girls are more likely to feel efficacious about, and so choose, careers in education, health, and social services (Bandura et al., 2001).

Effort and persistence   People with a high sense of self-efficacy are more likely to exert effort when they work at a task, and they are more likely to persist when they encounter obstacles. People with low self-efficacy about a task put less effort into it and give up more quickly in the face of difficulty.

---

[5]I urge you not to agonize over the difference between *self-concept* and *self-esteem,* because their meanings overlap quite a bit, and so they are often used interchangeably (Byrne, 2002; Harter, 1999; Pintrich & Schunk, 2002).

Self-efficacy seems to be most predictive of effort and persistence when people have not yet entirely mastered a new topic or skill—in other words, when they must still struggle to some extent (Schunk & Pajares, 2004). Once they've achieved mastery, there often is no *need* to exert effort, because completion of a task comes quickly and easily.

Learning and achievement   People with high self-efficacy tend to learn and achieve more than those with low self-efficacy, even when actual ability levels are the same (Bandura, 1986; Pajares, 1996; Schunk, 1989a; Valentine, DuBois, & Cooper, 2004; Zimmerman et al., 1992). In other words, when several individuals have equal ability, those who *believe* they can do a task are more likely to accomplish it than those who do not believe they are capable of success.

Ideally, learners should have a reasonably accurate sense of what they can and cannot accomplish, putting them in a good position to capitalize on their strengths and address their weaknesses (Försterling & Morgenstern, 2002; Wang & Lin, 2005). Yet a tad of overconfidence can be beneficial, in that it entices learners to take on challenging activities that will help them develop new skills and abilities (Assor & Connell, 1992; Bandura, 1997). Within this context, it is often useful to distinguish between **self-efficacy for learning** ("I can learn this if I put my mind to it") and **self-efficacy for performance** ("I already know how to do this") (Lodewyk & Winne, 2005; Schunk & Pajares, 2004). Self-efficacy for learning (for what one can *eventually* do with effort) should be on the optimistic side, while self-efficacy for performance should be more in line with current ability levels.

Learners are at a disadvantage when they underestimate their abilities. In such circumstances, they set unnecessarily low goals for themselves and give up easily in the face of small obstacles. But it's also possible to have too much of a good thing. When learners are *too* overconfident, they may set themselves up for failure by forming unrealistically high expectations or exerting insufficient effort to succeed (Bandura, 1997; Paris & Cunningham, 1996; Phillips & Zimmerman, 1990; Stevenson, Chen, & Uttal, 1990). And they will hardly be inclined to address weaknesses that they don't realize they have (McKeachie, 1987; Pintrich, 2003).

Factors in the Development of Self–Efficacy

According to social cognitive theorists (e.g., Bandura, 1986, 1997; Schunk, 1989a; Schunk, Hanson, & Cox, 1987), several factors affect the development of self-efficacy, including one's own previous successes and failures, the messages that others communicate, the successes and failures of others, and the successes and failures of the group as a whole.

Previous Successes and Failures

People feel more confident that they can succeed at a task—that is, they have greater self-efficacy—when they have succeeded at that task or at similar ones in the past (Bandura, 1986; Klein, 1990; Nicholls, 1984; Valentine et al., 2004). A student is more likely to believe he can learn to divide fractions if he has successfully mastered the process of multiplying fractions. Similarly, a student will be more confident about her ability to play field hockey or rugby if she has already developed skills in soccer. In some cases, learners' judgments of success are based on the progress they make over time. In other instances, their judgments are based on how well they perform in comparison with their peers (Butler, 1998a; Pintrich & Schunk, 2002; Schunk & Zimmerman, 1997).

Once people have developed a high sense of self-efficacy, an occasional failure is unlikely to dampen their optimism very much. In fact, when historically successful people encounter small setbacks on the way to achieving success, they learn that sustained effort and perseverance are key ingredients for that success; in other words, they develop **resilient self-efficacy** (Bandura, 1989). When people meet with *consistent* failure in performing a particular task, however, they tend to have little confidence in their ability to succeed at that task in the future. Each new failure confirms what they already "know" about the task: They can't do it.

It is not surprising, then, that students with a history of academic success have higher self-efficacy for academic tasks than students with lower school performance. For example, students with learning disabilities—students who typically have encountered failure after failure in classroom activities—often have low self-efficacy with regard to the things they study in school (Schunk, 1989c).

Messages from Others

To some extent, people's self-efficacy beliefs are enhanced when others praise good performance or provide assurances that success is possible. At school, statements such as "You can do this problem if you work at it" or "I'll bet Judy will play with you if you just ask her" do give students a slight boost in self-confidence. This boost is short-lived, however, unless students' efforts at a task ultimately meet with success (Schunk, 1989a).

We should note, too, that the messages learners receive are sometimes implied rather than directly stated, yet they can influence self-efficacy nonetheless. For example, by giving constructive criticism about how to improve a poorly written research paper—criticism that indirectly communicates the message that "I know you can do better, and here are some suggestions how"—a teacher may boost students' self-efficacy for writing research papers (Pintrich & Schunk, 2002; Tunstall & Gipps, 1996). In some cases, actions speak louder than words. For example, the teacher who provides a great deal of assistance to a struggling student—more assistance than the student really needs—is communicating the message that "I don't think you can do this on your own" (Schunk, 1989b).

Successes and Failures of Others

People often acquire information about their own self-efficacy by observing the successes and failures of other individuals, especially those who appear to be similar to themselves (Schunk, 1983, 1989c). As an example, students often consider the successes and failures of their peers, especially those of similar ability, when appraising their own chances of success on academic tasks. Thus, seeing a classmate model a behavior successfully is often more effective than seeing a teacher do it. In one research study (Schunk & Hanson, 1985), elementary school children having difficulty with subtraction were given 25 subtraction problems to complete. Those who had seen another student successfully complete the problems got an average of 19 correct, whereas those who saw a teacher complete the problems got only 13 correct, and those who saw no model at all solved only 8!

Curiously, it is sometimes better to watch a peer model who struggles with a task at first and then gradually masters it, rather than one who executes it perfectly at first shot (Kitsantas et al., 2000; Schunk et al., 1987; Zimmerman & Kitsantas, 2002). Presumably observing such a **coping model** shows learners that success does not necessarily come easily—that they must work and practice to achieve success—and allows them to observe the strategies that the model employs to gain proficiency.

Successes and Failures of the Group as a Whole

People may have greater self-efficacy when they work in a group than when they work alone, and especially when they achieve success as a group. Such **collective self-efficacy** is a function not only of people's perceptions of their own and others' capabilities but also of their perceptions of how effectively they can work together and coordinate their roles and responsibilities (Bandura, 1997, 2000).

To date, research on collective self-efficacy has focused primarily on adults (Bandura, 1997; Goddard, 2001; Goddard, Hoy, & Woolfolk Hoy, 2000; Tschannen-Moran, Woolfolk Hoy, & Hoy, 1998). For instance, when teachers at a school believe that, as a group, they can make a significant difference in the lives of their students, they influence students' achievement in several ways:

- They are more willing to experiment with new ideas and teaching strategies that can better help students learn.
- They have higher expectations regarding, and set higher goals for, students' performance.
- They put more effort into their teaching and are more persistent in helping students learn. (Bandura, 1997; Roeser, Marachi, & Gehlbach, 2002; Tschannen-Moran et al., 1998)

These effects should look familiar: Just as self-efficacy affects learners' choice of activities, goals, effort, and persistence, so, too, does it affect *teachers'* choices, goals, effort, and persistence. And probably as a result of these effects, students have higher self-efficacy for learning and actually *do* achieve at higher levels (Goddard, 2001; Goddard et al., 2000; Roeser et al., 2002; Tschannen-Moran et al., 1998).

We can reasonably assume that children, too, are likely to have higher self-efficacy when they work in groups, provided that those groups are functioning smoothly and effectively. We will consider strategies for fostering effective group work in chapter 14.

Yet children must also acquire skills for independent learning and performance. Social cognitive theorists believe that growing learners can and should ultimately take charge of their own behavior. We therefore turn to a topic gaining increasing prominence in psychological and educational literature—the topic of *self-regulation.*

SELF–REGULATION

As social cognitive theory has evolved over the years, it has increasingly emphasized the role of **self-regulation** of behavior (Bandura, 1977, 1982, 1986; Zimmerman, 1989; Zimmerman & Schunk, 2004). Through both direct and vicarious reinforcement and punishment, growing children gradually learn which behaviors are and are not acceptable to the people around them. Eventually, they develop their *own* ideas about appropriate and inappropriate behavior, and they choose their actions accordingly.

Social cognitive theorists are hardly the only ones who have considered the nature of self-regulation; behaviorists have addressed it (e.g., Belfiore & Hornyak, 1998), as have many cognitive and developmental theorists (e.g., see the discussion of Vygotsky's theory in chapter 11). Yet social cognitive theorists have, to a considerable degree, been responsible for laying the groundwork on which other theorists have built. In this chapter, we will, in a typically social cognitive manner, blend elements of behaviorism and cognitivism to explore the nature of self-regulated behavior.

Elements of Self–Regulation

From the perspective of social cognitive theorists, self-regulation entails at least four processes: setting standards and goals, self-observation, self-evaluation, and self-reaction (Bandura, 1986; Schunk, 1989c, 1998; Zimmerman & Schunk, 2004).

Setting Standards and Goals

As mature human beings, we tend to set standards for our own behavior; in other words, we establish criteria regarding what constitutes acceptable performance. We also establish certain goals that we value and toward which we direct many of our behaviors.

The kinds of performance standards and goals that people establish for themselves depend to some degree on the standards and goals they see other people adopt (Bandura, 1977, 1986). In other words, the behavior of *models* affects learners' standards and goals. In a study by Bandura and Kupers (1964), for example, children watched adult or child models reward themselves with candy and self-praise for their performance in a bowling game. Some of the children watched the models reward themselves only after achieving 20 points or more (reflecting very high performance); these models admonished themselves for anything up to 19 points. Other children observed models reward themselves after achieving as few as 10 points. All of the children then had the opportunity to play the game themselves and to help themselves to candy whenever they chose. Bandura and Kupers found that the children tended to reinforce themselves using performance standards very similar to those they had seen the models use.

People are most apt to adopt the kinds of standards that models similar to themselves in ability adopt (Bandura, 1977). They are unlikely to adopt the standards of models who are much more competent or who apply performance standards inconsistently (Bandura, 1977; Bandura & Whalen, 1966).

Self-Observation

An important part of self-regulation is to observe oneself in action. To make progress toward important goals, people must be aware of how well they are doing at present; in other words, they must know what parts of their performance are working well and what parts need improvement.

Self-Evaluation

People's behaviors are frequently judged by others—for instance, by relatives, teachers, classmates, friends, and the general public. Eventually, people begin to judge and evaluate their *own* behaviors based on the standards they hold for themselves.

Self-Reaction

As people become increasingly self-regulating, they begin to reinforce themselves—perhaps by feeling proud or telling themselves that they did a good job—when they accomplish their goals. They also begin to punish themselves—perhaps by feeling sorry, guilty, or ashamed—when they do something that does not meet their self-chosen performance standards. Such self-praise and self-criticism can be as influential in altering behavior as the reinforcements and punishments that others administer (Bandura, 1977, 1986).

To illustrate, consider Jason, a student who perceives himself to have average intelligence. Jason is likely to form standards for his own academic achievement that match the achievement of other "average" students; he is therefore likely to pat himself on the back for "B" work and to maintain

The author engages in self-regulation.

a similar level of effort on future tasks. In contrast, consider Joanna, a student whose close friends are the high achievers of the class. If Joanna believes that her ability is similar to that of her friends, she is likely to adopt high standards for herself and to admonish herself for the same B-level achievement of which Jason is so proud. Provided that the B does not appreciably undermine her self-efficacy, Joanna is likely to try harder on the same task the next time around (Bandura, 1989).

Promoting Self–Regulated Behavior

Writing a textbook is a major undertaking. As I sit here in my office tapping on my computer keyboard day after day, I sometimes wonder why in the world I ever committed myself to such a project when I could instead be in my warm, comfortable living room reading mystery novels or watching television game shows. Yet each day I drag myself to my office to produce a few more pages. How do I do it? I do it by reinforcing myself every time I finish a small section of the book. For example, as soon as I finished the section on self-efficacy you just read, I gave myself permission to go watch my favorite game show. Before I can watch another one, though, I need to finish this section on self-regulation.

Psychologists have identified several techniques for promoting self-regulated behavior. These techniques (sometimes called *self-control*[6] or *self-management*) include self-instructions, self-monitoring, self-reinforcement, and self-imposed stimulus control.

Self-Instructions

One effective strategy is to teach learners to repeat **self-instructions** that guide their behavior (Mace, Belfiore, & Shea, 1989; Meichenbaum, 1985; Schunk, 1989c). For instance, earlier in the chapter I described a study in which preschoolers more easily learned new dance moves by reminding themselves about specific response sequences (e.g., "slide, jump, slide, jump, run,

---

[6]Some theorists make a distinction between the terms *self-control* and *self-regulation*. For instance, Díaz, Neal, and Amaya-Williams (1990) define self-control as complying with someone else's standards for appropriate behavior even when the latter individual is absent, whereas self-regulation involves setting one's *own* standards for appropriate behavior. Schunk and Zimmerman (1997; Kitsantas et al., 2000; Zimmerman & Kitsantas, 1999) suggest that self-control is heavily dependent on comparing one's own performance with internal standards that have been acquired from a model's performance, whereas true self-regulation is more automatic and flexible, allowing adaptation to changing circumstances.

and stop") (Vintere et al., 2004, p. 309). Similarly, beginning tennis students improve the accuracy of their returns when they give themselves these four verbal cues:

- "Ball" (to remind them to keep their eyes on the ball)
- "Bounce" (to continue tracking the path of the ball)
- "Hit" (to focus on contacting the ball with the racket)
- "Ready" (to get into position for the next ball) (Ziegler, 1987)

Other studies show self-instructions to be effective in helping students acquire more effective approaches to academic tasks, develop better social skills, and keep their impulsive and aggressive behavior in check (Alberto & Troutman, 2003; Guevremont, Osnes, & Stokes, 1988; Hughes, 1988; Leon & Pepe, 1983; Meichenbaum, 1977).

Meichenbaum (1977) has successfully used five steps in teaching children how to give themselves instructions to guide their behavior:

1. *Cognitive modeling:* An adult model performs the desired task while verbalizing instructions that guide performance.
2. *Overt, external guidance:* The child performs the task while listening to the adult verbalize the instructions.
3. *Overt self-guidance:* The child repeats the instructions aloud while performing the task.
4. *Faded, overt self-guidance:* The child whispers the instructions while performing the task.
5. *Covert self-instruction:* The child silently thinks about the instructions while performing the task.

This sequence is graphically depicted in Figure 6.2. As you can see, the adult initially serves as a model not only for the behavior itself but also for self-instructions. Responsibility for performing the task *and* for guiding that performance is gradually turned over to the child.

	Task Performance	Task Instructions
Step 1: Cognitive modeling	The adult performs and models the desired behavior.	The adult verbalizes instructions.
Step 2: Overt, external guidance	The child performs the desired behavior.	The adult verbalizes instructions.
Step 3: Overt self-guidance	The child performs the desired behavior.	The child repeats the instructions aloud.
Step 4: Faded, overt self-guidance	The child performs the desired behavior.	The child whispers the instructions.
Step 5: Covert self-instruction	The child performs the desired behavior.	The child thinks silently about the instructions.

Figure 6.2
Meichenbaum's five steps for promoting self-regulated behavior.

Self-Monitoring

Another method that can help people control their own behavior is simply to have them observe and assess their own responses—**self-monitoring**—just as someone else might assess those responses in applied behavior analysis (see chapter 5). The mere recording of responses is often enough to alter the frequency of a behavior. For example, my family was once part of a research project in which randomly selected households recorded their television-watching habits over a period of several weeks. We were instructed to mark down every instance of television viewing—including the date, time of day, length of time, and programs watched—on a specially designed record sheet. Each time I thought about turning on the television set, I remembered all of the work I would have to go through to record my viewing, and, as often as not, I found something else to do instead. Thus, the simple process of having to record my television-watching behavior altered that behavior.

Self-monitoring can be instituted in a classroom setting as well. For example, in one study (Harris, 1986), students having difficulty keeping their minds on their spelling assignments were given tape recorders that emitted a small beep at random intervals about 45 seconds apart. Whenever students heard a beep, they asked themselves, "Was I paying attention?" This simple technique doubled their time on task and tripled their productivity on spelling assignments. Other studies have obtained similar results in terms of increased on-task behavior and assignment completion (Belfiore & Hornyak, 1998; Hallahan, Marshall, & Lloyd, 1981; Harris, 1986; Heins, Lloyd, & Hallahan, 1986; Mace et al., 1989; Mace & Kratochwill, 1988; Webber, Scheuermann, McCall, & Coleman, 1993).

Just as desirable behaviors can be increased, undesirable behaviors can be decreased through self-monitoring. For example, self-recording of a target behavior has been found to reduce such disruptive classroom behaviors as talking out of turn, leaving one's seat without permission, and hitting classmates (Bolstad & Johnson, 1972; Mace et al., 1989; Moletzsky, 1974; Webber et al., 1993). Through self-monitoring, learners become more consciously aware of how frequently they engage in certain unproductive behaviors, and such awareness can be a key factor in behavior improvement (Emmer & Gerwels, 2006).

Self-Reinforcement

People are often able to change their behavior through **self-reinforcement,** giving themselves a treat or special privilege when they behave in a desired fashion and withholding reinforcement when they do not (Mace et al., 1989; Mahoney & Thoresen, 1974; O'Leary & O'Leary, 1972; Rimm & Masters, 1974). For example, I am able to maintain my book-writing behavior by applying the Premack principle described in chapter 4: I let myself engage in easy, enjoyable activities only after I have completed more difficult ones.

When students learn to reinforce themselves for their accomplishments—perhaps by giving themselves some free time, helping themselves to a small treat, or simply praising themselves—their study habits and academic performance improve (Beneke & Harris, 1972; Greiner & Karoly, 1976; Hayes et al., 1985; Stevenson & Fantuzzo, 1986). In one research study (Stevenson & Fantuzzo, 1986), students who had been performing poorly in arithmetic were taught to give themselves points when they did well on their assignments; they could later use these points to "buy" a variety of items and privileges. Within a few weeks, these students were doing as well as their classmates on both in-class assignments and homework. In another study (Bandura & Perloff, 1967), self-reinforcement was just as effective in modifying student behaviors as reinforcement administered by a teacher.

Self-Imposed Stimulus Control

As you should recall from our discussion of instrumental conditioning in chapter 4, a response is under stimulus control when it is emitted in the presence of some stimuli but not in the presence of others. This idea can be translated into an effective means of promoting self-regulation (Mahoney & Thoresen, 1974); I call it **self-imposed stimulus control.** To increase a particular desired behavior, an individual might be instructed to seek out an environment in which that behavior is most likely to occur. For example, a student who wishes to increase the time actually spent studying each day should sit at a table in the library rather than on a bed at home. Conversely, to decrease an undesired behavior, an individual should engage in that behavior only in certain situations. For example, I once knew a professor who, in an effort to stop smoking, gradually reduced the number of locations in which he allowed himself to smoke. Eventually, he was able to smoke in only one place, facing a back corner of his office; at that point, he successfully stopped smoking.

We should note here that techniques designed to promote self-regulation work only when learners are motivated to change their own behavior. Under such circumstances, such techniques can help learners discover that they have some control, not only over their behavior but over their environment as well. Three precautions must be taken, however. First, people being trained in self-regulation strategies must have the capability for performing the desired behaviors; for example, students who want to modify their study habits will achieve higher grades only if they possess adequate academic skills to ensure success. Second, people must *believe* they can make the necessary behavior changes; in other words, they must have high self-efficacy (Schunk, 1998; Zimmerman & Schunk, 2004). And third, people must be cautioned not to expect too much of themselves too quickly. Many individuals would prefer overnight success, but shaping, either of oneself or of another, is usually a slow, gradual process. Just as the dieter will not lose 40 pounds in one week, it is equally unlikely that a habitually poor student will achieve honor roll status immediately. For self-regulation techniques to be effective, one's expectations for oneself must be practical and realistic.

The Cognitive Side of Self–Regulation

We have seen numerous indications that self-regulation involves cognitive processes as well as behavior. As a concrete example, in Meichenbaum's final step for teaching self-instructions, the learner does not verbalize, but merely *thinks* about, the instructions that a model has provided. More generally, such elements of self-regulation as setting standards for performance, self-evaluation, and self-reaction (e.g., feeling proud or ashamed) are probably more cognitive than behavioral in nature.

In recent years, psychologists have applied the concept of self-regulation more explicitly to the control of one's mental processes; in particular, they now talk about *self-regulated learning* as well as self-regulated behavior. For example, self-regulated learners set goals for a learning activity, choose study strategies that are likely to help them accomplish the goals, monitor their progress toward the goals, and change their study strategies if necessary. We will talk more about self-regulated learning when we discuss metacognition and study strategies in chapter 12, where we will draw from the work of both cognitive and social cognitive theorists.

EDUCATIONAL IMPLICATIONS OF SOCIAL COGNITIVE THEORY

Social cognitive theory has numerous implications for classroom practice. Let's look at some of the most important ones.

◆ *Students often learn a great deal simply by observing others.* According to many behaviorists (e.g., B. F. Skinner), people must make active responses for learning to occur. But in this chapter, we've seen many examples of how learning can also occur through observations of what other people do. Furthermore, students may learn what behaviors are and are not acceptable through their vicarious experiences—more specifically, by seeing others receive reinforcement or punishment for various responses. Accordingly, teachers and other school personnel must be consistent in the rewards and punishments they administer—not only from time to time but also from student to student.

◆ *Describing the consequences of behaviors can effectively increase appropriate behaviors and decrease inappropriate ones.* As you should recall, social cognitive theorists propose that reinforcement and punishment affect behavior only when learners are consciously aware of response–consequence contingencies. Thus promises of rewards for good behaviors and warnings of unpleasant consequences for misdeeds can be effective means of improving student behavior. In contrast, administering reinforcement or punishment when students do not recognize the relationship between an action and its consequence is unlikely to bring about behavior change.

◆ *Modeling provides an alternative to shaping for teaching new behaviors.* Behaviorists describe one effective means—shaping—for teaching a new response. But to shape a particular behavior, one must begin by reinforcing an existing behavior and then gradually modify that behavior through differential reinforcement; for complex behaviors, this process can be quite time consuming. Social cognitive theory offers a faster, more efficient means for teaching new behavior: modeling.

To promote effective learning from a model, a teacher must make sure that four essential conditions exist: attention, retention, motor reproduction, and motivation. First of all, the teacher must make sure that students pay attention to the model and especially to the relevant aspects of the model's behavior. Second, the teacher can facilitate students' retention of what they observe by helping them form appropriate memory codes (perhaps verbal labels or visual images) for their observations. Third, giving students opportunities to practice the behaviors they see and providing corrective feedback about their efforts will aid their motor reproduction of the responses they are modeling. Finally, the teacher must remember that students will display behaviors they have learned only if they have the motivation to do so. Many children are intrinsically motivated to perform, but others may require external incentives and reinforcers. (We'll consider numerous motivational strategies, with a particular focus on those that foster intrinsic motivation, in chapters 15 and 16.)

◆ *Teachers, parents, and other adults must model appropriate behaviors and take care that they don't model inappropriate ones.* Adults often possess characteristics (e.g., competence, prestige, power) that make them influential models for children. Accordingly, they must be careful that they model appropriate behaviors for the children with whom they interact. I am delighted when I see teachers and other adults show characteristics such as open-mindedness, empathy, and concern for physical fitness. I cringe when I see them express disdain for particular points of view, disregard the needs and concerns of other human beings, or smoke cigarettes.

A child I know once tried out for a role in a school Christmas pageant. Lisa went off to school on the morning of pageant tryouts, aware that students could each try out for only one part and thinking that she had a good chance of winning the role of Mrs. Claus. Lisa was convinced that the teacher would award the leading role of Santa Claus to a girl named Ann; however, because Ann was late that morning and the teacher had announced that latecomers would not be allowed to try out, Lisa instead tried out for Santa himself. When Ann arrived 10 minutes late, the teacher disregarded her rule about latecomers being ineligible, allowed Ann to try out for Santa Claus, and ultimately awarded the role to Ann. In doing so, this teacher, one of the school's most visible role models, modeled hypocrisy and favoritism.

As an educational psychologist who helps future teachers learn how to teach, my job is a particularly challenging one because I must practice what I preach. If I tell my students that immediate feedback, organization of information, vivid examples, hands-on experiences, and assessment practices that match instructional objectives are all important components of effective teaching, my students' learning will obviously be enhanced when I model all of those things as well. To say one thing but do another would be not only hypocritical but also counterproductive.

Through their daily interactions with students, teachers model not only behaviors but attitudes as well (Pugh, 2002; Rahm & Downey, 2002). For example, in a unit on adaptation and evolution in his high school zoology class, science teacher Kevin Pugh (2002) consistently modeled enthusiasm for science through statements such as these:

- "What we want to do this week is learn more about how every animal is truly an amazing design. Because every animal . . . is designed to survive and thrive in a particular environment. And when you learn how to see animals in terms of how they're adapted to their environment, every animal becomes an amazing creation" (p. 1108).
- "While driving here, I passed a bunch of Canadian geese and I started to think, I began to wonder, 'Why do they have a black head and white neck? What's the adaptive purpose?' " (p. 1110).
- "My personal perspective is science isn't worth much . . . if it doesn't sort of make the world more meaningful to look at; help you to understand things or make some part of your world more interesting. . . . When I teach, what I really want you to do is to try and be able to see things in a new way, in a different way" (p. 1110).

◆ *Exposure to a variety of other models further enhances students' learning.* Adult models need not be limited to children's teachers and parents. Other adults can be invited to visit classrooms on occasion; for example, police officers, prominent city officials, business people, and nurses might demonstrate appropriate behaviors and attitudes related to safety, good citizenship, responsibility, and health. Symbolic models can also be effective; for example, studying the lives of such individuals as Helen Keller, Martin Luther King, Jr., and Eleanor Roosevelt is a viable method of illustrating many desirable behaviors (e.g., Nucci, 2001).

Models don't simply demonstrate appropriate behaviors. Carefully chosen ones can also help break down traditional stereotypes regarding what different groups of people can and cannot do. For example, teachers might introduce students to male nurses, female engineers, African American physicians, Hispanic business executives, or athletes who are wheelchair bound. By exposing students to successful individuals of both genders, from many cultural and socioeconomic backgrounds, and with a variety of physical disabilities, teachers can help students realize that they themselves may also have the potential to accomplish great things.

♦ *Students must believe they are capable of accomplishing school tasks.* As we have seen, students' self-efficacy affects their learning and academic achievement. Yet students are likely to differ widely in their confidence about performing tasks successfully. For example, in adolescence, boys are likely to have higher self-efficacy than girls with regard to mathematics, science, and sports; meanwhile, girls are likely to have higher self-efficacy than boys for assignments in an English class (Dunning, Johnson, Ehrlinger, & Kruger, 2003; Wigfield, Eccles, & Pintrich, 1996).

To enhance students' self-efficacy related to school activities, teachers can make use of the factors that seem to promote self-efficacy. For instance, teachers can tell students that peers very similar to themselves have mastered the things they are learning. Teachers might also have students actually observe their peers successfully accomplishing tasks; it may be especially beneficial for students to see a peer struggling with a task or problem at first—something they themselves are likely to do—and then eventually mastering it. In addition, teachers can plan group activities in which students collaborate on challenging assignments. But most importantly, teachers can foster high self-efficacy by helping students achieve classroom success themselves—for example, by helping them master essential basic skills and providing guidance and support for tackling more advanced, difficult ones.

Changing students' self-efficacy one task or skill at a time is ultimately easier than trying to change their overall self-concepts or self-esteem (Bong & Skaalvik, 2003). Yet when students develop high self-efficacy regarding a number of different topics and subject areas, they increasingly gain confidence that, in general, they can master new domains. In other words, they may eventually develop a **generalized self-efficacy** that applies broadly to many areas of the school curriculum (Bong & Skaalvik, 2003; Schunk & Pajares, 2004).

♦ *Teachers should help students set realistic expectations for their accomplishments.* As growing children become increasingly self-regulating, they begin to adopt standards for their own behavior. Such standards are often based on those that people around them have adopted, and so they may in some cases be either overly optimistic or overly pessimistic (Paris & Cunningham, 1996; Phillips & Zimmerman, 1990). When a student's standards for performance are unrealistically high, as might be true for a perfectionist, continual disappointment and frustration are likely to result (Dixon, Dungan, & Young, 2003). When a student's standards are too low, underachievement will be the outcome. Teachers can best facilitate students' academic and social progress by helping them form optimistic self-expectations that are also reasonable given current ability levels and available instruction and support.

♦ *Self-regulation techniques provide effective methods for improving student behavior.* Earlier in the chapter, I described four techniques for promoting self-regulation: self-instructions, self-monitoring, self-reinforcement, and self-imposed stimulus control. When students are intrinsically motivated to change their own behaviors, such techniques can provide a viable alternative to behaviorist approaches.

As social cognitive theorists have so clearly shown, we cannot ignore the social context of the classroom. Students can and do learn from the models—the parents, teachers, and peers—that they see every day. Social cognitive theorists have also made it clear that we must consider cognitive as well as environmental factors when trying to explain how human beings learn and behave. As we move into cognitivism in the next chapter, we will begin to look at such cognitive factors more closely.

SUMMARY

Social cognitive theory focuses on the ways in which people learn from observing one another. This perspective reflects a blending of behaviorist concepts (e.g., reinforcement and punishment) and cognitive notions (e.g., awareness and expectations). Environmental and cognitive variables continually interact with one another and with behavior, such that each influences the others in reciprocal ways.

Many behaviors, beliefs, and attitudes are acquired through *modeling;* academic skills, aggression, and morality are three examples. Effective models are likely to be competent, prestigious, and powerful and to exhibit behaviors that are "gender-appropriate" and relevant to the observer's own situation. Four conditions are necessary for modeling to occur: attention, retention, motor reproduction, and motivation.

Individuals with high *self-efficacy*—those who believe they can perform successfully in particular activities or domains—are more likely to choose challenging activities, exert effort and persist at those activities, and exhibit high levels of achievement over the long run. Self-efficacy can be enhanced through encouraging messages, others' (especially peers') successes, group accomplishments, and, most importantly, one's own individual successes.

Social cognitive theorists propose that although the environment influences behavior, over time people begin to regulate their own behavior; people do so by developing their own standards for performance, observing and evaluating themselves on the basis of those standards, and reinforcing or punishing themselves (even if only mentally and emotionally) for what they have or have not done. Teachers can help their students become more self-regulating by teaching such techniques as self-instructions, self-monitoring, self-reinforcement, and self-imposed stimulus control.

Social cognitive theory offers numerous implications for educational practice. For example, describing response–reinforcement and response–punishment contingencies makes students aware of those contingencies; hence, such descriptions are likely to affect behavior before any consequences are ever imposed. When instruction involves teaching new skills, modeling provides an effective, and often more efficient, alternative to traditional behaviorist techniques. Modeling is not restricted to planned instruction, however: Teachers and other adults model a variety of behaviors, attitudes, and values in their daily interactions with students, and so they must be careful that their behaviors reflect fairness, acceptance of diverse viewpoints, a healthy lifestyle, and high ethical standards. And when teaching potentially challenging subject matter, teachers must give students reason to believe that they are truly capable of mastering that subject matter.

Part Four

Cognitive Views of Learning

CHAPTER 7

Introduction to Cognition and Memory

Since the 1960s, cognitivism (also known as *cognitive psychology*) has been the predominant perspective within which learning research has been conducted and theories of learning have evolved. As we begin to explore this perspective, you will undoubtedly notice a change in emphasis. In earlier chapters, we focused largely on the roles of environmental conditions (stimuli) and observable behaviors (responses) in learning, although social cognitive theory also provided a window into such mental phenomena as expectations, attention, and self-efficacy. At this point, we will begin to look more directly at **cognitive processes,** considering how people perceive, interpret, remember, and in other ways think about environmental events.

As you should recall, early behaviorists chose not to incorporate mental events into their learning theories, arguing that such events were impossible to observe and measure and so could not be studied objectively. During the 1950s and 1960s, however, many psychologists became increasingly dissatisfied with such a "thoughtless" approach to human learning. Major works with a distinctly cognitive flavor began to emerge; publications by Noam Chomsky (1957) in psycholinguistics and by Bruner, Goodnow, and Austin (1956) in concept learning are examples. Ulric Neisser's *Cognitive Psychology*, published in 1967, was a landmark book that helped to legitimize cognitive theory as a major alternative to behaviorism (Calfee, 1981). Increasingly, cognitivism began appearing in educational psychology literature as well, with Jerome Bruner

(1961a, 1961b, 1966) and David Ausubel (1963, 1968; Ausubel & Robinson, 1969) being two well-known early proponents. By the 1970s, the great majority of learning theorists had joined the cognitive bandwagon (Robins, Gosling, & Craik, 1999).

Yet the roots of cognitive psychology preceded the mass discontentment with strict S–R psychology by many years. Some cognitive learning theories, notably those of American psychologist Edward Tolman and the Gestalt psychologists of Germany, appeared in the early decades of the twentieth century. At about the same time, two developmental psychologists, Jean Piaget in Switzerland and Lev Vygotsky in Russia, described how children's thought processes change with age and speculated about underlying learning mechanisms that might make such change possible.

Equally important to the cognitive movement was research conducted in the early and middle decades of the twentieth century in an area known as *verbal learning*. Verbal learning theorists originally tried to apply a stimulus–response analysis to human language and verbal behavior, but they soon discovered that the complexities of human language-based learning were sometimes difficult to explain from a behaviorist perspective. Increasingly, verbal learning theorists began to incorporate cognitive processes into their explanations of research results.

In this chapter we'll look at both early and more recent cognitive views of human learning. We'll also begin to explore the nature of human memory—something that psychologists have studied almost exclusively from a cognitivist perspective. We'll look more closely at one major component of human memory—long-term memory—in chapters 8 through 10. We'll switch to a more developmental perspective of cognition in chapter 11, where we'll look at Piaget's and Vygotsky's work and at contemporary perspectives that have built on their ideas.

EDWARD TOLMAN'S PURPOSIVE BEHAVIORISM

Edward Chace Tolman (1932, 1938, 1942, 1959) was a prominent learning theorist during the heyday of behaviorism, yet his work had a distinctly cognitive flair. Like his behaviorist contemporaries, Tolman valued the importance of objectivity in research and used nonhuman species (especially rats) as the subjects of his research. Unlike his contemporaries, however, Tolman included internal mental phenomena in his explanations of how learning occurs. Following are examples of his ideas:[1]

◆ *Learning is an internal rather than external change.* Tolman proposed that learning is an internal process that isn't necessarily reflected in an organism's behavior. As an example, let's look at a study by Tolman and Honzik (1930) in which three groups of rats ran a difficult maze under different reinforcement conditions. Group 1 rats were reinforced with food each time they completed the maze. Group 2 rats received no reinforcement for successful performance. Group 3 rats were not reinforced during the first 10 days in the maze but began receiving reinforcement on the 11th day.

---

[1]Tolman's theory was described in greater depth in earlier editions of this book but has been condensed in this edition to make room for advancements in contemporary theories and research. My earlier, lengthier discussion is presented in the reading "Studying Cognitive Phenomena with Behaviorist Techniques: Tolman's Work" on the book's Companion Website at www.prenhall.com/ormrod.

The results of the experiment appear in Figure 7.1; the data points indicate the average number of wrong turns (errors) each group made while traveling the maze each day. Notice that the performance of Groups 2 and 3 improved somewhat (i.e., they made fewer wrong turns) even when they were not receiving reinforcement. Notice, too, that once the rats in Group 3 began receiving reinforcement, their performance in the maze equaled (in fact, it surpassed!) Group 1's performance. Apparently, Group 3 rats had learned as much as Group 1 rats during the first 10 days even though the two groups had been performing differently. Tolman used the term **latent learning** for such unobservable learning. In Tolman's view, reinforcement influences *performance* rather than learning, in that it increases the likelihood that a learned behavior will be exhibited. (As you may recall from chapter 6, social cognitive theorists have come to a similar conclusion.)

◆ *Behavior is purposive.* Tolman believed that learning should be viewed not as the formation of S–R connections but as a process of learning that certain events lead to other events (e.g., that following a particular path through a maze leads to reinforcement). He proposed that once an organism has learned that a behavior leads to a certain end result, the organism behaves in order to achieve that end. In other words, behavior has a *purpose,* that of goal attainment. Because Tolman stressed the goal-directed nature of behavior, his theory of learning is sometimes referred to as **purposive behaviorism.**

◆ *Expectations affect behavior.* According to Tolman, once an organism learns that certain behaviors produce certain kinds of results, it begins to form expectations about the outcomes of its behaviors. Rather than reinforcement affecting the response that it follows, the organism's *expectation* of reinforcement affects the response that it *precedes.* (Once again, we see a similarity with social cognitive theory.)

When an organism's expectations are not met, its behavior may be adversely affected. For example, in an experiment by Elliott (described in Tolman, 1932), rats received one of two reinforcers for running a maze: An experimental group received a favorite rat delicacy—bran

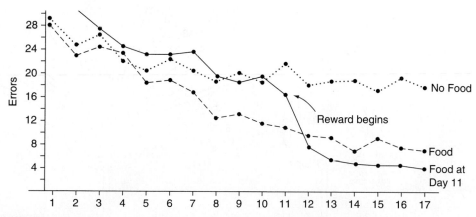

Figure 7.1
Maze performance of rats receiving food, no food, or food beginning on Day 11.
Adapted from "Introduction and Removal of Reward, and Maze Performance in Rats" by E. C. Tolman and C. H. Honzik, 1930, *University of California Publications in Psychology, 4,* p. 267. Copyright © 1930 by University of California Press. Adapted with permission.

mash—whereas a control group received relatively unenticing sunflower seeds. The experimental group ran the maze faster than the control group, apparently because they were expecting a yummier treat at the end of the maze. On the 10th day, the experimental group rats were switched to the sunflower seed reinforcement that the control group rats had been getting all along. After discovering the change in reinforcement, these rats began to move through the maze more slowly than they had previously, and even more slowly than the control rats. Because both groups were being reinforced identically at this point (i.e., with boring sunflower seeds), the inferior performance of the rats in the experimental group was apparently due to the change in reinforcement, resulting in a *depression effect* similar to what I described in chapter 4. As Tolman might put it, the rats' expectation of reinforcement was no longer being confirmed. As you or I might say, the rats were very disappointed with the treat awaiting them.

♦ *Learning results in an organized body of information.* In a series of studies, Tolman demonstrated that rats who run a maze learn more than just a set of independent responses. It appears that they also learn how the maze is arranged—the lay of the land, so to speak. For example, in a classic study by Tolman, Ritchie, and Kalish (1946), rats ran numerous times through a maze that looked like Maze 1 of Figure 7.2. They were then put in a situation similar to Maze 2 of Figure 7.2. Because the alley that had previously led to food was now blocked, the rats had to choose among 18 other alleys. Applying the behaviorist concept of generalization, we would expect the rats to make their running response to a stimulus very similar to the blocked alley. We would therefore predict that the rats would choose alleys near the blocked one, especially Alley 9 or Alley 10. However, few of the rats chose either of these routes. By far the most common choice was Alley 6, the one that presumably would provide a shortcut to the location in which the rats had come to expect food.

Based on such research, Tolman proposed that rats (and presumably many other species as well) develop **cognitive maps** of their environments: They learn where different parts of the

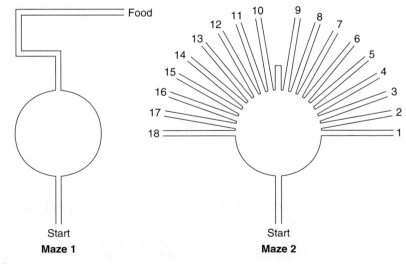

Figure 7.2
Mazes used by Tolman, Ritchie, and Kalish (1946).

environment are situated in relation to one another. Knowing how things are organized in space enables an organism to get from one place to another quickly and easily, often by the shortest possible route. The concept of a cognitive map (sometimes called a *mental map*) has continued to be a topic of research for more contemporary researchers, psychologists, and geographers alike (e.g., Downs & Stea, 1977; Foo, Warren, Duchon, & Tarr, 2005; García-Mira & Real, 2005; Salomon, 1979/1994).

In his research methods, Tolman was clearly influenced by behaviorists. But in developing his views about the organized nature of what organisms learn, Tolman was influenced by the ideas of the Gestalt psychologists of Germany, which we look at now.

GESTALT PSYCHOLOGY

During the early decades of the twentieth century, a perspective emerged in German psychology that was largely independent of behaviorism-dominated American psychology. This perspective, known as **Gestalt psychology,** was advanced by such theorists as Max Wertheimer (e.g., 1912, 1959), Wolfgang Köhler (e.g., 1925, 1929, 1947, 1959), and Kurt Koffka (1935). Gestalt psychologists emphasized the importance of organizational processes in perception, learning, and problem solving and believed that individuals were predisposed to organize information in particular ways. Following are several basic ideas to emerge from Gestalt psychology:

◆ *Perception is often different from reality.* The origin of Gestalt psychology is usually attributed to Wertheimer's (1912) description and analysis of an optical illusion known as the **phi phenomenon.** Wertheimer observed that when two lights blink on and off sequentially at a particular rate, they often appear to be only one light moving quickly back and forth. (You can see this effect in the blinking lights of many roadside signs.) The fact that an individual "sees" motion when observing stationary objects led Wertheimer to conclude that perception of an experience is sometimes different from the experience itself.

◆ *The whole is more than the sum of its parts.* Gestaltists believed that human experience cannot be successfully understood when various aspects of experience are studied in isolation from one another. For example, we perceive the illusion of movement in the phi phenomenon only when two or more lights are present; no motion is perceived in a single light. Similarly, we recognize a particular sequence of musical notes as being the melody of "Jingle Bells," but we hear the same song even when the key changes and so the specific notes that are played are different (Rachlin, 1995). A combination of stimuli may show a pattern not evident in any of the stimuli alone; to use a Gestaltist expression, the whole is more than the sum of its parts.

The importance of the interrelationships among elements in a situation can be seen in Köhler's (1929) **transposition** experiments with chickens. Hens were shown two sheets of gray paper, one a bit darker than the other. Grain was placed on both sheets, but the hens were allowed to feed only from the darker one. On a subsequent occasion, the hens were shown a sheet of paper the same shade as that on which they had previously been fed, along with a sheet of an even darker shade. In this second situation, the hens tended to go to the darker of the two sheets—in other words, to one on which they had *not* previously been reinforced. The hens had apparently learned something about the relationship between the two sheets of paper: Darker is better.

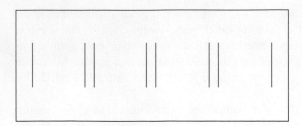

Figure 7.3a   **Figure 7.3b**

◆ *An organism structures and organizes experience.* The German word *Gestalt,* roughly translated, means "structured whole." Structure is not necessarily inherent in a situation; instead, an organism *imposes* structure. For example, if you look at Figure 7.3a, you probably perceive three pairs of lines with single lines at each end. Yet turn your attention to Figure 7.3b, in which the same lines appear within a particular context. You probably now see the lines differently—as four pairs forming the sides of four rectangles. The lines themselves are identical in both cases, but the way in which you organize them (i.e., how you group the lines together) is different. The "structure" of the lines is something that you yourself impose on each figure.

◆ *The organism is predisposed to organize experience in certain ways.* Gestaltists suggested that organisms (especially human beings) are predisposed to structure their experiences in similar, and therefore predictable, ways. They proposed several principles to describe how people organize their experiences. One of the dominant principles affecting how people organize information is the **law of proximity:** People tend to perceive as a unit those things that are close together in space. For example, look at the following dots:

● ● ●   ● ● ●   ● ● ●

Not only do you see nine dots, but you probably also perceive an arrangement of three groups of three dots each. That is, you see those dots that are in closer proximity to one another as somehow belonging together. In the same way, when you looked at Figure 7.3a, you perceived lines that were close together as forming pairs. And notice how you read and interpret the letter sequence ONEVERYHIGHWAY differently depending on whether they're grouped this way:

ONE VERY HIGH WAY

or this way:

ON EVERY HIGHWAY

Figure 7.4a

Figure 7.4b

Figure 7.5   Singing in the rain

Another organizational principle from Gestalt psychology is the **law of similarity:** People tend to perceive as a unit those things that are similar to one another. For example, look at the dots in Figure 7.4a. Can you see the letter Y among them? Perhaps not. But now look at the dots in Figure 7.4b. This time a letter Y is obvious. The arrangement of the dots is the same in both cases, but in the second case the dots forming the Y are all black, and you tend to perceive those similar black dots as a unit. Yet you probably haven't noticed other letters, such as E or H, that are also formed by some of the dots. As early as 6 or 7 months of age, children show evidence that they perceive the world in accordance with the law of similarity (Quinn, Bhatt, Brush, Grimes, & Sharpnack, 2002).

Still another Gestaltist principle is the **law of closure:** People tend to fill in missing pieces to form a complete picture. For example, when you looked at Figure 7.3b, you filled in missing segments of what appeared to be continuous straight lines to perceive four rectangles. Similarly, when you look at Figure 7.5, you are probably able to read "Singing in the rain," even though 50% of the print is missing. You simply fill in what isn't there.

Gestaltists further proposed that individuals always organize their experience as simply, concisely, symmetrically, and completely as possible, a principle known as the **law of Prägnanz** (i.e., "terseness" or "preciseness") (Koffka, 1935). For example, you are likely to see rectangles in Figure 7.3b because rectangles are simple, symmetric figures. It is unlikely that you would mentally fill in the missing pieces of that figure in a wild and crazy fashion such as that shown in Figure 7.6. The "KISS" principle that many successful product designers advocate ("Keep it simple, stupid!") is a modern-day adaptation of this law of Prägnanz.

◆ *Learning follows the law of Prägnanz.* According to Gestalt psychologists, learning involves the formation of **memory traces.** These memory traces are subject to the law of Prägnanz, so that over time they tend to become simpler, more concise, and more complete than the actual input. For example, after seeing the somewhat irregular objects in Figure 7.7, people are likely to remember them later as being a "circle" and a "square." As another example, consider a study by Tversky (1981), in which people studied maps and then drew them from memory. Distortions in people's reproductions often followed the law of Prägnanz: Curvy, irregular lines were straightened, slanted lines were represented as north–south or east–west lines, and map features were placed in better alignment with one another than they had been in the original maps.

Figure 7.6

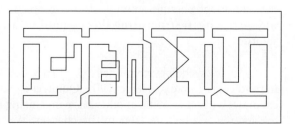

Figure 7.7
Irregularly shaped objects may
later be remembered as "circles"
or "squares."

◆ *Problem solving involves restructuring and insight.* As we noted in chapter 4, Thorndike (1898) described problem solving (such as that exhibited by cats in puzzle boxes) as a process of trial and error. Gestaltists proposed a very different view of how organisms solve problems. Köhler (1925), for instance, suggested that problem solving involves mentally combining and recombining various elements of a problem until a structure that solves the problem is achieved. He described numerous observations of chimpanzees solving problems through what he perceived to be the mental manipulation of the problem situation. In one situation, a chimp named Sultan was faced with a dilemma: Some fruit was placed far enough outside his cage that he couldn't reach it. Sultan had had earlier experiences in which he had used sticks to rake in fruit; however, the only stick inside the cage was too short. A longer stick was outside the cage, but, like the fruit, was beyond Sultan's reach. The following scenario ensued:

> Sultan tries to reach the fruit with the smaller of the two sticks. Not succeeding, he tears at a piece of wire that projects from the netting of his cage, but that, too, in vain. Then he gazes about him (there are always in the course of these tests some long pauses during which the animals scrutinize the whole visible area). He suddenly picks up the little stick, once more goes up to the bars, directly opposite to the long stick, scratches it towards him with the [short stick], seizes it, and goes with it to the point opposite the [fruit], which he secures. From the moment that his eyes fall upon the long stick, his procedure forms one consecutive whole, without hiatus. . . . (Köhler, 1925, p. 180)

In another situation, Sultan, again confronted with fruit placed outside the cage beyond his reach, had two hollow bamboo rods, one somewhat thinner than the other, and both too short to reach the fruit. After numerous "fruitless" attempts, he seemingly gave up and resorted to playing indifferently with the sticks. At one serendipitous point, Sultan found himself holding the two sticks end to end in such a way that they appeared to form a long, straight line. He immediately pushed the end of the thinner stick into the end of the thicker one (thus making a single long stick), ran over to the edge of the cage, and obtained the elusive bananas.

In neither of the situations I have just described did Sultan engage in the random trial-and-error learning that Thorndike had observed for cats. Instead, it appeared to Köhler as if Sultan thought about possible solutions to the problem, arranging the problem elements in various ways—that is, **restructuring** them—until he arrived at a sudden **insight** as to a problem solution.

Gestalt psychology continues to influence how cognitive psychologists conceptualize learning and cognition (e.g., Henle, 1985; Quinn et al., 2002; Vecera, Vogel, & Woodman, 2002). For example, we will examine another basic organizing principle—figure-ground—when we look at the nature of attention later in the chapter. We will see *closure* at work when we examine constructive processes in perception and memory in chapters 8 and 10. We will revisit the

Gestaltist idea of *insight* in our exploration of problem solving in chapter 13. And the general idea that people organize the things that they learn will come up repeatedly in our discussion of learning and cognition in the chapters to come.

VERBAL LEARNING RESEARCH

Beginning in the late 1920s, some researchers began to apply behaviorist principles to a uniquely human behavior: language. Such **verbal learning** research continued throughout the middle decades of the twentieth century (especially from the 1930s through the 1960s and early 1970s) and yielded many insights into the nature of human learning.

Central to verbal learning research were two learning tasks, serial learning and paired associate learning, that could easily be analyzed in terms of an S–R perspective. **Serial learning** involves learning a sequence of items in a particular order; the alphabet, the days of the week, and the planets in our solar system are examples. Verbal learning theorists explained serial learning in this way: The first item in the list is a stimulus to which the second item is learned as a response, the second item then serves as a stimulus to which the third item is the learned response, and so on.

Paired associate learning involves learning pairs of items. Learning foreign language vocabulary words and their English equivalents (e.g., *le papier* is French for "the paper") and learning state capitals (e.g., Juneau is the capital of Alaska) are two examples. Verbal learning theorists described paired associates as being distinct stimulus–response associations: The first item in each pair is the stimulus, and the second item is the response.

Increasingly, verbal learning studies yielded results that could not be easily explained in terms of simple S–R connections, and theorists began to introduce a variety of mental phenomena into their discussions of learning processes. In this section, I will describe some general learning principles that emerged from verbal learning research. Some of the findings are relatively easy to explain from a behaviorist perspective, but others are troublesome.

◆ *Serial learning is characterized by a particular pattern.* In a serial learning task, a **serial learning curve** is usually observed: People learn the first few items and last few items more quickly and easily than they learn the middle items (J. F. Hall, 1971; McCrary & Hunter, 1953; Roediger & Crowder, 1976). If we were to graph the speed with which the various items in a serial list are learned, we might obtain results similar to what you see in Figure 7.8. A common example is the way in which most children learn the alphabet: They learn the first letters (A, B, C, D) and the last letters (X, Y, Z) before they learn the middle letters (e.g., J, K, L, M).

The tendency for the first items in a serial learning curve to be learned quickly is called the **primacy effect.** The tendency for the last items to be learned quickly is called the **recency effect.** Verbal learning theorists explained both effects by proposing that the end points of the list (i.e., the first and last items) served as *anchors* to which the other items would then be attached in a stimulus-response fashion.

◆ *Overlearned material is more easily recalled at a later time.* What happens when you learn information perfectly and then continue to study it? This process of **overlearning,** in which you learn material to mastery and then practice it for additional study trials, enables you to remember

Figure 7.8
A typical serial learning curve.

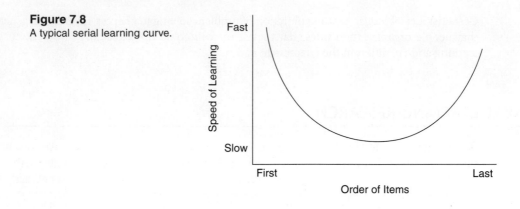

the information much more accurately at a later time (Krueger, 1929; Underwood, 1954). As you may recall from chapter 3, practice is important for learning, presumably because it strengthens stimulus–response connections.

◆ *Distributed practice is usually more effective than massed practice.* Imagine that you have to study for a test. You estimate that you need six hours to master the test material. Would you do better on the test if you studied for six hours all at once or if you broke your study time into smaller chunks—say, six one-hour sessions? Verbal learning researchers discovered that **distributed practice,** spreading study time out over several occasions, usually leads to better learning than **massed practice,** in which study time occurs all at once (Glenberg, 1976; Underwood, 1961; Underwood, Kapelak, & Malmi, 1976). In fact, the further apart the study sessions are, the better one's recall for the learned information is apt to be over the long run (Bahrick, Bahrick, Bahrick, & Bahrick, 1993). From a behaviorist perspective, massed practice might eventually lead to fatigue, which would cause the learner to begin practicing inappropriate responses.

◆ *Learning in one situation often affects learning and recall in another situation.* Imagine yourself having to learn two sets of paired associates. The first set looks like this:

Set 1
house—dragon
plant—sled
lamp—music
onion—pillow

The second one looks like this:

Set 2
house—paper
plant—clock
lamp—turkey
onion—chair

After you have first learned Set 1 and then learned Set 2, you are asked to recall the responses to each of the stimulus words in Set 1. Will you have difficulty? Probably so, because you learned different responses to those same words when you learned Set 2. You would have an easier time remembering the correct responses you learned in Set 1 if you had *not* had to learn the Set 2 responses as well.

Verbal learning researchers observed that when people learn two sets of paired associates in succession, their learning of the second set often diminishes their ability to recall the first set (J. F. Hall, 1971), a phenomenon known as **retroactive inhibition.** In fact, individuals in this situation often have difficulty remembering the second set as well (J. F. Hall, 1971), a phenomenon known as **proactive inhibition.** The tendency for a set of paired associates learned at one time to interfere with the recall of a set learned either earlier or later is especially likely to occur when the two sets have the same or similar stimulus words but different response words (Osgood, 1949).

Under different circumstances, learning one set of information may actually improve the recall of information learned at another time, a phenomenon that verbal learning theorists called either **retroactive facilitation** or **proactive facilitation,** depending on the order in which the two sets of information were learned (J. F. Hall, 1971). Facilitation is most likely to occur when two situations have similar or identical stimuli and when they have similar responses as well (Osgood, 1949). As an example, after learning the stimulus–response pair "house — dragon," you would probably learn "house — monster" fairly easily.

Verbal learning theorists (e.g., McGeoch, 1942; Melton & Irwin, 1940; Underwood, 1948) proposed that retroactive and proactive inhibition were major factors in *forgetting* verbal information; therefore, they were among the first to discuss theoretical ideas related to *memory.* Many contemporary cognitive psychologists also suggest that inhibition plays a significant role in memory and forgetting, although they are less likely to focus on specific S–R associations that may be involved.

◆ *Characteristics of the material affect the speed with which people can learn it.* Verbal learning researchers identified a number of characteristics that affect the ease of learning and remembering verbal material:

1. Items are more quickly learned when they are *meaningful*—that is, when they can be easily associated with other ideas (Cofer, 1971; Paivio, 1971). German psychologist Hermann Ebbinghaus (1913) stumbled on this principle well before the verbal learning movement was off and running in the Western hemisphere. Ebbinghaus, who served as his own subject of study for a number of experiments in serial learning, found that some words triggered associations that helped him remember the words more easily. He attempted to eliminate the influence of associations by using presumably meaningless **nonsense syllables** ("words" such as JAD, MON, and ZIV). Yet even many nonsense syllables often have meaningfulness and evoke associations, thus making them relatively easy to learn (J. F. Hall, 1971). For example, the nonsense syllable JAD might make you think of "jade," and the syllable MON might remind you of "money."

2. Items are easier to learn and remember when they are *pronounceable* (Di Vesta & Ingersoll, 1969; Underwood & Schulz, 1960). For example, the nonsense syllable DNK should be learned faster than BPX because most people can pronounce DNK more easily.

Some items are more
meaningful than others.

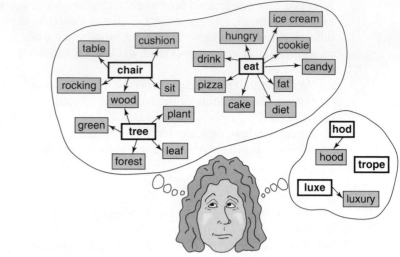

3. *Concrete* items are easier to learn and remember than abstract items (Gorman, 1961; Paivio, 1963); for example, items such as

   turtle, hammer, sandwich

are learned more easily than items such as

   truth, joy, experience

4. One probable reason that the concreteness of items makes them easier to learn and remember is that concrete items can be *mentally visualized*. In general, items that readily evoke mental images are more memorable than those that are hard to visualize (Paivio, 1971). For example, it is easier to form a mental image of a turtle than it is to form an image of truth. This phenomenon of visual imagery—very clearly a mental phenomenon—is quite difficult to explain from an S–R perspective.

♦ *People often impose meaning on new information.* The effect of meaningfulness just mentioned can be explained from an S–R perspective: When a stimulus word has many other words associated with it, one of those associations may in turn be associated with the response to be learned. What is more troublesome for an S–R approach is the fact that people will go out of their way to *make* information meaningful when they are trying to learn it. For example, when Bugelski (1962) asked adults to learn paired associates involving nonsense syllables, they invariably reported that they imposed meanings to help them learn the pairs. To illustrate, when given this pair:

DUP — TEZ

one person used the word *deputize* to help form the connection. Cognitive theories have emerged that probably better explain this tendency for human beings to search for meaning.

♦ *People organize what they learn.* When people are allowed to recall items of a serial learning task in any order (a task known as **free recall**), they typically do *not* recall the items in the original presentation order. Instead, their recall order often reflects an organizational scheme of some kind (Bousfield, 1953; Buschke, 1977; Jenkins & Russell, 1952). In a classic experiment by Bousfield (1953), college students were given a list of 60 words, 15 from each of four categories: animals, names, vegetables, and professions. Although the words were presented in a random order, the students tended to recall them in category clusters. For example, a typical recall order might have been something like this:

> camel, giraffe, zebra, donkey, Jason, Adam, Howard, pumpkin, cabbage, carrot, lettuce, radish, milkman, baker, dentist

People even try to organize seemingly unorganized material (Tulving, 1962). This tendency human beings have to insist on organizing what they learn is difficult to explain from behaviorist principles. As you will see in later chapters, however, it lends itself quite easily to an explanation based on cognitive learning theories.

   ◆ *People often use encoding strategies to help them learn.* As the earlier example of remembering *DUP—TEZ* as "deputize" illustrates, people often change, or *encode,* information in some way to make it easier to learn (Bugelski, 1962; Dallett, 1964; Underwood & Erlebacher, 1965). Furthermore, when experimenters specifically tell people to use a certain encoding strategy to help them learn information, learning improves (Bugelski, Kidd, & Segmen, 1968; J. F. Hall, 1971). For instance, when people are instructed in techniques for forming mental visual images, they are able to remember a list of words more accurately than individuals who have not been given such instructions (Bugelski et al., 1968).

   ◆ *People are more likely to learn general ideas than to learn words verbatim.* In fact, when people focus on learning ideas rather than on learning information word for word, their learning is faster and their recall more accurate (Briggs & Reed, 1943; English, Welborn, & Killian, 1934; Jones & English, 1926). Most verbal learning research focused on the learning of verbatim information. In doing so, it may very well have ignored the way in which human beings actually learn most verbal material.

   Clearly, verbal learning research provided us with a number of useful learning principles. It also gave us two learning tasks, serial and paired associate learning, that continue to be used in learning research. At the same time, in trying to stretch S–R models of learning to explain human verbal behavior, it began to demonstrate some weaknesses of the behaviorist perspective.

   In more recent decades, the focus of verbal learning research has been on how people learn meaningful verbal material (e.g., prose passages) rather than artificially constructed serial lists or paired associates. In fact, the term *verbal learning* was largely abandoned (e.g., the *Journal of Verbal Learning and Verbal Behavior* became the *Journal of Memory and Language* in 1985) as verbal learning researchers began to embrace cognitivist ideas.

INTRODUCTION TO CONTEMPORARY COGNITIVISM

We have just seen how, even during the heyday of behaviorism, researchers were laying a foundation for cognitive learning theories. During the 1960s, discontent with the inadequacies of behaviorism became more widespread. The behaviorist perspective could not easily explain why people often try to organize and make sense of new information and sometimes even alter its form. Learning theorists increasingly came to the realization that they had to bring mental events—cognition—into the picture.

General Assumptions of Cognitive Theories

The assumptions underlying contemporary cognitive theories of learning are radically different from those underlying behaviorism. What follow are some of the most central ones:

♦ *Some learning processes may be unique to human beings.* Because people possess abilities unique to the species (complex language is an example), the processes involved in learning are often quite different for human beings than they are for other animals. Accordingly, almost all research within the cognitivist perspective is conducted with human beings, and theories formulated from this research are typically not generalized to other species.

♦ *Learning involves the formation of mental representations or associations that are not necessarily reflected in overt behavior changes.* Like Tolman and social cognitive theorists, contemporary cognitive psychologists believe that learning involves an internal, mental change rather than the external behavior change that many behaviorists describe. Learning can, therefore, occur without being reflected in an individual's observed performance.

♦ *People are actively involved in the learning process.* Rather than being passive victims of environmental conditions, people are active participants in the learning process and in fact *control* their own learning. Individual learners themselves determine how they mentally process the events they experience, and these cognitive processes in turn determine what, if anything, is learned. To the extent that individual learners think differently about a situation, they will learn different things from it.

♦ *Knowledge is organized.* An individual's knowledge, beliefs, attitudes, and emotions are not isolated from one another but are instead all associated and interconnected. The learning process itself contributes to this organization. As you will discover in our later discussion of long-term memory, people usually learn most effectively when they relate new information to things they already know.

♦ *Objective, systematic observations of people's behavior should be the focus of scientific inquiry; however, inferences about unobservable mental processes can often be drawn from behavior.* Cognitive psychologists share with behaviorists the beliefs that the study of learning must be objective and that learning theories should be based on the results of empirical research. Also, like behaviorists, they recognize that they have no way of knowing that learning has occurred until they see a behavior change of some sort. Cognitivists differ from behaviorists in one critical respect, however: By observing the responses that people make to different stimulus conditions, they believe they can draw reasonable inferences about the nature of the internal mental events that lead to those responses. In fact, researchers have become increasingly ingenious in designing research studies that enable them to draw conclusions about specific cognitive processes.

A classic study by Bransford and Franks (1971) provides an example of inference drawing in cognitive research. In this experiment, undergraduate students listened to 24 sentences and answered simple questions about each one. The sentences were variations on four general ideas: a rock rolling down a hill, a man reading a newspaper, a breeze blowing, and ants eating jelly. To illustrate, the six sentences about the ants eating jelly were as follows:

The ants ate the sweet jelly which was on the table.
The ants in the kitchen ate the jelly which was on the table.
The ants in the kitchen ate the jelly.

The ants ate the sweet jelly.
The ants were in the kitchen.
The jelly was on the table.

The students then listened to a second set of 28 sentences (variations on the same four themes as before) and were asked to indicate whether or not each had been in the first set. Most of the sentences (24 out of 28) were *new* sentences; following are some examples:

The ants in the kitchen ate the sweet jelly which was on the table.
The ants in the kitchen ate the sweet jelly.
The ants ate the jelly which was on the table.
The jelly was sweet.

The students erroneously "recognized" most of these new sentences as being "old" ones. Sentences that contained a lot of information were especially likely to be recognized as having been heard before; for instance, "The ants in the kitchen ate the sweet jelly which was on the table" was more likely to be recognized than "The jelly was sweet." From such results, Bransford and Franks concluded that people abstract general ideas from the verbal information they receive (rather than learning it verbatim) and organize similar ideas together in their memories. Sentences in the experiment that included most or all of the information related to a single theme may have more closely resembled the students' organized memories and so seemed more familiar to them.

Obviously, Bransford and Franks did not directly observe the cognitive processes they described. Yet such processes seem to be reasonable explanations of the behaviors they *did* see.

Despite sharing certain common assumptions, cognitivists take somewhat different approaches in their attempts to portray how learning occurs. The predominant approach to the study of human learning, as reflected in ongoing research and journal space, is a group of theories collectively known as *information processing theory*. In recent years, however, two other perspectives—*constructivism* and *contextual theories*—have also gained popularity, especially among psychologists who concern themselves with instructional practice and other educational issues.

Information Processing Theory

Many cognitive theories focus on how people think about (i.e., *process*) the information they receive from the environment—how they perceive the stimuli around them, how they "put" what they've perceived into their memories, how they "find" what they've learned when they need to use it, and so on. Such theories are collectively known as **information processing theory.**

Early views of information processing, especially those that emerged in the 1960s, portrayed human learning as being similar to how computers process information. It soon became clear, however, that the computer analogy was overly simplistic—that people often think about and interpret information in ways that are difficult to explain in the rigid, algorithmic, one-thing-always-leads-to-another ways that characterize computers (Bereiter, 1997; Mayer, 1996a; Munakata, 2006; Reisberg, 1997). At this time, the general perspective known as information processing theory includes a variety of specific theories about how people mentally deal with the information they receive. Some of these theories are computerlike in nature, but many others are not.

Information processing researchers have been extremely helpful in identifying the many processes that human cognition involves. In doing so, however, they have sometimes zeroed in on trivial tasks that only remotely resemble typical human learning situations (Bjorklund, 1997; Hambrick & Engle, 2003). And although they have told us a great deal about *how* people learn, they have been less specific about exactly *what* is acquired in the learning process (Alexander, White, & Daugherty, 1997). But in my mind, the biggest weakness of information processing theory is that it has been better at dissection than at synthesis: It has yet to combine various cognitive processes into an integrated whole that explains, overall, how human beings think and behave.

Constructivism

In recent decades, it has become increasingly apparent that learners don't just absorb information as they encounter it. Instead, people do a great deal with the information they acquire, actively trying to organize and make sense of it, often in unique, idiosyncratic ways. Many cognitive theorists now portray learning more as *constructing* knowledge rather than directly acquiring it from the outside world (e.g., see Bransford, Brown, & Cocking, 1999; Marshall, 1992; Mayer, 1996a; Spivey, 1997; Windschitl, 2002). Some (but not all) theorists refer to this perspective as **constructivism** rather than information processing theory.

Early Gestalt psychologists clearly had a constructivist bent. For instance, construction is involved when learners perceive separate objects as being a unit (reflecting such principles as *proximity* or *similarity*) and when they fill in missing pieces in what they are looking at (reflecting the principle of *closure*). Tolman's concept of *cognitive map* has a constructivist flavor as well: Learners combine various spatial relationships they have learned into a general mental representation of how their environment is laid out. In these situations, we see the process of construction occurring separately within each learner, reflecting a perspective known as **individual constructivism.**

In other situations, people work together to make sense of their world. For instance, several students may form a study group when they have a difficult and confusing textbook; helping one another, they may be able to interpret and understand the book in ways that they cannot do on their own. As another example, astronomers have, over the course of several centuries, made increasingly better sense of the phenomena they've observed through their telescopes; the discipline of astronomy provides a view of the universe that innumerable scientists have pieced together over many centuries. Theories of learning that focus on how people work together, perhaps at a single sitting or perhaps over the course of many years, reflect a perspective known as **social constructivism.**

Constructivist perspectives have directed psychologists' attention to *what* is learned; the *schemas, scripts,* and *personal theories* to be described in chapter 9 are examples of the forms that learner-constructed knowledge might take. These perspectives also place the reins for directing learning squarely in the hands of the learner. Teachers cannot "pour" knowledge into the heads of students as they might pour lemonade into a glass; rather, students must make their own lemonade.

Yet constructivism, like information processing, has its drawbacks. To date, it offers only vague explanations of the cognitive processes that underlie learning (Mayer, 2004; Tarver, 1992). Furthermore, some constructivists take the idea of learner control too far, suggesting that teachers don't have—and perhaps *shouldn't* have—much influence over how students interpret subject matter and learn from classroom activities (e.g., see critiques by Hirsch, 1996; Marton & Booth, 1997; Mayer, 2004; S. M. Miller, 2003). In fact, a voluminous body of research (not to mention the countless personal experiences of students in elementary, secondary, and college classrooms) tells us that a wide variety of teaching methods, from teacher-directed lectures to more student-directed group discussions, very definitely *do* affect what students learn and how effectively they learn it. To use the "reins" metaphor once again, although learners are in the driver's seat in the learning process, teachers can provide a road map and offer suggestions about how to move the horse and wagon forward. To revert to the "lemonade" metaphor, teachers can supply the lemons, sugar, and water, as well as some directions about the relative proportions of each that will yield a tasty drink.

Contextual Theories

Some cognitivist theories place considerable emphasis on the importance of the immediate environment—the *context*—in learning (e.g., Greeno, Collins, & Resnick, 1996; Pea, 1993; Perkins, 1995; Sternberg & Wagner, 1994; Wenger, 1998). In general, such **contextual theories** suggest that learners often think and perform more "intelligently" when they can draw on a variety of environmental support systems that enable them to make sense of new situations and help them tackle challenging tasks and problems.

Sometimes environmental supports for learning and performance are concrete and easily observable. This is the case, for instance, when people use calculators, computers, diagrams, equations, or paper and pencil to help them analyze data or solve problems. In other instances, environmental supports are so abstract and pervasive in one's culture that they are taken for granted and easily overlooked as contextual factors affecting learning. Consider, for example, the concepts *north, south, east,* and *west.* Over the years, you have undoubtedly used these concepts frequently to help you find your way around town or around the planet. Despite their obvious relationship to Mother Earth, these concepts are creations that some cultures—and *only* some cultures—provide.

Contextual theories of learning have a variety of labels attached to them. Terms such as *situated learning, situated cognition, distributed learning,* and *distributed intelligence* all refer to situations in which learning and thinking are influenced by the physical and social contexts in which people are immersed. For example, the term *distributed intelligence* refers, in part, to the notion that we often perform more effectively when we think about and discuss ideas with others than when we think alone. When contextual perspectives focus specifically on the influence of culture in learning, the term *sociocultural theory* is often used. Sociocultural theory has its roots in Vygotsky's theory of cognitive development, and so we'll look at it more closely in our discussion of developmental perspectives in chapter 11.

With the exception of the work of Vygotsky and some of his Russian compatriots in the first half of the twentieth century, contextual views have been a fairly recent addition to the cognitivist scene. Accordingly, we do not yet have a large body of research that allows us to substantiate some theoretical claims and modify others. The benefit of contextual theories lies largely in how they bring our attention back to the importance of the immediate context—an idea that seemingly brings us back full circle to behaviorism. There is a very important difference, however. The emphasis here is not on concrete, observable stimuli that bring about relatively thought-free conditioning (a behaviorist view), but rather on general factors—physical, social, and cultural—that support very "thoughtful" learning.

Integrating Cognitive Perspectives

It is important to note that complete consensus does not exist, even among cognitivists, about how different cognitive theories can best be categorized (for various possibilities, see Bredo, 1997; Case, 1996; Derry, 1996; Greeno et al., 1996; Mayer, 1996a, 1996b; Reynolds, Sinatra, & Jetton, 1996). As one simple example, some theorists portray contemporary information processing theory as being decidedly constructivist in nature (Derry, 1996; Mayer, 1996a, 1996b; Phye, 1997; Prawat, 1996; Pressley, Wharton-McDonald, et al., 1997).

Despite the fuzziness of the boundaries between various cognitive perspectives, some psychologists and educators have insisted on drawing sharp distinctions among them. This tendency to dichotomize theoretical perspectives—to portray one as black and another as white, to suggest that one points strictly to "teacher-centered" instructional methods while another supports more "learner-centered" methods, and in some cases to imply that one is a "good guy" and another is a "bad guy"—drives me nuts. In recent years, a few of my colleagues in the field have expressed similar frustration (Bereiter & Scardamalia, 1996; Clancey, 1997; Harris & Alexander, 1998; Hynd, 1998b; Salomon, 1993; Sfard, 1998).

Having read countless books, articles, and papers about human learning over the past 40 years, I remain firmly convinced that ideas from information processing theory, constructivism, and contextual views, as well as ideas from theories we've already considered (e.g., social cognitive theory and recent, cognitively oriented behaviorist perspectives) all make significant contributions to our understanding of how human beings think and learn. Taken in combination, they give us a more complete understanding of human cognition than any single approach can offer alone.[2] Accordingly, we will be pulling from a variety of cognitive perspectives, in a somewhat eclectic manner, as we continue to explore how people think and learn in this and the next few chapters. However, we will organize much of our discussion around a view of human memory that has evolved largely from information processing research. We look at basic components of memory now.

AN INFORMATION PROCESSING VIEW OF HUMAN MEMORY

Imagine yourself taking an exam over the material in this chapter. Imagine, too, that as your instructor, I write ridiculously picky exam questions. You come to this question: "What was Edward C. Tolman's middle name?"[3] You know you read this information in the chapter, and you even wrote it down in your notebook, but despite your best efforts you cannot recall it now that you need it. After considering all of the names you can think of that begin with C, you finally

---

[2]For examples of how two or more theories might be combined, I refer you to Anderson, Greeno, Reder, and Simon (2000); Gauvain (2001); P. A. Ornstein and Haden (2001); Packer and Goicoechea (2000); and Zimmerman (1981).

[3]In reality, I would *never* give you such a question, for reasons you'll discover in chapter 10.

write "Charles"—although you're pretty sure it *wasn't* Charles—and turn in your exam. Immediately afterward, you congregate with your classmates in the hall and rehash the questions. "What was Tolman's middle name?" you ask. Your friend Harry responds smugly, "It was Chace. I can remember that easily because my sister married a guy named Marvin Chace." And then your friend Carol adds, "I learned the name by imagining Tolman *chacing* his rats down their mazes." You grit your teeth, thinking it ridiculous that Harry and Carol would do better than you on a question because of a coincidental brother-in-law or a silly visual image. But let's face it, your classmates remembered and you did not.

Learning a piece of information at one time does not guarantee that you will remember it later on. Information theorists have consistently made a distinction between *learning* and *memory*. And in their early, computer-analogy days, they began to use such computer lingo as *storage, encoding,* and *retrieval*—terms that have "stuck" despite the drift to non-computer-based views of human cognition.

Learning versus memory   *Learning* is viewed, quite simply, as the acquisition of new information or skills; as we defined it in chapter 1, it involves a long-term change in mental representations or associations as a result of experience. In contrast, **memory** is related to the ability to recall previously acquired information. In some instances, the word *memory* is used to refer to the process of retaining information for a period of time. In other instances, it is used to refer to a particular "location" (e.g., *working memory* or *long-term memory*) where acquired information is kept.

Storage   The process of "putting" new information in memory is known as **storage.** For example, if you can put this fact in your head:

Jeanne Ormrod's birthday is August 22.

then you are *storing* the information. We will talk a little bit about storage processes in this chapter, and we will examine some of them in depth in chapter 8.

Encoding   As people store information in memory, they usually modify it in some way; this process of **encoding**[4] often helps them store the information more easily. Sometimes encoding involves *changing the form* of the information. For example, I once had a combination lock for which the combination was 22-8-14. I quickly learned the first two numbers by encoding them as "the day and month of my birthday." In this case, I changed numerical information into a verbal form. Encoding may also involve *adding to* new information using one's existing knowledge of the world. For example, consider this information:

Jeanne Ormrod was born in Providence, Rhode Island.

On reading this, you might conclude that I am a native New Englander or that I am a U.S. citizen—inferences you might store along with the information I actually gave you. Yet another encoding process is one of *simplifying* information that has been presented—for example, by remembering the overall meaning or gist of a situation rather than the specific details of what happened. For example, you might remember that the author of one of your textbooks talked about her birthday but not remember the actual date.

----

[4]In our discussion of modeling in chapter 6, we noted that people can often remember a model's behavior more accurately when they form verbal or visual *memory codes* to help them remember the specific actions that the model has demonstrated. Such memory codes are examples of encoding in action.

Retrieval   The process by which people "find" information they have previously stored so they can use it again is called **retrieval**. For example, I am hoping that, come mid-August, you will retrieve the date of my birthday and send me a tasteful card. Because I get cards from few of my readers (and primarily from students in my own classes), we can conclude that retrieval is quite easy in some cases but more difficult in others. (An alternative hypothesis, of course, is that information retrieval is occurring but is not resulting in a behavior change.)

A Dual–Store Model of Memory

Late in the nineteenth century, Harvard psychologist William James (1890) proposed that human memory has three components: an after-image, a primary memory, and a secondary memory. James's model was largely ignored during the behaviorism-dominated early decades of the twentieth century, but the advent of cognitivism in the 1960s brought a renewed interest in human memory, and psychologists Richard Atkinson and Richard Shiffrin (1968, 1971) proposed a model of memory similar to that of James. This model, which laid the groundwork for what has become the most prevalent view of human memory today, is depicted in simplified form in Figure 7.9. Despite its three components, the model is known as a **dual-store model** because of its claim that short-term memory and long-term memory are distinctly different entities. As you will discover later in the chapter, not all psychologists buy into this claim.

In Atkinson and Shiffrin's model, information from the environment—input—first enters a *sensory register,* where it is held for a very short time (a few seconds at most). If the information is processed in a particular way, it moves on to *short-term memory.* Information is held in short-term memory for less than a minute, however, and must be processed further if it is to move on to *long-term memory.* Processing of information in short-term memory frequently involves the use of information from long-term memory as well (hence the two-way arrows between short-term and long-term memory in Figure 7.9). If a piece of information reaches the sensory register or short-term memory but is not then processed sufficiently for its transference to the next component of the memory system, the information is assumed to be lost from the memory system—in other words, it is forgotten. Whether information can be lost from long-term memory as well (note the dotted arrow and question mark in Figure 7.9) is still an open question that we will address in chapter 10.

The model of memory just described can be likened to an information selection and storage system similar to one you might use to store important documents at home. You undoubtedly acquire numerous pieces of paper over the course of a few months; among this mass of paper may be such items as newspapers, personal letters, bills, a driver's license, university transcripts, junk mail, and grocery store receipts. You probably discard some items (such as junk mail and grocery receipts) almost as soon as you get them; these things get no further than the "sensory

Figure 7.9
A simplified dual-store model of memory.

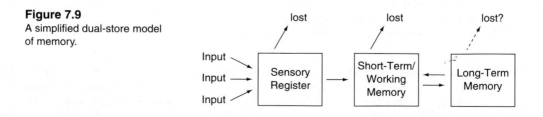

register" of your storage system. You need to deal with others (such as bills) briefly (e.g., you need to pay them) and then you can more or less forget them; they are processed for a short time in your system's "short-term storage." Still others (such as a driver's license and transcripts) may be important enough that you want to put them in some sort of "long-term storage" compartment—perhaps a wallet, file cabinet, or safe-deposit box—where you can find them later.

Over the years, learning theorists have continued to build on and modify Atkinson and Shiffrin's dual-store model. For example, they have theorized about the forms in which information is stored and the processes through which it is moved from short-term memory to long-term memory. But perhaps the most noticeable change is an increasing reference to short-term memory as a "working" memory that processes information in addition to storing it (hence, the term *working* in the second box of Figure 7.9). To be consistent with contemporary memory theorists, we will primarily use the term *working memory* from this point on.

In the pages that follow, we will examine the three components of the dual-store model and at various **control processes**—cognitive processes that directly affect memory's functioning—involved along the way. As we proceed, remember that the language we will use is sometimes metaphorical in nature (Roediger, 1980; Torgesen, 1996). For example, the three components of memory are not necessarily three separate "places" in the brain. Furthermore, when we talk about memory processes, we are not necessarily saying anything about neurological events. As you discovered in chapter 2, psychologists still have much to learn about how memory processes occur physiologically and how brain structure relates to psychological models of human memory. Occasionally I will suggest in footnotes where in the brain certain structures and functions may be located. But our emphasis here will be on what psychologists have learned about memory by studying human behavior and performance—for instance, what kinds of things people seem to be able to remember, and under what circumstances they remember most effectively—rather than by studying the anatomy and physiology of the brain.

Sensory Register

The first component of the dual-store model, the **sensory register**,[5] holds incoming information long enough for it to undergo preliminary cognitive processing. All of the environmental information we are capable of sensing probably stays with us in the sensory register for a very brief time. For example, if you have ever waved a flashlight or sparkler in the air on a dark night, you've undoubtedly noticed that the light leaves a trail behind it. This trail does not exist in the air itself; it is the result of your sensory register holding the light for a short time after you've seen it. As another example, when you sit in a classroom for an hour or more, your attention will almost inevitably wander away from the instructor at some point. You may have noticed that when you tune back in to what the instructor is saying, you can often recall two or three words that the instructor has said *before* you tuned back in. Virtually everything the instructor has uttered has probably been recorded in your sensory register despite your mental absence from class, but, alas, only those last two or three words are still there when you decide to be mentally "present" again.

---

[5]Theorists have given this component a variety of labels, including *sensory memory, brief sensory store, sensory buffer, iconic memory,* and *echoic memory.*

Characteristics of the Sensory Register

Let's look specifically at three characteristics of the sensory register: capacity, forms of storage, and duration.

Capacity   The capacity of the sensory register is, as far as psychologists can tell, unlimited. All of the environmental information that human beings are capable of sensing is probably stored briefly in the sensory register.

Forms of storage   Information appears to be stored in the sensory register in basically the same form in which it has been sensed: visual input is stored in a visual form, auditory input in an auditory form, and so on (Coltheart, Lea, & Thompson, 1974; Cowan, 1995; Howard, 1983; Turvey & Kravetz, 1970). At this point, information has not yet been understood or interpreted by the learner. In other words, the sensory register holds information *before* it is encoded.[6]

Duration   Information remains in the sensory register for only a very brief time, but measuring its exact duration is difficult. One problem in studying the characteristics of information in the sensory register is that when we ask people to report or in some other way process something that they've stored there, the information automatically moves on to working memory and so is no longer in the place where we want to study it!

In an early study, George Sperling (1960) designed an ingenious method to assess the duration of information in the sensory register. Recruiting adults to participate in his experiment, Sperling presented displays of three rows of four letters and digits each; following is a typical display:

```
7    1    V    F
X    L    5    3
B    4    W    7
```

Each display was presented for a fraction of a second, then participants were asked to recall either one particular row of symbols or all 12 symbols. When asked to recall a single row, people were able to do so with 76% accuracy; because they were not told *which* row they would need to recall until after the display had disappeared, they apparently remembered approximately 76% of the symbols they had seen. Yet when asked to recall all 12 symbols, they could do so with only 36% accuracy. Sperling's explanation of these results was that most of the symbols were stored initially but faded from memory before the participants had a chance to report them all. In a follow-up experiment, Sperling (1960) varied the amount of time that elapsed between the display and the signal indicating which row was to be remembered. People could recall little of a display after a delay of more than a quarter of a second.

From the results of research studies such as Sperling's, it appears that the duration of visual information in the sensory register is probably less than a second (G. R. Loftus & Loftus, 1976; Wingfield & Byrnes, 1981). Auditory information appears to last longer, with a possible duration of 2 to 4 seconds (Conrad & Hull, 1964; Darwin, Turvey, & Crowder, 1972; Moray, Bates, & Barnett, 1965).

---

[6]As we discovered in chapter 2, different parts of the brain seem to be responsible for processing different kinds of sensory input. We can reasonably guess, then, that the sensory register is not a single structure located in a particular spot in the brain. Rather, different areas may act as sensory registers for different sensory modalities.

Why might auditory input last longer than visual input? One possible explanation (e.g., Wingfield & Byrnes, 1981) is that a major source of auditory input—human speech—can be understood only within its sequential context. For example, consider this sentence:

I scream for ice cream.

You can interpret the first two words as either *I scream* or *ice cream*. Only when you hear the third word—*for*—can you begin to interpret the first two words accurately. The task of understanding speech, which is frequently filled with temporarily ambiguous sounds, is often easier if we can hold those sounds in memory in an uninterpreted form until we receive additional, clarifying information. As we human beings have acquired a greater capacity for language, then, evolution must also have given us a greater capacity to retain uninterpreted sequential auditory input.

Two factors probably account for the rapid disappearance of information from the sensory register (Breitmeyer & Ganz, 1976; G. R. Loftus & Loftus, 1976; Willingham, 2004). First, *interference* may be a factor: New information coming in effectively replaces (and thereby erases) the information already there. Many psychologists also believe that, even without new input, existing information in the sensory register simply fades away, or *decays,* over time. Regardless of the reasons for the sensory register's short duration, in most instances people don't need to store information there for very long. Important information is probably going to be processed sufficiently that it enters working memory. Unimportant information, like junk mail, is probably best dealt with by throwing it away.

Moving Information to Working Memory: The Role of Attention

If we want to move information from the sensory register into working memory, it appears that, at least in most cases, we must *pay attention* to it (Atkinson & Shiffrin, 1968; Cowan, 1995; Kulhavy, Peterson, & Schwartz, 1986). For example, as you read this book, you are probably attending to only a small part of the visual input that your eyes sense right now (I hope you are attending to the words on this page!). In the same way, you do not worry about all of the sounds you hear at any particular time; you select only certain sounds to pay attention to. In essence, information that an individual pays attention to moves on to working memory, whereas information that is not attended to may be lost from the memory system.

One reason people don't remember something they've seen or heard, then, is that they never really paid attention to it. If you are sitting in class with your mind a thousand miles away from the professor's lecture, you might say that you forgot what the instructor said, or you might say that you never heard it in the first place. The reality of the situation is somewhere in between: The lecture reached your sensory register but was not sufficiently processed to move on to your working memory.

Even when people pay attention to a particular stimulus, they don't necessarily attend to *important aspects* of the stimulus.[7] Such is especially the case with complex stimuli, such as reading materials (e.g., Faust & Anderson, 1967). Once, when I was teaching introductory psychology to first-year college students, a young woman who had failed my first two exams came to my office expressing frustration about her lack of success in my class. When I asked her to describe

---

[7]Behaviorists have referred to this issue as one of a *nominal stimulus* (what is presented to the learner) versus an *effective stimulus* (what the learner is actually attending to).

how she went about completing the assigned readings in the textbook, she told me, "Well, I start looking through the chapter, and when I get to a page that looks important, I read it." With further probing, I discovered that this young woman had been reading only about one out of every three pages assigned.

Factors Influencing Attention

Certain kinds of stimuli tend to draw attention, whereas other kinds do not (Cowan, 1995; Horstmann, 2002; Rakison, 2003; Sergeant, 1996). Following are some important factors affecting what people pay attention to and, therefore, what they store in working memory.

Motion   Imagine that you've agreed to meet some friends at a carnival. When you first see your friends in the crowd, you might wave one or both arms wildly about to get their attention. Moving objects are more likely to capture attention than stationery ones—a principle that holds true for infants and adults alike (Abrams & Christ, 2003; Bahrick, Gogate, & Ruiz, 2002).

Size   Which of the following letters first draw your eye?

A B c d E f G

You probably noticed the B and E before the other letters because of their larger size. Attention tends to be drawn to large objects, a principle that newspaper publishers apply when they typeset front-page headlines in large letters and that advertisers take advantage of when they put potentially unenticing information in fine print.

Intensity   More intense stimuli—bright colors and loud noises, for instance—attract attention. Teachers frequently speak more loudly than usual—"**Be quiet!**"—when they want to get students' attention. Similarly, toy manufacturers emphasize bright colors in the toys they produce, knowing that young children browsing store shelves will be more attracted to vivid reds and yellows than to subtle pinks and beiges.

Novelty   Stimuli that are novel or unusual in some way tend to draw people's attention. For example, look at the women in Figure 7.10. You probably find yourself attending more to the woman on the right than to the other three. A woman with two heads and three legs is not someone you see every day.

Figure 7.10
Novelty draws attention.

Incongruity   Objects that don't make sense within their context tend to capture people's attention. For example, read this sentence:

I took a walk to the rabbit this morning.

Did you spend more time looking at the word *rabbit* than at the other words? If so, it may have been because *rabbit* is incongruous with the rest of the sentence.

Emotion   Stimuli with strong emotional associations attract attention. A nude body flashing through a crowded room usually draws the attention (and astonished expressions) of just about everyone present. Words such as *blood* and *murder* also are attention getters because of their emotional overtones.

Personal significance   The factors I've just listed—size, intensity, novelty, incongruity, and emotion—tend to capture attention but don't necessarily hold it for very long. In contrast, personal significance——the meaning and relevance people find in an object or event—can both capture and *maintain* attention (Barkley, 1996a; Voss & Schauble, 1992; Vurpillot & Ball, 1979). When a student sits in front of a television set with an open textbook, the stimulus that the student attends to—the television or the book—depends in large part on which stimulus is more closely related to the student's motives at the time. If the textbook is interesting or if an important examination is scheduled for the next day, the student will attend to the book. But if a popular situation comedy or a cliff-hanging soap opera is on, or if the textbook is dry and unenticing, the student may very well forget that the text is even in the same room.

Social cues   Again imagine yourself at that carnival I mentioned earlier. You've now connected with your friends and are in line to ride through the Spook House. Suddenly many people in front of you gasp as they look up at the Death-Defying Triple Loop-the-Loop off to the right. Almost certainly you will follow their line of sight to discover why they are gasping. People are more likely to pay attention to things they see *others* looking at and reacting to (Baldwin, 2000; Gauvain, 2001; Kingstone, Smilek, Ristic, Friesen, & Eastwood, 2003). Even infants rely on such social cues, as you will discover in our discussion of *social referencing* in Chapter 11.[8]

Think, for a moment, about curriculum materials, including textbooks, that you have seen recently. Do they have characteristics that are likely to catch a student's eye? Do important words and concepts stand out, perhaps because they are larger or **more intense** or *unusual*? Are certain topics likely to grab a student's interest because they are interesting and relevant to the age group? If your answer to these questions is "no," then students may very well have difficulty attending to and learning from those materials.

Nature of Attention

What cognitive processes underlie people's ability to attend to certain aspects of the environment and to ignore others? On the surface, the answer might appear simple: "People just focus their eyes on what they want to pay attention to," you might think. Yet you can probably recall times when you have directed your eyes toward a specific object yet not paid attention to it at all:

---

[8]Here we see a good example of how information processing and contextual theories can be effectively integrated.

Perhaps you were listening intently to a piece of music or were deep in thought about something that wasn't anywhere in sight (e.g., see Mack, 2003).

Furthermore, people are able to focus the attention of at least one other sense—hearing—without having to physically orient themselves in a particular direction. For instance, you can go to a party at which numerous conversations are going on simultaneously and successfully attend to just one of them, regardless of where your ears are "aimed." You may be listening to the person standing directly in front of you, or, if that person has been rambling on for more than an hour about the difficulty he has growing rhubarb, you may instead tune in to a more interesting conversation a few feet to your right or left. Even though you may be looking directly at the rhubarb grower and nodding in mock agreement, your attention is somewhere else altogether.

The ability to attend to one spoken message while ignoring others—aptly called the **cocktail party phenomenon**—has been studied using a technique called **shadowing:** A person is asked to listen through earphones to two simultaneously spoken messages and to repeat one of the messages. Focusing in on one of the messages is fairly easy when the two people speaking have very different voices, are talking about different topics, and are presenting their messages from seemingly different directions. It becomes far more difficult—sometimes impossible—when the two voices, topics, or apparent locations of the speakers are similar (Cherry, 1953). Furthermore, people who shadow one of two messages notice very little of the other message; perhaps they notice whether the other speaker is male or female, but they can seldom report any of the words included in the unattended message and typically do not even notice whether the message is spoken in their native tongue (Cherry, 1953).

Given such findings, some early cognitivists (e.g., Broadbent, 1958) likened auditory attention to a *filter:* A listener uses physical characteristics to select one message and screen out others, much as a television tuner zeroes in on one frequency and shuts out the rest. Yet subsequent research has indicated that people do not totally filter out information from a supposedly unattended message. People who participate in shadowing experiments notice especially meaningful words (e.g., their own names) in the unattended message (Heatherton, Macrae, & Kelley, 2004; Treisman, 1964). They also hear words from that message if the words fit meaningfully into the attended message (Gray & Wedderburn, 1960; Treisman, 1964). For example, suppose you hear these two sentences simultaneously and are asked to shadow only the first one:

Speaker 1:   I bought candy at the plate today.
Speaker 2:   Put the rhubarb on my store, please.

You might very well "hear" the first speaker say, "I bought candy at the store today" (borrowing the word *store* from the second speaker) because such a sentence makes more sense than what the speaker really did say.

Although most psychologists now reject the idea that attention is like a filter, they continue to have difficulty pinning down its precise nature. It almost certainly involves both automatic responses (e.g., immediately turning to look in the direction of a loud, unexpected noise) and conscious control (e.g., deciding which conversation to listen to at a cocktail party).[9] It also involves learning to some degree; in particular, people learn that certain kinds of stimuli are important and that others can easily be ignored (Kruschke, 2003). In general, you might think of

---

[9]The hindbrain, midbrain, and forebrain all have some involvement in attention. The reticular formation, hippocampus, and frontal and parietal lobes of the cortex are especially important (see chapter 2).

Figure 7.11
The Peter-Paul goblet.

attention as being *focused cognitive processing of particular aspects of the environment* (Barkley, 1996a; Cowan, 1995; Johnston, McCann, & Remington, 1995).

Attention as a Limited Capacity

Perhaps life would be simpler if people didn't have to choose certain stimuli to pay attention to, but could instead attend to *everything* that they record in their sensory registers. Unfortunately, it turns out that people are incapable of attending to everything at once. For example, look at Figure 7.11. At first glance, you probably see a white goblet. But if you look at the black spaces on either side of the goblet, you should also be able to see two silhouettes ("Peter" and "Paul") staring at each other.

Now try this little exercise: See if you can focus on both the goblet and the two silhouettes at *exactly* the same time, so that you can clearly see the details of both. Can you do it? Most people are unable to attend to the goblet and the faces at exactly the same time, although they may be able to shift their focus from the goblet to the faces and back again very quickly.

The Peter–Paul goblet illustrates a phenomenon that early Gestalt psychologists called **figure–ground:** An individual can attend to one object (the **figure**) and notice the details of that object. Whatever the individual is not paying attention to (i.e., the background, or **ground**) is not carefully inspected: The individual may notice a few salient characteristics, such as color, but is likely to overlook more specific information about unattended objects.[10]

Gestalt psychologists proposed that people can pay attention to only one thing at a time—hence the difficulty most folks have in attending to both the goblet and the faces simultaneously. Other theorists (e.g., Shapiro, 1994; Treisman, 1964; Welford, 1977) have proposed something similar: People can only attend to one *complex* source of information at a time. In situations in which more than one stimulus requires attention, one's attention must be switched quickly back and forth from one to another.

But now consider a situation in which you are driving your car while also carrying on a conversation with a friend. Certainly you're attending to two things, the road and the conversation, at once. To account for such a situation, many theorists (e.g., Cowan, 1995; Pashler, 1992;

------

[10]For contemporary analyses of the figure–ground phenomenon, see Peterson (1994); Peterson and Gibson (1994); and Vecera, Vogel, and Woodman (2002).

Sergeant, 1996) describe attention as involving a **limited processing capacity,** with the number of stimuli being attended to depending on how much cognitive processing is required for each one. If you are engaging in a difficult task, such as learning how to drive a car with a standard transmission, you may very well need to devote your full attention to that task and so not hear a thing that your friend is telling you. However, if you are doing something more habitual or automatic, such as driving a standard transmission after years of driving experience, you can easily devote some attention to what your friend is saying. Many tasks, such as driving, become increasingly automatic over time, therefore requiring less and less of our attention (I'll say more about this phenomenon, known as *automaticity,* in chapter 8). Even so, when people carry on a conversation (say, on a cellular phone) while driving, they have slower reaction times and are less likely to notice traffic signals (Strayer & Johnston, 2001). Occasionally, people do become adept at splitting their attention among two complex tasks, but only when they have considerable practice in performing both tasks at the same time, ideally making the execution of one or both of them automatic (Hirst, Spelke, Reaves, Caharack, & Neisser, 1980; Lien, Ruthruff, & Johnson, 2006; Reisberg, 1997; Spelke, Hirst, & Neisser, 1976).

Regardless of how we view attention, one thing is clear: People's ability to attend to the stimuli around them is limited, such that they usually cannot attend to or otherwise learn from two complex situations at the same time. Thus, learners must be quite selective about the information they choose to process, and they must ignore (and so lose) a lot of the information they receive. As frustrating as it may sometimes seem, people simply cannot attend to, learn, and remember everything they encounter.

Attention is closely connected with working memory, although theorists continue to debate *how* closely the two are linked (e.g., Downing, 2000; Woodman, Vogel, & Luck, 2001). As you will see now, working memory controls attention to some extent, and it, like attention, has a limited capacity.

Working Memory

Atkinson and Shiffrin (1968) used the term *short-term memory* to refer to a storage mechanism that holds information for a brief time after it is attended to so that it can be mentally processed. But as I mentioned earlier, most theorists now believe that this component of memory is also where cognitive processing itself takes place, hence their more frequent use of the term **working memory** (e.g., Baddeley, 1986; Daneman & Carpenter, 1980; Han & Kim, 2004).

In essence, working memory is the component of memory in which "thinking" occurs. You might think of it as the "awareness" or "consciousness" of the memory system (e.g., Bellezza, 1986).[11] It identifies information in the sensory register that warrants attention, saves the information for a longer period of time, and processes it further. It may also hold and process information that it retrieves from long-term memory—information that will help in interpreting newly received environmental input.

---

[11]To a considerable degree, processes associated with the central executive appear to be located in the frontal lobes of the cortex. For instance, individuals with damage to their frontal lobes may have trouble controlling attention, planning a course of action, and inhibiting inappropriate responses (Baddeley, 2001; Byrnes, 2001; Kimberg, D'Esposito, & Farah, 1997).

Many theorists portray working memory as playing the role of **central executive**, controlling and monitoring the flow and use of information throughout the memory system (Baddeley, 1986, 2001; Barkley, 1996b; Cowan, 1995; Demetriou, Christou, Spanoudis, & Platsidou, 2002). As the brain continues to mature over the course of childhood and adolescence, this central executive function becomes increasing sophisticated and effective (Carlson, Davis, & Leach, 2005; Kuhn, 2006; Lyon & Krasnegor, 1996; Zelazo, Müller, Frye, & Marcovitch, 2003).

Characteristics of Working Memory

Working memory is quite different from the sensory register in terms of capacity, forms of storage, and duration.

Capacity   Unlike the sensory register, working memory appears to have a very limited capacity. After reviewing a number of early studies, George Miller (1956) characterized its capacity as the *magical number seven, plus or minus two:* People can hold from five to nine units of information in working memory at one time, with the average number of memorable units being about seven. Although the *number* of information units in working memory cannot be increased beyond 7 ± 2, Miller suggested, the *amount* of information in each unit can be increased. For example, in a discussion of working memory in an undergraduate psychology class, I once asked students to try to remember this string of digits:

$$5 \quad 1 \quad 8 \quad 9 \quad 3 \quad 4 \quad 2 \quad 7 \quad 6$$

Most students remembered somewhere between six and eight digits. A few remembered all nine by clumping them into groups of three like this:

$$5\text{--}1\text{--}8 \qquad 9\text{--}3\text{--}4 \qquad 2\text{--}7\text{--}6$$

This process of combining pieces of information in some way, called **chunking**, increases the amount of information that the limited space of working memory can hold. To use Miller's analogy, if you can hold only seven coins, you are far richer holding seven quarters, or even seven gold pieces, than seven pennies.

Miller's original assessment of 7 ± 2 is probably an overly simplistic view of working memory's capacity. The number of items that can be stored depends on how much information each item includes and how strong the associations are within the various "pieces" of each item (Alvarez & Cavanagh, 2004; Baddeley, 2001; Cowan, Chen, & Rouder, 2004). For example, Simon (1974) found that, although he himself could remember a list of 7 one- or two-syllable words, he could remember only 6 three-syllable words, 4 two-word phrases, and even fewer phrases of more than two words. In other words, the larger the chunks, the fewer of them working memory can hold at a time. Thus it may be difficult to identify the true capacity of working memory, at least in terms of a specific number of discrete items that can be stored there (J. R. Anderson, 1990).

Furthermore, there may be a trade-off between how much processing is necessary and how much information can be held in working memory: Cognitive processing may take up some of its capacity, leaving less room for information storage. As an example, try solving the following long-division problem in your head, without referring back to the page until after you've solved it:

$$37\overline{)4281}$$

Almost impossible, isn't it? You may have found that while you were dividing 37 into 42, you forgot the last two digits of the dividend. Although you probably had no trouble holding six numbers in your working memory, you may not have been able to hold all six while also doing something with them.

An additional point to keep in mind is that working memory capacity seems to differ somewhat from one individual to the next (Corno et al., 2002; Linderholm & van den Broek, 2002). For instance, younger children may have slightly less physical working memory "space" than older children do (Fry & Hale, 1996; Gathercole & Hitch, 1993; Kail, 1993). And on average, children with learning disabilities appear to have slightly less working memory capacity than their nondisabled peers (Swanson, Cooney, & O'Shaughnessy, 1998).

Forms of storage   Regardless of the form in which information is received, it appears that much of the information stored in working memory is encoded in an *auditory* form, especially when the information is language based (Alegria, 1998; Baddeley, 1986; Baddeley & Logie, 1992). For example, in a study by Conrad (1964), adults were shown six-letter sequences, with letters being presented visually, one at a time, at intervals of three-fourths of a second. As soon as the last letter of a sequence had been presented, participants in the study wrote down all six of the letters they had seen, guessing at any letters that they could not easily recall. When people recalled letters incorrectly, the letters they said they had seen were more likely to resemble the actual stimuli in terms of how they *sounded* than how they looked. For example, the letter *F* was "remembered" as the auditorially similar letter *S* 131 times but as the visually similar letter *P* only 14 times. Similarly, the letter *V* was remembered as *B* 56 times but as *X* only 5 times.

Yet working memory almost certainly includes ways of encoding information in other forms as well, including visual, spatial, and tactile forms (Baddeley, 1986, 2001; Harris, Miniussi, Harris, & Diamond, 2002; E. E. Smith, 2000). An example of visual encoding in working memory can be found in an ingenious experiment by Shepard and Metzler (1971) involving pictures of three-dimensional block configurations similar to those shown in Figure 7.12. In this experiment, adults compared pairs of these pictures and determined whether they represented the same three-dimensional configuration. For example, *a* and *b* in Figure 7.12 constitute a "match": If *b* were rotated 90 degrees clockwise, it would be identical to *a*. However, *a* and *c* are not a match: If *c* were rotated 90 degrees counterclockwise, it would become apparent that its top branch points in a different direction from that of *a*. Shepard and Metzler measured people's reaction time to each pair of figures, assuming that more extensive cognitive processing would be reflected in longer reaction times. Results were quite dramatic: Reaction times were almost entirely a function of how much a figure would have to be turned for it to be lined up with another figure. In other words, the participants were responding as if they were mentally "rotating" images, with more rotation resulting in a longer reaction time. Similar results were obtained when people compared rotated letters (Cooper & Shepard, 1973).

Figure 7.12
Figures similar to those used by Shepard and Metzler (1971).

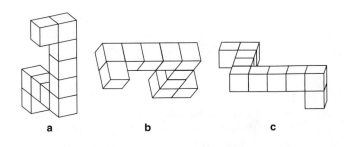

a   b   c

Many theorists believe that working memory actually involves two or more separate storage systems that specialize in different sensory modalities (Baddeley, 2001; Schacter, 1999; Shah & Miyake, 1996; E. E. Smith, 2000; Willingham, 2004).[12] As an example of these separate storage systems, Alan Baddeley (e.g., 1986, 2001) has suggested that a mechanism he calls a **phonological loop**[13] can keep a small amount of auditory information fresh through constant repetition (more about such repetition shortly). Meanwhile, a **visuospatial sketchpad** allows manipulation and short-term retention of visual material. Presumably, working memory also includes a "place" where information from multiple modalities can be integrated into an overall understanding of a particular situation (or episode); Baddeley (2001) calls this component the **episodic buffer.**

Having modality-specific storage mechanisms seems to help us "stretch" our working memory capacity somewhat. We have an easier time performing two tasks at the same time when one task involves primarily auditory information and the other task is more visual in nature—for instance, when we are asked simultaneously to judge whether a series of sentences are true or false (an auditory, verbal task) and to perform tasks similar to that in Figure 7.12 (Baddeley, 1999; Just et al., 2001; Mayer & Moreno, 1998). Even so, people in such situations do not devote the amount of mental "energy" to either of the tasks that they would use if they were doing only one of them (Just et al., 2001).

Duration   Working memory is just what its alternative name, *short-term memory,* implies: short. An experiment by Peterson and Peterson (1959) gives us some idea of how long information in working memory lasts. In this experiment, adults were told three consonant letters (e.g., *D X P*) and then immediately asked to count backward by threes from a three-digit number, which was different in each trial. At a signal that occurred anywhere from 3 to 18 seconds after the three consonants had been presented, the participants were asked to recall the consonants. When recall was delayed only 3 seconds, people were able to remember the letters with 80% accuracy; after an 18-second interval, however, their accuracy was only about 10%.

Considering research results such as those of Peterson and Peterson, psychologists believe that the duration of working memory is probably somewhere between 5 and 20 seconds. As is true for the sensory register, both decay and interference have been offered as explanations for the short time span of working memory. Some information stored in working memory may simply fade away (i.e., decay) if it is not processed further (Gold, Murray, Sekuler, Bennett, & Sekuler, 2005; Reitman, 1974). Other information may be replaced ("bumped out," as one of my professors used to put it) by new input (Cowan, Wood, Nugent, & Treisman, 1997; Keppel & Underwood, 1962; Melton, 1963; Reitman, 1974). For example, as a woman who for many years had a husband, three children, a dog, and two cats all living in the house, I found myself frequently being interrupted in the middle of tasks. If I had a batch of cookies in the oven, and Jeff asked me to make him a snack and Tina asked me to help her find something she'd misplaced, my

---

[12]Neurological evidence supports this idea: Tasks involving the processing of verbal, auditory information activate different parts of the brain than do tasks involving the processing of visual and spatial information (Awh et al., 1996; Goldman-Rakic, 1992; Jonides, Lacey, & Nee, 2005; MacAndrew, Klatzky, Fiez, McClelland, & Becker, 2002).

[13]In his early writings, Baddeley called this an *articulatory loop.* However, he changed the term to reflect the fact that it involves the *sounds* (phonemes) of speech but does not necessarily involve actual speaking (articulation).

cookies were very likely to be pushed from my working memory until I was confronted with new environmental input: the smell of something burning. My husband called me absentminded, but I knew better. My mind was definitely present, but the working component of it had a limited capacity, and new input interfered with the information already stored there. (We're now down to just me, my husband, two pets, and occasionally a kid or two; I find that the more of them who are in the house at once, the less I can concentrate on a single task, such as writing this book.)

Control Processes in Working Memory

Working memory, and especially its central executive component, appears to be the home of many processes important for learning, thinking, and behavior—for example, directing attention, making sense of situations, drawing inferences, reasoning, planning, making decisions, solving problems, and inhibiting irrelevant thoughts and actions (Baddeley, 2001; Carlson & Moses, 2001; Demetriou et al., 2002; Engle, 2002). But at least three control processes affect the functioning of working memory itself: organization, retrieval, and maintenance rehearsal.

Organization   Earlier, I described Miller's (1956) proposal that people can increase the amount of information they can hold in working memory by *chunking* it in some way. As they develop, children show an increasing tendency to chunk information, thereby enhancing the capacity of their working memories (Farnham-Diggory, 1972; Gathercole & Hitch, 1993).

Chunking is an organizational process, in that two or more pieces of information are combined. Information can be organized in a variety of ways. For example, consider again the nine-digit string I presented earlier:

5   1   8   9   3   4   2   7   6

I have already described one way of chunking this string: grouping it into three groups of three digits each. Another frequently observed organizational strategy is to impose a rhythm, or even a melody, on the numbers (Bower & Springston, 1970). Still another way of organizing the digits is to attach some meaning to them—a process that involves retrieving information that has previously been stored in long-term memory. For instance, when I gave the nine-digit string to my undergraduate class, a student named Dave, then a varsity football player, remembered all nine digits easily and claimed he could have added a few more to the list without difficulty. He explained his approach this way:

> Well, "51" is Jason, a guy who played center during my freshman year. "89" is Jeff, a wide receiver from my roommate's hometown. "34" is John, a current running back on my team—well, his number has changed, but I always think of him as "34." "2" is another Dave (not me), who's a wide receiver. And "76" is my good friend Dan. My number is 75, and so Dan's locker is next to mine.

By attaching meaning to the numbers, Dave also facilitated their storage in long-term memory. In chapter 8, we'll look at such *meaningful learning* more closely.

Retrieval   Retrieval of information from working memory is often quite easy and automatic. Yet to some degree, how quickly and easily something is retrieved may depend on how much information is stored there (Sternberg, 1966; Thomas, Milner, & Haberlandt, 2003). For example, in an early study by Sternberg (1966), college students were given a set of from one to six numbers, which the students presumably stored in working memory. Then an additional number was presented, and the students were asked whether that number had been among the original set. The time it took for students to answer the question depended almost entirely on the size of the number set already stored in working memory, with each successively larger set yielding a reaction time of about 40 milliseconds longer. From such results, it appears that retrieval of information from working memory may sometimes be a process of scanning all of the contents of working memory, successively and exhaustively, until the desired information is found.

Maintenance rehearsal   You look up a friend's telephone number and store it in your working memory; its seven digits are about the limit of what your working memory can hold. But then you find that someone else is using the telephone, and so you must wait to place your call. How do you keep your friend's number in working memory? If you are like most people, you probably repeat it to yourself over and over again.

Repeating information to keep it alive in working memory is a process known as **maintenance rehearsal,** which often takes the form of subvocal speech (Landauer, 1962; Sperling, 1967). Maintenance rehearsal provides a means for saving information from the forgetting processes of decay and interference; when such rehearsal isn't possible, information in working memory disappears quickly. As an example, recall Peterson and Peterson's (1959) examination of the duration of working memory described earlier. After participants in the experiment were given the three consonants they needed to remember, they were asked to count backward by threes until the signal for recall. Such backward counting kept them from rehearsing the three letters; otherwise, they might have kept them in working memory indefinitely simply by repeating them over and over as long as necessary.

There is apparently an upper limit to the amount of information people can keep in working memory simply through repetition, and this upper limit reflects how much can be repeated before some of it starts to fade (Baddeley, 1999). As an illustration, try remembering the following two lists of words. After reading the words in List 1 once or twice, cover the page and rehearse the words until you've written them all down on a piece of scrap paper:

List 1: beg, far, hum, late, kick, wheel

Now try the same thing with the following words:

List 2: caterpillar, university, ostentatious, alimony, calamity, interrogation

Each list has six items, but you probably found the first list easier to remember than the second because the words were shorter and so you could repeat them all fairly quickly. In contrast, you may have found that the words in the second list each took so long to pronounce that by the time you got to the end of the list, one or two of the earlier words were starting to fade away. This phenomenon—being able to remember a greater number of short items than longer items—is known as the *word length effect* (e.g., Baddeley, 2001). Here's where Baddeley's concept of *phonological loop* comes into play. Baddeley likens the phenomenon to the circus performer who tries to spin a number of plates at the same time: Just as the performer must periodically return to each plate to keep it spinning, so, too, must a learner frequently return to and repeat each word to keep it fresh in memory. In both cases, there's an upper limit to the number of items that can simultaneously be kept active.

Maintenance rehearsal is observed more frequently in older children and adults than in younger children (Bjorklund & Coyle, 1995; Gathercole & Hitch, 1993; Rosser, 1994), so it is probably to some degree a learned skill. I myself used rehearsal frequently in high school and college whenever I had difficulty remembering something I would be tested on—perhaps when I needed to know a complicated formula, a verbatim definition, or a list of seemingly unrelated items. I would continue to repeat the information to myself as test papers were distributed, then immediately write it in the margin so it would be there for me if I needed it.

Although maintenance rehearsal can indeed be a useful strategy for keeping information in working memory, teachers must remember that the information will disappear once rehearsal stops. If students are using maintenance rehearsal frequently, their teachers might suspect that they are having trouble storing that information in their long-term memories. Yet long-term memory is where important information ultimately *should* be stored.

Moving Information to Long-Term Memory: Connecting New Information with Prior Knowledge

Storage processes in the first two components of memory are fairly straightforward: Anything sensed is stored in the sensory register, and anything attended to is stored in working memory. Storage of information in long-term memory is not so simple. A dual-store model of memory tells us that further processing is necessary for information to go from working memory to long-term memory, and typically such processing involves combining new information with information already in long-term memory (recall the two-way arrows in between working and long-term memory in Figure 7.9). In other words, people store information in long-term memory most successfully when they relate it to things they already know (more on this point in chapter 8).

From the dual-store perspective, control processes that enable storage in long-term memory take place in working memory. As we've seen, working memory has a limited capacity and can handle only so much information at one time. The result is that long-term memory storage occurs slowly, and a great deal is lost from working memory along the way. In essence, working memory is the bottleneck in the memory system: It prevents most information from ever getting into long-term memory.

Long-Term Memory

Long-term memory is perhaps the most complex component of the human memory system. As such, it has been studied more extensively than either the sensory register or working memory, and psychologists have offered numerous theories about its nature. I will give you an overview of it here and then describe its characteristics and relevant control processes in more depth in the following three chapters.

Characteristics of Long-Term Memory

Much of the content of long-term memory relates to the nature of "how things are or were"—knowledge often referred to as **declarative knowledge.** But it also includes knowledge about "how to do things"—knowledge known as **procedural knowledge** (e.g., J. R. Anderson, 1983a, 1995). Its capacity is obviously much larger than that of working memory, its forms of storage appear to be more flexible, and its duration is, of course, quite a bit longer.

Capacity   As far as theorists can determine, the capacity of long-term memory is unlimited. In fact, as you will discover in chapter 8, the more information that is already stored there, the easier it is to store additional information.

Forms of storage   Information is probably encoded in long-term memory in a variety of ways. For example, language provides one basis for storing information, sensory images provide another, and nonverbal abstractions and meanings—general understandings of the world, if you will—provide still another. Over the long run, people rarely save information in the precise ways they encountered it in the environment. Rather than remember word-for-word sentences or precise mental images, people tend to remember the gist of what they see and hear, along with idiosyncratic interpretations and (often) minor or major distortions of reality.

Some of the knowledge in long-term memory is **explicit knowledge,** such that people can easily recall and explain it. But a great deal of it is, instead, **implicit knowledge** that affects people's behavior even though they cannot consciously retrieve and inspect it. We'll look closely at the nature of both explicit and implicit knowledge—as well as at the nature of both declarative and procedural knowledge—in chapter 9.

Another noteworthy characteristic of the knowledge in long-term memory is its *interconnectedness:* Related pieces of information tend to be associated together. Virtually every piece of information in long-term memory is probably directly or indirectly connected with every other piece.[14]

Duration   As you will learn in chapter 10, theorists disagree regarding the duration of long-term memory. Some theorists believe that information, once stored in long-term memory, remains there permanently, and that any "forgetting" is simply a *retrieval* problem. In contrast, others believe that information can disappear from long-term memory through a variety of forgetting processes—processes that may or may not kick in depending on how the information was initially stored and how often it is used. Ultimately, although some information may remain in long-term memory for long periods, there is probably no way to show conclusively that *all* information stored there remains permanently. The question about the duration of long-term memory is still an open one, and the best we can say is that long-term memory's duration is indefinitely *long.*

Speaking of retrieval from long-term memory, what was Edward C. Tolman's middle name? Did you perhaps remember your friend Harry's brother-in-law, Marvin *Chace*? Or did you think of Tolman *chacing* his rats down their mazes? As you will discover in chapter 10, the more ways that people store a piece of information in long-term memory, the better their chances of retrieving the information when they need it.

Challenges to the Dual–Store Model

Up to this point, we have been talking about the dual-store (three-component) model of memory almost as if it were "truth." But not all psychologists agree that it accurately represents how human memory functions. I myself sometimes wonder whether the three components are the

---

[14]As you should recall from chapter 2, most neurons in the brain have synaptic connections with hundreds of other neurons. Presumably many of these synapses account for the organized nature of long-term memory.

distinctly different entities that the model portrays. For example, recall my earlier point that auditory information in the sensory store may last as long as 2 to 4 seconds. Also recall how Baddeley's *phonological loop* can maintain a list of spoken words in working memory only to the extent that the list is short and consists of quickly pronounceable words—a list that can be repeated in, say, 2 to 4 seconds. In fact, Baddeley has suggested that auditory information stored in working memory tends to last only about 2 seconds unless it is rehearsed (Baddeley, 2001). It's possible, then, that maintenance rehearsal may in some cases act on and maintain information that is actually in a sensory-register type of mechanism.

A number of theorists have questioned the idea that working memory and long-term memory are the separate entities that the dual-store model portrays—that is, they have argued that both components are actually different aspects of a *single* (rather than dual) storage mechanism. Others have challenged a related idea: that active, conscious processing in working memory is really necessary for storage in long-term memory. We now look at some of the evidence related to each of these issues.

Are Working Memory and Long-Term Memory Really Different?

Let's return to the serial learning curve described earlier in the chapter. Given a list of items to remember, people can more easily recall the first few items in the list (the *primacy effect*) and the last few items (the *recency effect*) than the middle items (to refresh your memory, look once again at Figure 7.8). Using a dual-store model of memory to explain this curve (e.g., Norman, 1969), we might say that people process the first few items sufficiently to store them in long-term memory, and they continue to hold the last few items in working memory after the entire list has been presented. They lose many of the middle items because they don't have enough time to process them adequately before later items "bump them out" of working memory. Supporting this interpretation is the finding that when presentation rate is slowed down (allowing for more processing in working memory), the primacy effect increases, and when processing is prevented, the primacy effect disappears (Glanzer & Cunitz, 1966; Peterson & Peterson, 1962). In contrast, the recency effect seems to be more affected by the recall interval: The longer that recall of the list is delayed—decreasing the likelihood that any items are still in working memory—the less people are able to remember items at the end of the list (Glanzer & Cunitz, 1966; Postman & Phillips, 1965).

Yet other research studies have cast doubt on the idea that the recency effect in serial learning necessarily reflects the use of a working memory separate from long-term memory (Crowder, 1993; Greene, 1986; Reisberg, 1997; Wickelgren, 1973). For example, in a study by Thapar and Greene (1993), college students viewed a list of words presented two words at a time on a computer screen; they also performed a 20-second "distractor" task (mentally adding a series of digits) after each pair of words. The students remembered the last few words in the list much better than the middle words, even though, thanks to the distractor task, *none* of the words could possibly have still been in working memory. Considering results such as these, theorists have suggested that the serial learning curve can be explained as easily by a single-store model as by a dual-store model. One possible explanation is that items in a list are easier to remember if they are distinctive in some way. Items near the end of the list may be more memorable because of their positions: A learner may specifically identify a word as "the last one" or "the next-to-last one" (Greene, 1986; Wagner, 1996). A second possibility is simply that forgetting occurs rapidly at first and then slowly tapers off—a pattern that holds true for many different species and many different tasks (J. R. Anderson,

1995; Wickelgren, 1973; Wixted & Ebbesen, 1991). From this perspective, the recency effect may be the result of the fact that the last items of a list have not yet undergone that rapid decay.

Another source of evidence supporting the dual-store model is the finding that encoding seems to be somewhat different in working memory versus long-term memory, with the former being heavily dependent on verbatim auditory encoding and latter being more likely to involve gist and general meanings that are often nonverbal in nature. Yet forms of encoding in the two components overlap quite a bit. For instance, information in working memory sometimes takes the form of general meanings (Shulman, 1971, 1972), and information in long-term memory sometimes takes an acoustic form (T. O. Nelson & Rothbart, 1972). Furthermore, even the initial encoding of information (which presumably takes place in working memory) often draws on knowledge in long-term memory right from the get-go (Kirschner, Sweller, & Clark, 2006). For instance, people recognize words in print more quickly when the words are embedded in a meaningful context (Rayner, Foorman, Perfetti, Pesetsky, & Seidenberg, 2001). And they recognize spoken words much more quickly when the words are common ones they use every day (Wagner, 1996).

Still another body of evidence that has been used both for and against the working memory versus long-term memory distinction comes from people who have undergone certain brain injuries or neurosurgical procedures. Sometimes these individuals show an impairment of one kind of memory without a corresponding loss of function in the other (Atkinson & Shiffrin, 1968; Eysenck & Keane, 1990; Wagner, 1996; Zechmeister & Nyberg, 1982). Some individuals can recall events experienced before a brain trauma but are unable to retain new experiences. Such a disability may suggest either (a) a problem with working memory while long-term memory remains intact (a dual-store explanation); or (b) a problem in general storage processes (a single-store explanation). Other brain-injured individuals can recall new experiences long enough to talk briefly about them but cannot remember them a few minutes later or at any point thereafter. These might be cases in which (a) working memory is functioning but new information seemingly cannot be transferred into long-term memory (a dual-store explanation); or (b) general retrieval processes have been impaired (a single-store explanation).

To some degree, working memory and long-term memory processes seem to depend on different parts of the brain (Zola-Morgan & Squire, 1990). And different areas of the brain are active when people are trying to recall items from the beginning versus end of a serial list (Talmi, Grady, Goshen-Gottstein, & Moscovitch, 2005). Even so, as noted in chapter 2, most learning and thinking tasks—even very simple ones—tend to involve many parts of the brain. Certainly different parts of the brain specialize in different tasks, but a human being is likely to rely on many parts regardless of the circumstances.

Is Conscious Thought Necessary for Long-Term Memory Storage?

In the dual-store model, information must go through working memory before it can be stored in long-term memory. Working memory is, by definition, an active, conscious mechanism. It would seem, then, that a learner would have to be actively involved in storing virtually anything in long-term memory. This isn't always the case, however. Some kinds of information—once they've captured a person's attention—seem to be automatically stored in long-term memory even if not specifically selected for further processing (Frensch & Rünger, 2003; Zacks, Hasher, & Hock, 1986). For example, consider this question:

Which word occurs more frequently in English—*bacon* or *pastrami?*

You probably had no difficulty answering correctly that *bacon* is the more frequently occurring word. Hasher and Zacks (1984) found that people could easily answer such questions about the frequency of events even though they had never been concerned about counting them. Similarly, people could answer questions about where various events occurred without having intentionally processed such information. Such automatic storage of frequency information and locations begins quite early in life and may help establish a knowledge base on which future learning can build (Siegler & Alibali, 2005).

Much of this seemingly "nonconsciously" processed information becomes implicit (rather than explicit) knowledge. Quite possibly, the brain learns—and stores information in long-term memory—in at least two distinctly different ways. One is a very conscious way in which working memory plays an active role. Another is a more basic, "thoughtless" way that involves formation of simple stimulus–stimulus and stimulus–response associations similar to those of which behaviorists speak (Bachevalier, Malkova, & Beauregard, 1996; Frensch & Rünger, 2003; Siegel, 1999).

Complicating the picture even further is the possibility that thinking itself may sometimes occur outside the confines of working memory. A series of studies by Dutch researchers Dijksterhuis, Nordgren, and their colleagues indicates that complex problems—those involving far more information than working memory's limited capacity can handle—are often more effectively addressed when people don't actively think about them for a period of time (Dijksterhuis & Nordgren, 2006). Even when not consciously mulling over a complex problem, the researchers suggest, people may be slowly analyzing the problem, determining which aspects of the problem are more and less important to take into account, imprecisely estimating particular quantities, and integrating problem-relevant information into an overall summary. The result is that a complex problem is sometimes better solved when it remains outside of working memory's limited-capacity "limelight" for a while. The products of such nonconscious thinking are often implicit and hard to put a finger on. For instance, people might describe them as "intuition" or a "gut feeling" that they cannot easily explain (Dijksterhuis & Nordgren, 2006, p. 105).

Alternative Views of Human Memory

In attempts to address weaknesses of the dual-store model, some theorists have offered alternative models. Here we'll look at two of them: a levels-of-processing model and an activation model. Both of these theories emphasize cognitive processes involved in human memory rather than the possible structures that may comprise it.

Levels of Processing

The **levels-of-processing** model of human memory (Cermak & Craik, 1979; Craik & Lockhart, 1972) was the first major theoretical alternative to the dual-store model. According to this view, incoming information is processed by a **central processor** (similar to the *central executive* aspect of working memory I spoke of earlier) at any one of a number of different levels of complexity. This central processor has a limited capacity, in that it can hold only so much at one time; the information temporarily held there is what we are aware of at any given time.

How long and how well information is remembered depends on how thoroughly the central processor deals with it. Information that isn't processed at all leaves only a very brief impression (much as it does in the sensory register of the dual-store model). Information that is processed superficially, such that only surface characteristics (e.g., appearance, brightness) are attended to, may last a few seconds (much as it does in the dual-store model's working memory). Only when information undergoes "deep" processing—that is, when it is interpreted, understood, and related to previously learned information—do we remember it for any length of time.

An experiment by Turnure, Buium, and Thurlow (1976) illustrates how different levels of processing lead to different degrees of information recall. Children 4 and 5 years old were asked to remember pairs of common objects (e.g., remembering that *soap* and *jacket* go together). Children processed the information in one of five ways, as follows:

1. *Labels.* They repeated the names of the objects.
2. *Sentence generation.* They made up sentences that included both objects in a pair.
3. *Sentence repetition.* They repeated experimenter-generated sentences that stated a relationship between the two objects (e.g., "The soap is hiding in the jacket").
4. *"What" question.* They answered a question about a relationship between the objects (e.g., "What is the soap doing in the jacket?").
5. *"Why" question.* They answered a question concerning why a particular relationship existed between the objects (e.g., "Why is the soap hiding in the jacket?").

In this experiment, children learned most effectively when they were forced to think about (i.e., process) a relationship between the objects: The question-answering conditions (Conditions 4 and 5) led to the greatest recall of the word pairs. Repeating a sentence that expressed such a relationship (Condition 3) led to some recall; presumably repetition promoted some processing of the association between each pair. Least effective for learning were the first two conditions. In the labeling condition (Condition 1), no relationship between objects was processed, and children in the sentence-generation condition (Condition 2) often constructed sentences that did not effectively connect the two objects (e.g., "I have some soap and a jacket").

One element that frequently arises as an important factor in learning is **intention to learn:** People who intend to learn something are more likely to learn and remember it than people who do not specifically try to learn the information. Proponents of the levels-of-processing model have argued that people process information more thoroughly when they are intending to learn it but that the depth of processing, rather than intention to learn per se, affects the success of learning. In fact, research supports this point: When individuals process material deeply, they often learn it successfully even when they are not specifically *trying* to learn it (e.g., Postman, 1964). In other words, nonintentional learning (often called **incidental learning**) is just as effective as intentional learning if the degree of processing is equal in the two situations.

A study by Hyde and Jenkins (1969) provides an example of successful incidental learning as a result of deep processing. College students were shown a list of 24 words presented at a rate of one word every two seconds. Some students (a control group) were merely told to learn the words; thus, they would be intentionally learning the words. Different experimental groups received different instructions, as follows:

1. *Pleasantness rating.* Students were told to rate each word for its degree of pleasantness; for example, a word such as *love* might be rated as relatively pleasant, whereas *hate* might be rated as less pleasant.
2. *Counting letters.* Students were told to count the number of letters in each word.
3. *Counting letter Es.* Students were told to count the number of letter *Es* in each word.

At the same time, some of the students receiving each of the different instructions were told to learn the words as they went along; these students were presumably engaged in intentional learning of the words. Other students were not told to learn the words; for these students, any recall of the words would presumably be the result of incidental learning.

The different tasks that Hyde and Jenkins assigned should lead to different levels of processing. In counting all of the letters or the number of *Es* in a word, the learner would need to look only at the superficial characteristics of the word and would not have to interpret the word's meaning; thus, a counting task should lead to relatively shallow processing. In rating a word's pleasantness, the learner must examine the word's meaning; hence, deeper, semantic processing should result. Consistent with levels-of-processing theory, students who rated words for pleasantness remembered more words than students who counted letters. More interesting, however, is the fact that incidental learning students who rated the words for pleasantness generally remembered as many words as any of the intentional learning groups (in fact, they did *better* than the intentional counting groups). Here was a case where learning was facilitated simply by virtue of the fact that students had to focus on the underlying meaning of the material to be learned. Depth of processing, not intention to learn, was the critical factor affecting learning.

The levels-of-processing model has certainly had its impact on psychologists' conceptualizations of learning and memory; for instance, I often see learning theorists writing about processing information "deeply" or in a more "shallow" manner. Nevertheless, weaknesses of this approach have surfaced. For one thing, the idea of *depth* of processing is a vague notion that is difficult to define or measure in precise terms (Baddeley, 1978; Willingham, 2004). Furthermore, some research indicates that degree of learning is not always a function of the degree of processing in the way that the model predicts. For instance, the more frequently information is repeated, the better it can be remembered *regardless* of the depth of processing it has undergone (T. O. Nelson, 1977). Even more damaging, however, is the finding that, in some cases, superficial processing actually leads to *better* recall than deeper processing. In an experiment by Morris, Bransford, and Franks (1977), college students were given a series of words and asked (1) whether each word fit appropriately into a sentence (a task involving "deep" semantic processing) or (2) whether the word rhymed with another word (a task involving "superficial" phonetic processing). Students recalled more words on an unexpected recall test when they had processed them semantically; however, they were more successful at identifying rhymes of the original words when they had processed them phonetically. Stein (1978) has reported similar results.

Another view related to the levels-of-processing approach is that information processing is most effective not necessarily when it is semantic but rather when it is *elaborative*—that is, when the learner adds information to the material to be learned in such a way that the new material is encoded more precisely, more meaningfully, and more completely (Craik & Tulving, 1975; Ellis & Hunt, 1983). We will examine the process of elaboration in more detail in the next chapter.

Activation

Some theorists (e.g., J. R. Anderson, 1995; Collins & Loftus, 1975; Cowan, 1995; Kimberg, D'Esposito, & Farah, 1997; Woltz, 2003) have proposed that working and long-term memory are not necessarily separate entities but may instead simply reflect different **activation** states of a single memory. From this perspective, all information stored in memory is in either an active or an inactive state. Information that is currently active, which may include both incoming information and information previously stored in memory, is the information that a learner is paying attention to and processing—information that I have previously described as being in working

The author activates part of
her memory.

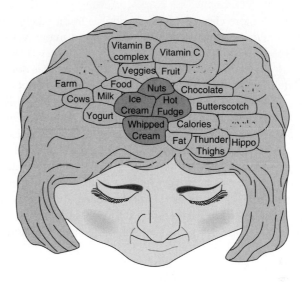

memory. As attention shifts, other pieces of information in memory become activated, and the
previously activated information gradually becomes inactive. The bulk of the information stored
in memory is in an inactive state, so that we are not consciously aware of it—I have previously
described this information as being in long-term memory.

A key idea in activation theory is that activation almost invariably spreads from one piece of
information to associated pieces. As evidence for this idea, theorists point to a phenomenon
called **priming.** A study by Ratcliff and McKoon (1981) provides an illustration. College students first studied a series of sentences (e.g., *The doctor hated the book*). After the students knew
the sentences well, they were shown a number of nouns, one at a time, and asked to identify
those that had been included in the sentences they learned earlier. Sometimes the nouns were
immediately preceded by another noun from the same sentence (e.g., they might see *book* right
after seeing *doctor*); when such was the case, the students correctly indicated having seen the second noun significantly faster than they would have otherwise. It's as if presentation of the first
noun activated memories associated with that noun and so made those other memories more
readily available. That is, activation of one noun stimulated, or *primed,* activation of the second.

Activation theorists aren't very specific about what activation actually *is* or how far it is apt
to spread (Willingham, 2004). (Some theorists hint that it might involve neurons stimulating one
another via synapses in the brain.) And activation theory doesn't help us understand why different kinds of stimuli (e.g., auditory versus visual, verbal versus spatial) seem to be processed in
somewhat different areas of the brain (Baddeley, 2001). Despite such limitations, activation theory is quite useful in understanding how people retrieve information from long-term memory.
Accordingly, we will encounter it again in later chapters, and especially in chapter 10.

Remembering That *The Map Is Not the Territory*

After writing the previous section on "Challenges to the Dual-Store Model," I took a short coffee
break to sweep my working memory clean of the difficult ideas I'd been wrestling with. (I do this
often during a writing project—I call it "letting the mental dust settle"—and find that it helps me

write more clearly.) My husband was in the kitchen as I was brewing my coffee, and so I mentioned my consternation about how so many research results don't fit easily into any single model of human memory.

His response was a helpful one: "The map is not the territory." As a geographer, he was partly telling me that no single map can completely or accurately represent the physical terrain it depicts. But he was also telling me—as was Alfred Korzybski, with whom the expression originated (e.g., Korzybski, 1933)—that no single human abstraction can entirely and truthfully represent its counterpart in reality. By their very nature, human abstractions are meant to *simplify* an aspect of life—to make it more understandable and manageable.

So it is with the dual-store model of memory (and any other model of memory, for that matter). Concepts such as working memory and long-term memory help us explain many of the phenomena we see in everyday human performance, and so psychologists continue to use them. We, too, will continue to use these concepts throughout the book, and you will find them to be extremely useful in summarizing much—but not all—of what we know about human thinking and learning.

GENERAL EDUCATIONAL IMPLICATIONS OF COGNITIVE THEORIES

We have much more to discover about cognitivist perspectives in the chapters ahead. But even at this point, we can make some generalizations and consider their implications for educational practice.

◆ *People control their own learning.* The behaviorist B. F. Skinner (1954, 1968) argued that students must make active responses in the classroom if they are to learn anything. Cognitivists share Skinner's view; however, they emphasize *mental* activity rather than physical activity. Students who are not mentally active in the classroom—those who do not attend to, think about, and in other ways cognitively process the subject matter at hand—will learn very little. For those who *do* become mentally engaged with the subject matter, the nature of their cognitive processes will determine what they learn and how effectively they learn it. As we will see in upcoming chapters, a variety of instructional strategies can help students mentally process classroom material in beneficial ways.

◆ *Memory is selective.* Because learners usually receive much more information than they can possibly process and remember, they must continually make choices about what things to focus on and what things to ignore. Unfortunately, teachers and textbooks often load students up with more details than any normal person can possibly remember (Calfee, 1981; E. D. Gagné, 1985). In such situations, students must inevitably select some information to the exclusion of other information, but they aren't always the best judges of what material is most important to learn.

Details are often effective means of illustrating, clarifying, and elaborating on the main points of a lecture or textbook. In this sense, they are indispensable. At the same time, teachers must help their students sort through essential and nonessential information so that the students don't lose sight of the forest because of the trees.

◆ *Attention is essential for learning.* Regardless of which model of memory we use, we know that attention is critical for long-term retention of information. Sometimes attention to a particular stimulus is all that is needed. In other cases (e.g., in reading a textbook) attention to a particular *part* of the stimulus is important. In general, people will *not* learn the things that they don't process in some way, and paying attention is the first step they must take.

There is an old saying, "You can lead a horse to water, but you can't make him drink." Ormrod's corollary is "The horse can't possibly drink if you don't at least lead him to the water." Helping students focus their attention on important information is the first step in helping them learn it: It gets them to the water trough.

Yet classrooms are usually lively environments with many stimuli competing for students' attention. For example, think of yourself in one of your college classes. Sometimes you pay attention to what the teacher is saying, but at other times your attention drifts to such things as the shape of the instructor's nose, the style of another student's clothes, the doodles in your notebook, or the plans you've made for the weekend. If adults cannot pay attention during every minute of a class session, how can we reasonably expect younger learners to do so?

Actually, the things that teachers do in the classroom make a big difference in the extent to which students pay attention to the topic at hand. Following are several effective strategies for capturing and holding students' attention:

- *Include variety in topics and presentation styles.* Repetition of the same topics and the same procedures day after day can lead to boredom and reduced attention (Zirin, 1974). Variety and novelty in the subject matter and mode of presentation will help keep students' attention focused on a lesson (Berlyne, 1960; Good & Brophy, 1994; Krapp, Hidi, & Renninger, 1992).

- *Provide frequent breaks, especially when working with young children.* After prolonged periods of sitting quietly and attentively, even adults are likely to become restless and distracted. Frequent breaks are especially important for students in the early and middle elementary grades. For example, children are often more attentive after recess than before, even if recess has involved playing quietly in the classroom rather than running around the schoolyard (Pellegrini & Bjorklund, 1997; Pellegrini, Huberty, & Jones, 1995).

- *Ask questions.* Questions are an excellent way of maintaining students' attention when it might otherwise wander off (Davis & O'Neill, 2004; Grabe, 1986; Marmolejo, Wilder, & Bradley, 2004). By periodically asking questions in class—perhaps by occasionally addressing questions to particular students, or perhaps by requiring everyone to answer with hand votes or preprinted *true* and *false* response cards—teachers can help students keep their attention where it should be. And by giving students questions they should try to answer as they read a textbook, teachers are likely to increase students' learning of content related to those questions (McCrudden et al., 2005). (We'll consider additional benefits of teacher questions in chapter 10.)

- *Minimize distractions when independent work is assigned.* Most students, especially younger ones, are better able to concentrate on challenging independent assignments when their work environment is relatively quiet and subdued (e.g., Higgins & Turnure, 1984).

- *Seat students near the teacher if they have difficulty staying on task.* Students are more likely to pay attention when they are placed at the front of the room and near the teacher (Doyle, 1986a; Schwebel & Cherlin, 1972). Front-row seats may be especially appropriate for students with a history of being easily distracted.

- *Monitor students' behaviors.* Behaviors often provide a clue to whether students are paying attention. For example, students should be directing their eyes at the teacher, textbook, or other appropriate stimulus and should be clearly working on the task at hand (Grabe, 1986; Piontkowski & Calfee, 1979; Samuels & Turnure, 1974).

- *People can process only a limited amount of information at a time.* We have characterized both attention and the "working" aspect of memory as having a limited capacity; in other words, people can pay attention to and think about only a small amount of information at any one time. Accordingly, getting information into long-term memory will be a slow process. Educators must remember this point in pacing their lectures and in choosing or creating their instructional materials. When too much information is presented too fast, students will simply not be able to remember it all.

- *The limited capacity of working memory is not necessarily a bad thing.* The working memory bottleneck forces learners to condense, organize, and synthesize the information they receive (e.g., R. M. Gagné & Driscoll, 1988). These processes may be in learners' best interest over the long run, as you will discover in our discussion of long-term memory storage in the next chapter.

SUMMARY

Cognitivism is currently the predominant theoretical perspective within which human learning is studied and explained. The roots of cognitive theory can be found in research and theories dating back to the 1920s and 1930s. For example, Edward Tolman, while conducting animal laboratory studies similar to those of behaviorists, included mental phenomena in his views of how learning occurs. Gestalt psychologists emphasized the importance of organizational processes in perception, learning, and problem solving, proposing that people are predisposed to organize information in particular ways. In the middle decades of the twentieth century, verbal learning theorists, who initially attempted to apply an S–R analysis to the study of human language-based learning, further stoked the fire of cognitivism by increasingly incorporating mental events into explanations of their research results.

Contemporary cognitivism emphasizes mental processes and proposes that many aspects of learning are probably unique to the human species. Cognitivists share behaviorists' belief that the study of learning must be objective and that learning theories should be based on empirical research; however, they suggest that by observing the responses people make to different stimulus conditions, they can draw inferences

about the cognitive processes that have led to various responses. Cognitivism encompasses several perspectives—information processing theory, constructivism, and contextual views—that all contribute to our understanding of how human beings think and learn.

Many cognitive theorists, especially those with an information processing bent, distinguish between *learning* (acquiring new information) and *memory* (saving information for a period of time); occasionally, they also use *memory* in reference to a particular "spot" (metaphorically speaking) where information is saved. Some information processing terminology is borrowed from computer lingo: *Storage* means "putting" information in memory, *encoding* involves changing information to store it more effectively, and *retrieval* is the process of "finding" information that was stored at an earlier time.

Currently the most prevalent view of human memory—a *dual-store model*—maintains that memory has three distinct components. The first component, the *sensory register*, holds virtually all incoming information for a very short time (a few seconds or less, depending on the modality). If the information held in the sensory register is not processed in some fashion—at a minimum, by being paid attention to—it may disappear from the memory system.

Information that is attended to moves on to *working memory* (also called short-term memory), where it is actively processed; in essence, working memory is the "thinking" center of the memory system. Working memory has a limited capacity; for example, most people can hold no more than five to nine digits there at a single time. Furthermore, information stored in working memory lasts only about 5 to 20 seconds unless it is processed further.

Information that undergoes additional processing (e.g., integration with previously stored information) moves on to the third component—*long-term memory*. Long-term memory appears to have the capacity to hold a great deal of information for a relatively long time.

Not all cognitive theorists believe that human memory has the three distinct components just described. Furthermore, some research evidence suggests that conscious processing in some sort of "working memory" is not always necessary for learning to occur. Accordingly, some psychologists have offered alternative views of human memory, perhaps focusing on *depth of processing* as an important factor affecting learning or perhaps suggesting that memory is one large entity of which only a tiny portion can be *activated* at a time. Nevertheless, the dual-store (three-component) model effectively accounts for many research results and so continues to be a popular mechanism for helping us understand the nature of human memory.

Despite the differing perspectives of memory that currently exist, we can make several generalizations about memory that have implications for classroom practice. For instance, what learners do "inside" makes a huge difference in what they learn and how well they remember it, and teachers can do many things to nudge students toward effective cognitive processes. Also, teachers must make sure that students are actively attending to classroom subject matter and, more specifically, to important parts of that material. Finally, teachers must recognize that learners can process only a limited amount of information at a time and so must be selective about the things they study. The processing bottleneck of the memory system is not necessarily a bad thing; it forces learners to condense and integrate information in ways that are often beneficial over the long run.

CHAPTER 8

Long–Term Memory I: Storage

Over the years, I've had a number of students approach me after receiving a low score on one of my exams. "I studied so *hard*!" a student might whine, displaying a look of frustrated desperation. "I studied twice as long as my roommate did, yet my roommate got an A while I got a C−!"

Storing information in long-term memory and retrieving it later can be a tricky business. If two roommates are equally motivated to achieve in my class, the difference between them may be the result of their storage and retrieval processes. After more than 30 years of talking with students about how they typically study, I have come to the conclusion that many are sadly uninformed about how best to learn and remember information.

Even when students effectively store information in their long-term memories, they don't always learn what their teachers *think* they are learning. For example, when my daughter Tina was in fourth grade, she came home one day complaining about a song she was learning in the school choir. "It has bad words in it, Mom," she told me. I was quite surprised to learn that she was talking about "America the Beautiful," but then she recited the guilty line from the second verse:

All the bastard cities gleam.

After shuddering in response to the richness of my daughter's vocabulary, I patiently explained to her that the line in question was actually "Alabaster cities gleam." Two weeks later the rest of the family went to hear Tina's choir performing in concert. As the children began to sing "America the Beautiful," 6-year-old Alex turned to me and whispered, "Why are they singing about *spaceship* skies?"

Long-term memory provides a mechanism for saving information over a relatively long period of time. It also provides a knowledge base from which to interpret new information. As we shall see, people frequently store incoming information in long-term memory by relating it to things they already know—in other words, to things already existing in long-term memory. Different people are likely to store the same information differently, then, because they have previously stored different kinds of information in their respective long-term memories. Alex had never heard the word *spacious* before, but *spaceship* was a frequent word in his world of science fiction cartoons. Similarly, Tina was unfamiliar with *alabaster*, but . . . well, let's not go there.

In this chapter, we will explore the multifaceted nature of long-term memory storage. We will first consider how storage is often constructive in nature and look at examples of construction in action. We will then examine cognitive processes that may be involved in long-term memory storage, as well as activities and characteristics that either facilitate or interfere with storage. Finally, we will identify strategies for promoting effective long-term memory storage in instructional settings. In the two subsequent chapters, we will look at the nature of the knowledge that people acquire and at the processes involved in retrieving that knowledge from long-term memory.

CONSTRUCTION IN STORAGE

Imagine, for a minute, that your mind worked like a videocassette recorder, such that you recorded everything you saw and heard. Your memory of an event would involve a simple process of finding and replaying the appropriate cassette, and you would be able to remember the event as completely and accurately as if you were reliving it. Studying for an exam would be easy, you might think—no need for reading the textbook more than once or for mindless repetition of meaningless facts.

Unfortunately, our minds are not accurate recorders of life events. As we discovered in the preceding chapter, we can process only a small amount of information in working memory at any one time, and so we quickly lose most of what we've stored in our sensory registers. In a manner of speaking, most of the information we receive from the environment goes in one ear (or eye) and out the other. In part because we retain such a small percentage of the information we receive, many learning theorists believe that long-term memory storage often involves a process of *construction,* whereby we use the bits and pieces of the information we do retain to build a reasonable understanding of the world around us.

Examples of Construction in Action

At any given point in time, our interpretation of the environment (**perception**) is usually both less and more than the information we actually receive from the environment (**sensation**). Perception is *less* than sensation because people cannot possibly interpret all of the information that bombards their sensory receptors at any given moment. Right now, as you are looking at this book, light waves are bouncing off of the page and hitting the light-sensitive cells in the retinas of your eyes. At the same time, you may also be receiving light waves from the table at which you are working, the carpet on the floor, and the pictures on the walls. Your ears are probably receiving numerous sound waves, perhaps from a radio, a nearby conversation, an air conditioner, or traffic outside your window. Perhaps a certain smell is drifting through the air, or a certain taste from your last meal lingers in your mouth. It is neither necessary nor possible for you to interpret *all* of these sensations, so you will attend to some of them and ignore the others.

But perception is also much *more* than sensation, because sensation alone provides insufficient information for an adequate interpretation of ongoing events. It appears that people use the data they receive from their sensory receptors to put together, or construct, an overall perception of any given situation (Neisser, 1967; Ornstein, 1972). As an example, consider the fact that our eyes do not provide a continual report of visual stimulation; rather, they jump from one focal point to another, taking periodic "snapshots" of the visual field. These jumps in focus, or **saccades**, occur four or five times a second, with visual sensation occurring primarily during the rest periods between them (Abrams, 1994; Irwin, 1996). If we receive only four or five snapshots of visual information each second, our visual world should appear jerky and erratic, much as an old-time movie does. The fact that we instead see smooth-flowing motion is due, in large part, to the mental "filling in" that occurs as our minds interpret visual sensations. (This principle should remind you of the Gestalt concept of *closure*.)

Even if human eyes functioned 100% of the time, they would typically provide an incomplete picture of the environment, and we would have to mentally fill in the information that we did not sense. For example, imagine walking into a bookstore and seeing the store clerk behind the counter. You probably sense only the clerk's head and upper torso, yet you perceive an entire person. You assume that the clerk has a lower torso and two legs, and in fact you would be quite surprised if you saw a very different lower body—a carved pumpkin, perhaps—as he emerged from behind the counter.

As another example of construction in perception, look at the three pictures in Figure 8.1. Most people perceive the picture on the left as being that of a woman, even though many of her features are missing. Enough features are visible—an eye and parts of the nose, mouth, chin, and hair—that you can construct a meaningful perception from them. Do the other two figures provide

People often make assumptions about what they don't see and may be quite surprised when such assumptions are inaccurate.

Figure 8.1
Can you construct a person from each of these pictures?
Reprinted from "Age in the Development of Closure Ability in Children" by C. M. Mooney, 1957, *Canadian Journal of Psychology, 11,* p. 220. Copyright 1957 by Canadian Psychological Association. Reprinted with permission.

enough information for you to construct two more faces? Construction of a face from the figure on the right may take you a while, but it can be done.

Consider, too, how much is missing from the spoken language that we hear. For example, let's say that you are in a noisy room and hear someone say:

I -an't -ear a thing in this -lace!

Although you haven't heard everything the person said, you may have enough information to perceive the sentence:

I can't hear a thing in this place!

Even when you do hear everything the speaker says, what you *really* hear is a continuousstreamofsoundwaves rather than . . . separate . . . words . . . spoken . . . like . . . this. Only when you are familiar with the particular language you are listening to can you mentally divide the one long sound you actually sense into separate words. For instance, you can easily understand the following sentence when you hear it:

I read a book.

even though the identical sentence in Mandarin Chinese would give you trouble:

Wŏkànshū.

To an individual fluent in Mandarin Chinese but not in English, the situation would be reversed; that person would "hear" this:

Ireadabook.

and this:

Wŏ kàn shū.

Figure 8.2
An architectural impossibility.
Art courtesy of Roly West (Roly is
the driver in each of the antique
cars at the bottom of the picture).

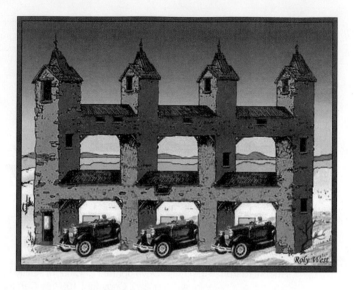

The constructive nature of perception allows us sometimes to be fooled in optical illusions. Consider, for example, the four-towered structure shown in Figure 8.2. If you look closely, you will notice that it's an architectural impossibility: If all of the corners are 90° angles (as they seem to be), then the two horizontal hallways couldn't possibly connect with the four towers in the ways depicted.

Curiously, once you have constructed meaning from what you have seen or heard, that meaning then seems so obvious to you. Furthermore, you tend to perceive the same pattern of sensory information in the same way at a future time; a particular construction of sensory input tends to stick. For example, if you were to close this book now and not pick it up again for a week or more, you would see the three faces in Figure 8.1 almost immediately, even if you had had difficulty perceiving them originally.

Different people may construct different interpretations of any given event. For instance, consider Tina's and Alex's rather unconventional interpretations of "America the Beautiful." As another example, take a close look at the picture in Figure 8.3. Describe to yourself what you see. Notice the shape of the head, the eye, the nose, the mouth, the jaw line. But just what is it that you *do* see? Is this a picture of a man? Or is it, perhaps, a picture of a rat or a mouse?

Figure 8.3
Reprinted from "The Role of
Frequency in Developing
Perceptual Sets" by B. R.
Bugelski & D. A. Alampay, 1961,
*Canadian Journal of Psychology,
15,* p. 206. Copyright 1961 by
Canadian Psychological
Association. Reprinted with
permission.

The man–rat picture in Figure 8.3 is an example of an **ambiguous stimulus,** something that readily lends itself to more than one possible construction. Some people perceive the figure as a bald man with an overbite, a strangely shaped ear, and a backward tilt to his head. Others instead perceive a rat or mouse with a very short front leg and a long tail curling beneath its body (Bugelski & Alampay, 1961).

As you can see, then, people often perceive the world in unique ways, and all may arrive at different conclusions about what they have seen and heard. As a result, several people witnessing the same event often store very different things in their long-term memories. We now look more closely at the processes involved in long-term memory storage.

LONG–TERM MEMORY STORAGE PROCESSES

Following is a short story, "The War of the Ghosts." Read it silently *one time only,* then cover the page and write down as much of the story as you can remember.

The War of the Ghosts

One night two young men from Egulac went down to the river to hunt seals, and while they were there it became foggy and calm. Then they heard war-cries, and they thought, "Maybe this is a war-party." They escaped to the shore, and hid behind a log. Now canoes came up, and they heard the noise of paddles, and saw one canoe coming up to them. There were five men in the canoe, and they said:

"What do you think? We wish to take you along. We are going up the river to make war on the people."

One of the young men said: "I have no arrows."

"Arrows are in the canoe," they said.

"I will not go along. I might be killed. My relatives do not know where I have gone. But you," he said, turning to the other, "may go with them."

So one of the young men went, but the other returned home.

And the warriors went on up the river to a town on the other side of Kalama. The people came down to the water, and they began to fight, and many were killed. But presently the young man heard one of the warriors say, "Quick, let us go home: that Indian has been hit." Now he thought: "Oh, they are ghosts." He did not feel sick, but they said he had been shot.

So the canoes went back to Egulac, and the young man went ashore to his house, and made a fire. And he told everybody and said, "Behold I accompanied the ghosts, and we went to fight. Many of our fellows were killed, and many of those who attacked us were killed. They said I was hit, and I did not feel sick."

He told it all, and then he became quiet. When the sun rose he fell down. Something black came out of his mouth. His face became contorted. The people jumped up and cried.

He was dead. (Bartlett, 1932, p. 65)

Now cover the story and write down everything you can remember of it.

Once you have finished, compare your reproduction with the original. What differences do you notice? Your reproduction is almost certainly shorter than the original, with numerous details omitted. Perhaps you added some things, consistent with the process of construction described earlier. But you probably maintained the gist of the story: You included its main ideas and events, mostly in their proper sequence.

Using this Native American ghost story, Frederic Bartlett (1932) conducted one of the earliest studies of the long-term memory of meaningful verbal information. Bartlett asked his students at England's Cambridge University to read the story two times, then to recall it at various times later on. Students' recollections differed from the actual story in a number of ways:

1. *The words themselves were changed.* In other words, recall was not verbatim.

2. *The focus was on significant events that contributed to the plot line.* Some details, especially those that were essential to the story and those that were particularly striking, were retained. Unimportant details and meaningless information, however, were omitted. For example, such details as "something black came out of his mouth" and "he was dead" were likely to be remembered; such details as "the young man . . . made a fire" and "a town on the other side of Kalama" were frequently forgotten.

3. *Parts of the story were distorted and additional information was inserted to make the story more logical and consistent with English culture.* For example, people rarely go "to the river to hunt seals," because seals are saltwater animals and most rivers have fresh water. Students might therefore say that the men went to the river to *fish.* Similarly, the supernatural element did not fit comfortably with the religious beliefs of most Cambridge students and was often altered. In the following recollection, written by a student six months after he had read the original story, several additions and distortions are evident:

   > Four men came down to the water. They were told to get into a boat and to take arms with them. They inquired, "What arms?" and were answered "Arms for battle." When they came to the battle-field they heard a great noise and shouting, and a voice said: "The black man is dead." And he was brought to the place where they were, and laid on the ground. And he foamed at the mouth. (Bartlett, 1932, pp. 71–72)

   The main idea of the story—a battle—is retained. But after six months, the story has been so distorted that it is barely recognizable.

4. *There was a tendency to explain as well as describe events in the story.* For example, one student insisted on explaining events in parentheses:

   > The young man did not feel sick (i.e., wounded), but nevertheless they proceeded home (evidently the opposing forces were quite willing to stop fighting). (Bartlett, 1932, p. 86)

Bartlett's findings illustrate several general principles of long-term memory storage. First, learners select some pieces of information to store and exclude others. Second, they are more likely to store underlying meanings than verbatim input. Third, they use their existing knowledge about the world (i.e., things they have already stored in long-term memory) to help them make sense of and understand new information. And fourth, some of that existing knowledge may be *added* to the new information, such that what is learned is more than, and perhaps qualitatively different from, the information actually presented.

In the preceding chapter, I introduced you to the distinction between declarative knowledge—knowledge about "how things are or were" (e.g., facts, figures, events in one's personal life)—and procedural knowledge—knowledge about "how to do things" (e.g., motor skills, problem-solving techniques, study strategies). Storing declarative knowledge and procedural knowledge may involve somewhat different, although overlapping, processes. In this section of the chapter, we will look at six cognitive processes that affect long-term memory storage—selection, rehearsal, meaningful learning, internal organization, elaboration, and visual imagery—with a particular focus on the acquisition of declarative knowledge. We will then look at how some of these processes may also be involved in the acquisition of procedural knowledge. Finally, we will examine evidence in support of the idea that new information in long-term memory sometimes requires a period of *consolidation* in order to endure over the long run.

Selection

As we saw in chapter 7, some attended-to information is automatically stored in long-term memory even if it is not specifically selected for further processing (recall our discussion of the frequencies of *bacon* versus *pastrami*). But most explicit knowledge—information that people *know* that they know and can easily explain—apparently must be encoded as well as attended to if it is to be stored effectively for the long run. Such encoding takes time and requires the active involvement of working memory, which, as noted in chapter 7, has a very limited capacity. One theorist (Simon, 1974) has estimated that each new piece of information takes about 10 seconds to encode. Using this estimate and the additional estimate that 30 new pieces of information might be presented in a minute of a typical classroom lecture, another theorist (E. D. Gagné, 1985) has estimated that students can process only six pieces of information per minute—*one-fifth* of the lecture content! Obviously, learners must be extremely selective about the information they choose to process and so must have a means of determining what is important and what is not.[1]

Although the selection process itself is largely directed by working memory (presumably by its central executive component), long-term memory also plays a critical role. People's knowledge about the world, their priorities, and their predictions about what environmental input is likely to be useful affect what they pay attention to and think about (Schwartz & Reisberg, 1991; Voss & Schauble, 1992). A student who has learned that a teacher's lecture content will probably reappear on an upcoming exam is apt to listen closely to what the teacher is saying. A student who has learned that a teacher's exam questions are based entirely on outside reading assignments or has decided that an active social life is more important than classroom achievement may instead attend to something more relevant or interesting—perhaps the flattering sweater worn by the student on her right.

Given the capacity and time constraints of human memory, how can teachers help students select important information? An obvious way is simply to tell students what information is important and what is not (Bjork, 1972; McCrudden, Schraw, & Hartley, 2006; Reynolds & Shirey, 1988). Another way is to build redundancy into lectures and instructional materials by repeating important points several times. For example, when I am presenting an important idea to my students, I typically present it several times. I state the idea once and then state it again using different words. I then illustrate it with at least two examples (often as many as five), and

---

[1]Some advocates for *speed-reading* programs claim that speed-reading greatly increases the amount of information that a person can learn and remember within a certain time period. Contemporary views of memory indicate that such outcomes are highly unlikely. In fact, research tells us that people's comprehension of text is significantly lower when they speed-read than when they read at a normal rate. Speed-reading is probably effective only when readers already know much of the information they are reading (Carver, 1971, 1990; Crowder & Wagner, 1992).

I present the idea itself once again. Notice the redundancy in the last four sentences—it should have been very difficult not to process my meaning at least once! (We'll identify additional strategies in our discussion of *signals* later in the chapter.)

Rehearsal

You should recall from the preceding chapter that **rehearsal**—repeating something over and over in a short time period (say, over the course of a minute or so)—provides a means of maintaining information in working memory indefinitely. In their early dual-store model of memory, Atkinson and Shiffrin (1971) proposed that rehearsal is also a method of storing information in long-term memory, and there is some evidence that they were right. Several studies have shown that people remember frequently rehearsed items better than less frequently rehearsed ones (T. O. Nelson, 1977; Rundus, 1971; Rundus & Atkinson, 1971).

Yet a number of theorists have argued that rehearsal leads to storage in long-term memory only if, in the process, the learner associates the new information with existing knowledge—in other words, if rehearsal also involves *meaningful learning* (Craik & Watkins, 1973; Klatzky, 1975; Watkins & Watkins, 1974). From their perspective, mere repetition of information—maintenance rehearsal—is sufficient to keep the information in working memory but *in*sufficient to move it on to long-term memory. Rehearsal that in some way helps learners make associations between the new information and things they already know—sometimes known as **elaborative rehearsal**—does facilitate storage in long-term memory. As an example, in a study by Craik and Watkins (1973), college students were asked to perform two tasks simultaneously: They had to keep one word in their working memories (by rehearsing it) while at the same time examining additional words to see if they met certain criteria. In this situation, the amount of rehearsal did *not* influence the extent to which the students were able to recall the words they had rehearsed; apparently the second task kept them busy enough that they were unable to make associations with the rehearsed words. When the additional words were presented at a slower rate, however, recall of the rehearsed words improved, presumably because the students could devote more working memory capacity to forming associations with the words.

Learning information primarily through repetition is sometimes called **rote learning** (Ausubel, Novak, & Hanesian, 1978; Hiebert & Lefevre, 1986; Mayer, 1996b). In rote learning, there is little or no attempt to make the information meaningful or to understand it in terms of things one already knows. If such information is stored in long-term memory at all, it is stored in relative isolation from other information. As you will discover when you read chapter 10, information stored in this unconnected fashion becomes difficult to retrieve.

So many times I have seen students engage in simple repetition as a means of trying to learn new information. This process, often referred to as "memorizing," emphasizes the learning of verbatim information rather than the learning of underlying meanings. Although young children (e.g., elementary school students) are especially likely to use this strategy when trying to learn new information (Cuvo, 1975; Gathercole & Hitch, 1993; Rosser, 1994), I have observed high school and college students using it as well. Teachers must help students understand that mere repetition is an inefficient means of storing information for the long run, if it even works at all. The four processes we turn to now—meaningful learning, internal organization, elaboration, and visual imagery—are clearly more effective methods of long-term memory storage.

Meaningful Learning

Look at this string of 15 letters:

MAIGUWRSENNFLOD

And now look at this string:

MEANINGFULWORDS

Both strings are the same length, and both contain exactly the same letters. Which string is easier to learn? No doubt you will agree that the second list is easier because you can relate it to words you already know. In the same way, my daughter Tina related a phrase from "America the Beautiful" to her existing knowledge about the world—which unfortunately included *bastard* but not *alabaster*)—as did my son Alex, who heard *spaceship skies* instead of *spacious skies*. By relating new information to knowledge already stored in their long-term memories, people find *meaning* in the information. Hence, this process is frequently known as **meaningful learning;** it is also what we are referring to when we talk about understanding or comprehension.

We learn information meaningfully by storing it in long-term memory in association with similar, related pieces of information. Meaningful learning appears to facilitate both storage and retrieval: The information is stored more quickly and remembered more easily (J. R. Anderson, 1995; Ausubel et al., 1978; Mayer, 1996b). To illustrate, consider the following passage from an experiment by Bransford and Johnson (1972):

> The procedure is actually quite simple. First you arrange things into different groups. Of course, one pile may be sufficient depending on how much there is to do. If you have to go somewhere else due to lack of facilities that is the next step, otherwise you are pretty well set. It is important not to overdo things. That is, it is better to do too few things at once than too many. In the short run this may not seem important, but complications can easily arise. A mistake can be expensive as well. At first the whole procedure will seem complicated. Soon, however, it will become just another facet of life. It is difficult to foresee any end to the necessity for this task in the immediate future, but then one never can tell. After the procedure is completed one arranges the materials into different groups again. Then they can be put into their appropriate places. Eventually they will be used once more and the whole cycle will then have to be repeated. However, that is part of life. (p. 722)

All of the words in this passage were undoubtedly familiar to you, yet you may have had some difficulty understanding what you were reading. If you didn't know what the passage was about, you would have had trouble relating it to things in your long-term memory. But now try reading the passage again, this time thinking of it as a description of washing clothes. Bransford and Johnson found that college students who knew the topic of the passage remembered twice as much as those who had no topic with which to connect things.

People can also store nonverbal material more easily when it has meaning for them. For example, in a study by Bower, Karlin, and Dueck (1975), students were asked to remember somewhat meaningless line drawings; examples of these "droodles" appear in Figure 8.4. Students who were given meaningful labels for such pictures, such as "a midget playing a trombone in a telephone booth" or "an early bird who caught a very strong worm" were more likely to remember them correctly a week later than students who weren't given such labels.

Relating new information to *oneself* can have a particularly dramatic effect on learning (Heatherton, Macrae, & Kelley, 2004). This point was clearly illustrated in a study by Rogers,

Figure 8.4
Droodles from Bower, Karlin, and Dueck (1975).
From "Comprehension and Memory for Pictures" by G. H. Bower, M. B. Karlin, and A. Dueck, 1975, *Memory and Cognition, 3,* p. 217. Reprinted by permission of Psychonomic Society, Inc.

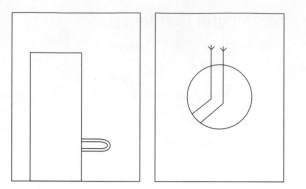

Kuiper, and Kirker (1977). College students were given a list of 40 adjectives (some words were presented in large type and some in small type) and asked to respond to one of four questions about each word. They were then unexpectedly asked to remember as many of the 40 adjectives as they could. Following are the four questions asked about different adjectives and the amount of incidental learning that resulted from answering each of them:

Question	Percentage Recalled
1. Does it have big letters?	3%
2. Does it rhyme with _____?	7%
3. Does it mean the same as _____?	13%
4. Does it describe you?	30%

When the students were required to relate the word to something they already knew (question 3), they remembered more than when they were asked to consider superficial characteristics of the word (questions 1 and 2). But when they were asked to relate the word to themselves (question 4), incidental learning was more than *twice* what it was for meaningful but not self-related processing.

Because meaningful learning allows new information to be organized with previously learned information, it is sometimes referred to as **external organization** (e.g., E. D. Gagné, 1985). Another equally important process is the organization of a new body of information within itself, as we shall see now.

Internal Organization

A body of new information is stored more effectively and remembered more completely when the various pieces are interconnected in some way—that is, when the information to be learned has **internal organization.** In fact, people seem to have a natural tendency to organize and integrate the information they receive. For instance, in our discussion of verbal learning research in chapter 7, we noted that people who are asked to remember a list of words often put the words into categories while learning them (e.g., remembering all of the animals together, all of the vegetables together, and so on). You may also recall the Bransford and Franks (1971) study described in chapter 7, in which students learned that "The ants in the kitchen ate the sweet jelly which was on the table" by integrating the content of several shorter sentences.

You have undoubtedly had teachers whose lectures were unorganized, with one point following another in an unpredictable sequence. As you might expect, material presented in

Figure 8.5
Example of a conceptual hierarchy from Bower et al. (1969). From "Hierarchical Retrieval Schemes in Recall of Categorized Word Lists" by G. H. Bower, M. C. Clark, A. M. Lesgold, and D. Winzenz, 1969, *Journal of Verbal Learning and Verbal Behavior, 8,* p. 324. Copyright 1969 by Academic Press. Reprinted by permission.

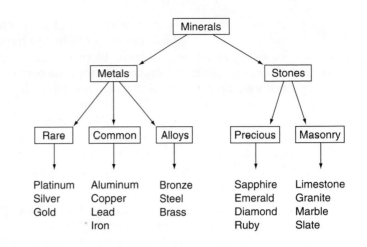

such an unorganized fashion is more difficult to learn than clearly organized material. An experiment by Bower, Clark, Lesgold, and Winzenz (1969) demonstrates just how dramatic the effects of internal organization can be. College students were given four study trials in which to learn 112 words that fell into four categories (e.g., minerals, plants, etc.). Some students had words arranged randomly, whereas other students had words arranged in four conceptual hierarchies (the minerals hierarchy in Figure 8.5 is an example). After one study trial, students who had studied the organized words could remember more than three times as many words as those who had studied the randomized words. After four study trials, the students in the organized group remembered all 112, whereas those in the random group remembered only 70.

Many good students spontaneously organize information as they learn it, and such learner-generated organization can be quite effective (Britton, Stimson, Stennett, & Gülgöz, 1998; Buschke, 1977; McDaniel & Einstein, 1989; Tulving, 1962). Furthermore, providing students with specific organizational schemes can often help students learn more effectively (Atkinson et al., 1999; DuBois, Kiewra, & Fraley, 1988; DuBois, Staley, Guzy, & DiNardo, 1995; Kiewra et al., 1988).

Elaboration

Suffering from cold symptoms? Consider this:

> Aren't you tired of sniffles and runny noses all winter? Tired of always feeling less than your best? Get through a whole winter without colds. Take Eradicold Pills as directed. (Harris, 1977, p. 605)

Do Eradicold Pills prevent colds? If you believe they do, then you have been the unwitting victim of **elaboration**: You added your own information to the passage you read and "learned" that information along with what you had actually read. In a study by Harris (1977), people who read the preceding passage asserted that Eradicold Pills prevented colds almost as frequently as those who read an explicit statement to that effect.

When people receive new information, they often impose their own interpretations on it—perhaps making assumptions, drawing inferences, and so on—and learn those interpretations right along with the information they've actually received. Elaboration, then, is a process of learning *more* than the material presented; I like to think of it as *learning between the lines.*[2] As an example, my son Jeff tells me that when he first heard the expression "losing one's voice" when he was in first or second grade, he concluded that people eventually lose their voices permanently. From this, he deduced that people are born with a finite amount of "voice" that they eventually use up. So as not to waste his own supply, he would mouth the words, rather than actually sing them, during his weekly choir sessions at school.

Numerous studies lead to the same conclusion: People frequently elaborate on the information they receive and later have difficulty distinguishing between the actual "truth" and their elaborations of it (e.g., Bower, Black, & Turner, 1979; Graesser & Bower, 1990; Johnson, Bransford, & Solomon, 1973; Loftus, 2003; Reder & Ross, 1983). As an illustration, read the following passage *one time only*:

> Nancy woke up feeling sick again and she wondered if she really were pregnant. How would she tell the professor she had been seeing? And the money was another problem.
>
> Nancy went to the doctor. She arrived at the office and checked in with the receptionist. She went to see the nurse, who went through the usual procedures. Then Nancy stepped on the scale and the nurse recorded her weight. The doctor entered the room and examined the results. He smiled at Nancy and said, "Well, it seems my expectations have been confirmed." When the examination was finished, Nancy left the office. (Owens, Bower, & Black, 1979, pp. 185–186)

Did the doctor tell Nancy she was pregnant? The fact is, he did not. Yet in a study conducted by Owens and his colleagues (1979), when students read the passage and then were asked a day later to recall information about it, they "remembered" considerably more than they had actually read. Many of their recalled elaborations were directly related to Nancy's suspected condition. Other students in the experiment read only the second paragraph of the passage and so didn't know that Nancy thought she was pregnant; these students added far fewer elaborations.

As was the case for my son Jeff when he heard the expression "losing one's voice," and as may also have been the case for you when you read about Eradicold Pills, elaboration sometimes leads to distortions and errors in what is learned. But most of the time, elaboration is a highly effective means of long-term memory storage: Elaborated information is typically learned and remembered far more easily than nonelaborated information (J. R. Anderson, 1990, 1995; Greeno, Collins, & Resnick, 1996; McDaniel & Einstein, 1989; Myers & Duffy, 1990; Pressley, 1982; van der Broek, 1990). As Anderson (1990) has pointed out, most elaborations reflect correct assumptions and interpretations of an event, not incorrect ones.

Elaboration appears to be especially effective when it helps to tie new information together—that is, when it also helps to organize it. For example, in studies by Stein, Bransford, and their colleagues (Stein & Bransford, 1979; Stein et al., 1982), fifth graders and college students were instructed to learn a series of sentences. Each sentence involved a particular kind of man and a particular activity; following are two examples:

The fat man read the sign.

The hungry man got into the car.

---

[2]*Meaningful learning* and *elaboration* might strike you as very similar processes, and theorists sometimes use the terms interchangeably. In my mind, it is helpful to distinguish between the two. Whereas meaningful learning involves *connecting* new information to existing knowledge, elaboration also involves *embellishing on* new information.

The sentences were elaborated with phrases added on to them—elaborations generated either by the experimenters or by the students themselves. Some of the elaborative phrases (*precise* elaborations) provided a connection between a man's characteristic and his activity, for example:

> The fat man read the sign warning about the thin ice.

> The hungry man got into the car to go to the restaurant.

Other elaborative phrases (*imprecise* elaborations) did not tie the characteristic and activity together; here are some examples:

> The fat man read the sign that was two feet high.

> The hungry man got into the car and drove away.

Precise elaborations were much more effective than imprecise ones in helping the students remember the sentences.

In some cases, learners elaborate on and integrate new information to the point where they construct an entirely new idea, concept, procedure, or line of reasoning. Oftentimes, learning something by constructing it *on one's own* makes it more memorable than having someone else present it in a prepackaged format. This phenomenon is known as the **generation effect.** Self-constructed knowledge (provided that it is accurate, of course) appears to be beneficial primarily in situations where learners engage in greater elaboration of new material than they might otherwise (McDaniel, Waddill, & Einstein, 1988; McNamara & Healy, 1995; Wiley & Voss, 1999).

Elaboration probably facilitates long-term memory for several reasons. First, elaborated information is less likely to be confused with other, similar information stored in long-term memory (Ellis & Hunt, 1983). Second, elaboration provides additional means through which the information can later be retrieved (J. R. Anderson, 1990, 1995); in a sense, it provides more places to "look" for the information. And third, elaboration may help with inferences about what the information was *likely* to have been when the information itself cannot be accurately recalled (J. R. Anderson, 1990).

Visual Imagery

Without looking back at Figure 8.4, can you recall what the "midget playing a trombone in a telephone booth" looked like? Can you remember the "early bird who caught a very strong worm"? If so, then you may have stored these things not only as the verbal labels I gave them but also in terms of **visual imagery**—that is, as mental "pictures" that captured how the figures actually looked.

As we will discover in the next chapter, theorists haven't completely pinned down the exact nature of visual imagery. Nevertheless, research consistently indicates that forming visual images can be a powerful means of storing information in long-term memory. People of all ages have a remarkably accurate memory for visual information (Brown & Campione, 1972; Bruck, Cavanagh, & Ceci, 1991; Levin & Mayer, 1993; Standing, 1973). For instance, in an experiment by Shepard (1967), college students looked at more than 600 pictures (color photos and illustrations from magazines), with an average inspection time of less than six seconds per picture. The students were then given pairs of dissimilar pictures and asked to identify which picture in each pair they had seen; they were able to do so with 98% accuracy. (In comparison, their accuracy on a similar task using words was only 88%.) Furthermore, images may be relatively enduring. For instance, in a study by Mandler and Ritchey (1977), people's memory for meaningfully organized pictures showed little decline over a 4-month period.

People's memory for visual material is often better than it is for strictly verbal material (Clark & Paivio, 1991; Dewhurst & Conway, 1994; Edens & McCormick, 2000; Shepard, 1967). In fact, people tend to remember information better when it is presented in *both* verbal and visual forms, rather than in only one form or the other (Kulhavy, Lee, & Caterino, 1985; Paivio, 1975, 1986; Sadoski & Paivio, 2001).

Especially when new material is concrete and easily visualizable, learners sometimes create their *own* mental images (e.g., Cooper, Tindall-Ford, Chandler, & Sweller, 2001; Gambrell & Bales, 1986; Sadoski & Quast, 1990; Thrailkill & Ormrod, 1994). For example, when students form visual images while reading stories or listening to explanations of school subject matter, they more effectively understand and remember what they have read or heard (Cothern, Konopak, & Willis, 1990; Dewhurst & Conway, 1994; Sadoski & Paivio, 2001). Furthermore, specifically instructing people to form visual images of what they are studying helps them learn the material more quickly and remember it more effectively (M. S. Jones, Levin, Levin, & Beitzel, 2000; Pressley, Johnson, Symons, McGoldrick, & Kurita, 1989). For instance, when students are instructed to form visual images connecting pairs of objects, memory for those pairs is enhanced (Bower, 1972). Accordingly, imagery provides the foundation for a number of memory strategies called *mnemonics,* which we'll consider in chapter 12.

Children's facility to form and manipulate visual images increases with age (Kosslyn, Margolis, Barrett, Goldknopf, & Daly, 1990; Pressley, 1977, 1982). Yet learners of all ages differ considerably in their ability to use visual imagery: Some form images quickly and easily, whereas others form them only slowly and with difficulty (Behrmann, 2000; Clark & Paivio, 1991; Kosslyn, 1985; Riding & Calvey, 1981).

It is important to note, however, that even for "good visualizers," visual images tend to be imprecise representations of external objects, with many details omitted, blurry, or altered (Chambers & Reisberg, 1985; Loftus & Bell, 1975; Reed, 1974; Sadoski & Paivio, 2001). They are sometimes distorted by a learner's general knowledge, as an early study by Carmichael, Hogan, and Walters (1932) illustrates. An experimenter asked adults to remember simple pictures like the ones shown on the left side of Figure 8.6. Two groups were given different sets of labels for the pictures, and the participants tended to remember the pictures in ways that more closely fit the specific labels they were given. For instance, as you can see in Figure 8.6, the first picture was reproduced differently depending on whether it had been labeled as eyeglasses or dumbbells. Similarly, recall of the second picture was influenced by its identity as a kidney bean or a canoe.

Because images tend to be incomplete and are sometimes inaccurate, they aren't always useful when precise, detailed information must be stored. For example, many educators have advocated the use of visual imagery in learning to spell (e.g., Harris, 1985; Radebaugh, 1985), and some research has provided support for this practice (Kernaghan & Woloshyn, 1994; Roberts & Ehri, 1983).

Figure 8.6

Experimental stimuli and examples of participants' reproductions, from Carmichael, Hogan, & Walters (1932). Adapted from "An Experimental Study of the Effect of Language on the Reproduction of Visually Perceived Form" by L. Carmichael, H. P. Hogan, and A. A. Walters, 1932, *Journal of Experimental Psychology, 15,* p. 80.

Original Stimuli

"eye glasses"   "dumbbells"

"kidney bean"   "canoe"

Examples of Reproductions

Although imagery may occasionally help spelling, one's visual image of a word will not necessarily include *all* of its letters (Ormrod & Jenkins, 1988). To illustrate, my mental image of the word *silhouette,* until I looked it up in the dictionary just now, was something along these lines:

sil꜀꜀꜀ette

I had an image of the word that was sufficient to recognize it when I read it but not sufficiently detailed for spelling it correctly.

Of the six long-term memory storage processes we've just examined, the last three—internal organization, elaboration, and visual imagery—are clearly constructive in nature. Each of them involves combining new information with things already in long-term memory. When we organize information, we often use a familiar framework (perhaps a hierarchy of well-known categories) to give new material a meaningful structure. When we elaborate, we use both new information and our existing knowledge to construct a reasonable interpretation of an event. When we use visual imagery, we often create those images for ourselves based on what we know about how objects typically appear.

How Procedural Knowledge Is Acquired

Some of the procedures people learn—for example, driving a car with a stick shift, planting flowers, spiking a volleyball—consist primarily of overt behaviors. Many others—for instance, writing an essay, solving for *x* in an algebraic equation, surfing the Internet—have a significant mental component as well. Most procedures probably involve a combination of physical behaviors and mental activities.

Procedural knowledge ranges from relatively simple actions (e.g., holding a pencil correctly or using scissors) to far more complex ones. Complex procedures are usually not learned in one fell swoop. Instead, they are acquired slowly over a period of time, often only with a great deal of practice (Beilock & Carr, 2003; Charness, Tuffiash, & Jastrzembski, 2004; Ericsson, 2003; Proctor & Dutta, 1995).

Researchers are just beginning to identify the storage processes involved in acquiring procedural knowledge. To some degree, of course, learners store physical procedures in terms of actual behaviors (Keele, 1981; Willingham, 1999; Willingham & Goedert-Eschmann, 1999). Yet some procedures, complex ones especially, may also be learned as declarative knowledge—in other words, as *information* about how to do something (J. R. Anderson, 1983a; Beilock & Carr, 2003). Learners may initially use such information to guide them as they execute a procedure (recall our discussion of self-instructions in chapter 6). To the extent that they must do so, however, their performance is likely to be slow and laborious and require a lot of concentration (i.e., it consumes considerable working memory capacity). As learners continue to practice the procedure, their performance gradually becomes faster, easier, and more efficient. People who show exceptional talent in a particular skill—say, in figure skating or playing the piano—typically practice a great deal, usually a minimum of three to four hours a day over a period of 10 years or more (Ericsson, 1996).

Exactly how the informational and behavioral aspects of procedural knowledge are interrelated in the learning process is not yet clear. Some theorists (e.g., J. R. Anderson, 1983a, 1987;

Beilock & Carr, 2003) has suggested that declarative knowledge is acquired first and, with practice, gradually *evolves* into procedural knowledge. Other theorists (Willingham & Goedert-Eschmann, 1999) have proposed that people simultaneously learn both information and behaviors in the process of acquiring a new procedure. However, people learn the information—that is, they learn explicit declarative knowledge—fairly quickly, whereas they learn the appropriate behaviors in a more gradual, *implicit* fashion. When the behaviors are still imperfect and unreliable, people use their declarative information to help them remember what they need to do, presumably by engaging in overt or subvocal self-instructions. Such verbal self-support becomes less necessary as they increasingly fine-tune and master the behavioral aspects of the procedure.

Some of the storage processes we've already discussed play a role in acquiring procedural knowledge as well as declarative knowledge. For instance, verbally rehearsing a sequence of steps in a motor skill enhances people's ability to perform the skill (Weiss & Klint, 1987). Illustrations or live demonstrations of a procedure, which presumably foster visual imagery, are also quite helpful (R. M. Gagné, 1985; Kitsantas et al., 2000; Zimmerman & Kitsantas, 1999). In fact, imagining *oneself* performing an action (e.g., executing a gymnastics skill or a basketball shot) can enhance acquisition of a procedure, although such imagined behaviors are obviously not as effective as actual practice (Feltz, Landers, & Becker, 1988; Kosslyn, 1985).

Does New Knowledge Require a Consolidation Period?

As we've seen, much procedural knowledge is acquired gradually over time. However, I've implied that long-term storage of declarative information can sometimes be quite rapid. For example, imagine that you encounter an intriguing new fact—*Attention is essential for learning*, let's say. You elaborate on this fact: "That explains why I never remember anything when I try to study while watching TV!" Through such elaboration, you're able to store the fact very quickly in long-term memory, where it immediately "sticks." But is the stick an immediate one? Some researchers don't think so.

In particular, some psychologists believe that the neural underpinnings of new memories needs some **consolidation** time—perhaps a few minutes or a few hours, or perhaps even longer (e.g., Lee, Everitt, & Thomas, 2004; Wixted, 2005; Woodman & Vogel, 2005). Considerable evidence for such consolidation comes from studies of **retrograde amnesia:** Accident victims who suffer serious head traumas often cannot remember events immediately leading up to their accidents, and sometimes they also forget events that occurred in the last few weeks, months, or even years before their accidents (Siegel, 1999; Wixted, 2005).

At this point, theorists can only speculate about the processes involved in the consolidation aspect of long-term storage. Possibly it involves some sort of low-level, unconscious activation or rehearsal (Siegel, 1999; Woodman & Vogel, 2005). It appears, too, that sleep plays a role in consolidation, although theorists disagree about exactly what that role might be (e.g., see Massimini et al., 2005; Stickgold, 2005).

FACTORS AFFECTING LONG-TERM MEMORY STORAGE

A number of factors affect how learners store information in long-term memory. In this section, we will consider cognitive factors—working memory, prior knowledge, prior misconceptions, and expectations—and behavioral factors—verbalization, enactment, repetition, and review—that appear to be especially influential.

Working Memory

As we have seen, long-term memory storage is most likely to be effective when new material is connected with existing knowledge. For learners to make a connection between a new piece of information and a piece of information that they already have, they must be *aware* of the relationship between the two. In other words, both pieces must be in working memory at the same time (Daneman, 1987; Kintsch & van Dijk, 1978; Mayer, Moreno, Boire, & Vagge, 1999; Nuthall, 2000).

An experiment by Hayes-Roth and Thorndyke (1979) illustrates this idea. In this experiment, students read one of two passages describing a fictional country. The same pieces of information appeared in both passages but in a different order: In one passage, related pieces of information appeared in sequential sentences, whereas in the other, they appeared in separate paragraphs. Students more frequently made connections between two related pieces of information (and thus could draw inferences from them) when those pieces of information were presented one right after the other, presumably because both items were more likely to be in working memory at the same time.

People don't necessarily have to experience two things in sequence to make connections between them, however. In many cases, new information reminds learners of something they already know, leading them to retrieve that knowledge to working memory. In other cases, a wise teacher might point out the relationships between the new information and previously learned material, thus encouraging retrieval of relevant prior knowledge.

The less working memory capacity learners have, of course, the less "room" they have to think about how various bits of information might fit together. For example, students with seemingly "smaller" working memories draw fewer inferences from what they read than do students with "bigger" ones (Linderholm & van den Broek, 2002; Oakhill, Cain, & Yuill, 1998).

Prior Knowledge

People can connect new information to prior knowledge only when they actually *have* knowledge that relates to what they're learning. One of the most important factors affecting long-term memory storage, then, is what a person *already knows* (Ausubel et al., 1978; Haskell, 2001; Novak, 1998; Shapiro, 2004). Learners who have a large body of information already stored in long-term memory have more ideas to which they can relate their new experiences and so can more easily engage in such processes as meaningful learning and elaboration. Learners who lack relevant knowledge must resort to inefficient rote-learning strategies. In other words, the rich (in knowledge) get richer, and the poor stay relatively poor.

Our prior knowledge about the world often affects our ability to encode even the most basic kinds of information. For example, when you see someone walking away from you, that person does not appear to shrink, even though the image on your retinas is in fact getting smaller. You have learned from experience that people do not shrink just because they move away from you, and so you make certain mental adjustments regarding people's sizes. What would happen if you had no such experience with perceiving people and other things at varying distances? Anthropologist Colin Turnbull (1961) observed exactly this situation while studying the Ba Mbuti pygmies, a tribe living in the thick jungle of the Congo rain forest. With no open spaces in their environment, the Ba Mbuti never had the opportunity to see objects more than a few feet away from them. Turnbull described an incident in which a member of the tribe, a man named Kenge, traveled for the first time to an area of open grasslands. When Kenge spied a herd of buffalo grazing in the far distance, he asked, "What insects are those?" and dismissed as folly Turnbull's reply that they were actually buffalo that were very far away. A short time later, as the men approached the buffalo by car, Kenge grew increasingly frightened as he watched the buffalo "grow" in size, fearful that a magic trick was being played on him.

Numerous studies have illustrated the importance of previous knowledge for encoding and storing new information (e.g., Alexander, Kulikowich, & Schulze, 1994; Dole, Duffy, Roehler, & Pearson, 1991; Gauntt, 1991; W. S. Hall, 1989; Machiels-Bongaerts, Schmidt, & Boshuizen, 1991; Novak & Musonda, 1991; Rouet, Favart, Britt, & Perfetti, 1997; Schneider, 1993). As an example, some of my colleagues and I once conducted a study of how well people from different disciplines learn and remember maps (Ormrod, Ormrod, Wagner, & McCallin, 1988). We asked faculty members and students in three disciplines—geography, sociology, and education—to study two maps and then reproduce them from memory. The first of these maps, shown in Figure 8.7, depicts a city arranged in accordance with usual citylike patterns; that is, its arrangement is *logical*. Notice how the downtown business district is located at a point where it can be easily reached from different directions (this is typical), and the mills, lumberyard, and low-income

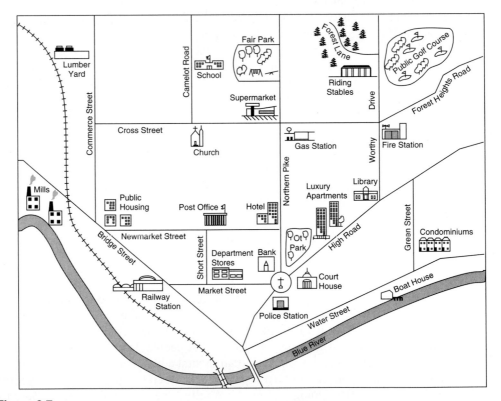

Figure 8.7
The logical city map from Ormrod et al. (1988).
Reprinted from "Reconceptualizing Map Learning" by J. E. Ormrod, R. K. Ormrod, E. D. Wagner, & R. C. McCallin, 1988, *American Journal of Psychology, 101,* p. 428. Reprinted with permission of the University of Illinois Press.

housing are situated near the railroad tracks (also typical). The second map, shown in Figure 8.8, is on a larger scale and depicts several political regions (countries, perhaps). Several things about this map make no sense; that is, its arrangement is *illogical*. Notice how a river originates in the plains and runs *up* into the mountains, transportation networks do not interconnect, and towns are not located at transportation junctions. My colleagues and I predicted that geographers would remember more of the logical city map than either sociologists or educators because they could use their knowledge of typical urban patterns to learn the map meaningfully. We also predicted that the geographers would have no advantage over folks in the other disciplines on the illogical "countries" map because geographic principles were largely inapplicable in making sense of the map. Our predictions were confirmed: Geographers showed better recall than the other two groups for the logical city map but not for the illogical countries map. Because we had asked the participants to "think aloud" as they studied the maps, we were also able to examine the strategies they employed. As we expected, the geographers learned the maps more meaningfully than the other groups, and all three groups learned the city map more meaningfully than the countries map. But our nongeographers used primarily rote-learning strategies, mostly in the form of simple repetition.

Other studies have yielded similar results. For example, children who know a lot about spiders remember more from reading a passage about spiders than do children who initially know very little (Pearson, Hansen, & Gordon, 1979). People who know a lot about baseball or basketball can remember more new facts about those sports and more about what happened in a particular game

Figure 8.8
The illogical country map from Ormrod et al. (1988).
Reprinted from "Reconceptualizing Map Learning" by J. E. Ormrod, R. K. Ormrod, E. D. Wagner, & R. C. McCallin, 1988, *American Journal of Psychology, 101*, p. 429. Reprinted with permission of the University of Illinois Press.

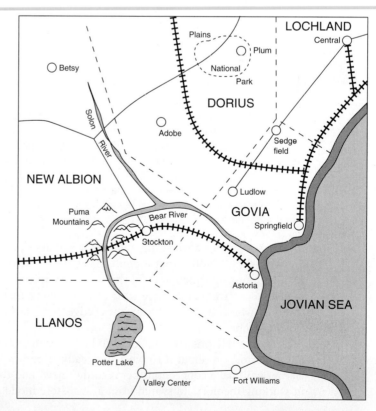

than can people who are relatively uninformed about the sports (Hall & Edmondson, 1992; Kuhara-Kojima & Hatano, 1991; Spilich, Vesonder, Chiesi, & Voss, 1979). Experts at the game of chess can remember the locations of chess pieces on a chessboard more accurately than chess novices, but only when the placement of pieces is logical within the framework of an actual game (Chase & Simon, 1973; deGroot, 1965). Second graders in Brazil who have experience as street vendors learn basic arithmetic more easily than students without street-vending experience (Saxe, 1988). Eighth graders who know a lot about American history engage in more elaborative processing when they read a history textbook (e.g., they are more likely to summarize the material, make inferences, and identify unanswered questions) than classmates who have less history knowledge (Hamman et al., 1995).

Although older children and adults usually learn most things more easily than younger children, we sometimes find the reverse to be true if younger children have more knowledge about the subject matter (Chi, 1978; Lindberg, 1991; Schneider, Körkel, & Weinert, 1990). For example, children who are expert chess players can better remember where chess pieces are on a chessboard than adults who are relative novices at chess (Chi, 1978). Similarly, 8-year-olds who know a lot about soccer remember more from a passage they read about soccer than 12-year-olds who know very little about the game (Schneider et al., 1990).

Because everyone has somewhat different knowledge about the world, people are likely to elaborate on the same information in different ways and, as a result, to learn different things. For example, how would you interpret this newspaper headline (from Leinhardt, 1992)?

VIKINGS CREAM DOLPHINS

Your interpretation might depend on whether you are more attuned to American football or to possible early Scandinavian cuisine (Leinhardt, 1992). And consider the following passage from a study conducted by Anderson, Reynolds, Schallert, and Goetz (1977):

> Rocky slowly got up from the mat, planning his escape. He hesitated a moment and thought. Things were not going well. What bothered him most was being held, especially since the charge against him had been weak. He considered his present situation. The lock that held him was strong but he thought he could break it. He knew, however, that his timing would have to be perfect. Rocky was aware that it was because of his early roughness that he had been penalized so severely—much too severely from his point of view. The situation was becoming frustrating; the pressure had been grinding on him for too long. He was being ridden unmercifully. Rocky was getting angry now. He felt he was ready to make his move. He knew that his success or failure would depend on what he did in the next few seconds. (Anderson et al., 1977, p. 372)

Is this story about a wrestling match? Or is it about a prison escape? Read the passage again, and you should notice that it could be about either one. Anderson and his colleagues found that students' interpretations of the story depended on their background: Physical education majors more frequently viewed it as a wrestling match, whereas music education majors (most of whom had little or no knowledge of wrestling) were more likely to interpret it as a prison escape.

It is entirely possible, however, to have existing knowledge about a topic and yet *not* relate new information about it to what is already stored in long-term memory. As noted earlier, a learner will make connections between the "new" and the "old" only if both are simultaneously in working memory. To switch from a dual-store model of memory to an activation model for a moment, we might say that both the new and the old must be *activated* at the same time. As we consider instructional strategies later in the chapter, we'll identify a variety of ways in which teachers might promote meaningful learning and elaboration by activating students' prior knowledge.

Prior Misconceptions

When people engage in elaboration, they use what they already know about a topic to expand on, and presumably make better sense of, new information. But what happens when people use inaccurate "knowledge"—**misconceptions**[3]—to elaborate? If people think that new information is clearly "wrong" within the context of what they currently believe about the world, they may ignore the information altogether. Alternatively, they may distort the information to be consistent with their "knowledge" and as a result learn something quite different from what they actually saw, heard, or read (Dole et al., 1991; Lipson, 1982; Porat, 2004; Roth & Anderson, 1988; Sneider & Pulos, 1983). In some instances, then, having *mis*information is more detrimental than having *no* information about a topic.

We saw one instance of such *mis*learning in Bartlett's (1932) study involving "The War of the Ghosts": Many students distorted the story to make it consistent with English culture. A study by Eaton, Anderson, and Smith (1984) provides another example. Fifth graders spent several weeks studying a unit on light in their science curriculum. A pretest had shown that many students had a particular misconception about light: They believed that people see things only because the light shines on them and makes them brighter. During the unit, the correct explanation of human sight was presented: Light reflects off objects and continues to travel *to the eye,* which then detects the light and so makes vision possible. Despite reading and hearing this information, most students retained their misconceptions about vision in a test given at the end of the unit. Only 24 to 30% of them correctly indicated in their answers that light must travel not only from the light source to the object but also from the object to the eye.

Prior misconceptions can wreak havoc even at the college level (Bishop & Anderson, 1990; Clement, 1982; Kendeou & van den Broek, 2005). For example, undergraduates who study the nature of vision in a psychology course—including the idea that light must travel from the object to the eye—often leave the course thinking that vision occurs because something travels in the *opposite* direction—that is, from the eye to the object (Winer, Cottrell, Gregg, Fournier, & Bica, 2002). Similarly, students in teacher education programs may disregard a professor's definitions for certain concepts (instead relying on their previous, often very different understandings of the concepts), and they are likely to ignore any recommendations for teaching practice that contradict their own beliefs about "good teaching" (Holt-Reynolds, 1992). I have seen such phenomena in some of my own undergraduate teacher education classes. For instance, some students stick to their existing definitions of such terms as *negative reinforcement* and *elaboration* even though I point out quite emphatically that a psychologist defines these words differently than a layperson does. And, despite the evidence I present regarding the effectiveness of meaningful learning, a few students continue to insist that rote learning is a better approach.

---

[3]Some theorists prefer terms such as *naive beliefs* or *naive conceptions* to reflect the fact that such inaccuracies, though not a good match with contemporary scientific understandings, may be reasonable conclusions from a child's early knowledge and experiences.

Teachers often present information to students with the assumption that the information will correct students' erroneous beliefs. Unfortunately, what often happens instead is that students stubbornly hold onto their preconceived notions about the world and distort the new information to fit those notions. As we examine the nature of *personal theories* in chapter 9, we'll look in greater depth at the kinds of misbeliefs children and adults are likely to have.

Expectations

Read this sentence:

> I pledge allegiance to the flag of the United Stetes of American, and to the Repulbic for which it stends, one nation, under God, indivsible, with liberty and justice for all.

You may have noticed one or two typographical errors in the passage. But did you catch them all? Altogether there were *five* mistakes, as italicized below:

> I pledge allegiance to the flag of the United St*e*tes of America*n*, and to the Repul*b*ic for which it st*e*nds, one nation, under God, indiv*s*ible, with liberty and justice for all.

If you didn't notice all of the errors—and many people don't—then your expectation of what words *should* have been there influenced your interpretation of the sentence. If you have seen and heard the U.S. Pledge of Allegiance as many times as I have, you know that the phrase "I pledge allegiance . . . " is usually followed by a certain sequence of words, and so you may have seen what you expected to see.

We often form expectations about the things we will see and hear—expectations based on our knowledge, and perhaps also on our misconceptions, about how the world typically operates. Such expectations can influence the ways in which we encode and store new information in long-term memory (Kaiser, McCloskey, & Proffitt, 1986; Schacter, 1999). In many cases we perceive and learn something more quickly when we have a good idea ahead of time about the information we are going to receive, perhaps because relevant portions of long-term memory have already been activated (recall the discussion of *priming* in chapter 7). The process of reading provides a good example. Beginning readers pay close attention to the letters on the page as they read and, as a result, often read slowly and comprehend little. More mature readers tend not to look as carefully at the printed page. Instead, they rely on such things as context, sentence syntax, prior knowledge about a topic, and expectations about what the author is trying to communicate in order to draw hasty, although usually accurate, conclusions about what is on the page. It is precisely because mature readers *do* jump to conclusions that they read so quickly and efficiently (Dole et al., 1991; Owens, 1996; Smith, 1988).

Yet such an efficient approach to reading has a potential drawback as well: Readers risk jumping to the *wrong* conclusions and misperceiving or misinterpreting what is on the page. They may have difficulty proofreading accurately, "seeing" correctly spelled words that are actually misspelled. And they may have trouble learning how to spell the many new vocabulary words (e.g., *psychology, environment, reinforcement*) that they encounter in their reading (Frith, 1978, 1980; Ormrod, 1985, 1986a, 1986b, 1986c). For example, people frequently misread my name—Jeanne Ormrod—as "Jeanne Orm*o*nd," an error that I find quite annoying. But let's face it: Ormrod is an unusual name, whereas Ormond is more common. One can almost not blame readers who see *Orm* . . . and just assume that the rest of the word is . . . *ond*. Using the first few letters of a word to identify the word is a common strategy in reading (Lima, 1993).

Earlier in the chapter, I introduced the concept of *ambiguous stimulus*, a stimulus that can be interpreted in more than one way. Ambiguous stimuli are especially likely to be encoded in accordance with people's expectations (Eysenck & Keane, 1990; Sherman & Bessenoff, 1999). For instance, when I show the man–mouse picture (Figure 8.3) to students in my classes, I consistently find that the great majority of students who have been led to expect a mouse—by previously viewing a picture that is clearly a rodent—do in fact see a mouse or rat. Students who have similarly been led to expect a man see the bald-headed man. And notice how your expectations concerning how people typically behave influence your initial interpretation of the first statement in this verbal exchange (from Gleitman, 1985, p. 432):

> "We're going to have my grandmother for Thanksgiving dinner."
> "You are? Well, we're going to have turkey."

The behaviors we see other people exhibit are often subject to numerous interpretations and so are prime examples of ambiguous stimuli. For example, if you see me smile at you (my behavior), you might draw any number of possible conclusions: I'm happy to see you, I'm *not* happy to see you but am being polite, I detest you but need a favor, I think the shirt you're wearing looks ridiculous, and so on. People tend to interpret others' behaviors in accordance with their own expectations (Juvonen, 1991; Nisbett & Bellows, 1977; Ritts, Patterson, & Tubbs, 1992; Snyder & Swann, 1978). They expect desirable behaviors from a person they like or admire and so are likely to perceive that person's behaviors in a positive light—a phenomenon known as the **halo effect**. In much the same way, they expect inappropriate behaviors from a person they dislike, and their perceptions of that person's behaviors are biased accordingly— we could call this the **horns effect**. As an example, imagine that Mr. Brighteyes, a teacher, has a student named Mary who consistently performs well in classwork, and another, Susan, who more typically turns in sloppy and incomplete work. Let's say that both girls turn in an assignment of marginal quality. Mr. Brighteyes is likely to *over*rate Mary's performance and *under*rate Susan's.

Many factors affect people's expectations, and hence their interpretations, of another's behaviors. For instance, people often expect higher-quality performance from people who are clean and well groomed than from people who are dirty and disheveled—hence the adage "Dress for success." Teachers expect well-behaved students to be more academically successful than poorly behaved students; thus, their judgments of a specific student's academic performance are likely to be influenced by the way the student behaves in the classroom (Bennett, Gottesman, Rock, & Cerullo, 1993). Stereotypes about people of different genders, races, ethnic backgrounds, and socioeconomic groups also have an effect (Darley & Gross, 1983; C. Reyna, 2000; Sherman & Bessenoff, 1999; Stephan & Stephan, 2000). An experiment by Darley and Gross (1983) provides an example. Undergraduate students were told that they were participating in a study on teacher evaluation methods and were asked to view a videotape of a fourth grader named Hannah. Two versions of the videotape were designed to give two different impressions about Hannah's socioeconomic status; Hannah's clothing, the kind of playground on which she played, and information about her parents' occupations indirectly conveyed to some students that she was from a low socioeconomic background and to others that she was from a high socioeconomic background. All students then watched Hannah taking an oral achievement test (on which she performed at grade level) and were asked to rate Hannah on a number of characteristics. Students who had been led to believe that Hannah came from wealthy surroundings rated her ability well above grade level, whereas students who believed she lived in an impoverished environment evaluated her as being below grade level. The two groups of students also rated Hannah differently in terms of her work habits, motivation, social skills, and general maturity.

Individuals' expectations and perceptions may even be influenced by other people's names. In an experiment by Harari and McDavid (1973), elementary school teachers were asked to grade essays written by 10-year-old children. Teachers who read an essay supposedly written by "Lisa" gave it a better grade than teachers who read the same essay but thought it was written by "Bertha." In the same way, "David" received better grades than "Hubert." Students' essays are prime examples of ambiguous stimuli, because the criteria for perceiving (grading) them are typically subjective and require considerable teacher judgment.

Verbalization

An activity that clearly facilitates long-term memory storage is **verbalization**—talking or writing about an experience that either has happened or is happening. Children often talk with their parents or teachers about past and current events, and their memory for those events is enhanced as a result (Haden, Ornstein, Eckerman, & Didow, 2001; Hemphill & Snow, 1996; McGuigan & Salmon, 2004; K. Nelson, 1996; Tessler & Nelson, 1994). For older children and adults, verbalization can also take the form of **self-explanation,** in which learners talk to themselves in an attempt to understand difficult subject matter. For example, when reading a challenging textbook chapter, students might paraphrase the parts they understand, identify parts with which they're having trouble (e.g., "This is confusing"), draw inferences from the ideas presented, and summarize what they've read. When students are encouraged to engage in overt self-explanation as they study something, they are more likely to elaborate on it and so better understand and remember the content (Atkinson, Derry, Renkl, & Wortham, 2000; de Bruin, Whittingham, Hillebrand, & Rikers, 2003; deLeeuw & Chi, 2003).

Writing provides yet another form of verbalization that can facilitate long-term memory storage. For instance, when students write about what they are reading in their textbooks—answering study questions, relating the material to things they already know, analyzing various points of view, and so on—they are more likely to engage in such storage processes as meaningful learning, organization, and elaboration (Benton, 1997; Burnett & Kastman, 1997; Durst & Newell, 1989; Greene & Ackerman, 1995; Konopak, Martin, & Martin, 1990; Marshall, 1987).

Enactment

By **enactment,** I mean engaging in an overt psychomotor behavior—actually *doing* something—that in some way reflects what is being learned. The importance of enactment has popped up in previous chapters under different guises: In our discussion of behaviorism (chapters 3 through 5), we noted the importance of *active responding* in learning, and in our discussion of social cognitive theory (chapter 6), we noted the importance of *motor reproduction* in modeling.

A wide variety of physical actions seem to promote long-term memory storage. Young children more easily remember geometric shapes when they can actually draw the shapes (Heindel & Kose, 1990). Children in the upper elementary grades better understand what they learn in science when they create illustrations of scientific concepts; for instance, they might show how the nervous system works by drawing a diagram of a neuron, or they might illustrate gravity, friction, and kinetic energy by drawing a picture of a roller coaster (Edens & Potter, 2001; Van Meter, 2001). Undergraduate students studying physics can better apply the things they learn about how pulley systems work when they can experiment with actual pulleys rather than when simply looking at diagrams of various pulley systems (Ferguson & Hegarty, 1995).

Physical enactment is, of course, especially helpful when people are learning complex motor skills—that is, when they are acquiring procedural knowledge. In such instances, people typically learn most effectively when they get regular feedback about how they are doing (R. M. Gagné, 1985; Proctor & Dutta, 1995). Sometimes such feedback follows directly from their performance; for instance, a new tennis player can see where he hits each ball, and a new driver knows that she needs more practice with a standard transmission if she keeps stalling the engine every time she tries to move the car forward. In other cases, however, people learn more effectively when a more advanced individual (e.g., a coach) commends them for proper form or gives them constructive suggestions on what they might do differently (Kladopoulos & McComas, 2001; Kluger & DeNisi, 1998; Schunk & Zimmerman, 1997).

As we discovered in chapter 4, behaviorists think of feedback as a form of *positive reinforcement*. And as we noted in chapter 6, social cognitive theorists propose that feedback affects learners' *self-efficacy*. Here we see a third role that feedback can play: a source of *information* that can help learners improve their performance. Whenever possible, teachers should provide such information immediately so that students can store it in working memory simultaneously with their recollection of what they have just done; in this way, the two are more easily integrated (J. R. Anderson, 1987).

Repetition and Review

As we've already seen, rehearsal is probably a relatively *in*effective way to promote long-term memory storage. In contrast to such short-lived rehearsal, reviewing and practicing information and procedures at periodic intervals over the course of a few weeks, months, or years clearly enhances retention and performance. This principle seems to hold true for people of all ages, even young infants (Anderson & Schooler, 1991; Belfiore, Skinner, & Ferkis, 1995; Dempster, 1991; Péladeau, Forget, & Gagné, 2003; Proctor & Dutta, 1995; Rovee-Collier, 1993; West & Stanovich, 1991).

In essence, recent researchers have supported early verbal learning theorists' finding that *overlearning* facilitates memory. A second verbal learning principle is also relevant here: Additional learning and practice sessions are typically more effective when they are spaced out over a period of time—that is, when they reflect *distributed practice* rather than *massed practice* (J. R. Anderson, 1990; Bahrick et al., 1993; Dempster, 1991). In the lingo of contemporary cognitive psychology, this phenomenon is known as the **spacing effect.** It is important to note that initial learning is sometimes a bit *slower* when it is spread out over time; its benefits are most clearly seen when we look at *long-term retention* rather than speed of initial learning (Bahrick et al., 1993; Rawson & Kintsch, 2005).

Mere exposure to information—no matter how often—is not enough, however. As is true for most learning, a person must, at a minimum, pay attention to the information. For instance, in one classic experiment, American college students were shown drawings of 15 different versions of a Lincoln penny. Despite the thousands of times that the students had seen and handled pennies, fewer than half of them could pick out the correct version (Nickerson & Adams, 1979). When searching for pennies, people don't need to look at minute details to distinguish them from other coins because their color alone is a surefire indicator.

By reviewing and practicing what we have learned over a period of time, we probably accomplish several things. First, we engage in additional processing—processing that may allow us to elaborate on learned information in new ways and so understand it more thoroughly (Dempster, 1991; McDaniel & Masson, 1985). Second, by reviewing the same information repeatedly, especially in different contexts, we form more and stronger associations with other things in memory; as a result, we can more readily recall the information when needed at a future time (J. R. Anderson, 1990, 1995; Calfee, 1981). Continued practice seems to have a third benefit as well: It promotes automaticity, our next topic of discussion.

Development of Automaticity

Schneider and Shiffrin (1977; Shiffrin & Schneider, 1977) have distinguished between two types of information processing: controlled and automatic. **Controlled processing** requires much of a learner's attention and is likely to use most or all of the learner's working memory capacity. In other words, controlled processing requires conscious thought and effort. An example is the cognitive processing necessary for learning to drive a car. I still remember the summer evening many years ago when my father tried to teach me to drive a standard shift in our 1951 Ford convertible (no, I'm not *that* old; the car was almost an antique at the time). Trying to steer the car in the right direction while simultaneously monitoring the speed and negotiating the stick shift and clutch consumed all of my attention and working memory capacity. In fact, my working memory must have been overflowing, because I kept forgetting to step on the clutch, thus jerking the car forward and almost catapulting my father into outer space. (Dad enrolled me in a drivers' education class the following morning.)

In contrast, **automatic processing**, also known as **automaticity**, occurs with little or no conscious attention or effort and requires little working memory capacity; it is, in a sense, "thoughtless." Controlled processes become increasingly automatic through repetition and practice (Beilock & Carr, 2003; Cheng, 1985; Schneider & Shiffrin, 1977; Shiffrin & Schneider, 1977). As I continued to drive that 1951 Ford, I gradually became more proficient, and I was able to devote less and less mental effort to the task of driving. With several months of persistent practice, I was cruising Main Street with my friends, tapping my fingers to early Beatles music on the radio, munching McDonald's french fries (12 cents a bag in those days), and watching the sidewalk for male classmates of particular interest. Even though my car had a standard transmission, driving had essentially become an automatic activity for me.

As you should recall from chapter 7, working memory has a limited capacity, and so people can usually attend to only one demanding task—one task that requires conscious, controlled processing—at a time. However, people can probably attend to several tasks simultaneously when each of them involves only automatic processing. How many mental activities they can conduct at the same time, then, depends on how automatically they can perform each activity.

Many academic tasks require performing a number of "subtasks" at more or less the same time. For successful performance of these tasks, some of the subtasks should probably be automatic (Lesgold, 1983; Mayer & Wittrock, 1996; Perfetti, 1983; Resnick, 1989; Resnick & Johnson, 1988). Consider the case of reading. Comprehending what one reads is often a difficult task involving controlled, conscious effort. If students are to understand what they read, basic reading processes such as letter and word identification must occur automatically. In fact, research is clear on this point: The more effort a student must devote to identifying the words on the page, the lower the student's comprehension of a passage is apt to be (Greene & Royer, 1994; LaBerge & Samuels, 1974; Perfetti & Lesgold, 1979).

Writing, too, is a multifaceted process that can easily exceed the limits of working memory unless some processes are automatic (Berninger, Fuller, & Whitaker, 1996; Flower & Hayes, 1981; McCutchen, 1996). Good writers devote most of their attention to the communicative aspect of writing—that is, to expressing their thoughts in a clear, logical, and organized fashion (Birnbaum, 1982; Pianko, 1979). Apparently, these individuals have already learned the mechanics of writing (spelling, grammar, punctuation, etc.) thoroughly enough to apply them automatically. In contrast, poor writers devote a considerable amount of attention to writing mechanics and so can give little thought to communicating their ideas clearly (Birnbaum, 1982; Pianko, 1979). Becoming a good writer, then, is at least partly a matter of automatizing basic skills. People can devote themselves to the task of clear self-expression only if they are not bogged down with concerns about subject-verb agreement or the correct spelling of *psychology*.

Similarly, some aspects of mathematics—especially basic math facts—need to become second nature (e.g., R. M. Gagné, 1983). For example, in my course on educational assessment, students must be able to solve problems such as the following before they can learn to interpret intelligence test (IQ) scores:

$$\frac{70-100}{15} = ?$$

To solve such a problem easily, my students must have certain arithmetic facts at their fingertips; in this case, they must be able to subtract 100 from 70 quickly and must automatically recognize that −30 divided by 15 equals −2. I have frequently observed that when my students must consciously and effortfully calculate a simple arithmetic problem, they lose sight of the overall task they are trying to accomplish.

Earlier in the chapter, I emphasized the importance of meaningful learning. Meaningful learning is certainly important for basic knowledge and skills. To the extent possible, students must be able to make sense of simple facts and procedures, relating them to other things already known about the world. At the same time, meaningful learning is not enough for things that must be recalled quickly and automatically. These things should be repeated and practiced often enough that they become second nature.

Yet automaticity has its downsides as well. For one thing, people may perform habitual actions without even thinking about them, to the point where they can't remember whether they've done them or not (Reason & Mycielska, 1982). For example, sometimes I know that I've fed the dog only by checking his dish to see if it's still damp, and sometimes I know that I've let the cat in for the night only by looking all around the house until I find her or, alternatively, by calling for her outside and waiting to see if she comes running. A more serious disadvantage of automaticity is that it increases the likelihood that an individual will quickly recall certain ideas or perform certain procedures when other, less automatic ideas or procedures are more useful (Langer, 2000; LeFevre, Bisanz, & Mrkonjic, 1988). People are far more flexible, and so far more likely to identify unique approaches to situations or creative solutions to problems, when they aren't automatically "locked in" to a particular response (Killeen, 2001; Langer, 2000). We'll revisit this issue in our discussion of *mental set* in problem solving in chapter 13.

PROMOTING EFFECTIVE STORAGE PROCESSES

I often hear educators and educational psychologists making the distinction between teacher-centered and learner-centered approaches to instruction. By *teacher-centered instruction,* they mean methods in which the instructor directly presents the material to be learned—for instance, through lectures, explanations, textbooks, and educational videos. Because teacher-centered methods often present information in essentially the same form that students are expected to learn it, they are sometimes called **expository instruction.** In contrast, *learner-centered instruction* encourages students to construct their *own* knowledge and understandings, although usually within the context of planned activities and some degree of teacher guidance. Discovery learning, whole-class and small-group discussions, cooperative learning, and group problem-solving activities are all examples of learner-centered instruction.

In my opinion, the terms *teacher-centered* and *learner-centered* are misnomers. Presumably students are at the center of *any* form of instruction, in that teachers design their lessons with students' learning, rather than their own learning, in mind. The key difference is not one of focus but rather one of *control:* Students direct the course of learning to a greater degree in learner-centered approaches than in teacher-centered approaches. Hence, I suggest that we use slightly different terminology. In **teacher-directed instruction**, the teacher calls most of the shots, choosing what topics will be addressed, directing the course of the lesson, and so on. In **learner-directed instruction,** students have considerable say in the issues they address and how to address them.

Historically, most instruction has been the teacher-directed variety. Yet some psychologists have criticized such instruction—especially the lecture method—as being a relatively ineffective pedagogical technique. For example, B. F. Skinner (e.g., 1968; Skinner & Epstein, 1982) proposed that learning occurs most effectively when students make active responses; because the typical classroom lecture does not allow much active responding, it is unlikely to promote learning. Jerome Bruner (e.g., 1961a, 1961b) has been similarly critical of lectures, suggesting that students can better understand ideas when they have concrete, firsthand experiences with those ideas, perhaps through hands-on discovery sessions.

In recent years, many educators and educational psychologists have called for an increasing use of learner-directed approaches, especially those in which students interact in large or small groups. A growing body of research indicates that such approaches can be highly effective. Because they are especially valuable for encouraging complex cognitive skills, we'll examine them in chapter 14, after we've had a chance to discuss metacognition and problem solving.

In the meantime, we should note that teacher-directed instruction has many advocates among contemporary cognitive theorists (e.g., Mayer, 2004; Pressley, with McCormick, 1995; Rosenshine & Stevens, 1986; Tarver, 1992; Weinert & Helmke, 1995). These theorists suggest that students listening to a teacher's explanation or lecture are not necessarily the passive nonresponders that Skinner portrayed. Instead, students, although perhaps not overtly active, are nevertheless *cognitively* active: They busily attend to and meaningfully interpret the information they hear. Ultimately, what matters most about any instructional method is not whether it is teacher- or learner-directed, but *how well it promotes effective storage processes.*

Unfortunately, some educators seem to forget this basic principle. All too often, classroom instruction and assessment methods emphasize the learning of classroom material at a verbatim level, with little or no regard for its underlying meaning (Doyle, 1983, 1986b; Fennema, Carpenter, & Peterson, 1989; Mac Iver, Reuman, & Main, 1995; Schoenfeld, 1985). Many school textbooks are equally guilty, presenting lists of facts with few interrelationships between them and without regard for what students know beforehand (Alleman & Brophy, 1992; Beck and McKeown, 1994, 2001; Berti, 1994; Calfee & Chambliss, 1988; Chambliss, Calfee, & Wong, 1990). To get a sense of what students may encounter in their textbooks, read the following textbook passage:

> *The Langurian and Pitok War.* In 1367 Marain and the settlements ended a 7-year war with the Langurian and Pitoks. As a result of this war Languria was driven out of East Bacol. Marain would now rule Laman and other lands that had belonged to Languria. This brought peace to the Bacolian settlements. The settlers no longer had to fear attacks from Laman. The Bacolians were happy to be a part of Marain in 1367. Yet a dozen years later, these same people would be fighting the Marish for independence, or freedom from United Marain's rule. This war was called the Freedom War or the Bacolian Revolution. A revolution changes one type of government or way of thinking and replaces it with another. (Beck & McKeown, 1994, p. 239)

Are you confused? I certainly am. The passage is from an actual American history textbook, albeit with a few modifications:

- *1763* has been changed to *1367*
- *Britain* has been changed to *Marain*
- *Colonies* has been changed to *settlements*
- *French* has been changed to *Langurian*
- *Indians* has been changed to *Pitoks*
- *North America* has been changed to *East Bacol*
- *Canada* has been changed to *Laman*
- *War for Independence* has been changed to *Freedom War*
- *American* has been changed to *Bacolian*

If I were to show you the original passage, you would understand it easily *if* you grew up in the United States or for some other reason already know about the French and Indian War and the American Revolution. But for many American fifth graders, the original passage is almost as confusing as the modified one I just presented, because they have little prior knowledge about the countries and events described (Beck & McKeown, 1994).

Perhaps as a result of instruction, textbooks, assignments, and evaluation methods that downplay the importance of learning classroom subject matter in a meaningful fashion, students often engage in rote learning (Novak & Musonda, 1991; Perkins & Simmons, 1988; Prawat, 1989). Yet even the most teacher-directed lesson can promote meaningful learning and other effective storage processes. Following are a number of principles that should guide instructional practice regardless of whether it is teacher-directed or learner-directed.

◆ *Meaningful learning can occur only when students have prior knowledge to which they can relate new ideas.* Students have considerable difficulty learning and remembering material that does not overlap with their existing knowledge. When students are observed processing material in a rote manner (e.g., rehearsing it), they probably either lack the appropriate background knowledge for learning the material effectively or are unaware of the relevant knowledge they *do* have. For example, American history textbooks frequently refer to the colonists' distress over Britain's "taxation without representation" policy, yet they don't always provide an adequate explanation of why this policy was so upsetting to the colonists (Beck & McKeown, 1994). Many adults can easily relate the idea of taxation without representation to their own frustrations with high taxes. Most fifth graders, however, have little if any experience on which to draw in understanding the colonists' situation.

Whenever they introduce a new topic, teachers must consider what knowledge students already have about the topic and begin instruction at that point. As an example, early mathematics instruction might build on informal counting procedures children have developed on their own (Fennema et al., 1989). Teachers can incorporate students' personal and cultural experiences into topics being introduced (Garcia, 1992). They can also have students apply new material within the context of everyday activities and problems—for example, by using mapping skills to map the school or neighborhood or studying metric units as part of a cooking class (Brophy & Alleman, 1991; Reesink, 1984).

When students seem to have very little knowledge about a particular topic, teachers might provide actual experiences to which the students can then relate new concepts. For example, a teacher might introduce the idea of *taxation without representation* by conducting an activity in which students are told to give valued objects to fellow students (only temporarily) without regard for their own wishes in the matter. I frequently use this create-an-experience strategy myself, not only in my classes but also in my books; asking you to read the passage about the Langurian and Pitok War a bit earlier was an example of the kinds of things I do. I then follow up by relating new concepts and principles to the experience my students or readers have just had.

Analogies that relate classroom subject matter to familiar concepts and situations can also be quite effective (Bulgren, Deshler, Schumaker, & Lenz, 2000; Donnelly & McDaniel, 1993; English, 1997b; Zook, 1991). Figure 8.9 presents examples of effective analogies for a variety of classroom topics. Analogies help students learn information more meaningfully and retrieve it more easily, particularly when the topic is a new one for students or when the material is fairly abstract. At the same time, teachers must be careful to point out ways in which the two things being compared are *different*. Otherwise, students may take an analogy too far and draw incorrect conclusions (Duit, 1990; Glynn, 1991; Sfard, 1997; Zook & Di Vesta, 1991).

Even when students do have existing knowledge to which they can relate new material, they frequently aren't aware of connections they might make (Paris & Lindauer, 1976; Spires & Donley, 1998; Spires, Donley, & Penrose, 1990; Stodolsky et al., 1991). Hence, theorists recommend that instruction include **prior knowledge activation**—some means of encouraging students to retrieve relevant knowledge from long-term memory to working memory. For example, teachers and students might discuss a topic in class before students begin a reading assignment about the topic (Hansen & Pearson, 1983; Wilson & Anderson, 1986). And when content learned earlier in the year (or perhaps in previous years) is important for understanding something new, teachers might provide a quick review of that content—a "refresher," if you will.

♦ *Students are more apt to engage in meaningful learning when they are explicitly encouraged to do so.* Students must approach new information with the attitude that they can understand and make sense of it. In other words, they must approach it with a **meaningful learning set** (Ausubel et al., 1978). Students are more likely to have this attitude when teachers emphasize understanding rather than verbatim recitation—for instance, when students know they will be expected to explain concepts in their own words rather than reproduce textbook definitions (Ausubel et al., 1978). But ultimately, students must have confidence that they *can* understand new material. Students who have learned through past experience that certain kinds of subject matter are confusing or incomprehensible are more likely to resort to a rote-learning approach (Ausubel & Robinson, 1969).

♦ *Students learn more effectively when a lesson begins with an advance organizer.* Earlier in the chapter, I distinguished between *internal organization*—how various ideas within a body of new

- If we think of the earth's history as a *24-hour day,* then humans have been in existence only for the last minute of that day. (Hartmann, Miller, & Lee, 1984)
- The growth of a glacier is like *pancake batter being poured into a frying pan*. As more and more substance is added to the middle, the edges spread farther and farther out. (courtesy of R. K. Ormrod)
- The Ural Mountains in Russia are like *the Appalachian Mountains in the United States*. They are old, worn-down mountains that served as temporary barriers to migration. (Andrews, 1987)
- The human circulatory system is similar to a *parcel delivery system*. "Red blood cells work like trucks, carrying needed materials from a central distribution point for delivery throughout the body. Arteries and veins are like roads, acting as access routes through which the various points of delivery are reached. The heart is like the warehouse or the central point in which vehicles are loaded and dispatched, and to which empty vehicles are returned to be reloaded." (Stepich & Newby, 1988, p. 136)
- Peristalsis, a process that moves food through the digestive system, is ". . . like *squeezing ketchup out of a single-serving packet*. You squeeze the packet near one corner and run your fingers along the length of the packet toward an opening at the other corner. When you do this, you push the ketchup through the packet, in one direction, ahead of your fingers, until it comes out of the opening." (Newby, Ertmer, & Stepich, 1994, p. 4, emphasis added)

- Any horizontal surface, such as a table, exerts force on an object that rests on it. You might think of the table as a *spring* that is compressed when something is put on top of it. The spring pushes up against the object. (D. E. Brown, 1992)
- The process of heat flow is similar to *falling dominos*. In both cases, one thing affects the thing next to it, which in turn affects the thing next to *it,* and so on. (Royer & Cable, 1976)
- Electricity going through a wire is like *people going through a tunnel*. Everything that enters at one end comes out at the other. (Gentner & Gentner, 1983)
- Tying a bowline knot is like *a rabbit guarding the territory around its home*. You hold the rope vertically and make a loop near the middle. The loop is the rabbit hole, the upper end of the rope is the tree, and the lower end is the rabbit. The rabbit goes up and out of the hole, around the tree, and back down the hole. (Hayes & Henk, 1986)
- A dual-store model of memory is like *the information selection and storage system you use at home*. Some things (e.g., junk mail) are discarded as soon as they arrive, others (e.g., bills) are dealt with only briefly, and still others (e.g., driver's license) are used regularly and saved for a long period of time (see chapter 7 of this book).
- Retrieval from long-term memory is like *looking for something in a large, dark room with only a small flashlight*. You can look at only one small spot at a time, and it is virtually impossible to look everywhere (Lindsay & Norman, 1977; see chapter 10 of this book).

Figure 8.9
Examples of analogies that promote connections between new ideas and things students already know.

information are interrelated—and *external organization*—how that information is related to what students already know. One means of facilitating both forms of organization is the use of **advance organizers** (Ausubel et al., 1978). An advance organizer is a general introduction to new material that is typically designed to accomplish either or both of two purposes. An **expository organizer** provides a rough overview or outline of the material, describing the general topics that will be presented and their relationship to one another; thus, it provides the beginnings of an internal organizational scheme. A **comparative organizer** shows how the new material relates to students' previous experiences, to information they have previously learned in school, or possibly to their own purposes for studying the material; it also points out similarities between the new information and the old. In this way, the organizer facilitates external organization (i.e., meaningful learning). An additional advantage of a comparative organizer is that it establishes a meaningful learning set: Students anticipate being able to make sense of the new material and thus are more likely to approach the learning task with meaningful learning in mind.

Research consistently demonstrates the effectiveness of advance organizers in facilitating student learning, especially when material is not clearly organized and students have trouble organizing it on their own (Ausubel et al., 1978; Corkill, 1992; Mayer, 1979a, 1979b). Advance organizers also appear to promote more meaningful learning and greater transfer of classroom material to new situations (Mayer, 1987).

Advance organizers are usually more effective when they are fairly concrete (Corkill, 1992; Mayer & Bromage, 1980; Zook, 1991). A variety of formats—overviews, outlines, analogies, examples, and thought-provoking questions—all appear to be effective (Alexander, Frankiewicz, & Williams, 1979; Corkill, 1992; Frase, 1975; Glynn & Di Vesta, 1977; Mayer, 1984; Zook, 1991). For example, here is how a teacher might introduce a lesson on radar by means of an analogy—a comparative advance organizer:

> Radar means the detection and location of remote objects by reflection of radio waves. The phenomenon of acoustic echoes is familiar. Sound waves reflected from a building or cliff are received back at the observer after a lapse of a short interval. The effect is similar to you shouting in a canyon and, seconds later, hearing a nearly exact replication of your voice. Radar uses exactly the same principle except that the waves involved are radio waves, not sound waves. These travel very much faster than sound waves, 186,000 miles per second, and can cover much longer distances. Thus, radar involves simply measuring the time between transmission of the waves and their subsequent return or echo, and then converting that to a distance measure. (Mayer, 1984, p. 30)

In some situations, an advance organizer might even take a graphic rather than strictly verbal form. For example, when introducing a unit on minerals, a hierarchical diagram similar to the one in Figure 8.5 might provide a helpful visual overview—an expository advance organizer.

♦ *Students often need guidance in determining what things are most important to learn.* When instruction provides a great deal of information, students may have trouble deciding which things are important and which things are not (Dole et al., 1991; Reynolds & Shirey, 1988). For example, students may focus their attention on interesting, relatively trivial details at the expense of less interesting but more important ideas (Alexander & Jetton, 1996; Garner, Alexander, Gillingham, Kulikowich, & Brown, 1991; Ward, 1991). Or they may look at the equations they see in a scientific proof while disregarding any verbal explanation of the equations (Dee-Lucas & Larkin, 1991).

A variety of **signals** pointing to important information can facilitate students' learning from expository forms of instruction (Armbruster, 1984; Lorch, Lorch, & Inman, 1993; Reynolds & Shirey, 1988). For example, writing key points on the chalkboard is a means of emphasizing those points. Underlining or italicizing important phrases and sentences in a textbook passage makes them more prominent (Hartley, Bartlett, & Branthwaite, 1980; McAndrew, 1983). Specific instructional objectives for a lesson let students know what they should focus on (McCrudden et al., 2006; also see chapter 5). Questions interspersed throughout a lecture or textbook passage draw students' attention to particular ideas (Anderson & Biddle, 1975; Andre, 1979; McDaniel & Einstein, 1989).

♦ *In as many ways as possible, students should interconnect the new ideas they are learning.* Expository instruction tends to be more effective when it presents new information in the basic organizational format in which students should store it in memory (Dansereau, 1995;

Tennyson & Cocchiarella, 1986; Tennyson, Tennyson, & Rothen, 1980; Wade, 1992). For example, teachers facilitate students' learning when they present ideas in a logical sequence, identify any hierarchical relationships that exist among concepts, and make cause-effect relationships clear. Showing how material should be organized and interrelated may be especially important for students who have little relevant background knowledge and for students who have a history of learning difficulties (Buckland, 1968; deLeeuw & Chi, 2003; Krajcik, 1991; Mayer, 1989).

One strategy for showing how the concepts and ideas of a lesson interrelate is a **concept map** or **knowledge map**—a diagram of the concepts or main ideas of a unit (often identified by circles) and the interrelationships among them (often designated by lines and by words or phrases that link two concepts or ideas together). As an illustration, Figure 8.10 presents a concept map that a teacher might use to organize some of the key concepts in a lesson on ancient Egyptian art. Such organizational maps can frequently help students learn, organize,

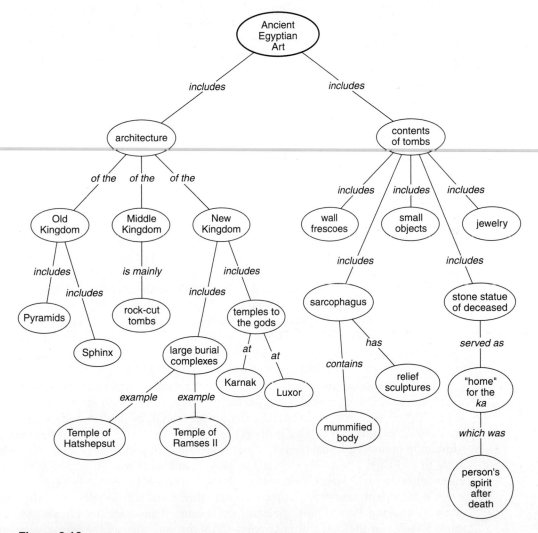

Figure 8.10
A possible concept map for a lesson on ancient Egyptian art.

and remember the things they hear in a lecture or read in a textbook (Krajcik, 1991; Linn, Songer, & Eylon, 1996; Novak, 1998; O'Donnell, Dansereau, & Hall, 2002).

◆ *Generally speaking, students learn and remember new material more effectively when they elaborate on it.* Students are more likely to remember classroom material over the long run if they expand on the material based on things they already know. As examples, they might draw an inference that has not been explicitly stated, speculate on the motives of historical figures, or think about how they might apply a scientific principle at home.

Many classroom activities can potentially promote student elaboration of classroom subject matter. For example, asking students to talk about a topic, perhaps within the context of a class discussion or cooperative learning activity, almost forces them to do *something* (mentally) with the material (Hiebert & Raphael, 1996; Reiter, 1994; Yager, Johnson, & Johnson, 1985). Asking students to write about what they are learning—perhaps in a research paper or on an essay question—enables them to pull their thoughts together and perhaps to identify and resolve gaps and inconsistencies in their understanding (Prawat, 1989). And when students tutor their classmates on subject matter they presumably know quite well, they learn it at an even higher level of understanding (Brown & Palincsar, 1987; Inglis & Biemiller, 1997; Semb, Ellis, & Araujo, 1993).

Teachers must remember, however, that elaboration can sometimes lead students to acquire erroneous ideas, especially if students already have misconceptions about the topic at hand. Teachers must continually monitor students' understanding of classroom material—perhaps by asking questions, assigning regular homework, or giving occasional quizzes—and then take steps to correct any misinterpretations that students' responses reveal. Some of their misconceptions may be "stubborn" ones that are not easily corrected; we will identify strategies for changing such misconceptions in our discussion of *conceptual change* in chapter 9.

◆ *Visual aids enhance long-term memory storage.* As we have seen, visual imagery can be a highly effective way of encoding information. It may be especially valuable when used in conjunction with other storage processes such as meaningful learning or elaboration. Thus, presenting information in visual form—through physical objects, pictures, maps, diagrams, graphs, live models, and so on—is often a helpful supplement to verbal material (Carney & Levin, 2002; Garry & Gerrie, 2005; Small, Lovett, & Scher, 1993; Verdi & Kulhavy, 2002; Verdi, Kulhavy, Stock, Rittschof, & Johnson, 1996; Waddill, McDaniel, & Einstein, 1988; Winn, 1991). Although you might think that adding visual aids to verbal material could overburden a limited-capacity working memory, in fact visuals seem to *reduce* the strain on working memory—apparently because they provide an external means of storing some of the information a learner is trying to make sense of (Butcher, 2006; Carlson, Chandler, & Sweller, 2003).

In most situations, visual aids should be simple, concise, and clear, presenting major ideas without overwhelming students with detail (Butcher, 2006; Shah & Hoeffner, 2002; Vekiri, 2002). Images in color seem to be more memorable than those in black and white, with the colors being an integral part of what learners encode (Spence, Wong, Rusan, & Rastegar, 2006). In addition to promoting visual imagery, many visual aids can also show students how major ideas relate to and affect one another; thus they provide one more way of helping students organize information (Levin & Mayer, 1993; Mayer, 1989; Winn, 1991).

It is important, however, that pictures and other visual aids be relevant to the material students are studying. For example, irrelevant visual material that is included in a reader or textbook solely to enhance the book's attractiveness can sometimes distract the learner's attention away from the more important part of the book—the text (Carney & Levin, 2002; Levin, Anglin, & Carney, 1987; Samuels, 1967, 1970).

- *A variety of instructional strategies promote acquisition of procedures.* Theorists have suggested several teaching strategies that seem to help students learn and remember procedures more effectively. For instance, teachers can demonstrate a procedure or show pictures of the specific behaviors it involves (R. M. Gagné, 1985). They can verbalize their own thoughts—thereby demonstrating *mental* procedures—as they engage in a complex task (recall our discussion of *cognitive modeling* in chapter 6). They can encourage students to use verbal rehearsal while learning a new skill—in other words, to repeat the required steps over and over to themselves (Weiss & Klint, 1987). And, of course, students will be more likely to remember a procedure when teachers give them a chance to carry it out themselves and provide feedback about their performance (Cohen, 1989; Heindel & Kose, 1990; Proctor & Dutta, 1995). When procedures are fairly complicated, teachers may want to break them down into smaller tasks and have students practice each one separately at first (J. R. Anderson et al., 1996; Beilock & Carr, 2003). Chapters 12 and 13 describe additional strategies for facilitating the acquisition of procedural knowledge related to metacognition and problem solving.

- *Students learn new material more effectively when they have sufficient time to process it well.* Effective long-term memory storage processes—meaningful learning, internal organization, elaboration, visual imagery—often take *time*. In learner-directed learning sessions, students have considerable control over how they spend their time, and so they can stop when they need to in order to think things through. But in teacher-directed learning sessions, the teacher is largely in control of the pacing and must be sure to give students the processing time they need. For example, when giving a lecture, teachers might lecture for 8 or 10 minutes and then give students a 2-minute interval in which to compare notes and clarify subject matter with one another (Rowe, 1987).

- *End-of-lesson summaries promote learning and retention.* As we noted in our earlier discussion of advance organizers, students tend to learn more effectively when they receive advance notice of the things they will be learning. Students also tend to benefit from summaries presented at the end of a verbal lecture or written passage: They learn more effectively when they hear or read a synopsis of the information they have just studied (Hartley & Trueman, 1982; Lorch et al., 1993).

Summaries probably serve multiple functions for students. Among other things, they can help students review material, determine which of the many ideas they have studied are most important, and pull key ideas into a more cohesive organizational structure.

- *Periodic review and practice enhances learning.* As we have seen, rehearsal of information within a short time span (e.g., less than a minute) is a relatively ineffective way to store information in long-term memory. But occasional repetition of learned information over a longer period of time (e.g., over the course of a few days, weeks, or months) *does* enhance storage and retention. Teachers might find it helpful, then, to have students review and practice important material throughout the school year, perhaps by integrating the material into the context of new lessons. Repetition is especially important for facts and skills that students need every day—for example, for basic number facts, words frequently encountered in reading, and rules of punctuation. (Computer software can sometimes make such drill and practice more palatable; e.g., see Lesgold [1983], Perfetti [1983], and Resnick & Johnson [1988].) Basic information and skills should certainly be learned as meaningfully as possible, but they should also be practiced until students can retrieve them quickly and automatically.

◆ *Learning quickly does not always mean learning better.* Earlier in the chapter, we noted that distributed practice sometimes leads to slower learning than massed practice but tends to promote greater retention of material over the long run. More generally, how *quickly* students learn something is not necessarily a good indication of how *well* they learn it (Bahrick et al., 1993; Phye, 2001; Salomon, 1979/1994; Schmidt & Bjork, 1992). To truly master a topic, students must relate it to things they already know, form many interconnections among its various parts, draw inferences about and in other ways elaborate on it, and perhaps learn certain aspects of it to automaticity. Such things take time—in some cases a great deal of time—but for important topics and skills, it is time well spent.

Furthermore, although a certain amount of feedback is essential for learning to take place, occasional rather than continual feedback about one's performance may sometimes promote performance over the long run, even though it may result in slower improvement initially (Schmidt & Bjork, 1992). It may be that learners need practice not only in performing certain tasks but also in retrieving relevant knowledge about each task and giving themselves feedback about their performance (Schmidt & Bjork, 1992).

Allowing students to make errors during instruction can be valuable as well. When students make errors along the way—and especially when they're given some guidance about how to *detect* and *correct* their errors—they become more comfortable with occasional mistakes and perform better over the long run (Keith & Frese, 2005; Mathan & Koedinger, 2005).

SOME FINAL REMARKS ABOUT LONG-TERM MEMORY STORAGE

Before we leave our discussion of long-term memory storage, we should note a few final points about storage processes:

◆ *Long-term memory storage is idiosyncratic.* Any two people store different information from the same situation, and for several reasons. First, they attend to different aspects of the situation, and so they store different information in their working memories. Second, they encode information in different ways; for example, some people store a great deal in a language-based form whereas others rely more heavily on visual imagery (Mayer & Massa, 2003). And third, they bring their unique background experiences to the situation so that the interpretations of what they observe are truly their own.

◆ *Storage of new information sometimes affects previously learned information as well.* Consistent with the process of elaboration, learners sometimes distort new material to fit their existing beliefs. Yet in other situations, a new piece of information may help learners recognize that something they stored earlier is inaccurate or that two previously learned pieces of information are related in a way they had not previously recognized.

◆ *The ways in which people store new information affect both the nature of the knowledge they possess and the ease with which they can retrieve that knowledge later on.* In the next two chapters, we will consider two other topics related to long-term memory: the nature of knowledge (chapter 9) and retrieval (chapter 10). As we address these topics, we will continually find that long-term memory storage processes are inextricably related both to what we know and how easily we can recall it at a future time.

SUMMARY

Many theorists believe that long-term memory storage processes are often constructive in nature. We typically store *less* than we have sensed because our working memories cannot hold all of the input that our sensory registers temporarily record. At the same time, we also store *more* than we have sensed, using the incomplete data we receive to construct a logical understanding of the events around us.

Long-term memory storage involves a variety of cognitive processes. *Selection* is the process of determining what information we should process further and what information is irrelevant to our needs. *Rehearsal* is repeating something over and over in a relatively meaningless (rote) fashion; its effectiveness in promoting long-term memory storage is questionable at best. *Meaningful learning* is connecting new material with similar ideas already stored in memory; in other words, it is a process of making sense of the material. *Internal organization* is the integration of various pieces of new information into a cohesive, interrelated whole. *Elaboration* involves imposing one's previously acquired knowledge and beliefs on new information. And *visual imagery* is encoding information in a mental "picture" that captures its physical appearance to some extent.

Most research investigating the effectiveness of long-term memory storage processes has involved declarative knowledge (e.g., facts, concepts, principles). But these processes may also play a role in the acquisition of procedural knowledge (e.g., motor skills, problem-solving strategies), in part because declarative knowledge can evolve into procedural knowledge and can also support learners' efforts in the early stages of acquiring a new skill. The neurological underpinnings of long-term storage of declarative and procedural knowledge alike may require some time—perhaps several minutes or hours, perhaps even longer—to *consolidate*.

Several cognitive factors affect long-term memory storage. People are likely to relate new material to their existing knowledge only when both things are in working memory at the same time. A greater amount of existing knowledge about a topic, provided that it is *accurate*, usually facilitates long-term memory storage. Expectations about what will be seen or heard often yield more rapid and efficient learning. However, misconceptions and inaccurate predictions about the topic under consideration sometimes lead to distortions in what is learned and remembered.

Overt behaviors can affect long-term memory storage as well. It is often helpful to talk about, write about, or physically enact aspects of the things that are being learned. Furthermore, although repetition of information within a period of a few seconds or minutes (rehearsal) is not an effective way of storing information in the first place, occasional repetition of information stretched out over time makes the information easier to remember over the long run. Knowledge and skills needed on a regular basis should, in many cases, be practiced over and over until they are learned to a level of *automaticity*—that is, until they can be retrieved and used quickly and effortlessly.

Contemporary psychologists have made a distinction between teacher-centered and learner-centered instruction; the two approaches might better be described as *teacher-directed* versus *learner-directed* instruction. Although some theorists have argued that one approach is better than the other, in fact the effectiveness of either approach depends on the cognitive processes it encourages students to engage in. Regardless of the instructional methods used, teachers can foster effective long-term memory storage processes in a wide variety of ways—for instance, by activating students' prior knowledge about a topic, helping students organize and integrate new material, giving signals about what is most important to learn and remember, encouraging students to draw inferences and in other ways elaborate on ideas, and providing numerous opportunities for practice and review.

CHAPTER 9

Long–Term Memory II: The Nature of Knowledge

Take a few minutes to answer the following questions:

1. What did you do yesterday?
2. In what kind of house or apartment did you live when you were 9 years old?
3. What is a *noun*?
4. How are rote learning and meaningful learning different?
5. What is the best mode of transportation around the town or city in which you live?
6. What prominent individuals would be good choices for leading your country in the next 2 or 3 decades?
7. How do you ride a bicycle?
8. When buying things at the grocery store, how do you decide which checkout line to go to?

9. What are some reasons why people own horses?
10. Why do many people prefer grass rather than gravel in their front yards?

These questions asked you about 10 very different topics, but I suspect that you could easily respond to most of them. Even if you always lose at Trivial Pursuit and would never dream of becoming a contestant on the television game show *Jeopardy,* you nevertheless have a great deal of information stored in your long-term memory. Some of what you know relates to your personal life experiences (see questions 1 and 2), but much more of it is general knowledge about the world. You've acquired some of your knowledge from teachers or textbooks (see questions 3 and 4), but you've probably picked up a vast amount on your own over the years. Some of your "knowledge" isn't necessarily fact but instead reflects your personal beliefs and preferences (see questions 5 and 6). Furthermore, you don't only know and believe things about your own past history and about the world around you, but you also know how to do a great many things (see questions 7 and 8). And you've pulled some of what you know and believe into more general understandings of why the world is the way it is (see questions 9 and 10).

As you will discover, theorists have gone in many directions in describing the possible nature of human knowledge, and it will be virtually impossible for us to roll all of their ideas into a tight little package. In this chapter we will distinguish among different kinds of knowledge, speculate on the possible forms in which knowledge might be encoded, and consider a variety of ways in which long-term memory might be organized. Later we will consider the overall quality of knowledge that people acquire and look at how expertise related to a particular field or discipline develops over the years.

THE VARIOUS KINDS OF KNOWLEDGE

In my overview of long-term memory in chapter 7, I introduced you to two general distinctions regarding the multifaceted nature of knowledge in long-term memory. Here we look at these distinctions—declarative versus procedural knowledge, and explicit versus implicit knowledge— in more detail.

Declarative and Procedural Knowledge

As I mentioned in chapter 7, **declarative knowledge** concerns the nature of "how things are or were." Such knowledge enables you to interpret what you see and hear around you, recognize important people and places in your life, and recall past events. Many theorists believe that declarative knowledge takes at least two distinct forms: **episodic memory**—one's memory of personal life experiences[1]—and **semantic memory**—one's general knowledge of the world independent of those experiences (e.g., Bauer, 2006; S. K. Johnson & Anderson, 2004; Tulving, 1983, 1991, 1993). These two forms of declarative knowledge are different in several important ways. For instance, we *remember* events we have experienced (episodic) but *know* things about

---

[1]Some theorists have developed the idea of episodic memory further, often using the term *autobiographic memory;* for example, see Bauer (2006), Eacott (1999), M. L. Howe (2003), and K. Nelson (1996).

the world (semantic). We can often recall when a particular event happened to us (episodic) but usually cannot recall when we acquired specific facts about the world (semantic). We are most likely to remember a certain life event when we are in the same place in which it happened, yet we can usually recall general information about the world regardless of where we are at the time. Our semantic memories typically stay with us longer than our episodic memories; for instance, we are far more likely to recall the typical menu items at a particular fast-food restaurant than to remember what we actually ordered at that restaurant a year ago last Tuesday. And to some degree, episodic and semantic memory appear to involve different parts of the cortex (Buckner & Petersen, 1996; Siegel, 1999).

In contrast to declarative knowledge, **procedural knowledge** involves knowing "how to do things" (J. R. Anderson, 1983a, 1995; Corno et al., 2002).[2] For example, you probably know how to ride a bicycle, wrap a gift, and add the numbers 57 and 94. To do such things successfully, you must adapt your actions to changing conditions; for instance, when riding a bike, you must be able to turn left or right if you see an object directly in your path, and you must be able to come to a complete stop when you reach your destination. Accordingly, as you will learn in our discussion of *productions* a bit later, procedural knowledge includes information about how to respond under different circumstances; that is, it includes **conditional knowledge**.

As you might guess, episodic, semantic, and procedural forms of knowledge are interconnected in long-term memory. For instance, when I think about what *dogs* are like (semantic knowledge), I may be reminded of how our former dog Anna once ate the leftover chocolate cake we brought home after Tina's birthday party at McDonald's (episodic knowledge), and I might be reminded, too, of how to put miniature snow boots on current dog Tobey's feet so that the boots stay on in deep snow (procedural knowledge). How was Anna able to get the chocolate cake? Why does Tobey need boots to walk in the snow? And why does putting on the boots in one way work better than putting them on in another? Perhaps there is yet another kind of knowledge—**conceptual knowledge**—that reflects our understanding of why certain events happened, why certain things are the way they are, and why certain procedures are effective but others are not (J. R. Anderson, 1995; Byrnes, 2001). Whether such knowledge is distinctively different from the other forms we've identified, or whether it simply reflects relationships among those other forms, is as yet unclear (Byrnes, 2001).

Explicit and Implicit Knowledge

How do you grow flowers from a packet of flower seeds? You can probably describe the process fairly accurately, explaining that you need to plant the seeds in soil, make sure they have plenty of sunlight, water them regularly, and so on. But how do you keep your balance when you ride a bicycle? How do you move your legs when you skip? What things do you do to form a grammatically correct sentence when you speak? Such questions are more difficult to answer: Even though such activities are probably second nature to you, you really can't put your finger on exactly what you do when you engage in them.

---

[2]When theorists talk about *skill learning,* in most cases they are talking about the acquisition of procedural knowledge.

Many theorists make a distinction between **explicit knowledge**—knowledge that we can easily recall and explain—and **implicit knowledge**—knowledge that we cannot consciously recall or explain but that nevertheless affects our behavior (e.g., Frensch & Rünger, 2003; Graf & Masson, 1993; Roediger, 1990; Siegler, 2000). Sometimes people have no conscious awareness that they have learned something, yet what they have learned clearly shows up in their actions. This is the case, for example, for people who have suffered certain types of brain damage (Bachevalier, Malkova, & Beauregard, 1996; Cermak, 1993; Gabrieli, Keane, Zarella, & Poldrack, 1997). There is also evidence that we acquire some implicit knowledge when we learn either a first or second language: We can produce grammatically correct sentences even though we cannot explain how we do it (Ellis, 1994; Reber, 1993).[3]

Sometimes memories are sufficiently "dim" that they affect us only in subtle ways. For example, when 9-year-olds look at pictures of classmates from their preschool days, they may have no conscious recollection of some of them, but their physiological responses suggest that they *do* recognize these children at some level (Newcombe & Fox, 1994). As another example, when college students are asked to specify which direction well-known cultural images face (e.g., when students in England are asked which way Queen Elizabeth faces on a 10-pence coin, and when students in Japan are asked which side the cartoon character Hello Kitty wears her bow on), they can rarely tell you. However, when forced to choose between the correct orientation and its mirror image, they guess correctly about 65 to 80% of the time—hardly stellar performance, but certainly better than chance (Kelly, Burton, Kato, & Akamatsu, 2001).

HOW INFORMATION IS ENCODED IN LONG–TERM MEMORY

Take a minute and think about a rose. What things come to mind? Perhaps words such as *flower, red, beautiful, long-stemmed,* or *expensive* pop into your head. Perhaps you can picture what a rose looks like or recall how it smells. Perhaps you can even feel a thorn prick your finger as you imagine yourself reaching out to clip a rose from its bush.

Information is probably encoded in long-term memory in a number of ways. For one thing, it may be encoded *symbolically,* represented in memory by words (e.g., "Roses are red, violets are blue"), mathematical expressions, or other symbolic systems. Sometimes environmental input is stored as an *image* that retains some of its physical characteristics; for example, a rose has a certain look and a particular smell. Input may also be represented as one or more *propositions,* such that its underlying abstract meaning is stored; for example, the fact that "a rose is a flower" may be stored as an abstract idea. Still another way in which information can be stored in long-term memory is *productions*—the procedures involved in performing a particular task; for example, one learns the procedure necessary for clipping a rose from a rose bush. These four ways of encoding information—symbols, imagery, propositions, and productions—appear frequently in theories of long-term memory, and so we will look at each of them more closely.

---

[3]The acquisition of explicit knowledge probably relies heavily on the hippocampus—that seahorse-shaped part of the limbic system I mentioned in chapter 2. Other brain structures—for instance, the cerebellum and amygdala—seem to be more instrumental in acquiring implicit knowledge (Nadel, 2005; Siegel, 1999).

Encoding in Terms of Symbols: Words, Numbers, Etc.

A **symbol** is something that represents an object or event, often without bearing much resemblance to that object or event. As human beings, we probably represent much of our experience as symbols—as words, numbers, maps, graphs, and so on (DeLoache, 1995; Flavell, Miller, & Miller, 2002; Salomon, 1979/1994).

There is no question that some information is stored in terms of actual words—in other words, as **verbal codes** (Bower, 1972; Brainerd & Reyna, 2002; Clark & Paivio, 1991; Salomon, 1979/1994).[4] Support for this idea comes both from everyday human experiences and from several theoretical perspectives. First, people have verbal labels for many of the objects and events in their lives; for instance, you think of this thing you are reading as a *book*. Second, people sometimes learn information in a verbatim fashion; Hamlet's soliloquy ("To be or not to be . . .") and the lyrics of "Jingle Bells" are examples of things that people typically learn word for word. Third, people often talk to themselves as a way of guiding themselves through new tasks and procedures (recall our discussion of *self-instructions* in chapter 6; Vygotsky's concept of *self-talk,* described in chapter 11, also reflects this idea). And finally, people use language to help them associate things in memory. For example, the French word for "dog" is *chien;* I remember this word by thinking "dog chain." Many of the principles that emerged from verbal learning research (e.g., the serial learning curve) probably apply primarily to information stored in a verbal code.

Encoding in Terms of Appearance: Imagery

Can you imagine your mother's face? the melody of a favorite song? the smell of a rose? If so, you are probably drawing on mental images. Many psychologists believe that people store images in several modalities, including visual, auditory, and olfactory (smelling).[5] However, research and theory have emphasized visual imagery, so that will be our focus here.

Visual imagery appears to be a distinct form of information storage (e.g., Bower, 1972; Farah, Hammond, Levine, & Calvanio, 1988; Kosslyn, 1994; Sadoski & Paivio, 2001).[6] Its exact nature is still an open question, but one thing is clear: A visual image is probably *not* a mental snapshot. Visual imagery appears to recruit some of the same cognitive processes as visual perception (Behrmann, 2000; Kosslyn, 1994; Peterson, Kihlstrom, Rose, & Glisky, 1992). In some instances, it may involve envisioning motion (e.g., mentally "seeing" a galloping horse or "scanning" various parts of a picture) or encoding spatial relationships among several distinct entities (Farah et al., 1988; Sadoski & Paivio, 2001).

---

[4]We previously encountered this idea in our discussion of social cognitive theory in chapter 6. At the time, we used Bandura's terminology, talking about words as one form of a *memory code.*

[5]For more on auditory imagery, see Intons-Peterson (1992), Intons-Peterson, Russell, and Dressel (1992), and Reisberg (1992).

[6]The idea that people store information in at least two different ways—verbally and visually—is the essence of Allan Paivio's *dual coding theory* (e.g., Clark & Paivio, 1991; Paivio, 1971, 1986; Sadoski & Paivio, 2001). Do not confuse dual coding theory with the *dual-store model* of memory described in chapter 7. Dual coding theory distinguishes between two forms of encoding in long-term memory, whereas the dual-store model distinguishes between working memory and long-term memory.

Oftentimes people's *gestures*—especially the ways they move their hands as they speak—reflect their attempts to communicate their visual images or knowledge of spatial relationships. For instance, my husband talks with his hands as much as with his mouth, and he consistently uses certain motions when he talks about certain kinds of things. Whenever he talks about something wavy in shape (e.g., a snake in the grass or a windy mountain road), he will move his hand forward in a snakelike manner. Whenever he talks about the size or shape of an object, he will use his hands to show its contour. (I once asked him to describe the dimensions of something while he was driving in the mountains of Colorado. Big mistake. He took both hands off the steering wheel to gesture while he described the object, and it was a miracle we didn't end up in a ditch.) Gestures often seem to represent aspects of visual or spatial encoding that are not necessarily reflected in what we say and may in some instances communicate implicit rather than explicit knowledge (Alibali, Bassok, Solomon, Syc, & Goldin-Meadow, 1999; Bassok, 1997; Goldin-Meadow, 1997, 2001; Koschmann & LeBaron, 2002; Krauss, 1998; Roth, 2001).

Encoding in Terms of Meanings: Propositions

People are more apt to remember the general meaning of what they see or hear than precise, word-for-word detail. For example, think about the section you just read on imagery. What do you remember about it? You probably don't remember the specific words you read, but you should be able to recall the general ideas of the section. (If you cannot, go back and read the section again!)

Some theorists (J. R. Anderson, 1995; E. D. Gagné, 1985; van Dijk & Kintsch, 1983; Kintsch, 1998) believe that meanings are stored as **propositions**—that is, as small units of knowledge concerning relationships among objects or events. To paraphrase John Anderson's (1990) definition, a proposition is the smallest unit of knowledge that (1) can stand as a separate statement or assertion and (2) can be judged as being either true or false. To illustrate, consider the following sentence:

Mary's uncle, whom she adores, owns a red Ferrari.

We can break this complex sentence into four smaller assertions, each containing part of its meaning:

1. Mary has an uncle.
2. Mary adores the uncle.
3. The uncle owns a Ferrari.
4. The Ferrari is red.

Each assertion is either true or false; if any one of them is false, the entire sentence is false. The four assertions are rough verbal analogs of the abstract propositions that may be stored in memory when the sentence itself is encountered.

Any proposition has two components. First, it includes one or more **arguments**—objects or events that are the topics of the proposition. Second, it involves a single **relation**—a description of an argument or a relationship among two or more arguments. For example, the assertion "Mary has an uncle" contains two arguments ("Mary" and "uncle") and one relation ("has"). Arguments are usually reflected by nouns and pronouns in a sentence, whereas relations are more typically reflected by verbs, adjectives, and adverbs.

Propositions provide a theoretical model of how meanings may be encoded. It is becoming increasingly clear that a great deal of the information individuals receive is stored primarily in terms of underlying meanings. For example, participants in research studies can often remember information verbatim if asked to do so immediately after the information has been presented. When recall is delayed, their ability to remember the exact input declines rapidly, yet they continue to remember its *meaning* fairly accurately (J. R. Anderson, 1990; Kintsch, 1977; Reder, 1982; Reyna, 1995).

Nonverbal visual information also appears to be stored at least partly in terms of meanings (Mandler & Johnson, 1976; Mandler & Parker, 1976; Mandler & Ritchey, 1977). An experiment by Mandler and Johnson (1976) illustrates this point well. In the experiment, college students looked at line drawings that included a number of different objects; for instance, one picture was a classroom scene that included a teacher, student, desk, bookshelf, flag, clock, globe, and large map. The students were then shown another set of pictures and asked whether each of the pictures was identical to a previous picture or had been changed in some way. Students were far more likely to notice changes in the pictures that reflected a change in the general meaning (e.g., a teacher was talking about a child's drawing instead of a world map) than in those that reflected a nonmeaningful change (e.g., the teacher's skirt and hairstyle were different).

Encoding in Terms of Actions: Productions

As already noted, some of our knowledge is *procedural:* We know how to perform various actions and activities. Some procedures are primarily *psychomotor*—that is, they involve particular movements of the arms, hands, legs, neck, and so on. Others are more cognitive in nature—that is, they involve mentally manipulating facts, figures, and the like.

Some theorists have suggested that procedural knowledge is encoded in the form of **productions** (J. R. Anderson, 1983a, 1987, 1990, 1995; E. D. Gagné, 1985). Productions can best be described as a set of IF–THEN rules. For example, productions for riding a bicycle would include rules such as these:

1. IF I want to speed up, THEN I pedal at a faster rate.
2. IF I want to slow down, THEN I pedal at a slower rate.
3. IF my route turns to the right, THEN I turn the handlebars in a clockwise direction.
4. IF my route turns to the left, THEN I turn the handlebars in a counterclockwise direction.
5. IF an object is directly in front of me, THEN I must turn either right or left.
6. IF I want to stop, THEN I squeeze the brakes on the handlebars.

Similarly, productions for adding 2 two-digit numbers would include these rules:

1. IF the sum of the digits in the "ones" column equals 9 or less, THEN I write that sum in the "ones" column of the answer space.
2. IF the sum of the digits in the "ones" column equals 10 or more, THEN I write the digit that appears in the "ones" column of that sum in the "ones" column of the answer space and carry the "1" to the "tens" column of the problem.
3. IF the sum of the digits in the "tens" column equals 9 or less, THEN I write that sum in the "tens" column of the answer space.

4. IF the sum of the digits in the "tens" column equals 10 or more, THEN I write the digit that appears in the "ones" column of that sum in the "tens" column of the answer space and write the "1" in the "hundreds" column of the answer space.

As you can see, the "IF" part of a production specifies the condition under which a particular behavior will occur, and the "THEN" part specifies what the behavior will be. Productions, then, provide a means through which individuals can be responsive to different environmental conditions. Although some psychologists have described such *conditional knowledge* as a form of knowledge distinct from the other forms I have already described, from this *production* perspective it is an integral part of procedural knowledge (Byrnes, 2001).

Whether procedural knowledge is encoded as productions or, instead, in some other form, it clearly requires integration of the various behavioral and mental components involved (Willingham, 1998, 2004). It also requires some sort of mental "supervisor," or central executive, to coordinate and guide the overall execution of the activity (Beilock & Carr, 2003; Keele, Cohen, & Ivry, 1990; Willingham, 2004).

Different Forms of Encoding Are Not Mutually Exclusive

We may store information using any one of the four methods of encoding I've just described—as symbols, images, propositions, or productions—or perhaps in some other way that theorists have not yet identified. Furthermore, we sometimes encode the same information simultaneously in two or more different ways—perhaps as both words (symbols) and underlying meanings (propositions), or perhaps as both words and images. When we encode the same information in two or more different ways, we often associate those codes in long-term memory (Heil, Rösler, & Hennighausen, 1994; Reisberg, 1997; Sadoski & Paivio, 2001; Sporer, 1991). For example, in an experiment by Pezdek (1977), college students frequently confused information they had seen in pictures with information they had read in sentences. As an illustration, some students first saw a picture of a car parked by a tree and then read the sentence, "The car by the tree had ski racks on it." These students tended to recognize a picture of a car with ski racks as being one they had seen before, even though the original picture had not included a rack; hence, they were probably storing the same information in both visual and verbal forms. Similarly, in the study by Carmichael, Hogan, and Walters (1932) that I described in the preceding chapter (the study in which people looked at figures given one of two labels; see Figure 8.6 as a reminder), people probably stored the stimulus figures both as images (e.g., two balls connected by a line) and as words (e.g., *eyeglasses* or *dumbbells*).

It appears, too, that different but related pieces of information are frequently stored in connection with one another (e.g., Brown & Schopflocher, 1998). We will now look more closely at such interconnections—in other words, at the general organization of long-term memory.

THE ORGANIZATION OF LONG–TERM MEMORY

Contemporary theories of long-term memory are **associationistic:** They propose that pieces of information stored in long-term memory are associated, or connected, with one another. To show you what I mean, get a piece of paper and try this exercise. In just a minute, you will read a common, everyday word. As soon as you read it, write down the first word that comes into your head. Then write down the first word that *that* word reminds you of. Continue writing down the first word that each successive word brings to mind until you have a list of 10 words.

Ready? Here is the word to get your mind rolling:

beach

Once you have completed your list of 10 words, examine it carefully. It should give you an idea of what ideas are associated with what other ideas in your long-term memory.

Here is the list that I constructed using the same procedure and my own long-term memory:

sand
castle
king
queen
Elizabeth
England
London
theater
Hair
nude

Some of my associations might be similar to yours. For example, beach–sand and king–queen are common associates. Others might be unique to me. For instance, the last five items on my list reflect my trip to London in my college days, when I attended a different theater production every night. The most memorable of the productions I saw was the musical *Hair,* in which several actors briefly appeared nude—quite a shocking and memorable sight in 1969.

Psychologists believe that virtually all pieces of information stored in long-term memory are directly or indirectly related to one another. Different learners relate and organize their long-term memories somewhat idiosyncratically because their past experiences have been different. Nevertheless, the organizational schemes that people use may share some common features. At least three models of long-term memory organization have been proposed: the hierarchy, the propositional network, and parallel distributed processing.

Long-Term Memory as a Hierarchy

An early view of long-term memory organization was that information was stored in a hierarchical arrangement, with more general, superordinate information at the top of the hierarchy and more specific, subordinate information below it (Ausubel, 1963, 1968; Ausubel & Robinson, 1969; Collins & Quillian, 1969, 1972). An example of such a hierarchy is my own knowledge of the animal kingdom, part of which is depicted in Figure 9.1. Notice how the most general category—animals—is at the top of the hierarchy. Next are two major categories of animals—vertebrates and invertebrates—followed by more and more subordinate categories, until finally specific instances of a category (e.g., Rin Tin Tin, Tippy, and Anna are all German shepherds) are reached. As you can see, part of my hierarchy would resemble that of a biologist (my classes of vertebrates, for instance), but other parts are uniquely my own.

In a classic study, Collins and Quillian (1969) demonstrated how long-term memory might be organized hierarchically. Adults were given a number of statements (e.g., "A canary can sing")

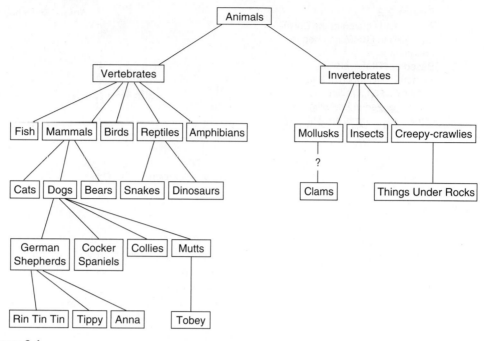

Figure 9.1
The author's hierarchical knowledge of the animal kingdom.

and asked to indicate whether they were true or false; people's reaction times to confirm or reject the statements were recorded. Following are some examples of true statements and approximate reaction times to them:

Statements About Category Membership	Reaction Times (msec)
A canary is a canary.	1000
A canary is a bird.	1160
A canary is an animal.	1240

Statements About Characteristics	Reaction Times (msec)
A canary can sing.	1300
A canary can fly.	1380
A canary has skin.	1470

Notice how the reaction times increased for the three sentences regarding category membership: Participants most quickly verified that a canary is a canary and least quickly verified that a canary is an animal. Now notice the different reaction times for the three statements concerning a canary's characteristics: Participants found the statement about singing easiest and the one about having skin most difficult. Collins and Quillian argued that the two sets of sentences are actually parallel, because most people associate singing directly with canaries, whereas they associate flying with birds and having skin with animals.

Collins and Quillian suggested that an individual's knowledge about categories and category characteristics is arranged in a hierarchical fashion similar to that depicted in Figure 9.2. To verify

Figure 9.2
A simplified version of the Collins and Quillian (1969) knowledge hierarchy.
Based on "Retrieval Time from Semantic Memory" by A. M. Collins & M. R. Quillian, 1969, *Journal of Verbal Learning and Verbal Behavior, 8,* pp. 240–247.

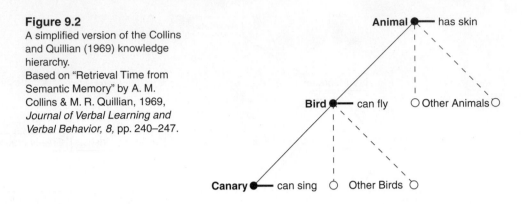

the statements, subjects had to locate the two components of the statement (e.g., "canary" and "skin") within their long-term memories and determine whether they were associated, either directly or indirectly. The farther apart the two components were in the hierarchy, the longer it would take to verify a statement (hence, the longer the reaction times).

Strictly hierarchical models of long-term memory have been the object of considerable criticism (Bourne, Dominowski, Loftus, & Healy, 1986; Loftus & Loftus, 1976; Wingfield & Byrnes, 1981). First, information is not always hierarchical in nature. Second, predictions consistent with hierarchically arranged information are not always confirmed. For example, just as people more quickly verify that a canary is a bird than they verify that a canary is an animal, we should expect that people would agree with the statement "A collie is a mammal" faster than the statement "A collie is an animal," because *collie* is closer to *mammal* than it is to *animal* in a logical hierarchy of animals. Yet the opposite holds true: People more quickly agree that a collie is an animal than that it is a mammal (Rips, Shoben, & Smith, 1973).

At this point, it appears that some information in long-term memory may be arranged hierarchically but that most information is probably organized less systematically. An alternative view of long-term memory, the propositional network, may provide a more useful and flexible theoretical model.

Long–Term Memory as a Propositional Network

A **network** model portrays memory as consisting of many pieces of information interconnected through a variety of associations. To illustrate, let's return again to my previous list of successive associations resulting from the word *beach*: sand, castle, king, queen, Elizabeth, England, London, theater, *Hair,* nude. Such a list might have been generated from a long-term memory network such as the one in Figure 9.3. Different individuals should have networks with somewhat different associations and so should generate different lists. Some individuals, depending on their experiences at the beach, might even associate *beach* and *nude* directly with each other!

One widely used model of long-term memory organization is the **propositional network** (J. R. Anderson, 1976, 1983a, 1983b, 1990; Anderson & Bower, 1973; E. D. Gagné, 1985; Lindsay & Norman, 1977; Norman & Rumelhart, 1975). A propositional network is one in

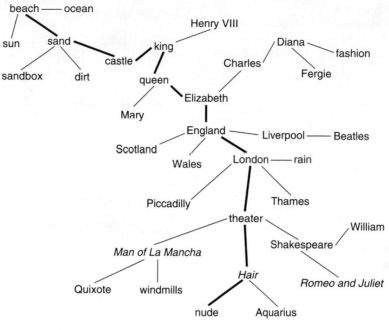

Figure 9.3
A hypothetical network of information in long-term memory.

which propositions and their interrelationships are stored in a networklike fashion. As an illustration, let's return to a sentence we considered earlier in the chapter:

Mary's uncle, whom she adores, owns a red Ferrari.

and to the four assertions it contains:

1. Mary has an uncle.
2. Mary adores the uncle.
3. The uncle owns a Ferrari.
4. The Ferrari is red.

The four assertions can be diagrammed as propositions, as shown in Figure 9.4. These diagrams, using Anderson's (1990) symbols, each show a proposition (symbolized by an oval) that encompasses one relation and one or more arguments.

As you should notice, the four diagrams in Figure 9.4 share three concrete entities (arguments); in particular, *Mary, uncle,* and *Ferrari* each appear in two or more propositions. Such commonalities allow the propositions to be linked in a network; an example is shown in Figure 9.5. A propositional network model of long-term memory is obviously more flexible than a hierarchical model. A hierarchy includes only superordinate–subordinate relationships; in contrast, a network can easily include a wide variety of relationships (e.g., possession, location, opposition).

Network models are often conceptualized as including not only propositions (meanings) but other memory codes (such as imagery and productions) as well (E. D. Gagné, 1985; Glass,

Figure 9.4
Diagrams of separate propositions.

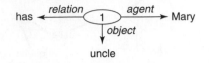

1. Mary has an uncle.

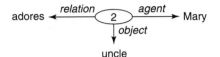

2. Mary adores the uncle.

3. The uncle owns a Ferrari.

4. The Ferrari is red.

Holyoak, & Santa, 1979; Paivio, 1986; Sadoski & Paivio, 2001). For example, you might have a visual image of a Ferrari stored in association with the information about Mary's uncle and his red sports car. Perhaps not too far away in the same network are productions related to driving automobiles.

In the preceding chapter, I described the process of *meaningful learning*—storing new information by relating it to knowledge already in long-term memory. Both hierarchical and propositional network models of memory give us an idea of how such meaningful learning might occur. For example, using a hierarchical model of long-term memory organization, Ausubel described meaningful learning as involving **subsumption**, whereby people place new information under an appropriate superordinate category in their knowledge hierarchy (Ausubel, 1963, 1968; Ausubel et al., 1978; Ausubel & Robinson, 1969). To illustrate, students are more likely to learn meaningful information about an animal called a skink if they are told that it is "a kind

Figure 9.5
A propositional network.

Mary's uncle, whom she adores, owns a red Ferrari.

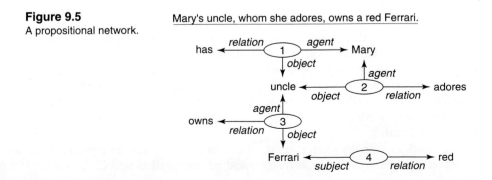

Figure 9.6
Meaningful learning
in a propositional
network.

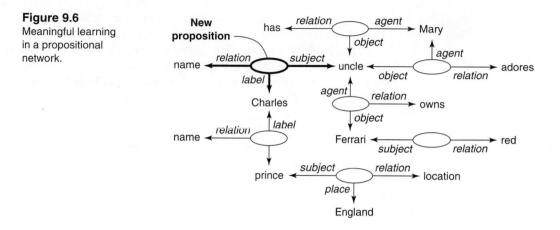

of lizard that looks like a snake" than if they are told that it is "brightly colored" or "a shy, seldom-seen creature." In the former case, they can store the concept *skink* under the more general concept *lizard;* in the latter two situations, they aren't really sure just *where* to put it.

Using a propositional network model of long-term memory, we can characterize meaningful learning as a process of storing new propositions with related propositions in the network. For example, let's assume that you have already stored propositions concerning Mary's uncle and his red Ferrari in a form similar to what I depicted in Figure 9.5. You then read the following sentence:

The uncle is named Charles.

You might connect this proposition to your existing propositions about the uncle and perhaps to propositions concerning another Charles that you know of, as illustrated in Figure 9.6.

A propositional network model of memory gives us greater flexibility in the nature of interrelationships than a strictly hierarchical model offers. The black-and-white nature of propositions—each one must be definitely true or false—is troublesome, however. Many aspects of human experience that are stored in long-term memory, such as an interpretation of a Shakespearian play or an emotional reaction to a work of art, cannot be easily classified as right or wrong (Eisner, 1994).

Parallel Distributed Processing

Until now, we have been speaking as if various bits of information are each stored in a single "place" in long-term memory. But let's return to a couple of research findings we encountered in our discussion of the brain in chapter 2. First, even when people think about something fairly simple—perhaps a single word—numerous areas of the cortex are activated. Second, let's revisit Lashley's (1929) work with maze-running rats. As Lashley gradually removed more and more of their brains, the rats gradually remembered less and less about mazes they had mastered; no single surgery marked a dramatic change from "knowing" to "not knowing" a maze. In both people and rats, and presumably in many other species as well, knowledge about a particular thing seems to be distributed across many parts of the brain.

With such findings in mind, some theorists have proposed that each piece of information is stored in the form of an integrated collection of entities, called **nodes,** that are located throughout long-term memory. Any single node may be associated with many different pieces of information. Each separate idea that you have stored in your long-term memory is represented, then, not as a single node but rather as a *unique network of interconnected nodes.* As one idea (network) is activated, other ideas that share some of its nodes may also be activated.

Such a view of long-term memory is often called **parallel distributed processing (PDP):** Pieces of information are stored in a *distributed* fashion throughout long-term memory, with numerous nodes being processed simultaneously—that is, in *parallel* (McClelland & Rumelhart, 1986; O'Brien, 1999; Plunkett, 1996; Rogers & McClelland, 2004; Rumelhart & McClelland, 1986). Parallel distributed processing is also known as **connectionism,** but it should not be confused with Edward Thorndike's connectionism described in chapter 4.

The parallel distributed processing model is useful for understanding the multidimensional nature of even the simplest of ideas (e.g., Rayner et al., 2001; Siegler & Alibali, 2005). For example, when we read the word

beach

in a textbook, we may simultaneously retrieve not only what it means but also how it sounds, how it is pronounced, and what a typical beach looks like. The model also helps us understand how we can often fill in missing information when a stimulus is incomplete: Enough nodes of an idea are activated that the entire network becomes activated.

Nevertheless, the PDP model is far from perfect (Fodor & Pylyshyn, 1988; Holyoak, 1987; Lachter & Bever, 1988; McClelland, 2001; Pinker & Prince, 1988; Sternberg, 1996). It tends to portray learning as a gradual process of strengthening and weakening associations and so does not explain how we can sometimes learn something very rapidly or, alternatively, quickly revise our beliefs about something in the face of contradictory information (Ratcliff, 1990; Schacter, 1989). Furthermore, some simple and highly automatized cognitive tasks seem to occur in fairly localized areas of the brain (Besner, 1999; Bowers, 2002). And although the PDP model was presumably developed to be consistent with research findings about brain functioning, its relationship to brain anatomy is a loose one at best (McClelland, 2001; Siegler & Alibali, 2005).

Regardless of how long-term memory is organized, it clearly *is* organized. To some extent, people organize all of the information they store in their long-term memories. To an even greater extent, they organize their knowledge regarding very specific objects, events, and topics. At this point, we look at several specific examples of how people might organize their experiences—in particular, *concepts, schemas, scripts, personal theories,* and *worldviews.* Of these, we will spend the most time looking at concepts, in part because they reflect simpler and more basic forms of organization and in part because researchers have been studying them for a longer time and so have a better understanding of them.

CONCEPTS

One night in late May many years ago, my son Jeff and I had a discussion about the seasons. It went something like this:

Jeff: When are spring and summer coming?
Mom: Spring is already here. Haven't you noticed how warm it is, and how the leaves are back on the trees, and how the birds are singing again?

Jeff:	Oh. Then when is summer coming?
Mom:	Well, you have only one more week of school, and then a couple of weeks after that, summer will be here.
Jeff:	Summer is when we go swimming, right?
Mom:	[I pause and think about how to answer.] Right.

As a 4-year-old, Jeff had not yet precisely defined the concepts of *spring* and *summer.* When I was a child, summer was a season of heat, humidity, and no school. As an adult, I now define it more formally as the 3-month period between the summer solstice and the autumn equinox. To Jeff, however, summer was simply the time when he could swim.

Children begin to categorize aspects of their world as early as 3 months of age (Behl-Chadha, 1996; Eimas & Quinn, 1994; Quinn, 2002, 2003), and their categories undoubtedly form the basis for their first concepts. Generally speaking, you might think of a **concept** as a class of objects or events that share one or more similarities (Flavell et al., 2002; Klausmeier, 1990; Oakes & Rakison, 2003; Schwartz & Reisberg, 1991). Some concepts are defined by readily observable characteristics and are fairly easy to learn. For example, the word *milk* refers to a white liquid with a particular taste. Similarly, the word *red* refers to a certain range of light wavelengths (although people disagree about exactly where "red" ends and "orange" begins). Other concepts are defined by less salient attributes, so are more slowly learned and more easily misconstrued. For instance, the four seasons of the year are "officially" designated by the occurrences of solstices and equinoxes that most people are unaware of, so many people erroneously define them in terms of different weather conditions. Still other concepts may be even harder to grasp because they are based on abstract, relativistic, and sometimes elusive criteria. For example, psychologists have wrestled with the concept of *intelligence* for many years and still cannot agree on what the term means.

Some theorists have found it useful to distinguish between two general kinds of concepts, which I will refer to as *concrete* versus *abstract* concepts (e.g., R. M. Gagné, 1985; Karpov, 2003; Mandler, 2003).[7] **Concrete concepts** are easily identified by physical appearance; *cow, red,* and *round* are examples. From a behaviorist perspective, concrete concepts may develop, at least in part, as a result of generalization: Once an organism has learned to respond in a certain way to one stimulus, it tends to respond in the same way to similar stimuli. In contrast, **abstract concepts** are difficult to conceptualize in terms of specific, observable characteristics; examples include *intelligence, charisma,* and *work.* Because generalization is unlikely to occur when objects or events don't *look* similar, abstract concepts are probably best acquired through formal instruction—at a minimum, by having a definition provided (R. M. Gagné, 1985; Karpov, 2003; Vygotsky, 1962). Consider the concept *cousin* as an example. There is no way to learn what a cousin is simply by looking at examples of cousins and noncousins; all will have one head, two arms, two legs, and so on. Instead, a person probably learns a definition that provides guidance in identifying cousins: A *cousin* is an offspring of a parent's sibling.

In some cases, people first learn a concept in a concrete form and then later acquire a more abstract understanding of it (R. M. Gagné, 1985; Liu, Golinkoff, & Sak, 2001; Rakison, 2003).

---

[7]Theorists use various labels for this or a similar distinction. For instance, instead of using the terms *concrete* versus *abstract,* Mandler (2003) talks about *perceptual* versus *conceptual* categories, and Vygotsky and his followers have used the terms *spontaneous* versus *scientific* concepts (e.g., Karpov, 2003; Vygotsky, 1962).

One cannot learn abstract (defined) concepts such as *cousin* through physical examination alone.

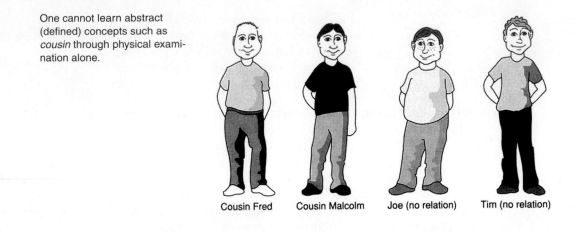

Cousin Fred   Cousin Malcolm   Joe (no relation)   Tim (no relation)

When I was a child, *summer* was a concrete concept for me: Heat, humidity, and no school were easily observable characteristics. I later acquired an abstract concept of summer as I learned how the seasons are determined by the tilt of the earth in relation to the sun. In a similar way, children first learn about a *circle* as a concrete concept (i.e., a "roundish" thing); later, perhaps in a high school geometry class, they may acquire an abstract definition (i.e., all points on a plane equidistant from another single point). And they will initially conceptualize various family members (cousins, uncles, etc.) in terms of things they can actually see, rather than in terms of the nature of the relationship (Keil, 1989). The following two conversations, each between an experimenter (E) and a child (C), illustrate:

[E:]	This man your daddy's age loves you and your parents and loves to visit and bring presents, but he's not related to your parents at all. He's not your mommy or daddy's brother or sister or anything like that. Could that be an uncle?
C:	Yes.
E:	What is an uncle?
C:	An uncle is that he brings you presents at Christmas.
E:	What else?
C:	An uncle is that he lets you come over to his house.
E:	Could I be your uncle?
C:	No . . . because I don't know you.
E:	If I got to know you and brought you presents, could I be your uncle?
C:	Yes. (Keil, 1989, pp. 71, 76)
[E:]	Suppose your mommy has all sorts of brothers, some very old and some very, very young. One of your mommy's brothers is so young he's only 2 years old. Could that be an uncle?
C:	No . . . because he's little and 2 years old.
E:	How old does an uncle have to be?
C:	About 24 or 25.
E:	If he's 2 years old, can he be an uncle?
C:	No . . . he can be a cousin. (Keil, 1989, pp. 71, 74, 76)

Most concepts are identified by a label—a word that symbolizes the concept and represents it in both thought and communication. For example, you have probably formed a concept that encompasses the many things you have seen with the following characteristics:

- Shorter and wider than most adult humans
- Covered with a short, bristly substance
- Appended at one end by an object similar in appearance to a paintbrush
- Appended at the other end by a lumpy thing with four pointy objects sticking upward (two soft and floppy, two hard and curved around)
- Held up from the ground by four spindly sticks, two at each end
- Usually observed in pastures or barns
- Almost always eating grass

You have no doubt attached a particular label to these similar-looking things: *cow.*

We haven't completely acquired a concept until we can correctly identify all positive and negative instances of it. A **positive instance** is a particular example of a concept. To illustrate, you and I are positive instances of the concept *person,* and this thing you are reading is a positive instance of the concept *book.* A **negative instance** is a nonexample of the concept. You and I are negative instances of the concept *cow,* and this book is a negative instance of the concept *pencil.*

People often have "sort-of" understandings of concepts, in that they cannot always accurately distinguish positive instances from negative instances. A child who vehemently denies that a Chihuahua is a dog has not completely learned the concept of *dog;* neither has the child who calls the neighbor's cow "doggie." Denying that a Chihuahua is a dog—**undergeneralization**— reflects an inability to recognize all positive instances. Identifying a cow as a dog—**overgeneralization**—reflects an inability to reject all negative instances. The various theories of concept learning that we will consider now can help us understand how such "sort-of" knowledge might exist.

Theories of Concept Learning

Some additional terms will be useful to us as we examine the various theories of concept learning that psychologists have proposed. In particular, I need to explain what I mean when I talk about *features* and *rules.*

Features (some theorists instead use the term **attributes**) are the characteristics of a concept's positive instances. For instance, my dog Tobey has numerous features worthy of note, including these:

- Hairy
- At one time, physiologically equipped to impregnate female dogs
- Wearing a red collar
- Likely to bark loudly at any negative instance of an Ormrod
- Presently located on my office floor

Some features are important for identifying positive instances of a concept, whereas others are not. **Defining features** are characteristics that must be present in all positive instances. For example, to be a dog, Tobey should have hair and, as a male member of the species, should have (or once have had) the capability of impregnating a female, who would then eventually give birth to live young. **Correlational features** are frequently found in positive instances but are not essential for concept membership. For example, most dogs bark and many dogs wear collars, but neither of these features is a characteristic of *all* dogs. **Irrelevant features** are characteristics that are unrelated to membership in the concept. Tobey's location on my office floor is totally irrelevant to his dogness.

Let's pause here for a brief exercise. Figure 9.7 presents eight positive instances and eight negative instances of the concept *gudge*. Can you identify one or more defining features of a gudge?

As you may have surmised, the two defining features of a gudge are that it be gray and square. A large black dot is a correlational feature: Black dots are found on six of the eight gudges but on only one nongudge. White dots and topside "whiskers" are irrelevant features, because they are found equally often on gudges and nongudges.

From some theoretical perspectives, learning a concept is a process of learning what features are important for identifying positive instances of the concept. In particular, one must learn that certain features are essential and that others are often present but *not* essential. Learning to differentiate between a concept's defining and correlational features often takes

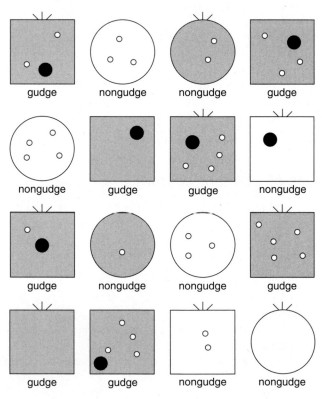

Figure 9.7
Positive and negative instances of a *gudge*.

time and experience (Keil, 1989; Mervis, 1987). For example, consider this question that Saltz (1971) posed to children:

> A father goes to work. On the way home from work in the evening he stops at a bar to have a drink. His friends there are drunkards and he becomes a drunkard too. Is he still a father? (Saltz, 1971, p. 28)

Saltz found that, even at the age of 8, most children denied that a drunkard could still be a father. Apparently, many young children believe that "goodness" defines fatherhood rather than correlating with it, a belief that they are likely to abandon only when they encounter enough "bad" positive instances of a father.

Some concepts have a single defining feature; others are apt to have two or more features that may or may not all need to be present at the same time. For instance, the concept *red* has one defining feature: a particular range of wavelengths. In contrast, the concept *gudge* has two that must both be present: square and gray. An *out* in baseball is an example of a concept for which no single defining feature is always present; for example, it can be three strikes while a player is at bat, the tagging of a player who is running from base to base, or a fly ball caught before it touches the ground. Concept **rules** specify how defining features are combined in delineating particular concepts. Early theorists (Bourne, 1967; Bruner, Goodnow, & Austin, 1956; Dodd & White, 1980; Klein, 1987; Saltz, 1971) identified a variety of possible concept rules, including these:

1. *Simple:* Only one particular feature must be present; for example, *red* is a specific range of wavelengths.
2. *Conjunctive:* Two or more features must all be present; for example, a *circle* must be two-dimensional and must have all points equidistant from a center point.
3. *Disjunctive:* Two or more defining features are not all present at the same time; for example, an *out* in baseball occurs in any one of several different situations.
4. *Relational:* The relationship between two or more features determines the concept; for example, the concept *between* requires three objects, two located on opposite sides of a third.

When early researchers examined the effects of various concept rules on learning, they discovered that simple rules (in which only one feature determines concept membership) are easiest to learn, conjunctive and disjunctive rules are moderately difficult, and relational rules are most difficult (Bourne, 1967; Haygood & Bourne, 1965; Neisser & Weene, 1962). Consistent with this finding is the fact that although children begin to form a few simple relational concepts (e.g., *above, below, between*) before age 1, they may continue to struggle with certain relational concepts until the early elementary grades (Owens, 1996; Palermo, 1973; Quinn, 2003). For example, many 7-year-olds do not fully understand what the concept *less* means.

With these "concepts about concepts" in mind, we now look at several views of concept learning that psychologists have proposed: buildup of associations, hypothesis testing, prototypes, feature lists, and exemplars.

Buildup of Associations

Consistent with their focus on stimuli and responses, early behaviorists tended to view a *concept* not as a mental entity but rather as a common response to a number of different stimuli (e.g., Kendler, 1961). In one early behaviorist theory, Clark Hull (1920) suggested that acquiring a concept is largely a process of building up associations between particular aspects of a stimulus and particular responses to that stimulus. To use contemporary terminology, Hull suggested that any instance of a concept has both defining and irrelevant features, and that a learner who correctly identifies a stimulus as being a positive instance is reinforced for responding to both its defining and irrelevant features. When correctly identifying a second positive instance, the learner is again reinforced for responding to the defining and irrelevant features. In repeated encounters with positive instances of the concept, the defining features are always the same; however, the irrelevant features differ from one occasion to the next. Thus, the response is more closely associated with the defining features than with irrelevant features, and so the organism learns to respond in the same way to the same (defining) features of different positive instances.

A demonstration exercise, in which you will learn the concept *mudge* using Figure 9.8, illustrates Hull's theory. Your first step is to get two index cards or similar-sized pieces of paper. Use one card to cover the right side of the figure. Now take the second card and cover the left side, exposing only the top section above the first horizontal line. You will see two objects, one of which is a mudge. Take a wild guess, and see if you can pick the mudge. Once you have made your selection, move your paper down the left column to the next horizontal line, revealing the correct answer. In this section you will also see two more objects; pick the one you think is the mudge. Keep moving your paper down the page, one section at a time, on each occasion getting your feedback and then selecting a likely mudge from the next pair of objects. Continue the process with the pairs in the right-hand column.

You have presumably learned that *mudge* is "large." Let's analyze this concept learning task from Hull's perspective. You were reinforced every time you chose a large square, you were never

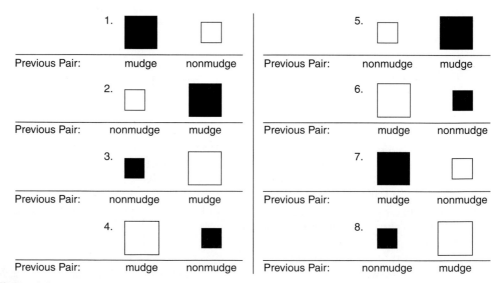

Figure 9.8
Identify the *mudge* in each pair.

reinforced for choosing a small square, and you were reinforced for choosing black, white, left, or right squares about half of the time. Thus, the occurrence of reinforcement for choosing boxes with different characteristics was as follows:

Characteristic	Amount of Reinforcement
large	100%
small	0%
black	50%
white	50%
left	50%
right	50%

Because it has been reinforced every time, the response of selecting "large" should be the strongest one for you, and you should therefore be most likely to choose a large square again, regardless of its color and position.

Although contemporary psychologists have largely abandoned simple stimulus-response explanations of human learning, many acknowledge that relatively "nonmental" associations may form the basis of some concepts, especially for infants and young children (Gelman & Kalish, 2006; Kuhn & Franklin, 2006; Younger, 2003; also see Kendler & Kendler, 1959). Well before their first birthday, children show an ability to detect commonly occurring patterns in the world around them: They realize that certain features tend to go together and other features do not. In a sense, infants are budding statisticians, unconsciously tabulating the frequencies of the various characteristics they observe and detecting correlations among some of them (Ariely, 2001; Gelman & Kalish, 2006; Younger, 2003). Such an ability may, for example, underlie infants' early understanding of words in their native language (Saffran, 2003).

Hypothesis Testing

Take a few minutes to learn the concept *studge* using Figure 9.9 and the two index cards you gathered for the *mudge* exercise. Cover the right side of the figure with one card, and cover all but the top section of the left side with the other card. In the exposed section in the upper left, you will see a rectangle with three gray circles inside; take a wild guess and decide whether the rectangle is a studge. Once you have made your guess, move the left card down to the next horizontal line, revealing the correct answer. In this section you will also see a second rectangle, one with a gray square inside; decide whether you think it is a studge. Keep moving the card down the left side of the figure, one section at a time, on each occasion getting your feedback and then deciding whether the next rectangle is a studge. Continue the process with the rectangles on the right side of the figure.

Now that you have finished, you have, I hope, learned that the concept *studge* is "two or three circles." Shape and number are defining features for the concept; color is irrelevant to studgeness. In learning about studges, perhaps you found yourself forming different hypotheses about what is and is not a studge. For instance, the first example was a studge. You may have used that positive instance to generate one or more hypotheses, such as the following:

- A studge is anything gray.
- A studge is round.
- A studge is three of something.
- A studge is three gray circles

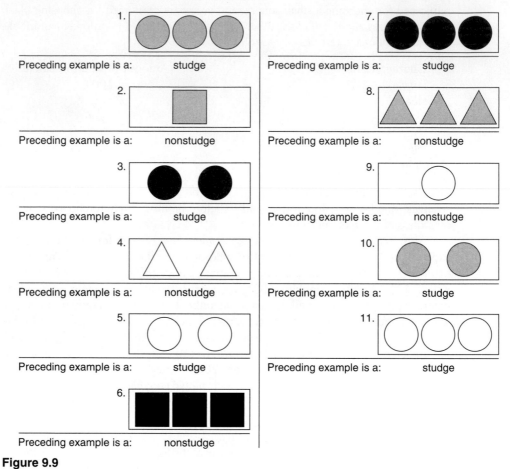

Figure 9.9
Positive and negative instances of a *studge*.

The second example in Figure 9.9 was a nonstudge, so, had you held the hypothesis that a studge is gray, you would have eliminated this hypothesis at that point. A hypothesis such as "three of something," however, would have been confirmed with the second example but disconfirmed with the third. Eventually you may have been left with only the correct, two-or-three-circles hypothesis.

In another early theory of concept learning, Bruner, Goodnow, and Austin (1956) proposed that concept learning is a process of forming various hypotheses about the features and rules that define a concept and then using positive and negative instances to confirm or reject each hypothesis. To support their theory, they used stimuli similar to my positive and negative instances of studges to study concept learning in adults. They gave participants in their study one positive instance of the concept and then asked them to try to select other positive instances from among an array of stimuli varying on four dimensions (shape, color, number of objects, and number of borders around the objects). By noting the selections that were made, Bruner and his colleagues observed several approaches that the participants used in formulating and testing their hypotheses. Some people appeared to test one hypothesis at a time, choosing stimuli that varied on only one feature from a previous positive instance. If they received feedback that confirmed their hypothesis, they continued to test it; if they received contradictory feedback, they would form a different hypothesis and begin to test that one. Other people appeared to hold several hypotheses in mind at the same time and test them simultaneously as they chose various stimuli. This latter strategy would, of course, be faster, but it would also place greater demands on working memory, hence leading to more errors. This tendency to test several hypotheses simultaneously was also observed by Levine (1966).

Studies of children's early vocabulary learning indicate that human beings are predisposed to favor some hypotheses over others. For example, when 2- and 3-year-olds hear a new word— *wudge,* perhaps—attached to a particular object in a group of objects, they are likely to think that the object's shape (rather than, say, its size or color) is a defining feature and so will identify similarly shaped objects as also being wudges (Diesendruck & Bloom, 2003; Gershkoff-Stowe & Smith, 2004). Another predisposition is to hypothesize that a new word refers to something for which one does not already have a label. For example, imagine that you see a collection of eight different objects and know the names of only five of them. If someone mentions an unfamiliar word—*brudge,* let's say—and asks you to find an example in the collection, chances are that you will choose one of the three previously unlabeled objects as being a brudge. Even most 3- and 4-year-olds make such a choice (Au & Glusman, 1990).

Although some hypothesis testing may very well occur when people learn concepts, it is certainly not the only process involved in concept learning. Experiments in which hypothesis testing has been observed have been criticized as being artificial and not resembling real-world concept learning conditions (Glass et al., 1979; Rosch, 1973a). People rarely encounter a situation in which they can pick possible examples of a concept in a systematic manner; more typically, they find a positive instance here, a negative instance there, and so on, in a somewhat haphazard fashion over a period of time. Furthermore, in several experiments (Brooks, 1978; Reber & Allen, 1978; Reber, Kassin, Lewis, & Cantor, 1980), people who were instructed to identify the rules underlying certain classification schemes (i.e., to form hypotheses) actually performed more poorly than people who were not so instructed. In these cases, the more successful learners were the less analytic ones: They simply remembered early positive instances and compared new examples with them. A different theory of concept learning—one involving the formation of prototypes—better explains such findings.

Prototypes

Eleanor Rosch (1973a, 1973b, 1977a; Rosch, Mervis, Gray, Johnson, & Boyes-Braem, 1976) and other theorists (Eysenck & Keane, 1990; Kemler Nelson, 1990; Wittgenstein, 1958) have argued that many real-world concepts are difficult to delineate in terms of defining features and precise rules. Objects can lack important features yet still be identified as positive instances of a particular concept. For example, a common feature of human beings is that they have two legs, but you can still recognize a person who has no legs as being a human. Similarly, although dogs typically have hair, a few breeds with little or no hair have recently emerged. Thus, people must often use correlational features rather than defining features to identify positive instances of a concept.

Furthermore, concepts may have fuzzy boundaries, so that in certain borderline cases correct identification of positive and negative instances is difficult (Labov, 1973; Oden, 1987; Rosch, 1973a, 1978; Zazdeh, Fu, Tanak, & Shimura, 1975). For instance, is a stroke a *disease*?

In a study by McCloskey and Glucksberg (1978), some people believed that it was and others did not. Is turquoise a shade of *blue* or a shade of *green*? My husband insists that turquoise is green, but I know better: It's blue.

Rosch (1973a, 1973b, 1977a, 1977b, 1978; Rosch & Mervis, 1975; Rosch et al., 1976) and others (Attneave, 1957; Tennyson & Cocchiarella, 1986; Walton & Bower, 1993) have proposed that people form concepts by developing a **prototype,** or representative example, of a typical member of that category. As an illustration, form an image in your mind of a *bird*. What probably comes to mind is a small creature, perhaps about the shape and size of a robin or sparrow. It is unlikely that you would instead imagine a penguin or an ostrich because these animals, although they are birds, are not as typically birdlike in appearance as robins and sparrows. Similarly, imagine a *vehicle*. Your image probably resembles a car or a truck rather than a canoe or hot-air balloon, because cars and trucks are more commonly observed instances of vehicles. Now imagine *red*. You probably picture a color similar to that red crayon you had when you were 5 rather than maroon or shocking pink.

A prototype is likely to incorporate features of the most typical, commonly observed positive instances of the concept. For instance, your prototype of a human being probably has two arms and two legs, stands upright, and is slightly less than 2 meters tall. Your prototype of a table is apt to be a rectangular flat surface held up by four legs, one of them at each of the four corners. You identify new objects as positive instances of a particular concept when you compare them with the concept prototype and find them to be sufficiently similar. A positive identification does not require that all features be present, however. Thus, you can still recognize a legless man as a human being, and you can still recognize a three-legged object as a table.

At least two sources of evidence support the idea that many concepts may be represented in memory in the form of prototypes. First, people easily identify positive instances of a concept that closely resemble the prototype but have difficulty identifying positive instances that are less similar (Glass, Holyoak, & O'Dell, 1974; Rips et al., 1973; Rosch, 1978; Wilkins, 1971). In one experiment (Rosch, 1973b), elementary school and undergraduate students identified as birds those creatures that looked particularly birdlike (e.g., robins and sparrows) more quickly than they identified creatures less similar to the prototype (e.g., chickens and ducks).

A second source of evidence for prototypes is the finding that people usually recognize positive instances they haven't previously encountered when those instances closely resemble a prototypical example. In fact, people recognize them more easily than positive instances they *have* encountered that do *not* closely match the prototype (Bomba & Siqueland, 1983; Franks & Bransford, 1971; Posner, Goldsmith, & Welton, 1967; Posner & Keele, 1968). For example, in an experiment by Franks and Bransford (1971), college students viewed a series of geometric patterns that involved one or more variations from a particular "base" pattern; the base pattern itself was not presented. The students were then shown another series of patterns (including the base pattern) and asked to identify which ones they had previously seen; they had actually seen *none* of these patterns earlier. Students were especially likely to "recognize" patterns that closely resembled the base pattern; they were most confident that they had seen the base pattern itself. Presumably, the base pattern represented the single best example of the various stimuli the students had originally seen and thus most closely approximated the pattern prototype they had formed.

Rosch and her colleagues (1976) have suggested that conceptual prototypes may be organized in a three-level hierarchy—a hierarchical organizational scheme similar to what I described earlier in the chapter. **Basic-level concepts** are the ones we use most frequently—for instance, the ones we use when we name objects (this is a *chair,* this is a *hat,* this is a *car,* and so on). **Superordinate concepts** are more general categories that encompass a number of basic-level concepts (e.g., chairs and tables are both *furniture,* hats and shoes are two kinds of *clothing,* and cars and trucks are *vehicles*). **Subordinate concepts** are more specific subdivisions of basic-level concepts (e.g., *rocking chairs* and *lawn chairs* are types of chairs, *berets* and *bowlers* are types of hats, and *Volkswagen Beetles* and *Ford Mustangs* are types of cars). You can think of the three levels as reflecting varying degrees of abstraction: The superordinate concepts are most abstract, and the subordinate concepts are most concrete.

At least when we consider concepts that have verbal labels—*words*—children learn basic-level concepts first, with superordinate and subordinate concepts coming a bit later (Gelman & Kalish, 2006; Mervis, Pani, & Pani, 2003). As children learn more about the category in question, they begin to make finer and finer discriminations among subcategories, especially when the adults around them introduce new words for the subcategories. As an example, after months of age-appropriate input from his parents, a 24-month-old boy named Ari knew 38 bird names—*penguin, peacock, chickadee, flamingo, grosbeak,* and so on. He overgeneralized or under-generalized some of the concepts—for instance, he once used *peacock* in reference to a pheasant—but overall he had pinned down the various kinds of birds exceedingly well for a 2-year-old (Mervis et al., 2003).

We probably cannot explain all human concept learning strictly in terms of the development of prototypes, however. For one thing, how we categorize an object depends on the context in which we find it. For instance, if a cuplike object contains flowers, we might identify it as a *vase* rather than a *cup;* if it contains mashed potatoes, we might instead identify it as a *bowl* (Labov, 1973; Schwartz & Reisberg, 1991). Furthermore, not all concepts lend themselves readily to a single prototypical representation (Eysenck & Keane, 1990; Hampton, 1981). For instance, I have a difficult time identifying a typical example of *music:* Classical, rock, jazz, and country-western are all quite different.

Feature Lists

Feature list theory (Bourne, 1982; Bourne et al., 1986; Neumann, 1974, 1977; Rips et al., 1973; Smith, Shoben, & Rips, 1974; Ward, Vela, & Haas, 1990) is in some ways similar to prototype theory but focuses more on a concept's defining and correlational features. From this perspective, learning a concept involves developing a **feature list** that includes the following:

- Relevant features, both defining and correlational, of the concept
- The probability that each of these features is likely to be present in any specific instance—that is, the frequency with which each feature occurs
- The relationships among the features—that is, the rules for their combination

Recognizing an object as a positive instance of a concept, then, is a matter of determining whether the object possesses enough relevant features. Prototypes are recognized more quickly than other positive instances only because they encompass most or all of the concept's relevant features.

A prediction from feature list theory is that negative instances will be erroneously identified as positive instances if a sufficient number of relevant features are present. Bourne (1982) confirmed this prediction in an experiment involving an *exclusive disjunctive* concept. Earlier in the chapter, I described a disjunctive concept as being one with two or more defining features that do not all need to be present at once (the example I gave was an *out* in baseball). An exclusive disjunctive concept is a subcategory of this kind of concept: An item possessing any of the defining features is a positive instance, but an item possessing all of them is not. (For example, a *pludge* is anything that is red or square, but things that are both red and square are non-pludges.) In an experiment involving college students, Bourne presented numerous positive and negative instances of an exclusive disjunctive concept that had two relevant features; an item that had one, but *only* one, of the features was a positive instance. Despite their training, when the students were later asked to identify examples of the concept, they were more likely to "recognize" those stimuli possessing both relevant features than those possessing only one of the two features.

As you discovered in chapter 7, we human beings have a natural tendency to pick up on the relative frequencies of various objects and events in our lives (recall how you knew that the word *bacon* occurs more frequently in the English language than *pastrami*). And consistent with our earlier discussion of buildup-of-associations views of concept learning, we also seem to acquire some knowledge about the statistical odds with which various features are likely to be present in positive instances of a concept (Ariely, 2001). Yet feature list theory is probably not the perfect explanation of concept learning, either: As we noted earlier, we cannot always identify the specific features on which concepts are based. To the extent that we can identify defining and correlational features, however, our awareness of them undoubtedly comprises part of our knowledge about concepts.

Exemplars

In some cases, our knowledge of a concept may be based more on a variety of examples—that is, on **exemplars**—than on a single prototype (Carmichael & Hayes, 2001; Reisberg, 1997; Ross & Spalding, 1994; Sadoski & Paivio, 2001). Exemplars can give us an idea of the variability we are likely to see in any category of objects or events. As an illustration, consider the concept *fruit.* Many things are likely to come to mind here: Apples, bananas, grapes, mangos, and kiwifruit are all possibilities. If you encounter a new instance of fruit—a blackberry, let's say—you could compare it with the variety of exemplars you have already stored and find one (a raspberry, perhaps) that is relatively similar.

It is possible that prototypes or exemplars are used to identify positive instances in clear-cut situations, whereas formal definitions (which include defining features) are used in other, more ambiguous ones (Andre, 1986; Glass & Holyoak, 1975; Glass et al., 1979). In some cases, it may also be true that children rely on prototypes or exemplars initially and then acquire a more general, abstract understanding (perhaps including a formal definition) later on (e.g., Liu et al., 2001). As a preschooler, my son Jeff adamantly denied that the concept *animal* includes people, fish, and insects. The belief that these organisms are nonanimals is a common phenomenon among young children, who often restrict their conception of animals to four-legged mammals (Carey, 1985; Kyle & Shymansky, 1989; Saltz, 1971). I suspect that Jeff's animal prototype might have resembled the family dog or perhaps the cows he often saw in the surrounding countryside. When he began studying the animal kingdom in school, he learned a biology-based definition of an animal that incorporates some of its major features: a form of life that derives its food from other organisms, responds immediately to its environment, and can move its body. At that point Jeff acknowledged that people, fish, and creepy-crawlies are legitimate animals. (If he were to study biology in depth at some future time, however, he might learn that biologists do not totally agree on a definition of *animal* and that true defining features of the concept are difficult to identify.)

Reconciling Theories of Concept Learning

Each of the theories of concept learning we've just examined certainly has an element of truth. As human beings, perhaps we represent any single concept in long-term memory as a prototype, a set of defining and correlational features, *and* a number of exemplars (e.g., Armstrong, Gleitman, & Gleitman, 1983). Infants and toddlers undoubtedly rely on unintentional, unconscious statistical tabulations as they begin to learn the words associated with various objects and events. And clearly there are times when we form and test hypotheses about the nature of particular concepts (I recall consciously struggling with the difference between a *brush* and a *comb* when I was a preschooler). As we strive to better understand the nature of concept learning, we do not necessarily need to choose just one theory as being the "right" one to the exclusion of the others. It is quite likely that different approaches to concept learning are more or less useful for different age groups, for different kinds of concepts, and at different points in the learning process (Feldman, 2003; Gelman & Kalish, 2006; Reisberg, 1997).

In our discussion of concepts, two factors have emerged as essential components of the concept learning process. First, people must learn the characteristics that determine concept membership (and discover which of those characteristics, if any, are truly definitive). Second, they must develop awareness of the degree of acceptable variation from best examples of the concept. For example, an ostrich is a bird even though it is much larger than the prototypical bird; however, a certain other creature that is the same size and also walks on two legs—a human being— falls outside of the bird category. In other words, to learn a concept completely, one must eventually learn its boundaries.

Factors Facilitating Concept Learning

Young children seem quite eager to learn new concepts, especially those that have verbal labels. Hearing a new word clues them in to the fact that others in their community find the word—and so also the concept that it represents—quite useful in everyday life (Goldstone & Johansen, 2003). And when children encounter a new, unfamiliar object, they are likely to ask "What is it?" and to press for information about what purpose the object serves (Kemler Nelson, Egan, & Holt, 2004).

The following principles capture important factors affecting concept learning and yield strategies for helping learners of all ages acquire new concepts:

• *Concepts are easier to learn when defining features are more salient than correlational and irrelevant features.* The more obvious a concept's defining features are—the more readily they capture a learner's attention—the easier the concept is to master, especially for young children (e.g., Rakison, 2003). As a young child, my son Jeff easily learned the correct meanings of *red, hot,* and *television,* presumably because the features that define these concepts are readily observable. However, he struggled with words such as *spring, summer, work,* and *university*—concepts whose defining features are not so apparent.

Because young children typically pay more attention to obvious features, their early understandings of concepts are apt to be based on such features. For example, in a study by DeVries (1969), children ranging in age from 3 to 6 played for a short time with a good-natured cat named Maynard. Then, as they watched, the experimenter placed a ferocious-looking dog mask on Maynard and asked them, "What is this animal now?" Many of the 3-year-olds asserted that Maynard was now a dog and refused to pet him. In contrast, the 6-year-olds could overlook the dog mask, recognizing that it did not change Maynard's catness. As children grow older, they begin to attend less to perceptually salient features and focus more on abstract qualities (Anglin, 1977; Keil, 1989; Rakison, 2003).

Salient correlational features can often be helpful in the early stages of concept learning, in part because they make positive instances easier to identify. For example, the concept *bird* is relatively easy to learn, because many characteristics—feathers, wings, beak, small size, and scrawny legs and feet—are either defining or correlational features. But learners who are overly dependent on correlational features will sometimes make errors. More specifically, they may either overgeneralize (i.e., identify something as an example of a concept when in fact it is not) or undergeneralize (i.e., overlook a true example of a concept). For instance, the concept *animal* is difficult for many children, because many of the salient features of positive instances—body covering, nature and number of limbs, facial features, shape, and size—are correlational rather than defining features. So, too, might a true understanding of the concept *art* be a tough one to acquire. Things that stand out about a particular work of art are characteristics such as shape, color, medium (e.g., paint or clay), and subject matter (e.g., people or objects), yet these characteristics are only tangentially related to what art *is*.

One logical strategy for enhancing concept learning, then, is to highlight a concept's defining features while downplaying its correlational and irrelevant ones. For instance, a science teacher who creates a line drawing to illustrate the concept of *insect* might make an insect's essential characteristics (e.g., six legs, three body parts) more noticeable by outlining them with dark, thick, lines. Similarly, a music teacher who wants to help students learn about *three-quarter time* might have them tap out the rhythm with drumsticks or their fingers as they listen to waltzes and other songs that have three beats to a measure.

◆ *Definitions facilitate concept learning* (Fukkink & de Glopper, 1998; R. M. Gagné, 1985; Tennyson & Cocchiarella, 1986). A good definition includes defining features plus any rules related to them (e.g., "all defining features must be present"). Furthermore, it describes the concept in terms of other concepts with which students are already familiar (R. M. Gagné, 1985). Definitions and other explicit descriptions may be especially helpful when concepts involve a number of defining features or reflect concepts involve conjunctive, disjunctive, or relational rules.

◆ *Numerous and varied positive instances help to illustrate a concept* (Clark, 1971; R. M. Gagné, 1985; Merrill & Tennyson, 1977, 1978; Tennyson & Cocchiarella, 1986). Through encountering many instances of concepts, people can form prototypes of the concepts. In some situations, in fact, providing a "best example" is more helpful than offering a definition. To illustrate, Park (1984) used two instructional methods to teach basic psychology concepts (e.g., *positive reinforcement* and *negative reinforcement*) to high school students. For some students, instruction focused on the defining features of the concepts; for others, it focused on illustrative examples of the concepts. Students for whom defining features were emphasized were better able to classify new examples during instruction. However, students who had been given examples of the concepts remembered more of what they had learned after instruction was completed. Ideally, of course, definitions and examples should be presented hand in hand, and in fact this combination of methods leads to more effective concept learning than either method alone (Dunn, 1983; Tennyson, Youngers, & Suebsonthi, 1983).

Concepts are better learned with many examples than with only one or two (Kinnick, 1990; Tennyson & Park, 1980; Tennyson & Tennyson, 1975). First examples should be simple and straightforward, with as few irrelevant features as possible (Clark, 1971; Merrill & Tennyson, 1977, 1978).

Later examples should be more difficult, with more irrelevant features present (Clark, 1971; Kinnick, 1990; Merrill & Tennyson, 1977). Ultimately, examples should illustrate the full range of the concept so that students do not undergeneralize (Merrill & Tennyson, 1978; Tennyson & Cocchiarella, 1986); for example, the concept *mammal* should be illustrated by whales and platypuses as well as by cats and dogs.

    ◆ *Negative instances are useful in demonstrating what a concept is* **not** (Clark, 1971; R. M. Gagné, 1985; Tennyson & Cocchiarella, 1986). Negative instances, especially when they are *near misses* to the concept, are helpful in defining the concept's limits and in preventing overgeneralization (Merrill & Tennyson, 1977; Winston, 1973). For example, in learning about dogs, students can be shown that such similar-looking animals as cats, goats, and cows are nondogs in order to learn just where to draw the line on dogness.

    ◆ *Positive and negative instances are more effective when presented simultaneously.* In their everyday lives, people typically learn concepts through **sequential presentation:** They encounter a series of positive and negative instances one at a time over a period of weeks, months, or years, and in the process they may gain information about what is and is not an example of the concept. But a faster way to learn concepts is **simultaneous presentation,** in which people can see a number of positive and negative instances all at once (Bourne, Ekstrand, & Dominowski, 1971; Ellis & Hunt, 1983; R. M. Gagné, 1985). One likely reason for the difference in effectiveness is that in sequential presentation, the learner must store in memory what is learned from each instance, and that information can be forgotten from one instance to the next. In simultaneous presentation, the information to be gleaned from positive and negative instances is available all at once, so demands on memory are not as great.

    ◆ *Classroom assessment tasks can enhance as well as monitor concept learning.* Do students truly understand what a concept is, or have they simply memorized a definition in a rote, meaningless fashion? To find out, teachers can ask students to select positive instances of the concept from among numerous possibilities (Kinnick, 1990; Merrill & Tennyson, 1977; Tennyson & Cocchiarella, 1986). One educator has called this strategy an *eg hunt,* a tongue-in-cheek variation of "e.g." (Thiagarajan, 1989). Students who have not completely mastered a concept will be unable to identify all positive and negative instances accurately, especially in borderline cases. For instance, in one study (P. Wilson, 1988), sixth and eighth graders were asked to define the concept

Concepts are best learned through a simultaneous presentation of both positive and negative instances.

Each of these is a dog.

None of these is a dog.

rectangle: Many of them defined a rectangle in such a way that squares were (appropriately) included. Yet, when shown a variety of shapes and asked to identify the rectangles, the great majority of students who had correctly defined the concept of rectangle nevertheless did *not* identify any squares as being positive instances.

In addition to asking students to identify positive and negative instances, teachers might also ask students to generate their *own* examples and applications of a concept. By doing so, teachers encourage students to check and refine their current understandings (Ellis & Hunt, 1983; Watts & Anderson, 1971). The benefits of self-generated examples and applications are illustrated in an experiment in which high school students received instruction in basic psychological concepts (Watts & Anderson, 1971). Students who were asked to apply the concepts to new situations remembered more of the material than students who were asked only to recall certain facts.

Concepts are perhaps the simplest ways in which we organize the world around us. But we also organize concepts into larger, more inclusive concepts, and often organize the more inclusive concepts into even *more* inclusive ones, and so on, in a hierarchical fashion (recall our earlier discussion of subordinate, basic-level, and superordinate concepts). Children become increasingly flexible in how they organize their concepts, perhaps thinking of a *muffin* as a type of *bread* on one occasion and as a type of *breakfast food* on another occasion, depending on the demands of the situation at hand (Nguyen & Murphy, 2003). In addition, children and adults alike integrate their concepts into more complex and comprehensive understandings of their world. Our next topics of discussion, *schemas* and *scripts,* are examples of how we might pull several concepts together.

SCHEMAS AND SCRIPTS

In contemporary cognitive theory, the term **schema** usually refers to a closely connected set of ideas (including concepts) related to a specific object or event (Bartlett, 1932; Dansereau, 1995; Derry, 1996; Rumelhart & Ortony, 1977; Willingham, 2004). For example, you probably have a schema for what a faculty member's *office* is typically like: It is usually a small room that contains a desk, one or more chairs, bookshelves with books, and other items useful in performing academic duties. You undoubtedly also have a schema about the nature of physical *substances*—a schema that includes ideas such as the following:

- A substance has a location: It is somewhere in particular.
- A substance is stable: It doesn't simply appear or disappear without cause.
- A substance is sensitive to gravity: It will fall toward the earth if nothing holds it up.
- A substance can move: For instance, it can be pushed. (Reiner, Slotta, Chi, & Resnick, 2000)

Our schemas often influence how we perceive and remember new situations. For instance, your schema of a faculty office might distort your later memory of what a particular office was actually like. In a study by Brewer and Treyens (1981), 30 college students were brought, one at a time, to a room they believed to be the experimenter's university office. After waiting in the office for less than a minute, they were taken to another room and asked to write down everything they could remember about the room. Most students correctly remembered things that one would expect to find in an office (e.g., a desk, a chair, and shelves). Relatively few of them remembered items not likely to be part of an office schema (e.g., a skull, a clown-shaped light switch, and a tennis racket). And 9 of the 30 students "remembered" books that weren't there at all!

People often form schemas about events as well as objects; such event schemas are sometimes called **scripts** (Bower, Black, & Turner, 1979; Dansereau, 1995; Schank, 1975; Schank & Abelson, 1977). As an illustration, consider the following situation:

> John was feeling bad today so he decided to go see the family doctor. He checked in with the doctor's receptionist, and then looked through several medical magazines that were on the table by his chair. Finally the nurse came and asked him to take off his clothes. The doctor was very nice to him. He eventually prescribed some pills for John. Then John left the doctor's office and headed home. (Bower et al., 1979, p. 190)

You probably had no trouble understanding the passage because you have been to a doctor's office yourself and have a script for how those visits usually go. You can therefore fill in a number of details that the passage doesn't ever tell you. You probably inferred that John must have *traveled* to the doctor's office, although the story omits this essential step. Likewise, you probably concluded that John took his clothes off in the examination room, *not* in the waiting room, even though the story never makes it clear where John did his striptease. As you can see, then, a person's mental script for an event will influence what information is "learned" from a given instance of the event. In a study by Bower and colleagues (1979), college students read the same passage you just read. The students in the experiment "remembered" reading about many activities that were likely to be part of a visit to the doctor (e.g., arriving at the doctor's office) but that they had in fact *not* read.

Other research provides further support for the idea that schemas and scripts influence how learners process, store, and remember new information. To illustrate, people have an easier time making sense of poems from various historical periods when they have well-developed schemas for poems written in each of those periods (Peskin, 1998). Many people (especially those with stereotypical schemas about how males and females behave) more accurately remember pictures and films that portray men and women behaving in a gender-stereotypical rather than counterstereotypical manner (Cordua, McGraw, & Drabman, 1979; Martin & Halverson, 1981; Signorella & Liben, 1984). People also have an easier time remembering events similar to those in their own culture, presumably because such events are consistent with recognizable scripts (Lipson, 1983; Reynolds, Taylor, Steffensen, Shirey, & Anderson, 1982; Steffensen, Joag-Dev, & Anderson, 1979). And consider the following story about two boys playing hooky:

> The two boys ran until they came to the driveway. "See, I told you today was good for skipping school," said Mark. "Mom is never home on Thursday," he added. Tall hedges hid the house from the road so the pair strolled across the finely landscaped yard. "I never knew your place was so big," said Pete. "Yeah, but it's nicer now than it used to be since Dad had the new stone siding put on and added the fireplace."
>
> There were front and back doors and a side door which led to the garage which was empty except for three parked 10-speed bikes. They went in the side door, Mark explaining that it was always open in case his younger sisters got home earlier than their mother.
>
> Pete wanted to see the house so Mark started with the living room. It, like the rest of the downstairs, was newly painted. Mark turned on the stereo, the noise of which worried Pete. "Don't worry, the nearest house is a quarter of a mile away," Mark shouted. Pete felt more comfortable observing that no houses could be seen in any direction beyond the huge yard.

The dining room, with all the china, silver, and cut glass, was no place to play so the boys moved into the kitchen where they made sandwiches. Mark said they wouldn't go to the basement because it had been damp and musty ever since the new plumbing had been installed. (Pichert & Anderson, 1977, p. 310)

You would probably remember different details from the story, depending on whether you read it from the perspective of a potential home buyer or a potential burglar (Anderson & Pichert, 1978). Different schemas and scripts come into play for buying versus burgling a home.

As we noted in chapter 7, the human memory system typically encounters more information than it can possibly handle. Schemas and scripts provide a means for reducing this information overload: They help people to focus their attention on things that are likely to be important and to ignore what is probably unimportant (Goetz, Schallert, Reynolds, & Radin, 1983; Martin & Halverson, 1981; Sweller, 1994; Wilson & Anderson, 1986). For example, when going to see the doctor, it is more important to check in with the receptionist than to study the pictures on the waiting room wall. Schemas also enable people to make sense of incomplete information (R. C. Anderson, 1984; Dansereau, 1995; Martin & Halverson, 1981; Rumelhart & Ortony, 1977; Wilson & Anderson, 1986). As a result, individuals may "remember" things that they never specifically encountered but instead filled in using their existing schemas and scripts (Bower et al., 1979; Farrar & Goodman, 1992; Flavell et al., 2002; Kardash, Royer, & Greene, 1988).

Schema theory has intuitive appeal as a way of helping us understand how we organize our experiences and use what we've learned to predict and interpret future experiences. It has been criticized for being somewhat vague, however; for example, theorists have not been very precise regarding what schemas and scripts actually *are* (Dansereau, 1995; Reynolds, Sinatra, & Jetton, 1996). Furthermore, although we can reasonably assume that people form and modify schemas and scripts based on the specific objects and events they encounter in their lives (Flavell et al., 2002; Pressley, with McCormick, 1995; Rumelhart, 1980), the cognitive processes that occur during this learning are not at all clear.

Schemas and scripts usually relate to relatively specific objects and events. Another concept—that of *personal theories*—can help us understand how people may organize their knowledge and beliefs on a much grander scale.

PERSONAL THEORIES

Many psychologists have speculated that people form general theories—coherent belief systems that encompass cause–effect relationships—about many aspects of the world around them, including physical phenomena, biological phenomena, social relationships, political entities, and mental events (e.g., Flavell, 2000; Haskell, 2001; Hatano & Inagaki, 1996; Kuhn, 2001b; Torney-Purta, 1994; Wellman & Gelman, 1992). To distinguish these theories from those that scientists formulate based on considerable research evidence, I'll refer to them as **personal theories**.[8]

This perspective of how people organize knowledge is sometimes known as **theory theory**. No, you're not seeing double here: We're discussing a theoretical perspective about people's everyday theories. As an illustration of this approach, take a minute to read the two scenarios in Figure 9.10 and answer the questions that each one poses.

---

[8]Some theorists instead call them *folk theories*.

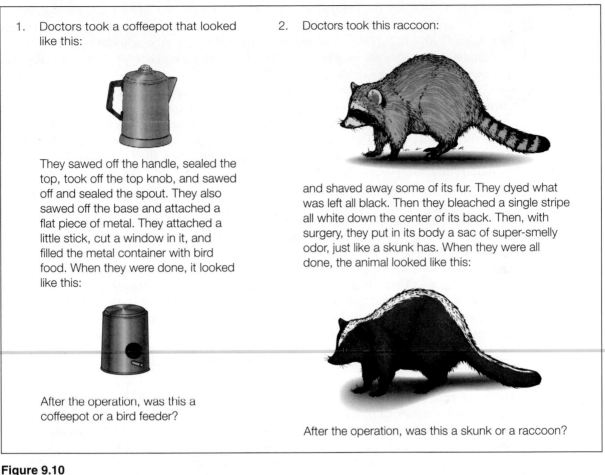

1. Doctors took a coffeepot that looked like this:

They sawed off the handle, sealed the top, took off the top knob, and sawed off and sealed the spout. They also sawed off the base and attached a flat piece of metal. They attached a little stick, cut a window in it, and filled the metal container with bird food. When they were done, it looked like this:

After the operation, was this a coffeepot or a bird feeder?

2. Doctors took this raccoon:

and shaved away some of its fur. They dyed what was left all black. Then they bleached a single stripe all white down the center of its back. Then, with surgery, they put in its body a sac of super-smelly odor, just like a skunk has. When they were all done, the animal looked like this:

After the operation, was this a skunk or a raccoon?

Figure 9.10
What the doctors did.
Both scenarios based on Keil, 1989, p. 184.

Chances are, you concluded that the coffeepot had been transformed into a bird feeder but that the raccoon was still a raccoon despite its radical surgery; even fourth graders come to these conclusions (Keil, 1986, 1989). Now how is it possible that the coffeepot could be made into something entirely different, whereas the raccoon could not?

The concepts that people form are influenced in part by the theories they have about how the world operates (Gelman & Kalish, 2006; Keil, 1994; Medin, 1989). For example, young children—even infants—seem to make a basic distinction between man-made objects (e.g., coffeepots and bird feeders) and biological entities (e.g., raccoons and skunks) (Greif, Kemler Nelson, Keil, & Gutierrez, 2006; Mandler, 2003; Poulin-Dubois, 1999). Furthermore, young children seem to conceptualize the two categories in fundamentally different ways: Man-made objects are defined largely by the *functions* they serve (e.g., keeping coffee warm or feeding birds), whereas biological entities are defined primarily by their origins (e.g., the parents who brought them into being or their DNA). Thus, when a coffeepot begins to hold birdseed rather than coffee, it becomes a bird feeder by virtue of the fact that its function has changed. But when a raccoon is surgically altered to look like a skunk, it still has raccoon parents and raccoon DNA and so cannot possibly *be* a skunk (Keil, 1987, 1989). Thinking along similar lines, even preschoolers will tell you that you cannot change a yellow finch into a bluebird by giving it a coat of blue paint or dressing it in a "bluebird" costume (Keil, 1989).

Theories about the world begin to emerge in the early months of life, long before children encounter formal scientific theories at school. For instance, in our discussion of *core knowledge* in chapter 2, we saw evidence that 3- to 4-month-old infants have already begun to form a theory about the physical world: They are surprised when solid objects seem to be suspended in midair or appear to pass directly through other objects. Apparently, then, their early theories of physics include rudimentary understandings of gravity and of the principle that only one object can occupy a particular place at a particular time (Baillargeon, 1994; Spelke, 1994; Wynn & Chiang, 1998).

As human beings grow older and encounter many new experiences and a great deal of new information, they continually expand on and revise their theories about the physical world, the biological world, and the social and mental aspects of human beings (e.g., Keil & Silberstein, 1996; Wellman & Gelman, 1992). Their personal theories about the world seem to guide them as they identify potential defining features of concepts they are learning (Gelman & Kalish, 2006; Gelman & Koenig, 2003; Keil, 1987, 1989; McCauley, 1987). For example, if you were trying to learn what a *horse* is, your knowledge that it's an animal would lead you to conclude that its location (in a stable, a pasture, a shopping mall, or wherever) is an irrelevant feature. In contrast, if you were trying to learn what the *equator* is, knowing that it's something on a map of the world should lead you to suspect that location is of the utmost importance.

More generally, personal theories help people organize and make sense of personal experiences, classroom subject matter, and other new information (Reiner et al., 2000; Wellman & Gelman, 1998). Although theory theory has been criticized for offering only vague descriptions of the nature, structure, and origins of a personal theory (K. Nelson, 1996; Siegler & Alibali, 2005), it is nevertheless quite useful in helping us understand why people sometimes misconstrue the world around them, as we shall see now.

Personal Theories Versus Reality

Some psychologists and educators have argued that we can never completely know what is "real" or "true" about the world because knowledge and reasoning processes are constructed and so are inherently man-made entities (e.g., Lakoff & Núñez, 1997; von Glasersfeld, 1995).[9] Be that as it may, some ways of understanding the world are certainly more *useful* than others: They align themselves fairly closely with our day-to-day observations, and they enable us to make predictions about future events with considerable accuracy (Chinn, 1998; Tobin & Tippins, 1993).

The personal theories that children form are not always consistent with the theories that experts in a particular field have developed (e.g., diSessa, 1996; Duit, 1991; Halldén, 1994;

---

[9]This perspective is sometimes called *radical constructivism*.

C. L. Smith, Maclin, Grosslight, & Davis, 1997). For example, what is *rain*? Here is one 7-year-old's explanation:

> Clouds think it's too hot, and one day they start sweating. I guess they start sweating and then the sweat falls on us. (Stepans, 1991, p. 95)

And what shape is the earth that the rain falls on? Some fifth graders might tell you that it's "round, like a thick pancake" (Vosniadou, 1994). Many Japanese children believe that plants and inanimate objects have "minds" similar to those of humans; although this idea isn't consistent with contemporary scientific thinking, it *is* consistent with certain aspects of Japanese culture (Hatano & Inagaki, 1996).

Even adults don't always have their facts straight (Losh, Tavani, Njoroge, Wilke, & McAuley, 2003). For example, my husband, who teaches geography at the college level, tells me that some of his students believe that rivers always run from north to south (after all, water can only run "downhill") and that the Great Lakes contain saltwater. I find misconceptions in my own college classes as well, such as the belief that negative reinforcement involves the presentation of an aversive stimulus (see chapter 4 for the correct explanation) and the belief that rote learning is more effective than meaningful learning (Lennon, Ormrod, Burger, & Warren, 1990). And many adults, especially before they take a course in physics, think that in order to keep an object moving through space, one must continually apply force to the object; this notion is inconsistent with physicists' principle of *inertia* (diSessa, 1996).

Figure 9.11 lists some of the misconceptions that researchers have observed in children, and in some cases in adults as well. People's erroneous notions about the world probably have a variety of sources. Sometimes misconceptions result from how things *appear* to be (Byrnes, 1996; diSessa, 1996; Duit, 1991); for example, from our perspective living here on the earth's surface, the sun looks as if it moves around the earth, rather than vice versa. Sometimes misconceptions are fostered by common expressions in language; for instance, we often talk about the sun "rising" and "setting" (Duit, 1991; Mintzes, Trowbridge, Arnaudin, & Wandersee, 1991; Roth & Anderson, 1988; Stepans, 1991). Sometimes people infer incorrect cause–effect relationships between two events simply because the events often occur at the same time (Byrnes, 1996; Keil, 1991). Perhaps even fairy tales and television cartoon shows play a role in promoting misconceptions (Glynn, Yeany, & Britton, 1991); as an example, after cartoon "bad guys" run off the edge of a cliff, they usually remain suspended in air until they realize there's nothing solid holding them up. And unfortunately it is sometimes the case that we acquire erroneous ideas because we have seen or heard them from others; in some instances, teachers or textbooks even give us such misinformation (Begg, Anas, & Farinacci, 1992; Duit, 1991).

When students have few if any misunderstandings about a particular phenomenon, helping them acquire more sophisticated theories about the phenomenon is a fairly straightforward process, as we'll see in the next section. When students have many well-engrained misconceptions about the topic, however, helping them acquire scientifically acceptable understandings is more difficult, as we'll discover in a later section on conceptual change.

Fostering Theory Development

Because personal theories (like all theories) are integrated bodies of knowledge, long-term memory storage processes that enhance such integration—for instance, meaningful learning, internal

In biology

- Plants "eat" soil, fertilizer, and water, just as people eat more "humanly" food (Roth & Anderson, 1988). (From the perspective of biology, plants produce their own food through the process of photosynthesis.)
- Vision involves something moving outward from the eye toward the object being seen (Winer & Cottrell, 1996; Winer et al., 2002). (In reality, the opposite is true: Light rays bounce off the object to the eye.)

In astronomy

- The earth is bigger than the sun and stars (Vosniadou, 1991).
- The sun revolves around the earth. It "rises" in the morning and "sets" in the evening, at which point it "goes" to the other side of the earth (Vosniadou, 1991; Vosniadou & Brewer, 1987).
- The earth is shaped like a round, flat disk (Nussbaum, 1985; Sneider & Pulos, 1983; Vosniadou, 1994; Vosniadou & Brewer, 1987).
- Space has an absolute "up" and "down"; people standing at the South Pole will fall off the earth (Sneider & Pulos, 1983).

In physics

- Objects exist for a purpose. For example, some rocks are pointy so that animals that live nearby can scratch themselves when they have an itch (Kelemen, 1999, 2004).
- Any moving object has a force acting on it. For example, a ball thrown in the air continues to be pushed upward by the force of the throw until it begins its descent (Carey, 1986; diSessa, 1996; Kyle & Shymansky, 1989). (In reality, force is needed only to change the direction or speed of an object; otherwise, *inertia* is at work.)

- If an astronaut were to open the hatch while traveling in outer place, he or she would be "sucked out" by the vacuum in space (Haskell, 2001). (In reality, the astronaut would be blown out by the air inside the spacecraft.)
- When an electric current lights up a lightbulb, it is "used up" (consumed) by the lightbulb and disappears (Kyle & Shymansky, 1989). (In reality, the current flows back to the power source from which it originated.)

In mathematics

- Multiplication always leads to a bigger number (De Corte, Greer, & Verschaffel, 1996). (This principle holds true only when the multiplier is larger than 1.)
- Division always leads to a smaller number (Tirosh & Graeber, 1990). (This principle holds true only when the divisor is larger than 1.)

In geography, history, and social studies

- The lines separating countries or states are marked on the earth (Gardner, Torff, & Hatch, 1996).
- Islands float on top of the ocean (Gardner et al., 1996).
- Christopher Columbus was the first person to believe that the world is round rather than flat (Hynd, 2003).
- People are poor only because they don't have enough money to buy a job. Giving a poor person a small amount of money will make the person rich (Delval, 1994).
- People can move from one social class to another by making superficial changes, perhaps by changing from rags to nice clothing, furs, and jewelry (Delval, 1994).

Figure 9.11
Examples of common misconceptions.

organization, and elaboration—are, of course, likely to enrich those theories. Psychologists and educators have offered additional suggestions as well:

♦ *Physical models can help learners tie ideas together.* In some cases, learners' personal theories include **mental models**—representations of how particular concepts and principles interrelate or how a specific system works—that reflect the structure of external reality (English, 1997a; Greeno, 1991; Halford, 1993; Perfetti, Britt, Rouet, Georgi, & Mason, 1994). Instructors can facilitate the formation of accurate models by presenting physical versions of them, perhaps in the form of a flowchart that shows how a computer program works, a diagram that shows how pulleys can help someone lift heavy objects more easily, or a three-dimensional double helix that depicts the structure of DNA (Carney & Levin, 2002; Mayer, 1989; Reiner et al., 2000).

♦ *Group interaction can enhance learners' theoretical understandings.* Often, learners acquire more sophisticated understandings when they discuss a phenomenon they have observed, exchange perspectives about it, and build on one another's ideas (e.g., O'Donnell & King, 1999). We'll look at the nature and benefits of group interactions more closely in chapter 14.

♦ *Some personal theories and mental models can be helpful even when they aren't entirely accurate.* Sometimes theories and models can help learners understand and predict phenomenon even though they don't precisely reflect what experts believe to be the "true" state of affairs. For instance, in chapter 7 I presented the dual-store model of memory, and I have continued to refer to working memory and long-term memory as distinctive entities. Not all research findings support the dual-store model (see the section "Challenges to the Dual-Store Model" in chapter 7), and my gut instincts tell me that it's almost certainly an oversimplification of how human cognition and memory operate. Nevertheless, the working-versus-long-term distinction is a very *useful* one that can often help us predict how students are likely to learn and perform in the classroom. Similarly, a *flow* model of how a warm substance heats a colder one (heat travels from one to the other) does not accurately capture the molecular nature of heat (molecules move more quickly in a warm substance than in a cold one). Yet the "heat flow" notion can often help students make reasonably accurate predictions about temperature and is especially useful when learners have only a limited ability to think abstractly about the nature of heat (Linn & Muilenburg, 1996; Reiner et al., 2000).

We mustn't take this idea too far, however. When learners' theories and models are substantially different from experts' views, they can wreak havoc with new learning. In such situations, conceptual change is clearly in order, as you'll discover shortly.

WORLDVIEWS

People's personal theories tend to be related to particular phenomena in particular domains—for instance, to basic understandings of how human memory works or how physical objects interact in space. In contrast, a **worldview** is a general set of beliefs and assumptions about reality—about "how things are and should be"—that influence understandings of a wide variety of phenomena (Koltko-Rivera, 2004). Following are examples:

- Life and the universe came into being through random acts of nature *or* as part of a divine plan and purpose.
- Objects in nature (rocks, trees, etc.) have some degree of "consciousness" *or* are incapable of conscious thought.

- Human beings are at the mercy of the forces of nature *or* must learn to live in harmony with nature *or* should strive to master the forces of nature.
- One's sense of well-being is best secured by relying on scientific principles and logical reasoning processes *or* by seeking guidance and support from sources beyond the realm of scientific and logical thought.
- People's successes and failures in life are the result of their own actions *or* divine intervention *or* fate *or* random occurrences. (Koltko-Rivera, 2004; Medin, 2005)

To a considerable degree, such beliefs and assumptions are probably culturally transmitted, with different cultures communicating somewhat different beliefs and assumptions through adults' day-to-day interactions with one another and with children (Astuti, Solomon, & Carey, 2004; Koltko-Rivera, 2004; Losh, 2003).

Worldviews are often such an integral part of everyday thinking that people take them for granted and usually aren't consciously aware of them. In many cases, then, worldviews encompass implicit rather than explicit knowledge. Nevertheless they influence learners' interpretations of everyday events and classroom subject matter. Consider these examples:

- After a major hurricane ripped through southern Florida in the summer of 1992, many fourth and fifth graders attributed the hurricane to natural causes, but some children—those who had heard alternative explanations from family members, neighbors, or church groups—believed that people's actions or supernatural forces also played a role in the hurricane's origins and destructiveness (O. Lee, 1999).
- When American high school students talk about American history, European Americans are likely to depict historical events as leading up to increasing freedom, equality, and democracy for its citizens. African Americans are more likely to depict historical events as contributing to or maintaining racist and oppressive attitudes and practices (T. Epstein, 2000).
- When American high school students read newspaper articles about the appropriateness or inappropriateness of prayer in public schools, some view the trend away from prayer as a sign of "progress" toward greater religious freedom. But others—those from deeply religious Christian families, for instance—view the same trend as a "decline" that reflects abandonment of the country's religious heritage (Mosborg, 2002).

On some occasions, learners' differing worldviews can and must be accommodated within the context of classroom lessons and activities. But in other instances, a certain worldview may impede learners' mastery of important classroom subject matter. In such situations, the challenge for teachers is one of bringing about *conceptual change,* our next topic of discussion.

THE CHALLENGE OF CONCEPTUAL CHANGE

In some cases, replacing one belief with another one is fairly straightforward. For instance, if you think that my birthday is January 1, I can simply tell you that, no, January 1st is *my brother's* birthday—*mine* is August 22—and you might very well make the mental adjustment. But when a belief or misconception is part of a larger theory or worldview, a major overhaul may sometimes be in order. The process of replacing one personal theory or belief system with another, presumably more adaptive one is known as **conceptual change**.[10] Don't let the term *conceptual* mislead you here: For the most part, we are talking about changing interrelated sets of ideas rather than merely specific, isolated concepts.

Research in classrooms indicates that learners of all ages often hold quite stubbornly to misconceptions and counterproductive beliefs about the world, even after considerable instruction that explicitly contradicts them (e.g., Anderson, Sheldon, & Dubay, 1990; Carey, 1986; Chambliss, 1994; Chinn & Brewer, 1993; Holt-Reynolds, 1992; Roth, 1990; Shuell, 1996; Winer, Cottrell, Gregg, Fournier, & Bica, 2002). Why are learners' counterproductive beliefs often so resistant to change? Theorists have offered several possible explanations:

◆ *People's existing beliefs affect their interpretations of new information.* Thanks to the processes of meaningful learning and elaboration—processes that usually facilitate learning—learners are more likely to interpret new information in ways that are consistent with what they already "know" about the world, to the point where they continue to believe what they have always believed (e.g., Kendeou & van den Broek, 2003; Porat, 2004). Generally speaking, maintaining existing perspectives, rather than considering alternative and possibly conflicting ones, seems to be the "default" mode in human cognition (De Lisi & Golbeck, 1999).

◆ *Most people have a confirmation bias.* Learners of all ages (college students included) tend to look for information that confirms their existing beliefs and to ignore or discredit any contradictory evidence—a phenomenon known as **confirmation bias** (Chinn & Brewer, 1993; Duit, 1991; Kuhn, Amsel, & O'Loughlin, 1988; Minstrell & Stimpson, 1996; Schauble, 1990). For example, when students in a high school science lab observe results that contradict what they expected to happen, they might complain that "Our equipment isn't working right" or "I can never do science anyway" (Minstrell & Stimpson, 1996).

◆ *People's existing beliefs are often consistent with their everyday experiences.* Truly accurate explanations of physical phenomena (e.g., commonly accepted principles or theories in physics) are often fairly abstract and difficult to relate to everyday reality (Alexander, 1997; Driver, Asoko, Leach, Mortimer, & Scott, 1994; Mintzes et al., 1991; Schmittau, 2003). For example, although the law of inertia tells us that force is needed to *start* an object in motion but not to *keep* it in motion, we know from experience that if we want to move a heavy object across the floor, we must keep on pushing it until we get it where we want it (Driver et al., 1994). Consider, too, Newton's second law: Force is a product of mass and acceleration ($F = ma$). This law tells us that acceleration must *always* accompany force—an idea that many people have difficulty relating to their own observations. A young woman taking an introductory college physics course expressed her confusion this way:

> I want it to be true, but there's just no way it is, you know . . . I don't know why I just started doubting myself because that stupid force formula. . . . I mean I want what seems logical to me to make sense with what I've learned and what you can, like, you know, like when we were talking about the formulas. I mean you learn these formulas and you apply them to all these problems. But when something that you know is true—I mean to me it makes so much sense that it's

---

[10]Some theorists use the term *conceptual change* in reference to *any* situation in which one belief or set of beliefs is replaced by another, even a situation as simple as revising a belief about a person's birthday. They may refer to more extensive changes (the "overhaul" variety) as *radical conceptual change, restructuring,* or *reconstruction.*

crazy to even debate it, that if you're pushing this with a constant force, and you see it moving, that it's not accelerating. (diSessa, Elby, & Hammer, 2003, pp. 275–276, emphasis removed)

◆ *Some erroneous beliefs are integrated into a cohesive whole, with many interrelationships existing among various ideas.* In such instances, changing misconceptions involves changing an entire organized body of knowledge—an entire theory or worldview—rather than a single belief (Chambliss, 1994; Derry, 1996; Duit, 1991; Koltko-Rivera, 2004). For example, the belief that the sun revolves around the earth may be part of a more general "earth-centered" view of things, perhaps one that includes the moon, stars, and various other heavenly bodies revolving around the earth as well. In reality, of course, the moon revolves around the earth, the earth revolves around the sun, and the other stars are not directly involved with the earth one way or the other. Yet the earth-centered view is a much easier one to understand and accept (on the surface, at least), and everything fits so nicely together.

◆ *People may fail to see an inconsistency between new information and their prior beliefs.* In many situations, people learn new information without letting go of their prior beliefs, so that two inconsistent ideas remain in long-term memory simultaneously (Chambliss, 1994; Keil & Silberstein, 1996; Mintzes et al., 1991; Winer & Cottrell, 1996). Sometimes this happens because people learn the new information at a rote level, without relating it to the things they already know and believe (Chambliss, 1994; Strike & Posner, 1992; Kendeou & van den Broek, 2005). In other cases, it may occur because existing beliefs take the form of implicit knowledge—knowledge that cannot consciously be accessed (Keil & Silberstein, 1996; Strike & Posner, 1992). In either situation, people do not realize that the new things they have learned contradict what they already believe, and they may continue to apply previously acquired beliefs when interpreting new situations (Champagne, Klopfer, & Gunstone, 1982; Hynd, 2003; Luque, 2003).

◆ *People may have a personal or emotional investment in their existing beliefs.* For one reason or another, people may be especially committed to certain beliefs, perhaps insisting that "This theory is what I believe in! Nobody can make me change it!" (Mason, 2003, p. 228). In some instances, their beliefs may be an integral part of their religion or culture (Hatano & Inagaki, 1996; Porat, 2004; Southerland & Sinatra, 2003). In other cases, people may interpret challenges to their belief systems as threats to their self-efficacy or overall self-esteem (Gregoire, 2003; Linnenbrink & Pintrich, 2003; Luque, 2003; Sherman & Cohen, 2002).

◆ *Sometimes people's existing beliefs are supported by their social environment.* To the extent that others in a learner's support network (e.g., one's family, peers, religious group, or political party) hold a particular set of beliefs, the learner will have less reason to abandon those beliefs (Hatano & Inagaki, 2003; Porat, 2004). We see the effect of social context even in highly educated academic communities. For instance, the dominance of behaviorism in North American psychology in the first few decades of the twentieth century encouraged most budding psychologists to take an S–R approach to learning and to reject quite adamantly any suggestion that they look at the decidedly nonobservable phenomenon called *thinking.*

Promoting Conceptual Change

When students have few existing beliefs about a particular topic, helping them acquire more sophisticated understandings can be relatively easy. When they have many naive beliefs and misconceptions about the topic, however, helping them master explanations consistent with current scientific thinking is apt to be more difficult. In the latter situation, teachers face a twofold challenge: They must not only help students learn new things but also help them *unlearn*, or at least *inhibit*, existing beliefs (Hynd, 2003). Theorists and researchers have offered several suggestions for getting students on the road to conceptual change:

◆ *Before instruction begins, teachers should determine what beliefs and misconceptions about a topic exist.* Teachers can more easily address students' counterproductive beliefs when they know what those beliefs *are* (P. K. Murphy & Alexander, 2004; Roth & Anderson, 1988; Stepans, 1991). Thus, a lesson might begin with informal questioning or a formal pretest to probe students' current views of the subject matter at hand. Teachers may need to ask a series of questions to get a clear understanding of what their students really believe. The following dialogue illustrates the kinds of probing questions that may be in order:

Adult:	What is rain?
Child:	It's water that falls out of a cloud when the clouds evaporate.
Adult:	What do you mean, "clouds evaporate"?
Child:	That means water goes up in the air and then it makes clouds and then, when it gets too heavy up there, then the water comes and they call it rain.
Adult:	Does the water stay in the sky?
Child:	Yes, and then it comes down when it rains. It gets too heavy.
Adult:	Why does it get too heavy?
Child:	'Cause there's too much water up there.
Adult:	Why does it rain?
Child:	'Cause the water gets too heavy and then it comes down.
Adult:	Why doesn't the whole thing come down?
Child:	Well, 'cause it comes down at little times like a salt shaker when you turn it upside down. It doesn't all come down at once 'cause there's little holes and it just comes out.
Adult:	What are the little holes in the sky?
Child:	Umm, holes in the clouds, letting the water out. (dialogue from Stepans, 1991, p. 94)

This conception of a cloud as a "salt shaker" of sorts is hardly consistent with the scientifically accepted view of how and why rain comes about. As teachers gain more experience teaching a particular topic over the years, they can begin to anticipate what students' prior beliefs and misbeliefs about that topic are likely to be (e.g., Hollon, Roth, & Anderson, 1991).

◆ *Students should learn correct information in a meaningful rather than rote fashion.* Students will notice inconsistencies between new information and prior beliefs only when they try to make connections between the new and the old. To use levels-of-processing terminology for a moment, students are most likely to modify their misconceptions in light of new data if they process those data *in depth*—in other words, if they become actively engaged in learning and truly try to understand the information being presented (D. E. Brown, 1992; Chinn & Brewer, 1993; Howe, Tolmie, Greer, & Mackenzie, 1995; Pintrich, Marx, & Boyle, 1993; Slusher & Anderson, 1996). Instruction is most likely to encourage meaningful learning, and therefore to promote conceptual change, when it focuses on a few key ideas rather than covering many topics superficially (diSessa, 1996; Roth & Anderson, 1988).

◆ *Students are more apt to revise their current way of thinking when they believe revision is in order.* Many theorists suggest that conceptual change is most likely to occur when learners encounter evidence that blatantly contradicts what they currently believe. Such contradictory evidence can create a sense of mental "discomfort"—something that some theorists call *disequilibrium* and others call *cognitive dissonance* (see chapters 11 and 15, respectively). As an example, one first-grade teacher wanted to challenge her students' belief that rocks always sink in water. She showed her class two stones, a small piece of granite and a considerably larger piece of pumice. Pumice, of course, results when molten lava cools; because it has many pockets of air, it is relatively light and so can float. Before the teacher dropped the stones into a container of water, she asked the class to make a prediction, and a girl named Brianna predicted that both stones would sink. The granite did sink, but the pumice floated. Brianna was noticeably agitated: *"No! No! that's not right! That doesn't go with my mind (student grabs her head) it just doesn't go with my mind"* (Hennessey, 2003, p. 121).

Theorists have offered several suggestions for how teachers might create mental disequilibrium and then encourage students to address it:

- Ask questions that challenge students' current beliefs.
- Present phenomena that students cannot adequately explain within their existing perspectives.
- Ask students to make predictions about what will happen in various circumstances—predictions that, given their present beliefs, are likely to be wrong.
- Encourage students to conduct experiments to test various hypotheses.
- Ask students to provide possible explanations for puzzling phenomena.
- Engage students in discussions of the pros and cons of various explanations.
- Show how one explanation of an event or phenomenon is more plausible (i.e., makes more sense) than others.
  (Andre & Windschitl, 2003; Chinn & Malhotra, 2002; Echevarria, 2003; Guzzetti, Snyder, Glass, & Gamas, 1993; Hatano & Inagaki, 2003; Howe et al., 1995; Pine & Messer, 2000; Posner, Strike, Hewson, & Gertzog, 1982; Prawat, 1989; Roth, 2002; C. L. Smith et al., 1997; Vosniadou & Brewer, 1987)

Such strategies must encompass a wide variety of instructional methods, including demonstrations, hands-on experiments, teacher explanations, and student discussions. There is certainly no single "best" instructional method for promoting conceptual change (Hynd, 1998b).

◆ *Students must explicitly compare their existing beliefs with alternative explanations.* Students are more likely to replace a misconception with a more accurate understanding, rather than to accept the accurate understanding while also *retaining* the misconception, if they are thinking about both ideas at the same time. In other words, the erroneous and accurate beliefs should both be in working memory simultaneously. Unfortunately, many textbook authors seem to be oblivious to this point: When they present new ideas in science or history, they neglect to point out that these ideas may be inconsistent with what students currently believe. The result is that students often do *not* shed their misconceptions in the face of contradictory information (deLeeuw & Chi, 2003; Kowalski, Taylor, & Guggia, 2004; McKeown & Beck, 1990; Otero, 1998; Southerland & Sinatra, 2003).

One strategy for encouraging students to compare various beliefs and explanations is to engage them in discussions about the pros and cons of each one (Prawat, 1989; C. L. Smith et al., 1997). Yet textbooks can present the pros and cons of various perspectives as well. One effective approach is **refutational text,** in which possible objections to a particular explanation are presented but then discredited (Hynd, 2003; Kowalski et al., 2004). In this way, students are persuaded to "buy into" the preferred explanation and also "inoculated" against accepting counterarguments they might encounter at a future time (Hynd, 2003).

◆ *Students must want to learn the correct explanation.* Students are most likely to engage in deep processing and meaningful learning when they are motivated to do so (Hatano & Inagaki, 1993; Lee & Anderson, 1993; Pintrich et al., 1993). At a minimum, they must be interested in the subject matter, believe it will help them achieve their personal goals, set their sights on mastering it, and have sufficient self-efficacy to believe that they *can* master it (Andre & Windschitl, 2003; Gregoire, 2003; Hynd, 2003; Patrick & Pintrich, 2001). Furthermore, students must not see the new, contradictory information as in some way threatening their self-esteem (Minstrell & Stimpson, 1996; Sherman & Cohen, 2002). And ideally, the classroom should be socially and emotionally supportive of conceptual change (Hatano & Inagaki, 2003). For instance, students must feel confident that their teacher and classmates will not ridicule them for expressing logical but incorrect ideas, and they must believe that the ultimate goal of a lesson is understanding the subject matter rather than simply performing well on a quiz or assignment. As we consider motivation in chapters 15 and 16, we'll identify strategies for accomplishing such things.

Some theorists have suggested that it may sometimes be easier to help students *understand* new explanations than to make students *believe* and *accept* them, especially when the subject matter involves controversial issues such as evolution, capital punishment, or abortion (Eagly, Kulesa, Chen, & Chaiken, 2001; Kuhn, Shaw, & Felton, 1997; Sinatra, Southerland, McConaughy, & Demastes, 2003; Southerland & Sinatra, 2003). Probably the most defensible approach when dealing with controversial issues is to help students understand the reasoning behind various perspectives, as well as the evidence for and against each one, but to acknowledge that students must ultimately come to conclusions consistent with their own moral and religious convictions (Sinatra et al., 2003; Southerland & Sinatra, 2003).

◆ *Throughout a lesson, students' understanding should be monitored for particularly tenacious misconceptions.* Because of human beings' natural tendency to reinterpret new information in light of what they already "know," some misconceptions may persist in spite of a teacher's best efforts. These misconceptions are sometimes blatantly incorrect; at other times, they may be sort-of-but-not-quite correct. To illustrate the latter situation, let's consider an example offered by Roth and Anderson (1988), once again dealing with students' understanding of vision. Students sometimes define *transparent* as "something you can see through." Although such a definition is consistent with how we generally speak about transparency, it may nevertheless reflect the erroneous belief that sight originates with the eye and goes outward to and through the transparent object. *Transparent* is more accurately defined as "something light passes through." In the following class discussion, the teacher probes students' reasoning about transparency, uncovers a potential misconception, and encourages students to offer a scientifically more accurate explanation:

Ms. Ramsey:	(Puts up transparency) Why can't the girl see around the wall?
Annie:	The girl can't see around the wall because the wall is opaque.
Ms. Ramsey:	What do you mean when you say the wall is opaque?
Annie:	*You can't see through it. It is solid.*
Brian:	(calling out) The rays are what can't go through the wall.
Ms. Ramsey:	I like that answer better. Why is it better?

Brian:	The rays of light bounce off the car and go to the wall. They can't go through the wall.
Ms. Ramsey:	Where are the light rays coming from originally?
Students:	The sun.
Annie:	*The girl can't see the car because she is not far enough out.*
Ms. Ramsey:	So you think her position is what is keeping her from seeing it. (She flips down the overlay with the answer.) Who was better?
Students:	Brian.
Ms. Ramsey:	(to Annie) Would she be able to see if she moved out beyond the wall?
Annie:	Yes.
Ms. Ramsey:	Why?
Annie:	*The wall is blocking her view.*
Ms. Ramsey:	Is it blocking her view? What is it blocking?
Student:	Light rays.
Ms. Ramsey:	Light rays that are doing what?
Annie:	If the girl moves out beyond the wall, then the light rays that bounce off the car are not being blocked. (Roth & Anderson, 1988, pp. 129–130)

Notice how Ms. Ramsey is not satisfied with Annie's original answer that the wall is opaque. With further questioning, it becomes clear that Annie's understanding of opaqueness is off target: She talks about the girl being unable to "see through" the wall rather than light's inability to pass through the wall. With Ms. Ramsey's continuing insistence on precise language, Annie eventually begins to bring light rays into her explanation (Roth & Anderson, 1988).

Assessment of students' comprehension is important *after* a lesson as well. Teachers are more likely to detect misconceptions when they ask students to *use* and *apply* the things they have learned (as Ms. Ramsey does in the conversation just presented) rather than simply to spit back facts, definitions, and formulas memorized at a rote level (Roth, 1990; Roth & Anderson, 1988).

As you have seen, teachers can do a variety of things to nudge learners toward conceptual change. Ultimately, however, learners themselves are in control of the cognitive processes (meaningful learning, internal organization, elaboration, etc.) that will enable them to make sense of new ideas and thereby acquire more accurate understandings. Their proficiency in directing their own learning efforts and their understanding of what it actually *means* to learn something are key elements in their ability to revise their thinking about classroom subject matter. Accordingly, we will revisit the topic of conceptual change after we have discussed metacognition in chapter 12.

Usually—but not always—learners abandon erroneous and counterproductive beliefs as they acquire considerable knowledge about a topic. We look now at how the quality of knowledge about a topic changes over time and may gradually evolve into true *expertise*.

DEVELOPMENT OF EXPERTISE

Obviously, people acquire an increasing amount of information in their long-term memories over time. Many people eventually acquire a great deal of information about a particular topic or subject matter, to the point where we can say they are *experts* in their field. It appears, however, that experts don't just know more than their peers; their knowledge is also *qualitatively* different from that of others. In particular, their knowledge tends to be tightly organized, with many interrelationships among the things that they know and with many abstract generalizations unifying more concrete details (Alexander & Judy, 1988; Bédard & Chi, 1992; Proctor & Dutta, 1995; Zeitz, 1994). Such qualities enable experts to retrieve the things they need more easily, to find parallels between seemingly diverse situations, and to solve problems more creatively and effectively (Chi, Glaser, & Rees, 1982; De Corte, Greer, & Verschaffel, 1996; Hatano & Oura, 2003; Rabinowitz & Glaser, 1985; Voss, Greene, Post, & Penner, 1983).

Patricia Alexander (1997, 1998, 2003, 2004) has suggested that there may be three somewhat distinct stages in the development of knowledge related to a particular subject matter. At the first stage, which she calls *acclimation,* learners familiarize themselves with a new content domain, much as someone might do by taking an introductory course in biology, economics, or art history. At this point, they pick up a lot of facts that they tend to store in relative isolation from one another. As a result of such "fragmented" learning, they are likely to hold on to many misconceptions that they may have acquired before they started studying the subject systematically.

At the second stage, which Alexander calls *competence,* learners acquire considerably more information about the subject matter, and they also acquire some general principles that help tie the information together. Because learners at the competence stage make numerous interconnections among the things they learn, they are likely to correct many of the specific misconceptions they have previously developed. Those misconceptions that remain, however, are apt to pervade much of their thinking about the subject. At the competence stage, learners' entire approach to the subject matter begins to resemble that of experts; for example, they may start to "think like a historian" or to engage in some of their own scientific research. Competence is something that people acquire only after studying a particular subject in depth, perhaps through an undergraduate major, a master's degree, or several years of professional experience.

At the final stage—*expertise*—we can say that learners have truly mastered their field. They know a great deal about the subject matter, and they have pulled much of their knowledge together into a tightly integrated whole. They now help lead the way in terms of conducting research, proposing new ways of looking at things, solving problems, and, in general, creating new knowledge. Expertise comes only after many years of studying and experience in a particular field; as a result, few learners ever reach this stage.

Because knowledge at the competence and expertise stages is fairly well integrated, any misconceptions at either of these stages may be especially resistant to change (Alexander, 1998). As an example, let's return to our discussion of verbal learning research in chapter 7. Initially, verbal learning researchers (most of them certainly experts in psychology) tried to explain human language-based learning within the context of behaviorism, the predominant theoretical perspective at the time. It was only after several *decades,* as evidence that behaviorist principles could *not* explain continued to mount up, that these researchers abandoned their S–R explanations for more cognitive ones.[11]

---

[11]More generally, such *paradigm shifts* in scientific communities occur only after considerable evidence and a great deal of discussion and debate. For a classic discussion of paradigm shifts, see T. Kuhn's (1970) *The Structure of Scientific Revolutions.*

Alexander points out that the development of expertise depends not only on the acquisition of knowledge but also on effective learning strategies and a strong interest in the subject matter. We will identify many effective learning strategies in chapter 12, and we will examine the specific benefits of interest in chapter 16.

GENERALIZATIONS ABOUT THE NATURE OF KNOWLEDGE

In this chapter we have considered a variety of perspectives about how knowledge in long-term memory might be encoded and organized. At this point, let's make some final generalizations about the nature of knowledge:

♦ *There can be considerable redundancy in how information is stored.* Earlier in the chapter, I mentioned a finding by Rips and colleagues (1973) that people can verify that "A collie is an animal" more quickly than they can verify that "A collie is a mammal." It is probably a more economical use of long-term memory "space" to remember that a collie is a mammal and that a mammal is an animal; people can then easily infer that a collie must be an animal. Yet it appears from these researchers' results that people store the fact that a collie is an animal as well—a fact that is redundant with other knowledge in long-term memory. Such redundancy may simply be a matter of convenience: If we have plenty of "room" in long-term memory, why not store the same information in the variety of ways in which we might need it later on?

As we've noted, too, the same information may be encoded in two or more different forms, for instance as both words and a visual image (recall the car with ski racks by the tree). Different forms of encoding facilitate different ways of thinking about a topic (Eisner, 1994; Salomon, 1979/1994). A picture may sometimes be worth a thousand words, depicting spatial relationships that are difficult to capture in any other way. Yet words and meanings may more easily allow us to interrelate similar ideas (perhaps through the propositions they have in common) in ways that spatial representations would not allow.

♦ *Most of our knowledge is a summary of our experiences rather than information about specific events.* The bulk of our knowledge appears to be semantic rather than episodic in nature: As we go through life, we continually combine our many specific experiences into a general knowledge of the world that is somewhat independent of those experiences.

Concepts are a good example of how we summarize the objects and events we encounter. As summaries of the things we have learned, concepts have several advantages:

1. *Concepts reduce the world's complexity* (Bruner, 1957; Sokal, 1977). Classifying similar objects and events makes life simpler and easier to understand. For example, when you drive along a country road, it is easier to think to yourself "There are some cows" than to think "There is a brown object, covered with bristly stuff, appended by a paintbrush and a lumpy thing, and held up by four sticks. Ah, yes, and I also see a black-and-white spotted object, covered with bristly stuff, appended by a paintbrush and a lumpy thing, and held up by four sticks. And over there is a brown-and-white spotted object. . . ."

2. *Concepts allow abstraction of the environment* (Bruner, 1966). An object covered with bristly stuff, appended by a paintbrush and a lumpy thing, and held up by four sticks is a very concrete thing. The concept *cow*, however, can be more abstract, incorporating

such characteristics as "female," "supplier of milk," and, to the dairy farmer, "economic asset." Concepts and their labels allow individuals to think about their experiences without necessarily having to consider all of their concrete, perceptual aspects.

3. *Concepts enhance the power of thought* (Bruner, 1966). When you are thinking about an object covered with bristly stuff, appended by a paintbrush and a lumpy thing, held up by four sticks, and so on, you can think of little else; to express this point in terms of contemporary memory theory, your working memory capacity is filled to the brim. But when you simply think *cow,* you can also think about *horse, dog, goat,* and *pig* at the same time.

4. *Concepts facilitate inferences and generalization to new situations* (Halford & Andrews, 2006; Mandler, 2000; Sloutsky, Lo, & Fisher, 2001; Welder & Graham, 2001). When we learn a concept, we associate certain characteristics with it. Then, when we encounter a new instance of the concept, we can draw on our knowledge of associated characteristics to make assumptions and inferences about the new instance. For example, if you see a herd of cattle as you drive through the country-side, you can assume that you are passing through either dairy or beef country, depending on whether you see large udders hanging down between two of the spindly sticks. If you purchase a potted flower, you know that you must water it regularly because of something you have learned about the concept *flower:* It needs water to live. Thanks to concepts, we don't have to learn from scratch in each new situation.

5. *Concepts make it easier for us to make connections among the things we know* (Bruner, 1957; Goldstone & Johansen, 2003). Once we have condensed and abstracted information into concepts, we can more easily make associations among those concepts in long-term memory. For instance, we can relate the concept *cow* to the concepts *bull* and *calf* in a familial sort of way and to *mammal, animal,* and *living thing* in a hierarchical fashion.

We must remember, however, that our summaries of the world will sometimes cause us to make mistakes. For example, when we identify a new stimulus as being a positive instance of a particular concept, we are likely to react to the stimulus as we would to any other instance of the concept. In the process, we may lose sight of the unique qualities of that particular stimulus. Furthermore, if we have identified a stimulus incorrectly, our response to it may be inappropriate. I remember as a young child trying to make a wagon using square pieces of wood for wheels. Calling those pieces of wood *wheels* was an inaccurate identification, and, as you can imagine, my wagon didn't move very far. Finally, in some situations we may *over*classify our experiences. For example, when we form **stereotypes** of certain groups of people (perhaps people of specific genders, races, or cultural backgrounds), we are apt to draw many incorrect inferences about how particular members of that group are apt to behave (Murray & Jackson, 1982/1983; Nelson & Miller, 1995; Oskamp, 2000).

 ◆ *In most situations, integrated knowledge is more useful than fragmented knowledge.* When we integrate the things we know, we are more likely to draw inferences that go beyond the specific things we have learned. Furthermore, as we will discover in the next chapter, organized information is easier to remember—in other words, to retrieve—than unorganized information.

Many contemporary learning theorists stress the importance of teaching an integrated body of knowledge—knowledge that includes general principles, cause–effect relationships, and so on—rather than simply teaching isolated facts. In the case of mathematics, for example, teachers should help students make associations between general concepts and principles of mathematics, on the one hand, and specific procedures for solving mathematical problems, on the other (Hiebert et al., 1997; Rittle-Johnson, Siegler, & Alibali, 2001). When students learn specific mathematical procedures (e.g., how to do long division, or how to add two fractions by finding a common denominator) in association with the overall "logic" of mathematics, they are more likely to apply problem-solving procedures appropriately and to recognize occasions when they have obtained illogical and therefore incorrect problem solutions.

◆ *The in-depth study of a few topics is often more beneficial than the superficial study of many topics.* Historically, many people have seen the role of schools as being one of promoting cultural literacy—that is, of helping children learn the many facts that a seemingly "educated" person should know (e.g., see Hirsch, 1996). Adults in Western countries are often chagrined when they hear how many children don't know the capital of France, can't list the planets of the solar system, or have no idea who wrote *Romeo and Juliet.*

Certainly schooling should, in part, be about helping children acquire a basic knowledge of the world and culture in which they live so that they can participate more fully and effectively in their society (Hirsch, 1996). Yet if schools focus exclusively on imparting isolated facts, an integrated body of knowledge about the world is unlikely to develop. In recent years, a number of theorists have suggested that teachers focus more on teaching a few topics in depth than on covering many topics at a superficial level (Berliner & Biddle, 1995; Brophy & Alleman, 1992; Gardner, 2000; Onosko & Newmann, 1994; Sizer, 1992). They advocate the idea that **less is more:** When students study *less* material so that they can study it more thoroughly, they learn it *more* completely and with greater understanding, and they are more likely to undergo conceptual change when such change is warranted.

SUMMARY

Long-term memory includes several different kinds of knowledge. *Declarative knowledge*—knowledge about "how things are or were"—includes both recollections of prior events in one's life (episodic memory) and general information about the world (semantic memory). In contrast, *procedural knowledge* involves "how to do things" and, often, awareness of the conditions under which various actions are called for (conditional knowledge). When learners integrate their declarative and procedural knowledge to address *why* questions—for instance, when they understand why it makes sense to engage in certain procedures on certain occasions—they also have *conceptual knowledge*. Some knowledge in long-term memory is *explicit,* in that people are consciously aware of it and can easily recall and explain it, whereas other knowledge is *implicit,* "hidden" from conscious view and mental inspection.

People probably encode information in a variety of ways, including symbols (e.g., verbal codes), imagery (e.g., visual images), meanings (e.g., propositions), and actions (e.g., productions), and information encoded in these different ways is interconnected. Some information may be organized in a hierarchical format that reflects superordinate and subordinate categories, but much more is probably organized as a network (perhaps consisting of interrelated propositions) that encompasses many different kinds of relationships. Building loosely on neurological research, some theorists have proposed that any single piece of information is represented in long-term memory in a distributed fashion, that is, as a network of scattered but interconnected nodes that activate simultaneously.

Concepts are classes of objects or events that share one or more common properties. Some concepts are concrete, in that they are easily identified by their physical appearance, whereas others are more abstract and difficult to pin down in terms of observable characteristics. Learning a concept often involves learning the features that determine which objects and events are members of the concept (i.e., positive instances) and which are nonmembers (i.e., negative instances). Drawing from several theories of concept learning, we can speculate that learning a concept may involve unconsciously learning a commonly occurring pattern in the world, testing hypotheses about the nature of a particular concept, forming a prototype of a typical positive instance, developing a feature list for the concept, and storing exemplars that represent the variability of positive instances. Teachers can help students master concepts in the classroom when they capitalize on factors that facilitate concept learning—for instance, when they provide definitions, highlight defining features, simultaneously present both positive and negative instances, and ask students to generate their own examples.

A *schema* is a closely connected set of ideas related to a specific object or event. A schema that summarizes how a common event typically transpires (e.g., what a visit to the doctor's office is usually like) is sometimes called a *script*. Schemas and scripts often influence how we process, store, and remember new situations; for example, they allow us to fill in missing information using our knowledge about how the world typically operates.

Some of the knowledge stored in long-term memory takes the form of *personal theories*, coherent belief systems that encompass cause–effect relationships about physical, biological, social, political, or mental phenomena. Personal theories influence concept learning by giving learners some idea about the features that are likely to be important. Such theories are not always accurate reflections of the world, however; they may include incomplete or inaccurate understandings.

Whereas personal theories tend to be related to particular phenomena in particular domains, *worldviews* encompass people's general beliefs and assumptions about reality—about "how things are and should be"—that influence understandings of a wide variety of phenomena. Although worldviews often lurk well below conscious awareness—that is, they are likely to reflect implicit rather than explicit knowledge—they can have a significant impact on how people interpret everyday events and classroom subject matter.

When students are starting from scratch about a new topic (i.e., when they have minimal information and few if any misconceptions about the topic), helping them acquire a good understanding of the topic can be relatively straightforward. For instance, teachers can present physical models that depict structures or cause–effect relationships, and they can encourage students to build on one another's ideas in small-group or whole-class discussions. But when students must replace existing misconceptions with more accurate explanations—that is, when they must undergo *conceptual change*—the teacher's task is more challenging, in part because students are likely to distort new information to be consistent with what they already believe and in part because students may have a personal, emotional, or social stake in keeping their existing conceptions. Theorists have offered numerous suggestions for promoting conceptual change; for instance, teachers should encourage meaningful learning of a few key ideas rather than rote learning of many isolated facts, and they must show students how new explanations are more plausible and useful than existing ones.

The development of *expertise* in a particular subject area involves acquiring an increasing amount of knowledge, making numerous interconnections within that knowledge base, and eventually integrating what has been learned into a cohesive whole. People typically become experts in their field only after many years of intensive study and practice.

Most of our knowledge probably represents a summary of our life experiences. For example, concepts summarize what we have learned about particular objects or events; as such, they reduce the complexity of the environment and facilitate generalization to new situations. By and large, integrated knowledge about a topic is more useful than knowledge of separate facts.

CHAPTER 10

Long–Term Memory III: Retrieval and Forgetting

Here are definitions of four words in the English language. Can you identify the specific words to which they refer?

- The fluid part of blood
- A picture form of writing used in ancient Egypt
- A game whose object is to snap small plastic disks into a container
- A small, hard-shelled, ocean-dwelling animal that attaches itself to rocks and ships

You probably identified some of these words almost without thinking. But there is a good chance that you could not retrieve all four instantaneously. For one or more of them, you may have found yourself looking around in your long-term memory, perhaps for a lengthy period of time, in "places" where a word might be located. (In case you could not retrieve all four words, they are *plasma, hieroglyphics, tiddlywinks,* and *barnacle.*)[1]

---

[1]Some of my readers, of course—especially those for whom English is a second or third language—may never have stored them in the first place.

Retrieving information from long-term memory is sometimes easy and automatic, at other times slow and strenuous, and at still other times virtually impossible. We tend to remember frequently used information without conscious effort. For instance, we can quickly retrieve the locations of our homes and the names of our close friends. It is more difficult to retrieve information that we seldom use. For example, we often have trouble remembering words that we rarely encounter in our everyday lives (words such as *hieroglyphics* and *barnacle*); in some cases, we may feel that such words are on the "tips of our tongues," yet we still cannot recall them (A. Brown, 1991; Brown & McNeill, 1966; also see Thompson, Emmorey, & Gollan, 2005). Similarly, we may experience difficulty in identifying people whom we have not seen recently or frequently (Yarmey, 1973).

In this chapter, we will look at how memory theorists believe long-term memory retrieval works and at how retrieval, like storage, is often constructive in nature. Later, we will explore several explanations of why we are sometimes unable to retrieve the things we think we have learned—in other words, why we forget. Finally, we will make use of our knowledge about retrieval to identify additional implications of memory theory for instructional practice.

HOW RETRIEVAL WORKS

How easily we retrieve something from long-term memory depends in large part on how well we stored it in the first place. Unlike working memory, which is functionally quite small, long-term memory is so large that an exhaustive inspection of it all is probably impossible. A search of long-term memory must therefore be selective, focusing only on certain "sections" (e.g., Hopkins & Atkinson, 1968). If the sought-after information is not stored in one of those sections, we will not retrieve it.

Our success in retrieving information from long-term memory depends to some extent on whether we initially stored the information in a well-organized fashion. To understand the role that organization plays in retrieval, let's first look at an analogous situation—your great-grandmother's attic. (I am going back three generations, because young families typically have homes without much attic space, and many grandparents seem to live in condominiums these days.) Granny probably kept many things in her attic, including furniture, books, old clothes, seldom-used cooking utensils, and holiday decorations. She may have been a very organized woman, one who stored all of the books in one place, all of the clothes in another, and all of the holiday decorations somewhere else. Alternatively, she may have been more haphazard, throwing things up there any old place, so that some cooking utensils were with books, others were with clothes, and still others were stuffed in an old dresser or on the top shelf of a dilapidated armoire. How Granny stored items in her attic undoubtedly affected her ability to find them later. If she stored things systematically (e.g., books with books and cooking utensils with cooking utensils), she would have been able to locate them easily when she needed them. But if she stored them in a helter-skelter fashion, she may have had to purchase new canning jars every summer because she couldn't track down her jars from any of the previous 13 years.

So it is with long-term memory. Retrieval is easier when related pieces of information are stored in close association with one another, because we then have a good idea about where to

An organized long-term memory makes things easier to retrieve.

find a certain piece of information. To illustrate, try answering this question about a concept I presented in an earlier chapter:

What is a discriminative stimulus?

You may be able to answer the question quickly and easily, or you may have to search your long-term memory for a while. Your ability to retrieve the answer depends partly on how well you have organized the information you acquired from previous chapters. The word *stimulus* should, of course, lead you to look among the many pieces of information you have stored about behaviorist learning theories. The word *discriminative* might suggest to you that you look more specifically in your information about discrimination. If your knowledge about discrimination is stored with what you know about antecedent stimuli (and it should be, because the two concepts are related), then you should find the answer to the question. A discriminative stimulus lets you know that a particular response is likely to be reinforced; it *sets the occasion* for a particular response-reinforcement contingency.

Lindsay and Norman (1977) have characterized long-term memory retrieval as being similar to looking for something in a large, dark room with only a small flashlight. Imagine that the electricity goes off in Granny's house on a dark, moonless night. Because Granny can no longer use either her electric can opener or her electric lights, she takes a flashlight up to the attic to find the manual can opener she put there last October. She switches on her flashlight and begins her search. Unfortunately, the flashlight cannot illuminate the whole attic at once. Instead, she must aim the light first at one spot, then at another, until eventually she finds the can opener. The necessity to search the attic one spot at a time will not be a problem if Granny knows the exact location of the can opener (e.g., in a drawer with other small cooking utensils), but she may search all night without success if she has no idea where she might have stashed the thing.

In much the same way, retrieval from long-term memory may be a process of looking in various small "locations" in memory, just one location at a time. Information that has been stored in a logical place (i.e., associated with similar ideas) will probably be found quickly. Information that has been stored haphazardly, in a rote-learning fashion, will turn up only after a great deal of searching, or possibly not at all.

Retrieval of information is also easier when learners engage in thought processes similar to those they previously used when storing the information—a phenomenon known as **encoding specificity** (Morris, Bransford, & Franks, 1977; Tulving, 1983). An experiment by Bower and Holyoak (1973) illustrates the importance of a match between the cognitive processes at work during storage and during retrieval. In this study, college students listened to a set of tape-recorded sounds and identified something that each sound might be (e.g., chirping crickets or soldiers clumping down stairs). Two weeks later, they listened to a second set of sounds, including some sounds they had heard previously and some new sounds as well. Once again they were asked to identify what each sound might be and to indicate whether they had heard that exact sound during the first session. When students labeled a sound in the same way in the second session as they had in the first session, they were likely to recognize it as being one they had heard before. When they labeled it in a different way in the two sessions (e.g., once as a bouncing ball and once as a heartbeat), they were less likely to recognize it as being a familiar one. Other students, who had labels provided for them by the experimenter, showed similar results.

Let's return to the activation model of memory described in chapter 7. According to this model, all information stored in memory is in either an active or inactive state. Information in an active state is what we might think of as being in working memory, whereas inactive information is in long-term memory. The activation model lends itself particularly well to an understanding of how long-term memory retrieval might work. From this perspective, our starting point in long-term memory might be an idea triggered by something in the environment. Retrieval is then a process of **spreading activation,** with the activation flowing through connections within the network of stored information (e.g., J. R. Anderson, 1990; Collins & Loftus, 1975; E. D. Gagné, 1985). Only a small part of the network can be activated at once, thus accounting for the limited-capacity, "flashlight" quality of retrieval. If the activation eventually spreads to that part of the network in which the information is located—something that is more likely to happen if similar ideas are closely associated in the network—we will retrieve the desired information.

Generally speaking, retrieval is easier for things we know well—things we have practiced a lot and use frequently—and particularly for things we have learned to automaticity. It's as if we go to those "places" often enough that we don't even have to think about where to go in order to find them.

In addition, retrieval is usually easier when we are relaxed rather than anxious about retrieving information, especially if we are looking for nonautomatized information (e.g., Ashcraft, 2002). Anxiety adversely affects retrieval: We don't search long-term memory in an "open-minded" manner, and so we reduce our chances of finding what we are seeking. As an analogy, think about what happens when you are looking for your car keys and are desperate to find them quickly because you are already late for an important appointment. As you begin to panic, your search strategies become less and less efficient. You look in the same places over and over again; you don't think creatively about the wide variety of places in which the keys might be lurking.

Retrieval Cues

Retrieval is obviously easier when we have a good idea where to "look" in long-term memory—that is, when we know which part of long-term memory to activate. Accordingly, hints about where to find information—**retrieval cues**—are often helpful. Essentially, retrieval cues are likely to activate the part of long-term memory where a desired piece of information can be found (recall the discussion of *priming* in chapter 7).

In chapter 8, you read a story called "The War of the Ghosts." Can you fill in the blank in this sentence from the story?

And the warriors went on up the river to a town on the other side of —.

See if you can remember the name of the town before you continue reading.

Any luck? If not, then perhaps you will recognize the town from among these four choices: (1) Bisantri, (2) Dormro, (3) Muckaruck, (4) Kalama. Is it any easier to fill in the blank now? It should be. Perhaps you have now correctly identified Kalama as the answer. In this question, I gave you a type of retrieval cue known as an **identity cue** (Bourne, Dominowski, Loftus, & Healy, 1986), because it was identical to the information you were trying to retrieve. Recognition tasks, such as multiple-choice tests, are often easier than recall tasks (e.g., Semb et al., 1993), presumably because of the identity cues that recognition tasks provide.

Now try this exercise. Read the following list of 24 words *one time only*. I will ask you to recall them as soon as you have finished.

tulip	pencil	spoon	bed	baker	ruby
hat	mountain	doctor	paper	daisy	shirt
chair	fork	diamond	canyon	knife	table
hill	soldier	rose	pen	shoe	emerald

Now that you have read all 24 words, cover the page and write as many of them as you can remember. *Do not look back at the list just yet.*

If you cannot remember all 24, see if these words and phrases help you:

clothing	professions
eating utensils	writing supplies
gemstones	furniture
flowers	land forms

These category names should help you remember more of the words, because all of the 24 words fall into one of the categories. Such **associate cues** are related to the words you were searching for; as such, they should direct your search toward relevant parts of your long-term memory.

A third kind of retrieval cue is an organizational structure, or **frame,** that systematically guides the search of long-term memory (e.g., Calfee, 1981). For example, in chapter 8 I described an experiment by Bower and his colleagues (1969) in which presenting words in an organized format (e.g., the "minerals" hierarchy shown in Figure 8.5), rather than in a random order, facilitated learning and recall. An overall organizational structure provides numerous cues that should focus retrieval efforts (e.g., "Hmmm, now that I've remembered the rare and common metals, I need to remember the alloys"). We find another example of a frame in the sentence

King Philip comes over for good spaghetti.

Biology students often tell me that they use this sentence—in particular, the first letters of the words in the sentence—to remember the categories in the biological classification system: *kingdom, phylum, class, order, family, genus,* and *species.* By reminding students of the letters that the various category names begin with, the sentence focuses their long-term memory search on terms that begin with those letters. The sentence essentially serves as a *superimposed meaningful structure,* a type of mnemonic we'll discuss in chapter 12.

Sometimes the physical environment in which something has been learned also facilitates retrieval (Godden & Baddeley, 1975; Smith, Glenberg, & Bjork, 1978). That is, it serves as a **contextual cue.** In an unusual demonstration of this principle, Godden and Baddeley (1975) had scuba divers learn 36 unrelated words in either of two environments: on shore or 20 feet below the water's surface. They were then asked to remember the words in either the same or a different environment. On a free recall task, the divers were able to recall more words when they were in the same environment in which they had learned the words than when they were in the other environment. Yet even if the environment itself is not the specific one in which we originally learned something, exposure to some of the characteristics of that environment—perhaps the same smells or the same background music—can help us remember (Balch, Bowman, & Mohler, 1992; Cann & Ross, 1989; Holland, Hendriks, & Aarts, 2005; Schab, 1990).[2]

Retrieval cues are apt to be most effective when we have associated them *frequently* with the specific information we are trying to remember (Tulving, 1968, 1975; Tulving & Thomson, 1971; Underwood, 1983). For example, when retrieving the list of 24 words I gave you earlier, once you remembered *table,* you should have had little trouble remembering *chair* as well (or vice versa), because the two words often occur together in conversation.

A downside of retrieval cues is that they may occasionally set boundaries on the areas of long-term memory we search. For instance, in a study by Brown (1968), an experimental group of college students was given a list of 25 U.S. states to read, while a control group had no such list. Both groups were then asked to recall as many of the 50 states as they could. Compared with the control group, the experimental group remembered more of the states they had previously read but *fewer* of the states they had *not* read. Thus, retrieval cues can hinder recall when they direct a learner's search to parts of long-term memory *other* than those that hold desired information.

CONSTRUCTION IN RETRIEVAL

Read the following passage *one time only:*

Carol Harris's Need for Professional Help

Carol Harris was a problem child from birth. She was wild, stubborn, and violent. By the time Carol turned eight, she was still unmanageable. Her parents were very concerned about her

---

[2]The physical context may even affect the "retrieval" of classically conditioned responses; see Bouton (1994) for an explanation.

mental health. There was no good institution for her problem in her state. Her parents finally decided to take some action. They hired a private teacher for Carol. (Sulin & Dooling, 1974)

Now cover the passage and answer this question: Did you read the statement "She was deaf, dumb, and blind" anywhere in the passage?

You probably answered "no" to my question. But do you think you might have been fooled if you had read the same passage with the name Helen Keller substituted for Carol Harris? Sulin and Dooling (1974) compared what happened when people read a Carol Harris version of the story versus when they read a Helen Keller version: Immediately after reading the passage, 20% of the "Helen Keller" group stated that the passage had included a statement about the woman being "deaf, dumb, and blind," yet no one in the "Carol Harris" group made that mistake. A week later, the number asserting they had read such a statement rose to 50% for the "Helen Keller" group but only to 5% for the "Carol Harris" group. In a follow-up study using the same passage, Dooling and Christiaansen (1977) found that people who read about Carol Harris, but who were told at recall a week later that the passage was really about Helen Keller, were also likely to "remember" the statement about her being "deaf, dumb, and blind." At retrieval time, the participants in the two studies were apparently using their prior knowledge about Helen Keller as well as their actual memory of what they had read. The longer the time interval between storage and retrieval, the greater the impact their prior knowledge had.

Such results indicate that long-term memory retrieval, like long-term memory storage, may involve constructive processes. People often retrieve only a portion of the information that has previously been presented to them, and they may fill in the "holes" based on what is logical or consistent with their existing knowledge and beliefs about themselves or about the world more generally (R. C. Anderson, 1984; Halpern, 1985; Heit, 1993; Kolodner, 1985; Loftus, 1991; Neisser, 1981; Spiro, 1980a, 1980b; Wilson & Anderson, 1986).

Construction can occur in retrieval of nonverbal as well as verbal material. For example, in chapter 8, I described research by Carmichael and colleagues (1932), in which people's reproductions of line drawings reflected the labels (e.g., eyeglasses or dumbbells) assigned to them (see Figure 8.6). The participants probably remembered only parts of those drawings and filled in the rest based on what they knew about the objects that the labels identified. Another example of constructive retrieval of nonverbal material can be found in the recall of a crime one has witnessed. Eyewitness testimony is sometimes an inaccurate representation of what actually happened (Buckhout, 1974; Lindsay, 1993; Loftus, 1991, 1992). Observers' descriptions of the crime may vary considerably, depending on prior knowledge about the individuals involved, expectations about what typically happens in such a situation, and additional information presented at a later time (more on the last point shortly).

Even especially vivid memories can be partly reconstructed and so have the potential to be inaccurate. As an example, think about where you were and what you were doing when, on September 11, 2001, you first heard about the attack on the World Trade Center. You can probably recall where you were and what you were doing in considerable detail. But how *accurate* is your recollection? Unless you have a videotape of yourself when you first heard the news, there is no way to be sure.

Neisser and Harsch (1992) studied college students' memory for another disaster, the crash of the space shuttle *Challenger* on January 28, 1986. (To refresh your memory, the *Challenger* plummeted into the ocean soon after liftoff, and seven astronauts perished, including Christa McAuliffe, the first teacher to travel into space.) Neisser and Harsch asked the students to describe the circumstances in which they heard the news both the morning after the incident and then again $2\frac{1}{2}$ years later. Even after more than 2 years, many students were quite confident about their recollections. Despite their confidence, some of them were way off base. For example, one student gave this account the morning after hearing about the disaster:

> I was in my religion class and some people walked in and started talking about [it]. I didn't know any details except that it had exploded and the schoolteacher's students had all been watching which I thought was so sad. Then after class I went to my room and watched the TV program talking about it and I got all the details from that. (Neisser & Harsch, 1992, p. 9)

The same student had this recollection $2\frac{1}{2}$ years later:

> When I first heard about the explosion I was sitting in my freshman dorm room with my roommate and we were watching TV. It came on a news flash and we were both totally shocked. I was really upset and I went upstairs to talk to a friend of mine and then I called my parents. (Neisser & Harsch, 1992, p. 9)

Our memories of experiencing or hearing about significant and emotion-laden events are often quite vivid, detailed ones with a seemingly "snapshot" quality to them; hence, psychologists call them **flashbulb memories** (Bohannon & Symons, 1992; Brewer, 1992; Brown & Kulik, 1977). Yet we shouldn't let such vividness lead us astray: Many flashbulb memories are quite accurate, but many others are not (Brewer, 1992; Rubin, 1992; Schmolck, Buffalo, & Squire, 2000; Talarico & Rubin, 2003).

Although constructive processes may be responsible for many errors in what we remember, construction usually facilitates long-term memory retrieval. When our memory of an event is incomplete, we can fill in details based on what makes sense (Halpern, 1985; Kintsch, Mandel, & Kozminsky, 1977; Kolodner, 1985; Reder, 1982). For example, an American student may not immediately remember which general surrendered at Appomattox at the end of the American Civil War; however, the student might reasonably assume that, because the South lost the war and General Robert E. Lee commanded the Southern troops, it was probably General Lee who surrendered at Appomattox. Similarly, a student trying to remember how to spell the word *ascertain* may surmise that, because the word is related in meaning to the word *certain,* it should be spelled similarly.

The Power of Suggestion: Effects of Subsequently Presented Information

Sometimes people's recollections are influenced not only by their prior knowledge but also by information presented to them sometime *after* they learned whatever they are retrieving. Generally speaking, this is a good thing: People *should* continually update their knowledge and understanding as new information comes in. In some cases, however—for instance, in eyewitness testimony—further information in the form of incorrect statements or misleading questions can be detrimental.

As an illustration of how constructive processes can lead people astray in eyewitness testimony, consider an experiment by Loftus and Palmer (1974). Five different groups of adults watched a film depicting a car accident, and then people in each group were asked one of five questions about how fast the car was going. The participants' estimates of the speed varied significantly, depending on how the question was worded (italics highlight the variations in wording):

Question Asked	Estimated Speed (mph)
About how fast were the cars going when they *contacted* each other?	31.8
About how fast were the cars going when they *hit* each other?	34.0
About how fast were the cars going when they *bumped* into each other?	38.1
About how fast were the cars going when they *collided* into each other?	39.3
About how fast were the cars going when they *smashed* into each other?	40.8

As you can see, the participants' reconstructions of the accident were influenced to some extent by the severity of the crash implied by the question they were asked.

As another example, let's consider what has become a classic study of eyewitness testimony in young children (Leichtman & Ceci, 1995). A man identified as "Sam Stone" briefly visited a preschool classroom; he commented on the story the teacher was reading to the children, strolled around the perimeter of the room, waved goodbye, and left. Later, an adult asked, "When Sam Stone got that bear dirty, did he do it on purpose or as an accident?" and "Was Sam Stone happy or sad that he got the bear dirty?" (p. 571). When asked these questions, many of the children recalled that Sam soiled a teddy bear, even though he never touched a stuffed animal during his visit. Susceptibility to leading questions was especially common in 3- and 4-year-olds; 5- and 6-year-olds were less likely to be swayed by the suggestive remarks (Leichtman & Ceci, 1995).

The results just described illustrate the **misinformation effect:** People's memory for an event may become distorted when they subsequently receive inaccurate information about the event (Bruck & Ceci, 1997; Lindsay, 1993; Loftus, 1992; Principe, Kanaya, Ceci, & Singh, 2006; Titcomb & Reyna, 1995; Toglia, 1996; Zaragoza & Mitchell, 1996). Apparently, people integrate the misinformation with their original knowledge of the event and use the two in combination to reconstruct what "must" have happened.

Constructing Entirely New "Memories"

In some cases, retrieval is almost entirely constructive, in that an individual is asked to provide information that has never actually been stored. For example, consider this arithmetic problem:

$$\frac{1}{2} \times 0 = ?$$

You may never have been given the answer to this specific problem, yet you no doubt learned long ago that anything times zero equals zero. Hence you are able to construct the correct answer:

$$\frac{1}{2} \times 0 = 0$$

Constructive retrieval enables individuals to produce information beyond what they have specifically stored. Such construction takes time, however (J. R. Anderson, 1985). In a study by Stazyk, Ashcraft, and Hamann (1982), students easily retrieved multiplication facts they had practiced many times and so quickly answered such problems as 2×3 and 4×6. However, they were slower to answer "zero" problems such as 2×0 and 0×6. Many students probably store a general rule for such problems (i.e., anything times zero equals zero) rather than specific answers to each problem, and they must therefore construct their answer from the rule each time such a problem is presented. When fast reaction times are essential (e.g., when numerous basic math facts are needed to solve complex problems), it is probably to a student's advantage to learn the specific information required rather than a more general rule from which the information can be derived.

Occasionally, new "memories" have little or no basis in fact. In particular, they are **false memories** for things that were never experienced (e.g., Loftus, 2003, 2004). For instance, asking people to picture an imaginary object or event increases the likelihood that, later on, they will remember actually experiencing it; young children have an especially difficult time distinguishing fact from fantasy (Foley, Harris, & Herman, 1994; Garry & Polaschek, 2000; Gonsalves et al., 2004; Mazzoni & Memon, 2003; Parker, 1995). And when people see photographs of themselves partaking in certain events—perhaps because an experimenter has electronically imposed their faces on photographs of people taking a hot-air balloon ride—they may later recall actually participating in the events (Garry & Gerrie, 2005).

False memories are common when stimuli might reasonably or logically have been encountered. For example, in word-list learning tasks, people may "remember" seeing words that they never actually saw but that are close associates of words they *did see*, presumably because the unseen words were activated during the learning session (Brainerd & Reyna, 1998; Roediger & McDermott, 2000; Seamon, Luo, & Gallo, 1998; Urbach, Windmann, Payne, & Kutas, 2005). Plausibility also increases false recall of nonexperienced events, especially for older children and adults (Ghetti & Alexander, 2004; Pezdek, Finger, & Hodge, 1997). For example, in a study by Pezdek and colleagues (1997), high school students were asked whether certain events happened when they were 8 years old. Some of the events actually did happen, but the experimenters fabricated two others, one involving a common religious ritual for Catholic children and another involving a common ritual for Jewish children. As you might guess, Catholic students were more likely to "remember" the Catholic event, whereas Jewish students were more apt to "remember" the Jewish one, and their scripts for such events allowed them to "recall" a fair number of details about what had transpired.

Remembering Earlier Recollections

In their study of memory about the *Challenger* disaster, Neisser and Harsch (1992) interviewed many students a third time, 3 years after the disaster itself and so 6 months after the second recall session. On this third occasion, most students essentially repeated their stories from 6 months earlier. When participants who inaccurately remembered the occasion were given hints as to the truth about where they had been and what they had been doing, they stuck with their prior misrecollections; furthermore, they were quite surprised when they were shown their original, morning-after descriptions. It appeared that these students were remembering not what had actually had happened but what they had previously *said* had happened.

As the Neisser and Harsch study illustrates, recalling an event that has happened to us often affects our later memory for the event, especially when we verbally describe the event

(Mazzoni & Kirsch, 2002; Paller, 2004; Schank & Abelson, 1995; Winograd & Neisser, 1992). Such **narratives** can definitely be constructive in nature. Author Marion Winik has described the process this way:

> Sometimes I think childhood memories are fabricated like pearls around a grain of sand. You know how it works: take one old photograph and the quick current of memory it sparks; add what you heard happened, what could have happened, what probably happened; then tell the story over and over until you get the details down. It doesn't take a degree in psychology to reverse-engineer your childhood based on the adult it produced.
>
>   Even if I've made it all up, it doesn't matter. I'm stuck with the past I believe in, even if it's wrong. (Winik, 1994, p. 40)

Many children acquire a rudimentary narrative structure before they are 2, and this structure enhances their memory of what they have experienced (Bauer & Mandler, 1990). As children get older, their narratives become more detailed and complete; for instance, they begin to talk not only about what happened but also about particular people's motives and intentions (Bauer, 2006; Gauvain, 2001). Some children construct more elaborate ones than others—in part because their parents encourage such elaboration—and their memories for events are better as a result (Bauer, 2006; Fivush & Nelson, 2004; Leichtman, Pillemer, Wang, Koreishi, & Han, 2000; K. Nelson & Fivush, 2004).

Self-Monitoring During Retrieval

In chapter 5 I described an aspect of self-regulation known as *self-monitoring*, in which people observe and assess their own behaviors. It appears that people may also engage in self-monitoring of a more "cognitive" sort when they retrieve information from long-term memory (Koriat & Goldsmith, 1996; Mazzoni & Kirsch, 2002). That is, they reflect on their recollections in an effort to determine whether they are remembering something accurately or inaccurately. For instance, as we have seen, people are more likely to believe a recollection is accurate when it is plausible—when it is consistent with what they know about themselves and about the world in general. They are also more likely to have confidence in the accuracy of a memory when it is vivid, detailed, and easy to retrieve—perhaps when it seems to "jump out" at them (Mazzoni & Kirsch, 2002). And because they know that their memories of long-ago events are typically quite "hazy," they will often agree that nonrecalled events in early childhood—including some that a researcher has made up—probably did happen (Ghetti & Alexander, 2004; Mazzoni & Kirsch, 2002). Consistent with what you will learn about *metacognition* in chapter 12, the ability to take such factors into account when self-monitoring the accuracy of one's memories seems to improve over the course of childhood (Ghetti & Alexander, 2004).

One difficulty in self-monitoring is **source monitoring**—remembering when or where a memory actually came into being (Carroll & Perfect, 2002; Payne, Neuschatz, Lampinen, & Lynn, 1997; Robinson & Whitcombe, 2003; Schacter, 1999). For example, memory expert Donald Thomson was once accused of raping a woman at the exact time he was engaged in a television interview about memory. The woman described Dr. Thomson in vivid detail and was certain he had been her attacker. In fact, she had watched the interview just before she was raped, and in the process of confusing her sources his face became an integral part of her recollection of the crime (Schacter, 1999; Thomson, 1988).

Faulty source monitoring is sometimes at the root of people's false memories of things they've imagined rather than actually experienced (Carroll & Perfect, 2002; Giles,

Gopnik, & Heyman, 2002). It can also lead to unintentional plagiarism of another person's ideas. For instance, in 1976 a U.S. court found former Beatle George Harrison guilty of copyright infringement after noting striking similarities between Harrison's song "My Sweet Lord" and an earlier piece by the Chiffons called "He's So Fine." Harrison recalled having heard the Chiffons' hit but had no conscious awareness that it might have been the source of his own tune (Carroll & Perfect, 2002).

Important Cautions in Probing People's Memories

Teachers, clinicians, law enforcement officers, attorneys, and other individuals who rely on people's memories to conduct their work must continually keep in mind the constructive nature of long-term memory retrieval. Sometimes human memory is reasonably accurate. But at other times a person's recollection can be seriously distorted or even completely fabricated. And a person's sense of confidence about a memory is not always a good indication of how accurate the memory actually is, especially when it comes to recognizing other people's faces (Perfect, 2002; Wells, Olson, & Charman, 2002).

Occasionally distortions and fabrications in memory are the result of the kinds of questions and feedback that professionals present (Giles et al., 2002; Gilstrap & Ceci, 2005; Wells & Bradfield, 1999; Wells et al., 2002; Zaragoza, Payment, Ackil, Drivdahl, & Beck, 2001). Leading questions such as "Where were you when So-And-So attacked you"?—which implies both that an attack occurred and that So-And-So was its perpetrator—are to be avoided at all costs, especially when the details of an event are largely unknown. Instead, professionals should ask open-ended questions such as "What did you see?" or "What happened next?" (e.g., Holliday, 2003). And they should refrain from repeatedly asking the same questions, insisting that people provide speculative answers to questions about which they're unsure, or implying that certain responses are correct or in some other way acceptable (Hirstein, 2005; Siegel, 1999; Wells et al., 2002).

Although people sometimes "remember" something they have never actually experienced, it is more often the case that they cannot retrieve something they *did* experience. We turn our attention now to explanations of why attempts at retrieval sometimes prove fruitless—in other words, to explanations of forgetting.

FORGETTING

In the early decades of cognitive psychology, many theorists thought that once information is stored in long-term memory, it remains there permanently in some form (Loftus & Loftus, 1980). Some evidence indicates that information may indeed remain in long-term memory for a very long time (Bahrick, 1984; Semb & Ellis, 1994). For instance, in a study by Bahrick (1984), individuals remembered a considerable amount of the Spanish they had learned in high school or college as many as 50 years before, even if they had not spoken Spanish since that time. Other evidence is found in experiments in which people *re*learn information they have previously learned but can no longer recall or recognize: These individuals learn the information more quickly than people who have not previously studied the same material (T. O. Nelson, 1971, 1978).

The observations of neurosurgeon Wilder Penfield (1958, 1959; Penfield & Roberts, 1959) have been cited as evidence for the permanence of long-term memory. Penfield sometimes operated on locally anesthetized but otherwise conscious patients. In doing so, he discovered that stimulating portions of the brain with a weak electric current could evoke vivid sensations. Patients would describe hearing a song, delivering a baby, or going to a circus as if the experience were actually happening to them at that very moment. They acted almost as if they were reliving previous events in their lives.

Unfortunately, Penfield never determined whether the events his patients "remembered" had actually occurred. A more difficult challenge for a permanence-of-memory view is that, although certainly some information lasts a long time, researchers have not yet demonstrated—and quite possibly *cannot* demonstrate—that *all* information stored in long-term memory remains there for the life of the individual (Eysenck & Keane, 1990; Willingham, 2004).

One thing about long-term memory is certainly clear: Over time, people recall less and less about the events they have experienced and the information they have acquired (J. R. Anderson, 1995; Wixted & Ebbesen, 1991). Theorists have offered a number of explanations about why we forget much of what we learn. Here we look at several possibilities: decay, interference, failure to retrieve, repression, construction error, and failure to store or consolidate. We then consider possible reasons why our earliest experiences are especially difficult to recall.

Decay

Increasingly, psychologists have come to believe that information can gradually fade away, or **decay,** and eventually disappear from memory altogether. Decay seems to be especially common when information is used rarely or not at all (Altmann & Gray, 2002; Byrnes, 2001; Loftus & Loftus, 1980; Schacter, 1999).

Some kinds of information are apparently more susceptible to decay than others. In particular, the exact details of an event—verbatim information, if you will—fade more quickly than the underlying meaning, or gist, of the event (Brainerd & Reyna, 1992, 2002; Cohen, 2000). We find an exception to this general rule when certain details capture key perceptual features of an event or are in some other way quite distinctive (Ausubel et al., 1978; Eysenck, 1979; Pansky & Koriat, 2004; Reisberg, 1997). Meanwhile, less distinctive ones are forgotten or become a general blur. To illustrate, when I think back to my early lessons in U.S. history, I remember the general idea behind the American Revolution: The colonists were fighting for independence from British rule. I also remember certain distinctive details; for example, the Battle of Bunker Hill is commemorated by a monument I visited frequently as a child, and the Boston Tea Party was a unique and colorful illustration of American dissatisfaction with British taxation policies. However, I have forgotten the details of many other events, because, to my young mind, they consisted of nondistinctive people and places.

Yet just as it may be impossible to determine whether information stays forever in long-term memory, it may be equally impossible to show conclusively that it disappears from memory altogether. For instance, perhaps a person who seemingly loses information simply never "looks" in the right place. It does appear, however, that unused memories weaken and become less accessible over time.

Interference

In chapter 7, I described the phenomena of proactive and retroactive inhibition: In both situations, learning one set of verbal material interferes with the ability to recall another set. Verbal learning theorists (McGeoch, 1942; Melton & Irwin, 1940; Postman & Underwood, 1973; Underwood, 1948) proposed that such inhibition is a major cause of forgetting verbal information. Some contemporary memory theorists agree, although they often use the term **interference** rather than inhibition (Altmann & Gray, 2002; Dempster & Corkill, 1999; Lustig, Konkel, & Jacoby, 2004; Schacter, 1999). In support of this explanation of forgetting, recall of word lists can be as high as 85% when sources of interference are removed from a serial learning task (Underwood, 1957).

An interference view of forgetting might best be described as a theory of confusion: An individual has learned numerous responses and gets them mixed up. An experiment by John Anderson (1974) helps us place interference within a contemporary cognitive framework. College students learned a long list of single-proposition sentences, each of which involved a person and a place; here are some examples:

A hippie is in the park.
A hippie is in the church.
A policeman is in the park.
A sailor is in the park.

The people and places appeared in varying numbers of sentences; some items (e.g., the policeman) appeared in only one sentence, whereas others (e.g., the park) appeared several times. The students studied the sentences until they knew them very well—more specifically, until they could respond to a long list of questions (e.g., "Who is in the park?" "Where are the hippies?") with 100% accuracy. At that point, they were given a new set of sentences and asked to indicate whether or not these had been in the first set. The more frequently the person and the place had appeared in the first set of sentences, the longer it took the students to determine whether the person and place had appeared *together* in that first set. Anderson (1974, 1976, 1983a, 1990) has explained these results as being a function of the numerous associations the students developed to the frequently appearing people and places. For example, the more frequently that certain places had been associated with *hippie* in the original set of sentences, the longer students would take to search among their associations with *hippie* to determine whether a new sentence about a hippie had been encountered before. Thus, multiple associations with a concept can slow down retrieval time for information connected with the concept—a phenomenon that Anderson calls the **fan effect.**

Interference is probably more relevant in the forgetting of rote-learned information than of meaningfully learned information (Good & Brophy, 1986). In other words, response competition and confusion are more likely to be a problem when associations between pieces of information are arbitrary rather than logical.

Failure to Retrieve

You can probably think of occasions when you couldn't remember something at first, yet recalled it later on. Clearly, then, the information was still in your long-term memory; you just couldn't retrieve it the first time around.

Using our "flashlight" analogy again, we might say failure to retrieve occurs when people neglect to "look" in the part of long-term memory that holds the desired information. Perhaps the information was initially stored in connection with ideas very different from those one is thinking of at the present time. Or perhaps the information was stored with very few connections to other ideas; as a result, even a broad search of memory doesn't focus the flashlight on (i.e., activate) it (J. R. Anderson, 1995). Given appropriate retrieval cues, however, people may eventually find what they are looking for (Tulving, 1975; Tulving & Psotka, 1971; Underwood, 1983).

Some instances of failure to retrieve involve forgetting to do something that needs to be done at a future time (Einstein & McDaniel, 2005). As an example, when I was considerably younger, I often forgot to turn off my car lights after driving to work on a foggy morning. I occasionally forgot important meetings. Sometimes I forgot to bring crucial handouts or transparencies to class. Yes, yes, I know what you're thinking: I was suffering from the absentminded professor syndrome.

It's not that I would lose information from my long-term memory. When I went to the parking lot at the end of the day and discovered that my car battery was dead, I would readily remember that I had turned on my car lights that morning. When I was reminded of an important meeting I'd missed or got to the point in a class session where I needed the handout I'd forgotten to bring, I would think, "Oh, yes, of course!" My problem was that I *forgot to retrieve* important information at the appropriate time. Fortunately, as I've learned more about memory, I've also developed a strategy to overcome my absentmindedness. I'll share it with you near the end of the chapter.

Repression

Earlier in the chapter, I mentioned that emotionally laden news sometimes results in a flashbulb memory—a vivid, detailed recollection of where we were and what we were doing when experiencing or learning about an especially significant event. But in some situations we may have an experience that is so painful or emotionally distressing that we tend either not to remember it at all or else to remember only isolated fragments of it (Arrigo & Pezdek, 1997; Loftus & Kaufman, 1992; Nadel & Jacobs, 1998). This phenomenon, often known as **repression**,[3] was first described by Sigmund Freud (1915/1957, 1922); more recently, several theorists have explained it within a contemporary cognitivist framework (Erdelyi, 1985; Erdelyi & Goldberg, 1979; B. P. Jones, 1993; Wegman, 1985). To describe repression in contemporary memoryterminology, painful information begins to produce anxiety whenever the relevant part of longterm memory is approached. Because anxiety itself is unpleasant, the memory search will tend to steer clear of the anxiety-arousing part of long-term memory. Thus, the painful memory, as well as any other information stored in close association with it, remains out of reach and so is essentially "forgotten."

Most victims of traumatic events can consciously recall the events (e.g., Goodman et al., 2003). Yet repression is occasionally observed in clinical settings (Erdelyi, 1985; Pezdek & Banks, 1996; Schooler, 2001). Over a series of therapy sessions, perhaps with the help of hypnosis (which induces relaxation), a client gradually recalls bits and pieces of a traumatic incident; eventually, the client may remember the entire event. Recalling the incident often relieves the symptoms for which the client has sought the therapist's assistance (Erdelyi & Goldberg, 1979). Unfortunately, however, many presumably repressed "memories" are never checked for accuracy; thus, they may or may not be based on something that actually occurred (Brandon, Boakes, Glaser, & Green, 1998; Loftus, 1993; McNally, 2003). For instance, although a hypnotic state may increase people's confidence

---

[3]Arrigo and Pezdek (1997) prefer the term *psychogenic amnesia,* which describes the nature of the phenomenon without offering the "repression" explanation of why it occurs.

and willingness to talk about past events, it doesn't necessarily improve their memory for what transpired (Dinges et al., 1992; Lynn, Lock, Myers, & Payne, 1997; Reisberg, 1997).

A few laboratory research studies support a possible role of repression in forgetting: People do seem to have less recall for information they willfully try *not* to think about (M. C. Anderson & Green, 2001; Davis, 1987; Davis & Schwartz, 1987; Eriksen & Kuethe, 1956; Levy & Anderson, 2002). Overall, however, the evidence for repression is more spotty in laboratory research than that found in therapeutic settings. It may be that events sufficiently traumatic to bring about repression cannot easily or ethically be created in a laboratory setting; it may also be that many adults simply do not repress painful information as a matter of course (Erdelyi, 1985; Goodman et al., 2003; B. P. Jones, 1993).

Construction Error

We have already seen how construction can lead to errors in recall. Construction can occur either at storage (i.e., learner-invented information is stored) or at retrieval (i.e., the learner "remembers" information that was never encountered). Construction at retrieval time is particularly likely to occur when there are holes in the information retrieved—holes possibly due to decay, interference, or unsuccessful retrieval. So, as you might expect, erroneous reconstruction of an event or a body of learned information is increasingly likely to occur as time goes on (Anderson & Pichert, 1978; Dooling & Christiaansen, 1977; Spiro, 1977).

Failure to Store or Consolidate

A final explanation of "forgetting" is the fact that some information may never have been completely stored in the first place (Bourne et al., 1986; Ellis & Hunt, 1983; Siegel, 1999). Perhaps we didn't pay attention to the information, so it never entered working memory. Or perhaps we didn't process it sufficiently to get it into long-term memory. Even if it *did* get into long-term memory, perhaps some outside factor—a serious accident, for instance—interfered with consolidation processes (see chapter 8).

In some instances, the brain may be able to store information only in ways that lead to implicit knowledge, which is not accessible to *conscious* retrieval. This is the case for people with certain kinds of brain injuries (Siegel, 1999; Wixted, 2005). And it partly explains why people have little or no recollection of their first few years of life, as we shall see now.

The Case of Infantile Amnesia

You probably remember very little of your infancy and early childhood. I remember a couple of snippets—for instance, I recall waiting patiently in my crib one morning until my parents woke up, and I recall being held lovingly by my Nana one day in her flower garden—but for all I know, these "memories" never really happened. I certainly don't remember the first birthday party my parents gave me at age 1, even though photographs suggest that it must have a very festive occasion. Generally speaking, people remember little or nothing about specific events in their lives that occurred before age 3—a phenomenon known as **infantile amnesia** (Newcombe, Drummey, Fox, Lie, & Ottinger-Albergs, 2000; Pillemer & White, 1989).

Children have *some* ability to remember information from a very early age, however. In fact, a study by DeCasper and Spence (1986) suggests that some memory capacity emerges even before birth. In this study, pregnant women read aloud a passage from a children's book (e.g., Dr. Seuss's *The Cat and the Hat*) twice a day for the final six weeks of their pregnancies. Later, their newborn babies were given pacifiers, and the babies' sucking rates (either fast or slow) determined whether they heard a recording of their mother reading the prebirth story or a different one. Even though the infants were only 2 or 3 days old, they began to adjust their sucking rate so that they could hear the familiar story—the one they had previously heard only while still in the womb!

Young infants clearly remember some of their postbirth experiences as well. For instance, when a ribbon connected to a mobile is tied to a baby's foot, even a 2-month-old easily learns that kicking makes the mobile move and remembers the connection over a period of several days—longer if the child has an occasional reminder (Rovee-Collier, 1999). Infants age 3 to 6 months show evidence that they remember the order in which they've see a sequence of three mobiles (Gulya, Rovee-Collier, Galluccio, & Wilk, 1998). At age 6 months, they can recall and imitate actions they have seen 24 hours earlier, and their memory for observed actions increases in duration in the months that follow (Bauer, 1995, 2006; Collie & Hayne, 1999). By the time children are 2 years old, they are highly accurate in identifying pictures they have seen previously (Brown & Scott, 1971; Perlmutter & Lange, 1978).

Much of what infants learn and remember appears to be in the form of *implicit knowledge*—knowledge that affects their behavior even though they cannot consciously recall it (Nadel, 2005; C. A. Nelson, 1995; Newcombe et al., 2000). Theorists have offered at least two plausible explanations for why we consciously recall so little of our early years. First, brain structures that are actively involved in explicit memories, such as the hippocampus and frontal cortex, are not fully developed at birth, and the frontal cortex in particular continues to mature in significant ways for several years thereafter (LeDoux, 1998; Nell, 2002; Newcombe et al., 2000). Second, as we have seen, talking about experiences enhances memory for them (recall our discussions of *verbalization* in chapter 8 and of *narratives* earlier in this chapter), but infants and toddlers don't have the language skills to talk about events. As they gain linguistic proficiency, and particularly when people around them engage them in conversations about what they are experiencing, their memories improve dramatically (Eacott, 1999; Haden, Ornstein, Eckerman, & Didow, 2001; K. Nelson, 1996; Simcock & Hayne, 2002). Presumably, talking about events enables them to encode the events in a verbal (language-based) form, making the events more easily retrievable at a later time.

Perhaps all of the explanations I've just presented are partially responsible for the universal human problem of forgetting. Yet forgetting isn't necessarily a bad thing. Many of the things we learn on any particular occasion have little use to us later (especially *much* later), and we rarely need to remember things *exactly* as we originally experienced them (Anderson & Schooler, 1991; Reisberg, 1997; Schacter, 1999). As Byrnes (2001) has put it, "our minds seem to be naturally equipped to retain only those events that repeat on a regular basis" (p. 59).

In classroom settings, however, students sometimes forget things related to important instructional objectives. In the final section of the chapter, we will pull together what we have learned about retrieval and forgetting, as well as about memory more generally, into several general principles that have implications for classroom practice.

GENERAL PRINCIPLES OF RETRIEVAL FOR INSTRUCTIONAL SETTINGS

In the preceding three chapters, we've identified numerous principles about memory and knowledge that have implications for classroom practice. Following are several additional ones that have particular relevance for retrieval of academic subject matter:

* *The internal organization of a body of information facilitates its retrieval.* When material is presented in an organized fashion—for instance, when hierarchical structures, cause–effect relationships, and so on are clearly specified—students are more likely to store it in a similar organizational network. And when information in long-term memory is organized, it can more easily be retrieved.

Some of my own students have found the following analogy useful in helping them understand the importance of organization for retrieval:

> Imagine 10,000 buttons scattered on a hardwood floor. Randomly choose two buttons and connect them with a thread. Now put this pair down and randomly choose two more buttons, pick them up, and connect them with a thread. As you continue to do this, at first you will almost certainly pick up buttons that you have not picked up before. After a while, however, you are more likely to pick at random a pair of buttons and find that you have already chosen one of the pair. So when you tie a thread between the two newly chosen buttons, you will find three buttons tied together. In short, as you continue to choose random pairs of buttons to connect with a thread, after a while the buttons start becoming interconnected into larger clusters. . . . (Kauffman, 1995, p. 56)

Eventually, you will form a single giant cluster of buttons. At this point, you can pick up almost any button in the pile and have most of the others follow. Now think of the buttons as being individual pieces of information related to a particular topic, and think of the threads as being your associations among those pieces. Eventually, you make enough associations that when you retrieve one idea about the topic, you can also retrieve, either directly or indirectly, most of the other things you know about it.[4]

* *How something is retrieved at one time affects how it will be retrieved later on.* As we've seen, retrieval can be quite constructive. We've seen, too, that people tend to remember things in the same way time after time. If they remember something incorrectly once, they're likely to remember it in the same incorrect way on a future occasion.

When students don't know appropriate interconnections to make among the ideas they are studying, they may pull the ideas together in a way that seems logical but isn't necessarily accurate (recall our discussion of *theory theory* in chapter 9). As an illustration, when a researcher asks fourth graders from Michigan why the Americas were once called the New World, a girl named Rita has this to say:

> Because they used to live in England, the British, and they didn't know about . . . they wanted to get to China 'cause China had some things they wanted. They had some cups or whatever—no, they had furs. They had fur and stuff like that and they wanted to have a shorter way to get to China so they took it and they landed in Michigan, but it wasn't called Michigan. I think it was the British that landed in Michigan and they were there first and so they tried to claim that land, but it didn't work out for some reason so they took some furs and

---

[4] I am indebted to one of my former students, Jason Cole, for originally making the analogy between Kauffman's scenario and the organization of memory.

brought them back to Britain and they sold them, but they mostly wanted it for the furs. So then the English landed there and they claimed the land and they wanted to make it a state, and so they got it signed by the government or whoever, the big boss, then they were just starting to make it a state so the British just went up to the Upper Peninsula and they thought they could stay there for a little while. Then they had to fight a war, then the farmers, they were just volunteers, so the farmers went right back and tried to get their family put together back again. (VanSledright & Brophy, 1992, p. 849)

Rita has taken bits and pieces of information she has learned in school and pulled them into a scenario that makes sense to her. In the process, she has made some creative connections indeed. For instance, she associates China with both cups (after all, many cups *are* made of china) and furs (which early traders actually obtained in western North America). Notice, too, how Rita maintains that the British found a shorter way to get to China—one that apparently went through Michigan. At the same time, Rita doesn't make at least one essential connection that would help her understand early American history—the fact that the "British" and the "English" were the same group of people.

Although Rita's description of American history has a few elements of truth, these elements have been combined to form an overall "knowledge" of history that could give any historian heart failure. If teachers want students to connect and remember classroom subject matter in a particular way, then, they should make the appropriate connections clear *right from the start.*

◆ *Information that must be retrieved within a particular context should be stored within that context.* People are most likely to retrieve information relevant to a situation when they have stored it in close association with other aspects of the situation. If they have stored it elsewhere, they are much less likely to stumble on it at times when it will be useful. Thus, information should be stored with retrieval in mind.

In light of this principle, teachers should give students numerous opportunities to relate classroom material to the various situations that are later likely to require its retrieval. For example, a student is more likely to retrieve mathematical ideas relevant to accounting, surveying, or engineering if the math teacher incorporates problems involving accounting, surveying, and engineering into instruction. Similarly, a student studying for a psychology test that stresses application will be better prepared if he or she uses study time to consider numerous situations in which psychological principles can be applied. Furthermore, students should have opportunities to use the things they learn in real-world contexts; we'll consider such *authentic activities* in chapters 11 and 13.

◆ *External retrieval cues minimize failure to retrieve.* Earlier I mentioned the common problem of *forgetting to retrieve*—in particular, forgetting to do something you need to do. The best way to address this problem, I've found, is to create an **external retrieval cue**—a physical reminder outside of (external to) the memory system. The classic example is a string around the finger: The string is tied in a spot impossible to overlook and serves as a reminder that something needs to be remembered.[5]

---

[5]An *external retrieval cue* should remind you of the concept of *cueing* (or *prompting*) described in chapter 4. Behaviorists think of cues as evoking desired responses, whereas cognitivists think of them as facilitating retrieval. The effect is the same—a desired behavior is more likely to occur—but the explanation of why the cue has an effect is different.

Finger strings are terribly unfashionable, but other external retrieval cues can be equally effective. Over the years, I've developed several that have made me one of the *least* absentminded professors on the planet. I keep a weekly calendar open by the telephone on my desk, and I write in it not only the meetings and appointments I need to go to but also the things I do regularly every week—teaching class Monday afternoons, playing racquetball Wednesday evenings, and so on. I write notes to myself about things I need to do on a particular day or accomplish by the end of the week, and I put them in plain sight on my desk. And if I need to be sure to bring something with me to class or an appointment, I put it on the floor between my desk and my office door, so that I will definitely see it as I leave. Essentially, what I'm doing is guaranteeing retrieval of the things I need to remember.

As we'll discover in chapter 12, children and adolescents are typically quite naive about how their memories work (and don't work), and teachers are in an excellent position to help them learn to use their memories most effectively. Teachers can, of course, provide occasional verbal reminders (e.g., "Don't forget to bring your permission slips back tomorrow!"). But ultimately, students should also be shown how to develop their *own* retrieval cues—appointment books, to-do lists, self-reminder sticky notes, and so on—so that they can eventually become responsible for their own retrieval.

◆ *Questions about previously learned material can promote both review and further elaboration.* In our discussion of instructional objectives in chapter 5, we made a distinction between lower-level skills and higher-level skills. This was essentially a distinction between simply *knowing* something versus *doing* something (mentally) with that knowledge—for example, applying, analyzing, synthesizing, or evaluating it. We can make a similar distinction between **lower-level questions** and **higher-level questions:** The former ask students to retrieve something pretty much as they have stored it in memory, whereas the latter ask students to elaborate on the retrieved information.

Teacher questioning is a widely used teaching technique (Cazden, 2001; Mehan, 1979), probably because it has several benefits. We noted one such benefit in chapter 7: Questions help to focus students' attention on classroom activities. Questions also provide a feedback mechanism through which teachers and students alike can discover how much students have learned from a current lesson or can remember from previous lessons (Airasian, 1994; Connolly & Eisenberg, 1990; Fox & LeCount, 1991). When questions focus students' attention on previously studied material, they encourage review of the material—review that should promote greater recall later on (Wixson, 1984). And higher-level questions have the additional advantage of encouraging students to go beyond the information itself and construct more sophisticated understandings (Aulls, 1998; Meece, 1994; Minstrell & Stimpson, 1996). As examples, consider these questions from a lesson on the telegraph:

> Was the need for a rapid communications system [in North America] greater during the first part of the nineteenth century than it had been during the latter part of the eighteenth century? Why do you think so? (Torrance & Myers, 1970, p. 214)

To answer these questions, students must recall what they know about the eighteenth and nineteenth centuries (including the increasing movement of European settlers to distant western territories) and pull that knowledge together in a way they have perhaps never done before.

All too often, however, teachers and instructional materials pose lower-level, fact-based questions, with few if any higher-level questions to facilitate student elaboration (Armbruster & Ostertag, 1993; Aulls, 1998; Harrop & Swinson, 2003; Raudenbush, Rowan, & Cheong, 1993; Tobin, 1987).

Such a state of affairs is unfortunate. Fact-based questions are certainly quite useful for helping students acquire and review basic knowledge and skills. Yet research indicates quite clearly that teachers and instructional materials (e.g., textbooks) promote greater student achievement when they ask higher-level questions in addition to lower-level ones—for instance, when they call for inferences, applications, justifications, and solutions to problems as well as asking for knowledge (Armbruster & Ostertag, 1993; Brophy, 1992b; Frederiksen, 1984b; Liu, 1990; Redfield & Rousseau, 1981).

♦ *Taxonomies of objectives can be useful reminders of the various ways in which students might be asked to think about and apply what they have learned.* In our discussion of instructional objectives in chapter 5, we looked at Bloom's early Taxonomy of Educational Objectives, which suggests six increasingly complex levels of behavior that teachers might encourage and assess (Bloom et al., 1956). More recently, a collaborative group of educational psychologists (L. W. Anderson et al., 2001) has revised the taxonomy, in part to reflect theoretical advances in learning and cognition. The revision is a two-dimensional taxonomy that includes six *cognitive processes,* each of which is potentially relevant to four different *types of knowledge* (see Figure 10.1). The six cognitive processes are similar to the six levels in Bloom's original taxonomy (see Figure 5.5 on page 108). However, the cognitive processes are described by verbs rather than nouns, and the last two, *evaluate* and *create,* reflect a reversal of Bloom's *synthesis* and *evaluation* levels. The four types of knowledge include two forms of declarative knowledge, *factual knowledge* and *conceptual knowledge,* as well as *procedural knowledge* and *metacognitive knowledge* (we'll look at the nature of the last one more closely in chapter 12).

The revised taxonomy includes six *cognitive processes,* each of which is potentially relevant to four different *types of knowledge.*

Cognitive Processes

1. **Remember:** recognizing or recalling information learned at an earlier time and stored in long-term memory
2. **Understand:** constructing meaning from instructional materials and messages (e.g., drawing inferences, identifying new examples, summarizing)
3. **Apply:** using knowledge in a familiar or new situation
4. **Analyze:** breaking information into its constituent parts, and perhaps identifying interrelationships among those parts
5. **Evaluate:** making judgments about information using certain criteria or standards
6. **Create:** putting knowledge and/or procedures together to form a coherent, structured, and possibly original whole

Types of Knowledge

A. **Factual knowledge:** knowing specific pieces of information (e.g., facts, terminology)
B. **Conceptual knowledge:** knowing more general structures and interrelationships among pieces of information (e.g., general principles, schemas, models, theories)
C. **Procedural knowledge:** knowing how to do something (e.g., using step-by-step algorithms, employing scientific research methods), and possibly applying certain criteria in choosing the procedure to use
D. **Metacognitive knowledge:** knowing about the nature of thinking and about effective learning strategies, and being aware of one's own cognitive processes

Figure 10.1
A two-dimensional revision of Bloom's taxonomy (L. W. Anderson et al., 2001).

The two dimensions of the revised taxonomy are intended to represent two continuums that progress from very simple cognitive processes and types of knowledge to more complex ones. The continuums are not hard and fast, however; for example, some forms of conceptual knowledge can be fairly complex and abstract, whereas some forms of procedural knowledge are quite simple and concrete (L. W. Anderson et al., 2001). Rather than nitpick about the extent to which certain cognitive processes or types of knowledge are truly more complex than others, a more useful perspective of the revised taxonomy is to regard it as a helpful reminder of the various kinds of knowledge that students might have and the various ways in which they might use and apply it in new tasks and situations.

◆ *Retrieval can take time.* Sometimes retrieval happens quickly and easily, especially for material that has been used repeatedly and possibly been learned to automaticity. But in other instances, searching long-term memory for information relevant to a particular question or task can take a considerable amount of time. People need even more time if they must pull together what they can recall to draw new inferences, make new comparisons, generate new applications, and so on.

In the classroom, then, it is unreasonable to expect students to formulate insightful, creative responses to higher-level questions in a split second. Yet when teachers ask students a question, they typically wait for only a very short time—often a second or less—and if students don't respond in that short time interval, teachers tend to speak again, perhaps by asking different students the same question, rephrasing the question, or even answering the question themselves (Jegede & Olajide, 1995; Rowe, 1974, 1987). Teachers are equally reluctant to let much time elapse after students answer questions or make comments in class; on average, they allow 1 second or less of silence before responding to a statement or asking another question (Jegede & Olajide, 1995; Rowe, 1987).

The amount of time teachers allow to pass after their own and students' questions and comments is known as **wait time.** In many instances, 1 second is probably *not* sufficient time for students to think about (process) the questions teachers ask and the comments classmates make in class. After all, they must retrieve the things they know and, in the case of higher-level questions, must construct a response they have not previously stored.

Research indicates that students benefit tremendously simply from being given a little time to think. For example, when teachers increase their wait time by allowing at least 3 seconds to elapse (instead of only one) after both their own questions and students' remarks, we see changes in student behavior such as the following (Mohatt & Erickson, 1981; Rowe, 1974, 1987; Tharp, 1989; Tobin, 1987):[6]

Increased student participation:

- Students talk more and are more likely to answer questions correctly.
- More students participate in class; previously quiet students (including many minority students) become more active contributors.
- Students are more likely to contribute spontaneously to a class discussion—for example, by asking questions and presenting their own perspectives.
- Students are more likely to talk *to one another* (as well as to their teacher) within the context of a classroom discussion.

---

[6]Note, however, that waiting *too* long may be detrimental because students' attention begins to drift elsewhere, so that important information is no longer in working memory (Duell, 1994).

Better quality of student responses:

- Students' responses are longer and more sophisticated.
- Students are more likely to support their responses with evidence or logic.
- Students are more likely to give a variety of responses to the same question.
- Students are more likely to speculate when they don't know an answer.

Better classroom performance:

- Students are less likely to feel confused by course content; they are more likely to feel confident that they can master the material.
- Students' motivation to learn class material increases.
- Students show higher achievement, especially for complex material.
- Discipline problems decrease (as one fifth-grade boy put it, "It's the first time in all my years in school that anybody cared what I really thought—not just what I am supposed to say" [Rowe, 1987, p. 40]).

We also see changes in teacher behavior when we increase wait time to at least three seconds. More specifically, we see changes such as the following (Rowe, 1974, 1987; Tobin, 1987):

Different kinds of questions:

- Teachers ask fewer simple questions (e.g., questions requiring the recall of facts).
- Teachers ask more complex questions (e.g., questions requiring students to elaborate or develop alternative explanations).

Increased flexibility in instruction:

- Teachers modify the direction of discussion to accommodate students' comments and questions.
- Teachers allow their classes to pursue a topic in greater depth than they originally anticipated.

Changes in expectations:

- Teachers' expectations for many students, especially previously low-achieving students, begin to improve.

In general, increasing wait time during class discussions and question–answer sessions benefits student learning in two ways (Tobin, 1987). First, it allows students more time to process information. Second, it appears to change the very nature of teacher–student discussions; for example, teachers are more likely to ask challenging, thought-provoking questions. In fact, the nature of the questions that teachers ask is probably as important as—and perhaps even more important than—the amount of wait time per se (Giaconia, 1988).

When the objective is recall of facts—when students need to retrieve information very quickly, to "know it cold"—then wait time during a question–answer session should be short. There is a definite advantage to rapid-fire drill and practice for skills that teachers want students to learn to a level of automaticity (Tobin, 1987). But when objectives include more complex processing of ideas and issues, longer wait time provides both teachers and students the time they need to retrieve relevant ideas and think them through.

◆ *Classroom assessments promote retrieval and review; they also influence storage processes.* As a college professor, I give regular quizzes—usually every 2 or 3 weeks in undergraduate classes and at least once a month in masters' level classes. I also give frequent out-of-class assignments in which students must apply what they are learning to their personal and professional lives. My assessments encourage review, of course, but they also encourage students to reflect on class-room material in new ways. Even my multiple-choice questions require students to elaborate on what they have learned, often by asking them to recognize new examples of concepts or to eval-uate various classroom strategies using principles of effective learning and memory.

My assessment practices don't just affect what students do at retrieval time, however. They also affect how students study classroom subject matter to begin with; in other words, they affect students' storage processes. Because my students know from Day 1 that I am going to assess their *understanding* and *application* of what they learn in my class, most of them focus on meaningful learning and elaboration when they listen, speak, read, and study. A few of them, alas, do what they've always done in other classes—they rote-memorize—and these students typically struggle on my quizzes and assignments until they either seek my assistance or else stumble on more effective approaches themselves.

Research tells us that classroom assessments, *when designed appropriately,* can enhance stu-dents' learning and memory in at least four ways:

1. *By promoting effective storage processes.* Students tend to read and study differently depending on how they expect their learning to be assessed (Frederiksen, 1984b; Frederiksen & Collins, 1989; Lundeberg & Fox, 1991). For example, students are likely to focus on memorizing isolated facts at a rote level if they believe a test will require verbatim recall. They are more likely to try to make sense of what they are studying—that is, to engage in meaningful learning—when they know they will have to put things in their own words. And they are more likely to elaborate on class mate-rial if such elaboration will be required at assessment time—for instance, if they known they will have to apply, analyze, or synthesize the material.

2. *By encouraging review before the assessment.* As we discovered in chapter 8, students have a better chance of remembering things over the long run if they review those things periodically. Preparing for assessments is one way of reviewing classroom mate-rial. For instance, most students study class material more and learn it better when they are told they will be tested on it than when they are simply told to learn it (Frederiksen, 1984b; Halpin & Halpin, 1982). We should note, however, that stu-dents typically spend more time studying the information they think will be on a assessment than the things they think an assessment won't cover (Corbett & Wilson, 1988; Frederiksen, 1984b; Frederiksen & Collins, 1989).

3. *By requiring review during the assessment itself.* Taking a test or completing an assign-ment is, in and of itself, an occasion for retrieving and reviewing learned information. Generally speaking, the very process of completing an assessment on classroom mate-rial helps students learn the material better (Dempster, 1991; Foos & Fisher, 1988; Frederiksen, 1984b; Nungester & Duchastel, 1982; Roediger & Karpicke, 2006). But once again, the nature of the assessment probably makes a difference here: Tasks that require students to go beyond the material itself (e.g., to draw inferences) are more likely to be effective than those that ask only for recall of previously learned facts (Foos & Fisher, 1988). And tasks that require a broad search of long-term memory

promote more comprehensive review than do relatively specific test questions (Frederiksen & Ward, 1978; Murnane & Raizen, 1988).

4. *By providing feedback.* Assessments provide a concrete mechanism for letting students know what things they have learned correctly and what things they have learned either *in*correctly or not at all. For example, when students get constructive comments on their essays—comments that point out the strengths and weaknesses of each response, indicate where answers are ambiguous or imprecise, suggest how an essay might be more complete or better organized, and so on—their understanding of class material and their writing skills are both likely to improve (Baron, 1987; Krampen, 1987).

When we look at typical classroom tests, we are most likely to see test items that focus on lower-level skills (e.g., knowledge of simple facts), perhaps because such items are the easiest ones to write (Frederiksen & Collins, 1989; Nickerson, 1989; Poole, 1994; Silver & Kenney, 1995). If teachers want students to do *more* than memorize facts, they must develop assessments that encourage students to process information in certain ways—perhaps to rephrase ideas in their own words, generate their own examples of concepts, relate principles and procedures to real-world situations, use class material to solve problems, or examine ideas with a critical eye. Sometimes, of course, well-constructed test items can encourage such processes. In many cases, however, teachers may want to use other kinds of assessment tasks—perhaps writing stories, keeping journals, collecting and synthesizing data, comparing contradictory historical accounts, critiquing government policies, creating portfolios—that more readily allow students to apply classroom subject matter to new problems and situations, including those in their own lives (Lester, Lambdin, & Preston, 1997; Mehrens, 1992; Paris & Paris, 2001; Shepard, 2000).

♦ *Long-term memory can probably never be a totally reliable record of information.* Long-term memory storage and retrieval are both constructive processes and so will always be fallible. Students' memories can never be complete, verbatim repositories of what they have studied at school or elsewhere. At the same time, students can certainly learn how to capitalize on the strengths of the human memory system and how to compensate for its weaknesses. As we'll see in the next two chapters, teachers and other adults play a significant role in helping children and adolescents learn and remember information in increasingly effective ways.

SUMMARY

Retrieval from long-term memory appears to be a process of searching its contents, in one "location" at a time, until the desired information is found. Retrieval is easier when information has previously been stored in connection with many other ideas in memory, when it has previously been learned to automaticity, or when relevant *retrieval cues* are present. Presumably interconnections among ideas, automaticity, and appropriate retrieval cues increase the probability that looked-for information will be activated.

Retrieval is often a constructive process: Some pieces of information are directly retrieved and other, nonretrieved details are filled in to create a logical, coherent (albeit sometimes incorrect) recollection. Recall of information and events can also be affected by information or misinformation (e.g., misleading questions) presented at a later time. People sometimes "remember" things they have never specifically learned, perhaps because they draw reasonable inferences from what they *have* learned or perhaps because related ideas in their long-term memories were activated during a learning experience. Describing a previous event in a particular way increases the likelihood that the learner will remember it in the same way on future occasions; in a sense, people remember their previous *recollections* of an event as much as (or even more than) they remember the event itself. As children get older, they increasingly reflect on the things they retrieve from long-term memory, and they begin to evaluate the quality of their recollections based on such factors as vividness and plausibility.

Theorists have offered a variety of explanations for why people "forget" things they have presumably learned, including *decay, interference, failure to retrieve, repression, construction error,* and *failure to completely store or consolidate* information. *Infantile amnesia*—remembering little or nothing about what happens during the first few years of life—may be a manifestation of the last of these explanations.

Forgetting is not necessarily a bad thing: We typically have little use for the trivial details of everyday life, and we rarely need to remember important information word for word.

Numerous instructional practices facilitate students' ability to retrieve the things they've learned. When students learn a new body of information in an organized manner, and when they also associate the information with contexts in which it is apt to be useful, they are more likely to retrieve ideas when potentially applicable or helpful. Yet retrieval is never guaranteed, and so *external retrieval cues* (e.g., "notes to self") can ensure that important things are remembered. Teacher questions and assessment practices can encourage retrieval and review. Lower-level questions and tasks may promote automaticity, but higher-level ones (those that ask students to infer, apply, justify, problem solve, etc.) are more likely to encourage further elaboration.

Part Five

Developmental Perspectives

CHAPTER 11

Developmental Perspectives on Cognition

In chapter 7, I described three general approaches that cognitive theorists have taken in conceptualizing learning: information processing theory, constructivism, and contextual theories. Our discussion of memory in the last three chapters has drawn primarily from information processing theory, albeit sometimes with a constructivist bent. Information processing theory had some roots in verbal learning research, which, in turn, was influenced by the S–R views of early behaviorists. Yet at the same time that behaviorists were dominating learning research in the early decades of the twentieth century, other researchers examining a somewhat different topic—child development—were coming to very different conclusions about what learning entails. One of these researchers, Swiss developmentalist Jean Piaget, proposed that through interacting with and reflecting on their physical and social worlds, children self-construct increasingly complex understandings and reasoning abilities with age. In making such a proposal, Piaget was a pioneer in *individual constructivism*. Meanwhile,

Russian psychologist Lev Vygotsky focused on the importance of society and culture for children's development. In particular, Vygotsky suggested, society and culture provide a wide variety of concepts, strategies, and other cognitive "tools" that children gradually begin to use in thinking about and dealing with everyday tasks and problems. Through his research and writings, Vygotsky laid much of the groundwork for a contextual view that has come to be known as the **sociocultural perspective.**

In this chapter we'll look at Piaget's and Vygotsky's views about learning and cognitive development, as well as at contemporary perspectives that their work has inspired. We'll also identify a variety of implications that Piagetian and Vygotskian approaches have for instructional practice.

PIAGET'S THEORY OF COGNITIVE DEVELOPMENT

During the 1920s, Jean Piaget began a research program in Geneva, Switzerland, that has probably had a greater impact on contemporary theories of cognitive development than that of any other single researcher. Trained as a biologist, Piaget also had interests in philosophy and was especially curious about the origins of knowledge, a branch of philosophy known as *epistemology*. To discover where knowledge comes from and the forms that it takes as it develops, Piaget and his colleagues undertook a series of studies that provided many unique insights into how children think and learn about the world around them (e.g., Inhelder & Piaget, 1958; Piaget, 1928, 1952b, 1959, 1970, 1971, 1972, 1980; Piaget & Inhelder, 1969).

Although Piaget's theory dates from the 1920s, its impact on psychological thought in the Western hemisphere was not widely felt until the 1960s, probably for several reasons. One likely reason is that Piaget, being Swiss, wrote in French, making his early work less accessible to English-speaking psychologists. Although his writings were eventually translated into English, his ideas initially gained widespread prominence and visibility largely through a summary of his early work written by the American psychologist John Flavell (1963).

A second reason that Piaget's research program was largely overlooked for more than three decades was his unconventional research methodology. Piaget used what he called the **clinical method:** He gave children a variety of tasks and problems, asking a series of questions about each one. He tailored his interviews to the particular responses that children gave, with follow-up questions varying from one child to the next. Such a procedure was radically different from the standardized, tightly controlled conditions typical of behaviorist animal research and was therefore unacceptable to many of Piaget's contemporaries in North America.

But perhaps the most critical reason that Piaget's theory did not immediately become part of the mainstream of psychological thought was its philosophical incompatibility with the behaviorist perspective that dominated the study of learning until the 1960s. Piaget focused on mental events—for example, on logical reasoning processes and the structure of knowledge—at a time when such mentalism was still being rejected by many learning theorists. The cognitivism that began to emerge in the 1960s was more receptive to Piagetian ideas.

Piaget's work is probably so popular today because it is such a global theory of intellectual development, incorporating such diverse topics as language; logical reasoning; moral judgments; and conceptions of time, space, and number. In addition, Piaget's unique studies with children, often involving cleverly designed problem situations, reveal a great deal about the nature of children's thought. In the next few pages, we'll examine Piagetian ideas that are especially relevant to our understanding of human learning and cognition.

Key Ideas in Piaget's Theory

Central to Piaget's theory are the following principles and concepts:

◆ *Children are active and motivated learners.* Piaget proposed that children are naturally curious about their world and actively seek out information to help them make sense of it (e.g., Piaget, 1952b). Rather than simply responding to the stimuli they encounter, children manipulate those stimuli and observe the effects of their actions. For example, consider Piaget's observation of his son Laurent at 16 months of age:

> Laurent is seated before a table and I place a bread crust in front of him, out of reach. Also, to the right of the child I place a stick about 25 cm. long. At first Laurent tries to grasp the bread without paying attention to the instrument, and then he gives up. I then put the stick between him and the bread. . . . Laurent again looks at the bread, without moving, looks very briefly at the stick, then suddenly grasps it and directs it toward the bread. But he grasped it toward the middle and not at one of its ends so that it is too short to attain the objective. Laurent then puts it down and resumes stretching out his hand toward the bread. Then, without spending much time on this movement, he takes up the stick again, this time at one of its ends . . . and draws the bread to him.
>
>   An hour later I place a toy in front of Laurent (out of his reach) and a new stick next to him. He does not even try to catch the objective with his hand; he immediately grasps the stick and draws the toy to him. (Piaget, 1952b, p. 335)

In this situation, Laurent is obviously experimenting with aspects of his environment to see what outcomes he can achieve. In Piaget's view, much of children's cognitive development is the result of such efforts to make sense of the world.

◆ *Children organize what they learn from their experiences.* Children don't just amass the things they learn into a collection of isolated facts. Instead, they pull their experiences together into an integrated view of how the world operates. For example, by observing that food, toys, and other objects always fall down (never up) when released, children begin to construct a basic understanding of gravity. As they interact with family pets, visit zoos, look at picture books, and so on, they develop an increasingly complex understanding of animals. Piaget depicted learning as a very *constructive* process: Children create (rather than simply absorb) their knowledge about the world.

In Piaget's terminology, the things that children learn and can do are organized as **schemes,** groups of similar actions or thoughts that are used repeatedly in response to the environment.[1] Initially, children's schemes are largely behavioral in nature, but over time they become increasingly mental and, eventually, abstract. For example, an infant might have a scheme for grasping and apply it in grabbing everything from bottles to rubber ducks. A teenager may have certain schemes related to logical thinking that might be applied to reasoning about a variety of social, political, or moral issues.

Piaget proposed that children use newly acquired schemes over and over in both familiar and novel situations. As children develop, new schemes emerge, and existing schemes are repeatedly practiced, occasionally modified, and sometimes integrated with one another into

---

[1]Don't confuse Piaget's *schemes* with the *schemas* I described in chapter 9, although both concepts reflect ways of organizing things that are learned. In fact, Piaget himself made a distinction between a *scheme* and a *schema* (plural for the latter is *schemata*), and he used *schema* in a different sense than contemporary cognitivists do (e.g., see Piaget, 1970, p. 705).

cognitive structures. A good deal of Piaget's theory focused on the development of the cognitive structures that govern logical reasoning—structures that Piaget called **operations.**

◆ *Interaction with the physical environment is critical for learning and cognitive development.* In the process of interacting with their environment, growing children develop and modify their schemes. For example, in the anecdote involving Laurent presented earlier, we see a toddler actively manipulating parts of his physical environment—more specifically, manipulating the stick and bread—and presumably learning that some objects can be used as tools to obtain other objects. By exploring and manipulating the world around them—by conducting many little "experiments" with objects and substances—children learn the nature of such physical characteristics as volume and weight, discover principles related to force and gravity, acquire a better understanding of cause–effect relationships, and so on.

◆ *Interaction with other people is equally critical for learning and development.* Although Piaget believed that children's knowledge and understandings of the world are largely self-constructed, nevertheless they have much to learn from interacting with others. For example, as you will discover shortly, preschoolers often have difficulty seeing the world from anyone's perspective but their own. Through social interactions, both positive (e.g., conversations) and negative (e.g., conflicts over such issues as sharing and fair play), young children gradually come to realize that different individuals see things differently and that their own view of the world is not necessarily a completely accurate or logical one. Elementary school children may begin to recognize logical inconsistencies in what they say and do when someone else points out the inconsistencies. And through discussions with peers or adults about social and political issues, high school students may slowly modify their newly emerging idealism about how the world "should" be.

◆ *Children adapt to their environment through the processes of assimilation and accommodation.* According to Piaget, children interact with their environment through two unchanging processes (he called them *functions*) known as assimilation and accommodation. **Assimilation** entails dealing with an object or event in a way that is consistent with an existing scheme. For example, an infant who sees Mama's flashy, dangling earrings may assimilate the earrings to his grasping scheme, clutching and pulling at them in much the same way that he grasps bottles. A second grader who has developed a scheme for adding two apples and three apples to make five apples may apply this scheme to a situation involving the addition of two dollars and three dollars.

Yet sometimes children cannot easily interpret a new object or event using existing schemes. In such situations, one of two forms of **accommodation** will occur: Children will either (a) modify an existing scheme to account for the new object or event or else (b) form an entirely new scheme to deal with it. For example, an infant who has learned to crawl must adjust her style of crawling when she meets a flight of stairs. And a child who encounters a long, snakelike creature with four legs may, after some research, reject the "snake" scheme—because snakes don't have legs—in favor of a new scheme: *skink.*

Assimilation and accommodation are complementary processes: Assimilation involves modifying one's perception of the environment to fit a scheme, and accommodation involves modifying a scheme to fit the environment. In Piaget's view, the two processes typically go hand in hand, with children interpreting new events within the context of their existing knowledge (assimilation) but also modifying their knowledge as a result of those events (accommodation).

As you might guess, *learning* is largely the result of accommodation—that is, of modifying existing schemes or forming new ones. Yet assimilation is almost always a necessary condition for accommodation to occur: You must be able to relate a new experience to what you already know before you can learn from it. As you discovered in chapter 8, this necessity for overlap between prior knowledge and new information is an important principle not only in Piaget's theory but in contemporary cognitive learning theories as well.

♦ *The process of equilibration promotes progression toward increasingly complex forms of thought.* Piaget suggested that children are sometimes in a state of **equilibrium:** They can comfortably interpret and respond to new events using existing schemes. But this equilibrium doesn't continue indefinitely. As children grow, they frequently encounter situations for which their current knowledge and skills are inadequate. Such situations create **disequilibrium,** a sort of mental "discomfort" that spurs them to try to make sense of what they observe. By replacing, reorganizing, or better integrating their schemes (in other words, through accommodation), children eventually are able to understand and address previously puzzling events. The movement from equilibrium to disequilibrium and back to equilibrium again is known as **equilibration.** In Piaget's view, equilibration and children's intrinsic desire to achieve equilibrium promote the development of more complex levels of thought and knowledge.

♦ *Children think in qualitatively different ways at different age levels.* A major feature of Piaget's theory is his description of four distinct stages of cognitive development, each with its own unique patterns of thought. Each stage builds on the accomplishments of any preceding stages, and so children progress through the four stages in the same, invariant sequence. In his early writings, Piaget suggested that the stages are *universal*—that they describe the cognitive development of children throughout the world.

Piaget speculated that children's progression through the four stages is limited by neurological maturation—that is, by genetically controlled developmental changes in the brain. In other words, a child is capable of moving from one stage to the next only when the brain matures sufficiently to enable the cognitive structures and thought processes associated with the next stage. As we discovered in chapter 2, the brain continues to develop throughout childhood and adolescence, and even in the early adult years. Quite possibly, this continuing neurological development, and especially the development of the frontal cortex, may allow growing human beings to think in increasingly sophisticated ways. Although some researchers have found evidence that significant neurological changes do occur at the typical transition ages for progression from one of Piaget's cognitive stages to the next (Epstein, 1978; Hudspeth, 1985), whether such changes are specifically related to the cognitive changes that Piaget described is still very much an open question.

As you will discover later in the chapter, many psychologists question the notion that cognitive development is either as stagelike or as universal as Piaget believed. Nevertheless, Piaget's stages provide helpful insights into the nature of children's thinking at different age levels, and so we will look at them more closely.

Piaget's Stages of Cognitive Development

Piaget's four stages are summarized in Table 11.1. The age ranges noted in the table are *averages:* Some children reach a stage a bit earlier, others a bit later. Also, children are occasionally in *transition* from one stage to the next, displaying characteristics of two adjacent stages at the same time.

Sensorimotor Stage (Birth Until Age 2)
According to Piaget, newborns' behaviors are little more than *reflexes*—biologically built-in responses to particular stimuli (e.g., sucking on a nipple)—that ensure their survival. But in the second month, infants begin to exhibit voluntary behaviors that they repeat over and over,

Table 11.1
Piaget's stages of cognitive development.

Stage and Age Range	General Description
Sensorimotor Stage (birth until about 2 years old)	Schemes primarily entail perceptions and behaviors. Children's understandings of the world are based largely on their physical interactions with it.
Preoperational Stage (2 until about 6 or 7 years old)	Many schemes now have a symbolic quality, in that children can think and talk about things beyond their immediate experience. Children begin to reason about events, although not always in ways that are "logical" by adult standards.
Concrete Operations Stage (6 or 7 until about 11 or 12 years old)	Children acquire cognitive structures that enable them to reason in logical, adultlike ways about concrete, reality-based situations. They also realize that their own perspectives are not necessarily shared by others.
Formal Operations Stage (11 or 12 through adulthood)	Children can now think logically about abstract, hypothetical, and contrary-to-fact situations. They acquire many capabilities essential for advanced reasoning in mathematics and science.

reflecting the development of perception- and behavior-based schemes—hence the label **sensorimotor stage.** Initially infants' voluntary behaviors focus almost exclusively on their own bodies (e.g., they might repeatedly put certain fingers in their mouths), but eventually their behaviors involve surrounding objects as well. For much of the first year, behaviors are largely spontaneous and unplanned.

Late in the first year, after repeatedly observing that certain actions lead to certain consequences, infants gradually acquire knowledge of cause–effect relationships in the world around them. At this point, they begin to engage in **goal-directed behavior,** acting in ways that they know will bring about desired results. At about the same time, they acquire **object permanence,** an understanding that physical objects continue to exist even when out of sight.

Piaget believed that for much of the sensorimotor period, children's thinking is restricted to objects in their immediate environment. But in the latter half of the second year, children develop **symbolic thought,** an ability to represent and think about objects and events in terms of internal, mental entities, or *symbols.* They may "experiment" with objects in their minds, first predicting what will happen if they do something to an object and then putting their plans into action. They may also recall and imitate behaviors they have seen other people exhibit—for instance, pretending to "talk" on a toy telephone. Such symbolic thinking marks the beginning of true thought as Piaget defined it.[2]

---

[2]The changes I've described in this section reflect six substages of the sensorimotor stage. For details, see the reading "Piaget's Sensorimotor Stage" on the book's Companion Website at www.prenhall.com/ormrod.

Preoperational Stage (Age 2 Until Age 6 or 7)

The ability to represent objects and events mentally (i.e., symbolic thought) gives children in the **preoperational stage** a more extended worldview than they had during the sensorimotor stage. One key source of symbols is language, which virtually explodes during the early part of the preoperational stage. The words in children's rapidly increasing vocabularies provide labels for newly developed mental schemes and serve as symbols that enable children to think about objects and events at different places and times. Furthermore, language enables children to communicate their thoughts and receive information from other people in ways that were not possible during the sensorimotor stage.

With the emergence of symbolic thought, then, young children are no longer restricted to the here-and-now and so can think and act far more flexibly than they did previously. They can now recall past events and envision future ones, and they begin to tie their experiences together into an increasingly complex understanding of the world.

Yet preoperational thinking has some definite limitations, especially as compared to the concrete operational thinking that appears later. For example, young children tend to confuse psychological phenomena (e.g., thoughts and emotions) with physical reality, a confusion manifested by such actions as attributing feelings to inanimate objects and insisting that monsters and bogeymen are lurking under the bed. They also tend to exhibit **egocentrism,** an inability to view situations from another person's perspective.[3] Young children may have trouble understanding how a thoughtless remark may have hurt someone else's feelings. And they may say things without considering the perspective of the listener—for instance, leaving out critical details as they tell a story and giving a fragmented version that a listener cannot possibly understand. Here we see one reason why, in Piaget's view, social interaction is so important for development. Only by getting repeated feedback from other people can children learn that their thoughts and feelings are unique to them—that their own perception of the world is not always shared by others.

When we consider adult forms of logical reasoning, preoperational children's thinking simply doesn't measure up. An example is difficulty with **class inclusion:** an ability to simultaneously classify an object as belonging both to a particular category and to one of its subcategories. Piaget provided an illustration in an interview with a 6-year-old boy that reflects the *clinical method* I described earlier. An adult begins the interview by showing the child a box containing about a dozen wooden beads, two of which are white and the rest brown. The following discussion ensues:

Adult:	Are there more wooden beads or more brown beads?
Child:	More brown ones, because there are two white ones.
Adult:	Are the white ones made of wood?
Child:	Yes.
Adult:	And the brown ones?
Child:	Yes.

---

[3]Don't confuse Piaget's definition of *egocentrism* with its more commonly used meaning. When we describe a person as being *egocentric* in everyday speech, we usually mean that the person is concerned only about his or her own needs and desires; hence, the term refers to a personality characteristic. In Piaget's theory, however, an egocentric child has a cognitive limitation, not a personality flaw: The child does not yet have the *ability* to look at the world from other people's perspectives.

Adult:	Then are there more brown ones or more wooden ones?
Child:	More brown ones.
Adult:	What color would a necklace made of the wooden beads be?
Child:	Brown and white. (Here [he] shows that he understands that all the beads are wooden.)
Adult:	And what color would a necklace made with the brown beads be?
Child:	Brown.
Adult:	Then which would be longer, the one made with the wooden beads or the one made with the brown beads?
Child:	The one with the brown beads.
Adult:	Draw the necklaces for me.

The child draws a series of black rings for the necklace of brown beads. He then draws a series of black rings plus two white rings for the necklace of wooden beads.

Adult:	Good. Now which will be longer, the one with the brown beads or the one with the wooden beads?
Child:	The one with the brown beads. (dialogue from Piaget, 1952a, pp. 163–164)

Another commonly cited example of the "illogic" of preoperational thinking is a young child's typical response to a **conservation of liquid** problem. Imagine three glasses: Glasses A and B are tall, thin, and filled to equal heights with water, while Glass C is short, fat, and empty, as is shown in the "before" part of Figure 11.1. Clearly Glasses A and B contain the same amount of water. But now the contents of Glass B are poured into Glass C, thereby creating the situation shown in the "after" part of Figure 11.1. Do Glass A and Glass C contain the same amount of water, or does one contain more?

Being a logical adult, you would probably conclude that the two glasses hold identical amounts of water (excluding a few drops that might have been lost during pouring). The preoperational child,

Figure 11.1
The water in Glass B ("before") is poured into Glass C ("after"). Does Glass C have the same amount of water that Glass B did?

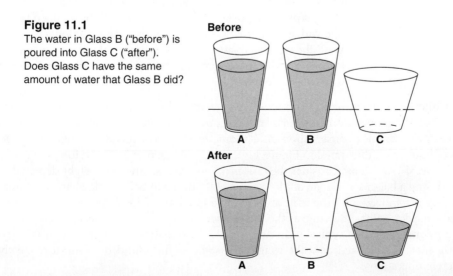

however, is likely to say that the glasses hold different amounts of water: Most will say that Glass A has more because it is taller, although a few will say that Glass C has more because it is fatter. The child's thinking depends more on perception than logic during the preoperational stage and so is susceptible to outward appearances: The glasses *look* different and so must *be* different.

As children approach the later part of the preoperational stage, perhaps at around age 4 or 5, they show early signs of being logical. For example, they sometimes draw correct conclusions about classification problems (e.g., the wooden beads problem) and conservation problems (e.g., the water glasses problem). But they base their reasoning on hunches and intuition rather than on any conscious awareness of underlying logical principles, and so they cannot yet explain *why* their conclusions are correct.

Concrete Operations Stage (Age 6 or 7 Until Age 11 or 12)

When children move into the **concrete operations stage**, their thinking processes begin to take the form of logical *operations* through which they can integrate various qualities and perspectives of an object or event. Such operational thought enables a number of more advanced abilities. For example, children now realize that their own perspectives and feelings are not necessarily shared by others and may reflect personal opinions rather than reality. Accordingly, they know they can sometimes be wrong and begin to seek out external validation for their ideas, asking such questions as "What do you think?" and "Did I get that problem right?"

Children in the concrete operations stage are capable of many forms of logical thought. For example, they are capable of **conservation**: They understand that if nothing is added or taken away, amount stays the same despite any changes in shape or arrangement. They also exhibit class inclusion—for instance, recognizing that brown beads can simultaneously be wooden beads. They can readily explain their reasoning, as the following interview with an 8-year-old about the wooden beads problem illustrates:

Adult:	Are there more wooden beads or more brown beads?
Child:	More wooden ones.
Adult:	Why?
Child:	Because the two white ones are made of wood as well.
Adult:	Suppose we made two necklaces, one with all the wooden beads and one with all the brown ones. Which one would be longer?
Child:	Well, the wooden ones and the brown ones are the same, and it would be longer with the wooden ones because there are two white ones as well. (dialogue from Piaget, 1952a, p. 176)

Children continue to develop their newly acquired logical thinking capabilities throughout the concrete operations stage. For instance, over time they become capable of dealing with increasingly complex conservation tasks. Some forms of conservation, such as the conservation of liquid task illustrated in Figure 11.1, appear at age 6 or 7. Other forms may not appear until several years later. Consider the task involving conservation of weight depicted in Figure 11.2. Using a balance scale, an adult shows a child that two balls of clay have the same weight. One ball is removed from the scale and smashed into a pancake shape. The child is then asked if the pancake weighs the same as the unsmashed ball or if the two pieces of clay weigh different amounts. Children typically do not achieve conservation of weight—that is, they do not realize that the flattened pancake weighs the same as the round ball—until relatively late in concrete operations.

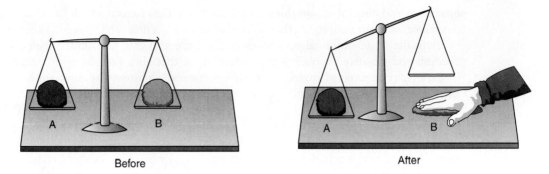

Figure 11.2
Balls A and B initially weigh the same ("before"). When Ball B is flattened into a pancake shape ("after"), how does its weight now compare with that of Ball A?

Despite their advancements in reasoning, children in the concrete operations stage are limited in one very important respect: They can apply their logical operations only to concrete, observable objects and events—hence the term *concrete* operations. They have difficulty dealing with abstract concepts and with hypothetical ideas that contradict reality as they know it. For example, the concrete operational child should readily agree with the logic that

> If all first graders are children,
> And if all children are people,
> Then all first graders are people.

yet will have trouble recognizing the logical validity of a similar problem that includes a contrary-to-fact premise:

> If all first graders are children,
> And if all children are hippopotamuses,
> Then all first graders are hippopotamuses.

Concrete operational children cannot easily distinguish between logic and reality, and, after all, first graders are *not* hippopotamuses.

Formal Operations Stage (Age 11 or 12 Through Adulthood)

Sometime around puberty, children enter the **formal operations stage.** At this point, they become capable of thinking and reasoning about things that have little or no basis in physical reality—abstract concepts, hypothetical ideas, contrary-to-fact statements, and so on. For example, they become able to see the underlying meanings of proverbs such as *A rolling stone gathers no moss* and *Don't put the cart before the horse.* They become better able to understand abstract concepts in mathematics, science, and social studies: *negative number, infinity, momentum, quark, republic, human rights,* and so on.

Other abilities essential to mathematical and scientific reasoning emerge as well. For instance, **proportional thinking** develops, through which children truly begin to understand proportions in the form of fractions, decimals, ratios, and so on. And children become capable of

separation and control of variables: In testing a hypothesis about which factor among many is responsible for a particular result, they will test one factor at a time while holding all others constant.

With the onset of formal operations children are also able to examine their own thought processes and evaluate the quality and logic of those thoughts. For example, a child might say, "Oops, I just contradicted myself, didn't I?" In essence, children who have reached the formal operations stage can apply mental operations to *other* mental operations—they can think about their thinking.

Because youngsters capable of formal operational reasoning can deal with hypothetical and contrary-to-fact ideas, they can envision how the world might be different from, and possibly better than, the way it actually is. Thus they may initially be quite idealistic about social, political, religious, and ethical issues. Many adolescents begin to show concern about world problems and devote some of their energy to worthy issues such as global warming, world hunger, or animal rights. However, they often offer recommendations for change that seem logical but aren't practical in today's world. For example, they may argue that racism would disappear overnight if people would just begin to "love one another," or they may propose that a nation should disband its armed forces and eliminate all its weaponry as a way of moving toward world peace. Piaget suggested that adolescent idealism reflects an inability to separate one's own logical abstractions from the perspectives of others and from practical considerations.[4] It is only through experience that adolescents eventually begin to temper their optimism with some realism about what is possible in a given time frame and with limited resources.

CURRENT PERSPECTIVES ON PIAGET'S THEORY

Some of Piaget's ideas about learning and motivation are quite compatible with contemporary views. Although Piaget was vague about how assimilation and accommodation might actually work (Flavell, Miller, & Miller, 2002; Klahr, 1982), most learning theorists embrace the principle that children's new learning builds on their prior knowledge. Many also believe that learning is, as Piaget proposed, a very constructive process (see chapter 8). Meanwhile, many motivation theorists share Piaget's beliefs that much of a human being's motivation for learning and development comes from within and that conflicting perceptions or ideas do, in fact, create mental discomfort (disequilibrium) that motivates further exploration and learning. It appears that children and adults alike are naturally inclined to try to make sense of—and as a result, can deal more effectively with—the people, objects, and events around them (see chapters 15 and 16).

Perhaps Piaget's greatest contribution to our understanding of learning and development was the nature of the *research questions* he asked and sought to answer about how children think and reason. As a result, his theory has inspired a great deal of research about cognitive development. In general, this research supports Piaget's proposed *sequence* in which different abilities emerge (Flavell et al., 2002). For example, the ability to reason about abstract ideas emerges only after children are already capable of reasoning about concrete objects and events, and the order

---

[4]Piaget suggested that the inability to separate logical abstractions from others' perspectives and practical considerations is another form of *egocentrism*—in this case, one that characterizes formal operations rather than preoperational thought.

in which various conservation tasks are mastered is much as Piaget described. Contemporary researchers question the *ages* at which various abilities actually appear, however. They are also finding that children's logical reasoning capabilities may vary considerably depending on their previous experiences, knowledge, and cultural background. And most seriously doubt that cognitive development is as stagelike as Piaget proposed.

Capabilities of Different Age-Groups

Infants and preschoolers are apparently more competent than Piaget's descriptions of the sensorimotor and preoperational stages suggest. For instance, infants show preliminary signs of object permanence as early as $2^{1}/_{2}$ months old and continue to firm up this understanding over a period of many months (Baillargeon, 2004; Cohen & Cashon, 2006). Preschoolers don't always show egocentrism: If we ask them to show us their artwork, they hold it so that we (rather than they) can see it (Newcombe & Huttenlocher, 1992). And under some circumstances they are capable of class inclusion and conservation (Donaldson, 1978; Gelman & Baillargeon, 1983; Rosser, 1994).

Piaget may have underestimated the capabilities of elementary school children as well. Many elementary students occasionally show some ability to think abstractly and hypothetically (Carey, 1985; Metz, 1995). Also, some elementary school children can separate and control variables, especially when asked to choose among several possible experiments or when given hints about the importance of controlling all variables except the one being tested (Barchfeld, Sodian, Thoermer, & Bullock, 2005; Danner & Day, 1977; Metz, 1995; Ruffman, Perner, Olson, & Doherty, 1993). And even first and second graders show some ability to understand and use simple proportions (e.g., fractions such as $^{1}/_{2}$, $^{1}/_{3}$, and $^{1}/_{4}$) if they can relate them to everyday objects (Empson, 1999; Van Dooren, De Bock, Hessels, Janssens, & Verschaffel, 2005).

Yet Piaget probably *over*estimated what adolescents can do. Formal operational thinking processes (e.g., proportional reasoning, separation and control of variables) emerge much more gradually than Piaget suggested, and even high school students don't use them as regularly as Piaget would have us believe (Flieller, 1999; Kuhn & Franklin, 2006; Schauble, 1996; Schliemann & Carraher, 1993; Tourniaire & Pulos, 1985). In fact, even *adults* don't always reason in the logical ways that supposedly characterize formal operational thought (Pascarella & Terenzini, 1991). For instance, when adults draw conclusions and inferences about real-world events, they may overrely on their existing knowledge about the world—thus having the same difficulty in separating logic from reality that children in concrete operations do (Kuhn & Franklin, 2006). Perhaps the rules of formal logic—the kind you might learn in a philosophy class—don't reflect the typical ways in which children or adults reason (Halford & Andrews, 2006; Kuhn & Franklin, 2006). To some degree, Piaget's formal operations stage may capture adults' capabilities under the best of circumstances rather than their normal, day-to-day reasoning processes (Sternberg, 2003).

Effects of Experience and Prior Knowledge

Piaget proposed that neurological maturation places significant constraints on children's reasoning abilities at any particular age. Although maturation certainly places limits on cognitive development (see chapter 2), Piaget may have overrated its importance in logical thought, especially for older children and adolescents. Explicit training and other experiences often help youngsters acquire reasoning abilities sooner than Piaget would have us believe (Brainerd, 2003; Kuhn, 2006).

For instance, children as young as age 4 or 5 begin to show conservation after having experience with conservation tasks, especially if they can actively manipulate the task materials and discuss their reasoning with someone who already exhibits conservation (Field, 1987; Halford & Andrews, 2006; Mayer, 1992). Similarly, instruction with concrete manipulatives can help children grasp the nature of proportions (Fujimura, 2001). Children ages 10 and 11 can more easily solve logical problems involving hypothetical ideas if they are taught relevant problem-solving strategies, and they become increasingly able to separate and control variables when they have numerous experiences that require them to do so (Kuhn & Franklin, 2006; S. Lee, 1985; Schauble, 1990).

Piaget also suggested that once children acquire a particular reasoning skill, they can apply it in virtually any context. However, it is becoming increasingly apparent that for people of all ages, the ability to think logically can vary considerably from one situation to the next, depending on knowledge, background experiences, and training relevant to the situation (Brainerd, 2003; Kuhn & Franklin, 2006). For instance, adolescents may demonstrate formal operational thought in one content domain while thinking more concretely in another (Klaczynski, 2001; Lovell, 1979; Tamburrini, 1982). Evidence of formal operations typically emerges in the physical sciences earlier than in such subjects as history and geography, perhaps because the latter subjects are further removed from students' everyday realities. And in general, adolescents and adults are apt to apply formal operational thought to topics about which they have a great deal of knowledge and yet think concretely about topics with which they are unfamiliar (Girotto & Light, 1993; Linn, Clement, Pulos, & Sullivan, 1989; Schliemann & Carraher, 1993).

One experience that promotes more advanced reasoning is formal education. Going to school and the specific nature of one's schooling are associated with mastery of concrete operational and formal operational tasks (Artman & Cahan, 1993; Flieller, 1999; Rogoff, 2003). For instance, you'll be happy to learn that taking college courses in a particular area (in human learning, perhaps?) leads to improvements in formal reasoning skills related to that area (Lehman & Nisbett, 1990).

Effects of Culture

Piaget suggested that his stages were universal, that they applied to children and adolescents around the globe. Yet research indicates that the course of cognitive development differs somewhat from one culture to another. For example, Mexican children whose families make pottery for a living acquire conservation skills much earlier than Piaget proposed (Price-Williams, Gordon, & Ramirez, 1969). Apparently, making pottery requires children to make frequent judgments about needed quantities of clay and water—judgments that must be fairly accurate regardless of the specific shape or form of the clay or water container. In other cultures, especially in some where children don't attend school, conservation appears several years later than it does in Western cultures, and formal operational reasoning may never appear at all (M. Cole, 1990; Fahrmeier, 1978). In such contexts, some logical reasoning skills may simply have little relevance to people's daily lives (J. G. Miller, 1997).

Views on Piaget's Stages

In light of all the evidence, does it still make sense to talk about discrete stages of cognitive development? Most contemporary developmental theorists doubt that cognitive development is as stagelike as Piaget proposed (Cohen & Cashon, 2006; Flavell, 1994; Kuhn & Franklin, 2006;

Siegler & Alibali, 2005). Children exhibit certain developmental *trends* in their thinking (e.g., a trend toward increasingly abstract thought), to be sure. But the sophistication of their reasoning in any given situation depends in large part on the particular context in which they find themselves and on their prior knowledge and experiences relative to the task at hand. Thus, children don't necessarily reason in consistently logical or illogical ways at any single point in time.

Yet some psychologists believe that, by entirely rejecting Piaget's notion of stages, we may be throwing the baby out with the bath water. We look at their perspectives now.

NEO–PIAGETIAN THEORIES OF COGNITIVE DEVELOPMENT

A few psychologists have combined some of Piaget's ideas with concepts from information processing theory to construct **neo-Piagetian theories** of how children's learning and reasoning capabilities change over time (e.g., Case, 1985; Case & Okamoto, 1996; Fischer & Immordino-Yang, 2006; Fischer, Knight, & Van Parys, 1993). Neo-Piagetian theorists do not always agree about the exact nature of children's thinking at different age levels or about the exact mechanisms that promote cognitive development. Nevertheless, several ideas are central to their thinking:

◆ *Cognitive development is constrained by the maturation of information processing mechanisms in the brain.* Neo-Piagetian theorists have echoed Piaget's belief that cognitive development depends somewhat on brain maturation. Recall, for example, the concept of *working memory,* that limited-capacity component of the human memory system in which active, conscious mental processing occurs. Children certainly use their working memories more effectively as they get older, courtesy of such processes as myelination, chunking, maintenance rehearsal, and automaticity (see chapters 2, 7, and 8). But the actual physical "space" of working memory may increase somewhat as well (Fry & Hale, 1996; Gathercole & Hitch, 1993; Kail, 1993). Neo-Piagetian theorists propose that children's more limited working memory capacity at younger ages restricts their ability to acquire and use complex thinking and reasoning skills. In a sense, it places a "ceiling" on what children can accomplish at any particular age (Case & Okamoto, 1996; Fischer & Bidell, 1991; Lautrey, 1993).

◆ *Children acquire cognitive structures that affect their thinking in particular content domains.* As we've seen, children's ability to think logically depends on their specific knowledge, experiences, and instruction related to the task at hand, and so the sophistication of their reasoning may vary considerably from one situation to another. With this point in mind, neo-Piagetian theorists reject Piaget's notion that children develop increasingly integrated systems of mental processes (operations) that they can apply equally to a wide variety of tasks and content domains. Instead, neo-Piagetians suggest, children acquire more specific systems (**structures**) of concepts and thinking skills that influence thinking and reasoning capabilities relative to specific topics or content domains.

◆ *Development in specific content domains can sometimes be characterized as a series of stages.* Although neo-Piagetian theorists reject Piaget's notion that a single series of stages characterizes all of cognitive development, they speculate that cognitive development in specific content domains often has a stagelike nature (e.g., Case, 1985; Case & Okamoto, 1996; Fischer & Bidell, 1991; Fischer & Immordino-Yang, 2006). Children's entry into a particular stage is marked by the acquisition of new abilities, which children practice and gradually master over time. Eventually, they integrate these abilities into more complex structures that mark their entry into a subsequent stage.

Even in a particular subject area, however, cognitive development is not necessarily a single series of stages through which children progress as if they were climbing rungs on a ladder. In some cases, development might be better characterized as progression along "multiple strands" of skills that occasionally interconnect, consolidate, or separate in a weblike fashion (Fischer & Immordino-Yang, 2006; Fischer et al., 1993). From this perspective, children may acquire more advanced levels of competence in a particular area through any one of several pathways. For instance, as they become increasingly proficient in reading, children may gradually develop their word decoding skills, their comprehension skills, and so on—and they may often combine these skills when performing a task—but the relative rates at which each skill is mastered will vary from one child to the next.

◆ *Formal schooling has a greater influence on cognitive development than Piaget believed.* Whereas Piaget emphasized the importance of children's informal interactions with their environment, neo-Piagetians argue that within the confines of children's neurological maturation and working memory capacity, formal instruction can definitely impact cognitive development (Case & Okamoto, 1996; Case et al., 1993; Fischer & Immordino-Yang, 2006; Griffin, Case, & Capodilupo, 1995). One prominent neo-Piagetian, Robbie Case, has been particularly adamant about the value of formal education for cognitive advancements. A closer look at his theory can give you a flavor for the neo-Piagetian approach.

Case's Theory

Robbie Case was a highly productive neo-Piagetian researcher at the University of Toronto until his untimely death in 2000. Central to his theory is the notion of **central conceptual structures,** integrated networks of concepts and cognitive processes that form the basis for much of children's thinking, reasoning, and learning in particular areas (Case & Okamoto, 1996; Case, Okamoto, Henderson, & McKeough, 1993). Over time, these structures undergo several major transformations, each of which marks a child's entry to the next higher stage of development.

Case speculated about the nature of children's central conceptual structures with respect to several domains, including number, spatial relationships, and social thought (Case & Okamoto, 1996). A central conceptual structure related to *number* underlies children's ability to reason about and manipulate mathematical quantities. This structure reflects an integrated understanding of how such mathematical concepts and operations as numbers, counting, addition, and subtraction are interconnected. A central conceptual structure related to *spatial relationships* underlies children's performance in such areas as drawing, construction and use of maps, replication of geometric patterns, and psychomotor activities (e.g., writing in cursive, hitting a ball with a racket). This structure enables children to align objects in space according to one or more reference points (e.g., the *x*- and *y*-axes used in graphing). And a central conceptual structure related to *social thought* underlies children's reasoning about interpersonal relationships, their knowledge of common scripts related to human interaction, and their comprehension of short stories and other works of fiction. This structure includes children's general beliefs about human beings' thoughts, desires, and behaviors. Case found evidence indicating that these three conceptual structures probably develop in a wide variety of cultural and educational contexts (Case & Okamoto, 1996).

From ages 4 to 10, Case suggested, parallel changes occur in children's central conceptual structures in each of the three areas, with such changes reflecting increasing integration and multidimensional reasoning over time (Case & Okamoto, 1996). We'll take the development of children's understanding of number as an example.

A Possible Central Conceptual Structure for Number

From Case's perspective, 4-year-olds understand the difference between "a little" and "a lot" and recognize that adding objects leads to more of them and subtracting objects leads to fewer of them. Such knowledge might take the form depicted in the top half of Figure 11.3.

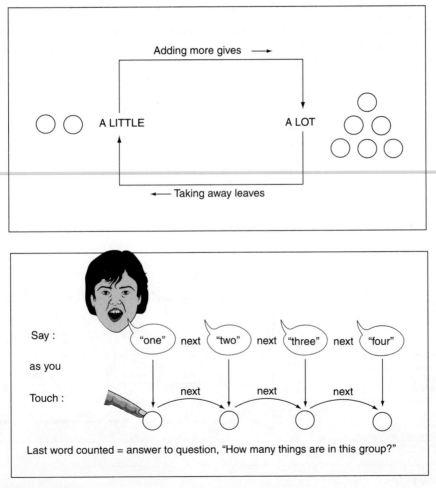

Figure 11.3
Hypothetical numerical structures at age 4.
From "The Role of Central Conceptual Structures in the Development of Children's Thought" by R. Case & Y. Okamoto, in collaboration with S. Griffin, A. McKeough, C. Bleiker, B. Henderson, & K. M. Stephenson, 1996, *Monographs of the Society for Research in Child Development, 61*(1, Serial No. 246), p. 6. Copyright 1996 by the Society for Research in Child Development. Adapted with permission from the Society for Research in Child Development.

Furthermore, many 4-year-olds can accurately count a small set of objects and conclude that the last number they count equals the total number of objects in the set. This process is depicted in the bottom half of Figure 11.3. Thus 4-year-olds can visually compare a group of 5 objects with a group of 6 objects and tell you that the latter group contains more objects, and they may also count accurately to either 5 or 6. Yet they cannot answer a question such as, "Which is more, 5 or 6?"—a question that involves knowledge of *both* more-versus-less and counting. It appears that they have not yet integrated their two understandings of number into a single conceptual framework.

By the time children are 6, they can easily answer simple "Which is more?" questions. Case proposed that at age 6, the two structures in Figure 11.3 have become integrated into the more comprehensive structure depicted in Figure 11.4. As illustrated in the figure, children's knowledge and reasoning about numbers now includes several key elements:

- Children understand and can say the verbal numbers "one," "two," "three," and so on.
- They recognize the written numerals 1, 2, 3, and so on.
- They have a systematic process for counting objects: They say each successive number as they touch each successive object in a group. Eventually, children count by mentally "tagging" (rather than physically touching) each object.
- They also use their fingers for representing small quantities (e.g., 3 fingers equals 3 objects). Their use of fingers for both counting objects and representing quantities may be a key means through which they integrate the two processes into a single conceptual structure.
- They equate movement toward higher numbers with such concepts as "a lot," "more," and "bigger." Similarly, they equate movement toward lower numbers with such concepts as "a little," "less," and "smaller."

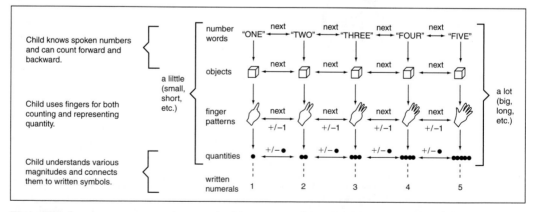

Figure 11.4
Hypothetical central conceptual structure at age 6.
Source: From "Differentiation, Integration, and Covariance Mapping as Fundamental Processes in Cognitive and Neurological Growth" by R. Case & M. P. Mueller, 2001, *Mechanisms of Cognitive Development: Behavioral and Neural Perspectives* (J. L. McClelland & R. S. Siegler, Eds.), p. 201. Mahwah, NJ: Erlbaum. Adapted with permission from Lawrence Erlbaum Associates.

- They understand that movement from one number to the next is equivalent to either adding one unit to the set or subtracting one unit from it, depending on the direction of movement.
- They realize that any change in one dimension (e.g., from 3 to 4) must be accompanied by an equivalent change along other dimensions (e.g., from "three" to "four," and from ••• to ••••).

In essence, the more comprehensive conceptual structure at age 6 forms a mental "number line" that children can use to facilitate their understanding and execution of such processes as addition, subtraction, and comparisons of quantities.

At age 8, Case proposed, children have sufficiently mastered this central conceptual structure that they can begin to use two number lines simultaneously to solve mathematical problems. For example, they can now answer such questions as, "Which number is bigger, 32 or 28?" and "Which number is closer to 25, 21 or 18?" Such questions require them to compare digits in both the 1s column and 10s column, with each comparison taking place along a separate number line. In addition, 8-year-olds presumably have a better understanding of operations that require transformations across columns, such as "carrying 1" to the 10s column during addition or "borrowing 1" from the 10s column during subtraction.

Finally, at about age 10, children become capable of generalizing the relationships of two number lines to the entire number system. They now understand how the various columns (1s, 10s, 100s, etc.) relate to one another and can expertly move back and forth among the columns. They can also treat the answers to mathematical problems as mental entities in and of themselves and so can answer such questions as "Which number is bigger, the difference between 6 and 9 or the difference between 8 and 3?"

Case tracked the development of children's central conceptual structure for number only until age 10. He acknowledged, however, that children's understanding of numbers continues to develop well into adolescence. For instance, he pointed out that teenagers often have trouble with questions such as "What is a half of a third?" and suggested that their difficulty results from an incomplete conceptual understanding of division and the results (e.g., fractions) that it yields.

IMPLICATIONS OF PIAGETIAN AND NEO–PIAGETIAN THEORIES

Piaget's theory and the subsequent research and theories it has inspired have numerous practical implications for educators and other professionals, as revealed in the following principles:

- *Children can learn a great deal through hands-on experiences with physical objects and natural phenomena.* Children of all ages learn many things by exploring their natural and human-made physical worlds (e.g., Flum & Kaplan, 2006). In infancy, such exploration might involve experimenting with objects that have visual and auditory appeal, such as rattles, stacking cups, and pull toys. At the preschool level, it might involve playing with water, sand, wooden blocks, and age-appropriate manipulative toys. During the elementary school years, it might entail throwing and catching balls, working with clay and watercolor paints, or constructing Popsicle-stick structures. Despite an increased capacity for abstract thought after puberty, adolescents also benefit from opportunities to manipulate and experiment with concrete materials—perhaps equipment in a science lab, cameras and film, food and cooking utensils, or wood and woodworking tools. Such opportunities allow teenagers to tie abstract scientific concepts to the concrete, physical world.

In educational settings, learning through exploration often goes by the term **discovery learning.** Piaget suggested that effective discovery learning should be largely a child-initiated and child-directed effort. Young children can certainly learn a great deal from their informal interactions with sand, water, and other natural substances (Hutt, Tyler, Hutt, & Christopherson, 1989). By and large, however, researchers are finding that youngsters benefit more from carefully planned and structured activities that help them construct appropriate interpretations (Hardy, Jonen, Möller, & Stern, 2006; Hickey, 1997; Mayer, 2004; B. Y. White & Frederiksen, 1998, 2005). The extent to which a discovery session needs to be structured depends somewhat on students' current knowledge and reasoning skills (de Jong & van Joolingen, 1998; Kuhn & Dean, 2004; B. Y. White & Frederiksen, 1998, 2005). For instance, high school students are more likely to profit from their own, self-directed experiments in a physics lab when they can test various hypotheses systematically through careful separation and control of variables and when they have appropriate concepts (*force, momentum,* etc.) with which to interpret their findings.

Teachers should keep in mind that discovery learning has a downside—one related to the *confirmation bias* phenomenon I mentioned in chapter 9. In particular, students may misinterpret what they observe, either learning the wrong thing or confirming their existing misconceptions about the world (Hammer, 1997; Schauble, 1990). Consider the case of Barry, an eleventh grader whose physics class was studying the idea that an object's mass and weight do *not,* in and of themselves, affect the speed at which the object falls. Students were asked to design and build an egg container that would keep an egg from breaking when dropped from a third-floor window. They were told that on the day of the egg drop, they would record the time it took for the eggs to reach the ground. Convinced that heavier objects fall faster, Barry added several nails to his egg's container. Yet when he dropped it, classmates timed its fall at 1.49 seconds, a time very similar to that for other students' lighter containers. He and his teacher had the following discussion about the result:

Teacher:	So what was your time?
Barry:	1.49. I think it should be faster.
Teacher:	Why?
Barry:	Because it weighed more than anybody else's and it dropped slower.
Teacher:	Oh really? And what do you attribute that to?
Barry:	That the people weren't timing real good. (Hynd, 1998a, p. 34)

◆ *Puzzling phenomena can create disequilibrium and spur children to acquire new understandings.* Events and information that conflict with youngsters' current understandings create disequilibrium that may motivate them to reevaluate and perhaps modify what they "know" to be true. For instance, if they believe that "light objects float and heavy objects sink" or that "wood floats and metal sinks," an instructor might present a common counterexample: a metal battleship (floating, of course) that weighs many tons. From Piaget's perspective, we are talking here about revising existing schemes; from the perspective of contemporary cognitive psychology, we are talking about *conceptual change.*

◆ *Interactions with peers can also promote more advanced understandings.* As noted earlier, Piaget proposed that interaction with peers helps children realize that others often view the world very differently than they do and that their own ideas are not always completely logical or accurate. Furthermore, interactions with age-mates that involve differences of opinion—**sociocognitive conflict**—can create disequilibrium that may spur children to reevaluate their current perspectives.

Many contemporary psychologists share Piaget's belief in the importance of sociocognitive conflict (e.g., Bell, Grossen, and Perret-Clermont, 1985; De Lisi & Golbeck, 1999; Webb & Palincsar, 1996). They have offered several reasons why interactions with peers may help promote cognitive growth:

- Peers speak at a level that children can understand.
- Whereas children may accept an adult's ideas without argument, they are more willing to disagree with and challenge the ideas of their peers.
- When children hear competing views held by peers—individuals who presumably have knowledge and abilities similar to their own—they may be motivated to reconcile the contradictions. (Champagne & Bunce, 1991; Damon, 1984; Hatano & Inagaki, 1991)

◆ *Children are more likely to reason in sophisticated ways when they work with familiar tasks and topics.* Earlier I mentioned that children and adolescents display more advanced reasoning skills when they work with subject matter they know well. We find an example in a study by Pulos and Linn (1981). In this study, 13-year-olds were shown the picture presented in Figure 11.5 and told, "These four children go fishing every week, and one child, Herb, always catches the most fish. The other children wonder why." If you look at the picture, it is obvious that Herb differs from the other children in several ways, including the kind of bait he uses, the length of his fishing rod, and

Figure 11.5
Fishing picture used in Pulos and Linn (1981).
Picture used with permission of Steven Pulos.

his location by the pond. Students who were avid fishermen more effectively separated and controlled variables for this situation than they did in a more traditional academic task—determining what one or more variables influence how quickly a pendulum swings back and forth—whereas the reverse was true for nonfishermen.

◆ *Piaget's clinical method can offer many insights into children's reasoning processes.* By presenting a variety of Piagetian tasks involving either concrete or formal operational thinking skills—tasks involving class inclusion, conservation, separation and control of variables, proportional reasoning, and so on—and observing students' responses to such tasks, teachers can gain valuable insights into how their students think and reason. Teachers need not stick to traditional Piagetian reasoning tasks, however. On the contrary, the clinical method is applicable to a wide variety of academic domains and subject matter. To illustrate, a teacher might present various kinds of maps (e.g., a road map of Pennsylvania, an aerial map of Chicago, a three-dimensional relief map of a mountainous area) and ask students to interpret what they see. Children in the primary grades (kindergarten, first grade, second grade) are apt to interpret many symbols on the maps in a concrete fashion. For instance, they might think that roads depicted in red are *actually* red. They might also have difficulty with the scale of a map, perhaps thinking that lines can't be roads because they're "too skinny for two cars to fit on" or that mountains depicted by bumps on a relief map aren't really mountains because "they aren't high enough" (Liben & Downs, 1989, p. 184). Understanding the concept of *scale* of a map requires proportional reasoning—an ability that doesn't emerge until after puberty—and so it is hardly surprising that young children would be confused by it.

◆ *Piaget's stages can provide some guidance about when certain abilities are likely to emerge, but they should not be taken too literally.* As we have seen, Piaget's four stages of cognitive development are not always accurate descriptions of children's and adolescents' thinking capabilities. Nevertheless, they do provide a rough idea about the reasoning skills youngsters are apt to have at various ages (Kuhn, 1997; Metz, 1997). For example, preschool teachers should not be surprised to hear young children arguing that the three pieces of a broken candy bar constitute more candy than a similar, unbroken bar (a belief that reflects lack of conservation). Elementary school teachers should recognize that their students are likely to have trouble with proportions (e.g., fractions, decimals) and with such abstract concepts as *historical time* in history, and *pi* (π) in mathematics (Barton & Levstik, 1996; Byrnes, 1996; Tourniaire & Pulos, 1985). And educators and other professionals who work with adolescents should expect to hear passionate arguments that reflect idealistic yet unrealistic notions about how society should operate.

Piaget's stages also provide guidance about strategies that are apt to be effective in teaching children at different age levels. For instance, given the abstract nature of historical time, elementary school teachers planning history lessons should probably minimize the extent to which they talk about specific dates before the recent past (Barton & Levstik, 1996). Also, especially in the elementary grades (and to a lesser degree in middle and high school), instructors should find ways to make abstract ideas more concrete for their students.

Yet teachers must remember that most reasoning skills probably emerge far more gradually than Piaget's stages would have us believe. For instance, students have some ability to think abstractly in elementary school but continue to have trouble with certain abstractions in high school, especially about topics they don't know much about. And they may be able to deal with simple proportions (e.g., $\frac{1}{2}$, $\frac{1}{3}$) in the elementary grades and yet struggle with problems involving complex proportions (e.g., $\frac{15}{27} \div \frac{19}{33}$) in the middle and secondary school years.

◆ *Children can succeed in a particular domain only when they have mastered basic concepts and skills central to that domain.* Some basic forms of knowledge provide the foundation on which a great deal of subsequent learning depends. Examples include knowledge and skills related to counting (recall our discussion of a central conceptual structure for number) and locating objects accurately in two-dimensional space (recall the central conceptual structure for spatial relationships). If children come to school without such knowledge and skills, they may be on a path to long-term academic failure unless educators actively intervene.

For example, as noted earlier, a central conceptual structure for number seems to emerge in a wide variety of cultures. Yet Robbie Case and his colleagues have found that some children—perhaps because they've had little or no prior experience with numbers and counting—begin school without a sufficiently developed conceptual structure for number to enable normal progress in a typical mathematics curriculum. Explicit instruction in such activities as counting, connecting specific number words (e.g., "three," "five") with specific quantities of objects, and making judgments about relative number (e.g., "Since this set [•••] has more than this set [••], we can say that 'three' has more than 'two'") leads to improved performance not only in these tasks but in other quantitative tasks as well (Case & Okamoto, 1996; Griffin et al., 1995).

The use of explicit instruction to promote cognitive development is more consistent with Lev Vygotsky's theory than with Piaget's. We turn to Vygotsky's ideas now.

VYGOTSKY'S THEORY OF COGNITIVE DEVELOPMENT

In Piaget's theory, learning and development are largely an individual enterprise: By assimilating and accommodating to new experiences, children develop increasingly more advanced and integrated schemes over time. Thus, Piaget's perspective depicts children as doing most of the mental "work" themselves. In contrast, Vygotsky believed that adults foster children's learning and development in an intentional and somewhat systematic manner. The kinds of instruction and guidance that adults give children depend, of course, on the particular society and culture in which the adults and children reside—hence the term *sociocultural theory*.[5]

Vygotsky conducted numerous studies of children's thinking from the 1920s until his premature death from tuberculosis in 1934. However, Western psychologists were largely unfamiliar with his work until several decades later, when his major writings were translated from Russian into English (e.g., Vygotsky, 1962, 1978, 1987a, 1997). Although Vygotsky never had the chance to develop his theory fully, his views are clearly evident in many theorists' discussions of learning and instruction today. In fact, while Piaget's influence has been on the wane in recent years (Bjorklund, 1997), Vygotsky's influence has become increasingly prominent.

Key Ideas in Vygotsky's Theory

Vygotsky acknowledged that biological factors (e.g., neurological maturation) play a role in development. Children bring certain characteristics and dispositions to the situations they encounter, and their responses vary accordingly. Furthermore, children's behaviors, which are influenced in part by inherited traits, affect the particular experiences that they have (Vygotsky, 1997). However, Vygotsky's primary focus was on the role of the environment—especially a

---

[5]You may also see the term *cultural–historical* theory used in reference to Vygotsky's ideas.

child's social and cultural environment—in fostering cognitive growth. Following are central concepts and principles in Vygotsky's theory:

♦ *Some cognitive processes are seen in a variety of species; others are unique to human beings.* Vygotsky distinguished between two kinds of processes, or *functions.* Many species exhibit **lower mental functions:** certain basic ways of learning and responding to the environment—discovering what foods to eat, how best to get from one location to another, and so on. But human beings are unique in their use of **higher mental functions:** deliberate, focused cognitive processes that enhance learning, memory, and logical reasoning. In Vygotsky's view, the potential for acquiring lower mental functions is biologically built in, but society and culture are critical for the development of higher mental functions.

♦ *Through both informal conversations and formal schooling, adults convey to children the ways in which their culture interprets and responds to the world.* To promote higher mental functions, adults share with children the *meanings* they attach to objects, events, and, more generally, human experience. In the process, they transform, or *mediate,* the situations children encounter. Meanings are conveyed through a variety of mechanisms, including language (spoken words, writing, etc.), mathematical symbols, art, music, literature, and so on.

Informal conversations are one common method through which adults pass along culturally appropriate ways of interpreting situations. But no less important in Vygotsky's eyes is formal education, in which teachers systematically impart the ideas, concepts, and terminology used in various academic disciplines (Vygotsky, 1962). Although Vygotsky, like Piaget, saw value in allowing children to make some discoveries themselves, he also saw value in having adults describe the discoveries of previous generations (Karpov & Haywood, 1998; Vygotsky, 1962).

Increasingly, contemporary developmental psychologists are recognizing the many ways in which culture shapes children's cognitive development. A society's culture ensures that each new generation benefits from the wisdom that preceding generations have accumulated. It guides children in certain directions by encouraging them to pay attention to particular stimuli (and not to others) and to engage in particular activities (and not in others). And it provides a "lens" through which children come to construct culturally appropriate interpretations of their experiences.

♦ *Every culture passes along physical and cognitive tools that make daily living more effective and efficient.* Not only do adults teach children specific ways of interpreting experience, but they also pass along specific tools that can help children tackle the various tasks and problems they are apt to face. Some tools, such as scissors, sewing machines, and computers, are physical objects. Others, such as writing systems, maps, and spreadsheets, involve symbols as well as physical entities. Still others, such as strategies for studying a textbook and mentally calculating change from a dollar, may have no physical basis at all. In Vygotsky's view, acquiring tools that are at leastly partly symbolic or mental in nature—**cognitive tools**—greatly enhances children's thinking abilities.

Different cultures pass along different cognitive tools. Thus Vygotsky's theory leads us to expect greater diversity among children than Piaget's theory does. For instance, recall a point made earlier in the chapter: Children acquire conservation skills at a younger age if conservation of clay and water is important for a family pottery business. Similarly, children are more likely to acquire map-reading skills if maps (perhaps of roads, subway systems, and shopping malls) are a prominent part of their community and family life (Trawick-Smith, 2003; Whiting & Edwards, 1988). And children are more apt to have a keen sense of time if cultural activities are tightly regulated by clocks and calendars (K. Nelson, 1996).

◆ *Thought and language become increasingly interdependent in the first few years of life.* One very important cognitive tool is language. For us as adults, thought and language are closely interconnected. We often think in terms of the specific words that our language provides; for example, when we think about household pets, words such as *dog* and *cat* are likely to pop up repeatedly in our heads. In addition, we usually express our thoughts when we converse with others; as we sometimes put it, we "speak our minds."

Vygotsky proposed that, in contrast to the state of affairs for adults, thought and language are distinctly separate functions for infants and young toddlers. In these early years of life, thinking occurs independently of language, and when language appears, it is first used primarily as a means of communication rather than as a mechanism of thought. But sometime around age 2, thought and language become intertwined: Children begin to express their thoughts when they speak, and they begin to think in terms of words.

When thought and language merge, children often talk to themselves and in doing so may appear to be speaking in the "egocentric" manner that Piaget described. In Vygotsky's view, such **self-talk** (also known as *private speech*) plays an important role in cognitive development. By talking to themselves, children learn to guide and direct their own behaviors through difficult tasks and complex maneuvers in much the same way that adults have previously guided them. Self-talk eventually evolves into **inner speech,** in which children "talk" to themselves mentally rather than aloud. They continue to direct themselves verbally through tasks and activities, but others can no longer see and hear them do it. We are essentially talking about *self-regulation* here—a concept we previously explored in chapter 6 and will take up once again in chapter 12.

Recent research has supported Vygotsky's views regarding the progression and role of self-talk and inner speech. The frequency of children's audible self-talk decreases during the preschool and early elementary years, but this decrease is at first accompanied by an increase in whispered mumbling and silent lip movements, presumably reflecting a transition to inner speech (Bivens & Berk, 1990; Owens, 1996; Winsler & Naglieri, 2003). Furthermore, self-talk increases when children are performing more challenging tasks, at which they must exert considerable effort to be successful (Berk, 1994; Schimmoeller, 1998). As you undoubtedly know from your own experience, even adults occasionally talk to themselves when they face new challenges.

◆ *Complex mental processes begin as social activities; as children develop, they gradually internalize the processes they use in social contexts and start to use them independently.* Vygotsky proposed that higher mental functions have their roots in social interactions. As children discuss objects, events, tasks, and problems with adults and other knowledgeable individuals—often within the context of everyday cultural activities—they gradually incorporate into their own thinking the ways in which the people around them talk about and interpret the world, and they begin to use the words, concepts, symbols, and strategies—in essence, the cognitive tools—that are typical for their culture.

The process through which social activities evolve into internal mental activities is called **internalization.** The progression from self-talk to inner speech just described illustrates this process: Over time, children gradually internalize adults' directions so that they are eventually giving *themselves* directions.

Not all higher mental functions emerge through children's interactions with adults, however. Some also develop as children interact with their peers. For example, children frequently argue with one another about a variety of matters—how best to carry out an activity, what games to play, who did what to whom, and so on. According to Vygotsky, childhood arguments help children discover that there are often several points of view about the same situation. Eventually, Vygotsky suggested, children internalize the "arguing" process and acquire the ability to look at a situation from several different angles on their own.

◆ *Children appropriate their culture's tools in their own idiosyncratic manner.* Children do not necessarily internalize *exactly* what they see and hear in a social context. Rather, they often transform ideas, strategies, and other cognitive tools to suit their own needs and purposes—thus, Vygotsky's theory has a constructivist element to it. The term **appropriation** is often used to refer to this process of internalizing but also adapting the ideas and strategies of one's culture for one's own use.

◆ *Children can accomplish more difficult tasks when they have the assistance of people more advanced and competent than themselves.* Vygotsky distinguished between two kinds of ability levels that characterize children's skills at any particular point in development. A child's **actual developmental level** is the upper limit of tasks that he or she can perform independently, without help from anyone else. A child's **level of potential development** is the upper limit of tasks that he or she can perform with the assistance of a more competent individual. To get a true sense of children's cognitive development, Vygotsky suggested, we should assess their capabilities both when performing alone *and* when performing with assistance.

Children can typically do more difficult things in collaboration with adults than they can do on their own. For instance, they can more quickly learn how to swing a tennis racket or baseball bat when adults are initially present to guide their movements. They can play more difficult piano pieces when adults help them locate some of the notes on the keyboard or provides suggestions about what fingers to use. They can solve more difficult mathematics problems when their teacher helps them identify critical problem components and potentially fruitful problem-solving strategies. And they can often read more complex prose within a reading group at school than they are likely to read independently at home.

◆ *Challenging tasks promote maximum cognitive growth.* The range of tasks that children cannot yet perform independently but *can* perform with the help and guidance of others is, in Vygotsky's terminology, the **zone of proximal development (ZPD).** A child's zone of proximal development includes learning and problem-solving abilities that are just beginning to emerge and develop—abilities that are in an immature, "embryonic" form. Naturally, any child's ZPD will change over time. As some tasks are mastered, more complex ones will appear to present new challenges.

Vygotsky proposed that children learn very little from performing tasks they can already do independently. Instead, they develop primarily by attempting tasks they can accomplish only in collaboration with a more competent individual—that is, when they attempt tasks within their zone of proximal development. In a nutshell, it is the challenges in life, rather than the easy successes, that promote cognitive development.

Whereas challenging tasks are beneficial, impossible tasks, which children cannot do even with considerable structure and assistance, are of no benefit whatsoever (Vygotsky, 1987b). (For example, it is pointless to ask a typical kindergartner to solve for x in an algebraic equation.) Thus, a child's ZPD sets a limit on what he is cognitively capable of learning.

CURRENT PERSPECTIVES ON VYGOTSKY'S THEORY

Vygotsky focused more on the processes through which children develop than on the characteristics that children of particular ages are likely to exhibit. He did identify stages of development but portrayed them in only the most general terms (e.g., see Vygotsky, 1997, pp. 214–216). In addition, Vygotsky's descriptions of developmental processes were often imprecise and empirically unsubstantiated (Gauvain, 2001; Haenan, 1996; Moran & John-Steiner, 2003; Wertsch, 1984). For these reasons, Vygotsky's theory has been more difficult for researchers to test and either verify or disprove than has the case for Piaget's theory.

Despite such weaknesses, many contemporary theorists and practitioners have found Vygotsky's theory both insightful and helpful. Although they have taken Vygotsky's notions in many directions, we can discuss much of their work within the context of several general ideas: social construction of meaning, scaffolding, participation in adult activities, apprenticeships, acquisition of teaching skills, and dynamic assessment.

Social Construction of Meaning

In recent years, contemporary theorists have elaborated on Vygotsky's proposal that adults help children attach meaning to the objects and events around them. They point out that an adult (e.g., a parent or teacher) often helps a child make sense of the world through joint discussion of a phenomenon or event that the two of them are mutually experiencing (Crowley & Jacobs, 2002; Eacott, 1999; Feuerstein, 1990; John-Steiner & Mahn, 1996). Such an interaction, sometimes called a **mediated learning experience**, encourages the child to think about the phenomenon or event in particular ways—to attach labels to it, recognize principles that underlie it, draw certain conclusions from it, and so on. As an example, consider the following exchange, in which a 5-year-old boy and his mother are talking about a prehistoric animal exhibit at a natural history museum:

Boy:	Cool. Wow, look. Look giant teeth. Mom, look at his giant teeth.
Mom:	He looks like a saber tooth. Do you think he eats meat or plants?
Boy:	Mom, look at his giant little tooth, look at his teeth in his mouth, so big.
Mom:	He looks like a saber tooth, doesn't he. Do you think he eats plants or meat?
Boy:	Ouch, ouch, ouch, ouch. (referring to sharp tooth)
Mom:	Do you think he eats plants or meat?
Boy:	Meat.
Mom:	How come?
Boy:	Because he has sharp teeth. (Growling noises) (Ash, 2002, p. 378)

Even without his mother's assistance, the boy would almost certainly have learned something about the characteristics of saber-tooth tigers from his museum visit. Yet Mom has helped her son make better sense of the experience than he might have done on his own, for instance by using the label *saber tooth* and helping him connect tooth characteristics to eating preferences. Notice how persistent Mom is in asking her son to make the tooth–food connection. She continues to ask her question about meat versus plants until the boy finally infers, correctly, that saber tooths must have been meat eaters.

In addition to co-constructing meanings with adults, children often talk among themselves to make sense of phenomena. Not only might peer-group discussions provoke the *sociocognitive conflict* of which I spoke earlier, but they can also help children make better sense of a situation than any one of them could make individually. As an example of how students in a classroom might work together to construct meaning, let's consider a discussion in a third-grade class taught by Keisha Coleman. The students are debating how they might solve the problem $-10 + 10 = ?$. They are using a number line like the following to facilitate their discussion.

Several students, including Tessa, agree that the solution is "zero" but disagree about how to use the number line to arrive at that answer. Excerpts from a discussion between Tessa and her classmate Chang (as facilitated by Ms. Coleman) follow:

Tessa:	You have to count numbers to the right. If you count numbers to the right, then you couldn't get to zero. You'd have to count to the left.
[Ms. Coleman]:	Could you explain a little bit more about what you mean by that? I'm not quite sure I follow you. . . .
Tessa:	Because if you went that way [points to the right] then it would have to be a higher number. . . .
Chang:	I disagree with what she's trying to say. . . . Tessa says if you're counting right, then the number is—I don't really understand. She said, "If you count right, then the number has to go smaller." I don't know what she's talking about. Negative ten plus ten is zero. . . . What do you mean by counting to the right?
Tessa:	If you count from ten up, you can't get zero. If you count from ten left, you can get zero.
Chang:	Well, negative ten is a negative number—smaller than zero.
Tessa:	I know.
Chang:	Then why do you say you can't get to zero when you're adding to negative ten, which is smaller than zero?
Tessa:	OHHHH! NOW I GET IT! This is positive. . . . You have to count right.
[Ms. Coleman]:	You're saying in order to get to zero, you have to count to the right? From where, Tessa?
Tessa:	Negative 10. (P. L. Peterson, 1992, pp. 165–166)

The class continues in its efforts to pin down precisely how to use the number line to solve the problem. Eventually, Tessa offers a revised and more complete explanation. Pointing to the appropriate location on the number line, she says, "You start at negative 10. Then you add 1, 2, 3, 4, 5, 6, 7, 8, 9, 10." She moves her finger one number to the right for each number she counts. She reaches the zero point on the number line when she counts "10" and concludes, "That equals zero" (P. L. Peterson, 1992, p. 168).

Many contemporary theorists have become convinced of the value of joint meaning-making discussions in helping children acquire more complex understandings of their physical, social, and academic worlds. The popularity of this perspective, which reflects the *social constructivist* view I introduced in chapter 7, has led to increasing advocacy for instructional practices involving student interaction (class discussions, cooperative learning activities, peer tutoring, etc.) in elementary and secondary classrooms. It is important to note, however, that children and adolescents sometimes acquire misinformation from one another (Good, McCaslin, & Reys, 1992). It is essential, then, that teachers monitor group discussions for and correct any misconceptions or misinterpretations that young people may pass on to their peers.

Scaffolding

Recall Vygotsky's suggestion that children are most likely to benefit from tasks and activities they can successfully accomplish only with the assistance and support of more competent individuals—that is, tasks within their zone of proximal development. Contemporary theorists have identified a variety of techniques—collectively known as **scaffolding**—that can help students accomplish challenging tasks in instructional contexts. One effective technique is to ask questions that get students thinking in appropriate ways about a task, as illustrated in the following dialogue:

Teacher:	[writes 6) 44 on the board] 11 divided by 6. What number times 6 is close to 44?
Child:	6.
Teacher:	What's 6 times 6? [writes 6]
Child:	36.
Teacher:	36. Can you get one that's any closer? [erasing the 6]
Child:	8.
Teacher:	What's 6 times 8?
Child:	64 . . . 48.
Teacher:	48. Too big. Can you think of something . . .
Child:	6 times 7 is 42. (Pettito, 1985, p. 251)

Additional forms of scaffolding are these:

- Help students develop a plan for dealing with a new task.
- Model the correct performance of a task.
- Divide a complex task into several smaller, simpler activities.
- Give specific guidelines for accomplishing the task.
- Provide a calculator, computer software (word processing programs, spreadsheets, etc.), or other technology that makes some aspects of the task easier.
- Keep students' attention focused on the relevant aspects of the task.
- Ask questions that get students thinking about the task in productive ways.
- Keep students motivated to complete the task.
- Remind students what their goals are in performing the task (e.g., what a problem solution should look like).
- Give frequent feedback about how students are progressing.
  (A. Collins, 2006; Gallimore & Tharp, 1990; Good et al., 1992; Lajoie & Derry, 1993; Lodewyk & Winne, 2005; P. F. Merrill et al., 1996; Rogoff, 1990; Rosenshine & Meister, 1992; Wood, Bruner, & Ross, 1976)

As students become more adept at performing a complex task, scaffolding is ideally modified to nurture newly emerging skills (Puntambekar & Hübscher, 2005). And over time it is gradually phased out, until the students can complete the task on their own.

Scaffolding in its various forms can be a highly effective way of helping learners acquire complex reasoning, metacognitive, and problem-solving skills (e.g., Hogan & Tudge, 1999; Hogan, Nastasi, & Pressley, 2000; Radziszewska & Rogoff, 1991; Rittle-Johnson & Koedinger, 2005; Rogoff, 1995). Accordingly, we'll revisit this concept in chapters 12 and 13.

Participation in Adult Activities

Virtually all cultures allow—and in fact usually require—children to be involved in adult activities to some degree. Children's early experiences are often at the fringe of an activity, and their involvement is mediated, scaffolded, and supervised through what is sometimes known as **guided participation** (Rogoff, 2003). From a Vygotskian perspective, gradual entry into adult activities increases the probability that children will engage in behaviors and thinking skills within their zone of proximal development. It also helps children tie newly acquired skills and thinking abilities to the specific contexts in which they are apt to be useful later on (Carraher, Carraher, & Schliemann, 1985; Light & Butterworth, 1993). As children acquire greater competence, they gradually take a more central role in a particular activity until, eventually, they are full-fledged participants (Gaskins, 1999; Guberman, 1999; Lave & Wenger, 1991).

Even for adults, entry into new activities is often a gradual process (Wenger, 1998). Imagine, for example, that you take a job at a large insurance company. You've never worked in the insurance business before, and so you have a lot to learn about what insurance contracts entail. But you also have to learn how your company operates—which people take responsibility for which tasks, what forms should be completed in different situations, where you can get answers to various questions, and so on. Little by little, the "old-timers" in your company will help you master everything you need to know, and eventually you yourself will become an old-timer who assists newcomers to the firm (Wenger, 1998).

Apprenticeships

An especially intensive form of guided participation is an **apprenticeship,** in which a novice works with an expert for a lengthy period to learn how to perform complex tasks within a particular domain. The expert provides considerable structure and guidance throughout the process, gradually removing scaffolding and giving the novice more responsibility as competence increases (A. Collins, 2006; Rogoff, 1990, 1991). Many cultures use apprenticeships as a way of teaching children particular skills and trades in the adult community—perhaps weaving, tailoring, or midwifery (Lave, 1991; Lave & Wenger, 1991; Rogoff, 1990). We also see apprenticeships frequently in music instruction—for instance, in teaching a student how to play a musical instrument (Elliott, 1995).

In an apprenticeship, a person learns not only the behaviors but also the language of a skill or trade (Lave & Wenger, 1991). For example, when master weavers teach apprentices their art, they might use such terms as *warp, weft, shuttle,* and *harness* to focus attention on a particular aspect of the process. Similarly, when teachers guide students through scientific experiments, they use words like *hypothesis, evidence,* and *theory* to help the students evaluate their procedures and results (Perkins, 1992).

Furthermore, an apprenticeship can show novices how experts typically *think* about a task or activity—a situation known as a **cognitive apprenticeship** (J. S. Brown et al., 1989; A. Collins, 2006; A. Collins, Brown, & Newman, 1989; Roth & Bowen, 1995). An example is the relationship between a university professor and a graduate student (Roth & Bowen, 1995). For instance, I used to teach a doctoral seminar called Cognition and Instruction, in which I assigned a gigantic collection of outside readings (the required articles and book chapters stacked up to a pile about 2 feet high). As a class we spent 2 or 3 hours over the course of the semester talking about how to read such a large amount of material productively. I shared such strategies as skimming, reading with particular goals in mind, and relating one theorist's perspectives to another's, and I provided a list of focus questions that students should try to answer as they read. Students were also required to complete a major research project by the end of the semester; I met with each of them periodically to help them narrow down their topic, identify fruitful directions to pursue, organize their thoughts, and consider possible conclusions.

Although apprenticeships can differ widely from one context to another, they typically have some or all of the following features (A. Collins, 2006; A. Collins et al., 1989):

- *Modeling:* The teacher carries out the task, simultaneously thinking aloud about the process, while the student observes and listens.
- *Coaching:* As the student performs the task, the teacher gives frequent suggestions, hints, and feedback.
- *Scaffolding:* The teacher provides various forms of support for the student, perhaps by simplifying the task, breaking it into smaller and more manageable components, or providing less complicated equipment.
- *Articulation:* The student explains what he or she is doing and why, allowing the teacher to examine the student's knowledge, reasoning, and problem-solving strategies.
- *Reflection:* The teacher asks the student to compare his or her performance with that of experts, or perhaps with an ideal model of how the task should be done.
- *Increasing complexity and diversity of tasks:* As the student gains greater proficiency, the teacher presents more complex, challenging, and varied tasks to complete.
- *Exploration:* The teacher encourages the student to frame questions and problems on his or her own, and in doing so to expand and refine acquired skills.

Apprenticeships are clearly labor intensive; as such, their use in the classroom is not always practical or logistically feasible (De Corte et al., 1996). At the same time, teachers can certainly use elements of an apprenticeship model to help their students develop more complex skills. For example, prompts such as the following help students think about writing tasks in the same ways that expert writers do (Scardamalia & Bereiter, 1985):

- "My purpose . . . "
- "My main point . . . "
- "An example of this . . . "
- "The reason I think so . . . "
- "To liven this up I'll . . . "
- "I'm not being very clear about what I just said, so . . . "
- "I'm getting off the topic, so . . . "
- "This isn't very convincing because . . . "
- "I can tie this together by . . . "

Such prompts provide the same sort of scaffolding that an expert writer might provide, and they help students develop more sophisticated writing strategies (Scardamalia & Bereiter, 1985).

Acquisition of Teaching Skills

As learners acquire new skills from more experienced members of their community, they may also learn how to teach those skills to someone else (Gauvain, 2001). With age and experience, they become increasingly adept at teaching others what they have learned. Let's look at an example involving the game of Monopoly. Four 8-year-old girls are playing the game while a researcher videotapes their interactions (Guberman, Rahm, & Menk, 1998). One girl, Carla, has limited math skills and little experience playing the game. On her first turn, she lands on Connecticut Avenue:

Nancy:	Do you want to buy it?
Carla:	Hmmmm . . . [There is a long pause and some unrelated discussion among the players.] How much is it again? Twelve hundred . . .
Nancy:	A hundred and twenty dollars.
Carla:	A hundred and twenty [She starts to count her money] . . . a hundred [She is referring to a $10 bill] . . .
Sarah:	You give her one of these and one of these. [She holds up first a $100 bill and then a $20 bill of her own money.] (Guberman et al., 1998, p. 436; format adapted)

Notice how Nancy and Sarah scaffold Carla's initial purchase. Nancy asks her to consider buying the property and tells her the purchase price. When it is clear that Carla is having trouble counting out $120 (she thinks a $10 bill is worth $100), Sarah gives her sufficient guidance that she can identify the needed bills by color alone. As Carla becomes more competent later in the game, the other girls reduce their support. For instance, at one point Carla lands on Virginia Avenue, with a purchase price of $160:

Carla hesitates making the payment, looking through her money. Eventually, she takes a $100 bill from her money and appears unsure how to continue.

Nancy:	Just a fifty and a ten.

Carla gives a $50 bill and a $10 bill to the banker. (Guberman et al., 1998, p. 437; format adapted)

When children and adults teach others, the "teachers" often benefit as much as the "students" (Fuchs, Fuchs, Mathes, & Simmons, 1997; Inglis & Biemiller, 1997; Webb & Palincsar, 1996). For instance, when students study something with the expectation that they will be teaching it to someone else, they are more motivated to learn it, find it more interesting, and learn it more effectively (Benware & Deci, 1984; Semb, Ellis, & Araujo, 1993). Furthermore, when children who are relatively weak in a particular skill (compared to their age-mates) have the opportunity to guide younger children in that skill, they develop greater ability to guide themselves as well, presumably because they internalize the directions they have been giving someone else (Biemiller, Shany, Inglis, & Meichenbaum, 1998).

Dynamic Assessment

As noted earlier, Vygotsky believed that we can get a more complete picture of children's cognitive development when we assess both their *actual developmental level* (the upper limit of tasks they can successfully accomplish on their own) and their *level of potential development* (the upper limit of tasks they can accomplish when they have the assistance of more competent individuals). When assessing children's cognitive abilities, however, most teachers focus almost exclusively on *actual* developmental level: They ask children to take tests, complete assignments, and so on, without help from anyone else. To assess children's level of potential development, some theorists have suggested an alternative known as **dynamic assessment,** which involves (a) identifying tasks that children cannot initially do independently, (b) providing in-depth instruction and practice in behaviors and cognitive processes related to the task, and then (c) determining the extent to which each child has benefited from the instruction (Feuerstein, 1979, 1980; Kozulin & Falik, 1995; Lidz & Gindis, 2003; Tzuriel, 2000). This approach often yields more optimistic evaluations of children's cognitive capabilities than traditional measures of cognitive ability and may be especially useful in assessing the abilities of children from diverse cultural backgrounds (Feuerstein, 1979; Swanson & Lussier, 2001; Tzuriel, 2000).

To date, we have little hard data about the validity and reliability of dynamic assessment techniques (Swanson & Lussier, 2001; Tzuriel, 2000). However, one advantage of these techniques is the rich body of qualitative information they can yield about how children approach a new learning task.

ADDING A SOCIOCULTURAL ELEMENT TO INFORMATION PROCESSING THEORY

In chapter 7, I briefly got on my soapbox and argued that an integration of theoretical perspectives can often yield a more complete understanding of human learning than any single theory can yield alone. Consistent with this view, some theorists have found it productive to integrate elements of information processing theory and sociocultural theory. In particular, they suggest, information processing theory may tell us a great deal about *what* changes over time, and sociocultural views (notions about mediated learning experiences, guided participation, and the like) may help us explain *how* those changes occur (Gauvain, 2001; Ornstein & Haden, 2001).

This blend of information processing and sociocultural approaches is still in its infancy, but researchers have made considerable progress in three areas: intersubjectivity, social construction of memory, and collaborative use of cognitive strategies.

Intersubjectivity

For two people to interact and communicate, they must have shared understandings on which to build. For instance, each member of the pair should have some awareness of what the other person sees, knows, thinks, and feels. Such mutual understanding is known as **intersubjectivity** (Newson & Newson, 1975; Rommetveit, 1985; Trevarthen, 1980). The beginnings of intersubjectivity are seen at about 2 months of age, when infants and their caregivers focus on and interact with each other, making eye contact, exchanging smiles, taking turns vocalizing, and so on (Adamson & McArthur, 1995; Kingstone, Smilek, Ristic, Friesen, & Eastwood, 2003).

Sometime around 9 or 10 months of age, intersubjectivity becomes more complex, taking the form of **joint attention.** At this point, an infant and caregiver can focus on a single object, with both members of the pair monitoring the *other's* attention to the object and coordinating their behaviors toward the object (Adamson & McArthur, 1995; Carpenter, Nagell, & Tomasello, 1998; Trevarthen & Hubley, 1978).

Early in the second year, infants also begin to show **social referencing**, looking at someone else for clues about how to respond to or feel about a particular object or event (Feinman, 1992; Klinnert, Emde, Butterfield, & Campos, 1986). Children are most likely to engage in social referencing when they encounter a new and uncertain situation. For example, in one study

(Klinnert, 1984), 1- and $1^1/_2$-year-old infants were shown three new toys to which their mothers had been instructed to respond with a happy, fearful, or neutral expression. Upon seeing each new toy, most infants looked at their mother and chose actions consistent with her response. They typically moved toward the toy if Mom showed pleasure but moved away from it if she showed fear.

As information processing theorists tell us, attention is critical to learning and cognitive development. As we bring the sociocultural perspective into the picture, we see that awareness of a *partner's* attention is critical as well (Baldwin, 2000; Gauvain, 2001). For instance, when an adult uses a word that an 18-month-old toddler has never heard before, the toddler will often look immediately at the speaker's face and follow the speaker's line of vision to the object being referenced. In this way, children probably learn many object labels (Baldwin, 2000). In general, a child can learn from a person with more experience only if both people are focusing on the same thing and *know* that they are sharing their focus. Because intersubjectivity is so critical for children's ability to learn from more experienced members of their community, it appears to be a universal phenomenon across cultures (Adamson & Bakeman, 1991).

Social Construction of Memory

In the section on "Social Construction of Meaning" earlier in the chapter, we saw how adults often help children construct meaning from events they are jointly experiencing. An adult can also help a child reconstruct events that the two of them have *previously* experienced and stored in their respective long-term memories. In some cases, talking about an event *after* it has transpired enhances memory even more than talking about it at the time it's happening (McGuigan & Salmon, 2004). Perhaps the delay in discussion gives children a chance to store and consolidate certain aspects of the event on their own, with the postevent discussion offering a chance to retrieve, and hence better remember, the experience (McGuigan & Salmon, 2004).

Almost as soon as children are old enough to talk, their parents begin to engage them in conversations about past events, helping them construct the *narratives* I spoke of in chapter 10 (Fivush, Haden, & Reese, 1996; Gauvain, 2001; Ratner, 1984). Initially, the parents do most of the work, reminiscing, asking questions, prompting recall, and so on, but by time children are 3, they, too, are active participants in the conversations (Fivush et al., 1996). As an example, consider the following dialogue, in which 6-year-old Kerry and her mother talk about a recent whale-watching expedition:

Mother:	And we went with, who'd we go with?
Kerry:	David.
Mother:	David. Who else?
Kerry:	And Nana and Papa.
Mother:	And who else? Daddy went too, didn't he?
Kerry:	Yeah.
Mother:	Yeah. Who else?
Kerry:	That's all.
Mother:	Oh, and Auntie Karen and Uncle Pete, right?
Kerry:	Yeah.
Mother:	And David's two brothers.
Kerry:	Mmhm.

Mother:	We went whale watching and um I think it turned out to be a disaster because it was rough out there and we got kind of seasick. We did see whales, but not as good as we wanted to.
Kerry:	I saw one.
Mother:	Yeah, we saw them. They're big, huh?
Kerry:	[Nods.]
Mother:	How many were there?
Kerry:	About thirteen.
Mother:	About thirteen! There were only two or three!
Kerry:	No, there wasn't, because they were runnin' back and forth like fifty times! (Hemphill & Snow, 1996, p. 182)

Such discussions, sometimes called **co-constructed narratives,** can help children make better sense of an event and perhaps apply labels to it (e.g., *whale watching, seasick*). By doing these things, children encode and so remember the event more effectively.

As we noted in chapter 10, talking about an event can occasionally lead to a distorted memory for it, especially if children are led to "recall" things that didn't actually happen. But as a general rule, conversations about past events are quite productive and have several benefits (Gauvain, 2001; Haskell, 2001; K. Nelson, 1996). First, as noted in our discussion of *verbalization* in chapter 8, children can better encode (and so better remember) the things they talk about. Second, because adults focus on certain aspects of events and not others, children learn what things are important to remember. Third, because adults are apt to interpret events in particular ways (e.g., finding some things amusing and others distasteful), children acquire perspectives and values appropriate for their culture. For example, when European American mothers recall past events with their 3-year-olds, they often speculate about the thoughts and feelings of the participants. In contrast, Asian mothers are more likely to talk about social norms and expectations, such as what someone should have done instead (Mullen & Yi, 1995). Such differences are consistent with the priorities and values of these cultures (Bauer, 2006; MacDonald, Uesiliana, & Hayne, 2000; Mullen & Yi, 1995).

Collaborative Use of Cognitive Strategies

In our discussion of cognitivist ideas in previous chapters, we've occasionally talked about mental processes as *strategies*—encoding strategies, study strategies, self-regulation strategies, and so on. Some cognitive processes are in fact quite strategic, in that people intentionally use them to accomplish certain goals. Sometimes children develop these strategies on their own. On other occasions they learn effective strategies by modeling how adults or peers approach subject matter (recall the discussion of *cognitive modeling* in chapter 6). A combination of information processing theory and sociocultural theory gives us a third alternative: Adults can engage children in activities that require collaborative use of particular strategies. Through joint discussion and use of strategies—typically with considerable adult guidance and scaffolding at first—children gradually internalize the strategies and begin using them independently (Freund, 1990; Gauvain, 1999, 2001).

As an example of the last approach, let's consider a study by Radziszewska and Rogoff (1988) in which 9- and 10-year-old children each worked with either a parent or a peer to plan a shopping trip that would involve stops at numerous locations. Each pair was asked to imagine

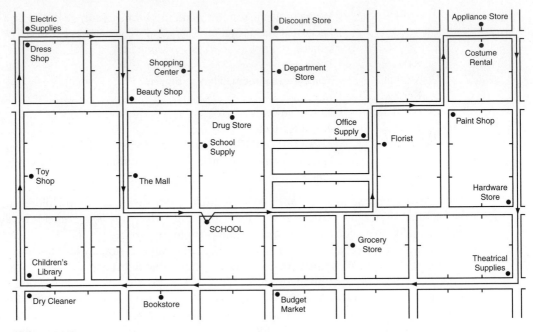

Figure 11.6
The imaginary town map used by Radziszewska and Rogoff (1988).
Reprinted from "Influence of Adult and Peer Collaborators on Children's Planning Skills" by B. Radziszewska &
B. Rogoff, 1988, *Developmental Psychology, 24,* p. 842. Copyright 1988 by the American Psychological
Association. Reprinted with permission.

that they needed to go on a shopping trip to get materials for a school play (masks, costumes, etc.). They were given a shopping list of 10 items and an imaginary town map (see Figure 11.6) and instructed to identify the shortest possible route (beginning and ending at school) by which they could obtain all 10 items. Child–parent and child–peer pairs alike were able to plot a course that would enable them to get the needed items, but on average, the child–parent pairs identified shorter routes (the route marked in Figure 11.6 is an example of a good route). Furthermore, the parents provided more strategic guidance and engaged the children in more collaborative decision making than the children's age-mates did. After two planning sessions with a partner, the children were asked to plan a third trip, this time independently. Those who had previously worked with a parent identified shorter, more efficient routes than those who had worked with a peer.

IMPLICATIONS OF VYGOTSKY'S THEORY AND ITS OFFSHOOTS

Vygotsky's work and the recent theoretical advances it has inspired have numerous implications for instructional practice. Following are examples:

♦ *Children can think more effectively when they acquire the basic cognitive tools of various activities and academic disciplines.* Virtually every activity in our society involves certain concepts and ways of thinking, and mastering them enables children to engage more successfully in the activity. For instance, children can become better musicians when they can read music and understand what *keys, chords,* and *thirds* are. They develop their carpentry skills when they know how to interpret blueprints and understand terms such as *plumb* and *right angle.* Furthermore, through such disciplines as science, mathematics, and social studies, our culture passes along key concepts (e.g., *galaxy, right triangle*), principles (e.g., *Pythagorean theorem, supply-and-demand*), symbols (e.g., H_2O, x^3), and visual representations (e.g., graphs, maps) that can help growing children interpret, organize and successfully deal with the physical and social worlds in which they live.

♦ *Children learn and remember more when they talk about their experiences.* Children begin to talk about their experiences almost as soon as they begin to speak, and by age 2 they do it fairly often (van den Broek, Bauer, & Bourg, 1997). Parents and teachers should join in the process: As we've seen, talking with children about joint experiences not only enhances children's memories of what they are seeing and doing but also helps children interpret their experiences in culturally appropriate ways.

♦ *Children should have opportunities to engage in activities that closely resemble those they will encounter in the adult world.* In industrialized societies, children are largely separated from the adult workplace, and so they have little exposure to the kinds of activities they will eventually need to perform when they themselves reach adulthood (Rogoff, 2003). Accordingly, many theorists recommend that teachers incorporate **authentic activities**—tasks identical or similar to those that children will eventually encounter in the outside world—into the school curriculum (e.g., Hickey, 1997; Greeno et al., 1996; Hiebert & Fisher, 1992; Lave, 1993). Given what we have learned about cognitive development and learning, we can speculate that such activities are likely to have several benefits. For one thing, when students work in a naturalistic context, using the physical and social resources (e.g., tools, peers) that such a context offers, students should be able to accomplish more than they might accomplish in relatively artificial and unscaffolded classroom tasks (Greeno et al., 1996). Second, complex authentic tasks can help students make meaningful connections among the various ideas and skills they have learned in the classroom. Finally, because authentic activities resemble real-world tasks and problems, they should help students make mental connections between the things they learn at school and out-of-school tasks (more about this point in chapter 13).

Authentic activities can be developed for virtually any area of the school curriculum. For example, teachers might have students:

- Write an editorial
- Participate in a debate
- Design an electrical circuit
- Conduct an experiment
- Write a computer program
- Create and distribute a class newsletter
- Perform in a concert
- Plan a family budget
- Converse in a foreign language
- Make a videotape
- Construct a museum display
- Develop a home page for the Internet

By placing classroom activities in real-world contexts, teachers can often enhance students' mastery of classroom subject matter (A. Collins et al., 1989; De Corte et al., 1996). For example, students may show greater improvement in writing skills when they practice writing stories, essays, and letters to real people, rather than completing short, artificial writing exercises (Hiebert & Fisher, 1992). Likewise, they may gain a more complete understanding of how to use and interpret maps when they construct their own maps than when they engage in workbook exercises involving map interpretation (Gregg & Leinhardt, 1994).

Theorists have suggested that an authentic activity is most likely to be effective when it has characteristics such as the following:

- It requires a fair amount of background knowledge about a particular topic; in other words, students must know the subject matter thoroughly and have learned it in a meaningful fashion.
- It promotes higher-level thinking skills; for example, it may involve synthesizing information, forming and testing hypotheses, solving problems, and drawing conclusions.
- It requires students to seek out information in a variety of contexts and perhaps from a variety of academic disciplines.
- It conveys high expectations for students' performance yet also encourages students to take risks and experiment with new strategies.
- Its final outcome is complex and somewhat unpredictable; there is not necessarily a single "right" response or answer. (Newmann & Wehlage, 1993; Paris & Turner, 1994)

It may occasionally be possible to assign authentic activities as homework; for example, teachers might ask students to write an editorial, design an electrical circuit, or plan a family budget while working at home in the evening. But many authentic activities may require considerable classroom dialogue, with students asking questions of one another, sharing their ideas, offering explanations of their thinking, and synthesizing their efforts into an integrated whole (Newmann & Wehlage, 1993; Paris & Turner, 1994). For example, creating a school newspaper, making a videotape, and conversing in a foreign language may be activities that students can perform only as a group. Furthermore, because authentic activities are typically more complex and open-ended than traditional classroom tasks, they may require considerable teacher scaffolding (Brophy, 1992a; Hickey, 1997). For such reasons, many authentic activities can be accomplished more effectively in class than at home, or perhaps through a combination of group work during class and independent work after school hours.

We should note, however, that it is not necessarily desirable to fill the entire school day with complex, authentic tasks. For one thing, students can often master basic skills more effectively when they practice them in relative isolation from other activities (J. R. Anderson, Reder, & Simon, 1996). For example, when learning to play the violin, students need to master their fingering before they join an orchestra, and when learning to play soccer, they need to practice dribbling and passing before they play in a game. Second, some authentic tasks may be too expensive and time consuming to warrant their use on a regular basis in the classroom (Griffin & Griffin, 1994). It is probably most important that classroom tasks encourage students to engage in such cognitive processes as meaningful learning, organization, and elaboration—processes that promote long-term retention and application of classroom subject matter—than that tasks always be authentic in nature (J. R. Anderson et al., 1996).

♦ *Group learning activities can help children internalize cognitive strategies.* As we've seen, Vygotsky suggested that children are apt to internalize—and so eventually use independently—the processes they first use in social interaction. Group study sessions, class discussions about literature, debates about controversial issues, and collaborative problem-solving tasks—all of these can help children acquire more sophisticated strategies, as we'll discover in the next three chapters.

♦ *Children often acquire better strategies when they collaborate with adults on complex tasks.* Although children internalize many important skills through interactions with their age-mates, they are likely to acquire more sophisticated strategies—and acquire them more quickly—when adults rather than peers assist them in their efforts (Gauvain, 1999; McCaslin & Good, 1996; Radziszewska & Rogoff, 1988, 1991). Generally speaking, adults suggest and model more effective strategies, give more helpful guidance, and are more willing to let children take charge of a complex task at appropriate times.

♦ *Challenging tasks, especially when sufficiently scaffolded, are likely to foster maximum cognitive development.* To promote cognitive development, teachers and other adults must present some tasks and assignments that a child can perform successfully only with assistance—that is, tasks within the child's zone of proximal development. Children at any single age level are apt to have different zones of proximal development and so may need different tasks and assignments. In other words, instruction is most effective when it is individually tailored to children's unique strengths and limitations.

♦ *Children's abilities should be assessed under a variety of work conditions.* To get a good handle on children's cognitive development, teachers ultimately need to know not only what the children can and cannot do, but also under what conditions they are most likely to accomplish various tasks successfully (Calfee & Masuda, 1997). By asking children to work under varying conditions—sometimes independently, sometimes in collaboration with one or more peers, and sometimes with adult instruction and support—teachers can get a better sense of the tasks that are in each child's zone of proximal development.

COMPARING PIAGETIAN AND VYGOTSKIAN PERSPECTIVES

Piaget's and Vygotsky's theories have some ideas in common that continue to appear in more contemporary views of cognitive development. Yet they also have important differences that have led modern researchers to probe more deeply into the mechanisms through which children's cognitive processes develop.

Common Themes

If we look beyond the very different vocabulary Piaget and Vygotsky used to describe the phenomena they observed, we notice four themes that their theories share: qualitative changes in the nature of thought, challenge, readiness, and the importance of social interaction.

Qualitative changes in the nature of thought   Both Piaget and Vygotsky pointed out that children acquire more complex reasoning processes over time. Piaget described such development in terms of four qualitatively different stages, whereas Vygotsky spoke in terms of the internalization of many different mental functions. Regardless of whose perspective we take, we come to the same conclusion: Children think differently at different ages.

Challenge   We see the importance of challenge most clearly in Vygotsky's concept of the *zone of proximal development:* Children benefit most from tasks they can perform only with the assistance of more competent individuals. Yet challenge—albeit of a somewhat different sort—also lies at the heart of Piaget's theory: Children develop more sophisticated knowledge and thought processes only when they encounter phenomena they cannot adequately understand using their existing schemes—in other words, phenomena that create *disequilibrium.*

Readiness   According to both theories, any child will be cognitively ready for some experiences but not ready for others. From Piaget's perspective, children can accommodate to new objects and events only when they can also assimilate them into existing schemes. That is, there must be some overlap between the "new" and the "old." In addition, Piaget argued that children cannot learn from an experience until they have begun the transition into a stage that allows them to deal with and conceptualize that experience appropriately.

Vygotsky, too, proposed that there are limits on the tasks that children can reasonably handle at any particular time. As children acquire some capabilities, other, slightly more advanced ones begin to emerge, initially in an immature form. Children's newly forming abilities fall within their zone of proximal development and can be fostered through adult assistance and guidance.

Importance of social interaction   In Piaget's eyes, the people in a child's life can present information and arguments that create disequilibrium and foster greater perspective taking. For instance, when young children disagree with one another, they begin to realize that different people may have different yet equally valid viewpoints, and they gradually shed the egocentrism that characterizes the preoperational stage.

In Vygotsky's view, social interactions provide the very foundation for thought processes: Children internalize the processes they use when they converse with others until, ultimately, they can use them independently. Furthermore, tasks within the ZPD can, by definition, be accomplished only when others assist in children's efforts—perhaps directly in face-to-face interactions, or perhaps indirectly through study guides, tutoring software, or other concrete forms of scaffolding.

Key Theoretical Differences

Following are four questions that capture key differences between Piaget's and Vygotsky's theories of cognitive development.

To what extent is language essential for learning and cognitive development?   According to Piaget, language provides verbal labels for many of the concepts and other schemes that children have already developed. It is also the primary means through which children interact with others and so can begin to incorporate multiple perspectives into their thinking. In Piaget's view, however, much of cognitive development occurs independently of language.

For Vygotsky, however, language is absolutely critical for learning and cognitive development. Children's thought processes are internalized versions of social interactions that are largely verbal in nature. Through two language-based phenomena—self-talk and inner speech—children begin to guide their own behaviors in ways that others have previously guided them. Furthermore, in their conversations with adults, children learn the meanings that their culture ascribes to particular events and gradually begin to interpret the world in cultural-specific ways.

The truth of the matter probably lies somewhere between Piaget's and Vygotsky's perspectives. Piaget clearly underestimated the importance of language: Children acquire more complex understandings of physical phenomena and events not only through their own interactions with the world but also (as Vygotsky suggested) by learning how others interpret those phenomena and events. On the other hand, Vygotsky may have overstated the case for language. Some concepts clearly emerge *before* children have verbal labels to attach to them (Halford & Andrews, 2006; Oakes & Rakison, 2003). Furthermore, verbal exchanges may be less important for cognitive development in some cultures than in others. For instance, adults in some rural communities in Guatemala and India place heavy emphasis on gestures and demonstrations, rather than on verbal instructions, to teach and guide children (Rogoff, Mistry, Göncü, & Mosier, 1993).

What kinds of experiences promote learning and development?   Piaget maintained that children's independent, self-motivated explorations of the physical world form the basis for many developing schemes, and children often construct these schemes with little guidance from others. In contrast, Vygotsky argued for activities that are facilitated and interpreted by more competent individuals. The distinction, then, is one of self-exploration versus guided exploration and instruction.

Children almost certainly benefit from both kinds of experiences—opportunities to manipulate and experiment with physical phenomena on their own and opportunities to draw upon the wisdom of prior generations (Brainerd, 2003; Karpov & Haywood, 1998). But as it turns out, *perception* of the physical world may be more important than actual physical manipulation of it. For example, children with significant physical disabilities make major cognitive advancements despite fairly limited hands-on experiences with physical objects (Bebko, Burke, Craven, & Sarlo, 1992). And "manipulation" of objects in a "virtual world" that educational computer software provides can also be highly effective (Moreno, 2006). In one way or another, however, children must have some sort of experience with the physical world—encounters with various physical phenomena (e.g., pressure, inertia, oscillation), exposure to cause–effect relationships, and so on—if they are to get a good sense of how it works.

What kinds of social interactions are most valuable?   Both theorists saw value in interacting with people of all ages. However, Piaget emphasized the benefits of interactions with peers (who could create conflict), whereas Vygotsky placed greater importance on interactions with adults and other more advanced individuals (who could support children in challenging tasks and help them make appropriate interpretations).

Some contemporary theorists have proposed that interactions with peers and interactions with adults play different roles in children's cognitive development (Damon, 1984; Rogoff, 1991; Webb & Palincsar, 1996). When children's development requires that they abandon old perspectives in favor of new, more complex ones, the sociocultural conflict that often occurs among age-mates (and the multiple perspectives that emerge from it) may be optimal for bringing about such change. But when children's development instead requires that they learn new skills, the thoughtful, patient guidance of a competent adult may be more beneficial (Gauvain, 2001; Radziszewska & Rogoff, 1991).

How influential is culture?   In Piaget's mind, the nature of children's logical thinking skills and the progression of these skills over time are largely independent of the specific cultural context in which children are raised. But in Vygotsky's view, culture is of paramount importance in determining the specific thinking skills that children acquire. Vygotsky was probably more on target here. Earlier in the chapter, I presented evidence to indicate that children's reasoning skills do not necessarily appear at the same ages in different cultures. In fact, some reasoning skills (especially those involving formal operational thought) may never appear at all.

We must keep in mind, however, that there isn't necessarily a single "best" or "right" way for a culture to promote cognitive development (Rogoff, 2003). Despite their diverse instructional practices, virtually all of the world's cultures have developed myriad strategies for helping growing children acquire the knowledge and skills they will need to be successful participants in the local adult society.

Obviously neither Piaget nor Vygotsky was completely right or completely wrong. Both offered groundbreaking insights into the nature of children's learning and thinking, and both have had a profound influence on contemporary views of learning, cognition, and cognitive development. In fact, Piaget's and Vygotsky's theories complement each other to some extent, with the former helping us understand how children often reason on their own and the latter providing ideas about how adults can help them reason more effectively.

SUMMARY

Jean Piaget portrayed children as active and motivated learners who, through numerous interactions with their physical and social environments, construct an increasingly complex understanding of the world around them. He proposed that cognitive development proceeds through four stages: (1) the sensorimotor stage (when cognitive functioning is based primarily on behaviors and perceptions); (2) the preoperational stage (when symbolic thought and language become prevalent, but reasoning is "illogical" by adult standards); (3) the concrete operations stage (when logical reasoning capabilities emerge but are limited to concrete objects and events); and (4) the formal operations stage (when thinking about abstract, hypothetical, and contrary-to-fact ideas becomes possible).

Developmental researchers have found that Piaget probably underestimated the capabilities of infants, preschoolers, and elementary school children and overestimated the capabilities of adolescents. Researchers have found, too, that children's reasoning on particular tasks depends somewhat on their prior knowledge, background experiences, and formal schooling relative to those tasks. The great majority of developmentalists now doubt that cognitive development can really be characterized as a series of general stages that pervade children's thinking in diverse content domains. A few theorists, known as neo-Piagetians, propose that children acquire more specific systems of concepts and thinking skills relevant to particular domains and that these systems may change in a stagelike manner. Many others suggest that, instead, children exhibit gradual trends in a variety of abilities. However, virtually all contemporary theorists acknowledge the value of Piaget's research methods and his views about motivation, the construction of knowledge, and the appearance of qualitative changes in cognitive development.

At about the same time that Piaget was conducting his research in Switzerland, Russian psychologist Lev Vygotsky was developing a very different, sociocultural theory of how children develop. Vygotsky proposed that adults promote children's cognitive development by communicating the meanings that their culture assigns to objects and events, passing along physical and cognitive tools that make everyday tasks and problems easier, and assisting children with challenging tasks. In Vygotsky's view, social activities are often precursors to, and form the basis for, complex mental processes: Children initially use new skills in the course of interacting with adults or peers and slowly internalize and modify these skills for their own, independent use.

Contemporary theorists have extended Vygotsky's theory in several directions. For instance, some suggest that adults can help children benefit from their experiences through joint construction of meanings, guided participation, and cognitive apprenticeships. Others recommend that adults engage children in authentic, adultlike tasks, initially providing enough scaffolding that youngsters can accomplish the tasks successfully and gradually withdrawing it as proficiency increases. Still others have effectively combined Vygotsky's ideas with information processing theory to explore the roles of intersubjectivity, social construction of memory, and adult–child collaboration in children's learning and development.

Piaget's and Vygotsky's views of cognitive development share several common themes, including principles related to qualitative change, challenge, readiness, and social interaction. However, the two perspectives differ with regard to the role that language plays in cognitive development, the relative value of free exploration versus more structured and guided activities, the relative importance of interactions with peers versus adults, and the influence of culture.

CHAPTER 12

Metacognition, Self-Regulated Learning, and Study Strategies

When I look back on my days as a high school student, I think about how I used to learn, or at least *tried* to learn, and I shudder. Although I was a reasonably good student, my ideas about how I could best study were incredibly naive. For example, I remember sitting on my bed "reading" my history textbook at night: My eyes dutifully went down each page, focusing briefly on every line, but my mind was many miles away. After completing a reading assignment, I often couldn't remember a thing I had read, yet I had the crazy notion that my supposed knowledge of history would miraculously come to mind at test time (it didn't). I remember, too, studying vocabulary words for my class in Mandarin Chinese: I truly believed that simply repeating the words over and over again would get them through my thick skull. In retrospect, the only subject I learned well was mathematics, because the various mathematical concepts and principles I studied seemed quite logical based on what I already knew.

When I went to college, I continued to bumble along, spending too much time in mindless reading and taking notes in class that I can now make very little sense of (I have to wonder how much they helped me even then). It was only after a great deal of studying experience and considerable trial and error that I began to realize how important it was that I pay attention to course material with my mind as well as my eyes and that I try to understand the things I was studying.

How, as a metacognitively naive high school student, the author read her history textbook.

A critical turning point of World War II was . . .
hmmm,
wonder what I should wear to school tomorrow . . .
December 7, 1941 . . .
I'm really angry at what Marjorie said to me in P.E. today . . .
next time I'll say something nasty back to her . . .
I bet I can come up with something clever . . .
let's see . . .
goodness, I've finished the first part of the chapter already.

As you have been reading this book, I hope you have been learning a great deal about how *you* learn and remember; perhaps you have also been modifying your approach to your own learning tasks. For example, you may now be trying to pay closer attention to what you read in textbooks and what you hear in class. You may also be focusing more on understanding, organizing, and elaborating on your course material. In any case, I hope you are not reading this book the way I used to read my history text.

People's knowledge of their own learning and cognitive processes, as well as their regulation of those processes to enhance learning and memory, are collectively known as **metacognition.**[1] The more metacognitively sophisticated students are, the better their school learning and achievement are likely to be. Unfortunately, many students of all ages (even many adults) appear to know little about effective ways to learn and remember (Dryden & Jefferson, 1994; Mayer, 1996b; Pintrich & De Groot, 1990; Schofield & Kirby, 1994; J. W. Thomas, 1993a).

Metacognition is closely related to that *central executive* I spoke of in chapter 7. You might think of it as the "manager" or "coach" of a person's learning (Schoenfeld, 1985): It guides information processing and monitors the effectiveness of the various strategies a learner is applying to a particular learning task. But just as the coach of a basketball team might be either quite knowledgeable about playing basketball or instead harbor some very counterproductive misconceptions about how best to play the game, so, too, can a learner's metacognitive knowledge be either a help or a hindrance in the learning process.

In this chapter, we will look at the many things that people's metacognitive knowledge and skills may include. We will revisit social cognitive theorists' notion of self-regulation, this time

---

[1]You may occasionally see terms such as *metamemory* and *hypercognition*.

applying it to an understanding of how learners regulate their learning and cognitive processes in the pursuit of specific learning tasks. We will examine numerous learning and study strategies that appear to promote effective learning and retention of classroom material and consider how students' *epistemological beliefs*—their beliefs about the nature of knowledge and learning—influence how they study and learn. We will discover that students' learning strategies improve with age but that students don't always use effective strategies even when they may be capable of doing so. Finally, we will identify instructional practices that can help students become metacognitively more sophisticated, and thus better able to learn and achieve in the classroom, over the long run.

METACOGNITIVE KNOWLEDGE AND SKILLS

Metacognition includes knowledge and skills such as the following:

- Being aware of what one's own learning and memory capabilities are and of what learning tasks can realistically be accomplished (e.g., recognizing that it probably isn't possible to memorize everything in a 200-page reading assignment in a single evening)
- Knowing which learning strategies are effective and which are not (e.g., realizing that meaningful learning is more likely to lead to long-term retention than rote learning)
- Planning an approach to a learning task that is likely to be successful (e.g., finding a place to study where there will be few distractions)
- Using effective learning strategies (e.g., taking detailed notes when lecture material is likely to be difficult to remember)
- Monitoring one's present knowledge state (e.g., recognizing when information has been learned and when it has not)
- Knowing effective strategies for retrieval of previously stored information (e.g., thinking about the context in which a certain piece of information was probably learned)

In essence, then, metacognition is *thinking about thinking*. As you can see, it involves some fairly complex (and often abstract) ideas and processes. Many of these ideas and processes are not specifically taught in the classroom. Thus, it should not surprise you to learn that students typically acquire metacognitive knowledge and skills slowly and only after many challenging learning experiences, nor should it be surprising that some students develop few if any effective study strategies at all.

As an example of metacognition, let's consider what happens when students study their textbooks. Their reading in this situation is not just a process of identifying the words on the page, nor is it just making sense of the sentences and paragraphs in which those words appear. Students are also trying to store the information they read in long-term memory so that they can retrieve it later on. In other words, they are *reading for learning*.

What specifically do students do when they read for learning? Good readers—those who understand and effectively remember what they read—do many of the following:

- Clarify their purpose for reading something
- Read differently depending on whether they want to ascertain the gist of a passage, learn the passage's content thoroughly and in great detail, or simply read for pleasure

- Determine what is most important to learn and remember, and focus their attention and efforts on that material
- Try to make sense of and elaborate on (e.g., draw inferences from and identify logical relationships within) what they read
- Bring their prior knowledge into play in understanding and elaborating on what they read
- Envision possible examples and applications of the ideas presented
- Make predictions about what they are likely to read next in a passage
- Ask themselves questions that they try to answer as they read
- Periodically check themselves to make sure they understand and remember what they have read
- Try to clarify any seemingly ambiguous points
- Persist in their efforts to understand when they initially have trouble understanding something
- Read for possible conceptual change—in other words, read with the understanding that the ideas they encounter may be inconsistent with things they currently believe
- Critically evaluate what they read
- Summarize what they have read
  (Baker, 1989; Barnett, 1999; Brown & Palincsar, 1987; Brown, Palincsar, & Armbruster, 1984; Chan, Burtis, & Bereiter, 1997; Dole et al., 1991; Hacker, 1998b; Myers & Duffy, 1990; Palincsar & Brown, 1989; Roth & Anderson, 1988; Schraw & Bruning, 1995; vander Broek, 1990)

In contrast, poor readers—those who have trouble learning and remembering the things they read—use few of the strategies I've just listed. For example, they have little focus and sense of purpose as they read a passage (Brown & Palincsar, 1987). They have

How the author *should* have read her history textbook.

A critical turning point of World War II was the Japanese attack on Pearl Harbor on December 7, 1941 . . . why would the attack on Pearl Harbor have been so important for the outcome of the war? . . . probably because it forced the United States to enter the war, greatly increasing the number of ships, guns, and troops available to the Allies.

difficulty drawing inferences from the ideas they encounter (Oakhill, 1993). They rarely ask themselves questions about the material, predict what's coming next, clarify ambiguous statements, or summarize what they've read (Palincsar & Brown, 1984). They overlook inconsistencies among ideas within the text, as well as inconsistencies between those ideas and their prior beliefs about the world (Brown & Palincsar, 1987; Roth & Anderson, 1988). And, in general, poor readers seem to have little metacognitive awareness of the things they should do mentally as they read (Baker, 1989). As examples, consider three high school students' descriptions of how they studied:

- I stare real hard at the page, blink my eyes and then open them—and cross my fingers that it will be right here (points at head).
- It's easy. If [the teacher] says study, I read it twice. If she says read, it's just once through.
- I just read the first line in each paragraph—it's usually all there. (Brown & Palincsar, 1987, p. 83)

As you might guess, these students did *not* learn very effectively from the things they were reading (Brown & Palincsar, 1987).

Not all students are so metacognitively naive. For example, as 9-year-old Eamon describes what he does when he encounters new ideas in science, he seems to have a fairly good understanding of meaningful learning and the dynamic nature of knowledge:

I try to look for a fit. Like if it doesn't fit with any . . . of the ideas that I have in my head I just leave it and wait for other ideas to come in so that I can try to fit them together with my ideas. Maybe they will go with my ideas and then another idea will come in and I can fit it together with that idea and my understanding just keeps on enlarging. An idea usually does fit. (Hennessey, 2003, p. 123)

It appears, then, that Eamon has some explicit knowledge of his own thought processes: He can actively think about and describe them. Yet a good deal of metacognition may be *implicit:* People often regulate their learning processes without conscious awareness that they are doing so.[2]

The process of metacognition is consistent with social cognitive theorists' notion of *self-regulation:* It provides the mechanism through which people begin to regulate one aspect of their lives—their own learning. Let's look more closely at what self-regulated learning involves.

SELF-REGULATED LEARNING

In our discussion of self-regulation in chapter 6, we discovered that as children grow older, most of them begin to set standards and goals for their own performance. They then choose behaviors that they think will help them meet such standards and goals, and they evaluate the effects of their actions.

Social cognitive theorists and cognitivists alike have begun to portray effective learning in a similar manner—as a process of setting goals, choosing learning strategies that are likely to help

---

[2]Some theorists propose that metacognition includes both explicit and implicit knowledge, but others suggest that we should use the term only to refer to knowledge and processes of which people are consciously aware (e.g., Brown, Bransford, Ferrera, & Campione, 1983; diSessa et al., 2003; Hacker, 1998a). I will use the term in its broader sense, which encompasses both explicit and implicit knowledge.

one achieve those goals, and then evaluating the results of one's efforts (Paris & Cunningham, 1996; Schunk & Zimmerman, 1994; Winne, 1995a; Zimmerman, 1998, 2004). Yet increasingly, theorists have begun to realize that effective learning includes control of one's motivation and emotions as well. Thus, **self-regulated learning** typically includes most or all of the following:

♦ *Goal setting:* Identifying one or more desired end results for a learning activity. Self-regulated learners know what they want to accomplish when they read or study; for instance, they may want to learn specific facts, get an overall understanding of the ideas being presented, or simply acquire sufficient knowledge to do well on a classroom exam (Mayer, 1996b; Nolen, 1996; Winne & Hadwin, 1998; Wolters, 1998). Typically, they tie their goals for a particular learning activity to their longer-term goals and aspirations (Zimmerman, 1998, 2004). And especially as they reach college, they may set deadlines for themselves as a way of making sure they don't leave important learning tasks until the last minute (Ariely & Wertenbroch, 2002).

♦ *Planning:* Determining how best to use the time available for a learning task. Self-regulated learners plan ahead with regard to a learning task and use their time effectively to accomplish their goals (Zimmerman, 1998; Zimmerman & Risemberg, 1997). Typically they devote more time to more difficult material, although they may sometimes review easy material to make sure they still know it, and they may intentionally ignore material they think is *so* difficult that they can't possibly master it in the time they have (Metcalfe, 2002; Son & Metcalfe, 2000; Son & Schwartz, 2002).

♦ *Self-motivation:* Maintaining motivation to complete a learning task. Self-regulated learners are likely to have high self-efficacy regarding their ability to accomplish a learning task (Schunk & Pajares, 2004; Zimmerman & Risemberg, 1997). They also show considerable self-discipline, putting work before pleasure (delaying gratification)—for instance, by diligently completing assigned tasks in class and at home (Duckworth & Seligman, 2005; Trautwein & Köller, 2004). And they use a variety of strategies to keep themselves on task—perhaps embellishing on the task to make it more fun, reminding themselves of the importance of doing well, giving themselves a self-efficacy "pep talk" ("I did well before, so I can certainly do well again!"), visualizing their eventual success, or promising themselves a reward when they are finished (Corno, 1993; Wolters, 2000, 2003a; Wolters & Rosenthal, 2000).

♦ *Attention control:* Maximizing attention on the learning task. Self-regulated learners try to focus their attention on the subject matter at hand and to clear their minds of potentially distracting thoughts and emotions (Harnishfeger, 1995; Kuhl, 1985; Winne, 1995a; Wolters, 2003a).

♦ *Application of learning strategies:* Selecting and using appropriate ways of cognitively processing the material to be learned. Self-regulated learners have a wide variety of learning strategies at their disposal, and they use different ones depending on the specific goal they want to accomplish. For example, they read a magazine article differently depending on whether they are reading it for entertainment or studying for an exam (Linderholm, Gustafson, van den Broek, & Lorch, 1997; Schunk & Zimmerman, 1997; Winne, 1995a; Wolters, 2003a).

♦ *Self-monitoring:* Checking periodically to see whether progress is being made toward the goal(s) of a learning activity. Self-regulated learners continually monitor their progress during a learning activity, and they change their learning strategies or modify their goals if necessary (Butler & Winne, 1995; Carver & Scheier, 1990; Thiede, Anderson, & Therriault, 2003; Zimmerman, 1998).

◆ *Appropriate help-seeking:* Seeking assistance that might faciliate learning. Self-regulated learning doesn't always involve learning independently. Self-regulated learners know when they need an expert's help to master certain topics or skills, and on such occasions they actively seek it out (Aleven, Stahl, Schworm, Fischer, & Wallace, 2003; Karabenick & Sharma, 1994; A. M. Ryan, Pintrich, & Midgley, 2001).

◆ *Self-evaluation:* Assessing the final outcome of one's efforts. Self-regulated learners determine whether what they have learned is sufficient for the goal(s) they have set for themselves (Butler & Winne, 1995; Schraw & Moshman, 1995; Zimmerman & Schunk, 2004).

◆ *Self-reflection:* Determining the extent to which one's learning strategies have been successful and efficient, and possibly identifying alternatives that may be more effective in future learning situations (Kuhn, 2001b; Winne & Stockley, 1998; Zimmerman, 1998, 2004).

When students are self-regulated learners, they set higher academic goals for themselves, learn more effectively, and achieve at higher levels in the classroom (Bronson, 2000; Butler & Winne, 1995; Winne, 1995a; Zimmerman & Bandura, 1994; Zimmerman & Risemberg, 1997). Unfortunately, few students acquire a high level of self-regulation, perhaps in part because traditional instructional practices do little to promote it (Paris & Ayres, 1994; Zimmerman & Bandura, 1994).

The Roots of Self–Regulated Learning

To some extent, self-regulated learning probably develops from opportunities to engage in independent, self-directed learning activities appropriate for the age group (Corno & Mandinach, 2004; Paris & Paris, 2001; Vye et al., 1998; Zimmerman, 2004). Regular exposure to self-regulating models—adults and peers who set high standards for their own performance, effectively keep themselves on task, and so on—may play a role as well (Corno & Mandinach, 2004; Zimmerman, 2004).

But if we take Vygotsky's perspective for a moment, we might reasonably suspect that self-regulated learning also has roots in socially regulated learning (Stright, Neitzel, Sears, & Hoke-Sinex, 2001; Vygotsky, 1962). At first, other people (e.g., parents or teachers) might help children learn by setting goals for a learning activity, keeping children's attention focused on the learning task, suggesting effective learning strategies, monitoring learning progress, and so on. Over time, children assume increasing responsibility for these processes; that is, they begin to set their *own* learning goals, stay on task with little prodding from others, identify potentially effective strategies, and evaluate their own learning.

How might children make the transition from other-regulated learning to self-regulated learning? A possible answer can be found in our previous discussion of collaborative use of cognitive strategies in chapter 11. From a Vygotskian perspective, a reasonable bridge between other-regulated learning and self-regulated learning is **co-regulated learning**, in which an adult and one or more children share responsibility for directing the various aspects of the learning process (Bodrova & Leong, 1996; McCaslin & Good, 1996; McCaslin & Hickey, 2001). For instance, the adult and children might agree on the specific goals of a learning endeavor, or the adult might describe the criteria that indicate successful learning and then have children evaluate their own performance in light of those criteria. Initially, the adult might provide considerable structure, or scaffolding, for the children's learning efforts; in a true Vygotskian fashion, such scaffolding is gradually removed as children become more effectively self-regulating.

Later in the chapter, we will consider several strategies that teachers can use to facilitate the development of self-regulation in students at a variety of age levels. Before we can do so, however, we must find out more about what metacognitive processes entail. At this point, let's consider what research has to say about effective learning and study strategies.

EFFECTIVE LEARNING AND STUDY STRATEGIES

In my descriptions of cognitive theories in earlier chapters, I have often alluded to people's strategies for learning, studying, solving problems, and so on. Perhaps we should stop for a moment to consider what we actually mean by the term *strategy*. Sometimes people engage in effective storage processes with little conscious awareness of what they are doing (Kintsch, 1998; Stanovich, 1999). For instance, as you read an enjoyable novel, you may automatically relate events in the story to similar events in your own life. But generally speaking, when psychologists use the terms **learning strategy** and **study strategy**, they are talking about the *intentional* use of one or more cognitive processes to accomplish a particular learning task (Alexander, Graham, & Harris, 1998; Siegler & Alibali, 2005; Snowman, 1986).[3]

People do a lot of things "in their heads" when they want to learn and remember new material, but some strategies are clearly more effective than others. In the next few pages, we will consider research findings regarding several effective learning and study strategies. The first three—meaningful learning, elaboration, and organization—are long-term memory storage processes that we initially encountered in chapter 8. The others—note taking, identifying important information, summarizing, comprehension monitoring, and mnemonics—are additional strategies that researchers have consistently found to be valuable techniques in academic learning tasks.

Meaningful Learning and Elaboration

In chapter 8, I described *meaningful learning* as a process of relating new material to knowledge already stored in long-term memory and *elaboration* as a process of using prior knowledge to interpret and expand on that new material. Both processes involve making connections between new information and the things we already know, and both processes clearly facilitate our learning as we study (Dole et al., 1991; Pressley & Hilden, 2006; Waters, 1982; Weinstein, 1978; Wittrock & Alesandrini, 1990).

A study by Van Rossum and Schenk (1984) illustrates this point well. College students studied and took notes on a historical passage, then took a test on the contents of the passage and answered questions about how they had studied. Approximately half of the students described rote-learning

---

[3]Snowman (1986) has suggested that we distinguish between more general *learning strategies* (overall plans for accomplishing a learning task) and *learning tactics* (more specific techniques executed during the learning task itself). For the most part, the strategies I describe in this chapter are of the more specific, tactical type.

approaches to studying; they interpreted the objective of the assignment as one of memorizing facts (as one student described it, "learning everything by heart"). The other half described meaningful and elaborative approaches to the study process: They attempted to understand, interpret, abstract meaning, and apply what they read. One student's self-report illustrates the latter approach:

> First I read the text roughly through and try to form a picture of the content. The second time I read more accurately and try through the structure of the text to make the small connections in and between the paragraphs. The third or fourth time I try to repeat to myself, without looking at the text, the main lines of the argument, emphasizing reasonings. This is my usual way to study texts. (Van Rossum & Schenk, 1984, p. 77)

There were no differences between the two groups of students in their performance on multiple-choice questions that assessed their knowledge of facts in the passage. However, students who used meaningful learning strategies performed better on multiple-choice questions that required drawing inferences and produced better-integrated and qualitatively superior responses on an essay test over the same material.

Students appear to learn classroom subject matter very differently depending on whether they are trying to remember facts or generate applications—in other words, depending on whether they are trying to elaborate on what they learn. In a study conducted by one of my doctoral students, Rose McCallin (McCallin, Ormrod, & Cochran, 1997), undergraduate education majors who were enrolled in two educational psychology classes completed a questionnaire that assessed their approach to learning the course material. Some students described themselves as wanting to learn specific teaching techniques; in other words, they wanted to be told exactly what they should do as teachers in the classroom. Other students described themselves as preferring to understand psychological principles of human learning and behavior so that they could develop their *own* classroom procedures. Following the course's unit on educational testing and measurement, McCallin gave the students a list of basic concepts in educational assessment and asked them to draw a diagram (concept map) that showed how the concepts were related to one another. Students with a tell-me-what-to-do attitude tended to depict relationships among concepts that were simplistically factual or procedural (e.g., "*Raw scores* are used to compute a *mean*"). In contrast, students with a let-me-apply-it-myself attitude described conceptual interrelationships that reflected more sophisticated processing, including hierarchical structures, cause-effect relationships, and deductive reasoning (e.g., "*Reliability* affects the *standard error of measurement*"). Although McCallin did not study how well the students remembered course material after the semester was over, we could reasonably predict that the latter kind of students—those who developed a well-integrated and elaborated understanding of the topic in question so that they could apply it themselves—would be able to retrieve and reconstruct the course material more effectively. And, for reasons that you will discover in our discussion of transfer and problem solving in the next chapter, such students should also be able to apply principles of educational psychology more readily to new situations and problems.

Organization

In chapter 8, we examined evidence for the importance of *internal organization*—finding connections and interrelationships within a body of new information—for long-term memory storage. Making oneself aware of the inherent organizational structure of new material facilitates learning; so, too, does imposing an organizational structure on material when a structure doesn't initially exist (Britton et al., 1998; Gauntt, 1991; Kail, 1990; Wade, 1992).

Nevertheless, students often fail to construct appropriate organizational structures for information presented in lectures and written materials. Rather than recognizing and taking advantage of the interrelationships inherent in a body of information, students frequently "organize" various ideas simply as a list of unrelated facts (Meyer, Brandt, & Bluth, 1980). Furthermore, students are less likely to organize learning material as it becomes more difficult for them (Kletzien, 1988).

Students can use several techniques to help them organize classroom material effectively. One common approach is to create an outline of the major topics and ideas. When students learn how to outline the things they hear in lectures and read in textbooks, their classroom learning often improves (McDaniel & Einstein, 1989; Wade, 1992). Curiously, however, good students are *less* likely to outline classroom material than their more "average" classmates (Baker, 1989). It may be that better students organize material easily enough in their heads that paper-and-pencil outlines aren't necessary.

A second approach involves creating a graphic representation of the information to be learned—perhaps a map, flow chart, pie chart, or matrix (Dansereau, 1995; B. F. Jones, Pierce, & Hunter, 1988/1989; Scevak, Moore, & Kirby, 1993; Van Patten, Chao, & Reigeluth, 1986). For example, high school students can remember historical events more effectively when they put information about important events on a map depicting where each event took place (Scevak et al., 1993). As another example, consider how students might better remember the sequence in which various historical events took place. A number of years ago, my son Alex (then a high school senior) and I took an undergraduate art history course at my university. The first unit of the course covered a 40,000-year span, including prehistoric art (e.g., cave paintings), Mesopotamian art (e.g., the Gates of Ishtar), and ancient Egyptian art (e.g., the pyramids at Giza). As we studied for our first test, Alex and I had a hard time keeping the time periods of all of the cultures and artistic styles straight. We finally constructed a time line, depicted in Figure 12.1, that organized what was happening when and kept us from going into severe numbers shock. The time line didn't necessarily help us make better sense of events, but it did help us keep track of them. It also provided a way for us to encode the information visually as well as verbally (B. F. Jones et al., 1988/1989).

Another graphic technique for organizing information is concept mapping (Krajcik, 1991; Mintzes, Wandersee, & Novak, 1997; Novak & Gowin, 1984). In chapter 8, I described a *concept map* as a way that teachers can depict the overall organizational structure of a lesson or unit (refer back to Figure 8.10 as an example). Yet students can also create their *own* concept maps for a lesson. Figure 12.2 shows concept maps constructed by two fifth-grade students after they watched a slide-show lecture on Australia. Notice how very different the knowledge of the two children appears to be, even though both children received the same information.

Self-constructed concept maps often facilitate students' classroom performance, probably for several reasons (Holley & Dansereau, 1984; Mintzes et al., 1997; Novak, 1998; Novak & Gowin, 1984). By focusing on how concepts relate to one another, students organize material better. They are also more likely to notice how new concepts are related to things they already know; thus, they are more likely to learn the material meaningfully. And, like such graphic techniques as maps and time lines, concept maps can help students encode information in long-term memory visually as well as verbally. Concept maps are especially helpful to low-achieving students, perhaps because they provide a means of helping these students process information in ways that high-achieving

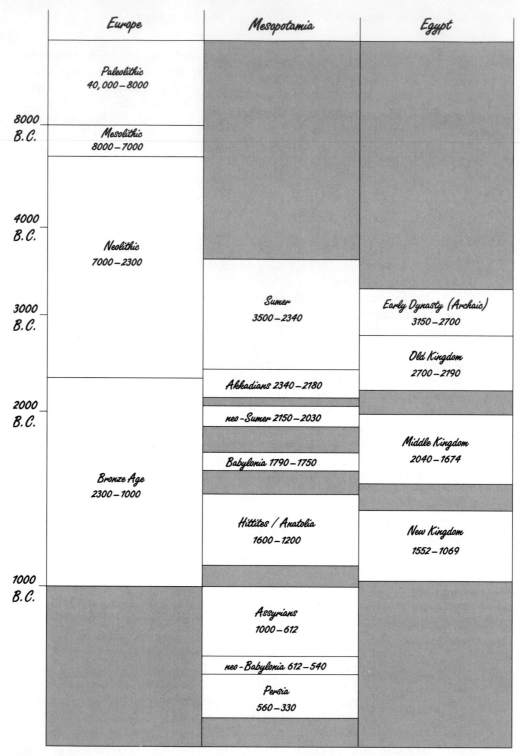

Figure 12.1
The Ormrod time line for prehistoric, Mesopotamian, and ancient Egyptian art.

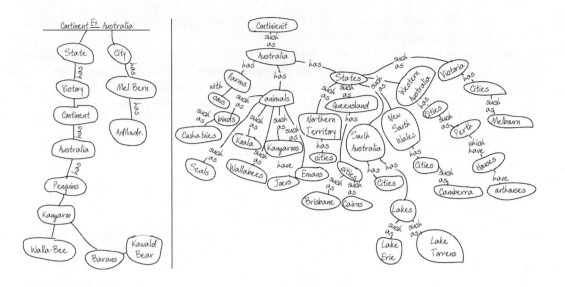

Figure 12.2

Concept maps constructed by two fifth-grade students after watching a slide lecture on Australia.

From *Learning How to Learn* (pp. 100–101) by J. D. Novak & D. B. Gowin, 1984, Cambridge, England: Cambridge University Press. Copyright 1984 by Cambridge University Press. Reprinted with the permission of Cambridge University Press.

students do more regularly (Dansereau, 1995; Lambiotte, Dansereau, Cross, & Reynolds, 1989; Mintzes et al., 1997; Stensvold & Wilson, 1990).

Student-constructed concept maps can provide information to teachers as well as to students; in particular, such maps may indicate possible misconceptions and "holes" in students' understanding (Novak, 1998; Novak & Gowin, 1984; Novak & Musonda, 1991). If you look carefully at the concept map on the left side of Figure 12.2, you should detect several misconceptions that the student has about Australia. For example, Adelaide is *not* part of Melbourne; it is a different city altogether! If geographic knowledge about Australia is an instructional objective, then this student clearly needs further instruction to correct such misinformation.

Note Taking

In general, taking notes on information presented in lectures and textbooks is positively correlated with student learning (Benton, Kiewra, Whitfill, & Dennison, 1993; Cohn, Hult, & Engle, 1990; Peverly, Brobst, Graham, & Shaw, 2003; Shrager & Mayer, 1989). Note taking probably serves two functions for students (Di Vesta & Gray, 1972; Kiewra, 1989). For one thing, it facilitates *encoding* of material: By writing information and looking at it on paper, students are likely to encode it both verbally and visually. As evidence for the encoding function of note taking, students remember more when they take notes even if they have no opportunity to review the notes (Howe, 1970; Weinstein & Mayer, 1986). In addition, notes serve as a form of concrete *external storage* for information presented in class: Given the notorious fallibility of long-term memory (see chapter 10), pen and paper often provide a dependable alternative (Benton et al., 1993). Once lecture content is recorded on paper, it can be reviewed at regular intervals later on.

In my own classes, I have often observed how very different the notes of different students can be, even though all of the students sit through the same class sessions. Some students write extensively; others write very little. Some students try to capture all of the main ideas of a lecture or explanation, whereas others copy only the specific words I write on the board— mostly terms and their definitions. Some students include details and examples in their notes; others do not.

Not surprisingly, the effectiveness of note taking depends on the type of notes taken. Notes are more useful when they are relatively complete representations of the presented material (Benton et al., 1993; Cohn et al., 1990; Kiewra, 1989). They are more likely to promote learning when they represent an encoding of the information that is consistent with the objectives of the instructional unit; hence, those objectives should be clear to students (Barnett, Di Vesta, & Rogozinski, 1981; Snowman, 1986). Notes are also more likely to be effective when they summarize main ideas and include details that support those ideas (Brown, Campione, & Day, 1981; Doctorow, Wittrock, & Marks, 1978; Kiewra, 1985; Peverly et al., 2003; Taylor, 1982). And notes that go beyond the material—those that include students' own elaborations of it—may be especially beneficial (Barnett et al., 1981; Kiewra, 1989; King, 1992).

Another effective technique is reorganizing and elaborating on notes that were previously taken during a lecture or reading assignment (DuBois, Kiewra, & Fraley, 1988; Kiewra, 1985; Kiewra et al., 1988; Shimmerlick & Nolan, 1976). Especially in a lecture, students have no control over how fast information is presented and may not have time to process everything meaningfully. In such a case, students may need to focus merely on writing information during class and then organizing and encoding it appropriately afterward.

Unfortunately, many students (especially those at the junior high and high school, rather than college, levels) have difficulty understanding their own notes when they use them to review class material at a later time (Yokoi, 1997). Teachers can do some very simple things to improve the quality and completeness of the notes that students take. Writing important ideas on the chalkboard may be helpful: Students are far more likely to write down those things that their

The effectiveness of note taking depends on the type of notes taken.

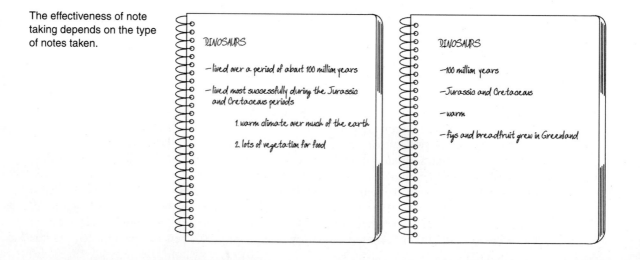

teacher writes. Emphasizing important ideas (e.g., by repeating them) also increases the likeli-hood that students will record the ideas on paper. Furthermore, providing some kind of general organizational framework—a skeletal outline, a compare-and-contrast matrix, or the like—facilitates students' ability to organize information in ways that the teacher envisions (Benton et al., 1993; Kiewra, 1989; Pressley, Yokoi, Van Meter, Van Etten, & Freebern, 1997; Van Meter, Yokoi, & Pressley, 1994; Yokoi, 1997).

Identifying Important Information

Students frequently encounter more information than they can possibly store in long-term memory within a reasonable time period. As a result, they must determine which things are most important for them to learn and study—for instance, they must separate main ideas from trivial details (Dole et al., 1991; Reynolds & Shirey, 1988). The task is often a challenging one, in part because the relative "importance" of different ideas is ultimately determined by the teacher, who may have a different per-spective on the material than students do (Alexander & Jetton, 1996; Broekkamp, Van Hout-Wolters, Rijlaarsdam, & van den Bergh, 2002; Schellings, Van Hout-Wolters, & Vermunt, 1996).

The various *signals* that are present in a lecture or textbook (e.g., specified objectives of a les-son, boldfaced or italicized words, ideas written on the chalkboard) can help students discrimi-nate between important and unimportant information (recall our discussion of signals near the end of chapter 8). In some instances, however, students may overlook or misinterpret such signals; in other instances, existing signals may be few and far between. In the absence of useful signals, students often have trouble identifying the main points of a lecture or reading assign-ment; this is particularly true when they have little background knowledge about the subject matter they are studying (Byrnes, 1996; Dole et al., 1991; Garner et al., 1991). Many students use relatively inadequate methods of selecting information—for example, focusing on first sen-tences of paragraphs or on distinctive pieces of information (such as definitions and formulas)—and often miss critical ideas as a result (Mayer, 1984; Pallock & Surber, 1997; Surber, 2001).

Once students become proficient at identifying important information, then underlining or highlighting the information—at least in materials that students own, such as class notes and purchased textbooks—is likely to be beneficial. I encourage my own students to underline or highlight the important points that their textbooks present; doing so is less time consuming than taking notes on a book's content, and it keeps specific information within its larger context. But underlining and highlighting are probably effective only when used sparingly to emphasize main ideas and essential details (Snowman, 1986). Highlighting an entire page, as if with a paint roller, can hardly be of much value.

Summarizing

Students are sometimes encouraged to summarize the material they read and hear—for instance, by condensing and integrating it, deriving abstract representations of it, or identify-ing suitable headings to label it. Doing so seems to facilitate learning and retention of the material (Dole et al., 1991; Jonassen, Hartley, & Trueman, 1986; King, 1992; Rinehart, Stahl, & Erickson, 1986; Wade-Stein & Kintsch, 2004; Wittrock & Alesandrini, 1990).

Unfortunately, many students have difficulty adequately summarizing the things they read and hear (Anderson & Hidi, 1988/1989; Brown & Palincsar, 1987; Byrnes, 1996;

Jonassen et al., 1986). If we think about it, we realize that developing a good summary is not an easy task at all: Students must discriminate between important and unimportant information, identify main ideas that may or may not be explicitly stated, and organize critical elements into a cohesive whole (Anderson & Hidi, 1988/1989; Greene & Ackerman, 1995; Spivey, 1997). In classrooms, students must also have some sense of how they are going to be evaluated and tailor their summaries to the evaluation criteria (Snowman, 1986).

Theorists have offered several suggestions for helping students create good summaries of classroom subject matter:

- Have students first practice developing summaries for short, easy, and well-organized passages (perhaps those only a few paragraphs in length), then gradually introduce longer and more difficult texts for them to summarize.
- When students are writing a summary, suggest that they:
  - Identify or invent a topic sentence for each paragraph or section.
  - Identify superordinate concepts or ideas that subsume several more specific points.
  - Find supporting information for each main idea.
  - Delete trivial and redundant information.
- Have students compare and discuss their summaries, considering what ideas they thought were important and why. (Anderson & Hidi, 1988/1989; Brown & Day, 1983; Rinehart et al., 1986; Rosenshine & Meister, 1992)

Such strategies do seem to help students to write better summaries and, ultimately, to learn and remember classroom material more effectively (Bean & Steenwyk, 1984; Pressley, with McCormick, 1995; Rinehart et al., 1986).

Comprehension Monitoring

Students who learn most effectively typically check themselves periodically to be sure they are understanding and remembering what they hear in class or read in a textbook. They also take steps to remediate any comprehension difficulties they have—for example, by asking questions or rereading a passage. In other words, good students engage in **comprehension monitoring**[4] (Baker, 1989; Dole et al., 1991; Hacker, Dunlosky, & Graesser, 1998; Haller, Child, & Walberg, 1988; Otero & Kintsch, 1992).

Unfortunately, many students of all ages *don't* carefully monitor their comprehension as they sit in class or read a textbook (Baker & Brown, 1984; Flavell, 1979; Hacker, Bol, Horgan, & Rakow, 2000; Otero, 1998). As a result, they are often ignorant about what they know and what they don't know, and they may think they understand something they actually *mis*understand. In other words, they have an **illusion of knowing**[5] (Baker, 1989; Brown, 1978; Butler & Winne, 1995; Hacker, 1998b; Voss & Schauble, 1992). Students are especially likely to have an illusion of knowing something when they have little prior knowledge about the subject matter or when the material is especially difficult for them (Hacker, 1998a; Maki, 1998; Stone, 2000; Winne & Jamieson-Noel, 2001). Illusions of knowing are also more common when students have overly

---

[4]Theorists are talking about a similar idea when they use the terms *metacomprehension, self-regulated comprehension, calibration, judgment of learning,* and *metamnemonic evaluation.*

[5]You may also see the term *secondary ignorance.*

simplistic ideas of what it means to "know" something (more on this idea in the upcoming section on epistemological beliefs).

When students think they know classroom material, they are likely to stop studying it. Thus, students who have only the *illusion* of knowing it will stop studying prematurely (Dunning, Heath, & Suls, 2004; Horgan, 1990; Voss & Schauble, 1992). And they are likely to be quite puzzled when, as a result, they perform poorly on an exam or assignment (Hacker et al., 2000; Horgan, 1990). For example, students occasionally approach me to express their confusion about why they did so poorly on an exam when they "knew" the information so well. When I ask these students specific questions about the material, I usually find that they don't really have a good grasp of it at all.

One strategy for facilitating students' comprehension monitoring is to have them draw pictures or diagrams of the material they are studying (Van Meter, 2001); such a strategy may be especially useful for topics that involve spatial arrangements or cause–effect relationships. Another approach is to have students formulate questions before a lesson or reading assignment that they then answer as they go along (Bragstad & Stumpf, 1982; Robinson, 1961; Rosenshine, Meister, & Chapman, 1996; E. L. Thomas & Robinson, 1972). For instance, before reading a textbook, a student might turn each heading and subheading into a question to be answered and then read sections of text with the intention of finding answers to the questions (Robinson, 1961). Such **self-questioning** is probably even more effective when students do it *throughout* a lesson or reading assignment (Brozo, Stahl, & Gordon, 1985; Dole et al., 1991; Haller et al., 1988; Wong, 1985). For example, undergraduate students who ask themselves questions as they take notes during a class lecture take better notes, understand the material better, and remember it longer (King, 1992; Spires, 1990).

By asking themselves questions periodically, students are more likely to know when they know something and when they do not. After reviewing research on the effectiveness of self-questioning, however, Snowman (1986) concluded that positive effects are limited to the acquisition of facts, without any noticeable impact on more sophisticated behaviors such as application or evaluation

Students are not always accurate judges of what they know and what they do not.

of those facts. This may be because most students ask themselves primarily fact-based questions (e.g., "When did Columbus reach the New World?") rather than higher-level questions (e.g., "Why did Columbus risk his life to find a new route to India?"), perhaps because they have learned to expect mostly fact-based questions on their classroom examinations (Jackson, Ormrod, & Salih, 1996, 1999). To promote meaningful learning, elaboration, and, in general, higher-level processing of information, teachers might encourage students to continually ask themselves questions such as the following:

- Explain why (how) . . .
- What is the main idea of . . . ?
- How would you use . . . to . . . ?
- What is a new example of . . . ?
- What do you think would happen if . . . ?
- What is the difference between . . . and . . . ?
- How are . . . and . . . similar?
- What conclusions can you draw about . . . ?
- How does . . . affect . . . ?
- What are the strengths and weaknesses of . . . ?
- What is the best . . . and why?
- How is . . . related to . . . that we studied earlier?
   (King, 1992, p. 309)

Ideally, students should assess their understanding of class material at some later time as well. People are often inaccurate and overly optimistic judges of how much they will be able to remember about something they have just read (Nelson & Dunlosky, 1991; Pressley, Borkowski, & Schneider, 1987; Weaver & Kelemen, 1997). In a simple illustration of this principle (Nelson & Dunlosky, 1991), undergraduate students studied a series of 60 paired associates (e.g., *ocean–tree*) for 8 seconds apiece. Students were asked how confident they were that in 10 minutes' time they would be able to remember the second word in each pair when cued with the first; this question was sometimes asked immediately after a word pair had been presented (the immediate condition) and sometimes asked after several minutes had elapsed (the delayed condition). After studying all 60 pairs, students were tested for their actual ability to recall the second word in every pair. Their estimates of how much they would remember were far more accurate for word pairs in the delayed condition than for pairs in the immediate condition; in the immediate condition, students believed they would remember many more pairs than they actually did. The problem with judging one's knowledge of something immediately after studying it, Nelson and Dunlosky reasoned, is that the information is still in working memory and therefore can easily be retrieved. Ideally, students need to judge the likelihood that they can retrieve information from long-term memory as well—something they can judge only when they monitor their comprehension after several minutes, hours, or days have elapsed.

Mnemonics

Most of the strategies we've discussed so far are based on the assumption that the material makes sense and can be logically organized. But if you reflect back on your own educational experiences, you can probably recall many situations in which you had trouble learning important information because it didn't hang together in any logical way. Perhaps the troublesome material consisted of long lists of items, unfamiliar vocabulary words in a foreign language, or particular rules of grammar, spelling, or mathematics. **Mnemonics**—memory "tricks"—are devices that facilitate the learning and recall of many forms of hard-to-remember material. Here we will look at three general types of mnemonics: verbal mediation, visual imagery, and superimposed meaningful structures.

Verbal Mediation

Imagine you are trying to learn that the German word *Handschuh* means *glove*. Playing off how the word sounds phonetically, you might remember this word by thinking of a glove as a "shoe for the hand." Such a mnemonic is an example of **verbal mediation,** in which two words or ideas are associated by a word or phrase (the verbal mediator) that connects them. Here are some examples of verbal mediators for other German vocabulary words:

German Word	English Meaning	Mediator
der Hund	dog	hound
das Schwein	pig	swine
die Gans	goose	gander
der Stier	bull	steer

Notice that in every case, the verbal mediator bridges the gap between the German word and its English equivalent. By storing the mediator, you can make a connection between the two words.

Verbal mediators clearly facilitate learning (e.g., Bugelski, 1962), and their use is not necessarily restricted to the learning of foreign vocabulary words. For example, here is a mnemonic sometimes seen in spelling instruction:

The principal is my pal.

Retrieving this sentence will enable a student to remember that the correct spelling for a school administrator is "princi*pal*" rather than "princi*ple*." And as a high school student, my daughter remembered the chemical symbol for gold—Au—by thinking "*Ay, you* stole my *gold* watch!"

Visual Imagery

As we discovered in chapter 8, a visual image is a powerful storage mechanism that can be formed quickly and retained for a relatively long time. Accordingly, visual imagery forms the basis for a number of effective mnemonic devices. Three common ones are the method of loci, the pegword method, and the keyword method.

Method of loci   In the days of the Greek and Roman empires, orators used a particular technique to help them remember the major ideas they wished to include in their hours-long harangues at the forum (lecture notes were apparently not used very often in those days). The orators would think about a familiar route they walked frequently—the route from home to the forum, for example—and about the significant landmarks along the way—perhaps a bridge, a large tree, and a brothel, in that order. Then, when planning a speech, they would translate each key point into some sort of concrete, observable object and form a visual image of each successive key point located at a particular landmark along the familiar route. As an illustration, let's say that the first three points in an orator's speech were the frequent traffic jams near the forum, the importance of a mass transit system in downtown Rome, and the consequent necessity for a tax increase. He might store images such as these: (1) numerous horses and pedestrians entangled in a traffic jam on the bridge (first landmark), (2) a gigantic, 30-person chariot perched among the branches of the large tree (second landmark), and (3) several toga-clad prostitutes pitching coins at a tax collector from the upstairs window of the brothel (third landmark). Later, when pontificating at the forum, the orator would take a mental walk along his familiar route; as he passed each landmark, he would readily retrieve the image of that landmark and the object symbolizing the next major point of his speech. In this manner, he could easily remember all of the main ideas of the oration and their correct order.

This **method of loci** (*loci* is the Latin word for *places*) is clearly an effective mnemonic technique (Christen & Bjork, 1976; Groninger, 1971; Snowman, 1986) and lends itself readily to the storage and retention of lists of items. For example, in a study by Groninger (1971), some participants learned a list of 25 words using the method of loci while others learned the words simply by grouping them. People using the method of loci learned the words faster and remembered more of them on a free recall task five weeks later. Both groups performed equally well, however, when asked to recognize (rather than recall) the words; thus, it appears that the benefit of the method of loci may lie in the imagery-based retrieval cues it provides.

Pegword method   The **pegword method** is another technique for effectively learning a list of items and their relative positions (Bower, 1972; Bugelski, Kidd, & Segmen, 1968; Higbee, 1976; Mastropieri & Scruggs, 1989, 1992). This method consists of using a well-known or easily learned list of items that then serves as a series of "pegs" on which another list is "hung" through visual imagery. To illustrate, the following poem is sometimes used as a pegboard:

> One is a bun.
> Two is a shoe.
> Three is a tree.
> Four is a door.
> Five is a hive.
> Six is sticks.
> Seven is heaven.
> Eight is a gate.
> Nine is a line; and
> Ten is a hen.
> (Miller, Galanter, & Pribram, 1960, p. 135)

This poem should be an easy one to remember because its lines are composed of the numbers 1 through 10 in conjunction with rhyming nouns. Now suppose you need to remember a list of items in a certain order. You take the first item on your list and form a visual image of it interacting with the noun that rhymes with *one* (in this case, *bun*), then take the second list item and imagine it interacting with the noun that rhymes with *two* (shoe), and so on. Images can be formed quickly and typically need not be practiced to be remembered.

Consider this food chain as an example of a list you might learn using the "One is a bun" poem:

> *Algae* in a lake are eaten by
> *Water fleas,* which are eaten by
> *Minnows,* which are eaten by
> *Larger fish,* which are eaten by
> *Eagles.*

Using the pegword method, you form an image of algae and a bun together—perhaps a hamburger bun covered with green algae. Similarly, you visualize water fleas in conjunction with a shoe—perhaps you see a shoe filled with water and several water fleas doing the backstroke across the surface. For the last three items of the food chain, you might form images of a tree with minnows hanging down like fruit, a door with a large fish stuffed through the keyhole, and an eagle wearing a beehive for a hat. Remembering the food chain, then, is simply a matter of thinking "One is a bun," conjuring up the image of the bun with algae, then thinking "Two is a shoe," retrieving the shoe image, and so on.[6]

Keyword method   I have already described the use of verbal mediation in learning foreign language words. But as you may have noticed, the German words I chose for my illustrations of verbal mediation closely resembled English words. More often, however, words in a foreign language don't have an obvious relationship to their English meanings. In such situations, the **keyword method** provides an effective alternative. This technique, which is actually a combination of verbal mediation and visual imagery, involves two steps: (1) identifying an English word or phrase (the keyword) that sounds similar to the foreign word and then (2) forming a visual image of the English sound-alike word with the English meaning. For example, consider how we might remember these German words:

German Word	English Meaning	Keyword(s)	Visual Image
das Pferd	horse	Ford	A *horse* driving a *Ford*
das Kaninchen	rabbit	can on chin	A *rabbit* with a *can on* its *chin*
der Waschbär	raccoon	wash, bar	A *raccoon washing* with a *bar* of soap
das Stachelschwein	porcupine	stash, swine	A *porcupine stash*ing nuts under a pig (*swine*)

The keyword method has been shown to be an effective instructional device in teaching both English and foreign language vocabulary words (Atkinson, 1975; M. S. Jones et al., 2000; Levin, McCormick, Miller, Berry, & Pressley, 1982). It is also useful in teaching such paired associates as names and faces, states and their capitals, cities and their products, and famous people and their creations (Carney & Levin, 2000; Carney, Levin, & Stackhouse, 1997; Pressley,

Using a keyword to remember that a horse is a *Pferd*.

---

[6]My cousin Natalie Powell, who worked at Gallaudet College for many years, has given me a version of "One is a bun" that students who are deaf can use: *One is you, two is vegetable, three is rooster, four is football, five is paper, six is water, seven is smoking, eight is pumpkin, nine is Indian, ten is nut.* Each number is matched with a word that involves similar hand movements in American Sign Language.

Levin, & Delaney, 1982; Rummel, Levin, & Woodward, 2003). Furthermore, older students (such as eighth graders) often spontaneously apply this mnemonic to new learning tasks once they have been trained in its use (Carney & Levin, 2000; B. F. Jones & Hall, 1982; M. S. Jones et al., 2000; Mastropieri & Scruggs, 1989). Although only concrete objects can actually be visualized, the technique can be used with more abstract words as well, provided that they can be adequately represented by a concrete object. For example, consider the Spanish word for *love: amor.* This word might be learned by picturing a heart (symbolizing *love*) wearing a suit of *armor* (the keyword).

Identifying keywords when numbers are involved can be a bit trickier; for example, you might have trouble identifying sound-alike words for numbers such as 239 or 1861. To address this problem, Lorayne and Lucas (1974) suggested that learners use specific consonant sounds as substitutes for different digits and then create words using those sounds. As an illustration, imagine that you want to remember that the painting on the left side of Figure 12.3 was painted by Jean-Louis-Ernest Meissonier in 1861. To remember the artist's name, you can use the keyword *messenger.* To remember the date, you can create a word using the number–letter equivalents on the right side of Figure 12.3. To keep things simple, we'll assume that you already know that Meissonier lived in the 1800s and so will address only the last two digits of the year. If we use *J* to represent the 6 and *T* to represent the 1, we can form a second keyword, *jet.* Now, form a visual image of the man as a *messenger* who has just walked down the steps from his *jet* in the background (Carney & Levin, 1994). Although this approach may seem complicated, in fact college students learn it fairly easily, and using it helps them remember the artists and dates of paintings more easily than they would otherwise (Carney & Levin, 1994).

When encouraging students to use mnemonics based on visual imagery, teachers must keep three things in mind. First, many young children cannot generate effective images on their own and so probably need to have pictures provided for them (Mayer, 1987). Second, for imagery to be an effective means of remembering a connection between two items (e.g., between a tree and a mass transit system, or between love and *amor*), the two items must be incorporated into the same image in an *interacting* fashion (Bower, 1972; Dempster & Rohwer, 1974). Thus, while an image of a heart wearing armor is an effective way of remembering the Spanish word for *love,* an image of a heart placed beside a suit of armor probably is not. Third, as noted in chapter 8, imagery does not preserve details very effectively; therefore, it may not help one remember such specific information as the exact shape of a heart or the number of dents on a suit of armor.

Superimposed Meaningful Structure

One of my most vivid memories from my years as an undergraduate psychology major is being required to learn the 12 cranial nerves: olfactory, optic, oculomotor, trochlear, trigeminal, abducens, facial, auditory, glossopharyngeal, vagus, spinal accessory, and hypoglossal. It is not the nerves themselves that I remember but rather how painfully difficult it was to learn them all in their correct order. I had little luck drilling the list into my thick skull (I was using the tried-and-not-so-true method of rehearsal) until a friend passed along this mnemonic:

On old Olympus's towering top, a Finn and German viewed some hops.

Notice that the first letters of the words in the sentence correspond with the first letters of the 12 cranial nerves: Just like in the list of nerves, the first three words in the sentence begin with *O,*

Number-Letter Equivalents

1 = T or D

2 = N

3 = M

4 = R

5 = L

6 = J, soft G, SH, or CH

7 = K, hard C, or hard G

8 = F or V

9 = P or B

10 = S, Z, or soft C

To remember that this masterpiece was painted by Jean-Louis-Ernest *Meissonier* in 18*61*, form a visual image of the man as a *messenger* who has just walked down the steps from his *jet* (*J* for 6 and *T* for 1) in the background (Carney & Levin, 1994). (Number-letter equivalents are from Lorayne & Lucas, 1974).

Figure 12.3
Using the keyword method to remember the artist and year of a masterpiece.

Source: A Cavalier: Time of Louis XIII, 1861, Jean-Louis-Ernest Meissonier. By kind permission of the Trustees of the Wallace Collection, London.

the next two begin with *T,* and so on. And the sentence, though a bit strange, is fairly easy to remember because of the structure provided by its rhythm and rhyme.

"On old Olympus" illustrates a mnemonic I call a **superimposed meaningful structure.**[7] The technique is simple: The learner imposes a familiar structure on the body of information to be learned. That structure can be a sentence, story, rhythm, acronym, or anything else already familiar to the learner. For instance, during a recent trip to visit my brother-in-law in England, I stumbled

---

[7]I have also seen the terms *semantic elaboration* and *acrostic* used in reference to this technique.

on the following mnemonic for remembering the kings and queens of England, beginning with King William I and ending with Queen Elizabeth II:

> Willie, Willie, Harry, Steve,
> Harry, Dick, John, Harry Three.
> Edward One, Two, Three, Dick Two,
> Henry Four, Five, Dick the Bad,
> Harrys twain and Ned, the lad.
> Mary, Lizzie, James, the Vain,
> Charlie, Charlie, James again.
> William and Mary, Anne o' Gloria,
> Four Georgies, William, and Victoria.
> Edward Seven, Georgie Five,
> Edward, George, and Liz (alive).

Figure 12.4 lists additional examples of mnemonics, some for declarative information and others for procedures.

Superimposed meaningful structures clearly facilitate memory for lists of items (Bower & Clark, 1969; Bulgren, Schumaker, & Deshler, 1994). As an example, let's look at an experiment by Bower and Clark (1969). Two groups of college students learned 12 lists of 10 nouns: Group 1 learned each list by using repetition, whereas Group 2 composed narrative stories that included all 10 words of each list. Following is an example of a Group 2 story (the nouns to be remembered are in capital letters):

> A LUMBERJACK DARTed out of a forest, SKATEd around a HEDGE past a COLONY of DUCKS. He tripped on some FURNITURE, tearing his STOCKING while hastening toward the PILLOW where his MISTRESS lay. (Bower & Clark, 1969, p. 182)

After the students had learned each of the 12 lists perfectly, they were then asked to recall all 120 words (the first word of each list was given as a retrieval cue). Students in Group 1 (repetition) recalled only 13% of the words; in contrast, students in Group 2 (stories) recalled 93%!

It should be clear by now that mnemonics can be extremely helpful learning aids. As you may have noticed, their effectiveness lies in their conformity with a few critical principles of storage and retrieval. First, they often impose a structure or organization on the material to be learned. Second, they help the learner relate the new material to information already stored in long-term memory (e.g., to the number system or a familiar poetic meter). And third, they provide retrieval cues (such as the *associate cues* and *frames* described in chapter 10) that help learners find the information at a later time.

In the past few pages, we have identified a number of effective learning and study strategies. Some of these, such as outlining, taking notes, and writing summaries, are **overt strategies;** in other words, they are behaviors that we can actually see. Others—such as elaborating, identifying important information, and monitoring comprehension—are **covert strategies;** they are internal mental processes that we often can*not* see. Ultimately, it is probably the ways in which students process the information they receive—the covert strategies—that determine how effectively they learn and remember the information (Kardash & Amlund, 1991).

What kinds of learning and study strategies are we likely to see in students of different ages? We now look at trends in the development of metacognitive knowledge and skills.

The Mnemonic	What It Represents
	For Declarative Information
ROY G. BIV	The spectrum: red, orange, yellow, green, blue, indigo, violet
HOMES	The five Great Lakes: Huron, Ontario, Michigan, Erie, Superior
Every good boy does fine.	The lines on the treble clef: E G B D F
Every awesome dude gets babes easily.	The strings on a guitar: E A D G B E
While watching hippos, wear waterproof white hats.[a]	The pattern of whole and half steps in a major scale in Western music: whole, whole, half, whole, whole, whole, half.
Campbell's ordinary soup does make Peter pale.	The geologic time periods of the Paleozoic era: Cambrian, Ordovician, Silurian, Devonian, Mississippian, Pennsylvanian, Permian
When the "mites" go up, the "tites" go down.	The distinction between stalagmites and stalactites
A "boot"	The shape of Italy
A "bearskin rug"	The shape of France
George Ellen's old grandmother rode a pig home yesterday.	The correct spelling of *geography*
I before E, except after C.	The correct spelling of words such as *receive*
Thirty days has September	The number of days in each month
	For Procedural Information
Righty, tighty; lefty, loosy.	Turning a screw (clockwise to tighten it, counterclockwise to loosen it)
BEEF	Good form for a free throw in basketball: *b*alance the ball, *e*lbows in, *e*levate the arms, *f*ollow through
FOIL	Multiplying a mathematical expression of the form (a*x* + b) (c*x* + d): Multiply the *f*irst terms in each set of parentheses, then the *o*uter terms, the *i*nner terms, and finally the *l*ast terms

Figure 12.4
Examples of superimposed meaningful structures.

[a] I thank an anonymous student for the "Every awesome dude . . . " mnemonic and Lee Boissonneault for the "While watching hippos . . . " mnemonic.

DEVELOPMENT OF METACOGNITIVE KNOWLEDGE AND SKILLS

Developmental psychologists have observed several trends in the development of metacognition:

♦ *Children become increasingly aware of the nature of thinking.* In chapter 9, we examined *theory theory,* a perspective that focuses on the personal theories that children develop about various aspects of their world. "Theory theorists" propose that children develop personal theories not only about their physical and social worlds but also about their internal, psychological world. More specifically, children develop a **theory of mind**, which includes increasingly complex understandings of their own and others' mental states—thoughts, beliefs, perspectives, feelings, motives, and so on (e.g., Flavell, 2000; Lillard, 1998; Wellman, 1990).

Young children have only a limited ability to look inward at their own thinking and knowledge (Flavell, Green, & Flavell, 2000). Although many preschoolers have the words *know, remember,* and *forget* in their vocabularies, they don't fully grasp the nature of these mental phenomena. For instance, 3-year-olds use the term *forget* simply to mean "not knowing" something, regardless of whether they knew the information at an earlier time (Lyon & Flavell, 1994). When 4- and 5-year-old children are taught a new piece of information, they may say that they've known it for quite some time (Taylor, Esbensen, & Bennett, 1994).

During the elementary and secondary school years, children and adolescents become better able to reflect on their own thought processes and so are increasingly aware of the nature of thinking and learning (Flavell et al., 2002; Wellman & Hickling, 1994). To some extent, adults may foster such development by talking about the mind's activities—for instance, by referring to "thinking a lot" or describing someone's mind as "wandering" (Wellman & Hickling, 1994).

◆ *Children become increasingly realistic about their memory capabilities and limitations.* Young children tend to be overly optimistic about how much they can remember. As they grow older and encounter a wide variety of learning tasks, they discover that some things are more difficult to learn than others (Bjorklund & Green, 1992; Flavell et al., 2002). They also begin to realize that their memories are not perfect—that they cannot possibly remember everything they see or hear. For example, in a study by Flavell, Friedrichs, and Hoyt (1970), four age groups of children (ranging from preschoolers to fourth graders) were shown strips of paper picturing from 1 to 10 objects and asked to predict how many objects they thought they could remember at a time (a working memory task). The children were then tested to determine how many objects they actually could remember. All four groups of children tended to overestimate their working memory capacities, but the estimates of the older children were more realistic. For example, kindergarten children predicted that they could remember an average of 8.0 objects but in fact remembered only 3.6. In contrast, the fourth graders estimated that they could remember 6.1 objects and actually recalled 5.5 (a much closer prediction).

◆ *Children become increasingly aware of and use effective learning and memory strategies.* Young children have little metacognitive awareness of effective strategies. Even when they can verbally describe which learning and memory strategies are effective and which are not, they tend to use relatively ineffective ones when left to their own devices. In contrast, older children are more likely to have a variety of strategies, to apply them broadly and flexibly, and to know when to use each one (Alexander et al., 1998; A. L. Brown et al., 1983; Flavell et al., 2002; Schneider & Lockl, 2002; Siegler & Alibali, 2005). Consider these research findings as examples:

- When asked to study and remember numerous bits of information, 6- and 7-year olds allocate their study time somewhat haphazardly, without regard for the difficulty of each item. In contrast, 9- and 10-year-olds focus their efforts on the more difficult items (Masur, McIntyre, & Flavell, 1973; Schneider & Lockl, 2002).
- Rehearsal is rare in preschoolers but increases in frequency and effectiveness throughout the elementary school years (Gathercole & Hitch, 1993; Kunzinger, 1985; K. Nelson, 1996). At age 7 or 8, children often rehearse information spontaneously, but they tend to repeat each item they need to remember in isolation from the others. When they reach age 9 or 10, they begin to use *cumulative rehearsal,* reciting the entire list at once and continuing to add any new items.

- Children increasingly organize the things they need to remember, perhaps by putting items into categories (Hacker, 1998a; Moely, 1977; Siegler & Alibali, 2005). They also become more flexible in their organizational strategies, especially as they reach adolescence (Plumert, 1994).
- The use of elaboration continues to increase throughout the school years (Flavell et al., 2002; Kail, 1990; Schneider & Pressley, 1989). For example, 10th graders are more likely than 8th graders to use elaboration when trying to remember paired associates (e.g., *doctor–machine, acorn–bathtub*) (Waters, 1982). Sixth graders often draw inferences from the things they read, whereas first graders rarely do (Chan, Burtis, Scardamalia, & Bereiter, 1992).

Certainly such trends are due, in part, to children's growing experience with a wide variety of learning tasks. But the increasing capacity of working memory and the increasing maturity of that central executive I spoke of in chapter 7 may also play a role (Borkowski & Burke, 1996; Pressley & Hilden, 2006).

- *Children engage in more comprehension monitoring as they get older.* Young children (e.g., those in the early elementary grades) often think they know or understand something before they actually do. As a result, they don't study things they need to learn as much as they should, and they often don't ask questions when they receive incomplete or confusing information (Dufresne & Kobasigawa, 1989; Flavell et al., 1970; Markman, 1977; McDevitt, Spivey, Sheehan, Lennon, & Story, 1990). Children's ability to monitor their own comprehension improves throughout the school years, and so children and adolescents become more aware of when they actually know something (Hacker, 1998a; Schneider & Lockl, 2002; van Kraayenoord & Paris, 1997). Yet even many college students have difficulty assessing their own knowledge accurately; for instance, they often overestimate how well they will perform or have performed on an exam (Dunning et al., 2004; Hacker et al., 2000; Schneider & Lockl, 2002; Sinkavich, 1995).

- *Some learning processes may be used unconsciously and automatically at first but become more conscious and deliberate with development.* It is not unusual to see young learners organizing or elaborating on the things they are learning without being consciously aware that they are doing so (Bjorklund, 1987; Flavell et al., 2002; Howe & O'Sullivan, 1990). For example, young children may automatically group things into categories as a way of learning them more effectively; only later do they *try* to categorize the things they need to learn (Bjorklund, 1987). Thus, children's learning processes become more intentional—and therefore more *strategic*—with age.

The specific learning strategies that students use depend, to some extent, on their beliefs about the nature of the knowledge they are trying to acquire, as well as about the nature of learning itself. Such *epistemological beliefs* are our next topic.

EPISTEMOLOGICAL BELIEFS

Earlier in the chapter, I described how, as a high school student, I believed that I was reading my history textbook even when I was thinking about something else and that I could effectively study my Chinese vocabulary words by repeating them aloud to myself a few times. It is clear that I had a very naive notion of what learning involves: I thought it was a relatively mindless process that would magically happen regardless of how much effort I invested.

I also had some pretty shaky beliefs about what "knowledge" is. I thought that the academic disciplines I was studying—history, science, literature—were pretty much set in stone, with definite right and wrong ways of looking at things. Experts didn't know everything just yet (e.g., they still hadn't figured out how to cure the common cold), but that knowledge was "out there" somewhere and they would eventually find it. In the meantime, it was my job as a student to acquire as many facts as I could. I wasn't quite sure what I would do with them all, but I knew, deep down, that they would somehow make me a better person.

As people who learn new things every day, we all have ideas about what "knowledge" and "learning" are—ideas that are collectively known as **epistemological beliefs**.[8] In many cases, such beliefs are pulled together into cohesive, although not necessarily accurate, personal theories about human learning and cognition (Hofer & Pintrich, 1997; Kuhn, 2000; Lampert, Rittenhouse, & Crumbaugh, 1996). Included in these theories are beliefs about such things as:

- *The certainty of knowledge:* Whether knowledge is a fixed, unchanging, absolute "truth" *or* a tentative, dynamic entity that will continue to evolve over time[9]
- *The simplicity and structure of knowledge:* Whether knowledge is a collection of discrete and isolated facts *or* a set of complex and interrelated ideas
- *The source of knowledge:* Whether knowledge comes from outside of learners (i.e., from a teacher or another "authority" of some kind) *or* is derived and constructed by learners themselves
- *The criteria for determining truth:* Whether an idea is accepted as true when it is communicated by an expert *or* when it is logically evaluated based on available evidence
- *The speed of learning:* Whether knowledge is acquired quickly if at all (in which case learners either know something or they don't, in an all-or-none fashion) *or* is acquired gradually over a period of time (in which case learners can partially know something)
- *The nature of learning ability:* Whether people's ability to learn is fixed at birth (i.e., inherited) *or* can improve over time with practice and use of better strategies (Bendixen & Rule, 2004; Elder, 2002; Hammer, 1994; Hofer, 2004; Hofer & Pintrich, 1997; King & Kitchener, 2002; Linn, Songer, & Eylon, 1996; Schommer, 1994a; Wood & Kardash, 2002)

Keep in mind that epistemological beliefs are not as "either–or" as I have just described them. Some theorists have suggested that the elements I've listed probably reflect *continuums* rather than strict dichotomies (Baxter Magolda, 2002; King & Kitchener, 2002; Kuhn & Weinstock, 2002; Marton & Booth, 1997).

Whether and in what ways people's various beliefs about knowledge and learning hang together as an integrated belief system is a matter of considerable debate (Buehl & Alexander, 2001; diSessa, Elby, & Hammer, 2003; Hofer, 2004; Hofer & Pintrich, 2002; Qian & Alvermann, 1995; Schommer-Aikins, 2002, 2004). Concerns about research methodologies fuel this debate. Researchers obtain information about learners' beliefs primarily from interviews and questionnaires, yet some theorists suspect that learners' true beliefs may be implicit rather than

---

[8]You may also see such terms as *personal epistemology, intuitive epistemology, epistemic cognition, ways of knowing,* or *meta-knowing* (diSessa et al., 2003; Hofer, 2002; Kuhn, 1999).

[9]The belief that there is an ultimate "truth" that experts will eventually determine is sometimes called *logical positivism.* This view contrasts sharply with *radical constructivism,* a perspective maintaining that there is no "reality" separate from people's constructed understandings and beliefs.

explicit and so are far removed from conscious awareness (diSessa et al., 2003; Hammer & Elby, 2002; Schraw & Moshman, 1995). In addition, the particular measures and statistical methods used seems to influence the kinds of beliefs and interrelationships among them that researchers identify (Schraw, Bendixen, & Dunkle, 2002).

Increasingly, theorists are beginning to realize that people's epistemological beliefs are somewhat context- and situation-specific (Andre & Windschitl, 2003; Bell & Linn, 2002; Louca, Elby, Hammer, & Kagey, 2004; Schommer-Aikins, 2002, 2004; Schraw, 2000). For example, even though you and I may believe that scientific views of the world will probably continue to evolve over time (thus believing that knowledge is somewhat uncertain), we know that other things are fairly black and white. Two plus two equals four, the capital of France is Paris, and William Shakespeare wrote *Romeo and Juliet;* these facts are unlikely to change any time in the foreseeable future. Furthermore, learners' epistemological beliefs may be specific to particular content domains. Following are some examples:

- Many students believe that knowledge in some disciplines is more certain than knowledge in others. For example, they may believe that knowledge in mathematics, the natural sciences, and history is pretty much a "sure thing," whereas knowledge in some social sciences—psychology, for one—is more tentative (De Corte, Op't Eynde, & Verschaffel, 2002; Estes, Chandler, Horvath, & Backus, 2003; Haenen, Schrijnemakers, & Stufkens, 2003; Hofer, 2000; Schommer, 1994b).

- Many students think that learning mathematics and physics means memorizing procedures and formulas and finding the "right" answer. Furthermore, there is usually only one "correct" way to solve a problem and one "correct" answer to it (De Corte et al., 2002; Hammer, 1994; Muis, 2004).

- Many students think that when they work on math problems, they will either solve the problems within a few minutes or else not solve them at all. Many also think that when an answer to a math problem isn't a whole number, it is probably wrong (Muis, 2004; Schoenfeld, 1988).

Developmental and Cultural Differences in Epistemological Beliefs

Learners' epistemological beliefs often change over time. For example, young children typically believe in the certainty of knowledge: They are likely to think that there is an absolute truth about almost any topic out there somewhere (Astington & Pelletier, 1996; Hofer & Pintrich, 1997; Kuhn & Weinstock, 2002). As they reach the middle school and high school years, some (but by no means all) of them begin to realize that knowledge is a subjective entity and that different perspectives on a topic may be equally valid (Belenky, Clinchy, Goldberger, & Tarule, 1986/1997; Kuhn & Weinstock, 2002; Perry, 1968; Perkins & Ritchhart, 2004; Schommer, 1997). Other changes may also occur at the high school level. For example, students in 12th grade are more likely than 9th graders to believe that knowledge consists of complex interrelationships (rather than discrete facts), that learning happens slowly (rather than quickly), and that learning ability can improve with practice (rather than being fixed at birth) (Schommer, 1997).

For some people—especially those who pursue higher education—epistemological beliefs evolve even further in adulthood. Increasingly, these individuals come to view knowledge and "truth" as tentative, uncertain entities. And particularly if they continue on to graduate school, they begin to appreciate the need for analyzing and evaluating other people's claims and arguments (even those of experts) using logic and solid evidence (Baxter Magolda, 2002, 2004; Hofer & Pintrich, 1997; Kuhn, 2001a; Kuhn & Park, 2005; Schommer-Aikins, Hopkins, Anderson, & Drouhard, 2005).

Although the acquisition of abstract thought is almost certainly a prerequisite for more advanced epistemological beliefs, environmental factors also play a role in their development. Even young children may hear adults contradict one another—for instance, a teacher might contradict something a parent has said—and so must begin to ponder the credibility of different authority figures (Hofer, 2004). By early adolescence, children show considerable variability in their epistemological beliefs, apparently at least partly as a result of exposure to others' beliefs about the certainty and origins of knowledge and related issues (Haerle, 2004; Kuhn, Daniels, & Krishnan, 2003).

Researchers have also begun to uncover cultural differences in learners' epistemological beliefs. For instance, beginning in middle school, students in the United States are more likely to question the validity of an authority figure's claims than are students in the Far East. In contrast, students in Far Eastern countries (e.g., Japan and Korea) are likely to believe that knowledge is cut and dried and can be effectively gained from authority figures (Kuhn & Park, 2005; Qian & Pan, 2002). Yet Asian learners appear to have the advantage in another respect: Compared to their American counterparts (who sometimes expect quick results with little work), Asian college students are more likely to believe that mastering complex academic topics is often a slow, effortful process requiring diligence, persistence, and a combination of rote and meaningful learning (Dahlin & Watkins, 2000; Li, 2005; Li & Fischer, 2004; Marton & Booth, 1997; Tweed & Lehman, 2002). Some differences exist even among Western cultures. For example, college students in Ireland are more likely than American students to view learning as a complex and constructive process that results in somewhat tentative understandings of a topic. Their peers in the United States are more likely to view learning as a process of attending carefully to presented information and memorizing it as a set of isolated facts (McDevitt, Sheehan, Cooney, Smith, & Walker, 1994).

Effects of Epistemological Beliefs

Students' epistemological beliefs clearly influence how they study and learn. Following are some specific effects that different beliefs are likely to have:

- *Beliefs regarding the certainty of knowledge:* When students believe that knowledge related to a topic is a fixed, certain entity, they are apt to jump to quick and potentially inaccurate conclusions based on the information they receive. In contrast, when students view knowledge as something that continues to evolve and doesn't necessarily include definitive right and wrong answers, they are apt to enjoy cognitively challenging tasks, engage in meaningful learning, read course material critically, undergo conceptual change when it is warranted, and recognize that some issues are controversial and not easily resolved (Kardash & Howell, 2000; Kardash & Scholes, 1996; Mason, 2003; Patrick & Pintrich, 2001; Schommer, 1994a).
- *Beliefs regarding the simplicity and structure of knowledge:* Students who believe that knowledge is a collection of discrete facts are apt to use rote-learning processes when they study and to hold on to their misconceptions about a topic. They also tend to believe that they "know" the material they are studying if they can recall basic facts and definitions. In contrast, students who believe that knowledge is a complex set of interrelated ideas are likely

to engage in meaningful learning, organization, and elaboration when they study and likely to evaluate the success of their learning efforts in terms of how well they understand and can apply what they've learned (Hammer, 1994; Hofer & Pintrich, 1997; Mason, 2003; Purdie & Hattie, 1996; Schommer-Aikins, 2002).

- *Beliefs regarding the source of knowledge:* Students who believe that knowledge originates outside of the learner and is passed along directly by authority figures are apt to be fairly passive learners, perhaps listening quietly to explanations without trying to clarify confusing ideas, or perhaps exerting little effort when lessons consist of discovery activities and class discussions rather than lectures. In contrast, students who believe that knowledge is something that one constructs for oneself are apt to be cognitively engaged in learning activities, make interconnections among ideas, read and listen critically, work to make sense of seemingly contradictory pieces of information, undergo conceptual change, and get emotionally involved with the things they are studying (Chan et al., 1997; Haseman, 1999; Hogan, 1997; McDevitt et al., 1990; Schommer, 1994b; Schraw & Bruning, 1995).

- *Beliefs regarding the criteria for determining truth:* When students believe that something is probably true if it comes from an "expert" of some sort, they are likely to accept information from authority figures without question. But when they believe that ideas should be judged on their logical and scientific merit (rather than on their source), they are likely to critically evaluate new information on the basis of available evidence (King & Kitchener, 2002). The following interview with a student, concerning the belief that the Egyptians (rather than, say, an earlier civilization or extraterrestrials) built the pyramids, illustrates the latter perspective:

Interviewer:	Can you ever say you know for sure about this issue?
Student:	It . . . is very far along the continuum of what is probable.
Interviewer:	Can you say that one point of view is right and one is wrong?
Student:	Right and wrong are not comfortable categories to assign to this kind of item. It's more or less likely or reasonable, more or less in keeping with what the facts seem to be. (dialogue from King & Kitchener, 1994, p. 72)

As students grow older, and especially as they move into higher levels of education (e.g., graduate school), they become increasingly adept at distinguishing between weak and strong evidence for a particular idea or point of view (Kuhn, 2001a).

- *Beliefs regarding the speed of learning:* When students believe that learning happens quickly in an all-or-none fashion, they are likely to believe that they have learned something before they really have, perhaps after only a single reading of their textbooks; they are also likely to give up quickly in the face of failure and to express discouragement or dislike regarding the topic they are studying. In contrast, when students believe that learning is a gradual process that often takes time and effort, they are likely to use a wide variety of learning strategies as they study and to persist until they have made sense of the ideas presented (Butler & Winne, 1995; Kardash & Howell, 2000; Schommer, 1990, 1994b).

- *Beliefs regarding the nature of learning ability:* As you might guess, students' beliefs about the nature of learning ability are correlated with their persistence in learning. If they think that learning ability is a fixed commodity, they will quickly give up on challenging tasks. In contrast, if they think that their ability to learn something is under their control, they will pursue a variety of supportive learning activities and try, try again until they have mastered the subject matter (Hartley & Bendixen, 2001; Schommer, 1994a, 1994b).

Not surprisingly, students with developmentally more advanced epistemological beliefs—for example, those who believe that knowledge is complex and uncertain and that learning is often a slow, gradual process—achieve at higher levels in the classroom (Buehl & Alexander, 2005; Kardash & Sinatra, 2003; Schommer, 1994a). Furthermore, higher levels of academic achievement may bring about more advanced views about knowledge and learning (Schommer, 1994b; Strike & Posner, 1992). The more students can get beyond the "basics" and explore the far reaches of a discipline—whether it be science, mathematics, history, literature, or some other domain—the more they will discover that learning involves acquiring an integrated and cohesive set of ideas, that even experts don't know everything about a topic, and that truly complete and accurate "knowledge" of how the world operates may ultimately be an unattainable goal.

It is important to note here that students are not the only ones who can have relatively naive beliefs about the nature of knowledge and learning. Some *teachers* appear to have naive beliefs as well. Some teachers seem to believe that knowledge about a particular subject matter is a fixed and well-defined entity, that students need to "absorb" this knowledge in isolated bits and pieces, and that learning is a process of mindless memorization and rehearsal (L. M. Anderson, 1997; Hofer & Pintrich, 1997; Patrick & Pintrich, 2001; Schommer, 1994b). Such beliefs are likely to influence the ways that teachers teach and assess their students. For example, teachers holding these beliefs will be more likely to focus on lower-level skills in their instructional objectives, classroom activities, assignments, and tests (Grossman, 1990; Hofer & Pintrich, 1997). Fortunately, teachers often acquire more sophisticated beliefs about their subject matter as they gain experience in the classroom (Corkill, Bouchard, & Bendixen, 2002).

THE INTENTIONAL LEARNER

Earlier I described learning and study strategies as involving the *intentional* use of certain cognitive processes to learn. Truly effective learning, it appears, involves **intentional learning,** in which a learner is actively and consciously engaged in cognitive and metacognitive activities directed specifically at thinking about and learning something (Bereiter, 1997; Bereiter & Scardamalia, 1989; Langer, 1997, 2000; Sinatra & Pintrich, 2003a).[10] Intentional learners have particular goals they want to accomplish as they learn, and they make use of the many self-regulatory strategies they have at their disposal to achieve those goals. Long gone is that reactive responder to environmental stimuli whom we encountered in the early days of behaviorism. Instead, we now have the learner squarely in the driver's seat with an itinerary, a road map, and considerable knowledge about how to drive the car.

Without a doubt, intentional learning involves both automatic and controlled processes. Many of the basic components of learning—retrieving word meanings, connecting new ideas to very similar information already in long-term memory, and so on—have been practiced to a level of automaticity, and so the learner carries them out with little thought or effort. But overseeing the process is a very conscious, goal-directed individual who brings into play a variety of strategies—deciding what to focus on, trying to make sense of ambiguous text passages, drawing inferences for one's own life circumstances, and the like—as necessary (diSessa et al., 2003; Kintsch, 1998; Sinatra & Pintrich, 2003b).

---

[10]The concepts *mindful learning* and *mindfulness* (Langer, 1997, 2000) reflect a similar idea.

Intentional learning may be especially important when learners need to overhaul their current understandings of a topic or issue—in other words, when they must undergo *conceptual change* (Bendixen & Rule, 2004; Gunstone, 1994; Sinatra & Pintrich, 2003a). Intentional learning brings into play several processes that are critical for revising one's understandings in any significant fashion (Luque, 2003; Mason, 2003). First, intentional learners actively attend to and think about the new information, and so they are more likely to notice discrepancies with what they currently believe. Second, they are eager to acquire mastery of the subject matter, and so they exert considerable effort to make sense of it. Third, they bring to the table a variety of learning and self-regulatory strategies—elaboration, self-motivation, self-monitoring, and so on—that maximize their chances for revising their beliefs in line with what they are hearing or reading. But in addition to such processes, intentional learners must have epistemological beliefs consistent with the notion of conceptual change. More specifically, they must believe that knowledge about a topic continues to evolve and improve over time and that learning something *well* can take time, effort, and perseverance (Southerland & Sinatra, 2003).

Intentional learning is the ideal situation. Unfortunately, what is more typical is that students don't regularly, consistently, or actively use effective learning and self-regulatory strategies. We now look at reasons why.

WHY STUDENTS DON'T ALWAYS USE EFFECTIVE STRATEGIES

As we have seen, many students continue to use ineffective learning and study strategies (e.g., rote memorization) throughout their academic careers. Given what you have learned about metacognition up to this point, can you generate some hypotheses about why this might be so? In this section, I will suggest several possible reasons why effective learning strategies emerge slowly if at all. You will, I hope, find some of your own ideas in my list.

♦ *Students are uninformed or misinformed about effective strategies.* In a recent study in Philadelphia (B. L. Wilson & Corbett, 2001), researchers interviewed middle school students in a low-income neighborhood. Many of the students aspired to professional careers (doctor, lawyer, teacher, etc.) but were hardly on track toward their goals: They misbehaved in class, inconsistently completed homework, and often skipped school. They had little idea about what it would take to do well in school. The following interview with one boy illustrates their naïveté:

Interviewer:	Are you on track to meet your goals?
Student:	No. I need to study more.
Interviewer:	How do you know that?
Student:	I just know by some of my grades. [mostly Cs]
Interviewer:	Why do you think you will be more inclined to do it in high school?
Student:	I don't want to get let back. I want to go to college.
Interviewer:	What will you need to do to get better grades?
Student:	Just do more and more work. I can rest when the school year is over. (dialogue from B. L. Wilson & Corbett, 2001, p. 23)

Many students, even those at the high school and college levels, are metacognitively naive about how they can best learn (Alexander & Judy, 1988; Barnett, 2001; Palmer & Goetz, 1988; J. W. Thomas, 1993a; Wood, Motz, & Willoughby, 1997). Some students, like the boy in the interview, believe that all they need to do to learn information better is to exert more effort—that is, to *try harder*—with little regard for how they should mentally process the information (O'Sullivan & Joy, 1990; Pressley, Borkowski, & Schneider, 1987). When I present a unit on cognitive psychology to my undergraduate educational psychology class, my description of such basic strategies as organizing information and relating it to familiar concepts and experiences appears to be a major revelation to about half of my students; sadly, too many of them have always viewed learning as being best approached through rote memorization. Furthermore, many students believe (incorrectly) that trying to learn information meaningfully—that is, trying to understand and make sense of the things they study—interferes with their ability to do well on classroom tests that emphasize rote memorization and knowledge of isolated facts (Crooks, 1988).

Undoubtedly a key reason why students have little knowledge about effective learning strategies is that schools rarely *teach* such strategies (Hamman, Berthelot, Saia, & Crowley, 2000; Pressley & Hilden, 2006; Pressley et al., 1990; Wood et al., 1997). Yet when left to discover strategies on their own, students typically acquire effective ones slowly if at all, and some develop counterproductive misconceptions about how best to learn (Pressley & Hilden, 2006). Sometimes even *teachers* foster misconceptions, perhaps with maxims like this one: "Repeat a sentence out loud three times and write it down three times, and then it's yours forever" (Matlin, 2004).

◆ *Students have epistemological beliefs that lead them to underestimate or misrepresent a learning task.* Students are unlikely to use effective strategies if they believe that the learning task at hand is an easy one or that their success in learning is unrelated to the effort they put forth (Butler & Winne, 1995; Winne, 1995a). And as we have already seen, they will certainly not engage in such processes as meaningful learning, organization, and elaboration if they think that "knowledge" is nothing more than a collection of unrelated facts.

◆ *Students mistakenly believe that they are already using effective strategies.* Perhaps because they are not monitoring their comprehension or perhaps because they have defined learning in an overly simplistic manner, many low-achieving students erroneously believe that their current approach to learning and studying is a good one (Loranger, 1994; Starr & Lovett, 2000). In some cases, feedback that students are *not* mastering the material will spur them to adopt more effective strategies, at least for the short run (Starr & Lovett, 2000). In other instances, however, students may attribute their poor performance to factors outside of themselves—perhaps to poor instruction or a "picky" test (we'll discuss the nature and effects of such *attributions* in chapter 16).

◆ *Students have little relevant prior knowledge on which they can draw.* Students who use ineffective learning and study strategies tend to know less about the subject matter they are studying, and less about the world in general, than students who use effective strategies (Alexander & Judy, 1988; Chi, 1981; Schneider, 1993). For example, students may know too little about a topic to determine what is important and what is not (Alexander & Jetton, 1996; Carpenter & Just, 1986; McDaniel & Einstein, 1989). They may have few concepts or experiences to which they can relate new material in a meaningful fashion; thus, they have greater difficulty comprehending the things they read (Dole et al., 1991; Hall, 1989; Wilson & Anderson, 1986; Woloshyn, Pressley, & Schneider, 1992). And they are likely to have fewer organizational frameworks and schemas that they can impose on what might otherwise appear to be an unrelated set of facts (Carpenter & Just, 1986; Pressley & Hilden, 2006).

◆ *Assigned learning tasks do not lend themselves to sophisticated strategies.* In some situations, teachers may assign tasks for which effective strategies are either counterproductive or impossible. For example, when teachers assign simple tasks that involve lower-level skills (e.g., when they insist that facts and definitions be learned verbatim), students are unlikely to engage in such processes as meaningful learning and elaboration (J. W. Thomas, 1993a; Turner, 1995; Van Meter et al., 1994). When teachers expect a great deal of material to be mastered for each test, students may have to devote the limited time that they have to getting a general "impression" of everything rather than to developing an in-depth understanding and integration of the subject matter (J. W. Thomas, 1993b). When teachers tell students exactly what questions will be asked on a particular classroom test or assignment, students are likely to focus only on material related to those questions, without regard for the larger context in which the material appears (J. W. Thomas, 1993a).

    ◆ *Students have goals that are inconsistent with effective learning.* Students are not always interested in learning for understanding; instead, they may be more interested in remembering information only long enough to get a passing grade, or they may want to complete an assigned task in as little time and with as little effort as possible. Effective learning strategies may be largely irrelevant to such motives (Mayer, 1996b; Nolen, 1996).

    ◆ *Students think that sophisticated learning strategies require too much effort to make them worthwhile.* If students believe that certain strategies involve too much time and effort, they are unlikely to use them, no matter how effective the strategies might be (Guttentag, 1984; Palmer & Goetz, 1988; Pressley et al., 1990). In many cases, students seem to be unaware of how much a few simple strategies can help them learn and remember classroom material (Pressley, Levin, & Ghatala, 1984; Zimmerman, 1994). In other instances, they may have little experience with a particular strategy; thus, they have learned few (if any) of the strategy's components to automaticity, and so using it effectively *does* require a great deal of effort (Alexander et al., 1998; Siegler & Alibali, 2005).

    ◆ *Students have low self-efficacy about their ability to learn in an academic setting.* Some students, especially those with a history of academic failure, develop the belief that they are incapable of learning regardless of what they do. Such students may believe (erroneously) that *no* strategy is likely to make any appreciable difference in their school achievement (Alexander et al., 1998; Palmer & Goetz, 1988; Borkowski & Burke, 1996).

Teachers often assume that students will use the same relatively sophisticated study strategies that they themselves use—an assumption that is clearly unwarranted in many cases. But can metacognitive knowledge and skills be taught? Most psychologists believe that they can, and furthermore that they *should,* be taught. Let's look at some approaches to teaching metacognitive knowledge and skills.

PROMOTING EFFECTIVE LEARNING AND STUDY STRATEGIES

As students move through the grade levels—from elementary school to middle or junior high school, then to high school, and perhaps eventually on to college—their learning tasks become increasingly complex and challenging (e.g., Eccles & Midgley, 1989; J. E. Wilson, 1988). For example, students must remember more information, do more with it (in terms of application, problem solving, critical analysis, etc.), and understand it at a more abstract level. Thus, there is a greater need for sophisticated learning and study strategies as the years go by (Baker, 1989).

Many learning theorists suggest that schools should provide explicit instruction in how to study and learn. Such instruction is often essential if students are to acquire more advanced learning strategies—comprehension monitoring, critical evaluation of ideas, and so on—that they aren't likely to develop on their own (Rawson & Kintsch, 2005). And it may be especially valuable for at-risk students—those with a history of academic difficulties and a high probability of dropping out of school before graduation (Alderman, 1990; Brown & Palincsar, 1987; Weinstein, Hagen, & Meyer, 1991). In this final section of the chapter, we will examine research regarding the effectiveness of study skills training. We will also consider specific classroom strategies for promoting and enhancing students' metacognitive knowledge and skills.

Effectiveness of Study Skills Training Programs

Initially, most programs designed to enhance metacognitive knowledge and skills were at the college level (J. E. Wilson, 1988). But such programs eventually found their way into the high school, junior high, and upper elementary grades, and short, strategy-specific training sessions have been offered for children as young as age 4 or 5. The collective results of research studies indicate that learners at all levels *can* be taught more effective learning and study strategies, with consequent improvements in their memory, classroom performance, and academic achievement. Such training appears to be especially beneficial for low-achieving students (Baker, 1989; Carr & Schneider, 1991; DuBois, Staley, Guzy, & DiNardo, 1995; Fletcher & Bray, 1996; Haller et al., 1988; Hattie, Biggs, & Purdie, 1996; Holley & Dansereau, 1984; Kulik, Kulik, & Shwalb, 1983; Lange & Pierce, 1992; Mastropieri & Scruggs, 1989; Shrager & Mayer, 1989; Wade, 1983; C. E. Weinstein, Goetz, & Alexander, 1988).

Effective study skills programs tend to be multifaceted, teaching a wide variety of learning and study strategies. For example, successful reading-for-learning instruction is likely to teach students to (1) determine their purpose in reading a particular passage and modify their reading behavior accordingly, (2) activate background information and experiences relevant to the topic, (3) identify and attend to main ideas, (4) draw inferences from the things they read, and (5) monitor their reading comprehension as they go along. And general learning and study strategies programs typically include instruction about meaningful learning, organizational strategies, elaboration, mnemonics, note taking, and summarizing. Aside from such commonalities, training programs often differ markedly from one another; I invite you to explore some of the possibilities by consulting the references listed in the preceding paragraph.

Guidelines for Promoting Effective Strategies

Theorists and researchers have identified a number of practices that should promote the development of more sophisticated metacognitive knowledge and skills. Following are some guidelines to keep in mind:

◆ *Students learn strategies more effectively when the strategies are taught within the context of specific subject domains and actual academic learning tasks* (Hattie et al., 1996; Paris & Paris, 2001; Pressley, El-Dinary, Marks, Brown, & Stein, 1992; Pressley, Harris, & Marks, 1992). As students encounter specific academic content, they should simultaneously learn ways to study the content. For example, when presenting new information in class, a teacher might (1) suggest how students can organize their notes, (2) describe mnemonics for things that are difficult to remember, and (3) ask various students to summarize the ideas presented. When assigning textbook pages to be read at home, a teacher might (4) suggest that students consider what they know about a topic *before* they begin reading about it, (5) ask students to use headings and subheadings to make predictions about upcoming content, and (6) provide questions for students to ask themselves as they read.

◆ *Students can use sophisticated learning strategies only when they have a knowledge base to which they can relate new material* (Brown et al., 1981; Greene, 1994; Weinstein & Mayer, 1986). The knowledge and skills that students bring to a lesson affect their ability to learn new information meaningfully, identify main ideas, and engage in such elaborative activities as drawing inferences and clarifying ambiguities. Teachers must be careful not to present difficult material until students have mastered the prerequisite knowledge and skills essential for a genuine understanding of the material.

◆ *Students should learn a wide variety of strategies, as well as the situations in which each one is appropriate* (Mayer & Wittrock, 1996; Nist, Simpson, Olejnik, & Mealey, 1991; Paris, 1988; Pressley, El-Dinary, et al., 1992; Pressley, Harris, & Marks, 1992). Different strategies are useful in different situations; for instance, meaningful learning may be more effective for learning general principles within a discipline, whereas mnemonics may be more effective for learning hard-to-remember pairs and lists. Organizing ideas in a hierarchical fashion may be appropriate for one unit (e.g., see Figure 8.5); organizing them in a two-dimensional matrix may be appropriate for another (e.g., see Figure 4.2).

◆ *Effective strategies should be practiced with a variety of tasks and on an ongoing basis* (Brown & Palincsar, 1987; A. Collins, Brown, & Newman, 1989; Pressley, El-Dinary, et al., 1992; Pressley, Harris, & Marks, 1992). When students learn a strategy only within the context of one particular task, they are unlikely to use the strategy in other contexts (Pressley et al., 1990). But when they learn to apply the same strategy to many different tasks over a long period, they are apt to recognize the strategy's value and to generalize its use to new situations. Effective strategy instruction is clearly not a one-shot deal.

◆ *Strategy instruction should include covert as well as overt strategies* (Kardash & Amlund, 1991). Certainly students stand to benefit from guidance about how to take notes from a lecture, underline the material they read in their textbooks, and write summaries of the material they study. But the sophisticated cognitive processes that underlie these behaviors—learning meaningfully, organizing, elaborating, comprehension monitoring, and so on—are ultimately the most important strategies for students to acquire.

◆ *Teachers can model effective strategies by thinking aloud about new material* (Brown & Palincsar, 1987; Pressley, El-Dinary, et al., 1992; Pressley, Harris, & Marks, 1992). When teachers think aloud about the content their classes are studying (e.g., "I remember that *Au* is the symbol for gold by remembering, '*Ay, you* stole my gold watch!'" or "Hmm . . . it seems to me that Napoleon's military tactics were similar to those of the ancient Assyrians"), they give their students specific, concrete examples of how to process information effectively.

◆ *Students can also benefit from reflecting on and describing their current study strategies.* Even at the college level, low achievers don't always have much metacognitive insight into how they approach classroom learning tasks (May & Etkina, 2002). And when they *can* put their finger on what they do (mentally) as they study, low achievers are apt to describe rote-memorization approaches rather than such strategies as integration of ideas and critical evaluation of the information and explanations presented (May & Etkina, 2002). Regularly encouraging students to think about how they know something or how they went about learning it—as well as about how they might learn it more effectively—can sometimes help them bring implicit metacognitive strategies to the surface for careful scrutiny and reflection (May & Etkina, 2002; Miller, Heafner, Massey, & Strahan, 2003).

◆ *Teachers should scaffold students' initial attempts at using new strategies, gradually phasing out the scaffolding as students become more proficient.* In chapter 11, I introduced the concept of *scaffolding,* whereby a competent individual (e.g., a teacher) guides and supports a learner's early attempts at a difficult task; as the learner becomes more skilled at performing the task independently, such support is gradually removed. Many of the metacognitive activities we have considered in this chapter (e.g., note taking, comprehension monitoring, summarizing) are challenging tasks indeed, and some teacher scaffolding to facilitate them is clearly in order (Graham & Harris, 1996; Katayama & Robinson, 2000; Pontecorvo, 1993; Pressley, Harris, & Marks, 1992; Rogoff, 1990).

In this chapter we've already seen several examples of how teachers can scaffold students' learning and study strategies. For instance, teachers can provide a general organizational framework that students can follow while taking notes. They can provide examples of questions that students can use to monitor their comprehension as they read (e.g., "Explain why . . . " or "What is a new example of . . . ?"). They can provide guidance about how to develop a good summary (e.g., "Identify or invent a topic sentence" or "Find supporting information for each main idea"). Such scaffolding is most likely to be helpful when students are studying subject matter they find difficult to comprehend yet *can* comprehend if they apply appropriate metacognitive strategies (Pressley, El-Dinary, et al., 1992). As students become more proficient in the use of these strategies, instruction can gradually proceed through increasingly more challenging material (Rosenshine & Meister, 1992).

As we noted in chapter 11, teachers can often scaffold complex classroom tasks through the use of computer tools—word processing programs, spreadsheets, and the like. In recent years, researchers have discovered that appropriately designed software can also scaffold students' learning strategies and self-regulated learning in computer-based instruction and online research (Azevedo, 2005; Graesser, McNamara, & VanLehn, 2005; Quintana, Zhang, & Krajcik, 2005; B. Y. White & Frederiksen, 2005). For instance, as students study science topics in a hypermedia program—one that allows them to choose among many possible pathways and information sources—computer software might occasionally encourage them to set goals for their learning or ask them to identify causal relationships among concepts (Graesser et al., 2005). As students search the Internet for resources about a particular topic, software might occasionally remind them about their goal(s) in conducting the research or about the criteria they should use to evaluate the content of a particular Web site (Quintana et al., 2005).

◆ *Students can often learn effective strategies by working cooperatively with their classmates.* A rapidly growing body of research indicates that group learning activities, especially when structured in particular ways, can promote more sophisticated cognitive processing. One effective approach is to teach students to ask one another, and then answer higher-level questions about the material they are studying—for instance, "Why is it that such-and-such is true?" Such an approach may take the form of either *guided peer questioning* or *reciprocal teaching,* both of which we'll examine in chapter 14.

◆ *Students must understand why new strategies are helpful.* Research indicates that strategy instruction is more successful when students not only learn effective strategies but also learn *how* and *why* these strategies are effective (Hattie et al., 1996; Paris & Paris, 2001; Pressley, Borkowski, & Schneider, 1987; Pressley & Hilden, 2006). In my own classes, I sometimes do little "experiments," presenting information that is difficult to learn and remember, then giving some students a mnemonic for learning the information but giving other students no guidance at all. We find out how much students in each group can recall by writing students' "test" scores on the board, and then we compare the two sets of numbers. The performance of the two groups is usually so dramatically different that my students readily acknowledge the usefulness of the mnemonic I've taught them.

Earlier I mentioned that students often don't realize just how ineffective their current strategies are. In several studies, Pressley and his colleagues trained students at a variety of age levels (ranging from 10 years to adulthood) to use keyword mnemonics to learn lists of vocabulary words (Pressley, Levin, & Ghatala, 1984, 1988; Pressley, Ross, Levin, & Ghatala, 1984). Although the students mastered the technique, many of them chose *not* to use it for a similar learning task later on. Students who were explicitly asked to consider just how much the key-word method had helped them learn the earlier words were far more likely to use it again in the new learning task. In a similar manner, teachers might occasionally need to show their students in a very concrete fashion (perhaps by using an ungraded quiz) just how little they are actually learning and remembering using their current ineffective strategies and how much more they can learn using a different approach.

◆ *Students should have epistemological beliefs that are consistent with effective strategies.* As we have seen, students' epistemological beliefs influence the learning strategies they use. Study strategies training, in and of itself, will not necessarily change those beliefs (Schraw & Moshman, 1995). Because students' beliefs about the nature of knowledge and learning may be in the form of implicit rather than explicit knowledge, they may be especially resistant to change (Schraw & Moshman, 1995).

Not only do epistemological beliefs affect students' ability to undergo conceptual change, but in fact revising epistemological beliefs involves conceptual change in and of itself. To nudge students toward increasingly sophisticated epistemological understandings, then, teachers must encourage students to reflect not only about their learning strategies but also about their underlying beliefs regarding the nature of knowledge and learning (Hofer, 2004). Teachers should also create situations in which students find reason to doubt—and so feel dissatisfied with—their current beliefs (Bendixen & Rule, 2004; Hofer, 2002). Piaget would have called such dissatisfaction *disequilibrium;* more recently, it has been called **epistemic doubt** (Bendixen, 2002; Bendixen & Rule, 2004).

One possible way to change students' epistemological beliefs is to talk specifically about the nature of knowledge and learning—for instance, to describe learning as an active, ongoing process of finding interconnections among ideas and eventually constructing one's own understanding of the world (Schommer, 1994b). But probably an even more effective approach is to provide classroom experiences that lead students to discover that knowledge must by necessity be a dynamic (rather than static) entity and to realize that successful learning sometimes occurs only through effort and persistence. For example, teachers can have students address complex issues and problems that have no clear-cut right or wrong answers (Kardash & Scholes, 1996; King & Kitchener, 2002; Schommer, 1994b). They can teach strategies for gathering data and testing competing hypotheses (Andre & Windschitl, 2003; King & Kitchener, 2002; C. L. Smith,

Maclin, Houghton, & Hennessey, 2000). They can ask students to compare several explanations of a particular phenomenon and consider the validity and strength of evidence supporting each one (Andre & Windschitl, 2003; King & Kitchener, 2002; Linn et al., 1996). And they can show students, perhaps by presenting puzzling phenomena, that students' current understandings—and in some cases even those of experts in the field—do not yet adequately explain all of human experience (Chan et al., 1997; Vosniadou, 1991).

Teachers must be careful how far they take such strategies, however. When students are firmly rooted in their *learning-involves-facts-that-I-can-get-only-from-an-expert* beliefs, they may find little of value in—and so may gain little from—lessons that emphasize diverse perspectives and offer few solid answers (Andre & Windschitl, 2003).

♦ *Students should acquire mechanisms for monitoring and evaluating their own learning.* As we noted earlier, self-regulated learners monitor their progress throughout a learning task and then evaluate their ultimate success in mastering the material they have been studying. In addition to teaching students self-questioning (a technique that facilitates comprehension monitoring), theorists have offered several recommendations for promoting self-monitoring and self-evaluation in students:

- Have students set specific goals and objectives for a study session and then describe achievements in relation to each one (Eilam, 2001; Mithaug & Mithaug, 2003; Morgan, 1985).
- Ask students to keep ongoing records of their performance and to reflect on their learning in writing assignments, journals, or portfolios (Belfiore & Hornyak, 1998; Paris & Paris, 2001; Perry, 1998).
- Provide specific criteria that students can use to judge their performance; possibly include students in the development of these criteria (Paris & Ayres, 1994; Windschitl, 2002; Winne, 1995b).
- Provide self-tests that students can use to assess their current understandings of class material (Dunlosky, Rawson, & McDonald, 2002; Nietfeld & Cao, 2004).
- On some occasions, delay teacher feedback so that students first have the opportunity to evaluate their own performance (Butler & Winne, 1995; Schroth, 1992).
- Encourage students to evaluate their performance realistically, and then reinforce them (e.g., with praise or extra-credit points) when their evaluations match the teacher's (McCaslin & Good, 1996; Nietfeld & Cao, 2004; Schraw, Potenza, & Nebelsick-Gullet, 1993; Zuckerman, 1994).

Even 5- and 6-year-olds can be encouraged to reflect on their performance and progress, perhaps through questions such as "What were we doing that we're proud of?" and "What can we do that we didn't do before?" (Mithaug & Mithaug, 2003; Perry, VandeKamp, Mercer, & Nordby, 2002, p. 10). By engaging frequently in self-monitoring and self-evaluation of classroom assignments, students should eventually develop appropriate standards for their performance and regularly apply the standards to the things they accomplish—true hallmarks of a self-regulated learner.

♦ *Students must believe that, with sufficient effort and appropriate strategies, they **can** learn and understand challenging material.* Strategy instruction must give students a sense of self-efficacy about their ability to learn classroom material (McCombs, 1988; Palmer & Goetz, 1988; Paris, 1988; Shapley, 1994). And it must show them that their success in learning *is*, in fact, related to the specific strategies they use (Butler & Winne, 1995; Pressley, Borkowski, & Schneider, 1987; Pressley, El-Dinary, et al., 1992).

Once students believe that they can learn academic subject matter successfully, they are more likely to *want* to learn it. Self-efficacy is one key ingredient in students' motivation to achieve in the classroom, for reasons we'll identify in chapter 15.

By teaching students the metacognitive knowledge and skills they need to learn challenging classroom material, teachers not only help students learn that specific material more successfully but also help them become more effective learners over the long run. And it is the long run for which teachers must ultimately prepare their students.

Yet even with effective learning and self-regulatory skills, and even with high self-efficacy, students will not necessarily become intentional, "thoughtful" learners who gain maximum benefit from their classroom experiences. Ultimately, *motivating* students to learn is as important as *helping them learn how to learn.* Thus, the motivational strategies we identify in chapters 15 and 16 will be an important complement to the instructional strategies we've identified here.

SUMMARY

People's knowledge of effective learning and cognitive processes and their use of such processes to enhance learning are collectively known as *metacognition*. Students with more advanced metacognitive knowledge and skills typically achieve at higher levels in the classroom.

The most successful students are *self-regulated learners*: They set goals for their performance, plan how best to use their learning time, focus their attention on learning tasks, keep themselves motivated as they study, use effective learning strategies, monitor their progress, evaluate the final outcome of their efforts, and reflect on the overall effectiveness of their approach in order to improve future learning efforts. Some self-regulated learning skills may be self-developed, but many probably emerge when other people model them or when students work with more experienced learners (e.g., teachers) to co-regulate a learning task.

Effective learning and study strategies include meaningful learning, elaboration, organizing, note taking, identifying important information, summarizing, comprehension monitoring, and, when necessary, using mnemonics for hard-to-remember facts and lists. Most important are the internal mental processes (covert strategies) that students use; any observable study behaviors (overt strategies) are likely to be effective only when the covert strategies that underlie them are productive. Children show increasing metacognitive sophistication as they grow older and gain more experience with academic learning tasks; nevertheless, many students at the high school and college levels are sadly uninformed or misinformed about how best to learn.

Learners' *epistemological beliefs* are the things they believe about the nature of knowledge (e.g., whether it is static or dynamic, whether it involves isolated facts or a cohesive body of interrelated ideas, whether it comes from an outside authority or is constructed within) and the nature of learning (e.g., whether it occurs in an all-or-none fashion or slowly over a period of time, and whether it is determined more by inherited ability or more by effort and strategies). Students' epistemological beliefs influence the approaches they take to learning tasks and the criteria they use to decide when they have learned something successfully. Such beliefs continue to evolve throughout students' educational careers, with particularly sophisticated ones typically not emerging until the undergraduate or graduate school years.

Ideally, students should be *intentional* learners. That is, they should be actively and consciously engaged in the learning process, should identify particular goals to accomplish as they study, and should bring a wide variety of learning and self-regulatory strategies to any study session. Intentional learning is especially important when students must undergo considerable conceptual change in order to truly understand the subject matter.

There are numerous reasons why students don't use effective strategies to learn classroom subject matter. For example, students may be uninformed about effective strategies or have overly simplistic beliefs about what "knowing" something means. They may have insufficient prior knowledge about a topic to enable meaningful learning and elaboration, or assigned classroom tasks may not lend themselves to such strategies. Students may be uninterested in mastering classroom subject matter or, alternatively, may believe that they cannot master it regardless of what they do.

Research indicates that training in effective learning and study strategies can significantly enhance students' classroom achievement. Theorists and researchers have offered a number of suggestions for promoting more sophisticated metacognitive knowledge and skills. For example, instruction regarding effective learning strategies is more successful when presented within the context of specific academic content rather than as a topic separate from academic subject areas. Strategy instruction is also more successful when students have numerous opportunities to practice specific strategies and when teachers and classmates scaffold early efforts. Students must develop epistemological beliefs consistent with effective learning strategies, and they must acquire mechanisms for monitoring and evaluating their learning efforts. Ultimately, students must discover that, with sufficient effort and appropriate strategies, they *can* learn and understand challenging classroom material.

CHAPTER 13

Transfer and Problem Solving

I n my many years of college teaching, the course I've taught most frequently is an undergraduate course in educational psychology for students who are preparing to become elementary or secondary teachers. In various class sessions, I introduce such topics as contemporary memory theory, instrumental conditioning, cognitive development, motivation, classroom management, and educational assessment. Many of my students seem to learn the material well: They carry on informed discussions in class and demonstrate comprehension and application on assignments and exams. But I always wonder about what happens to these students after they finish my course. Do the things they've learned in my class make a difference in the way they eventually teach their own students? Do they really apply the concepts I've taught them? Do principles and theories of educational psychology help them solve classroom problems?

When something you learn in one situation affects how you learn or perform in another situation, **transfer** is occurring. Sometimes you transfer knowledge and skills you have previously learned to solve a problem; hence, **problem solving** is a form of transfer.

Ideally, transfer and problem solving should be two of our educational system's top priorities. Schools at all levels, from preschools to doctoral programs, teach knowledge and skills with the assumption that students will somehow apply what they've learned to the "real world." Yet the things people learn in school do not always seem to transfer to new situations and new problems. Some adults cannot use basic addition and subtraction procedures to balance their checkbooks. Some teachers reinforce inappropriate behaviors in their classrooms, ignoring the basic behaviorist principles they learned in their undergraduate psychology classes. Many psychologists agree that, in general, much school learning seems to yield **inert knowledge** that students never use outside of the classroom (Haskell, 2001; Perkins & Salomon, 1989; Renkl et al., 1996; Whitehead, 1929).

In this chapter, we will examine concepts, principles, theories, and research related to both transfer and problem solving. We'll also consider a variety of factors that either facilitate or interfere with the successful application of acquired knowledge and skills to new situations and problems. At the end of the chapter, we'll look at implications for educational practice.

TRANSFER

Transfer is a part of everyday life: People continually encounter new situations and draw on previously acquired knowledge and skills to deal with them. In fact, transfer is an essential component of human functioning. Without it, people would have to start from scratch about how to behave in every new circumstance and would spend much of their time in trial-and-error learning.

If you think back to our discussions of classical and instrumental conditioning in chapters 3 and 4, you might realize that we have already talked about transfer to some extent. In those chapters we considered the phenomenon of *generalization:* After an organism learns a response to one stimulus, it often makes the same response to similar stimuli. Generalization is clearly an instance of transfer because learning in one stimulus situation influences behavior in a slightly different situation. But here we will hardly be limiting ourselves to the behaviorist perspective. As you will discover in the upcoming pages, most contemporary explanations of transfer are decidedly cognitivist in nature.

Types of Transfer

Transfer can involve declarative knowledge, procedural knowledge, or a combination of the two (Haskell, 2001). For instance, when the word *HOMES* helps you remember the names of the five Great Lakes, one piece of declarative knowledge helps you learn or remember several other pieces. When your knowledge of how to throw a baseball helps you cast a fishing line, your existing procedural knowledge is assisting you in learning a new procedure. When your understanding of the base-10 number system helps you during the "borrowing" process in a subtraction problem, your declarative knowledge is guiding your execution of a procedure. Transfer can go in the reverse direction as well—from procedural knowledge to declarative knowledge—as I recently found out in an attempt at waterskiing. I had water-skied quite a bit as a teenager and young adult and fancied myself a reasonably skillful skier. After a 20-year hiatus, I tried skiing once again when in my mid-fifties. I discovered that the boat had a hard time pulling me up and had to go much faster—too fast for my comfort zone—to keep me on the water's surface. I had, alas, gained 30 pounds during that ski-free hiatus. My newly acquired declarative knowledge—more poundage necessitates more speed—has spurred a renewed commitment to minimize my junk food intake.

In addition to acknowledging that different instances of transfer can involve different kinds of knowledge, theorists have made several distinctions among types of transfer: positive versus negative, vertical versus lateral, near versus far, and specific versus general. Let's look briefly at each of these distinctions.

Positive Versus Negative Transfer

When learning in one situation facilitates learning or performance in another situation, we say that **positive transfer** is at work. Learning basic arithmetic procedures should enable a person to balance a checkbook. Learning principles of instrumental conditioning and self-regulation should help a teacher keep students on task in the classroom. The processes of meaningful learning and elaboration are also instances of positive transfer, because previously learned information is used in understanding and remembering new ideas (Ausubel et al., 1978; Brooks & Dansereau, 1987; Voss, 1987). "Old" information can help meaningful and elaborative learning in a variety of ways—perhaps by serving as a conceptual framework to which new material is attached, helping a learner fill in holes when new ideas are ambiguous or incomplete, or providing an analogy that makes abstract ideas easier to understand.

In contrast, when something learned in one situation hinders a person's ability to learn or perform in a second situation, **negative transfer** is operating. For example, people accustomed to driving a standard transmission who find themselves driving a car with an automatic transmission often step on a clutch that isn't there. People who learn a second language typically apply patterns of speech production characteristic of their native tongue, thus giving them a foreign accent; they may also mistakenly apply spelling patterns from their native language (Fashola, Drum, Mayer, & Kang, 1996; Schmidt & Young, 1987). Students accustomed to memorizing facts in other college courses often don't perform well on my own application-oriented exams.

An example of a situation in which negative transfer frequently rears its ugly head is in work with decimals: Students often erroneously apply mathematical rules they have learned for whole numbers (Ni & Zhou, 2005). For example, when asked to compare two decimals such as these:

$$2.34 \text{ versus } 2.8$$

students sometimes apply the rule that "more digits mean a larger number" and so conclude that 2.34 is the larger of the two decimal numbers (Behr & Harel, 1988). Another rule inappropriately transferred to decimals is this whole-number rule: "When a number is divided, the result is a smaller number." Even college students show negative transfer of this rule; for instance, many assert that the answer to this problem:

$$5 \div 0.65$$

is a number smaller than 5 (Tirosh & Graeber, 1990). The answer is actually about 7.69, a *larger* number.

As you can see, then, transfer isn't always a good thing. At the end of the chapter, we'll look at ways to maximize positive transfer while minimizing negative transfer.

Vertical Versus Lateral Transfer

In some subject areas, topics build on one another in a hierarchical fashion, so that a learner must almost certainly know one topic before moving to the next. For example, an elementary school student should probably master principles of addition before moving to multiplication, because multiplication is an extension of addition. Similarly, a medical student must have expertise in human anatomy before studying surgical techniques: It's difficult to perform an appendectomy if you can't find the appendix. **Vertical transfer** refers to such situations: A learner acquires new knowledge or skills by building on more basic information and procedures.

In other cases, knowledge of one topic may affect learning a second topic even though the first is not a prerequisite to the second. Knowledge of French isn't essential for learning Spanish, yet knowing French should facilitate learning Spanish because many words are similar in the two languages. When knowledge of the first topic is not essential to learning the second one but is helpful in learning it just the same, we say that **lateral transfer** is occurring.

Near Versus Far Transfer

Near transfer involves situations or problems that are similar in both superficial characteristics and underlying relationships. For example, consider the following problem:

> An automotive engineer has designed a car that can reach a speed of 50 miles per hour within 5 seconds. What is the car's rate of acceleration?

Let's assume that you have learned how to solve this problem by applying the formula $v = a \times t$ (velocity = acceleration $\times$ time elapsed). You then encounter this problem:

> A car salesperson tells a customer that a particular model of car can reach a speed of 40 miles per hour within 8 seconds. What is the car's rate of acceleration?

The two problems have similar surface characteristics (they both involve cars) and similar underlying structures (they both involve the relationship among velocity, acceleration, and time).

But now imagine that after solving the first problem, you instead encounter this problem:

> A zoologist reports that a cheetah she has been observing can attain a speed of 60 kilometers per hour within a 10-second period. How quickly can the cheetah increase its speed?

Although the general structure is the same as before (once again, the $v = a \times t$ formula applies), we have now switched topics (from cars to cheetahs) and units of measurement (from miles-per-hour to kilometers-per-second). **Far transfer** involves two situations that are similar in one or more underlying relationships but *different* in their surface features. It may also involve looking at a relationship from a different angle—for instance, calculating a cheetah's acceleration rate when time period and final speed are known. An even "farther" instance of transfer might involve taking the $v = a \times t$ formula outside the classroom altogether—say, to a race track or zoologist's laboratory.

Specific Versus General Transfer

Both near and far transfer are instances of **specific transfer.** In specific transfer, the original learning task and the transfer task overlap in some way. For example, having knowledge about a human being's anatomy should help a veterinary student learn a dog's anatomy because the two species have many parallel anatomical features. A student who knows Spanish should easily learn Portuguese because the two languages have similar vocabulary and syntax.

In **general transfer,** the original task and the transfer task are different in both content and structure. For example, if knowledge of Latin helps a student learn physics, or if the study habits acquired in a physics course facilitate the learning of sociology, then general transfer is occurring.

Research clearly shows that near transfer is more common than far transfer and that specific transfer is more common than general transfer (Bassok, 1997; Di Vesta & Peverly, 1984; Gray & Orasanu, 1987; Perkins & Salomon, 1989). In fact, the question of whether general transfer can occur at all has been the subject of much debate over the years. We turn now to both early and contemporary theories of transfer, which vary considerably in their perspectives of what things transfer and when.

Theories of Transfer

How does transfer occur? We'll look first at an early view of transfer—one that predates twentieth-century learning theories—and then see what both behaviorists and cognitivists have had to say about how and when transfer takes place.

A Historical Perspective: Formal Discipline

In days of yore, serious scholars often studied rigorous and difficult topics—for instance, Latin, Greek, and formal logic—that are not as frequently studied today. Although these subject areas may have had no specific applicability to everyday tasks, scholars believed that learning such subjects would nevertheless improve people's learning and performance in many aspects of their lives. As recently as the middle of the twentieth century, students were given frequent practice in memorizing things (poems, for example), apparently as a method of improving their general learning capabilities. Such practices reflect the notion of **formal discipline:** Just as you exercise muscles to develop strength, you exercise your mind to learn more quickly and deal with new situations more effectively.

The theory of formal discipline, a predominant view in educational circles in the nineteenth century and early decades of the twentieth century, emphasized the importance and likelihood of general transfer, the idea being that learning in one situation improves learning and performance in another situation regardless of how different the two situations might be. As human learning began to be studied empirically, however, this notion of "mind as muscle" was soon discarded. For example, William James[1] (1890) memorized a new poem each day over the course of several weeks, assuming that he would begin to learn poems more quickly with practice. Yet he found that his poem learning did not improve; if anything, he learned his later poems more *slowly* than his early ones. More recently, researchers have found that learning computer programming— a skill requiring precise, detailed thinking about a logical sequence of events—does *not* facilitate people's logical thinking in areas unrelated to computer use (Mayer & Wittrock, 1996; Perkins & Salomon, 1989). The consensus of contemporary learning theorists is that general transfer, in the extreme sense portrayed by the formal discipline perspective, probably does not occur (e.g., Haskell, 2001; Salthouse, 2006).

An Early Behaviorist Theory: Thorndike's Identical Elements

Early in the twentieth century, the behaviorist Edward Thorndike (1903, 1924) proposed a theory of transfer that emphasized specific transfer: Transfer occurs only to the extent that the original and transfer tasks have *identical elements*—that is, the extent to which specific stimulus–response associations in the two tasks are the same. In an early study supporting his view (Thorndike & Woodworth, 1901), people received extensive training in estimating the areas of rectangles. The training improved people's subsequent ability to estimate the areas

---

[1]As you may recall, William James was the Harvard psychologist who, back in 1890, suggested that human memory has three components. Atkinson and Shiffrin's dual-store model (described in chapter 7) was based in part on James's ideas.

of rectangles and other two-dimensional forms (e.g., triangles and circles). However, training had less of an impact on the judgment of nonrectangular shapes, presumably because nonrectangles had elements both similar and dissimilar to the elements of rectangles. In a later study, Thorndike (1924) examined the interrelationships of high school students' academic achievement in various curricular areas. Achievement in one subject area appeared to facilitate students' achievement in another only when the two subjects were similar. For example, arithmetic achievement was related to performance in a bookkeeping course, but Latin proficiency was not. Thorndike concluded that the value of studying specific topics was due not to the benefits of mental exercise but to "the special information, habits, interests, attitudes, and ideals which they demonstrably produce" (Thorndike, 1924, p. 98).

A Later Behaviorist Perspective: Similarity of Stimuli and Responses

Since Thorndike's work, behaviorist views of transfer have focused on how transfer is affected by stimulus and response characteristics in both the original and transfer situations. As an illustration, consider these four lists of paired associates:

List 1	List 2	List 3	List 4
lamp–shoe	lamp–sock	rain–shoe	lamp–goat
boat–fork	boat–spoon	bear–fork	boat–shop
wall–lawn	wall–yard	sofa–lawn	wall–rice
corn–road	corn–lane	book–road	corn–fish

Imagine that you first learn List 1 and then are asked to learn List 2. Will your knowledge of the pairs in List 1 help you learn the pairs in List 2? Based on the results of verbal learning studies (Hall, 1966, 1971), the answer is yes: The stimulus words are identical in the two situations and the responses are similar, so positive transfer from one list to the other is likely to occur.

Now, however, imagine that you have to learn List 1 and then List 3. Will prior learning of List 1 help with List 3? The answer again is yes (Hall, 1966, 1971). Even though the stimulus words are very different, the responses in List 3 are identical to those of List 1—hence they have already been learned—and merely need to be attached to the new stimuli.

But now let's now suppose that, after learning List 1, you need to learn List 4. Here is a case in which very different responses from those of List 1 must be learned to the very same stimuli. Learning List 1 is likely to make learning List 4 more difficult because you will sometimes remember the List 1 response instead of the List 4 response (Hall, 1966, 1971), and negative transfer will result.

In general, principles of transfer that have emerged from behaviorist literature (Osgood, 1949; Thyne, 1963) include the following:

1. When stimuli and responses are similar in the two situations, maximal positive transfer will occur.
2. When stimuli are different and responses are similar, some positive transfer will occur.
3. When stimuli are similar and responses are different, negative transfer will occur.

As an example of the last principle, I remember one year as a high school student when my class schedule included second-period Latin and third-period French. The word for "and" (*et*) is spelled the same in both languages but pronounced very differently ("et" in Latin and "ay" in French), hence meeting the conditions for negative transfer (similar stimuli, different responses).

On several occasions I blurted out an "et" in my French class—a response that inevitably evoked a disgusted scowl from my French teacher.

As learning theorists have moved away from behaviorist perspectives to more cognitive explanations of how human beings learn, they have spoken less and less of specific stimulus–response connections. Nevertheless, we see hints of behaviorist notions even in today's conceptions of transfer. For example, similarity between something already learned and the demands of a new situation clearly *is* an important factor affecting the extent to which transfer occurs. And one cognitive psychologist (J. R. Anderson, 1987) has proposed that transfer occurs to the extent that procedures (productions) used in one situation apply to a second situation— a cognitive variation on Thorndike's theory of identical elements.

An Information Processing Perspective: Importance of Retrieval

As was evident in our earlier discussion of *inert knowledge,* simply knowing something doesn't necessarily mean that learners will use it later on. From an information processing perspective, people are likely to transfer previously learned information and skills to a new situation only if they retrieve what they've learned at the appropriate time (Cormier, 1987; Haskell, 2001; Prawat, 1989). To make a connection between their current situation and any prior knowledge that might be relevant, people must have both things in working memory at the same time. Given the low probability that any particular piece of information will be retrieved, as well as the limited capacity of working memory, many potentially relevant pieces of information may very well *not* be transferred in situations in which they would be helpful.

The presence or absence of retrieval cues in the transfer situation will influence what relevant knowledge, if any, is retrieved to working memory. A new event is more likely to call to mind previously learned information when aspects of the event and the needed information are closely associated in long-term memory. This will be the case, for instance, if learners previously anticipated the transfer situation when first storing the information.

A Contextual Perspective: Situated Learning

Some cognitive theorists have proposed that most learning is context specific—that it is "situated" in the environment in which it takes place. Such **situated learning** is unlikely to result in transfer to new contexts, especially those very different from the ones in which learning originally occurred (J. S. Brown, Collins, & Duguid, 1989; Greeno, Moore, & Smith, 1993; Lave & Wenger, 1991; Light & Butterworth, 1993; Wagner, 2006).

Some knowledge and skills may indeed be context bound (Butterworth, 1993; Hirschfeld & Gelman, 1994; Snow, 1994). For example, children who sell candy, gum, and other items on the street may readily use basic mathematical procedures when calculating total prices or computing change for a customer and yet not transfer such procedures to classroom math lessons (Carraher, Carraher, & Schliemann, 1985; Schliemann & Carraher, 1993). Carpenters may learn mathematical concepts such as *parallel* and *perpendicular* within the context of carpentry yet not realize that their knowledge is applicable in other situations requiring the same concepts (Millroy, 1991). Furthermore, as we discovered in our discussion of Piaget's theory in chapter 11, children can often apply logical thinking skills (e.g., proportional reasoning, or separation and control of variables) to situations with which they have had previous experience yet *not* be able to use them in less familiar contexts.

Even at school, skills don't necessarily transfer from one classroom to another (Bassok & Holyoak, 1990, 1993). A study by Saljo and Wyndham (1992) provides an illustration. High school students were asked to figure out how much postage they should put on an envelope weighing a particular amount, and they were given a table of postage rates that would enable them to determine the correct amount. When students were given the task in a social studies class, most of them used the postage table to find the answer. But when students were given the task in a math class, most of them ignored the postage table and tried to *calculate* the postage in some manner, sometimes figuring it to several decimal places. Thus, the students in the social studies class were more likely to solve the problem correctly; as a former social studies teacher myself, I suspect that they were well accustomed to looking for information in tables and charts in that context. In contrast, many of the students in the math class drew on strategies they associated with that class (using formulas and performing calculations) and so overlooked the more efficient and accurate approach.

It is important to note here that not all cognitivists believe that learning is as situated as some of their colleagues claim (e.g., see J. R. Anderson, Reder, & Simon, 1996, 1997; Bereiter, 1997; Perkins, 1992). Critics argue that in its present form, situated learning theory is too vague to allow us to predict exactly when transfer will and will not take place (J. R. Anderson et al., 1997; Renkl, Mandl, & Gruber, 1996). They also point out that people often do use the things they have learned in school in real-world situations; for example, most individuals in our society engage in reading and simple mathematics—two sets of skills they've probably learned at school—in many nonschool contexts (J. R. Anderson et al., 1996).

A key factor here appears to be the extent to which students *perceive* a content domain to be applicable to a wide variety of circumstances. Unfortunately, students all too often view their school learning as being relevant *only* to school (Gick & Holyoak, 1987; Mayer & Wittrock, 1996; Perkins & Simmons, 1988; Sternberg & Frensch, 1993). For example, when baking cookies, an 11-year-old might ask a parent, "Do two one-quarters make two fourths? I know it does in math but what about in cooking?" (Pugh & Bergin, 2005, p. 16). Fortunately, most students eventually learn that math has wide applicability, perhaps because teachers ask students to apply mathematical principles to a wide variety of situations and problems. The same isn't necessarily true for other disciplines, however. For instance, many elementary students don't recognize that the things they learn in science are useful in solving real-world problems (Rakow, 1984). And although college students often transfer skills they learn in algebra to a physics class, they rarely transfer skills in the other direction, from physics to algebra (Bassok, 1997).

A Contemporary View of General Transfer: Learning to Learn

We have already seen two extreme perspectives regarding general transfer. Advocates of formal discipline argued that learning rigorous and demanding subject matter facilitates virtually all future learning tasks because it strengthens and "disciplines" the mind. At the other extreme, Thorndike argued that learning in one situation will transfer to another situation only to the extent that the two situations have identical elements. Current perspectives about general transfer are somewhere in between: General transfer is not as common as specific transfer, but learning occurring at one time can facilitate learning at another time if, in the process, the individual *learns how to learn.*

In several early studies of learning to learn, Harry Harlow (1949, 1950, 1959) found that monkeys and young children became progressively faster at discrimination-learning tasks. More recently, a number of studies have examined the transfer value of metacognitive knowledge and skills. As we noted in chapter 12, effective study methods and habits often do generalize from one subject matter to another (see also Brooks & Dansereau, 1987; De Corte, 2003; A. L. Brown, 1978; Pressley, Snyder, & Cariglia-Bull, 1987).

Going Beyond Transfer of Knowledge: Emotional Reactions and Motivation May Transfer as Well

Despite their differences, all the views of transfer we've examined so far have one thing in common: As long as two tasks have at least *some* overlap in the information or skills required—even if the skills in question are general metacognitive ones rather than topic-specific ones—the possibility of transfer from one situation to the other exists. Yet transfer isn't necessarily limited to cognitive and metacognitive acquisitions. For instance, recall how, in my discussion of classical conditioning in chapter 3, Little Albert generalized (transferred) his fear of a white rat to other fuzzy white things. Just as emotional reactions may transfer to new situations, so, too, may motivation transfer. For instance, the kinds of goals that students learn to set for themselves in a learning task—perhaps to truly master the subject matter, on the one hand, or to rote-memorize just enough to "get by" on a class assignment or quiz—are apt to carry over as students move from one classroom environment to a very different one (Pugh & Bergin, 2005, 2006; Pugh, Linnenbrink, Kelly, Manzey, & Stewart, 2006; Volet, 1999). And in some cases, students may develop a general desire to apply what they learn in the classroom—they have a "spirit of transfer," if you will—that consistently reappears in later instructional contexts (Haskell, 2001; Pugh & Bergin, 2005, 2006). We'll return to this idea in our discussion of *dispositions* in chapter 15.

Factors Affecting Transfer

Learners are, of course, more likely to transfer something they learn when they approach a learning task with a conscious intention to apply it. But several other factors also influence the probability of transfer, as reflected in the following principles:

- *Meaningful learning promotes better transfer than rote learning.* We have previously seen that meaningfully learned information is more easily stored and retrieved than information learned at a rote level. Now we see an additional advantage of meaningful learning: It promotes positive transfer (Ausubel et al., 1978; Brooks & Dansereau, 1987; Mayer & Wittrock, 1996; Prawat, 1989). For example, in a study by Brownell and Moser (1949, cited in Mayer, 1977), third-grade students were taught the idea of borrowing in subtraction in a presumably meaningful manner: Two-digit numbers were represented by individual sticks and groups of 10 sticks bundled together, with borrowing represented by the untying of one group of 10. These students solved a variety of subtraction problems more successfully than students taught the same information simply through verbally presented rules. Along a similar vein, in an experiment by Mayer and Greeno (1972), two groups of college students received one of two methods of instruction on a formula related to basic probability theory. Group 1 received instruction that focused on the formula itself, whereas Group 2 received instruction that emphasized the relationship of the formula to students' general knowledge. Group 1 students were better able to apply the formula to problems similar to those they had studied during instruction, but Group 2 students were better able to use the formula in ways that had not specifically been covered in instruction—that is, they could transfer the formula to a wider variety of situations. Apparently, Group 2 students had made more connections between the new material and existing information in their long-term memories, and those connections enabled them to transfer probability theory in ways that Group 1 students could not.

- *The more thoroughly something is learned, the more likely it is to be transferred to a new situation.* Research is clear on this point: The probability of transfer increases when students know something *well* (Brophy, 1992b; Cormier & Hagman, 1987; Haskell, 2001; Voss, 1987).

Acquiring knowledge and skills thoroughly takes time. In fact, some conditions that make initial learning slower and more difficult may actually be beneficial both for retention (see chapter 8) and for transfer over the long run. For example, increasing the variability of the tasks learners are asked to practice during instruction—having them perform several different tasks or several variations on the same task within a single instructional unit—lowers their performance initially but enhances their ability to transfer what they have learned to new situations later on (Chen, 1999; Schmidt & Bjork, 1992).

Clearly, then, there is a trade-off between expediency and transfer. Teachers who teach a few things in depth are more likely to promote transfer than those who teach many things quickly— the *less is more* principle I introduced in chapter 9. Students should demonstrate thorough mastery of material if they will be expected to apply the material in future situations.

◆ *The more similar two situations are, the more likely it is that something learned in one situation will be applied to the other situation.* Behaviorists have argued that similarity of either stimuli or responses is necessary for transfer to occur. Cognitivists have proposed instead that because transfer depends on retrieval of relevant information at the appropriate time, the *perceived* similarity rather than actual similarity of the two situations is important (Bassok & Holyoak, 1993; Di Vesta & Peverly, 1984; Haskell, 2001; Voss, 1987). Either way, one thing is clear: Similarity between two situations makes a difference.

◆ *Principles are more easily transferred than discrete facts.* General principles and rules are more applicable than specific facts and information (Cheng, Holyoak, Nisbett, & Oliver, 1986; Fong, Krantz, & Nisbett, 1986; Gick & Holyoak, 1987; Judd, 1932; Perkins & Salomon, 1987; Perry, 1991; Singley & Anderson, 1989). For example, if you have read chapter 4, then you can probably recall the essence of operant conditioning: *A response that is followed by a reinforcer is strengthened and is therefore more likely to occur again.* This principle is easily transferable to a wide variety of situations, whereas specific facts that I mentioned in the same chapter (e.g., who did what research study and when) are not. Similarly, when students are trying to understand such current events as revolutions and international wars, general principles of history—for example, the principle that two groups of people often engage in battle when other attempts at reaching a mutually satisfying state of affairs have failed—are probably more applicable than precise knowledge of World War II battles. And when students study geography, general map interpretation skills—for instance, determining why various features are located where they are—are probably more useful than the names and locations of specific rivers, mountain ranges, and state capitals (Bochenhauer, 1990). General and perhaps somewhat abstract principles are especially helpful when a new situation does not, on the surface, appear to be similar to previous experiences and yet shares underlying structural or conceptual similarities with those experiences—in other words, when the new situation requires *far transfer* (J. R. Anderson et al., 1996; Perkins, 1995; Perkins & Salomon, 1989).[2]

---

[2]Perkins and Salomon (1989) have made a distinction between low-road transfer and high-road transfer. *Low-road transfer* occurs when a new situation is superficially quite similar to prior experiences, such that relevant knowledge and skills are readily retrieved. But in *high-road transfer,* people must make a conscious and deliberate connection between a new situation and their previous experiences; such a connection is often made on the basis of an underlying, abstract principle. In other words, low-road transfer is most likely to occur in situations involving near transfer, whereas high-road transfer is required in situations involving far transfer.

◆ *Numerous and varied examples and opportunities for practice increase the extent to which information and skills will be applied in new situations.* As situated learning theorists have reminded us, new knowledge is often stored in association with the contexts in which it has been acquired, and revisiting such contexts increases the chances of retrieving that knowledge. The more examples and practice situations in which particular information and skills are encountered, then, the greater the likelihood that transfer will occur (J. R. Anderson et al., 1996; Cormier, 1987; Cox, 1997; Gick & Holyoak, 1987; Kotovsky & Fallside, 1989; Perkins, 1995; Schmidt & Bjork, 1992; see Bassok & Holyoak, 1993, for an exception). For instance, when students are learning basic arithmetic principles, they might be asked to apply those principles in determining best buys at a grocery store, dividing items equitably among friends, running a lemonade stand, and so on. Arithmetic will then be associated in long-term memory with all of these situations, and when the need arises to determine which of two grocery products yields the most for the money, relevant arithmetic procedures should be readily retrieved.

◆ *The probability of transfer decreases as the time interval between the original task and the transfer task increases* (Gick & Holyoak, 1987). Here is another principle that is probably a result of retrieval: Information that has been learned recently is more likely, and more able, to be retrieved than information acquired further back in time (recall our discussion of *decay* in chapter 10).

◆ *Transfer increases when the cultural environment encourages and expects transfer.* Not only have behaviorists, information processing theorists, and situated learning theorists weighed in on the topic of transfer, but so, too, have sociocultural theorists (Haskell, 2001; Rogoff, 2003). In particular, these theorists suggest that teachers and other experts who regularly point out similarities among seemingly diverse tasks and situations and who communicate the importance of transfer increase the chances that learners will apply what they learn to new situations. Such a culture often exists in the workplace: New employees are expected to use newly acquired declarative and procedural knowledge in a wide variety of work situations (Haskell, 2001; Wenger, 1998). It is also evident in some classrooms, but is probably not as pervasive as it should be. All too often, it seems, students are encouraged to acquire school subject matter for mysterious purposes (e.g., "You'll need to know this in college" or "It will come in handy later in life") but given little insight about when and in what ways it will be useful. We'll consider strategies for creating and enhancing a culture of transfer near the end of the chapter.

How and when do people transfer information they have learned to find solutions to problems? It is to this topic—problem solving—that we turn next.

PROBLEM SOLVING

Can you solve these three problems?

1. What number is obtained when 3,354 is divided by 43?
2. How can a middle-aged educational psychologist be helped to control her junk food habit?
3. How can two groups of people of differing political or religious persuasions and a mutual lack of trust be convinced to curtail their proliferation of military weapons and instead work toward cooperation and peaceful coexistence?

The world presents us with many different kinds of problems. Some, such as Problem 1, are straightforward: All of the information necessary for a solution is presented, and the solution is definitely right or wrong. Others, such as Problem 2, may necessitate seeking out additional information (e.g., does the educational psychologist keep physically active, or does she sit around the house all day reading mystery novels and watching television game shows?), and there may be two or more solutions to the problem (e.g., self-reinforcement for altered eating habits, six months on a tropical island with no grocery stores). Still others, such as Problem 3, may be so complicated that, even after considerable research and creative thought, no easy solution emerges (as I write this, events in the Middle East come to mind). Different kinds of problems require different procedures and different solutions; this multifaceted nature of problem solving has made the theoretical study of problem solving a very challenging endeavor indeed.

Any problem has at least three components (Glass et al., 1979; Wickelgren, 1974):

- **Goal:** The desired end state—what a problem solution will hopefully accomplish
- **Givens:** Pieces of information that are provided when the problem is presented
- **Operations:** Actions that can be performed to approach or reach the goal

Operations are frequently described in terms of *productions,* the "IF–THEN" conditional actions described in chapter 9 (e.g., see J. R. Anderson, 1983a, 1987). When one or more operations can be applied to reach the goal state, the problem is successfully solved.

Problems vary greatly in terms of how well their components are specified and made clear. Many theorists have found it helpful to distinguish between well-defined and ill-defined problems, a distinction that actually reflects a continuum of problem structure rather than a rigid dichotomy (Frederiksen, 1984a). At one extreme is the **well-defined problem,** one for which the desired end result is clearly stated, all of the necessary information is readily available, and a particular sequence of operations will (if properly executed) lead to a correct solution. At the other extreme is the **ill-defined problem,** one in which the goal is ambiguous, some essential information is lacking, and no guaranteed means of reaching the goal exists. Well-defined problems often have only one right solution, whereas ill-defined problems often have several possible solutions that vary in terms of their relative "rightness" or acceptability. The problem of dividing 3,354 by 43 is well defined, while that of military disarmament is ill defined (e.g., the goal of "cooperation and peaceful coexistence" is ambiguous).[3] As you might guess, ill-defined problems are typically more difficult to solve and require more complex problem-solving strategies than well-defined problems.

Unfortunately, researchers have focused more on well-defined problems (often somewhat artificial ones) than on the ill-defined problems that life so often presents (Eysenck & Keane, 1990; Rosenshine, Meister, & Chapman, 1996; Zimmerman & Campillo, 2003). You will probably notice this bias as we proceed with our discussion of problem solving. Nevertheless, most of the theories and principles I will present presumably apply to both kinds of problems. And in fact, later in the chapter we will find that one strategy for solving ill-defined problems is to define them more specifically and concretely—in other words, to make them well defined.

---

[3]For a detailed discussion of ill-defined problems in international relations, see Voss, Wolfe, Lawrence, and Engle (1991).

Theories of Problem Solving

Behaviorists and cognitivists alike have offered theories of how human beings and other animal species solve problems. Here we will look briefly at early behaviorist and cognitivist views of problem solving. We will then draw largely from information processing theory as we explore more contemporary explanations.

Early Behaviorist Views: Trial-and-Error Learning and Response Hierarchies

In chapter 4, you read about Thorndike's (1898) classic work with a cat in a puzzle box. The cat needed to solve a problem: how to get out of a confining situation. It explored the box, manipulating the various parts, and eventually triggered a mechanism that opened the door. Once again the cat was put back into the box, and once again it tried different behaviors until it triggered the release mechanism. On each succeeding occasion, escape from the box took less time than it had previously. The cat's approach to the problem situation appeared to be one of trial and error, with the correct solution being followed by a desired consequence (escape from the box).

A trial-and-error approach is often observed in the problem-solving behavior of children. For example, consider the way many young children assemble jigsaw puzzles: They try to fit different pieces into the same spot, often without considering each piece's shape and appearance, until eventually they find a piece that fits. Such an approach to problem solving is a workable one if there are only a limited number of possibilities one can try. Otherwise, it can be quite time consuming, with no guarantee of finding a successful solution (Chi & Glaser, 1985).

In trial-and-error learning, humans and animals alike may discover that they can potentially solve a particular problem in a variety of ways, with some ways having greater success rates—that is, they are reinforced more often—than others. The result is that the stimuli comprising the problem are apt to be associated with several responses, with some associations being stronger than others (Davis, 1966; Hull, 1938; Mayzner & Tresselt, 1958, 1966; Skinner, 1966a). Such a **response hierarchy** can be graphically depicted like this (thicker arrows indicate stronger associations):

When encountering a particular stimulus situation, the organism first makes the response with the strongest association to the stimulus (R_1). If that response doesn't lead to success, the organism makes the response with the second strongest association (R_2), then the third strongest response (R_3), and so on until (perhaps) success is achieved. To illustrate, as my daughter Tina was growing up, she was often confronted with the same problem: getting permission from her parents to do something we didn't want her to do. Given this problem, she typically tried three different responses, usually in the same order. First she would smile sweetly and describe how much she wanted to engage in the forbidden activity (such a response, apparently, was associated most strongly with this particular problem situation). If that tactic was unproductive, she would speak indignantly about how her parents never let her do anything. As a last resort, she would run off to her room, slamming her door and shouting that her parents hated her. Tina never did learn that some problems, such as gaining permission to engage in forbidden activities, would be solved over her parents' dead bodies.

In their emphasis on trial-and-error learning and response hierarchies, early behaviorists obviously focused on the role that stimulus–response connections play in problem solving. Although such an approach can sometimes be used to explain problem-solving behavior, contemporary theorists have largely abandoned it to focus more on the mental processes involved in problem solving. Consistent with this trend, we, too, will abandon behaviorism at this point and embrace a more cognitively oriented perspective for the rest of our discussion.

Early Cognitivist Views: Insight and Stages of Problem Solving

In chapter 7, I described Gestalt psychologist Wolfgang Köhler's (1925) observations of chimpanzee behavior in problem-solving situations. Köhler observed little trial-and-error behavior of the form that Thorndike had described. Rather, it appeared to him that the chimpanzees carefully examined the components of a problem situation (sizing things up, so to speak) and mentally combined and recombined those components until they eventually found a winning combination. At this point of *insight,* the chimps would immediately move into action, performing the required responses in a deliberate manner until the problem was solved. From such observations, Köhler (1925, 1929) concluded that problem solving was a process of mentally *restructuring* a problem situation until insight into the problem's solution was reached.

Another early cognitive approach to problem solving was to identify the mental stages—perhaps including insight—through which problem solving might proceed. For example, Wallas (1926) identified four steps in problem solving:

1. *Preparation:* Defining the problem and gathering information relevant to its solution
2. *Incubation:* Thinking about the problem at a subconscious level while engaging in other activities
3. *Inspiration:* Having a sudden insight into the solution of the problem
4. *Verification:* Checking to be certain that the solution is correct

Whereas Wallas suggested that certain aspects of problem solving might be out of the mental "limelight," Polya (1957) proposed four steps that rely heavily on conscious, controlled mental activities:

1. *Understanding the problem:* Identifying the problem's knowns (givens) and unknowns and, if appropriate, using suitable notation, such as mathematical symbols, to represent the problem
2. *Devising a plan:* Determining appropriate actions to take to solve the problem
3. *Carrying out the plan:* Executing the actions that have been determined to solve the problem and checking their effectiveness
4. *Looking backward:* Evaluating the overall effectiveness of the approach to the problem, with the intention of learning something about how similar problems may be solved on future occasions

Unfortunately, Wallas and Polya derived their portrayals of problem solving more from introspection and informal observation than from controlled experimentation, and they were somewhat vague about how each of their four steps could be accomplished (Lester, 1985; Mayer, 1992; Schoenfeld, 1992). For example, Wallas's notion of incubation revealed little about how to behave to facilitate the occurrence of inspiration. Similarly, Polya recommended devising a plan with little consideration of just how one would go about doing that. For such reasons, early stage theories of problem solving were of limited usefulness in helping psychologists determine what specific cognitive processes are involved in solving problems.

Yet early cognitivist views have clearly had an impact on contemporary explanations of how people solve problems. As we shall soon see, problem solving sometimes involves deliberate and controlled mental processes (similar to those that Polya described) and at other times involves less conscious processes (about which Wallas speculated). Furthermore, people sometimes reconceptualize (restructure) problems with which they're wrestling and, in doing so, can occasionally reach solutions of the sudden-insight variety.

Information Processing Theory

Most contemporary theories focus less on the steps people follow in solving problems and more on the specific cognitive processes they use to reach problem solutions. The bulk of current research in problem solving reflects inquiry into the nature of these processes. In the following section, we will look at them in detail.

Cognitive Factors in Problem Solving

The ability to solve problems successfully depends on a number of factors related to the human information processing system. Here we will focus on several factors: working memory capacity, encoding and storage processes, long-term memory retrieval, the knowledge base relevant to the problem, and metacognition. As we go along, we'll identify several differences between problem-solving experts and novices within a particular content domain, discovering reasons why some people solve problems quickly, easily, and effectively, whereas others solve them either with great difficulty or not at all.

Working Memory Capacity

As you should recall, working memory is the component of memory in which the active, conscious processing of information occurs. Yet this component has a limited capacity: It can hold and process only a small amount of information at a time. If the information and processes necessary to solve a problem exceed working memory capacity—or perhaps if irrelevant thoughts consume some of that capacity—the problem cannot be solved (J. R. Anderson, 1987; Hambrick & Engle, 2003; Johnstone & El-Banna, 1986; Salthouse, 1991; Tourniaire & Pulos, 1985). For example, you may remember from chapter 7 how difficult it can be to solve long-division problems in your head.

The working memory limitation can be overcome in problem-solving situations in a couple of ways. First, some of the information necessary to solve the problem can be stored externally (e.g., by writing it down on paper) or perhaps even processed externally (e.g., by using a calculator). Second, as I suggested in chapter 8, some skills involved in problem solving should be learned well enough that they become automatic, thus requiring only minimal working memory capacity.

Encoding and Storage of the Problem

Consider this classic children's riddle:

> As I was going to St. Ives,
> I met a man with seven wives.
> Every wife had seven sacks.
> Every sack had seven cats.
> Every cat had seven kits.
> Kits, cats, sacks, wives.
> How many were going to St. Ives?

Many people take this logical approach to the problem: 1 traveler plus 1 man plus 7 wives plus 7^2 sacks (49) plus 7^3 cats (343) plus 7^4 kits (2,401) equal a total of 2,802 going to St. Ives. People who solve the problem in this way have encoded the problem incorrectly. In particular, they have overlooked the first line of the riddle: "As *I* was going to St. Ives." The problem statement doesn't tell us where the polygamist was taking his harem and menagerie—perhaps to St. Ives, perhaps not.

One critical factor in problem solving is *what* specific information is stored in memory (Chi, Glaser, & Farr, 1988; Glaser, 1987; Sternberg & Davidson, 1982, 1983; Whitten & Graesser, 2003). A difficulty you may have had with the St. Ives problem is that you encountered a lot of irrelevant information (all the kits, cats, sacks, and wives, plus the man who accompanied them), and you may have stored that information instead of or in addition to more essential data. Irrelevant information can be distracting, thus interfering with problem solving. For example, when my daughter Tina was in elementary and middle school, she often had trouble with math problems that included superfluous facts. She behaved almost as if she had learned that she needed to use *all* of the information she was given. This attitude may have been the result of her prior school experiences: Most of the problems she had previously encountered (especially word problems in mathematics) presented only the information needed to solve the problem—no more, no less.

A second critical factor is *how* a problem is encoded and stored in memory (Mayer, 1986; Ormrod, 1979; Prawat, 1989; Resnick, 1989; Schwartz, 1971; Sternberg & Davidson, 1982). For instance, consider this problem:

> A man who lived in a small town in the U.S. married 20 different women of the same town. All are still living and he has never divorced one of them. Yet he has broken no law. Can you explain? (Pretz, Naples, & Sternberg, 2003, p. 18)

The trick here lies in how you encode the word *marry*—whether you interpret it as entering into wedlock with a woman (in which case the problem seemingly has no solution) *or* as performing a marriage ceremony for two other people (in which case the solution is obvious). As another example, consider these two ways of presenting the same situation:

- There are 5 birds and 3 worms. How many more birds are there than worms?
- There are 5 birds and 3 worms. How many birds won't get a worm?

First graders often struggle with the first problem and yet solve the second one quite easily (Hudson, 1983). The first problem requires students to store *relational* information—how one thing compares to another. Relational information seems to be difficult to encode, even for adults. For instance, Mayer (1982) examined undergraduate students' ability to remember problems such as this one:

> A truck leaves Los Angeles en route to San Francisco at 1 P.M. A second truck leaves San Francisco at 2 P.M. en route to Los Angeles going along the same route. Assume the two cities are 465 miles apart and that the trucks meet at 6 P.M. If the second truck travels at 15 mph faster than the first truck, how fast does each truck go? (Mayer, 1982, p. 202)

The students in Mayer's study had considerable difficulty remembering relational information (e.g., one truck traveling *15 mph faster* than another): They made three times as many errors in recalling relational aspects of problems as they did in recalling basic assertions (e.g., two cities being 465 miles apart).

How people encode a problem—and therefore how they solve it—is partly a function of how they classify the problem to begin with. People are apt to have a variety of **problem schemas**—knowledge about certain types of problems that can be solved in certain ways—that they use in problem classification (Cooper & Sweller, 1987; L. S. Fuchs et al., 2004; Gick & Holyoak, 1983). For example, consider this problem:

> Ana went shopping. She spent $3.50 and then counted her money when she got home. She had $2.35 left. How much did Ana have when she started out? (Resnick, 1989, p. 165)

If you retrieve and apply an *addition* schema as you read the problem, you will probably get the correct answer of $5.85. However, if the word *left* in the problem leads you to classify the problem as one requiring subtraction (because many subtraction problems ask questions such as "How many are *left*?"), you may very well get the incorrect answer of $1.15 (Resnick, 1989).

Problem classification comes into play when solving social problems as well. Consider this situation:

> The students in Alice's ninth-grade social studies class have been working in pairs on an assigned project; their teacher has said that he will give a prize for the best project that a pair completes. Alice is now complaining to her younger sister Louisa that her partner, Meg, no longer wants to work with her; Meg thinks Alice is too bossy. Louisa suggests that the best course of action is simply for Alice and Meg to buckle down and finish the project so that they can win the prize. Alice, however, is thinking that she should instead talk with Meg and promise that she will be less bossy. (based on Berg & Calderone, 1994)

Louisa and Alice are classifying the problem in different ways here, and so they arrive at different solutions. In Louisa's eyes, the problem is one of completing the project. Alice sees the problem quite differently—as one of resolving an interpersonal conflict (Berg & Calderone, 1994).

Expert and novice problem solvers within a particular content domain seem to classify problems differently (Anzai, 1991; Chi et al., 1988; De Corte, Greer, & Verschaffel, 1996; Di Vesta & Peverly, 1984; Larkin, 1983; Novick, 1988; Schoenfeld & Herrmann, 1982). Experts generally classify a problem on the basis of abstract concepts and underlying principles and patterns. They seem to have a well-developed set of problem schemas that they use to represent different kinds of problems. Novices, however, tend to focus on specific, concrete aspects of a problem and so are apt to retrieve information related only to those aspects. As an illustration, Schoenfeld and Herrmann (1982) compared the ways that mathematics professors and students categorized a variety of math problems. Professors classified them on the basis of abstract principles related to problem solution: Those solved by analogy were grouped together, as were those solved by contradiction, and so on. In contrast, students classified the problems on the basis of more superficial characteristics, such as whether they contained polynomial expressions or whether they included figures from plane geometry. After a course in mathematics, the students were asked to repeat the classification task; at this point, they began to classify the problems as their professors had.

Experts may also spend more time defining ill-defined problems before attempting to solve them (Mitchell, 1989; Swanson, O'Connor, & Cooney, 1990; Voss, Tyler, & Yengo, 1983; Voss, Wolfe, Lawrence, & Engle, 1991). Consider this problem as an example:

> Imagine that the year is 1983 and that you are the Minister of Agriculture in the Soviet Union. Crop productivity has been low for the past several years, and people are beginning to go hungry. What would you do to increase crop production? (based on Voss, Greene, Post, & Penner, 1983; Voss, Tyler, & Yengo, 1983)

Take a few minutes to jot down some of your ideas.

How much time did you spend defining the problem? Chances are, you didn't spend much time at all; you probably went right to work thinking about possible problem solutions. If you were a political scientist specializing in the Soviet Union, however, you might have spent considerable time identifying various aspects of the problem—perhaps considering Soviet political policies, the amount of land available for farming, and so on—before thinking about how you might solve it (Mitchell, 1989; Voss, Greene, et al., 1983; Voss, Tyler, & Yengo, 1983).

Mental sets in encoding   People are often predisposed to approach and encode problems in particular ways—a phenomenon known as **mental set**.[4] Here is a problem for which people are often the victims of mental set:

> How can you throw a tennis ball so that it goes a short distance, comes to a complete stop, then reverses its direction? You may not bounce the ball against a surface, nor may you attach any other object (such as a string) to it. (based on M. Gardner, 1978)

I once gave this problem to a masters-level learning theories class, and only a handful of my 35 students could solve it. Most of them worked on the assumption that the ball had to be thrown horizontally (some even said that they encoded the problem as a visual image of a pitcher). Once you break this mental set, the answer is quite simple: You throw the ball *up*.

As another example of mental set, consider this "candle" problem similar to one used by Duncker (1945):

> You are in a room with a bulletin board firmly affixed to the wall. Your task is to stand a candle upright beside the bulletin board about 4 feet above the floor. You do not want the candle touching the bulletin board, because the candle's flame must not singe the bulletin board. Instead, you need to place the candle about a centimeter away. How can you accomplish the task, given the materials shown in Figure 13.1.

Develop a solution for the problem before you continue reading.

When I present this problem as a hands-on activity in my graduate classes, students typically identify three different solutions. One solution is to stab the knitting needle through

---

[4]Gestalt psychologists introduced this idea, using the term *Einstellung*.

Figure 13.1
Using some or all of these materials, how can you stand a candle upright beside the bulletin board so that you can safely light it? (Based on Duncker, 1945)

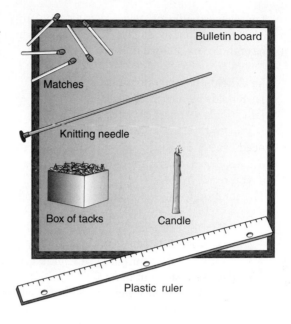

Bulletin board

Matches

Knitting needle

Box of tacks

Candle

Plastic ruler

the candle and into the bulletin board; this action almost invariably splits the candle and gouges the bulletin board. A second solution is to form a horizontal surface with the ruler, propping it against the bulletin board with thumbtacks (perhaps also sticking the knitting needle in the bulletin board just below it), and then place the candle on top; however, the precariously placed ruler usually falls to the floor once the candle is added. Only a third solution works: Take the thumbtacks out of the box, use the tacks to attach the box to the bulletin board, then affix the candle to the top side of the box (with either melted wax or a tack). The solution is obvious once you think about it, but many people have difficulty with the problem because they encode the box as a container and fail to consider its other possible functions.

The tendency to think of objects as having only one function, thereby overlooking other possible uses, is a form of mental set known as **functional fixedness** (Birch & Rabinowitz, 1951; Duncker, 1945; Maier & Janzen, 1968). The degree to which individuals experience functional fixedness depends, in part, on situational conditions. People more easily solve the candle problem if the tacks are presented *outside* of the box, presumably because they are less likely to think of the box only as a container (Duncker, 1945). The problem is also easier to solve if the box itself is labeled "BOX" (Glucksberg & Weisberg, 1966), possibly because the label draws attention to the box as something that can be used in solving the problem.

Mental set and functional fixedness are partly the result of past experience: If a particular approach to a problem has worked in the past, a person is likely to continue using it and perhaps learn it to a level of automaticity. The person is then likely to apply this approach, often in a relatively "mindless" fashion, even in situations where it is inappropriate or unnecessarily cumbersome. (Recall our discussion of automaticity's downsides in chapter 8.)

Luchins's experiments with water jar problems (1942; Luchins & Luchins, 1950) illustrate just how strongly one's past experiences can influence problem solving. Imagine, if you will, that you have three jars of three different sizes:

Jar A holds 20 ounces of water.
Jar B holds 59 ounces of water.
Jar C holds 4 ounces of water.

You need exactly 31 ounces of water. Assuming that you have an unlimited water supply, how can you get the exact amount of water using only the three jars you have? Try to find a solution before you read further.

The solution to the water jar problem is as follows:

1. Fill jar B. This gives you 59 ounces of water.
2. Pour water from jar B into jar A until A is full. This leaves 39 ounces in jar B.
3. Pour water from jar B into jar C until C is full. This leaves 35 ounces in jar B.
4. Pour the water out of jar C.
5. Once again pour water from B into C. At this point you have 31 ounces in jar B, the exact amount you need.

Mathematically speaking, the solution to the problem is

$$B - A - 2C$$

Luchins (1942) gave participants in his study a series of such problems, with the answer always being the same: $B - A - 2C$. He then presented the following three problems:

Jar A holds:	Jar B holds:	Jar C holds:	Obtain this amount:
23	49	3	20
15	39	3	18
28	76	3	25

Almost everyone solved the first two problems using the same formula as before: $B - A - 2C$. They had difficulty solving the third problem because the standard formula did not apply. But notice that all three can be solved quite easily: The solution for the first and third problems is $A - C$, and that for the second problem is $A + C$. The participants in Luchins's study (who were professors and graduate students—hardly mental slouches!) were victims of a problem-solving mental set established through prior experience.

In most situations, one's predisposition to approach similar problems in similar ways facilitates successful problem solving (Maier, 1945). A mental set influences the way in which a problem is encoded in memory, however, and this encoding in turn influences the parts of long-term memory that are searched for potentially relevant information and procedures. If a problem's encoding steers an individual in the wrong "direction" in long-term memory, then it hinders problem-solving performance (Alexander & Judy, 1988; Mayer, 1992; Stein, 1989). Let's now consider retrieval from long-term memory as yet another cognitive factor affecting problem-solving success.

Retrieval from Long-Term Memory

To use previously acquired knowledge to solve a problem, people must retrieve it while they are thinking about the problem. Thus, the factors that facilitate long-term memory retrieval—meaningful learning, organization and integration of new ideas, and so on—facilitate problem-solving success as well (Ausubel et al., 1978).

When people search long-term memory for knowledge relevant to a problem, they begin by looking in logical "places." They tend to retrieve familiar ideas first, identifying original or unusual problem solutions later or not at all (Bourne et al., 1986). They also tend to retrieve information closely associated with aspects of the problem situation; for example, people more easily solve the candle problem when they have previously learned a paired-associate list that includes the pair *candle–box* (Bassok, 2003; Weisberg, DiCamillo, & Phillips, 1979). Hints that provide important retrieval cues can be helpful, at least if individuals perceive their relevance (Bassok & Holyoak, 1993; Bourne et al., 1986; Gick & Holyoak, 1987). For example, the solution of anagrams such as this one:

Unscramble these letters to form a real word: NEEPLATH

is easier when you know that the solution belongs to a particular category such as *animals* (Safren, 1962). (The solution, by the way, is *elephant.*)

As I mentioned in chapter 10, anxiety can interfere with retrieval by restricting the part of long-term memory that is searched. Anxious individuals are therefore apt to have difficulty solving problems whose solutions are not readily apparent. For example, Glucksberg (1962) asked four groups of people to solve a candle problem similar to that presented in Figure 13.1. For two groups, the tacks were out of the box (an easy version of the problem), and for the other two groups, the tacks were in the box (a more difficult version). Two groups were given no reason to be anxious about solving the problem; their success or failure in finding a solution had no consequences. The other two groups had an incentive to make them more eager and anxious about finding a solution: The fastest 25% of the problem solvers would receive $5, and the fastest individual of all would receive $25 (a tidy sum back in 1962). Following are the mean reaction times (in minutes) for the four groups of problem solvers; larger numbers indicate greater difficulty in solving the problem:

	Easy version	Difficult version
Low anxiety	4.99	7.41
High anxiety	3.67	11.08

When the box was empty, its use as a platform for the candle was obvious, and anxiety facilitated problem solving. But when the box was already being used as a container, anxiety made the problem even more difficult to solve than it already was.

The effects of anxiety on problem solving seem to be reduced or eliminated when individuals know where to search in long-term memory. Although high-anxiety individuals typically perform more poorly than low-anxiety individuals on problem-solving tasks, performance of the two groups is similar when memory aids that promote appropriate retrieval are provided (Gross & Mastenbrook, 1980; Leherissey, O'Neil, & Hansen, 1971).

The value of incubation in long-term memory retrieval   In his early theory of problem solving, Wallas (1926) listed **incubation** as an important step in problem solving. Many contemporary cognitive theorists have also vouched for its importance, especially in dealing with difficult problems (e.g., Davidson, 2003; Dijksterhuis & Nordgren, 2006; Ellis & Hunt, 1983; Pretz et al., 2003). For one thing, some of the factors that interfere with problem solving, such as fatigue, anxiety, and counterproductive mental sets, may dissipate during the incubation period. And in the intervening time period, a person can search long-term memory more broadly—perhaps simply by "wandering aimlessly" through various areas (not necessarily with any conscious purpose or intent) and unexpectedly "stumbling" on potentially helpful information. Upon encountering this new information, the person may see its relevance for the previously unsolved problem, encode the problem differently than before (i.e., restructuring it), and so tackle it differently as well. In some cases, the recoding may yield an almost an instantaneous solution, resulting in that sudden *insight* phenomenon of which I spoke earlier (Ash & Wiley, 2006; Davidson, 2003; Dijksterhuis & Nordgren, 2006; Pretz et al., 2003).

In my own experience as a textbook writer, I have found incubation to be a highly effective strategy. Probably the biggest problem I face when I write is figuring out how best to organize the ever-expanding body of research findings related to learning and motivation. As my field continues to grow and evolve, I find that some organizational structures I've used in previous editions of this book are no longer useful in a later edition, and so I begin to experiment with alternative arrangements. Yet my mind seems to be able to handle only so much mini-paradigm-shifting in any single day. Oftentimes the best thing I can do is to turn off my computer in midafternoon, walk the dog, perhaps watch a television game show or two, and essentially let the "mental dust" settle. When I return to my computer the following morning, I often have fresh ideas that did not occur to me the day before.

If information relevant to a problem is to be retrieved from long-term memory, it must obviously be *in* long-term memory to begin with. So another factor affecting problem-solving success is an individual's knowledge base in a particular content domain, as we shall see now.

Knowledge Base

Successful (expert) problem solvers have a more complete and better organized knowledge base for the problems they solve (Anzai, 1991; Bédard & Chi, 1992; Chi, Glaser, & Rees, 1982; Lawson & Chinnappan, 1994). For example, using the concept mapping technique described in chapters 8 and 12, Cochran (1988) examined the achievement (much of which involved problem solving) of high school physics students studying a unit on electricity. The higher achievers were students who had better organized information about electrical concepts in long-term memory. Not only did these students know better which concepts should be associated with which other concepts, but they also knew the particular relationships that different concepts had with one another. In contrast, low achievers were often uncertain about just how the different aspects of electricity fit together and often misconstrued relationships among concepts. By having more information relative to a specific content domain, as well as more interconnections among various bits of information, expert problem solvers can more quickly and easily retrieve the things they need to solve a problem, and they can draw inferences that may facilitate problem solution (J. R. Anderson, 1993; Bédard & Chi, 1992; Chi et al., 1982; Hiebert & Lefevre, 1986; Stein, 1989).

Successful problem solvers also appear to have more knowledge of specific strategies they can use to solve problems within their area of expertise. For instance, once they have categorized a problem as falling into a particular category or being consistent with a certain problem schema, they readily apply certain procedures to solve it (Chi & Glaser, 1985; Gick, 1986; Mayer, 1986; Prawat, 1989; Reed, 1993). And they have often learned basic problem-solving procedures to automaticity (Chi et al., 1988; Glaser, 1987). Novice problem solvers, lacking the rich knowledge base of experts, are more likely to engage in ineffective problem-solving strategies—for example, resorting to trial and error, persevering with unproductive procedures, making unwarranted assumptions, and applying procedures and equations in a rote, meaningless fashion (Perkins & Simmons, 1988).

Metacognition

Metacognition plays a key role in problem solving. In particular, successful problem solvers must

- Believe that they are capable of solving the problem successfully.
- Understand that some problems may take considerable time and effort to accomplish.
- Analyze a problem into its component parts.
- Select appropriate problem-solving strategies.
- Plan a course of action.
- Monitor progress toward a solution, and change strategies if necessary.
  (Cardelle-Elawar, 1992; Davidson & Sternberg, 1998; De Corte et al., 1996; Dominowski, 1998; Geary, 2006; Kilpatrick, 1985; Lesgold & Lajoie, 1991; Lester, 1985; Pfeiffer, Feinberg, & Gelber, 1987; Schoenfeld, 1992; Silver, 1982; Zimmerman & Campillo, 2003)

The more metacognitively engaged people are in the problems they are tackling, the more likely they are to be flexible in their choice of strategies, to solve complex problems successfully, and to transfer effective problem-solving strategies to new situations (Delclos & Harrington, 1991; Dominowski, 1998; King, 1991).

As an illustration of the roles metacognition might play, consider this train of thought regarding a particular problem:

> I'm sloppy at doing [a particular kind of problem]; I'd better go slow. This is complicated. I should go through the steps carefully. This method isn't working. I'll try something else. I need to vocalize what I'm doing to help me keep on track. I need to write these steps out. (Lester, 1985, p. 63)

This individual, while obviously not an expert at solving the problem in question, is bringing several beneficial metacognitive skills to bear on the problem—for example, acknowledging the need to go slowly and carefully, recognizing when a strategy is unproductive, and identifying specific behaviors that may facilitate problem-solving success.

Unfortunately, students sometimes have epistemological beliefs that interfere with effective problem solving. In the case of mathematics, for instance, many students believe that successful problem solving is largely a matter of luck, that a problem can have only one right answer, that there's only one way to solve any particular problem, and that a problem is either solvable within a few minutes' time or else not solvable at all (De Corte et al., 1996; Geary, 1994; Schoenfeld, 1992). When students have naive beliefs about the nature of a subject area or about knowledge more generally—perhaps thinking that there is a single "right" answer to virtually any issue— they are especially likely to have difficulty addressing ill-defined problems (P. M. King & Kitchener, 2004; Schraw, Dunkle, & Bendixen, 1995).

We have spoken of the need to have appropriate strategies for solving particular problems and to regulate (metacognitively) the effectiveness of those strategies in achieving a problem solution. We now look at what such strategies might entail.

Problem–Solving Strategies

Problem-solving strategies fall into two general categories: algorithms and heuristics.

Algorithms

As I mentioned previously, well-defined problems can typically be solved using a particular sequence of operations. For example, you can solve the problem 43 $\overline{)3,354}$ using either of two procedures: (1) apply prescribed methods of long division or (2) push the appropriate series of buttons on a calculator. Either approach leads to the correct answer: 78. Similarly, you can make a tasty pumpkin pie if you follow a recipe to the letter in terms of ingredients, measurements, and oven temperature. Such specific, step-by-step procedures for solving problems are called **algorithms.** Algorithms are typically domain specific: They are useful with particular problems in a particular content area but are, for the most part, inapplicable to problems in other areas.

Let's consider some of the algorithms that children use when they are given an arithmetic problem such as this one:

If I have 2 apples and you give me 4 more apples, how many apples do I have altogether?

Young children can often solve such problems even if they have not yet had specific instruction in addition at school (Carpenter & Moser, 1984). A strategy that emerges early in development is simply to put up two fingers and then four additional fingers and count all the fingers to reach the solution of "6 apples." Somewhat later, children may begin to use a *min* strategy, whereby they start with the larger number (for the apple problem, they would start with 4) and then add on, one by one, the smaller number (e.g., counting "four apples … then five, six … six apples altogether") (Siegler & Jenkins, 1989). Still later, of course, children learn the basic addition facts (e.g., "2 + 4 = 6") that enable them to answer simple addition problems without having to count at all. As new strategies emerge, children may initially have trouble using them effectively, and so they may often resort to the earlier, less efficient, but more dependable ones. Eventually, they acquire sufficient proficiency with their new strategies that they can comfortably leave the less efficient ones behind (Siegler & Alibali, 2005).

Sometimes, when a single algorithm is insufficient to solve a problem, several algorithms in combination can lead to a correct solution (R. M. Gagné, 1985). Mathematics problems (e.g., algebraic equations, geometric proofs) are frequently solved through a combination of algorithms. But combining algorithms is not necessarily as easy as it sounds (e.g., Mayer & Wittrock, 1996). In some cases, individuals may have to learn, through either formal classroom instruction or informal experiences, the process of combining algorithms. A study by Scandura (1974) illustrates this point. Elementary school children were taught trading rules such as these:

n caramels $= n + 1$ toy soldiers
n toy soldiers $= n + 2$ pencils

They were then asked to make trades that involved combining two of these rules (e.g., trading caramels for pencils). Children who were unable to combine rules successfully were identified, and half of them were given specific instruction on how to combine the rules. Subsequently, all of these instructed children effectively combined the trading rules (one of them first required additional instruction), whereas none of the children in an untrained control group were able to do so.

Heuristics

Not all problems can be solved with algorithms. For instance, no specific algorithms exist for eliminating a junk food addiction or establishing world peace. And in other situations, algorithms may exist but be too time consuming to be practical. For example, although an algorithm exists for determining the best move in a game of checkers, people tend not to use it because of its impracticality. This algorithm is as follows: Consider every possible move, then consider every possible next move that the opponent could make in response to each of those moves, then consider every follow-up move that could be made in response to each of *those* moves, and so on until the winner is projected for every conceivable series of moves (Samuel, 1963). Such an algorithm would take either a sophisticated computer programmer or a lifetime of complete dedication to a single game of checkers.

When algorithms for a particular problem are either nonexistent or impractical, people tend to use **heuristics**—general problem-solving strategies that may or may not yield a correct solution. Following are several examples.

Brainstorming   In brainstorming, one initially tries to generate a large number of possible approaches to a problem without regard for how realistic or practical they might be. Only after generating a lengthy set of possibilities—perhaps including some seemingly bizarre, outlandish ones—does one evaluate them to determine their likely usefulness and effectiveness. This postponement of evaluation increases the odds that an individual will conduct a broad search of long-term memory and, perhaps, stumble on an unusual or creative solution for a challenging problem (Halpern, 1997; Osborn, 1963; Runco & Chand, 1995). For instance, brainstorming is often used in trying to resolve international conflicts, sometimes with success and sometimes without.

Means–ends analysis   In means–ends analysis, one breaks a problem into two or more subproblems and then works successively on each of them. For example, imagine that an infant sees an attractive toy beyond her reach. A string is attached to the toy; its other end is attached to a cloth closer at hand. Between the cloth and the infant is a foam rubber barrier. Many 12-month-old infants can put two and two together and realize that to accomplish the goal (getting the toy), they must first do several other things. Accordingly, they remove the barrier, pull the cloth toward them, grab the string, and reel in the toy (Willatts, 1990).

Means–ends analysis appears to be a relatively common method of solving problems (Greeno, 1973; Newell & Simon, 1972) and is most likely to be used when the final goal is clearly specified (Sweller & Levine, 1982). However, a potential disadvantage of this approach is that, by attending to only one subgoal at a time, a person may lose sight of the problem as a whole (Sweller & Levine, 1982).

Working backward   In some cases it's helpful to begin at the problem goal and then work in reverse, one step at a time, toward the initial problem state (Chi & Glaser, 1985; Newell, Shaw, & Simon, 1958; Wickelgren, 1974). In each step backward, the individual identifies one or more conditions that would produce the present condition. In a sense, working backward is the opposite approach to that of means–ends analysis.

Working backward is frequently used in solving algebra and geometry proofs. Students are given an initial situation—a formula or geometric configuration with certain characteristics—and then are asked to prove, through a series of mathematically logical steps, how another formula or another characteristic (the goal) must also be true. Sometimes it is easier to move logically from the goal backward to the initial state; mathematically speaking, this approach is just as valid.

Using visual imagery   In chapter 7, we noted that working memory may include a *visuospatial sketchpad* that allows short-term storage and manipulation of visual material. And in chapters 8 and 9, we discovered that visual imagery provides a potentially powerful means of storing information in long-term memory. So when problems are easily visualizable or have an obvious spatial structure, people sometimes use visual imagery to solve them (English, 1997b; Geary, 2006; Hegarty & Kozhevnikov, 1999; Kosslyn, 1985). For instance, when conducting research for my doctoral dissertation, I discovered that people are more likely to use visual imagery in tackling easily visualizable problems such as this one

> The plate is higher than the napkin.
> The cup is lower than the napkin.
> Which is lowest?

than in tackling less visualizable ones such as this one

> Wednesday is hotter than Tuesday.
> Thursday is colder than Tuesday.
> Which is coldest?

I found, too, that the chances of visual imagery increase when the problem solver must hold a fair amount of information in working memory at once—information that, if stored verbally, might exceed working memory capacity (J. O. Ellis, 1975; Ormrod, 1979).

Drawing an analogy   See if you can solve the following problem:

> Suppose you are a doctor faced with a patient who has a malignant tumor in his stomach. It is impossible to operate on the patient, but unless the tumor is destroyed the patient will die. There is a kind of ray that can be used to destroy the tumor. If the rays reach the tumor all at once at a sufficiently high intensity, the tumor will be destroyed. Unfortunately, at this intensity the healthy tissue that the rays pass through on the way to the tumor will also be destroyed. At lower intensities the rays are harmless to healthy tissue, but they will not affect the tumor either. What type of procedure might be used to destroy the tumor with the rays, and at the same time avoid destroying the healthy tissue? (Gick & Holyoak, 1980, pp. 307–308)

If you are having trouble solving the problem, then consider this situation:

> A general wishes to capture a fortress located in the center of a country. There are many roads radiating outward from the fortress. All have been mined so that, while small groups of men can pass over the roads safely, any large force will detonate the mines. A full-scale direct attack is therefore impossible. The general's solution is to divide his army into small groups, send each group to the head of a different road, and have the groups converge simultaneously on the fortress. (Gick & Holyoak, 1980, p. 309)

Now go back to the tumor problem. Perhaps the general's strategy in capturing the fortress has given you an idea about how to destroy the tumor. It can be destroyed by shooting a number of low-intensity rays from different directions, such that they all converge on the tumor simultaneously. College students are more likely to solve the tumor problem when they have first read the solution to the fortress problem, because the two problems can be solved in analogous ways (Gick & Holyoak, 1980).

Drawing an analogy between a problem situation and another situation often provides insights into how a problem can be solved (A. L. Brown, Kane & Echols, 1986; Clement, 1987; English, 1997b; Holyoak, 1985; Mayer & Wittrock, 1996; Schultz & Lochhead, 1991). For example, a student might solve a math problem by studying a similar, "worked out" problem— one that has already been solved correctly using a particular procedure (R. K. Atkinson, Derry, Renkl, & Wortham, 2000; Mwangi & Sweller, 1998; Reimann & Schult, 1996; Zhu & Simon, 1987). As another example, consider a problem that the Greek scientist Archimedes confronted sometime around 250 B.C.:

> King Hiero asked a goldsmith to make him a gold crown and gave the craftsman the gold he should use. When he received the finished crown, he suspected that the goldsmith had cheated him by replacing some of the gold with silver, a cheaper metal. The only way to determine the goldsmith's honesty was to compare the crown's weight against its volume. Any metal has a particular volume for any given weight, and that ratio is different for each metal. The crown could be weighed easily enough. But how could its volume be measured?

Archimedes was pondering the problem one day as he stepped into a bathtub. He watched the bathwater rise and, through analogy (and perhaps visual imagery as well), immediately identified a solution to the king's problem: The crown's volume could be determined by placing it in a container of water and measuring the amount of water that was displaced.

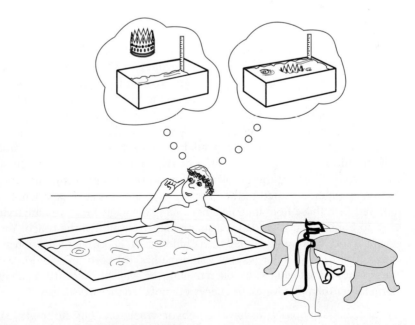

Analogies are sometimes helpful in solving problems.

Children show some ability to draw analogies by their first birthday and become capable of increasingly complex ones as they grow older (Siegler & Alibali, 2005). Using an analogy is not a surefire approach, however: Problem solvers may make an incorrect analogy or draw inappropriate parallels and so solve a problem incorrectly as a result (Bassok, 2003; Mayer & Wittrock, 1996; Novick, 1988). But the major stumbling block is that without an expert's guidance, the chances of retrieving and recognizing a helpful analogy are typically quite slim. People of all ages rarely use analogies to tackle a problem unless its analogue has similar superficial features that make its relevance obvious (Bassok, 2003; Mayer & Wittrock, 1996; Reed, Ernst, & Banerji, 1974). For instance, after learning the solution to the fortress problem (splitting the troops into small groups), many college students don't see its relationship to the tumor problem (Gick & Holyoak, 1980). They are more likely to make the connection when the parallels are readily apparent—for instance, when the analogous problem involves a lab assistant simultaneously shooting low-intensity laser beams from different directions to repair an expensive lightbulb (Holyoak & Koh, 1987).

Shortcut heuristics: Representativeness and availability   Some problem-solving heuristics are executed quickly and simply but, unfortunately, not always dependably. Two examples are representativeness and availability (Halpern, 1997; Kahneman & Tversky, 1972; Klaczynski, 2001; Mayer, 1992; Tversky & Kahneman, 1973). **Representativeness** involves jumping to conclusions about a solution based on obvious characteristics of the problem. Let me illustrate by adapting a problem used by Kahneman and Tversky (1973). Imagine that I have a stack of 100 personality profiles of 30 engineers and 70 lawyers, all of whom are successful in their careers. I pull this description randomly from the pile:

> Jack is a 45-year-old man. He is married and has four children. He is generally conservative, careful, and ambitious. He shows no interest in political and social issues and spends most of his free time on his many hobbies, which include home carpentry, sailing, and mathematical puzzles. (Kahneman & Tversky, 1973, p. 241)

Now for the problem: What is the probability that this man is one of the 30 engineers?

The probability that the man is an engineer is 30%, because the stack of 100 personality profiles contained profiles of 30 engineers. Yet many people in Kahneman and Tversky's study gave a higher figure; they jumped to a conclusion based on obvious characteristics about Jack that many people associate stereotypically with engineers (e.g., conservative views and enjoyment of mathematical puzzles).

A second shortcut heuristic, **availability,** is a strategy whereby a problem is solved based only on information that comes immediately to mind (i.e., is retrieved) when the problem is encountered. Typically, the problem will be solved using recently acquired information rather than information acquired in the distant past, because recent experiences are more likely to be retrieved than those from long ago. For example, imagine that you are trying to decide whether to go to California or Florida for a sunny March vacation at the beach. You learned many years ago that Florida has more rainfall than California. In February, just as you are about to make your choice, you hear on the news that California has just been drenched in a heavy rainstorm. You may easily book a flight to Florida, retrieving the available information about the California rainstorm rather than the overall frequency of rainfall in the two states.

Because many problems have no right or wrong solutions, no single "best" strategy may exist for solving them. And in any case, different strategies are appropriate in different situations. But sometimes people use strategies at the wrong times, often because they've learned such strategies at a rote, meaningless level. Let's look at what happens when individuals use problem-solving strategies meaninglessly.

Meaningless Versus Meaningful Problem Solving

See if you can solve this problem before you read further:

> The number of quarters a man has is seven times the number of dimes he has. The value of the dimes exceeds the value of the quarters by two dollars and fifty cents. How many has he of each coin? (Paige & Simon, 1966, p. 79)

If you found an answer to the problem—any answer at all—then you overlooked an important point: Quarters are worth more than dimes. If there are more quarters than dimes, the value of the dimes cannot possibly be greater than the value of the quarters. The fact is, the problem makes no sense, and so it cannot be solved.

When people learn algorithms at a rote level, without understanding their underlying logic, they may sometimes apply the algorithms "unthinkingly" and inappropriately (De Corte et al., 1996; Perkins & Simmons, 1988; Prawat, 1989; Resnick, 1989). As a result, they may obtain illogical or physically impossible results. Consider the following instances of meaningless mathematical problem solving as examples:

- A student is asked to figure out how many chickens and how many pigs a farmer has if the farmer has 21 animals with 60 legs in all. The student adds 21 and 60, reasoning that, because the problem says "how many in all," addition is the logical operation (Lester, 1985).
- A student uses subtraction whenever a word problem contains the word *left*—even when a problem actually requiring addition includes the phrase "John left the room to get more apples" (Schoenfeld, 1982).
- Middle school students are asked to calculate how many 40-person buses are needed to transport 540 people to a baseball game. The majority give an answer that includes a fraction, without acknowledging that in the case of buses, only whole numbers are possible (Silver, Shapiro, & Deutsch, 1993).

All too often, when schools teach problem solving, they focus on teaching algorithms for well-defined problems but neglect to help students understand why the algorithms work and how they can be used with real-world problems (Carr & Biddlecomb, 1998; Cooney, 1991; Perkins & Salomon, 1989; Porter, 1989; Silver et al., 1993). For example, perhaps you can remember learning how to solve a long-division problem, but you probably don't remember learning *why* you multiply the divisor by each digit in your answer and write the product in a particular location below the dividend. Or perhaps you were taught a "key word" method for solving word problems: Words such as *altogether* indicate addition, and words such as *left* mean subtraction. This approach is a meaningless one indeed and often leads to erroneous solutions.

How can teachers help students engage in more meaningful problem solving? And, in general, how can they help students become more expert at problem solving and other forms of transfer? We identify several answers to these questions in the next section.

FACILITATING TRANSFER AND PROBLEM SOLVING IN THE CLASSROOM

As we noted earlier in the chapter, students often fail to see the relevance of what they have learned in school to new school tasks or to out-of-school problems. Thus, a major objective of our educational system—positive transfer—is not being achieved as successfully as we would like. At the same time, students sometimes erroneously apply what they have learned to situations in which it is not appropriate—a case of negative transfer.

Learning theorists still have much to learn about the complex processes of transfer and problem solving. Nevertheless, theories and research in both areas provide numerous suggestions for educational practice:

◆ *Students need to learn information meaningfully and thoroughly.* Most theorists agree that a solid knowledge base is a prerequisite for successful transfer and problem solving (e.g., Frederiksen, 1984a; Haskell, 2001; Hiebert & Lefevre, 1986). In the process of acquiring this knowledge base, students should develop a multitude of interconnections and relationships among the concepts and ideas they learn. They should also discover the potential relevance of such concepts and ideas for the various situations they may encounter later on (Bereiter, 1995; Brophy & Alleman, 1991; Perkins, 1995; Perkins & Salomon, 1987; Prawat, 1989; Sternberg & Frensch, 1993).

Unfortunately, many school curricula include long lists of topics that must be taught, the result being that no single topic is taught very thoroughly (Brophy & Alleman, 1992; Porter, 1989). Breadth of coverage occurs at the expense of depth of coverage—and at the expense of successful transfer and problem solving as well.

◆ *Students should also learn problem-solving strategies in a meaningful manner.* All too often, students learn problem-solving algorithms as procedures separate from anything they have previously learned about the world. For example, they may learn mathematics—its symbols, principles, and algorithms—in total isolation from the concrete physical world they regularly deal with (Carpenter, 1985; Davis, 1987; Hiebert & Wearne, 1993; Resnick, 1989). When students learn an algorithm in a rote, meaningless fashion, they are likely to use it mechanically, thoughtlessly, and often incorrectly, and they are *un*likely to recognize many of the situations in which it might legitimately be applied (Greeno, 1991; Hiebert & Wearne, 1993; Kilpatrick, 1985; Perkins & Simmons, 1988).

Rather than simply learning algorithms at a rote level, students should understand *why* they do the things they do in order to solve problems. In other words, they should connect abstract, symbol-based procedures to things they already know about the subject matter and to concrete reality (Carpenter, 1985; Geary, 1994; Prawat, 1989; Resnick, 1989; Rittle-Johnson & Alibali, 1999; Rittle-Johnson, Siegler, & Alibali, 2001).

Following are examples of how teachers might help students meaningfully learn and apply various problem-solving strategies:

- Teach general schemas for classifying different kinds of problems, and give students practice in using the schemas in a wide variety of contexts (L. S. Fuchs et al., 2003b, 2004; Gerjets & Scheiter, 2003).
- While demonstrating a particular strategy, ask students to explain why the strategy is a good one (Calin-Jageman & Ratner, 2005; Renkl & Atkinson, 2003).
- When teaching a complex mathematical formula, present it using words and symbols that help students connect its components to concepts with which they're already familiar (R. K. Atkinson, Catrambone, & Merrill, 2003).

◆ *Discovery activities and expository instruction both play important roles in learning problem-solving skills.* Young children typically engage in a great deal of trial and error in their early play activities. Through such activities, they may discover the properties of a wide variety of objects, and these discoveries increase the likelihood that they will, at a later time, successfully solve problems with the objects (Christie & Johnsen, 1983; P. K. Smith & Dutton, 1979; Sylva, Bruner, & Genova, 1976).

Once children begin to encounter problems related to academic subject matter, occasional opportunities to discover problem-solving strategies on their own can also be valuable. In particular, instructional approaches that emphasize *guided* discovery sometimes facilitate better transfer of problem-solving skills to new situations (Hiebert et al., 1997; Kline & Flowers, 1998; Mayer, 1974; McDaniel & Schlager, 1990; Shymansky, Hedges, & Woodworth, 1990). Discovery learning is probably most useful when

- Problems are ill structured
- Students have good self-regulation skills and a solid knowledge base on which to build
- Students' discovery efforts are supplemented with teacher explanations and careful monitoring of students' understandings
  (Doyle, 1983; Frederiksen, 1984a; Schwartz & Martin, 2004)

Yet students do not always develop appropriate problem-solving strategies on their own, and even when they do, they may develop incorrect or counterproductive procedures. For well-structured problems that can be solved by a specific algorithm—especially problems that might initially exceed students' working memory capacity—and for students relatively unsophisticated about a particular topic, direct instruction of the algorithm is often more effective (Frederiksen, 1984a; R. M. Gagné, 1985; Kirschner, Sweller, & Clark, 2006).

◆ *Students should have a mental set for transfer.* We noted earlier that mental sets in problem solving—predispositions to solve problems in particular ways—sometimes interfere with successful problem solving. Yet a *general* mental set to transfer school learning—a predisposition to use and apply the things learned in the classroom—is clearly beneficial (Stein, 1989; Sternberg & Frensch, 1993). Teachers can promote such a mental set by creating a **culture of transfer**—a learning environment in which applying school subject matter to new situations, cross-disciplinary contexts, and real-world problems is both the expectation and the norm (Haskell, 2001). For example, teachers should frequently point out how academic content can be applied to a variety of situations both in and out of school (Cox, 1997; Perkins & Salomon, 1989; Sternberg & Frensch, 1993; Voss, 1987). And they can encourage students to be constantly thinking "How might I use this information?" as they listen, read, and study (Perkins, 1992; Stein, 1989; Sternberg & Frensch, 1993).

◆ *Some prerequisite skills should be practiced until they are learned to the level of automaticity.* Remember that problem solving occurs in working memory, a component of the memory system that has a limited capacity for holding and processing information at any single time. To the extent that students can process the simple and familiar aspects of a problem automatically, thereby using only a minimal amount of working memory capacity, they can devote more "space" to the problem's difficult and novel aspects (Frederiksen, 1984a; Geary, 1994; Gerjets & Scheiter, 2003; Mayer, 1985; Perkins & Salomon, 1987; Resnick, 1989).

◆ *Practice doesn't necessarily make perfect, but it does make successful transfer and problem solving more likely.* As mentioned earlier in the chapter, numerous and diverse examples and practice opportunities promote associations in long-term memory between new information and a variety of relevant situations; hence, the information is more likely to be retrieved when it is needed later on. Furthermore, to the extent that students must use a concept or procedure in a slightly different way each time they apply it, they are more likely to develop a general (perhaps abstract) understanding of it—one that doesn't depend on obvious surface features of the situation—and they are less likely to develop mental sets that limit their flexibility in applying it (Carr & Biddlecomb, 1998; Chen, 1999). As an example, try to solve each of the following problems:

- Mary needs to locate her wood stove 6 inches from the wall. She does not have a ruler with her. However, she has three sticks that measure 15, 7, and 2 inches, respectively. Using these, how can she get the right distance (6 inches)?
- John needs exactly 20 cups of fertilizer to spray his backyard. He has a bucket of fertilizer but only three jars that hold 9, 8, and 3 cups, respectively. How can he get 20 cups of fertilizer?
- One day Chef Smith needed to get 7 ounces of flour for his cooking but had only a balance scale and three weights of 9, 5, and 3 ounces available to him. How did he get exactly 7 ounces of flour? (all three problems from Chen, 1999, p. 715)

As you may have realized, all three problems can be solved using the same general strategy that Luchins's water jar problems require, in particular using three known amounts that, when added or subtracted, can yield a needed fourth amount. But notice how each problem has different surface features, including different forms of measurement (length, volume, weight) and different contexts and goals (positioning a stove, measuring fertilizer for gardening, weighing flour for cooking). Furthermore, each problem requires a different solution ($A - B - C$, $A + B + C$, $A - B + C$). Learning a problem-solving strategy with such varied problems is apt to take longer than learning it with very similar problems (e.g., with a series of water jar problems), but learners will then apply the strategy more broadly and flexibly (Chen, 1999).

Occasionally, teachers should present problems in a somewhat mixed-up order (rather than having students solve a set of problems that all require the same procedure), so that students have practice classifying problems before solving them (Geary, 1994; Mayer, 1985; Mayfield & Chase, 2002). Ideally, too, students should have opportunities to apply newly learned strategies to real-life problems as well as more traditional word problems (De Corte et al., 1996; Lave, 1988, 1993). For instance, a teacher might have students predict how much helium they would need to put in a balloon to make it float in the air or calculate the volume of a cylindrical punch bowl to determine whether it's large enough to hold a certain amount of punch for a class party.

♦ *Students should have experience identifying problems for themselves.* Teachers usually provide the problems they want their students to solve. But beyond the classroom—for instance, at home and in the world of employment—people must often identify and define for themselves the problems that stand in their way. Some theorists suggest that students may benefit from getting a head start on such **problem finding** in the classroom (Brown & Walter, 1990; Eisner, 1994; Hiebert et al., 1996; Porter, 1989; Resnick, Bill, Lesgold, & Leer, 1991). For example, in a math lesson, students might be given data describing the quantities and prices of items in a grocery store and asked to generate a number of questions that could be answered by those data. Or, in a history lesson, students might be given a scenario of an American Civil War battle in progress, instructed to identify the problems facing either the North or the South, and asked to propose possible solutions.

◆ *To minimize negative transfer, differences between two ideas should be emphasized.* Insects and spiders are similar stimuli—they are both small arthropods with exoskeletons and a generally creepy-crawly nature—and so students may inappropriately transfer what they know about one group of creepy-crawlies to the other. For similar stimuli, negative transfer can be reduced if differences rather than similarities are emphasized (Sternberg & Frensch, 1993). For instance, insects and spiders are different in a number of ways (e.g., six legs vs. eight legs, three body parts vs. two, antennae vs. no antennae), and if emphasized, these differences could reduce negative transfer from one concept to the other. Additionally, if negative transfer between two ideas is anticipated, it can be reduced by teaching each in a different environment (Bilodeau & Schlosberg, 1951; Greenspoon & Ranyard, 1957) for example, by teaching students about insects while sitting in the classroom and teaching them about spiders while on a field trip to the natural history museum.

◆ *Instruction in general problem-solving skills (both cognitive and metacognitive) can be helpful.* As I indicated in chapter 12, training in study skills can be effective and appears to improve classroom learning and achievement. Similarly, teaching general problem-solving strategies can enhance students' ability to solve problems successfully (Cardelle-Elawar, 1992; E. D. Gagné, 1985; Kramarski & Mevarech, 2003; Mayer, 1987; Schoenfeld, 1979, 1992; Simon, 1980). A study by Herrnstein, Nickerson, de Sánchez, and Swets (1986) provides some optimism about the effectiveness of training problem-solving skills: Seventh-grade Venezuelan students who took a year-long course in reasoning, problem-solving, and decision-making skills showed greater improvement in both the specific skills taught and general intellectual ability than did students in an untrained control group. Yet we should note here that, just as study strategies may be better learned when taught within the context of specific academic content areas (see chapter 12), so, too, may general problem-solving strategies be more effectively learned when connected with content domains to which they are applicable (Mayer, 1992; Resnick, 1987; Schoenfeld & Herrmann, 1982).

Several problem-solving strategies we've already identified—for instance, brainstorming, incubation, and forming visual images of problem components—are apt to be transferable to a wide variety of problem situations. Another useful strategy is talking aloud about a problem and about the problem-solving steps being applied. Doing so can enhance students' ability to identify appropriate approaches and to guide and monitor their own progress (in a metacognitive sense) toward solutions (Berardi-Coletta, Buyer, Dominowski, & Rellinger, 1995; Crowley & Siegler, 1999; deLeeuw & Chi, 2003; Vygotsky, 1962; see Lane & Schooler, 2004, for an exception). Still another strategy is using paper and pencil to diagram a problem or list its components; this tactic may help students encode a problem more concretely and see the interrelationships among various elements more clearly (Anzai, 1991; Fuson & Willis, 1989; Lindvall, Tamburino, & Robinson, 1982; Mayer, 1992; Prawat, 1989; Schultz & Lochhead, 1991; Wickelgren, 1974). And specific instruction in metacognitive and self-regulating problem-solving strategies—identifying one's final goal, monitoring one's progress toward the goal, and so on—can enhance problem-solving effectiveness in children and adults alike (Desoete, Roeyers, & De Clercq, 2003; L. S. Fuchs et al., 2003a).

◆ *Students should learn strategies for defining ill-defined problems.* Most problems presented in classroom situations are well defined (Frederiksen, 1984a; Sternberg et al., 2000). Students are asked to identify the protagonist and antagonist in a story, use a dictionary to find two different pronunciations of the word *wind,* or calculate how many pieces of candy six boys can each have if there are 18 pieces altogether. In contrast, most real-world problems are ill defined. People need to find viable means of home financing, decide what life insurance policy to purchase (if any), and maintain friendly and productive relationships with obnoxious co-workers.

Ill-defined problems often require an individual to search outside sources to find relevant and potentially helpful information (Simon, 1978). Students should therefore be well versed in techniques for finding information through such resources as libraries, computer databases, and government agencies. They should also learn techniques for more precisely defining ill-defined problems; for example, one helpful technique is to break a larger problem into a number of sub-problems and to define and impose constraints on each of those subproblems (Chi & Glaser, 1985; Reitman, 1964; Simon, 1973). Finally, to the extent that students possess a solid knowledge base related to the subject matter in question, they will be better able to define the problems they encounter (Bédard & Chi, 1992; Frederiksen, 1984a).

♦ *Students' early attempts to solve difficult problems should be scaffolded.* In chapter 12, we noted the importance of scaffolding students' early attempts to use sophisticated metacognitive strategies. Appropriate scaffolding can facilitate problem-solving performance as well (e.g., R. K. Atkinson, Renkl, & Merrill, 2003; Heller & Hungate, 1985; Perry & Winne, 2004; Rittle-Johnson & Koedinger, 2005). Teachers can do several things to help students in initial attempts at challenging problems: They can simplify early problems, model problem solutions (e.g., by providing worked-out examples), ask probing questions that encourage students to consider certain aspects of a problem, point out errors along the way, and in general keep students' frustration at a reasonable level. They can also give students questions to ask themselves as they proceed through a problem (King, 1991; Schoenfeld, 1992); here are some examples:

> What (exactly) are you doing? Can you describe it precisely? Why are you doing it? How does it fit into your solution? (Schoenfeld, 1992, p. 356)

As students become more adept at solving problems on their own, such scaffolding can be gradually phased out.

♦ *The development of effective problem-solving strategies can often be facilitated through cooperative group problem solving.* Numerous theorists have suggested that a cooperative learning environment may be ideal for promoting successful problem solving (e.g., Brenner et al., 1997; Carr & Biddlecomb, 1998; Hiebert et al., 1997; Palincsar & Herrenkohl, 1999; Qin, Johnson, & Johnson, 1995). By discussing concepts and principles relevant to the problem solution, students may identify more interrelationships among things they know and clarify things about which they are confused (Kilpatrick, 1985; Noddings, 1985). By thinking aloud about how to solve a problem, they may gain a better understanding of what they are mentally doing (Schoenfeld, 1985; Whimbey & Lochhead, 1986). And by observing the more effective strategies that their classmates sometimes use, they may begin to adopt those strategies themselves, leaving their own, less efficient strategies behind (Mayer, 1985; Noddings, 1985; Schoenfeld, 1985). As an illustration of the last point, consider this incident in a cooperative problem-solving setting:

> A youngster suggested that the group should "add, subtract, and multiply these two numbers" and then see which answer "looked" best. Other members of the group were shocked and said, "Donna! We can't do that. We have to figure it out." Donna tried that strategy only once more and then it disappeared from her public repertoire. (Noddings, 1985, pp. 350–351)

In chapter 14, we'll identify many specific strategies for facilitating effective group learning and problem solving.

♦ *Authentic activities can increase the probability that students will transfer knowledge, skills, and problem-solving strategies to real-world contexts.* In chapter 11, we discovered that authentic activities—activities similar to those that students will eventually encounter in the outside world—can help students make meaningful connections between school subject matter and out-of-school tasks. Quite possibly, authentic activities can also help break students out of the situated-learning "rut"—that is, they can help students realize that the information and skills they learn in school are applicable and useful *beyond* school (A. Collins et al., 1989; Rogoff, 2003).

Researchers often find that authentic activities enhance problem-solving skills. For example, preschoolers acquire and use new problem-solving strategies when they actively participate in realistic problem situations while watching the children's television program *Blue's Clues* (Crawley, Anderson, Wilder, Williams, & Santomero, 1999). Older children and adolescents are more likely to transfer scientific principles (e.g., nutritional values of different food groups, design of solar-powered airplanes) to real-life situations if, while they are studying, they are asked to plan a trip to the desert rather than if they are simply told they will be tested on the material (Bransford, Franks, Vye, & Sherwood, 1989).

We find a technology-based version of authentic problem-solving activities in the *Adventures of Jasper Woodbury* series,[5] in which middle school students encounter a number of real-life problem situations presented through videodisc technology. In one episode, "Journey to Cedar Creek," Jasper has just purchased an old boat and is hoping to pilot it home the same day. Because the boat has no running lights, he must figure out whether he can get home by sunset, and because he has spent all his cash and used his last check, he must determine whether he has enough gas to make the trip. Throughout the video, all the information students need to answer these questions is embedded in authentic contexts (e.g., a marine radio announces time of sunset, and mileage markers are posted at various landmarks along the river), but students must sift through a lot of irrelevant information to find it. In another episode, *The Right Angle,* teenager Paige Littlefield is searching for a cave in which her Native American grandfather left her a special gift before he died. The grandfather gave her directions that require knowledge and use of geometric principles (e.g., "From the easternmost point of Black Hawk Bluff, travel at a bearing of 25° until you are almost surrounded by rock towers. Go to Flat Top Tower. ... You will know Flat Top Tower because at a distance of 250 feet from the northern side of its base, the angle of elevation of its top is 45°"). Using the grandfather's directions and a topographical map of Paige's ancestral home region, students must locate the cave. There are numerous ways to approach each Jasper problem, and students work in small groups to brainstorm and carry out possible problem solutions. Students of all ability levels find the *Jasper* series highly motivating, and they transfer what they learn from one problem when solving similar problems (Cognition and Technology Group at Vanderbilt, 1990; Learning Technology Center at Vanderbilt, 1996).

In some instructional contexts, a great deal of learning occurs within the context of solving problems. In such **problem-based learning (PBL)**, students are given complex, real-world problems to tackle (usually in small groups) and must acquire new knowledge and skills in order to solve them. At the present time, problem-based learning is used primarily at the undergraduate and graduate levels, most notably in medical schools (Capon & Kuhn, 2004; Derry, 2006; Hmelo-Silver, 2004, 2006; Savery & Duffy, 2001). Recent evaluations of this approach have yielded mixed results. On the upside, students in PBL classrooms often integrate new concepts and ideas more completely than do students who receive more traditional instruction (Capon & Kuhn, 2004; Gijbels, Dochy, Van den Bossche, & Segers, 2005). On the downside,

---

[5]For online information about the series, visit http://peabody.vanderbilt.edu and enter "Jasper Woodbury" in the search box.

however, the complex problems that typify PBL sometimes exceed students' working memory capacities, thereby leaving no "room" for students to actually learn the new material they are working with (Kirschner et al., 2006). And in some cases students may connect new concepts only to the particular problem with which they are working—thereby *promoting* rather than curtailing situated learning (Bereiter & Scardamalia, 2006; Kirschner et al., 2006). It appears that problem-based learning is most often successful when students' efforts are sufficiently scaffolded to guide them in productive directions and to help them realize that successful problem solutions are well within their reach (Hmelo-Silver, 2006).

♦ *Classroom evaluation practices should include measures of transfer and problem solving.* As noted in chapter 10, traditional classroom assessment practices too often emphasize the learning of specific facts and procedures. Certainly basic knowledge and skills are important; among other things, they form the foundation for more sophisticated academic behaviors. But when teachers' instructional objectives also include transfer and problem solving, classroom assessment tasks should ask students to demonstrate the ability to apply classroom subject matter to a variety of situations (Foos & Fisher, 1988; Massialas & Zevin, 1983; Sternberg & Frensch, 1993). This practice can help successful transfer and problem solving become common phenomena rather than rare occurrences.

Teaching for effective transfer and problem solving takes time. Too often, schools seem to rush through a curriculum at the expense of providing sufficient practice at any single point along the way. Educators should probably slow down and give students time to use and apply the information and skills they learn. Under such conditions, students are likely to accomplish more over the long run.

SUMMARY

Transfer is the process of applying information and skills learned in one situation to learning or performance in another situation. Although most instances of transfer are beneficial, once in a while learning something at one time can negatively impact learning or performance at a later time. Over the years, views of what things transfer and when have varied considerably. Early educators took a "mind as muscle" view, assuming that studying any rigorous subject matter was likely to strengthen the mind and so facilitate future learning and performance. In contrast, early behaviorists proposed that similarity of stimuli or responses (or both) is essential for transfer to occur. More recently, cognitivists have suggested that people are most apt to apply what they've learned if their present context encourages retrieval of potentially useful prior knowledge *or* if they've acquired general learning strategies, motives, and dispositions that they bring to bear on virtually any learning task. Regardless of which theoretical perspective we take, it appears that transfer from one situation to another is most likely to occur when the two situations have *something* in common or require similar skills or attitudes on the part of the learner. Among the factors that facilitate transfer are thorough and meaningful learning, a wide variety of examples and opportunities for practice, and a general classroom culture that encourages transfer.

Problem solving is a form of transfer, in that previously learned information is applied to resolve a problem situation. Behaviorists and cognitive theorists have offered several theories of problem solving. Cognitive theories—which focus on such factors as working memory, encoding, retrieval, prior knowledge base, and metacognition—predominate at the present time. Some problems can be solved through specific *algorithms,* procedures that guarantee correct solutions. But many others may be solved only through more general *heuristics,* approaches without guaranteed outcomes (e.g., conducting a means–ends analysis, using visual imagery, drawing analogies). People typically apply problem-solving procedures more effectively and appropriately when they understand the logic behind the procedures.

Theory and research yield numerous suggestions for promoting transfer and problem solving in classroom settings. For example, a school's prescribed curriculum should make it possible for teachers to teach a few things thoroughly and meaningfully rather than many things superficially and at a rote level (the "less is more" idea). Students should have a *mental set* for transfer; that is, they should approach school subject matter with the idea that they may be able to use it on future occasions. Under some circumstances—for instance, when students' efforts are appropriately structured and scaffolded—such techniques as discovery learning, cooperative learning, and authentic activities can facilitate the development and transfer of effective problem-solving skills. Ideally, teachers should not only *teach* for transfer and problem solving but also emphasize it in their assessment practices.

CHAPTER 14

Social Processes in Knowledge Construction

M uch of our discussion of learning thus far has focused on the things that happen *to* and *inside of* individual people as they learn. Yet human beings are, by nature, very social creatures, and a great deal of their learning depends on the people around them. For instance, as Vygotsky pointed out, in virtually all cultures the members of previous generations—parents, teachers, and so on—are largely responsible for helping growing children acquire the accumulated wisdom of their culture.

Peers, too, are key players in human learning. We touched on this point in our discussion of developmental perspectives in chapter 11. When we looked at Piaget's theory, we found that interactions with age-mates (whether they be amicable conversations or not-so-amicable conflicts) are essential for helping children understand that others may have different—and sometimes more viable—perspectives of the world. Later in that chapter, we considered Vygotsky's proposal that complex mental processes begin as social activities—that children gradually internalize ways of thinking that they first use in social settings.

In this chapter we will look more closely at the roles that peers play in learning. We will also examine several instructional methods (class discussions, reciprocal teaching, cooperative learning, peer tutoring, communities of learners, and use of computer-mediated communication technologies) that involve significant interaction with peers.

HOW INTERACTIONS WITH PEERS CAN PROMOTE THINKING AND LEARNING

Increasingly, psychologists and educators are recognizing the value of having students work together to construct meaning about classroom subject matter—for instance, to explore, explain, discuss, and debate certain topics either in small groups or as an entire class. Following is an example of what might happen when learners tackle new subject matter and problems as a group:

> A third-grade class was working on the following problem: Bugs Bunny has 75 carrots. If he eats 5 carrots each day, for how many days does he have food? Most students solved the problem by writing 5s until they reached 75 and then counting the number of 5s. Maria solved the problem by writing $10 \times 5 = 50$, $5 \times 5 = 25$, and $10 + 5 = 15$. After the different methods had been presented, the class discussed the ways in which Maria's method was different from the others. Some students decided it was basically the same because Maria had added fives too, just in groups. The teacher then asked Maria why she chose 10 fives to start and not, say, 7 fives. Maria said she knew the answer to 10×5 so it was easy. This class discussion may look rather innocuous, but it had a significant effect on the way many students thought about division. After the discussion, a number of students began division problems by looking for multiples of the divisor, often choosing multiples or powers of 10. These were important breakthroughs in students' understandings and in the development of better methods. (Hiebert et al., 1997, pp. 44–45)

When learners work together in such a manner, they are, in essence, engaging in **distributed cognition**: They spread the learning task across many minds and can draw on multiple knowledge bases and ideas (Hewitt & Scardamalia, 1998; Kuhn, 2001b; Palincsar & Herrenkohl, 1999; Rogoff, 2003; Salomon, 1993).

Working with peers can be especially beneficial when students might gain a better understanding of a topic by tossing around diverse ideas, considering the strengths and weaknesses of each one, and revising current knowledge and beliefs in light of new evidence and insights. In such circumstances, interactions among age-mates can facilitate thinking and learning in numerous ways. In particular, peer group interactions related to a particular topic, task, or problem can

- Encourage students to clarify and organize their ideas sufficiently to explain and justify them to others
- Provide opportunities for students to elaborate on what they have learned—for example, by drawing inferences, generating hypotheses, and asking questions
- Expose students to new and possibly more sophisticated understandings and cognitive strategies
- Enable students to monitor their comprehension and possibly discover flaws and inconsistencies in their thinking
- Help students discover how people from different cultural and ethnic backgrounds may interpret the world in different, yet perhaps equally valid, ways
- Encourage students to find common ground in diverse perspectives and so perhaps to arrive at a more complex understanding than any single learner could arrive at independently
- Foster more advanced epistemological beliefs—for instance, an increasing recognition that acquiring "knowledge" involves acquiring an integrated set of ideas about a topic and that such knowledge is likely to evolve gradually over a lengthy period of time

- Introduce students to processes that experts in a discipline use to advance the frontiers of knowledge—for instance, presenting evidence in support of one's conclusions and examining the strengths and weaknesses of various explanations
- Promote the development of effective persuasion and argumentation skills
(L. M. Anderson, 1993; R. C. Anderson et al., 2001; Banks, 1991; Bell & Linn, 2002; Bielaczyc & Collins, 2006; Carr & Biddlecomb, 1998; Chinn, 2006; A. M. Clark et al., 2003; Derry, DuRussel, & O'Donnell, 1998; Fosnot, 1996; Hatano & Inagaki, 1993, 2003; Hiebert & Raphael, 1996; K. Hogan, Nastasi, & Pressley, 2000; A. King, 1999; Lampert, Rittenhouse, & Crumbaugh, 1996; Paris & Paris, 2001; Patrick & Middleton, 2002; Reiter, 1994; Schwarz, Neuman, & Biezuner, 2000; Stevens & Slavin, 1995; Webb & Palincsar, 1996)

Working with peers has other benefits as well. In line with Vygotsky's theory, students are likely to internalize—and eventually use independently—the study skills they initially use in collaboration with others (Applebee, Langer, Nystrand, & Gamoran, 2003; A. M. Clark et al., 2003; Webb & Palincsar, 1996). Furthermore, when students have the opportunity to work without constant teacher oversight, they are more willing to explore, experiment with, and in other ways take risks with new material (K. Hogan et al., 2000). And many students find interactive learning sessions highly motivating, in part because they can address their social needs at the same time that they're studying classroom subject matter (Hacker & Bol, 2004; Saville, Zinn, Neef, Van Norman, & Ferreri, 2006; Stevens & Slavin, 1995). One fourth grader described the motivational benefits of small-group discussions this way:

> I like it when we get to argue, because I have a big mouth sometimes, and I like to talk out in class, and I get really tired of holding my hand up in the air. Besides, we only get to talk to each other when we go outside at recess, and this gives us a chance to argue in a nice way. (A. M. Clark et al., 2003, p. 194)

We'll look at the social aspects of motivation more closely in chapters 15 and 16.

It is important to note, however, that peer-interactive approaches to instruction also have their downsides:

- Students may have insufficient expertise to tackle a task or problem without adult assistance. Even if they do have the expertise, they may have insufficient teaching and communication skills to help others understand their reasoning.
- Some students may be so anxious about making a bad impression on peers (e.g., by saying something "dumb") that they have trouble focusing on the overall discussion.
- Some student groups may have difficulty working together effectively and keeping themselves on task for any length of time.
- Students of high social status may dominate discussions, with other students acquiescing to their opinions and suggestions.
- Students may become annoyed or frustrated and begin to "tune out" if they perceive a discussion to be going in irrelevant or counterproductive directions.
- Students sometimes pass along misconceptions and illogical reasoning processes to their peers.
- If students believe that authority figures are the source of all knowledge and that "knowing" something means accumulating many facts (recall our discussion of *epistemological beliefs* in chapter 12), they may see little purpose in discussing controversial issues with classmates.

(Andre & Windschitl, 2003; Derry, DuRussel, & O'Donnell, 1998; Do & Schallert, 2004; Ellis & Rogoff, 1986; D. M. Hogan & Tudge, 1999; K. Hogan et al., 2000; Levy, Kaplan, & Patrick, 2000; Stacey, 1992; Wiley & Bailey, 2006; Wittenbaum & Park, 2001)

For such reasons, students probably learn most effectively with some teacher guidance and structure even when instructional methods are largely peer-interactive and student-directed. In the pages ahead, we'll consider a variety of forms that such guidance and structure might take.

CLASS DISCUSSIONS

Proponents of social constructivism argue that learners often work together to construct meaningful interpretations of their world (see chapter 7). Class discussions in which students feel that they can speak freely, asking questions and presenting their ideas and opinions in either a whole-class or small-group context, obviously provide an important mechanism for promoting such socially constructed understandings (Bruning, Schraw, & Ronning, 1995; De Corte et al., 1996; Fosnot, 1996; Greeno et al., 1996; Hiebert & Fisher, 1992; Marshall, 1992; Webb & Palincsar, 1996; White & Rumsey, 1994).

Class discussions lend themselves readily to a variety of academic disciplines. For example, students may discuss various interpretations of classic works of literature, addressing questions that have no easy or "right" answers; when they do so, they are more likely to relate what they are reading to their personal lives and thereby to understand it better (Applebee et al., 2003; Eeds & Wells, 1989; McGee, 1992; S. M. Miller, 2003). In history classes, students may study and discuss various documents related to a single historical event and so begin to recognize that history is not necessarily as cut-and-dried as traditional history textbooks portray it (Leinhardt, 1994; van Drie, van Boxtel, & van der Linden, 2006). In social studies, discussing controversial topics (e.g., capital punishment) can help students understand that diverse viewpoints on an issue may all have some legitimacy (Kuhn et al., 1997). In science classes, discussions of various and conflicting theoretical explanations of observed phenomena may help students come to grips with the idea that science is not "fact" as much as it is a dynamic and continually evolving understanding of the world (Bereiter, 1994). And in mathematics, class discussions that focus on alternative approaches to solving the same problem can promote a more meaningful understanding of mathematical principles and lead to better transfer of those principles to new situations and problems (Cobb et al., 1991; Hiebert & Wearne, 1992, 1996; Lampert, 1990).

Guidelines for Promoting Effective Discussions

Although students typically do most of the talking in classroom discussions, teachers nevertheless play a critical role. Theorists have offered several guidelines for how teachers can promote effective classroom discussions:

♦ *Class discussions should focus on topics that lend themselves to multiple perspectives, explanations, or approaches* (Hiebert & Raphael, 1996; Lampert, 1990; S. M. Miller, 2003; Onosko, 1996). Controversial topics appear to have several benefits: Students are more likely to express their views, seek out new information that resolves seemingly contradictory data, reevaluate their own positions on the issues under discussion, and develop a meaningful and well-integrated understanding of the subject matter (Applebee et al., 2003; Cohen, 1994; Johnson & Johnson, 1985a; Smith, Johnson, & Johnson, 1981).

◆ *Students should have sufficient prior knowledge about a topic to discuss it intelligently.* Such knowledge might come either from previous class sessions or from students' personal experiences (Bruning et al., 1995). In many cases, it is likely to come from studying a particular topic in depth (Onosko, 1996).

◆ *The classroom atmosphere should be conducive to open debate and the constructive evaluation of ideas.* Students are more likely to share their ideas and opinions if their teacher is supportive of multiple viewpoints and if disagreeing with classmates is socially acceptable. To promote such an atmosphere in the classroom, teachers might

- Communicate the message that understanding a topic at the end of a discussion is more important than having the "correct" answer at the beginning of the discussion.
- Communicate the beliefs that asking questions reflects curiosity, that differing perspectives on a controversial topic are both inevitable and healthy, and that changing one's opinion on a topic can be a sign of thoughtful reflection about the topic under discussion.
- Encourage students to try to understand one another's reasoning and explanations.
- Suggest that students build on one another's ideas whenever possible.
- Encourage students to be open in their agreement or disagreement with their classmates—in other words, to "agree to disagree."
- Depersonalize challenges to a student's line of reasoning by framing questions in a third-person voice—for example, by asking, "What if someone were to respond to your claim by saying . . . ?"
- Occasionally ask students to defend a position that is in direct opposition to what they actually believe.
- Require students to develop compromise solutions that take into account opposing perspectives.
  (Cobb & Yackel, 1996; Hatano & Inagaki, 1993, 2003; Herrenkohl & Guerra, 1998; K. Hogan et al., 2000; Lampert et al., 1996; Onosko, 1996; Perkins & Ritchhart, 2004; Reiter, 1994)

◆ *Small-group discussions encourage a greater number of students to participate.* Many students may speak more openly when their audience is a handful of classmates rather than the class as a whole; the difference is especially noticeable for females (A. M. Clark et al., 2003; Théberge, 1994). On some occasions, teachers may want to have students discuss an issue in small groups first, thereby allowing students to voice and gain support for their ideas in a relatively private context, and then bring students together for a whole-class discussion (Onosko, 1996).

◆ *Class discussions are often more effective when they are structured in some way.* Providing a structure for a class discussion—perhaps asking questions to get students thinking about particular issues, setting a particular goal toward which students should work, or assigning different roles to different class members (e.g., some evaluate the quality of evidence presented, others evaluate the validity of conclusions, etc.)—often increases the productivity of a discussion (Beck & McKeown, 2001; Calfee, Dunlap, & Wat, 1994; Herrenkohl & Guerra, 1998; Palincsar & Herrenkohl, 1999). Before conducting an experiment, a science teacher might ask students to make predictions about what will happen in the experiment and to explain and defend why they think their predictions are correct. Later, after students have observed the outcome of the experiment, the teacher might ask them to explain what happened and why (Hatano & Inagaki, 1991; Herrenkohl & Guerra, 1998). Another strategy, useful when the topic under discussion is an especially controversial one, might be to follow a sequence such as this one:

1. The class is divided into groups of four students apiece. Each group of four subdivides into two pairs.
2. Within a group, each pair of students studies a particular position on the issue and presents its position to the other two students.
3. The group of four has an open discussion of the issue, giving each student an opportunity to argue persuasively for his or her own position.
4. Each pair presents the perspective of the *opposing* side as sincerely and persuasively as possible.
5. The group strives for consensus on a position that incorporates all of the evidence presented (Deutsch, 1993).

◆ *Students may have more productive discussions when they are given guidance about how to behave.* Teachers must take steps to ensure that students' reactions to one another's ideas are not disparaging or mean spirited (A. M. Clark et al., 2003; Onosko, 1996; Windschitl, 2002). For example, they might provide rules such as the following for acceptable behavior during small-group or whole-class discussions:

- Encourage everyone to participate and listen to everyone's ideas.
- Restate what someone else has said if you don't understand.
- Be critical of ideas rather than people.
- Try to pull ideas from both sides together in a way that makes sense.
- Focus not on winning but on resolving the issue in the best possible way.
- Change your mind if the arguments and evidence presented indicate that you should do so. (based on Deutsch, 1993)

◆ *Teachers should monitor both the content and behaviors of small discussion groups and take corrective actions if necessary.* If students seem to be buying into their peers' misconceptions about the subject matter at hand, a gentle intervention (e.g., "Lydia thinks that [such-and-such]. Do the rest of you agree with that?") may steer a discussion in a more productive direction. And if students make hurtful remarks to peers, a reminder about the rules for behavior—and in some cases a request for an apology—may be in order.

◆ *Some type of closure should be provided at the end of the discussion.* Although students may sometimes come to consensus about a topic at the end of a class discussion, agreement is not always possible. Nevertheless, a class discussion should have some form of closure that helps students tie various ideas together. For instance, when I conduct discussions about controversial topics in my own classes, I spend a few minutes at the end of class identifying and summarizing the key issues that students have raised. Another strategy is to have students explain how a discussion has helped them understand a topic more fully (Onosko, 1996).

As you have seen, class discussions can help students think about and process classroom subject matter more completely. Such discussions can have an additional advantage as well: They can promote more effective learning strategies during reading and listening activities (A. L. Brown & Reeve, 1987; Cross & Paris, 1988; Palincsar & Brown, 1989; Paris & Winograd, 1990). One particular form of discussion—*reciprocal teaching*—is especially effective in this regard.

RECIPROCAL TEACHING

Annemarie Palincsar and Ann Brown (1984) have identified four key strategies that good readers typically use:

- *Summarizing:* They identify the gist and main ideas of what they read.
- *Questioning:* They ask themselves questions to make sure they understand what they are reading, thereby monitoring their comprehension as they proceed through reading material.
- *Clarifying:* They take steps to clarify confusing or ambiguous parts of the text, perhaps by rereading or imposing their own knowledge on those things.
- *Predicting:* They anticipate what they are likely to read next based on cues in the text (e.g., headings) and ideas that have previously been presented.

Palincsar and Brown noted that poor readers—students who learn little from textbooks and other things they read—rarely summarize, question, clarify, or predict. For example, many students cannot adequately summarize a typical *fifth*-grade textbook until high school or even junior college (A. L. Brown & Palincsar, 1987; Palincsar & Brown, 1984).

Yet summarizing, questioning, clarifying, and predicting are activities that typically occur internally rather than externally; they are cognitive processes rather than observable behaviors. Palincsar and Brown reasoned that students might acquire these strategies more easily if they first practiced them out loud and in cooperation with their classmates. In **reciprocal teaching** (A. L. Brown & Palincsar, 1987; Palincsar, 2003; Palincsar & Brown, 1984, 1989; Palincsar & Herrenkohl, 1999), a classroom teacher and several students meet in a group to read a section of text, stopping periodically to discuss that text as they proceed. Initially, the teacher leads the discussion, asking questions about the text to promote summarizing, questioning, clarifying, and predicting. But gradually, he or she turns the role of "teacher" over to different students, who then take charge of the discussion and ask one another the same kinds of questions their teacher has modeled. Eventually, students can read and discuss a text almost independently of the teacher, working together to construct its meaning and checking one another for comprehension and possible misunderstandings.

Reciprocal teaching sessions often begin with students making predictions about what they will read based on the title of a passage and their prior knowledge of a topic. Then, as they proceed through the text, they periodically stop to check their comprehension (e.g., by asking one another fact-based and inferential questions), clarify any potentially ambiguous statements or unfamiliar vocabulary, summarize what they have read, and predict what may be coming next. After finishing the passage, the "teacher" summarizes it, with other students possibly adding to and elaborating on the summary.

As an illustration, let's look at a reciprocal teaching session for a group of 6 first graders reading a passage about snowshoe rabbits. In this particular case, the classroom teacher reads the text in small segments (at higher grade levels, the students themselves take turns reading). After each segment, the teacher pauses while students discuss and process the segment. As you read the dialogue, look for examples of summarizing, questioning, clarifying, and predicting (there is at least one instance of each):

The children were reading about the snowshoe rabbit and it was the 16th day of dialogue. The teacher had just read a segment of text describing the season in which baby rabbits are born and the ways in which the mother rabbit cares for her babies. A student named Kam is the dialogue leader.

Kam:	When was the babies born?
Teacher:	That's a good question to ask. Call on someone to answer that question.
Kam:	Robby? Milly?
Milly:	Summer.
Teacher:	What would happen if the babies were born in the winter? Let's think.

Several children make a number of responses including: "The baby would be very cold." "They would need food." "They don't have no fur when they are just born."

Kam:	I have another question. How does she get the babies safe?
Kris:	She hides them.
Kam:	That's right but something else . . . .
Teacher:	There is something very unusual about how she hides them that surprised me. I didn't know this.
Travis:	They are all in a different place.
Teacher:	Why do you think she does this?
Milly:	Probably because I heard another story and when they're babies they usually eat each other or fight with each other
Teacher:	That could be! And what about when that lynx comes?

Several children comment that that would be the end of all the babies.

Travis:	If I was the mother, I would hide mine, I would keep them all together.
Kris:	If the babies are hidden and the mom wants to go and look at them how can she remember where they are?
Teacher:	Good question. Because she does have to find them again. Why? What does she bring them?
Milly:	She needs to bring food. She probably leaves a twig or something.
Teacher:	Do you think she puts out a twig like we mark a trail?

Several children disagree and suggest that she uses her sense of smell. One child, recalling that the snowshoe rabbit is not all white in the winter, suggests that the mother might be able to tell her babies apart by their coloring.

Teacher:	So we agree that the mother rabbit uses her senses to find her babies after she hides them. Kam, can you summarize for us now?
Kam:	The babies are born in the summer . . . .
Teacher:	The mother . . . .
Kam:	The mother hides the babies in different places.
Teacher:	And she visits them . . . .
Kam:	To bring them food.
Travis:	She keeps them safe.

Teacher:	Any predictions?
Milly:	What she teaches her babies . . . like how to hop.
Kris:	They know how to hop already.
Teacher:	Well, let's read and see.

(dialogue courtesy of A. Palincsar)

Reciprocal teaching provides a mechanism through which both teacher and students can model effective reading and learning strategies. When we consider that we are encouraging effective cognitive processes by first having students practice them aloud in group sessions, we realize that Vygotsky's theory is also at work here: Students should eventually internalize the processes that they first use in their discussions with others. Furthermore, the structured nature of a reciprocal teaching session scaffolds students' efforts to make sense of the things they read and hear. For instance, if you look back at the previous dialogue for a moment, you may notice how the teacher models elaborative questions and connections to prior knowledge ("What would happen if the babies were born in the winter?"; "Do you think she puts out a twig like we mark a trail?") and provides general guidance and occasional hints about how students should process the passage about snowshoe rabbits ("Kam, can you summarize for us now?"; "And she visits them . . . "). Also notice in the dialogue how students support one another in their efforts to process what they are reading; consider this exchange as an example:

Kam:	I have another question. How does she get the babies safe?
Kris:	She hides them.
Kam:	That's right but something else . . . .

Effectiveness of Reciprocal Teaching

Studies of reciprocal teaching have yielded significant and often dramatic improvements in students' reading and listening comprehension (Alfassi, 1998; A. L. Brown & Palincsar, 1987; Campione, Shapiro, & Brown, 1995; Hart & Speece, 1998; McGee, Knight, & Boudah, 2001; Palincsar, 1986; Palincsar & Brown, 1984, 1989; Rosenshine & Meister, 1994). Furthermore, students continue to show the benefits of this approach for at least six months after instruction (A. L. Brown & Palincsar, 1987). In an early study of reciprocal teaching (Palincsar & Brown, 1984), 6 seventh-grade students with a history of reading difficulty participated in 20 reciprocal teaching sessions, each lasting about 30 minutes. Despite the relatively short intervention, the students showed changes such as the following:

- They became increasingly able to process reading material in an effective manner—for example, by summarizing and questioning—and to do so independently of their classroom teacher.
- They demonstrated increasingly better comprehension of the passages they were reading. Average scores on daily comprehension tests increased from 30% before instruction to 70 to 80% (a level similar to that for average readers) after instruction.
- Three months after the reciprocal teaching intervention, their scores on a standardized reading comprehension test reflected an improvement in reading comprehension typically observed after 15 months of traditional schooling—more than a year's worth!

- They generalized their new reading strategies to other classes; for instance, they showed improved performance in their science and social studies classes, sometimes even surpassing the levels of their classmates (A. L. Brown & Palincsar, 1987; Palincsar & Brown, 1984).

A reciprocal teaching approach to reading instruction has been used successfully with a wide variety of students, ranging from third graders to college students. Furthermore, it can be used to foster more effective listening comprehension beginning in first grade (the snowshoe rabbit dialogue presented earlier is an example). And it can be employed with an entire classroom of students almost as easily as in a small group. Although teachers are often very skeptical of such a radically different approach to teaching and learning, their enthusiasm grows once they have tried it themselves (A. L. Brown & Palincsar, 1987; Palincsar & Brown, 1989). And as students gain increasing proficiency in this approach, they begin to use it more flexibly and creatively (Palincsar & Herrenkohl, 1999).

COOPERATIVE LEARNING

In **cooperative learning**[1] students work in small groups to achieve a common goal. Cooperative learning groups vary in duration, depending on the task to be accomplished. On some occasions, groups are formed on a short-term basis to accomplish specific tasks—perhaps to study new material, solve a problem, or complete an assigned project. On other occasions, groups are formed to work toward long-term classroom goals. For instance, **base groups** are cooperative groups that last an entire semester or school year; they provide a means through which students can clarify assignments for one another, help one another with class notes, and provide one another with a general sense of support and belonging in the classroom (Johnson & Johnson, 1991).

We find justification for cooperative learning in a number of theoretical perspectives. From a behaviorist point of view, rewards for group success are consistent with the notion of a group contingency. From the standpoint of social cognitive theory, students are likely to have higher self-efficacy for performing a task when they know that they will have the help of other group members; furthermore, students can model effective learning and problem-solving strategies for one another. And from the perspective of contemporary cognitivist ideas, students who collaborate on a learning task create scaffolding for one another's efforts and may co-construct more sophisticated ideas and strategies than any single group member might be able to construct alone.

---

[1]Some theorists distinguish between *cooperative* learning and *collaborative* learning, although different theorists draw the line somewhat differently (e.g., see Palincsar & Herrenkohl, 1999; Smith & MacGregor, 1992; Teasley & Roschelle, 1993). Part of their reasoning, I suspect, is that the term *cooperative learning* has historically been associated with particular theorists and particular instructional strategies (e.g., Johnson & Johnson, 1991; Slavin, 1983a, 1990a). Here I am using *cooperative learning* more broadly to refer to any instructional method in which students work together in a somewhat structured format to achieve a shared learning goal.

Common Features of Cooperative Learning

Cooperative learning is not simply a process of putting students in groups and setting them loose to work together on an assignment. Oftentimes students will be more accustomed to learning on an individual basis, or perhaps even to competing with classmates, than they are to engaging in cooperative endeavors. For a cooperative learning approach to be successful, teachers must structure classroom activities in such a way that cooperation is not only helpful for academic success but in fact even necessary for it (Johnson & Johnson, 1991). Following are several features that enhance the effectiveness of cooperative groups:

◆ *Students work in small, teacher-assigned groups.* Groups are typically comprised of two to six members; groups of three to four students can be especially effective (Hatano & Inagaki, 1991; Lou et al., 1996). In most cases, the teacher forms the groups, choosing combinations of students that are likely to be most productive (Johnson & Johnson, 1991). Many advocates of cooperative learning suggest that each group be relatively heterogeneous in makeup—that each group include high achievers and low achievers, boys and girls, and children of various ethnic backgrounds (Johnson & Johnson, 1991; Shachar & Sharan, 1994; Stevens & Slavin, 1995). Research on this practice yields mixed results, however, as we shall see shortly.

◆ *Groups have one or more common goals toward which to work.* At the beginning of a cooperative group activity, each group should have a clear and concrete understanding of what it needs to accomplish (Johnson & Johnson, 1991). For instance, in **project-based learning**, students begin with a "driving question" they need to answer (e.g., "Can good friends make me sick?") and then, with appropriate teacher scaffolding and technological tools, conduct an in-depth inquiry to address the question (Krajcik & Blumenfeld, 2006, p. 322; Mergendoller, Markham, Ravitz, & Larmer, 2006; Polman, 2004).

◆ *Students are given clear guidelines about how to behave.* Without instruction about appropriate group behaviors, students may act in a decidedly uncooperative manner; for example, they may try to dominate discussions, ridicule one another's ideas, or exert pressure to complete the task in a particular way (Blumenfeld, Marx, Soloway, & Krajcik, 1996; Webb & Palincsar, 1996). Instruction on group skills such as the following seems to increase cooperative and productive group behaviors:

- Listening to others politely and attentively
- Making sure everyone has an equal chance to participate and that everyone eventually understands the material
- Asking clear, precise questions when one doesn't understand
- Giving encouragement to others, and offering assistance as needed
- Offering feedback that is specific, kind, and constructive (e.g., "I'm curious why you chose to begin with this . . . " or "Have you considered including . . . ?")
- Addressing differences of opinion amicably and constructively (Berger, 2003, p. 94; Cohen, 1994; Deutsch, 1993; Gillies & Ashman, 1998; Johnson & Johnson, 1991; Lotan, 2006; Lou et al., 1996; O'Donnell & O'Kelly, 1994; Webb & Farivar, 1994, 1999; Webb & Palincsar, 1996)

◆ *Group members depend on one another for their success.* Group tasks should be structured so that each student's success depends on the help and participation of other group members. Furthermore, each student must believe it is to his or her advantage that other group members do well (Deutsch, 1993; Johnson & Johnson, 1991; Lou et al., 1996; Schofield, 1995; Slavin, 1983a). Tasks that involve creative problem solving and have more than one right answer are especially likely to encourage students to work cooperatively with one another (Blumenfeld et al., 1996). In some situations, each student might have a unique and essential function within the group, perhaps serving as group leader, critic, bookkeeper, peace-keeper, summarizer, or the like (A. L. Brown & Palincsar, 1989; Johnson & Johnson, 1991; Lotan, 2006). In other situations, the **jigsaw** technique is useful: New information is divided equally among all group members, and each student must teach his or her portion to the other group members (Aronson, 1997).

♦ *A structure is provided to encourage productive learning behaviors.* When students are novices at cooperative learning, it is often helpful to give them a structure—perhaps a set of steps, or "script," to follow—that guides their interaction (Fantuzzo, King, & Heller, 1992; Gillies, 2003; Meloth & Deering, 1994; Webb & Palincsar, 1996). For instance, in **scripted cooperation,** students work in pairs to read and study expository text (Dansereau, 1988; O'Donnell, 1999). One member of the pair might act as "recaller," summarizing the contents of a textbook passage. The other student acts as "listener," correcting any errors and recalling additional important information. For the next passage, the two students switch roles. Such an approach can help students improve such learning strategies as elaboration, summarizing, and comprehension monitoring (Dansereau, 1988).

The particular structure a teacher provides influences the kind of learning that results—for instance, whether students focus on learning facts, on the one hand, or engage in higher-level thinking skills, on the other. In one approach, which some theorists call **guided peer questioning** and others call **elaborative interrogation,** student pairs are given a structure that encourages them to ask one another higher-level questions about classroom material (Kahl & Woloshyn, 1994; A. King, 1997, 1999; A. King, Staffieri, & Adelgais, 1998; Ozgungor & Guthrie, 2004; Woloshyn, Pressley, & Schneider, 1992). More specifically, they are given "starters" such as these for constructing questions:

- Describe . . . in your own words.
- Explain why . . .
- What is the difference between . . . and . . . ?
- How could . . . be used to . . . ? (A. King, 1999, p. 93)

Students then use a series of such questions to probe and promote their partner's understanding. The following exchange shows two fifth graders using guided peer questioning as they study material about tide pools and tidal zones:

Janelle:	What do you think would happen if there weren't certain zones for certain animals in the tide pools?
Katie:	They would all be, like, mixed up—and all the predators would kill all the animals that shouldn't be there and then they just wouldn't survive. 'Cause the food chain wouldn't work—'cause the top of the chain would eat all the others and there would be no place for the bottom ones to hide and be protected. And nothing left for them to eat.
Janelle:	O.K. But what about the ones that had camouflage to hide them? (King, 1999, p. 95)

We join the two girls again later in the session; at this point, Katie is now asking the questions:

Katie:	How are the upper tide zone and the lower tide zone different?
Janelle:	They have different animals in them. Animals in the upper tide zone and splash zone can handle being exposed—have to be able to use the rain and sand and wind and sun—and they don't need that much water and the lower tide animals do.
Katie:	And they can be softer 'cause they don't have to get hit on the rocks.
Janelle:	Also predators. In the spray zone it's because there's predators like us people and all different kinds of stuff that can kill the animals and they won't survive, but the lower tide zone has not as many predators.
Katie:	But wait! Why do the animals in the splash zone have to survive? (King, 1999, p. 97)

Clearly, Janelle and Katie have become skilled at asking and answering higher-level questions. At the end of the second dialogue, we even see Katie questioning a basic assumption of the discussion—that animals in the splash zone need to survive.

◆ *The teacher serves primarily as a resource and monitor.* During cooperative learning activities, the teacher monitors each group to be sure that interactions are productive and socially appropriate (Johnson & Johnson, 1991; Meloth & Deering, 1999; Webb & Farivar, 1999). The teacher may also provide assistance in situations in which group members are unable to provide information or insights critical for accomplishing the group's goal. Too much intervention can be counterproductive, however: Students tend to talk less with one another when their teacher joins the group (Cohen, 1994).

◆ *Students are individually accountable for their achievement.* Each student demonstrates individual mastery or accomplishment of the group's goal—for example, by taking a quiz or having primary responsibility for a certain aspect of the group's final product. Individual accountability decreases the likelihood that some students will do most or all of the work while others get a free ride (Finn, Pannozzo, & Achilles, 2003; Johnson & Johnson, 1991; Karau & Williams, 1995; Slavin, 1983b, 1990a; Webb & Palincsar, 1996).

◆ *Students are rewarded for group success.* In addition to being accountable for their own learning and achievement, group members are typically rewarded in some way for the success of the group as a whole (Lou et al., 1996; Slavin, 1983b, 1990a). Group rewards often promote higher achievement overall, perhaps because students have a vested interest in helping one another learn and so make a concerted effort to help fellow group members understand the material being studied (Slavin, 1983b; Stevens & Slavin, 1995).

It is important to note, however, that not all researchers have found group rewards to be beneficial. In particular, students may sometimes learn better when they focus on using effective learning strategies than when they focus on obtaining a group reward (Meloth & Deering, 1992, 1994). More generally, the effects of extrinsic reinforcers can be a mixed bag, as you will discover in chapter 15.

◆ *At the completion of an activity, each group evaluates its effectiveness.* Once a cooperative group has accomplished its goal, it looks analytically and critically (often with the assistance of the teacher) at the ways in which it has functioned effectively and the ways in which it needs to improve (Cohen, 1994; Deutsch, 1993; Johnson & Johnson, 1991).

How Heterogeneous Should Cooperative Groups Be?

As I mentioned earlier, cooperative groups are often quite heterogeneous with respect to students' achievement levels, with high and low achievers being asked to work together. In recent years, some theorists have begun to question this practice (Cohen & Lotan, 1995; L. S. Fuchs, Fuchs, Hamlett, & Karns, 1998; Kumar, Gheen, & Kaplan, 2002; Lotan, 2006; O'Donnell & O'Kelly, 1994; S. E. Peterson, 1993). One potential problem with *very* heterogeneous grouping is that ability differences among students become more obvious. High-ability students may dominate discussions and work efforts and may discourage low-ability students from fully participating. Low-ability students may be reluctant to ask for help in understanding the material being studied, or they may simply sit back and let other group members do most or all of the work. And if a group fails to achieve its goal, the high performers in the group may resent and blame those who contributed little or nothing to the group's efforts.

Findings regarding the achievement gains of students in heterogeneous ability groupings have been somewhat mixed. Some studies indicate that heterogeneous groups benefit both high-ability students, who can sharpen their understanding of class material by explaining it to classmates, and low-ability students, who benefit from hearing such explanations (Cohen, 1994; L. S. Fuchs et al., 1996; Lou et al., 1996; Stevens & Slavin, 1995; Webb & Palincsar, 1996). Yet other studies indicate that high-ability students do not always gain much from working with their low-ability peers; in fact, these students occasionally even lose ground (Lou et al., 1996; Tudge, 1990; Webb, Nemer, Chizhik, & Sugrue, 1998). And middle-ability students may sometimes do better when grouped with *either* high-ability students (who can help them learn) or low-ability students (whom they can help learn), rather than being placed in the middle of a wide range of student abilities (Lou, Abrami, & d'Apollonia, 2001; Lou et al., 1996; McCaslin & Good, 1996; Webb & Palincsar, 1996).

The social dynamics within particular groups—the extent to which students stay on task, the extent to which low-ability students actively participate, the quality of help that high-ability students offer their classmates, and so on—appear to be an important factor in the effectiveness of heterogeneous groups (Osman, Duffy, Chang, & Lee, 2006; Webb & Mastergeorge, 2003; Webb, Nemer, & Zuniga, 2002). As an example, let's consider a seventh-grade classroom in which students were working in small groups to solve math problems such as this one:

> Find the cost of a 5-minute telephone call to prefix 756 (first minute costs $0.19; each additional minute costs $0.12). (Webb & Mastergeorge, 2003, p. 390)

Students in one group worked independently on the problem and then discovered that they had arrived at different answers. An exchange between a middle-ability student and a high-ability student (whom we'll call Student 1 and Student 2, respectively) followed:

Student 1:	*I got 79.* [On his paper appear the calculations 12 × 5 + 19.]
Student 2:	No, it's 12 times 4.
Student 1:	*Where'd you get 4 at?*
Student 2:	4 minutes and the additional minute is 19 cents. I got 0.67.
Student 1:	*5 minute call, enn . . . Where'd you get 4?*
Student 2:	Look, look. OK, 12 times 4, right? And then the minute, that's the 19 cents in the extra minute, which makes 5.
Student 1:	*Ah-ha.*

Student 2:	Because it says after each additional minute, so that means it will be 12 times 4. And then you add 19 cents, which is the additional time. You put 12 times 4.
Student 1:	*Times 4.*
Student 2:	And then you get the answer, and then you add 19 cents.
Student 1:	*Oh boy. Now I get it. Smart! Too smart.* (dialogue from Webb & Mastergeorge, 2003, p. 390)

Several elements of this exchange may facilitate Student 1's learning. Student 2 immediately notices Student 1's error and gives corrective feedback. Student 1 asks for an explanation of the correct answer, and Student 2 willingly provides one. Student 1 persists in his requests until he finally "gets it," at which point he acknowledges his understanding.

Two strategies I mentioned earlier—assigning different roles to different group members and providing scripts for interaction—are possible ways of equalizing the participation of students who have varying abilities. A third approach is to assign projects that require such a wide range of talents and skills that every group member is likely to have something unique and useful to contribute to the group's overall success (Cohen, 1994; Lotan, 2006; Schofield, 1995).

Effectiveness of Cooperative Learning Activities

Numerous research studies indicate that cooperative learning activities, when designed and structured appropriately, are effective in many ways. On average, students of all ability levels show higher academic achievement. Females, members of minority groups, and students at risk for academic failure are especially likely to show increased achievement (Barron, 2000; Ginsburg-Block & Fantuzzo, 1998; Lou et al., 1996; Mathes, Torgesen, & Allor, 2001; Nichols, 1996b; Qin, Johnson, & Johnson, 1995; Rohrbeck, Ginsburg-Block, Fantuzzo, & Miller, 2003; Shachar & Sharan, 1994; Stevens & Slavin, 1995). Cooperative learning activities may also promote higher-level thinking skills: Students essentially "think aloud," modeling various learning and problem-solving strategies for one another and developing greater metacognitive awareness as a result (Good et al., 1992; Paris & Winograd, 1990).

The benefits of cooperative learning activities are not limited to gains in learning and achievement. Students have higher self-efficacy about their chances of being successful, express more intrinsic motivation to learn school subject matter, participate more actively in classroom activities, and exhibit more self-regulated learning. They better understand the perspectives of others and more frequently engage in prosocial behavior, making decisions about how to divide a task fairly and equitably, resolving interpersonal conflicts, and encouraging and supporting one another's learning. Furthermore, they are more likely to believe that they are liked and accepted by their classmates, and increased numbers of friendships across racial and ethnic groups, as well as between students with and without disabilities, are likely to form (Deutsch, 1993; Good et al., 1992; Johnson & Johnson, 1985b, 1987; Lou et al., 1996, 2001; Marsh & Craven, 1997; Nichols, 1996a, 1996b; Slavin, 1983a, 1990a; Stevens & Slavin, 1995; Webb & Palincsar, 1996).

Some potential disadvantages of cooperative learning should be noted, however. Students may sometimes be more interested in achieving a group reward with the least possible effort and so will focus more on getting the "right" answer than on ensuring that all group members understand the subject matter being studied (Good et al., 1992; Hatano & Inagaki, 1991; Linn et al., 1996). The students who do most of the work and most of the talking may learn more than other group members, and they may harbor negative feelings about peers who contribute little if anything to the group effort (Blumenfeld, 1992; Gayford, 1992; Lotan, 2006; Webb, 1989). Students may occasionally agree to use an incorrect strategy or method that a particular group member has suggested. And in some cases, students may simply not have the skills to help one another learn (O'Donnell & O'Kelly, 1994; Webb & Mastergeorge, 2003). Clearly, then, teachers must keep a close eye on the discussions that cooperative groups have and the products that they create, providing additional structure and guidance when necessary to promote maximal learning and achievement.

One of the reasons that cooperative learning is so often effective is that students tutor one another in the subject matter they are studying. Such peer tutoring is our next topic of discussion.

PEER TUTORING

Teachers cannot always devote as much time as they would like to one-on-one instruction with their students. In such situations, **peer tutoring**,[2] whereby students who have mastered a topic teach those who have not, can provide an effective alternative for teaching fundamental knowledge and skills (A. L. Brown & Palincsar, 1987; Durkin, 1995; Greenwood, Carta, & Hall, 1988; Pigott et al., 1986).

In some cases, peer tutoring leads to greater academic gains than more traditional forms of instruction (Greenwood et al., 1988). One possible reason for its effectiveness is that it provides a context in which struggling students may be more comfortable asking questions when they don't understand something. In one study (Graesser & Person, 1994), students asked 240 times as many questions during peer tutoring as they did during whole-class instruction!

Peer tutoring typically benefits the tutors as well as those being tutored (Biemiller, Shany, Inglis, & Meichenbaum, 1998; D. Fuchs, Fuchs, Mathes, & Simmons, 1997; Greenwood et al., 1988; Semb et al., 1993; Webb & Palincsar, 1996). When students study material with the expectation that they will be teaching it to someone else, they are more motivated to learn it, find it more interesting, process it in a more meaningful fashion, and remember it longer (Benware & Deci, 1984; Semb et al., 1993). Furthermore, in the process of directing and guiding other students' learning and problem solving, tutors may, in a Vygotskian fashion, internalize these processes and so become better able to direct and guide their *own* learning and problem solving; in other words, peer tutoring may foster greater self-regulation (Biemiller et al., 1998). Peer tutoring has nonacademic benefits as well: Cooperation and other social skills improve, classroom behavior problems diminish, and friendships develop between students of different ethnic groups and between students with and without disabilities (Greenwood et al., 1988).

---

[2]Some theorists use the term *peer tutoring* when referring to structured learning sessions in which students of equal ability ask one another questions about classroom subject matter. I have incorporated the literature about such tutoring in my earlier discussion of cooperative learning. I am restricting my use of the term here to situations in which one learner has greater expertise in the subject matter than another.

Guidelines for Facilitating Effective Tutoring

Peer tutoring, like other interactive approaches to instruction, is most effective when teachers follow certain guidelines in its use. Following are several suggestions for using peer tutoring effectively:

◆ *Teachers should be sure that their tutors have mastered the material being taught and use sound instructional techniques.* Good tutors have a meaningful understanding of the subject matter they are teaching and provide explanations that focus on such understanding. In contrast, poor tutors are likely to describe procedures without explaining why the procedures are useful (L. S. Fuchs et al., 1996). Good tutors also use teaching strategies that are likely to promote learning: They ask questions, give hints, scaffold responses when necessary, provide feedback, and so on (Lepper, Aspinwall, Mumme, & Chabey, 1990).

Students don't always have the knowledge and skills that will enable them to become effective tutors, especially in the elementary grades (Greenwood et al., 1988; Kermani & Moallem, 1997; Wood, Wood, Ainsworth, & O'Malley, 1995). It is essential, then, that tutoring sessions be limited to subject matter that the student tutors know well. Training in effective tutoring skills is also helpful. For example, student tutors might be shown how to establish a good relationship with the students they are tutoring, how to break a task into simple steps, how and when to give feedback, and so on (Fueyo & Bushell, 1998; Inglis & Biemiller, 1997; Kermani & Moallem, 1997).

◆ *Structured interactions can enhance the effectiveness of peer tutoring.* Studies by Lynn and Douglas Fuchs and their colleagues (D. Fuchs et al., 1997; L. S. Fuchs et al., 1996; Mathes et al., 2001) indicate that providing a structure for tutoring sessions can help elementary students effectively tutor their classmates in reading comprehension skills. In one study (D. Fuchs et al., 1997), 20 second- through sixth-grade classes participated in a project called Peer-Assisted Learning Strategies (PALS). In each class, students were ranked with regard to their reading performance, and the ranked list was divided in half. The first-ranked student in the top half of the list was paired with the first-ranked student in the bottom half of the list, the second student in the top half was paired with the second student in the bottom half, and so on down the list; through this procedure, students who were paired together had moderate but not extreme differences in reading level. Each pair read material at the level of the weaker reader and engaged in the following activities:

- *Partner reading with retell:* The stronger reader read aloud for 5 minutes, and then the weaker reader read the same passage of text. Reading something that had previously been read presumably enabled the weaker reader to read the material easily. After the double reading, the weaker reader described the material that the pair had just read.
- *Paragraph summary:* The students both read a passage one paragraph at a time. Then, with help from the stronger reader, the weaker reader tried to identify the subject and main idea of the paragraph.
- *Prediction relay:* Both students read a page of text, and then, with help from the stronger reader, the weaker reader would summarize the text and also make a prediction about what the next page would say. The students would read the following page, and then the weaker reader would confirm or disconfirm the prediction, summarize the new page, make a new prediction, and so on.

Such a procedure enabled students in the PALS program to make significantly greater progress in reading than students who had more traditional reading instruction, even though the amount of class time devoted to reading instruction was similar for both groups. The researchers speculated that the superior performance of the PALS students was probably because they had more frequent opportunities to make verbal responses to the things they were reading, received more frequent feedback about their performance, and, in general, were more frequently encouraged to use effective reading strategies.

◆ *Teachers must be careful that their use of higher-ability students to tutor lower-ability students is not excessive or exploitive.* As we have seen, tutors often gain just as much from tutoring sessions as the students they are tutoring. When students teach something to a classmate, they must pull their knowledge together sufficiently to explain it in a way that someone else can understand; in the process, they review, organize, and elaborate on the things they have learned. Nevertheless, teachers must not assume that high-achieving students will always learn from a tutoring session; they should regularly monitor the effects of a peer tutoring program to make sure that all students are reaping its benefits.

◆ *Teachers can use peer tutoring to help students with special educational needs.* Peer tutoring has been used effectively to help students with learning disabilities, physical disabilities, and other special educational needs (Cushing & Kennedy, 1997; DuPaul, Ervin, Hook, & McGoey, 1998; D. Fuchs et al., 1997). In one study (Cushing & Kennedy, 1997), low-achieving students were assigned as regular tutors for classmates who had moderate or severe intellectual or physical disabilities. The student tutors clearly benefited from their tutoring assignments: They became more attentive in class, completed classroom tasks more frequently, and participated in class more regularly. I suspect that the opportunity to tutor classmates less capable than themselves may have enhanced their own self-efficacy for learning classroom subject matter, which in turn would encourage them to engage in the kinds of behaviors that would ensure (rather than interfere with) academic success.

◆ *Tutoring does not necessarily need to be limited to same-age pairs.* In many instances, students at one grade level can effectively tutor students at a lower grade level; for example, fourth or fifth graders can tutor students in kindergarten or first grade (Biemiller et al., 1998; A. L. Brown & Campione, 1994; Kermani & Moallem, 1997). Such a practice is consistent with Vygotsky's belief that older and more competent individuals are invaluable in promoting the cognitive development of younger children. Furthermore, low-ability students who tutor younger children on skills they themselves have mastered have the opportunity to regulate others' learning and, in the process, can internalize those regulation strategies for their own use (Biemiller et al., 1998).

COMMUNITIES OF LEARNERS

One important prerequisite for interactive instructional methods is a *sense of community*—a sense that teacher and students have shared goals, respect and support one another's efforts, and believe that everyone makes an important contribution to classroom learning (Hom & Battistich, 1995; Kim, Solomon, & Roberts, 1995; Lickona, 1991; Watson & Battistich, 2006). One way to create this sense of community is to transform the classroom into a **community of learners** in which teacher and students actively and cooperatively work to help one another learn

(A. L. Brown & Campione, 1994, 1996; A. Collins, 2006; Engle & Conant, 2002; Rogoff, 2003). A classroom that operates as a community of learners is likely to have certain characteristics:

- All students are active participants in classroom activities.
- Students draw on many resources—textbooks, magazines, the Internet, and one another—in their efforts to learn about a topic.
- Discussion and collaboration among two or more students are common occurrences and play a key role in learning.
- Diversity in students' interests and rates of progress is expected and respected.
- Students and teacher coordinate their efforts at helping one another learn; no one has exclusive responsibility for teaching others.
- Everyone is a potential resource for the others; different individuals are likely to serve as resources on different occasions, depending on the topics and tasks at hand.
- The teacher provides some guidance and direction for classroom activities, but students may also contribute guidance and direction.
- Mechanisms are in place through which students can share what they've learned with others.
- Constructive questioning and critique of one another's work is commonplace.
- The process of learning is emphasized as much as, and sometimes more than, the finished product.
(Bielaczyc & Collins, 1999; A. L. Brown & Campione, 1994, 1996; Campione et al., 1995; Rogoff, 1994, 2003; Rogoff, Matusov, & White, 1996; Scardamalia & Bereiter, 2006)

Underlying a community of learners is the guiding principle that students and teacher(s) alike are committed to·advancing the collective knowledge, skills, and understanding of all members of the classroom. Essentially, the class is engaged in **knowledge building**—authentically advancing the frontiers of the group's knowledge about a topic, much as adult researchers do in their efforts to advance understandings in various academic and professional disciplines (Bereiter & Scardamalia, 2006; Bielaczyc & Collins, 1999, 2006; Scardamalia & Bereiter, 2006). In the process, students create not only tangible products but also **conceptual artifacts**—theories, models, plans, problem-solving strategies, and other cognitive tools that they can use, evaluate, and possibly modify over time (Bereiter & Scardamalia, 2006; Scardamalia & Bereiter, 2006).

Ann Brown and Joseph Campione (1994) have described one simple example of how a community of learners might be structured. In this situation, students were divided into five groups to study five subtopics falling within a general theme; for instance, subtopics for the theme *changing populations* were *extinct, endangered, artificial, assisted,* and *urbanized.* Each group conducted research and prepared teaching materials related to its subtopic; in essence, they became the class experts on the subtopic. The class then reassembled into five new groups that included at least one representative from each of the previous groups; within these groups, the students taught one another the things they had learned.

Communities of learners typically incorporate a variety of interactive instructional strategies, including class discussions, cooperative learning, peer tutoring, and perhaps reciprocal teaching (A. L. Brown & Campione, 1996). (The *changing populations* unit just described reflects the *jigsaw* technique described earlier in the section on cooperative learning.) In addition, older students or subject-matter experts may occasionally sit in on group discussions and gently guide the students as they prepare their teaching materials—for example, asking "Remember that the reader hasn't read about echo location; is this enough to make it clear?" (A. L. Brown & Campione, 1996).

Researchers have not yet systematically compared the academic achievement of communities of learners with the achievement of more traditional classes, but case studies indicate that classes structured as communities of learners have several positive effects. These classes appear to promote higher-level thinking processes, including metacognitive reflections (e.g., "Other students can't understand _____ until they already know _____"), for extended periods of time (A. L. Brown & Campione, 1994, 1996). They can also promote more advanced epistemological beliefs—for instance, students are more likely to realize that there is probably no such thing as knowing everything that can possibly be known about a topic (Scardamalia & Bereiter, 2006). And they can be highly motivating: Students often insist on going to school even when they are ill, and they are disappointed when summer vacation begins (Rogoff, 1994). Communities of learners may be especially useful as a way of encouraging students with diverse backgrounds, cultural perspectives, and specialized talents to make unique and valued contributions to the classroom learning environment (Bielaczyc & Collins, 2006; Garcia, 1994).

At the same time, communities of learners have a couple of potential weaknesses (A. L. Brown & Campione, 1994; Hynd, 1998b). For one thing, what students learn will inevitably be limited to the knowledge that they themselves acquire and share with one another. Second, students may occasionally pass on their misconceptions to their classmates. Obviously, then, teachers who structure their classrooms as communities of learners must carefully monitor student interactions to make sure that instructional objectives are being achieved and that students ultimately acquire accurate understandings of the subject matter they are studying.

Guidelines for Creating Effective Learning Communities

Many of the principles and guidelines I've offered for class discussions and cooperative learning are relevant to communities of learning as well. For instance, the classroom atmosphere should be one in which students feel comfortable sharing ideas, disagreeing with one another, and occasionally changing their minds. The final goal of a learning task should be clear, and students' efforts should be structured and scaffolding sufficiently to enable students to reach that goal. And students should realize that helping their classmates learn is ultimately in everyone's best interest. In addition, the following guidelines may be helpful:

◆ *Students should focus on complex problems that need solving.* Ideally, communities of learners focus on significant issues and problems—those that have personal meaning to students and are potentially relevant to the well-being of the world at large (Brophy, 2004; Engle & Conant, 2002). The *changing populations* theme mentioned earlier is an example of a topic that many students are likely to view as important to themselves personally and to society as a whole.

◆ *Students should learn basic skills in persuasion and argumentation.* In a community of learners, students often bring diverse ideas and perspectives to bear on a topic, and they must learn to state and defend their positions in a way that convinces others. For instance, they should present solid evidence for their claims, and they must be able to critique (tactfully) any opposing claims that their classmates offer (Cazden, 2001; Engle & Conant, 2002). Such skills are most likely to develop when encouraged, modeled, scaffolded, and regularly practiced (Halpern, 1998; Klahr & Chen, 2003; Kuhn & Franklin, 2006; Kuhn & Udell, 2003; Kuhn & Weinstock, 2002).

◆ *Students must be committed to working effectively, and must learn* **how** *to work effectively, with all of their classmates.* Students inevitably bring their existing relationships with classmates—including some counterproductive perceptions and emotional "baggage"—to a community of learners. Teachers must often take active steps to help students discover the many unique abilities and other strengths that every community member can contribute to the overall learning effort (Brophy, 2004; Cazden, 2001).

COMPUTER-MEDIATED COMMUNICATION TECHNOLOGIES

Effective student interactions don't necessarily have to be face to face. Through such mechanisms as electronic mail (e-mail), Web-based chat rooms, and electronic bulletin boards, computer technology enables students to communicate with their peers (either in their own classroom or elsewhere), exchange perspectives, and brainstorm and build on one another's ideas (Bielaczyc & Collins, 2006; Brown & Paulus, 2002; Derry, 2006; Fabos & Young, 1999; J. Schacter, 2000). Technology also allows subject-matter experts to be pulled occasionally into the conversation (A. L. Brown & Campione, 1996; Winn, 2002).

We find an example of how technology can enhance student interaction and knowledge building in software created at the University of Toronto. This software, called Knowledge Forum,[3] enables students to communicate regularly using a classwide or cross-institution database and essentially creates a computer-based community of learners (Hewitt & Scardamalia, 1996, 1998; Lamon, Chan, Scardamalia, Burtis, & Brett, 1993; Scardamalia & Bereiter, 2006). Using the database, students share their questions, ideas, notes, writing products, and graphic constructions. Their classmates (and sometimes a subject-matter expert as well) respond regularly, perhaps by giving feedback, building on ideas, offering alternative perspectives, or synthesizing what has been learned.

Initial observations of this approach have been encouraging: Students are concerned about truly understanding classroom subject matter rather than simply "getting things done," actively try to relate new material to what they already know (i.e., they engage in meaningful learning and elaboration), and show greater ability to remember, synthesize, and apply classroom subject matter (Bereiter & Scardamalia, 2006; Lamon et al., 1993; Scardamalia & Bereiter, 2006). Students also build regularly on one another's ideas. As an example, consider how two students (identifying themselves by the initials AR and AD) respond online to another student's (JA's) question, "How does heat affect solids?" Scaffolded by the software, students use such the headings "My theory" and "I need to understand" to structure their discussion and enhance their metacognitive awareness of the tentative, dynamic nature of their current understandings:

JA: *My theory:*   I think that heat makes solids burn or melt. I think that my prediction is right because I've seen solds [sic] melt and burn.

AR: *My theory:*   I think that if a solid comes in contact with heat, it becomes hot. I also think it might change colour. Generally if any solid comes in contact with heat then it becomes hot. I think that the solid

---

[3]An early version of this software was known as Computer Supported Intentional Learning Environment, or CSILE (pronounced like the name *Cecil*). You can learn more about Knowledge Forum at http://www.KnowledgeForum.com.

AD:

would become hot faster if it could conduct energy well. If an object didn't conduct energy well then it would heat up, but take a longer time than an object that conducts energy well. It might change colour because we think that if something is very hot it is white or red and sort of hot it is orange or yellow. There might be some truth to this.

My theory: I think that it depends on how much heat there is. I also think that it depends on what sort of solid it is. For instance, the heat that might melt rubber might not melt metal. (This last sentece [sic] might be wrong, I'm just using it as an example.)

I need to understand: What makes wood burn instead of melt?

My theory: I think that it might have something to do with wood being organic, because I can't think of anything that is organic, and would melt. (Hewitt & Scardamalia, 1998, p. 85; format adapted)

Such technology-based discussions give students the time they may need to reflect on one another's ideas; hence, they allow that *wait time* I spoke of in chapter 10. And they may be especially valuable for students who are shy or for other reasons feel uncomfortable communicating with classmates in a more public fashion (Hewitt & Scardamalia, 1998).

Students find their online interactions highly enjoyable and motivating (Lamon et al., 1993). And ultimately, students are more likely to process information effectively, and so understand it better, if they are truly motivated to learn it. Up to now, we've talked about motivation only occasionally and in passing, but in fact motivation is *critical* to the learning process. In the final two chapters of the book, we'll look at the nature of motivation more closely; we'll also consider many teaching strategies that can keep students regularly engaged in, and perhaps even excited about, studying classroom subject matter.

SUMMARY

Human beings are a very social species; accordingly, their learning is often a very social enterprise. Interactions with peers about instructional topics have many advantages; for instance, they may (a) encourage learners to organize and elaborate on ideas, (b) promote the development of argumentation skills, (c) expose learners to diverse and possibly more sophisticated understandings and strategies, and (d) foster more advanced epistemological beliefs. Interactive approaches to instruction have some downsides, however (e.g., learners may pass along misconceptions and inappropriate strategies to their peers), and so usually require some teacher structure and guidance.

In a *class discussion,* students must clarify and organize their ideas and opinions sufficiently to express them to others, and they may acquire a more accurate and complete understanding of a topic after hearing what their classmates have to say. Class discussions are often more effective when they address complex or controversial issues about which students have some prior knowledge, when the classroom atmosphere supports open debate and constructive evaluation of ideas, and when sufficient structure is imposed to encourage all students to participate.

Reciprocal teaching is an approach to instruction in which students learn to ask one another certain kinds of questions about textbook content and other reading material. Reciprocal teaching significantly enhances students' reading comprehension skills, in large part by fostering more effective metacognitive skills (e.g., making predictions, summarizing what has been learned).

In *cooperative learning,* students work in small groups to accomplish specific goals. Successful cooperative learning groups have several key features: Students (1) have clear goals and guidelines for appropriate behavior, (2) must coordinate their efforts and support one another's learning in order to be successful, (3) are individually accountable for what they have learned, and (4) are rewarded for the overall success of their group. Research consistently confirms the effectiveness of cooperative learning activities, although it yields conflicting data about how heterogeneous groups should be in order to maximize learning.

Peer tutoring involves two students at either the same grade level or different grade levels. Tutors and tutees typically both benefit from tutoring sessions; this is especially true when tutors have a good command of the subject matter and use sound instructional techniques or when tutoring sessions are structured to promote effective instruction.

A *community of learners* is a classroom in which teacher and students actively and cooperatively work to help one another master complex, meaningful topics and issues; it often incorporates other interactive approaches such as class discussions and cooperative learning. Although the teacher provides some guidance and direction for classroom activities, students assume much of the responsibility for acquiring information about a topic and facilitating one another's learning.

Modern computer technology—for instance, in the form of *computer-mediated communication technology*—provides a way for student discussion and collaboration to go beyond classroom walls. It can also enhance interaction within a single classroom, for instance by providing a common database in which students can share their questions, insights, essays, and stories and by enabling students to build regularly on one another's ideas.

CHAPTER 15

Motivation and Affect

Over the years, I have learned how to do a great many things. For instance, I have learned how to teach and write about psychology. I have learned how to find my favorite junk food in the supermarket and my favorite television game show in *TV Guide*. I have learned how to control my tongue and temper in a university committee meeting. I have learned how to mow the lawn, file a tax return, cook lima beans, clean the garage, and pick up after slovenly children.

Yet you don't see me doing all of these things on a regular basis. I engage in some activities (e.g., writing about psychology, eating junk food, and watching television game shows) because I like doing them. I engage in others (e.g., behaving myself at committee meetings, filing tax returns, and mowing the lawn) not because I enjoy them but because they bring me things I *do* enjoy, such as productive relationships with university colleagues, IRS refunds, or a well-kept backyard. But there are some things that I rarely do because they aren't fun and they reap me few if any rewards. For example, you won't find me cooking lima beans (abominable little things), cleaning the garage (the cars don't care one way or the other), or picking up children's messy bedrooms (a never-ending battle). And there are additional things that I've never learned at all because I've seen little point in doing so. Batting averages of professional baseball players, locations for the "petite" sizes in ladies' clothing at Sears, and strategies for walking barefoot on hot coals all fall into this category.

Motivation—an internal state that arouses us to action, pushes us in particular directions, and keeps us engaged in certain activities—is the key ingredient here. Even if we are perfectly capable of learning something (and I am, mind you, quite capable of learning where to find virtually any clothing size at Sears), motivation often determines whether and to what extent we actually learn it, especially if the behaviors and cognitive processes necessary for learning are voluntary and under our control.[1] Furthermore, once we *have* learned how to do something, motivation is in large part responsible for whether we continue to do it.

We have touched on the importance of motivation in previous chapters—for instance, within the context of reinforcement in chapter 4, modeling in chapter 6, conceptual change in chapter 9, and self-regulated learning in chapter 12. In the final two chapters of the book, we'll look more closely at the nature in motivation. In this chapter, we'll consider how motivation influences behavior, cognition, and learning, and we'll see that two fundamentally different kinds of motivation, extrinsic and intrinsic, may have somewhat different effects. We'll also explore various theories about basic human needs—needs that characterize virtually everyone—and possible individual differences in motivation. We'll then turn our attention to a close companion of motivation—*affect* (emotion)—and look at the many ways in which it is involved in learning and behavior.

As we proceed, keep in mind that *learners are almost always motivated in one way or another.* For example, students in a typical sixth-grade classroom have a variety of motives (Lee & Anderson, 1991). Some will almost certainly want to learn the subject matter being presented in class. Others may be more interested in getting good grades, outperforming their classmates, pleasing their teacher and parents, or simply completing assignments as quickly and painlessly as possible. Such motives all have an *approach* quality to them: Underlying them is a desire to achieve certain outcomes. Yet students may sometimes behave in order to *avoid* certain situations—an assigned task with which they're likely to struggle, perhaps, or a social interaction in which they think they'll be bullied by peers. In general, teachers should never question *whether* their students are motivated. Instead, they should try to determine *in what ways* their students are motivated.

Keep in mind, too, that although learners certainly bring certain motives with them to the classroom, *motivation is partly a function of the learning environment*—a phenomenon known as **situated motivation** (Graham & Weiner, 1996; Greeno et al., 1996; Paris & Turner, 1994; Rueda & Moll, 1994). In school classrooms, many factors are likely to influence students' motivation. For instance, the kinds of instructional materials that a teacher uses (whether they are interesting, challenging, relevant to students' needs, and so on), the extent to which students find themselves having to compete with one another, and the ways in which students are evaluated are all likely to play a role (Boykin, 1994; Paris & Turner, 1994; Stipek, 1996). At the end of the chapter, we'll identify a number of strategies teachers can use to enhance students' motivation to master academic subject matter. As we explore cognitive factors in motivation—expectancies, values, goals, attributions, and so on—in chapter 16, we'll identify many additional strategies. Ultimately, I hope you discover that motivation is not something that people "turn on" and "turn off" at will. Rather, it is the result of numerous factors, some of which are in learners' control but many more of which are the result of learners' past and present environmental circumstances.

---

[1]Classical conditioning is an example of learning in which motivation plays little if any role. As you should recall from chapter 3, classical conditioning involves the acquisition of an involuntary response as a result of encountering two stimuli at approximately the same time. In such a situation, the learner has control neither of the stimulus pairing nor of the response, and conscious cognitive processes are often not involved.

GENERAL EFFECTS OF MOTIVATION

Children and adults alike aren't always consciously aware of the particular motives that drive their actions (Pintrich, 2003). Yet motivation consistently reveals itself through its effects on people's behaviors, as reflected in the following principles:

◆ *Motivation increases an individual's energy and activity level* (Maehr & Meyer, 1997; Pintrich et al., 1993; Vernon, 1969). It influences the extent to which an individual is likely to engage in a certain activity intensively and vigorously or half-heartedly and lackadaisically.

◆ *Motivation directs an individual toward certain goals* (Dweck & Elliott, 1983; Eccles & Wigfield, 1985; Maehr & Meyer, 1997). Motivation affects the choices people make and the consequences they find reinforcing. In chapter 16 we'll identify a variety of goals toward which people may strive.

◆ *Motivation promotes initiation of certain activities and persistence in those activities* (Eccles & Wigfield, 1985; Maehr & Meyer, 1997; Pintrich et al., 1993; Stipek, 1993). Motivation increases the likelihood that people will begin something on their own initiative, persist in the face of difficulty, and resume a task after a temporary interruption. In other words, motivation often manifests itself in considerable **personal investment** in a particular activity or domain (Maehr & McInerney, 2004; Maehr & Meyer, 1997).

Educators have long recognized that **time on task** is an important factor affecting school learning and achievement (Brophy, 1988; Davis & Thomas, 1989). The more time students spend engaged in a particular learning activity, the more academically successful they will be. Although time on task is partly determined by how teachers plan and schedule the school day—that is, by how much time they devote to different topics and activities—it is also determined to some extent by students' motivation to study and persist with those topics both in and outside of school.

◆ *Motivation affects the learning strategies and other cognitive processes an individual brings to bear on a task* (Dweck & Elliott, 1983; Eccles & Wigfield, 1985). Time on task is, in and of itself, insufficient for successful learning (e.g., Son & Schwartz, 2002). As contemporary cognitive theories tell us, certain mental processes—paying attention, learning meaningfully, elaborating, monitoring comprehension, identifying inconsistencies between new information and prior knowledge, and so on—are essential for effective learning and long-term retention of new information and skills. In other words, learners must be actively *thinking about* what they are seeing, hearing, and doing. Such **cognitive engagement** is one of the benefits of a high level of motivation (Christenson & Thurlow, 2004; Fredricks, Blumenfeld, & Paris, 2004; Lee & Anderson, 1993; Pugh & Bergin, 2006).

Yet not all forms of motivation have exactly the same effect on human learning and performance. In fact, extrinsic motivation and intrinsic motivation yield somewhat different results, as we shall see now.

EXTRINSIC VERSUS INTRINSIC MOTIVATION

At the beginning of the chapter, I mentioned that I engage in some activities because they bring about desirable consequences (i.e., they are extrinsically reinforced), whereas I engage in others simply because they are enjoyable. Just as behaviorists distinguish between extrinsic and intrinsic reinforcement, motivation theorists distinguish between extrinsic and intrinsic motivation.

Extrinsic motivation exists when the source of motivation lies outside of the individual and the task being performed. For example, I file an income tax return every year partly because I usually get a refund when I do so and partly because I will be fined (i.e., punished) if I *don't* file. For many years I attended university committee meetings because university service was part of my job description and I was quite dependent on my monthly paycheck (in my current position, attending committee meetings is, thank goodness, rarely required). I give my house a thorough cleaning when preparing to host a party because I would hate for my friends to discover I'm a slob.

In contrast, **intrinsic motivation** exists when the source of motivation lies within the individual and task: The individual finds the task enjoyable or worthwhile in and of itself. For instance, I frequently read books and articles about human learning and motivation because they continue to shed new light on topics that are, to me, utterly fascinating. I watch television game shows because I enjoy playing along as a home viewer. I eat junk food because it tastes good (an unfortunate consequence is that I have no need for the petite sizes at Sears).

Extrinsic motivation can certainly promote successful learning and productive behavior, as evidenced by the effectiveness of applied behavior analysis (see chapter 5). Extrinsic reinforcement for engaging in a particular activity increases an individual's time on task, and performance is likely to improve as a result (Emmer & Evertson, 1981). Extrinsic motivation in the classroom has its drawbacks, however: Extrinsically motivated students may exert only the minimal behavioral and cognitive effort they need to execute a task successfully (occasionally this may mean copying someone else's work), and they may stop an activity as soon as reinforcement ceases (Brophy, 2004; Flink, Boggiano, Main, Barrett, & Katz, 1992; Lee, 1991).

Intrinsic motivation has numerous advantages over extrinsic motivation. For any particular task, intrinsically motivated learners are more likely to:

- Pursue the task on their own initiative, without having to be prodded or cajoled
- Be cognitively engaged in the task (e.g., by keeping attention focused on it)
- Undertake more challenging aspects of the task
- Strive for true understanding of the subject matter (e.g., by engaging in meaningful rather than rote learning)
- Undergo conceptual change when such change is warranted
- Show creativity in performance
- Persist in the face of failure
- Experience pleasure, sometimes even exhilaration, in what they are doing
- Regularly evaluate their own progress, often using their own criteria
- Seek out additional opportunities to pursue the task
- Achieve at high levels
  (Brophy, 1986; Corpus, McClintic-Gilberg, & Hayenga, 2006; Csikszentmihalyi, 1990, 1996; Csikszentmihalyi & Nakamura, 1989; Flink et al., 1992; Gottfried, 1990; Harter, 1981; Hennessey, 1995; Hennessey & Amabile, 1987; Lee & Anderson, 1993; Maehr, 1984; Pintrich et al., 1993; Reeve, 2006; Russ, 1993; Schweinle, Turner, & Meyer, 2004; Spaulding, 1992; Stipek, 1993)

Csikszentmihalyi (1990, 1996; Csikszentmihalyi & Nakamura, 1989) has used the term **flow** to describe an intense form of intrinsic motivation, characterizing it as a state of complete absorption, focus, and concentration in a challenging activity, to the point that the individual loses track of time and completely ignores other tasks.

Obviously, intrinsic motivation is the optimal state of affairs in the classroom. At the same time, we should not assume that the presence of extrinsic versus intrinsic motivation must be an either-or situation. On many occasions, learners may be *both* extrinsically and intrinsically motivated (Hidi & Harackiewicz, 2000; Lepper, Corpus, & Iyengar, 2005). Furthermore, even a single motive can have both extrinsic and intrinsic aspects; for example, students may strive for good grades not only for the external rewards that such grades bring but also for verification that they have mastered the subject matter (Hynd, 2003). And as we will discover in our discussion of *internalized motivation* in chapter 16, some motives have a partly extrinsic, partly intrinsic nature.

BASIC HUMAN NEEDS

Over the years, theorists have offered varying perspectives about needs that might be universal across the human species. Here we focus on early perspectives (drives, need for arousal, and Maslow's hierarchy of needs) and more recent ones (needs for competence, self-worth, self-determination, and relatedness) that are especially relevant to instructional settings. As you will see, some of these perspectives shed light on when students are most likely to have intrinsic motivation to learn in the classroom.

Drive Reduction

Drive theory (Freud, 1915/1949; Hull, 1943, 1951, 1952; Woodworth, 1918) is based on the notion that people and other animals (*organisms*) try to maintain physiological homeostasis; in other words, they try to keep their bodies at an optimal state of functioning. A **drive** is an internal state of need within an organism: Something necessary for optimal functioning (e.g., food, water, warmth, or rest) is missing. When a drive exists, the organism behaves in ways that reduce the need and bring the body back into balance. For example, a hungry person eats, a thirsty person drinks, a cold person seeks out a source of heat, and a tired person goes to bed. If a response that reduces the need is not immediately possible, the organism shows a general increase in activity—activity that may eventually lead to an encounter with a need-reducing stimulus.

Although early psychologists of many theoretical persuasions found value in the concept of drive, advancements in drive theory emerged largely through the work of behaviorists. From a behaviorist perspective, a reinforcer is effective to the extent that it reduces a need state, thereby simultaneously reducing drive. For example, a drink of water is reinforcing only if an organism is thirsty, and a source of heat is reinforcing only if an organism is cold. Behaviors that reduce a need state—behaviors that are reinforced—are likely to be repeated when the same need emerges at some later time.

Probably the most widely cited version of drive theory is that of behaviorist Clark Hull (1943, 1951, 1952).[2] In 1943, Hull proposed that drive is based on physiological needs such as hunger and thirst. All of these needs contribute to the general drive state of the organism; drive

---

[2]Hull incorporated his view of drives into a larger theory of learning, which you can learn about in the reading "Beyond Pavlov, Thorndike, and Skinner: Other Early Behaviorist Theories" on the book's Companion Website at www.prenhall.com/ormrod.

itself is not specific to a particular need. Hull further proposed that the strength (or intensity) of a behavior is a function of both *habit strength* (i.e., the degree to which associations between a particular stimulus and response have been learned) and drive:

Strength of behavior = Habit × Drive

In such a multiplicative relationship, both habit (prior learning) and drive must be present. If either is zero, the strength of the behavior—the likelihood that it will occur—is also zero.

Hull based his notion of *habit times drive* on experiments conducted by two of his students (Perin, 1942; Williams, 1938). In these experiments, rats were placed in Skinner boxes and trained to press a bar for a food reinforcer. Different groups of rats received varying amounts of training, with a greater number of reinforced responses presumably leading to greater habit strength. Later, after going without food for either 3 hours (low drive) or 22 hours (high drive), the rats were once again placed in Skinner boxes, and their frequency of bar pressing was recorded under nonreinforcement (extinction) conditions. The hungrier rats pressed the bar many more times than the less hungry rats; similarly, rats who had received more training pressed the bar more often than those who had undergone little training. Rats with little drive (3 hours of food deprivation) and low habit strength (5 training trials) pressed the bar, on average, only once.

In 1951, Hull revised his thinking in two significant ways. First, he observed that some behaviors serve no apparent biological purpose. He therefore proposed that some drives are **acquired drives:** They develop when previously neutral stimuli are associated with drive-reducing stimuli such as food. To illustrate, one might become "driven" by a need for approval if approval has previously been associated with candy and other tasty treats. From this perspective, reinforcement results from reduction of one's drive rather than reduction of specific physiological needs.

In addition, Hull took into account research by Crespi (1942) and others indicating that reinforcers may affect performance rather than learning. (We examined Crespi's study in chapter 4. To refresh your memory, rats running down a runway for food began to run faster when the amount of reinforcement was increased; they began to run more slowly when the amount of reinforcement was decreased.) Accordingly, Hull introduced the concept of *incentive* into his theory, acknowledging that behaviors are influenced by the characteristics of a goal object—for example, by the amount of food at the end of a runway. Incentive became a third essential ingredient for a behavior to occur, as follows:

Strength of behavior = Habit × Drive × Incentive

When any of these three factors—habit strength, drive, or incentive—is absent, the behavior is not exhibited.

Other theorists have since expanded on Hull's notion that the characteristics of goal objects (incentives) are motivating forces in behavior (Mowrer, 1960; Overmier & Lawry, 1979; Spence, 1956). In their view, **incentive motivation** serves as a mediator (M) between stimuli and responses, affecting which stimuli are responded to and which are not. Symbolically, we could describe the relationship this way:

$$S \rightarrow M_{incentive} \rightarrow R$$

For example, I find a bag of Cheetos quite enticing after several hours of food-free book writing (thus leading to a reach-in-and-grab-a-handful response). However, the same bag provokes no response whatsoever right after a Thanksgiving dinner, when I have stuffed myself with turkey, mashed potatoes, and pumpkin pie.

Incentives undoubtedly play a role in human motivation. Just as Crespi's rats ran faster when they knew that mass quantities of food lay waiting at the end of the runway, so, too, do we humans apparently work harder when incentives are more attractive (Klinger, 1975, 1977). When our progress toward a particular goal object is temporarily stymied, we often intensify our efforts (Klinger, 1975). And when our progress is permanently blocked, we are likely to respond with immature behavior or aggression (Barker, Dembo, & Lewin, 1941; Dollard, Doob, Miller, Mowrer, & Sears, 1939; Hinton, 1968; Johnson, 1972).

Incentives remain in vogue as a probable source of motivation (see the discussion of social cognitive theory in chapter 6), and behaviorists acknowledge that different objects and events may be more or less reinforcing depending on whether an organism has been deprived of them for any significant period (McGill, 1999; Michael, 1993, 2000). But theorists have largely abandoned drives in their discussions of motivation (Bolles, 1975; Graham & Weiner, 1996). For one thing, learning sometimes occurs in the absence of any apparent drive reduction (Sheffield & Roby, 1950; Sheffield, Roby, & Campbell, 1954; Sheffield, Wulff, & Backer, 1951). For example, male rats will make responses that allow them to mount receptive female rats, even though they are pulled away from the females before they can consummate their affectionate relationship and reduce their sexual drive (Sheffield et al., 1951). Second, a great deal of human behavior seems to be aimed at accomplishing long-term goals rather than satisfying short-term needs (Pintrich & Schunk, 2002). Third, organisms sometimes behave in ways that actually increase their drive states (Olds & Milner, 1954; Rachlin, 1991; Sheffield, 1966a, 1966b). For instance, when rats have electrodes implanted in particular areas of their brains (called "pleasure centers"), they eagerly press a bar to obtain electrical stimulation of those areas, and they continue in their bar pressing until they're exhausted (Olds & Milner, 1954). In much the same way, we humans voluntarily increase our drive states by going to scary movies, reading suspense novels, and riding roller coasters. Some of us are even **sensation seekers,** putting ourselves in risky or dangerous situations on a regular basis for the physiological thrills that such situations yield (Zuckerman, 1994). Perhaps such sensation seeking is an extreme form of a more basic need, a need for arousal.

Arousal

Psychologists use the term **arousal** to refer to the level of internal energy an organism is currently experiencing. Organisms experiencing low levels of arousal are relaxed, perhaps even asleep. Organisms experiencing high levels of arousal are highly energized, perhaps to the point of being excessively anxious. Some research indicates that people have a basic need for stimulation; in other words, they have a **need for arousal.**[3]

As an example, let's consider a classic study by Heron (1957). Male college students were given $20 a day (quite an incentive in the 1950s) to stay as long as they were willing to do so in a boring environment—and I mean a *really* boring environment. Aside from occasional brief breaks for eating and other biological necessities, the students spent the time lying on a bed in a small

---

[3]Occasionally one of my students assumes that this term refers to sexual activity. On the contrary, *need for arousal* refers to a basic need for stimulation of *any* kind.

cubicle in which the only sound was the continuous hum of an air conditioner. They wore plastic visors that allowed them to see only diffused, unpatterned light (making them functionally blind) and thick gloves and cardboard sleeves that prevented them from feeling different shapes and textures (minimizing the information they could gain from touching things). Naturally, many students began by catching up on their sleep. Students spent their first few waking hours thinking about college coursework, personal issues, past experiences, and so on. Eventually, they ran out of things to think about and so simply let their minds wander aimlessly. As time went on, cognitive functioning deteriorated: The students had trouble concentrating, reported distorted perceptual processes (e.g., the room seemed to move, and objects appeared to change size and shape), and generally seemed quite disoriented. Some began to hallucinate, perhaps seeing a row of cartoon-like men with open mouths or a line of marching squirrels with bags over their shoulders, or perhaps hearing a music box playing or a church choir singing. Some also reported feelings of touch or movement: "One had a feeling of being hit in the arm by pellets fired from a miniature rocket ship he saw" (p. 54). More generally, people seem to have exceptional difficulty functioning under conditions of *sensory deprivation* for any length of time (Solomon et al., 1961).

Some theorists have suggested that not only do people have a basic need for stimulation but they also strive for a certain *optimal level* of arousal (e.g., Berlyne, 1960). Too little stimulation is unpleasant, but so is too much. For example, you may enjoy watching a television game show or listening to music, but you would probably rather not have three television sets, five compact disk players, and a live rock band all blasting in your living room at once. Different people have different optimal levels: Some are sensation seekers whereas others prefer a quieter existence. I, for one, like things a bit on a dull side. Although I certainly enjoy a suspenseful mystery novel on occasion, you'll never catch me riding a roller coaster or bungee jumping.

I've seen very little reference to need for arousal in the motivation literature in recent years, but this simple concept does seem to explain some of the things we see in classrooms. For instance, it explains why students create their own excitement (perhaps passing notes or playing practical jokes on one another) when their teacher drones on at length about a dry topic. (In a sociology class I took as a first-year college student, the girl who sat next to me kept a running tally of how many times the professor cleared his throat. This simple activity kept us both amused, which was fortunate, because the professor certainly did not.) Furthermore, more cognitive versions of the same idea—*stimulation seeking* and the *need for cognition*—have recently appeared on the scene, as we'll see in our discussion of *dispositions* later in the chapter.

Maslow's Hierarchy of Needs

Another early perspective of motivation was that of Abraham Maslow (1959, 1973a, 1973b, 1987). Maslow's theory is a central feature of **humanism,** a movement in psychology that gained prominence in the 1960s and 1970s. Humanism has its roots in counseling psychology and focuses its attention on how individuals acquire emotions, attitudes, values, and interpersonal skills. Humanist perspectives tend to be grounded more in philosophy than in research, but they provide useful insights into human motivation nevertheless.

In an attempt to pull together his informal observations of human behavior, Maslow proposed that people have five different sets of needs:

1. *Physiological needs.* People are motivated to satisfy needs related to their immediate physical survival—needs for food, water, oxygen, warmth, exercise, rest, and so on.

For example, if you've been sitting still in class for a long time, you may find yourself getting restless and fidgety, and if you're hungry, you may think more about your growling stomach than about a professor's lecture. Maslow's physiological needs are essentially the same as those of Hull's early drive theory.

2. *Safety needs.* People have a need to feel safe and secure in their environment. Although they may enjoy an occasional surprise, generally speaking they prefer structure and order in their lives. For example, most students like to know what things are expected of them and prefer classroom routines that are somewhat predictable.

3. *Love and belongingness needs.* People seek affectionate relationships with others and like to feel that they "belong" and are accepted as part of a group. For example, a 9-year-old may place great importance on having a "best friend." And many young adolescents take great pains to fit in with the cool crowd—for example, by wearing a certain hairstyle or buying clothes with a certain brand name conspicuously displayed on them.

4. *Esteem needs.* People need to feel good about themselves (**need for self-esteem**) and to believe that others also feel positively about them (**need for esteem from others**). To develop positive self-esteem, individuals strive for achievement and mastery of their environment. To attain the esteem and respect of others, they behave in ways that gain them recognition, appreciation, and prestige. For example, a second grader can partially satisfy the need for self-esteem by reading a book "all by myself" or by achieving a special merit badge in Cub Scouts or Campfire Girls. A high school student may try to satisfy the need for esteem from others by running for student council treasurer or becoming a star athlete. When their esteem needs are satisfied, people are self-confident and have a sense of self-worth; when these needs go unmet, people feel weak and inferior.

5. *Need for self-actualization.* People have a need to **self-actualize**—to develop and become all they are capable of becoming (also see Rogers, 1951, 1961). Individuals striving toward self-actualization seek out new activities as a way of expanding their horizons and want to learn simply for the sake of learning. For example, people seeking self-actualization might be driven by their own curiosity to learn everything they can about a particular topic, or they might pursue an active interest in ballet both as a means of developing muscle tone and as an outlet for creative self-expression.

Maslow proposed that the five sets of needs form a hierarchy, as illustrated in Figure 15.1. When two or more of these needs are unmet, people tend to satisfy them in a particular sequence. They begin with the lowest needs in the hierarchy, satisfying physiological needs first, safety needs next, and so on, addressing higher needs only after lower needs have been attended to. For example, a boy with a need for exercise (a physiological need) may become excessively restless in class even though he is scolded by his teacher for his hyperactivity (thereby *not* satisfying his need for esteem from others). A girl with an unfulfilled need for love and belonging may choose not to enroll in intermediate algebra—a class that would satisfy her desire to learn more math—if the peers whose friendships she most values tell her the class is only for nerds and various other uncool individuals. I once met a boy living in a Philadelphia ghetto who had a strong interest in learning yet often stayed home from school to avoid the

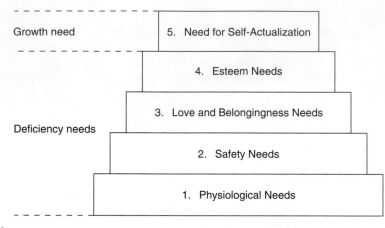

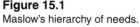

Figure 15.1
Maslow's hierarchy of needs.

violent gangs that hung out on the street corner. This boy's need for safety took precedence over any higher needs he might have had.

According to Maslow, the first four needs in the hierarchy—physiological, safety, love and belonging, and esteem needs—result from things that a person *lacks;* hence, Maslow called them **deficiency needs.** Deficiency needs can be met only by external sources—by people or events in one's environment. Furthermore, once these needs are fulfilled, there is no reason to satisfy them further. In contrast, self-actualization is a **growth need:** Rather than addressing a deficiency in a person's life, it enhances the person's growth and development and thus is rarely satisfied completely. Self-actualizing activities tend to be intrinsically motivated: People engage in them because doing so gives them pleasure and satisfies their desire to know and grow.

Needs that are satisfied most of the time have little effect on behavior. For example, many people in our society routinely satisfy their physiological and safety needs. The needs for love and esteem are more likely to go unfulfilled; hence, people may direct much of their effort toward developing self-respect and gaining the acceptance and respect of others. People are likely to strive for self-actualization only when all four deficiency needs are at least partially met. Once they are regularly focusing on self-actualization, however, they may occasionally disregard more basic needs, perhaps foregoing meals or jeopardizing their personal safety in pursuit of what is, in their minds, a noble cause.

In Maslow's view self-actualized individuals have a number of noteworthy characteristics. For example, they are independent, spontaneous, creative, and sympathetic to the plights of others. They perceive themselves, other people, and the world in general in an objective, realistic light, and they are quite comfortable with who they are. They typically have a mission in life—an important problem that they are concerned about solving. Maslow suggested that few people—probably less than 1% of the population—become fully self-actualized, and then only in the later years of life.

Despite its intuitive appeal, Maslow's hierarchy has been criticized on several counts. For one thing, little hard evidence exists to substantiate the hierarchical nature of human motivation.

Maslow derived his theory from his informal, subjective observations of presumably "self-actualized" personal friends and from published descriptions of such historical figures as Thomas Jefferson and Abraham Lincoln; it would be almost impossible for other investigators to confirm that these individuals had the characteristics Maslow identified. Furthermore, self-actualization is so rare that the hierarchy may not provide an accurate description of people in general (Petri, 1991). Finally, people's various motives are probably too diverse to be boiled down into such a short list of basic needs (Pintrich & Schunk, 2002). (You'll get a better sense of this diversity as we proceed through this and the following chapter.)

At the same time, aspects of Maslow's theory clearly have some merit. It makes sense that people will worry about their physiological well-being and personal safety before they try to address more social needs. And Maslow's notions of *esteem needs* and *love and belonging needs* are clearly reflected in contemporary theories about self-worth and relatedness—topics we turn to in upcoming sections.

Competence and Self-Worth

Maslow has hardly been the only one to suggest that people have a need to think positively about themselves. In 1959, Robert White proposed that human beings (and, he suggested, many other species as well) have a basic need for **competence**—a need to believe that they can deal effectively with their environment. In recent years, other theorists have echoed this belief, asserting that the need for competence is a fundamental human need (e.g., Boggiano & Pittman, 1992; Connell & Wellborn, 1991; Reeve, Deci, & Ryan, 2004; Ryan & Deci, 2000).

To achieve a sense of competence, young children spend a great deal of time engaged in exploring and attempting to master the world. As an illustration, let's look once again at an example I presented in chapter 11, in which Jean Piaget's son Laurent tried to reach a piece of bread that was beyond his reach:

> Laurent is seated before a table and I place a bread crust in front of him, out of reach. Also, to the right of the child I place a stick about 25 cm. long. At first Laurent tries to grasp the bread without paying attention to the instrument, and then he gives up. I then put the stick between him and the bread. . . . Laurent again looks at the bread, without moving, looks very briefly at the stick, then suddenly grasps it and directs it toward the bread. But he grasped it toward the middle and not at one of its ends so that it is too short to attain the objective. Laurent then puts it down and resumes stretching out his hand toward the bread. Then, without spending much time on this movement, he takes up the stick again, this time at one of its ends. . . and draws the bread to him. (Piaget, 1952b, p. 335)

Laurent was only 16 months old at the time, yet he clearly had an intrinsic desire to master at least one aspect of his environment. According to White (1959), the need for competence has biological significance and probably evolved with our species: It pushes people to develop ways of dealing more effectively with environmental conditions and thus increases their chances of survival.

Martin Covington (1992, 2004) has proposed that *protecting* one's sense of competence—something he calls **self-worth**—is one of people's highest priorities. Obviously, achieving success on a regular basis is one way of maintaining, perhaps even enhancing, this self-worth. But consistent success isn't always possible, especially when people face challenging tasks. In such situations, an alternative way to maintain self-worth is to *avoid failure,* because failure gives the impression of low ability (Covington, 1992; Covington & Müeller, 2001; Urdan & Midgley, 2001). Failure avoidance manifests itself in a variety of ways; for instance, people may refuse to engage in an activity, downplay its importance, set very low expectations for themselves, or refuse to abandon existing beliefs in the face of considerable contradictory evidence[4] (Covington, 1992; Harter, 1990; Martin, Marsh, & Debus, 2001; Sherman & Cohen, 2002).

In some situations, however, people can't avoid tasks at which they expect to do poorly, and so they use alternative strategies to protect their self-worth. Sometimes they make excuses that seemingly justify their poor performance (Covington, 1992; Urdan & Midgley, 2001). Yet they may also do things that actually *undermine* their chances of success—a phenomenon known as **self-handicapping.** Self-handicapping takes a variety of forms, including these:

- *Setting unattainably high goals:* Working toward goals that even the most able individuals couldn't achieve
- *Taking on too much:* Assuming so many responsibilities that a person could not possibly accomplish them all successfully
- *Creating impediments:* Concocting obstructions or additional requirements that make a task almost impossible to accomplish
- *Procrastinating:* Putting a task off until success is virtually impossible
- *Reducing effort:* Putting forth an obviously insufficient amount of effort to succeed
- *Cheating in class:* Presenting others' work as one's own
- *Using alcohol or drugs:* Taking substances that will inevitably reduce performance (E. M. Anderman, Griesinger, & Westerfield, 1998; Covington, 1992; D. Y. Ford, 1996; Jones & Berglas, 1978; Riggs, 1992; Urdan & Midgley, 2001; Urdan, Midgley, & Anderman, 1998; Wolters, 2003a)

It might seem paradoxical that people who want to be successful would engage in such behaviors. But if people believe they are unlikely to succeed at a particular task, they increase their chances of *justifying* their lack of success (and therefore they maintain self-worth) by acknowledging that, under the circumstances, success wasn't very likely to begin with (Covington, 1992; Jones & Berglas, 1978; Riggs, 1992). Curiously, some people are more likely to perform at their best, and less likely to display self-handicapping behaviors, when their chances of success are slim or when a task is in a seemingly "unimportant" domain (Covington, 1992; Urdan, Ryan, Anderman, & Gheen, 2002). In such situations, failure is not interpreted as indicating low ability and so doesn't threaten people's sense of self-worth.

To date, most research on self-worth theory and self-handicapping has focused on academic tasks and accomplishments. Some theorists suggest, however, that academic achievement isn't always the most important thing affecting people's sense of self-worth; for many people, such factors as social success or physical appearance may be more influential (Eccles, Wigfield, & Schiefele, 1998). Also troubling is the finding that people sometimes seem more comfortable maintaining *consistent* self-perceptions, even if those self-perceptions are negative ones (Hay, Ashman, van Kraayenoord, & Stewart, 1999). Yet in most instances, positive self-perceptions do appear to be a high priority.

Revisiting self-efficacy   On the surface, the concepts of competence and self-worth are similar to the concept of *self-efficacy* that we examined in chapter 6. In theory, however, there are two key

---

[4]Hence, the need to protect one's self-worth may be one reason why people don't undergo *conceptual change.*

differences between the needs for competence and self-worth, on the one hand, and self-efficacy, on the other. First, in line with our discussion here, having a sense of competence and self-worth may be a basic human need. In contrast, social cognitive theorists have suggested that self-efficacy is certainly a *good* thing, but they don't go so far as to speculate that it is an essential driving force of human nature. Second, competence and self-worth have been conceived as being fairly general, overarching self-perceptions (i.e., what you think about yourself overall), whereas self-efficacy is more task specific.

But now let's muddy the waters a bit. To some degree, how competent you think you are overall is apt to affect the confidence with which you approach a particular task, and how self-efficacious you feel about performing a task is apt to contribute in some way to your overall sense of competence and self-worth. Furthermore, in my own reading of the motivation literature, I find that theorists sometimes use the term *sense of competence* (or something similar) when talking about fairly specific tasks or situations, and they sometimes use the term *self-efficacy* to refer to a fairly general self-perception (e.g., Bandura, 1997).

One point on which everyone agrees is that one's sense of confidence—both about accomplishing specific tasks and about dealing with life in general—is an important variable influencing motivation, especially *intrinsic motivation.* Conversely, feelings of incompetence lead to decreased interest and motivation (e.g., Boggiano & Pittman, 1992; Harter et al., 1992; Mac Iver, Stipek, & Daniels, 1991; Reeve et al., 2004; Ryan & Deci, 2000).

As we discussed self-efficacy in chapter 6, we identified several variables that help learners believe they can succeed at a task, including encouraging messages, the successes of peers, and, most importantly, their *own* successes (either individually or as part of a group) at a task or activity. The last of these—actual successes—are, of course, the most powerful. Sometimes learners' successes are obvious; winning a bicycle race and constructing a sturdy bookcase from a set of instructions are examples. But many others are not so clear-cut, and in such instances feedback is often helpful. Curiously, even class grades and other extrinsic reinforcers can promote *intrinsic* motivation to the extent that they signal successful performance and therefore enhance learners' self-efficacy and overall sense of competence (Cameron, 2001; Covington, 2000; Hynd, 2003; Schunk & Zimmerman, 1997).

Self–Determination

Some psychologists suggest that people not only want to feel competent, but they also want to have some sense of *autonomy* regarding the things they do and the directions their lives take. In other words, human beings may have a basic need for **self-determination** (d'Ailly, 2003; deCharms, 1972; Deci & Ryan, 1992; Reeve et al., 2004; Ryan & Deci, 2000; Vansteenkiste, Zhou, Lens, & Soenens, 2005). For instance, when we think "I *want* to do this" or "I would *find it valuable* to do that," we have a high sense of self-determination. In contrast, when we think "I *have to*" or "I *should*," we are telling ourselves that someone or something else is making decisions for us.

Numerous motivation theorists have proposed that learners are more likely to be intrinsically motivated when they have a sense of self-determination about their present circumstances. For instance, when present conditions and events confirm learners' feelings of self-determination, learners are likely to

- Experience pleasure in activities, and voluntarily engage in them for long periods
- Think meaningfully and creatively about tasks and problems

- Undertake challenges that maximize long-term learning and development
- Achieve at high levels
- Stay in school rather than dropping out
  (Amabile & Hennessey, 1992; deCharms, 1972; Deci, 1992; Deci & Ryan, 1985, 1987; Hagger, Chatzisarantis, Barkoukis, Wang, & Baranowski, 2005; Hardré & Reeve, 2003; Reeve et al., 2004; Standage, Duda, & Ntoumanis, 2003; Vansteenkiste, Lens, & Deci, 2006; Wang & Stiles, 1976)

In contrast, when environmental circumstances and events lead people to conclude that they have little involvement in determining the course of their lives, they may comply with external demands but are unlikely to have much intrinsic motivation (Deci & Ryan, 1987). As an example, I think back to 1989 in the months after the Berlin Wall came down: Many East German workers reportedly showed little initiative or stick-to-itiveness on the job, quite possibly because they had for so long been told exactly what to do and what not to do under the Communist regime. Furthermore, when people's reasons for doing something lie outside of themselves, they are likely to undertake the easy things they know they can do rather than challenges at which they might fail (Stipek, 1993). Often, too, they may feel depressed and have a diminished sense of self-worth (Vansteenkiste et al., 2006).

Several variables appear to influence people's sense of self-determination one way or the other, including choices, threats and deadlines, controlling statements, extrinsic rewards, surveillance, and evaluation. After examining these variables, we'll also see how people can sometimes put a positive spin on controlling circumstances.

Choices   Let's return to a point I made in chapter 5: Children and adults alike seem to prefer having some choice in the reinforcers for which they work. From the perspective of self-determination, this finding makes perfect sense. In general, people have a greater sense of self-determination—and so are more intrinsically motivated—when they are able to make choices, within reasonable limits, about the things they do and the outcomes for which they will work (Deci & Ryan, 1987, 1992; Morgan, 1984; Stipek, 1993). For example, in an early study by Lewin, Lippitt, and White (1939), 10-year-old boys participating in after-school recreational programs were in one of three experimental conditions. In the *autocratic* group, adults made all of the decisions about what the boys would do. In the *laissez-faire* group, the boys did as they pleased, with little if any adult input. In the *democratic* group, the adults and boys engaged in group decision making about daily activities. The boys were most productive in the democratic setting: They showed greater initiative and on-task behavior related to group projects, and they were less likely to act aggressively toward their peers. Other researchers have found similar results in classroom settings: When students have choices (again, within appropriate limits) about the activities in which they engage, they show greater interest and involvement in their classwork, and they display fewer off-task behaviors (Dunlap et al., 1994; Foster-Johnson, Ferro, & Dunlap, 1994; Morgan, 1984; Paris & Turner, 1994; Powell & Nelson, 1997; Stipek, 1996; Vaughn & Horner, 1997).

We must qualify the effects of choices in a couple of ways, however. First, choices are likely to enhance sense of self-determination only if they are *real* choices—that is, if they truly allow a selection among several possible courses of action. Choices have little effect on motivation when they are highly constrained—say, when a teacher gives students a "choice" between two or three equally unappealing tasks (Reeve, Nix, & Hamm, 2003; Stefanou, Perencevich, DiCintio, & Turner, 2004).

Second, cultural differences have been observed in the importance of choices. In particular, although many American children find choice-making opportunities highly motivating, those from Asian-American families often prefer that people they trust (parents, teachers, respected peers, etc.) make the choices for them (Iyengar & Lepper, 1999). Perhaps the latter see trusted others as people who can make *wise* choices—choices that will ultimately lead to higher levels of learning and competence.

Threats and deadlines   Threats (e.g., "Do this or else!") and deadlines (e.g., "This is due by January 15—no exceptions!") are typically experienced as controlling people's behaviors. As a result, they reduce self-determination and intrinsic motivation (Clifford, 1990; Deci & Ryan, 1987).

Controlling statements   Some of the things people say to us, even though they aren't threatening in nature, nevertheless convey the message that others control our fate and so may undermine our sense of self-determination (Amabile & Hennessey, 1992; Boggiano, Main, & Katz, 1988; Koestner, Ryan, Bernieri, & Holt, 1984). As an example, in an experiment by Koestner and colleagues (1984), first and second graders were asked to paint a picture of a house in which they would like to live. The children were given the materials they needed—a paintbrush, a set of watercolor paints, two sheets of paper, and several paper towels—and then told some rules about how to proceed. For some children (the controlling-limits condition), restrictions described things that they could and could not do, as follows:

> Before you begin, I want to tell you some things that you will have to do. They are rules that we have about painting. You have to keep the paints clean. You can paint only on this small sheet of paper, so don't spill any paint on the big sheet. And you must wash out your brush and wipe it with a paper towel before you switch to a new color of paint, so that you don't get the colors all mixed up. In general, I want you to be a good boy (girl) and don't make a mess with the paints. (Koestner et al., 1984, p. 239)

For other children (the informational-limits condition), restrictions were presented only as information, like this:

> Before you begin, I want to tell you some things about the way painting is done here. I know that sometimes it's really fun to just slop the paint around, but here the materials and room need to be kept nice for the other children who will use them. The smaller sheet is for you to paint on, the larger sheet is a border to be kept clean. Also, the paints need to be kept clean, so the brush is to be washed and wiped in the paper towel before switching colors. I know that some kids don't like to be neat all the time, but now is a time for being neat. (Koestner et al., 1984, p. 239)

Each child was allowed 10 minutes of painting time. The experimenter then took the child's painting to another room, saying he would return in a few minutes. As he departed, he placed two more sheets of paper on the child's table, saying, "You can paint some more on this piece of paper if you like, or, if you want, you can play with the puzzles over on that table." In the experimenter's absence, the child was surreptitiously observed, and painting time was measured. Children in the informational-limits condition spent more time painting (so were apparently more intrinsically motivated to paint), and their paintings were judged to be more creative, than was true for their counterparts in the controlling-limits condition.

Extrinsic rewards   In chapter 5, I expressed the concern that using extrinsic reinforcement may undermine the intrinsic reinforcement that an activity provides. Extrinsic reinforcers are most likely to have this adverse effect when people perceive them as controlling or manipulating their behavior rather than as providing information about their progress.[5] Thus, they are unlikely to be beneficial, at least over the long run, if people interpret them as bribes or as limits on their freedom (Deci, Koestner, & Ryan, 2001; Lepper & Hodell, 1989; Reeve, 2006; Ryan, Mims, & Koestner, 1983). This principle may, in part, be the result of the message that an external reward communicates: that a task is not worth doing for its own sake (Hennessey, 1995; Stipek, 1993).

A reward for desirable behavior appears to have *no* adverse effects when learners interpret it as communicating that they are skillful or in some other way have *competence* (Cameron & Pierce, 2005; Cameron, Pierce, Banko, & Gear, 2005; Reeve et al., 2004). Nor does it undermine intrinsic motivation when it's unexpected—for instance, when scientists win the Nobel Prize for groundbreaking research findings—or when it's not contingent on specific behaviors (Cameron, 2001; Deci et al., 2001; Reeve, 2006).[6]

Surveillance and evaluation   People who know they are going to be evaluated based on their performance have a lower sense of self-determination and, as a result, are less intrinsically motivated. This is especially likely to be the case when the task at hand is a difficult one (Deci & Ryan, 1992; Harter et al., 1992; Hennessey, 1995; Reeve et al., 2004; Stipek, 1996). In fact, the mere presence of a potential evaluator is apt to undermine intrinsic motivation (Clifford, 1990; Deci & Ryan, 1987). For example, even though I have a mediocre singing voice, I like to sing and will often do so

Feelings of self-determination and intrinsic motivation are often greater when potential evaluators are absent from the scene.

---

[5]To my knowledge, theorists haven't specifically talked about the informational or controlling messages that *punishment* might communicate, but we can logically deduce that a similar pattern exists here as well. Certainly punishment can be presented in either of two ways—as a means of control or as a source of information about appropriate behavior. As we discovered in chapter 5, punishment is more effective when it is accompanied by reasons (information) about why the punished behavior is unacceptable.

[6]A potential downside of noncontingent reinforcement is that it may in some cases lead to superstitious behavior (see chapter 4).

when no one else is around to hear me (e.g., when I'm mowing the lawn or driving alone on business). But my intrinsic motivation to sing vanishes when anyone else is in earshot.

In chapter 10, we discovered that formal classroom assessments (e.g., assignments and tests) often promote long-term memory storage. Among other things, they encourage students to review classroom material more regularly and process information more thoroughly. But here we see a disadvantage of formal assessments: They may undermine students' intrinsic motivation to learn (Benware & Deci, 1984; Grolnick & Ryan, 1987; Hatano & Inagaki, 2003; Spaulding, 1992; Stipek, 1993). A study by Benware and Deci (1984) illustrates this point well. College students studied an article about brain functioning under either of two conditions: Some studied it with the expectation of being tested on it, while others studied it with the expectation that they would have to teach the material to someone else (a presumably nonevaluative situation). Compared with those in the first group, students in the second group enjoyed their learning experience more, found the material more interesting, and learned it in a more meaningful (rather than rote) fashion. Grolnick and Ryan (1987) have found similar results with fifth graders.

Curiously, people can undermine their own sense of self-determination simply by *imagining* that others may be evaluating their performance (Deci & Ryan, 1992; Ryan, 1982). For example, in a study by Ryan (1982), undergraduate students worked on a series of hidden-figure puzzles, in which they had to find shapes of particular objects embedded within the context of more complex drawings. Some students were told that the task was an indication of "creative intelligence." Even though these students were not specifically told that their performance would be evaluated, they were less likely than students in a control group to continue doing the puzzles in a free-choice situation later on. The mere idea that the task was indicative of intelligence may have led these students to consider how an outside person might evaluate their performance and, accordingly, to have less intrinsic motivation for engaging in the task (Deci & Ryan, 1992; Ryan, 1982).

We should keep in mind that no amount of self-determination is going to make us feel intrinsically motivated to do something if we don't also have a sense of competence. To show you what I mean, let's consider a study by Spaulding (1992, pp. 54–55). Seventh-grade students, including some who believed themselves to be competent writers and some who did not, were asked to write an essay concerning what they had learned in English class that year. Some students were asked to write it for their teacher, someone they believed would evaluate their work; hence, this group experienced low self-determination. Other students were asked to write the essay for the researcher so that she could tell future teachers what kinds of things students study in English; without the threat of evaluation looming over them, these students presumably experienced relatively high self-determination. As the students wrote their essays, Spaulding measured their task engagement (and, indirectly, their intrinsic motivation) in several ways. Students who believed themselves to be competent writers showed greater intrinsic motivation in the high self-determination condition—that is, when writing for the researcher. In contrast, students who believed they were poor writers were more engaged in the task when writing for the teacher. Apparently, self-determination in the absence of perceived competence did not promote intrinsic motivation.

Putting a Positive Spin on Controlling Circumstances

Sometimes people—adults, at least—respond to circumstances beyond their control by identifying ways to take charge of aspects of their lives despite existing constraints on their freedom. Because they cannot change their environment, they instead change *themselves* to better adapt to it—a phenomenon known as **secondary control** (N. C. Hall, Chipperfield, Perry, Ruthig, & Goetz, 2006; N. C. Hall, Goetz, Haynes, Stupnisky, & Chipperfield, 2006; Rothbaum, Weisz, & Snyder, 1982).

One common secondary-control strategy is to reinterpret an aversive event as something that can ultimately work in one's best interest—that is, to invoke the adage "Every cloud has a silver lining." Another is to take proactive steps to improve one's circumstances and, in the process, gain more control. For example, a college student might interpret a low grade on a difficult exam as a "wake-up call" to study harder or seek extra help. Parents of a child with a mental disability might become active, productive members of organizations such as the Autism Society of America or the National Alliance for the Mentally Ill. In part by helping people maintain their sense of self-determination, secondary control strategies enhance motivation to achieve at school and elsewhere, as well as psychological well-being more generally (N. C. Hall, Chipperfield, et al., 2006; N. C. Hall, Perry, Ruthig, Hladkyi, & Chippenfield, 2006; van Winkel, Ruthig, Stupnisky, Haynes, & Perry, 2006).

Relatedness

To some extent, we are all social creatures: We live, work, and play with our fellow human beings. Some theorists have proposed that people of all ages have a fundamental need to feel socially connected and to secure the love and respect of others. In other words, people have a **need for relatedness** (Connell, 1990; Connell & Wellborn, 1991; Reeve et al., 2004; Ryan & Deci, 2000). As is true for the need for competence, the need for relatedness may be important from an evolutionary standpoint: People who live in cohesive, cooperative social groups are more likely to survive than people who go it alone (Wright, 1994).

In the classroom, students' need for relatedness may manifest itself in a wide variety of behaviors. Many children and adolescents place high priority on interacting with friends, often at the expense of getting their schoolwork done (Dowson & McInerney, 2001; Doyle, 1986a; Wigfield, Eccles, Mac Iver, Reuman, & Midgley, 1991). They may also be concerned about projecting a favorable public image—that is, by looking smart, popular, athletic, or "cool" to others (Juvonen, 2000). And some may exhibit their need for relatedness by showing concern for other people's welfare or helping peers who are struggling with classroom assignments (M. E. Ford, 1996; Dowson & McInerney, 2001). The need for relatedness seems to be especially high in the middle school years (Brown, Eicher, & Petrie, 1986; Juvonen, 2000; A. M. Ryan & Patrick, 2001). Young adolescents tend to be overly concerned about what others think, prefer to hang out in tight-knit groups, and are especially susceptible to peer influence.

People seem to be more intrinsically motivated to accomplish new tasks when their need for relatedness has been addressed. For instance, students are more eager to engage in classroom activities and master academic subject matter when they believe their teachers truly care about them and support them in their efforts to learn (H. A. Davis, 2003; Furrer & Skinner, 2003; Roeser, Eccles, & Sameroff, 2000). Their motivation in the classroom also increases when their classmates support them in their learning (see chapter 14, especially the discussion of *communities of learners*). Other people's love and respect can enhance learners' intrinsic motivation indirectly as well as directly—in particular, by communicating high expectations for performance and in other ways boosting an overall sense of competence and self-worth (L. H. Anderman, Patrick, Hruda, & Linnenbrink, 2002; Newberg & Sims, 1996; Patrick, Anderman, & Ryan, 2002).

In chapter 16, the need for relatedness will show up in our discussions of *performance goals, social goals,* and *image management.* Yet although the need for relatedness may, to some extent, be a universal phenomenon, some people seem to have a greater need for interpersonal relationships than others (Kupersmidt, Buchele, Voegler, & Sedikides, 1996). In the next section, we look at these and other individual differences in motivation.

INDIVIDUAL DIFFERENCES IN MOTIVATION

Up to this point, we've been talking about forms of motivation that might characterize all of us at one time or another. But some theorists suggest that motivation takes the form of relatively enduring personality characteristics that people have to a greater or lesser extent. For example, I mentioned earlier that some people tend to be sensation seekers, whereas others prefer not to live so much "on the edge."

Theories that propose fairly stable individual differences in motivation are known as **trait theories** of motivation. Historically, researchers have focused considerable attention on individual differences in people's needs for affiliation, approval, and achievement. In recent years, they've also begun to look in depth at dispositions that predispose people to think or learn in particular ways. We'll look at these four individual difference variables here. We'll identify additional individual differences as we consider such topics as interest, goals, and attributions in chapter 16.

Need for Affiliation

The **need for affiliation** is the degree to which a person wants and needs friendly relationships with others (Boyatzis, 1973; Connell & Wellborn, 1991; M. E. Ford & Nichols, 1991; Hill, 1987; McClelland, 1984). For example, as high school students, my oldest two children couldn't stand the thought of being home "alone" (i.e., with their parents) on a Friday or Saturday night and so always found something to do with their friends. When they *were* home on a weeknight, they spent long hours talking to friends on the telephone, to the point where schoolwork sometimes didn't get done. In contrast, my youngest child, Jeff, has always been able to work or play alone quite happily for hours at a time.

Students' needs for affiliation will be reflected in the choices they make at school (Boyatzis, 1973; E. G. French, 1956; Sansone & Smith, 2002; Wigfield, Eccles, & Pintrich, 1996). For instance, students with a low need for affiliation may prefer to work alone, whereas students with a high need for affiliation more often prefer to work in small groups. When choosing work partners, students with a low affiliation need are apt to choose classmates whom they believe will be competent at an assigned task; students with a high affiliation need are likely to choose their friends even if these friends are relatively incompetent. In high school, students with a low need for affiliation are likely to choose a class schedule that meets their own interests and ambitions, whereas students with a high need for affiliation tend to choose one that enables them to be with their friends. As you can see, then, a high need for affiliation can sometimes interfere with maximal classroom learning and achievement (Urdan & Maehr, 1995; Wentzel & Wigfield, 1998).

Need for Approval

Another need in which we see individual differences is the **need for approval**, a desire to gain the acceptance and positive judgments of other people (Boyatzis, 1973; Crowne & Marlowe, 1964; Juvonen & Weiner, 1993; Urdan & Maehr, 1995). Many elementary school students have a strong desire to attain the approval of their teacher; at the secondary level, students are more apt to seek the approval of peers (Harter, 1999; Juvonen & Weiner, 1993; Urdan & Maehr, 1995). Cultural background may influence whether children and adolescents prefer adult or peer approval, however. For instance, many teenagers from Asian cultures highly value the approval of adult authority figures (e.g., Dien, 1998).

People with a high need for approval are often those with low self-esteem (Crowne & Marlowe, 1964). They may go out of their way to behave in ways they think will please others, sometimes compromising any standards that they themselves may have regarding appropriate behavior (Berndt & Keefe, 1996; Crowne & Marlowe, 1964). They are likely to engage in and persist at school tasks primarily to gain their teacher's praise, and they may self-handicap in activities at which they expect to do poorly (H. A. Davis, 2003; Harter, 1975; S. C. Rose & Thornburg, 1984). Especially in adolescence, students with a high need for approval give in easily to peer pressure, for fear that they might otherwise be rejected (Crowne & Marlowe, 1964; Wentzel & Wigfield, 1998). Such efforts are often counterproductive, however: Perhaps because they are trying *too* hard to be liked, students with a high need for approval tend to be relatively unpopular with peers (Boyatzis, 1973; Crowne & Marlowe, 1964).

Some adolescents may be so preoccupied with peer approval that they base their own sense of self-worth largely on what their peers think—or at least on what *they think* their peers think—of them (Dweck, 2000; Harter, 1999; Harter, Stocker, & Robinson, 1996). Teenagers who have such **contingent self-worth** are often on an emotional roller coaster, feeling elated one day and devastated the next, depending on how friends and classmates have recently treated them.

Need for Achievement

The **need for achievement,** sometimes called **achievement motivation,** is the need for excellence for its own sake, without regard for any external rewards that one's accomplishments might bring (Atkinson, 1957, 1964; Atkinson & Feather, 1966; McClelland, Atkinson, Clark, & Lowell, 1953; Vernon, 1969; Veroff, McClelland, & Ruhland, 1975). For example, a person with a high need for achievement might work diligently to maintain a 4.0 grade point average, practice long hours to become a professional basketball player, or play Monopoly with a vengeance.

People with a high need for achievement are realistic about the tasks they can accomplish, and they persist at tasks that are challenging yet achievable (Vernon, 1969; Veroff et al., 1975). They rarely rest on their laurels; instead, they set increasingly high standards for excellence as their current standards are met (Veroff et al., 1975). And they are willing and able to delay gratification: They put off small, immediate rewards for the larger rewards that their long-term efforts are likely to bring (French, 1955; Vernon, 1969; Veroff et al., 1975).

An early and widely cited theory of achievement motivation is that of John Atkinson and his associates (Atkinson, 1957, 1964; Atkinson & Birch, 1978; Atkinson & Feather, 1966; Atkinson & Raynor, 1978). These theorists proposed that the tendency to strive for achievement is a function of two related needs: the **motive for success,** or M_s (the desire to do well and accomplish goals), and the **motive to avoid failure,** or M_{af} (anxiety about failing to accomplish goals and reluctance to engage in activities that may lead to failure). For many people, one of these needs is stronger than the other, and achievement behavior depends on which need predominates.

Individuals with a stronger motive for success tend to seek and tackle moderately difficult tasks—those that are challenging yet can feasibly be accomplished. Because these individuals have a relatively low motive to avoid failure, they don't worry about the mistakes they may make or the stumbling blocks they may encounter. Furthermore, they recognize that success on difficult tasks is more noteworthy than success on easy tasks.

In contrast, individuals with a stronger motive to avoid failure typically forego such risks in favor of a sure thing. They steer clear of the moderately difficult tasks that their high M_s counterparts select. Instead, they often choose tasks they can almost certainly accomplish. Even though their success on such tasks may be meaningless, they are nevertheless able to avoid the failure they fear. Curiously, though, high M_{af} individuals sometimes choose extremely difficult tasks, those at which they cannot possibly succeed. When they fail at such tasks, they have a built-in explanation—after all, the task was impossible—and so the failure is easily rationalized. This tendency to choose very difficult tasks should remind you of the self-handicapping phenomenon I described earlier.

Atkinson and Litwin (1960) demonstrated the hypothesized effects of M_s and M_{af} in a concrete fashion. Their study involved a ring toss game: throwing rings to land around an upright peg. Male undergraduate students, some of whom had been identified as having a higher M_s and others as having a higher M_{af}, were told that they could stand wherever they wished, within a 15-foot range, as they attempted to throw 10 rings, one at a time, around the peg. The great majority of the high M_s students opted to stand about 8 to 12 feet away from the peg (thus taking on a moderate challenge). Of the high M_{af} students, only half stood in the 8- to 12-foot range; the other half stood either within 7 feet of the peg (thus making the task an easy one) or at least 13 feet away from it (thus making it extremely difficult). Isaacson (1964) found the same pattern in the course selections of college students: Those with a higher M_s tended to choose classes of moderate difficulty, whereas those with a higher M_{af} chose either very easy or very difficult classes.

More recently, Covington and Omelich (1991) have suggested that various combinations of high and low M_s and M_{af} (they use the terms *need to approach success* and *need to avoid failure*) result in four kinds of learners—overstrivers, optimists, failure avoiders, and failure accepters—that are described in Table 15.1. Of the four, the optimists (who are concerned about success but not about failure) are apt to be the most effective learners because they engage in the very behaviors and cognitive processes that make learning possible. The other three groups are more concerned about protecting their sense of self-worth than in mastering new knowledge and skills.

Table 15.1
Characteristics of learners with high versus low needs to approach success and avoid failure (based on Covington & Omelich, 1991).

		Motive for Success (M_s)	
		High	Low
Motive to Avoid Failure (M_{af})	High	*Overstrivers* are exceptionally hard working (perhaps too much so), in part to prevent failure. They take failures very hard.	*Failure avoiders* engage in self-handicapping behaviors to minimize the likelihood that failures will reflect low ability.
	Low	*Optimists* are self-confident about their ability to learn. They engage in behaviors and cognitive processes that maximize learning.	*Failure accepters* become increasingly convinced of their low ability as their excuses for failure become decreasingly plausible. They apply minimal effort on learning tasks.

In its earliest conceptualization, the need for achievement was thought to be a general trait that people exhibit consistently in a variety of activities across many domains. More recently, however, many theorists have proposed that this need may instead be somewhat specific to particular tasks and environments. Most contemporary psychologists now think of achievement motivation as reflecting specific *achievement goals,* as we'll discover in chapter 16.

Dispositions

A **disposition** is a general, relatively stable inclination to approach learning and problem-solving situations in a particular way.[7] Dispositions are intentional rather than accidental, and they encompass cognition, motivation, and personality characteristics (Kardash & Scholes, 1996; Kuhn, 2001a; Perkins & Ritchhart, 2004; Stanovich, 1999). Following are examples of productive dispositions that theorists have identified:

- *Stimulation seeking:* Eagerly interacting with one's physical and social environment in order to encounter new experiences and information
- *Need for cognition:* Regularly seeking and engaging in challenging cognitive tasks
- *Conscientiousness:* Consistently addressing assigned tasks in a careful, focused, and responsible manner
- *Learned industriousness:* Persisting and persevering even when considerable effort is required
- *Open-mindedness:* Flexibly considering alternative perspectives and multiple sources of evidence, and suspending judgment for a time rather than leaping to an immediate conclusion[8]
- *Spirit of transfer:* Processing information meaningfully, with regard for how it might be applied in future situations
- *Critical thinking:* Consistently evaluating information or arguments in terms of their accuracy, logic, and credibility, rather than accepting them at face value
- *Consensus seeking:* Seeking a synthesis of diverse perspectives, rather than assuming that perspectives must necessarily be mutually exclusive
- *Future time perspective:* Predicting and considering the long-term consequences of various courses of action
  (Cacioppo et al., 1996; Eccles et al., 1998; Eisenberger, 1992; Giancarlo & Facione, 2001; Halpern, 1997; Haskell, 2001; Husman & Freeman, 1999; Kardash & Scholes, 1996; Onosko & Newmann, 1994; Raine, Reynolds, & Venables, 2002; Southerland & Sinatra, 2003; Stanovich, 1999; Toplak & Stanovich, 2002; Trautwein, Lüdtke, Schnyder, & Niggli, 2006; Wiggins, 1996)

---

[7]Theorists are addressing a similar idea when they talk about *habits of mind.*

[8]Open-mindedness can be contrasted with a *need for closure,* whereby learners strive to draw rapid conclusions about what is and is not true. Learners with a need for closure tend to have relatively unsophisticated epistemological beliefs (e.g., knowledge is an accumulation of facts that can best be obtained from authority figures) and to process information in relatively superficial ways (DeBacker & Crowson, 2006).

Research on the nature and effects of dispositions is still in its infancy, but it is becoming increasingly clear that dispositions can be important factors affecting learning, motivation, and achievement. In fact, dispositions often "overrule" ability (e.g., as reflected in IQ scores) in their influence on people's long-term achievement (Dai & Sternberg, 2004; Kuhn & Franklin, 2006; Perkins & Ritchhart, 2004). For instance, children who, at age 3, are eager to seek out physical and social stimulation are, at age 11, better readers and higher achievers at school (Raine et al., 2002). Adolescents who are conscientious are more likely to do their homework (Trautwein et al., 2006). People who have a strong future time perspective are more motivated to engage in activities that will help them achieve their future goals (Husman & Freeman, 1999; Raynor, 1981). People with a high need for cognition learn more from what they read and are more likely to base conclusions on sound evidence and logical reasoning (Cacioppo et al., 1996; Dai, 2002). People who critically evaluate new evidence and are receptive to and open-minded about diverse perspectives show more advanced reasoning capabilities; they are also more likely to undergo conceptual change when warranted (Southerland & Sinatra, 2003; Stanovich, 1999).

Researchers have not yet systematically addressed the origins of various dispositions. Perhaps inherited temperamental differences (e.g., in stimulation seeking) are involved (Raine et al., 2002). Epistemological beliefs—for instance, the belief that knowledge is fixed and unchanging, on the one hand, or dynamic and continually evolving, on the other—may also play a role (King & Kitchener, 2002; Kuhn, 2001b; Mason, 2003; Schommer-Aikins, Hopkins, Anderson, & Drouhard, 2005). And quite possibly, teachers' actions in the classroom—for instance, whether they encourage inquisitive exploration, risk taking, and critical thinking with respect to classroom topics—make a difference (Flum & Kaplan, 2006; Kuhn, 2001b, 2006). In the following classroom interaction, a teacher actually seems to *discourage* any disposition to think analytically and critically about classroom material:

Teacher:	Write this on your paper . . . it's simply memorizing this pattern. We have meters, centimeters, and millimeters. Let's say. . . write millimeters, centimeters, and meters. We want to make sure that our metric measurement is the same. If I gave you this decimal, let's say .234 m (yes, write that). In order to come up with .234 m in centimeters, the only thing that is necessary is that you move the decimal. How do we move the decimal? You move it to the right two places. (Jason, sit up please.) If I move it to the right two places, what should .234 m look like, Daniel, in centimeters? What does it look like, Ashley?
Ashley:	23.4 cm.
Teacher:	Twenty-three point four. Simple stuff. In order to find meters, we're still moving that decimal to the right, but this time, boys and girls, we're only going to move it one place. So, if I move this decimal one place, what is my answer for millimeters? (dialogue from Turner, Meyer, et al., 1998, p. 741)

Undoubtedly, this teacher means well: She wants her students to know how to convert from one unit of measurement to another. But notice the attitude she engenders: "Write this. . . it's simply memorizing this pattern."

AFFECT AND ITS EFFECTS

When we talk about motivation, it is difficult not to talk about **affect**—the feelings, emotions, and general moods that a learner brings to bear on a task—at the same time.[9] For example, earlier in the chapter we noted that intrinsically motivated individuals typically find pleasure in what they are doing. Yet too much motivation—perhaps wanting something too much—may lead to an intense sense of anxiety. Pleasure, anxiety, excitement, pride, depression, anger, guilt— all of these are forms of affect. Affect is interrelated with motivation, learning, and cognition in a variety of ways, as we shall see now.

How Affect Is Related to Motivation

From an evolutionary perspective, the brain's immediate emotional responses to certain events— fearfully darting beyond striking range of a poisonous snake, say, or responding angrily to a neighbor who threatens violence—has helped human beings survive and thrive over the centuries (Damasio, 1994; Öhman & Mineka, 2003). But affect plays a role in the planful, thoughtful aspects of human motivation as well. For example, as people set goals for themselves, they are more likely to be optimistic about what they can accomplish if they are feeling cheerful rather than depressed (Harter, 1988). They also consider how they are apt to feel later on—in particular, how good a success will feel (e.g., making them happy or proud) and how bad a failure will feel (e.g., making them sad or ashamed) (Mellers & McGraw, 2001). And when they're in a good mood in an instructional setting, they're more likely to cognitively engage with new material and work hard to make sense of it (Linnenbrink & Pintrich, 2004; Pekrun, Goetz, Titz, & Perry, 2002).

As a general rule, people act in ways that help them feel happy and comfortable rather than sad, confused, or angry (Csikszentmihalyi, Rathunde, & Whalen, 1993; Isaacowitz, 2006). As they study, they occasionally encounter ideas that conflict with their current beliefs. Such discrepancies can cause considerable mental discomfort—a state of affairs that Piaget called *disequilibrium* but many contemporary theorists call **cognitive dissonance.** This dissonance typically motivates learners to try to resolve the discrepancies in some way—perhaps revising existing beliefs (thus undergoing *conceptual change*) or perhaps ignoring the new information—so that they can return to a more contented frame of mind (Buehl & Alexander, 2001; Harmon-Jones, 2001; Pintrich et al., 1993).

How Affect Is Related to Learning and Cognition

Historically, a significant weakness of cognitivist and social–cognitive perspectives of learning has been their general disregard for the affective aspects of mental processes (Dai, 2005; Hidi, Renninger, & Krapp, 2004; Pintrich, 2003). Yet affect is clearly intermingled with learning and cognition (Gray, 2004; Linnenbrink & Pintrich, 2004; Meyer & Turner, 2002; Ochsner & Lieberman, 2001). For example, while learning how to perform a task, we simultaneously learn

---

[9]Some theorists use the terms *affect* and *emotion* almost interchangeably. But others suggest that we use *emotion* to refer only to short-term states and *affect* in a broader sense to include both short-term states and longer-term moods and predispositions (Forgas, 2000; Linnenbrink & Pintrich, 2002; Rosenberg, 1998).

whether we like doing it (Zajonc, 1980). Problem solving is easier when we enjoy what we are doing, and successful attempts at learning and problem solving often bring on feelings of excitement, pleasure, and pride (Carver & Scheier, 1990; Harter, 1999; McLeod & Adams, 1989; Snow, Corno, & Jackson, 1996). Our failed attempts at a task are likely to make us feel frustrated or anxious, especially if the task is an easy one, and we are apt to develop a dislike for the task (Carver & Scheier, 1990; Shepperd & McNulty, 2002; Stodolsky, Salk, & Glaessner, 1991).

As we are thinking about, learning, or remembering something, our very thoughts and memories may have emotional overtones—a phenomenon known as **hot cognition** (e.g., Hoffman, 1991; Lazarus, 1991). Often the nature of the material we are trying to learn induces hot cognition and, as a result, affects cognitive processing. When information is emotionally charged, we are more likely to pay attention to it (Edwards & Bryan, 1997; Phelps, Ling, & Carrasco, 2006). We are also more likely to continue to think about it and repeatedly elaborate on it (Bower, 1994; Heuer & Reisberg, 1992; Siegel, 1999). Yet our ability to draw inferences from it and respond appropriately to it is sometimes hampered, at least in comparison with our ability to think logically about nonemotional topics (Blanchette & Richards, 2004; Damasio, 1994).

The emotional nature of what we have stored in long-term memory may influence our ability to retrieve it later on. Although we may occasionally repress extremely painful memories (see chapter 10), in general we can more easily retrieve information with high emotional content than we can recall relatively nonemotional information (Bauer, 2006; Bower, 1994; Reisberg, 1997; Russ, 1993; Talarico, LaBar, & Rubin, 2004). As one example, recall our discussion of *flashbulb memories* in chapter 10. As another, let's consider an experiment by Heuer and Reisberg (1990). Undergraduate students looked at a series of slides that depicted one of two stories. Both stories involved a boy and his mother visiting the boy's father at work. For some students (the emotional-content group), the father was a surgeon operating on an accident victim; among other things, these students saw slides of surgery in progress (with a person's internal organs in full view) and the badly scarred legs of a child. For other students (the neutral-content group), the father was an auto mechanic repairing a broken-down car; these students saw the internal workings of the car, including a piece that was clearly broken. Two weeks later, all of the students were given an unexpected quiz about the things they had observed. Students who had seen the emotion-laden sequence remembered both the general gist of the story and many of the tiny details depicted in the slides far more accurately than did students who had seen the neutral sequence. In fact, although they did not expect to be tested on what they had seen, students in the emotional-content group remembered more than students who had watched the neutral sequence and specifically been *told* to remember its plot and details. The superior memories of the "surgery" students were probably due not only to the vividly gory visual material but also to the fact that a human being was in distressed circumstances (e.g., see Cahill & McGaugh, 1995).

General mood states, too, can affect learning and memory. When we are in a good mood (e.g., when we feel happy or excited, rather than sad or depressed), we are more likely to pay attention to information, relate it to things we already know, and creatively elaborate on it (Bower, 1994; Hertel, 1994; Hettena & Ballif, 1981; Isen, Daubman, & Gorgoglione, 1987; Oatley & Nundy, 1996; N. Schwarz & Skurnik, 2003; Snow et al., 1996). A good mood is also likely to help us retrieve things we have previously stored in long-term memory (Oatley & Nundy, 1996). But in addition, we can sometimes retrieve information from long-term memory more successfully when our mood at the time of retrieval is the same as our mood when we initially stored the information—an effect known as **mood-dependent memory** (Bower, 1994; Bower & Forgas, 2001; Eich, 1995).

People often remember more
when information packs an
emotional wallop.

The Serial Killer,
the Relentless
Nymphomaniac,
and Me

Some cognitive theorists have suggested that affective responses to objects and events are integral parts of the network of associations that comprises long-term memory (Bower & Forgas, 2001).[10] Just as people can easily categorize things on the basis of concepts or schemas, so, too, can they easily categorize them on the basis of affect—what things make them happy, sad, angry, and so on (Bower & Forgas, 2001). Affective responses may, in fact, be an important source of *information* that learners have about objects and events (Clore, Gasper, & Garvin, 2001; N. Schwarz & Skurnik, 2003; Smith & Kirby, 2001). For instance, it is quite helpful to know that reading a good book will be a source of pleasure but that spending time with a verbally abusive relative will not.

In some circumstances, the affective components of a memory are so intense that they are easily retrieved, perhaps to the point where they are hard to ignore and unlikely to be confused with other memories[11] (Bower & Forgas, 2001; M. E. Ford, 1996; Schacter, 1999). In other cases, affective components may be sufficiently subtle that learners aren't consciously aware of them; that is, they are *implicit* rather than explicit knowledge (Bower & Forgas, 2001; Ito & Cacioppo, 2001; Winkielman & Berridge, 2004). Occasionally, people show physiological responses to a stimulus that they have no conscious recollection of at all; in such situations, previous affective responses to that stimulus are the *only* things that appear to remain in memory (Nadel & Jacobs, 1998; Zajonc, 2000).

Probably the most widely studied form of affect, at least within the context of human learning and cognition, is anxiety. Behaviorists have discovered that anxiety can be classically conditioned and sometimes leads to avoidance learning (see chapters 3 and 4). Cognitivists have

---

[10]Neurological evidence supports this view. Areas of the brain associated with emotion (e.g., the limbic system) communicate regularly with those responsible for "colder" aspects of cognition (e.g., the frontal cortex), and they sound an alarm when a potentially important stimulus warrants immediate attention (Dai & Sternberg, 2004; Schupp, Junghöfer, Weike, & Hamm, 2003; Siegel, 1999).

[11]Using the terminology of chapter 10, emotionally intense memories are less prone to *interference* from other memories (Bower & Forgas, 2001).

documented anxiety's negative effects on such cognitive processes as long-term memory retrieval and problem solving (see chapters 10 and 13). Anxiety has other effects as well—some beneficial and others not, as we will see now.

Anxiety

Anxiety is a feeling of uneasiness and apprehension about a situation, typically one with an uncertain outcome. Fear and anxiety are related concepts, in that both reflect the high end of the *arousal* continuum. Yet they have one critical difference that sets them apart: Fear is a response to a specific threat, whereas anxiety is vague and relatively unfocused. For example, people are *afraid* of certain things, but they don't always know exactly what they're *anxious* about (Lazarus, 1991).

Anxiety probably has two components: worry and emotionality (Liebert & Morris, 1967; Tryon, 1980; Zeidner, 1998). **Worry** is the cognitive aspect of anxiety, which includes troubling thoughts and beliefs about one's ability to deal with a situation. **Emotionality** is the affective aspect, which includes such physiological responses as muscular tension (e.g., stomach "butter-flies"), increased heart rate, and perspiration, as well as such behavioral responses as restlessness and pacing.

Psychologists have found it useful to distinguish between two types of anxiety. **State anxiety** is a temporary condition elicited by a particular stimulus. For example, you might experience state anxiety when working on an especially challenging math problem or when thinking about an upcoming exam in a notoriously difficult class. In contrast, **trait anxiety** is a relatively stable state of affairs, such that an individual is chronically anxious in certain situations. For instance, you might have general mathematics anxiety or test anxiety, becoming anxious whenever you encounter numbers or think about exams.

Effects of Anxiety

Early studies focused on the effects of anxiety on learning and performance. More recently, with the advent of cognitivism, studies have investigated the effects that anxiety is likely to have on cognitive processes. Let's examine the evidence in each of these areas.

Effects on learning and performance   Earlier I mentioned that people may strive to seek an optimal level of arousal, a "comfort zone" somewhere between too little and too much. But what is optimal may depend not only on the individual but also on the task at hand. Early researchers found that arousal affects learning and performance in a curvilinear ("inverted U") fashion (Broadhurst, 1959; Fiske & Maddi, 1961; Hebb, 1955; Yerkes & Dodson, 1908). More specifi-cally, a small degree of arousal (e.g., a low level of anxiety) facilitates learning and performance. A high degree of arousal (e.g., high anxiety) may facilitate learning and performance when the task is easy but is likely to interfere when the task is more difficult. For any task, there is proba-bly some optimal level of arousal (reflected by the top point of the inverted U) at which learning and performance are maximized (see Figure 15.2).

A classic experiment with mice by Yerkes and Dodson (1908) provides a concrete illustration of how arousal level and task difficulty interact. Each mouse was placed in a chamber from which it could escape by either of two doors. The wall opposite the doors was slowly moved to make the chamber smaller and smaller, until the mouse was eventually forced to escape through one door or the other. One door led to a safe, comfortable "nest box"; the other led to electric shock. The

Figure 15.2
The inverted U curve, depicting a curvilinear relationship between arousal and performance.

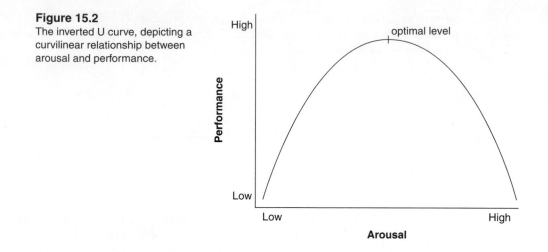

experimenters provided a clue to help the mouse determine which door was which: The doorway leading to the nest box was consistently lighter in color than the doorway leading to shock.

For different groups of mice, the experimenters varied arousal level by the amount of shock they administered—mild, intense, or somewhere in between—when the "wrong" door was entered. They varied task difficulty by varying the relative similarity or difference between the two doorways: some mice had to choose between white and black (an easy task), others chose between light and dark gray (a moderately difficult task), and still others chose between similar shades of gray (a very difficult, although not impossible, task).

The experimenters established a criterion of 30 correct door choices in a row as an indication that a mouse had successfully learned the discrimination. Figure 15.3 shows the average number of learning trials for mice in each condition; because the y-axis reflects quality of performance (speed of learning), groups needing fewer trials to reach the criterion appear higher in the figure than groups with more trials. Notice how the mice with an easy choice performed best under high arousal (intense shock) conditions. Those with a moderately difficult task performed better with moderate arousal (moderate shock). Those with an extremely difficult discrimination performed best when shock and arousal were relatively low.

This principle—that easy tasks are best accomplished with a relatively high level of arousal but more difficult tasks are better accomplished with a low or moderate level—is often known as the **Yerkes–Dodson law.** The principle holds true not only for mice but for human beings as well. A high level of anxiety enhances performance on easy and automatic tasks, such as running a mile or reciting the alphabet; here we have a case of **facilitating anxiety.** But the same high level interferes with performance on a difficult task, such as writing a psychology textbook or speaking before a large audience; in this situation, we have **debilitating anxiety.**

We often find the Yerkes–Dodson law at work in classroom tasks. For example, students who experience a small amount of muscular tension during mathematical problem solving are more successful problem solvers than students who experience no tension at all (Bloom & Broder, 1950). Highly anxious students sometimes perform better than low-anxiety students on tasks requiring verbatim recall of simple information; however, they perform comparatively poorly on tasks requiring flexible, creative thought (Kirkland, 1971). Low levels of anxiety throughout the course of instruction may facilitate students' learning; a high degree of anxiety at

Figure 15.3
Arousal level interacts with task difficulty, resulting in different optimal levels for different tasks. From data reported in "The relation of strength of stimulus to rapidity of habit-formation" by R. M. Yerkes and J. D. Dodson, 1908, *Journal of Comparative Neurology and Psychology, 18,* pp. 459–482.

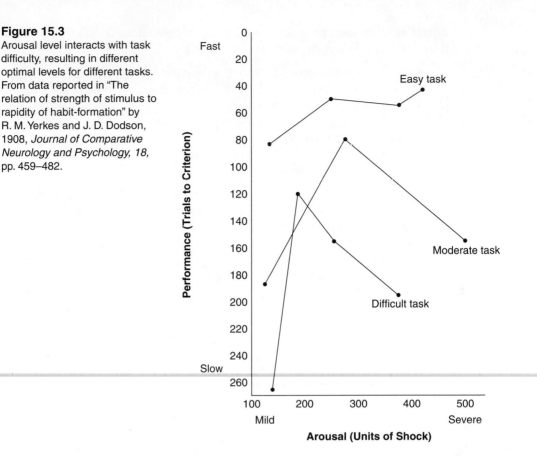

the tail end of instruction (e.g., at final exam time) is likely to be counterproductive (Kirkland, 1971). And the same degree of anxiety about a test may enhance the performance of high-ability students, for whom the test is easy, while lowering the performance of low-ability students, for whom the test is more difficult (Spielberger, 1966).

A useful distinction in this context is the difference between threat and challenge (Combs, Richards, & Richards, 1976). A **threat** is a situation in which learners believe they have little chance of success—they see failure as an almost inevitable outcome. In contrast, a **challenge** is a situation in which learners believe they can probably succeed if they try hard enough. Students are likely to have debilitating anxiety when they perceive a situation to be threatening. They respond to challenges more favorably; for example, they are likely to be highly motivated to do their best, and they express considerable excitement and satisfaction when they succeed (Cobb, Yackel, & Wood, 1989; Csikszentmihalyi et al., 1993; Natriello & Dornbusch, 1984; Thompson & Thompson, 1989).

For most students, school tasks are (and should be) challenging more often than easy. Accordingly, we should expect students with lower levels of anxiety to perform more effectively in the classroom, which is in fact the case: Students with relatively low trait anxiety achieve greater academic success (e.g., higher grade point averages) than their peers of equal ability who have high trait anxiety (Gaudry & Spielberger, 1971; Stipek, 1993; Tobias, 1980).

Effects on cognition   Imagine yourself sitting in class taking an exam. Here are some possible thoughts running through your mind as you do so:

- Oh, yes, my professor introduced this concept last week. It refers to. . .
- Here is something we didn't specifically talk about in class. Let me see if I can relate it to something we *did* talk about. . .
- The best way to solve this problem might be to. . .
- These questions are getting harder and harder. . .
- Oh, no, I only have 10 minutes left. I can't possibly finish. . .
- What if I fail this test? It's required for my program. . .

The first three thoughts are clearly relevant to the task at hand and should help you do your best on the exam. In contrast, the last three are irrelevant to your task: You are spending your time worrying rather than thinking about how to answer the test questions. As you should recall from our discussion of attention and working memory in chapter 7, people can attend to and process only a small amount of information at any one time. The more time and attention they devote to worrying about a test they are taking, the less capacity they have for dealing with and responding to the test itself.

Anxiety interferes with an individual's attention to a task (Easterbrook, 1959; Eysenck, 1992; Tobias, 1980; Wine, 1980). And because "worrying" thoughts take up a certain amount of working memory capacity, anxiety also interferes with effective cognitive processing (Mueller, 1980; Naveh-Benjamin, 1991; Tobias, 1985; Turner, Thorpe, & Meyer, 1998). Such effects are especially common when the task at hand is a difficult one (e.g., when it involves problem solving) and when it involves considerable retrieval of information from long-term memory (Ashcraft, 2002; Beilock & Carr, 2005; Beilock, Kulp, Holt, & Carr, 2004; Tobias, 1980).

In general, anxiety's debilitative effect is a distractive one: When performing a difficult task, highly anxious people are more likely to think irrelevant thoughts, be diverted by irrelevant stimuli, and exhibit irrelevant responses (Ashcraft, 2002; Beilock et al., 2004; Wine, 1980).

Common Sources of Anxiety

People can be anxious about a variety of things. For example, they may be concerned about their personal appearance (King & Ollendick, 1989). They may worry about how they perform in comparison with others and about what their peers might think of them as a result (Hill & Wigfield, 1984; King & Ollendick, 1989). They may feel uncomfortable when they encounter ideas that conflict with what they currently believe; recall our earlier discussion of *cognitive dissonance* (Bendixen, 2002; Harmon-Jones, 2001). They are likely to feel insecure when entering a new, unknown, and perhaps unsettling situation—for instance, when, as young adolescents, they make the transition from elementary school to junior high school (Bergamo & Evans, 2005; Eccles & Midgley, 1989; Tomback, Williams, & Wentzel, 2005). Adolescence brings additional sources of anxiety as well, including the high expectations that many secondary school teachers have for students' performance, the increasingly challenging nature of class material, and general concerns about what the future will bring (Eccles & Midgley, 1989; Phelan, Yu, & Davidson, 1994; Snow et al., 1996). And, in general, people are likely to become anxious whenever their sense of self-worth or self-efficacy is threatened—for instance, when they know they are being evaluated or when they receive some form of feedback that portrays them in an unflattering light (Covington, 1992; Eccles et al., 1998).

Two forms of trait anxiety—mathematics anxiety and test anxiety—have been the focus of considerable study. Let's look at what research tells us about each of these.

Mathematics anxiety Of all the subjects taught in schools, none seems to elicit as much anxiety for as many students as mathematics. Mathematics anxiety has both worry and emotionality components. First, math-anxious people firmly believe that they are incapable of succeeding at mathematical tasks. Second, they have negative emotional reactions to math: They fear and dislike it, often intensely (Wigfield & Meece, 1988).

One possible reason why students become anxious about math is that, as we noted in our discussion of classical conditioning (chapter 3), school curricula sometimes introduce mathematical concepts and procedures before students are cognitively ready to handle them. For example, developmentalists have proposed that the abilities to understand proportions and to deal with abstract ideas don't usually emerge until early adolescence and then continue to develop for several years after that (Schliemann & Carraher, 1993; Tourniaire & Pulos, 1985; also see the discussion of Piaget's theory in chapter 11). Yet we often expose students to such proportions as fractions and ratios, and to such abstract ideas as negative numbers and pi (π), in the upper elementary and early junior high school years. If students are asked to deal with mathematical tasks they can't understand, many of them will undoubtedly encounter frustration and failure. And when students associate frequent failure with math, we can expect them to develop a dislike for the subject and a belief that they are incapable of doing well in it.

As you might expect, students with high math anxiety do more poorly in mathematics classes than students with low math anxiety; furthermore, highly math-anxious students are less likely to enroll in additional math classes of their own volition (Ashcraft, 2002; Eccles & Jacobs, 1986; McCoy, 1990; Meece, Wigfield, & Eccles, 1990). Such differences between high-math-anxious and low-math-anxious students appear even when the two groups of students have done equally well in previous math classes. In fact, math anxiety may have a greater influence on students' future plans for taking (or not taking) mathematics than do their previous achievement levels and history of success in math (Eccles & Jacobs, 1986). Math anxiety, which is more common in girls than in boys even when achievement levels are the same, may be a key reason why so few girls pursue advanced study or careers in mathematics (Ashcraft, 2002; Eccles & Jacobs, 1986; Fennema, 1980). And for students of both genders, math anxiety may discourage pursuit of careers in science (Chipman, Krantz, & Silver, 1992).

Test anxiety Most of us get a little bit anxious about tests, and, as we have already seen, a small amount of anxiety can actually help us do better on them. But some students become extremely anxious in test-taking situations, and these students typically get lower test scores than their less anxious classmates (Cassady & Johnson, 2002; Chapell et al., 2005; Hembree, 1988; Hill, 1984). Such students appear to be concerned primarily about the *evaluative* aspect of tests: They are terribly concerned that someone else (such as their teacher) will make negative judgments about them (Harter, Whitesell, & Kowalski, 1992; Phillips, Pitcher, Worsham, & Miller, 1980; Wine, 1980). Test anxiety interferes not only with retrieval at the time of the test, but also with encoding and storage when learners are studying for the test (Cassady & Johnson, 2002). Thus, highly test-anxious students don't just "test" poorly; they also learn poorly.

Test anxiety is rare in the early grades but increases throughout the elementary school years (Kirkland, 1971; S. B. Sarason, 1972). Many secondary and upper elementary students have test anxiety that interferes with their test performance, especially when taking *high-stakes* tests whose results influence decisions about promotion, graduation, and other significant consequences

(Chabrán, 2003). Debilitative test anxiety is particularly common in students from minority groups, students with disabilities, and students with a history of academic failure (Kirkland, 1971; Phillips et al., 1980).

Anxiety may be at the root of a phenomenon known as **stereotype threat,** in which individuals from stereotypically low-achieving groups (e.g., females, certain minority groups) perform more poorly on tests than they otherwise would simply because they are aware that their group traditionally *does* do poorly (Steele, 1997). When people are aware of the unflattering stereotype—and especially when they know that the task they are performing reflects their ability in an important domain—worrisome thoughts intrude into working memory, heart rate and other physiological correlates of anxiety go up, and performance goes down (J. Aronson et al., 1999; Cadinu, Maass, Rosabianca, & Kiesner, 2005; Inzlicht & Ben-Zeev, 2003; McKown & Weinstein, 2003; Osborne & Simmons, 2002). We are less likely to see the negative effects of stereotype threat when people don't interpret their performance on a task as an indication of their competence, ability, and overall status in comparison with peers (Dweck, Mangels, & Good, 2004; Josephs, Newman, Brown, & Beer, 2003; McKown & Weinstein, 2003).

To perform most effectively in the classroom, learners should be motivated to do their best yet not be overly anxious about their performance. In the final section of this chapter, we will consider some general strategies for promoting students' motivation to achieve academic success and for keeping anxiety and other emotions at productive levels.

CREATING A MOTIVATING CLASSROOM ENVIRONMENT

All too often, I hear people (including some teachers) complain that students "just aren't motivated" to learn. But one thing should be clear by now: Motivation to learn classroom subject matter is not necessarily something that students bring to school with them—it can also be something that teachers *instill* in students (recall our earlier discussion of *situated motivation*). The school environment—including the specific instructional techniques teachers use—definitely does have an impact on students' desire to learn and achieve in the classroom (e.g., Brophy, 2004; J. T. Guthrie et al., 2004; Reeve, 2006).

The principles and theories we've examined in this chapter offer several ideas about how instructional practices can promote motivation:

◆ *Students learn more effectively and engage in more productive classroom behaviors when they are intrinsically rather than extrinsically motivated to learn and achieve.* Historically, parents, teachers, and society in general have emphasized the extrinsic advantages of classroom success (Harter, 1992; Spaulding, 1992). For example, parents give their children money and privileges for good report cards. Schools award athletic letters for sports participation. Teachers and guidance counselors point out that students will gain admission to college, find more employment opportunities, and earn higher salaries if they obtain their high school diplomas. Yet as we have seen, *intrinsically* motivated students are more likely to exhibit initiative, independence, ambition, meaningful learning, and enjoyment regarding academic activities than is true for their extrinsically motivated counterparts, and they ultimately achieve at higher levels in the classroom.

Unfortunately, children's intrinsic need to learn and achieve at school tends to decrease as they progress through the school grades, and it may be especially low when they make the often anxiety-arousing transition from elementary school to junior high school (Eccles et al., 1998; Gottfried, Fleming, & Gottfried, 2001; Lepper, Corpus, & Iyengar, 2005). Furthermore, children's very conception of what achievement *is* changes as they develop: As they progress through the elementary school years, they increasingly define success as doing better than their peers, rather than as mastering knowledge and skills per se (Eccles et al., 1998; Feld, Ruhland, & Gold, 1979; Ruble, 1980).

Researchers have identified a variety of strategies that appear to promote intrinsic motivation to learn classroom subject matter. Talking about intrinsic rather than extrinsic motives for pursuing classroom activities is one effective approach (Amabile & Hennessey, 1992; Graham & Weiner, 1996). For example, a teacher might say, "It's always nice to get good grades, but it's more important that you understand what you are studying and enjoy what you are doing," or, "You must be very proud of yourself for passing the district writing test." Adults who model intrinsic motivation—for instance, by visibly pursuing their own interests or expressing intrinsic enjoyment of something they are doing (e.g., saying "I feel wonderful" after generously doing something for someone else)—promote observers' intrinsic motivation for the same activities (Bryan, 1971; Csikszentmihalyi et al., 1993). And relating classroom topics to students' own lives, experiences, needs, and feelings (e.g., in geography, identifying students who have roots in the regions being studied, or, in history, having students imagine how they might have felt leaving home at age 12 to work as an apprentice) increases the likelihood that students will genuinely want to learn about those topics (Brophy, 1986; Wlodkowski & Ginsberg, 1995; Zahorik, 1994).

◆ *Students are more likely to be intrinsically motivated when they feel confident they can succeed at classroom tasks.* Throughout the book, we've identified many strategies for promoting students' academic success. For example, we have found that students learn classroom subject matter more successfully when teachers facilitate effective cognitive processing—for instance, by providing advance organizers, visual aids, and mnemonics. We have also discovered that some learning and study strategies promote more effective learning and memory than others and that students can learn to use such strategies. And we've seen that students often have more success on classroom tasks when they work with classmates rather than alone.

Yet not *all* successes enhance learners' sense of competence. To see what I mean, take a minute to do this little exercise:

Write the numbers 1 to 10 on a piece of paper. See if you can do it in less than 10 seconds.

Were you successful? If so, how good did your success make you feel? I just did the task in about 4 seconds' time but had little reason to feel particularly proud. After all, I'm 58 years old; if I can't write these numbers quickly and accurately by now, something must be terribly wrong.

Success on easy tasks, although virtually guaranteed, does little to enhance our self-efficacy and overall sense of competence. Sure, we can do it, but so can anyone else. However, challenges are not so easily accomplished: Perhaps we have failed to accomplish them in the past, or perhaps we know others who have failed. When we successfully meet a challenge, we must obviously be pretty competent folks. Success on a challenging task, then, gives learners feelings of satisfaction that are not possible with an easier task. Furthermore, because it enhances their feelings of competence, success in a challenging situation increases their intrinsic motivation (Clifford, 1990; Deci & Ryan, 1992; Dweck, 2000).

Too much of a challenge, however, can be discouraging. With this point in mind, teachers should help students develop a reasonable perspective as to what success is—for instance, daily or monthly improvement qualifies, but consistent perfection isn't realistic. And teachers can cast students' errors in an appropriate light—as inevitable minor stumbling blocks on the road to success—and make sure that, despite such errors, students eventually do succeed with effort, persistence, and appropriate strategies. Ultimately, students maximize their progress when they don't agonize over how well they're doing or not doing—when they instead focus their attention on actually mastering the task at hand (Brophy, 2004).

♦ *Students' intrinsic motivation also increases when they have some degree of autonomy in classroom activities.* For both pedagogical and logistical reasons, students often have little control over the things that happen in school. For example, society's needs and school district curricula typically dictate the kinds of knowledge and skills that students must master. The use of the same facilities and resources by many different students requires adherence to certain schedules. To keep students' attention focused on school tasks, teachers must maintain some semblance of order in the classroom.

Yet some degree of autonomy is essential for enhancing students' sense of self-determination and intrinsic motivation (e.g., Hardré, Crowson, & DeBacker, in press; Hardré & Reeve, 2003; Jones & Greene, 2003). Teachers can do numerous little things to give students a sense of self-determination about classroom activities. For instance, they can solicit students' input about how lessons might be improved and what rules might be appropriate for classroom behavior (Keller, 1987; Stefanou et al., 2004). They can provide opportunities for students to learn independently, perhaps through small-group work or computer-assisted instruction (Stefanou et al., 2004; Swan, Mitrani, Guerrero, Cheung, & Schoener, 1990). They can provide rationales regarding how certain boring, tedious activities are apt to benefit students over the long run (Reeve, 2006). And when evaluation is useful in promoting academic progress, teachers can provide mechanisms (e.g., checklists, feedback sheets) through which students can evaluate themselves (McCaslin & Good, 1996; Spaulding, 1992; Wlodkowski, 1978).

As noted earlier, a key factor affecting learners' sense of self-determination is having choices about what to do. Learners are more likely to have a sense of "ownership" about activities they have chosen for themselves (Schraw, Flowerday, & Lehman, 2001). Opportunities for choice-making must, of course, be within reasonable limits and take into account students' developmental readiness to make appropriate decisions (Brophy, 2004; Lane, Falk, & Wehby, 2006). For instance, when a particular objective can be accomplished in two or more different ways, teachers might give students a choice about how best to proceed or in what manner to demonstrate mastery (Hennessey & Amabile, 1987; Spaulding, 1992; Stefanou et al., 2004). And when extrinsic reinforcers are used as a way of encouraging students to perform dull but necessary tasks, teachers can preserve students' sense of self-determination by giving them choices regarding the specific reinforcers they can earn by completing the tasks (Spaulding, 1992).

Giving students autonomy does *not* mean removing all structure from classroom activities (H. A. Davis, 2003; deCharms, 1984; Reeve et al., 2004). Some structure—for instance, in the form of scaffolding that supports students' efforts to learn—is essential for promoting students' sense of self-efficacy and competence. In addition, a certain amount of structure can enhance students' sense of self-determination. For instance, if teachers clearly communicate expectations for academic performance (e.g., by providing evaluation criteria in advance), students know exactly what they must do to be successful (Reeve, 2006). Teachers can inform students well ahead of time about upcoming deadlines, so that students can budget their time accordingly (Spaulding, 1992). And teachers can establish general routines and procedures that students should typically follow as they work, thereby minimizing the need to give explicit instructions for each and every assignment (Spaulding, 1992).

◆ *Extrinsic motivation can also promote learning.* Although intrinsic motivation is the optimal situation, extrinsic motivation is not necessarily a bad thing, and it is certainly better than *no* motivation to learn and achieve. Oftentimes, students are motivated both by an intrinsic desire to master classroom subject matter and by the external rewards that such mastery brings—the good grades, public recognition, access to desirable educational opportunities and careers, and so on (Cameron, 2001; Covington, 2000; Hidi & Harackiewicz, 2000). Furthermore, many students (older ones especially) have multiple demands on their time, to the point where they must place priority on activities that bring them good grades and other outcomes important to their future well-being (e.g., C. S. Ryan & Hemmes, 2005).

As we have noted on previous occasions, extrinsic reinforcement may be most useful when desired behaviors will apparently not occur any other way. Learners may initially find a new activity boring, difficult, or frustrating and therefore need external encouragement to persist (Cameron, 2001; Deci et al., 2001; Hidi & Harackiewicz, 2000). In such circumstances, teachers should ideally reinforce students not just for doing something but for doing it *well*—that is, for engaging in behaviors and cognitive processes that will maximize achievement over the long run (e.g., Eisenberger & Cameron, 1996). With continuing practice, students' competence and skill are likely to improve, and they may eventually begin to find the activity intrinsically rewarding.

It is important to note, too, that students' intrinsic motivation to learn classroom material is not likely to appear overnight but instead will emerge slowly over time, especially if students have previously been accustomed to receiving extrinsic reinforcement for their efforts. When working with extrinsically motivated students, a reasonable approach is to increase emphasis on the intrinsic rewards of learning while only gradually weaning students from their dependence on external reinforcers (Covington, 1992; Lepper, 1981; Stipek, 1996).

◆ *Feedback and other forms of extrinsic reinforcement should maintain or enhance students' sense of competence and self-determination.* In chapter 4, we talked about positive feedback as a form of reinforcement; from an operant conditioning perspective, feedback has a *direct* effect on behavior. In chapter 6 and 8, we noted that feedback can also enhance performance *indirectly* by giving learners information about how they can improve. As we have seen in this chapter, motivation theorists suggest that feedback has an additional indirect effect on behavior: It enhances performance to the extent that it affirms an individual's sense of competence and overall self-worth.

In contrast, positive feedback is *unlikely* to be beneficial when it either (a) diminishes one's sense of competence or (b) communicates an attempt to control one's behavior and so undermines one's sense of self-determination (Burnett, 2001; Deci & Ryan, 1992; Reeve et al., 2004). For example, I respond to my children more favorably when they tell me

Boy, Mom, these brownies you made are really good. (*a competence-enhancing statement*)

than when they say

It's a good thing you finally baked something around here, Ma. All my friends' mothers do it all the time. (*a controlling statement*)

Compliments about things I do well are always welcome. But statements about what "good" parents are supposed to do make me feel as if I'm not really in charge in my own home. Besides, I have no intention of letting my children tell *me* how to behave.

Even *negative* feedback can be effective when it promotes competence and self-determination (R. Butler, 1988; Corno & Rohrkemper, 1985; Reeve, 2006; Tunstall & Gipps, 1996). If it provides information about how to improve in the future, thereby implying that the individual can eventually be successful, it is likely to promote intrinsic motivation. If it instead conveys the message that a learner is incompetent or imposes a feeling of outside control, it is apt to undermine any intrinsic motivation to continue engaging in a task.

◆ *Students are more likely to focus on their schoolwork when their nonacademic needs have been met* (Brophy, 2004; Fredricks et al., 2004). Our earlier discussions of drives, Maslow's hierarchy, and the need for relatedness point to a number of nonacademic needs that students are likely to have. On some occasions, students may have physiological needs; for instance, they may be hungry, thirsty, tired, or restless. Students may feel uncertain or insecure about what will happen to them in class, in the schoolyard, or on the way to and from school. And many students will have a strong desire to interact with other people (classmates and teachers alike) and ideally gain the companionship, acceptance, approval, and respect of those around them. The need for self-worth has nonacademic implications as well, in that students are apt to judge themselves not only on the basis of what they can do but also on the basis of how other people treat them and respond to their actions.

Teachers can do a number of simple things to ensure that students' physiological needs are met. For example, they can help students from low-income families apply for free lunch programs. They can alternate quiet, sedentary tasks with opportunities for physical activity. They can refer students with apparently untreated illnesses to the school nurse. And they should certainly include restroom breaks and trips to the drinking fountain in the daily schedule.

To meet students' need for safety and security at school and to keep students' anxiety about academic tasks and activities at a reasonable, facilitative level, teachers must create an environment that is somewhat orderly and predictable (Brophy, 1987; Dowaliby & Schumer, 1973; Grimes & Allinsmith, 1970; Klein, 1975). They should clearly describe expectations not only for academic performance but also for classroom behavior. They should deal with misbehaviors in a fair and consistent fashion. They should provide opportunities for students to voice any questions and concerns that may arise. And they must actively address bullying and other circumstances that may jeopardize students' physical or psychological well-being.

Students' needs for love, belonging, affiliation, and approval—in general, their need for relatedness—can be met in a variety of ways. Teacher–student relationships are, by their very nature, somewhat businesslike; after all, both teachers and students have a job to do. At the same time, teachers can express their interest and affection for students through the many little things they do throughout the day—for example, by acknowledging birthdays and other special occasions, taking students' ideas and opinions seriously, and offering a supportive and nonjudgmental ear when a particular student seems angry or depressed. Teachers should also provide opportunities for students to interact frequently with their classmates—for example, through such group-oriented instructional techniques as discussions, cooperative learning, reciprocal teaching, and role playing. Recall, too, the *sense of community* I described in chapter 14: Students are more likely to be academically successful—and more likely to stay in school rather than drop out—when they believe that their teachers and peers like and respect them and when they feel that they are valued members of the classroom (Certo, Cauley, & Chafin, 2002; Goodenow, 1993; Hymel, Comfort, Schonert-Reichl, & McDougall, 1996; Osterman, 2000; Patrick et al., 2002; Watson & Battistich, 2006).

To help students gain the esteem of others and maintain their own sense of self-worth, teachers can acknowledge students' accomplishments both in and out of class. They can schedule activities in such a way that all students are able to demonstrate their particular strengths at some point during the school day or at special events after school (e.g., Jenlink, 1994). They can "brag" about their students' accomplishments in many subtle ways—for example, by posting students' art projects on the wall, describing noteworthy achievements at parent–teacher conferences, and sending occasional good-news reports home to parents. But most importantly—I am probably beginning to sound like a broken record here—teachers must have high expectations for students' performance and do everything they can to help students *meet* those expectations (L. H. Anderman et al., 2002).

◆ *Dispositions that involve actively and thoughtfully engaging with school subject matter should promote more effective cognitive processing and learning over the long run.* To date, researchers have focused more on how students differ in their dispositions than on how to *promote certain dispositions.* But we can reasonably assume that teachers who encourage and model productive dispositions—for instance, by presenting thought-provoking questions, asking students to evaluate the quality of scientific evidence, insisting that students defend their opinions with sound rationales, teaching strategies for constructing persuasive arguments, and consistently exhibiting their own open-mindedness about diverse perspectives—get students off to a good start (e.g., see Baron, 1987; Derry, Levin, Osana, & Jones, 1998; Halpern, 1998; Kuhn, 2001b; Perkins & Ritchhart, 2004).

◆ *Learning is—and should be—an affective as well cognitive enterprise.* There is no reason that academic subject matter need be dry and emotionless. On the contrary, students will probably remember more if they have feelings about the things they study. For example, a scientific discovery might be exciting. A look at social injustices might make students angry. A poem might convey peace and serenity. One simple way that teachers can promote positive affect is to model their own enthusiasm and excitement about classroom subject matter—perhaps by bringing in newspaper articles and other outside materials they have run across, presenting material in an animated or even impassioned fashion, and sharing the particular questions and issues about which they themselves are concerned (Brophy, 1987, 1999; Perry, 1985; Wlodkowski, 1978).

Although students might occasionally feel outrage about certain historical events or current social phenomena, in general they should associate pleasure and other forms of positive affect with classroom activities. For example, although teachers don't necessarily want to give the impression that schoolwork is all fun and games, they can occasionally incorporate a few gamelike features into classroom tasks and activities (Brophy, 1986, 2004)—perhaps by using a television game show format during a review session (this strategy also addresses social needs) or having students act as detectives in interpreting archeological artifacts. And, in general, teachers must make sure that most of students' experiences with any task or subject matter, and especially their *early* experiences, are positive and nonthreatening ones (Wlodkowski, 1978).

◆ *Classroom assessments are more effective motivators when students perceive them as means of enhancing future achievement rather than as judgments of ability and worth.* Under the right circumstances, tests and other forms of classroom assessment can serve as effective motivators (albeit extrinsic ones) for academic learning. For example, most students study class material more and learn it better when they are told that their learning will be assessed than when they are simply told to learn it (Blumenfeld, Hamilton, Bossert, Wessels, & Meece, 1983; Frederiksen, 1984b; Halpin & Halpin, 1982). Classroom assessments are especially effective as motivators when they challenge students to perform at their very best (Natriello & Dornbusch, 1984). However, we should note several situations in which an assessment will definitely *not* motivate students to do well or, even worse, may motivate them to do *poorly:*

- When they believe they will be penalized for doing too well—for example, when they think they will receive more challenging work (e.g., extra readings or more difficult assignments) if they attain a high score
- When they think they will lose the esteem of their peers for doing too well—for example, when they are afraid of becoming nerds or "school girls"
- When they think their teacher's high standards for performance on the assessment are impossible to attain
- When they consistently perform at lower levels than most of their classmates
- When they believe an assessment is a poor reflection of what they know
  (Natriello, 1987; Natriello & Dornbusch, 1984; Paris, Lawton, Turner, & Roth, 1991; Paris & Turner, 1994; Sax, 1989)

Thus, a classroom assessment tool is most likely to serve as a motivator for learning when students perceive it to be a valid measure of instructional objectives, when they believe that successful performance on the assessment is possible, and when they are confident that successful performance will be rewarded rather than punished.

But as we discovered in our discussion of test anxiety, many students are so concerned about performing well on classroom assessments that they become overly anxious when encountering them. There are probably several reasons why high school and upper elementary students experience debilitative anxiety in assessment situations. Perhaps teachers too often imply that an upcoming assessment is an event to be feared or revered. Perhaps teachers too often stress the dire consequences of failing. Perhaps teachers and other school personnel make too many major decisions—about grades, scholarships, admission to special programs, and so on—based on the results of a single test score (recall our earlier discussion of high-stakes tests).

Researchers and practitioners have offered numerous suggestions for keeping students' anxiety about classroom assessments at a facilitative level:

- Help students master class material and effective study strategies to the point where successful performance on an assessment is highly probable.
- Keep an assessment short enough that students can easily complete it within the allotted time.
- Encourage students to do their best without creating unnecessary anxiety about the consequences of doing poorly.
- Provide whatever support (scaffolding) is appropriate to help students perform successfully on a classroom assessment task (e.g., give pretests for practice and feedback, allow students to use notes or other resources when there is no inherent value in committing certain kinds of information to memory.
- Base students' classroom grades on many sources of data (e.g., numerous small assessments) instead of on only one or two test scores.
- Minimize (and ideally eliminate) opportunities for students to compare their performance with that of classmates.
  (Brophy, 1986; Covington, 1992; Gaudry & Spielberger, 1971; Gaynor & Millham, 1976; Hill, 1984; Hill & Wigfield, 1984; Kirkland, 1971; Leherissey, O'Neil, & Hansen, 1971; Naveh-Benjamin, 1991; I. G. Sarason, 1980; S. B. Sarason, 1972; Sax, 1989; Sieber, Kameya, & Paulson, 1970; Stipek, 1993; Wine, 1980).

Above all, teachers and students alike must keep tests and other forms of classroom assessment in the proper context—as means of promoting learning and achievement, especially over the long run, rather than as means of making judgments about students' ability and worth. Evaluation procedures should provide frequent and informative feedback to students about what they have mastered and how they can improve (Brophy, 1986; Spaulding, 1992; Wine, 1980). Such procedures should also allow for the mistakes that are an inevitable part of the learning process. When students know they will have a chance to correct their errors, they are more likely to take on challenging, risky tasks (Brophy, 1986; Wlodkowski, 1978).

SUMMARY

Motivation is an internal state that arouses us to action, pushes us in certain directions, and keeps us engaged in certain activities. Motivation determines the extent to which we exhibit the particular responses we have learned; it also affects whether and in what ways we process the information we receive. *Intrinsic motivation* is ultimately more beneficial than *extrinsic motivation;* for example, intrinsically motivated individuals do things on their own initiative, maintain attention on tasks, and process information in meaningful ways. Yet intrinsic and extrinsic motivation are not necessarily mutually exclusive; often learners are simultaneously both intrinsically and extrinsically motivated.

Numerous theorists have speculated about the nature of human beings' basic, universal needs. Early *drive* theorists believed that members of many species (including people) behave in ways that satisfy their physiological needs and maintain homeostasis; a bit later, theorists modified drive theory to include *incentives,* suggesting that characteristics of goal objects mediate a stimulus–response relationship and thereby affect which stimuli are responded to and which are not. In addition to maintaining homeostasis, people may also have a need for stimulation, or *arousal:* People who have little access to environmental stimulation for extended periods show significant disruptions in perception and thinking. From the perspective of *Maslow's hierarchy,* people have five different sets of needs (ranging from physiological needs to self-actualization) that they strive to meet in a particular order.

More recently, some researchers have found evidence that people have a need to believe they are competent, capable individuals and may paradoxically undermine their own success as a way of protecting their sense of *self-worth*. People may also have a need for *self-determination*—a sense that they have some autonomy and control regarding the course that their lives will take. A third basic need that has emerged in contemporary research literature is the need for *relatedness*—a need to interact with and feel psychologically connected to others. Some motivation theorists have suggested that learners are more intrinsically motivated to learn new information and skills when all of these needs—competence and self-worth, self-determination, and relatedness—have been adequately addressed.

Trait theorists have found individual differences in human motivation. For instance, people seem to vary in their needs for affiliation, approval, and achievement. In addition, some learners have *dispositions*—general inclinations to approach learning and problem-solving situations in particular ways—that enhance their cognitive engagement and learning success.

Related to motivation is the concept of *affect*—the feelings, emotions, and moods that an individual brings to bear on a task. Affect influences motivation; for example, people choose their goals in part based on how they think they will feel if they achieve or don't achieve those goals. Affect also influences learning; for example, people can typically store and retrieve information with emotional overtones more easily than they can recall relatively nonemotional information. Of the various forms that affect may take, *anxiety* is the one that researchers have investigated most thoroughly. Anxiety tends to facilitate performance on easy tasks, but high levels interfere with performance on difficult tasks, presumably by interfering with effective cognitive processing and in other ways distracting people from what they are doing.

Theory and research on human motivation and affect yield numerous implications for promoting learning and achievement in the classroom. For instance, teachers should emphasize the intrinsically motivating aspects of school learning yet remember that extrinsic rewards can also be effective motivators when necessary. They can promote intrinsic motivation in part by addressing students' needs for competence and self-determination in classroom activities, as well as such nonacademic needs as those for physical well-being and supportive interpersonal relationships. Teachers should also keep in mind that certain emotions (e.g., enjoyment, excitement, and in some cases anger) can enhance classroom learning, whereas others (especially fear and anxiety) often interfere with students' concentration and performance.

CHAPTER 16

Cognitive Factors in Motivation

Within the past few decades, psychologists have radically changed their approach to the study of human motivation. Although physiological needs and drives certainly influence people's behavior, talk of such needs and drives has largely gone by the wayside. Concrete, extrinsic reinforcers play less of a role in conceptions of human learning and behavior than they did in the 1960s and 1970s. Most contemporary theorists now describe human motivation as being a function of cognitive processes—interpreting events, forming expectations about future success, setting goals toward which to strive, and so on. Not only does motivation *affect* cognition (see chapter 15), but in many respects motivation *is* cognition.

In our discussions of competence, self-worth, and self-determination in chapter 15, we have seen how certain aspects of cognition—in particular, perceptions of oneself and one's circumstances—are a key ingredient in human motivation. In this chapter we will consider additional cognitive factors, including interest, expectancies, values, goals, and attributions. Later, we will consider how learners become increasingly able to *self-regulate* their motivations and emotions, and we will discover that some behaviors that are initially motivated extrinsically may become *internalized* over time, to the point where an individual eventually engages in them freely and willingly. Finally, we will identify strategies for promoting cognitive processes that enhance motivation in instructional settings.

INTEREST

When we say that people have **interest** in a particular topic or activity, we mean that they find the topic or activity intriguing and enticing. Interest, then, is one form of intrinsic motivation (Hidi, Renninger, & Krapp, 2004). Positive affect accompanies interest; for example, people pursuing a task in which they are interested experience such feelings as pleasure, excitement, and liking (Hidi & Anderson, 1992; Hidi & Renninger, 2006; Schiefele, 1998).

Theorists distinguish between two general types of interest. Some interests reside within the individual; people tend to have personal preferences regarding the topics they pursue and the activities in which they engage. Such **personal interests**[1] are relatively stable and manifest themselves in consistent patterns in choice making over time. For example, my husband has a strong interest in football and so can often be found in front of the television set on Saturdays, Sundays, and Monday and Thursday evenings from September to January. (Fortunately, these are not the times when my favorite game shows are broadcast.) And each of my children has shown unique personal interests from an early age. When Tina was growing up, she spent many hours either talking to or talking about boys, and as a college student, she lived in a coeducational "fraternity" house with a ratio of three males to every female. For many years, Alex had a thing for critters; he was fascinated with ants as a toddler, and he had an intense interest in various kinds of reptiles (lizards, snakes, dinosaurs) throughout the elementary and middle school years. Jeff has always been a Lego man, in his younger days putting all of his allowance toward Lego sets and spending many hours in the basement designing architectural wonders. Even now as a young adult, when he's home he occasionally retreats to the basement to expand on his latest creation.

In contrast to personal interest, **situational interest** is evoked by something in the environment—something that is perhaps new, unusual, or surprising (Hidi & Renninger, 2006). For instance, as I was driving through the plains of eastern Colorado one day many years ago, I saw what looked like a llama out of the corner of my eye. Well, I knew quite well that the Colorado plains are cattle and horse country, not llama country, so I slowed down to take a closer look, eventually confirming the unlikely llama hypothesis. For a few minutes, I was more interested in identifying the strange creature I saw than in getting to my destination. In much the same way, you might have your interest temporarily piqued by a traffic accident at the side of the road, a strange-but-true tidbit in the newspaper, or a large, brightly wrapped gift with your name on it.

Effects of Interest

In general, interest promotes more effective information processing. People who are interested in a topic devote more attention to it and become more cognitively engaged in it (Hidi et al., 2004; McDaniel, Waddill, Finstad, & Bourg, 2000; Schiefele & Wild, 1994). They are also more likely

---

[1]You may also see the term *individual interests*.

to process information in a meaningful, organized, and elaborative fashion—for instance, by relating it to things they already know, interrelating ideas, drawing inferences, forming visual images, generating their own examples, and identifying potential applications (Hidi & Anderson, 1992; Pintrich & Schrauben, 1992; Schiefele, 1991, 1992; Schraw & Lehman, 2001; Tobias, 1994). And provided that they are not too attached to particular perspectives about a topic, they are more likely to undergo conceptual change if they encounter information that contradicts their existing understandings (Andre & Windschitl, 2003; Linnenbrink & Pintrich, 2003).

As you might guess, then, students who are interested in the material they are studying are more likely to remember it over the long run and so can build on it in future learning (Garner, Brown, Sanders, & Menke, 1992; Hidi & Renninger, 2006; Scholes & Kardash, 1996; Wigfield, 1994). As a result, interested students show higher academic achievement (Hidi & Harackiewicz, 2000; Krapp, Hidi, & Renninger, 1992; Schiefele, Krapp, & Winteler, 1992).

The *type* of interest undoubtedly makes a difference, however. Situational interest is sometimes of the "catch" variety: It engages you for a short time (as the llama did me), but you quickly move on to something else, and so cognitive processing and learning are likely to be limited (Mitchell, 1993). Other instances of situational interest are of the "hold" variety: You stay with a task or topic for a lengthy period—say, for an hour or more (Mitchell, 1993). "Hold" situational interest and long-term personal interests are ultimately more beneficial than "catch" interest. Whereas the latter may temporarily capture a learner's attention, the former—especially personal interests—provide the impetus that ultimately sustains involvement in an activity over the long run (Alexander, Kulikowich, & Schulze, 1994; Harackiewicz, Barron, Tauer, Carter, & Elliot, 2000; Mitchell, 1993).

Factors Promoting Interest

Researchers have identified numerous sources of situational interest (Hidi & Renninger, 2006; Renninger, Hidi, & Krapp, 1992; Schank, 1979; Schraw & Lehman, 2001; Zahorik, 1994). Some topics—for instance, death, destruction, danger, romance, and sex—appear to be inherently interesting for human beings. Things that are new, different, or unexpected often generate interest, as do things with a high activity level or intense emotions. Children and adolescents also tend to be intrigued by topics related to people and culture (e.g., disease, violence, holidays), nature (e.g., dinosaurs, weather, the sea), and current events (e.g., television shows, popular music, substance abuse, gangs). Works of fiction and fantasy (novels, short stories, movies, etc.) are more engaging when they include themes and characters with which people can personally identify. Nonfiction is more interesting when it is concrete and easy to understand and when relationships among ideas are clear. And, for children at least, challenging tasks are often more interesting than easy ones (Danner & Lonky, 1981; Harter, 1978)—a fortunate state of affairs if, as Lev Vygotsky proposed, challenges promote cognitive growth.

Researchers know less about the origins of personal interest, in part because research studies would probably have to track events in people's lives over a lengthy period. Many personal interests probably come from people's prior experiences with various topics and activities. For example, objects or events that initially invoke situational interest may provide the seed from which a sustained personal interest eventually grows (Alexander, 1997; Hidi & Harackiewicz, 2000; Hidi & Renninger, 2006). Parents may sometimes nurture their children's budding interests by providing relevant books and experiences (Leibham, Alexander, Johnson,

Neitzel, & Reis-Henrie, 2005). Learners may eventually find that acquiring greater knowledge and skill in a particular area enhances their sense of self-efficacy and competence, thereby generating intrinsic motivation. To some extent, interest and knowledge seem to perpetuate each other: Personal interest in a topic fuels a quest to learn more about the topic, and the increasing knowledge that one gains may in turn promote greater interest (Alexander, 1997; Hidi & Renninger, 2006; Kintsch, 1980; Tobias, 1994).

EXPECTANCIES AND VALUES

Some theorists (e.g., Atkinson, 1964; Dweck & Elliott, 1983; Eccles [Parsons], 1983; Feather, 1982; Wigfield, 1994; Wigfield & Eccles, 2000, 2002) have proposed that motivation for performing a task is a function of two variables, both of which are fairly subjective. First, a person must have a high expectation, or **expectancy,** for success. This concept overlaps with social cognitive theorists' concept of *self-efficacy* (Buehl & Alexander, 2004; Wigfield, Tonks, & Eccles, 2004) but also takes into account such outside factors as task difficulty and availability of outside support. Equally important, and equally subjective, is **value:** A person must believe that there are direct or indirect benefits in performing a task.

Effects of Expectancies and Values

Children in the preschool and early elementary school years often pursue activities they find interesting and enjoyable, regardless of their expectancies for success (Wigfield, 1994; Wigfield et al., 2004). For older children and adults, however, intrinsically motivated behavior occurs only when both high expectancy and high value are present. For example, as a doctoral student in educational psychology in the 1970s, I found value in human learning theory and had a high expectancy that I could master it; thus, I was motivated to learn as much as I could about how human beings learn. I value good music, too, but have a low expectancy for becoming an accomplished musician (I haven't yet learned basic piano playing skills to automaticity despite five years of lessons), so I don't work very hard or very often at my music. I'm much better at cooking lima beans than I am at piano playing, but I never cook them because I find no value in eating them. And there are some things that, for me, are associated with both low expectancy and low value; playing violent video games and walking barefoot on hot coals are two activities that spring to mind.

To some degree, expectancies and values are related to different aspects of people's behavior and performance (Durik, Vida, & Eccles, 2006; Mac Iver, Stipek, & Daniels, 1991; Wigfield & Eccles, 2002). Values affect the choices people make (e.g., students' course selections). In contrast, expectancies are related to people's effort and achievement (e.g., students' grade point averages).

Factors Influencing Expectancies and Values

People's expectancies are probably the result of several variables. Prior successes and failures in a particular domain make a difference, of course; for example, people will lower their expectations after experiencing a series of failures (Dweck, Goetz, & Strauss, 1980). But other factors affect expectancy level as well, including the perceived difficulty of a task, the quality of instruction, the availability of resources and support, one's general work habits, and the amount of effort that will probably be necessary (Dweck & Elliott, 1983; M. E. Ford, 1996; Wigfield & Eccles, 1992; Zimmerman, Bandura, & Martinez-Pons, 1992). From such factors, an individual comes to a conclusion—perhaps correct, perhaps not—about the likelihood of success.

Expectancy-value theorists have suggested four key reasons why value might be high or low: importance, utility, interest, and cost (Eccles [Parsons], 1983; Wigfield & Eccles, 1992, 2000). Some activities are valued because they are associated with desirable personal qualities; that is, they are viewed as *important*. For example, a boy who wants to be smart and thinks that smart people do well in school will place a premium on academic success. Other activities have high value because they are seen as means to a desired goal; that is, they have *utility*. For example, much as my daughter Tina found mathematics confusing and frustrating, she struggled through 4 years of high school math classes because many colleges require that much math (also see Bong, 2001). Still other activities are valued simply because they bring pleasure and enjoyment; in other words, they are *interesting*. For example, junk food doesn't help me achieve any of my long-range goals (in fact, it interferes with my goal of losing 15 pounds this year), but it surely does taste good.

Meanwhile, the *cost* factor may explain occasions in which a person sees little or no value in an activity. For example, I could undoubtedly improve my piano-playing skills with lessons and practice, but right now I have more important things to which I need to devote my time and energy. Other activities may be associated with too many bad feelings. For example, I can't imagine hang gliding or bungee jumping because I am deathly afraid of heights. And anything likely to threaten one's self-esteem is a "must" to avoid (Harter, 1990; Wigfield, 1994). For example, you may know individuals who rarely make the first move with people they would like to date for fear of being rejected.[2]

In addition to the importance, utility, interest, and cost factors, *culture* undoubtedly influences values as well. In particular, the people in one's life may, through everyday communications and activities, continually convey the belief that certain things (e.g., achieving at high levels in the classroom) are worth doing in their own right (Hickey & Granade, 2004; Hufton, Elliot, & Illushin, 2002; Wigfield et al., 2004). When we address the topic of *internalized motivation* later in the chapter, we'll identify one possible mechanism through which children adopt the values of the people around them.

Expectancies and values also influence *each other* (Eccles et al., 1998). More specifically, people who don't expect to do well in a particular activity may find reasons to devalue it. And people who don't value an activity are less likely to work hard at it and so have lower expectancies about their performance. As children move through the grade levels, they increasingly attach value to activities for which they have high expectancy for success and to activities they think will help them meet long-term goals. Meanwhile, they begin to *de*value the things they do poorly (Jacobs, Lanza, Osgood, Eccles, & Wigfield, 2002; Wigfield, 1994). Sadly, students' expectancies

---

[2]In chapter 5, I mentioned that learners sometimes engage in a cost–benefit analysis when deciding whether to engage in certain, potentially reinforceable behaviors. Such an analysis fits comfortably within an expectancies/values framework. In particular, we can expect that people will *not* exhibit a behavior if they think they will have to exert an inordinate amount of effort to achieve success or if they place little value on the activity and its consequences (Eccles [Parsons], 1984; Eccles & Wigfield, 1985; Feather, 1982; Paris & Byrnes, 1989).

and values related to many school-related domains (e.g., math, English, music, and sports) decline markedly over the school years (Eccles et al., 1998; Jacobs et al., 2002; Wigfield et al., 1991, 2004).

GOALS

As we discovered in our discussions of social cognitive theory and metacognition in chapters 6 and 12, setting goals is an important part of self-regulated behavior and learning. People's internal goals and standards for success motivate them to move in particular directions. Self-regulated learners know what they want to accomplish when they read or study, they direct their thoughts and learning strategies accordingly, and they continually monitor their progress toward the goals they have set for themselves (Carver & Scheier, 1990; Schunk & Zimmerman, 1994). Goal attainment results in considerable self-satisfaction; it also leads to greater self-efficacy and higher standards for future performance (Bandura, 1986, 1989). We must note, however, that goals are beneficial only to the extent that they are accomplishable. If they are unrealistically high—for instance, if learners expect error-free perfection—consistent failure to achieve them may result in excessive stress, frustration, or depression (Bandura, 1986; Blatt, 1995; Dixon, Dungan, & Young, 2003).

Goals figure prominently in theories of motivation. In our discussion of motivation's general effects in the preceding chapter, we noted that motivation revolves around the accomplishment of certain goals, with such goals influencing both the choices people make and the consequences they find reinforcing. People's goals also influence their cognitive processing; for instance, goals affect the extent to which learners become cognitively engaged in particular tasks and the cognitive strategies they use to study and learn (E. M. Anderman & Maehr, 1994; Brickman, Miller, & Roedel, 1997; Locke & Latham, 2002; Nolen, 1996; Winne & Marx, 1989).

Researchers have identified a wide variety of goals that people may set for themselves. Following are examples:

- Gaining physical comfort and personal well-being
- Obtaining extrinsic, concrete rewards
- Finding novelty and adventure
- Mastering new topics or skills
- Gaining a better understanding of the world
- Achieving and maintaining a sense of competence and self-worth
- Engaging in activities requiring intellectual or artistic challenge and creativity
- Doing well in school (e.g., getting good grades)
- Making a good impression on others
- Gaining the recognition or approval of superiors or peers
- Bringing honor to one's family or social group
- Developing productive interpersonal relationships
- Developing long-term, intimate relationships (e.g., getting married, having children)
- Helping others
- Doing better than others in competitive situations
- Becoming a productive member of society
- Achieving a desired career

- Gaining material wealth
- Gaining social or political power
- Achieving a sense of spiritual understanding or harmony
  (Boekaerts, de Koning, & Vedder, 2006; Brophy, 2004; Cacioppo, Petty, Feinstein, & Jarvis, 1996; Durkin, 1995; M. E. Ford, 1996; Lee & Anderson, 1991; McInerney, Roche, McInerney, & Marsh, 1997; Schutz, 1994; Urdan & Maehr, 1995; Wentzel, 1989; Wolters, 1998)

Some of these goals are well within conscious awareness. Others may lie below the surface, out of conscious "sight" but influencing people's behavior nevertheless (Shah, 2005).

Most human beings have and strive to achieve many of the goals just listed. For example, I achieve some degree of physical comfort by occasionally popping Cheetos into my mouth, I strive to affirm my high sense of self-worth by playing along at home as I watch television game shows, and I try to make a good impression in front of family and friends (or at least try not to look like a complete klutz) as I attempt parallel turns on the ski slope. But many of us have **core goals**—general goals of considerable priority for us at any given point in time—that seem to drive much of what we do (Schutz, 1994). For instance, my number one goal for many years has been to be a productive member of society—to leave the world a better place than I found it—and many of my behaviors (e.g., trying to raise socially responsible children, supporting my friends through difficult times, and writing books that can help teachers and other professionals understand and apply psychological principles) have in one way or another been directed toward that end.

Here we will focus on research findings related to several kinds of goals: achievement goals, work-avoidance goals, social goals, and career goals. We will then look at strategies people use for coordinating their efforts toward multiple goals.

Achievement Goals

As I mentioned in the preceding chapter, the need for achievement (also known as achievement motivation) was originally conceptualized as a general characteristic that people exhibit consistently across a variety of tasks and in many domains. But some contemporary psychologists have proposed that achievement motivation takes one of several forms, depending on the specific goal an individual has in mind. To illustrate, let's consider what three girls might be thinking during the first day of a basketball unit in a physical education class:

Jane: This is my chance to show all the girls what a great basketball player I am. If I stay near the basket, Joan and June will keep passing to me, and I'll score a lot of points. I can really impress Coach and my friends.

Joan: Boy, I hope I don't screw this up. If I shoot at the basket and miss, I'll look like a real jerk. Maybe I should just stay outside the three-point line and keep passing to Jane and June.

June: I'd really like to become a better basketball player. I can't figure out why I don't get more of my shots into the basket. I'll ask Coach to give me feedback about how I can improve my game. Maybe some of my friends will have suggestions, too.

All three girls want to play basketball well but for different reasons. Jane is concerned mostly about her performance—that is, about looking good in front of her coach and classmates—and so she wants to maximize opportunities to demonstrate her skill on the court. Joan is also concerned about the impression she'll make, but she just wants to make sure she *doesn't* look *bad*. Unlike Jane and Joan, June isn't even thinking about how her performance will appear to others. Instead, she is interested mainly in developing her skill—in mastering the game of basketball—and doesn't expect herself to be an expert on the first day. For June, making mistakes is an inevitable part of learning a new skill, not a source of embarrassment or humiliation.

June's approach to basketball illustrates a **mastery goal**[3]—a desire to achieve competence by acquiring additional knowledge or mastering new skills. In contrast, Jane and Joan are each setting a **performance goal**[4]—a desire to present oneself as competent in the eyes of others. More specifically, Jane has a **performance-approach goal:** She wants to look good and receive favorable judgments from others. Meanwhile, Joan has a **performance-avoidance goal:** She wants *not* to look bad and receive unfavorable judgments. In some cases, performance goals have an element of social comparison: People are concerned about how their accomplishments compare to those of their peers (Elliot & McGregor, 2000; Elliot & Thrash, 2001; Midgley et al., 1998). In essence, a mastery goal focuses on the *task*, whereas a performance goal focuses on the *self* (Grant & Dweck, 2003; Maehr & Kaplan, 2000; Nicholls, 1992).[5]

Mastery goals, performance-approach goals, and performance-avoidance goals are not necessarily mutually exclusive. People may simultaneously have two kinds, or even all three (E. M. Anderman & Maehr, 1994; Covington & Müeller, 2001; Hidi & Harackiewicz, 2000; Meece & Holt, 1993). For example, returning to our basketball example, we could imagine another girl, Jeanne, who wants to improve her basketball skills *and* look good in front of peers *and* not come across as a klutz.

Effects of Achievement Goals

A considerable body of research indicates that mastery goals are the optimal situation. In fact, research findings regarding mastery goals versus performance-avoidance goals are similar to those for motive for success versus motive to avoid failure (see chapter 15). As Table 16.1 illustrates, students with mastery goals tend to engage in the very activities that will help them learn: They pay attention in class, process information in ways that promote effective long-term memory storage, and learn from their mistakes. Furthermore, students with mastery goals have a healthy perspective about learning, effort, and failure: They realize that learning is a process of trying hard and continuing to persevere even in the face of temporary setbacks. Consequently, it is usually these students who learn the most from their classroom experiences.

---

[3]Theorists are referring to a similar idea when they talk about *learning goals, task goals, task involvement,* or *task orientation.* Psychologists sometimes like to stick to certain terminology to indicate the particular theoretical traditions on which they are building (Murphy & Alexander, 2000). However, the inconsistency in terms can be frustrating for newcomers to the field, because it interferes with their ability to synthesize what they are seeing in the research literature. As I present research findings in this section, I will be drawing on multiple programs of research and basically ignoring any subtle distinctions that theorists assign to the terms they use.

[4]You may also see the terms *ability goals, ego involvement,* or *ego orientation.*

[5]Some theorists have speculated that mastery goals can, like performance goals, be either approach oriented or avoidance oriented in nature (Elliot, 1999; Jagacinski, Kumar, & Boe, 2003; Linnenbrink & Pintrich, 2002; K. E. Ryan, Ryan, Arbuthnot, & Samuels, 2005). However, research on this distinction has been limited, and so we will not consider it here.

Table 16.1
Characteristics of people with mastery versus performance goals.

People with Mastery Goals	People with Performance Goals (Especially Those with Performance-Avoidance Goals)
Are more likely to be interested in and intrinsically motivated to learn school subject matter; show considerable cognitive engagement in classroom topics	Are more likely to be extrinsically motivated (i.e., motivated by expectations of external reinforcement and punishment) and more likely to cheat to obtain good grades
Believe that competence develops over time through practice and effort	Believe that competence is a stable characteristic (people either have talent or they don't); think that competent people shouldn't have to try very hard
Exhibit more self-regulated learning and behavior	Exhibit less self-regulation
Use learning strategies that promote understanding and transfer of course material (e.g., meaningful learning, elaboration, comprehension monitoring)	Use learning strategies that promote only rote learning (e.g., repetition, copying, word-for-word memorization); may procrastinate in their studying
Choose tasks that maximize opportunities for learning; seek out challenges	Choose tasks that maximize opportunities for demonstrating competence; avoid tasks and actions (e.g., asking for help) that might make them look incompetent
Are more likely to undergo conceptual change when confronted with convincing evidence that contradicts current beliefs	Are less likely to undergo conceptual change, in part because they are less likely to notice the discrepancy between new information and existing beliefs
React to easy tasks with feelings of boredom or disappointment	React to success on easy tasks with feelings of pride or relief
Seek feedback that accurately describes their ability and helps them improve	Seek feedback that flatters them
Willingly collaborate with peers when doing so is apt to enhance learning	Are willing to collaborate with peers primarily when collaboration offers opportunities to look competent or enhance social status
Evaluate their own performance in terms of the progress they make	Evaluate their own performance in terms of how they compare with others
Interpret failure as a sign that they need to exert more effort	Interpret failure as a sign of low ability and therefore predictive of continuing failure in the future
View errors as a normal and useful part of the learning process; use errors to improve performance	View errors as a sign of failure and incompetence; engage in self-handicapping to provide apparent justification for errors and failures
Persist in efforts to learn, even in the face of failure	Give up easily when they fail and avoid tasks that have previously led to failure
Are satisfied with their performance if they try hard and make progress, even if their efforts result in failure	Are satisfied with their performance only if they succeed
View a teacher as a resource and guide to help them learn	View a teacher as a judge and as a rewarder or punisher

(Continued)

Table 16.1
(Continued)

People with Mastery Goals	People with Performance Goals (Especially Those with Performance-Avoidance Goals)
Remain relatively calm during tests and classroom assignments	Are often quite anxious about tests and other assessments
As students, are more likely to feel comfortable at school and become actively involved in school activities	As students, are more likely to distance themselves from the school environment; may suffer from chronic depression
Achieve at higher levels	Achieve at lower levels

Sources: Ablard & Lipschultz, 1998; C. Ames & Archer, 1988; R. Ames, 1983; E. M. Anderman et al., 1998; E. M. Anderman & Maehr, 1994; Bandalos, Finney, & Geske, 2003; DeBacker & Crowson, 2006; Dweck, 1986, 2000; Dweck & Elliott, 1983; Dweck, Mangels, & Good, 2004; Entwisle & Ramsden, 1983; L. S. Fuchs et al., 1997; Gabriele & Montecinos, 2001; Grant & Dweck, 2003; Hardré et al., in press; Jagacinski & Nicholls, 1984, 1987; Kaplan & Midgley, 1999; Levy, Kaplan, & Patrick, 2004; Levy-Tossman & Kaplan, 2004; Linnenbrink & Pintrich, 2002, 2003; McGregor & Elliot, 2002; Meece, 1994; Middleton & Midgley, 1997; Midgley, 2002; Moran, Urdan, & Passarelli, 2003; Murphy & Alexander, 2000; Newman & Schwager, 1995; Nolen, 1996; Pugh, Linnenbrink, Kelly, Manzey, & Stewart, 2006; Rawsthorne & Elliot, 1999; A. M. Ryan, Pintrich, & Midgley, 2001; Schiefele, 1991, 1992; Senko & Harackiewicz, 2005; Shernoff & Hoogstra, 2001; Sideridis, 2005; Skaalvik, 1997; Southerland & Sinatra, 2003; Turner, Thorpe, & Meyer, 1998; Urdan, 2004; Wolters, 2004.

In contrast, students with performance goals—especially those with performance-*avoidance* goals—may stay away from some of the very tasks that, because of their challenging nature, would do the most to promote mastery of new skills. Furthermore, these students often experience debilitating anxiety about tests and other classroom tasks. Performance-*approach* goals are a mixed bag: They sometimes have very positive effects, spurring students on to achieve at high levels, especially in combination with mastery goals and high self-efficacy (Hardré, Crowson, & DeBacker, in press; Kaplan, Middleton, Urdan, & Midgley, 2002; Linnenbrink, 2005; Pintrich, 2000; Senko & Harackiewicz, 2005). Yet by themselves, performance-approach goals may be less beneficial than mastery goals: To achieve them, students may use relatively superficial learning strategies (e.g., rote memorization), exert only the minimal effort necessary to achieve desired outcomes, engage in self-handicapping, and perhaps cheat on classroom assessments (E. M. Anderman, Griesinger, & Westerfield, 1998; Brophy, 1987; Midgley, Kaplan, & Middleton, 2001). Performance-approach goals appear to be most detrimental when students are younger (e.g., in the elementary grades), have relatively low ability in the subject area, and have low self-efficacy for classroom tasks (Hidi & Harackiewicz, 2000; Kaplan, 1998; Kaplan & Midgley, 1997; Midgley et al., 2001).[6]

---

[6]Early studies contrasting the effects of mastery goals versus performance goals did not distinguish between performance-approach and performance-avoidance goals. Although most motivation theorists now make the distinction in their research, they have not yet reached consensus about the benefits and liabilities of performance-approach goals, probably in part because they have defined and measured such goals differently and in part because they have studied different populations of learners (Brophy, 2004; Grant & Dweck, 2003; Harackiewicz, Barron, Pintrich, Elliot, & Thrash, 2002; Kaplan, 1998).

Some learners seem to choose mastery goals over performance goals fairly consistently (e.g., L. A. Turner & Johnson, 2003; Senko & Harackiewicz, 2005). These people can be thought of as having a strong **motivation to learn**—a tendency to find learning activities meaningful and worthwhile and therefore to attempt to get the maximum benefit from them (Brophy, 1986, 2004; McCombs, 1988). This concept puts a new twist on the concept of achievement motivation: People want to engage in the cognitive processes that lead to successful learning as well as the behaviors that lead to observable achievements.

Origins of Achievement Goals

In some cases, mastery goals come from within. People are more likely to have mastery goals when they have high interest in, and high self-efficacy and optimism about, learning something (Bandura, 1997; P. K. Murphy & Alexander, 2000; Schiefele, 1992; Snyder et al., 2002). For example, when my son Alex was 12, his interest in lizards led him to subscribe to an adult-level herpetology magazine and read every issue from cover to cover. Similarly, people interested in antique automobiles might tinker with a Model T engine until they know the engine inside and out. And people interested in gymnastics might spend a good portion of their free time at the gym practicing, practicing, practicing.

Yet the instructional environment can encourage mastery goals as well (M. A. Church, Elliot, & Gable, 2001; Corpus, Tomlinson, & Stanton, 2004; Kaplan et al., 2002; Newman, 1998).[7] For instance, teachers might describe the intrinsic benefits of learning a skill, focus students' attention on the progress being made, or communicate their own goal of having students understand rather than rote-memorize classroom subject matter. In fact, insisting that students understand—a **press for understanding**—may be especially helpful (Middleton & Midgley, 2002; J. C. Turner, Meyer, et al., 1998). For example, teachers might continually ask students to explain and justify their reasoning, and they might refuse to accept substandard work that reflects little thought or effort (Middleton & Midgley, 2002).

Unfortunately, however, performance goals seem to be far more prevalent than mastery goals among today's students, at least those in the secondary grades (Blumenfeld, 1992; Elliot & McGregor, 2000; Harter, 1992). Most students, if they are motivated to succeed in their schoolwork, are primarily concerned about getting good grades, and they prefer short, easy tasks to lengthier, more challenging ones. Performance goals are also common in team sports, where the focus is often more on winning and gaining public recognition than on developing new skills and improving over time (Roberts, Treasure, & Kavussanu, 1997).

In some instances, students adopt performance goals as a means of avoiding failure, protecting their sense of self-worth, or—especially if their need for relatedness is high—enhancing relationships with peers (L. H. Anderman & Anderman, 1999; Covington, 1992; Elliot & McGregor, 2000; Urdan & Mestas, 2006). In other cases, students realize that performing at high levels—in particular, getting good grades—is critical for their future educational and professional opportunities (Covington & Müeller, 2001).

Many common teaching and coaching practices also contribute to the development of performance goals (L. H. Anderman & Anderman, 1999; M. A. Church et al., 2001; Kaplan et al., 2002;

---

[7]Some motivation theorists use the term *achievement goal orientations* in reference to goals that come from within and *achievement goal structures* in reference to goals that are presented or encouraged by the instructional environment (e.g., Midgley, 2002; Wolters, 2004).

Newman, 1998; Roberts et al., 1997). Posting "best" papers on the wall, scoring tests on a curve, displaying grades for everyone to see, focusing on surpassing other schools and teams, reminding students that good grades are important for college admissions—all of these strategies, though undoubtedly well intended, encourage learners to focus their attention more on "looking good" than on learning.

Even simply *attending* school may increase youngsters' focus on performance goals. Before children reach school age, they seem to focus primarily on mastery goals (e.g., Dweck & Elliott, 1983). But when they begin school at age 5 or 6, two things happen that orient them more toward performance goals (Dweck & Elliott, 1983). First, they suddenly have many peers around them to whom they can compare their own behavior; as a result, they may begin to define success more in terms of doing better than their classmates than in terms of task mastery. Second, whereas they have previously dealt primarily with physical tasks (e.g., learning to walk, fasten buttons, and ride a tricycle), they are now being asked to deal with tasks of an intellectual and somewhat abstract nature (e.g., learning to read, write, and add). The value of these school tasks may not be readily apparent to them, and their efforts in accomplishing them might therefore seem unnecessarily laborious. Furthermore, they may have greater difficulty assessing their progress on such tasks, to the point where they must rely on others (e.g., teachers) to make judgments about their competence. As learners approach adolescence, yet another factor kicks in: They are much more likely to worry about what others think of them than they were in their early years (Elkind, 1981; Hartup, 1983; Juvonen, 2000; Midgley, 1993).

Yet school is hardly the only environment influencing the acquisition of various achievement goals. Parents may encourage their toddlers and preschoolers to attempt and persist at challenging activities, on the one hand, or consistently chastise them for poor performance, on the other (L. A. Turner & Johnson, 2003). Furthermore, through the particular behaviors and values that are sanctioned and discouraged, different cultures may predispose children toward certain kinds of goals (Elliot, Chirkov, Kim, & Sheldon, 2001; Freeman, Gutman, & Midgley, 2002; Kaplan et al., 2002). For instance, cultures with a strong competitive element—as tends to be true in North American and some western European countries—may lead children to focus on performance goals. And cultures that instill in children a fear of bringing shame to themselves or their families—as is sometimes true in Asian families—can lead children to adopt performance-avoidance goals.

In recent years, achievement goal theory has largely dominated discussions of motivation in educational research journals (e.g., *Journal of Educational Psychology*). With such a strong presence, psychologists have observed its weaknesses as well as its strengths. Some theorists have argued that mastery and performance goals are heterogeneous categories that encompass more specific goals—goals related to achieving particular outcomes, comparing favorably with peers, validating one's sense of competence, and so on (Brophy, 2004, 2005; Grant & Dweck, 2003). The actual effects of various goals seem to depend on the nature of the particular task and context at hand (Elliot, Shell, Henry, & Maier, 2005). Furthermore, relationships between students' achievement goals and their classroom achievement tend to be weak ones at best, probably because students have many nonachievement-oriented goals that also influence their classroom performance (Boekaerts et al., 2006; Brophy, 2004). And in fact, when students are simply asked to describe what they want to accomplish at school (rather than to respond to researcher-written statements on questionnaires), many seem to be more concerned about work-avoidance and social goals than about achievement goals (Brophy, 2005; Cramblet & Denzine, 2006; Dowson & McInerney, 2001). Such goals are our next two topics.

Work–Avoidance Goals

As we have just seen, students sometimes want to avoid looking bad as they perform classroom tasks. But on other occasions, they may want to avoid having to do classroom tasks *at all,* or at least they will try to put as little effort as possible into those tasks. In other words, they may have a **work-avoidance goal** (Dowson & McInerney, 2001; Gallini, 2000; Nicholls, Cobb, Yackel, Wood, & Wheatley, 1990).

To date, much of the research on work-avoidance goals has focused on the middle school grades, where such goals seem to be fairly common (Dowson & McInerney, 2001; Gallini, 2000). Students with work-avoidance goals use a variety of strategies to minimize their workload. For instance, they may engage in off-task behavior, solicit help on easy tasks and problems, pretend that they don't understand something even when they *do,* complain loudly about challenging assignments, and select the least taxing alternatives whenever choices are given (Dowson & McInerney, 2001). They rarely use effective learning strategies or pull their weight in small-group activities (Dowson & McInerney, 2001; Gallini, 2000). At the college level—which gives students considerable leeway in how they schedule their time—students with work-avoidance goals are apt to put off doing their work until an assignment's due date is imminent (Wolters, 2003b).

Given the paucity of research findings on work-avoidance goals at present, we can only speculate about how these goals originate. In some instances, peers may encourage and model work-avoidance behaviors (Nolen, 1996). But we can reasonably guess that students are also likely to adopt such goals when they find little value in academic subject matter, have low self-efficacy for learning it, and see no long-term payoffs for mastering it (e.g., Garner, 1998; Wolters, 2003b). In other words, students are most likely to have work-avoidance goals when they have neither intrinsic nor extrinsic motivation to achieve instructional objectives. Students with work-avoidance goals may thus be teachers' biggest challenges, and teachers will have to use a wide variety of motivational strategies—probably including extrinsic reinforcers—to get them truly engaged in, and eventually committed to mastering, academic subject matter.

Social Goals

In chapter 15, we noted that most students make social relationships a high priority, and in fact all human beings probably have some need for relatedness. Learners are apt to have a variety of social goals, perhaps including the following:

- Forming and maintaining friendly or intimate relationships with others
- Gaining other people's approval
- Achieving status and prestige among peers (e.g., being one of the "popular kids")
- Meeting social obligations and keeping interpersonal commitments
- Becoming part of a cohesive, mutually supportive group
- Being a "good citizen" (e.g., following classroom rules and not unnecessarily distracting classmates from assigned tasks)
- Assisting and supporting others, and ensuring their welfare
- Being a source of honor and pride for one's family or community
  (Chen & Uttal, 1988; Dowson & McInerney, 2001; M. E. Ford, 1996; Hicks, 1997; Hinkley, McInerney, & Marsh, 2001; Li, 2005; Patrick, Anderman, & Ryan, 2002; Schutz, 1994)

The nature of students' social goals clearly affect their classroom behavior and academic performance. If students want to gain their teacher's attention and approval, they are apt to strive for good grades and in other ways shoot for performance goals (Hinkley et al., 2001). If they are seeking friendly relationships with classmates or are concerned about others' welfare, they may eagerly and actively engage in such activities as cooperative learning and peer tutoring; concern for others' welfare may also foster mastery goals (L. H. Anderman & Anderman, 1999; Dowson & McInerney, 2001). However, if students are particularly concerned about their social status, they may be willing to cooperate with classmates only if doing so maintains or enhances their standing in the eyes of peers (Levy-Tossman & Kaplan, 2004). And if they want to gain the approval of *low-achieving* peers, they may exert little effort in their studies and possibly even adopt work-avoidance goals (B. Brown, 1990; M. E. Ford & Nichols, 1991).

Career Goals

Most children and adolescents include career goals among their long-term goals. Young children set such goals with little thought and change them frequently; for instance, a 6-year-old may want to be a firefighter one week and a professional basketball player the next. By late adolescence, some (though by no means all) have reached some tentative and relatively stable decisions about the career paths they want to pursue (e.g., Marcia, 1980).

In earlier decades boys set higher aspirations for themselves than girls did, especially in domains that were stereotypically masculine (Deaux, 1984; Durkin, 1995; Lueptow, 1984). Perhaps things are changing, however: One recent study found *girls* to have higher career aspirations (Lapan, Tucker, Kim, & Kosciulek, 2003). Even in poor, inner-city neighborhoods, many adolescents aspire to professional careers, perhaps in medicine, law, teaching, or computer science (B. L. Wilson & Corbett, 2001). (How equipped they are to *achieve* their aspirations is another matter; for instance, look once again at the interview with an inner-city middle school student on p. 381 of chapter 12.)

Despite high aspirations, many young people, especially those raised in fairly traditional cultures, tend to limit themselves to gender-stereotypical careers (Lippa, 2002; Olneck, 1995; S. M. Taylor, 1994). Even as traditional boundaries between what professions are "appropriate" for men and women are slowly melting away, the majority of college students enrolled in engineering programs continue to be men, and the majority of education majors continue to be women. Certainly gender stereotypes are not the only things affecting learners' career goals; self-efficacy, expectancies, and values are also involved.

Coordinating Multiple Goals

At any one time, people are apt to be working toward several goals. At school, for instance, students may be simultaneously concerned about learning and understanding classroom subject matter, earning the good grades so important for college admissions, and enhancing social relationships with peers.

Addressing multiple goals simultaneously can be a challenging task indeed. People use a variety of strategies to juggle their diverse goals (Covington, 2000; Dodge, Asher, & Parkhurst, 1989; McCaslin & Good, 1996). They may engage in activities that allow them to address more than one goal—for instance, joining a student study group as a way of satisfying both achievement goals and social goals. Alternatively, they may pursue some goals while putting others on the "back burner." For example, they might complete assignments important for class grades while temporarily ignoring more enticing topics. Likewise, as I pursue the goal of completing this book, I leave dirty dishes in the sink, thereby ignoring my lower-priority goal of having a clean house. People may also modify their ideas of what it means to achieve a particular goal. For example, as I have become increasingly busy with my professional writing in recent years (thereby, I hope, satisfying my desire to make the world a better place), my definition of a clean house has deteriorated rapidly from being a spotless, Martha Stewart–like home to one in which family members can eventually find a pathway through the clutter on the floor.

People are most successful when their multiple goals all lead them in the same direction (M. E. Ford, 1992; Linnenbrink, 2005; Wentzel, 1999). Yet in some situations, accomplishing one goal is simply incompatible with accomplishing another. For example, achieving at a high level in the classroom may interfere with one's ability to maintain a friendship with a peer who doesn't value academic achievement (Berndt & Perry, 1990; Dodge et al., 1989; Phelan et al., 1994). On such occasions, people may have little choice but to abandon one goal in favor of another, at least for the time being (Boekaerts et al., 2006; McCaslin & Good, 1996; Shah, 2005). Quite possibly, human beings' evolutionary heritage comes into play here, leading people to forsake the "luxuries" of one's culture (e.g., learning to read) for more basic needs (e.g., maintaining social connectedness with others) (Geary, 1998).

Although we have identified several cognitive factors affecting motivation, we have largely ignored a very important one: the extent to which people make a *connection* between what they do and what happens to them. Certainly people are more eager to pursue an activity when they think their behaviors will help them achieve their goals. But some individuals fail to recognize existing contingencies between the behaviors they exhibit and the consequences that result. To what sources do people attribute the events that occur in their lives? To what things do they give credit when they succeed? What things do they blame when they fail? Our discussion of attributions in the next section will shed light on these questions.

ATTRIBUTIONS

You have undoubtedly gotten As on some of the classroom exams you have taken. On those occasions, why do you think you did so well? Did you study hard? Were the exams easy? Did you luck out and guess right about topics you knew little about? Or is it simply that you are an incredibly intelligent human being?

Now let's consider those exams on which you haven't done as well. On what did you blame your failures? Did you spend too little time studying, or did you perhaps study the wrong things? Were the exams too difficult? Were the questions poorly worded, so that you misinterpreted many that you should have answered correctly? Were you too tired or ill to think clearly? Or do you just not have what it takes?

People's various explanations for success and failure—their beliefs about what causes what—are **attributions.** People are often eager to identify the probable causes of things that happen to them, especially when events are unexpected—for instance, when they get a low score on a classroom assignment after thinking they have done a good job (Stupnisky, Perry, Hall, & van Winkel, 2006;

Weiner, 1986, 2000). Forming attributions is just one of the many ways in which human beings try to make better sense of their world (Tollefson, 2000; Weiner, 2000). In this case, people are trying to identify cause–effect relationships regarding events that affect them personally.

People are apt to explain events in a variety of ways. For instance, school children may attribute their successes and failures in the classroom to such things as effort, ability, luck, task difficulty, health, mood, physical appearance, or teachers' or peers' behaviors (Schunk, 1990). Attributions are as much a function of *perception* as of reality; thus, they are often distorted in line with existing beliefs about oneself and about how the world operates (Dweck, 1978; Dweck & Elliott, 1983; Paris & Byrnes, 1989). For example, your poor performance on exams in years past may very well have been the result of ineffective study strategies; like many students, you may have tried to learn class material in a rote, meaningless fashion (you obviously hadn't read this book yet!). But because you thought of yourself as a smart person and believed that you *had* studied adequately, you perhaps instead attributed your low scores to the exceptional difficulty or "pickiness" of your tests or to arbitrary and irrational evaluations by teachers.

People's attributions appear to vary in terms of three key dimensions: locus, stability, and controllability (Weiner, 1984, 1986, 2000, 2004).[8]

Locus ("place"): Internal versus external   We sometimes attribute the causes of events to *internal* things—that is, to factors within ourselves. Thinking that a good grade is the result of your hard work and believing that a poor grade is the result of your lack of ability are examples of internal attributions. At other times, we attribute events to *external* things—to factors outside of ourselves. Concluding that you received a scholarship because you were lucky and interpreting a friend's scowl as being due to her bad mood (rather than to anything you might have done to deserve the scowl) are examples of external attributions.

Some theorists have referred to the "locus" dimension as *locus of control*. However, Weiner (1986, 2000) has pointed out that *locus* and *control* are probably two distinctly different aspects of an attribution. For instance, one's singing ability may be internal but in many people's eyes is not entirely controllable.

Temporal stability: Stable versus unstable   Sometimes we think that events are a result of *stable* factors—things that probably won't change much in the near future. For example, if you believe that you do well in school because of inherited ability or that you have trouble making friends because you have a funny-looking nose, then you're attributing events to stable, relatively unchangeable causes. But sometimes we instead believe that events are the result of *unstable* factors—to things that can change from one time to the next. Thinking that winning a tennis game was simply a fluke and believing you got a bad test grade because your tennis game left you too exhausted to do well on the test are examples of attributions involving unstable factors.

Controllability: Controllable versus uncontrollable   On some occasions we attribute events to *controllable* factors—to things we (or perhaps someone else) can influence and change. For example, if you believe that a classmate invited you to lunch because you always smile and say nice things to her, and if you think you probably failed a test simply because you didn't study the

---

[8]In earlier writings, Weiner suggested two additional dimensions: *cross-situational generality* (global versus specific) and *intentionality* (intentional versus intentional). More recently, however, he has focused primarily on locus, stability, and controllability (Weiner, 2000, 2004).

right things, then you are attributing these events to controllable factors. On other occasions, we attribute events to *uncontrollable* factors—to things over which neither we nor others have influence. For example, if you think that you were chosen for a title role in *Romeo and Juliet* because you have the "right face" for the part, or that you played a lousy game of basketball because you had a mild case of the flu, then you are attributing these events to uncontrollable factors.

Attribution theory's notion of controllability overlaps with, yet is also somewhat different from, the concept of *self-determination* (Deci & Ryan, 1987). Attribution to controllable factors involves a belief that we can influence and alter environmental events and circumstances. In contrast, self-determination involves a belief that we can autonomously choose our behaviors and, ultimately, our fate. In other words, controllable attributions reflect control of one's *environment,* whereas self-determination reflects long-term control of one's *actions.*

The controllability dimension possibly has two subcomponents (Weisz & Cameron, 1985). First, one must believe that there is a *contingency* between the behavior and the outcome—in other words, that a particular behavior can cause a certain event to occur. Second, one must have a sense of *competence* (i.e., self-efficacy) that one is actually capable of performing the necessary behavior. A person is apt to believe that an event is uncontrollable if either one of these components is missing. For example, a student may know that good grades will result from making correct responses in class but may not believe that he or she has the ability to make those responses; in this situation there is a sense of contingency but no sense of competence (Weisz, 1986). As another example, a person from a minority group may have high self-efficacy for achieving a particular goal yet feel that the racial prejudice and discrimination of others will, nevertheless, make success impossible; in this case there is a sense of competence but no sense of contingency (Pintrich & Schunk, 2002; Sue & Chin, 1983).

We can analyze virtually any attribution in terms of the three dimensions just described. For example, viewing success on a task as being the result of inherited ability is an internal, stable, and uncontrollable attribution. Believing failure on a task was a case of bad luck is an external, unstable, and uncontrollable attribution. Table 16.2 analyzes eight common attributions in terms of the three dimensions.

As you look at Table 16.2, you might think to yourself that "ability can change with practice, so is unstable and controllable" or that "teachers' attitudes toward students often depend on how students behave in the classroom, so are really the result of internal, unstable, and student-controllable factors." Perhaps you are right, but keep in mind that people's *beliefs* about the locus, stability, and controllability of their attributions, not the reality of the situation, are what affect future behavior (Dweck & Leggett, 1988; Weiner, 1994).

What about *effort* (trying or not trying hard) and *luck* (either good or bad)? Are these temporary states of affairs, or are they more enduring qualities that tend to bless or haunt us time after time? People occasionally think of effort and luck as being relatively stable, enduring characteristics; for instance, they may believe that people are consistently lucky or unlucky (Weiner, 1986). To be consistent with much of the literature in attribution theory, however, in our discussions here we will treat both effort and luck as unstable, temporary factors.

And what about *intelligence?* Whether intelligence is actually a stable or unstable characteristic is a matter of considerable controversy among psychologists, and nonpsychologists—adults and children like—are similarly divided on the matter. Some people have an **entity view:** They believe that intelligence is a "thing" that is fairly permanent and unchangeable. Others have an **incremental view:** They believe that intelligence can and does improve with effort and practice

Table 16.2
Analyzing various attributions in terms of the three dimensions.

Success or Failure Attributed to	Locus	Stability	Controllability
Inherited ability	Internal	Stable	Uncontrollable
Personality	Internal	Stable	Uncontrollable
Effort	Internal	Unstable	Controllable
Health	Internal	Unstable	Uncontrollable
Energy level	Internal	Unstable	Uncontrollable
Task difficulty	External	Stable	Uncontrollable for oneself; possibly controllable for a teacher
Teacher's attitudes	External	Stable	Uncontrollable for oneself; controllable for the teacher
Luck or chance	External	Unstable	Uncontrollable

(Dweck, 2000; Dweck & Leggett, 1988; Weiner, 1994).[9] Because I cannot offer a definitive answer about the nature of intelligence, I have omitted it from Table 16.2; I have instead included "inherited" ability, which is presumably stable and uncontrollable.

Effects of Attributions

Attributions appear to have a significant influence on many aspects of people's functioning, including their performance and achievement in classroom settings (Davis, Ajzen, Saunders, & Williams, 2002; Dweck et al., 2004; Graham, 1994; Weiner, 1984, 1986, 2000). Attributions have fairly predictable effects on people's emotional responses, impacts of reinforcement and punishment, self-efficacy and expectancies, effort and persistence, learning strategies, and future choices and goals. We'll consider each of these in turn.

Emotional responses to events   People are, of course, happy when they succeed. But do they also feel *proud* of their accomplishments? When they believe that their successes are the result of another person's actions or some other outside force, they are apt to feel grateful rather than proud.[10] Individuals feel pride and satisfaction about their successes only when they attribute the successes to internal causes—that is, to things for which they themselves are responsible (Hareli & Weiner, 2002; Weiner, Russell, & Lerman, 1978, 1979).

---

[9]Entity versus incremental views of intelligence are examples of *epistemological beliefs*—in particular, beliefs about the nature of learning ability (see chapter 12).

[10]One recent study suggests that when college students believe that their teachers (rather than themselves) have control over the grades they receive, some feel *entitled* to good grades rather than grateful for them (Achacoso, Summers, & Schallert, 2002).

Along a similar vein, people usually feel a certain amount of sadness after a failure. When they believe that failure is the result of external causes—to events and people outside of themselves—they are apt to feel angry and resentful. When they instead believe that their failure is caused by their own lack of ability or effort, they are apt to feel guilty or ashamed (Eccles & Wigfield, 1985; Hareli & Weiner, 2002; Neumann, 2000; Weiner et al., 1978, 1979). People who attribute failure to internal causes, and especially to their lack of ability, often have lower self-esteem as a result (Covington, Spratt, & Omelich, 1980). If they think of intelligence as a fairly permanent entity over which they have no control, consistent failure may lead to long-term depression (Dweck, 2000).

Impacts of reinforcement and punishment   How people interpret the reinforcements and punishments they experience—for example, whether they think an event is the result of something that they themselves have done or instead the result of something that has been done *to* them—influences the long-term effects that reinforcement and punishment are likely to have. Consistent with our discussion of social cognitive theory in chapter 6, reinforcement and punishment can be effective only when people realize that *their own behavior*—something over which they have control—has been the cause of such consequences (Bandura, 1986).

Self-efficacy and expectancies   When people attribute their successes and failures to stable factors, they will expect their future performance in a given domain to be similar to their current performance. In this situation, success leads to an anticipation of future success, and failure breeds an expectation of more failure to come. In contrast, when people attribute their successes and failures to *un*stable factors—for example, to effort, strategies, or luck—then their current success rate will have less influence on their expectation for future success (Dweck, 1978; Fennema, 1987; Hong, Chiu, & Dweck, 1995; Weiner, 1986, 2000).

To be productively optimistic about their future performance—that is, to have high self-efficacy and expectancies for future success, and also to *achieve* that success—learners should attribute their past successes partly to stable, dependable factors such as natural talent and a consistently supportive environment (thus, they will know that success wasn't a fluke) and partly to unstable but controllable factors such as effort and strategies (thus, they will continue to work hard). At the same time, they should attribute their past failures primarily to unstable factors they can control and change (Dweck, 2000; Eccles [Parsons], 1983; Murray & Jackson, 1982/1983; Pomerantz & Saxon, 2001; Weiner, 1984).

With the preceding points in mind, let's return to the phenomenon of *stereotype threat*, which I described in chapter 15. If we bring attributions into the mix, we can reasonably expect that members of stereotypically low-achieving groups (e.g., females, members of certain minority groups) will be most likely to have low self-efficacy about tests of ability—and so more likely to experience anxiety that adversely affects their test scores—if they have an entity view of intelligence. If they believe that the ability being assessed is a relatively permanent thing beyond their control, their anxiety is apt to go up and so their test scores will go down. If, instead, they realize that ability can and does change with effort, practice, and appropriate strategies—and so is unrelated to their group membership—they are less likely to become the victims of stereotype threat (Dweck, 2000; Dweck et al., 2004).

Effort and persistence   When people believe that their failures are due to their own lack of effort—that they *do* have the ability to succeed if they try hard enough—they are likely to exert more effort in future situations and to persist in the face of difficulty. When they instead attribute failure to a lack of innate ability (they couldn't do it even if they tried), they give up easily and sometimes cannot even perform tasks they have previously done successfully (Brophy, 1986; Dweck, 1978; Eccles [Parsons], 1983; Feather, 1982; Weiner, 1984). Students with a history of academic failure are especially likely to attribute their class-room difficulties to low ability, and they often stop trying as a result (Pressley, Borkowski, & Schneider, 1987).

Attributions and effort sometimes interact in unproductive ways. Let's once again focus in on people with an entity view of intelligence. "Entity" individuals tend to believe that ability and effort are inversely related: Success with little effort reflects high ability, and success that comes only with a great deal of effort is a sign of low ability (Barker & Graham, 1987; Covington & Omelich, 1979; Dweck & Elliott, 1983; Eccles [Parsons], 1983; Graham, 1990). Such beliefs are especially prevalent when people have performance goals rather than mastery goals (see Table 16.1). For such individuals, effort is probably a double-edged sword that can cause harm either way it swings (Covington & Omelich, 1979; Covington et al., 1980; Eccles & Wigfield, 1985). In particular, those who perceive themselves as having low ability are in a no-win situation. If they don't try hard, failure is inevitable. If they *do* try hard and fail anyway, they look "stupid," at least in their own eyes. Thus, many of them don't try very hard (one form of *self-handicapping*), perhaps as a way of saving face and hiding their self-perceived low ability (Covington & Beery, 1976; Dweck, 1986; Eccles & Wigfield, 1985; Jagacinski & Nicholls, 1990; Murray & Jackson, 1982/1983). They may also decide that the activity isn't worth doing—in other words, they attach little value to it (Covington & Beery, 1976; Eccles & Wigfield, 1985).

In general, people are most likely to exert effort and persist after a failure when they attribute the failure to internal, unstable, and controllable variables (Clifford, 1984; Curtis & Graham, 1991; Dweck, 2000; Pressley, Borkowski, & Schneider, 1987). Blaming lack of effort alone can backfire, however. Individuals who try hard and still fail are likely to reach the conclusion that they have low ability—that they simply don't have what it takes. Therefore, it is more beneficial for people to attribute failure to strategies as well—to believe that they could succeed if they did things *differently* (Curtis & Graham, 1991; Pressley, Borkowski, & Schneider, 1987). Such attri-butions often characterize good students, who know that they need not only to work hard but also to work strategically (Brophy, 1987; Pressley, Borkowski, & Schneider, 1987; Weinstein, Hagen, & Meyer, 1991).

Learning strategies   People's attributions and resulting expectations for future performance clearly affect the cognitive strategies they apply to learning tasks. Students who expect to succeed in the classroom and believe that academic success is a result of their own doing are more likely to apply effective study strategies, especially when trained in their use, and they are more likely to approach problem-solving tasks in a logical, systematic, and meaningful fashion (Dweck et al., 2004; Palmer & Goetz, 1988; Pressley, Borkowski, & Schneider, 1987; Tyler, 1958). These stu-dents are also more likely to be self-regulated learners and to seek help when they need it (more on help seeking later in the chapter). In contrast, students who expect failure and believe that their academic performance is largely out of their hands often reject effective learning and problem-solving strategies in favor of rote-learning approaches.

Future choices and goals   As you might expect, individuals whose attributions lead them to expect success in a particular subject area are more likely to pursue that area—for instance, by enrolling in more courses in the same discipline (Dweck, 1986; Stipek & Gralinski, 1990; Weiner, 1986). Individuals who believe their chances for future success in an activity are slim will avoid the activity whenever possible. And when learners don't continue to pursue an activity, they can't possibly get better at it.

People's attributions also affect the achievement goals they set for themselves. Once again, their beliefs about intelligence—whether it is a relatively permanent entity or, alternatively, an ability that can change incrementally over time—come into play (Dweck, 2000; Dweck et al., 2004). In particular, if people believe that ability is something that they either have or don't have (rather than something they can increase with hard work), they are apt to set performance goals and assess their "inborn" talent by comparing themselves with others. In contrast, people who subscribe to an incremental view are apt to set mastery goals and assess their ability by monitoring their progress over time. For instance, in a series of studies conducted by Dweck and her associates (described by Dweck, 2000), middle school students were told that they could choose one of three tasks, which were described as follows:

1. One that's "easy enough so you won't make mistakes"
2. One that's "like something you're good at but hard enough to show you're smart"
3. One that's "hard, new and different—you might get confused and make mistakes, but you might learn something new and useful" (Dweck, 2000, p. 21)

Students with entity views were more likely to choose either Task 1 (consistent with a performance-avoidance goal) or Task 2 (consistent with a performance-approach goal). In contrast, students with incremental views more often chose Task 3 (consistent with a mastery goal).

Factors Influencing the Nature of Attributions

Why do different people attribute the same events to different causes? For instance, why does one person believe that a failure is merely a temporary setback due to an inappropriate strategy, while another attributes the same failure to low ability, and still another believes it to be the result of someone else's capricious and unpredictable actions? We now look at variables related to the acquisition of different attributions.

Age

Preschoolers don't have a clear understanding of how various possible causes—effort, ability, luck, task difficulty, and so on—might play a role in their successes and failures (Eccles et al., 1998; Heyman, Gee, & Giles, 2003; Nicholls, 1990). But as children get older, they become increasingly able to distinguish among these factors. For instance, at about age 6, they begin to recognize that effort and ability are separate qualities that are positively correlated: People who try hardest have the greatest ability, and effort is the primary determiner of success (Nicholls, 1990). Thus, children in the early elementary grades tend to believe they have the ability to do well in school if they expend a reasonable amount of effort (Dweck & Elliott, 1983; Lockhart, Chang, & Story, 2002; Stipek & Gralinski, 1990).

Sometime around age 9, they begin to understand that effort and ability often compensate for one another and that people with less ability may have to exert greater effort to achieve the same outcome as their more able peers (Nicholls, 1990). By age 13 or so, they make a clear distinction between effort and ability: They realize that people differ both in their inherent ability to perform a task and in the amount of effort they exert on a task. At this point, they also know that ability and effort can compensate for each other but that a lack of ability sometimes precludes success no matter *how* much effort a person puts forth (Nicholls, 1990). With age, then, learners increasingly acquire an entity view of intelligence (Dweck, 1999). If they are usually successful at classroom tasks, they will have high self-efficacy about such tasks. If failures are frequent, their self-efficacy may plummet (Dweck, 1986; Eccles [Parsons], 1983; Schunk, 1990; E. A. Skinner, 1995).

This state of affairs can lead to a **self-fulfilling prophecy**—a situation in which a person's expectations about future events create conditions through which those expectations become reality. (We'll call it *Self-Fulfilling Prophecy #1* to distinguish it from a second phenomenon we'll examine later.) As we discovered in chapter 6, people with low self-efficacy choose less challenging tasks and give up more easily than their more self-confident peers. And as a result, they will have fewer opportunities to discover that success *can* come with effort. Further compounding the problem is the fact that some children with low self-efficacy attribute the successes they do achieve to external factors and their failures to internal factors, thereby giving themselves little credit for the things they do well and blaming themselves for the things they do poorly (Ickes & Layden, 1978).

Situational Cues

Characteristics specific to the situation at hand—especially those that are easily noticed—can influence the attributions people make (Lassiter, 2002; Schunk, 1990; Weiner, 1984). Features of the task being performed are one influential characteristic; for example, complex math problems (e.g., those that include more numbers) are perceived as being more difficult, and so failure to solve them can readily be attributed to task difficulty rather than to internal causes (Schunk, 1990). The performance of peers provides another cue; for example, a failure is apt to be attributed to task difficulty if everyone else is failing, whereas it is more likely to be attributed to an internal source (such as lack of ability) if others are succeeding (Schunk, 1990; Weiner, 1984).

Patterns of Past Successes and Failures

The attributions that people form result partly from their previous success and failure experiences in a particular activity or domain (Klein, 1990; Paris & Byrnes, 1989; Pressley, Borkowski, & Schneider, 1987; Schunk, 1990; Stipek, 1993). Those who have previously tried and succeeded are more likely to believe that success is the result of internal factors, such as effort or high ability. Those who have tried and failed, or who have had an inconsistent pattern of successes and failures, are likely to believe that success is due to something beyond their control—perhaps to an ability they don't possess or to such external factors as a tough break or poor instruction.

People's *perceptions* of the pattern make a difference as well. For example, children are more likely to attribute events to internal, controllable causes when adults reinforce their successes but don't punish their failures. Conversely, children are more likely to make external attributions when adults punish failures and ignore successes (Katkovsky, Crandall, & Good, 1967). To some degree, extrinsic consequences for successes and failures may call children's attention to—and so help them remember—what they have or have not been able to do. But in addition, it seems likely that children are more willing to accept responsibility for their failures if others don't made a big deal of them and so don't call children's general competence into question.

When we consider classroom learning, metacognition also comes into play. In chapter 12, we discovered that students often think they have learned things they actually have *not* learned; in other words, they have an *illusion of knowing*. When these students consistently do poorly on exams, they cannot attribute their performance to internal factors; after all, they studied hard and so "know" the material. Instead, they are likely to attribute poor performance to such external factors as bad luck, exam difficulty, or teacher capriciousness (Horgan, 1990).

Verbal and Nonverbal Messages from Others

Just as people form attributions regarding the causes of their own performance, so, too, do they form attributions for *other people's* performance.[11] For instance, I recall a conversation I had not too long ago with a well-educated man whose training was in mechanical engineering rather than psychology or education. We were discussing the fact that, on average, children in inner-city schools achieve at lower levels than children in suburban schools. Knowing that I was an educational psychologist, the man asked me why I thought there was such a difference in performance levels. I said that there were apt to be a number of reasons, probably including smaller school budgets, larger class sizes, more obligations and fewer resources at home, poor nutrition and health care, fear for personal safety, a higher proportion of children with learning disabilities and other special needs, and so on. The man seemed quite surprised. "I always thought the kids just weren't *motivated*," he said. Notice how my attributions for the low achievement were largely external ones, whereas his sole attribution—students' motivation—was strictly internal.

The three dimensions described earlier—locus, stability, and controllability—are as relevant to people's attributions for others as they are to their self-attributions. Probably the most important one from an interpersonal standpoint is *controllability* (Weiner, 2000). The reasons I offered for the low achievement of many inner-city students—fewer resources, poor nutrition, a dangerous environment, and so on—all involved things beyond the students' control. In contrast, my conversational partner believed that the students performed poorly only because they didn't *want* to do well; in other words, high achievement was well within their grasp if they simply flipped that mythical motivation on-off switch.

Other people—parents, teachers, peers, and so on—communicate their attributions for learners' successes and failures in a variety of ways. In some cases, they communicate attributions verbally and explicitly (Henderlong & Lepper, 2000; Mueller & Dweck, 1998). For example, consider the things a teacher might say about a student's success:

- "That's wonderful. Your hard work has really paid off, hasn't it?"
- "You've done very well. It's clear that you really know how to study."
- "You did it! You're so smart!"
- "Terrific! This is certainly your lucky day!"

---

[11]A lengthy discussion of people's attributions for *others'* successes and failures was included in the fourth edition of this book. I've shortened the discussion considerably in this edition. If you'd like to learn more about both the nature and origins of people's attributions for their fellow human beings, look for the reading "Interpersonal Attributions" on the book's Companion Website at www.prenhall.com/ormrod.

Also consider the statements a teacher might make about a student's failure:

- "Why don't you practice a little more and then try again?"
- "Let's see whether we can come up with some study strategies that might work better for you."
- "Hmmm, maybe this just isn't something you're good at. Perhaps we should try a different activity."
- "Maybe you're just having a bad day."

All of these are well-intended comments, presumably designed to make a student feel good. But notice the different attributions they imply. In some cases success or failure is attributed to controllable (and therefore changeable) behaviors—that is, to hard work or lack of practice or to the use of effective or ineffective study strategies. But in other cases success or failure is attributed to uncontrollable ability—that is, to being smart or not "good at" something. And in still other cases an outcome is attributed to external, uncontrollable causes—that is, to a lucky break or a bad day.

People also communicate their attributions—and indirectly, their beliefs about a learner's ability level—through the emotions they convey and the extent to which they praise or criticize performance (Graham, 1990, 1991, 1997; Hareli & Weiner, 2002; C. Reyna & Weiner, 2001; Weiner, 2000). Frequent praise is often a message that learners' successes are the result of their efforts. However, by praising a learner for *easy* tasks, people may simultaneously convey the message that success wasn't expected—in other words, that a learner has low ability. Here, then, we see a perspective very different from that of behaviorism. Behaviorists propose that, as reinforcement, praise should increase the behavior it follows. From the standpoint of attribution theory, however, praise can be counterproductive for easy tasks. If it communicates low ability, learners may be unwilling to exert much effort on later tasks. Praise for effort is likely to be effective only when learners *have* exerted the effort.

Reactions to a learner's failures communicate attributions as well. When people criticize, express anger about, and perhaps punish a learner's poor performance, they convey the message that the learner has sufficient ability to master the task and simply isn't trying hard enough. But when people express pity or sympathy for the same performance, they communicate their belief that the learner's uncontrollable low ability is the reason for the failure.

Yet another way in which adults communicate their attributions is through the amount and kinds of help they provide. For example, teacher assistance, though often a valuable source of scaffolding on difficult tasks, may be counterproductive if students don't really need it. When students struggle temporarily with a task, unsolicited help from their teacher may communicate the message that they have low ability and little control over their own successes and failures. In contrast, allowing students to struggle on their own for a reasonable amount of time (not to the point of counterproductive frustration, of course) conveys the belief that students do have the ability to succeed on their own (Graham, 1990, 1997; Graham & Barker, 1990; Stipek, 1996; Weiner, 1984).

Research indicates that children's attributions for their performance are often similar to the attributions that adults assign to that performance (Dweck, Davidson, Nelson, & Enna, 1978; Eccles et al., 1998; Lueptow, 1984; Parsons, Adler, & Kaczala, 1982; Schunk, 1982). For instance, when parents and teachers communicate their belief that children are incapable of mastering a task, children are likely to attribute their failures to low ability and may therefore conclude that there is little to be gained by trying harder (Butler, 1994; Weiner, 2000; Yee & Eccles, 1988).

Culture

People's cultural backgrounds influence their attributions as well, particularly with respect to the controllability dimension. For example, members of some religious groups may place their fates in the hands of God, *karma,* or some other metaphysical force (Losh, 2003; also see the discussion of *worldviews* in chapter 9). As another example, students from Asian backgrounds are more likely to attribute classroom success and failure to unstable factors—effort in the case of academic achievement, and temporary situational factors in the case of appropriate or inappropriate behaviors—than students brought up in mainstream Western culture (Li & Fischer, 2004; Lillard, 1997; Steinberg, 1996; Weiner, 2004).[12] In contrast to many Western students, who are apt to think that a preexisting "intelligence" affects one's ability to learn, many Asian students reverse the cause and effect: Learning leads to intelligence (Li, 2003).

Some studies indicate a greater tendency for African American students—even those with high self-efficacy for academic subject matter—to believe they have little control over whether they achieve academic success (Graham, 1989; Holliday, 1985; Weiner, 2004). Racial prejudice may contribute to such an attribution: Some students may begin to believe that, because of the color of their skin, they have little chance of success no matter what they do (Sue & Chin, 1983; van Laar, 2000; Weiner, 2004).

Gender

Gender differences in attributions sometimes appear in research studies (Carr & Jessup, 1997; Deaux, 1984; Durkin, 1987; Dweck, 1978; Fennema, 1987; Huston, 1983; Stipek & Gralinski, 1990). In these instances, males are more likely to attribute their successes to ability and their failures to lack of effort, thus assuming the attitude that *I know I can do this because I have the ability.* Females show the reverse pattern: They attribute their successes to effort and their failures to lack of ability, believing that *I don't know if I can keep on doing it, because I'm not very good at this type of thing.* Such differences, which can appear even when boys' and girls' previous levels of achievement are equivalent, are most frequently observed in stereotypically male domains such as mathematics and sports (Eccles & Jacobs, 1986; Fennema, 1987; Stipek, 1984; Vermeer, Boekaerts, & Seegers, 2000). Typically they reflect general beliefs in society at large about what males and females are usually "good at" (Eccles et al., 1993; Herbert, Stipek, & Miles, 2003) and so may be the result of messages others have consistently communicated.

Self-Protective Bias

As a general rule, people tend to form attributions that maintain or enhance their sense of self-worth. For instance, we tend to attribute our successes to internal causes (e.g., to high ability or hard work) and our failures to external causes (e.g., to bad luck or another person's thoughtless or irresponsible behavior) (Igoe & Sullivan, 1991; Marsh, 1990; Weiner, 1992;

---

[12]Such attributions are often, but not always, a benefit. For instance, if students attribute their failures as well as their successes to effort, and if they place high priority on bringing honor to their families (as is true for many Asian students), then consistent failure can lead to feelings of humiliation and depression (Dweck, 2000).

Weisz & Cameron, 1985; Whitley & Frieze, 1985). By patting ourselves on the back for the things we do well and putting the blame elsewhere for poor performance, we are able to maintain positive self-perceptions (Katkovsky et al., 1967; Paris & Byrnes, 1989). This self-protective bias is not always in our best interest, however: If we inaccurately attribute our failures to factors outside of ourselves, we are unlikely to change our behavior in ways that will lead to greater success (Seligman, 1991; Zimmerman, 2004).

Curiously, people may think they're in control even in situations where they are not, and this belief can enhance their optimism on future occasions (S. C. Thompson, 1999). For instance, we might believe we have a better chance of winning the lottery if we pick the numbers ourselves rather than letting the computer pick them for us. In fact, only one behavior affects our chances of winning the lottery: actually buying a ticket. Every possible sequence of numbers has an equal chance of being the winning combination, regardless of how the numbers were selected.

Image Management

The attributions that individuals communicate to others do not always reflect their true beliefs about the sources of their successes and failures. As children get older, they discover that different kinds of attributions elicit different kinds of reactions from other people (Hareli & Weiner, 2002; Juvonen, 2000). To maintain positive interpersonal relationships (and thereby satisfy their need for relatedness), they begin to modify their attributions for the particular audience at hand. This phenomenon is sometimes called *face-saving,* but I suggest using the broader term **image management.**

Teachers, parents, and other adults are often sympathetic and forgiving when children fail because of something beyond their control (illness, lack of ability, etc.) but frequently get angry when children fail simply because they didn't try very hard. By the time children reach fourth grade, most of them are aware of this fact and so may verbalize attributions that are likely to elicit favorable reactions (Juvonen, 1996, 2000; Weiner, 1995). To illustrate, a student who knows very well that she did poorly on an assignment because she didn't put forth her best effort may distort the truth, telling her teacher that she "can't seem to make sense of this stuff" or "wasn't feeling well."

Children become equally adept at tailoring their attributions for the ears of their peers. Generally speaking, fourth graders believe that their peers value diligence and hard work, and so they are likely to tell their classmates that they did well on an assignment because they worked hard. By eighth grade, however, many students believe that their peers will disapprove of those who exert much effort on academic tasks, and so they often prefer to convey the impression that they *aren't* working very hard—for instance, that they "didn't study very much" for an important exam or "just lucked out" when they have performed at a high level (Howie, 2002; Juvonen, 1996, 2000).

For a variety of reasons, then, different people may interpret the same events in very different ways. Over time, learners gradually develop predictable patterns of attributions and expectations for their future performance. Some remain optimistic, confident that they can master new tasks and succeed in a variety of endeavors. But others, either unsure of their own chances for success or else convinced that they *cannot* succeed, display a growing sense of futility. Theorists have characterized this difference among people as being a difference in *explanatory style.*

Explanatory Style: Mastery Orientation Versus Learned Helplessness

A person's **explanatory style**[13] is the general way in which the person interprets daily events and consequences. Some people typically attribute their accomplishments to their own abilities and efforts; they have an I-can-do-it attitude known as a **mastery orientation.** Other people attribute successes to outside and uncontrollable factors and believe that their failures reflect a relatively permanent lack of ability; they have an I-can't-do-it-even-if-I-try attitude known as **learned helplessness** (Dweck, 2000; Eccles & Wigfield, 1985; Mikulincer, 1994; C. Peterson, Maier, & Seligman, 1993). You should think of this distinction as a continuum rather than a complete dichotomy. You might also look at it as a difference between *optimists* and *pessimists* (C. Peterson, 1990; Seligman, 1991).

As an illustration, consider these two boys, keeping in mind that both boys have the same ability level:

- Jerry is an enthusiastic, energetic learner. He enjoys working hard at school activities and takes obvious pleasure in doing well. He is always looking for a challenge and especially likes to solve the brainteaser problems that his teacher assigns as extra-credit work each day. He can't always solve the problems, but he takes failure in stride and is eager for more problems the following day.
- Jason is an anxious, fidgety student. He doesn't seem to have much confidence in his ability to accomplish school tasks successfully. In fact, he is always underestimating what he can do; even when he has succeeded, he doubts that he can do it again. He seems to prefer filling out worksheets that help him practice skills he's already mastered rather than attempting new tasks and problems. As for those daily brainteasers, he sometimes takes a stab at them, but he gives up quickly if the answer isn't obvious.

Jerry exhibits a mastery orientation: He clearly has his life (and his attributions) under control, and he is optimistic about his future performance. In contrast, Jason displays learned helplessness: He believes that challenging tasks are out of his reach and beyond his control, and he expects failure rather than success.

Researchers have identified a number of ways in which people with a mastery orientation differ from those with learned helplessness. In an academic context, those with a mastery orientation tend to perform better on classroom tasks than we would predict from their aptitude test scores and previous grade point averages (Seligman, 1991). In an athletic context, optimists bounce back from a lost game more readily, and overcome injuries more quickly, than do equally capable but more pessimistic athletes (C. Peterson, 1990). In general, people with a mastery orientation behave in ways that lead to higher achievement over the long run: They set ambitious goals, seek challenging situations, and persist in the face of failure. People with learned helplessness behave very differently: Because they underestimate their own ability, they set performance goals they can easily accomplish, avoid the challenges likely to maximize their learning and growth, and respond to failure in counterproductive ways (e.g., giving up quickly) that almost guarantee future failure (Dweck, 2000; Graham, 1989; C. Peterson, 1990; Seligman, 1991).

---

[13]You may also see the term *attributional style*.

They are also hampered by anxiety-related thoughts, which leave limited working memory capacity for concentrating on the task at hand (Mikulincer, 1994).

Extreme cases of learned helplessness typically manifest themselves in three ways (Maier & Seligman, 1976). First, there is a *motivational* effect: The individual is slow to exhibit responses that will yield desirable outcomes or enable escape from aversive situations. Second is a *cognitive* effect: The individual has difficulty learning new behaviors that would improve environmental circumstances. The third effect is an *emotional* one: The individual tends to be passive, withdrawn, anxious, and depressed.

Preschoolers occasionally show signs of learned helplessness about a particular task if they consistently encounter failure when attempting it (Burhans & Dweck, 1995). By age 5 or 6, some children begin to show a consistent tendency either to persist at a task and express confidence that they can master it, on the one hand, or to abandon a task quickly and say they don't have the ability to do it, on the other (Ziegert, Kistner, Castro, & Robertson, 2001). As a general rule, however, children younger than 8 rarely exhibit extreme forms of learned helplessness, perhaps because they still believe that success is largely the result of their own efforts (Eccles et al., 1998; Paris & Cunningham, 1996). By early adolescence, feelings of helplessness are more common: Some middle schoolers believe they cannot control the things that happen to them and are at a loss for strategies about how to avert future failures (Paris & Cunningham, 1996; C. Peterson et al., 1993). By the time people reach adulthood, learned helplessness often manifests itself in chronic depression (Seligman, 1975, 1991).

Roots of Learned Helplessness

I first described Seligman and Maier's (1967) classic study of learned helplessness in chapter 1, but a memory refresher and additional details are probably in order. In the first phase of the experiment, dogs received numerous painful and unpredictable shocks. Some dogs were able to escape the shocks by pushing a panel in the cage, whereas other dogs could not escape the shocks regardless of what they did. The following day, each dog was placed in a box that was divided into two compartments by a barrier. While in this box, the dog was presented with a series of tone-shock combinations, with a tone always preceding a shock; the dog could avoid the shock by jumping over the barrier into the other compartment as soon as it heard the tone. Dogs that had been able to escape the shocks on the first day quickly learned to avoid the shocks on the second day. In contrast, dogs that had previously been unable to escape displayed learned helplessness: They made few attempts to escape, instead simply sitting still and whining as the shocks were presented. Seligman and Maier's study suggests that when aversive events occur repeatedly, and when an organism cannot avoid, escape from, or otherwise terminate them, the organism will eventually give up and passively accept them.

People, too, begin to exhibit symptoms of learned helplessness when they cannot control the occurrence of aversive events (Hiroto, 1974; Hiroto & Seligman, 1975; C. Peterson et al., 1993). Such may be the case for school children who consistently have difficulty completing academic tasks (Dweck, 1986; Holliday, 1985; Jacobsen, Lowery, & DuCette, 1986; Stipek & Kowalski, 1989). As an example, consider the child with a learning disability. Often remaining unidentified as a student with special educational needs, the child may encounter repeated failure in academic work, despite reasonable efforts to succeed, and so may eventually stop trying. I have also seen the learned helplessness phenomenon in presumably nondisabled students when I talk with them about certain subject areas. Many students, for example, attribute their mathematics anxiety to the fact that, as elementary school students, they could not comprehend how to solve certain problems no matter what they did or how hard they tried. Others show learned helplessness in the area of spelling: Even when they know they have spelled a word incorrectly, they do not try to correct the spelling, excusing their behavior by such statements as "I'm just a bad speller" or "I never could spell very well" (Ormrod & Wagner, 1987).

How adults behave in their interactions with children can contribute to feelings of helplessness as well. For instance, mothers of children with early signs of learned helplessness are less likely to provide assistance when their children tackle challenging tasks, and they're *more* likely to suggest giving up in the face of difficulty, than mothers of mastery-oriented children (Hokoda & Fincham, 1995). Giving children negative feedback without also providing suggestions about how to improve—especially when the feedback calls into question children's overall competence and worth—can also instill helplessness (Dweck, 2000; Kamins & Dweck, 1999). Curiously, *praise for successes* can eventually lead to helplessness if the praise focuses on children's natural, inherited talents (thus fostering an entity view of ability) and the children then experience subsequent failures in the same domain (Dweck, 2000; Kamins & Dweck, 1999).

Helplessness can even develop when people observe *other* individuals having little control over their lives (Brown & Inouye, 1978; C. Peterson et al., 1993). In some cases, entire groups can begin to feel helpless when group members are asked to work together on tasks that, despite their best efforts, they cannot accomplish (Simkin, Lederer, & Seligman, 1983). When people have a history of experiences in which they *have* had control of their successes and failures, however, they are less likely to succumb to learned helplessness in the face of temporarily uncontrollable events (C. Peterson et al., 1993). (This last point should remind you of our discussion of *resilient self-efficacy* in chapter 6.)

Under some circumstances, learned helplessness may actually be a roundabout way in which people actually try to *maintain* a sense of control in chronically adverse conditions (Hall, Hladkyj, Ruthig, Pekrun, & Perry, 2002; Hall, Hladkyj, Taylor, & Perry, 2000; Rothbaum, Weisz, & Snyder, 1982). Because they are unable to change their environment, they instead accept their circumstances, recognize their limitations, acknowledge that factors beyond themselves (fate, God, etc.) are ultimately in charge, and try to identify the silver lining in their unhappy situation.

One of the outcomes of a mastery orientation, and of controllable attributions more generally, is an increased tendency to self-regulate one's own learning. In fact, truly effective learners regulate not only their approach to a learning task but also their motivation and affect. We now look at the interplay among motivation, affect, and self-regulation.

MOTIVATION, AFFECT, AND SELF-REGULATION

In chapter 15, we discovered how motivation and affect are interrelated with each other and with learning and cognition. Motivation and affect also influence, and are influenced by, self-regulation. Furthermore, the development of self-regulation often includes *internalizing* the motives, values, and goals of others.

How Motivation and Affect Influence Self-Regulation

As we discovered at the beginning of chapter 15, motivated individuals—and especially *intrinsically* motivated individuals—are more likely to initiate and persist at activities, more likely to be cognitively engaged in what they are doing, and more likely to use effective strategies in a learning task. Thus, motivation—and again, especially intrinsic motivation—sets the stage for self-regulation.

People are more likely to be self-regulated learners when they feel confident that they can be successful at a learning task and when they believe they can control the direction their lives are taking. In other words, self-regulated learners have a sense of both competence (self-efficacy) and self-determination (Corno & Rohrkemper, 1985; McCombs, 1996; Paris & Turner, 1994; Schunk, 1995; Zimmerman & Risemberg, 1997). In addition, self-regulated learners tend to set mastery goals for their performance and to attribute successful outcomes to things they themselves have done (e.g., work hard and use good strategies) (R. Ames, 1983; Blazevski, McEvoy, & Pintrich, 2003; Zimmerman, 1998).

One aspect of self-regulated learning in which motivation and affect figure prominently is *help-seeking* behavior. Why do some students willingly seek others' assistance when they need it, whereas other struggling students consistently ignore opportunities and offers for assistance? Researchers have found that students are *less* likely to seek help (either from teachers or from peers) when they

- Perceive requests for help as threatening their sense of competence and self-worth
- Believe that asking for help will undermine their sense of autonomy and self-determination (in some instances, they may also think they can learn more if they persist on their own)[14]
- Have performance goals (rather than mastery goals) in combination with low ability
- Have an entity (rather than incremental) view of intelligence
- Are concerned about making a good impression on others and think that a request for help might make them look stupid
- Worry that requests for help may be disparaged and rejected
  (Aleven, Stahl, Schworm, Fischer, & Wallace, 2003; R. Ames, 1983; Butler, 1998b; Mangels, 2004; Newman & Schwager, 1992; A. M. Ryan, Hicks, & Midgley, 1997; A. M. Ryan, Pintrich, & Midgley, 2001; Skaalvik & Valas, 2001; Turner, Husman, & Schallert, 2002)

How Self–Regulation Influences Motivation and Affect

Not only do motivational factors influence self-regulated learning, but self-regulated learners also *control* their motivation to some degree. They do so in a variety of ways:

- *Aligning assigned tasks with areas of interest.* When they have leeway in learning activities, they intentionally choose alternatives that interest them (Covington, 2000). For example, when thinking about research projects for an upcoming science fair, they might develop a project that relates to a current interest in lizards or a long-term goal of becoming a dentist.
- *Setting goals.* They set short-term as well as long-term goals for themselves (Locke & Latham, 2002; Zimmerman, 1998). For instance, they might tell themselves, "I need to finish reading this chapter on motivation before I go to lunch." By setting and reaching short-term goals, they also enhance their self-efficacy (Wolters, 2003a).

---

[14]Culture may also be a factor here. Many Western societies encourage students to be independent learners as much as possible and to minimize reliance on others (Karabenick & Sharma, 1994).

- *Focusing on productive attributions.* They identify factors within themselves over which they have considerable control, such as good strategies (Wolters, 2003a). For instance, while tackling a difficult geometry problem, they might think, "I've solved these kinds of problems before. What approaches did I use that worked for me?"
- *Minimizing enticing distractions.* They create or find an environment in which they can concentrate as they study (Kuhl, 1987; Wolters, 2003a; Wolters & Rosenthal, 2000). For instance, they might turn off the television while studying in the living room, or they might retreat to a quiet corner of the library.
- *Reminding themselves of the importance of doing well.* They engage in self-talk that emphasizes reasons for completing a task or performing at high levels (Wolters, 2003a; Wolters & Rosenthal, 2000). For instance, they might say, "I can help others in my study group understand this only if I understand it myself" or "Getting an A on this test is important for my GPA."
- *Enhancing the appeal of a task.* They devise ways to make a boring task more interesting and enjoyable (Sansone, Weir, Harpster, & Morgan, 1992; Wolters, 2003a; Wolters & Rosenthal, 2000). For example, they might try to make the task into a game of some sort, or they might embellish their written work with artful illustrations.
- *Self-imposing consequences.* They promise themselves, and then follow through on, rewards for doing well; they may also punish themselves in some way if they fail (Wolters, 2003a; Wolters & Rosenthal, 2000; also see the sections "Self-Reaction" and "Self-Reinforcement" in chapter 6). For example, they might treat themselves to a night at the movies with friends if, but only if, they get at least a B on an assignment.

Although emotions are not as easy to control as motivation, self-regulated learners rein in unproductive ones as much as they can. For instance, they try to put worrisome thoughts out of their minds while they study (Wolters, 2003a; Zeidner, 1998). They try to think of upcoming exams as being challenges that they can overcome rather than as threatening events that foreshadow almost certain doom (Richards & Gross, 2000). And they bounce back quickly after a discouraging failure, renewing their efforts and finding reasons for optimism that they will be successful the next time (Corno, 1993; Turner et al., 2002).

Internalized Motivation

As I mentioned in chapter 12, my son Alex and I once enrolled in an undergraduate course in art history. We were both taking the course primarily to gain a better understanding of the many works of art we'd seen in museums over the years. Alex also had a second reason for taking the course: to earn credit toward his high school diploma. Alex, of course, had to get a passing grade in the course. As for me, it mattered little whether I got an A or an F. Yet I diligently studied for every test, often foregoing things I'd rather have been doing, such as reading a mystery novel or watching a television game show. Why did I do it? Although I enjoyed attending class, studying the material before a test was definitely *not* an intrinsically motivating activity for me; the textbook had lots of beautiful pictures, but its prose was about as interesting and engaging as the telephone book. Nor was there any obvious extrinsic motivation for me to study; the grade I got in the course would in no way affect my future physical, financial, or emotional well-being. The bottom line was that, in my many years as a student, I had acquired a desire to achieve good grades, more or less for their own sake.

In our discussion so far, we have thought of intrinsic versus extrinsic motivation as an either-or state of affairs. In fact, there is a third possibility. The concept of **internalized motivation** refers to situations in which, over time, people gradually adopt behaviors that other individuals value, without regard for the external consequences that such behaviors may or may not bring (Deci & Ryan, 1995; Deci, Vallerand, Pelletier, & Ryan, 1991; Harter, 1992; Ryan & Connell, 1989; Ryan, Connell, & Grolnick, 1992).[15]

Deci and Ryan (1995, 2000; Deci et al., 1991; Ryan et al., 1992) have proposed that internalized motivation may evolve in the following sequence:

1. *External regulation.* The individual is motivated to behave, or else *not* to behave, in certain ways based primarily on the external consequences that will follow various behaviors; in other words, the individual is extrinsically motivated. For instance, students may do schoolwork primarily to avoid being punished for poor grades, and they are likely to need a lot of prodding to complete assigned tasks.

2. *Introjection.* The individual behaves in particular ways to gain the approval of others; for example, a student may willingly complete an easy, boring assignment as a means of gaining a teacher's approval. At this point, we see some internal pressure to engage in desired behaviors; for instance, the individual may feel guilty if he or she violates certain standards or rules for behavior. However, the person does not fully understand the rationale behind such standards and rules. Instead, the primary motives appear to be avoiding a negative self-evaluation and protecting one's sense of self-worth.

3. *Identification.* The individual now sees certain behaviors as being personally important or valuable. For instance, a student is likely to value learning and academic success for their own sake, to perceive assigned classroom tasks as being essential for learning, and to need little prodding to get assigned work done.

4. *Integration.* The individual has fully accepted the desirability of certain behaviors and integrated them into an overall system of motives and values. For example, a student might have acquired a keen interest in science as a possible career—an interest that will be evident in many things the student does on a regular basis.

Internalized motivation is an important aspect of self-regulated learning. It fosters a general work ethic—including that *motivation to learn* I spoke of earlier—in which the learner spontaneously engages in activities that, although not always fun or immediately gratifying, are essential for reaching long-term goals (Harter, 1992; McCombs, 1996; Ryan et al., 1992; Stipek, 1993).

Be careful that you don't equate *integrated motivation* with *intrinsic motivation.* Certainly they are both associated with a high degree of self-determination, and they can ultimately have similar effects on behavior. However, intrinsic motivation comes from within the individual or is inherent in the task being performed, whereas integrated motivation has its roots in other people's messages about what things are important and valuable (Reeve et al., 2004; Stefanou, Perencevich, DiCintio, & Turner, 2004). In some cases, integrated motivation or identified motivation (number 3 in the sequence) may actually be preferable to intrinsic motivation, in that

---

[15]This concept should remind you of Vygotsky's notion of *internalization* (see chapter 11).

learners will sustain their efforts even after the intrinsic appeal of an activity wears thin (Walls & Little, 2005).

Ryan and his colleagues (1992) have suggested that three conditions promote the development of internalized motivation:

- *The learner operates within the context of a warm, responsive, and supportive environment.* The learner feels a sense of relatedness to, and regard for, important other people in his or her environment (also see Wentzel & Wigfield, 1998).
- *The learner has some autonomy.* The people who are largely directing the learner's behavior (e.g., parents, teachers) exert no more control than necessary, as a way of maximizing the extent to which the learner maintains a sense of self-determination. And, over time, those people gradually relinquish control to the learner.
- *The learner operates within a certain degree of structure.* The environment provides information about expected behaviors and why they are important. Response–consequence contingencies are clearly identified.

Fostering the development of internalized motivation, then, involves a delicate balancing act between giving the learner sufficient opportunities for experiencing self-determination and providing some guidance about how the learner should behave. In a sense, adults scaffold desired behaviors at first, gradually reducing the scaffolding as the learner exhibits the behaviors more easily and frequently.

ENCOURAGING COGNITION THAT MOTIVATES

In this chapter we've considered several cognitive factors that influence motivation, including interests, expectancies, values, goals, and attributions. With these factors in mind, I offer several general principles that can guide teachers' efforts to enhance students' motivation—and consequently also their learning and achievement—in the classroom.

- *Students learn more when they find classroom material interesting as well as informative.* Almost all students learn more when a topic is interesting; students with little background knowledge in the topic are especially likely to benefit (Alexander, 1997; Garner, Alexander, Gillingham, Kulikowich, & Brown, 1991). Yet students often report that they find little of interest in classroom subject matter, especially once they reach the middle school and high school grades (Gentry, Gable, & Rizza, 2002; Larson, 2000; Mac Iver, Reuman, & Main, 1995).

Certainly teachers should capitalize on students' personal interests whenever possible (Alexander et al., 1994; Brophy, 1986, 1987; Wlodkowski, 1978). But situational interest factors—especially of the "hold" rather than "catch" variety—can also be incorporated into classroom topics and activities. For example, students typically enjoy opportunities to respond actively during a learning activity—perhaps by manipulating and experimenting with physical objects, creating new products, discussing controversial issues, or teaching something they've learned to peers (Andre & Windschitl, 2003; Brophy, 2004; Hidi, Weiss, Berndorff, & Nolan, 1998; Zahorik, 1994). They enjoy subject matter to which they can relate on a personal level—for instance, math lessons that involve favorite foods, works of literature that feature characters with whom students can readily identify, or history textbooks that portray historical figures as real people with distinctly human qualities (Anand & Ross, 1987; Levstik, 1994; Pugh & Bergin, 2006).

Students are often curious about things that are new and different and about events that are surprising and puzzling (Brophy, 1987; Lepper & Hodell, 1989; Sheveland, 1994; Stipek, 1993). They like to engage in fantasy and make-believe—for example, playing out the roles of key figures in historical events or imagining what it must be like to be weightless in space (Brophy, 1987, 2004; Lepper & Hodell, 1989). And they may eagerly seek out answers to questions they have themselves posed about a new topic (Brophy, 2004; Hidi & Renninger, 2006).

Keep in mind, however, that adding interesting but *irrelevant* information may sometimes be counterproductive, distracting students' attention from more important material. For instance, consider the following passage:

> Some insects live alone, and some live in large families. Wasps that live alone are called solitary wasps. A Mud Dauber Wasp is a solitary wasp. Click beetles live alone. When a click beetle is on its back, it flips itself into the air and lands right side up while it makes a clicking noise. Ants live in large families. There are many kinds of ants. Some ants live in trees. Black Ants live in the ground. (Garner, Gillingham, & White, 1989, p. 46)

If you are like me, you may have found the sentence about an upside-down beetle making a clicking noise as it rights itself to be the one interesting detail in an otherwise ho-hum passage. Such **seductive details** are apt to draw your attention and get you more cognitively engaged in what you are reading. If they are relevant to the topic you are reading about, they may enhance your understanding (Harp & Mayer, 1998; Sadoski & Paivio, 2001; Schraw, 1998). But if they distract your attention away from more central ideas or activate the wrong schemas in your long-term memory, they are likely to interfere with your overall learning (Garner et al., 1992; Harp & Mayer, 1998; Wade, 1992). In the preceding paragraph about insects, the description of a click beetle's strategy for turning itself over is definitely irrelevant to the paragraph's main idea (the social versus solitary nature of different insects) and so is unlikely to contribute to your learning (Garner et al., 1989). Seductive details are most distracting for readers who have only limited background knowledge about a topic and therefore have little basis for determining what is and what is not important (Alexander & Jetton, 1996; Garner et al., 1991).

◆ *Students tend to be more optimistic about their chances of success when they have environmental support for their efforts.* In chapters 6 and 15 we identified a number of strategies for enhancing students' self-efficacy for accomplishing classroom tasks. But as we discovered in our earlier discussion of expectancies, learners' expectations for success depend not only on their own perceived abilities but also on the availability of people who can guide them and resources that can make some parts of a task easier. Hence we see that appropriate scaffolding is apt to promote motivation as well as learning and development (Brophy, 2004). Not only does scaffolding enhance students' expectancies for success, but it may also enhance their interest in school subject matter (Hidi & Renninger, 2006).

◆ *Students are more motivated to learn classroom subject matter when they believe it has value for them personally.* Some classroom activities will be naturally fun, interesting, or otherwise intrinsically motivating for students. But others—perhaps occasional drill and practice to promote automaticity of basic skills, or perhaps intensive study of dry but essential topics—may have little obvious appeal. Teachers can do many things to help students find value in school activities. For example, they can identify the specific knowledge and skills that students will acquire from an instructional unit (Keller, 1987). They can show how things learned in the classroom will help address students' present concerns and long-term goals (C. Ames, 1992;

Brophy & Alleman, 1991; Ferrari & Elik, 2003). They can demonstrate how they themselves value academic activities—for example, by sharing their fascination with certain topics, modeling critical evaluation of new ideas, and describing how they use the things they've learned in school (Brophy, 1999, 2004; Brophy & Alleman, 1991; Kuhn, 2006). And they should refrain from asking students to engage in activities with little long-term benefit—memorizing trivial facts for no good reason, reading material that is clearly beyond students' comprehension level, and so on (Brophy, 1987).

The three factors that promote the development of internalized motivation—a responsive and supportive environment, age-appropriate autonomy, and a certain amount of structure—should also help learners acquire values that other people believe are important for long-term well-being. And in general, teachers should help students discover for themselves that studying school subject matter isn't just a means to concrete ends (a better job, higher salary, etc.) but in fact has many intangible rewards—better understanding of world events, more informed decision making, and so on (Brophy, 2004; Finke & Bettle, 1996). Ideally, then, students should come to value learning for its own sake.

◆ *Students learn more effectively when they set goals for themselves.* When we talked about instructional objectives in chapter 5, we were essentially talking about goals that teachers set for their students. But it is equally important that students set their *own* goals regarding what they want to accomplish at school (Wentzel, 1999). Not only are self-chosen goals an important part of self-regulated learning, but they can also help students make appropriate choices, direct students' efforts as they work in the classroom, and contribute to students' sense of self-determination. And ultimately, students are more likely to work toward—and so more likely to accomplish—goals they have set for themselves rather than those that others have imposed on them (Schunk, 1985).

Although teachers should certainly encourage students to develop long-term goals for themselves—perhaps to go to college or become an environmental scientist—such goals are often too general and abstract to guide students' immediate behaviors (Bandura, 1997; Husman & Freeman, 1999). Many students (younger ones especially) initially respond more favorably to fairly specific, concrete, short-term goals—perhaps learning a certain number of spelling words or solving a certain number of mathematics problems (Bandura & Schunk, 1981; Good & Brophy, 1994; Schunk & Rice, 1989). By setting and working for a series of short-term goals—sometimes known as **proximal goals**—students get regular feedback about the progress they are making, develop a greater sense of self-efficacy that they can master school subject matter, and achieve at higher levels (Bandura, 1997; Kluger & DeNisi, 1998; Page-Voth & Graham, 1999; Wolters, 2003a).

◆ *In general, mastery goals lead to better learning than performance goals.* To some degree, performance goals (e.g., completing assigned tasks, earning high grades and test scores) are inevitable in today's schools and in society at large (Butler, 1989; Elliot & McGregor, 2000). Furthermore, children and adolescents will invariably look to their peers' performance as one means of evaluating their *own* performance, and many aspects of the adult world (gaining admission to college, seeking employment, working in private industry, playing professional sports, etc.) are inherently competitive in nature. But ultimately, mastery goals are the ones most likely to promote effective learning and achievement over the long run. Mastery goals are especially motivating when they are specific ("I want to learn how to ride a bicycle"), challenging ("Writing a limerick looks difficult, but I'm sure I can do it"), and short-term ("I'm going to learn to count to 100 in French by the end of the month") (Alderman, 1990; Brophy, 1987; Mac Iver et al., 1995).

Recently, some theorists (Schunk & Swartz, 1993; Schunk & Zimmerman, 1997; Zimmerman & Kitsantas, 1997) have proposed that different kinds of mastery goals may be more useful at different points in learning, especially when learners are trying to learn a skill of some sort (e.g., writing a good paragraph, playing basketball, throwing darts). Initially, learners may want to work toward a **process goal,** perfecting the form or procedure that the skill involves without regard to the final outcome. As the desired form or procedure becomes more automatized, they may then want to shift their attention to a **product goal,** striving for a certain standard of performance (e.g., getting a certain percentage of balls in the basket or a certain number of darts in the center of the target).[16]

Through their own behaviors, teachers can demonstrate that improving and mastering knowledge and skills are the objectives most important for students to accomplish. For example, they can express their *own* belief that learning, understanding, and improving are ultimately more important than getting good grades, winning competitions, and so on (Roberts et al., 1997; Wentzel, 1999). They can suggest that students look to their peers not as a comparison group for evaluating their own performance, but rather as a source of information and assistance (Urdan, Ryan, Anderman, & Gheen, 2002). They can communicate the idea that mistakes are a normal part of learning and therefore to be expected (Ames, 1992; Dweck & Elliott, 1983; Perry & Winne, 2004). They can provide mechanisms and criteria through which students may easily record and assess academic progress (Good & Brophy, 1994; Spaulding, 1992). Rather than simply reporting test scores or letter grades, they can give specific feedback about how students can improve (Brophy, 1986; Butler, 1987; Graham & Weiner, 1996; Spaulding, 1992). And teachers should *not* repeatedly remind students that classwork will be evaluated and graded (Stipek, 1993; Thomas & Oldfather, 1997). Focusing learners' attention on mastery goals, especially when those goals relate to learners' own lives, may especially benefit students from diverse ethnic backgrounds and students at risk for academic failure (Alderman, 1990; Garcia, 1992; Maehr & Anderman, 1993).

◆ *Classroom activities are more effective when they enable students to meet several goals at once.* As we've seen, students are more productive when they can accomplish multiple goals simultaneously. For instance, students might work toward mastery goals by learning and practicing new skills within the context of group projects (thus meeting their social goals) and with evaluation criteria that allow for risk taking and mistakes (thus not interfering with performance goals). Students are *un*likely to strive for mastery goals when assignments ask little of them (thereby not enhancing their sense of competence), when they must compete with one another for resources or high test scores (possibly thwarting attainment of social goals), and when any single failure has a significant impact on final grades (impeding progress toward performance goals).

Within this context, we should note that performance-approach goals can be quite beneficial when students strive for them in conjunction with mastery goals (Linnenbrink, 2005; Senko & Harackiewicz, 2005). They become problematic primarily when they are incompatible with mastery goals—for instance, when a desire to get a good grade prompts a student to cheat rather than understand the subject matter (Dweck, 2000).

◆ *Optimistic teacher attributions and expectations regarding students' achievement boost students'* **actual** *achievement.* As we discovered in chapter 8, people often draw from their existing knowledge

---

[16]On the surface, such goals might look like performance goals. However, the focus is on *mastery* of a skill, not on how one's performance appears to others.

and beliefs to form expectations about what they are likely to see and hear. Those expectations, in turn, influence what people *do* see and hear, or at least what they *think* they see and hear. Expectations are especially influential when an event is ambiguous—that is, when it can be interpreted in multiple ways.

Many of students' day-to-day behaviors in the classroom lend themselves to a variety of interpretations. What teachers conclude from these behaviors—including the attributions teachers make about students' successes and failures—depends on how they have previously sized up different students' motivation levels, abilities, and so on. For example, imagine that a student, Linda, fails to finish a classroom assignment on time. Her teacher, Mr. Jones, might possibly conclude that Linda (1) didn't try very hard, (2) used her time poorly, or (3) wasn't capable of doing the task. Which conclusion Mr. Jones draws will depend on his prior beliefs about Linda—for instance, whether he thinks she (1) is lazy and unmotivated, (2) is both motivated and capable of doing the work but has not yet acquired effective self-regulation skills, or (3) has little innate capacity for learning (reflecting an entity view of intelligence).

Teachers' attributions for students' current behaviors affect their expectations for students' future performance. Their expectations, in turn, affect future attributions (Weiner, 2000). And their attributions and expectations both affect the teaching strategies they use with particular students. For example, if Mr. Jones thinks Linda is "unmotivated," he might use some sort of incentive—perhaps offering some free time at the end of the day—to entice her into completing assignments on time. If, instead, he thinks Linda lacks the necessary self-regulation skills for independent work, he might strive to teach her such skills—perhaps instructing her in the self-monitoring I described in chapter 6. But if he thinks Linda has insufficient intelligence to master classroom topics, he may do little if anything to help her along.

When teachers form optimistic attributions and expectations for students—for instance, when they believe that students can perform at high levels when conditions are right—they create a warmer classroom climate, interact with students more frequently, provide more opportunities for students to respond, and give more positive and more specific feedback; they also present more course material and more challenging topics. In contrast, when teachers have low expectations for certain students—for instance, when they believe they can do little to change students' seemingly "low intelligence" or "poor motivation"—they offer fewer opportunities for speaking in class, ask easier questions, give less feedback about students' responses, present few if any challenging assignments, and overlook good performance when it occurs (Babad, 1993; Good & Brophy, 1994; Graham, 1990, 1991; Rosenthal, 1994, 2002).

Most children and adolescents are well aware of their teachers' differential treatment of individual students, and they use such treatment to draw logical inferences about their own abilities (Butler, 1994; Good & Nichols, 2001; Weinstein, 1993). Furthermore, their behavior may begin to mirror their self-perceptions. For instance, when teachers repeatedly communicate low-ability messages, students may exert little effort on academic tasks, or they may frequently misbehave in class (Marachi, Friedel, & Midgley, 2001; Murdock, 1999). In some cases, then, teachers' attributions and expectations can lead to a self-fulfilling prophecy: What teachers expect students to achieve becomes what students actually *do* achieve. (We'll call this *Self-Fulfilling Prophecy #2.*) Teacher attributions and expectations appear to have a greater influence in the early elementary school years (grades 1 and 2), in the first year of secondary school, and, more generally, within the first few weeks of school—in other words, at times when students are entering new and unfamiliar school environments (Jussim, Eccles, & Madon, 1996; Kuklinski & Weinstein, 2001; Raudenbush, 1984; Rosenthal, 1994, 2002; Weinstein, Madison, & Kuklinski, 1995).

Obviously, then, teachers are most effective when they have optimistic attributions and expectations regarding students' performance. Following are several strategies teachers can use to acquire and maintain such optimism:

- *Look for strengths in every student.* Sometimes students' weaknesses are all too evident. But it is essential that teachers also look for the many unique qualities and strengths that students inevitably bring to the classroom—perhaps exceptional leadership skills in working with classmates or considerable creativity in story telling (e.g., (Carrasco, 1981; Hale-Benson, 1986).

- *Learn more about students' backgrounds and home environments.* Teachers are most likely to have low expectations for students' performance when they hold rigid stereotypes about students from certain ethnic or socioeconomic groups, often as a result of ignorance about students' cultures and home environments (Alexander, Entwisle, & Thompson, 1987; McLoyd, 1998; Snow et al., 1996). When teachers have a clear picture of their students' activities, habits, values, and families, they are far more likely to think of their students as *individuals* than as stereotypical members of a particular group.

- *Assume that ability can and often does improve with time, practice, and high-quality instructional practices.* In other words, teachers should take an incremental view, rather than an entity view, of students' intelligence and other abilities (Pintrich & Schunk, 2002).

- *Assess students' progress objectively and frequently.* Because expectations for students' performance often color teachers' informal estimates of how well students are progressing, teachers need to identify more objective ways of assessing learning and achievement. When such assessments occur regularly, they provide ongoing information to guide instruction (Goldenberg, 1992).[17]

- *Remember that teachers can definitely make a difference.* Teachers are more likely to have high expectations for students when they are confident in their *own* ability to promote learning and academic success (Ashton, 1985; Weinstein et al., 1995).

In their daily interactions with students, teachers must also take pains to communicate optimistic attributions about students' performance (Brophy, 2004; Dweck, 2000; Schunk, 1990). For instance, when a student succeeds at a task, a teacher might attribute the success to a combination of natural ability, effort, and good strategies (e.g., "Obviously you're good at this, and you've been working very hard on the new writing techniques you learned"). And when a student has difficulty with a task, attributions to controllable factors such as effort and strategies are most beneficial (e.g., "Perhaps you need to study a little more next time, and here are some suggestions on how you might study a little differently . . . "). When students' failures are consistently attributed to a lack of effort or ineffective strategies, rather than to low ability or uncontrollable external factors, and when increased effort or new strategies *do* in fact produce success, then students work harder, persist longer in the face of failure, and seek help when they need it (Dweck & Elliott, 1983; Eccles & Wigfield, 1985; Graham, 1991; Paris & Paris, 2001).

Equally important is to communicate that ability in particular domains can improve over time, especially with hard work and practice. In other words, teachers should consistently convey

---

[17]Here I am not talking about the high-stakes tests of which I spoke in chapters 5 and 15 (such tests yield only global measures of achievement), but rather about teacher-constructed assignments and tests that can provide detailed information about the knowledge and skills that students have and have not acquired.

an incremental and domain-specific view of intelligence (Brophy, 2004; Dweck, 2000). Such a message can often alleviate the negative impact of stereotype threat (Aronson, Fried, & Good, 2002; Johns, Schmader, & Martens, 2005).

◆ *Systematic attribution retraining can positively impact students' attributions.* A number of studies have shown that, for school-age children at least, attributions can be altered, with more persistence in the face of failure being the result (Andrews & Debus, 1978; Chapin & Dyck, 1976; Dweck, 1975; Fowler & Peterson, 1981; Robertson, 2000). In these **attribution retraining** studies, children are asked to engage in a particular task (e.g., reading difficult sentences, solving arithmetic problems, or constructing geometric puzzles), with occasional failures interspersed among more frequent successes. Within this context, one viable approach for changing attributions is for an adult to interpret each success in terms of the effort a child has exerted and each failure in terms of insufficient effort (Chapin & Dyck, 1976; Dweck, 1975; Fowler & Peterson, 1981). Another effective approach is to reinforce children for attributing their *own* successes and failures to effort or a lack thereof (Andrews & Debus, 1978; Fowler & Peterson, 1981).

Early studies focused on effort attributions, but as we've already noted, effort attributions are not always the most beneficial ones for learners to acquire. Attributions to effective and ineffective learning strategies (for success and failure, respectively) are often more productive than effort attributions, particularly when such attribution retraining accompanies a study strategies training program (Pressley, Borkowski, & Schneider, 1987; Reid & Borkowski, 1987; Weinstein et al., 1991).

Teachers must keep in mind that students' views of themselves and their abilities are not likely to change dramatically overnight (Hilt, 2005; Meece, 1994; Paris, 1990). Thus, efforts to help students acquire productive attributions must be an ongoing endeavor rather than a one-shot intervention.

◆ *Most of the time, and for most students, noncompetitive activities are more motivating than competitive ones.* Competition is a pervasive element of our society. In the business world, the people who have the best ideas, make the most money, or work the longest hours are (usually) the ones who get ahead. We often see competition in recreation, too—for instance, in the card games we play and the athletic events we watch on television. And our democratic political system is based on competition in the most basic sense: Those who get the most votes are the ones who end up in office.

Competition is prevalent in schools as well. For example, when teachers grade on the curve, their grades reflect how students stack up against one another, and so only a few are apt to get As. When students take college aptitude tests, their test scores (e.g., percentile ranks) reflect their relative standing within a national peer group. Participation in school sports can be quite competitive even before students meet other teams on the playing field: Especially in the high school grades, students must compete among themselves to make a team and achieve first-string status. In any one of these situations, "success" doesn't mean absolute mastery of a task; instead, it means outperforming others.

People can be quite motivated by competition *if* they believe they have a reasonable chance of winning (Brophy, 1986; Deci & Ryan, 1992; Krampen, 1987; Stipek, 1996). For example, the "good behavior game" described in chapter 5, in which two groups of students compete for privileges based on good behavior, leads to marked improvements in students' classroom behavior. Although there's an element of competition in this situation, both teams can win if their behavior warrants it. When competition requires that only some people can win and others must lose, however, several undesirable side effects are apt to result:

- *Competition promotes performance goals rather than mastery goals* (C. Ames, 1984; Hagen, 1994; Nicholls, 1984; Spaulding, 1992; Stipek, 1996). When the key to success is doing better than everyone else, learners inevitably focus their attention on how good they appear to others rather than on how much they are learning. And they define success as being better than everyone else rather than as improving their abilities and skills over time.
- *Competition promotes attributions to ability rather than to effort* (C. Ames, 1984; Nicholls, 1984; Stipek, 1993). Many people lose in competitive situations even when they exert a great deal of effort. They quite logically reach the conclusion that effort is not enough—that some sort of natural ability is the critical ingredient for success. Their failures, then, are due to their lack of that elusive ability, and they become pessimistic about their future chances for success.
- *For the losers, competition promotes a low sense of competence and diminishes self-worth* (C. Ames, 1984; C. Ames & Ames, 1981; Covington & Müeller, 2001). When people define success as mastery of a task or improvement in an activity over time, success is likely to come frequently and so will enhance self-efficacy. But when people instead define success as coming out on top, most will inevitably be losers. In the face of such "failure," they may understandably begin to believe themselves to be incompetent, and some may engage in self-handicapping as a way of protecting their sense of self-worth (Martin, Walsh, Williamson, & Debus, 2003).

As a result of such factors, competitive classroom environments typically lead to lower achievement for most students. Not only do students earn lower grades, they also show less creativity and develop more negative attitudes toward school (Amabile & Hennessey, 1992; Covington, 1992; Graham & Golen, 1991; Krampen, 1987). Competitive classroom environments may be especially detrimental to female students (Eccles, 1989; Inglehart, Brown, & Vida, 1994).

Teachers can take a variety of steps to minimize comparison and competition among students. For example, they can keep students' performance on classroom tasks private and confidential, minimizing the degree to which students are even aware of classmates' performance levels (Schunk, 1990; Spaulding, 1992). At any one time, they can have different students doing different tasks (Stipek, 1996). They can assess students' performance independently of how well classmates are doing and encourage students to assess their own performance in a similar manner (Spaulding, 1992; Wlodkowski, 1978). When little competitions among students (e.g., debates, team math games) do seem appropriate, teachers can make sure that all students or teams have a reasonable (and, if possible, equal) chance of winning (Brophy, 2004; Linnenbrink, 2005) and not make a big deal about who the ultimate winners are.

- ◆ *Challenges heighten motivation and minimize boredom* (Deci & Ryan, 1992; Hidi & Renninger, 2006; Pekrun, Goetz, Zirngibl, & Perry, 2003; Shernoff, Schneider, & Csikszentmihalyi, 2001; J. C. Turner, Meyer, et al., 1998). Learners typically become bored with easy tasks yet are frustrated by tasks at which they always seem to fail. Challenges provide a happy medium: They have those unexpected little twists and turns that maintain interest, but success is possible with persistence and the right strategies.

An important benefit of a challenge is that it promotes productive attributions (Clifford, 1990; Eisenberger, 1992; Lan et al., 1994; C. Peterson, 1988, 1990). When learners succeed at a very easy task—one on which they have exerted very little effort—they are likely to attribute their success to the fact that, hey, anybody can do it. When learners succeed at an *extremely* difficult task—something they thought themselves incapable of doing—they might attribute their success to good luck or somebody else's assistance. However, when they succeed at a challenging task—one they know they can do if they try long and hard enough—they cannot explain their success as being the result of task ease, and they have little reason to attribute their performance to luck or assistance. Their best alternative is to attribute their hard-won success to their own efforts and clever strategies. And such an attribution should bolster their self-efficacy and sense of competence and, perhaps, their overall sense of self-worth.

Throughout the book I've alluded to the effects of challenging tasks, not only for motivation, but also for development and learning (e.g., see the discussions of Piaget's and Vygotsky's theories in chapter 11 and the discussion of metacognition in chapter 12). When are learners most likely to take on new risks and challenges? Theorists suggest that conditions such as these are optimal:

- Standards for success are realistic for each individual.
- Scaffolding is sufficient to make success possible.
- There are few, if any, penalties for errors.
- Rewards cannot be obtained by engaging in easier tasks, or rewards are greater for challenging tasks than they are for easy ones.
- Learners believe that success will probably be the result of their own knowledge, skills, efforts, and strategies (i.e., learners have internal attributions).
- Learners have a sense of competence and a sense of self-determination.
  (Brophy & Alleman, 1992; Clifford, 1990; Corno & Rohrkemper, 1985; Deci & Ryan, 1985; Dweck & Elliott, 1983; Lan et al., 1994; Perry, VandeKamp, Mercer, & Nordby, 2002; Stipek, 1993)

A moment ago, I stated that success on challenging tasks promotes feelings of competence. But the last of the conditions I just listed indicates that the reverse is also true: Competence increases the challenges that people undertake. In other words, we have a happily "vicious" cycle here: Challenge promotes competence, and competence promotes a desire for more challenge.

Yet the school day shouldn't necessarily be one challenge after another. Such a state of affairs would be absolutely exhausting, and probably quite discouraging as well. Instead, teachers should probably strike a balance between easy tasks—those that will boost students' self-confidence over the short run—and the challenging tasks so critical for a long-term sense of competence and self-efficacy (Keller, 1987; Spaulding, 1992; Stipek, 1993, 1996).

A TARGET Mnemonic for Motivational Strategies

Many motivational strategies can be summed up in six words: task, autonomy, recognition, grouping, evaluation, and time (J. L. Epstein, 1989; Maehr & Anderman, 1993). This multifaceted TARGET approach to motivation is presented in Table 16.3. If you look closely at the entries in the table, you'll find that they reflect many of the concepts we've addressed in our two chapters on motivation and affect, including intrinsic and extrinsic motivation, competence and self-worth, self-determination, relatedness, hot cognition, interests, expectancies, values, expectations, goals, and attributions. And especially if you look at Column 2, you'll be convinced, as I am, that teachers clearly *can* make a difference—in fact, a very sizable one—not only in promoting students' learning but in enhancing their motivation as well.

Table 16.3
Six TARGET principles of motivation.

Principle	Examples of Classroom Practices
Classroom **tasks** affect motivation.	• Present new topics through tasks that students find interesting, engaging, and perhaps emotionally charged. • Encourage meaningful rather than rote learning. • Relate activities to students' lives and goals. • Provide sufficient support that students can be successful.
The amount of **autonomy** students have affects motivation, especially intrinsic motivation.	• Give students some choice about what and how they learn. • Teach self-regulation strategies. • Solicit students' opinions about classroom practices and policies. • Have students take leadership roles in some activities.
The amount and nature of the **recognition** students receive affect motivation.	• Acknowledge not only academic successes but also personal and social successes. • Commend students for improvement as well as for mastery. • Provide concrete reinforcers for achievement only when students are not intrinsically motivated to learn. • Show students how their own efforts and strategies are directly responsible for their successes.
The **grouping** procedures in the classroom affect motivation.	• Provide frequent opportunities for students to interact (e.g., cooperative learning activities, peer tutoring). • Plan activities to which all students can make valuable contributions. • Teach the social skills that students need to interact effectively with peers. • Create an atmosphere of mutual caring, respect, and support.
The forms of **evaluation** in the classroom affect motivation.	• Make evaluation criteria clear; specify them in advance. • Minimize or eliminate competition for grades (e.g., don't grade "on a curve"). • Give specific feedback about what students are doing well. • Give concrete suggestions for how students can improve.
How teachers schedule **time** affects motivation.	• Give students enough time to gain mastery of important topics and skills. • Let students' interests dictate some activities. • Include variety in the school day (e.g., intersperse high-energy activities among more sedentary ones).

Sources: J. L. Epstein, 1989; Maehr & Anderman, 1993.

SUMMARY

Cognition plays a significant role in many aspects of human motivation. One influential factor that has both cognitive and affective components is *interest,* which can take either of two forms. *Situational interest* is temporary and evoked by something in the immediate environment. *Personal interest* is more stable and resides within the individual. Learners who are interested in the topic they are studying engage in more effective information processing and so remember the subject matter better over the long run. Teachers can often get students actively engaged in classroom subject matter both by capitalizing on individual personal interests and by evoking situational interest—for instance, by conducting hands-on activities or assigning fiction and nonfiction to which students can relate on a personal level.

Some motivation theorists have proposed that motivation for performing any particular task depends on two subjective variables. First, people must have an *expectancy* that they will be successful; their expectations for success will depend not only on their own skill level but also on such outside factors as the quality of instruction and the availability of resources and support. Second, people must *value* the task: They must believe that there are direct or indirect benefits to performing it—perhaps achieving a desired goal, impressing others, or simply having fun. In the classroom, students must believe that they will have the support they need to master something; they must also see how school subject matter has value for them personally.

Learners have a wide variety of goals that may either contribute to or interfere with learning in instructional settings. Students who have *mastery goals* want to acquire additional knowledge or skills. Those who have *performance goals* either want to look competent in the eyes of others (a *performance-approach goal*) or else not to look incompetent (a *performance-avoidance goal*). The three kinds of goals are not necessarily mutually exclusive (a person might have two, or even all three), but generally speaking, learners with mastery goals are more likely to recognize that competence comes only through effort and practice,

to choose activities that maximize opportunities for learning, and to use errors constructively to improve future performance. Other common goals include *work-avoidance goals* (i.e., getting by with minimal effort), *social goals* (i.e., gaining and maintaining relationships with others), and *career goals*. Sometimes people can work toward two or more goals simultaneously; at other times, achieving one goal prevents them from satisfying others. Ideally, teachers should focus students' attention primarily on mastery goals, and they should encourage students to set some of their own goals, including short-term, concrete ones that will give them a sense of accomplishment and enable them to see the progress they are making.

Attributions—the cause–effect explanations that people construct for things that happen to them—are yet another cognitive factor affecting motivation. Attributions influence many aspects of behavior and cognition, including emotional reactions to success and failure, expectations for future success, expenditure of effort, learning strategies, and future choices and goals. People's attributions emerge from many sources. Their history of success and failure certainly has an influence; for instance, if they consistently fail no matter what they do, they are apt to attribute such failure to something stable and uncontrollable, such as lack of natural talent. But other factors make a difference as well, including situational cues (e.g., the apparent difficulty of a task), the attributions that other people communicate either verbally or nonverbally, the beliefs and worldviews of one's culture, and self-protective biases. As children grow older, and especially as they reach adolescence or adulthood, many develop a general explanatory style, perhaps an I-can-do-it attitude (*mastery orientation*) that promotes effort, persistence, and preference for challenge, or perhaps an I-*can't*-do-it attitude (*learned helplessness*) that leads them to set easy goals and to give up quickly in the face of obstacles. Through both what they say and what they do, teachers should communicate attributions that lead students to be optimistic about achieving success on classroom tasks.

Just as effective learners self-regulate their cognitive processes, so, too, do they intentionally try to bring productive motives and emotions to a learning situation, for instance by setting specific goals for a learning task, devising ways to make boring tasks more interesting, and trying to put worrisome thoughts out of mind. Self-regulation is also reflected in the phenomenon of *internalized motivation:* People gradually begin to value and adopt the behaviors that those around them value and encourage. Teachers and other adults can foster internalized motivation by creating a warm and supportive environment, giving learners some autonomy in what they do and learn, and providing sufficient structure to promote success.

References

Ablard, K. E., & Lipschultz, R. E. (1998). Self-regulated learning in high-achieving students: Relations to advanced reasoning, achievement goals, and gender. *Journal of Educational Psychology, 90,* 94–101.

Abrams, R. A. (1994). The forces that move the eyes. *Current Directions in Psychological Science, 3,* 65–67.

Abrams, R. A., & Christ, S. E. (2003). Motion onset captures attention. *Psychological Science, 14,* 427–432.

Achacoso, M. V., Summers, J. J., & Schallert, D. L. (2002, April). *Entitlement as an attributional belief: A new venue for a model of academic motivation.* Paper presented at the annual meeting of the American Educational Research Association, New Orleans, LA.

Adamson, L. B., & Bakeman, R. (1991). The development of shared attention during infancy. In R. Vasta (Ed.), *Annals of child development* (Vol. 8, pp. 1–41). London: Kingsley.

Adamson, L. B., & McArthur, D. (1995). Joint attention, affect, and culture. In C. Moore & P. J. Dunham (Eds.), *Joint attention: Its origins and role in development* (pp. 205–221). Hillsdale, NJ: Erlbaum.

Adolphs, R., & Damasio, A. R. (2001). The interaction of affect and cognition: A neurobiological perspective. In J. P. Forgas (Ed.), *Handbook of affect and social cognition* (pp. 27–49). Mahwah, NJ: Erlbaum.

Airasian, P. W. (1994). *Classroom assessment* (2nd ed.). New York: McGraw-Hill.

Alberto, P. A., & Troutman, A. C. (2003). *Applied behavior analysis for teachers* (6th ed.). Upper Saddle River, NJ: Merrill/Prentice Hall.

Alderman, K. (1990). Motivation for at-risk students. *Educational Leadership, 48*(1), 27–30.

Alegria, J. (1998). The origin and functions of phonological representations in deaf people. In C. Hulme & R. M. Joshi (Eds.), *Reading and spelling: Development and disorders.* Mahwah, NJ: Erlbaum.

Aleven, V., Stahl, E., Schworm, S., Fischer, F., & Wallace, R. (2003). Help seeking and help design in interactive learning environments. *Review of Educational Research, 73,* 277–320.

Alexander, P. A. (1997). Mapping the multidimensional nature of domain learning: The interplay of cognitive, motivational, and strategic forces. In P. R. Pintrich & M. L. Maehr (Eds.), *Advances in motivation and achievement* (Vol. 10). Greenwich, CT: JAI Press.

Alexander, P. A. (1998). Positioning conceptual change within a model of domain literacy. In B. Guzzetti & C. Hynd (Eds.), *Perspectives on conceptual change: Multiple ways to understand knowing and learning in a complex world* (pp. 55–76). Mahwah, NJ: Erlbaum.

Alexander, P. A. (2003). The development of expertise: The journey from acclimation to proficiency. *Educational Researcher, 32*(8), 10–14.

Alexander, P. A. (2004). A model of domain learning: Reinterpreting expertise as a multidimensional, multistage process. In D. Y. Dai & R. J. Sternberg (Eds.), *Motivation, emotion, and cognition: Integrative perspectives on intellectual functioning and development* (pp. 273–298). Mahwah, NJ: Erlbaum.

Alexander, K., Entwisle, D., & Thompson, M. (1987). School performance, status relations, and the structure of sentiment: Bringing the teacher back in. *American Sociological Review, 52,* 665–682.

Alexander, L., Frankiewicz, R., & Williams, R. (1979). Facilitation of learning and retention of oral instruction using advance and post organizers. *Journal of Educational Psychology, 71,* 701–707.

Alexander, P. A., Graham, S., & Harris, K. R. (1998). A perspective on strategy research: Progress and prospects. *Educational Psychology Review, 10,* 129–154.

Alexander, P. A., & Jetton, T. L. (1996). The role of importance and interest in the processing of text. *Educational Psychology Review, 8,* 89–121.

Alexander, P. A., & Judy, J. E. (1988). The interaction of domain-specific and strategic knowledge in academic performance. *Review of Educational Research, 38,* 375–404.

Alexander, P. A., Kulikowich, J. M., & Schulze, S. K. (1994). How subject-matter knowledge affects recall and interest. *American Educational Research Journal, 31,* 313–337.

Alexander, P. A., White, C. S., & Daugherty, M. (1997). Analogical reasoning and early mathematical learning. In L. D. English (Ed.), *Mathematical reasoning: Analogies, metaphors, and images* (pp. 117–147). Mahwah, NJ: Erlbaum.

Alfassi, M. (1998). Reading for meaning: The efficacy of reciprocal teaching in fostering reading comprehension in high school students in remedial reading classes. *American Educational Research Journal, 35,* 309–332.

Alford, G. S., & Rosenthal, T. L. (1973). Process and products of modeling in observational concept attainment. *Child Development, 44,* 714–720.

Alibali, M. W., Bassok, M., Solomon, K. O., Syc, S. E., & Goldin-Meadow, S. (1999). Illuminating mental representations through speech and gesture. *Psychological Science, 10,* 327–333.

Alland, A. (1983). *Playing with form.* New York: Columbia University Press.

Alleman, J., & Brophy, J. (1992). Analysis of the activities in a social studies curriculum. In J. Brophy (Ed.), *Advances in research on teaching: Vol. 3. Planning and managing learning tasks and activities.* Greenwich, CT: JAI Press.

Allen, K. D. (1998). The use of an enhanced simplified habit-reversal procedure to reduce disruptive outbursts during athletic performance. *Journal of Applied Behavior Analysis, 31,* 489–492.

Altmann, E. M., & Gray, W. D. (2002). Forgetting to remember: The functional relationship of decay and interference. *Psychological Science, 13,* 27–33.

Alvarez, G. A., & Cavanagh, P. (2004). The capacity of visual short-term memory is set both by visual information load and by number of objects. *Psychological Science, 15,* 106–111.

Amabile, T. M., & Hennessey, B. A. (1992). The motivation for creativity in children. In A. K. Boggiano & T. S. Pittman (Eds.), *Achievement and motivation: A social-developmental perspective.* Cambridge, England: Cambridge University Press.

Amedi, A., Merabet, L. B., Bermpohl, F., & Pascual-Leone, A. (2005). The occipital cortex in the blind: Lessons about plasticity and vision. *Current Directions in Psychological Science, 14,* 306–311.

Ames, C. (1984). Competitive, cooperative, and individualistic goal structures: A cognitive-motivational analysis. In R. Ames & C. Ames (Eds.), *Research on motivation in education: Vol. 1. Student motivation.* Orlando: Academic Press.

Ames, C. (1992). Classrooms: Goals, structures, and student motivation. *Journal of Educational Psychology, 84,* 261–271.

Ames, C., & Ames, R. (1981). Competitive versus individualistic goal structures: The salience of past performance information for causal attributions and affect. *Journal of Educational Psychology, 73,* 411–418.

Ames, C., & Archer, J. (1988). Achievement goals in the classroom: Students' learning strategies and motivation processes. *Journal of Educational Psychology, 80,* 260–267.

Ames, R. (1983). Help-seeking and achievement orientation: Perspectives from attribution theory. In A. Nadler, J. Fisher, & B. DePaulo (Eds.), *New directions in helping* (Vol. 2). New York: Academic Press.

Amrein, A. L., & Berliner, D. C. (2002a, December). *An analysis of some unintended and negative consequences of high-stakes testing* (Report EPSL-0211–125-EPRU). Tempe: Educational Policy Study Laboratory, Arizona State University. Retrieved April 28, 2003, from http://www.asu.edu/educ/epsl/EPRU/epru_2002_Research_Writing.htm

Amrein, A. L., & Berliner, D. C. (2002b, March 28). High-stakes testing, uncertainty, and student learning. *Education Policy Analysis Archives, 10*(18). Retrieved April 9, 2002, from http://epaa.asu.edu/epaa/v10n18/.

Amrein, A. L., & Berliner, D. C. (2002c). The impact of high-stakes tests on student academic performance: An analysis of NAEP results in states with high-stakes tests and ACT, SAT, and AP test results in states with high school graduation exams. Retrieved April 28, 2003, from Arizona State University, Education Policy Studies Laboratory Web site: http://www.asu.edu/educ/epsl/EPRU/epru_2002_Research_Writing.htm.

Anand, P., & Ross, S. (1987). A computer-based strategy for personalizing verbal problems in teaching mathematics. *Educational Communication and Technology Journal, 35,* 151–162.

Anderman, E. M., Griesinger, T., & Westerfield, G. (1998). Motivation and cheating during early adolescence. *Journal of Educational Psychology, 90,* 84–93.

Anderman, E. M., & Maehr, M. L. (1994). Motivation and schooling in the middle grades. *Review of Educational Research, 64,* 287–309.

Anderman, L. H., & Anderman, E. M. (1999). Social predictors of changes in students' achievement goal orientation. *Contemporary Educational Psychology, 25,* 21–37.

Anderman, L. H., Patrick, H., Hruda, L. Z., & Linnenbrink, E. A. (2002). Observing classroom goal structures to clarify and expand goal theory. In C. Midgley (Ed.), *Goals, goal structures, and patterns of adaptive learning* (pp. 243–278). Mahwah, NJ: Erlbaum.

Anderson, C. A., Berkowitz, L., Donnerstein, E., Huesmann, L. R., Johnson, J. D., Linz, D., Malamuth, N. M., & Wartella, E. (2003). The influence of media violence on youth. *Psychological Science in the Public Interest, 4,* 81–110.

Anderson, C. A., & Bushman, B. J. (2001). Effects of violent video games on aggressive behavior, aggressive cognition, aggressive affect, physiological arousal, and prosocial behavior: A meta-analytic review of the scientific literature. *Psychological Science, 12,* 353–359.

Anderson, C. W., Sheldon, T. H., & Dubay, J. (1990). The effects of instruction on college nonmajors' conceptions of respiration and photosynthesis. *Journal of Research in Science Teaching, 27,* 761–776.

Anderson, D. R. (2003). The Children's Television Act: A public policy that benefits children. *Applied Developmental Psychology, 24,* 337–340.

Anderson, J. R. (1974). Retrieval of propositional information from long-term memory. *Cognitive Psychology, 6,* 451–474.

Anderson, J. R. (1976). *Language, memory, and thought.* Hillsdale, NJ: Erlbaum.

Anderson, J. R. (1983a). *The architecture of cognition.* Cambridge, MA: Harvard University Press.

Anderson, J. R. (1983b). A spreading activation theory of memory. *Journal of Verbal Learning and Verbal Behavior, 22,* 261–295.

Anderson, J. R. (1985). *Cognitive psychology and its implications* (2nd ed.). New York: W. H. Freeman.

Anderson, J. R. (1987). Skill acquisition: Compilation of weak-method problem solutions. *Psychological Review, 94,* 192–210.

Anderson, J. R. (1990). *Cognitive psychology and its implications* (3rd ed.). New York: W. H. Freeman.

Anderson, J. R. (1993). Problem solving and learning. *American Psychologist, 48,* 35–44.

Anderson, J. R. (1995). *Learning and memory: An integrated approach.* New York: Wiley.

Anderson, J. R., & Bower, G. H. (1973). *Human associative memory.* Washington, DC: Winston.

Anderson, J. R., Greeno, J. G., Reder, L. M., & Simon, H. A. (2000). Perspectives on learning, thinking, and activity. *Educational Researcher, 29*(4), 11–13.

Anderson, J. R., Reder, L. M., & Simon, H. A. (1996). Situated learning and education. *Educational Researcher, 25*(4), 5–11.

Anderson, J. R., Reder, L. M., & Simon, H. A. (1997). Situative versus cognitive perspectives: Form versus substance. *Educational Researcher, 26*(1), 18–21.

Anderson, J. R., & Schooler, L. J. (1991). Reflections of the environment in memory. *Psychological Science, 2,* 396–408.

Anderson, L. M. (1993). Auxiliary materials that accompany textbooks: Can they promote "higher-order" learning? In B. K. Britton, A. Woodward, & M. Binkley (Eds.), *Learning from textbooks: Theory and practice.* Hillsdale, NJ: Erlbaum.

Anderson, L. M. (1997, March). Taking students' entering knowledge and beliefs seriously when teaching about learning and teaching. In H. Borko (Chair), *Educational psychology and teacher education: Perennial issues.* Symposium conducted at the annual meeting of the American Educational Research Association, Chicago.

Anderson, L. W., Krathwohl, D. R., Airasian, P. W., Cruikshank, K. A., Mayer, R. E., Pintrich, P. R., Raths, J., & Wittrock, M. C. (Eds.) (2001). *A taxonomy for learning, teaching, and assessing: A revision of Bloom's taxonomy of educational objectives.* New York: Longman.

Anderson, M. C., & Green, C. (2001). Suppressing unwanted memories by executive control. *Nature, 410,* 366–369.

Anderson, P., Rothbaum, B. O., & Hodges, L. F. (2003). Virtual reality exposure in the treatment of social anxiety. *Cognitive and Behavioral Practice, 10,* 240–247.

Anderson, R. C. (1984). Role of reader's schema in comprehension, learning, and memory. In R. C. Anderson, J. Osborn, & R. J. Tierney (Eds.), *Learning to read in American schools: Basal readers and content texts.* Hillsdale, NJ: Erlbaum.

Anderson, R. C., & Biddle, B. (1975). On asking people questions about what they are reading. In G. H. Bower (Ed.), *Psychology of learning and motivation* (Vol. 9). New York: Academic Press.

Anderson, R. C., Nguyen-Jahiel, K., McNurlen, B., Archodidou, A., Kim, S.-Y., Reznitskaya, A., Tillmanns, M., & Gilbert, L. (2001). The snowball phenomenon: Spread of ways of talking and ways of thinking across groups of children. *Cognition and Instruction, 19,* 1–46.

Anderson, R. C., & Pichert, J. W. (1978). Recall of previously unrecallable information following a shift in perspective. *Journal of Verbal Learning and Verbal Behavior, 17,* 1–12.

Anderson, R. C., Reynolds, R. E., Schallert, D. L., & Goetz, E. T. (1977). Frameworks for comprehending discourse. *American Educational Research Journal, 14,* 367–381.

Anderson, V., & Hidi, S. (1988/1989). Teaching students to summarize. *Educational Leadership, 46*(4), 26–28.

Andre, T. (1979). Does answering higher-level questions while reading facilitate productive learning? *Review of Educational Research, 49,* 280–318.

Andre, T. (1986). Problem solving and education. In G. D. Phye & T. Andre (Eds.), *Cognitive classroom learning: Understanding, thinking, and problem solving.* Orlando: Academic Press.

Andre, T., & Windschitl, M. (2003). Interest, epistemological belief, and intentional conceptual change. In G. M. Sinatra & P. R. Pintrich (Eds.), *Intentional conceptual change* (pp. 173–197). Mahwah, NJ: Erlbaum.

Andrews, A. C. (1987). The analogy theme in geography. *Journal of Geography, 86,* 194–197.

Andrews, G. R., & Debus, R. L. (1978). Persistence and the causal perception of failure: Modifying cognitive attributions. *Journal of Educational Psychology, 70,* 154–166.

Anglin, J. M. (1977). *Word, object, and conceptual development.* New York: W. W. Norton.

Anker, A. L., & Crowley, T. J. (1982). Use of contingency contracts in specialty clinics for cocaine abuse. *National Institute on Drug Abuse: Research Monograph Series, 4,* 452–459.

Anzai, Y. (1991). Learning and use of representations for physics expertise. In K. A. Ericsson & J. Smith (Eds.), *Toward a general theory of expertise: Prospects and limits.* Cambridge, England: Cambridge University Press.

Appel, J. B., & Peterson, N. J. (1965). Punishment: Effects of shock intensity on response suppression. *Psychological Reports, 16,* 721–730.

Applebee, A. N., Langer, J. A., Nystrand, M. & Gamoran, A. (2003). Discussion-based approaches to developing understanding: Classroom instruction and student performance in middle and high school English. *American Educational Research Journal, 40,* 685–730.

Ardoin, S. P., Martens, B. K., & Wolfe, L. A. (1999). Using high-probability instructional sequences with fading to increase student compliance during transitions. *Journal of Applied Behavior Analysis, 32,* 339–351.

Ariely, D. (2001). Seeing sets: Representation by statistical properties. *Psychological Science, 12,* 157–162.

Ariely, D., & Wertenbroch, K. (2002). Procrastination, deadlines, and performance: Self-control by precommitment. *Psychological Science, 13,* 219–224.

Arlin, M. (1984). Time, equality, and mastery learning. *Review of Educational Research, 54,* 65–86.

Armbruster, B. B. (1984). The problem of "inconsiderate text." In G. G. Duffy, L. R. Roehler, & J. Mason (Eds.), *Comprehension instruction: Perspectives and suggestions.* New York: Longman.

Armbruster, B. B., & Ostertag, J. (1993). Questions in elementary science and social studies textbooks. In B. K. Britton, A. Woodward, & M. Binkley (Eds.), *Learning from textbooks: Theory and practice.* Hillsdale, NJ: Erlbaum.

Armstrong, S. L., Gleitman, L. R., & Gleitman, H. G. (1983). What some concepts might not be. *Cognition, 13,* 263–308.

Aronfreed, J. (1968). Aversive control of socialization. In W. J. Arnold (Ed.), *Nebraska*

Symposium on Motivation. Lincoln: University of Nebraska Press.

Aronfreed, J., & Reber, A. (1965). Internalized behavioral suppression and the timing of social punishment. *Journal of Personality and Social Psychology, 1,* 3–16.

Aronson, E. (1997). *The jigsaw classroom: Building cooperation in the classroom* (2nd ed.). New York: Longman.

Aronson, J., Fried, C. B., & Good, C. (2002). Reducing the effects of stereotype threat on African American college students by shaping theories of intelligence. *Journal of Experimental Social Psychology, 38,* 113–125.

Aronson, J., Lustina, M. J., Good, C., Keough, K., Steele, C. M., & Brown, J. (1999). When white men can't do math: Necessary and sufficient factors in stereotype threat. *Journal of Experimental Social Psychology, 35,* 29–46.

Arrigo, J. M., & Pezdek, K. (1997). Lessons from the study of psychogenic amnesia. *Current Directions in Psychological Science, 6,* 148–152.

Artman, L., & Cahan, S. (1993). Schooling and the development of transitive inference. *Developmental Psychology, 29,* 753–759.

Ash, D. (2002). Negotiations of thematic conversations about biology. In G. Leinhardt, K. Crowley, & K. Knutson (Eds.), *Learning conversations in museums* (pp. 357–400). Mahwah, NJ: Erlbaum.

Ash, I. K., & Wiley, J. (2006). The nature of restructuring in insight: An individual-differences approach. *Psychonomic Bulletin & Review, 13*(1), 66–73.

Ashcraft, M. H. (2002). Math anxiety: Personal, educational, and cognitive consequences. *Current Directions in Psychological Science, 11,* 181–184.

Ashton, P. (1985). Motivation and the teacher's sense of efficacy. In C. Ames & R. Ames (Eds.), *Research on motivation in education: Vol. 2. The classroom milieu.* San Diego, CA: Academic Press.

Assor, A., & Connell, J. P. (1992). The validity of students' self-reports as measures of performance affecting self-appraisals. In D. H. Schunk & J. L. Meece (Eds.), *Student perceptions in the classroom.* Hillsdale, NJ: Erlbaum.

Astington, J. W., & Pelletier, J. (1996). The language of mind: Its role in teaching and learning. In D. R. Olson & N. Torrance (Eds.), *The handbook of education and human development: New models of learning, teaching, and schooling.* Cambridge, MA: Blackwell.

Astuti, R., Solomon, G. E. A., & Carey, S. (2004). Constraints on conceptual development. *Monographs of the Society for Research in Child Development, 69*(3, Serial No. 277).

Atance, C. M., & Meltzoff, A. N. (2006). Preschoolers' current desires warp their choices for the future. *Psychological Science, 17,* 583–587.

Atkinson, J. W. (1957). Motivational determinants of risk-taking behavior. *Psychological Review, 64,* 359–372.

Atkinson, J. W. (1958). *Motives in fantasy, action, and sobriety.* Princeton, NJ: Van Nostrand.

Atkinson, J. W. (1964). *Introduction to motivation.* Princeton, NJ: Van Nostrand.

Atkinson, J. W., & Birch, D. (1978). *Introduction to motivation* (2nd ed.). New York: Van Nostrand.

Atkinson, J. W., & Feather, N. T. (Eds.) (1966). *A theory of achievement motivation.* New York: Wiley.

Atkinson, J. W., & Litwin, G. H. (1960). Achievement motive and test anxiety conceived as motive to approach success and motive to avoid failure. *Journal of Abnormal and Social Psychology, 60,* 52–63.

Atkinson, J. W., & Raynor, J. O. (1978). *Personality, motivation, and achievement.* Washington, DC: Hemisphere.

Atkinson, R. C. (1975). Mnemotechnics in second-language learning. *American Psychologist, 30,* 821–828.

Atkinson, R. C., & Shiffrin, R. M. (1968). Human memory: A proposed system and its control processes. In K. W. Spence & J. T. Spence (Eds.), *The psychology of learning and motivation: Advances in research and theory* (Vol. 2). New York: Academic Press.

Atkinson, R. C., & Shiffrin, R. M. (1971). The control of short-term memory. *Scientific American, 225*(2), 82–90.

Atkinson, R. K., Catrambone, R., & Merrill, M. M. (2003). Aiding transfer in statistics: Examining the use of conceptually oriented equations and elaborations during subgoal learning. *Journal of Educational Psychology, 95,* 762–773.

Atkinson, R. K., Derry, S. J., Renkl, A., & Wortham, D. (2000). Learning from examples: Instructional principles from the worked examples research. *Review of Educational Research, 70,* 181–214.

Atkinson, R. K., Levin, J. R., Kiewra, K. A., Meyers, T., Kim, S., Atkinson, L. A., Renandya, W. A., & Hwang, Y. (1999). Matrix and mnemonic text-processing adjuncts: Comparing and combining their components. *Journal of Educational Psychology, 91,* 342–357.

Atkinson, R. K., Renkl, A., & Merrill, M. M. (2003). Transitioning from studying examples to solving problems: Effects of self-explanation prompts and fading worked-out steps. *Journal of Educational Psychology, 95,* 774–783.

Attneave, A. (1957). Transfer of experience with a class schema to identification learning of patterns and shapes. *Journal of Experimental Psychology, 54,* 81–88.

Au, T. K., & Glusman, M. (1990). The principle of mutual exclusivity in word learning: To honor or not to honor? *Child Development, 61,* 1474–1490.

Aulls, M. W. (1998). Contributions of classroom discourse to what content students learn during curriculum enactment. *Journal of Educational Psychology, 90,* 56–69.

Austin, J. L. (2000). Behavioral approaches to college teaching. In J. Austin and J. E. Carr (Eds.), *Handbook of applied behavior analysis* (pp. 449–471). Reno, NV: Context Press.

Austin, J., Alvero, A. M., & Olson, R. (1998). Prompting patron safety belt use at a restaurant. *Journal of Applied Behavior Analysis, 31,* 655–657.

Ausubel, D. P. (1963). *The psychology of meaningful verbal learning.* New York: Grune & Stratton.

Ausubel, D. P. (1968). *Educational psychology: A cognitive view.* New York: Holt, Rinehart & Winston.

Ausubel, D. P., Novak, J. D., & Hanesian, H. (1978). *Educational psychology: A cognitive view* (2nd ed.). New York: Holt, Rinehart & Winston.

Ausubel, D. P., & Robinson, F. G. (1969). *School learning: An introduction to educational psychology.* New York: Holt, Rinehart & Winston.

Awh, E., Jonides, J., Smith, E. E., Schumacher, E. H., Koeppe, R. A., & Katz, S. (1996). Dissociation of storage and rehearsal in verbal working memory: Evidence from positron emission tomography. *Psychological Science, 7,* 25–31.

Ayllon, T., Layman, D., & Kandel, H. J. (1975). A behavioral-educational alternative to drug control of hyperactive children. *Journal of Applied Behavior Analysis, 8,* 137–146.

Azevedo, R. (2005). Computer environments as metacognitive tools for enhancing learning. *Educational Psychologist, 40,* 193–197.

Azrin, N. H. (1960). Effects of punishment intensity during variable-interval reinforcement. *Journal of the Experimental Analysis of Behavior, 3,* 123–142.

Azrin, N. H., & Holz, W. C. (1966). Punishment. In W. K. Honig (Ed.), *Operant behavior: Areas of research and application.* New York: Appleton-Century-Crofts.

Babad, E. (1993). Teachers' differential behavior. *Educational Psychology Review, 5,* 347–376.

Baccus, J. R., Baldwin, M. W., & Packer, D. J. (2004). Increasing implicit self-esteem through classical conditioning. *Psychological Science, 15,* 498–502.

Bachevalier, J., Malkova, L., & Beauregard, M. (1996). Multiple memory systems: A neuropsychological and developmental perspective. In G. R. Lyon & N. A. Krasnegor (Eds.), *Attention, memory, and executive function.* Baltimore: Paul H. Brookes.

Bach-y-Rita, P. (1981). Brain plasticity as a basis for therapeutic procedures. In P. Bach-y-Rita (Ed.), *Recovery of function: Theoretical considerations for brain injury rehabiliation.* Baltimore: University Park Press.

Baddeley, A. D. (1978). The trouble with levels: A reexamination of Craik and Lockhart's framework for memory research. *Psychological Review, 85,* 139–152.

Baddeley, A. D. (1986). *Working memory.* Oxford, England: Clarendon Press.

Baddeley, A. D. (1999). *Essentials of human memory.* Philadelphia: Psychology Press.

Baddeley, A. D. (2001). Is working memory still working? *American Psychologist, 56,* 851–864.

Baddeley, A. D., & Logie, R. (1992). Auditory imagery and working memory. In D. Reisberg (Ed.), *Auditory imagery.* Hillsdale, NJ: Erlbaum.

Bahrick, H. P. (1984). Semantic memory content in permastore: Fifty years of memory for Spanish learned in school. *Journal of Experimental Psychology: General, 113,* 1–29.

Bahrick, H. P., Bahrick, L. E., Bahrick, A. S., & Bahrick, P. E. (1993). Maintenance of foreign language vocabulary and the spacing effect. *Psychological Science, 4,* 316–321.

Bahrick, L. E., Gogate, L. J., & Ruiz, I. (2002). Attention and memory for faces and actions in infancy: The salience of actions over faces in dynamic events. *Child Development, 73,* 1629–1643.

Baillargeon, R. (1994). How do infants learn about the physical world? *Current Directions in Psychological Science, 3,* 133–140.

Baillargeon, R. (2004). Infants' physical worlds. *Current Directions in Psychological Science, 13,* 89–94.

Baker, L. (1989). Metacognition, comprehension monitoring, and the adult reader. *Educational Psychology Review, 1,* 3–38.

Baker, L., & Brown, A. L. (1984). Metacognitive skills of reading. In D. Pearson (Ed.), *Handbook of reading research.* New York: Longman.

Baker, L., Scher, D., & Mackler, K. (1997). Home and family influences on motivations for reading. *Educational Psychologist, 32,* 69–82.

Balch, W., Bowman, K., & Mohler, L. (1992). Music-dependent memory in immediate and delayed word recall. *Memory and Cognition, 20,* 21–28.

Baldwin, D. A. (2000). Interpersonal understanding fuels knowledge acquisition. *Current Directions in Psychological Science, 9,* 40–45.

Bandalos, D. L., Finney, S. J., & Geske, J. A. (2003). A model of statistics performance based on achievement goal theory. *Journal of Educational Psychology, 95,* 604–616.

Bandura, A. (1965a). Behavioral modification through modeling practices. In L. Krasner & L. Ullman (Eds.), *Research in behavior modification.* New York: Holt, Rinehart & Winston.

Bandura, A. (1965b). Influence of models' reinforcement contingencies on the acquisition of imitative responses. *Journal of Personality and Social Psychology, 1,* 589–595.

Bandura, A. (1969). *Principles of behavior modification.* New York: Holt, Rinehart & Winston.

Bandura, A. (1973). *Aggression: A social learning analysis.* Englewood Cliffs, NJ: Prentice Hall.

Bandura, A. (1977). *Social learning theory.* Englewood Cliffs, NJ: Prentice Hall.

Bandura, A. (1982). Self-efficacy mechanism in human agency. *American Psychologist, 37,* 122–147.

Bandura, A. (1986). *Social foundations of thought and action: A social cognitive theory.* Englewood Cliffs, NJ: Prentice Hall.

Bandura, A. (1989). Human agency in social cognitive theory. *American Psychologist, 44,* 1175–1184.

Bandura, A. (1997). *Self-efficacy: The exercise of control.* New York: Freeman.

Bandura, A. (2000). Exercise of human agency through collective efficacy. *Current Directions in Psychological Science, 9,* 75–78.

Bandura, A. (2006). Toward a psychology of human agency. *Perspectives on Psychological Science, 1,* 164–180.

Bandura, A., Barbaranelli, C., Caprara, G. V., & Pastorelli, C. (2001). Self-efficacy beliefs as shapers of children's aspirations and career trajectories. *Child Development, 72,* 187–206.

Bandura, A., Grusec, E., & Menlove, F. L. (1967). Vicarious extinction of avoidance behavior. *Journal of Personality and Social Psychology, 5,* 16–23.

Bandura, A., Jeffery, R. W., & Bachicha, D. L. (1974). Analysis of memory codes and cumulative rehearsal in observational learning. *Journal of Research in Personality, 7,* 295–305.

Bandura, A., & Kupers, C. J. (1964). Transmission of patterns of self-reinforcement through modeling. *Journal of Abnormal and Social Psychology, 69,* 1–9.

Bandura, A., & McDonald, F. J. (1963). Influences of social reinforcement and the behavior of models in shaping children's moral judgments. *Journal of Abnormal and Social Psychology, 67,* 274–281.

Bandura, A., & Menlove, F. L. (1968). Factors determining vicarious extinction of avoidance behavior through symbolic modeling. *Journal of Personality and Social Psychology, 5,* 16–23.

Bandura, A., & Perloff, B. (1967). Relative efficacy of self-monitored and externally imposed reinforcement systems. *Journal of Personality and Social Psychology, 7,* 111–116.

Bandura, A., Ross, D., & Ross, S. A. (1961). Transmission of aggression through imitation of aggressive models. *Journal of Abnormal and Social Psychology, 63,* 575–582.

Bandura, A., Ross, D., & Ross, S. A. (1963). Imitation of film-mediated aggressive models. *Journal of Abnormal and Social Psychology, 66,* 3–11.

Bandura, A., & Schunk, D. (1981). Cultivating competence, self-efficacy, and intrinsic interest through proximal self-motivation. *Journal of Personality and Social Psychology, 41,* 586–598.

Bandura, A., & Walters, R. H. (1963). *Social learning and personality development.* New York: Holt, Rinehart & Winston.

Bandura, A., & Whalen, C. K. (1966). The influence of antecedent reinforcement and divergent modeling cues on patterns of self-reward. *Journal of Personality & Social Psychology, 3,* 373–382.

Bangert-Drowns, R. L., Kulik, C. C., Kulik, J. A., & Morgan, M. (1991). The instructional effect of feedback in test-like events. *Review of Educational Research, 61,* 213–238.

Banks, J. A. (1991). Multicultural literacy and curriculum reform. *Educational Horizons, 69*(3), 135–140.

Barbetta, P. M. (1990). GOALS: A group-oriented adapted levels system for children with behavior disorders. *Academic Therapy, 25,* 645–656.

Barbetta, P. M., Heward, W. L., Bradley, D. M., & Miller, A. D. (1994). Effects of immediate and delayed error correction on the acquisition and maintenance of sight words by students with developmental disabilities. *Journal of Applied Behavior Analysis, 27,* 177–178.

Barch, D. M. (2003). Cognition in schizophrenia: Does working memory work? *Current Directions in Psychological Science, 12,* 146–150.

Barchfeld, P., Sodian, B., Thoermer, C., & Bullock, M. (2005, April). *The development of experiment generation abilities from primary school to late adolescence.* Poster presented at the biennial meeting of the Society for Research in Child Development, Atlanta, GA.

Barker, G. P., & Graham, S. (1987). Developmental study of praise and blame as attributional cues. *Journal of Educational Psychology, 79,* 62–66.

Barker, R. H., Dembo, T., & Lewin, K. (1941). Frustration and regression: An experiment with young children. *University of Iowa Studies in Child Welfare, 18,* 1–314.

Barkley, R. A. (1996a). Critical issues in research on attention. In G. R. Lyon & N. A. Krasnegor (Eds.), *Attention, memory, and executive function.* Baltimore: Paul H. Brookes.

Barkley, R. A. (1996b). Linkages between attention and executive functions. In G. R. Lyon & N. A. Krasnegor (Eds.), *Attention, memory, and executive function.* Baltimore: Paul H. Brookes.

Barnett, J. E. (1999, April). *Adaptive studying across disciplines: A think-aloud study.* Paper presented at the annual meeting of the American Educational Research Association, Montreal.

Barnett, J. E. (2001, April). *Study strategies and preparing for exams: A survey of middle and high school students.* Paper presented at the annual meeting of the American Educational Research Association, Seattle, WA.

Barnett, J. E., Di Vesta, F. J., & Rogozinski, J. T. (1981). What is learned in note taking? *Journal of Educational Psychology, 73,* 181–192.

Baron, A., Kaufman, A., & Stauber, K. A. (1969). Effects of instructions and reinforcement feedback on human operant behavior maintained by fixed-interval reinforcement. *Journal of the Experimental Analysis of Behavior, 12,* 701–712.

Baron, J. B. (1987). Evaluating thinking skills in the classroom. In J. B. Baron & R. J. Sternberg (Eds.), *Teaching thinking skills: Theory and practice.* New York: W. H. Freeman.

Barrish, H. H., Saunders, M., & Wolf, M. M. (1969). Good behavior game: Effects of individual contingencies for group consequences on disruptive behavior in a classroom. *Journal of Applied Behavior Analysis, 2,* 119–124.

Barron, B. (2000). Problem solving in video-based microworlds: Collaborative and individual outcomes of high-achieving sixth-grade students. *Journal of Educational Psychology, 92,* 391–398.

Barth, R. (1979). Home-based reinforcement of school behavior: A review and analysis. *Review of Educational Research, 49,* 436–458.

Bartlett, F. C. (1932). *Remembering: A study in experimental and social psychology.* Cambridge, England: Cambridge University Press.

Barton, K. C., & Levstik, L. S. (1996). "Back when God was around and everything": Elementary children's understanding of historical time. *American Educational Research Journal, 33,* 419–454.

Bassok, M. (1997). Two types of reliance on correlations between content and structure in reasoning about word problems. In L. D. English (Ed.), *Mathematical reasoning: Analogies, metaphors, and images* (pp. 221–246). Mahwah, NJ: Erlbaum.

Bassok, M. (2003). Analogical transfer in problem solving. In J. E. Davidson & R. J. Sternberg (Eds.),

The psychology of problem solving (pp. 343–369). Cambridge, England: Cambridge University Press.

Bassok, M., & Holyoak, K. (1990, April). *Transfer of solution procedures between quantitative domains.* Paper presented at the annual meeting of the American Educational Research Association, Boston.

Bassok, M., & Holyoak, K. J. (1993). Pragmatic knowledge and conceptual structure: Determinants of transfer between quantitative domains. In D. K. Detterman & R. J. Sternberg (Eds.), *Transfer on trial: Intelligence, cognition, and instruction.* Norwood, NJ: Ablex.

Bates, J. A. (1979). Extrinsic reward and intrinsic motivation: A review with implications for the classroom. *Review of Educational Research, 49,* 557–576.

Bauer, P. J. (1995). Recalling past events: From infancy to early childhood. In R. Vasta (Ed.), *Annals of child development: A research annual* (Vol. 11, pp. 25–71). London: Jessica Kingsley.

Bauer, P. J. (2002). Long-term recall memory: Behavioral and neuro-developmental changes in the first 2 years of life. *Current Directions in Psychological Science, 11,* 137–141.

Bauer, P. J. (2006). Event memory. In W. Damon & R. M. Lerner (Series Eds.), D. Kuhn, & R. Siegler (Vol. Eds.), *Handbook of child psychology: Vol. 1. Cognition, perception, and language* (6th ed.). New York: Wiley.

Bauer, P. J., & Mandler, J. M. (1990). Remembering what happened next: Very young children's recall of event sequences. In R. Fivush & J. A. Hudson (Eds.), *Knowing and remembering in young children* (pp. 9–29). Cambridge, England: Cambridge University Press.

Bauer, P. J., Wiebe, S. A., Carver, L. J., Waters, J. M., & Nelson, C. A. (2003). Developments in long-term explicit memory late in the first year of life: Behavioral and electrophysiological indices. *Psychological Science, 14,* 629–635.

Baumrind, D. (1983). Rejoinder to Lewis's reinterpretation of parental firm control effects: Are authoritative families really harmonious? *Psychological Bulletin, 94,* 132–142.

Baumrind, D., Larzelere, R. E., & Cowan, P. A. (2002). Ordinary physical punishment: Is it harmful? Comment on Gershoff (2002). *Psychological Bulletin, 128*(4), 580–589.

Baxter Magolda, M. B. (2002). Epistemological reflection: The evolution of epistemological assumptions from age 18 to 30. In B. K. Hofer & P. R. Pintrich (Eds.), *Personal epistemology: The psychology of beliefs about knowledge and knowing* (pp. 89–102). Mahwah, NJ: Erlbaum.

Baxter Magolda, M. B. (2004). Evolution of a constructivist conceptualizationn of epistemological reflection. *Educational Psychologist, 39,* 31–42.

Bay-Hinitz, A. K., Peterson, R. F., & Quilitch, H. R. (1994). Cooperative games: A way to modify aggressive and cooperative behaviors in young children. *Journal of Applied Behavior Analysis, 27,* 435–446.

Bean, T. W., & Steenwyk, F. L. (1984). The effect of three forms of summarization instruction on sixth graders' summary writing and comprehension. *Journal of Reading Behavior, 16,* 297–306.

Bebko, J. M., Burke, L., Craven, J., & Sarlo, N. (1992). The importance of motor activity in sensorimotor development: A perspective from children with physical handicaps. *Human Development, 35*(4), 226–240.

Beck, I. L., & McKeown, M. G. (1994). Outcomes of history instruction: Paste-up accounts. In M. Carretero & J. F. Voss (Eds.), *Cognitive and instructional processes in history and the social sciences* (pp. 237–256). Mahwah, NJ: Erlbaum.

Beck, I. L., & McKeown, M. G. (2001). Inviting students into the pursuit of meaning. *Educational Psychology Review, 13,* 225–241.

Becker, W. C. (1971). *Parents are teachers.* Champaign, IL: Research Press.

Bédard, J., & Chi, M. T. H. (1992). Expertise. *Current Directions in Psychological Science, 1,* 135–139.

Beeman, M. J., & Chiarello, C. (1998). Complementary right- and left-hemisphere language comprehension. *Current Directions in Psychological Science, 7,* 2–8.

Begg, I., Anas, A., & Farinacci, S. (1992). Dissociation of processes in belief: Source recollection, statement familiarity, and the illusion of truth. *Journal of Experimental Psychology: General, 121,* 446–458.

Behl-Chadha, G. (1996). Basic-level and superordinate-like categorical representations in early infancy. *Cognition, 60,* 105–141.

Behr, M., & Harel, G. (1988, April). Cognitive conflict in procedure applications. In D. Tirosh (Chair), *The role of inconsistent ideas in learning mathematics.* Symposium conducted at the annual meeting of the American Educational Research Association, New Orleans, LA.

Behrmann, M. (2000). The mind's eye mapped onto the brain's matter. *Current Directions in Psychological Science, 9,* 50–54.

Beilock, S. L., & Carr, T. H. (2003). From novice to expert performance: Memory, attention, and the control of complex sensorimotor skills. In A. M. Williams, N. J. Hodges, M. A. Scott, & M. L. J. Court (Eds.), *Skill acquisition in sport: Research, theory, and practice.* New York: Routledge.

Beilock, S. L., & Carr, T. H. (2005). When high-powered people fail: Working memory and "choking under pressure" in math. *Psychological Science, 16,* 101–105.

Beilock, S. L., Kulp, C. A., Holt, L. E., & Carr, T. H. (2004). More on the fragility of performance: Choking under pressure in mathematical problem solving. *Journal of Experimental Psychology: General, 133,* 584–600.

Belenky, M., Clinchy, B., Goldberger, N. R., & Tarule, J. (1997). *Women's ways of knowing: The development of self, mind, and voice.* New York: Basic Books. (Originally published 1986)

Belfiore, P. J., & Hornyak, R. S. (1998). Operant theory and application to self-monitoring in adolescents. In D. H. Schunk and B. J. Zimmerman (Eds.), *Self-regulated learning: From teaching to self-reflective practice.* New York: Guilford Press.

Belfiore, P. J., Lee, D. L., Vargas, A. U., & Skinner, C. H. (1997). Effects of high-preference single-digit mathematics problem completion on multiple-digit mathematics problem performance. *Journal of Applied Behavior Analysis, 30,* 327–330.

Belfiore, P. J., Skinner, C. H., & Ferkis, M. A. (1995). Effects of response and trial repetition on sight-word training for students with learning disabilities. *Journal of Applied Behavior Analysis, 28,* 347–348.

Bell, N., Grossen, M., & Perret-Clermont, A. (1985). Sociocognitive conflict and intellectual growth. In M. W. Berkowitz (Ed.), *Peer conflict and psychological growth.* San Francisco: Jossey-Bass.

Bell, P., & Linn, M. C. (2002). Beliefs about science: How does science instruction contribute? In B. K. Hofer & P. R. Pintrich (Eds.), *Personal epistemology: The psychology of beliefs about knowledge and knowing* (pp. 321–346). Mahwah, NJ: Erlbaum.

Bellezza, F. S. (1986). Mental cues and verbal reports in learning. In G. H. Bower (Ed.), *The psychology of learning and motivation: Advances in research and theory* (Vol. 20). Orlando, FL: Academic Press.

Bem, S. L. (1987). Gender schema theory and its implications for child development: Raising gender-aschematic children in a gender-schematic society. In P. Shaver & C. Hendrick (Eds.), *Sex and gender* (pp. 251–271). Thousand Oaks, CA: Sage.

Bendixen, L. (2002). A process model of epistemic belief change. In B. K. Hofer & P. R. Pintrich (Eds.), *Personal epistemology: The psychology of beliefs about knowledge and knowing* (pp. 191–208). Mahwah, NJ: Erlbaum.

Bendixen, L. D., & Rule, D. C. (2004). An integrative approach to personal epistemology: A guiding model. *Educational Psychologist, 39,* 69–80.

Beneke, W. N., & Harris, M. B. (1972). Teaching self-control of study behavior. *Behaviour Research and Therapy, 10,* 35–41.

Bennett, R. E., Gottesman, R. L., Rock, D. A., & Cerullo, F. (1993). Influence of behavior perceptions and gender on teachers' judgments of students' academic skill. *Journal of Educational Psychology, 85,* 347–356.

Benton, S. L. (1997). Psychological foundations of elementary writing instruction. In G. D. Phye (Ed.), *Handbook of academic learning: Construction of knowledge.* San Diego, CA: Academic Press.

Benton, S. L., Kiewra, K. A., Whitfill, J. M., & Dennison, R. (1993). Encoding and external-storage effects on writing processes. *Journal of Educational Psychology, 85,* 267–280.

Benware, C., & Deci, E. L. (1984). Quality of learning with an active versus passive motivational set. *American Educational Research Journal, 21,* 755–765.

Berardi-Coletta, B., Buyer, L. S., Dominowski, R. L., & Rellinger, E. A. (1995). Metacognition and problem solving: A process-oriented approach. *Journal of Experimental Psychology: Learning, Memory, and Cognition, 21,* 205–223.

Bereiter, C. (1994). Implications of postmodernism for science, or, science as progressive discourse. *Educational Psychologist, 29*(1), 3–12.

Bereiter, C. (1995). A dispositional view of transfer. In A. McKeough, J. Lupart, & A. Marini (Eds.), *Teaching for transfer: Fostering generalization in learning.* Mahwah, NJ: Erlbaum.

Bereiter, C. (1997). Situated cognition and how to overcome it. In D. Kirshner & J. A. Whitson (Eds.), *Situated cognition: Social, semiotic, and psychological perspectives.* Mahwah, NJ: Erlbaum.

Bereiter, C., & Scardamalia, M. (1989). Intentional learning as a goal of instruction. In L. B. Resnick (Ed.), *Knowing, learning and instruction: Essays in honour of Robert Glaser* (pp. 361–392). Mahwah, NJ: Erlbaum.

Bereiter, C., & Scardamalia, M. (1996). Rethinking learning. In D. R. Olson & N. Torrance (Eds.), *The handbook of education and human development: New models of learning, teaching, and schooling.* Cambridge, MA: Blackwell.

Bereiter, C., & Scardamalia, M. (2006). Education for the Knowledge Age: Design-centered models of teaching and instruction. In P. A. Alexander & P. H. Winne (Eds.), *Handbook of educational psychology* (2nd ed., pp. 695–713). Mahwah, NJ: Erlbaum.

Berg, C. A., & Calderone, K. S. (1994). The role of problem interpretations in understanding the development of everyday problem solving. In R. J. Sternberg & R. K. Wagner (Eds.), *Mind in context: Interactionist perspectives on human intelligence.* Cambridge, England: Cambridge University Press.

Bergamo, M., & Evans, M. A. (2005, April). *Rules of surviving peer relationships: Advice from middle school students.* Poster presented at the annual meeting of the American Educational Research Association, Montreal.

Berger, R. (2003). *An ethic of excellence: Building a culture of craftsmanship with students.* Portsmouth, NH: Heinemann.

Berk, L. E. (1994). Why children talk to themselves. *Scientific American, 271,* 78–83.

Berkowitz, L., & LePage, A. (1967). Weapons as aggression-eliciting stimuli. *Journal of Personality and Social Psychology, 7,* 202–207.

Berliner, D. C. (1989). The place of process-product research in developing the agenda for research on teacher thinking. *Educational Psychologist, 24,* 325–344.

Berliner, D. C. (1997, March). Discussant's comments. In H. Borko (Chair), *Educational psychology and teacher education: Perennial issues.* Symposium conducted at the annual meeting of the American Educational Research Association, Chicago.

Berliner, D. C. (2005, April). *Ignoring the forest, blaming the trees: Our impoverished view of educational reform.* Paper presented at the annual meeting of the American Educational Research Association, Montreal.

Berliner, D. C., & Biddle, B. J. (1995). *The manufactured crisis: Myths, fraud, and the attack on America's public schools.* Reading, MA: Addison-Wesley.

Berlyne, D. E. (1960). *Conflict, arousal, and curiosity.* New York: McGraw-Hill.

Berndt, T. J., & Keefe, K. (1996). Friends' influence on school adjustment: A motivational analysis. In J. Juvonen & K. R. Wentzel (Eds.), *Social motivation: Understanding children's school adjustment* (pp. 248–278). Cambridge, England: Cambridge University Press.

Berndt, T., & Perry, T. (1990). Distinctive features and effects of early adolescent friendships. In R. Montemayor, G. Adams, & T. Gullotta (Eds.), *From childhood to adolescence: A transitional period?* Newbury Park, CA: Sage.

Berninger, V. W., Fuller, F., & Whitaker, D. (1996). A process model of writing development across the life span. *Educational Psychology Review, 8,* 193–218.

Bersh, P. J. (1951). The influence of two variables upon the establishment of a secondary reinforcer for operant responses. *Journal of Experimental Psychology, 41,* 62–73.

Berti, A. E. (1994). Children's understanding of the concept of the state. In M. Carretero & J. F. Voss (Eds.), *Cognitive and instructional processes in history and the social sciences* (pp. 49–75). Mahwah, NJ: Erlbaum.

Besner, D. (1999). Basic processes in reading: Multiple routines in localist and connectionist models. In R. M. Klein & P. A. McMullen (Eds.), *Converging methods for understanding reading and dyslexia* (pp. 413–458). Cambridge, MA: MIT Press.

Bialystok, E. (1994a). Representation and ways of knowing: Three issues in second language acquisition. In N. C. Ellis (Ed.), *Implicit and explicit learning of languages.* London: Academic Press.

Bialystok, E. (1994b). Towards an explanation of second language acquisition. In G. Brown, K. Malmkjær, A. Pollitt, & J. Williams (Eds.), *Language and understanding.* Oxford, England: Oxford University Press.

Bielaczyc, K., & Collins, A. (1999). Learning communities in classrooms: A reconceptualization of educational practice. In C. M. Reigeluth (Ed.), *Instructional-design theories and models: A new paradigm of instructional theory* (pp. 269–292). Mahwah, NJ: Erlbaum

Bielaczyc, K., & Collins, A. (2006). Fostering knowledge-creating communities. In A. M. O'Donnell, C. E. Hmelo-Silver, & G. Erkens (Eds.), *Collaborative learning, reasoning, and technology* (pp. 37–60). Mahwah, NJ: Erlbaum.

Biemiller, A., Shany, M., Inglis, A., & Meichenbaum, D. (1998). Factors influencing children's acquisition and demonstration of self-regulation on academic tasks. In D. H. Schunk & B. J. Zimmerman (Eds.), *Self-regulated learning: From teaching to self-reflective practice* (pp. 203–224). New York: Guilford Press.

Bilodeau, I. M., & Schlosberg, H. (1951). Similarity in stimulating conditions as a variable in retroactive inhibition. *Journal of Experimental Psychology, 41,* 199–204.

Binder, L. M., Dixon, M. R., & Ghezzi, P. M. (2000). A procedure to teach self-control to children with attention deficit hyperactivity disorder. *Journal of Applied Behavior Analysis, 33,* 233–237.

Birch, H. G., & Rabinowitz, H. S. (1951). The negative effect of previous experience on productive thinking. *Journal of Experimental Psychology, 41,* 121–125.

Birnbaum, J. C. (1982). The reading and composing behaviors of selected fourth- and seventh-grade students. *Research in the Teaching of English, 16,* 241–260.

Bishop, B. A., & Anderson, C. W. (1990). Student conceptions of natural selection and its role in evolution. *Journal of Research in Science Teaching, 27,* 415–427.

Bivens, J. A., & Berk, L. E. (1990). A longitudinal study of the development of elementary school children's private speech. *Merrill-Palmer Quarterly, 36,* 443–463.

Bjork, R. A. (1972). Theoretical implications of directed forgetting. In A. W. Melton & E. Martin (Eds.), *Coding processes in human memory.* Washington, DC: V. H. Winston.

Bjorklund, D. F. (1987). How age changes in knowledge base contribute to the development of children's memory: An interpretive review. *Developmental Review, 7,* 93–130.

Bjorklund, D. F. (1997). In search of a metatheory for cognitive development (or, Piaget is dead and I don't feel so good myself). *Child Development, 68,* 144–148.

Bjorklund, D. F., & Coyle, T. R. (1995). Utilization deficiencies in the development of memory strategies. In F. E. Weinert & W. Schneider (Eds.), *Research on memory development: State of the art and future directions.* Hillsdale, NJ: Erlbaum.

Bjorklund, D. F., & Green, B. L. (1992). The adaptive nature of cognitive immaturity. *American Psychologist, 47,* 46–54.

Black, J. E., Isaacs, K. R., Anderson, B. J., Alcantara, A. A., & Greenough, W. T. (1990). Learning causes synaptogenesis, whereas motor activity causes angiogenesis, in cerebellar cortex of adult rats. *Proceedings of the National Academy of Sciences, 87,* 5568–5572.

Blanchard, F. A., Lilly, T., & Vaughn, L. A. (1991). Reducing the expression of racial prejudice. *Psychological Science, 2,* 101–105.

Blanchette, I., & Richards, A. (2004). Reasoning about emotional and neutral materials: Is logic affected by emotion? *Psychological Science, 15,* 745–752.

Blatt, S. J. (1995). The destructiveness of perfectionism: Implication for treatment of depression. *American Psychologist, 50,* 1103–1020.

Blazevski, J. L., McEvoy, A. P., & Pintrich, P. R. (2003, April). *The relation of achievement goals to cognitive regulation, persistence, and achievement.* Paper presented at the annual meeting of the American Educational Research Association, Chicago.

Block, J. H. (1980). Promoting excellence through mastery learning. *Theory into Practice, 19*(1), 66–74.

Blok, H., Oostdam, R., Otter, M. E., & Overmaat, M. (2002). Computer-assisted instruction in support of beginning reading instruction: A review. *Review of Educational Research, 72,* 101–103.

Bloom, B. S. (1968). Mastery learning. In *Evaluation comment* (Vol. 1, No. 2). Los Angeles: University of California at Los Angeles, Center for the Study of Evaluation of Instructional Programs.

Bloom, B. S. (1981). *All our children learning*. New York: McGraw-Hill.

Bloom, B. S., & Broder, L. J. (1950). *Problem-solving processes of college students*. Chicago: University of Chicago Press.

Bloom, B. S., Englehart, M. B., Furst, E. J., Hill, W. H., & Krathwohl, D. R. (1956). *Taxonomy of educational objectives. The classification of educational goals. Handbook I: Cognitive domain*. New York: Longmans Green.

Bloom, L., & Tinker, E. (2001). The intentionality model and language acquisition. *Monographs of the Society for Research in Child Development, 66*(4, Serial No. 267).

Blumenfeld, P. C. (1992). The task and the teacher: Enhancing student thoughtfulness in science. In J. Brophy (Ed.), *Advances in research on teaching: Vol. 3. Planning and managing learning tasks and activities*. Greenwich, CT: JAI Press.

Blumenfeld, P. C., Hamilton, V. L., Bossert, S., Wessels, K., & Meece, C. (1983). Teacher talk and student thought: Socialization into the student role. In J. Levine & U. Wang (Eds.), *Teacher and student perceptions: Implications for learning*. Hillsdale, NJ: Erlbaum.

Blumenfeld, P. C., Marx, R. W., Soloway, E., & Krajcik, J. (1996). Learning with peers: From small group cooperation to collaborative communities. *Educational Researcher, 25*(8), 37–40.

Bochenhauer, M. H. (1990, April). *Connections: Geographic education and the National Geographic Society*. Paper presented at the annual meeting of the American Educational Research Association, Boston.

Bodrova, E., & Leong, D. J. (1996). *Tools of the mind: The Vygotskian approach to early childhood education*. Upper Saddle River, NJ: Merrill/Prentice Hall.

Boekaerts, M., de Koning, E., & Vedder, P. (2006). Goal-directed behavior and contextual factors in the classroom: An innovative approach to the study of multiple goals. *Educational Psychologist, 41*, 33–51.

Boggiano, A. K., Main, D. S., & Katz, P. A. (1988). Children's preference for challenge: The role of perceived competence and control. *Journal of Personality and Social Psychology, 54*, 134–141.

Boggiano, A. K., & Pittman, T. S. (Eds.) (1992). *Achievement and motivation: A social-developmental perspective*. Cambridge, England: Cambridge University Press.

Bohannon, J. N., III, & Symons, V. L. (1992). Flashbulb memories: Confidence, consistency, and quantity. In E. Winograd & U. Neisser (Eds.), *Affect and accuracy in recall: Studies of "flashbulb" memories*. Cambridge, England: Cambridge University Press.

Bolles, R. C. (1975). *Theory of motivation* (2nd ed.). New York: Harper & Row.

Bolstad, O., & Johnson, S. (1972). Self-regulation in the modification of disruptive classroom behavior. *Journal of Applied Behavior Analysis, 5*, 443–454.

Bomba, P. C., & Siqueland, E. R. (1983). The nature and structure of infant form categories. *Journal of Experimental Child Psychology, 35*, 294–328.

Bong, M. (2001). Between- and within-domain relations of academic motivation among middle and high school students: Self-efficacy, task-value, and achievement goals. *Journal of Educational Psychology, 93*, 23–34.

Bong, M., & Clark, R. E. (1999). Comparison between self-concept and self-efficacy in academic motivation research. *Educational Psychologist, 34*, 139–153.

Bong, M., & Skaalvik, E. M. (2003). Academic self-concept and self-efficacy: How different are they really? *Educational Psychology Review, 15*, 1–40.

Borkowski, J. G., & Burke, J. E. (1996). Theories, models, and measurements of executive functioning. In G. R. Lyon & N. A. Krasnegor (Eds.), *Attention, memory, and executive function* (pp. 235–261). Baltimore: Brookes.

Born, D. G., & Davis, M. L. (1974). Amount and distribution of study in a personalized instruction course and in a lecture course. *Journal of Applied Behavior Analysis, 7*, 365–375.

Bortfeld, H., & Whitehurst, G. J. (2001). Sensitive periods in first language acquisition. In D. B. Bailey, Jr., J. T. Bruer, F. J. Symons, & J. W. Lichtman (Eds.), *Critical thinking about critical periods* (pp. 173–192). Baltimore: Brookes.

Bourbeau, P. E., Sowers, J., & Close, D. E. (1986). An experimental analysis of generalization of banking skills from classroom to bank settings in the community. *Education and Training of the Mentally Retarded, 21*, 98–107.

Bourne, L. E., Jr. (1967). Learning and utilization of conceptual rules. In B. Kleinmuntz (Ed.), *Concepts and the structure of memory*. New York: Wiley.

Bourne, L. E., Jr. (1982). Typicality effects in logically defined concepts. *Memory and Cognition, 10*, 3–9.

Bourne, L. E., Jr., Dominowski, R. L., Loftus, E. F., & Healy, A. F. (1986). *Cognitive processes* (2nd ed.). Englewood Cliffs, NJ: Prentice Hall.

Bourne, L. E., Jr., Ekstrand, D. R., & Dominowski, R. L. (1971). *The psychology of thinking*. Englewood Cliffs, NJ: Prentice Hall.

Bousfield, W. A. (1953). The occurrence of clustering in the recall of randomly arranged associates. *Journal of General Psychology, 49*, 229–240.

Bouton, M. E. (1994). Context, ambiguity, and classical conditioning. *Current Directions in Psychological Science, 3*, 49–53.

Bower, G. H. (1972). Mental imagery and associative learning. In L. W. Gregg (Ed.), *Cognition in learning and memory*. New York: Wiley.

Bower, G. H. (1994). Some relations between emotions and memory. In P. Ekman & R. J. Davidson (Eds.), *The nature of emotion: Fundamental questions*. New York: Oxford University Press.

Bower, G. H., Black, J. B., & Turner, T. J. (1979). Scripts in memory for text. *Cognitive Psychology, 11*, 177–220.

Bower, G. H., & Clark, M. C. (1969). Narrative stories as mediators for serial learning. *Psychonomic Science, 14*, 181–182.

Bower, G. H., Clark, M. C., Lesgold, A. M., & Winzenz, D. (1969). Hierarchical retrieval schemes in recall of categorized word lists. *Journal of Verbal Learning and Verbal Behavior, 8*, 323–343.

Bower, G. H., & Forgas, J. P. (2001). Mood and social memory. In J. P. Forgas (Ed.), *Handbook of affect and social cognition* (pp. 95–120). Mahwah, NJ: Erlbaum.

Bower, G. H., & Hilgard, E. R. (1981). *Theories of learning* (5th ed.). Englewood Cliffs, NJ: Prentice Hall.

Bower, G. H., & Holyoak, K. J. (1973). Encoding and recognition memory for naturalistic sounds. *Journal of Experimental Psychology, 101*, 360–366.

Bower, G. H., Karlin, M. B., & Dueck, A. (1975). Comprehension and memory for pictures. *Memory and Cognition, 3*, 216–220.

Bower, G. H., McLean, J., & Meachem, J. (1966). Value of knowing when reinforcement is due. *Journal of Comparative and Physiological Psychology, 62*, 184–192.

Bower, G. H., & Springston, F. (1970). Pauses as recoding points in letter series. *Journal of Experimental Psychology, 83*, 421–430.

Bowers, J. S. (2002). Challenging the widespread assumption that connectionism and distributed representations go hand-in-hand. *Cognitive Psychology, 45*, 413–445.

Bowers, F. E., Woods, D. W., Carlyon, W. D., & Friman, P. C. (2000). Using positive peer reporting to improve the social interactions and acceptance of socially isolated adolescents in residential care: A systematic replication. *Journal of Applied Behavior Analysis, 33*, 239–242.

Bowman, L. G., Piazza, C. C., Fisher, W. W., Hagopian, L. P., & Kogan, J. S. (1997). Assessment of preference for varied versus constant reinforcers. *Journal of Applied Behavior Analysis, 30*, 451–458.

Boyatzis, R. E. (1973). Affiliation motivation. In D. C. McClelland & R. S. Steele (Eds.), *Human motivation: A book of readings*. Morristown, NJ: General Learning Press.

Boykin, A. W. (1994). Harvesting talent and culture: African-American children and educational reform. In R. J. Rossi (Ed.), *Schools and students at risk: Context and framework for positive change*. New York: Teachers College Press.

Braaksma, M. A. H., Rijlaarsdam, G., & van den Bergh, H. (2002). Observational learning and the effects of model-observer similarity. *Journal of Educational Psychology, 94*, 405–415.

Bragstad, B. J., & Stumpf, S. M. (1982). *A guidebook for teaching study skills and motivation*. Boston: Allyn & Bacon.

Brainerd, C. J. (2003). Jean Piaget, learning research, and American education. In B. J. Zimmerman & D. H. Schunk (Eds.), *Educational psychology: A century of contributions* (pp. 251–287). Mahwah, NJ: Erlbaum.

Brainerd, C. J., & Reyna, V. F. (1992). Explaining "memory free" reasoning. *Psychological Science, 3*, 332–339.

Brainerd, C. J., & Reyna, V. F. (1998). When things that were never experienced are easier to "remember" than things that were. *Psychological Science, 9*, 484–489.

Brainerd, C. J., & Reyna, V. F. (2002). Fuzzy-trace theory and false memory. *Current Directions in Psychological Science, 11*, 164–169.

Brandon, S., Boakes, J., Glaser, D., & Green, R. (1998). Recovered memories of childhood sexual abuse: Implications for clinical practice. *British Journal of Psychiatry, 172,* 296–307.

Bransford, J. D., Brown, A. L., & Cocking, R. R. (Eds.) (1999). *How people learn: Brain, mind, experience, and school.* Washington, DC: National Academy Press.

Bransford, J. D., & Franks, J. J. (1971). The abstraction of linguistic ideas. *Cognitive Psychology, 2,* 331–350.

Bransford, J. D., Franks, J. J., Vye, N. J., & Sherwood, R. D. (1989). New approaches to instruction: Because wisdom can't be told. In S. Vosniadou & A. Ortony (Eds.), *Similarity and analogical reasoning* (pp. 470–497). Cambridge, England: Cambridge University Press.

Bransford, J. D., & Johnson, M. K. (1972). Contextual prerequisites for understanding: Some investigations of comprehension and recall. *Journal of Verbal Learning and Verbal Behavior, 11,* 717–726.

Braukmann, C. J., Ramp, K. K., & Wolf, M. M. (1981). Behavioral treatment of juvenile delinquency. In S. W. Bijou & R. Ruiz (Eds.), *Behavior modification: Contributions to education.* Hillsdale, NJ: Erlbaum.

Bredo, E. (1997). The social construction of learning. In G. D. Phye (Ed.), *Handbook of academic learning: Construction of knowledge.* San Diego, CA: Academic Press.

Breitmeyer, B. B., & Ganz, L. (1976). Implications of sustained and transient channels for theories of visual pattern masking, saccadic suppression, and information processing. *Psychological Review, 83,* 1–36.

Brenner, M. E., Mayer, R. E., Moseley, B., Brar, T., Durán, R., Reed, B. S., & Webb, D. (1997). Learning by understanding: The role of multiple representations in learning algebra. *American Educational Research Journal, 34,* 663–689.

Bressler, S. L. (2002). Understanding cognition through large-scale cortical networks. *Current Directions in Psychological Science, 11,* 58–61.

Brewer, W. F. (1992). The theoretical and empirical status of the flashbulb memory hypothesis. In E. Winograd & U. Neisser (Eds.), *Affect and accuracy in recall: Studies of "flashbulb" memories.* Cambridge, England: Cambridge University Press.

Brewer, W. F., & Treyens, J. C. (1981). Role of schemata in memory for places. *Cognitive Psychology, 13,* 207–230.

Brickman, S., Miller, R. B., & Roedel, T. D. (1997, March). *Goal valuing and future consequences as predictors of cognitive engagement.* Paper presented at the annual meeting of the American Educational Research Association, Chicago.

Briggs, L. J., & Reed, H. B. (1943). The curve of retention for substance material. *Journal of Experimental Psychology, 32,* 513–517.

Britton, B. K., Stimson, M., Stennett, B., & Gülgöz, S. (1998). Learning from instructional text: Test of an individual differences model. *Journal of Educational Psychology, 90,* 476–491.

Broadbent, D. E. (1958). *Perception and communication.* London: Pergamon Press.

Broadhurst, P. L. (1959). The interaction of task difficulty and motivation: The Yerkes–Dodson law revived. *Acta Psychologia, 16,* 321–338.

Broekkamp, H., Van Hout-Wolters, B. H. A. M., Rijlaarsdam, G., & van den Bergh, H. (2002). Importance in instructional text: Teachers' and students' perceptions of task demands. *Journal of Educational Psychology, 94,* 260–271.

Bronfenbrenner, U. (1970). *Two worlds of childhood: U.S. and U.S.S.R.* New York: Russell Sage Foundation.

Bronfenbrenner, U. (1999). Is early intervention effective? Some studies of early education in familial and extra-familial settings. In A. Montagu (Ed.), *Race and IQ* (expanded ed., pp. 343–378). New York: Oxford University Press.

Bronson, M. B. (2000). *Self-regulation in early childhood: Nature and nurture.* New York: Guilford Press.

Brooke, R. R., & Ruthren, A. J. (1984). The effects of contingency contracting on student performance in a PSI class. *Teaching of Psychology, 11,* 87–89.

Brooks, L. R. (1978). Nonanalytic concept formation and memory for instances. In E. Rosch & B. B. Lloyd (Eds.), *Cognition and categorization.* Hillsdale, NJ: Erlbaum.

Brooks, L. W., & Dansereau, D. F. (1987). Transfer of information: An instructional perspective. In S. M. Cormier & J. D. Hagman (Eds.), *Transfer of learning: Contemporary research and applications.* San Diego, CA: Academic Press.

Brophy, J. E. (1986). *On motivating students.* Occasional Paper No. 101, Institute for Research on Teaching, Michigan State University, East Lansing.

Brophy, J. E. (1987). Synthesis of research on strategies for motivating students to learn. *Educational Leadership, 45*(2), 40–48.

Brophy, J. E. (1988). Research linking teacher behavior to student achievement: Potential implications for instruction of Chapter 1 students. *Educational Psychologist, 23,* 235–286.

Brophy, J. E. (1992a). Conclusions: Comments on an emerging field. In J. Brophy (Ed.), *Advances in research on teaching: Vol. 3. Planning and managing learning tasks and activities.* Greenwich, CT: JAI Press.

Brophy, J. E. (1992b). Probing the subtleties of subject-matter teaching. *Educational Leadership, 49*(7), 4–8.

Brophy, J. E. (1999). Toward a model of the value aspects of motivation in education: Developing appreciation for particular learning domains and activities. *Educational Psychologist, 34,* 75–85.

Brophy, J. (2004). *Motivating students to learn* (2nd ed.). Mahwah, NJ: Erlbaum.

Brophy, J. (2005). Goal theorists should move on from performance goals. *Educational Psychologist, 40,* 167–176.

Brophy, J. E., & Alleman, J. (1991). Activities as instructional tools: A framework for analysis and evaluation. *Educational Researcher, 20*(4), 9–23.

Brophy, J. E., & Alleman, J. (1992). Planning and managing learning activities: Basic principles. In J. Brophy (Ed.), *Advances in research on teaching: Vol. 3. Planning and managing learning tasks and activities.* Greenwich, CT: JAI Press.

Brothers, K. J., Krantz, P. J., & McClannahan, L. E. (1994). Office paper recycling: A function of container proximity. *Journal of Applied Behavior Analysis, 27,* 153–160.

Brown, A. (1991). A review of the tip-of-the-tongue experience. *Psychological Bulletin, 109,* 204–223.

Brown, A. L. (1978). Knowing when, where, and how to remember: A problem of metacognition. In R. Glaser (Ed.), *Advances in instructional psychology,* Hillsdale, NJ: Erlbaum.

Brown, A. L., Bransford, J. D., Ferrera, R. A., & Campione, J. C. (1983). Learning, remembering, and understanding. In J. Flavell & E. Mankman (Eds.), *Carmichael's manual of children psychology* (Vol. 1). New York: Wiley.

Brown, A. L., & Campione, J. C. (1972). Recognition memory for perceptually similar pictures in preschool children. *Journal of Experimental Psychology, 95,* 55–62.

Brown, A. L., & Campione, J. C. (1994). Guided discovery in a community of learners. In K. McGilly (Ed.), *Classroom lessons: Integrating cognitive theory and classroom practice.* Cambridge, MA: MIT Press/Bradford.

Brown, A. L., & Campione, J. C. (1996). Psychological theory and the design of innovative learning environments: On procedures, principles, and systems. In L. Schauble & R. Glaser (Eds.), *Innovations in learning: New environments for education.* Mahwah, NJ: Erlbaum.

Brown, A. L., Campione, J., & Day, J. (1981). Learning to learn: On training students to learn from texts. *Educational Researcher, 10*(2), 14–21.

Brown, A. L., & Day, J. D. (1983). Macrorules for summarizing texts: The development of expertise. *Journal of Verbal Learning and Verbal Behavior, 22,* 1–14.

Brown, A. L., Kane, M. J., & Echols, K. (1986). Young children's mental models determine analogical transfer across problems with a common goal structure. *Cognitive Development, 1,* 103–122.

Brown, A. L., & Palincsar, A. S. (1987). Reciprocal teaching of comprehension strategies: A natural history of one program for enhancing learning. In J. Borkowski & J. D. Day (Eds.), *Cognition in special education: Comparative approaches to retardation, learning disabilities, and giftedness.* Norwood, NJ: Ablex.

Brown, A. L., & Palincsar, A. S. (1989). Guided, cooperative learning and individual knowledge acquisition. In L. B. Resnick (Ed.), *Knowing, learning, and instruction: Essays in honor of Robert Glaser.* Hillsdale, NJ: Erlbaum.

Brown, A. L., Palincsar, A. S., & Armbruster, B. B. (1984). Instructing comprehension fostering activities in interactive learning situations. In H. Mandl, N. Stein, & T. Trabasso (Eds.), *Learning and comprehension of text.* Hillsdale, NJ: Erlbaum.

Brown, A. L., & Reeve, R. A. (1987). Bandwidths of competence: The role of supportive contexts in learning and development. In L. S. Liben (Ed.), *Development and learning: Conflict or congruence?* Hillsdale, NJ: Erlbaum.

Brown, A. L., & Scott, M. S. (1971). Recognition memory for pictures in preschool children. *Journal of Experimental Child Psychology, 11,* 401–412.

Brown, B. (1990). Peer groups. In S. Feldman & G. Elliott (Eds.), *At the threshold: The developing adolescent* (pp. 171–196). Cambridge, MA: Harvard University Press.

Brown, B. B., Eicher, S. A., & Petrie, S. (1986). The importance of peer group ("crowd") affiliation in adolescence. *Journal of Adolescence, 9,* 73–96.

Brown, D. E. (1992). Using examples and analogies to remediate misconceptions in physics: Factors influencing conceptual change. *Journal of Research in Science Teaching, 29,* 17–34.

Brown, I., & Inouye, D. K. (1978). Learned helplessness through modeling: The role of perceived similarity in competence. *Journal of Personality and Social Psychology, 36,* 900–908.

Brown, J. (1968). Reciprocal facilitation and impairment of free recall. *Psychonomic Science, 10,* 41–44.

Brown, J. S., Collins, A., & Duguid, P. (1989). Situated cognition and the culture of learning. *Educational Researcher, 18*(1), 32–42.

Brown, N. R., & Schopflocher, D. (1998). Event clusters: An organization of personal events in autobiographical memory. *Psychological Science, 9,* 470–475.

Brown, R., & Herrnstein, R. J. (1975). *Psychology.* Boston: Little, Brown.

Brown, R., & Kulik, J. (1977). Flashbulb memories. *Cognition, 5,* 73–99.

Brown, R., & McNeill, D. (1966). The "tip of the tongue" phenomenon. *Journal of Verbal Learning and Verbal Behavior, 5,* 325–337.

Brown, R. D., & Bjorklund, D. F. (1998). The biologizing of cognition, development, and education: Approach with cautious enthusiasm. *Educational Psychology Review, 10,* 355–373.

Brown, S. I., & Walter, M. I. (1990). *The art of problem posing* (2nd ed.). Hillsdale, NJ: Erlbaum.

Brown, V. R., & Paulus, P. B. (2002). Making group brainstorming more effective: Recommendations from an associative memory perspective. *Current Directions in Psychological Science, 11,* 208–212.

Brown, W. H., Bryson-Brockmann, W., & Fox, J. J. (1986). The usefulness of J. R. Kantor's setting event concept for research on children's social behavior. *Child and Family Behavior Therapy, 8*(2), 15–25.

Brown, W. H., Fox, J. J., & Brady, M. P. (1987). Effects of spatial density on 3- and 4-year-old children's socially directed behavior during freeplay: An investigation of a setting factor. *Education and Treatment of Children, 10,* 247–258.

Brozo, W. G., Stahl, N. A., & Gordon, B. (1985). Training effects of summarizing, item writing, and knowledge of information sources on reading test performance. In J. A. Niles & R. V. Lalik (Eds.), *Issues in literacy.* Rochester, NY: National Reading Conference.

Bruck, M., Cavanagh, P., & Ceci, S. (1991). Fortysomething: Recognizing faces at one's 25th reunion. *Memory and Cognition, 19,* 221–228.

Bruck, M., & Ceci, S. J. (1997). The suggestibility of young children. *Current Directions in Psychological Science, 6,* 75–79.

Bruer, J. T. (1997). Education and the brain: A bridge too far. *Educational Researcher, 26*(8), 4–16.

Bruer, J. T. (1999). *The myth of the first three years: A new understanding of early brain development and lifelong learning.* New York: Free Press.

Bruer, J. T., & Greenough, W. T. (2001). The subtle science of how experience affects the brain. In D. B. Bailey, Jr., J. T. Bruer, F. J. Symons, & J. W. Lichtman (Eds.), *Critical thinking about critical periods* (pp. 209–232). Baltimore: Brookes.

Bruner, J. S. (1957). On going beyond the information given. In *Contemporary approaches to cognition.* Cambridge, MA: Harvard University Press.

Bruner, J. S. (1961a). The act of discovery. *Harvard Educational Review, 31,* 21–32.

Bruner, J. S. (1961b). *The process of education.* Cambridge, MA: Harvard University Press.

Bruner, J. S. (1966). *Toward a theory of instruction.* New York: W. W. Norton.

Bruner, J. S., Goodnow, J., & Austin, G. (1956). *A study of thinking.* New York: Wiley.

Bruning, R. H., Schraw, G. J., & Ronning, R. R. (1995). *Cognitive psychology and instruction* (2nd ed.). Englewood Cliffs, NJ: Prentice Hall/Merrill.

Bryan, J. H. (1971). Model affect and children's imitative altruism. *Child Development, 42,* 2061–2065.

Bryan, J. H. (1975). Children's cooperation and helping behaviors. In E. M. Hetherington (Ed.), *Review of child development research* (Vol. 5). Chicago: University of Chicago Press.

Buckhout, R. (1974). Eyewitness testimony. *Scientific American, 231*(6), 23–31.

Buckland, P. R. (1968). The ordering of frames in a linear program. *Programmed Learning and Educational Technology, 5,* 197–205.

Buckner, R. L., & Petersen, S. E. (1996). What does neuroimaging tell us about the role of prefrontal cortex in memory retrieval? *Seminars in the Neurosciences, 8,* 47–55.

Buehl, M. M., & Alexander, P. A. (2001). Beliefs about academic knowledge. *Educational Psychology Review, 13,* 385–418.

Buehl, M. M., & Alexander, P. A. (2004, April). *Modeling the relations between students' domain-specific epistemological beliefs, motivation, and task performance.* Paper presented at the American Educational Research Association, San Diego, CA.

Buehl, M. M., & Alexander, P. A. (2005). Motivation and performance differences in students' domain-specific epistemological belief profiles. *American Educational Research Journal, 42,* 697–726.

Bufford, R. K. (1976). Evaluation of a reinforcement procedure for accelerating work rate in a self-paced course. *Journal of Applied Behavior Analysis, 9,* 208.

Bugelski, B. R. (1962). Presentation time, total time, and mediation in paired-associate learning. *Journal of Experimental Psychology, 63,* 409–412.

Bugelski, B. R., & Alampay, D. A. (1961). The role of frequency in developing perceptual sets. *Canadian Journal of Psychology, 15,* 205–211.

Bugelski, B. R., Kidd, E., & Segmen, J. (1968). Image as a mediator in one-trial paired-associate learning. *Journal of Experimental Psychology, 76,* 69–73.

Bulgren, J. A., Deshler, D. D., Schumaker, J. B., & Lenz, B. K. (2000). The use and effectiveness of analogical instruction in diverse secondary content classrooms. *Journal of Educational Psychology, 92,* 426–441.

Bulgren, J. A., Schumaker, J. B., & Deshler, D. D. (1994). The effects of a recall enhancement routine on the test performance of secondary students with and without learning disabilities. *Learning Disabilities Research and Practice, 9,* 2–11.

Burhans, K. K., & Dweck, C. S. (1995). Helplessness in early childhood: The role of contingent worth. *Child Development, 66,* 1719–1738.

Burnett, P. (2001). Elementary students' preferences for teacher praise. *Journal of Classroom Interaction, 36,* 16–23.

Burnett, R. E., & Kastman, L. M. (1997). Teaching composition: Current theories and practices. In G. D. Phye (Ed.), *Handbook of academic learning: Construction of knowledge.* San Diego, CA: Academic Press.

Buschke, H. (1977). Two-dimensional recall: Immediate identification of clusters in episodic and semantic memory. *Journal of Verbal Learning and Verbal Behavior, 16,* 201–215.

Bushell, D., Wrobel, P. A., & Michaelis, M. L. (1968). Applying "group" contingencies to the classroom study behavior of preschool children. *Journal of Applied Behavior Analysis, 1,* 55–61.

Bussey, K., & Bandura, A. (1992). Self-regulatory mechanisms governing gender development. *Child Development, 63,* 1236–1250.

Butcher, K. R. (2006). Learning from text with diagrams: Promoting mental model development and inference generation. *Journal of Educational Psychology, 98,* 182–197.

Butler, D. L., & Winne, P. H. (1995). Feedback and self-regulated learning: A theoretical synthesis. *Review of Educational Research, 65,* 245–281.

Butler, R. (1987). Task-involving and ego-involving properties of evaluation: Effects of different feedback conditions on motivational perceptions, interest, and performance. *Journal of Educational Psychology, 79,* 474–482.

Butler, R. (1988). Enhancing and undermining intrinsic motivation: The effects of task-involving and ego-involving evaluation on interest and performance. *British Journal of Educational Psychology, 58,* 1–14.

Butler, R. (1989). Mastery versus ability appraisal: A developmental study of children's observations of peers' work. *Child Development, 60,* 1350–1361.

Butler, R. (1994). Teacher communication and student interpretations: Effects of teacher responses to failing students on attributional inferences in two age groups. *British Journal of Educational Psychology, 64,* 277–294.

Butler, R. (1998a). Age trends in the use of social and temporal comparison for self-evaluation: Examination of a novel developmental hypothesis. *Child Development, 69*, 1054–1073.

Butler, R. (1998b). Determinants of help seeking: Relations between perceived reasons for classroom help-avoidance and help-seeking behaviors in an experimental context. *Journal of Educational Psychology, 90*, 630–644.

Butterworth, G. (1993). Context and cognition in models of cognitive growth. In P. Light & G. Butterworth (Eds.), *Context and cognition: Ways of learning and knowing*. Hillsdale, NJ: Erlbaum.

Byrne, B. M. (2002). Validating the measurement and structure of self-concept: Snapshots of past, present, and future research. *American Psychologist, 57*, 897–909.

Byrnes, J. P. (1996). *Cognitive development and learning in instructional contexts*. Boston: Allyn & Bacon.

Byrnes, J. P. (2001). *Minds, brains, and learning: Understanding the psychological and educational relevance of neuroscientific research*. New York: Guilford Press.

Byrnes, J. P., & Fox, N. A. (1998). The educational relevance of research in cognitive neuroscience. *Educational Psychology Review, 10*, 297–342.

Cacioppo, J. T., Petty, R. E., Feinstein, J. A., & Jarvis, W. B. G. (1996). Dispositional differences in cognitive motivation: The life and times of individuals varying in need for cognition. *Psychological Bulletin, 119*, 197–253.

Cadinu, M., Maass, A., Rosabianca, A., & Kiesner, J. (2005). Why do women underperform under stereotype threat? Evidence for the role of negative thinking. *Psychological Science, 16*, 572–578.

Cahill, L., Haier, R. J., Fallon, J., Alkire, M., Tang, C., Keator, D., Wu, J., & McGaugh, J. (1996). Amygdala activity at encoding correlated with long-term, free recall of emotional information. *Proceedings of the National Academy of Sciences, 93*, 8016–8321.

Cahill, L., & McGaugh, J. L. (1995). A novel demonstration of enhanced memory associated with emotional arousal. *Consciousness and Cognition, 4*, 410–421.

Cairns, H. S. (1996). *The acquisition of language* (2nd ed.). Austin, TX: Pro-Ed.

Calfee, R. (1981). Cognitive psychology and educational practice. In D. C. Berliner (Ed.), *Review of Research in Education* (Vol. 9). Washington, DC: American Educational Research Association.

Calfee, R., & Chambliss, M. J. (1988, April). *The structure of social studies textbooks: Where is the design?* Paper presented at the annual meeting of the American Educational Research Association, New Orleans.

Calfee, R., Dunlap, K., & Wat, A. (1994). Authentic discussion of texts in middle grade schooling: An analytic-narrative approach. *Journal of Reading, 37*, 546–556.

Calfee, R. C., & Masuda, W. V. (1997). Classroom assessment as inquiry. In G. D. Phye (Ed.), *Handbook of classroom assessment: Learning, achievement, and adjustment*. San Diego, CA: Academic Press.

Calin-Jageman, R. J., & Ratner, H. H. (2005). The role of encoding in the self-explanation effect. *Cognition and Instruction, 23*, 523–543.

Cameron, J. (2001). Negative effects of reward on intrinsic motivation—A limited phenomenon: Comment on Deci, Koestner, and Ryan (2001). *Review of Educational Research, 71*, 29–42.

Cameron, J., & Pierce, W. D. (2005). *Rewards for performance, cognitive processes, and intrinsic motivation*. Paper presented at the annual meeting of the American Educational Research Association, San Francisco, CA.

Cameron, J., Pierce, W. D., Banko, K. M., & Gear, A. (2005). Achievement-based rewards and intrinsic motivation: A test of cognitive mediators. *Journal of Educational Psychology, 97*, 641–655.

Campbell, F. A., & Ramey, C. T. (1995). Cognitive and school outcomes for high-risk African-American students at middle adolescence: Positive effects of early intervention. *American Educational Research Journal, 32*, 742–772.

Campione, J. C., Shapiro, A. M., & Brown, A. L. (1995). Forms of transfer in a community of learners: Flexible learning and understanding. In A. McKeough, J. Lupart, & A. Marini (Eds.), *Teaching for transfer: Fostering generalization in learning*. Mahwah, NJ: Erlbaum.

Cann, A., & Ross, D. (1989). Olfactory stimuli as context cues in human memory. *American Journal of Psychology, 102*, 91–102.

Capon, N., & Kuhn, D. (2004). What's so good about problem-based learning? *Cognition and Instruction, 22*, 61–79.

Cardelle-Elawar, M. (1992). Effects of teaching metacognitive skills to students with low mathematics ability. *Teaching and Teacher Education, 8*, 109–121.

Carey, R. G., & Bucher, B. D. (1986). Positive practice overcorrection: Effects of reinforcing correct performance. *Behavior Modification, 10*, 73–92.

Carey, S. (1985). *Conceptual change in childhood*. Cambridge, MA: MIT Press.

Carey, S. (1986). Cognitive science and science education. *American Psychologist, 41*, 1123–1130.

Carlson, N. R. (1999). *Foundations of physiological psychology*. Boston: Allyn & Bacon.

Carlson, R., Chandler, P., & Sweller, J. (2003). Learning and understanding science instructional material. *Journal of Educational Psychology, 95*, 629–640.

Carlson, S. M., Davis, A. C., & Leach, J. C. (2005). Less is more: Executive function and symbolic representation in preschool children. *Psychological Science, 16*, 609–616.

Carlson, S. M., & Moses, L. J. (2001). Individual differences in inhibitory control and children's theory of mind. *Child Development, 72*, 1032–1053.

Carmichael, C. A., & Hayes, B. K. (2001). Prior knowledge and exemplar encoding in children's concept acquisition. *Child Development, 72*, 1071–1090.

Carmichael, L., Hogan, H. P., & Walters, A. A. (1932). An experimental study of the effect of language on the reproduction of visually

perceived form. *Journal of Experimental Psychology, 15*, 73–86.

Carney, R. N., & Levin, J. R. (1994). Combining mnemonic strategies to remember who painted what when. *Contemporary Educational Psychology, 19*, 323–339.

Carney, R. N., & Levin, J. R. (2000). Mnemonic instruction, with a focus on transfer. *Journal of Educational Psychology, 92*, 783–790.

Carney, R. N., & Levin, J. R. (2002). Pictorial illustrations *still* improve students' learning from text. *Educational Psychology Review, 14*, 5–26.

Carney, R. N., Levin, J. R., & Stackhouse, T. L. (1997). The face-name mnemonic strategy from a different perspective. *Contemporary Educational Psychology, 22*, 399–412.

Carpenter, P. A., & Just, M. A. (1986). Cognitive processes in reading. In J. Orasanu (Ed.), *Reading comprehension: From research to practice*. Hillsdale, NJ: Erlbaum.

Carpenter, T. P. (1985). Learning to add and subtract: An exercise in problem solving. In E. A. Silver (Ed.), *Teaching and learning mathematical problem solving: Multiple research perspectives*. Hillsdale, NJ: Erlbaum.

Carpenter, T. P., & Moser, J. M. (1984). The acquisition of addition and subtraction concepts in grades one through three. *Journal for Research in Mathematics Education, 15*, 179–202.

Carpenter, M., Nagell, K., & Tomasello, M. (1998). Social cognition, joint attention, and communicative competence from 9 to 15 months of age. *Monographs of the Society for Research in Child Development, 63*(Serial No. 255). Chicago: University of Chicago Press.

Carr, M., & Biddlecomb, B. (1998). Metacognition in mathematics from a constructivist perspective. In D. J. Hacker, J. Dunlosky, & A. C. Graesser (Eds.), *Metacognition in educational theory and practice* (pp. 69–91). Mahwah, NJ: Erlbaum.

Carr, M., & Jessup, D. (1997). Gender differences in first grade mathematics strategy use: Social, metacognitive, and attributional differences. *Journal of Educational Psychology, 89*, 318–328.

Carr, M., & Schneider, W. (1991). Long-term maintenance of organizational strategies in kindergarten children. *Contemporary Educational Psychology, 16*, 61–75.

Carraher, T. N., Carraher, D. W., & Schliemann, A. D. (1985). Mathematics in the streets and in the schools. *British Journal of Developmental Psychology, 3*, 21–29.

Carrasco, R. L. (1981). Expanded awareness of student performance: A case study in applied ethnographic monitoring in a bilingual classroom. In H. T. Trueba, G. P. Guthrie, & K. H. Au (Eds.), *Culture and the bilingual classroom: Studies in classroom ethnography*. Rowley, MA: Newbury House.

Carroll, J. B. (1963). A model of school learning. *Teachers College Record, 64*, 723–733.

Carroll, J. B. (1989). The Carroll model: A 25-year retrospective and prospective view. *Educational Researcher, 18*(1), 26–31.

Carroll, M., & Perfect, T. J. (2002). Students' experiences of unconscious plagiarism: Did I beget or forget? In T. J. Perfect & B. L. Schwartz (Eds.), *Applied metacognition* (pp. 146–166). Cambridge, England: Cambridge University Press.

Carver, C. S., & Scheier, M. F. (1990). Origins and functions of positive and negative affect: A control-process view. *Psychological Review, 97,* 19–35.

Carver, R. P. (1971). *Sense and nonsense in speed reading.* Silver Springs, MD: Revrac.

Carver, R. P. (1990). *Reading rate: A review of research and theory.* San Diego, CA: Academic Press.

Case, R. (1985). *Intellectual development: Birth to adulthood.* Orlando, FL: Academic Press.

Case, R. (1996). Changing views of knowledge and their impact on educational research and practice. In D. R. Olson & N. Torrance (Eds.), *The handbook of education and human development: New models of learning, teaching, and schooling.* Cambridge, MA: Blackwell.

Case, R., & Mueller, M. P. (2001). Differentiation, integration, and covariance mapping as fundamental processes in cognitive and neurological growth. In J. L. McClelland & R. S. Siegler (Eds.), *Mechanisms of cognitive development: Behavioral and neural perspectives* (pp. 185–219). Mahwah, NJ: Erlbaum.

Case, R., & Okamoto, Y., in collaboration with Griffin, S., McKeough, A., Bleiker, C., Henderson, B., & Stephenson, K. M. (1996). The role of central conceptual structures in the development of children's thought. *Monographs of the Society for Research in Child Development, 61*(1–2, Serial No. 246).

Case, R., Okamoto, Y., Henderson, B., & McKeough, A. (1993). Individual variability and consistency in cognitive development: New evidence for the existence of central conceptual structures. In R. Case & W. Edelstein (Eds.), *The new structuralism in cognitive development: Theory and research on individual pathways.* Basel, Switzerland: Karger.

Cassady, J. C., & Johnson, R. E. (2002). Cognitive test anxiety and academic performance. *Contemporary Educational Psychology, 27,* 270–295.

Castro-Caldas, A., Miranda, P. C., Carmo, I., Reis, A., Leote, F., Ribeiro, C., & Ducla-Soares, E. (1999). Influence of learning to read and write on the morphology of the corpus callosum. *European Journal of Neurology, 6,* 23–28.

Catania, A. C. (1985). The two psychologies of learning: Blind alleys and nonsense syllables. In S. Koch & D. E. Leary (Eds.), *A century of psychology as science.* New York: McGraw-Hill.

Catania, A. C., & Reynolds, G. S. (1968). A quantitative analysis of the responding maintained by interval schedules of reinforcement. *Journal of the Experimental Analysis of Behavior, 11,* 327–383.

Cazden, C. B. (2001). *Classroom discourse: The language of teaching and learning* (2nd ed.). Portsmouth, NH: Heinemann.

Cermak, L. S. (1993). Automatic versus controlled processing and the implicit task performance of amnesic patients. In P. Graf & M. E. J. Masson (Eds.), *Implicit memory: New directions in cognition, development, and neuropsychology.* Hillsdale, NJ: Erlbaum.

Cermak, L. S., & Craik, F. I. M. (Eds.) (1979). *Levels of processing in human memory.* Hillsdale, NJ: Erlbaum.

Certo, J., Cauley, K. M., & Chafin, C. (2002, April). *Students' perspectives on their high school experience.* Paper presented at the annual meeting of the American Educational Research Association, New Orleans, LA.

Chabrán, M. (2003). Listening to talk from and about students on accountability. In M. Carnoy, R. Elmore, & L. S. Siskin (Eds.), *The new accountability: High schools and high-stakes testing* (pp. 129–145). New York: Routledge Falmer.

Chalmers, D. J. (1996). *The conscious mind: In search of a fundamental theory.* New York: Oxford University Press.

Chambers, D., & Reisberg, D. (1985). Can mental images be ambiguous? *Journal of Experimental Psychology: Human Perception and Performance, 11,* 317–328.

Chambliss, M. J. (1994). Why do readers fail to change their beliefs after reading persuasive text? In R. Garner & P. A. Alexander (Eds.), *Beliefs about text and instruction with text.* Hillsdale, NJ: Erlbaum.

Chambliss, M. J., Calfee, R. C., & Wong, I. (1990, April). *Structure and content in science textbooks: Where is the design?* Paper presented at the annual meeting of the American Educational Research Association, Boston.

Champagne, A. B., & Bunce, D. M. (1991). Learning-theory-based science teaching. In S. M. Glynn, R. H. Yeany, & B. K. Britton (Eds.), *The psychology of learning science.* Hillsdale, NJ: Erlbaum.

Champagne, A. B., Klopfer, L. E., & Gunstone, R. F. (1982). Cognitive research and the design of science instruction. *Educational Psychologist, 17,* 31–53.

Chan, C., Burtis, J., & Bereiter, C. (1997). Knowledge building as a mediator of conflict in conceptual change. *Cognition and Instruction, 15,* 1–40.

Chan, C. K. K., Burtis, P. J., Scardamalia, M., & Bereiter, C. (1992). Constructive activity in learning from text. *American Educational Research Journal, 29,* 97–118.

Chapell, M. S., Blanding, Z. B., Silverstein, M. E., Takahashi, M., Newman, B., Gubi, A., & McCann, N. (2005). Test anxiety and academic performance in undergraduate and graduate students. *Journal of Educational Psychology, 97,* 268–274.

Chapin, M., & Dyck, D. G. (1976). Persistence in children's reading behavior as a function of N length and attribution retraining. *Journal of Abnormal Psychology, 85,* 511–515.

Charness, N., Tuffiash, M., & Jastrzembski, T. (2004). Motivation, emotion, and expert skill acquisition. In D. Y. Dai & R. J. Sternberg (Eds.), *Motivation, emotion, and cognition: Integrative perspectives on intellectual functioning and development* (pp. 299–319). Mahwah, NJ: Erlbaum.

Chase, W. G., & Simon, H. A. (1973). Perception in chess. *Cognitive Psychology, 4,* 55–81.

Chen, Z. (1999). Schema induction in children's analogical problem solving. *Journal of Educational Psychology, 91,* 703–715.

Chen, C., & Uttal, D. H. (1988). Cultural values, parents' beliefs, and children's achievement in the United States and China. *Human Development, 31,* 351–358.

Cheng, P. W. (1985). Restructuring versus automaticity: Alternative accounts of skill acquisition. *Psychological Review, 92,* 414–423.

Cheng, P. W., Holyoak, K. J., Nisbett, R. E., & Oliver, L. M. (1986). Pragmatic versus syntactic approaches to training deductive reasoning. *Cognitive Psychology, 18,* 293–328.

Cherry, E. C. (1953). Some experiments on the recognition of speech, with one and with two ears. *Journal of the Acoustical Society of America, 25,* 975–979.

Cheyne, J. A., & Walters, R. H. (1970). Punishment and prohibition: Some origins of self-control. In T. M. Newcomb (Ed.), *New directions in psychology.* New York: Holt, Rinehart & Winston.

Chi, M. T. H. (1978). Knowledge structures and memory development. In R. S. Siegler (Ed.), *Children's thinking: What develops?* Hillsdale, NJ: Erlbaum.

Chi, M. T. H. (1981). Knowledge development and memory performance. In M. P. Friedman, J. P. Das, & N. O'Connor (Eds.), *Intelligence and learning.* New York: Plenum Press.

Chi, M. T. H., & Glaser, R. (1985). Problem-solving ability. In R. J. Sternberg (Ed.), *Human abilities: An information-processing approach.* New York: W. H. Freeman.

Chi, M. T. H., Glaser, R., & Farr, M. J. (Eds.) (1988). *The nature of expertise.* Hillsdale, NJ: Erlbaum.

Chi, M. T. H., Glaser, R., & Rees, E. (1982). Expertise in problem solving. In R. J. Sternberg (Ed.), *Advances in the psychology of human intelligence.* Hillsdale, NJ: Erlbaum.

Chinn, C. A. (1998). A critique of social constructivist explanations of knowledge change. In B. Guzzetti & C. Hynd (Eds.), *Perspectives on conceptual change: Multiple ways to understand knowing and learning in a complex world* (pp. 77–115). Mahwah, NJ: Erlbaum.

Chinn, C. A. (2006). Learning to argue. In A. M. O'Donnell, C. E. Hmelo-Silver, & G. Erkens (Eds.), *Collaborative learning, reasoning, and technology* (pp. 355–383). Mahwah, NJ: Erlbaum.

Chinn, C. A., & Brewer, W. F. (1993). The role of anomalous data in knowledge acquisition: A theoretical framework and implications for science instruction. *Review of Educational Research, 63,* 1–49.

Chinn, C. A., & Malhotra, B. A. (2002). Children's responses to anomalous scientific data: How is conceptual change impeded? *Journal of Educational Psychology, 94,* 327–343.

Chipman, S. F., Krantz, D. H., & Silver, R. (1992). Mathematics anxiety and science careers among able college women. *Psychological Science, 3,* 292–295.

Chomsky, N. (1957). *Syntactic structures.* The Hague: Mouton.

Chomsky, N. (1959). Review of B. F. Skinner's *Verbal behavior, Language, 35,* 26–58.

Chomsky, N. (1972). *Language and mind* (Enl. ed.). San Diego, CA: Harcourt Brace Jovanovich.

Christen, F., & Bjork, R. A. (1976). *On updating the loci in the method of loci.* Paper presented at the annual meeting of the Psychonomic Society, St. Louis, MO.

Christenson, S. L., & Thurlow, M. L. (2004). School dropouts: Prevention, considerations, interventions, and challenges. *Current Directions in Psychological Science, 13,* 36–39.

Christie, J. F., & Johnsen, E. P. (1983). The role of play in social-intellectual development. *Review of Educational Research, 53,* 93–115.

Christmann, E., Badgett, J., & Lucking, R. (1997). Microcomputer-based computer-assisted instruction within differing subject areas: A statistical deduction. *Journal of Educational Computing Research, 16,* 281–296.

Church, M. A., Elliot, A. J., & Gable, S. L. (2001). Perceptions of classroom environment, achievement goals, and achievement outcomes. *Journal of Educational Psychology, 93,* 43–54.

Church, R. M. (1993). Human models of animal behavior. *Psychological Science, 4,* 170–173.

Cipani, E. (2002). *Positive behavioral support: Five plans for teachers.* Upper Saddle River, NJ: Merrill/Prentice Hall.

Cizek, G. J. (2003). *Detecting and preventing classroom cheating: Promoting integrity in assessment.* Thousand Oaks, CA: Corwin.

Clancey, W. J. (1997). *Situated cognition: On human knowledge and computer representations.* Cambridge, England: Cambridge University Press.

Clark, A.-M., Anderson, R. C., Kuo, L., Kim, I., Archodidou, A., & Nguyen-Jahiel, K. (2003). Collaborative reasoning: Expanding ways for children to talk and think in school. *Educational Psychology Review, 15,* 181–198.

Clark, D. C. (1971). Teaching concepts in the classroom: A set of teaching prescriptions derived from experimental research. *Journal of Educational Psychology, 62,* 253–278.

Clark, J. M., & Paivio, A. (1991). Dual coding theory and education. *Educational Psychology Review, 3,* 149–210.

Clarke, H. F., Dalley, J. W., Crofts, H. S., Robbins, T. W., & Roberts, A. C. (2004). Cognitive inflexibility after prefrontal serotonin depletion. *Science, 304,* 878–880.

Clement, J. (1982). Students' preconceptions in elementary mechanics. *American Journal of Physics, 50,* 66–71.

Clement, J. (1987). Overcoming students' misconceptions in physics: The role of anchoring intuitions and analogical validity. In *Proceedings of the Second International Seminar on Misconceptions and Educational Strategies in Science and Mathematics* (Vol. 3). Ithaca, NY: Cornell University.

Clifford, M. M. (1984). Thoughts on a theory of constructive failure. *Educational Psychologist, 19,* 108–120.

Clifford, M. M. (1990). Students need challenge, not easy success. *Educational Leadership, 48*(1), 22–26.

Clore, G. L., Gasper, K., & Garvin, E. (2001). Affect as information. In J. P. Forgas (Ed.), *Handbook of affect and social cognition* (pp. 121–144). Mahwah, NJ: Erlbaum.

Coates, B., & Hartup, W. W. (1969). Age and verbalization in observational learning. *Developmental Psychology, 1,* 556–562.

Cobb, P., Wood, T., Yackel, E., Nicholls, J., Wheatley, G., Trigatti, B., & Perlwitz, M. (1991). Assessment of a problem centered second-grade mathematics project. *Journal for Research in Mathematics Education, 22,* 3–29.

Cobb, P., & Yackel, E. (1996). Constructivist, emergent, and sociocultural perspectives in the context of developmental research. *Educational Psychologist, 31,* 175–190.

Cobb, P., Yackel, E., & Wood, T. (1989). Young children's emotional acts while engaged in mathematical problem solving. In D. B. McLeod & V. M. Adams (Eds.), *Affect and mathematical problem solving: A new perspective.* New York: Springer-Verlag.

Cochran, K. F. (1988, April). *Cognitive structure representation in physics.* Paper presented at the annual meeting of the American Educational Research Association, New Orleans, LA.

Cofer, C. (1971). Properties of verbal materials and verbal learning. In J. Kling & L. Riggs (Eds.), *Woodworth and Schlosberg's experimental psychology.* New York: Holt, Rinehart & Winston.

Cognition and Technology Group at Vanderbilt (1990). Anchored instruction and its relationship to situated cognition. *Educational Researcher, 19*(6), 2–10.

Cohen, E. G. (1994). Restructuring the classroom: Conditions for productive small groups. *Review of Educational Research, 64,* 1–35.

Cohen, E. G., & Lotan, R. A. (1995). Producing equal-status interaction in the heterogeneous classroom. *American Educational Research Journal, 32,* 99–120.

Cohen, G. (2000). Hierarchical models in cognition: Do they have psychological reality? *European Journal of Cognitive Psychology, 12*(1), 1–36.

Cohen, L. B., & Cashon, C. H. (2006). Infant cognition. In W. Damon & R. M. Lerner (Series Eds.), D. Kuhn, & R. Siegler (Vol. Eds.), *Handbook of child psychology: Vol. 1. Cognition, perception, and language* (6th ed.). New York: Wiley.

Cohen, R. L. (1989). Memory for action events: The power of enactment. *Educational Psychology Review, 1,* 57–80.

Cohn, S., Hult, R. E., & Engle, R. W. (1990, April). *Working memory, notetaking, and learning from a lecture.* Paper presented at the annual meeting of the American Educational Research Association, Boston.

Cole, M. (1990). Cognitive development and formal schooling: The evidence from cross-cultural research. In L. C. Moll (Ed.), *Vygotsky and education* (pp. 89–110). New York: Cambridge University Press.

Cole, M. (2006). Culture and cognitive development in phylogenetic, historical and ontogenetic perspective. In W. Damon & R. M. Lerner (Series Eds.), D. Kuhn, & R. Siegler (Vol. Eds.), *Handbook of child psychology: Vol. 2. Cognition, perception, and language* (6th ed.). New York: Wiley.

Cole, N. S. (1990). Conceptions of educational achievement. *Educational Researcher, 19*(3), 2–7.

Coleman, C. L., & Holmes, P. A. (1998). The use of noncontingent escape to reduce disruptive behaviors in children with speech delays. *Journal of Applied Behavior Analysis, 31,* 687–690.

Collie, R., & Hayne, H. (1999). Deferred imitation by 6- and 9-month-old infants: More evidence for declarative memory. *Developmental Psychobiology, 35,* 83–90.

Collier, G., Hirsh, E., & Hamlin, P. H. (1972). The ecological determinants of reinforcement in the rat. *Physiology and Behavior, 9,* 705–716.

Collier, V. (1989). How long? A synthesis of research on academic achievement in a second language. *TESOL Quarterly, 23,* 509–523.

Collins, A. (2006). Cognitive apprenticeship. In R. K. Sawyer (Ed.), *The Cambridge handbook of the learning sciences* (pp. 47–60). Cambridge, England: Cambridge University Press.

Collins, A., Brown, J. S., & Newman, S. E. (1989). Cognitive apprenticeship: Teaching the crafts of reading, writing, and mathematics. In L. B. Resnick (Ed.), *Knowing, learning, and instruction: Essays in honor of Robert Glaser.* Hillsdale, NJ: Erlbaum.

Collins, A. M., & Loftus, E. F. (1975). A spreading-activation theory of semantic processing. *Psychological Review, 82,* 407–428.

Collins, A. M., & Quillian, M. R. (1969). Retrieval time from semantic memory. *Journal of Verbal Learning and Verbal Behavior, 8,* 240–247.

Collins, A. M., & Quillian, M. R. (1972). How to make a language user. In E. Tulving & W. Donaldson (Eds.), *Organization of memory.* New York: Academic Press.

Coltheart, M., Lea, C. D., & Thompson, K. (1974). In defense of iconic memory. *Quarterly Journal of Experimental Psychology, 26,* 633–641.

Colwill, R. M. (1993). An associative analysis of instrumental learning. *Current Directions in Psychological Science, 2,* 111–116.

Colwill, R. M., & Rescorla, R. A. (1986). Associative structures in instrumental learning. In G. H. Bower (Ed.), *The psychology of learning and motivation* (Vol. 20). Orlando, FL: Academic Press.

Combs, A. W., Richards, A. C., & Richards, F. (1976). *Perceptual psychology: A humanistic approach to the study of persons.* New York: Harper & Row.

Conklin, C. A. (2006). Environments as cues to smoke: Implications for human extinction-based research and treatment. *Experimental and Clinical Psychopharmacology, 14,* 12–19.

Conklin, H. M., & Iacono, W. G. (2002). Schizophrenia: A neurodevelopmental perspective. *Current Directions in Psychological Science, 11,* 33–37.

Connell, J. P. (1990). Context, self, and action: A motivational analysis of self-system processes across the life span. In D. Cicchetti & M. Beeghly (Eds.), *The self in transition: Infancy to childhood.* Chicago: University of Chicago Press.

Connell, J. P., & Wellborn, J. G. (1991). Competence, autonomy, and relatedness: A motivational analysis of self-system processes. In M. R. Gunnar & L. A. Sroufe (Eds.), *Self processes and development: The Minnesota Symposia on Child Psychology* (Vol. 23). Hillsdale, NJ: Erlbaum.

Connolly, F. W., & Eisenberg, T. E. (1990). The feedback classroom: Teaching's silent friend. *T.H.E. Journal, 17*(5), 75–77.

Conrad, R. (1964). Acoustic confusions in immediate memory. *British Journal of Psychology, 55*, 75–84.

Conrad, R., & Hull, A. J. (1964). Information, acoustic confusion, and memory span. *British Journal of Psychology, 55*, 429–432.

Conyers, C., Miltenberger, R., Maki, A., Barenz, R., Jurgens, M., Sailer, A., Haugen, M., & Kopp, B. (2004). A comparison of response cost and differential reinforcement of other behavior to reduce disruptive behavior in a preschool classroom. *Journal of Applied Behavior Analysis, 37*, 411–415.

Cook, V., & Newson, M. (1996). *Chomsky's universal grammar: An introduction* (2nd ed.). Oxford, England: Blackwell.

Cooney, J. B. (1991). Reflections on the origin of mathematical intuition and some implications for instruction. *Learning and Individual Differences, 3*, 83–107.

Cooper, H. (1989). Synthesis of research on homework. *Educational Leadership, 47*(3), 85–91.

Cooper, G., & Sweller, J. (1987). Effects of schema acquisition and rule automation on mathematical problem-solving transfer. *Journal of Educational Psychology, 79*, 347–362.

Cooper, G., Tindall-Ford, S., Chandler, P., & Sweller, J. (2001). Learning by imagining procedures and concepts. *Journal of Experimental Psychology: Applied, 7*, 68–82.

Cooper, L. A., & Shepard, R. N. (1973). The time required to prepare for a rotated stimulus. *Memory and Cognition, 1*, 246–250.

Corbett, H. D., & Wilson, B. (1988). Raising the stakes in statewide mandatory minimum competency testing. *Politics of Education Association Yearbook*, 27–39.

Cordua, G. D., McGraw, K. O., & Drabman, R. S. (1979). Doctor or nurse: Children's perception of sex typed occupations. *Child Development, 50*, 590–593.

Corkill, A. J. (1992). Advance organizers: Facilitators of recall. *Educational Psychology Review, 4*, 33–67.

Corkill, A. J., Bouchard, L., & Bendixen, L. D. (2002, April). *Epistemic beliefs as a measure of dispositions: Comparing preservice and practicing teachers.* Paper presented at the annual meeting of the American Educational Research Association, New Orleans, LA.

Cormier, S. M. (1987). The structural processes underlying transfer of training. In S. M. Cormier & J. D. Hagman (Eds.), *Transfer of learning: Contemporary research and applications.* San Diego, CA: Academic Press.

Cormier, S. M., & Hagman, J. D. (1987). Introduction. In S. M. Cormier & J. D. Hagman (Eds.), *Transfer of learning: Contemporary research and applications.* San Diego, CA: Academic Press.

Corno, L. (1993). The best-laid plans: Modern conceptions of volition and educational research. *Educational Researcher, 22*, 14–22.

Corno, L. (1996). Homework is a complicated thing. *Educational Researcher, 25*(8), 27–30.

Corno, L., Cronbach, L. J., Kupermintz, H., Lohman, D. F., Mandinach, E. B., Porteus, A. W., & Talbert, J. E. (2002). *Remaking the concept of aptitude: Extending the legacy of Richard E. Snow.* Mahwah, NJ: Erlbaum.

Corno, L., & Mandinach, E. B. (2004). What we have learned about student engagement in the past twenty years. In D. M. McNerney & S. Van Etten (Eds.), *Big theories revisited* (pp. 299–328). Greenwich, CT: Information Age.

Corno, L., & Rohrkemper, M. M. (1985). The intrinsic motivation to learn in classrooms. In C. Ames & R. Ames (Eds.), *Research on motivation in education: Vol. 2. The classroom milieu.* Orlando, FL: Academic Press.

Corno, L., Cronbach, L. J., Kupermintz, H., Lohman, D. F., Mandinach, E. B., Porteu, A. W., & Talbert, J. E. (2002). *Remaking the concept of aptitude: Extending the legacy of Richard E. Snow.* Mahwah, NJ: Erlbaum.

Corpus, J. H., McClintic-Gilberg, M. S., & Hayenga, A. O. (2006, April). *Understanding intrinsic and extrinsic motivation: Age differences and links to children's beliefs and goals.* Paper presented at the annual meeting of the American Educational Research Association, San Francisco, CA.

Corpus, J. H., Tomlinson, T. D., & Stanton, P. R. (April, 2004). *Does social-comparison praise undermine children's intrinsic motivation?* Paper presented at the American Educational Research Association, San Diego, CA.

Corte, H. E., Wolf, M. M., & Locke, B. J. (1971). A comparison of procedures for eliminating self-injurious behavior of retarded adolescents. *Journal of Applied Behavior Analysis, 4*, 201–214.

Cothern, N. B., Konopak, B. C., & Willis, E. L. (1990). Using readers' imagery of literary characters to study text meaning construction. *Reading Research and Instruction, 30*, 15–29.

Covington, M. V. (1992). *Making the grade: A self-worth perspective on motivation and school reform.* Cambridge, England: Cambridge University Press.

Covington, M. V. (2000). Intrinsic versus extrinsic motivation in schools: A reconciliation. *Current Directions in Psychological Science, 9*, 22–25.

Covington, M. V. (2004). Self-worth theory goes to college: Or do our motivation theories motivate? In D. M. McNerney & S. Van Etten (Eds.), *Big theories revisited* (pp. 91–114). Greenwich, CT: Information Age.

Covington, M. V., & Beery, R. M. (1976). *Self-worth and school learning.* New York: Holt, Rinehart & Winston.

Covington, M. V., & Müeller, K. J. (2001). Intrinsic versus extrinsic motivation: An approach/avoidance reformulation. *Educational Psychology Review, 13*, 157–176.

Covington, M. V., & Omelich, C. L. (1979). Effort: The double-edged sword in school achievement. *Journal of Educational Psychology, 71*, 169–182.

Covington, M. V., & Omelich, C. L. (1991). Need achievement revisited: Verification of Atkinson's original 2 × 2 model. In C. D. Spielberger, I. G. Sarason, Z. Kulcsar, & G. L. Van Heck (Eds.), *Stress and emotion* (Vol. 14). New York: Hemisphere.

Covington, M. V., Spratt, M., & Omelich, C. (1980). Is effort enough or does diligence count too? Student and teacher reactions to effort stability in failure. *Journal of Educational Psychology, 72*, 717–729.

Cowan, N. (1995). *Attention and memory: An integrated framework.* New York: Oxford University Press.

Cowan, N., Chen, Z., & Rouder, J. N. (2004). Constant capacity in an immediate serial-recall task: A logical sequel to Miller (1956). *Psychological Science, 15*, 634–640.

Cowan, N., Wood, N. L., Nugent, L. D., & Treisman, M. (1997). There are two word-length effects in verbal short-term memory: Opposed effects of duration and complexity. *Psychological Science, 8*, 290–295.

Cox, B. D. (1997). The rediscovery of the active learner in adaptive contexts: A developmental-historical analysis of transfer of training. *Educational Psychologist, 32*, 41–55.

Cox, C. D., Cox, B. S., & Cox, D. J. (2005). Long-term benefits of prompts to use safety belts among drivers exiting senior communities. *Journal of Applied Behavior Analysis, 38*, 533–536.

Craft, M. A., Alberg, S. R., & Heward, W. L. (1998). Teaching elementary students with developmental disabilities to recruit teacher attention in a general education classroom: Effects on teacher praise and academic productivity. *Journal of Applied Behavior Analysis, 31*, 399–415.

Craik, F. I. M., & Lockhart, R. S. (1972). Levels of processing: A framework for memory research. *Journal of Verbal Learning and Verbal Behavior, 11*, 671–684.

Craik, F. I. M., & Tulving, E. (1975). Depth of processing and the retention of words in episodic memory. *Journal of Experimental Psychology: General, 104*, 268–294.

Craik, F. I. M., & Watkins, M. J. (1973). The role of rehearsal in short-term memory. *Journal of Verbal Learning and Verbal Behavior, 12*, 598–607.

Cramblet, L. D., & Denzine, G. M. (2006, April). *Converging evidence that college students do not spontaneously generate performance goals in normative terms.* Paper presented at the annual meeting of the American Educational Research Association, San Francisco.

Crawley, A. M., Anderson, D. R., Wilder, A., Williams, M., & Santomero, A. (1999). Effects of repeated exposures to a single episode of the television program *Blue's Clues* on the viewing behaviors and comprehension of preschool children. *Journal of Educational Psychology 91*, 630–637.

Crespi, L. P. (1942). Quantitative variation of incentive and performance in the white rat. *American Journal of Psychology, 55*, 467–517.

Crill, W. E., & Raichle, M. E. (1982). Clinical evaluation of injury and recovery. In

J. G. Nicholls (Ed.), *Repair and regeneration of the nervous system*. New York: Springer-Verlag.

Critchfield, T. S., Haley, R., Sabo, B., Colbert, J., & Macropolis, G. (2003). A half century of scalloping in the work habits of the United States Congress. *Journal of Applied Behavior Analysis, 36,* 465–486.

Critchfield, T. S., & Kollins, S. H. (2001). Temporal discounting: Basic research and the analysis of socially important behavior. *Journal of Applied Behavior Analysis, 34,* 101–122.

Cromer, R. F. (1993). Language growth with experience without feedback. In P. Bloom (Ed.), *Language acquisition: Core readings.* Cambridge, MA: MIT Press.

Crooks, T. J. (1988). The impact of classroom evaluation practices on students. *Review of Educational Research, 58,* 438–481.

Crosbie, J., & Kelly, G. (1994). Effects of imposed postfeedback delays in programmed instruction. *Journal of Applied Behavior Analysis, 27,* 483–491.

Cross, D. R., & Paris, S. G. (1988). Developmental and instructional analyses of children's metacognitive and reading comprehension. *Journal of Educational Psychology, 80,* 131–142.

Crowder, N. A., & Martin, G. (1961). *Trigonometry.* Garden City, NY: Doubleday.

Crowder, R. G. (1993). Short-term meory: Where do we stand? *Memory and Cognition, 21,* 142–145.

Crowder, R. G., & Wagner, R. K. (1992). *The psychology of reading: An introduction* (2nd ed.). New York: Oxford University Press.

Crowley, K., & Jacobs, M. (2002). Building islands of expertise in everyday family activity. In G. Leinhardt, K. Crowley, & K. Knutson (Eds.), *Learning conversations in museums* (pp. 333–356). Mahwah, NJ: Erlbaum.

Crowley, K., & Siegler, R. S. (1999). Explanation and generalization in young children's strategy learning. *Child Development, 70,* 304–316.

Crowley, T. J. (1984). Contingency contracting treatment of drug-abusing physicians, nurses, and dentists. *National Institute on Drug Abuse: Research Monograph Series, 46,* 68–83.

Crowne, D. P., & Marlowe, D. (1964). *The approval motive: Studies in evaluative dependence.* New York: Wiley.

Csikszentmihalyi, M. (1990). *Flow: The psychology of optimal experience.* New York: Harper & Row.

Csikszentmihalyi, M. (1996). *Creativity: Flow and the psychology of discovery and invention.* New York: HarperCollins.

Csikszentmihalyi, M., & Nakamura, J. (1989). The dynamics of intrinsic motivation: A study of adolescents. In C. Ames & R. Ames (Eds.), *Research on motivation in education: Vol. 3. Goals and cognitions.* Orlando, FL: Academic Press.

Csikszentmihalyi, M., Rathunde, K., & Whalen, S. (1993). *Talented teenagers: A longitudinal study of their development.* New York: Cambridge University Press.

Curtis, K. A., & Graham, S. (1991, April). *Altering beliefs about the importance of strategy: An attributional intervention.* Paper presented at the annual meeting of the American Educational Research Association, Chicago.

Curtiss, S. (1977). *Genie: A psycholinguistic study of a modern-day "wild child."* New York: Academic Press.

Cushing, L. S., & Kennedy, C. H. (1997). Academic effects of providing peer support in general education classrooms on students without disabilities. *Journal of Applied Behavior Analysis, 30,* 139–151.

Cuvo, A. J. (1975). Developmental differences in rehearsal and free recall. *Journal of Experimental Child Psychology, 19,* 65–78.

Dahlin, B., & Watkins, D. (2000). The role of repetition in the processes of memorizing and understanding: A comparison of the views of Western and Chinese secondary students in Hong Kong. *British Journal of Educational Psychology, 70,* 65–84.

Dai, D. Y. (2002, April). *Effects of need for cognition and reader beliefs on the comprehension of narrative text.* Paper presented at the annual meeting of the American Educational Research Association, New Orleans, LA.

Dai, D. Y. (2005, April). Introductory remarks. In D. Y. Dai (Chair), *Beyond cognitivism: Where are we now?* Symposium presented at the annual meeting of the American Educational Research Association, Montreal.

Dai, D. Y., & Sternberg, R. J. (2004). Beyond cognitivism: Toward an integrated understanding of intellectual functioning and development. In D. Y. Dai & R. J. Sternberg (Eds.), *Motivation, emotion, and cognition: Integrative perspectives on intellectual functioning and development* (pp. 3–38). Mahwah, NJ: Erlbaum.

d'Ailly, H. (2003). Children's autonomy and perceived control in learning: A model of motivation and achievement in Taiwan. *Journal of Educational Psychology, 95,* 84–96.

Dallett, K. M. (1964). Implicit mediators in paired-associate learning. *Journal of Verbal Learning and Verbal Behavior, 3,* 209–214.

Damasio, A. R. (1994). *Descartes' error: Emotion, reason, and the human brain.* New York: Avon Books.

D'Amato, M. R. (1955). Secondary reinforcement and magnitude of primary reinforcement. *Journal of Comparative and Physiological Psychology, 48,* 378–380.

D'Amato, M. R. (1970). *Experimental psychology: Methodology, psychophysics, and learning.* New York: McGraw-Hill.

Damon, W. (1984). Peer education: The untapped potential. *Journal of Applied Developmental Psychology, 5,* 331–343.

Daneman, M. (1987). Reading and working memory. In J. R. Beech & A. M. Colley (Eds.), *Cognitive approaches to reading.* Chichester, England: Wiley.

Daneman, M., & Carpenter, P. A. (1980). Individual differences in working memory and reading. *Journal of Verbal Learning and Verbal Behavior, 19,* 450–466.

Danner, F. W., & Day, M. C. (1977). Eliciting formal operations. *Child Development, 48,* 1600–1606.

Danner, F. W., & Lonky, E. (1981). A cognitive-developmental approach to the effects of rewards on intrinsic motivation. *Child Development, 52,* 1043–1052.

Dansereau, D. F. (1988). Cooperative learning strategies. In C. E. Weinstein, E. T. Goetz, & P. A. Alexander (Eds.), *Learning and study strategies: Issues in assessment, instruction, and evaluation.* San Diego, CA: Academic Press.

Dansereau, D. F. (1995). Derived structural schemas and the transfer of knowledge. In A. McKeough, J. Lupart, & A. Marini (Eds.), *Teaching for transfer: Fostering generalization in learning.* Mahwah, NJ: Erlbaum.

Darley, J. M., & Gross, P. H. (1983). A hypothesis-confirming bias in labeling effects. *Journal of Personality and Social Psychology, 44,* 20–33.

Darling-Hammond, L. (1991). The implications of testing policy for quality and equality. *Phi Delta Kappan, 73,* 220–225.

Darwin, C. J., Turvey, M. T., & Crowder, R. G. (1972). An auditory analogue of the Sperling partial report procedure: Evidence for brief auditory storage. *Cognitive Psychology, 3,* 255–267.

Davidson, J. E. (2003). Insights about insightful problem solving. In J. E. Davidson & R. J. Sternberg (Eds.), *The psychology of problem solving* (pp. 149–175). Cambridge, England: Cambridge University Press.

Davidson, J. E., & Sternberg, R. J. (1998). Smart problem solving: How metacognition helps. In D. J. Hacker, J. Dunlosky, & A. C. Graesser (Eds.), *Metacognition in educational theory and practice* (pp. 47–68). Mahwah, NJ: Erlbaum.

Davis, G. A. (1966). Current status of research and theory in human problem solving. *Psychological Bulletin, 66,* 36–54.

Davis, G. A., & Thomas, M. A. (1989). *Effective schools and effective teachers.* Boston: Allyn & Bacon.

Davis, H. A. (2003). Conceptualizing the role and influence of student-teacher relationships on children's social and cognitive development. *Educational Psychologist, 38,* 207–234.

Davis, L. L., & O'Neill, R. E. (2004). Use of response cards with a group of students with learning disabilities including those for whom English is a second language. *Journal of Applied Behavior Analysis, 37,* 219–222.

Davis, P. J. (1987). Repression and the inaccessibility of affective memories. *Journal of Personality and Social Psychology, 53,* 585–593.

Davis, P. J., & Schwartz, G. E. (1987). Repression and the inaccessibility of affective memories. *Journal of Personality and Social Psychology, 52,* 155–162.

Davis, L. E., Ajzen, I., Saunders, J., & Williams, T. (2002). The decision of African American students to complete high school: An application of the theory of planned behavior. *Journal of Educational Psychology, 94,* 810–819.

Deaux, K. (1984). From individual differences to social categories: Analysis of a decade's research on gender. *American Psychologist, 39,* 105–116.

DeBacker, T. K., & Crowson, H. M. (2006). Influences on cognitive engagement and achievement: Personal epistemology and achievement motives. *British Journal of Educational Psychology, 76,* 535–551.

de Bruin, A., Whittingham, J., Hillebrand, C., & Rikers, R. (2003, April). *The effect of self-explanations and anticipations on acquiring chess skill in novices.* Paper presented at the annual meeting of the American Educational Research Association, Chicago.

DeCasper, A. J., & Spence, M. J. (1986). Prenatal maternal speech influences newborns' perception of speech sounds. *Infant Behavior and Development, 9,* 133–150.

deCharms, R. (1972). Personal causation training in the schools. *Journal of Applied Social Psychology, 2,* 95–113.

deCharms, R. (1984). Motivation enhancement in educational settings. In R. Ames & C. Ames (Eds.), *Research on motivation in education: Vol. 1. Student motivation.* Orlando, FL: Academic Press.

Deci, E. L. (1971). Effects of externally mediated rewards on intrinsic motivation. *Journal of Personality and Social Psychology, 18,* 105–115.

Deci, E. L. (1992). The relation of interest to the motivation of behavior: A self-determination theory perspective. In K. A. Renninger, S. Hidi, & A. Krapp (Eds.), *The role of interest in learning and development.* Hillsdale, NJ: Erlbaum.

Deci, E. L., Koestner, R., & Ryan, R. M. (2001). Extrinsic rewards and intrinsic motivation in education: Reconsidered once again. *Review of Educational Research, 71,* 1–27.

Deci, E. L., & Ryan, R. M. (1985). *Intrinsic motivation and self-determination in human behavior.* New York: Plenum Press.

Deci, E. L., & Ryan, R. M. (1987). The support of autonomy and the control of behavior. *Journal of Personality and Social Psychology, 53,* 1024–1037.

Deci, E. L., & Ryan, R. M. (1992). The initiation and regulation of intrinsically motivated learning and achievement. In A. K. Boggiano & T. S. Pittman (Eds.), *Achievement and motivation: A social-developmental perspective.* Cambridge, England: Cambridge University Press.

Deci, E. L., & Ryan, R. M. (1995). Human autonomy: The basis for true self-esteem. In M. H. Kernis (Ed.), *Efficacy, agency, and self-esteem.* New York: Plenum Press.

Deci, E. L., Vallerand, R. J., Pelletier, L. G., & Ryan, R. M. (1991). Motivation and education: The self-determination perspective. *Educational Psychologist, 26,* 325–346.

De Corte, E. (2003). Transfer as the productive use of acquired knowledge, skills, and motivations. *Current Directions in Psychological Science, 12,* 142–146.

De Corte, E., Greer, B., & Verschaffel, L. (1996). Mathematics teaching and learning. In D. C. Berliner & R. C. Calfee (Eds.), *Handbook of educational psychology.* New York: Macmillan.

De Corte, E., Op't Eynde, P., & Verschaffel, L. (2002). "Knowing what to believe": The relevance of students' mathematical beliefs for mathematics education. In B. K. Hofer & P. R. Pintrich (Eds.), *Personal epistemology: The psychology of beliefs about knowledge and knowing* (pp. 297–320). Mahwah, NJ: Erlbaum.

Dee-Lucas, D., & Larkin, J. H. (1991). Equations in scientific proofs: Effects on comprehension. *American Educational Research Journal, 28,* 661–682.

DeGrandpre, R. J. (2000). A science of meaning: Can behaviorism bring meaning to psychological science? *American Psychologist, 55,* pp. 721–739.

deGroot, A. D. (1965). *Thought and choice in chess.* The Hague: Mouton.

de Jong, T., & van Joolingen, W. R. (1998). Scientific discovery learning with computer simulations of conceptual domains. *Review of Educational Research, 68,* 179–201.

Delclos, V. R., & Harrington, C. (1991). Effects of strategy monitoring and proactive instruction on children's problem-solving performance. *Journal of Educational Psychology, 83,* 35–42.

deLeeuw, N., & Chi, M. T. H. (2003). Self-explanation: Enriching a situation model or repairing a domain model? In G. M. Sinatra & P. R. Pintrich (Eds.), *Intentional conceptual change* (pp. 55–78). Mahwah, NJ: Erlbaum.

De Lisi, R., & Golbeck, S. L. (1999). Implications of Piagetian theory for peer learning. In A. M. O'Donnell & A. King (Eds.), *Cognitive perspectives on peer learning* (pp. 3–37). Mahwah, NJ: Erlbaum.

DeLoache, J. S. (1995). Early understanding and use of symbols: The model model. *Current Directions in Psychological Science, 4,* 109–113.

Delval, J. (1994). Stages in the child's construction of social knowledge. In M. Carretero & J. F. Voss (Eds.), *Cognitive and instructional processes in history and the social sciences* (pp. 77–102). Mahwah, NJ: Erlbaum.

Demetriou, A., Christou, C., Spanoudis, G., & Platsidou, M. (2002). The development of mental processing: Efficiency, working memory, and thinking. *Monographs of the Society for Research in Child Development, 67* (1, Serial No. 268).

Dempster, F. N. (1991). Synthesis of research on reviews and tests. *Educational Leadership, 48*(7), 71–76.

Dempster, F. N. (1992). The rise and fall of the inhibitory mechanism: Toward a unified theory of cognitive development and aging. *Developmental Review, 12,* 45–75.

Dempster, F. N., & Corkill, A. J. (1999). Interference and inhibition in cognition and behavior: Unifying themes for educational psychology. *Educational Psychology Review, 11,* 1–88.

Dempster, F. N., & Rohwer, W. D. (1974). Component analysis of the elaborative encoding effect in paired-associate learning. *Journal of Experimental Psychology, 103,* 400–408.

Derry, S. J. (1996). Cognitive schema theory in the constructivist debate. *Educational Psychologist, 31,* 163–174.

Derry, S. J. (2006). eStep as a case of theory-based Web course design. In A. M. O'Donnell, C. E. Hmelo-Silver, & G. Erkens (Eds.), *Collaborative learning, reasoning, and technology* (pp. 171–196). Mahwah, NJ: Erlbaum.

Derry, S. J., DuRussel, L. A., & O'Donnell, A. M. (1998). Individual and distributed cognitions in interdisciplinary teamwork: A developing case study and emerging theory. *Educational Psychology Review, 10,* 25–56.

Derry, S. J., Levin, J. R., Osana, H. P., & Jones, M. S. (1998). Developing middle school students'

statistical reasoning abilities through simulation gaming. In S. P. Lajoie (Ed.), *Reflections on statistics: Learning, teaching, and assessment in grades K–12* (pp. 175–195). Mahwah, NJ: Erlbaum.

Desoete, A., Roeyers, H., & De Clercq, A. (2003). Can offline metacognition enhance mathematical problem solving? *Journal of Educational Psychology, 95,* 188–200.

Deutsch, M. (1993). Educating for a peaceful world. *American Psychologist, 48,* 510–517.

DeVries, R. (1969). Constancy of generic identity in the years three to six. *Monographs of the Society for Research in Child Development, 34* (Whole No. 127).

Dewhurst, S. A., & Conway, M. A. (1994). Pictures, images, and recollective experience. *Journal of Experimental Psychology: Learning, Memory, and Cognition, 20,* 1088–1098.

Diamond, M., & Hopson, J. (1998). *Magic trees of the mind.* New York: Dutton.

Díaz, R. M., Neal, C. J., & Amaya-Williams, M. (1990). The social origins of self-regulation. In L. C. Moll (Ed.), *Vygotsky and education: Instructional implications and applications of sociohistorical psychology.* Cambridge, England: Cambridge University Press.

Dien, T. (1998). Language and literacy in Vietnamese American communities. In B. Pérez (Ed.), *Sociocultural contexts of language and literacy.* Mahwah, NJ: Erlbaum.

Diesendruck, G., & Bloom, P. (2003). How specific is the shape bias? *Child Development, 74,* 168–178.

Dijksterhuis, A., & Nordgren, L. F. (2006). A theory of unconscious thought. *Perspectives on Psychological Science, 1,* 95–109.

Dinges, D. F., Whitehouse, W. G., Orne, E. C., Powell, J. W., Orne, M. T., & Erdelyi, M. H. (1992). Evaluating hypnotic memory enhancement (hypermnesia and reminiscence) using multitrial forced recall. *Journal of Experimental Psychology: Learning, Memory, and Cognition, 18,* 1139–1147.

diSessa, A. A. (1996). What do "just plain folk" know about physics? In D. R. Olson & N. Torrance (Eds.), *The handbook of education and human development: New models of learning, teaching, and schooling.* Cambridge, MA: Blackwell.

diSessa, A. A., Elby, A., & Hammer, D. (2003). J's epistemological stance and strategies. In G. M. Sinatra & P. R. Pintrich (Eds.), *Intentional conceptual change* (pp. 237–290). Mahwah, NJ: Erlbaum.

Di Vesta, F. J., & Gray, S. G. (1972). Listening and notetaking. *Journal of Educational Psychology, 63,* 8–14.

Di Vesta, F. J., & Ingersoll, G. M. (1969). Influence of pronounceability, articulation, and test mode on paired-associate learning by the study-recall procedure. *Journal of Experimental Psychology, 79,* 104–108.

Di Vesta, F. J., & Peverly, S. T. (1984). The effects of encoding variability, processing activity and rule example sequences on the transfer of conceptual rules. *Journal of Educational Psychology, 76,* 108–119.

Dixon, F. A., Dungan, D. E., & Young, A. (2003, April). *An empirical typology of perfectionism in* students who attend a Christian liberal arts university. Paper presented at the annual meeting of the American Educational Research Association, Chicago.

Dixon, M. R., & Cummings, A. (2001). Self-control in children with autism: Response allocation during delays to reinforcement. *Journal of Applied Behavior Analysis, 34,* 491–495.

Dixon, M. R., Rehfeldt, R. A., & Randich, L. (2003). Enhancing tolerance to delayed reinforcers: The role of intervening activities. *Journal of Applied Behavior Analysis, 36,* 263–266.

Do, S. L., & Schallert, D. L. (2004). Emotions and classroom talk: Toward a model of the role of affect in students' experiences of classroom discussions. *Journal of Educational Psychology, 96,* 619–634.

Doctorow, M., Wittrock, M. C., & Marks, C. (1978). Generative processes in reading comprehension. *Journal of Educational Psychology, 70,* 109–118.

Dodd, D. H., & White, R. M. (1980). *Cognition: Mental structures and processes.* Boston: Allyn & Bacon.

Dodge, K. A., Asher, S. R., & Parkhurst, J. T. (1989). Social life as a goal-coordination task. In C. Ames & R. Ames (Eds.), *Research on motivation in education: Vol. 3. Goals and cognitions.* San Diego, CA: Academic Press.

Dole, J. A., Duffy, G. G., Roehler, L. R., & Pearson, P. D. (1991). Moving from the old to the new: Research on reading comprehension instruction. *Review of Educational Research, 61,* 239–264.

Dollard, J. C., Doob, L., Miller, N., Mowrer, O., & Sears, R. (1939). *Frustration and aggression.* New Haven, CT: Yale University Press.

Dominowski, R. L. (1998). Verbalization and problem solving. In D. J. Hacker, J. Dunlosky, & A. C. Graesser (Eds.), *Metacognition in educational theory and practice* (pp. 25–45). Mahwah, NJ: Erlbaum.

Donahoe, J., & Vegas, R. (2004). Pavlovian conditioning: The CS-UR relation. *Journal of Experimental Psychology: Animal Behavior Processes, 30,* 17–33.

Donaldson, M. (1978). *Children's minds.* New York: W. W. Norton.

Donnelly, C. M., & McDaniel, M. A. (1993). Use of analogy in learning scientific concepts. *Journal of Experimental Psychology: Learning, Memory, and Cognition, 19,* 975–987.

Dooling, D. J., & Christiaansen, R. E. (1977). Episodic and semantic aspects of memory for prose. *Journal of Experimental Psychology: Human Learning and Memory, 3,* 428–436.

Dorris, M. (1989). *The broken cord.* New York: Harper & Row.

Doupe, A. J., & Kuhl, P. (1999). Birdsong and human speech: Common themes and mechanisms. *Annual Review of Neuroscience, 22,* 567–631.

Dowaliby, F. J., & Schumer, H. (1973). Teacher-centered versus student-centered mode of college classroom instruction as related to manifest anxiety. *Journal of Educational Psychology, 64,* 125–132.

Downing, P. E. (2000). Interactions between visual working memory and selective attention. *Psychological Science, 11,* 467–473.

Downs, R. M., & Stea, D. (1977). *Maps in minds.* New York: Harper & Row.

Dowson, M., & McInerney, D. M. (2001). Psychological parameters of students' social and work avoidance goals: A qualitative investigation. *Journal of Educational Psychology, 93,* 35–42.

Doyle, W. (1983). Academic work. *Review of Educational Research, 53,* 159–199.

Doyle, W. (1986a). Classroom organization and management. In M. C. Wittrock (Ed.), *Handbook of research on teaching* (3rd ed.). New York: Macmillan.

Doyle, W. (1986b). Content representation in teachers' definitions of academic work. *Journal of Curriculum Studies, 18,* 365–379.

Doyle, W. (1990). Classroom management techniques. In O. C. Moles (Ed.), *Student discipline strategies: Research and practice.* Albany: State University of New York Press.

Drabman, R. S. (1976). Behavior modification in the classroom. In W. E. Craighead & M. J. Mahoney (Eds.), *Behavior modification principles, issues, and applications.* Boston: Houghton Mifflin.

Dreikurs, R. (1998). *Maintaining sanity in the classroom: Classroom management techniques* (2nd ed.). Bristol, PA: Hemisphere.

Drevno, G. E., Kimball, J. W., Possi, M. K., Heward, W. L., Gardner, R., III, & Barbetta, P. M. (1994). Effects of active student responding during error correction on the acquisition, maintenance, and generalization of science vocabulary by elementary students: A systematic replication. *Journal of Applied Behavior Analysis, 27,* 179–180.

Driver, R., Asoko, H., Leach, J., Mortimer, E., & Scott, P. (1994). Constructing scientific knowledge in the classroom. *Educational Researcher, 23*(7), 5–12.

Dryden, M. A., & Jefferson, P. (1994, April). *Use of background knowledge and reading achievement among elementary school students.* Paper presented at the annual meeting of the American Educational Research Association, New Orleans, LA.

DuBois, N. F., Kiewra, K. A., & Fraley, J. (1988, April). *Differential effects of a learning strategy course.* Paper presented at the annual meeting of the American Educational Research Association, New Orleans, LA.

DuBois, N. F., Staley, R., Guzy, L., & DiNardo, P. (1995, April). *Durable effects of a study skills course on academic achievement.* Paper presented at the annual meeting of the American Educational Research Association, San Francisco.

Duckworth, A. L., & Seligman, M. E. P. (2005). Self-discipline outdoes IQ in predicting academic performance of adolescents. *Psychological Science, 16,* 939–944.

Duell, O. K. (1994). Extended wait time and university student achievement. *American Educational Research Journal, 31,* 397–414.

Dufresne, A., & Kobasigawa, A. (1989). Children's spontaneous allocation of study time: Differential and sufficient aspects. *Journal of Experimental Child Psychology, 47,* 274–296.

Duit, R. (1990, April). *On the role of analogies, similes, and metaphors in learning science.* Paper presented at the annual meeting of the American Educational Research Association, Boston.

Duit, R. (1991). Students' conceptual frameworks: Consequences for learning science. In S. M. Glynn, R. H. Yeany, & B. K. Britton (Eds.), *The psychology of learning science.* Hillsdale, NJ: Erlbaum.

DuNann, D. G., & Weber, S. J. (1976). Short- and long-term effects of contingency managed instruction on low, medium, and high GPA students. *Journal of Applied Behavior Analysis, 9,* 375–376.

Duncker, K. (1945). On problem solving. *Psychological Monographs, 58* (Whole No. 270).

Dunlap, G., dePerczel, M., Clarke, S., Wilson, D., Wright, S., White, R., & Gomez, A. (1994). Choice making to promote adaptive behavior for students with emotional and behavioral challenges. *Journal of Applied Behavior Analysis, 27,* 505–518.

Dunlosky, J., Rawson, K. A., & McDonald, S. L. (2002). Influence of practice tests on the accuracy of predicting memory performance for paired associates, sentences, and text material. In T. J. Perfect & B. L. Schwartz (Eds.), *Applied metacognition* (pp. 68–92). Cambridge, England: Cambridge University Press.

Dunn, C. S. (1983). The influence of instructional methods on concept learning. *Science Education, 67,* 647–656.

Dunning, D., Heath, C., & Suls, J. M. (2004). Flawed self-assessment: Implications for health, education, and the workplace. *Psychological Science in the Public Interest, 5,* 69–106.

Dunning, D., Johnson, K. Ehrlinger, J., & Kruger, J. (2003). Why people fail to recognize their own incompetence. *Current Directions in Psychological Science, 12,* 83–87.

DuPaul, G. J., Ervin, R. A., Hook, C. L., & McGoey, K. E. (1998). Peer tutoring for children with attention deficit hyperactivity disorder: Effects on classroom behavior and academic performance. *Journal of Applied Behavior Analysis, 31,* 579–592.

Durik, A., M., Vida, M., & Eccles, J. S. (2006). Task values and ability beliefs as predictors of high school literacy choices: A developmental analysis. *Journal of Educational Psychology, 98,* 382–393.

Durkin, K. (1987). Social cognition and social context in the construction of sex differences. In M. A. Baker (Ed.), *Sex differences in human performance.* Chichester, England: Wiley.

Durkin, K. (1995). *Developmental social psychology: From infancy to old age.* Cambridge, MA: Blackwell.

Durst, R. K., & Newell, G. E. (1989). The uses of function: James Britton's category system and research on writing. *Review of Educational Research, 59,* 375–394.

Dweck, C. S. (1975). The role of expectations and attributions in the alleviation of learned helplessness. *Journal of Personality and Social Psychology, 31,* 674–685.

Dweck, C. S. (1978). Achievement. In M. E. Lamb (Ed.), *Social and personality development.* New York: Holt, Rinehart & Winston.

Dweck, C. S. (1986). Motivational processes affecting learning. *American Psychologist, 41,* 1040–1048.

Dweck, C. S. (1999). *Self-theories: Their role in motivation, personality, and development.* Philadelphia: Taylor & Francis.

Dweck, C. S. (2000). *Self-theories: Their role in motivation, personality, and development.* Philadelphia: Psychology Press.

Dweck, C. S., Davidson, W., Nelson, S., & Enna, B. (1978). Sex differences in learned helplessness: II. The contingencies of evaluative feedback in the classroom; III. An experimental analysis. *Developmental Psychology, 14,* 268–276.

Dweck, C. S., & Elliott, E. S. (1983). Achievement motivation. In E. M. Hetherington (Ed.), *Handbook of child psychology: Vol. 4. Socialization, personality, and social development* (4th ed.). New York: Wiley.

Dweck, C. S., Goetz, T. E., & Strauss, N. L. (1980). Sex differences in learned helplessness: IV. An experimental and naturalistic study of failure generalization and its mediators. *Journal of Personality and Social Psychology, 38,* 441–452.

Dweck, C. S., & Leggett, E. L. (1988). A social-cognitive approach to motivation and personality. *Psychological Review, 95,* 256–273.

Dweck, C. S., Mangels, J. A., & Good, C. (2004). Motivational effects on attention, cognition, and performance. In D. Y. Dai & R. J. Sternberg (Eds.), *Motivation, emotion, and cognition: Integrative perspectives on intellectual functioning and development* (pp. 41–55). Mahwah, NJ: Erlbaum.

Dyer, H. S. (1967). The discovery and development of educational goals. *Proceedings of the 1966 Invitational Conference on Testing Problems.* Princeton, NJ: Educational Testing Service.

Eacott, M. J. (1999). Memory for the events of early childhood. *Current Directions in Psychological Science, 8,* 46–49.

Eagly, A. H., Kulesa, P., Chen, S., & Chaiken, S. (2001). Do attitudes affect memory? Tests of the congeniality hypothesis. *Current Directions in Psychological Science, 10,* 5–9.

Easterbrook, J. A. (1959). The effect of emotion on cue utilization and the organization of behavior. *Psychological Review, 66,* 183–201.

Eaton, J. F., Anderson, C. W., & Smith, E. L. (1984). Students' misconceptions interfere with science learning: Case studies of fifth-grade students. *Elementary School Journal, 84,* 365–379.

Ebbinghaus, H. (1913). *Memory: A contribution to experimental psychology* (H. A. Ruger & C. E. Bussenius, Trans.). New York: Teachers College. (Original work published 1885)

Eccles, J. S. (1989). Bringing young women to math and science. In M. Crawford & M. Gentry (Eds.), *Gender and thought: Psychological perspectives.* New York: Springer-Verlag.

Eccles, J. S., & Jacobs, J. E. (1986). Social forces shape math attitudes and performance. *Signs: Journal of Women in Culture and Society, 11,* 367–380.

Eccles, J. S., Jacobs, J., Harold, R., Yoon, K. S., Arbreton, A., & Freedman-Doan, C. (1993). Parents and gender-related socialization during the middle childhood and adolescent years. In S. Oskamp & M. Costanzo (Eds.), *Gender issues in contemporary society.* Newbury Park, CA: Sage.

Eccles, J. S., & Midgley, C. (1989). Stage-environment fit: Developmentally appropriate classrooms for young adolescents. In C. Ames & R. Ames (Eds.), *Research on motivation in education: Vol. 3. Goals and cognition.* New York: Academic Press.

Eccles, J. S., & Wigfield, A. (1985). Teacher expectations and student motivation. In J. B. Dusek (Ed.), *Teacher expectancies.* Hillsdale, NJ: Erlbaum.

Eccles (Parsons), J. (1983). Expectancies, values, and academic behaviors. In J. T. Spence (Ed.), *Achievement and achievement motivation.* San Francisco: W. H. Freeman.

Eccles (Parsons), J. (1984). Sex differences in mathematics participation. In M. Steinkamp & M. Maehr (Eds.), *Women in science.* Greenwich, CT: JAI Press.

Eccles, J. S., Wigfield, A., & Schiefele, U. (1998). Motivation to succeed. In W. Damon (Editor-in-Chief) and N. Eisenberg (Volume Editor), *Handbook of child psychology* (5th ed., Vol. 3). New York: Wiley.

Echevarria, M. (2003). Anomalies as a catalyst for middle school students' knowledge construction and scientific reasoning during science inquiry. *Journal of Educational Psychology, 95,* 357–374.

Ecott, C. L., & Critchfield, T. S. (2004). Noncontingent reinforcement, alternative reinforcement, and the matching law: A laboratory demonstration. *Journal of Applied Behavior Analysis, 37,* 249–265.

Edens, K. M., & McCormick, C. B. (2000). How do adolescents process advertisements? The influence of ad characteristics, processing objective, and gender. *Contemporary Educational Psychology, 25,* 450–463.

Edens, K. M., & Potter, E. F. (2001). Promoting conceptual understanding through pictorial representation. *Studies in Art Education, 42,* 214–233.

Edwards, K., & Bryan, T. S. (1997). Judgmental biases produced by instructions to disregard: The (paradoxical) case of emotional information. *Personality and Social Psychology Bulletin, 23,* 849–864.

Eeds, M., & Wells, D. (1989). Grand conversations: An explanation of meaning construction in literature study groups. *Research in the Teaching of English, 23,* 4–29.

Eich, R. (1995). Searching for mood dependent memory. *Psychological Science, 6,* 67–75.

Eilam, B. (2001). Primary strategies for promoting homework performance. *American Educational Research Journal, 38,* 691–725.

Eimas, P. D., & Quinn, P. C. (1994). Studies on the formation of perceptually based basic-level categories in young infants. *Child Development, 65,* 903–917.

Einstein, G. O., & McDaniel, M. A. (2005). Prospective memory: Multiple retrieval processes. *Current Directions in Psychological Science, 14,* 286–290.

Eisenberg, N., Martin, C. L., & Fabes, R. A. (1996). Gender development and gender effects. In D. C. Berliner & R. C. Calfee (Eds.), *Handbook of educational psychology.* New York: Macmillan.

Eisenberger, R. (1992). Learned industriousness. *Psychological Review, 99,* 248–267.

Eisenberger, R., & Cameron, J. (1996). Detrimental effects of reward: Reality or myth? *American Psychologist, 51,* 1153–1166.

Eisner, E. W. (1994). *Cognition and curriculum reconsidered.* New York: Teachers College Press.

Elbert, T., Pantev, C., & Taub, E. (1995). Increased cortical representation of the fingers of the left hand in string players. *Science, 270,* 305–307.

Elder, A. D. (2002). Characterizing fifth grade students' epistemological beliefs in science. In B. K. Hofer & P. R. Pintrich (Eds.), *Personal epistemology: The psychology of beliefs about knowledge and knowing* (pp. 347–363). Mahwah, NJ: Erlbaum.

Elkind, D. (1981). *Children and adolescents: Interpretive essays on Jean Piaget* (3rd ed.). New York: Oxford University Press.

Ellingson, S. A., Miltenberger, R. G., Stricker, J. M., Garlinghouse, M. A., Roberts, J., Galensky, T. L., & Rapp, J. T. (2000). Analysis and treatment of finger sucking. *Journal of Applied Behavior Analysis, 33,* 41–52.

Elliot, A. J. (1999). Approach and avoidance motivation and achievement goals. *Educational Psychologist, 34,* 169–189.

Elliot, A. J., Chirkov, V. I., Kim, Y., & Sheldon, K. M. (2001). A cross-cultural analysis of avoidance (relative to approach) personal goals. *Psychological Science, 12,* 505–510.

Elliot, A. J., & McGregor, H. A. (2000, April). Approach and avoidance goals and autonomous-controlled regulation: Empirical and conceptual relations. In A. Assor (Chair), *Self-determination theory and achievement goal theory: Convergences, divergences, and educational implications.* Symposium conducted at the annual meeting of the American Educational Research Association, New Orleans.

Elliot, A. J., Shell, M. M., Henry, K. B., & Maier, M. A. (2005). Achievement goals, performance contingencies, and performance attainment: An experimental test. *Journal of Educational Psychology, 97,* 630–640.

Elliot, A. J., & Thrash, T. M. (2001). Achievement goals and the hierarchical model of achievement motivation. *Educational Psychology Review, 13,* 139–156.

Elliott, D. J. (1995). *Music matters: A new philosophy of music education.* New York: Oxford University Press.

Elliott, R., & Vasta, R. (1970). The modeling of sharing: Effects associated with vicarious reinforcement, symbolization, age, and generalization. *Journal of Experimental Child Psychology, 10,* 8–15.

Elliott, S. N., & Busse, R. T. (1991). Social skills assessment and intervention with children and adolescents. *School Psychology International, 12,* 63–83.

Ellis, H. C., & Hunt, R. R. (1983). *Fundamentals of human memory and cognition* (3rd ed.). Dubuque, IA: Wm. C. Brown.

Ellis, J. O. (1975). *Cognitive processes in logical problem-solving: The three-term series problem.* Unpublished doctoral dissertation, The Pennsylvania State University, University Park.

Ellis, N. C. (Ed.) (1994). *Implicit and explicit learning of languages.* London: Academic Press.

Ellis, S., & Rogoff, B. (1986). Problem solving in children's management of instruction. In E. C. Mueller & C. R. Cooper (Eds.), *Process and outcome in peer relationships* (pp. 301–325). Orlando, FL: Academic Press.

Emmer, E. T. (1987). Classroom management and discipline. In V. Richardson-Koehler (Ed.), *Educators' handbook: A research perspective.* White Plains, NY: Longman.

Emmer, E. T., & Evertson, C. M. (1981). Synthesis of research on classroom management. *Educational Leadership, 38,* 342–347.

Emmer, E. T., & Gerwels, M. C. (2006). Classroom management in middle and high school classrooms. In C. M. Evertson & C. S. Weinstein (Eds.), *Handbook of classroom management: Research, practice, and contemporary issues* (pp. 407–437). Mahwah, NJ: Erlbaum.

Empson, S. B. (1999). Equal sharing and shared meaning: The development of fraction concepts in a first-grade classroom. *Cognition and Instruction, 17,* 283–342.

Emshoff, J. G., Redd, W. H., & Davidson, W. S. (1976). Generalization training and the transfer of treatment effects with delinquent adolescents. *Journal of Behavior Therapy and Experimental Psychiatry, 7,* 141–144.

Engerman, J. A., Austin, J., & Bailey, J. S. (1997). Prompting patron safety belt use at a supermarket. *Journal of Applied Behavior Analysis, 30,* 577–579.

Engle, R. W. (2002). Working memory capacity as executive attention. *Current Directions in Psychological Science, 11,* 19–23.

Engle, R. A., & Conant, F. R. (2002). Guiding principles for fostering productive disciplinary engagement: Explaining an emergent argument in a community of learners classroom. *Cognition and Instruction, 20,* 399–483.

English, H. B., Welborn, E. L., & Killian, C. D. (1934). Studies in substance memorization. *Journal of General Psychology, 11,* 233–260.

English, L. D. (1997a). Analogies, metaphors, and images: Vehicles for mathematical reasoning. In L. D. English (Ed.), *Mathematical reasoning: Analogies, metaphors, and images* (pp. 3–18). Mahwah, NJ: Erlbaum.

English, L. D. (Ed.) (1997b). *Mathematical reasoning: Analogies, metaphors, and images.* Mahwah, NJ: Erlbaum.

Entwisle, N. J., & Ramsden, P. (1983). *Understanding student learning.* London: Croom Helm.

Epstein, H. (1978). Growth spurts during brain development: Implications for educational policy and practice. In J. Chall & A. Mirsky (Eds.), *Education and the brain: The 77th yearbook of the National Society for the Study of Education, Part II.* Chicago: University of Chicago Press.

Epstein, R. (1991). Skinner, creativity, and the problem of spontaneous behavior. *Psychological Science, 2,* 362–370.

Epstein, J. L. (1989). Family structures and student motivation. In R. E. Ames & C. Ames (Eds.), *Research on motivation in education: Vol. 3. Goals and cognitions* (pp. 259–295). New York: Academic Press.

Epstein, T. (2000). Adolescents' perspectives on racial diversity in U.S. history: Case studies from an urban classroom. *American Educational Research Journal, 37,* 185–214.

Erdelyi, M. H. (1985). *Psychoanalysis: Freud's cognitive psychology.* New York: W. H. Freeman.

Erdelyi, M. H., & Goldberg, B. (1979). Let's not sweep repression under the rug: Toward a cognitive psychology of repression. In J. F. Kihlstrom & F. J. Evans (Eds.), *Functional disorders of memory.* Hillsdale, NJ: Erlbaum.

Ericsson, K. A. (1996). *The road to excellence: The acquisition of expert performance in the arts and science, sports, and games.* Mahwah, NJ: Erlbaum.

Ericsson, K. A. (2003). The acquisition of expert performance as problem solving. In J. E. Davidson & R. J. Sternberg (Eds.), *The psychology of problem solving* (pp. 31–83). Cambridge, England: Cambridge University Press.

Eriksen, C. W., & Kuethe, J. L. (1956). Avoidance conditioning of verbal behavior without awareness: A paradigm of repression. *Journal of Abnormal and Social Psychology, 53,* 203–209.

Estes, W. K. (1969). New perspectives on some old issues in association theory. In N. J. Mackintosh & W. K. Honig (Eds.), *Fundamental issues in associative learning.* Halifax, Canada: Dalhousie University Press.

Estes, D., Chandler, M., Horvath, K. J., & Backus, D. W. (2003). American and British college students' epistemological beliefs about research on psychological and biological development. *Applied Developmental Psychology, 23,* 625–642.

Evans, G. W., & Oswalt, G. L. (1968). Acceleration of academic progress through the manipulation of peer influence. *Behaviour Research and Therapy, 6,* 189–195.

Evertson, C. M., & Weinstein, C. S. (2006). Classroom management as a field of inquiry. In C. M. Evertson & C. S. Weinstein (Eds.), *Handbook of classroom management: Research, practice, and contemporary issues* (pp. 3–15). Mahwah, NJ: Erlbaum.

Eysenck, M. W. (1979). Depth, elaboration, and distinctiveness. In L. S. Cermak & F. I. M. Craik (Eds.), *Levels of processing in human memory.* Hillsdale, NJ: Erlbaum.

Eysenck, M. W. (1992). *Anxiety: The cognitive perspective.* Hove, England: Erlbaum.

Eysenck, M. W., & Keane, M. T. (1990). *Cognitive psychology: A student's handbook.* Hove, England: Erlbaum.

Fabos, B., & Young, M. D. (1999). Telecommunication in the classroom: Rhetoric versus reality. *Review of Educational Research, 69,* 217–259.

Fahrmeier, E. D. (1978). The development of concrete operations among the Hausa. *Journal of Cross-Cultural Psychology, 9,* 23–44.

Fantuzzo, J. W., King, J., & Heller, L. R. (1992). Effects of reciprocal peer tutoring on mathematics and school adjustment: A component analysis. *Journal of Educational Psychology, 84,* 331–339.

Farah, M. J., Hammond, K. M., Levine, D. N., & Calvanio, R. (1988). Visual and spatial mental imagery: Dissociable systems of representation. *Cognitive Psychology, 20,* 439–462.

Farnham-Diggory, S. (1972). The development of equivalence systems. In S. Farnham-Diggory (Ed.), *Information processing in children.* New York: Academic Press.

Farrar, M. J., & Goodman, G. S. (1992). Developmental changes in event memory. *Child Development, 63,* 173–187.

Farwell, L. A., & Smith, S. S. (2001). Using brain MERMER testing to detect knowledge despite efforts to conceal. *Journal of Forensic Sciences, 46*(1), 1–9.

Fashola, O. S., Drum, P. A., Mayer, R. E., & Kang, S. (1996). A cognitive theory of orthographic transitioning: Predictable errors in how Spanish-speaking children spell English words. *American Educational Research Journal, 33,* 825–843.

Faust, G. W., & Anderson, R. C. (1967). Effects of incidental material in a programmed Russian vocabulary lesson. *Journal of Educational Psychology, 58,* 3–10.

Feather, N. T. (1982). *Expectations and actions: Expectancy-value models in psychology.* Hillsdale, NJ: Erlbaum.

Feinman, S. (1992). *Social referencing and the social construction of reality in infancy.* New York: Plenum Press.

Feld, S., Ruhland, D., & Gold, M. (1979). Developmental changes in achievement motivation. *Merrill-Palmer Quarterly, 25,* 43–60.

Feldman, J. (2003). The simplicity principle in human concept learning. *Current Directions in Psychological Science, 12,* 227–232.

Feltz, D. L., Chaase, M. A., Moritz, S. E., & Sullivan, P. J. (1999). A conceptual model of coaching efficacy: Preliminary investigation and instrument development. *Journal of Educational Psychology, 91,* 765–776.

Feltz, D. L., Landers, D. M., & Becker, B. J. (1988). A revised meta-analysis of the mental practice literature on motor skill performance. In D. Druckman & J. A. Swets (Eds.), *Enhancing human performance: Issues, theories, and techniques: Background papers.* Washington, DC: National Research Council.

Fennema, E. (1980). Sex-related differences in mathematics achievement: Where and why. In L. H. Fox, L. Brody, & D. Tobin (Eds.), *Women and the mathematical mystique.* Baltimore: Johns Hopkins University Press.

Fennema, E. (1987). Sex-related differences in education: Myths, realities, and interventions. In V. Richardson-Koehler (Ed.), *Educators' handbook: A research perspective.* New York: Longman.

Fennema, E., Carpenter, T. P., & Peterson, P. L. (1989). Learning mathematics with understanding: Cognitively guided instruction. In

J. Brophy (Ed.), *Advances in research on teaching* (Vol. 1). Greenwich, CT: JAI Press.

Fenning, P. A., & Bohanon, H. (2006). Schoolwide discipline policies: An analysis of discipline codes of conduct. In C. M. Evertson & C. S. Weinstein (Eds.), *Handbook of classroom management: Research, practice, and contemporary issues* (pp. 1021–1039). Mahwah, NJ: Erlbaum.

Ferguson, E. L., & Hegarty, M. (1995). Learning with real machines or diagrams: Application of knowledge to real-world problems. *Cognition and Instruction, 13,* 129–160.

Ferrari, M., & Elik, N. (2003). Influences on intentional conceptual change. In G. M. Sinatra & P. R. Pintrich (Eds.), *Intentional conceptual change* (pp. 21–54). Mahwah, NJ: Erlbaum.

Ferster, C. B., & Skinner, B. F. (1957). *Schedules of reinforcement.* Englewood Cliffs, NJ: Prentice Hall.

Feuerstein, R. (1979). *The dynamic assessment of retarded performers: The Learning Potential Assessment Device, theory, instruments, and techniques.* Baltimore: University Park Press.

Feuerstein, R. (1980). *Instrumental enrichment: An intervention program for cognitive modifiability.* Baltimore: University Park Press.

Feuerstein, R. (1990). The theory of structural cognitive modifiability. In B. Z. Presseisen (Ed.), *Learning and thinking styles: Classroom interaction.* Washington, DC: National Education Association.

Field, D. (1987). A review of preschool conservation training: An analysis of analyses. *Developmental Review, 7,* 210–251.

Field, T. F., Woodson, R., Greenberg, R., & Cohen, D. (1982). Discrimination and imitation of facial expressions by neonates. *Science, 218*(8), 179–181.

Finke, R. A., & Bettle, J. (1996). *Chaotic cognition: Principles and applications.* Mahwah, NJ: Erlbaum.

Finn, J. D., Pannozzo, G. M., & Achilles, C. M. (2003). The "why's" of class size: Student behavior in small classes. *Review of Educational Research, 73,* 321–368.

Fischer, K. W., & Bidell, T. (1991). Constraining nativist inferences about cognitive capacities. In S. Carey & R. Gelman (Eds.), *The epigenesis of mind: Essays on biology and cognition.* Hillsdale, NJ: Erlbaum.

Fischer, K. W., & Immordino-Yang, M. H. (2006). Cognitive development and education: From dynamic general structure to specific learning and teaching. In W. Damon & R. M. Lerner (Series Eds.), D. Kuhn, & R. Siegler (Vol. Eds.), *Handbook of child psychology: Vol. 1. Cognition, perception, and language* (6th ed.). New York: Wiley.

Fischer, K. W., Knight, C. C., & Van Parys, M. (1993). Analyzing diversity in developmental pathways: Methods and concepts. In R. Case & W. Edelstein (Eds.), *The new structuralism in cognitive development: Theory and research on individual pathways.* Basel, Switzerland: Karger.

Fischer, S. M., Iwata, B. A., & Mazaleski, J. L. (1997). Noncontingent delivery of arbitrary reinforcers as treatment for self-injurious behavior. *Journal of Applied Behavior Analysis, 30,* 239–249.

Fisher, W. W., & Mazur, J. E. (1997). Basic and applied research on choice responding. *Journal of Applied Behavior Analysis, 30,* 387–410.

Fiske, D. W., & Maddi, S. R. (1961). *Functions of varied experience.* Homewood, IL: Dorsey.

Fivush, R., Haden, C., & Reese, E. (1996). Remembering, recounting, and reminiscing: The development of autobiographical memory in social context. In D. C. Rubin (Ed.), *Remembering our past: Studies in autobiographical memory* (pp. 341–359). Cambridge, England: Cambridge University Press.

Fivush, R., & Nelson, K. (2004). Culture and language in the emergence of autobiographical memory. *Psychological Science, 15,* 573–577.

Flaherty, C. F. (1985). *Animal learning and cognition.* New York: Alfred Knopf.

Flaherty, C. F., Uzwiak, A. J., Levine, J., Smith, M., Hall, P., & Schuler, R. (1980). Apparent hypoglycemic conditioned responses with exogenous insulin as the unconditioned stimulus. *Animal Learning and Behavior, 8,* 382–386.

Flavell, J. H. (1963). *The developmental psychology of Jean Piaget.* New York: Van Nostrand Reinhold.

Flavell, J. H. (1979). Metacognition and cognitive monitoring: A new area of cognitive-developmental inquiry. *American Psychologist, 34,* 906–911.

Flavell, J. H. (1994). Cognitive development: Past, present, and future. In R. D. Parke, P. A. Ornstein, J. J. Rieser, & C. Zahn-Waxler (Eds.), *A century of developmental psychology.* Washington, DC: American Psychological Association.

Flavell, J. H. (2000). Development of children's knowledge about the mental world. *International Journal of Behavioral Development, 24*(1), 15–23.

Flavell, J. H., Friedrichs, A. G., & Hoyt, J. D. (1970). Developmental changes in memorization processes. *Cognitive Psychology, 1,* 324–340.

Flavell, J. H., Green, F. L., & Flavell, E. R. (2000). Development of children's awareness of their own thoughts. *Journal of Cognitive Development, 1,* 97–112.

Flavell, J. H., Miller, P. H., & Miller, S. A. (2002). *Cognitive development* (4th ed.). Upper Saddle River, NJ: Prentice Hall.

Flege, J. E., Munro, M. J., & MacKay, I. R. A. (1995). Effects of age of second-language learning on the production of English consonants. *Speech Communication, 16*(1), 1–26.

Fletcher, K. L., & Bray, N. W. (1996). External memory strategy use in preschool children. *Merrill-Palmer Quarterly, 42,* 379–396.

Fletcher-Flinn, C. M., & Gravatt, B. (1995). The efficacy of computer-assisted instruction (CAI): A meta-analysis. *Journal of Educational Computing Research, 12,* 219–242.

Flieller, A. (1999). Comparison of the development of formal thought in adolescent cohorts aged 10 to 15 years (1967–1996 and 1972–1993). *Developmental Psychology, 35,* 1048–1058.

Flink, C., Boggiano, A. K., Main, D. S., Barrett, M., & Katz, P. A. (1992). Children's achievement-related behaviors: The role of extrinsic and intrinsic motivational orientations. In A. K. Boggiano & T. S. Pittman (Eds.), *Achievement and motivation: A social-developmental perspective.* Cambridge, England: Cambridge University Press.

Flood, W. A., Wilder, D. A., Flood, A. L., & Masuda, A. (2002). Peer-mediated reinforcement plus prompting as treatment for off-task behavior in children with attention deficit hyperactivity disorder. *Journal of Applied Behavior Analysis, 35,* 199–204.

Flower, L. S., & Hayes, J. R. (1981). A cognitive process theory of writing. *College Composition and Communication, 32,* 365–387.

Flum, H., & Kaplan, A. (2006). Exploratory orientation as an educational goal. *Educational Psychologist, 41,* 99–110.

Fodor, J. A., & Pylyshyn, Z. W. (1988). Connectionism and cognitive architecture: A critical analysis. *Cognition, 28,* 3–71.

Foley, M. A., Harris, J., & Herman, S. (1994). Developmental comparisons of the ability to discriminate between memories for symbolic play enactments. *Developmental Psychology, 30,* 206–217.

Fong, G. T., Krantz, D. H., & Nisbett, R. E. (1986). The effects of statistical training on thinking about everyday problems. *Cognitive Psychology, 18,* 253–292.

Foo, P., Warren, W. H., Duchon, A., & Tarr, M. J. (2005). Do humans integrate routes into a cognitive map? Map- versus landmark-based navigation of novel shortcuts. *Journal of Experimental Psychology: Learning, Memory, and Cognition, 31,* 195–215.

Foos, P. W., & Fisher, R. P. (1988). Using tests as learning opportunities. *Journal of Educational Psychology, 80,* 179–183.

Ford, D. Y. (1996). *Reversing underachievement among gifted black students.* New York: Teachers College Press.

Ford, M. E. (1992). *Motivating humans: Goals, emotions, and personal agency beliefs.* Newbury Park, CA: Sage.

Ford, M. E. (1996). Motivational opportunities and obstacles associated with social responsibility and caring behavior in school contexts. In J. Juvonen & K. R. Wentzel (Eds.), *Social motivation: Understanding children's school adjustment* (pp. 126–153). Cambridge, England: Cambridge University Press.

Ford, M. E., & Nichols, C. W. (1991). Using goal assessments to identify motivational patterns and facilitate behavioral regulation and achievement. In M. Maehr & P. R. Pintrich (Eds.), *Advances in motivation and achievement: Vol. 7. Goals and self-regulatory processes.* Greenwich, CT: JAI Press.

Forgas, J. P. (2000). The role of affect in social cognition. In J. Forgas (Ed.), *Feeling and thinking: The role of affect in social cognition* (pp. 1–28). New York: Cambridge University Press.

Försterling, F., & Morgenstern, M. (2002). Accuracy of self-assessment and task performance: Does it pay to know the truth? *Journal of Educational Psychology, 94,* 576–585.

Forsyth, J. P., & Eifert, G. H. (1998). Phobic anxiety and panic: An integrative behavioral account of their origin and treatment. In J. J. Plaud & G. H. Eifert (Eds.), *From behavior theory to behavior therapy* (pp. 38–67). Needham Heights, MA: Allyn & Bacon.

Fosnot, C. T. (1996). Constructivism: A psychological theory of learning. In C. T. Fosnot (Ed.), *Constructivism: Theory, perspectives, and practice.* New York: Teachers College Press.

Foster-Johnson, L., Ferro, J., & Dunlap, G. (1994). Preferred curriculum activities and reduced problem behaviors in students with intellectual disabilities. *Journal of Applied Behavior Analysis, 27,* 493–504.

Fowler, J. W., & Peterson, P. L. (1981). Increasing reading persistence and altering attributional style of learned helpless children. *Journal of Educational Psychology, 73,* 251–260.

Fowler, S. A., & Baer, D. M. (1981). "Do I have to be good all day?" The timing of delayed reinforcement as a factor in generalization. *Journal of Applied Behavior Analysis, 14,* 13–24.

Fox, E. J. (2004). The personalized system of instruction: A flexible and effective approach to mastery learning. In D. J. Moran & R. W. Malott (Eds.), *Evidence-based educational methods* (pp. 201–221). San Diego, CA: Elsevier.

Fox, P. W., & LeCount, J. (1991, April). *When more is less: Faculty misestimation of student learning.* Paper presented at the annual meeting of the American Educational Research Association, Chicago.

Foxx, R. M., & Azrin, N. H. (1973). The elimination of autistic self-stimulatory behavior by overcorrection. *Journal of Applied Behavior Analysis, 6,* 1–14.

Foxx, R. M., & Bechtel, D. R. (1983). Overcorrection: A review and analysis. In S. Axelrod & J. Apsche (Eds.), *The effects of punishment on human behavior.* New York: Academic Press.

Foxx, R. M., & Shapiro, S. T. (1978). The timeout ribbon: A nonexclusionary timeout procedure. *Journal of Applied Behavior Analysis, 11,* 125–136.

Frankel, F., & Simmons, J. Q. (1985). Behavioral treatment approaches to pathological unsocialized physical aggression in young children. *Journal of Child Psychiatry, 26,* 525–551.

Franks, J. J., & Bransford, J. D. (1971). Abstraction of visual patterns. *Journal of Experimental Psychology, 90,* 65–74.

Frase, L. T. (1975). Prose processing. In G. H. Bower (Ed.), *The psychology of learning and motivation* (Vol. 9). New York: Academic Press.

Frederiksen, J. R., & Collins, A. (1989). A systems approach to educational testing. *Educational Researcher, 18*(9), 27–32.

Frederiksen, N. (1984a). Implications of cognitive theory for instruction in problem-solving. *Review of Educational Research, 54,* 363–407.

Frederiksen, N. (1984b). The real test bias: Influences of testing on teaching and learning. *American Psychologist, 39,* 193–202.

Frederiksen, N., & Ward, W. C. (1978). Measures for the study of creativity in scientific problem solving. *Applied Psychological Measurement, 2,* 1–24.

Fredricks, J. A., Blumenfeld, P. C., & Paris, A. H. (2004). School engagement: Potential of the concept, state of the evidence. *Review of Educational Research, 74,* 59–109.

Freeland, J. T., & Noell, G. H. (1999). Maintaining accurate math responses in elementary school students: The effects of delayed intermittent reinforcement and programming common stimuli. *Journal of Applied Behavior Analysis, 32,* 211–215.

Freeman, K. E., Gutman, L. M., & Midgley, C. (2002). Can achievement goal theory enhance our understanding of the motivation and performance of African American young adolescents? In C. Midgley (Ed.), *Goals, goal structures, and patterns of adaptive learning* (pp. 175–204). Mahwah, NJ: Erlbaum.

French, E. G. (1955). Some characteristics of achievement motivation. *Journal of Experimental Psychology, 50,* 232–236.

French, E. G. (1956). Motivation as a variable in work partner selection. *Journal of Abnormal and Social Psychology, 53,* 96–99.

Frensch, P. A., & Rünger, D. (2003). Implicit learning. *Current Directions in Psychological Science, 12,* 13–18.

Freud, S. (1922). *Beyond the pleasure principle.* London: International Psychoanalytic Press.

Freud, S. (1949). Instincts and their vicissitudes. In *Collected papers of Sigmund Freud* (Vol. 4). (J. Riviere, Trans.). London: Hogarth. (Original work published 1915)

Freud, S. (1957). Repression. In J. Strachey (Ed.), *The standard edition of the complete psychological works of Sigmund Freud* (Vol. 14). London: Hogarth Press. (Original work published 1915)

Freund, L. (1990). Maternal regulation of children's problem solving behavior and its impact on children's performance. *Child Development, 61,* 113–126.

Friedrich, L. K., & Stein, A. H. (1973). Aggressive and pro-social television programs and the natural behavior of preschool children. *Society for Research in Child Development Monographs, 38* (Whole No. 151).

Friman, P. C., & Poling, A. (1995). Making life easier with effort: Basic findings and applied research on response effort. *Journal of Applied Behavior Analysis, 28,* 583–590.

Frith, U. (1978). From print to meaning and from print to sound, or how to read without knowing how to spell. *Visible Language, 12,* 43–54.

Frith, U. (1980). Unexpected spelling problems. In U. Frith (Ed.), *Cognitive processes in spelling.* London: Academic Press.

Frost, J. L., Shin, D., & Jacobs, P. J. (1998). Physical environments and children's play. In O. N. Saracho & B. Spodek (Eds.), *Multiple perspectives on play in early childhood education.* Albany: State University of New York Press.

Fry, A. F., & Hale, S. (1996). Processing speed, working memory, and fluid intelligence. *Psychological Science, 7,* 237–241.

Fuchs, D., Fuchs, L. S., Mathes, P. G., & Simmons, D. C. (1997). Peer-assisted learning strategies: Making classrooms more responsive to diversity. *American Educational Research Journal, 34,* 174–206.

Fuchs, L. S., Fuchs, D., Hamlett, C. L., & Karns, K. (1998). High-achieving students' interactions and performance on complex mathematical tasks as a function of homogeneous and heterogeneous pairings. *American Educational Research Journal, 35,* 227–267.

Fuchs, L. S., Fuchs, D., Karns, K., Hamlett, C. L., Dutka, S., & Katzaroff, M. (1996). The relation between student ability and the quality and effectiveness of explanations. *American Educational Research Journal, 33,* 631–664.

Fuchs, L. S., Fuchs, D., Karns, K., Hamlett, C. L., Katzaroff, M., & Dutka, S. (1997). Effects of task-focused goals on low-achieving students with and without learning disabilities. *American Educational Research Journal, 34,* 513–543.

Fuchs, L. S., Fuchs, D., Prentice, K., Burch, M., Hamlett, C. L., Owen, R., Hosp, M., & Jancek, D. (2003b). Explicitly teaching for transfer: Effects on third-grade students' mathematical problem solving. *Journal of Educational Psychology, 95,* 295–305.

Fuchs, L. S., Fuchs, D., Prentice, K., Burch, M., Hamlett, C. L., Owen, R., & Schroeter, K. (2003a). Enhancing third-grade students' mathematical problem solving with self-regulated learning strategies. *Journal of Educational Psychology, 95,* 306–315.

Fuchs, L. S., Fuchs, D., Prentice, K., Hamlett, C. L., Finelli, R., & Courey, S. J. (2004). Enhancing mathematical problem solving among third-grade students with schema-based instruction. *Journal of Educational Psychology, 96,* 635–647.

Fueyo, V., & Bushell, D., Jr. (1998). Using number line procedures and peer tutoring to improve the mathematics computation of low-performing first graders. *Journal of Applied Behavior Analysis, 31,* 417–430.

Fujimura, N. (2001). Facilitating children's proportional reasoning: A model of reasoning processes and effects of intervention on strategy change. *Journal of Educational Psychology, 93,* 589–603.

Fukkink, R. G., & de Glopper, K. (1998). Effects of instruction in deriving word meanings from context: A meta-analysis. *Review of Educational Research, 68,* 450–469.

Fuller, M. L. (2001). Multicultural concerns and classroom management. In Grant, C. A., & Gomez, M. L., *Campus and classroom: Making schooling multicultural* (2nd ed., pp. 109–134). Upper Saddle River, NJ: Merrill/Prentice Hall.

Furrer, C., & Skinner, E. (2003). Sense of relatedness as a factor in children's academic engagement and performance. *Journal of Educational Psychology, 95,* 148–162.

Furst, E. J. (1981). Bloom's taxonomy of educational objectives for the cognitive domain: Philosophical and educational issues. *Review of Educational Research, 51,* 441–453.

Fuson, K. C., & Willis, G. B. (1989). Second graders' use of schematic drawings in solving addition and subtraction word problems. *Journal of Educational Psychology, 81,* 514–520.

Gabriele, A. J., & Montecinos, C. (2001). Collaborating with a skilled peer: The influence of achievement goals and perceptions of partner's competence on the participation and learning of low-achieving students. *Journal of Experimental Education, 69,* 152–178.

Gabrieli, J. D. E., Keane, M. M., Zarella, M. M., & Poldrack, R. A. (1997). Preservation of implicit memory for new associations in global amnesia. *Psychological Science, 8,* 326–329.

Gagne, E. D. (1985). *The cognitive psychology of school learning.* Boston: Little, Brown.

Gagné, R. M. (1983). Some issues in the psychology of mathematics instruction. *Journal of Research in Mathematics Education, 14*(1), 7–18.

Gagné, R. M. (1985). *The conditions of learning and theory of instruction* (4th ed.). New York: Holt, Rinehart & Winston.

Gagné, R. M., & Driscoll, M. P. (1988). *Essentials of learning for instruction* (2nd ed.). Englewood Cliffs, NJ: Prentice Hall.

Gallimore, R., & Tharp, R. (1990). Teaching mind in society: Teaching, schooling, and literate discourse. In L. C. Moll (Ed.), *Vygotsky and education: Instructional implications and applications of sociohistorical psychology.* Cambridge, England: Cambridge University Press.

Gallini, J. (2000, April). *An investigatin of self-regulation developments in early adolescence: A comparison between non at-risk and at-risk students.* Paper presented at the annual meeting of the American Educational Research Association, New Orleans, LA.

Gallistel, C. R., & Gibbon, J. (2001). Computational versus associative models of simple conditioning. *Current Directions in Psychological Science, 10,* 146–150.

Gambrell, L. B., & Bales, R. J. (1986). Mental imagery and the comprehension-monitoring performance of fourth- and fifth-grade poor readers. *Reading Research Quarterly, 21,* 454–464.

Garb, J. L., & Stunkard, A. J. (1974). Taste aversions in man. *American Journal of Psychiatry, 131,* 1204–1207.

Garcia, E. E. (1992). "Hispanic" children: Theoretical, empirical, and related policy issues. *Educational Psychology Review, 4,* 69–93.

Garcia, E. E. (1994). *Understanding and meeting the challenge of student cultural diversity.* Boston: Houghton Mifflin.

Garcia, J., & Koelling, R. A. (1966). The relation of cue to consequence in avoidance learning. *Psychonomic Science, 4,* 123–124.

García-Mira, R., & Real, J. E. (2005). Environmental perception and cognitive maps. *International Journal of Psychology, 40,* 1–2.

Garcia-Palacios, A., Hoffman, H., Carlin, A., Furness, T. A., III, & Botella, C. (2002). Virtual reality in the treatment of spider phobia: A controlled study. *Behaviour Research and Therapy, 40,* 983–993.

Gardner, H. (2000). *The disciplined mind: Beyond facts and standardized tests, the K–12 education that every child deserves.* New York: Penguin Books.

Gardner, H., Torff, B., & Hatch, T. (1996). The age of innocence reconsidered: Preserving the best of the progressive traditions in psychology and education. In D. R. Olson & N. Torrance (Eds.), *The handbook of education and human development: New models of learning, teaching, and schooling.* Cambridge, MA: Blackwell.

Gardner, M. (1978). *Aha! Insight.* New York: Scientific American.

Garner, R. (1998). Epilogue: Choosing to learn or not-learn in school. *Educational Psychology Review, 10,* 227–237.

Garner, R., Alexander, P. A., Gillingham, M. G., Kulikowich, J. M., & Brown, R. (1991). Interest and learning from text. *American Educational Research Journal, 28,* 643–659.

Garner, R., Brown, R., Sanders, S., & Menke, D. J. (1992). "Seductive details" and learning from text. In K. A. Renninger, S. Hidi, & A. Krapp (Eds.), *The role of interest in learning and development.* Hillsdale, NJ: Erlbaum.

Garner, R., Gillingham, M. G., & White, C. S. (1989). Effects of "seductive details" on macroprocessing and microprocessing in adults and children. *Cognition and Instruction, 6,* 41–57.

Garnier, H. E., Stein, J. A., & Jacobs, J. K. (1997). The process of dropping out of high school: A 19-year perspective. *American Educational Research Journal, 34,* 395–419.

Garry, M., & Gerrie, M. P. (2005). When photographs create false memories. *Current Directions in Psychological Science, 14,* 321–325.

Garry, M., & Polaschek, D. L. L. (2000). Imagination and memory. *Current Directions in Psychological Science, 9,* 6–10.

Gaskins, S. (1999). Children's daily lives in a Mayan village: A case study of culturally constructed roles and activities. In A. Göncü (Ed.), *Children's engagement in the world: Sociocultural perspectives* (pp. 25–61). Cambridge, England: Cambridge University Press.

Gasper, K. L. (1980). The student perspective. *Teaching Political Science, 7,* 470–471.

Gathercole, S. E., & Hitch, G. J. (1993). Developmental changes in short-term memory: A revised working memory perspective. In A. F. Collins, S. E. Gathercole, M. A. Conway, & P. E. Morris (Eds.), *Theories of memory.* Hove, England: Erlbaum.

Gaudry, E., & Spielberger, C. D. (Eds.) (1971). *Anxiety and educational achievement.* Sydney, Australia: Wiley.

Gauntt, H. L. (1991, April). *The roles of prior knowledge of text structure and prior knowledge of content in the comprehension and recall of expository text.* Paper presented at the annual meeting of the American Educational Research Association, Chicago.

Gauvain, M. (1999). Everyday opportunities for the development of planning skills: Sociocultural and family influences. In A. Göncü (Ed.), *Children's engagement in the world: Sociocultural perspectives* (pp. 173–201). Cambridge, England: Cambridge University Press.

Gauvain, M. (2001). *The social context of cognitive development.* New York: Guilford Press.

Gayford, C. (1992). Patterns of group behavior in open-ended problem solving in science classes of 15-year-old students in England. *Internal Journal of Science Education, 14,* 41–49.

Gaynor, J., & Millham, J. (1976). Student performance and evaluation under variant teaching and testing methods in a large college course. *Journal of Educational Psychology, 68,* 312–317.

Geary, D. C. (1994). *Children's mathematical development: Research and practical applications.* Washington, DC: American Psychological Association.

Geary, D. C. (1998). What is the function of mind and brain? *Educational Psychology Review, 10,* 377–387.

Geary, D. C. (2006). Development of mathematical understanding. In W. Damon & R. M. Lerner (Series Eds.), D. Kuhn, & R. Siegler (Vol. Eds.), *Handbook of child psychology: Vol. 1. Cognition, perception, and language* (6th ed.). New York: Wiley.

Geckeler, A. S., Libby, M. E., Graff, R. B., & Ahearn, W. H. (2000). Effects of reinforcer choice measured in single-operant and concurrent-schedule procedures. *Journal of Applied Behavior Analysis, 33,* 347–351.

Gelman, R., & Baillargeon, R. (1983). A review of some Piagetian concepts. In J. H. Flavell & E. M. Markman (Eds.), *Handbook of child psychology: Vol. 3. Cognitive development.* New York: Wiley.

Gelman, S. A., & Kalish, C. W. (2006). Conceptual development. In W. Damon & R. M. Lerner (Series Eds.), D. Kuhn, & R. Siegler (Vol. Eds.), *Handbook of child psychology: Vol. 1. Cognition, perception, and language* (6th ed.). New York: Wiley.

Gelman, S. A., & Koenig, M. A. (2003). Theory-based categorization in early childhood. In D. H. Rakison & L. M. Oakes (Eds.), *Early category and concept development: Making sense of the blooming, buzzing confusion* (pp. 330–359). Oxford, England: Oxford University Press.

Gentile, J. R., & Lalley, J. P. (2003). *Standards and mastery learning: Aligning teaching assessment so all children can learn.* Thousand Oaks, CA: Corwin Press.

Gentner, D., & Gentner, D. R. (1983). Flowing waters or teeming crowds: Mental models of electricity. In D. Gentner & A. L. Stevens (Eds.), *Mental models.* Hillsdale, NJ: Erlbaum.

Gentry, M., Gable, R. K., & Rizza, M. G. (2002). Students' perceptions of classroom activities: Are there grade-level and gender differences? *Journal of Educational Psychology, 94,* 539–544.

Gerjets, P., & Scheiter, K. (2003). Goal configurations and processing strategies as moderators between instructional design and cognitive load: Evidence from hypertext-based instruction. *Educational Psychologist, 38,* 33–41.

Gershkoff-Stowe, L., & Smith, L. B. (2004). Shape and the first hundred nouns. *Child Development, 75,* 1098–1114.

Gerst, M. S. (1971). Symbolic coding processes in observational learning. *Journal of Personality and Social Psychology, 19,* 7–17.

Ghetti, S., & Alexander, K. W. (2004). "If it happened, I would remember it": Strategic use of event memorability in the rejection of false autobiographical events. *Child Development, 75,* 542–561.

Giaconia, R. M. (1988). Teacher questioning and wait-time (Doctoral dissertation, Stanford University, 1988). *Dissertation Abstracts International, 49,* 462A.

Giancarlo, C. A., & Facione, P. A. (2001). A look across four years at the disposition toward critical thinking among undergraduate students. *The Journal of General Education, 50,* 29–55.

Gick, M. L. (1986). Problem-solving strategies. *Educational Psychologist, 21,* 99–120.

Gick, M. L., & Holyoak, K. J. (1980). Analogical problem solving. *Cognitive Psychology, 12,* 306–355.

Gick, M. L., & Holyoak, K. J. (1983). Schema induction and analogical transfer. *Cognitive Psychology, 15,* 1–38.

Gick, M. L., & Holyoak, K. J. (1987). The cognitive basis of knowledge transfer. In S. M. Cormier & J. D. Hagman (Eds.), *Transfer of learning: Contemporary research and applications.* San Diego, CA: Academic Press.

Giedd, J. N., Blumenthal, J., Jeffries, N. O., Rajapakse, J. C., Vaituzis, A. C., Liu, H., Berry, Y. C., Tobin, M., Nelson, J., & Castellanos, F. X. (1999a). Development of the human corpus callosum during childhood and adolescence: A longitudinal MRI study. *Progress in Neuro-Psychopharmacology and Biological Psychiatry, 23,* 571–588.

Giedd, J. N., Jeffries, N. O., Blumenthal, J., Castellanos, F. X., Vaituzis, A. C., Fernandez, T., Hamburger, S. D., Liu, H., Nelson, J., Bedwell, J., Tran, L., Lenane, M., Nicolson, R., & Rapoport, J. L. (1999b). Childhood-onset schizophrenia: Progressive brain changes during adolescence. *Biological Psychiatry, 46,* 892–898.

Gijbels, D., Dochy, F., Van den Bossche, P., & Segers, M. (2005). Effects of problem-based learning: A meta-analysis from the angle of assessment. *Review of Educational Research, 75,* 27–61.

Giles, J. W., Gopnik, A., & Heyman, G. D. (2002). Source monitoring reduces the suggestibility of preschool children. *Psychological Science, 13,* 288–291.

Gillies, R. M. (2003). The behaviors, interactions, and perceptions of junior high school students during small-group learning. *Journal of Educational Psychology, 95,* 137–147.

Gillies, R. M., & Ashman, A. F. (1998). Behavior and interactions of children in cooperative groups in lower and middle elementary grades. *Journal of Educational Psychology, 90,* 746–757.

Gilstrap, L. L., & Ceci, S. J. (2005). Reconceptualizing children's suggestibility: Bi-directional and temporal properties. *Child Development, 76,* 40–53.

Ginsburg-Block, M. D., & Fantuzzo, J. W. (1998). An evaluation of the relative effectiveness of NCTM standards-based interventions for low-achieving urban elementary students. *Journal of Educational Psychology, 90,* 560–569.

Girotto, V., & Light, P. (1993). The pragmatic bases of children's reasoning. In P. Light & G. Butterworth (Eds.), *Context and cognition: Ways of learning and knowing.* Hillsdale, NJ: Erlbaum.

Glanzer, M., & Cunitz, A. R. (1966). Two storage mechanisms in free recall. *Journal of Verbal Learning and Verbal Behavior, 5,* 351–360.

Glaser, R. (1987). Thoughts on expertise. In C. Schooler & W. Schaie (Eds.), *Cognitive functioning and social structure over the life course.* Norwood, NJ: Ablex.

Glass, A. L., & Holyoak, K. J. (1975). Alternative conceptions of semantic memory. *Cognition, 3,* 313–339.

Glass, A. L., Holyoak, K. J., & O'Dell, C. (1974). Production frequency and the verification of quantified statements. *Journal of Verbal Learning and Verbal Behavior, 13,* 237–254.

Glass, A. L., Holyoak, K. J., & Santa, J. L. (1979). *Cognition.* Reading, MA: Addison-Wesley.

Gleitman, H. (1985). Some trends in the study of cognition. In S. Koch & D. E. Leary (Eds.), *A century of psychology as science.* New York: McGraw-Hill.

Glenberg, A. (1976). Monotonic and nonmonotonic lag effects in paired-associate and recognition memory paradigms. *Journal of Verbal Learning and Verbal Behavior, 15,* 1–16.

Glover, J., & Gary, A. L. (1976). Procedures to increase some aspects of creativity. *Journal of Applied Behavior Analysis, 9,* 79–84.

Glucksberg, S. (1962). The influence of strength of drive on functional fixedness and perceptual recognition. *Journal of Experimental Psychology, 63,* 36–41.

Glucksberg, S., & Weisberg, R. W. (1966). Verbal behavior and problem solving: Some effects of labeling in a functional fixedness problem. *Journal of Experimental Psychology, 71,* 659–664.

Glynn, S. M. (1991). Explaining science concepts: A teaching-with-analogies model. In S. M. Glynn, R. H. Yeany, & B. K. Britton (Eds.), *The psychology of learning science.* Hillsdale, NJ: Erlbaum.

Glynn, S. M., & Di Vesta, F. J. (1977). Outline and hierarchical organization as aids for study and retrieval. *Journal of Educational Psychology, 69,* 89–95.

Glynn, S. M., Yeany, R. H., & Britton, B. K. (1991). A constructive view of learning science. In S. M. Glynn, R. H. Yeany, & B. K. Britton (Eds.), *The psychology of learning science.* Hillsdale, NJ: Erlbaum.

Goddard, R. D. (2001). Collective efficacy: A neglected construct in the study of schools and student achievement. *Journal of Educational Psychology, 93,* 467–476.

Goddard, R. D., Hoy, W. K., & Woolfolk Hoy, A. (2000). Collective teacher efficacy: Its meaning, measure, and impact on student achievement. *American Educational Research Journal, 37,* 479–507.

Godden, D. R., & Baddeley, A. D. (1975). Context-dependent memory in two natural environments: On land and underwater. *British Journal of Psychology, 66,* 325–332.

Goetz, E. T., Schallert, D. L., Reynolds, R. E., & Radin, D. I. (1983). Reading in perspective: What real cops and pretend burglars look for in a story. *Journal of Educational Psychology, 75,* 500–510.

Gogtay, N., Giedd, J. N., Lusk, L., Hayashi, K. M., Greenstein, D., Vaituzis, A. C., Nugent, T. F., III, Herman, D. H., Clasen, L. S., Toga, A. W., Rapoport, J. L., & Thompson, P. M. (2004). Dynamic mapping of human cortical development during childhood through early adulthood. *Proceedings of the National Academy of Sciences of the United States of America, 101,* 8174–8179.

Gold, J. M., Murray, R. F., Sekuler, A. B., Bennett, P. J., & Sekuler, R. (2005). Visual memory decay is deterministic. *Psychological Science, 16,* 769–774.

Goldenberg, C. (1992). The limits of expectations: A case for case knowledge about teacher expectancy effects. *American Educational Research Journal, 29,* 517–544.

Goldin-Meadow, S. (1997). When gestures and words speak differently. *Current Directions in Psychological Science, 6,* 138–143.

Goldin-Meadow, S. (2001). Giving the mind a hand: The role of gesture in cognitive change. In J. L. McClelland & R. S. Siegler (Eds.), *Mechanisms of cognitive development: Behavioral and neural perspectives* (pp. 5–31). Mahwah, NJ: Erlbaum.

Goldman-Rakic, P. S. (1986). Setting the stage: Neural development before birth. In S. L. Friedman, K. A. Klivington, & R. W. Peterson (Eds.), *The brain, cognition, and education.* Orlando, FL: Academic Press.

Goldman-Rakic, P. S. (1992). Working memory and the mind. *Scientific American, 90,* 111–117.

Goldstein, N. E., Arnold, D. H., Rosenberg, J. L., Stowe, R. M., & Ortiz, C. (2001). Contagion of aggression in day care classrooms as a function of peer and teacher responses. *Journal of Educational Psychology, 93,* 708–719.

Goldstone, R. L., & Johansen, M. K. (2003). Final commentary: Conceptual development from origins to asymptotes. In D. H. Rakison & L. M. Oakes (Eds.), *Early category and concept development: Making sense of the blooming, buzzing confusion* (pp. 403–418). Oxford, England: Oxford University Press.

Gonsalves, B., Reber, P. J., Gitelman, D. R., Parrish, T. B., Mesulam, M.-M., & Paller, K. A. (2004). Neural evidence that vivid imagining can lead to false remembering. *Psychological Science, 15,* 655–660.

Good, T. L., & Brophy, J. E. (1986). *Educational psychology: A realistic approach.* New York: Longman.

Good, T. L., & Brophy, J. E. (1994). *Looking in classrooms* (6th ed.). New York: HarperCollins.

Good, T. L., McCaslin, M. M., & Reys, B. J. (1992). Investigating work groups to promote problem solving in mathematics. In J. Brophy (Ed.), *Advances in research on teaching: Vol. 3. Planning and managing learning tasks and activities.* Greenwich, CT: JAI Press.

Good, T. L., & Nichols. S. L. (2001). Expectancy effects in the classroom: A special focus on improving the reading performance of minority students in first-grade classrooms. *Educational Psychologist, 36,* 113–126.

Goodenow, C. (1993). Classroom belonging among early adolescent students: Relationships to motivation and achievement. *Journal of Early Adolescence, 13*(1), 21–43.

Goodman, C. S., & Tessier-Lavigne, M. (1997). Molecular mechanisms of axon guidance and target recognition. In W. M. Cowan, T. M. Jessell, & S. L. Zipursky (Eds.), *Molecular and cellular approaches to neural development* (pp. 108–137). New York: Oxford University Press.

Goodman, G. S., Ghetti, S., Quas, J. A., Edelstein, R. S., Alexander, K. W., Redlich, A. D., Cordon, I. M., & Jones, D. P. H. (2003). A prospective study of memory for child sexual abuse: New findings relevant to the repressed-memory controversy. *Psychological Science, 14,* 113–118.

Gootman, M. E. (1998). Effective in-house suspension. *Educational Leadership, 56*(1), 39–41.

Gopnik, M. (Ed.) (1997). *The inheritance and innateness of grammars.* New York: Oxford University Press.

Gorman, A. M. (1961). Recognition memory for nouns as a function of abstractness and frequency. *Journal of Experimental Psychology, 61,* 23–29.

Gottfried, A. E. (1990). Academic intrinsic motivation in young elementary school children. *Journal of Educational Psychology, 82,* 525–538.

Gottfried, A. E., Fleming, J. S., & Gottfried, A. W. (2001). Continuity of academic intrinsic motivation from childhood through late adolescence: A longitudinal study. *Journal of Educational Psychology, 93,* 3–13.

Gould, E., Beylin, A., Tanapat, P., Reeves, A., & Shors, T. J. (1999). Learning enhances adult neurogenesis in the hippocampal formation. *Nature Neuroscience, 2,* 260–265.

Grabe, M. (1986). Attentional processes in education. In G. D. Phye & T. Andre (Eds.), *Cognitive classroom learning: Understanding, thinking, and problem solving.* Orlando, FL: Academic Press.

Graesser, A. C., & Bower, G. H. (Eds.) (1990). *Inferences and text comprehension. The psychology of learning and motivation: Advances in research and theory* (Vol. 25). Orlando, FL: Academic Press.

Graesser, A. C., McNamara, D. S., & VanLehn, K. (2005). Scaffolding deep comprehension strategies through Point&Query, AutoTutor, and iSTART. *Educational Psychologist, 40,* 225–234.

Graesser, A. C., & Person, N. K. (1994). Question asking during tutoring. *American Educational Research Journal, 31,* 104–137.

Graf, P., & Masson, M. E. J. (Eds.) (1993). *Implicit memory: New directions in cognition, development, and neuropsychology.* Hillsdale, NJ: Erlbaum.

Graham, S. (1989). Motivation in Afro-Americans. In G. L. Berry & J. K. Asamen (Eds.), *Black students: Psychosocial issues and academic achievement.* Newbury Park, CA: Sage.

Graham, S. (1990). Communicating low ability in the classroom: Bad things good teachers sometimes do. In S. Graham & V. S. Folkes (Eds.), *Attribution theory: Applications to achievement, mental health, and interpersonal conflict.* Hillsdale, NJ: Erlbaum.

Graham, S. (1991). A review of attribution theory in achievement contexts. *Educational Psychology Review, 3,* 5–39.

Graham, S. (1994). Classroom motivation from an attributional perspective. In H. F. O'Neil, Jr., & M. Drillings (Eds.), *Motivation: Theory and research.* Hillsdale, NJ: Erlbaum.

Graham, S. (1997). Using attribution theory to understand social and academic motivation in African American youth. *Educational Psychologist, 32,* 21–34.

Graham, S., & Barker, G. (1990). The downside of help: An attributional-developmental analysis of helping behavior as a low ability cue. *Journal of Educational Psychology, 82,* 7–14.

Graham, S., & Golen, S. (1991). Motivational influences on cognition: Task involvement, ego involvement, and depth of information processing. *Journal of Educational Psychology, 83,* 187–194.

Graham, S., & Harris, K. R. (1996). Addressing problems in attention, memory, and executive functioning. In G. R. Lyon & N. A. Krasnegor (Eds.), *Attention, memory, and executive function* (pp. 349–365). Baltimore: Brookes.

Graham, S., & Weiner, B. (1996). Theories and principles of motivation. In D. C. Berliner & R. C. Calfee (Eds.), *Handbook of educational psychology.* New York: Macmillan.

Granger, R. H., Jr., & Schlimmer, J. C. (1986). The computation of contingency in classical conditioning. In G. H. Bower (Ed.), *The psychology of learning and motivation: Advances in research and theory* (Vol. 20). Orlando: Academic Press.

Grant, H., & Dweck, C. S. (2003). Clarifying achievement goals and their impact. *Journal of Personality and Social Psychology, 85,* 541–553.

Gray, J. A., & Wedderburn, A. A. I. (1960). Grouping strategies with simultaneous stimuli. *Quarterly Journal of Experimental Psychology, 12,* 180–184.

Gray, J. R. (2004). Integration of emotion and cognitive control. *Current Directions in Psychological Science, 13,* 46–48.

Gray, W. D., & Orasanu, J. M. (1987). Transfer of cognitive skills. In S. M. Cormier & J. D. Hagman (Eds.), *Transfer of learning: Contemporary research and applications.* San Diego, CA: Academic Press.

Green, L., Fry, A. F., & Myerson, J. (1994). Discounting of delayed rewards: A life-span comparison. *Psychological Science, 5,* 33–36.

Green, L., & Rachlin, H. (1977). Pigeon's preferences for stimulus information: Effects of amount of information. *Journal of the Experimental Analysis of Behavior, 27,* 255–263.

Greene, B. A. (1994, April). *Instruction to enhance comprehension of unfamiliar text: Should it focus on domain-specific or strategy knowledge?* Paper presented at the annual meeting of the American Educational Research Association, New Orleans, LA.

Greene, B. A., & Royer, J. M. (1994). A developmental review of response time data that support a cognitive components model of reading. *Educational Psychology Review, 6,* 141–172.

Greene, R. L. (1986). Sources of recency effects in free recall. *Psychological Bulletin, 99,* 221–228.

Greene, S., & Ackerman, J. M. (1995). Expanding the constructivist metaphor: A rhetorical perspective on literacy research and practice. *Review of Educational Research, 65,* 383–420.

Greeno, J. G. (1973). The structure of memory and the process of solving problems. In R. L. Solso (Ed.), *Contemporary issues in cognitive psychology. The Loyola Symposium.* Washington, DC: Winston.

Greeno, J. G. (1991). A view of mathematical problem solving in school. In M. U. Smith (Ed.), *Toward a unified theory of problem solving: Views from the content domains.* Hillsdale, NJ: Erlbaum.

Greeno, J. G., Collins, A. M., & Resnick, L. B. (1996). Cognition and learning. In D. C. Berliner & R. C. Calfee (Eds.), *Handbook of educational psychology.* New York: Macmillan.

Greeno, J. G., Moore, J. L., & Smith, D. R. (1993). Transfer of situated learning. In D. K. Detterman & R. J. Sternberg (Eds.), *Transfer on trial: Intelligence, cognition, and instruction.* Norwood, NJ: Ablex.

Greenough, W. T., Black, J. E., & Wallace, C. S. (1987). Experience and brain development. *Child Development, 58,* 539–559.

Greenough, W. T., Juraska, J. M., & Volkmar, F. R. (1979). Maze training effects on dendritic branching in occipital cortex of adult rats. *Behavioral and Neural Biology, 26,* 287–297.

Greenspoon, J., & Ranyard, R. (1957). Stimulus conditions and retroactive inhibition. *Journal of Experimental Psychology, 53,* 55–59.

Greenwood, C. R., Carta, J. J., & Hall, R. V. (1988). The use of peer tutoring strategies in classroom management and educational instruction. *School Psychology Review, 17,* 258–275.

Greer, R. D. (1983). Contingencies of the science and technology of teaching and pre-behavioristic research practices in education. *Educational Researcher, 12*(1), 3–9.

Gregg, M., & Leinhardt, G. (1994, April). *Constructing geography.* Paper presented at the annual meeting of the American Educational Research Association, New Orleans, LA.

Gregoire, M. (2003). Is it a challenge or a threat? A dual-process model of teachers' cognition and appraisal processes during conceptual change. *Educational Psychology Review, 15,* 147–179.

Greif, M. L., Kemler Nelson, D. G., Keil, F. C., & Gutierrez, F. (2006). What do children want to know about animals and artifacts? Domain-specific requests for information. *Psychological Science, 17,* 455–459.

Greiner, J. M., & Karoly, P. (1976). Effects of self-control training on study activity and academic performance: An analysis of self-monitoring, self-reward, and systematic planning components. *Journal of Counseling Psychology, 23,* 495–502.

Griffin, M. M., & Griffin, B. W. (1994, April). *Some can get there from here: Situated learning, cognitive style, and map skills.* Paper presented at the annual meeting of the American Educational Research Association, New Orleans, LA.

Griffin, S. A., Case, R., & Capodilupo, A. (1995). Teaching for understanding: The importance of the central conceptual structures in the elementary mathematics curriculum. In A. McKeough, J. Lupart, & A. Marini (Eds.), *Teaching for transfer: Fostering generalization in learning.* Mahwah, NJ: Erlbaum.

Grimes, J. W., & Allinsmith, W. (1970). Compulsivity, anxiety, and school achievement. In P. H. Mussen, J. J. Conger, & J. Kagan (Eds.), *Readings in child development and personality.* New York: Harper & Row.

Grolnick, W. S., & Ryan, R. M. (1987). Autonomy in children's learning: An experimental and individual difference investigation. *Journal of Personality and Social Psychology, 52,* 890–898.

Groninger, L. D. (1971). Mnemonic imagery and forgetting. *Psychonomic Science, 23,* 161–163.

Gronlund, N. E. (2000). *How to write and use instructional objectives* (6th ed.). Upper Saddle River, NJ: Merrill/Prentice Hall.

Gross, T. F., & Mastenbrook, M. (1980). Examination of the effects of state anxiety on problem-solving efficiency under high and low memory conditions. *Journal of Educational Psychology, 72,* 605–609.

Grossman, P. L. (1990). *The making of a teacher: Teacher knowledge and teacher education.* New York: Teachers College Press.

Guberman, S. R. (1999). Supportive environments for cognitive development: Illustrations from children's mathematical activities outside of school. In A. Göncü (Ed.), *Children's engagement in the world: Sociocultural perspectives* (pp. 202–227). Cambridge, England: Cambridge University Press.

Guberman, S. R., Rahm, J., & Menk, D. W. (1998). Transforming cultural practices: Illustrations from children's game play. *Anthropology and Education Quarterly, 29,* 419–445.

Guevremont, D. C., Osnes, P. G., & Stokes, T. F. (1988). The functional role of preschoolers' verbalization in the generalization of self-instructional training. *Journal of Applied Behavior Analysis, 21,* 45–55.

Gulya, M., Rovee-Collier, C., Galluccio, L., & Wilk, A. (1998). Memory processing of a serial list by young infants. *Psychological Science, 9,* 303–307.

Gunnoe, M. L., & Mariner, C. L. (1997). Toward a developmental-contextual model of the effects of parental spanking on children's aggression. *Archives of Pediatrics and Adolescent Medicine, 151,* 768–775.

Gunstone, R. F. (1994). The importance of specific science content in the enhancement of metacognition. In P. J. Fensham, R. F. Gunstone, & R. T. White (Eds.), *The content of science: A constructivist approach to its teaching and learning.* London: Falmer Press.

Guskey, T. R. (1985). *Implementing mastery learning.* Belmont, CA: Wadsworth.

Gustafsson, J., & Undheim, J. O. (1996). Individual differences in cognitive functions. In D. C. Berliner & R. C. Calfee (Eds.), *Handbook of educational psychology.* New York: Macmillan.

Guthrie, E. R. (1935). *The psychology of learning.* New York: Harper & Row.

Guthrie, J. T., Wigfield, A., Barbosa, P., Perencevich, K. C., Taboada, A., Davis, M. H., Scafiddi, N. T., & Tonks, S. (2004). Increasing reading comprehension and engagement through concept-oriented reading instruction. *Journal of Educational Psychology, 96,* 403–423.

Guttentag, R. E. (1984). The mental effort requirement of cumulative rehearsal: A developmental study. *Journal of Experimental Child Psychology, 37,* 92–106.

Guzzetti, B. J., Snyder, T. E., Glass, G. V., & Gamas, W. S. (1993). Promoting conceptual change in science: A comparative meta-analysis of instructional interventions from reading education and science education. *Reading Research Quarterly, 28,* 117–159.

Hacker, D. J. (1998a). Definitions and empirical foundations. In D. J. Hacker, J. Dunlosky, & A. C. Graesser (Eds.), *Metacognition in educational theory and practice* (pp. 1–23). Mahwah, NJ: Erlbaum.

Hacker, D. J. (1998b). Self-regulated comprehension during normal reading. In D. J. Hacker, J. Dunlosky, & A. C. Graesser (Eds.), *Metacognition in educational theory and practice* (pp. 165–191). Mahwah, NJ: Erlbaum.

Hacker, D. J., & Bol, L. (2004). Metacognitive theory: Considering the social-cognitive influences. In D. M. McInerney & S. Van Etten (Eds.), *Big theories revisited* (pp. 275–297). Greenwich, CT: Information Age.

Hacker, D. J., Bol, L., Horgan, D. D., & Rakow, E. A. (2000). Test prediction and performance in a classroom context. *Journal of Educational Psychology, 92,* 160–170.

Hacker, D. J., Dunlosky, J., & Graesser, A. C. (Eds.) (1998). *Metacognition in educational theory and practice* (pp. 145–164). Mahwah, NJ: Erlbaum.

Haden, C. A., Ornstein, P. A., Eckerman, C. O., & Didow, S. M. (2001). Mother-child conversational interactions as events unfold: Linkages to subsequent remembering. *Child Development, 72,* 1016–1031.

Haenan, J. (1996). Piotr Gal'perin's criticism and extension of Lev Vygotsky's work. *Journal of Russian and East European Psychology, 34*(2), 54–60.

Haenen, J., Schrijnemakers, H., & Stufkens, J. (2003). Sociocultural theory and the practice of teaching historical concepts. In A. Kozulin, B. Gindis, V. S. Ageyev, & S. M. Miller (Eds.), *Vygotsky's educational theory in cultural context* (pp. 246–266). Cambridge, England: Cambridge University Press.

Haerle, F. (2004, April). *Personal epistemologies of elementary school students: Their beliefs about knowledge and knowing.* Paper presented at the American Educational Research Association, San Diego, CA.

Hagen, A. S. (1994, April). *Achievement motivation processes and the role of classroom context.* Paper presented at the annual meeting of the American Educational Research Association, New Orleans, LA.

Hagger, M. S., Chatzisarantis, N. L. D., Barkoukis, V., Wang, C. K. J., & Baranowski, J. (2005). Perceived autonomy support in physical education and leisure-time physical activity: A cross-cultural evaluation of the trans-contextual model. *Journal of Educational Psychology, 97,* 376–390.

Hagopian, L. P., Crockett, J. L., van Stone, M., DeLeon, I. G., & Bowman, L. G. (2000). Effects of noncontingent reinforcement on problem behavior and stimulus engagement: The role of satiation, extinction, and alternative reinforcement. *Journal of Applied Behavior Analysis, 33,* 433–449.

Haier, R. J. (2001). PET studies of learning and individual differences. In J. L. McClelland & R. S. Siegler (Eds.), *Mechanisms of cognitive development: Behavioral and neural perspectives* (pp. 123–145). Mahwah, NJ: Erlbaum.

Hale-Benson, J. E. (1986). *Black children: Their roots, culture, and learning styles.* Baltimore: Johns Hopkins University Press.

Halford, G. S. (1993). *Children's understanding: The development of mental models.* Hillsdale, NJ: Erlbaum.

Halford, G. S., & Andrews, G. (2006). Reasoning and problem solving. In W. Damon & R. M. Lerner (Series Eds.), D. Kuhn, & R. Siegler (Vol. Eds.), *Handbook of child psychology: Vol. 2. Cognition, perception, and language* (6th ed.). New York: Wiley.

Hall, J. F. (1966). *The psychology of learning.* Philadelphia: J. B. Lippincott.

Hall, J. F. (1971). *Verbal learning and retention.* Philadelphia: J. B. Lippincott.

Hall, N. C., Chipperfield, J. G., Perry, R. P., Ruthig, J. C., & Goetz, T. (2006). Primary and secondary control in academic development: Gender-specific implications for stress and health in college students. *Anxiety, Stress, and Coping: An International Journal, 19,* 189–210.

Hall, N. C., Hladkyj, S., Ruthig, J. C., Pekrun, R. H., & Perry, R. P. (2002, April). *The role of action control in moderating primary versus secondary control strategy use in college students.* Paper presented at the annual meeting of the American Educational Research Association, New Orleans, LA.

Hall, N. C., Goetz, T., Haynes, T. L., Stupnisky, R. H., & Chipperfield, J. G. (2006, April). *Self-regulation of primary and secondary control: Optimizing control striving in an academic achievement setting.* Paper presented at the annual meeting of the American Educational Research Association, San Francisco.

Hall, N. C., Hladkyj, S., Taylor, J. R., & Perry, R. P. (2000, April). *Primary and secondary control: Empirical links to academic motivation, achievement, and failure.* Paper presented at the annual meeting of the American Educational Research Association, New Orleans, LA.

Hall, N. C., Perry, R. P., Ruthig, J. C., Hladkyi, S., & Chipperfield, J. C. (2006). Primary and secondary control in achievement settings: A longitudinal field study of academic motivation, emotions, and performance. *Journal of Applied Social Psychology, 36,* 1430–1470.

Hall, R. V., Axelrod, S., Foundopoulos, M., Shellman, J., Campbell, R. A., & Cranston,

S. S. (1971). The effective use of punishment to modify behavior in the classroom. *Educational Technology, 11*(4), 24–26. Reprinted in K. D. O'Leary & S. O'Leary (Eds.) (1972). *Classroom management: The successful use of behavior modification.* New York: Pergamon.

Hall, R. V., Cristler, C., Cranston, S. S., & Tucker, B. (1970). Teachers and parents as researchers using multiple baseline designs. *Journal of Applied Behavior Analysis, 3,* 247–255.

Hall, V. C., & Edmondson, B. (1992). Relative importance of aptitude and prior domain knowledge on immediate and delayed posttests. *Journal of Educational Psychology, 84,* 219–223.

Hall, W. S. (1989). Reading comprehension. *American Psychologist, 44,* 157–161.

Hallahan, D. P., Marshall, K. J., & Lloyd, J. W. (1981). Self-recording during group instruction: Effects of attention to task. *Learning Disabilities Quarterly, 4,* 407–413.

Halldén, O. (1994). On the paradox of understanding history in an educational setting. In G. Leinhardt, I. L. Beck, & C. Stainton (Eds.), *Teaching and learning in history.* Hillsdale, NJ: Erlbaum.

Haller, E. P., Child, D. A., & Walberg, H. J. (1988). Can comprehension be taught? A quantitative synthesis of "metacognitive" studies. *Educational Researcher, 17*(9), 5–8.

Halpern, D. F. (1985). The influence of sex-role stereotypes on prose recall. *Sex Roles, 12,* 363–375.

Halpern, D. F. (1997). *Critical thinking across the curriculum: A brief edition of thought and knowledge.* Mahwah, NJ: Erlbaum.

Halpern, D. F. (1998). Teaching critical thinking for transfer across domains: Dispositions, skills, structure, training, and metacognitive monitoring. *American Psychologist, 53,* 449–455.

Halpin, G., & Halpin, G. (1982). Experimental investigations of the effects of study and testing on student learning, retention, and ratings of instruction. *Journal of Educational Psychology, 74,* 32–38.

Hambrick, D. Z., & Engle, R. W. (2003). The role of working memory in problem solving. In J. E. Davidson & R. J. Sternberg (Eds.), *The psychology of problem solving* (pp. 176–206). Cambridge, England: Cambridge University Press.

Hamman, D., Berthelot, J., Saia, J., & Crowley, E. (2000). Teachers' coaching of learning and its relation to students' strategic learning. *Journal of Educational Psychology, 92,* 342–348.

Hamman, D., Shell, D. F., Droesch, D., Husman, J., Handwerk, M., Park, Y., & Oppenheim, N. (1995, April). *Middle school readers' on-line cognitive processes: Influence of subject-matter knowledge and interest during reading.* Paper presented at the annual meeting of the American Educational Research Association, San Francisco.

Hammer, D. (1994). Epistemological beliefs in introductory physics. *Cognition and Instruction, 12,* 151–183.

Hammer, D. (1997). Discovery learning and discovery teaching. *Cognition and Instruction, 15,* 485–529.

Hammer, D., & Elby, A. (2002). On the form of a personal epistemology. In B. K. Hofer &

P. R. Pintrich (Eds.), *Personal epistemology: The psychology of beliefs about knowledge and knowing* (pp. 169–190). Mahwah, NJ: Erlbaum.

Hampton, J. A. (1981). An investigation of the nature of abstract concepts. *Memory and Cognition, 9,* 149–156.

Han, S.-H., & Kim, M.-S. (2004). Visual search does not remain efficient when executive working memory is working. *Psychological Science, 15,* 623–628.

Hansen, J., & Pearson, P. D. (1983). An instructional study: Improving the inferential comprehension of good and poor fourth-grade readers. *Journal of Educational Psychology, 75,* 821–829.

Harackiewicz, J. M., Barron, K. E., Pintrich, P. R., Elliot, A. J., & Thrash, T. M. (2002). Revision of achievement goal theory: Necessary and illuminating. *Journal of Educational Psychology, 94,* 638–645.

Harackiewicz, J. M., Barron, K. E., Tauer, J. M., Carter, S. M., & Elliot, A. J. (2000). Short-term and long-term consequences of achievement goals: Predicting interest and performance over time. *Journal of Educational Psychology, 92,* 316–330.

Harari, H., & McDavid, J. W. (1973). Name stereotypes and teachers' expectations. *Journal of Educational Psychology, 65,* 222–225.

Hardré, P. L., & Reeve, J. (2003). A motivational model of rural students' intentions to persist in, versus drop out of, high school. *Journal of Educational Psychology, 05,* 347–356.

Hardré, P. L., Crowson, H. M., & DeBacker, T. K. (in press). A multi-theory study of high school students' beliefs, perceptions, goals and academic motivation. *Journal of Experimental Education.*

Hardy, I., Jonen, A., Möller, K., & Stern, E. (2006). Effects of instructional support within constructivist learning environments for elementary school students' understanding of "floating and sinking." *Journal of Educational Psychology, 98,* 307–326.

Hareli, S., & Weiner, B. (2002). Social emotions and personality inferences: A scaffold for a new direction in the study of achievement motivation. *Educational Psychologist, 37,* 183–193.

Haring, N. G., & Liberty, K. A. (1990). Matching strategies with performance in facilitating generalization. *Focus on Exceptional Children, 22*(8), 1–16.

Harlow, H. F. (1949). The formation of learning sets. *Psychological Review, 56,* 51–65.

Harlow, H. F. (1950). Analysis of discrimination learning by monkeys. *Journal of Experimental Psychology, 40,* 26–39.

Harlow, H. F. (1959). Learning set and error factor theory. In S. Koch (Ed.), *Psychology: A study of science.* New York: McGraw-Hill.

Harlow, H. F., & Zimmerman, R. R. (1959). Affectional responses in the infant monkey. *Science, 130,* 421–432.

Harmon-Jones, E. (2001). The role of affect in cognitive-dissonance processes. In J. P. Forgas (Ed.), *Handbook of affect and social cognition* (pp. 237–255). Mahwah, NJ: Erlbaum.

Harnishfeger, K. K. (1995). The development of cognitive inhibition: Theories, definitions,

and research evidence. In F. N. Dempster & C. J. Brainerd (Eds.), *Interference and inhibition in cognition.* San Diego, CA: Academic Press.

Harp, S. F., & Mayer, R. E. (1998). How seductive details do their damage: A theory of cognitive interest in science learning. *Journal of Educational Psychology, 90,* 414–434.

Harris, J. A., Miniussi, C., Harris, I. M., & Diamond, M. E. (2002). Transient storage of a tactile memory trace in primary somatosensory cortex. *Journal of Neuroscience, 22,* 8720–8725.

Harris, J. R. (1998). *The nurture assumption: Why children turn out the way they do.* New York: Free Press.

Harris, K. R. (1986). Self-monitoring of attentional behavior versus self-monitoring of productivity: Effects of on-task behavior and academic response rate among learning disabled children. *Journal of Applied Behavior Analysis, 19,* 417–423.

Harris, K. R., & Alexander, P. A. (1998). Integrated, constructivist education: Challenge and reality. *Educational Psychology Review, 10,* 115–127.

Harris, M. (1992). *Language experience and early language development: From input to uptake.* Hove, England: Erlbaum.

Harris, M. (1985). Visualization and spelling competence. *Journal of Developmental Education, 9*(2), 2–5, 31.

Harris, M. J., & Rosenthal, R. (1985). Mediation of interpersonal expectancy effects: 31 meta-analyses. *Psychological Bulletin, 97,* 363–386.

Harris, R. J. (1977). Comprehension of pragmatic implications in advertising. *Journal of Applied Psychology, 62,* 603–608.

Harris, V. W., & Sherman, J. A. (1973). Use and analysis of the "Good Behavior Game" to reduce disruptive classroom behavior. *Journal of Applied Behavior Analysis, 6,* 405–417.

Harrop, A., & Swinson, J. (2003). Teachers' questions in the infant, junior and secondary school. *Educational Studies, 29*(1), 49–57.

Harrow, A. J. (1972). *A taxonomy of the psychomotor domain: A guide for developing behavioral objectives.* New York: David McKay.

Hart, E. R., & Speece, D. L. (1998). Reciprocal teaching goes to college: Effects for postsecondary students at risk for academic failure. *Journal of Educational Psychology, 90,* 670–681.

Harter, S. (1975). Mastery motivation and the need for approval in older children and their relationship to social desirability response tendencies. *Developmental Psychology, 11,* 186–196.

Harter, S. (1978). Pleasure derived from optimal challenge and the effects of extrinsic rewards on children's difficulty level choices. *Child Development, 49,* 788–799.

Harter, S. (1981). A model of mastery motivation in children: Individual differences and developmental change. In W. A. Collins (Ed.), *The Minnesota symposia on child psychology: Vol. 14. Aspects of the development of competence.* Hillsdale, NJ: Erlbaum.

Harter, S. (1988). The construction and conservation of the self: James and Cooley revisited. In D. K. Lapsley & F. C. Power (Eds.), *Self, ego, and identity: Integrative approaches* (pp. 43–69). New York: Springer-Verlag.

Harter, S. (1990). Causes, correlates, and the functional role of global self-worth: A life-span perspective. In R. J. Sternberg & J. Kolligian, Jr. (Eds.), *Competence considered*. New Haven, CT: Yale University Press.

Harter, S. (1992). The relationship between perceived competence, affect, and motivational orientation within the classroom: Processes and patterns of change. In A. K. Boggiano & T. S. Pittman (Eds.), *Achievement and motivation: A social-developmental perspective*. Cambridge, England: Cambridge University Press.

Harter, S. (1999). *The construction of the self: A developmental perspective*. New York: Guilford Press.

Harter, S., Stocker, C., & Robinson, N. S. (1996). The perceived directionality of the link between approval and self-worth: The liabilities of a looking glass self-orientation among young adolescents. *Journal of Research on Adolescence, 6*, 285–308.

Harter, S., Whitesell, N. R., & Kowalski, P. (1992). Individual differences in the effects of educational transitions on young adolescents' perceptions of competence and motivational orientation. *American Educational Research Journal, 29*, 777–807.

Hartley, J., Bartlett, S., & Branthwaite, A. (1980). Underlining can make a difference—sometimes. *Journal of Educational Research, 73*, 218–224.

Hartley, J., & Trueman, M. (1982). The effects of summaries on the recall of information from prose: Five experimental studies. *Human Learning, 1*, 63–82.

Hartley, K., & Bendixen, L. D. (2001). Educational research in the Internet age: Examining the role of individual characteristics. *Educational Researcher, 30*(9), 22–26.

Hartmann, W. K., Miller, R., & Lee, P. (1984). *Out of the cradle: Exploring the frontiers beyond earth*. New York: Workman.

Hartup, W. W. (1983). Peer relations. In P. H. Mussen (Series Ed.) & E. M. Hetherington (Vol. Ed.), *Handbook of child psychology: Vol. 4. Socialization, personality, and social development* (pp. 103–196). New York: Wiley.

Haseman, A. L. (1999, April). *Cross talk: How students' epistemological beliefs impact the learning process in a constructivist course*. Paper presented at the annual meeting of the American Educational Research Association, Montreal.

Hasher, L., & Zacks, R. T. (1984). Automatic processing of fundamental information. *American Psychologist, 39*, 1372–1388.

Haskell, R. E. (2001). *Transfer of learning: Cognition, instruction, and reasoning*. San Diego, CA: Academic Press.

Hatano, G., & Inagaki, K. (1991). Sharing cognition through collective comprehension activity. In L. B. Resnick, J. M. Levine, & S. D. Teasley (Eds.), *Perspectives on socially shared cognition*. Washington, DC: American Psychological Association.

Hatano, G., & Inagaki, K. (1993). Desituating cognition through the construction of conceptual knowledge. In P. Light & G. Butterworth (Eds.), *Context and cognition: Ways of learning and knowing*. Hillsdale, NJ: Erlbaum.

Hatano, G., & Inagaki, K. (1996). Cognitive and cultural factors in the acquisition of intuitive biology. In D. R. Olson & N. Torrance (Eds.), *The handbook of education and human development: New models of learning, teaching, and schooling*. Cambridge, MA: Blackwell.

Hatano, G., & Inagaki, K. (2003). When is conceptual change intended? A cognitive-socio-cultural view. In G. M. Sinatra & P. R. Pintrich (Eds.), *Intentional conceptual change* (pp. 407–427). Mahwah, NJ: Erlbaum.

Hatano, G., & Oura, Y. (2003). Commentary: Reconceptualizing school learning using insight from expertise research. *Educational Researcher, 32*(8), 26–29.

Hattie, J., Biggs, J., & Purdie, N. (1996). Effects of learning skills interventions on student learning: A meta-analysis. *Review of Educational Research, 66*, 99–136.

Hay, I., Ashman, A. F., van Kraayenoord, C. E., & Stewart, A. L. (1999). Identification of self-verification in the formation of children's academic self-concept. *Journal of Educational Psychology, 91*, 225–229.

Hayes, D. A., & Henk, W. A. (1986). Understanding and remembering complex prose augmented by analogic and pictorial illustration. *Journal of Reading Behavior, 18*, 63–78.

Hayes, K. J., & Hayes, C. (1952). Imitation in a home-raised chimpanzee. *Journal of Comparative and Physiological Psychology, 45*, 450–459.

Hayes, S. C., Rosenfarb, I., Wulfert, E., Munt, E. D., Korn, Z., & Zettle, R. D. (1985). Self-reinforcement effects: An artifact of social standard setting? *Journal of Applied Behavior Analysis, 18*, 201–214.

Hayes-Roth, B., & Thorndyke, P. W. (1979). Integration of knowledge from text. *Journal of Verbal Learning and Verbal Behavior, 18*, 91–108.

Haygood, R. C., & Bourne, L. E., Jr. (1965). Attribute- and rule-learning aspects of conceptual behavior. *Psychological Review, 72*, 175–195.

Hayne, H., Barr, R., & Herbert, J. (2003). The effect of prior practice on memory reactivation and generalization. *Child Development, 74*, 1615–1627.

Heatherton, T. F., Macrae, C. N., & Kelley, W. M. (2004). What the social brain sciences can tell us about the self. *Current Directions in Psychological Science, 13*, 190–193.

Hebb, D. O. (1955). Drives and the c. n. s. (conceptual nervous system). *Psychological Review, 62*, 243–254.

Heck, A., Collins, J., & Peterson, L. (2001). Decreasing children's risk taking on the playground. *Journal of Applied Behavior Analysis, 34*, 349–352.

Hegarty, M., & Kozhevnikov, M. (1999). Types of visual-spatial representations and mathematical problem solving. *Journal of Educational Psychology, 91*, 684–689.

Heil, M., Rösler, F., & Hennighausen, E. (1994). Dynamics of activation in long-term memory: The retrieval of verbal, pictorial, spatial, and color information. *Journal of Experimental Psychology: Learning, Memory, and Cognition, 20*, 169–184.

Heindel, P., & Kose, G. (1990). The effects of motoric action and organization on children's memory. *Journal of Experimental Child Psychology, 50*, 416–428.

Heins, E. D., Lloyd, J. W., & Hallahan, D. P. (1986). Cued and noncued self-recording of attention to task. *Behavior Modification, 10*, 235–254.

Heit, E. (1993). Modeling the effects of expectations on recognition memory. *Psychological Science, 4*, 244–251.

Heller, J. I., & Hungate, H. N. (1985). Implications for mathematics instruction of research on scientific problem solving. In E. A. Silver (Ed.), *Teaching and learning mathematical problem solving: Multiple research perspectives*. Hillsdale, NJ: Erlbaum.

Helmke, A. (1989). Affective student characteristics and cognitive development: Problems, pitfalls, perspectives. *International Journal of Educational Research, 13*, 915–932.

Hembree, R. (1988). Correlates, causes, effects, and treatment of test anxiety. *Review of Educational Research, 58*, 47–77.

Hemphill, L., & Snow, C. (1996). Language and literacy development: Discontinuities and differences. In D. R. Olson & N. Torrance (Eds.), *The handbook of education and human development: New models of learning, teaching, and schooling*. Cambridge, MA: Blackwell.

Henderlong, J., & Lepper, M. R. (2000, April). *The effects of praise on children's motivation: Person, product, and process feedback*. Paper presented at the annual meeting of the American Educational Research Association, New Orleans, LA.

Henle, M. (1985). Rediscovering Gestalt psychology. In S. Koch & D. E. Leary (Eds.), *A century of psychology as science*. New York: McGraw-Hill.

Hennessey, B. A. (1995). Social, environmental, and developmental issues and creativity. *Educational Psychology Review, 7*, 163–183.

Hennessey, B. A., & Amabile, T. M. (1987). *Creativity and learning*. Washington, DC: National Education Association.

Hennessey, M. G. (2003). Metacognitive aspects of students' reflective discourse: Implications for intentional conceptual change teaching and learning. In G. M. Sinatra & P. R. Pintrich (Eds.), *Intentional conceptual change* (pp. 103–132). Mahwah, NJ: Erlbaum.

Herbert, J. J., & Harsh, C. M. (1944). Observational learning by cats. *Journal of Comparative Psychology, 37*, 81–95.

Herbert, J., Stipek, D., & Miles, S. (2003, April). *Gender differences in perceptions of ability in elementary school students: The role of parents, teachers and achievement*. Paper presented at the annual meeting of the American Educational Research Association, Chicago.

Heron, W. (1957). The pathology of boredom. *Scientific American, 196*(1), 52–56.

Herrenkohl, L. R., & Guerra, M. R. (1998). Participant structures, scientific discourse, and student engagement in fourth grade. *Cognition and Instruction, 16*, 431–473.

Herrnstein, R. J. (1969). Method and theory in the study of avoidance. *Psychological Review, 76*, 49–69.

Herrnstein, R. J. (1977). The evolution of behaviorism. *American Psychologist, 32,* 593–603.

Herrnstein, R. J., Nickerson, R. S., de Sánchez, M., & Swets, J. A. (1986). Teaching thinking skills. *American Psychologist, 41,* 1279–1289.

Hertel, P. T. (1994). Depression and memory: Are impairments remediable through attentional control? *Current Directions in Psychological Science, 3,* 190–193.

Hess, R. D., & McDevitt, T. M. (1984). Some cognitive consequences of maternal intervention techniques: A longitudinal study. *Child Development, 55,* 2017–2030.

Hess, R. D., & McDevitt, T. M. (1989). Family. In E. Barnouw (Ed.), *International encyclopedia of communications.* New York: Oxford University Press.

Hettena, C. M., & Ballif, B. L. (1981). Effects of mood on learning. *Journal of Educational Psychology, 73,* 505–508.

Heuer, F., & Reisberg, D. (1990). Vivid memories of emotional events: The accuracy of remembered minutiae. *Memory and Cognition, 18,* 496–506.

Heuer, F., & Reisberg, D. (1992). Emotion, arousal, and memory for detail. In S. Christianson (Ed.), *Handbook of emotion and memory.* Hillsdale, NJ: Erlbaum.

Hewitt, J., & Scardamalia, M. (1996, April). *Design principles for the support of distributed processes.* Paper presented at the annual meeting of the American Educational Research Association, New York.

Hewitt, J., & Scardamalia, M. (1998). Design principles for distributed knowledge building processes. *Educational Psychology Review, 10,* 75–96.

Heyman, G. D., Gee, C. L., & Giles, J. W. (2003). Preschool children's reasoning about ability. *Child Development, 74,* 516–534.

Hickey, D. T., & Granade, J. B. (2004). The influence of sociocultural theory on our theories of engagement and motivation. In D. M. McNerney & S. Van Etten (Eds.), *Big theories revisited* (pp. 223–247). Greenwich, CT: Information Age.

Hickey, D. T. (1997). Motivation and contemporary socio-constructivist instructional perspectives. *Educational Psychologist, 32,* 175–193.

Hicks, L. (1997). Academic motivation and peer relationships—how do they mix in an adolescent world? *Middle School Journal, 28,* 18–22.

Hidi, S., & Anderson, V. (1992). Situational interest and its impact on reading and expository writing. In K. A. Renninger, S. Hidi, & A. Krapp (Eds.), *The role of interest in learning and development.* Hillsdale, NJ: Erlbaum.

Hidi, S., & Harackiewicz, J. M. (2000). Motivating the academically unmotivated: A critical issue for the 21st century. *Review of Educational Research, 70,* 151–179.

Hidi, S., & Renninger, K. A. (2006). The four-phase model of interest development. *Educational Psychologist, 41,* 111–127.

Hidi, S., Renninger, K. A., & Krapp, A. (2004). Interest, a motivational variable that combines affecting and cognitive functioning. In D. Y. Dai & R. J. Sternberg (Eds.), *Motivation, emotion,* and cognition: Integrative perspectives on intellectual functioning and development (pp. 89–115). Mahwah, NJ: Erlbaum.

Hidi, S., Weiss, J., Berndorff, D., & Nolan, J. (1998). The role of gender, instruction, and a cooperative learning technique in science education across formal and informal settings. In L. Hoffman, A. Krapp, K. Renninger, & J. Baumert (Eds.), *Interest and learning: Proceedings of the Seeon Conference on interest and gender* (pp. 215–227). Kiel, Germany: IPN.

Hiebert, E. H., & Fisher, C. W. (1992). The tasks of school literacy: Trends and issues. In J. Brophy (Ed.), *Advances in research on teaching: Vol. 3. Planning and managing learning tasks and activities.* Greenwich, CT: JAI Press.

Hiebert, E. H., & Raphael, T. E. (1996). Psychological perspectives on literacy and extensions to educational practice. In D. C. Berliner & R. C. Calfee (Eds.), *Handbook of educational psychology.* New York: Macmillan.

Hiebert, J., Carpenter, T. P., Fennema, E., Fuson, K., Human, P., Murray, H., Olivier, A., & Wearne, D. (1996). Problem solving as a basis for reform in curriculum and instruction: The case of mathematics. *Educational Researcher, 25*(4), 12–21.

Hiebert, J., Carpenter, T. P., Fennema, E., Fuson, K. C., Wearne, D., Murray, H., Olivier, A., & Human, P. (1997). *Making sense: Teaching and learning mathematics with understanding.* Portsmouth, NH: Heinemann.

Hiebert, J., & Lefevre, P. (1986). Conceptual and procedural knowledge in mathematics: An introductory analysis. In J. Hiebert (Ed.), *Conceptual and procedural knowledge: The case of mathematics.* Hillsdale, NJ: Erlbaum.

Hiebert, J., & Wearne, D. (1992). Links between teaching and learning place value with understanding in first grade. *Journal for Research in Mathematics Education, 23,* 98–122.

Hiebert, J., & Wearne, D. (1993). Instructional tasks, classroom discourse, and students' learning in second-grade arithmetic. *American Educational Research Journal, 30,* 393–425.

Hiebert, J., & Wearne, D. (1996). Instruction, understanding, and skill in multidigit addition and subtraction. *Cognition and Instruction, 14,* 251–283.

Higbee, K. L. (1976). Can young children use mnemonics? *Psychological Reports, 38,* 18.

Higgins, A. T., & Turnure, J. E. (1984). Distractibility and concentration of attention in children's development. *Child Development, 55,* 1799–1810.

Hill, C. A. (1987). Affiliation motivation: People who need people . . . but in different ways. *Journal of Personality and Social Psychology, 52,* 1008–1018.

Hill, K. T. (1984). Debilitating motivation and testing: A major educational problem, possible solutions, and policy applications. In R. Ames & C. Ames (Eds.), *Research on motivation in education: Vol. 1. Student motivation.* New York: Academic Press.

Hill, K. T., & Wigfield, A. (1984). Test anxiety: A major educational problem and what can be done about it. *Elementary School Journal, 85,* 105–126.

Hilt, L. M. (2005, April). *The effects of attribution retraining on class performance, achievement motivation, and attributional style in high school students.* Poster presented at the biennial meeting of the Society for Research in Child Development, Atlanta, GA.

Hinkley, J. W., McInerney, D. M., & Marsh, H. W. (2001, April). *The multifaceted structure of school achievement motivation: A case for social goals.* Paper presented at the annual meeting of the American Educational Research Association, Seattle, WA.

Hinton, B. L. (1968). Environmental frustration and creative problem solving. *Journal of Applied Psychology, 52,* 211–217.

Hiroto, D. S. (1974). Locus of control and learned helplessness. *Journal of Experimental Psychology, 102,* 187–193.

Hiroto, D. S., & Seligman, M. E. P. (1975). Generality of learned helplessness in man. *Journal of Personality and Social Psychology, 31,* 311–327.

Hirsch, E. D., Jr. (1996). *The schools we need and why we don't have them.* New York: Doubleday.

Hirschfeld, L. A., & Gelman, S. A. (Eds.) (1994). *Mapping the mind: Domain specificity in cognition and culture.* Cambridge, England: Cambridge University Press.

Hirsh-Pasek, K., & Golinkoff, R. M. (1996). *The origins of grammar: Evidence from early language comprehension.* Cambridge, MA: MIT Press.

Hirst, W., Spelke, E., Reaves, C., Caharack, G., & Neisser, U. (1980). Dividing attention without alternation or automaticity. *Journal of Experimental Psychology: General, 109,* 98–117.

Hirstein, W. (2005). *Brain fiction: Self-deception and the riddle of confabulation.* Cambridge, MA: MIT Press/Bradford.

Hmelo-Silver, C. E. (2004). Problem-based learning: What and how do students learn? *Educational Psychology Review, 16,* 235–266.

Hmelo-Silver, C. E. (2006). Design principles for scaffolding technology-based inquiry. In A. M. O'Donnell, C. E. Hmelo-Silver, & G. Erkens (Eds.), *Collaborative learning, reasoning, and technology* (pp. 147–170). Mahwah, NJ: Erlbaum.

Hoch, H., McComas, J. J., Johnson, L., Faranda, N., & Guenther, S. L. (2002). The effects of magnitude and quality of reinforcement on choice responding during play activities. *Journal of Applied Behavior Analysis, 35,* 171–181.

Hofer, B. K. (2000). Dimensionality and disciplinary differences in personal epistemology. *Contemporary Educational Psychology, 25,* 378–405.

Hofer, B. K. (2002). Personal epistemology as a psychological and educational construct: An introduction. In B. K. Hofer & P. R. Pintrich (Eds.), *Personal epistemology: The psychology of beliefs about knowledge and knowing* (pp. 3–14). Mahwah, NJ: Erlbaum.

Hofer, B. K. (2004). Epistemological understanding as a metacognitive process: Thinking aloud during online searching. *Educational Psychologist, 39,* 43–55.

Hofer, B. K., & Pintrich, P. R. (1997). The development of epistemological theories: Beliefs about knowledge and knowing and their relation to learning. *Review of Educational Research, 67*, 88–140.

Hofer, B. K., & Pintrich, P. R. (Eds.) (2002). *Personal epistemology: The psychology of beliefs about knowledge and knowing.* Mahwah, NJ: Erlbaum.

Hoffman, M. L. (1975). Altruistic behavior and the parent–child relationship. *Journal of Personality and Social Psychology, 31*, 937–943.

Hoffman, M. L. (1991). Empathy, social cognition, and moral action. In W. M. Kurtines & J. L. Gewirtz (Eds.), *Moral behavior and development: Vol. 1. Theory.* Hillsdale, NJ: Erlbaum.

Hogan, D. M., & Tudge, J. R. H. (1999). Implications of Vygotsky's theory for peer learning. In A. M. O'Donnell & A. King (Eds.), *Cognitive perspectives on peer learning* (pp. 39–65). Mahwah, NJ: Erlbaum.

Hogan, K. (1997, March). *Relating students' personal frameworks for science learning to their cognition in collaborative contexts.* Paper presented at the annual meeting of the American Educational Research Association, Chicago.

Hogan, K., Nastasi, B. K., & Pressley, M. (2000). Discourse patterns and collaborative scientific reasoning in peer and teacher-guided discussions. *Cognition and Instruction, 17*, 379–432.

Hokoda, A., & Fincham, F. D. (1995). Origins of children's helplessness and mastery achievement patterns in the family. *Journal of Educational Psychology, 87*, 375–385.

Holland, R. W., Hendriks, M., & Aarts, H. (2005). Smells like clean spirit: Nonconscious effects of scent on cognition and behavior. *Psychological Science, 16*, 689–693.

Holley, C. D., & Dansereau, D. F. (1984). *Spatial learning strategies: Techniques, applications, and related issues.* Orlando, FL: Academic Press.

Holliday, B. G. (1985). Towards a model of teacher–child transactional processes affecting black children's academic achievement. In M. B. Spencer, G. K. Brookins, & W. R. Allen (Eds.), *Beginnings: The social and affective development of black children.* Hillsdale, NJ: Erlbaum.

Holliday, R. E. (2003). Reducing misinformation effects in children with cognitive interviews: Dissociating recollection and familiarity. *Child Development, 74*, 728–751.

Hollis, K. L. (1997). Contemporary research on Pavlovian conditioning: A "new" functional analysis. *American Psychologist, 52*, 956–965.

Hollon, R. E., Roth, K. J., & Anderson, C. W. (1991). Science teachers' conceptions of teaching and learning. In J. Brophy (Ed.), *Advances in research on teaching: Vol. 2. Teachers' knowledge of subject matter as it relates to their teaching practice.* Greenwich, CT: JAI Press.

Holt-Reynolds, D. (1992). Personal history-based beliefs as relevant prior knowledge in course work. *American Educational Research Journal, 29*, 325–349.

Holyoak, K. J. (1985). The pragmatics of analogical transfer. In G. H. Bower (Ed.), *The psychology of learning and motivation: Advances in research and theory* (Vol. 19). Orlando, FL: Academic Press.

Holyoak, K. J. (1987). Review of parallel distributed processing. *Science, 236*, 992.

Holyoak, K. J., & Koh, K. (1987). Surface and structural similarity in analogical transfer. *Memory and Cognition, 15*, 332–340.

Hom, A., & Battistich, V. (1995, April). *Students' sense of school community as a factor in reducing drug use and delinquency.* Paper presented at the annual meeting of the American Educational Research Association, San Francisco.

Homme, L. E., Csanyi, A. P., Gonzales, M. A., & Rechs, J. R. (1970). *How to use contingency contracting in the classroom.* Champaign, IL: Research Press.

Homme, L. E., deBaca, P. C., Devine, J. V., Steinhorst, R., & Rickert, E. J. (1963). Use of the Premack principle in controlling the behavior of nursery school children. *Journal of the Experimental Analysis of Behavior, 6*, 544.

Hong, Y., Chiu, C., & Dweck, C. S. (1995). Implicit theories of intelligence: Reconsidering the role of confidence in achievement motivation. In M. H. Kernis (Ed.), *Efficacy, agency, and self-esteem.* New York: Plenum Press.

Hopkins, R. H., & Atkinson, R. C. (1968). Priming and the retrieval of names from long-term memory. *Psychonomic Science, 11*, 219–220.

Horgan, D. (1990, April). *Students' predictions of test grades: Calibration and metacognition.* Paper presented at the annual meeting of the American Educational Research Association, Boston.

Horstmann, G. (2002). Evidence for attentional capture by a surprising color singleton in visual search. *Psychological Science, 13*, 499–505.

Howard, D. V. (1983). *Cognitive psychology: Memory, language, and thought.* New York: Macmillan.

Howe, C., Tolmie, A., Greer, K., & Mackenzie, M. (1995). Peer collaboration and conceptual growth in physics: Task influences on children's understanding of heating and cooling. *Cognition and Instruction, 13*, 483–503.

Howe, M. J. A. (1970). Using students' notes to examine the role of the individual learner in acquiring meaningful subject matter. *Journal of Educational Research, 64*, 61–63.

Howe, M. L. (2003). Memories from the cradle. *Current Directions in Psychological Science, 12*, 62–65.

Howe, M. L., & O'Sullivan, J. T. (1990). The development of strategic memory: Coordinating knowledge, metamemory, and resources. In D. F. Bjorklund (Ed.), *Children's strategies: Contemporary views of cognitive development.* Hillsdale, NJ: Erlbaum.

Howie, J. D. (2002, April). *Effects of audience, gender, and achievement level on adolescent students' communicated attributions and affect in response to academic success and failure.* Paper presented at the annual meeting of the American Educational Research Association, New Orleans, LA.

Hubbs-Tait, L., Nation, J. R., Krebs, N. F., & Bellinger, D. C. (2005). Neurotoxicants, micronutrients, and social environments: Individual and combined effects on children's development. *Psychological Science in the Public Interest, 6*, 57–121.

Hubel, D. H., & Wiesel, T. N. (1970). The period of susceptibility to the physiological effects of unilateral eye closure in kittens. *Journal of Physiology, 206*, 419–436.

Hubel, D. H., Wiesel, T. N., & Levay, S. (1977). Plasticity of ocular dominance columns in monkey striate cortex, *Philosophical Transactions of the Royal Society of London, B 278*, 307–409.

Hudson, T. (1983). Correspondences and numerical differences between disjoint sets. *Child Development, 54*, 84–90.

Hudspeth, W. J. (1985). Developmental neuropsychology: Functional implications of quantitative EEG maturation [Abstract]. *Journal of Clinical and Experimental Neuropsychology, 7*, 606.

Huff, J. A. (1988). Personalized behavior modification: An in-school suspension program that teaches students how to change. *School Counselor, 35*, 210–214.

Hufton, N., Elliott, J., & Illushin, L. (2002). Achievement motivation across cultures: Some puzzles and their implications for future research. *New Directions for Child and Adolescent Development, 96*, 65–85.

Hughes, J. N. (1988). *Cognitive behavior therapy with children in schools.* New York: Pergamon.

Hull, C. L. (1920). Quantitative aspects of the evolution of concepts: An experimental study. *Psychological Monographs, 28* (Whole No. 123).

Hull, C. L. (1938). The goal-gradient hypothesis applied to some "field-force" problems in the behavior of young children. *Psychological Review, 45*, 271–299.

Hull, C. L. (1943). *Principles of behavior: An introduction to behavior theory.* New York: Appleton-Century-Crofts.

Hull, C. L. (1951). *Essentials of behavior.* New Haven, CT: Yale University Press.

Hull, C. L. (1952). *A behavior system: An introduction to behavior theory concerning the individual organism.* New Haven, CT: Yale University Press.

Humphreys, L. G. (1939). Acquisition and extinction of verbal expectations in a situation analogous to conditioning. *Journal of Experimental Psychology, 25*, 294–301.

Hundert, J. (1976). The effectiveness of reinforcement, response cost, and mixed programs on classroom behaviors. *Journal of Applied Behavior Analysis, 9*, 107.

Husman, J., & Freeman, B. (1999, April). *The effect of perceptions of instrumentality on intrinsic motivation.* Paper presented at the annual meeting of the American Educational Research Association, Montreal.

Huston, A. C. (1983). Sex-typing. In E. M. Hetherington (Ed.), *Handbook of child psychology: Vol. 4. Socialization, personality, and social development* (4th ed.). New York: Wiley.

Huston, A. C., Watkins, B. A., & Kunkel, D. (1989). Public policy and children's television. *American Psychologist, 44*, 424–433.

Hutt, S. J., Tyler, S., Hutt, C., & Christopherson, H. (1989). *Play, exploration, and learning: A natural history of the pre-school.* London: Routledge.

Huttenlocher, P. R. (1979). Synaptic density in human frontal cortex–developmental changes and effects of aging. *Brain Research, 163*, 195–205.

Huttenlocher, P. R. (1990). Morphometric study of human cerebral cortex development. *Neuropsychologia, 28*, 517–527.

Huttenlocher, P. R. (1993). Morphometric study of human cerebral cortex development. In M. H. Johnson (Ed.), *Brain development and cognition: A reader.* Cambridge, MA: Blackwell.

Huttenlocher, P. R., & Dabholkar, A. S. (1997). Regional differences in synaptogenesis in human cerebral cortex. *Journal of Comparative Neurology, 387*, 167–178.

Hyde, T. S., & Jenkins, J. J. (1969). Differential effects of incidental tasks on the organization of recall of a list of highly associated words. *Journal of Experimental Psychology, 82*, 472–481.

Hymel, S., Comfort, C., Schonert-Reichl, K., & McDougall, P. (1996). Academic failure and school dropout: The influence of peers. In J. Juvonen & K. R. Wentzel (Eds.), *Social motivation: Understanding children's school adjustment* (pp. 313–345). Cambridge, England: Cambridge University Press.

Hynd, C. (1998a). Conceptual change in a high school physics class. In B. Guzzetti & C. Hynd (Eds.), *Perspectives on conceptual change: Multiple ways to understand knowing and learning in a complex world* (pp. 27–36). Mahwah, NJ: Erlbaum.

Hynd, C. (1998b). Observing learning from different perspectives: What does it mean for Barry and his understanding of gravity?. In B. Guzzetti & C. Hynd (Eds.), *Perspectives on conceptual change: Multiple ways to understand knowing and learning in a complex world* (pp. 235–244). Mahwah, NJ: Erlbaum.

Hynd, C. (2003). Conceptual change in response to persuasive messages. In G. M. Sinatra & P. R. Pintrich (Eds.), *Intentional conceptual change* (pp. 291–315). Mahwah, NJ: Erlbaum.

Iacoboni, M., & Woods, R. P. (1999). Cortical mechanisms of human imitation. *Science, 286*, 2526–2528.

Ickes, W. J., & Layden, M. A. (1978). Attributional styles. In J. Harvey, W. Ickes, & R. Kidd (Eds.), *New directions in attributional research* (Vol. 2). Hillsdale, NJ: Erlbaum.

Igoa, C. (1995). *The inner world of the immigrant child.* Mahwah, NJ: Erlbaum.

Igoe, A. R., & Sullivan, H. (1991, April). *Gender and grade-level differences in student attributes related to school learning and motivation.* Paper presented at the annual meeting of the American Educational Research Association, Chicago.

Inglehart, M., Brown, D. R., & Vida, M. (1994). Competition, achievement, and gender: A stress theoretical analysis. In P. R. Pintrich, D. R. Brown, & C. E. Weinstein (Eds.), *Student motivation, cognition, and learning: Essays in honor of Wilbert J. McKeachie.* Hillsdale, NJ: Erlbaum.

Inglis, A., & Biemiller, A. (1997, March). *Fostering self-direction in mathematics: A cross-age tutoring program that enhances math problem solving.* Paper presented at the annual meeting of the American Educational Research Association, Chicago.

Inhelder, B., & Piaget, J. (1958). *The growth of logical thinking from childhood to adolescence* (A. Parsons & S. Milgram, Trans.). New York: Basic Books.

Intons-Peterson, M. J. (1992). Components of auditory imagery. In D. Reisberg (Ed.), *Auditory imagery.* Hillsdale, NJ: Erlbaum.

Intons-Peterson, M. J., Russell, W., & Dressel, S. (1992). The role of pitch in auditory imagery. *Journal of Experimental Psychology: Human Perception and Performance, 18*, 233–240.

Inzlicht, M., & Ben-Zeev, T. (2003). Do high-achieving female students underperform in private? The implications of threatening environments on intellectual processing. *Journal of Educational Psychology, 95*, 796–805.

Irwin, D. E. (1996). Integrating information across saccadic eye movements. *Current Directions in Psychological Science, 5*, 94–100.

Isaacowitz, D. M. (2006). Motivated gaze: The view from the gazer. *Current Directions in Psychological Science, 15*, 68–72.

Isaacson, R. L. (1964). Relation between achievement, test anxiety, and curricular choices. *Journal of Abnormal and Social Psychology, 68*, 447–452.

Isen, A., Daubman, K. A., & Gorgoglione, J. M. (1987). The influence of positive affect on cognitive organization: Implications for education. In R. E. Snow & M. J. Farr (Eds.), *Aptitude, learning and instruction* (Vol. 3). Hillsdale, NJ: Erlbaum.

Ito, T. A., & Cacioppo, J. T. (2001). Affect and attitudes: A social neuroscience approach. In J. P. Forgas (Ed.), *Handbook of affect and social cognition* (pp. 50–74). Mahwah, NJ: Erlbaum.

Iwata, B. A. (1987). Negative reinforcement in applied behavior analysis: An emerging technology. *Journal of Applied Behavior Analysis, 20*, 361–378.

Iwata, B. A., & Bailey, J. S. (1974). Reward versus cost token systems: An analysis of the effects on students and teacher. *Journal of Applied Behavior Analysis, 7*, 567–576.

Iwata, B. A., Dorsey, M. F., Slifer, K. J., Bauman, K. E., & Richman, G. S. (1994). Toward a functional analysis of self-injury. *Journal of Applied Behavior Analysis, 27*, 197–209. (Reprinted from *Analysis and Intervention in Developmental Disabilities, 2*, 3–20, 1982)

Iwata, B. A., Pace, G. M., Cowdery, G. E., & Miltenberger, R. G. (1994). What makes extinction work: An analysis of procedural form and function. *Journal of Applied Behavior Analysis, 27*, 131–144.

Iyengar, S. S., & Lepper, M. R. (1999). Rethinking the value of choice: A cultural perspective on intrinsic motivation. *Journal of Personality and Social Psychology, 76*, 349–366.

Jackson, D. L., Ormrod, J. E., & Salih, D. J. (1996, April). *The nature of students' metacognitive processes, as reflected in their self-generated questions and class notes.* Paper presented at the annual meeting of the American Educational Research Association, New York.

Jackson, D. L., Ormrod, J. E., & Salih, D. J. (1999, April). *Promoting students' achievement by teaching them to generate higher-order self-questions.* Paper presented at the annual meeting of the American Educational Research Association, Montreal.

Jacob, B. A. (2003). Accountability, incentives, and behavior: The impact of high-stakes testing in the Chicago Public Schools. *Education Next, 3*(1). Retrieved March 10, 2004, from http://www.educationnext.org/unabridged/20031/jacob.pdf

Jacobs, J. E., Lanza, S., Osgood, D. W., Eccles, J. S., & Wigfield, A. (2002). Changes in children's self-competence and values: Gender and domain differences across grades one through twelve. *Child Development, 73*, 509–527.

Jacobsen, B., Lowery, B., & DuCette, J. (1986). Attributions of learning disabled children. *Journal of Educational Psychology, 78*, 59–64.

Jacobsen, L. K., Giedd, J. N., Berquin, P. C., Krain, A. L., Hamburger, S. D., Kumra, S., & Rapoport, J. L. (1997a). Quantitative morphology of the cerebellum and fourth ventricle in childhood-onset schizophrenia. *American Journal of Psychiatry, 154*, 1663–1669.

Jacobsen, L. K., Giedd, J. N., Castellanos, F. X., Vaituzis, A. C., Hamburger, S. D., Kumra, S., Lenane, M. C., & Rapoport, J. L. (1997b). Progressive reduction of temporal lobe structures in childhood-onset schizophrenia. *American Journal of Psychiatry, 155*, 678–685.

Jagacinski, C. M., Kumar, S., & Boe, J. L. (2005, April). *The 2 × 2 structure of achievement goal orientations: Applications in the college classroom.* Paper presented at the annual meeting of the American Educational Research Association, Chicago.

Jagacinski, C. M., & Nicholls, J. (1984). Conceptions of ability and related affects in task involvement and ego involvement. *Journal of Educational Psychology, 76*, 909–919.

Jagacinski, C. M., & Nicholls, J. (1987). Competence and affect in task involvement and ego involvement: The impact of social comparison information. *Journal of Educational Psychology, 79*, 107–114.

Jagacinski, C. M., & Nicholls, J. G. (1990). Reducing effort to protect perceived ability: "They'd do it but I wouldn't." *Journal of Educational Psychology, 82*, 15–21.

James, W. (1890). *Principles of psychology.* New York: Holt.

Jegede, O. J., & Olajide, J. O. (1995). Wait-time, classroom discourse, and the influence of sociocultural factors in science teaching. *Science Education, 79*, 233–249.

Jenkins, J. J., & Russell, W. A. (1952). Associative clustering during recall. *Journal of Abnormal and Social Psychology, 47*, 818–821.

Jenlink, C. L. (1994, April). *Music: A lifeline for the self-esteem of at-risk students.* Paper presented at the annual meeting of the American Educational Research Association, New Orleans, LA.

Johns, M., Schmader, T., & Martens, A. (2005). Knowing is half the battle: Teaching stereotype threat as a means of improving women's math performance. *Psychological Science, 16,* 175–179.

Johnson, B. M., Miltenberger, R. G., Knudson, P., Emego-Helm, K., Kelso, P., Jostad, C., & Langley, L. (2006). A preliminary evaluation of two behavioral skills training procedures for teaching abduction-prevention skills to schoolchildren. *Journal of Applied Behavior Analysis, 39,* 25–34.

Johnson, D. W., & Johnson, R. T. (1985a). Classroom conflict: Controversy versus debate in learning groups. *American Educational Research Journal, 22,* 237–256.

Johnson, D. W., & Johnson, R. T. (1985b). Motivational processes in cooperative, competitive, and individualistic learning situations. In C. Ames & R. Ames (Eds.), *Research on motivation in education: Vol. 2. The classroom milieu.* Orlando, FL: Academic Press.

Johnson, D. W., & Johnson, R. T. (1987). *Learning together and alone: Cooperative, competitive, and individualistic learning* (2nd ed.). Englewood Cliffs, NJ: Prentice Hall.

Johnson, D. W., & Johnson, R. T. (1991). *Learning together and alone: Cooperative, competitive, and individualistic learning* (3rd ed.). Upper Saddle River, NJ: Prentice Hall.

Johnson, J. S., & Newport, E. L., (1989). Critical period effects in second language learning. *Cognitive Psychology, 21,* 60–99.

Johnson, M. H., & de Haan, M. (2001). Developing cortical specialization for visual-cognitive function: The case of face recognition. In J. L. McClelland & R. S. Siegler (Eds.), *Mechanisms of cognitive development: Behavioral and neural perspectives* (pp. 253–270). Mahwah, NJ: Erlbaum.

Johnson, M. K., Bransford, J. D., & Solomon, S. K. (1973). Memory for tacit implications of sentences. *Journal of Experimental Psychology, 98,* 203–205.

Johnson, R. N. (1972). *Aggression in man and animals.* Philadelphia: Saunders.

Johnson, S. K., & Anderson, M. C. (2004). The role of inhibitory control in forgetting semantic knowledge. *Psychological Science, 15,* 448–453.

John-Steiner, V., & Mahn, H. (1996). Sociocultural approaches to learning and development: A Vygotskian framework. *Educational Psychologist, 31,* 191–206.

Johnston, J. C., McCann, R. S., & Remington, R. W. (1995). Chronometric evidence for two types of attention. *Psychological Science, 6,* 365–369.

Johnstone, A. H., & El-Banna, H. (1986). Capacities, demands, and processes—a predictive model for science education. *Education in Chemistry, 23,* 80–84.

Jonassen, D. H., Hannum, W. H., & Tessmer, M. (1989). *Handbook of task analysis procedures.* New York: Praeger.

Jonassen, D. H., Hartley, J., & Trueman, M. (1986). The effects of learner-generated versus text-provided headings on immediate and delayed recall and comprehension: An exploratory study. *Human Learning, 5,* 139–150.

Jones, B. F., & Hall, J. W. (1982). School applications of the mnemonic keyword method as a study strategy by eighth graders. *Journal of Educational Psychology, 74,* 230–237.

Jones, B. F., Pierce, J., & Hunter, B. (1988/1989). Teaching students to construct graphic representations. *Educational Leadership, 46*(4), 20–25.

Jones, B. P. (1993). Repression: The evolution of a psychoanalytic concept from the 1890's to the 1990's. *Journal of the American Psychoanalytic Association, 41*(1), 63–93.

Jones, E. E., & Berglas, S. (1978). Control of attributions about the self through self-handicapping strategies: The appeal of alcohol and the role of underachievement. *Personality and Social Psychology Bulletin, 4,* 200–206.

Jones, H. E., & English, H. B. (1926). Notional vs. rote memory. *American Journal of Psychology, 37,* 602–603.

Jones, K. M., Drew, H. A., & Weber, N. L. (2000). Noncontingent peer attention as treatment for disruptive classroom behavior. *Journal of Applied Behavior Analysis, 33,* 343–346.

Jones, M. C. (1924). The elimination of children's fears. *Journal of Experimental Psychology, 7,* 382–390.

Jones, M. S., Levin, M. E., Levin, J. R., & Beitzel, B. D. (2000). Can vocabulary-learning strategies and pair-learning formats be profitably combined? *Journal of Educational Psychology, 92,* 256–262.

Jones, V. (1996). Classroom management. In J. Sikula, T. J. Buttery, & E. Guyton (Eds.), *Handbook of research on teacher education* (2nd ed., pp. 503–521). New York: Macmillan.

Jones, J. E., & Greene, B. A. (2003, April). *Autonomy support, motivation, self-regulation, and perceived competence: Influences on achievement in a training context.* Paper presented at the annual meeting of the American Educational Research Association, Chicago.

Jonides, J., Lacey, S. C., & Nee, D. E. (2005). Processes of working memory in mind and brain. *Current Directions in Psychological Science, 14,* 2–5.

Jordan, A. B. (2003). Children remember prosocial program lessons but how much are they learning? *Applied Developmental Psychology, 24,* 341–345.

Josephs, R. A., Newman, M. L., Brown, R. P., & Beer, J. M. (2003). Status, testosterone, and human intellectual performance: Stereotype threat as status concern. *Psychological Science, 14,* 158–163.

Judd, C. H. (1932). Autobiography. In C. Murchison (Ed.), *History of psychology in autobiography* (Vol. 2). Worcester, MA: Clark University Press.

Jussim, L., Eccles, J., & Madon, S. (1996). Social perception, social stereotypes, and teacher expectations: Accuracy and the quest for the powerful self-fulfilling prophecy. In L. Berkowitz (Ed.), *Advances in experimental social psychology.* New York: Academic Press.

Just, M. A., Carpenter, P. A., Keller, T. A., Emery, L., Zajac, H., & Thulborn, K. R. (2001). Interdependence of nonoverlapping cortical systems in dual cognitive tasks. *NeuroImage, 14,* 417–426.

Juvonen, J. (1991, April). *The effect of attributions and interpersonal attitudes on social emotions and behavior.* Paper presented at the annual meeting of the American Educational Research Association, Chicago.

Juvonen, J. (1996). Self-presentation tactics promoting teacher and peer approval: The function of excuses and other clever explanations. In J. Juvonen & K. R. Wentzel (Eds.), *Social motivation: Understanding children's school adjustment* (pp. 43–65). Cambridge, England: Cambridge University Press.

Juvonen, J. (2000). The social functions of attributional face-saving tactics among early adolescents. *Educational Psychology Review, 12,* 15–32.

Juvonen, J., & Weiner, B. (1993). An attributional analysis of students' interactions: The social consequences of perceived responsibility. *Educational Psychology Review, 5,* 325–345.

Kahl, B., & Woloshyn, V. E. (1994). Using elaborative interrogation to facilitate acquisition of factual information in cooperative learning settings: One good strategy deserves another. *Applied Cognitive Psychology, 8,* 465–478.

Kahneman, D., & Tversky, A. (1972). Subjective probability: A judgment of representativeness. *Cognitive Psychology, 3,* 430–454.

Kahneman, D., & Tversky, A. (1973). On the psychology of prediction. *Psychological Review, 80,* 237–251.

Kail, R. (1990). *The development of memory in children* (3rd ed.). New York: W. H. Freeman.

Kail, R. (1993). The role of a global mechanism in developmental change in speed of processing. In M. L. Howe & R. Pasnak (Eds.), *Emerging themes in cognitive development: Vol. 1. Foundations.* New York: Springer-Verlag.

Kaiser, M. K., McCloskey, M., & Proffitt, D. R. (1986). Development of intuitive theories of motion: Curvilinear motion in the absence of external forces. *Developmental Psychology, 22,* 67–71.

Kamin, L. J. (1956). The effects of termination of the CS and avoidance of the US on avoidance learning. *Journal of Comparative and Physiological Psychology, 49,* 420–424.

Kamin, L. J., Brimer, C. J., & Black, A. H. (1963). Conditioned suppression as a monitor of fear of the CS in the course of avoidance training. *Journal of Comparative and Physiological Psychology, 56,* 497–501.

Kamins, M. L., & Dweck, C. S. (1999). Person versus process praise and criticism: Implications for contingent self-worth and coping. *Developmental Psychology, 35,* 835–847.

Kaplan, A. (1998, April). *Task goal orientation and adaptive social interaction among students of diverse cultural backgrounds.* Paper presented at the annual meeting of the American Educational Research Association, San Diego, CA.

Kaplan, A., & Midgley, C. (1997). The effect of achievement goals: Does level of perceived academic competence make a difference? *Contemporary Educational Psychology, 22,* 415–435.

Kaplan, A., & Midgley, C. (1999). The relationship between perceptions of the classroom goal structure and early adolescents' affect in school: The mediating role of coping strategies. *Learning and Individual Differences, 11,* 187–212.

Kaplan, A., Middleton, M. J., Urdan, T., & Midgley, C. (2002). Achievement goals and goal structures. In C. Midgley (Ed.), *Goals, goal structures, and patterns of adaptive learning* (pp. 21–53). Mahwah, NJ: Erlbaum.

Karabenick, S. A., & Sharma, R. (1994). Seeking academic assistance as a strategic learning resource. In P. R. Pintrich, D. R. Brown, & C. E. Weinstein (Eds.), *Student motivation, cognition, and learning: Essays in honor of Wilbert J. McKeachie.* Hillsdale, NJ: Erlbaum.

Karau, S. J., & Williams, K. D. (1995). Social loafing: Research findings, implications, and future directions. *Current Directions in Psychological Science, 4,* 134–140.

Kardash, C. A. M., & Amlund, J. T. (1991). Self-reported learning strategies and learning from expository text. *Contemporary Educational Psychology, 16,* 117–138.

Kardash, C. A. M., & Howell, K. L. (2000). Effects of epistemological beliefs and topic-specific beliefs on undergraduates' cognitive and strategic processing of dual-positional text. *Journal of Educational Psychology, 92,* 524–535.

Kardash, C. A. M., Royer, J. M., & Greene, B. A. (1988). Effects of schemata on both encoding and retrieval of information from prose. *Journal of Educational Psychology, 80,* 324–329.

Kardash, C. A. M., & Scholes, R. J. (1996). Effects of pre-existing beliefs, epistemological beliefs, and need for cognition on interpretation of controversial issues. *Journal of Educational Psychology, 88,* 260–271.

Kardash, C. A. M., & Sinatra, G. M. (2003, April). *Epistemological beliefs and dispositions: Are we measuring the same construct?* Paper presented at the annual meeting of the American Educational Research Association, Chicago.

Karpov, Y. V. (2003). Development through the lifespan. In A. Kozulin, B. Gindis, V. S. Ageyev, & S. M. Miller (Eds.), *Vygotsky's educational theory in cultural context.* Cambridge, England: Cambridge University Press.

Karpov, Y. V., & Haywood, H. C. (1998). Two ways to elaborate Vygotsky's concept of mediation: Implications for instruction. *American Psychologist, 53,* 27–36.

Katayama, A. D., & Robinson, D. H. (2000). Getting students "partially" involved in note-taking using graphic organizers. *Journal of Experimental Education, 68,* 119–133.

Katkovsky, W., Crandall, V. C., & Good, S. (1967). Parental antecedents of children's beliefs in internal-external control of reinforcements in intellectual achievement situations. *Child Development, 38,* 765–776.

Kauffman, S. (1995). *At home in the universe: The search for laws of self-organization and complexity.* New York: Oxford University Press.

Kaufman, A., Baron, A., & Kopp, R. E. (1966). Some effects of instructions on human operant behavior. *Psychonomic Monograph Supplements, 1,* 243–250.

Kazdin, A. E. (1972). Response cost: The removal of conditional reinforcers for therapeutic change. *Behavior Therapy, 3,* 533–546.

Kazdin, A. E., & Benjet, C. (2003). Spanking children: Evidence and issues. *Current Directions in Psychological Science, 12,* 99–103.

Keele, S. W. (1981). Behavioral analysis of movement. In J. W. Brookhart, V. B. Mountcastle, & V. B. Brooks (Eds.), *Handbook of physiology: Vol. II. Motor control* (pp. 1391–1414). Bethesda, MD: American Physiological Society.

Keele, S. W., Cohen, A., & Ivry, R. (1990). Motor programs: Concepts and issues. In M. Jeannerod (Ed.), *Attention and performance XIII* (pp. 77–110). Mahwah, NJ: Erlbaum.

Keil, F. C. (1986). The acquisition of natural kind and artifact terms. In W. Demopolous & A. Marras (Eds.), *Language learning and concept acquisition.* Norwood, NJ: Ablex.

Keil, F. C. (1987). Conceptual development and category structure. In U. Neisser (Ed.), *Concepts and conceptual development: Ecological and intellectual factors in categorization.* Cambridge, England: Cambridge University Press.

Keil, F. C. (1989). *Concepts, kinds, and cognitive development.* Cambridge, MA: MIT Press.

Keil, F. C. (1991). Theories, concepts, and the acquisition of word meaning. In S. A. Gelman & J. P. Byrnes (Eds.), *Perspectives on language and thought: Interrelations in development.* Cambridge, England: Cambridge University Press.

Keil, F. C. (1994). The birth and nurturance of concepts by domains: The origins of concepts of living things. In L. A. Hirschfeld & S. A. Gelman (Eds.), *Mapping the mind: Domain specificity in cognition and culture.* Cambridge, England: Cambridge University Press.

Keil, F. C., & Silberstein, C. S. (1996). Schooling and the acquisition of theoretical knowledge. In D. R. Olson & N. Torrance (Eds.), *The handbook of education and human development: New models of learning, teaching, and schooling.* Cambridge, MA: Blackwell.

Keith, N., & Frese, M. (2005). Self-regulation in error management training: Emotion control and metacognition as mediators of performance effects. *Journal of Applied Psychology, 90,* 677–691.

Kelemen, D. (1999). Why are rocks pointy? Children's preference for teleological explanations of the natural world. *Developmental Psychology, 35,* 1440–1452.

Kelemen, D. (2004). Are children "intuitive theists"? Reasoning about purpose and design in nature. *Psychological Science, 15,* 295–301.

Kellam, S. G., Rebok, G. W., Ialongo, N., & Mayer, L. S. (1994). The course and malleability of aggressive behavior from early first grade into middle school: Results of a developmental epidemiology-based preventive trial. *Journal of Child Psychology and Psychiatry and Allied Disciplines, 35,* 259–281.

Keller, F. S. (1968). Goodbye teacher. *Journal of Applied Behavior Analysis, 1,* 79–89.

Keller, F. S. (1974). An international venture in behavior modification. In F. S. Keller & E. Ribes-Inesta (Eds.), *Behavior modification:*

Applications to education. New York: Academic Press.

Keller, J. M. (1987). Development and use of the ARCS model of instructional design. *Journal of Instructional Development, 10*(3), 2–10.

Kelley, M. L., & Carper, L. B. (1988). Home-based reinforcement procedures. In J. C. Witt, S. N. Elliott, & F. M. Gresham (Eds.), *Handbook of behavior therapy in education.* New York: Plenum Press.

Kelly, S. W., Burton, A. M., Kato, T., & Akamatsu, S. (2001). Incidental learning of real-world regularities. *Psychological Science, 12,* 86–89.

Kemler Nelson, D. G. (1990). When experimental findings conflict with everyday observations: Reflections on children's category learning. *Child Development, 61,* 606–610.

Kemler Nelson, D. G., Egan, L. C., & Holt, M. B. (2004). When children ask, "What is it?" what do they want to know about artifacts? *Psychological Science, 15,* 384–389.

Kendeou, P., & van den Broek, P. (2005). The effects of readers' misconceptions on comprehension of scientific text. *Journal of Educational Psychology, 97,* 235–245.

Kendler, T. S. (1961). Concept formation. *Annual Review of Psychology, 13,* 447–472.

Kendler, T. S., & Kendler, H. H. (1959). Reversal and nonreversal shifts in kindergarten children. *Journal of Experimental Psychology, 58,* 56–60.

Keppel, G., & Underwood, B. J. (1962). Proactive inhibition in short-term retention of single items. *Journal of Verbal Learning and Verbal Behavior, 1,* 153–161.

Kermani, H., & Moallem, M. (1997, March). *Cross-age tutoring: Exploring features and processes of peer-mediated learning.* Paper presented at the annual meeting of the American Educational Research Association, Chicago.

Kernaghan, K., & Woloshyn, V. E. (1994, April). *Explicit versus implicit multiple strategy instruction: Monitoring grade one students' spelling performances.* Paper presented at the annual meeting of the American Educational Research Association, New Orleans, LA.

Kiewra, K. A. (1985). Investigating notetaking and review: A depth of processing alternative. *Educational Psychologist, 20,* 23–32.

Kiewra, K. A. (1989). A review of note-taking: The encoding-storage paradigm and beyond. *Educational Psychology Review, 1,* 147–172.

Kiewra, K. A., DuBois, N. F., Christian, D., McShane, A., Meyerhoffer, M., & Roskelly, D. (1988, April). *Theoretical and practical aspects of taking, reviewing, and borrowing conventional, skeletal, or matrix lecture notes.* Paper presented at the annual meeting of the American Educational Research Association, New Orleans, LA.

Killeen, P. R. (1991). Behavior's time. In G. H. Bower (Ed.), *The psychology of learning and motivation: Advances in research and theory* (Vol. 27). San Diego, CA: Academic Press.

Killeen, P. R. (2001). The four causes of behavior. *Current Directions in Psychological Science, 10,* 136–140.

Kilpatrick, J. (1985). A retrospective account of the past 25 years of research on teaching mathematical problem solving. In E. A. Silver (Ed.), *Teaching and learning mathematical problem solving: Multiple research perspectives.* Hillsdale, NJ: Erlbaum.

Kim, D., Solomon, D., & Roberts, W. (1995, April). *Classroom practices that enhance students' sense of community.* Paper presented at the annual meeting of the American Educational Research Association, San Francisco.

Kim, J. S., & Sunderman, G. L. (2005). Measuring academic proficiency under the No Child Left Behind Act: Implications for educational equity. *Educational Researcher, 34*(8), 3–13.

Kimberg, D. Y., D'Esposito, M., & Farah, M. J. (1997). Cognitive functions in the prefrontal cortex—working memory and executive control. *Current Directions in Psychological Science, 6,* 185–192.

Kimble, G. A. (2000). Behaviorism and unity in psychology. *Current Directions in Psychological Science, 9,* 208–212.

King, A. (1991). Effects of training in strategic questioning on children's problem-solving performance. *Journal of Educational Psychology, 83,* 307–317.

King, A. (1992). Comparison of self-questioning, summarizing, and notetaking-review as strategies for learning from lectures. *American Educational Research Journal, 29,* 303–323.

King, A. (1997). ASK to THINK—TEL WHY: A model of transactive peer tutoring for scaffolding higher level complex learning. *Educational Psychologist, 32,* 221–235.

King, A. (1999). Discourse patterns for mediating peer learning. In A. M. O'Donnell & A. King (Eds.), *Cognitive perspectives on peer learning* (pp. 87–115). Mahwah, NJ: Erlbaum.

King, A., Staffieri, A., & Adelgais, A. (1998). Mutual peer tutoring: Effects of structuring tutorial interaction to scaffold peer learning. *Journal of Educational Psychology, 90,* 134–152.

King, N. J., & Ollendick, T. H. (1989). Children's anxiety and phobic disorders in school settings: Classification, assessment, and intervention issues. *Review of Educational Research, 59,* 431–470.

King, P. M., & Kitchener, K. S. (1994). *Developing reflective judgment: Understanding and promoting intellectual growth and critical thinking in adolescents and adults.* San Francisco: Jossey-Bass.

King, P. M., & Kitchener, K. S. (2002). The reflective judgment model: Twenty years of research on epistemic cognition. In B. K. Hofer & P. R. Pintrich (Eds.), *Personal epistemology: The psychology of beliefs about knowledge and knowing* (pp. 37–61). Mahwah, NJ: Erlbaum.

King, P. M., & Kitchener, K. S. (2004). Reflective judgment: Theory and research on the development of epistemic assumptions through adulthood. *Educational Psychologist, 39,* 5–18.

Kingstone, A., Smilek, D., Ristic, J., Friesen, C. K., & Eastwood, J. D. (2003). Attention, researchers! It is time to take a look at the real world. *Current Directions in Psychological Science, 12,* 176–180.

Kinnick, V. (1990). The effect of concept teaching in preparing nursing students for clinical practice. *Journal of Nursing Education, 29,* 362–366.

Kintsch, W. (1977). Reading comprehension as a function of text structure. In A. S. Reber & D. L. Scarborough (Eds.), *Toward a psychology of reading.* New York: Wiley.

Kintsch, W. (1980). Learning from text, levels of comprehension, or: Why anyone would read a story anyway. *Poetics, 9,* 87–98.

Kintsch, W. (1998). *Comprehension: A paradigm for cognition.* Cambridge, England: Cambridge University Press.

Kintsch, W., Mandel, T. S., & Kozminsky, E. (1977). Summarizing scrambled stories. *Memory and Cognition, 5,* 547–552.

Kintsch, W., & van Dijk, T. A. (1978). Toward a model of text comprehension and production. *Psychological Review, 85,* 363–394.

Kirkland, M. C. (1971). The effect of tests on students and schools. *Review of Educational Research, 41,* 303–350.

Kirschner, P. A., Sweller, J., & Clark, R. E. (2006). Why minimal guidance during instruction does not work: An analysis of the failure of constructivist, discovery, problem-based, experiential, and inquiry-based teaching. *Educational Psychologist, 41,* 75–86.

Kitsantas, A., Zimmerman, B. J., & Cleary, T. (2000). The role of observation and emulation in the development of athletic self-regulation. *Journal of Educational Psychology, 92,* 811–817.

Klaczynski, P. A. (2001). Analytic and heuristic processing influences on adolescent reasoning and decision-making. *Child Development, 72,* 844–861.

Kladopoulos, C. N., & McComas, J. J. (2001). The effects of form training on foul-shooting performance in members of a women's college basketball team. *Journal of Applied Behavior Analysis, 34,* 329–332.

Klahr, D. (1982). Non-monotone assessment of monotone development: An information processing analysis. In S. Strauss & R. Stavy (Eds.), *U-shaped behavioral growth* (pp. 63–86). New York: Academic Press.

Klahr, D., & Chen, Z. (2003). Overcoming the positive-capture strategy in young children: Learning about indeterminacy. *Child Development, 74,* 1275–1296.

Klatzky, R. L. (1975). *Human memory.* San Francisco: W. H. Freeman.

Klausmeier, H. J. (1990). Conceptualizing. In B. F. Jones & L. Idol (Eds.), *Dimensions of thinking and cognitive instruction.* Hillsdale, NJ: Erlbaum.

Kleim, J. A., Swain, R. A., Armstrong, K. A., Napper, R. M. A., Jones, T. A., & Greenough, W. T. (1998). Selective synaptic plasticity within the cerebellar cortex following complex motor skill learning. *Neurobiology of Learning and Memory, 69,* 274–289.

Klein, J. D. (1990, April). *The effect of interest, task performance, and reward contingencies on self-efficacy.* Paper presented at the annual meeting of the American Educational Research Association, Boston.

Klein, P. S. (1975). Effects of open vs. structured teacher–student interaction on creativity of children with different levels of anxiety. *Psychology in the Schools, 12,* 286–288.

Klein, S. B. (1987). *Learning: Principles and applications.* New York: McGraw-Hill.

Kletzien, S. B. (1988, April). *Achieving and nonachieving high school readers' use of comprehension strategies for reading expository text.* Paper presented at the annual meeting of the American Educational Research Association, New Orleans, LA.

Kline, K., & Flowers, J. (1998, April). *A comparison of fourth graders' proportional reasoning in reform and traditional classrooms.* Paper presented at the annual meeting of the American Educational Research Association, San Diego, CA.

Klinger, E. (1975). Consequences of commitment to and disengagement from incentives. *Psychological Review, 82,* 1–25.

Klinger, E. (1977). *Meaning and void: Inner experience and the incentives in people's lives.* Minneapolis: University of Minnesota Press.

Klinnert, M. D. (1984). The regulation of infant behavior by maternal facial expression. *Infant Behavior and Development, 7,* 447–465.

Klinnert, M. D., Emde, R. N., Butterfield, P., & Campos, J. J. (1986). Social referencing: The infant's use of emotional signals from a friendly adult with mother present. *Developmental Psychology, 22,* 427–434.

Kluger, A. N., & DeNisi, A. (1998). Feedback interventions: Toward the understanding of a double-edged sword. *Current Directions in Psychological Science, 7,* 67–72.

Knutson, J. S., Simmons, D. C., Good, R., III, & McDonagh, S. H. (2004). Specially designed assessment and instruction for children who have not responded adequately to reading intervention. *Assessment for Effective Intervention, 29*(4), 47–58.

Koestner, R., Ryan, R. M., Bernieri, F., & Holt, K. (1984). Setting limits on children's behavior: The differential effects of controlling vs. informational styles on intrinsic motivation and creativity. *Journal of Personality, 52,* 233–248.

Koffka, K. (1935). *Principles of Gestalt psychology.* New York: Harcourt, Brace.

Koger, S. M., Schettler, T., & Weiss, B. (2005). Environmental toxins and developmental disabilities: A challenge for psychologists. *American Psychologist, 60,* 243–255.

Köhler, W. (1925). *The mentality of apes.* London: Routledge & Kegan Paul.

Köhler, W. (1929). *Gestalt psychology.* New York: Liveright.

Köhler, W. (1947). *Gestalt psychology: An introduction to new concepts in modern psychology.* New York: Liveright.

Köhler, W. (1959). Gestalt psychology today. *American Psychologist, 14,* 727–734.

Kolb, B., Gibb, R., & Robinson, T. E. (2003). Brain plasticity and behavior. *Current Directions in Psychological Science, 12,* 1–5.

Kolb, B., & Whishaw, I. Q. (1990). *Fundamentals of human neuropsychology* (3rd ed.). New York: Freeman.

Kolodner, J. (1985). Memory for experience. In G. H. Bower (Ed.), *The psychology of learning and motivation: Advances in research and theory* (Vol. 19). Orlando, FL: Academic Press.

Koltko-Rivera, M. E. (2004). The psychology of worldviews. *Review of General Psychology, 8,* 3–58.

Konopak, B. C., Martin, S. H., & Martin, M. A. (1990). Using a writing strategy to enhance sixth-grade students' comprehension of content material. *Journal of Reading Behavior, 22,* 19–37.

Koriat, A., & Goldsmith, M. (1996). Monitoring and control processes in the strategic regulation of memory accuracy. *Psychological Review, 103,* 490–517.

Korzybski, A. (1933). *Science and sanity: An introduction to non-Aristotelean systems and general semantics.* Lancaster, PA: International Non-Aristotelian Library.

Koschmann, T., & LeBaron, C. (2002). Learner articulation as interactional achievement: Studying the conversation of gesture. *Cognition and Instruction, 20,* 249–282.

Kosslyn, S. M. (1985). Mental imagery ability. In R. J. Sternberg (Ed.), *Human abilities: An information-processing approach.* New York: W. H. Freeman.

Kosslyn, S. M. (1994). *Image and brain: The resolution of the imagery debate.* Cambridge, MA: MIT Press.

Kosslyn, S. M., Margolis, J. A., Barrett, A. M., Goldknopf, E. J., & Daly, P. F. (1990). Age differences in imagery ability. *Child Development, 61,* 995–1010.

Kotovsky, K., & Fallside, D. (1989). Representation and transfer in problem solving. In D. Klahr & K. Kotovsky (Eds.), *Complex information processing: The impact of Herbert A. Simon.* Hillsdale, NJ: Erlbaum.

Kowalski, P. S., Taylor, A. K., & Guggia, A. E. (April, 2004). *Ability, effort, and refutational text as factors influencing change in students' psychological misconceptions.* Paper presented at the American Educational Research Association, San Diego, CA.

Kozulin, A., & Falik, L. (1995). Dynamic cognitive assessment of the child. *Current Directions in Psychological Science, 4,* 192–196.

Krajcik, J. S. (1991). Developing students' understanding of chemical concepts. In S. M. Glynn, R. H. Yeany, & B. K. Britton (Eds.), *The psychology of learning science.* Hillsdale, NJ: Erlbaum.

Krajcik, J. S., & Blumenfeld, P. C. (2006). In R. Sawyer (Ed.), *The Cambridge handbook of the learning sciences* (pp. 317–333). New York: Cambridge University Press.

Kramarski, B., & Mevarech, Z. R. (2003). Enhancing mathematical reasoning in the classroom: The effects of cooperative learning and metacognitive training. *American Educational Research Journal, 40,* 281–310.

Krampen, G. (1987). Differential effects of teacher comments. *Journal of Educational Psychology, 79,* 137–146.

Krapp, A., Hidi, S., & Renninger, K. A. (1992). Interest, learning, and development. In K. A. Renninger, S. Hidi, & A. Krapp (Eds.), *The role of interest in learning and development.* Hillsdale, NJ: Erlbaum.

Krathwohl, D. R. (1994). Reflections on the taxonomy: Its past, present, and future. In L. W. Anderson & L. A. Sosniak (Eds.), *Bloom's taxonomy: A forty-year perspective. Ninety-third yearbook of the National Society for the Study of Education, Part II.* Chicago: National Society for the Study of Education.

Krathwohl, D. R., Bloom, B. S., & Masia, B. B. (1964). *Taxonomy of educational objectives. Handbook II: Affective domain.* New York: David McKay.

Krauss, R. M. (1998). Why do we gesture when we speak? *Current Directions in Psychological Science, 7,* 54–60.

Kritch, K. M., & Bostrow, D. E. (1998). Degree of constructed-response interaction in computer-based programmed instruction. *Journal of Applied Behavior Analysis, 31,* 387–398.

Krueger, W. C. F. (1929). The effect of overlearning on retention. *Journal of Experimental Psychology, 12,* 71–78.

Krumboltz, J. D., & Krumboltz, H. B. (1972). *Changing children's behavior.* Englewood Cliffs, NJ: Prentice Hall.

Kruschke, J. K. (2003). Attention in learning. *Current Directions in Psychological Science, 12,* 171–175.

Kuhara-Kojima, K., & Hatano, G. (1991). Contribution of content knowledge and learning ability to the learning of facts. *Journal of Educational Psychology, 83,* 253–263.

Kuhl, J. (1985). Volitional mediators of cognition-behavior consistency: Self-regulatory processes and actions versus state orientation. In J. Kuhl & J. Beckmann (Eds.), *Action control: From cognition to behavior.* Berlin, Germany: Springer-Verlag.

Kuhl, J. (1987). Action control: The maintenance of motivational states. In F. Halisch & J. Kuhl (Eds.), *Motivation, intention, and volition.* Berlin, Germany: Springer-Verlag.

Kuhl, P. K., Conboy, B. T., Padden, D., Nelson, T., & Pruitt, J. (2005). Early speech perception and later language development: Implications for the "critical period." *Language Learning and Development, 1,* 237–264.

Kuhl, P. K., Tsao, F.-M., & Liu, H.-M. (2003). Foreign-language experience in infancy: Effects of short-term exposure and social interaction on phonetic learning. *Proceedings of the National Academy of Sciences, 100,* 9096–9101.

Kuhl, P. K., Williams, K. A., & Lacerda, F. (1992). Linguistic experience alters phonetic perceptions in infants by 6 months of age. *Science, 255,* 606–608.

Kuhn, D. (1997). Constraints or guideposts? Developmental psychology and science education. *Review of Educational Research, 67,* 141–150.

Kuhn, D. (1999). A developmental model of critical thinking. *Educational Researcher, 28,* 16–26.

Kuhn, D. (2000). Metacognitive development. *Current Directions in Psychological Science, 9,* 178–181.

Kuhn, D. (2001a). How do people know? *Psychological Science, 12,* 1–8.

Kuhn, D. (2001b). Why development does (and does not) occur: Evidence from the domain of inductive reasoning. In J. L. McClelland & R. S. Siegler (Eds.), *Mechanisms of cognitive development: Behavioral and neural perspectives* (pp. 221–249). Mahwah, NJ: Erlbaum.

Kuhn, D. (2006). Do cognitive changes accompany developments in the adolescent brain? *Perspectives on Psychological Science, 1,* 59–67.

Kuhn, D., Amsel, E., & O'Loughlin, M. (1988). *The development of scientific thinking skills.* San Diego, CA: Academic Press.

Kuhn, D., Daniels, S., & Krishnan, A. (2003, April). *Epistemology and intellectual values as core metacognitive constructs.* Paper presented at the annual meeting of the American Educational Research Association, Chicago.

Kuhn, D., & Dean, D. (2004). Metacognition as a conceptual bridge between cognitive psychology and educational practice. *Theory into Practice, 43,* 268–273.

Kuhn, D., & Franklin, S. (2006). The second decade: What develops (and how)? In W. amon & R. M. Lerner (Series Eds.), D. Kuhn, & R. Siegler (Vol. Eds.), *Handbook of child psychology: Vol. 1. Cognition, perception, and language* (6th ed.). New York: Wiley.

Kuhn, D., & Park, S.-H. (2005). Epistemological understanding and the development of intellectual values. *International Journal of Educational Research, 43,* 111–124.

Kuhn, D., Shaw, V., & Felton, M. (1997). Effects of dyadic interaction on argumentative reasoning. *Cognition and Instruction, 15,* 287–315.

Kuhn, D., & Udell, W. (2003). The development of argument skills. *Child Development, 74,* 1245–1260.

Kuhn, D., & Weinstock, M. (2002). What is epistemological thinking and why does it matter? In B. K. Hofer & P. R. Pintrich (Eds.), *Personal epistemology: The psychology of beliefs about knowledge and knowing* (pp. 121–144). Mahwah, NJ: Erlbaum.

Kuhn, T. (1970). *The structure of scientific revolutions* (2nd ed.). Chicago: University of Chicago Press.

Kuklinski, M. R., & Weinstein, R. S. (2001). Classroom and developmental differences in a path model of teacher expectancy effects. *Child Development, 72,* 1554–1578.

Kulhavy, R. W., Lee, J. B., & Caterino, L. C. (1985). Conjoint retention of maps and related discourse. *Contemporary Educational Psychology, 10,* 28–37.

Kulhavy, R. W., Peterson, S., & Schwartz, N. H. (1986). Working memory: The encoding process. In G. D. Phye & T. Andre (Eds.), *Cognitive classroom learning: Understanding, thinking, and problem solving.* Orlando, FL: Academic Press.

Kulik, C. C., Kulik, J. A., & Bangert-Drowns, R. L. (1990). Effectiveness of mastery learning programs: A meta-analysis. *Review of Educational Research, 60,* 265–299.

Kulik, C. C., Kulik, J. A., & Shwalb, B. J. (1983). College programs for high-risk and disadvantaged students: A meta-analysis of findings. *Review of Educational Research, 53,* 397–414.

Kulik, C. C., Schwalb, B. J., & Kulik, J. A. (1982). Programmed instruction in secondary education: A meta-analysis of evaluation findings. *Journal of Educational Research, 75*(3), 133–138.

Kulik, J. A., Cohen, P. A., & Ebeling, B. J. (1980). Effectiveness of programmed instruction in higher education: A meta-analysis of findings. *Educational Evaluation and Policy Analysis, 2*(6), 51–64.

Kulik, J. A., & Kulik, C. C. (1988). Timing of feedback and verbal learning. *Review of Educational Research, 58*, 79–97.

Kulik, J. A., Kulik, C. C., & Cohen, P. A. (1979). A meta-analysis of outcome studies of Keller's Personalized System of Instruction. *American Psychologist, 34*, 307–318.

Kulik, J. A., Kulik, C. C., & Cohen, P. A. (1980). Effectiveness of computer-based college teaching: A meta-analysis of findings. *Review of Educational Research, 50*, 525–544.

Kumar, R., Gheen, M. H., & Kaplan, A. (2002). Goal structures in the learning environment and students' disaffection from learning and schooling. In C. Midgley (Ed.), *Goals, goal structures, and patterns of adaptive learning* (pp. 143–173). Mahwah, NJ: Erlbaum.

Kunzinger, E. L., III. (1985). A short-term longitudinal study of memorial development during early grade school. *Developmental Psychology, 21*, 642–646.

Kupersmidt, J. B., Buchele, K. S., Voegler, M. E., & Sedikides, C. (1996). Social self-discrepancy: A theory relating peer relations problems and school maladjustment. In J. Juvonen & K. R. Wentzel (Eds.), *Social motivation: Understanding children's school adjustment* (pp. 66–97). Cambridge, England: Cambridge University Press.

Kyle, W. C., & Shymansky, J. A. (1989, April). Enhancing learning through conceptual change teaching. *NARST News, 31*, 7–8.

LaBerge, D., & Samuels, S. J. (1974). Toward a theory of automatic information processing in reading. *Cognitive Psychology, 6*, 293–323.

Labov, W. (1973). The boundaries of words and their meanings. In C.-J. N. Bailey & R. W. Shuy (Eds.), *New ways of analyzing variations in English*. Washington, DC: Georgetown University Press.

Lachter, J., & Bever, T. G. (1988). The relation between linguistic structure and associative theories of language learning—A critique of some connectionist learning models. *Cognition, 28*, 195–247.

Lajoie, S. P., & Derry, S. J. (Eds.) (1993). *Computers as cognitive tools*. Hillsdale, NJ: Erlbaum.

Lakoff, G., & Núñez, R. E. (1997). The metaphorical structure of mathematics: Sketching out cognitive foundations for a mind-based mathematics. In L. D. English (Ed.), *Mathematical reasoning: Analogies, metaphors, and images* (pp. 21–89). Mahwah, NJ: Erlbaum.

Lambiotte, J. G., Dansereau, D. F., Cross, D. R., & Reynolds, S. B. (1989. Multirelational semantic maps. *Educational Psychology Review, 1*, 331–367.

Lamon, M., Chan, C., Scardamalia, M., Burtis, P. J., & Brett, C. (1993, April). *Beliefs about learning and constructive processes in reading: Effects of a computer supported intentional learning environment (CSILE)*. Paper presented at the annual meeting of the American Educational Research Association, Atlanta, GA.

Lampert, M. (1990). When the problem is not the question and the solution is not the answer: Mathematical knowing and teaching.

American Educational Research Journal, 17, 29–63.

Lampert, M., Rittenhouse, P., & Crumbaugh, C. (1996). Agreeing to disagree: Developing sociable mathematical discourse. In D. R. Olson & N. Torrance (Eds.), *The handbook of education and human development: New models of learning, teaching, and schooling*. Cambridge, MA: Blackwell.

Lan, W. Y., Repman, J., Bradley, L., & Weller, H. (1994, April). *Immediate and lasting effects of criterion and payoff on academic risk taking*. Paper presented at the annual meeting of the American Educational Research Association, New Orleans, LA.

Landauer, T. K. (1962). Rate of implicit speech. *Perceptual and Motor Skills, 15*, 646.

Landrum, T. J., & Kauffman, J. M. (2006). Behavioral approaches to classroom management. In C. M. Evertson & C. S. Weinstein (Eds.), *Handbook of classroom management: Research, practice, and contemporary issues* (pp. 47–71). Mahwah, NJ: Erlbaum.

Lane, S. M., & Schooler, J. W. (2004). Skimming the surface: Verbal overshadowing of analogical retrieval. *Psychological Science, 15*, 715–719.

Lane, K., Falk, K., & Wehby, J. (2006). Classroom management in special education classrooms and resource rooms. In C. M. Evertson & C. S. Weinstein (Eds.), *Handbook of classroom management: Research, practice, and contemporary issues* (pp. 439–460). Mahwah, NJ: Erlbaum.

Lange, G., & Pierce, S. H. (1992). Memory-strategy learning and maintenance in preschool children. *Developmental Psychology, 28*, 453–462.

Langer, E. J. (1997). *The power of mindful learning*. Reading, MA: Addison-Wesley.

Langer, E. J. (2000). Mindful learning. *Current Directions in Psychological Science, 9*, 220–223.

Lapan, R. T., Tucker, B., Kim, S.-K., & Kosciulek, J. F. (2003). Preparing rural adolescents for post-high school transitions. *Journal of Counseling and Development, 81*, 329–342.

Laraway, S., Snycerski, S., Michael, J., & Poling, A. (2003). Motivating operations and terms to describe them: Some further refinements. *Journal of Applied Behavior Analysis, 36*, 407–414.

Larkin, J. H. (1983). The role of problem representation in physics. In D. Gentner & A. L. Stevens (Eds.), *Mental models*. Hillsdale, NJ: Erlbaum.

Larson, R. W. (2000). Toward a psychology of positive youth development. *American Psychologist, 55*, pp. 170–183.

Lashley, K. S. (1929). *Brain mechanisms and intelligence*. Chicago: University of Chicago Press.

Lassiter, G. D. (2002). Illusory causation in the courtroom. *Current Directions in Psychological Science, 11*, 204–208.

Lautrey, J. (1993). Structure and variability: A plea for a pluralistic approach to cognitive development. In R. Case & W. Edelstein (Eds.), *The new structuralism in cognitive development: Theory and research on individual pathways*. Basel, Switzerland: Karger.

Lave, J. (1988). *Cognition in practice: Mind, mathematics, and culture in everyday life*. Cambridge, England: Cambridge University Press.

Lave, J. (1991). Situating learning in communities of practice. In L. B. Resnick, J. M. Levine, &

S. D. Teasley (Eds.), *Perspectives on socially shared cognition*. Washington, DC: American Psychological Association.

Lave, J. (1993). Word problems: A microcosm of theories of learning. In P. Light & G. Butterworth (Eds.), *Context and cognition: Ways of learning and knowing*. Hillsdale, NJ: Erlbaum.

Lave, J., & Wenger, E. (1991). *Situated learning: Legitimate peripheral participation*. Cambridge, England: Cambridge University Press.

Lawson, M. J., & Chinnappan, M. (1994). Generative activity during geometry problem solving: Comparison of the performance of high-achieving and low-achieving high school students. *Cognition and Instruction, 12*, 61–93.

Lazarus, R. S. (1991). *Emotion and adaptation*. New York: Oxford University Press.

Learning Technology Center at Vanderbilt (1996). *Jasper in the Classroom* [videodisc]. Mahwah, NH: Erlbaum.

LeBlanc, L. A., Coates, A. M., Daneshvar, S., Charlop-Christy, M. H., Morris, C., & Lancaster, B. M. (2003). Using video modeling and reinforcement to teach perspective-taking skills to children with autism. *Journal of Applied Behavior Analysis, 36*, 253–257.

LeDoux, J. (1998). *The emotional brain*. London: Weidenfeld and Nicholson.

LeDoux, J. (2003). The emotional brain, fear, and the amygdala. *Cellular and Molecular Neurobiology, 23*, 727–738.

Lee, O. (1991, April). *Motivation to learn subject matter content: The case of science*. Paper presented at the annual meeting of the American Educational Research Association, Chicago.

Lee, O. (1999). Science knowledge, world views, and information sources in social and cultural contexts: Making sense after a natural disaster. *American Educational Research Journal, 36*, 187–219.

Lee, O., & Anderson, C. W. (1991, April). *Student motivation in middle school science classrooms*. Paper presented at the annual meeting of the American Educational Research Association, Chicago.

Lee, O., & Anderson, C. W. (1993). Task engagement and conceptual change in middle school science classrooms. *American Educational Research Journal, 30*, 585–610.

Lee, S. (1985). Children's acquisition of conditional logic structure: Teachable? *Contemporary Educational Psychology, 10*, 14–27.

Lee, J. L. C., Everitt, B. J., & Thomas, K. L. (2004). Independent cellular processes for hippocampal memory consolidation and reconsolidation. *Science, 304*, 839–843.

LeFevre, J., Bisanz, J., & Mrkonjic, J. (1988). Cognitive arithmetic: Evidence for obligatory activation of arithmetic facts. *Memory and Cognition, 16*, 45–53.

Leff, R. (1969). Effects of punishment intensity and consistency on the internalization of behavioral suppression in children. *Developmental Psychology, 1*, 345–356.

Leherissey, B. L., O'Neil, H. F., Jr., & Hansen, D. N. (1971). Effects of memory support on state anxiety and performance in computer-assisted learning. *Journal of Educational Psychology, 62*, 413–420.

Lehman, D. R., & Nisbett, R. E. (1990). A longitudinal study of the effects of undergraduate training on reasoning. *Developmental Psychology, 26,* 952–960.

Leibham, M. E., Alexander, J. M., Johnson, K. E., Neitzel, C. L., & Reis-Henrie, F. P. (2005). Parenting behaviors associated with the maintenance of preschoolers' interests: A prospective longitudinal study. *Journal of Applied Developmental Psychology, 26,* 397–414.

Leichtman, M. D., & Ceci, S. J. (1995). The effects of stereotypes and suggestions on preschoolers' reports. *Developmental Psychology, 31,* 568–578.

Leichtman, M. D., Pillemer, D. B., Wang, Q., Koreishi, A., & Han, J. J. (2000). When Baby Maisy came to school: Mothers' interview styles and preschoolers' event memories. *Cognitive Development, 15,* 99–114.

Leinhardt, G. (1992). What research on learning tells us about teaching. *Educational Leadership, 49*(7), 20–25.

Leinhardt, G. (1994). History: A time to be mindful. In G. Leinhardt, I. L. Beck, & C. Stainton (Eds.), *Teaching and learning in history.* Hillsdale, NJ: Erlbaum.

Lejuez, C. W., Schaal, D. W., & O'Donnell, J. (1998). Behavioral pharmacology and the treatment of substance abuse. In J. J. Plaud & G. H. Eifert (Eds.), *From behavior theory to behavior therapy* (pp. 116–135). Needham Heights, MA: Allyn & Bacon.

Lenneberg, E. (1967). *Biological foundations of language.* New York: Wiley.

Lennon, R., Ormrod, J. E., Burger, S. F., & Warren, E. (1990, October). *Belief systems of teacher education majors and their possible influences on future classroom performance.* Paper presented at the annual meeting of the Northern Rocky Mountain Educational Research Association, Greeley, CO.

Lentz, F. E. (1988). Reductive procedures. In J. C. Witt, S. N. Elliott, & F. M. Gresham (Eds.), *Handbook of behavior therapy in education.* New York: Plenum Press.

Leon, J. A., & Pepe, H. J. (1983). Self-instructional training: Cognitive behavior modification for remediating arithmetic deficits. *Exceptional Children, 50,* 54–60.

Lepper, M. R. (1981). Intrinsic and extrinsic motivation in children: Detrimental effects of superfluous social controls. In W. A. Collins (Ed.), *Minnesota Symposia on Child Psychology* (Vol. 14). Hillsdale, NJ: Erlbaum.

Lepper, M. R., Aspinwall, L. G., Mumme, D. L., & Chabey, R. W. (1990). Self-perception and social-perception processes in tutoring: Subtle social control strategies of expert tutors. In J. M. Olson & M. P. Zanna (Eds.), *Self-inference processes: The Ontario Symposium.* Hillsdale, NJ: Erlbaum.

Lepper, M. R., Corpus, J. H., & Iyengar, S. S. (2005). Intrinsic and extrinsic motivational orientations in the classroom: Age differences and academic correlates. *Journal of Educational Psychology, 97,* 184–196.

Lepper, M. R., Greene, D., & Nisbett, R. E. (1973). Understanding children's intrinsic interest with extrinsic reward: A test of the "overjustification" hypothesis. *Journal of Personality and Social Psychology, 28,* 129–137.

Lepper, M. R., & Hodell, M. (1989). Intrinsic motivation in the classroom. In C. Ames & R. Ames (Eds.), *Research on motivation in education: Vol. 3. Goals and cognitions.* San Diego, CA: Academic Press.

Lerman, D. C., & Iwata, B. A. (1995). Prevalence of the extinction burst and its attenuation during treatment. *Journal of Applied Behavior Analysis, 28,* 93–94.

Lerman, D. C., Iwata, B. A., & Wallace, M. D. (1999). Side effects of extinction: Prevalence of bursting and aggression during the treatment of self injurious behavior. *Journal of Applied Behavior Analysis, 32,* 1–8.

Lerman, D. C., Kelley, M. E., Vorndran, C. M., Kuhn, S. A. C., & LaRue, R. H., Jr. (2002). Reinforcement magnitude and responding during treatment with differential reinforcement. *Journal of Applied Behavior Analysis, 35,* 29–48.

Lerman, D. C., & Vorndran, C. M. (2002). On the status of knowledge for using punishment: Implications for treating behavior disorders. *Journal of Applied Behavior Analysis, 35,* 431–464.

Lesgold, A. M. (1983). A rationale for computer-based reading instruction. In A. C. Wilkinson (Ed.), *Classroom computers and cognitive science.* New York: Academic Press.

Lesgold, A. M., & Lajoie, S. (1991). Complex problem-solving in electronics. In R. J. Sternberg & P. A. Frensch (Eds.), *Complex problem solving: Principles and mechanisms.* Hillsdale, NJ: Erlbaum.

Lester, F. K., Jr. (1985). Methodological considerations in research on mathematical problem-solving instruction. In E. A. Silver (Ed.), *Teaching and learning mathematical problem solving: Multiple research perspectives.* Hillsdale, NJ: Erlbaum.

Lester, F. K., Jr., Lambdin, D. V., & Preston, R. V. (1997). A new vision of the nature and purposes of assessment in the mathematics classroom. In G. D. Phye (Ed.), *Handbook of classroom assessment: Learning, achievement, and adjustment.* San Diego, CA: Academic Press.

Leuner, B., Mendolia-Loffredo, S., Kozorovitskiy, Y., Samburg, D., Gould, E., & Shors, T. J. (2004). Learning enhances the survival of new neurons beyond the time when the hippocampus is required for memory. *Journal of Neuroscience, 24,* 7477–7481.

Levay, S., Wiesel, T. N., & Hubel, D. H. (1980). The development of ocular dominance columns in normal and visually deprived monkeys, *Journal of Comparative Neurology, 19,* 11–51.

Levin, H. M. (1998). Educational performance standards and the economy. *Educational Researcher, 27*(4), 4–10.

Levin, J. R., Anglin, G. J., & Carney, R. N. (1987). On empirically validating functions of pictures in prose. In D. M. Willows & H. A. Houghton (Eds.), *The psychology of illustration: I. Basic research.* New York: Springer-Verlag.

Levin, J. R., & Mayer, R. E. (1993). Understanding illustrations in text. In B. K. Britton, A. Woodward, & M. Binkley (Eds.), *Learning from textbooks: Theory and practice.* Hillsdale, NJ: Erlbaum.

Levin, J. R., McCormick, C. B., Miller, G. E., Berry, J. K., & Pressley, M. (1982). Mnemonic versus nonmnemonic vocabulary learning strategies for children. *American Educational Research Journal, 19,* 121–136.

Levine, M. (1966). Hypothesis behavior by humans during discrimination learning. *Journal of Experimental Psychology, 71,* 331–338.

Levstik, L. S. (1994). Building a sense of history in a first-grade classroom. In J. Brophy (Ed.), *Advances in research on teaching: Vol. 4. Case studies of teaching and learning in social studies.* Greenwich, CT: JAI Press.

Levy, B. J., & Anderson, M. C. (2002). Inhibitory processes and the control of memory retrieval. *Trends in Cognitive Sciences, 6,* 299–305.

Levy, I., Kaplan, A., & Patrick, H. (2000, April). *Early adolescents' achievement goals, intergroup processes, and attitudes towards collaboration.* Paper presented at the annual meeting of the American Educational Research Association, New Orleans, LA.

Levy, I., Kaplan, A., & Patrick, H. (2004). Early adolescents' achievement goals, social status, and attitudes towards cooperation with peers. *Social Psychology of Education, 7,* 127–159.

Levy-Tossman, I., & Kaplan, A. (April, 2004). *Goal orientation and intergroup processes in school: A person-centered longitudinal investigation.* Paper presented at the American Educational Research Association, San Diego, CA.

Lewin, K., Lippitt, R., & White, R. (1939). Pattern of aggressive behavior in experimentally created "social climates." *Journal of Social Psychology, 10,* 271–299.

Lewis, D. J., & Maher, B. A. (1965). Neural consolidation and electroconvulsive shock. *Psychological Review, 72,* 225–239.

Lhyle, K. G., & Kulhavy, R. W. (1987). Feedback processing and error correction. *Journal of Educational Psychology, 79,* 320–322.

Li, J. (2003). U.S. and Chinese beliefs about learning. *Journal of Educational Psychology, 95,* 258–267.

Li, J. (2005). Mind or virtue: Western and Chinese beliefs about learning. *Current Directions in Psychological Science, 14,* 190–194.

Li, J., & Fischer, K. W. (2004). Thought and affect in American and Chinese learners' beliefs about learning. In D. Y. Dai & R. J. Sternberg (Eds.), *Motivation, emotion, and cognition: Integrative perspectives on intellectual functioning and development* (pp. 385–418). Mahwah, NJ: Erlbaum.

Liao, Y. K. (1992). Effects of computer-assisted instruction on cognitive outcomes: A meta-analysis. *Journal of Research on Computing in Education, 24,* 367–380.

Liben, L. S., & Downs, R. M. (1989). Understanding maps as symbols: The development of map concepts in children. In H. W. Reese (Ed.), *Advances in child development and behavior* (Vol. 22), pp. 145–201. San Diego, CA: Harcourt Brace Jovanovich.

Lichtman, J. W. (2001). Developmental neurobiology overview: Synapses, circuits, and plasticity. In D. B. Bailey, Jr., J. T. Bruer, F. J. Symons, &

J. W. Lichtman (Eds.), *Critical thinking about critical periods* (pp. 27–42). Baltimore: Brookes.

Lickona, T. (1991). Moral development in the elementary school classroom. In W. M. Kurtines & J. L. Gewirtz (Eds.), *Moral behavior and development: Vol. 3. Application*. Hillsdale, NJ: Erlbaum.

Lidz, C. S., & Gindis, B. (2003). Dynamic assessment of the evolving cognitive functions in children. In A. Kozulin, B. Gindis, V. S. Ageyev, & S. M. Miller (Eds.), *Vygotsky's educational theory in cultural context* (pp. 99–116). Cambridge, England: Cambridge University Press.

Liebert, R. M., & Morris, L. W. (1967). Cognitive and emotional components of test anxiety: A distinction and some initial data. *Psychological Reports, 20,* 975–978.

Lien, M.-C., Ruthruff, E., & Johnston, J. C. (2006). Attentional limitations in doing two tasks at once: The search for exceptions. *Current Directions in Psychological Science, 15,* 89–93.

Light, P., & Butterworth, G. (Eds.) (1993). *Context and cognition: Ways of learning and knowing*. Hillsdale, NJ: Erlbaum.

Lightfoot, D. (1999). *The development of language: Acquisition, change, and evolution*. Malden, MA: Blackwell.

Lillard, A. S. (1997). Other folks' theories of mind and behavior. *Psychological Science, 8,* 268–274.

Lillard, A. S. (1998). Ethnopsychologies: Cultural variations in theories of mind. *Psychological Bulletin, 123,* 3–33.

Lima, S. D. (1993). Word-initial letter sequences and reading. *Current Directions in Psychological Science, 2,* 139–142.

Lindberg, M. A. (1991). A taxonomy of suggestibility and eyewitness memory: Age, memory process, and focus of analysis. In J. L. Doris (Ed.), *The suggestibility of children's recollections*. Washington, DC: American Psychological Association.

Linderholm, T., Gustafson, M., van den Broek, P., & Lorch, R. F., Jr. (1997, March). *Effects of reading goals on inference generation*. Paper presented at the annual meeting of the American Educational Research Association, Chicago.

Linderholm, T., & van den Broek, P. (2002). The effects of reading purpose and working memory capacity on the processing of expository text. *Journal of Educational Psychology, 94,* 778–784.

Lindsay, D. S. (1993). Eyewitness suggestibility. *Current Directions in Psychological Science, 2,* 86–89.

Lindsay, P. H., & Norman, D. A. (1977). *Human information processing*. New York: Academic Press.

Lindvall, C. M., Tamburino, J. L., & Robinson, L. (1982, March). *An exploratory investigation of the effect of teaching primary grade children to use specific problem-solving strategies in solving simple story problems*. Paper presented at the annual meeting of the American Educational Research Association, New York.

Linn, M. C., Clement, C., Pulos, S., & Sullivan, P. (1989). Scientific reasoning during adolescence: The influence of instruction in science knowledge and reasoning strategies. *Journal of Research in Science Teaching, 26,* 171–187.

Linn, M. C., & Muilenburg, L. (1996). Creating lifelong science learners: What models form a firm foundation? *Educational Researcher, 25*(5), 18–24.

Linn, M. C., Songer, N. B., & Eylon, B. (1996). Shifts and convergences in science learning and instruction. In D. C. Berliner & R. C. Calfee (Eds.), *Handbook of educational psychology*. New York: Macmillan.

Linn, R. L. (2003). Accountability: Responsibility and reasonable expectations. *Educational Researcher, 32,* 3–13.

Linnenbrink, E. A. (2005). The dilemma of performance-approach goals: The use of multiple goal contexts to promote students' motivation and learning. *Journal of Educational Psychology, 97,* 197–213.

Linnenbrink, E. A., & Pintrich, P. R. (2002). Achievement goal theory and affect: An asymmetrical bidirectional model. *Educational Psychologist, 37,* 69–78.

Linnenbrink, E. A., & Pintrich, P. R. (2003). Achievement goals and intentional conceptual change. In G. M. Sinatra & P. R. Pintrich (Eds.), *Intentional conceptual change* (pp. 347–374). Mahwah, NJ: Erlbaum.

Linnenbrink, E. A., & Pintrich, P. R. (2004). Role of affect in cognitive processing in academic contexts. In D. Y. Dai & R. J. Sternberg (Eds.), *Motivation, emotion, and cognition: Integrative perspectives on intellectual functioning and development* (pp. 57–87). Mahwah, NJ: Erlbaum.

Lippa, R. A. (2002). *Gender, nature, and nurture*. Mahwah, NJ: Erlbaum.

Lipsitt, L. P., & Kaye, H. (1964). Conditioned sucking in the human newborn. *Psychonomic Science, 1,* 29–30.

Lipson, M. Y. (1982). Learning new information from text: The role of prior knowledge and reading ability. *Journal of Reading Behavior, 14,* 243–261.

Lipson, M. Y. (1983). The influence of religious affiliation on children's memory for text information. *Reading Research Quarterly, 18,* 448–457.

Littlewood, W. T. (1984). *Foreign and second language learning: Language-acquisition research and its implications for the classroom*. Cambridge, England: Cambridge University Press.

Liu, J., Golinkoff, R. M., & Sak, K. (2001). One cow does not an animal make: Young children can extend novel words at the superordinate level. *Child Development, 72,* 1674–1694.

Liu, L. G. (1990, April). *The use of causal questioning to promote narrative comprehension and memory*. Paper presented at the annual meeting of the American Educational Research Association, Boston.

Locke, E. A., & Latham, G. P. (2002). Building a practically useful theory of goal setting and task motivation: A 35-year odyssey. *American Psychologist, 57,* 705–717.

Locke, J. L. (1993). *The child's path to spoken language*. Cambridge, MA: Harvard University Press.

Lockhart, K. L., Chang, B., & Story, T. (2002). Young children's beliefs about the stability of traits: Protective optimism? *Child Development, 73,* 1408–1430.

Lodewyk, K. R., & Winne, P. H. (2005). Relations among the structure of learning tasks, achievement, and changes in self-efficacy in secondary students. *Journal of Educational Psychology, 97,* 3–12.

Loftus, E. F. (1991). Made in memory: Distortions in recollection after misleading information. In G. H. Bower (Ed.), *The psychology of learning and motivation: Advances in research and theory* (Vol. 27). San Diego, CA: Academic Press.

Loftus, E. F. (1992). When a lie becomes memory's truth: Memory distortion after exposure to misinformation. *Current Directions in Psychological Science, 1,* 121–123.

Loftus, E. F. (1993). The reality of repressed memories. *American Psychologist, 48,* 518–537.

Loftus, E. F. (2003). Make-believe memories. *American Psychologist, 58,* 867–873.

Loftus, E. F. (2004). Memories of things unseen. *Current Directions in Psychological Science, 13,* 145–147.

Loftus, E. F., & Kaufman, L. (1992). Why do traumatic experiences sometimes produce good memory (flashbulbs) and sometimes no memory (repression)? In E. Winograd & U. Neisser (Eds.), *Affect and accuracy in recall: Studies of "flashbulb" memories*. Cambridge, England: Cambridge University Press.

Loftus, E. F., & Loftus, G. R. (1980). On the permanence of stored information in the human brain. *American Psychologist, 35,* 409–420.

Loftus, E. F., & Palmer, J. C. (1974). Reconstruction of automobile destruction: An example of the interaction between language and memory. *Journal of Verbal Learning and Verbal Behavior, 13,* 585–589.

Loftus, G. R., & Bell, S. M. (1975). Two types of information in picture memory. *Journal of Experimental Psychology: Human Learning and Perception, 104,* 103–113.

Loftus, G. R., & Loftus, E. F. (1976). *Human memory: The processing of information*. New York: Wiley.

Logue, A. W. (1979). Taste aversion and the generality of the laws of learning. *Psychological Bulletin, 86,* 276–296.

Loranger, A. L. (1994). The study strategies of successful and unsuccessful high school students. *Journal of Reading Behavior, 26,* 347–360.

Lorayne, H., & Lucas, J. (1974). *The memory book*. New York: Stein and Day.

Lorch, R. F., Jr., Lorch, E. P., & Inman, W. E. (1993). Effects of signaling topic structure on text recall. *Journal of Educational Psychology, 85,* 281–290.

Losh, S. C. (2003). On the application of social cognition and social location to creating causal explanatory structures. *Educational Research Quarterly, 26*(3), 17–33.

Losh, S. C., Tavani, C. M., Njoroge, R., Wilke, R., & McAuley, M. (2003). What does education *really* do? Educational dimensions and pseudoscience support in the American general public, 1979–2001. *Skeptical Inquirer, 27*(5), 30–35.

Lotan, R. A. (2006). Managing groupwork in heterogeneous classrooms. In C. M. Evertson & C. S. Weinstein (Eds.), *Handbook of classroom management: Research, practice, and contemporary issues* (pp. 525–539). Mahwah, NJ: Erlbaum.

Lou, Y., Abrami, P. C., & d'Apollonia, S. (2001). Small group and individual learning with technology: A meta-analysis. *Review of Educational Research, 71,* 449–521.

Lou, Y., Abrami, P. C., Spence, J. C., Poulsen, C., Chambers, B., & d'Apollonia, S. (1996). Within-class grouping: A meta-analysis. *Review of Educational Research, 66,* 423–458.

Louca, L., Elby, A., Hammer, D., & Kagey, T. (2004). Epistemological resources: Applying a new epistemological framework to science instruction. *Educational Psychologist, 39,* 57–68.

Lovell, K. (1979). Intellectual growth and the school curriculum. In F. B. Murray (Ed.), *The impact of Piagetian theory: On education, philosophy, psychiatry, and psychology.* Baltimore: University Park Press.

Lovitt, T. C., Guppy, T. E., & Blattner, J. E. (1969). The use of free-time contingency with fourth graders to increase spelling accuracy. *Behaviour Research and Therapy, 7,* 151–156.

Luchins, A. S. (1942). Mechanization in problem solving: The effect of Einstellung. *Psychological Monographs, 54* (Whole No. 248).

Luchins, A. S., & Luchins, E. H. (1950). New experimental attempts at preventing mechanization in problem solving. *Journal of General Psychology, 42,* 279–297.

Ludwig, T. D., Gray, T. W., & Rowell, A. (1998). Increasing recycling in academic buildings: A systematic replication. *Journal of Applied Behavior Analysis, 31,* 683–686.

Lueptow, L. B. (1984). *Adolescent sex roles and social change.* New York: Columbia University Press.

Luna, B., & Sweeney, J. A. (2004). The emergence of collaborative brain function: fMRI studies of the development of response inhibition. *Annals of the New York Academy of Sciences, 1021,* 296–309.

Lundeberg, M. A., & Fox, P. W. (1991). Do laboratory findings on test expectancy generalize to classroom outcomes? *Review of Educational Research, 61,* 94–106.

Luque, M. L. (2003). The role of domain-specific knowledge in intentional conceptual change. In G. M. Sinatra & P. R. Pintrich (Eds.), *Intentional conceptual change* (pp. 133–170). Mahwah, NJ: Erlbaum.

Lustig, C., Konkel, A., & Jacoby, L. L. (2004). Which route to recovery? Controlled retrieval and accessibility bias in retroactive interference. *Psychological Science, 15,* 729–735.

Luyben, P. D., Hipworth, K., & Pappas, T. (2003). Effects of CAI on the academic performance and attitudes of college students. *Teaching of Psychology, 30,* 154–158.

Lynn, S. J., Lock, T. G., Myers, B., & Payne, D. G. (1997). Recalling the unrecallable: Should hypnosis be used to recover memories in psychotherapy? *Current Directions in Psychological Science, 6,* 79–83.

Lyon, T. D., & Flavell, J. H. (1994). Young children's understanding of "remember" and "forget." *Child Development, 65,* 1357–1371.

Lyon, G. R., & Krasnegor, N. A. (Eds.) (1996). *Attention, memory, and executive function.* Baltimore: Brookes.

MacAndrew, D. K., Klatzky, R. L., Fiez, J. A., McClelland, J. L., & Becker, J. T. (2002). The phonological-similarity effect differentiates between two working memory tasks. *Psychological Science, 13,* 465–468.

MacDonald, S., Uesiliana, K., & Hayne, H. (2000). Cross-cultural and gender differences in childhood amnesia. *Memory, 8,* 365–376.

Mace, F. C., Belfiore, P. J., & Shea, M. C. (1989). Operant theory and research on self-regulation. In B. J. Zimmerman & D. H. Schunk (Eds.), *Self-regulated learning and academic achievement: Theory, research, and practice.* New York: Springer-Verlag.

Mace, F. C., Hock, M. L., Lalli, J. S., West, B. J., Belfiore, P., Pinter, E., & Brown, D. K. (1988). Behavioral momentum in the treatment of noncompliance. *Journal of Applied Behavior Analysis, 21,* 123–141.

Mace, F. C., & Kratochwill, T. R. (1988). Self-monitoring. In J. C. Witt, S. N. Elliott, & F. M. Gresham (Eds.), *Handbook of behavior therapy in education.* New York: Plenum Press.

Mace, F. C., Page, T. J., Ivancic, M. T., & O'Brien, S. (1986). Effectiveness of brief time-out with and without contingent delay: A comparative analysis. *Journal of Applied Behavior Analysis, 19,* 79–86.

Macfarlane, A. (1978). What a baby knows. *Human Nature, 1,* 74–81.

Machiels-Bongaerts, M., Schmidt, H. G., & Boshuizen, H. P. A. (1991, April). *The effects of prior knowledge activation on free recall and study time allocation.* Paper presented at the annual meeting of the American Educational Research Association, Chicago.

Mac Iver, D. J., Reuman, D. A., & Main, S. R. (1995). Social structuring of the school: Studying what is, illuminating what could be. In J. T. Spence, J. M. Darley, & D. J. Foss (Eds.), *Annual review of psychology* (Vol. 46, pp. 375–400). Palo Alto, CA: Annual Review, Inc.

Mac Iver, D., Stipek, D. J., & Daniels, D. (1991). Explaining within-semester changes in student effort in junior high school and senior high school courses. *Journal of Educational Psychology, 83,* 201–211.

Mack, A. (2003). Inattentional blindness: Looking without seeing. *Current Directions in Psychological Science, 12,* 180–184.

MacPherson, E. M., Candee, B. L., & Hohman, R. J. (1974). A comparison of three methods for eliminating disruptive lunchroom behavior. *Journal of Applied Behavior Analysis, 7,* 287–297.

Maehr, M. L. (1984). Meaning and motivation: Toward a theory of personal investment. In R. Ames & C. Ames (Eds.), *Research on motivation in education: Vol. 1. Student motivation.* Orlando, FL: Academic Press.

Maehr, M. L., & Anderman, E. M. (1993). Reinventing schools for early adolescents: Emphasizing task goals. *Elementary School Journal, 93,* 593–610.

Maehr, M. L., & Kaplan, A. (2000, April). It might be all about self: Self-consciousness as an organizing scheme for integrating understandings from self-determination theory and achievement goal theory. In A. Assor (Chair), *Self-determination theory and achievement goal theory: Convergences, divergences, and educational implications.* Symposium conducted at the annual meeting of the American Educational Research Association, New Orleans, LA.

Maehr, M. L., & McInerney, D. M. (2004). Motivation as personal investment. In D. M. McNerney & S. Van Etten (Eds.), *Big theories revisited* (pp. 61–90). Greenwich, CT: Information Age.

Maehr, M. L., & Meyer, H. A. (1997). Understanding motivation and schooling: Where we've been, where we are, and where we need to go. *Educational Psychology Review, 9,* 371–409.

Magee, S. K., & Ellis, J. (2000). Extinction effects during the assessment of multiple problem behaviors. *Journal of Applied Behavior Analysis, 33,* 313–316.

Mager, R. F. (1962). *Preparing instructional objectives.* Belmont, CA: Fearon.

Mager, R. F. (1972). *Goal analysis.* Belmont, CA: Fearon.

Mager, R. F. (1984). *Preparing instructional objectives* (2nd ed.). Belmont, CA: David S. Lake.

Mahoney, M. J., & Thoresen, C. E. (1974). *Self-control: Power to the person.* Monterey, CA: Brooks-Cole.

Maier, N. R. F. (1945). Reasoning in humans III: The mechanisms of equivalent stimuli and of reasoning. *Journal of Experimental Psychology, 35,* 349–360.

Maier, N. R. F., & Janzen, J. C. (1968). Functional values as aids and distractors in problem solving. *Psychological Reports, 22,* 1021–1034.

Maier, S. F., & Seligman, M. E. P. (1976). Learned helplessness: Theory and evidence. *Journal of Experimental Psychology: General, 105,* 3–46.

Maki, R. H. (1998). Test predictions over text material. In D. J. Hacker, J. Dunlosky, & A. C. Graesser (Eds.), *Metacognition in educational theory and practice* (pp. 117–144). Mahwah, NJ: Erlbaum.

Mandler, J. M. (2000). Perceptual and conceptual processes in infancy. *Journal of Cognition and Development, 1,* 3–36.

Mandler, J. M. (2003). Conceptual categorization. In D. H. Rakison & L. M. Oakes (Eds.), *Early category and concept development: Making sense of the blooming, buzzing confusion* (pp. 103–131). Oxford, England: Oxford University Press.

Mandler, J. M., & Johnson, N. S. (1976). Some of the thousand words a picture is worth. *Journal of Experimental Psychology: Human Learning and Memory, 2,* 529–540.

Mandler, J. M., & Parker, R. E. (1976). Memory for descriptive and spatial information in complex pictures. *Journal of Experimental Psychology: Human Learning and Memory, 2,* 38–48.

Mandler, J. M., & Ritchey, G. H. (1977). Long-term memory for pictures. *Journal of Experimental Psychology: Human Learning and Memory, 3,* 386–396.

Mangels, J. (2004, May). *The influence of intelligence beliefs on attention and learning: A neuro-physiological approach.* Invited address presented at the annual meeting of the American Psychological Society, Chicago.

Marachi, R., Friedel, J., & Midgley, C. (2001, April). *"I sometimes annoy my teacher during math": Relations between student perceptions of the teacher and disruptive behavior in the classroom.* Paper presented at the annual meeting of the American Educational Research Association, Seattle, WA.

Marcia, J. E. (1980). Identity in adolescence. In J. Adelson (Ed.), *Handbook of adolescent psychology.* New York: Wiley.

Markman, E. M. (1977). Realizing that you don't understand: A preliminary investigation. *Child Development, 48,* 986–992.

Marmolejo, E. K., Wilder, D. A., & Bradley, L. (2004). A preliminary analysis of the effects of response cards on student performance and participation in an upper division university course. *Journal of Applied Behavior Analysis, 37,* 405–410.

Marsh, H. W. (1990). A multidimensional, hierarchical model of self-concept: Theoretical and empirical justification. *Educational Psychology Review, 2,* 77–172.

Marsh, H. W., & Craven, R. (1997). Academic self-concept: Beyond the dustbowl. In G. D. Phye (Ed.), *Handbook of classroom assessment: Learning, achievement, and adjustment.* San Diego, CA: Academic Press.

Marshall, H. H. (Ed.) (1992). *Redefining student learning: Roots of educational change.* Norwood, NJ: Ablex.

Marshall, J. (1987). The effects of writing on students' understanding of literary texts. *Research in the Teaching of English, 21,* 30–63.

Martin, A. J., Marsh, H. W., & Debus, R. L. (2001). A quadripolar need achievement representation of self-handicapping and defensive pessimism. *American Educational Research Journal, 38,* 583–610.

Martin, A. J., Marsh, H. W., Williamson, A., & Debus, R. L. (2003). Self-handicapping, defensive pessimism, and goal orientation: A qualitative study of university students. *Journal of Educational Psychology, 95,* 617–628.

Martin, C. L., & Halverson, C. F. (1981). A schematic processing model of sex typing and stereotyping in children. *Child Development, 52,* 1119–1134.

Martin, I., & Levey, A. B. (1987). Learning what will happen next: Conditioning, evaluation, and cognitive processes. In G. Davey (Ed.), *Cognitive processes and Pavlovian conditioning in humans.* Chichester, England: Wiley.

Martin, S. S., Brady, M. P., & Williams, R. E. (1991). Effects of toys on the social behavior of preschool children in integrated and nonintegrated groups: Investigation of

a setting event. *Journal of Early Intervention, 15,* 153–161.

Marton, F., & Booth, S. (1997). *Learning and awareness.* Mahwah, NJ: Erlbaum.

Maslow, A. H. (1959). *New knowledge in human values.* New York: Harper & Row.

Maslow, A. H. (1973a). Self-actualizing people: A study of psychological health. In R. J. Lowry (Ed.), *Dominance, self-esteem, self-actualization: Germinal papers of A. H. Maslow.* Monterey, CA: Brooks-Cole.

Maslow, A. H. (1973b). Theory of human motivation. In R. J. Lowry (Ed.), *Dominance, self-esteem, self-actualization: Germinal papers of A. H. Maslow.* Monterey, CA: Brooks-Cole.

Maslow, A. H. (1987). *Motivation and personality* (3rd ed.). New York: Harper & Row.

Mason, L. (2003). Personal epistemologies and intentional conceptual change. In G. M. Sinatra & P. R. Pintrich (Eds.), *Intentional conceptual change* (pp. 199–236). Mahwah, NJ: Erlbaum.

Massialas, B. G., & Zevin, J. (1983). *Teaching creatively: Learning through discovery.* Malabar, FL: Robert E. Krieger.

Massimini, M., Ferrarelli, F., Huber, R., Esser, S. K.,& Tononi, G. (2005). Breakdown of cortical effective connectivity during sleep. *Science, 310,* 1768–1769.

Mast, V. K., Fagen, J. W., Rovee-Collier, C. K., & Sullivan, M. W. (1984). Immediate and long-term memory for reinforcement context: The development of learned expectancies in early infancy. *Child Development, 51,* 700–707.

Mastropieri, M. A., & Scruggs, T. E. (1989). Constructing more meaningful relationships: Mnemonic instruction for special populations. *Educational Psychology Review, 1,* 83–111.

Mastropieri, M. A., & Scruggs, T. E. (1992). Science for students with disabilities. *Review of Educational Research, 62,* 377–411.

Masur, E. F., McIntyre, C. W., & Flavell, J. H. (1973). Developmental changes in apportionment of study time among items in a multitrial free recall task. *Journal of Experimental Child Psychology, 15,* 237–246.

Mathan, S. A., & Koedinger, K. R. (2005). Fostering the intelligent novice: Learning from errors with metacognitive tutoring. *Educational Psychologist, 40,* 257–265.

Mathes, P. G., Torgesen, J. K., & Allor, J. H. (2001). The effects of peer-assisted literacy strategies for first-grade readers with and without additional computer-assisted instruction. *American Educational Research Journal, 38,* 371–410.

Mathews, J. R., Friman, P. C., Barone, V. J., Ross, L. V., & Christophersen, E. R. (1987). Decreasing dangerous infant behaviors through parent instruction. *Journal of Applied Behavior Analysis, 20,* 165–169.

Matlin, M. W. (2004, April 22). *"But I thought I got an A!": Metacognition and the college student.* Invited address presented in the Department of Psychology, University of New Hampshire, Durham.

Maxmell, D., Jarrett, O. S., & Dickerson, C. (1998, April). *Are we forgetting the children's needs? Recess through the children's eyes.* Paper

presented at the annual meeting of the American Educational Research Association, San Diego, CA.

May, D. B., & Etkina, E. (2002). College physics students' epistemological self-reflection and its relationship to conceptual learning. *Physics Education Research: A Supplement to the American Journal of Physics, 70,* 1249–1258.

Mayer, G. R., & Butterworth, T. N. (1979). A preventive approach to school violence and vandalism: An experimental study. *Personnel Guidance Journal, 57,* 436–441.

Mayer, R. E. (1974). Acquisition processes and resilience under varying testing conditions for structurally different problem solving procedures. *Journal of Educational Psychology, 66,* 644–656.

Mayer, R. E. (1977). *Thinking and problem solving: An introduction to human cognition and learning.* Glenview, IL: Scott, Foresman.

Mayer, R. E. (1979a). Can advance organizers influence meaningful learning? *Review of Educational Research, 49,* 371–383.

Mayer, R. E. (1979b). Twenty years of research on advance organizers: Assimilation theory is still the best predictor of results. *Instructional Science, 8,* 133–167.

Mayer, R. E. (1982). Memory for algebra story problems. *Journal of Educational Psychology, 74,* 199–216.

Mayer, R. E. (1984). Aids to text comprehension. *Educational Psychologist, 19,* 30–42.

Mayer, R. E. (1985). Implications of cognitive psychology for instruction in mathematical problem solving. In E. A. Silver (Ed.), *Teaching and learning mathematical problem solving: Multiple research perspectives.* Hillsdale, NJ: Erlbaum.

Mayer, R. E. (1986). Mathematics. In R. F. Dillon & R. J. Sternberg (Eds.), *Cognition and instruction.* San Diego, CA: Academic Press.

Mayer, R. E. (1987). *Educational psychology: A cognitive approach.* Boston: Little, Brown.

Mayer, R. E. (1989). Models for understanding. *Review of Educational Research, 59,* 43–64.

Mayer, R. E. (1992). *Thinking, problem solving, cognition* (2nd ed.). New York: W. H. Freeman.

Mayer, R. E. (1996a). Learners as information processors: Legacies and limitations of educational psychology's second metaphor. *Educational Psychologist, 31,* 151–161.

Mayer, R. E. (1996b). Learning strategies for making sense out of expository text: The SOI model for guiding three cognitive processes in knowledge construction. *Educational Psychology Review, 8,* 357–371.

Mayer, R. E. (1998). Does the brain have a place in educational psychology? *Educational Psychology Review, 10,* 389–396.

Mayer, R. E. (2004). Should there be a three-strikes rule against pure discovery learning? *American Psychologist, 59,* 14–19.

Mayer, R. E., & Bromage, B. (1980). Different recall protocols for technical texts due to advance organizers. *Journal of Educational Psychology, 72,* 209–225.

Mayer, R. E., & Greeno, J. G. (1972). Structural differences between learning outcomes produced by different instructional methods. *Journal of Educational Psychology, 63,* 165–173.

Mayer, R. E., & Massa, L. J. (2003). Three facets of visual and verbal learners: Cognitive ability, cognitive style, and learning preference. *Journal of Educational Psychology, 95*, 833–846.

Mayer, R. E., & Moreno, R. (1998). A split-attention effect in multimedia learning: Evidence for dual processing systems in working memory. *Journal of Educational Psychology, 90*, 312–320.

Mayer, R. E., Moreno, R., Boire, M., & Vagge, S. (1999). Maximizing constructivist learning from multimedia communications by minimizing cognitive load. *Journal of Educational Psychology, 91*, 638–643.

Mayer, R. E., & Wittrock, M. C. (1996). Problem-solving transfer. In D. C. Berliner & R. C. Calfee (Eds.), *Handbook of educational psychology*. New York: Macmillan.

Mayfield, K. H., & Chase, P. N. (2002). The effects of cumulative practice on mathematics problem solving. *Journal of Applied Behavior Analysis, 35*, 105–123.

Mayzner, M. S., & Tresselt, M. E. (1958). Anagram solution times: A function of letter-order and word frequency. *Journal of Experimental Psychology, 56*, 350–376.

Mayzner, M. S., & Tresselt, M. E. (1966). Anagram solution times: A function of multiple-solution anagrams. *Journal of Experimental Psychology, 71*, 66–73.

Mazur, J. E. (1993). Predicting the strength of a conditioned reinforcer: Effects of delay and uncertainty. *Current Directions in Psychological Science, 2*, 70–74.

Mazzoni, G., & Kirsch, I. (2002). Autobiographical memories and beliefs: A preliminary metacognitive model. In T. J. Perfect & B. L. Schwartz (Eds.), *Applied metacognition* (pp. 121–145). Cambridge, England: Cambridge University Press.

Mazzoni, G., & Memon, A. (2003). Imagination can create false autobiographical memories. *Psychological Science, 14*, 186–188.

McAllister, W. R., & McAllister, D. E. (1965). Variables influencing the conditioning and the measurement of acquired fear. In W. F. Prokasy (Ed.), *Classical conditioning*. New York: Appleton-Century-Crofts.

McAndrew, D. A. (1983). Underlining and note-taking: Some suggestions from research. *Journal of Reading, 27*, 103–108.

McAshan, H. H. (1979). *Competency-based education and behavioral objectives*. Englewood Cliffs, NJ: Educational Technology.

McCall, R. B., & Plemons, B. W. (2001). The concept of critical periods and their implications for early childhood services. In D. B. Bailey, Jr., J. T. Bruer, F. J. Symons, & J. W. Lichtman (Eds.), *Critical thinking about critical periods* (pp. 267–287). Baltimore: Brookes.

McCallin, R. C., Ormrod, J. E., & Cochran, K. C. (1997, March). *Algorithmic and heuristic learning sets and their relationship to cognitive structure*. Paper presented at the annual meeting of the American Educational Research Association, Chicago.

McCaslin, M., & Good, T. L. (1996). The informal curriculum. In D. C. Berliner & R. C. Calfee (Eds.), *Handbook of educational psychology*. New York: Macmillan.

McCaslin, M., & Hickey, D. T. (2001). Self-regulated learning and academic achievement: A Vygotskian view. In B. Zimmerman & D. Schunk (Eds.), *Self-regulated learning and academic achievement: Theory, research, and practice* (2nd ed., pp. 227–252). Mahwah, NJ: Erlbaum.

McCauley, R. N. (1987). The role of theories in a theory of concepts. In U. Neisser (Ed.), *Concepts and conceptual development: Ecological and intellectual factors in categorization*. Cambridge, England: Cambridge University Press.

McClelland, D. C. (1984). *Motives, personality, and society. Selected papers*. New York: Praeger.

McClelland, D. C., Atkinson, J. W., Clark, R. A., & Lowell, E. L. (1953). *The achievement motive*. New York: Appleton-Century-Crofts.

McClelland, J. L. (2001). Failures to learn and their remediation: A Hebbian account. In J. L. McClelland & R. S. Siegler (Eds.), *Mechanisms of cognitive development: Behavioral and neural perspectives* (pp. 97–121). Mahwah, NJ: Erlbaum.

McClelland, J. L., & Rumelhart, D. E. (1986). *Parallel distributed processing* (Vol. 2). Cambridge, MA: MIT Press.

McCloskey, M. E., & Glucksberg, S. (1978). Natural categories: Well-defined or fuzzy sets? *Memory and Cognition, 6*, 462–472.

McClowry, S. G. (1998). The science and art of using temperament as the basis for intervention. *School Psychology Review, 27*, 551–563.

McCombs, B. L. (1988). Motivational skills training: Combining metacognitive, cognitive, and affective learning strategies. In C. E. Weinstein, E. T. Goetz, & P. A. Alexander (Eds.), *Learning and study strategies: Issues in assessment, instruction, and evaluation*. San Diego, CA: Harcourt Brace Jovanovich.

McCombs, B. L. (1996). Alternative perspectives for motivation. In L. Baker, P. Afflerbach, & D. Reinking (Eds.), *Developing engaged readers in school and home communities*. Hillsdale, NJ: Erlbaum.

McCoy, L. P. (1990, April). *Correlates of mathematics anxiety*. Paper presented at the annual meeting of the American Educational Research Association, Boston.

McCrary, J. W., & Hunter, W. S. (1953). Serial position curves in verbal learning. *Science, 117*, 131–134.

McCrudden, M. T., Schraw, G., & Hartley, K. (2006). The effect of general relevance instructions on shallow and deeper learning and reading time. *Journal of Experimental Education, 74*, 293–310.

McCrudden, M. T., Schraw, G., & Kambe, G. (2005). The effect of relevance instructions on reading time and learning. *Journal of Educational Psychology, 97*, 88–102.

McCutchen, D. (1996). A capacity theory of writing: Working memory in composition. *Educational Psychology Review, 8*, 299–325.

McDaniel, M. A., & Einstein, G. O. (1989). Material-appropriate processing: A contextualist approach to reading and studying strategies. *Educational Psychology Review, 1*, 113–145.

McDaniel, M. A., Maier, S. F., & Einstein, G. O. (2002). "Brain-specific" nutrients: A memory cure? *Psychological Science in the Public Interest, 3*(1), 12–38.

McDaniel, M. A., & Masson, M. E. J. (1985). Altering memory representations through retrieval. *Journal of Experimental Psychology: Learning, Memory, and Cognition, 11*, 371–385.

McDaniel, M. A., & Schlager, M. S. (1990). Discovery learning and transfer of problem-solving skills. *Cognition and Instruction, 7*, 129–159.

McDaniel, M. A., Waddill, P. J., & Einstein, G. O. (1988). A contextual account of the generation effect: A three-factor theory. *Journal of Memory and Language, 27*, 521–536.

McDaniel, M. A., Waddill, P. J., Finstad, K., & Bourg, T. (2000). The effects of text-based interest on attention and recall. *Journal of Educational Psychology, 92*, 492–502.

McDevitt, T. M., Sheehan, E. P., Cooney, J. B., Smith, H. V., & Walker, I. (1994). Conceptions of listening, learning processes, and epistemologies held by American, Irish, and Australian university students. *Learning and Individual Differences, 6*, 231–256.

McDevitt, T. M., Spivey, N., Sheehan, E. P., Lennon, R., & Story, R. (1990). Children's beliefs about listening: Is it enough to be still and quiet? *Child Development, 55*, 810–820.

McDonald, R. V., & Siegel, S. (2004). The potential role of drug onset cues in drug dependence and withdrawal. *Experimental and Clinical Psychopharmacology, 12*, 23–26.

McGee, K. D., Knight, S. L., & Boudah, D. J. (2001, April). *Using reciprocal teaching in secondary inclusive English classroom instruction*. Paper presented at the annual meeting of the American Educational Research Association, Seattle, WA.

McGee, L. M. (1992). An exploration of meaning construction in first graders' grand conversations. In C. K. Kinzer & D. J. Leu (Eds.), *Literacy research, theory, and practice: Views from many perspectives*. Chicago: National Reading Conference.

McGeoch, J. A. (1942). *The psychology of human learning*. New York: David McKay.

McGill, P. (1999). Establishing operations: Implications for the assessment, treatment, and prevention of problem behavior. *Journal of Applied Behavior Analysis, 32*, 393–418.

McGregor, H. A., & Elliot, A. J. (2002). Achievement goals as predictors of achievement-relevant processes prior to task engagement. *Journal of Educational Psychology, 94*, 381–395.

McGuigan, F., & Salmon, K. (2004). The time to talk: The influence of the timing of adult-child talk on children's event memory. *Child Development, 75*, 669–686.

McHale, M. A., Brooks, Z., & Wolach, A. H. (1982). Incentive shifts with different massed and spaced trial cues. *Psychological Record, 32*, 85–92.

McInerney, D. M., Roche, L. A., McInerney, V., & Marsh, H. W. (1997). Cultural perspectives on school motivation: The relevance and application of goal theory. *American Educational Research Journal, 34,* 207–236.

McKeachie, W. J. (1987). Cognitive skills and their transfer: Discussion. *International Journal of Educational Research, 11,* 707–712.

McKenzie, H. S., Clark, M., Wolf, M. M., Kothera, R., & Benson, C. (1968). Behavior modification of children with learning disabilities using grades as tokens and allowances as back up reinforcers. *Exceptional Children, 34,* 745–752.

McKeown, M. G., & Beck, I. L. (1990). The assessment and characterization of young learners' knowledge of a topic in history. *American Educational Research Journal, 27,* 688–726.

McKerchar, P. M., & Thompson, R. H. (2004). A descriptive analysis of potential reinforcement contingencies in the preschool classroom. *Journal of Applied Behavior Analysis, 37,* 431–444.

McKown, C., & Weinstein, R. S. (2003). The development and consequences of stereotype consciousness in middle childhood. *Child Development, 74,* 498–515.

McLaughlin, T. F., & Malaby, J. (1972). Intrinsic reinforcers in a classroom token economy. *Journal of Applied Behavior Analysis, 5,* 263–270.

McLaughlin, T. F., & Williams, R. L. (1988). The token economy. In J. C. Witt, S. N. Elliott, & F. M. Gresham (Eds.), *Handbook of behavior therapy in education.* New York: Plenum Press.

McLeod, D. B., & Adams, V. M. (Eds.) (1989). *Affect and mathematical problem solving: A new perspective.* New York: Springer-Verlag.

McLoyd, V. C. (1998). Socioeconomic disadvantage and child development. *American Psychologist, 53,* 185–204.

McNally, R. J. (2003). Recovering memories of trauma: A view from the laboratory. *Current Directions in Psychological Science, 12,* 32–35.

McNamara, D. S., & Healy, A. F. (1995). A generation advantage for multiplication skill training and nonword vocabulary acquisition. In A. F. Healy & L. E. Bourne, Jr. (Eds.), *Learning and memory of knowledge and skills: Durability and specificity.* Thousand Oaks, CA: Sage.

McNamara, E. (1987). Behavioural approaches in the secondary school. In K. Wheldall (Ed.), *The behaviourist in the classroom.* London: Allen & Unwin.

Medin, D. L. (1989). Concepts and conceptual structure. *American Psychologist, 44,* 1469–1481.

Medin, D. L. (2005, August). *Role of culture and expertise in cognition.* Invited address presented at the annual meeting of the American Psychological Association, Washington, DC.

Meece, J. L. (1994). The role of motivation in self-regulated learning. In D. H. Schunk & B. J. Zimmerman (Eds.), *Self-regulation of learning and performance: Issues and educational applications.* Hillsdale, NJ: Erlbaum.

Meece, J. L., & Holt, K. (1993). A pattern analysis of students' achievement goals. *Journal of Educational Psychology, 85,* 582–590.

Meece, J. L., Wigfield, A., & Eccles, J. S. (1990). Predictors of math anxiety and its influence on young adolescents' course enrollment intentions and performance in mathematics. *Journal of Educational Psychology, 82,* 60–70.

Meehl, P. E. (1950). On the circularity of the law of effect. *Psychological Bulletin, 47,* 52–75.

Mehan, H. (1979). *Social organization in the classroom.* Cambridge, MA: Harvard University Press.

Mehrens, W. A. (1992). Using performance assessment for accountability purposes. *Educational Measurement: Issues and Practices, 11*(1), 3–9.

Meichenbaum, D. (1977). *Cognitive-behavior modification: An integrative approach.* New York: Plenum Press.

Meichenbaum, D. (1985). Teaching thinking: A cognitive–behavioral perspective. In S. F. Chipman, J. W. Segal, & R. Glaser (Eds.), *Thinking and learning skills: Vol. 2. Research and open questions.* Hillsdale, NJ: Erlbaum.

Mellers, B. A., & McGraw, A. P. (2001). Anticipated emotions as guides to choice. *Current Directions in Psychological Science, 10,* 210–214.

Mellers, B. A., Schwartz, A., Ho, K., & Ritov, H. (1997). Decision affect theory: Emotional reactions to the outcomes of risky options. *Psychological Science, 8,* 423–429.

Meloth, M. S., & Deering, P. D. (1992). Effects of two cooperative conditions on peer-group discussions, reading comprehension, and metacognition. *Contemporary Educational Psychology, 17,* 175–193.

Meloth, M. S., & Deering, P. D. (1994). Task talk and task awareness under different cooperative learning conditions. *American Educational Research Journal, 31,* 138–165.

Meloth, M. S., & Deering, P. D. (1999). The role of the teacher in promoting cognitive processing during collaborative learning. In A. M. O'Donnell & A. King (Eds.), *Cognitive perspectives on peer learning* (pp. 235–255). Mahwah, NJ: Erlbaum.

Melton, A. W. (1963). Implications of short-term memory for a general theory of memory. *Journal of Verbal Learning and Verbal Behavior, 2,* 1–21.

Melton, A. W., & Irwin, J. M. (1940). The influence of degree of interpolated learning on retroactive inhibition and the overt transfer of specific responses. *American Journal of Psychology, 53,* 173–203.

Meltzoff, A. N. (1988a). Infant imitation after a 1-week delay: Long-term memory for novel acts and multiple stimuli. *Developmental Psychology, 24,* 470–476.

Meltzoff, A. N. (1988b). Infant imitation and memory: Nine-month-old infants in immediate and deferred tests. *Child Development, 59,* 217–225.

Meltzoff, A. N., & Moore, M. K. (1977). Imitation of facial and manual gestures by human neonates. *Science, 198,* 75–78.

Mergendoller, J. R., Markham, T., Ravitz, J., & Larmer, J. (2006). Pervasive management of project based learning: Teachers as guides and facilitators. In C. M. Evertson & C. S. Weinstein (Eds.), *Handbook of classroom management: Research, practice, and contemporary issues* (pp. 583–615). Mahwah, NJ: Erlbaum.

Merrill, M. D., & Tennyson, R. D. (1977). *Concept teaching: An instructional design guide.* Englewood Cliffs, NJ: Educational Technology.

Merrill, M. D., & Tennyson, R. D. (1978). Concept classification and classification errors as a function of relationships between examples and non-examples. *Improving Human Performance, 7,* 351–364.

Merrill, P. F., Hammons, K., Vincent, B. R., Reynolds, P. L., Christensen, L., & Tolman, M. N. (1996). *Computers in education* (3rd ed.). Needham Heights, MA: Allyn & Bacon.

Mervis, C. B. (1987). Child-basic object categories and early lexical development. In U. Neisser (Ed.), *Concepts and conceptual development: Ecological and intellectual factors in categorization.* Cambridge, England: Cambridge University Press.

Mervis, C. B., Pani, J. R., & Pani, A. M. (2003). Transaction of child cognitive-linguistic abilities and adult input in the acquisition of lexical categories at the basic and subordinate levels. In D. H. Rakison & L. M. Oakes (Eds.), *Early category and concept development: Making sense of the blooming, buzzing confusion* (pp. 242–274). New York: Oxford University Press.

Merzenich, M. M. (2001). Cortical plasticity contributing to child development. In J. L. McClelland & R. S. Siegler (Eds.), *Mechanisms of cognitive development: Behavioral and neural perspectives* (pp. 67–95). Mahwah, NJ: Erlbaum.

Metcalfe, J. (2002). Is study time allocated selectively to a region of proximal learning? *Journal of Experimental Psychology: General, 131,* 349–363.

Metz, K. E. (1995). Reassessment of developmental constraints on children's science instruction. *Review of Educational Research, 65,* 93–127.

Metz, K. E. (1997). On the complex relation between cognitive developmental research and children's science curricula. *Review of Educational Research, 67,* 151–163.

Meyer, B. J. F., Brandt, D. H., & Bluth, G. J. (1980). Use of top-level structure in text: Key for reading comprehension of ninth-grade students. *Reading Research Quarterly, 16,* 72–103.

Meyer, D. K., & Turner, J. C. (2002). Discovering emotion in classroom motivation research. *Educational Psychologist, 37,* 107–114.

Meyer, K. A. (1999). Functional analysis and treatment of problem behavior exhibited by elementary school children. *Journal of Applied Behavior Analysis, 32,* 229–232.

Michael, J. (1993). Establishing operations. *The Behavior Analyst, 16,* 191–206.

Michael, J. (2000). Implications and refinements of the establishing operation concept. *Journal of Applied Behavior Analysis, 33,* 401–410.

Michael, J. L. (1974). The essential components of effective instruction and why most college teaching is not. In F. S. Keller & E. Ribes-Inesta (Eds.),

Behavior modification: Applications to education. New York: Academic Press.

Middleton, M. J., & Midgley, C. (1997). Avoiding the demonstration of lack of ability: An under-explored aspect of goal theory. *Journal of Educational Psychology, 89,* 710–718.

Middleton, M. J., & Midgley, C. (2002). Beyond motivation: Middle school students' perceptions of press for understanding in math. *Contemporary Educational Psychology, 27,* 373–391.

Midgley, C. (1993). Motivation and middle level schools. In M. Maehr & P. R. Pintrich (Eds.), *Advances in motivation and achievement* (Vol. 8, pp. 217–274). Greenwich, CT: JAI Press.

Midgley, C. (Ed.) (2002). *Goals, goal structures, and patterns of adaptive learning.* Mahwah, NJ: Erlbaum.

Midgley, C., Kaplan, A., & Middleton, M. (2001). Performance-approach goals: Good for what, for whom, under what circumstances, and at what cost? *Journal of Educational Psychology, 93,* 77–86.

Midgley, C., Kaplan, A., Middleton, M., Maehr, M., Urdan, T., Anderman, L., Anderman, E., & Roeser, R. (1998). The development and validation of scales assessing students' achievement goal orientations. *Contemporary Educational Psychology, 23,* 113–131.

Mikulincer, M. (1994). *Human learned helplessness: A coping perspective.* New York: Plenum Press.

Miller, D. L., & Kelley, M. L. (1994). The use of goal setting and contingency contracting for improving children's homework performance. *Journal of Applied Behavior Analysis, 27,* 73–84.

Miller, G. A. (1956). The magical number seven, plus or minus two: Some limits on our capacity for processing information. *Psychological Review, 63,* 81–97.

Miller, G. A., Galanter, E., & Pribram, K. H. (1960). *Plans and the structure of behavior.* New York: Holt, Rinehart & Winston.

Miller, J. G. (1997). A cultural-psychology perspective on intelligence. In R. J. Sternberg & E. L. Grigorenko (Eds.), *Intelligence, heredity, and environment* (pp. 269–302). Cambridge, England: Cambridge University Press.

Miller, N. E. (1948). Studies of fear as an acquirable drive: I. Fear as motivation and fear-reduction as reinforcement in the learning of new responses. *Journal of Experimental Psychology, 38,* 89–101.

Miller, N. E., & Dollard, J. C. (1941). *Social learning and imitation.* New Haven, CT: Yale University Press.

Miller, R. B., & Steward, W. M. (2003, April). *Perceived instrumentality and affective self-reactions to academic performance.* Paper presented at the annual meeting of the American Educational Research Association, Chicago.

Miller, R. R., & Barnet, R. C. (1993). The role of time in elementary associations *Current Directions in Psychological Science, 2,* 106–111.

Miller, S. D., Heafner, T., Massey, D., & Strahan, D. B. (2003, April). *Students' reactions to teachers' attempts to create the necessary conditions to promote the acquisition of self-regulation skills.* Paper presented at the annual meeting of the American Educational Research Association, Chicago.

Miller, S. M. (2003). How literature discussion shapes thinking: ZPDs for teaching/learning habits of the heart and mind. In A. Kozulin, B. Gindis, V. S. Ageyev, & S. M. Miller (Eds.), *Vygotsky's educational theory in cultural context* (pp. 289–316). Cambridge, England: Cambridge University Press.

Millroy, W. L. (1991). An ethnographic study of the mathematical ideas of a group of carpenters. *Learning and Individual Differences, 3,* 1–25.

Mineka, S., & Zinbarg, R. (2006). A contemporary learning theory perspective on the etiology of anxiety disorders: It's not what you thought it was. *American Psychologist, 61,* 10–26.

Minstrell, J., & Stimpson, V. (1996). A classroom environment for learning: Guiding students' reconstruction of understanding and reasoning. In L. Schauble & R. Glaser (Eds.), *Innovations in learning: New environments for education.* Mahwah, NJ: Erlbaum.

Mintzes, J. J., Trowbridge, J. E., Arnaudin, M. W., & Wandersee, J. H. (1991). Children's biology: Studies on conceptual development in the life sciences. In S. M. Glynn, R. H. Yeany, & B. K. Britton (Eds.), *The psychology of learning science.* Hillsdale, NJ: Erlbaum.

Mintzes, J. J., Wandersee, J. H., & Novak, J. D. (1997). Meaningful learning in science: The human constructivist perspective. In G. D. Phye (Ed.), *Handbook of academic learning: Construction of knowledge.* San Diego, CA: Academic Press.

Mitchell, J. B. (1989). Current theories on expert and novice thinking: A full faculty considers the implications for legal education. *Journal of Legal Education, 39,* 275–297.

Mitchell, M. (1993). Situational interest: Its multifaceted structure in the secondary school mathematics classroom. *Journal of Educational Psychology, 85,* 424–436.

Mithaug, D. K., & Mithaug, D. E. (2003). Effects of teacher-directed versus student-directed instruction on self-management of young children with disabilities. *Journal of Applied Behavior Analysis, 36,* 133–136.

Moely, B. E. (1977). Organizational factors in the development of memory. In R. V. Kail & J. W. Hagen (Eds.), *Perspectives on the development of memory and cognition.* Hillsdale, NJ: Erlbaum.

Mohatt, G., & Erickson, F. (1981). Cultural differences in teaching styles in an Odawa school: A sociolinguistic approach. In H. T. Trueba, G. P. Guthrie, & K. H. Au (Eds.), *Culture and the bilingual classroom: Studies in classroom ethnography.* Rowley, MA: Newbury House.

Moletzsky, B. (1974). Behavior recording as treatment: A brief note. *Behavior Therapy, 5,* 107–111.

Mooney, C. M. (1957). Age in the development of closure ability in children. *Canadian Journal of Psychology, 11,* 219–226.

Moran, S., & John-Steiner, V. (2003). Creativity in the making: Vygotsky's contemporary contribution to the dialectic of development and creativity. In R. K. Sawyer, V. John-Steiner, S. Moran, R. J. Sternberg, D. H. Feldman, J. Nakamura, & M. Csikszentmihalyi, *Creativity and development* (pp. 61–90). Oxford, England: Oxford University Press.

Moran, K. B., Urdan, T., & Passarelli, S. J. (2003, April). *Changes in academic value and self-handicapping: The influence of goals and classroom goal structures.* Paper presented at the annual meeting of the American Educational Research Association, Chicago.

Moray, N., Bates, A., & Barnett, R. (1965). Experiments on the four-eared man. *Journal of the Acoustical Society of America, 38,* 196–201.

Moreno, R. (2006). Learning in high-tech and multimedia environments. *Current Directions in Psychological Science, 15,* 63–67.

Morgan, M. (1984). Reward-induced decrements and increments in intrinsic motivation. *Review of Educational Research, 54,* 5–30.

Morgan, M. (1985). Self-monitoring of attained subgoals in private study. *Journal of Educational Psychology, 77,* 623–630.

Morris, C. D., Bransford, J. D., & Franks, J. J. (1977). Levels of processing versus transfer appropriate processing. *Journal of Verbal Learning and Verbal Behavior, 16,* 519–533.

Morris, E. K. (1982). Some relationships between interbehavioral psychology and radical behaviorism. *Behaviorism, 10,* 187–216.

Morris, R. J. (1985). *Behavior modification with exceptional children: Principles and practices.* Glenview, IL: Scott, Foresman.

Morris, R. J., Kratochwill, T. R., & Aldridge, K. (1988). Fears and phobias. In J. C. Witt, S. N. Elliott, & F. M. Gresham (Eds.), *Handbook of behavior therapy in education.* New York: Plenum Press.

Mosborg, S. (2002). Speaking of history: How adolescents use their knowledge of history in reading the daily news. *Cognition and Instruction, 20,* 323–358.

Mowrer, O. H. (1938). Preparatory set (expectancy): A determinant in motivation and learning. *Psychological Review, 45,* 62–91.

Mowrer, O. H. (1939). A stimulus-response analysis and its role as a reinforcing agent. *Psychological Review, 46,* 553–565.

Mowrer, O. H. (1956). Two-factor learning theory reconsidered, with special reference to secondary reinforcement and the concept of habit. *Psychological Review, 63,* 114–128.

Mowrer, O. H. (1960). *Learning theory and behavior.* New York: Wiley.

Mowrer, O. H., & Lamoreaux, R. R. (1942). Avoidance conditioning and signal duration: A study of secondary motivation and reward. *Psychological Monographs, 54* (Whole No. 247).

Mueller, J. H. (1980). Test anxiety and the encoding and retrieval of information. In I. G. Sarason (Ed.), *Test anxiety: Theory, research, and applications.* Hillsdale, NJ: Erlbaum.

Mueller, C. M., & Dweck, C. S. (1998). Intelligence praise can undermine motivation and performance. *Journal of Personality and Social Psychology, 75,* 33–52.

Mueller, M. M., Edwards, R. P., & Trahant, D. (2003). Translating multiple assessment techniques into an intervention selection model for classrooms. *Journal of Applied Behavior Analysis, 36,* 563–573.

Mueller, M. M., Sterling-Turner, H. E., & Scattone, D. (2001). Functional assessment of hand flapping in a general education classroom. *Journal of Applied Behavior Analysis, 34,* 233–236.

Muis, K. R. (2004). Personal epistemology and mathematics: A critical review and synthesis of research. *Review of Educational Research, 74,* 317–377.

Mullen, M. K., & Yi, S. (1995). The cultural context of talk about the past: Implications for the development of autobiographical memory. *Cognitive Development, 10,* 407–419.

Mumme, D. L., & Fernald, A. (2003). The infant as onlooker: Learning from emotional reactions observed in a television scenario. *Child Development, 74,* 221–237.

Munakata, Y. (2006). Information processing approaches to development. In W. Damon & R. M. Lerner (Series Eds.), D. Kuhn, & R. Siegler (Vol. Eds.), *Handbook of child psychology: Vol. 2. Cognition, perception, and language* (6th ed.). New York: Wiley.

Murata, A., Fadiga, L., Fogassi, L., Gallese, V., Raos, V., & Rizzolatti, G. (1997). Object representation in the ventral premotor cortex (area F5) of the monkey. *Journal of Neurophysiology, 78,* 2226–2230.

Murdock, T. B. (1999). The social context of risk: Status and motivational predictors of alienation in middle school. *Journal of Educational Psychology, 91,* 62–75.

Murnane, R. J., & Raizen, S. A. (Eds.) (1988). *Improving indicators of the quality of science and mathematics education in grades K–12.* Washington, DC: National Academy Press.

Murphy, P. K., & Alexander, P. A. (2000). A motivated exploration of motivation terminology. *Contemporary Educational Psychology, 25,* 3–53.

Murphy, P. K., & Alexander, P. A. (2004). Persuasion as a dynamic, multidimensional process: An investigation of individual and intraindividual differences. *American Educational Research Journal, 41,* 337–363.

Murphy, E. S., McSweeney, F. K., Smith, R. G., & McComas, J. J. (2003). Dynamic changes in reinforcer effectiveness: Theoretical, methological, and practical implications for applied research. *Journal of Applied Behavior Analysis, 36,* 421–438.

Murray, C. B., & Jackson, J. S. (1982/1983). The conditioned failure model of black educational underachievement. *Humboldt Journal of Social Relations, 10,* 276–300.

Mwangi, W., & Sweller, J. (1998). Learning to solve compare word problems: The effect of example format and generating self-explanations. *Cognition and Instruction, 16,* 173–199.

Myers, J. L., & Duffy, S. A. (1990). Causal inferences and text memory. In A. C. Graessner & G. H. Bower (Eds.), *Inferences and text comprehension. The psychology of learning and motivation: Advances in research and theory* (Vol. 25). Orlando, FL: Academic Press.

Nadel, L. (2005, August). *Memory, stress, and the brain: In Miller's footsteps.* Invited address presented at the annual meeting of the American Psychological Association, Washington, DC.

Nadel, L., & Jacobs, W. J. (1998). Traumatic memory is special. *Current Directions in Psychological Science, 7,* 154–157.

Natriello, G. (1987). The impact of evaluation processes on students. *Educational Psychologist, 22,* 155–175.

Natriello, G., & Dornbusch, S. M. (1984). *Teacher evaluative standards and student effort.* New York: Longman.

Naveh-Benjamin, M. (1991). A comparison of training programs intended for different types of text-anxious students: Further support for an information-processing model. *Journal of Educational Psychology, 83,* 134–139.

Neef, N. A., Marckel, J., Ferreri, S. J., Bicard, D. F., Endo, S., Aman, M. G., Miller, K. M., Jung, S., Nist, L., & Armstrong, N. (2005). Behavioral assessment of impulsivity: A comparison of children with and without attention deficit hyperactivity disorder. *Journal of Applied Behavior Analysis, 38,* 23–37.

Neisser, U. (1967). *Cognitive psychology.* New York: Appleton-Century-Crofts.

Neisser, U. (1981). John Dean's memory: A case study. *Cognition, 9,* 1–22.

Neisser, U., & Harsch, N. (1992). Phantom flashbulbs: False recollections of hearing the news about *Challenger.* In E. Winograd & U. Neisser (Eds.), *Affect and accuracy in recall: Studies of "flashbulb" memories.* Cambridge, England: Cambridge University Press.

Neisser, U., & Weene, P. (1962). Hierarchies in concept formation. *Journal of Experimental Psychology, 64,* 644–645.

Nell, V. (2002). Why young men drive dangerously: Implications for injury prevention. *Current Directions in Psychological Science, 11,* 75–79.

Nelson, C. A. (1995). The ontogeny of human memory: A cognitive neuroscience perspective. *Developmental Psychology, 31,* 723–738.

Nelson, C. A. (2005, April). *Brain development and plasticity: Examples from the study of early institutional rearing.* Invited address at the Developmental Science Teaching Institute at the biennial meeting of the Society for Research in Child Development, Atlanta, GA.

Nelson, K. (1996). *Language in cognitive development: The emergence of the mediated mind.* Cambridge, England: Cambridge University Press.

Nelson, K., & Fivush, R. (2004). The emergence of autobiographical memory: A social cultural developmental theory. *Psychological Review, 111,* 486–511.

Nelson, L. J., & Miller, D. T. (1995). The distinctiveness effect in social categorization: You are what makes you unusual. *Psychological Science, 6,* 246–249.

Nelson, T. O. (1971). Savings and forgetting from long-term memory. *Journal of Verbal Learning and Verbal Behavior, 10,* 568–576.

Nelson, T. O. (1977). Repetition and depth of processing. *Journal of Verbal Learning and Verbal Behavior, 16,* 151–171.

Nelson, T. O. (1978). Detecting small amounts of information in memory: Savings for non-recognized items. *Journal of Experimental Psychology: Human Learning and Memory, 4,* 453–468.

Nelson, T. O., & Dunlosky, J. (1991). When people's judgments of learning (JOLs) are extremely accurate at predicting subsequent recall: The "delayed-JOL effect." *Psychological Science, 2,* 267–270.

Nelson, T. O., & Rothbart, R. (1972). Acoustic savings for items forgotten from long-term memory. *Journal of Experimental Psychology, 93,* 357–360.

Neumann, P. G. (1974). An attribute frequency model for the abstraction of prototypes. *Memory and Cognition, 2,* 241–248.

Neumann, P. G. (1977). Visual prototype formation with discontinuous representation of dimensions of variability. *Memory and Cognition, 5,* 187–197.

Neumann, R. (2000). The causal influences of attributions on emotions: A procedural priming approach. *Psychological Science, 11,* 179–182.

Neville, H. J., & Bruer, J. T. (2001). Language processing: How experience affects brain organization. In D. B. Bailey, Jr., J. T. Bruer, F. J. Symons, & J. W. Lichtman (Eds.), *Critical thinking about critical periods* (pp. 151–172). Baltimore: Brookes.

Nevin, J. A., Mandell, C., & Atak, J. R. (1983). The analysis of behavioral momentum. *Journal of the Experimental Analysis of Behavior, 39,* 49–59.

Newberg, N. A., & Sims, R. B. (1996). Contexts that promote success for inner-city students. *Urban Education, 31,* 149–176.

Newby, T. J., Ertmer, P. A., & Stepich, D. A. (1994, April). *Instructional analogies and the learning of concepts.* Paper presented at the annual meeting of the American Educational Research Association, New Orleans, LA.

Newcombe, N. S., Drummey, A. B., Fox, N. A., Lie, E., & Ottinger-Albergs, W. (2000). Remembering early childhood: How much, how, and why (or why not). *Current Directions in Psychological Science, 9,* 55–58.

Newcombe, N. S., & Fox, N. A. (1994). Infantile amnesia: Through a glass darkly. *Child Development, 65,* 31–40.

Newcombe, N., & Huttenlocher, J. (1992). Children's early ability to solve perspective-taking problems. *Developmental Psychology, 28,* 635–643.

Newell, A., Shaw, J. C., & Simon, H. A. (1958). Elements of a theory of human problem solving. *Psychological Review, 65,* 151–166.

Newell, A., & Simon, H. A. (1972). *Human problem solving.* Englewood Cliffs, NJ: Prentice Hall.

Newman, R. S. (1998). Students' help seeking during problem solving: Influences of personal and contextual achievement goals. *Journal of Educational Psychology, 90,* 644–658.

Newman, R. S., & Schwager, M. T. (1992). Student perceptions and academic help seeking. In D. Schunk & J. Meece (Eds.), *Student perceptions in the classroom*. Hillsdale, NJ: Erlbaum.

Newmann, F. M., & Wehlage, G. G. (1993). Five standards of authentic instruction. *Educational Leadership, 50*(7), 8–12.

Newport, E. L. (1990). Maturational constraints on language learning. *Cognitive Science, 14*, 11–28.

Newson, J., & Newson, E. (1975). Intersubjectivity and the transmission of culture: On the origins of symbolic functioning. *Bulletin of the British Psychological Society, 28*, 437–446.

Nguyen, S. P., & Murphy, G. L. (2003). An apple is more than just a fruit: Cross-classification in children's concepts. *Child Development, 74*, 1783–1806.

Ni, Y., & Zhou, Y.-D. (2005). Teaching and learning fraction and rational numbers: The origins and implications of whole number bias. *Educational Psychologist, 40*, 27–52.

Nicholls, J. G. (1984). Conceptions of ability and achievement motivation. In R. Ames & C. Ames (Eds.), *Research on motivation in education: Vol. 1. Student motivation*. Orlando, FL: Academic Press.

Nicholls, J. G. (1990). What is ability and why are we mindful of it? A developmental perspective. In R. J. Sternberg & J. Kolligian (Eds.), *Competence considered*. New Haven, CT: Yale University Press.

Nicholls, J. G. (1992). Students as educational theorists. In D. Schunk & J. L. Meece (Eds.), *Student perception in the classroom*. Hillsdale, NJ: Erlbaum.

Nicholls, J. G., Cobb, P., Yackel, E., Wood, T., & Wheatley, G. (1990). Students' theories of mathematics and their mathematical knowledge: Multiple dimensions of assessment. In G. Kulm (Ed.), *Assessing higher order thinking in mathematics*. Washington, DC: American Association for the Advancement of Science.

Nichols, J. D. (1996a). Cooperative learning: A motivational tool to enhance student persistence, self-regulation, and efforts to please teachers and parents. *Educational Research and Evaluation, 2*, 246–260.

Nichols, J. D. (1996b). The effects of cooperative learning on student achievement and motivation in a high school geometry class. *Contemporary Educational Psychology, 21*, 467–476.

Nichols, J. D., Ludwin, W. G., & Iadicola, P. (1999). A darker shade of gray: A year-end analysis of discipline and suspension data. *Equity and Excellence in Education, 32*(1), 43–55.

Nickerson, R. S. (1989). New directions in educational assessment. *Educational Researcher, 18*(9), 3–7.

Nickerson, R. S., & Adams, M. J. (1979). Long-term memory for a common object. *Cognitive Psychology, 1*, 287–307.

Nietfeld, J. L., & Cao, L. (April, 2004). *The effect of distributed monitoring exercises and feedback on performance and monitoring accuracy*. Paper presented at the American Educational Research Association, San Diego, CA.

Nikopoulos, C. K., & Keenan, M. (2004). Effects of video modeling on social initiations by children with autism. *Journal of Applied Behavior Analysis, 37*, 93–96.

Nisbett, R. E., & Bellows, N. (1977). Verbal reports about causal influences on social judgments: Private access versus public theories. *Journal of Personality and Social Psychology, 35*, 613–624.

Nisbett, R. E., & Wilson, T. D. (1977). Telling more than we can know: Verbal reports on mental processes. *Psychological Review, 84*, 231–259.

Nist, S. L., Simpson, M. L., Olejnik, S., & Mealey, D. L. (1991). The relation between self-selected study processes and test performance. *American Educational Research Journal, 28*, 849–874.

Noddings, N. (1985). Small groups as a setting for research on mathematical problem solving. In E. A. Silver (Ed.), *Teaching and learning mathematical problem solving: Multiple research perspectives*. Hillsdale, NJ: Erlbaum.

Nolen, S. B. (1996). Why study? How reasons for learning influence strategy selection. *Educational Psychology Review, 8*, 335–355.

Norman, D. A. (1969). *Memory and attention: An introduction to human information processing*. New York: Wiley.

Norman, D. A., & Rumelhart, D. E. (1975). *Explorations in cognition*. San Francisco: W. H. Freeman.

Northup, J. (2000). Further evaluation of the accuracy of reinforcer surveys: A systematic replication. *Journal of Applied Behavior Analysis, 33*, 335–338.

Northup, J., Broussard, C., Jones, K. George, T., Vollmer, T. R., & Herring, M. (1995). The differential effects of teachers and peer attention on the disruptive classroom behavior of three children with a diagnosis of attention deficit hyperactivity disorder. *Journal of Applied Behavior Analysts, 28*, 227–228.

Novak, J. D. (1998). *Learning, creating, and using knowledge: Concept maps as facilitative tools in schools and corporations*. Mahwah, NJ: Erlbaum.

Novak, J. D., & Gowin, D. B. (1984). *Learning how to learn*. Cambridge, England: Cambridge University Press.

Novak, J. D., & Musonda, D. (1991). A twelve-year longitudinal study of science concept learning. *American Educational Research Journal, 28*, 117–153.

Novick, L. R. (1988). Analogical transfer, problem similarity, and expertise. *Journal of Experimental Psychology: Learning, Memory, and Cognition, 14*, 510–520.

Nucci, L. P. (2001). *Education in the moral domain*. Cambridge, England: Cambridge University Press.

Nungester, R. J., & Duchastel, P. C. (1982). Testing versus review: Effects on retention. *Journal of Educational Psychology, 74*, 18–22.

Nussbaum, J. (1985). The earth as a cosmic body. In R. Driver (Ed.), *Children's ideas of science*. Philadelphia: Open University Press.

Nuthall, G. (2000). The anatomy of memory in the classroom: Understanding how students acquire memory processes from classroom activities in science and social studies units. *American Educational Research Journal, 37*, 247–304.

Oakes, L. M., & Rakison, D. H. (2003). Issues in the early development of concepts and categories: An introduction. In D. H. Rakison & L. M. Oakes (Eds.), *Early category and concept development: Making sense of the blooming, buzzing confusion* (pp. 3–23). Oxford, England: Oxford University Press.

Oakhill, J. (1993). Children's difficulties in reading comprehension. *Educational Psychology Review, 5*, 223–237.

Oakhill, J., Cain, K., & Yuill, N. (1998). Individual differences in children's comprehension skill: Toward an integrated model. In C. Hulme & R. M. Joshi (Eds.), *Reading and spelling: Development and disorders*. Mahwah, NJ: Erlbaum.

Oatley, K., & Nundy, S. (1996). Rethinking the role of emotions in education. In D. R. Olson & N. Torrance (Eds.), *The handbook of education and human development: New models of learning, teaching, and schooling*. Cambridge, MA: Blackwell.

O'Brien, G. (1999). A connectionist theory of phenomenal experience. *Behavioral and Brain Sciences, 22*, 127–196.

Ochsner, K. N., & Lieberman, M. D. (2001). The emergence of social cognitive neuroscience. *American Psychologist, 56*, 717–734.

Oden, G. C. (1987). Concept, knowledge, and thought. *Annual Review of Psychology, 38*, 203–227.

O'Donnell, A. M. (1999). Structuring dyadic interaction through scripted cooperation. In A. M. O'Donnell & A. King (Eds.), *Cognitive perspectives on peer learning* (pp. 179–196). Mahwah, NJ: Erlbaum.

O'Donnell, A. M., Dansereau, D. F., & Hall, R. H. (2002). Knowledge maps as scaffolds for cognitive processing. *Educational Psychology Review, 14*, 71–86.

O'Donnell, A. M., & King, A. (Eds.) (1999). *Cognitive perspectives on peer learning*. Mahwah, NJ: Erlbaum.

O'Donnell, A. M., & O'Kelly, J. (1994). Learning from peers: Beyond the rhetoric of positive results. *Educational Psychology Review, 6*, 321–349.

Öhman, A., & Mineka, S. (2003). The malicious serpent: Snakes as a prototypical stimulus for an evolved module of fear. *Current Directions in Psychological Science, 12*, 5–9.

Olds, J., & Milner, P. (1954). Positive reinforcement produced by electrical stimulation of septal area and other regions of rat brain. *Journal of Comparative and Physiological Psychology, 47*, 419–427.

O'Leary, K. D., Kaufman, K. F., Kass, R. E., & Drabman, R. S. (1970). The effects of loud and soft reprimands on the behavior of disruptive students. *Exceptional Children, 37*, 145–155.

O'Leary, K. D., & O'Leary, S. G. (Eds.) (1972). *Classroom management: The successful use of behavior modification.* New York: Pergamon Press.

Olneck, M. R. (1995). Immigrants and education. In J. A. Banks & C. A. M. Banks (Eds.), *Handbook of research on multicultural education.* New York: Macmillan.

Olson, M. A., & Fazio, R. H. (2001). Implicit attitude formation through classical conditioning. *Psychological Science, 12,* 413–417.

Onosko, J. J. (1996). Exploring issues with students despite the barriers. *Social Education, 60*(1), 22–27.

Onosko, J. J., & Newmann, F. M. (1994). Creating more thoughtful learning environments. In J. N. Mangieri & C. C. Block (Eds.), *Creating powerful thinking in teachers and students: Diverse perspectives.* Fort Worth, TX: Harcourt Brace.

Ormrod, J. E. (1979). Cognitive processes in the solution of three-term series problems. *American Journal of Psychology, 92,* 235–255.

Ormrod, J. E. (1985). Proofreading *The Cat in the Hat:* Evidence for different reading styles of good and poor spellers. *Psychological Reports, 57,* 863–867.

Ormrod, J. E. (1986a). Differences between good and poor spellers in reading style and short-term memory. *Visible Language, 20,* 437–447.

Ormrod, J. E. (1986b). Learning to spell: Three studies at the university level. *Research in the Teaching of English, 20,* 160–173.

Ormrod, J. E. (1986c). Learning to spell while reading: A follow-up study. *Perceptual and Motor Skills, 63,* 652–654.

Ormrod, J. E., & Jenkins, L. (1988, April). *Study strategies for learning spelling: What works and what does not.* Paper presented at the annual meeting of the American Educational Research Association, New Orleans, LA.

Ormrod, J. E., Ormrod, R. K., Wagner, E. D., & McCallin, R. C. (1988). Reconceptualizing map learning. *American Journal of Psychology, 101,* 425–433.

Ormrod, J. E., & Wagner, E. D. (1987, October). *Spelling conscience in undergraduate students: Ratings of spelling accuracy and dictionary use.* Paper presented at the annual meeting of the Northern Rocky Mountain Educational Research Association, Park City, UT.

Ornstein, P. A., & Haden, C. A. (2001). Memory development or the *development* of memory? *Current Directions in Psychological Science, 10,* 202–205.

Ornstein, R. (1972). *The psychology of consciousness.* San Francisco: W. H. Freeman.

Ornstein, R. (1997). *The right mind: Making sense of the hemispheres.* San Diego, CA: Harcourt Brace.

Osborn, A. F. (1963). *Applied imagination* (3rd ed.). New York: Scribner.

Osborne, J. G. (1969). Free-time as a reinforcer in the management of classroom behavior. *Journal of Applied Behavior Analysis, 2,* 113–118.

Osborne, J. W., & Simmons, C. M. (2002, April). *Girls, math, stereotype threat, and anxiety: Physiological evidence.* Paper presented at the annual meeting of the American Educational Research Association, New Orleans, LA.

Osgood, C. E. (1949). The similarity paradox in human learning: A resolution. *Psychological Review, 56,* 132–143.

Oskamp, S. (Ed.) (2000). *Reducing prejudice and discrimination.* Mahwah, NJ: Erlbaum.

Osman, G., Duffy, T. M., Chang, J.-Y., & Lee, J. E. (2006, April). *Learning through collaboration: Student perspectives.* Paper presented at the annual meeting of the American Educational Research Association, San Francisco.

Osterman, K. F. (2000). Students' need for belonging in the school community. *Review of Educational Research, 70,* 323–367.

O'Sullivan, J. T., & Joy, R. M. (1990, April). *Children's theories about reading difficulty: A developmental study.* Paper presented at the annual meeting of the American Educational Research Association, Boston.

Otero, J. (1998). Influence of knowledge activation and context on comprehension monitoring of science texts. In D. J. Hacker, J. Dunlosky, & A. C. Graesser (Eds.), *Metacognition in educational theory and practice* (pp. 145–164). Mahwah, NJ: Erlbaum.

Otero, J., & Kintsch, W. (1992). Failures to detect contradictions in a text: What readers believe versus what they read. *Psychological Science, 3,* 229–235.

Overmier, J. B., & Lawry, J. A. (1979). Pavlovian conditioning and the mediation of behavior. In G. H. Bower (Ed.), *The psychology of learning and motivation* (Vol. 13). New York: Academic Press.

Owens, J., Bower, G. H., & Black, J. B. (1979). The "soap opera" effect in story recall. *Memory and Cognition, 7,* 185–191.

Owens, R. E., Jr. (1996). *Language development* (4th ed.). Boston: Allyn & Bacon.

Ozgungor, S., & Guthrie, J. T. (2004). Interactions among elaborative interrogation, knowledge, and interest in the process of constructing knowledge from text. *Journal of Educational Psychology, 96,* 437–443.

Packard, R. G. (1970). The control of "classroom attention": A group contingency for complex behavior. *Journal of Applied Behavior Analysis, 3,* 13–28.

Packer, M. J., & Goicoechea, J. (2000). Sociocultural and constructivist theories of learning: Ontology, not just epistemology. *Educational Psychologist, 35,* 227–241.

Page-Voth, V., & Graham, S. (1999). Effects of goal setting and strategy use on the writing performance and self-efficacy of students with writing and learning problems. *Journal of Educational Psychology, 91,* 230–240.

Paige, J. M., & Simon, H. A. (1966). Cognitive processes in solving algebra word problems. In B. Kleinmuntz (Ed.), *Problem solving.* New York: Wiley.

Paivio, A. (1963). Learning of adjective-noun paired associates as a function of adjective-noun word order and noun abstractness. *Canadian Journal of Psychology, 17,* 370–379.

Paivio, A. (1971). *Imagery and verbal processes.* New York: Holt, Rinehart & Winston.

Paivio, A. (1975). Coding distinctions and repetition effects in memory. In G. H. Bower (Ed.), *The psychology of learning and motivation* (Vol. 9). New York: Academic Press.

Paivio, A. (1986). *Mental representations: A dual-coding approach.* New York: Oxford University Press.

Pajares, F. (1996). Self-efficacy beliefs in academic settings. *Review of Educational Research, 66,* 543–578.

Palermo, D. S. (1973). More about less: A study of language comprehension. *Journal of Verbal Learning and Verbal Behavior, 12,* 211–221.

Palincsar, A. S. (1986, April). *Interactive cognition to promote listening comprehension.* Paper presented at the annual meeting of the American Educational Research Association, San Francisco.

Palincsar, A. S. (2003). Ann L. Brown: Advancing a theoretical model of learning and instruction. In B. J. Zimmerman & D. H. Schunk (Eds.), *Educational psychology: A century of contributions* (pp. 459–475). Mahwah, NJ: Erlbaum.

Palincsar, A. S., & Brown, A. L. (1984). Reciprocal teaching of comprehension-fostering and comprehension-monitoring activities. *Cognition and Instruction, 1,* 117–175.

Palincsar, A. S., & Brown, A. L. (1989). Classroom dialogues to promote self-regulated comprehension. In J. Brophy (Ed.), *Advances in research on teaching* (Vol. 1). Greenwich, CT: JAI Press.

Palincsar, A. S., & Herrenkohl, L. R. (1999). Designing collaborative contexts: Lessons from three research programs. In A. M. O'Donnell & A. King (Eds.), *Cognitive perspectives on peer learning* (pp. 151–177). Mahwah, NJ: Erlbaum.

Paller, K. A. (2004). Electrical signals of memory and of the awareness of remembering. *Current Directions in Psychological Science, 13,* 49–55.

Pallock, L., & Surber, J. R. (1997, March). *Effect of topic frequency and importance on recall of text.* Paper presented at the annual meeting of the American Educational Research Association, Chicago.

Palmer, D. J., & Goetz, E. T. (1988). Selection and use of study strategies: The role of the studier's beliefs about self and strategies. In C. E. Weinstein, E. T. Goetz, & P. A. Alexander (Eds.), *Learning and study strategies: Issues in assessment, instruction, and evaluation.* San Diego, CA: Academic Press.

Pansky, A., & Koriat, A. (2004). The basic-level convergence effect in memory distortions. *Psychological Science, 15,* 52–59.

Papka, M., Ivry, R. B., & Woodruff-Pak, D. S. (1997). Eyeblink classical conditioning and awareness revisited. *Psychological Science, 8,* 404–408.

Paris, S. G. (1988). Models and metaphors of learning strategies. In C. E. Weinstein, E. T. Goetz, & P. A. Alexander (Eds.), *Learning and study strategies: Issues in assessment, instruction, and evaluation.* San Diego, CA: Academic Press.

Paris, S. G. (1990, April). Discussant's comments. In B. McCombs (Chair), *Theoretical perspectives on socialization and children's development of self-regulated learning.* Symposium presented at the annual meeting of the American Educational Research Association, Boston.

Paris, S. G., & Ayres, L. R. (1994). *Becoming reflective students and teachers with portfolios and authentic assessment*. Washington, DC: American Psychological Association.

Paris, S. G., & Byrnes, J. P. (1989). The constructivist approach to self-regulation and learning in the classroom. In B. J. Zimmerman & D. H. Schunk (Eds.), *Self-regulated learning and academic achievement: Theory, research, and practice*. New York: Springer-Verlag.

Paris, S. G., & Cunningham, A. E. (1996). Children becoming students. In D. C. Berliner & R. C. Calfee (Eds.), *Handbook of educational psychology*. New York: Macmillan.

Paris, S. G., Lawton, T. A., Turner, J. C., & Roth, J. L. (1991). A developmental perspective on standardized achievement testing. *Educational Researcher, 20*(5), 12–20, 40.

Paris, S. G., & Lindauer, B. K. (1976). The role of inference in children's comprehension and memory. *Cognitive Psychology, 8*, 217–227.

Paris, S. G., & Paris, A. H. (2001). Classroom applications of research on self-regulated learning. *Educational Psychologist, 36*, 89–101.

Paris, S. G., & Turner, J. C. (1994). Situated motivation. In P. R. Pintrich, D. R. Brown, & C. E. Weinstein (Eds.), *Student motivation, cognition, and learning: Essays in honor of Wilbert J. McKeachie*. Hillsdale, NJ: Erlbaum.

Paris, S. G., & Winograd, P. (1990). How metacognition can promote academic learning and instruction. In B. F. Jones & L. Idol (Eds.), *Dimensions of thinking and cognitive instruction*. Hillsdale, NJ: Erlbaum.

Park, O. (1984). Example comparison strategy versus attribute identification strategy in concept learning. *American Educational Research Journal, 21*, 145–162.

Parke, R. D. (1972). Some effects of punishment on children's behavior. In W. W. Hartup (Ed.), *The young child* (Vol. 2). Washington, DC: National Association for the Education of Young Children.

Parke, R. D. (1977). Some effects of punishment on children's behavior—revisited. In E. M. Hetherington & R. D. Parke (Eds.), *Contemporary readings in child psychology*. New York: McGraw-Hill.

Parke, R. D., & Deur, J. L. (1972). Schedule of punishment and inhibition of aggression in children. *Developmental Psychology, 7*, 266–269.

Parker, J. (1995). Age differences in source monitoring of performed and imagined actions on immediate and delayed tests. *Journal of Experimental Child Psychology, 60*, 84–101.

Parrish, J. M., Cataldo, M. F., Kolko, D. J., Neef, N. A., & Egel, A. L. (1986). Experimental analysis of response covariations among compliant and inappropriate behaviors. *Journal of Applied Behavior Analysis, 19*, 241–254.

Parsons, J. E., Adler, T. F., & Kaczala, C. M. (1982). Socialization of achievement attitudes and beliefs: Parental influences. *Child Development, 53*, 310–321.

Parsons, J. E., Kaczala, C. M., & Meece, J. L. (1982). Socialization of achievement attitudes and beliefs: Classroom influences. *Child Development, 53*, 322–339.

Pascarella, E. T., & Terenzini, P. T. (1991). *How college affects students: Findings and insights from twenty years of research*. San Francisco: Jossey-Bass.

Pashler, H. (1992). Attentional limitations in doing two tasks at the same time. *Current Directions in Psychological Science, 1*, 44–48.

Patrick, H., & Middleton, M. J. (2002). Turning the kaleidoscope: What we see when self-regulated learning is viewed with a qualitative lens. *Educational Psychologist, 37*, 27–39.

Patrick, H., & Pintrich, P. R. (2001). Conceptual change in teachers' intuitive conceptions of learning, motivation, and instruction: The role of motivational and epistemological beliefs. In B. Torff & R. J. Sternberg (Eds.), *Understanding and teaching the intuitive mind: Student and teacher learning* (pp. 117–143). Mahwah, NJ: Erlbaum.

Patrick, H., Anderman, L. H., & Ryan, A. M. (2002). Social motivation and the classroom social environment. In C. Midgley (Ed.), *Goals, goal structures, and patterns of adaptive learning* (pp. 85–108). Mahwah, NJ: Erlbaum.

Paus, T., Zijdenbos, A., Worsley, K., Collins, D. L., Blumenthal, J., Giedd, J. N., Rapoport, J. L., & Evans, A. C. (1999). Structural maturation of neural pathways in children and adolescents: In vivo study. *Science, 283*, 1908–1911.

Pavlov, I. P. (1927). *Conditioned reflexes* (G. V. Anrep, Trans.). London: Oxford University Press.

Payne, D. G., Neuschatz, J. S., Lampinen, J. M., & Lynn, S. J. (1997). Compelling memory illusions: The qualitative characteristics of false memories. *Current Directions in Psychological Science, 6*, 56–60.

Pea, R. D. (1993). Practices of distributed intelligence and designs for education. In G. Salomon (Ed.), *Distributed cognitions: Psychological and educational considerations*. Cambridge, England: Cambridge University Press.

Pear, J. J., & Crone-Todd, D. E. (1999). Personalized system of instruction in cyberspace. *Journal of Applied Behavior Analysis, 32*, 205–209.

Pearson, P. D., Hansen, J., & Gordon, C. (1979). The effect of background knowledge on young children's comprehension of explicit and implicit information. *Journal of Reading Behavior, 11*(3), 201–209.

Pekrun, R., Goetz, T., Titz, W., & Perry, R. P. (2002). Academic emotions in students' self-regulated learning and achievement: A program of qualitative and quantitative research. *Educational Psychologist, 37*, 91–105.

Pekrun, R., Goetz, T., Zirngibl, A., & Perry, R. (2003, April). *Students' academic emotions and their flow experiences, interest, motivation to learn, and engagement in academic tasks*. Paper presented at the annual meeting of the American Educational Research Association, Chicago.

Péladeau, N., Forget, J., & Gagné, F. (2003). Effect of paced and unpaced practice on skill application and retention: How much is enough? *American Educational Research Journal, 40*, 769–801.

Pellegrini, A. D., & Bjorklund, D. F. (1997). The role of recess in children's cognitive performance. *Educational Psychologist, 32*, 35–40.

Pellegrini, A. D., Huberty, P. D., & Jones, I. (1995). The effects of recess timing on children's playground and classroom behaviors. *American Educational Research Journal, 32*, 845–864.

Penfield, W. (1958). Some mechanisms of consciousness discovered during electrical stimulation of the brain. *Proceedings of the National Academy of Sciences, 44*, 51–66.

Penfield, W. (1959). Consciousness, memory, and man's conditioned reflexes. In K. Pribram (Ed.), *On the biology of learning*. New York: Harcourt, Brace, & World.

Penfield, W., & Roberts, L. (1959). *Speech and brain-mechanisms*. Princeton, NJ: Princeton University Press.

Perfect, T. J. (2002). When does eyewitness confidence predict performance? In T. J. Perfect & B. L. Schwartz (Eds.), *Applied metacognition* (pp. 95–120). Cambridge, England: Cambridge University Press.

Perfetti, C. A. (1983). Reading, vocabulary, and writing: Implications for computer-based instruction. In A. C. Wilkinson (Ed.), *Classroom computers and cognitive science*. New York: Academic Press.

Perfetti, C. A., Britt, M. A., Rouet, J.-F., Georgi, M. C., & Mason, R. A. (1994). How students use texts to learn and reason about historical uncertainty. In M. Carretero & J. F. Voss (Eds.), *Cognitive and instructional processes in history and the social sciences* (pp. 257–283). Mahwah, NJ: Erlbaum.

Perfetti, C. A., & Lesgold, A. M. (1979). Coding and comprehension in skilled reading and implications for reading instruction. In L. B. Resnick & P. Weaver (Eds.), *Theory and practice of early reading* (Vol. 1). Hillsdale, NJ: Erlbaum.

Perin, C. T. (1942). Behavior potentiality as a joint function of the amount of training and the degree of hunger at the time of extinction. *Journal of Experimental Psychology, 30*, 93–113.

Perin, C. T. (1943). A quantitative investigation of the delay-of-reinforcement gradient. *Journal of Experimental Psychology, 32*, 37–51.

Perkins, D. (1992). *Smart schools: From training memories to educating minds*. New York: Free Press/Macmillan.

Perkins, D. (1995). *Outsmarting IQ: The emerging science of learnable intelligence*. New York: Free Press.

Perkins, D., & Ritchhart, R. (2004). When is good thinking? In D. Y. Dai & R. J. Sternberg (Eds.), *Motivation, emotion, and cognition: Integrative perspectives on intellectual functioning and development* (pp. 351–384). Mahwah, NJ: Erlbaum.

Perkins, D. N., & Salomon, G. (1987). Transfer and teaching thinking. In D. N. Perkins, J. Lochhead, & J. Bishop (Eds.), *Thinking: The second international conference*. Hillsdale, NJ: Erlbaum.

Perkins, D. N., & Salomon, G. (1989). Are cognitive skills context-bound? *Educational Researcher, 18*(1), 16–25.

Perkins, D. N., & Simmons, R. (1988). Patterns of misunderstanding: An integrative model for science, math, and programming. *Review of Educational Research, 58,* 303–326.

Perlmutter, M., & Lange, G. A. (1978). A developmental analysis of recall-recognition distinctions. In P. A. Ornstein (Ed.), *Memory development in children.* Hillsdale, NJ: Erlbaum.

Perone, M., & Baron, A. (1980). Reinforcement of human observing behavior by a stimulus correlated with extinction or increased effort. *Journal of the Experimental Analysis of Behavior, 34,* 239–261.

Perry, A. C., & Fisher, W. W. (2001). Behavioral economic influences on treatments designed to decrease destructive behavior. *Journal of Applied Behavior Analysis, 34,* 211–215.

Perry, D. G., & Perry, L. C. (1983). Social learning, causal attribution, and moral internalization. In J. Bisanz, G. L. Bisanz, & R. Kail (Eds.), *Learning in children: Progress in cognitive development research.* New York: Springer-Verlag.

Perry, M. (1991). Learning and transfer: Instructional conditions and conceptual change. *Cognitive Development, 6,* 449–468.

Perry, N. E. (1998). Young children's self-regulated learning and contexts that support it. *Journal of Educational Psychology, 90,* 715–729.

Perry, N. E., VandeKamp, K. O., Mercer, L. K., & Nordby, C. J. (2002). Investigating teacher–student interactions that foster self-regulated learning. *Educational Psychologist, 37,* 5–15.

Perry, N. E., & Winne, P. H. (2004). Motivational messages from home and school: How do they influence young children's engagement in learning? In D. M. McNerney & S. Van Etten (Eds.), *Big theories revisited* (pp. 199–222). Greenwich, CT: Information Age.

Perry, R. P. (1985). Instructor expressivenss: Implications for improving teaching. In J. G. Donald & A. M. Sullivan (Eds.), *Using research to improve teaching* (pp. 35–49). San Francisco: Jossey-Bass.

Perry, W. G., Jr. (1968). *Forms of intellectual and ethical development in the college years.* Cambridge, MA: President and Fellows of Harvard College.

Peskin, J. (1998). Constructing meaning when reading poetry: An expert-novice study. *Cognition and Instruction, 16,* 235–263.

Peterson, C. (1988, August). *Explanatory style and academic performance.* Paper presented at the annual meeting of the American Psychological Association, Atlanta, GA.

Peterson, C. (1990). Explanatory style in the classroom and on the playing field. In S. Graham & V. S. Folkes (Eds.), *Attribution theory: Applications to achievement, mental health, and interpersonal conflict.* Hillsdale, NJ: Erlbaum.

Peterson, C., Maier, S. F., & Seligman, M. E. P. (1993). *Learned helplessness: A theory for the age of personal control.* New York: Oxford University Press.

Peterson, L. R., & Peterson, M. J. (1959). Short-term retention of individual items. *Journal of Experimental Psychology, 58,* 193–198.

Peterson, L. R., & Peterson, M. J. (1962). Minimal paired-associate learning. *Journal of Experimental Psychology, 63,* 521–527.

Peterson, M. A. (1994). Object recognition processes can and do operate before figure–ground organization. *Current Directions in Psychological Science, 3,* 105–111.

Peterson, M. A., & Gibson, B. S. (1994). Must figure–ground organization precede object recognition? An assumption in peril. *Psychological Science, 5,* 253–259.

Peterson, M. A., Kihlstrom, J. F., Rose, P. M., & Glisky, M. L. (1992). Mental images can be ambiguous: Reconstruals and reference-frame reversals. *Memory and Cognition, 20,* 107–123.

Peterson, P. L. (1992). Revising their thinking: Keisha Coleman and her third-grade mathematics class. In H. H. Marshall (Ed.), *Redefining student learning: Roots of educational change.* Norwood, NJ: Ablex.

Peterson, S. E. (1993). The effects of prior achievement and group outcome on attributions and affect in cooperative tasks. *Contemporary Educational Psychology, 18,* 479–485.

Petri, H. L. (1991). *Motivation: Theory, research, and applications* (3rd ed.). Belmont, CA: Wadsworth.

Pettito, A. L. (1985). Division of labor: Procedural learning in teacher-led small groups. *Cognition and Instruction, 2,* 233–270.

Peverly, S. T., Brobst, K. E., Graham, M., & Shaw, R. (2003). College adults are not good at self-regulation: A study on the relationship of self-regulation, note taking, and test taking. *Journal of Educational Psychology, 95,* 335–346.

Pezdek, K. (1977). Cross-modality semantic integration of sentence and picture memory. *Journal of Experimental Psychology: Human Learning and Memory, 3,* 515–524.

Pezdek, K., & Banks, W. P. (Eds.) (1996). *The recovered memory/false memory debate.* San Diego, CA: Academic Press.

Pezdek, K., Finger, K., & Hodge, D. (1997). Planting false childhood memories: The role of event plausibility. *Psychological Science, 8,* 437–441.

Pfeiffer, K., Feinberg, G., & Gelber, S. (1987). Teaching productive problem solving attitudes. In D. Berger, K. Pezdek, & W. Banks (Eds.), *Applications in cognitive psychology: Problem solving education and computing.* Hillsdale, NJ: Erlbaum.

Pfiffner, L. J., & Barkley, R. A. (1998). Treatment of ADHD in school settings. In R. A. Barkley, *Attention-deficit hyperactivy disorder: A handbook for diagnosis and treatment* (2nd ed., pp. 458–490). New York: Guilford Press.

Pfiffner, L. J., & O'Leary, S. G. (1987). The efficacy of all-positive management as a function of the prior use of negative consequences. *Journal of Applied Behavior Analysis, 20,* 265–271.

Pfiffner, L. J., & O'Leary, S. G. (1993). School-based psychological treatments. In J. L. Matson (Ed.), *Handbook of hyperactivity in children* (pp. 234–255). Boston: Allyn & Bacon.

Pfiffner, L. J., Rosén, L. A., & O'Leary, S. G. (1985). The efficacy of an all-positive approach to classroom management. *Journal of Applied Behavior Analysis, 18,* 257–261.

Phelan, P., Yu, H. C., & Davidson, A. L. (1994). Navigating the psychosocial pressures of adolescence: The voices and experiences of high school youth. *American Educational Research Journal, 31,* 415–447.

Phelps, E. A., Ling, S., & Carrasco, M. (2006). Emotion facilitates perception and potentiates the perceptual benefits of attention. *Psychological Science, 17,* 292–299.

Phillips, B. N., Pitcher, G. D., Worsham, M. E., & Miller, S. C. (1980). Test anxiety and the school environment. In I. G. Sarason (Ed.), *Test anxiety: Theory, research, and applications.* Hillsdale, NJ: Erlbaum.

Phillips, D. A., & Zimmerman, M. (1990). The developmental course of perceived competence and incompetence among competent children. In R. J. Sternberg & J. Kolligian (Eds.), *Competence considered.* New Haven, CT: Yale University Press.

Phillips, E. L., Phillips, E. A., Fixsen, D. L., & Wolf, M. M. (1971). Achievement place: Modification of the behaviors of predelinquent boys within a token economy. *Journal of Applied Behavior Analysis, 4,* 45–59.

Phye, G. D. (1997). Learning and remembering: The basis for personal knowledge construction. In G. D. Phye (Ed.), *Handbook of academic learning: Construction of knowledge.* San Diego, CA: Academic Press.

Phye, G. D. (2001). Problem-solving instruction and problem-solving transfer: The correspondence issue. *Journal of Educational Psychology, 93,* 571–578.

Piaget, J. (1928). *Judgment and reasoning in the child* (M. Warden, Trans.). New York: Harcourt, Brace.

Piaget, J. (1952a). *The child's conception of number* (C. Gattegno & F. M. Hodgson, Trans.). London: Routledge & Kegan Paul.

Piaget, J. (1952b). *The origins of intelligence in children* (M. Cook, Trans.). New York: W. W. Norton.

Piaget, J. (1959). *The language and thought of the child* (3rd ed.) (M. Gabain, Trans.). New York: Humanities Press.

Piaget, J. (1970). Piaget's theory. In P. H. Mussen (Ed.), *Carmichael's manual of psychology.* New York: Wiley.

Piaget, J. (1971). *Psychology and epistemology: Towards a theory of knowledge* (A. Rosin, Trans.). New York: Viking.

Piaget, J. (1972). *The principles of genetic epistemology* (W. Mays, Trans.). New York: Basic Books.

Piaget, J. (1980). *Adaptation and intelligence: Organic selection and phenocopy* (S. Eames, Trans.). Chicago: University of Chicago Press.

Piaget, J., & Inhelder, B. (1969). *The psychology of the child* (H. Weaver, Trans.). New York: Basic Books.

Pianko, S. (1979). A description of the composing processes of college freshmen writers. *Research in the Teaching of English, 13,* 5–22.

Piazza, C. C., Bowman, L. G., Contrucci, S. A., Delia, M. D., Adelinis, J. D., & Goh, H.-L.

(1999). An evaluation of the properties of attention as reinforcement for destructive and appropriate behavior. *Journal of Applied Behavior Analysis, 32,* 437–449.

Pichert, J. W., & Anderson, R. C. (1977). Taking different perspectives on a story. *Journal of Educational Psychology, 69,* 309–315.

Piersel, W. C. (1987). Basic skills education. In C. A. Maher & S. G. Forman (Eds.), *A behavioral approach to education of children and youth.* Hillsdale, NJ: Erlbaum.

Pigott, H. E., Fantuzzo, J. W., & Clement, P. W. (1986). The effects of reciprocal peer tutoring and group contingencies on the academic performance of elementary school children. *Journal of Applied Behavior Analysis, 19,* 93–98.

Piliavin, I. M., Piliavin, J. A., & Rodin, J. (1975). Costs, diffusion, and the stigmatized victim. *Journal of Personality and Social Psychology, 32,* 429–438.

Piliavin, J. A., Dovidio, J. F., Gaertner, S. L., & Clark, R. D., III (1981). Responsive bystanders: The process of intervention. In J. Grzelak & V. Derlega (Eds.), *Living with other people: Theory and research on cooperation and helping.* New York: Academic Press.

Pillemer, D. B., & White, S. H. (1989). Childhood events recalled by children and adults. In H. W. Reese (Ed.), *Advances in child development and behavior* (Vol. 21). New York: Academic Press.

Pine, K. J., & Messer, D. J. (2000). The effect of explaining another's actions on children's implicit theories of balance. *Cognition and Instruction, 18,* 35–51.

Pinker, S. (1993). Rules of language. In P. Bloom (Ed.), *Language acquisition: Core readings.* Cambridge, MA: MIT Press.

Pinker, S., & Prince, A. (1988). On language and connectionism: Analysis of a parallel distributed processing model of language acquisition. *Cognition, 28,* 73–193.

Pinkston, E. M., Reese, N. M., LeBlanc, J. M., & Baer, D. M. (1973). Independent control of a preschool child's aggression and peer interaction by contingent teacher attention. *Journal of Applied Behavior Analysis, 6,* 223–224.

Pintrich, P. R. (2000). Multiple goals, multiple pathways: The role of goal orientation in learning and achievement. *Journal of Educational Psychology, 92,* 544–555.

Pintrich, P. R. (2003). A motivational science perspective on the role of student motivation in learning and teaching contexts. *Journal of Educational Psychology, 95,* 667–686.

Pintrich, P. R., & De Groot, E. V. (1990). Motivational and self-regulated learning components of classroom academic performance. *Journal of Educational Psychology, 82,* 33–40.

Pintrich, P. R., Marx, R. W., & Boyle, R. A. (1993). Beyond cold conceptual change: The role of motivational beliefs and classroom contextual factors in the process of conceptual change. *Review of Educational Research, 63,* 167–199.

Pintrich, P. R., & Schrauben, B. (1992). Students' motivational beliefs and their cognitive engagement in academic tasks. In D. Schunk &

J. Meece (Eds.), *Students' perceptions in the classroom: Causes and consequences.* Hillsdale, NJ: Erlbaum.

Pintrich, P. R., & Schunk, D. H. (2002). *Motivation in education: Theory, research, and applications* (2nd ed.). Upper Saddle River, NJ: Merrill/Prentice Hall.

Piontkowski, D., & Calfee, R. (1979). Attention in the classroom. In G. A. Hale & M. Lewis (Eds.), *Attention and cognitive development.* New York: Plenum Press.

Piotrowski, J., & Reason, R. (2000). The national literacy strategy and dyslexia: A comparison of teaching methods and materials. *Support for Learning, 15*(2), 51–57.

Plumert, J. M. (1994). Flexibility in children's use of spatial and categorical organizational strategies in recall. *Developmental Psychology, 30,* 738–747.

Plummer, S., Baer, D. M., & LeBlanc, J. M. (1977). Functional considerations in the use of procedural time out and an effective alternative. *Journal of Applied Behavior Analysis, 10,* 689–706.

Plunkett, K. (1996). *Connectionism and development: Neural networks and the study of change.* New York: Oxford University Press.

Poche, C., Yoder, P., & Miltenberger, R. (1988). Teaching self-protection to children using television techniques. *Journal of Applied Behavior Analysis, 21,* 253–261.

Polman, J. L. (2004). Dialogic activity structures for project based learning environments. *Cognition and Instruction, 22,* 431–466.

Polya, G. (1957). *How to solve it.* Garden City, NY: Doubleday.

Pomerantz, E. M., & Saxon, J. L. (2001). Conceptions of ability as stable and self-evaluative processes: A longitudinal examination. *Child Development, 72,* 152–173.

Pontecorvo, C. (1993). Social interaction in the acquisition of knowledge. *Educational Psychology Review, 5,* 293–310.

Poole, D. (1994). Routine testing practices and the linguistic construction of knowledge. *Cognition and Instruction, 12,* 125–150.

Popham, W. J. (1995). *Classroom assessment: What teachers need to know.* Boston: Allyn & Bacon.

Porat, D. A. (2004). *It's not written here, but this is what happened:* Students' cultural comprehension of textbook narratives on the Israeli-Arab conflict. *American Educational Research Journal, 41,* 963–996.

Porter, A. (1989). A curriculum out of balance: The case of elementary school mathematics. *Educational Researcher, 18*(5), 9–15.

Posner, G. J., & Rudnitsky, A. N. (1986). *Course design: A guide to curriculum development for teachers* (3rd ed.). New York: Longman.

Posner, G. J., Strike, K. A., Hewson, P. W., & Gertzog, W. A. (1982). Accommodation of a scientific conception: Toward a theory of conceptual change. *Science Education, 66,* 211–227.

Posner, M. I., Goldsmith, R., & Welton, K. E., Jr. (1967). Perceived distance and the classification of distorted patterns. *Journal of Experimental Psychology, 73,* 28–38.

Posner, M. I., & Keele, S. W. (1968). On the genesis of abstract ideas. *Journal of Experimental Psychology, 77,* 353–363.

Postman, L. (1964). Short-term memory and incidental learning. In A. W. Melton (Ed.), *Categories of human learning.* New York: Academic Press.

Postman, L., & Phillips, L. (1965). Short-term temporal changes in free recall. *Quarterly Journal of Experimental Psychology, 17,* 132–138.

Postman, L., & Underwood, B. J. (1973). Critical issues in interference theory. *Memory and Cognition, 1,* 19–40.

Poulin-Dubois, D. (1999). Infants' distinction between animate and inanimate objects: The origins of naïve psychology. In P. Rochat (Ed.), *Early social cognition* (pp. 257–280). Mahwah, NJ: Erlbaum.

Powell, S., & Nelson, B. (1997). Effects of choosing academic assignments on a study with attention deficit hyperactivity disorder. *Journal of Applied Behavior Analysis, 30,* 181–183.

Prawat, R. S. (1989). Promoting access to knowledge, strategy, and disposition in students: A research synthesis. *Review of Educational Research, 59,* 1–41.

Prawat, R. S. (1992). From individual differences to learning communities—our changing focus. *Educational Leadership, 49*(7), 9–13.

Prawat, R. S. (1996). Constructivisms, modern and postmodern. *Educational Psychologist, 31,* 215–225.

Premack, D. (1959). Toward empirical behavior laws: I. Positive reinforcement. *Psychological Review, 66,* 219–233.

Premack, D. (1963). Rate differential reinforcement in monkey manipulation. *Journal of Experimental Analysis of Behavior, 6,* 81–89.

Prentice, N. M. (1972). The influence of live and symbolic modeling on prompting moral judgments of adolescent delinquents. *Journal of Abnormal Psychology, 80,* 157–161.

Pressley, M. (1977). Imagery and children's learning: Putting the picture in developmental perspective. *Review of Educational Research, 47,* 586–622.

Pressley, M. (1982). Elaboration and memory development. *Child Development, 53,* 296–309.

Pressley, M., & Hilden, K. (2006). Cognitive strategies: Production deficiencies and successful strategy instruction everywhere. In W. Damon & R. M. Lerner (Series Eds.), D. Kuhn, & R. Siegler (Vol. Eds.), *Handbook of child psychology: Vol. 2. Cognition, perception, and language* (6th ed.). New York: Wiley.

Pressley, M., Borkowski, J. G., & Schneider, W. (1987). Cognitive strategies: Good strategy users coordinate metacognition and knowledge. In R. Vasta & G. Whitehurst (Eds.), *Annals of child development* (Vol. 5). New York: JAI Press.

Pressley, M., El-Dinary, P. B., Marks, M. B., Brown, R., & Stein, S. (1992). Good strategy instruction is motivating and interesting. In K. A. Renninger, S. Hidi, & A. Krapp (Eds.), *The role of interest in learning and development.* Hillsdale, NJ: Erlbaum.

Pressley, M., Harris, K. R., & Marks, M. B. (1992). But good strategy instructors are constructivists! *Educational Psychology Review, 4,* 3–31.

Pressley, M., Johnson, C. J., Symons, S., McGoldrick, J., & Kurita, J. (1989). Strategies that improve children's memory and comprehension of what is read. *Elementary School Journal, 90,* 3–32.

Pressley, M., Levin, J. R., & Delaney, H. D. (1982). The mnemonic keyword method. *Review of Educational Research, 52,* 61–91.

Pressley, M., Levin, J. R., & Ghatala, E. S. (1984). Memory strategy monitoring in adults and children. *Journal of Verbal Learning and Verbal Behavior, 23,* 270–288.

Pressley, M., Levin, J. R., & Ghatala, E. S. (1988). Strategy-comparison opportunities promote long-term strategy use. *Contemporary Educational Psychology, 13,* 157–168.

Pressley, M. (with McCormick, C. B.) (1995). *Advanced educational psychology: For educators, researchers, and policymakers.* New York: HarperCollins.

Pressley, M., Ross, K. A., Levin, J. R., & Ghatala, E. S. (1984). The role of strategy utility knowledge in children's strategy decision making. *Journal of Experimental Child Psychology, 38,* 491–504.

Pressley, M., Snyder, B. L., & Cariglia-Bull, T. (1987). How can good strategy use be taught to children? Evaluation of six alternative approaches. In S. M. Cormier & J. D. Hagman (Eds.), *Transfer of learning: Contemporary research and applications.* San Diego, CA: Academic Press.

Pressley, M., Wharton-McDonald, R., Rankin, J., El-Dinary, P. B., Brown, R., Afflerbach, P., Mistretta, J., & Yokoi, L. (1997). Elementary reading instruction. In G. D. Phye (Ed.), *Handbook of academic learning: Construction of knowledge.* San Diego, CA: Academic Press.

Pressley, M., Woloshyn, V., Lysynchuk, L. M., Martin, V., Wood, E., & Willoughby, T. (1990). A primer of research on cognitive strategy instruction: The important issues and how to address them. *Educational Psychology Review, 2,* 1–58.

Pressley, M., Yokoi, L., Van Meter, P., Van Etten, S., & Freebern, G. (1997). Some of the reasons why preparing for exams is so hard: What can be done to make it easier? *Educational Psychology Review, 9,* 1–38.

Pretz, J. E., Naples, A. J., & Sternberg, R. J. (2003). Recognizing, defining, and representing problems. In J. E. Davidson & R. J. Sternberg (Eds.), *The psychology of problem solving* (pp. 3–30). Cambridge, England: Cambridge University Press.

Pribram, K. H. (1997). The work in working memory: Implications for development. In N. A. Krasnegor, G. R. Lyon, & P. S. Goldman-Rakic (Eds.), *Development of the prefrontal cortex: Evolution, neurobiology, and behavior* (pp. 359–378). Baltimore: Brookes.

Price-Williams, D. R., Gordon, W., & Ramirez, M. (1969). Skill and conservation. *Developmental Psychology, 1,* 769.

Principe, G. F., Kanaya, T., Ceci, S. J., & Singh, M. (2006). Believing is seeing: How rumors can engender false memories in preschoolers. *Psychological Science, 17,* 243–248.

Proctor, R. W., & Dutta, A. (1995). *Skill acquisition and human performance.* Thousand Oaks, CA: Sage.

Pugh, K. J. (2002). Teaching for transformative experiences in science: An investigation of the effectiveness of two instructional elements. *Teachers College Record, 104,* 1101–1137.

Pugh, K. J., & Bergin, D. A. (2005). The effect of schooling on students' out-of-school experience. *Educational Researcher, 34*(9), 15–23.

Pugh, K. J., & Bergin, D. A. (2006). Motivational influences on transfer. *Educational Researcher, 41,* 147–160.

Pugh, K. J., Linnenbrink, E. A., Kelly, K. L., Manzey, C., & Stewart, V. C. (2006, April). *Motivation, learning, and transformative experience: A study of deep engagement in science.* Paper presented at the annual meeting of the American Educational Research Association, San Francisco.

Pulos, S., & Linn, M. C. (1981). Generality of the controlling variables scheme in early adolescence. *Journal of Early Adolescence, 1,* 26–37.

Puntambekar, S., & Hübscher, R. (2005). Tools for scaffolding students in a complex learning environment: What have we gained and what have we missed? *Educational Psychologist, 40,* 1–12.

Purdie, N., & Hattie, J. (1996). Cultural differences in the use of strategies for self-regulated learning. *American Educational Research Journal, 33,* 845–871.

Qian, G., & Alvermann, D. (1995). Role of epistemological beliefs and learned helplessness in secondary school students' learning science concepts from text. *Journal of Educational Psychology, 87,* 282–292.

Qian, G., & Pan, J. (2002). A comparison of epistemological beliefs and learning from science text between American and Chinese high school students. In B. K. Hofer & P. R. Pintrich (Eds.), *Personal epistemology: The psychology of beliefs about knowledge and knowing* (pp. 365–385). Mahwah, NJ: Erlbaum.

Qin, Z., Johnson, D. W., & Johnson, R. T. (1995). Cooperative versus competitive efforts and problem solving. *Review of Educational Research, 65,* 129–143.

Quartz, S. R., & Sejnowski, T. J. (1997). The neural basis of cognitive development: A constructivist manifesto. *Behavioral and Brain Sciences, 20,* 537–596.

Quinn, P. C. (2002). Category representation in young infants. *Current Directions in Psychological Science, 11,* 66–70.

Quinn, P. C. (2003). Concepts are not just for objects: Categorization of spatial relation information by young infants. In D. H. Rakison & L. M. Oakes (Eds.), *Early category and concept development: Making sense of the blooming, buzzing confusion.* Oxford, England: Oxford University Press.

Quinn, P. C., Bhatt, R. S., Brush, D., Grimes, A., & Sharpnack, H. (2002). Development of form similarity as a Gestalt grouping principles in infancy. *Psychological Science, 13,* 320–328.

Quintana, C., Zhang, M., & Krajcik, J. (2005). A framework for supporting metacognitive aspects of online inquiry through software-based scaffolding. *Educational Psychologist, 40,* 235–244.

Rabinowitz, M., & Glaser, R. (1985). Cognitive structure and process in highly competent performance. In F. D. Horowitz & M. O'Brien (Eds.), *The gifted and the talented: Developmental perspectives.* Washington, DC: American Psychological Association.

Rachlin, H. (1991). *Introduction to modern behaviorism* (3rd ed.). New York: W. H. Freeman.

Rachlin, H. (1995) The value of temporal patterns in behavior. *Current Directions in Psychological Science, 4,* 188–192.

Radebaugh, M. R. (1985). Children's perceptions of their spelling strategies. *The Reading Teacher, 38,* 532–536.

Radke-Yarrow, M., Zahn-Waxler, C., & Chapman, M. (1983). Children's prosocial dispositions and behavior. In E. M. Hetherington (Ed.), *Handbook of child psychology: Vol. 4. Socialization, personality, and social development.* New York: Wiley.

Radziszewska, B., & Rogoff, B. (1988). Influence of adult and peer collaborators on children's planning skills. *Developmental Psychology, 24,* 840–848.

Radziszewska, B., & Rogoff, B. (1991). Children's guided participation in planning imaginary errands with skilled adult or peer partners. *Developmental Psychology, 27,* 381–389.

Rahm, J., & Downey, J. (2002). "A scientist can be anyone!": Oral histories of scientists can make "real science" accessible to youth. *Clearing House, 75,* 253–257.

Raine, A., Reynolds, C., & Venables, P. H. (2002). Stimulation seeking and intelligence: A prospective longitudinal study. *Journal of Personality and Social Psychology, 82,* 663–674.

Rakison, D. H. (2003). Parts, motion, and the development of the animate–inanimate distinction in infancy. In D. H. Rakison & L. M. Oakes (Eds.), *Early category and concept development: Making sense of the blooming, buzzing confusion* (pp. 159–192). Oxford, England: Oxford University Press.

Rakow, S. J. (1984). What's happening in elementary science: A national assessment. *Science and Children, 21*(4), 39–40.

Ramey, C. T. (1992). High-risk children and IQ: Altering intergenerational patterns. *Intelligence, 16,* 239–256.

Rapport, M. D., & Bostow, D. E. (1976). The effects of access to special activities on performance in four categories of academic tasks with third-grade students. *Journal of Applied Behavior Analysis, 9,* 372.

Rapport, M. D., Murphy, H. A., & Bailey, J. S. (1982). Ritalin vs. response cost in the control of hyperactive children: A within-subject comparison. *Journal of Applied Behavior Analysis, 15,* 205–216.

Ratcliff, R. (1990). Connectionist models of recognition memory: Constraints imposed by learning and forgetting functions. *Psychological Review, 97,* 285–308.

Ratcliff, R. A., & McKoon, G. (1981). Does activation really spread? *Psychological Review, 88,* 454–462.

Ratner, H. H. (1984). Memory demands and the development of young children's memory. *Child Development, 55,* 2173–2191.

Raudenbush, S. W. (1984). Magnitude of teacher expectancy effects on pupil IQ as a function of credibility induction: A synthesis of findings from 18 experiments. *Journal of Educational Psychology, 76,* 85–97.

Raudenbush, S. W., Rowan, B., & Cheong, Y. F. (1993). Higher order instructional goals in secondary schools: Class, teacher, and school influences. *American Educational Research Journal, 30,* 523–553.

Rawson, K. A., & Kintsch, W. (2005). Rereading effects depend on time of test. *Journal of Educational Psychology, 97,* 70–80.

Rawsthorne, L. J., & Elliot, A. J. (1999). Achievement goals and intrinsic motivation: A meta-analytic review. *Personality and Social Psychology Review, 3,* 326–344.

Rayner, K., Foorman, B. R., Perfetti, C. A., Pesetsky, D., & Seidenberg, M. S. (2001). How psychological science informs the teaching of reading. *Psychological Science in the Public Interest, 2,* 31–74.

Raynor, J. O. (1981). Future orientation and achievement motivation: Toward a theory of personality functioning and change. In G. Ydewalle & W. Lens (Eds.), *Cognition in human motivation and learning* (pp. 199–231). Hillsdale, NJ: Erlbaum.

Rayport, S. G. (1992). Cellular and molecular biology of the neuron. In S. C. Yudofsky & R. E. Hales (Eds.), *The American psychiatric press textbook of neuropsychiatry* (2nd ed., pp. 3–28). Washington, DC: American Psychiatric Press.

Reason, J., & Mycielska, K. (1982). *Absentminded? The psychology of mental lapses and everyday errors.* Upper Saddle River, NJ: Prentice Hall.

Reber, A. S. (1993). *Implicit learning and tacit knowledge: An essay on the cognitive unconscious.* New York: Oxford University Press.

Reber, A. S., & Allen, R. (1978). Analogical and abstraction strategies in synthetic grammar learning: A functionalist interpretation. *Cognition, 6,* 189–221.

Reber, A. S., Kassin, S. M., Lewis, S., & Cantor, B. (1980). On the relationship between implicit and explicit modes in the learning of a complex rule structure. *Journal of Experimental Psychology: Human Learning and Memory, 6,* 492–502.

Reder, L. M. (1982). Plausibility judgment versus fact retrieval: Alternative strategies for sentence verification. *Psychological Review, 89,* 250–280.

Reder, L. M., & Ross, B. H. (1983). Integrated knowledge in different tasks: Positive and negative fan effects. *Journal of Experimental Psychology: Human Learning and Memory, 8,* 55–72.

Redfield, D. L., & Rousseau, E. W. (1981). A meta-analysis of experimental research on teacher questioning behavior. *Review of Educational Research, 51,* 237–245.

Reed, S. (1974). Structural descriptions and the limitations of visual images. *Memory and Cognition, 2,* 329–336.

Reed, S. K. (1993). A schema-based theory of transfer. In D. K. Detterman & R. J. Sternberg (Eds.), *Transfer on trial: Intelligence, cognition, and instruction.* Norwood, NJ: Ablex.

Reed, S. K., Ernst, G. W., & Banerji, R. (1974). The role of analogy in transfer between similar problem states. *Cognitive Psychology, 6,* 436–450.

Reese, H. W., & Lipsitt, L. P. (1970). *Experimental child psychology.* New York: Academic Press.

Reesink, C. J. (1984). Metric munchies. *Science and Children, 21*(7), 16–17.

Reeve, J. (2006). Extrinsic rewards and inner motivation. In C. M. Evertson & C. S. Weinstein (Eds.), *Handbook of classroom management: Research, practice, and contemporary issues* (pp. 645–664.). Mahwah, NJ: Erlbaum.

Reeve, J., Deci, E. L., & Ryan, R. M. (2004). Self-determination theory: A dialectical framework for understanding sociocultural influences on student motivation. In D. M. McNerney & S. Van Etten (Eds.), *Big theories revisited* (pp. 31–60). Greenwich, CT: Information Age.

Reeve, J., Nix, G., & Hamm, D. (2003). Testing models of the experience of self-determination in intrinsic motivation and the conundrum of choice. *Journal of Educational Psychology, 95,* 375–392.

Reid, M. K., & Borkowski, J. G. (1987). Causal attributions of hyperactive children: Implications for training strategies and self-control. *Journal of Educational Psychology, 79,* 296–307.

Reimann, P., & Schult, T. J. (1996). Turning examples into cases: Acquiring knowledge structures for analogical problem solving. *Educational Psychologist, 31,* 123–132.

Reiner, M., Slotta, J. D., Chi, M. T. H., & Resnick, L. B. (2000). Naïve physics reasoning: A commitment to substance-based conceptions. *Cognition and Instruction, 18,* 1–34.

Reisberg, D. (Ed.) (1992). *Auditory imagery.* Hillsdale, NJ: Erlbaum.

Reisberg, D. (1997). *Cognition: Exploring the science of the mind.* New York: W. W. Norton.

Reiser, R. A., & Sullivan, H. J. (1977). Effects of self-pacing and instructor-pacing in a PSI course. *Journal of Educational Research, 71,* 8–12.

Reissland, N. (1988). Neonatal imitation in the first hour of life: Observations in rural Nepal. *Developmental Psychology, 24,* 464–469.

Reiter, S. N. (1994). Teaching dialogically: Its relationship to critical thinking in college students. In P. R. Pintrich, D. R. Brown, & C. E. Weinstein (Eds.), *Student motivation, cognition, and learning: Essays in honor of Wilbert J. McKeachie.* Hillsdale, NJ: Erlbaum.

Reitman, J. S. (1974). Without surreptitious rehearsal, information in short-term memory decays. *Journal of Verbal Learning and Verbal Behavior, 13,* 365–377.

Reitman, W. R. (1964). Heuristic decision procedures, open constraints, and the structure of ill-defined problems. In M. W. Shelley & G. L. Bryan (Eds.), *Human judgments and optimality.* New York: Wiley.

Renkl, A., & Atkinson, R. K. (2003). Structuring the transition from example study to problem solving in cognitive skill acquisition: A cognitive load perspective. *Educational Psychologist, 38,* 15–22.

Renkl, A., Mandl, H., & Gruber, H. (1996). Inert knowledge: Analyses and remedies. *Educational Psychologist, 31,* 115–121.

Renninger, K. A., Hidi, S., & Krapp, A. (Eds.) (1992). *The role of interest in learning and development.* Hillsdale, NJ: Erlbaum.

Repp, A. C., Barton, L., & Brulle, A. (1983). A comparison of two procedures for programming the differential reinforcement of other behavior. *Journal of Applied Behavior Analysis, 16,* 435–445.

Repp, A. C., & Deitz, S. M. (1974). Reducing aggressive and self-injurious behavior of institutionalized retarded children through reinforcement of other behaviors. *Journal of Applied Behavior Analysis, 7,* 313–325.

Rescorla, R. A. (1967). Pavlovian conditioning and its proper control procedures. *Psychological Review, 74,* 71–80.

Rescorla, R. A. (1987). A Pavlovian analysis of goal-directed behavior. *American Psychologist, 42,* 119–129.

Rescorla, R. A. (1988). Pavlovian conditioning: It's not what you think it is. *American Psychologist, 43,* 151–160.

Resnick, D. P., & Resnick, L. B. (1996). Performance assessment and the multiple functions of educational measurement. In M. B. Kane & R. Mitchell (Eds.), *Implementing performance assessment: Promises, problems, and challenges* (pp. 23–38). Mahwah, NJ: Erlbaum.

Resnick, L. B. (1987). *Education and learning to think.* Washington, DC: National Academy Press.

Resnick, L. B. (1989). Developing mathematical knowledge. *American Psychologist, 44,* 162–169.

Resnick, L. B., Bill, V. L., Lesgold, S. B., & Leer, M. N. (1991). Thinking in arithmetic class. In B. Means, C. Chelemer, & M. S. Knapp (Eds.), *Teaching advanced skills to at-risk students.* San Francisco: Jossey-Bass.

Resnick, L. B., & Johnson, A. (1988). Intelligent machines for intelligent people: Cognitive theory and the future of computer-assisted learning. In R. S. Nickerson & P. P. Zodhiates (Eds.), *Technology in education: Looking toward 2020.* Hillsdale, NJ: Erlbaum.

Reyna, C. (2000). Lazy, dumb, or industrious: When stereotypes convey attribution information in the classroom. *Educational Psychology Review, 12,* 85–110.

Reyna, C., & Weiner, B. (2001). Justice and utility in the classroom: An attributional analysis of the goals of teachers' punishment and intervention strategies. *Journal of Educational Psychology, 93,* 309–319.

Reyna, V. F. (1995). Interference effects in memory and reasoning: A fuzzy-trace theory analysis. In F. N. Dempster & C. J. Brainerd (Eds.), *Interference and inhibition in cognition.* San Diego, CA: Academic Press.

Reynolds, G. S. (1975). *A primer of operant conditioning* (Rev. ed.). Glenview, IL: Scott, Foresman.

Reynolds, R. E., & Shirey, L. L. (1988). The role of attention in studying and learning. In C. E. Weinstein, E. T. Goetz, & P. A. Alexander (Eds.), *Learning and study strategies: Issues in assessment, instruction, and evaluation.* San Diego, CA: Academic Press.

Reynolds, R. E., Sinatra, G. M., & Jetton, T. L. (1996). Views of knowledge acquisition and representation: A continuum from experience centered to mind centered. *Educational Psychologist, 31,* 93–104.

Reynolds, R. E., Taylor, M. A., Steffensen, M. S., Shirey, L. L., & Anderson, R. C. (1982). Cultural schemata and reading comprehension. *Reading Research Quarterly, 17,* 353–366.

Richards, J. M., & Gross, J. J. (2000). Emotion regulation and memory: The cognitive costs of keeping one's cool. *Journal of Personality and Social Psychology, 79,* 410–424.

Riding, R. J., & Calvey, I. (1981). The assessment of verbal-imagery learning styles and their effect on the recall of concrete and abstract prose passages by 11-year-old children. *British Journal of Psychology, 72,* 59–64.

Riggs, J. M. (1992). Self-handicapping and achievement. In A. K. Boggiano & T. S. Pittman (Eds.), *Achievement and motivation: A social-developmental perspective.* Cambridge, England: Cambridge University Press.

Rimm, D. C., & Masters, J. C. (1974). *Behavior therapy: Techniques and empirical findings.* New York: Academic Press.

Rinehart, S. D., Stahl, S. A., & Erickson, L. G. (1986). Some effects of summarization training on reading and studying. *Reading Research Quarterly, 21,* 422–438.

Ringdahl, J. E., Vollmer, T. R., Borrero, J. C., & Connell, J. E. (2001). Fixed-time schedule effects as a function of baseline reinforcement rate. *Journal of Applied Behavior Analysis, 34,* 1–15.

Ringdahl, J. E., Winborn, L. C., Andelman, M. S., & Kitsukawa, K. (2002). The effects of noncontingently available alternative stimuli on functional analysis outcomes. *Journal of Applied Behavior Analysis, 35,* 407–410.

Rips, L. J., Shoben, E. J., & Smith, E. E. (1973). Semantic distance and the verification of semantic relations. *Journal of Verbal Learning and Verbal Behavior, 12,* 1–20.

Rittle-Johnson, B., & Alibali, M. W. (1999). Conceptual and procedural knowledge of mathematics: Does one lead to the other? *Journal of Educational Psychology, 91,* 175–189.

Rittle-Johnson, B., & Koedinger, K. R. (2005). Designing knowledge scaffolds to support mathematical problem solving. *Cognition and Instruction, 23,* 313–349.

Rittle-Johnson, B., Siegler, R. S., & Alibali, M. W. (2001). Developing conceptual understanding and procedural skill in mathematics: An iterative process. *Journal of Educational Psychology, 93,* 346–362.

Ritts, V., Patterson, M. L., & Tubbs, M. E. (1992). Expectations, impressions, and judgments of physically attractive students: A review. *Review of Educational Research, 62,* 413–426.

Roberts, G. C., Treasure, D. C., & Kavussanu, M. (1997). Motivation in physical activity

contexts: An achievement goal perspective. *Advances in Motivation and Achievement, 10,* 413–447.

Roberts, K. T., & Ehri, L. C. (1983). Effects of two types of letter rehearsal on word memory in skilled and less skilled beginning readers. *Contemporary Educational Psychology, 8,* 375–390.

Roberts, T., & Kraft, R. (1987). Reading comprehension performance and laterality: Evidence for concurrent validity of dichotic, haptic, and EEG laterality measures. *Neuropsychologia, 25,* 817–828.

Robertson, J. S. (2000). Is attribution training a worthwhile classroom intervention for K–12 students with learning difficulties? *Educational Psychology Review, 12,* 111–134.

Robins, R. W., Gosling, S. D., & Craik, K. H. (1999). An empirical analysis of trends in psychology. *American Psychologist, 54,* pp. 117–128.

Robinson, F. P. (1961). *Effective study.* New York: Harper & Row.

Robinson, N. M., & Robinson, H. B. (1961). A method for the study of instrumental avoidance conditioning with children. *Journal of Comparative and Physiological Psychology, 54,* 20–23.

Robinson, E.J., & Whitcombe, E. L. (2003). Children's suggestibility in relation to their understanding about sources of knowledge. *Child Development, 74,* 48–62.

Robinson, S. L., & Griesemer, S. M. R. (2006). Helping individual students with problem behavior. In C. M. Evertson & C. S. Weinstein (Eds.), *Handbook of classroom management: Research, practice, and contemporary issues* (pp. 787–802). Mahwah, NJ: Erlbaum.

Robinson, T. R., Smith, S. W., Miller, M. D., & Brownell, M. T. (1999). Cognitive behavior modification of hyperactivity–impulsivity and aggression: A meta-analysis of school-based studies. *Journal of Educational Psychology, 91,* 195–203.

Roediger, H. L. (1980). Memory metaphors in cognitive psychology. *Memory and Cognition, 8,* 231–246.

Roediger, H. L., III (1990). Implicit memory: Retention without remembering. *American Psychologist, 45,* 1043–1056.

Roediger, H. L. (2004, March). What happened to behaviorism? *APS Observer, 17*(3), 5, 40–42.

Roediger, H. L., & Crowder, R. G. (1976). A serial position effect in recall of United States presidents. *Bulletin of the Psychonomic Society, 8,* 275–278.

Roediger, H. L., III, & Karpicke, J. D. (2006). Test-enhanced learning: Taking memory tests improves long-term retention. *Psychological Science, 17,* 249–255.

Roediger, H. L., III, & McDermott, K. B. (2000). Tricks of memory. *Current Directions in Psychological Science, 9,* 123–127.

Roeser, R. W., Eccles, J. S., & Sameroff, A. J. (2000). School as a context of early adolescents' academic social–emotional development: A summary of research findings. *The Elementary School Journal, 100,* 443–471.

Roeser, R. W., Marachi, R., & Gehlbach, H. (2002). A goal theory perspective on teachers'

professional identities and the contexts of teaching. In C. Midgley (Ed.), *Goals, goal structures, and patterns of adaptive learning* (pp. 205–241). Mahwah, NJ: Erlbaum.

Rogers, C. R. (1951). *Client-centered therapy: Its current practice, implication, and theory.* Boston: Houghton Mifflin.

Rogers, C. R. (1961). *On becoming a person: A therapist's view of psychotherapy.* Boston: Houghton Mifflin.

Rogers, T. B., Kuiper, N. A., & Kirker, W. S. (1977). Self-reference and the encoding of personal information. *Journal of Personality and Social Psychology, 35,* 677–688.

Rogers, T. T., & McClelland, J. L. (2004). *Semantic cognition: A parallel distributed processing approach.* Cambridge, MA: MIT Press.

Rogoff, B. (1990). *Apprenticeship in thinking: Cognitive development in social context.* New York: Oxford University Press.

Rogoff, B. (1991). Social interaction as apprenticeship in thinking: Guidance and participation in spatial planning. In L. B. Resnick, J. M. Levine, & S. D. Teasley (Eds.), *Perspectives on socially shared cognition.* Washington, DC: American Psychological Association.

Rogoff, B. (1994, April). *Developing understanding of the idea of communities of learners.* Paper presented at the annual meeting of the American Educational Research Association, New Orleans, LA.

Rogoff, B. (1995). Observing sociocultural activity on three planes: Participatory appropriation, guided participation, and apprenticeship. In J. V. Wertsch, P. del Rio, & A. Alvarez (Eds.), *Sociocultural studies of mind.* Cambridge, England: Cambridge University Press.

Rogoff, B. (2003). *The cultural nature of human development.* Oxford, England: Oxford University Press.

Rogoff, B., Matusov, E., & White, C. (1996). Models of teaching and learning: Participation in a community of learners. In D. R. Olson & N. Torrance (Eds.), *The handbook of education and human development: New models of learning, teaching, and schooling.* Cambridge, MA: Blackwell.

Rogoff, B., Mistry, J., Göncü, A., & Mosier, C. (1993). Guided participation in cultural activity by toddlers and caregivers. *Monographs of the Society for Research in Child Development, 58* (8, Serial No. 236).

Rohrbeck, C. A., Ginsburg-Block, M. D., Fantuzzo, J. W., & Miller, T. R. (2003). Peer-assisted learning interventions with elementary school students: A meta-analytic review. *Journal of Educational Psychology, 95,* 240–257.

Romaniuk, C., Miltenberger, R., Conyers, C., Jenner, N., Jurgens, M., & Ringenberg, C. (2002). The influence of activity choice on problem behaviors maintained by escape versus attention. *Journal of Applied Behavior Analysis, 35,* 349–362.

Rommetveit, R. (1985). Language acquisition as increasing linguistic structuring of experience and symbolic behavior control. In J. V. Wertsch (Ed.), *Culture, communication, and cognition: Vygotskian perspectives* (pp. 183–204). Cambridge, England: Cambridge University Press.

Rortvedt, A. K., & Miltenberger, R. G. (1994). Analysis of a high-probability instructional sequence and time-out in the treatment of child noncompliance. *Journal of Applied Behavior Analysis, 27,* 327–330.

Rosales-Ruiz, J., & Baer, D. M. (1997). Behavioral cusps: A developmental and pragmatic concept for behavior analysis. *Journal of Applied Behavior Analysis, 30,* 533–544.

Rosch, E. H. (1973a). Natural categories. *Cognitive Psychology, 4,* 328–350.

Rosch, E. H. (1973b). On the internal structure of perceptual and semantic categories. In T. E. Moore (Ed.), *Cognitive development and the acquisition of language.* New York: Academic Press.

Rosch, E. H. (1977a). Classification of real-world objects: Origins and representations in cognition. In P. N. Johnson-Laird & P. C. Wason (Eds.), *Thinking: Readings in cognitive science.* Cambridge, MA: Cambridge University Press.

Rosch, E. H. (1977b). Human categorization. In N. Warren (Ed.), *Advances in cross-cultural psychology* (Vol. 1). London: Academic Press.

Rosch, E. H. (1978). Principles of categorization. In E. Rosch & B. Lloyd (Eds.), *Cognition and categorization.* Hillsdale, NJ: Erlbaum.

Rosch, E. H., & Mervis, C. B. (1975). Family resemblances: Studies in the internal structure of categories. *Cognitive Psychology, 7,* 573–605.

Rosch, E. H., Mervis, C. B., Gray, W. D., Johnson, D. M., & Boyes-Braem, P. (1976). Basic objects in natural categories. *Cognitive Psychology, 8,* 382–439.

Rose, S. C., & Thornburg, K. R. (1984). Mastery motivation and need for approval in young children: Effects of age, sex, and reinforcement condition. *Educational Research Quarterly, 9*(1), 34–42.

Rosenberg, E. L. (1998). Levels of analysis and the organization of affect. *Review of General Psychology, 2,* 247–270.

Rosenshine, B., & Meister, C. (1992). The use of scaffolds for teaching higher-level cognitive strategies. *Educational Leadership, 49*(7), 26–33.

Rosenshine, B., & Meister, C. (1994). Reciprocal teaching: A review of the research. *Review of Educational Research, 64,* 479–530.

Rosenshine, B., Meister, C., & Chapman, S. (1996). Teaching students to generate questions: A review of the intervention studies. *Review of Educational Research, 66,* 181–221.

Rosenshine, B., & Stevens, R. (1986). Teaching functions. In M. C. Wittrock (Ed.), *Handbook of research on teaching* (3rd ed.). New York: Macmillan.

Rosenthal, R. (1994). Interpersonal expectancy effects: A 30-year perspective. *Current Directions in Psychological Science, 3,* 176–179.

Rosenthal, R. (2002). Covert communication in classrooms, clinics, courtrooms, and cubicles. *American Psychologist, 57,* 839–849.

Rosenthal, T. L., Alford, G. S., & Rasp, L. M. (1972). Concept attainment, generalization, and retention through observation and verbal coding. *Journal of Experimental Child Psychology, 13,* 183–194.

Rosenthal, T. L., & Bandura, A. (1978). Psychological modeling: Theory and practice. In S. L. Garfield & A. E. Begia (Eds.), *Handbook of psychotherapy and behavior change: An empirical analysis* (2nd ed.). New York: Wiley.

Rosenthal, T. L., & Zimmerman, B. J. (1978). *Social learning and cognition.* New York: Academic Press.

Ross, B. H., & Spalding, T. L. (1994). Concepts and categories. In R. J. Sternberg (Ed.), *Handbook of perception and cognition* (Vol. 12). New York: Academic Press.

Rosser, R. (1994). *Cognitive development: Psychological and biological perspectives.* Boston: Allyn & Bacon.

Rotenberg, K. J., & Mayer, E. V. (1990). Delay of gratification in Native and White children: A cross-cultural comparison. *International Journal of Behavioral Development, 13,* 23–30.

Roth, K. (1990). Developing meaningful conceptual understanding in science. In B. F. Jones & L. Idol (Eds.), *Dimensions of thinking and cognitive instruction.* Hillsdale, NJ: Erlbaum.

Roth, K. (2002). Talking to understand science. In J. Brophy (Ed.), *Social constructivist teaching: Affordances and constraints* (pp. 197–262). New York: Elsevier.

Roth, K., & Anderson, C. (1988). Promoting conceptual change learning from science textbooks. In P. Ramsden (Ed.), *Improving learning: New perspectives.* London: Kogan Page.

Roth, W., & Bowen, G. M. (1995). Knowing and interacting: A study of culture, practices, and resources in a grade 8 open-inquiry science classroom guided by a cognitive apprenticeship metaphor. *Cognition and Instruction, 13,* 73–128.

Roth, W.-M. (2001). Gestures: Their role in teaching and learning. *Review of Educational Research, 71,* 365–392.

Rothbaum, F., Weisz, J. R., & Snyder, S. S. (1982). Changing the world and changing the self: A two-process model of perceived control. *Journal of Personality and Social Psychology, 42,* 5–37.

Rouet, J.-F., Favart, M., Britt, M. A., & Perfetti, C. A. (1997). Studying and using multiple documents in history: Effects of discipline expertise. *Cognition and Instruction, 15,* 85–106.

Rovee-Collier, C. (1993). The capacity for long-term memory in infancy. *Current Directions in Psychological Science, 2,* 130–135.

Rovee-Collier, C. (1999). The development of infant memory. *Current Directions in Psychological Science, 8,* 80–85.

Rowe, M. B. (1974). Wait-time and rewards as instructional variables, their influence on language, logic, and fate control: Part I. Wait time. *Journal of Research in Science Teaching, 11,* 81–94.

Rowe, M. B. (1987). Wait time: Slowing down may be a way of speeding up. *American Educator, 11*(1), 38–43, 47.

Royer, J. M., & Cable, G. W. (1976). Illustrations, analogies, and facilitation of transfer in prose learning. *Journal of Educational Psychology, 68,* 205–209.

Rubin, D. C. (1992). Constraints on memory. In E. Winograd & U. Neisser (Eds.), *Affect and accuracy in recall: Studies of "flashbulb" memories.* Cambridge, England: Cambridge University Press.

Ruble, D. N. (1980). A developmental perspective on theories of achievement motivation. In L. J. Fyans, Jr. (Ed.), *Achievement motivation: Recent trends in theory and research.* New York: Plenum Press.

Rueda, R., & Moll, L. C. (1994). A sociocultural perspective on motivation. In H. F. O'Neil, Jr., & M. Drillings (Eds.), *Motivation: Theory and research.* Hillsdale, NJ: Erlbaum.

Ruef, M. B., Higgins, C., Glaeser, B., & Patnode, M. (1998). Positive behavioral support: Strategies for teachers. *Intervention in School and Clinic, 34*(1), 21–32.

Rueger, D. B., & Liberman, R. P. (1984). Behavioral family therapy for delinquent substance-abusing adolescents. *Journal of Drug Abuse, 14,* 403–418.

Ruffman, T., Perner, J., Olson, D. R., & Doherty, M. (1993). Reflecting on scientific thinking: Children's understanding of the hypothesis-evidence relation. *Child Development, 64,* 1617–1636.

Rumberger, R. W. (1995). Dropping out of middle school: A multilevel analysis of students and schools. *American Educational Research Journal, 32,* 583–625.

Rumelhart, D. E. (1980). Schemata: The building blocks of cognition. In R. J. Spiro, B. C. Bruce, & W. F. Brewer (Eds.), *Theoretical issues in reading comprehension.* Hillsdale, NJ: Erlbaum.

Rumelhart, D. E., & McClelland, J. L. (1986). *Parallel distributed processing* (Vol. 1). Cambridge, MA: MIT Press.

Rumelhart, D. E., & Ortony, A. (1977). The representation of knowledge in memory. In R. C. Anderson, R. J. Spiro, & W. E. Montague (Eds.), *Schooling and the acquisition of knowledge.* Hillsdale, NJ: Erlbaum.

Rummel, N., Levin, J. R., & Woodward, M. M. (2003). Do pictorial mnemonic text-learning aids give students something worth writing about? *Journal of Educational Psychology, 95,* 327–334.

Runco, M. A., & Chand, I. (1995). Cognition and creativity. *Educational Psychology Review, 7,* 243–267.

Rundus, D. (1971). Analysis of rehearsal processes in free recall. *Journal of Experimental Psychology, 89,* 63–77.

Rundus, D., & Atkinson, R. C. (1971). Rehearsal processes in free recall: A procedure for direct observation. *Journal of Verbal Learning and Verbal Behavior, 9,* 99–105.

Rusch, F., & Close, D. (1976). Overcorrection: A procedural evaluation. *AAESPH Review, 1,* 32–45.

Rushton, J. P. (1975). Generosity in children: Immediate and long-term effects of modeling, preaching, and moral judgment. *Journal of Personality and Social Psychology, 31,* 459–466.

Rushton, J. P. (1980). *Altruism, socialization, and society.* Englewood Cliffs, NJ: Prentice Hall.

Rushton, J. P. (1982). Social learning theory and the development of prosocial behavior. In N. Eisenberg (Ed.), *The development of prosocial behavior.* New York: Academic Press.

Russ, S. W. (1993). *Affect and creativity: The role of affect and play in the creative process.* Hillsdale, NJ: Erlbaum.

Ryan, A. M., Hicks, L., & Midgley, C. (1997). Social goals, academic goals, and avoiding seeking help in the classroom. *Journal of Early Adolescence, 17,* 152–171.

Ryan, A. M., & Patrick, H. (2001). The classroom social environment and changes in adolescents' motivation and engagement during middle school. *American Educational Research Journal, 38,* 437–460.

Ryan, A. M., Pintrich, P. R., & Midgley, C. (2001). Avoiding seeking help in the classroom: Who and why? *Educational Psychology Review, 13,* 93–114.

Ryan, C. S., & Hemmes, N. S. (2005). Effects of the contingency for homework submission on homework submission and quiz performance in a college course. *Journal of Applied Behavior Analysis, 38,* 79–88.

Ryan, K. E., Ryan, A. M., Arbuthnot, K., & Samuels, M. (2005, April). *Students' motivation for standardized math exams: Insights from students.* Paper presented at the annual meeting of the American Educational Research Association, Montreal.

Ryan, R. M. (1982). Control and information in the intrapersonal sphere: An extension of cognitive evaluation theory. *Journal of Personality and Social Psychology, 43,* 450–461.

Ryan, R. M., & Connell, J. P. (1989). Perceived locus of causality and internalization: Examining reasons for acting in two domains. *Journal of Personality and Social Psychology, 57,* 749–761.

Ryan, R. M., Connell, J. P., & Grolnick, W. S. (1992). When achievement is *not* intrinsically motivated: A theory of internalization and self-regulation in school. In A. K. Boggiano & T. S. Pittman (Eds.), *Achievement and motivation: A social–developmental perspective.* Cambridge, England: Cambridge University Press.

Ryan, R. M., & Deci, E. L. (2000). Self-determination theory and the facilitation of intrinsic motivation, social development, and well-being. *American Psychologist, 55,* 68–78.

Ryan, R. M., Mims, V., & Koestner, R. (1983). Relation of reward contingency and interpersonal context to intrinsic motivation: A review and test using cognitive evaluation theory. *Journal of Personality and Social Psychology, 45,* 736–750.

Ryan, S., Ormond, T., Imwold, C. & Rotunda, R. J. (2002). The effects of a public address system on the off-task behavior of elementary physical education students. *Journal of Applied Behavior Analysis, 35,* 305–308.

Sadoski, M., & Paivio, A. (2001). *Imagery and text: A dual coding theory of reading and writing.* Mahwah, NJ: Erlbaum.

Sadoski, M., & Quast, Z. (1990). Reader response and long-term recall for journalistic text: The roles of imagery, affect, and importance. *Reading Research Quarterly, 25,* 256–272.

Saffran, J. R. (2003). Statistical language learning: Mechanisms and constraints. *Current Directions in Psychological Science, 12,* 110–114.

Safren, M. A. (1962). Associations, sets, and the solution of word problems. *Journal of Experimental Psychology, 64,* 40–45.

Saljo, R., & Wyndham, J. (1992). Solving everyday problems in the formal setting: An empirical study of the school as context for thought. In S. Chaiklin & J. Lave (Eds.), *Understanding practice.* New York: Cambridge University Press.

Salomon, G. (1993). No distribution without individuals' cognition: A dynamic interactional view. In G. Salomon (Ed.), *Distributed cognitions: Psychological and educational considerations* (pp. 111–138). Cambridge, England: Cambridge University Press.

Salomon, G. (1994). *Interaction of media, cognition, and learning.* Hillsdale, NJ: Erlbaum. (Originally published 1979)

Salthouse, T. A. (1991). Mediation of adult age differences in cognition by reductions in working memory and speed of processing. *Psychological Science, 2,* 179–183.

Salthouse, T. A. (2006). Mental exercise and mental aging: Evaluating the validity of the "use it or lose it" hypothesis. *Perspectives on Psychological Science, 1,* 68–87.

Saltz, E. (1971). *The cognitive bases of human learning.* Homewood, IL: Dorsey.

Samuel, A. L. (1963). Some studies in machine learning using the game of checkers. In E. A. Feigenbaum & J. Feldman (Eds.), *Computers and thought.* New York: McGraw-Hill.

Samuels, S. J. (1967). Attentional processes in reading: The effect of pictures in the acquisition of reading responses. *Journal of Educational Psychology, 58,* 337–342.

Samuels, S. J. (1970). Effects of pictures on learning to read, comprehension and attitudes. *Review of Educational Research, 40,* 397–407.

Samuels, S. J., & Turnure, J. E. (1974). Attention and reading achievement in first-grade boys and girls. *Journal of Educational Psychology, 66,* 29–32.

Sansone, C., & Smith, J. (2002). Interest and self-regulation: The relation between having to and wanting to. In C. Sansone & J. Harackiewicz (Ed.), *Intrinsic and extrinsic motivation: The search for optimal motivation and performance* (pp. 341–372). San Diego, CA: Academic Press.

Sansone, C., Weir, C., Harpster, L., & Morgan, C. (1992). Once a boring task always a boring task? Interest as a self-regulatory mechanism. *Journal of Personality and Social Psychology, 63,* 379–390.

Sapolsky, R. M. (1999). Glucocorticoids, stress, and their adverse neurological effects: Relevance to aging. *Experimental Gerontology, 34,* 721–732.

Sarason, I. G. (1980). Introduction to the study of test anxiety. In I. G. Sarason (Ed.), *Test anxiety: Theory, research, and applications.* Hillsdale, NJ: Erlbaum.

Sarason, S. B. (1972). What research says about test anxiety in elementary school children. In A. R. Binter & S. H. Frey (Eds.), *The psychology of the elementary school child.* Chicago: Rand McNally.

Sasso, G. M., & Rude, H. A. (1987). Unprogrammed effects of training high-status peers to interact with severely handicapped children. *Journal of Applied Behavior Analysis, 20,* 35–44.

Savery, J. R., & Duffy, T. M. (2001). Problem based learning: An instructional model and its constructivist framework. CRLT Technical Report No. 16–01, Center for Research on Learning and Technolgoy, Indiana University. Retrieved March 9, 2005, from http://cee.indiana.edu/publications/journals/TR16–01.pdf

Saville, B. K., Zinn, T. E., Neef, N. A., Van Norman, R., & Ferreri, S. J. (2006). A comparison of interteaching and lecture in the college classroom. *Journal of Applied Behavior Analysis, 39,* 49–61.

Sawyer, R. J., Graham, S., & Harris, K. R. (1992). Direct teaching, strategy instruction, and strategy instruction with explicit self-regulation: Effects on the composition skills and self-efficacy of students with learning disabilities. *Journal of Educational Psychology, 84,* 340–352.

Sax, G. (1989). *Principles of educational and psychological measurement and evaluation* (3rd ed.). Belmont, CA: Wadsworth.

Saxe, G. B. (1988). Candy selling and math learning. *Educational Researcher, 17*(6), 14–21.

Scandura, J. M. (1974). Role of higher order rules in problem solving. *Journal of Experimental Psychology, 102,* 984–991.

Scardamalia, M., & Bereiter, C. (1985). Fostering the development of self-regulation in children's knowledge processing. In S. F. Chipman, J. W. Segal, & R. Glaser (Eds.), *Thinking and learning skills: Vol. 2. Research and open questions.* Hillsdale, NJ: Erlbaum.

Scardamalia, M., & Bereiter, C. (2006). Knowledge building: Theory, pedagogy, and technology. In R. K. Sawyer (Ed.), *The Cambridge handbook of the learning sciences* (pp. 97–115). Cambridge, England: Cambridge University Press.

Scevak, J. J., Moore, P. J., & Kirby, J. R. (1993). Training students to use maps to increase text recall. *Contemporary Educational Psychology, 18,* 401–413.

Schab, F. (1990). Odors and the remembrance of things past. *Journal of Experimental Psychology: Learning, Memory, and Cognition, 16,* 648–655.

Schacter, D. L. (1989). Memory. In M. I. Posner (Ed.), *Foundations of cognitive science* (pp. 683–725). Cambridge, MA: MIT Press.

Schacter, D. L. (1999). The seven sins of memory: Insights from psychology and neuroscience. *American Psychologist, 54,* 182–203.

Schacter, J. (2000). Does individual tutoring produce optimal learning? *American Educational Research Journal, 37,* 801–829.

Schank, R. C. (1975). *Conceptual information processing.* New York: Elsevier.

Schank, R. C. (1979). Interestingness: Controlling inferences. *Artificial Intelligence, 12,* 273–297.

Schank, R. C., & Abelson, R. P. (1977). *Scripts, plans, goals, and understanding: An inquiry into human knowledge structures.* Hillsdale, NJ: Erlbaum.

Schank, R. C., & Abelson, R. P. (1995). Knowledge and memory: The real story. In R. S. Wyer, Jr. (Ed.), *Advances in social cognition, Vol. 8; Knowledge and memory: The real story.* Hillsdale, NJ: Erlbaum.

Schauble, L. (1990). Belief revision in children: The role of prior knowledge and strategies for generating evidence. *Journal of Experimental Child Psychology, 49,* 31–57.

Schauble, L. (1996). The development of scientific reasoning in knowledge-rich contexts. *Developmental Psychology, 32,* 102–119.

Schellings, G. L. M., Van Hout-Wolters, B., & Vermunt, J. D. (1996). Individual differences in adapting to three different tasks of selecting information from texts. *Contemporary Educational Psychology, 21,* 423–446.

Schiefele, U. (1991). Interest, learning, and motivation. *Educational Psychologist, 26,* 299–323.

Schiefele, U. (1992). Topic interest and levels of text comprehension. In K. A. Renninger, S. Hidi, & A. Krapp (Eds.), *The role of interest in learning and development.* Hillsdale, NJ: Erlbaum.

Schiefele, U. (1998). Individual interest and learning: What we know and what we don't know. In L. Hoffman, A. Krapp, K. Renninger, & J. Baumert (Eds.), *Interest and learning: Proceedings of the Seeon Conference on interest and gender* (pp. 91–104). Kiel, Germany: IPN.

Schiefele, U., Krapp, A., & Winteler, A. (1992). Interest as a predictor of academic achievement: A meta-analysis of research. In K. A. Renninger, S. Hidi, & A. Krapp (Eds.), *The role of interest in learning and development.* Hillsdale, NJ: Erlbaum.

Schiefele, U., & Wild, K. (1994, April). *Motivational predictors of strategy use and course grades.* Paper presented at the annual meeting of the American Educational Research Association, New Orleans, LA.

Schimmoeller, M. A. (1998, April). *Influence of private speech on the writing behaviors of young children: Four case studies.* Paper presented at the annual meeting of the American Educational Research Association, San Diego, CA.

Schliefer, M., & Douglas, V. I. (1973). Effects of training on the moral judgment of young children. *Journal of Personality and Social Psychology, 28,* 62–67.

Schliemann, A. D., & Carraher, D. W. (1993). Proportional reasoning in and out of school. In P. Light & G. Butterworth (Eds.), *Context and cognition: Ways of learning and knowing.* Hillsdale, NJ: Erlbaum.

Schloss, P. J., & Smith, M. A. (1994). *Applied behavior analysis in the classroom.* Boston: Allyn & Bacon.

Schmidt, R. A., & Bjork, R. A. (1992). New conceptualizations of practice: Common principles in three paradigms suggest new concepts for training. *Psychological Science, 3,* 207–217.

Schmidt, R. A., & Young, D. E. (1987). Transfer of movement control in motor skill learning. In S. M. Cormier & J. D. Hagman (Eds.), *Transfer of learning: Contemporary research and applications.* San Diego, CA: Academic Press.

Schmittau, J. (2003). Cultural–historical theory and mathematics education. In A. Kozulin, B. Gindis, V. S. Ageyev, & S. M. Miller (Eds.), *Vygotsky's educational theory in cultural context* (pp. 225–245). Cambridge, England: Cambridge University Press.

Schmolck, H., Buffalo, E. A., & Squire, L. R. (2000). Memory distortions develop over time: Recollections of the O. J. Simpson trial verdict after 15 and 32 months. *Psychological Science, 11,* 39–45.

Schneider, W. (1993). Domain-specific knowledge and memory performance in children. *Educational Psychology Review, 5,* 257–273.

Schneider, W., Körkel, J., & Weinert, F. E. (1990). Expert knowledge, general abilities, and text processing. In W. Schneider & F. E. Weinert (Eds.), *Interactions among aptitudes, strategies, and knowledge in cognitive performance.* New York: Springer-Verlag.

Schneider, W., & Lockl, K. (2002). The development of metacognitive knowledge in children and adolescents. In T. J. Perfect & B. L. Schwartz (Eds.), *Applied metacognition* (pp. 224–257). Cambridge, England: Cambridge University Press.

Schneider, W., & Pressley, M. (1989). *Memory development between 2 and 20.* New York: Springer-Verlag.

Schneider, W., & Shiffrin, R. M. (1977). Controlled and automatic human information processing: I. Detection, search, and attention. *Psychological Review, 84,* 1–66.

Schoenfeld, A. H. (1979). Explicit heuristic training as a variable in problem solving performance. *Journal for Research in Mathematics Education, 10,* 173–187.

Schoenfeld, A. H. (1982). Measures of problem-solving performance and problem-solving instruction. *Journal for Research in Mathematics Education, 13,* 31–49.

Schoenfeld, A. H. (1985). Metacognitive and epistemological issues in mathematical understanding. In E. A. Silver (Ed.), *Teaching and learning mathematical problem solving: Multiple research perspectives.* Hillsdale, NJ: Erlbaum.

Schoenfeld, A. H. (1988). When good teaching leads to bad results: The disasters of "well-taught" mathematics courses. *Educational Psychologist, 23,* 145–166.

Schoenfeld, A. H. (1992). Learning to think mathematically: Problem solving, metacognition, and sense-making in mathematics. In D. A. Grouws (Ed.), *Handbook of research on mathematics teaching and learning.* New York: Macmillan.

Schoenfeld, A. H., & Herrmann, D. J. (1982). Problem perception and knowledge structure in expert and novice mathematical problem solvers. *Journal of Experimental Psychology: Learning, Memory, and Cognition, 8,* 484–494.

Schofield, J. W. (1995). Improving intergroup relations among students. In J. A. Banks & C. A. M. Banks (Eds.), *Handbook of research on multicultural education.* New York: Macmillan.

Schofield, N. J., & Kirby, J. R. (1994). Position location on topographical maps: Effects of task factors, training, and strategies. *Cognition and Instruction, 12,* 35–60.

Scholes, R. J., & Kardash, C. M. (1996, April). *The effect of topic interest on the relationship between text-based interest and importance in text comprehension.* Paper presented at the annual meeting of the American Educational Research Association, New York.

Schommer, M. (1990). Effects of beliefs about the nature of knowledge on comprehension. *Journal of Educational Psychology, 82,* 498–504.

Schommer, M. (1994a). An emerging conceptualization of epistemological beliefs and their role in learning. In R. Garner & P. A. Alexander (Eds.), *Beliefs about text and instruction with text.* Hillsdale, NJ: Erlbaum.

Schommer, M. (1994b). Synthesizing epistemological belief research: Tentative understandings and provocative confusions. *Educational Psychology Review, 6,* 293–319.

Schommer, M. (1997). The development of epistemological beliefs among secondary students: A longitudinal study. *Journal of Educational Psychology, 89,* 37–40.

Schommer-Aikins, M. (2002). An evolving theoretical framework for an epistemological belief system. In B. K. Hofer & P. R. Pintrich (Eds.), *Personal epistemology: The psychology of beliefs about knowledge and knowing* (pp. 103–118). Mahwah, NJ: Erlbaum.

Schommer-Aikins, M. (2004). Explaining the epistemological belief system: Introducing the embedded systemic odel and coordinated research approach. *Educational Psychologist, 39,* 19–29.

Schommer-Aikins, M., Hopkins, L., Anderson, C., & Drouhard, B. (2005, April). *Epistemological beliefs and need for cognition of traditional and non-traditional students.* Paper presented at the annual meeting of the American Educational Research Association, Montreal.

Schooler, J. W. (2001). Discovering memories of abuse in the light of meta-awareness. *Journal of Aggression, Maltreatment, and Trauma, 4,* 105–136.

Schraw, G. (1998). Processing and recall differences among seductive details. *Journal of Educational Psychology, 90,* 3–12.

Schraw, G. (2000). Reader beliefs and meaning construction in narrative text. *Journal of Educational Psychology, 92,* 96–106.

Schraw, G., Bendixen, L. D., & Dunkle, M. E. (2002). Development and validation of the Epistemic Belief Inventory (EBI). In B. K. Hofer & P. R. Pintrich (Eds.), *Personal epistemology: The psychology of beliefs about knowledge and knowing* (pp. 261–275). Mahwah, NJ: Erlbaum.

Schraw, G., & Bruning, R. (1995, April). *Reader beliefs and reading comprehension.* Paper presented at the annual meeting of the American Educational Research Association, San Francisco.

Schraw, G., Dunkle, M. E., & Bendixen, L. D. (1995). Cognitive processes in well-defined and ill-defined problem solving. *Applied Cognitive Psychology, 9,* 523–538.

Schraw, G., Flowerday, T., & Lehman, S. (2001). Increasing situational interest in the classroom. *Educational Psychology Review, 13,* 211–224.

Schraw, G., & Lehman, S. (2001). Situational interest: A review of the literature and directions for future research. *Educational Psychology Review, 13,* 23–52.

Schraw, G., & Moshman, D. (1995). Meta-cognitive theories. *Educational Psychology Review, 7,* 351–371.

Schraw, G., Potenza, M. T., & Nebelsick-Gullet, L. (1993). Constraints on the calibration of performance. *Contemporary Educational Psychology, 18,* 455–463.

Schroth, M. L. (1992). The effects of delay of feedback on a delayed concept formation transfer task. *Contemporary Educational Psychology, 17,* 78–82.

Schultz, K., & Lochhead, J. (1991). A view from physics. In M. U. Smith (Ed.), *Toward a unified theory of problem solving: Views from the content domains.* Hillsdale, NJ: Erlbaum.

Schunk, D. H. (1981). Modeling and attributional effects on children's achievement: A self-efficacy analysis. *Journal of Educational Psychology, 73,* 93–105.

Schunk, D. H. (1982). Effects of effort attributional feedback on children's perceived self-efficacy and achievement. *Journal of Educational Psychology, 74,* 548–556.

Schunk, D. H. (1983). Developing children's self-efficacy and skills: The roles of social comparative information and goal setting. *Contemporary Educational Psychology, 8,* 76–86.

Schunk, D. H. (1985). Participation in goal setting: Effects on self-efficacy and skills of learning disabled children. *Journal of Special Education, 19,* 307–317.

Schunk, D. H. (1987). Peer models and children's behavioral change. *Review of Educational Research, 57,* 149–174.

Schunk, D. H. (1989a). Self-efficacy and achievement behaviors. *Educational Psychology Review, 1,* 173–208.

Schunk, D. H. (1989b). Self-efficacy and cognitive skill learning. In C. Ames & R. Ames (Eds.), *Research on motivation in education: Vol. 3. Goals and cognitions.* San Diego, CA: Academic Press.

Schunk, D. H. (1989c). Social cognitive theory and self-regulated learning. In B. J. Zimmerman & D. H. Schunk (Eds.), *Self-regulated learning and academic achievement: Theory, research, and practice.* New York: Springer-Verlag.

Schunk, D. H. (1990, April). *Socialization and the development of self-regulated learning: The role of attributions.* Paper presented at the annual meeting of the American Educational Research Association, Boston.

Schunk, D. H. (1995). Inherent details of self-regulated learning include student perceptions. *Educational Psychologist, 30,* 213–216.

Schunk, D. H. (1998). Teaching elementary students to self-regulate practice of mathematical skills with modeling. In D. H. Schunk & B. J. Zimmerman (Eds.), *Self-regulated learning: From teaching to self-reflective practice* (pp. 137–159). New York: Guilford Press.

Schunk, D. H., & Hanson, A. R. (1985). Peer models: Influence on children's self-efficacy and achievement. *Journal of Educational Psychology, 77,* 313–322.

Schunk, D. H., Hanson, A. R., & Cox, P. D. (1987). Peer-model attributes and children's achievement behaviors. *Journal of Educational Psychology, 79,* 54–61.

Schunk, D. H., & Pajares, F. (2004). Self-efficacy in education revisited: Empirical and applied evidence. In D. M. McNerney & S. Van Etten (Eds.), *Big theories revisited* (pp. 115–138). Greenwich, CT: Information Age.

Schunk, D. H., & Rice, J. (1989). Learning goals and children's reading comprehension. *Journal of Reading Behavior, 21,* 279–293.

Schunk, D. H., & Swartz, C. W. (1993). Goals and progress feedback: Effects on self-efficacy and writing achievement. *Contemporary Educational Psychology, 18,* 337–354.

Schunk, D. H., & Zimmerman, B. J. (Eds.) (1994). *Self-regulation of learning and performance: Issues and educational applications.* Hillsdale, NJ: Erlbaum.

Schunk, D. H., & Zimmerman, B. J. (1997). Social origins of self-regulatory competence. *Educational Psychologist, 32,* 195–208.

Schupp, H. T., Junghöfer, M., Weike, A. I., & Hamm, A. O. (2003). Emotional facilitation of sensory processing in the visual cortex. *Psychological Science, 14,* 7–13.

Schutz, P. A. (1994). Goals as the transactive point between motivation and cognition. In P. R. Pintrich, D. R. Brown, & C. E. Weinstein (Eds.), *Student motivation, cognition, and learning: Essays in honor of Wilbert J. McKeachie.* Hillsdale, NJ: Erlbaum.

Schwartz, B., & Reisberg, D. (1991). *Learning and memory.* New York: W. W. Norton.

Schwartz, D. L., & Martin, T. (2004). Inventing to prepare for future learning: The hidden efficiency of encouraging original student production in statistics instruction. *Cognition and Instruction, 22,* 129–184.

Schwartz, S. H. (1971). Modes of representation and problem solving: Well evolved is half solved. *Journal of Experimental Psychology, 91,* 347–350.

Schwarz, B. B., Neuman, Y., & Biezuner, S. (2000). Two wrongs may make a right . . . if they argue together! *Cognition and Instruction, 18,* 461–494.

Schwarz, N., & Skurnik, I. (2003). Feeling and thinking: Implications for problem solving. In J. E. Davidson & R. J. Sternberg (Eds.), *The psychology of problem solving* (pp. 263–290). Cambridge, England: Cambridge University Press.

Schwebel, A. I., & Cherlin, D. L. (1972). Physical and social distancing in teacher-pupil relationships. *Journal of Educational Psychology, 63,* 543–550.

Schweinle, A., Turner, J. C., & Meyer, D. K. (April, 2004). *Student motivation and affect in the classroom context.* Paper presented at the American Educational Research Association, San Diego, CA.

Seamon, J. G., Luo, C. R., & Gallo, D. A. (1998). Creating false memories of words with or without recognition of list items: Evidence for nonconscious processes. *Psychological Science, 9,* 20–26.

Seitz, V., Rosenbaum, L. K., & Apfel, N. H. (1985). Effects of family support intervention: A ten-year follow-up. *Child Development, 56,* 376–391.

Seligman, M. E. P. (1975). *Helplessness.* San Francisco: W. H. Freeman.

Seligman, M. E. P. (1991). *Learned optimism.* New York: Alfred Knopf.

Seligman, M. E. P., & Campbell, B. A. (1965). Effects of intensity and duration of punishment on extinction of an avoidance response. *Journal of Comparative and Physiological Psychology, 59,* 295–297.

Seligman, M. E. P., & Maier, S. F. (1967). Failure to escape traumatic shock. *Journal of Experimental Psychology, 74,* 1–9.

Semb, G. B., & Ellis, J. A. (1994). Knowledge taught in school: What is remembered? *Review of Educational Research, 64,* 253–286.

Semb, G. B., Ellis, J. A., & Araujo, J. (1993). Long-term memory for knowledge learned in school. *Journal of Educational Psychology, 85,* 305–316.

Senko, C., & Harackiewicz, J. M. (2005). Regulation of achievement goals: The role of competence feedback. *Journal of Educational Psychology, 97,* 320–336.

Sergeant, J. (1996). A theory of attention: An information processing perspective. In G. R. Lyon & N. A. Krasnegor (Eds.), *Attention, memory, and executive function* (pp. 57–69). Baltimore: Brookes.

Sfard, A. (1997). Commentary: On metaphorical roots of conceptual growth. In L. D. English (Ed.), *Mathematical reasoning: Analogies, metaphors, and images* (pp. 339–371). Mahwah, NJ: Erlbaum.

Sfard, A. (1998). On two metaphors for learning and the dangers of choosing just one. *Educational Researcher, 27*(2), 4–13.

Shabani, D. B., Katz, R. C., Wilder, D. A., Beauchamp, K., Taylor, C. R., & Fischer, K. J. (2002). Increasing social initiations in children with autism: Effects of a tactile prompt. *Journal of Applied Behavior Analysis, 35,* 79–83.

Shachar, H., & Sharan, S. (1994). Talking, relating, and achieving: Effects of cooperative learning and whole-class instruction. *Cognition and Instruction, 12,* 313–353.

Shafto, F., & Sulzbacher, S. (1977). Comparing treatment tactics with a hyperactive preschool child: Stimulant medication and programmed teacher intervention. *Journal of Applied Behavior Analysis, 10,* 13–20.

Shah, J. Y. (2005). The automatic pursuit and management of goals. *Current Directions in Psychological Science, 14,* 10–13.

Shah, P., & Hoeffner, J. (2002). Review of graph comprehension research: Implications for instruction. *Educational Psychology Review, 14,* 47–69.

Shah, P., & Miyake, A. (1996). The separability of working memory resources for spatial thinking and language processing: An individual differences approach. *Journal of Experimental Psychology: General, 125,* 4–27.

Shapiro, A. M. (2004). How including prior knowledge as a subject variable may change outcomes of learning research. *American Educational Research Journal, 41,* 159–189.

Shapiro, K. L. (1994). The attentional blink: The brain's "eyeblink." *Current Directions in Psychological Science, 3,* 86–89.

Shapley, K. S. (1994, April). *Metacognition, motivation, and learning: A study of middle school students' use and development of self-regulated learning strategies.* Paper presented at the annual meeting of the American Educational Research Association, New Orleans, LA.

Sheffield, F. D. (1966a). A drive-induction theory of reinforcement. In R. N. Haber (Ed.), *Current research in motivation.* New York: Holt, Rinehart & Winston.

Sheffield, F. D. (1966b). New evidence on the drive-induction theory of reinforcement. In R. N. Haber (Ed.), *Current research in motivation.* New York: Holt, Rinehart & Winston.

Sheffield, F. D., & Roby, T. B. (1950). Reward value of a non-nutritive sweet taste. *Journal of Comparative and Physiological Psychology, 43,* 471–481.

Sheffield, F. D., Roby, T. B., & Campbell, B. A. (1954). Drive reduction versus consummatory behavior as determinants of reinforcement. *Journal of Comparative and Physiological Psychology, 47,* 349–354.

Sheffield, F. D., Wulff, J. J., & Backer, R. (1951). Reward value of copulation without sex drive reduction. *Journal of Comparative and Physiological Psychology, 44,* 3–8.

Shepard, L. A. (2000). The role of assessment in a learning culture. *Educational Researcher, 29*(7), 4–14.

Shepard, R. N. (1967). Recognition memory for words, sentences, and pictures. *Journal of Verbal Learning and Verbal Behavior, 6,* 156–163.

Shepard, R. N., & Metzler, J. (1971). Mental rotation of three-dimensional objects. *Science, 171,* 701–703.

Shepperd, J. A., & McNulty, J. K. (2002). The affective consequences of expected and unexpected outcomes. *Psychological Science, 13,* 85–88.

Sherman, D. K., & Cohen, G. L. (2002). Accepting threatening information: Self-affirmation and the reduction of defensive biases. *Current Directions in Psychological Science, 11,* 119–123.

Sherman, J. W., & Bessenoff, G. R. (1999). Stereotypes as source-monitoring cues: On the interaction between episodic and semantic memory. *Psychological Science, 10,* 106–110.

Shernoff, D. J., & Hoogstra, L. A. (2001). Continuing motivation beyond the high school classroom. In M. Michaelson & J. Nakamura (Eds.), *Supportive frameworks for youth engagement* (pp. 73–87). San Francisco: Jossey-Bass.

Shernoff, D. J., Schneider, B., & Csikszentmihalyi, M. (2001, April). *An assessment of multiple influences on student engagement in high school classrooms.* Paper presented at the annual meeting of the American Educational Research Association, Seattle, WA.

Sheveland, D. E. (1994, April). *Motivational factors in the development of independent readers.* Paper presented at the annual meeting of the American Educational Research Association, New Orleans, LA.

Shiffrin, R. M., & Schneider, W. (1977). Controlled and automatic human information processing: II. Perceptual learning, automatic attending, and a general theory. *Psychological Review, 84,* 127–190.

Shimmerlick, S. M., & Nolan, J. D. (1976). Reorganization and the recall of prose. *Journal of Educational Psychology, 68,* 779–786.

Shimoff, E., Catania, A. C., & Matthews, B. A. (1981). Uninstructed human responding: Sensitivity of low-rate performance to schedule contingencies. *Journal of the Experimental Analysis of Behavior, 36,* 207–220.

Shrager, L., & Mayer, R. E. (1989). Note-taking fosters generative learning strategies in novices. *Journal of Educational Psychology, 81,* 263–264.

Shuell, T. J. (1996). Teaching and learning in a classroom context. In D. C. Berliner & R. C. Calfee (Eds.), *Handbook of educational psychology.* New York: Macmillan.

Shulman, H. G. (1971). Similarity effects in short-term memory. *Psychological Bulletin, 75,* 399–415.

Shulman, H. G. (1972). Semantic confusion errors in short-term memory. *Journal of Verbal Learning and Verbal Behavior, 11,* 221–227.

Shulman, L. S., & Quinlan, K. M. (1996). The comparative psychology of school subjects. In D. C. Berliner & R. C. Calfee (Eds.), *Handbook of educational psychology.* New York: Macmillan.

Shymansky, J. A., Hedges, L. V., & Woodworth, G. (1990). A reassessment of the effects of inquiry-based science curricula of the 60's on student performance. *Journal of Research in Science Teaching, 27,* 127–144.

Sideridis, G. D. (2005). Goal orientation, academic achievement, and depression: Evidence in favor of a revised goal theory framework. *Journal of Educational Psychology, 97,* 366–375.

Sieber, J. E., Kameya, L. I., & Paulson, F. L. (1970). Effect of memory support on the problem-solving ability of test-anxious children. *Journal of Educational Psychology, 61,* 159–168.

Siegel, D. J. (1999). *The developing mind: How relationships and the brain interact to shape who we are.* New York: Guilford.

Siegel, S. (1975). Evidence from rats that morphine tolerance is learned response. *Journal of Comparative and Physiological Psychology, 89,* 498–506.

Siegel, S. (1979). The role of conditioning in drug tolerance and addiction. In J. D. Keehn (Ed.), *Psychopathology in animals: Research and clinical implications.* New York: Academic Press.

Siegel, S. (2005). Drug tolerance, drug addiction, and drug anticipation. *Current Directions in Psychological Science, 14,* 296–300.

Siegel, S., & Andrews, J. M. (1962). Magnitude of reinforcement and choice behavior in children. *Journal of Experimental Psychology, 63,* 337–341.

Siegel, S., Baptista, M. A. S., Kim, J. A., McDonald, R. V., & Weise-Kelly, L. (2000). Pavlovian psychopharmacology: The associative basis of tolerance. *Experimental and Clinical Psychopharmacology, 10,* 162–183.

Siegel, S., Hinson, R. E., Krank, M. D., & McCully, J. (1982). Heroin "overdose" death: Contribution of drug-associated environmental cues. *Science, 216,* 436–437.

Siegler, R. S. (2000). Unconscious insights. *Current Directions in Psychological Science, 9,* 79–83.

Siegler, R. S., & Alibali, M. W. (2005). *Children's thinking* (4th ed.). Upper Saddle River, NJ: Prentice Hall.

Siegler, R. S., & Jenkins, E. (1989). *How children discover new strategies.* Hillsdale, NJ: Erlbaum.

Sigman, M., & Whaley, S. E. (1998). The role of nutrition in the development of intelligence. In U. Neisser (Ed.), *The rising curve: Long-term gains in IQ and related measures* (pp. 155–182). Washington, DC: American Psychological Association.

Signorella, M. L., & Liben, L. S. (1984). Recall and reconstruction of gender-related pictures: Effects of attitude, task difficulty, and age. *Child Development, 55,* 393–405.

Silver, E. A. (1982). Knowledge organization and mathematical problem solving. In F. K. Lester & J. Garofalo (Eds.), *Mathematical problem solving: Issues in research.* Philadelphia: The Franklin Institute Press.

Silver, E. A., & Kenney, P. A. (1995). Sources of assessment information for instructional guidance in mathematics. In T. Romberg (Ed.), *Reform in school mathematics and authentic assessment.* Albany: State University of New York Press.

Silver, E. A., Shapiro, L. J., & Deutsch, A. (1993). Sense making and the solution of division problems involving remainders: An examination of middle school students' solution processes and their interpretations of solutions. *Journal of Research in Mathematics Education, 24,* 117–135.

Silverman, W. K., & Kearney, C. A. (1991). *Educational Psychology Review, 3,* 335–361.

Simcock, G., & Hayne, H. (2002). Breaking the barrier? Children fail to translate their preverbal memories into language. *Psychological Science, 13,* 225–231.

Simkin, D. K., Lederer, J. P., & Seligman, M. E. P. (1983). Learned helplessness in groups. *Behaviour Research and Therapy, 21,* 613–622.

Simon, H. A. (1973). The structure of ill-structured problems. *Artificial Intelligence, 4,* 181–201.

Simon, H. A. (1974). How big is a chunk? *Science, 183,* 482–488.

Simon, H. A. (1978). Information-processing theory of human problem solving. In W. K. Estes (Ed.), *Handbook of learning and cognitive processes: Vol. 5. Human information processing.* Hillsdale, NJ: Erlbaum.

Simon, H. A. (1980). Problem solving and education. In D. T. Tuma & F. Reif (Eds.), *Problem-solving and education: Issues in teaching and research.* Hillsdale, NJ: Erlbaum.

Simon, S. J., Ayllon, T., & Milan, M. A. (1982). Behavioral compensation: Contrastlike effects in the classroom. *Behavior Modification, 6,* 407–420.

Sinatra, G. M., & Pintrich, P. R. (Eds.) (2003a). *Intentional conceptual change.* Mahwah, NJ: Erlbaum.

Sinatra, G. M., & Pintrich, P. R. (2003b). The role of intentions in conceptual change learning. In G. M. Sinatra & P. R. Pintrich (Eds.), *Intentional conceptual change* (pp. 1–18). Mahwah, NJ: Erlbaum.

Sinatra, G. M., Southerland, S. A., McConaughy, F., & Demastes, J. (2003). Intentions and beliefs in students' understanding and acceptance of biological evolution. *Journal of Research on Science Teaching, 40,* 510–528.

Singley, M. K., & Anderson, J. R. (1989). *The transfer of cognitive skill.* Cambridge, MA: Harvard University Press.

Sinkavich, F. J. (1995). Performance and meta-memory: Do students know what they don't know? *Instructional Psychology, 22,* 77–87.

Siskin, L. S. (2003). When an irresistable force meets an immovable object: Core lessons about high schools and accountability. In M. Carnoy, R. Elmore, & L. S. Siskin (Eds.), *The new accountability: High schools and high-stakes testing* (pp. 175–194). New York: Routledge Falmer.

Sizer, T. R. (1992). *Horace's school: Redesigning the American high school.* Boston: Houghton Mifflin.

Skaalvik, E. M. (1997). Self-enhancing and self-defeating ego orientation: Relations with task avoidance orientation, achievement, self-perceptions, and anxiety. *Journal of Educational Psychology, 89,* 71–81.

Skaalvik, E. M., & Valas, H. (2001, April). *Student help seeking: Relations with academic self-concept and goal-orientation.* Paper presented at the annual meeting of the American Educational Research Association, Seattle, WA.

Skiba, R., & Raison, J. (1990). Relationship between the use of timeout and academic achievement. *Exceptional Children, 57,* 36–46.

Skiba, R. J., & Rausch, M. K. (2006). Zero tolerance, suspension, and expulsion: Questions of equity and effectiveness. In C. M. Evertson & C. S. Weinstein (Eds.), *Handbook of classroom management: Research, practice, and contemporary issues* (pp. 1063–1089). Mahwah, NJ: Erlbaum.

Skinner, B. F. (1938). *The behavior of organisms: An experimental analysis.* Englewood Cliffs, NJ: Prentice Hall.

Skinner, B. F. (1948). Superstition in the pigeon. *Journal of Experimental Psychology, 38,* 168–172.

Skinner, B. F. (1953). *Science and human behavior.* New York: Macmillan.

Skinner, B. F. (1954). The science of learning and the art of teaching. *Harvard Educational Review, 24,* 86–97.

Skinner, B. F. (1958). Reinforcement today. *American Psychologist, 13,* 94–99.

Skinner, B. F. (1966a). An operant analysis of problem solving. In B. Kleinmuntz (Ed.), *Problem solving: Research, method and theory.* New York: Wiley.

Skinner, B. F. (1966b). What is the experimental analysis of behavior? *Journal of the Experimental Analysis of Behavior, 9,* 213–218.

Skinner, B. F. (1968). *The technology of teaching.* New York: Appleton-Century-Crofts.

Skinner, B. F. (1971). *Beyond freedom and dignity.* New York: Alfred Knopf.

Skinner, B. F. (1973). The free and happy student. *Phi Delta Kappan, 55,* 13–16.

Skinner, B. F. (1989). The origins of cognitive thought. *American Psychologist, 44,* 13–18.

Skinner, B. F., & Epstein, R. (1982). *Skinner for the classroom.* Champaign, IL: Research Press.

Skinner, E. A. (1995). *Perceived control, motivation, and coping.* Thousand Oaks, CA: Sage.

Slater, A., Mattock, A., & Brown, E. (1990). Size constancy at birth: Newborn infants' responses to retinal and real size. *Journal of Experimental Child Psychology, 49,* 314–322.

Slavin, R. E. (1983a). *Cooperative learning.* New York: Longman.

Slavin, R. E. (1983b). When does cooperative learning increase student achievement? *Psychological Bulletin, 94,* 429–445.

Slavin, R. E. (1990a). *Cooperative learning: Theory, research, and practice.* Upper Saddle River, NJ: Prentice Hall.

Slavin, R. E. (1990b). Mastery learning re-reconsidered. *Review of Educational Research, 60,* 300–302.

Sloutsky, V. M., Lo, Y.-F., & Fisher, A. V. (2001). How much does a shared name make things similar? Linguistic labels, similarity, and the development of inductive inference. *Child Development, 72,* 1695–1709.

Slusher, M. P., & Anderson, C. A. (1996). Using causal persuasive arguments to change beliefs and teach new information: The mediating role of explanation availability and evaluation bias in the acceptance of knowledge. *Journal of Educational Psychology, 88,* 110–122.

Small, S. L., Flores, D. K., & Noll, D. C. (1998). Different neural circuits subserve reading before and after therapy for acquired dyslexia. *Brain and Language, 62,* 298–308.

Small, M. Y., Lovett, S. B., & Scher, M. S. (1993). Pictures facilitate children's recall of unillustrated expository prose. *Journal of Educational Psychology, 85,* 520–528.

Smith, B. L., & MacGregor, J. T. (1992). What is collaborative learning? In A. Goodsell, M. Maher, & V. Tinto (Eds.), *Collaborative learning: A sourcebook for higher education.* University Park: National Center on Postsecondary Teaching, Learning, and Assessment, The Pennsylvania State University.

Smith, C. A., & Kirby, L. D. (2001). Affect and cognitive appraisal processes. In J. P. Forgas (Ed.), *Handbook of affect and social cognition* (pp. 75–92). Mahwah, NJ: Erlbaum.

Smith, C. L., Maclin, D., Grosslight, L., & Davis, H. (1997). Teaching for understanding: A study of students' preinstruction theories of matter and a comparison of the effectiveness of two approaches to teaching about matter and density. *Cognition and Instruction, 15,* 317–393.

Smith, C. L., Maclin, D., Houghton, C., & Hennessey, M. G. (2000). Sixth-grade students' epistemologies of science: The impact of school science experiences on epistemological development. *Cognition and Instruction, 18,* 349–422.

Smith, E. E. (1988). Concepts and thought. In R. J. Sternberg & E. E. Smith (Eds.), *The psychology of human thought.* New York: Cambridge University Press.

Smith, E. E. (2000). Neural bases of human working memory. *Current Directions in Psychological Science, 9,* 45–49.

Smith, E. E., Shoben, E. J., & Rips, L. J. (1974). Structure and process in semantic memory: A feature model of semantic decisions. *Psychological Review, 81,* 214–241.

Smith, K., Johnson, D. W., & Johnson, R. T. (1981). Can conflict be constructive? Controversy versus concurrence seeking in learning groups. *Journal of Educational Psychology, 73,* 651–663.

Smith, P. K., & Dutton, S. (1979). Play and training on direct and innovative problem-solving. *Child Development, 50,* 830–836.

Smith, R. E., & Smoll, F. L. (1997). Coaching the coaches: Youth sports as a scientific and applied behavioral setting. *Current Directions in Psychological Science, 6*(1), 16–21.

Smith, S. M., Glenberg, A., & Bjork, R. A. (1978). Environmental context and human memory. *Memory and Cognition, 6,* 342–353.

Sneider, C., & Pulos, S. (1983). Children's cosmographies: Understanding the earth's shape and gravity. *Science Education, 67,* 205–221.

Snow, R. E. (1989). Aptitude-treatment interaction as a framework for research on individual differences in learning. In P. L. Ackerman, R. J. Sternberg, & R. Glaser (Eds.), *Learning and individual differences: Advances in theory and research.* New York: W. H. Freeman.

Snow, R. E. (1994). Abilities in academic tasks. In R. J. Sternberg & R. K. Wagner (Eds.), *Mind in context: Interactionist perspectives on human intelligence.* Cambridge, England: Cambridge University Press.

Snow, R. E., Corno, L., & Jackson, D., III (1996). Individual differences in affective and conative functions. In D. C. Berliner & R. C. Calfee (Eds.), *Handbook of educational psychology.* New York: Macmillan.

Snowman, J. (1986). Learning tactics and strategies. In G. D. Phye & T. Andre (Eds.), *Cognitive classroom learning: Understanding, thinking, and problem solving.* Orlando, FL: Academic Press.

Snyder, C. R., Shorey, H. S., Cheavens, J., Pulvers, K. M., Adams, V. H., III, & Wiklund, C. (2002). Hope and academic success in college. *Journal of Educational Psychology, 94,* 820–826.

Snyder, M., & Swann, W. B. (1978). Behavioral confirmation in social interaction: From social perception to social reality. *Journal of Experimental Social Psychology, 14,* 148–162.

Sokal, R. R. (1977). Classification: Purposes, principles, progress, prospects. In P. N. Johnson-Laird & P. C. Wason (Eds.), *Thinking: Readings in cognitive science.* Cambridge, England: Cambridge University Press.

Solnick, J. V., Rincover, A., & Peterson, C. R. (1977). Some determinants of the reinforcing and punishing effects of timeout. *Journal of Applied Behavior Analysis, 10,* 415–424.

Solomon, P., Kubzansky, P. E., Leiderman, P. H., Mendelson, J. H., Trumbull, R., & Wexler, D. (1961). *Sensory deprivation: A symposium held at Harvard Medical School.* Cambridge, MA: Harvard University Press.

Son, L. K., & Metcalfe, J. (2000). Metacognitive and control strategies in study-time allocation. *Journal of Experimental Psychology: Learning, Memory, and Cognition, 26,* 204–221.

Son, L. K., & Schwartz, B. L. (2002). The relation between metacognitive monitoring and control. In T. J. Perfect & B. L. Schwartz (Eds.), *Applied metacognition* (pp. 15–38). Cambridge, England: Cambridge University Press.

Southerland, S. A., & Sinatra, G. M. (2003). Learning about biological evolution: A special case of intentional conceptual change. In G. M. Sinatra & P. R. Pintrich (Eds.), *Intentional conceptual change* (pp. 317–345). Mahwah, NJ: Erlbaum.

Sowell, E. R., & Jernigan, T. L. (1998). Further MRI evidence of late brain maturation: Limbic volume increases and changing asymmetries during childhood and adolescence. *Developmental Neuropsychology, 14,* 599–617.

Sowell, E. R., Thompson, P. M., Holmes, C. J., Jernigan, T. L., & Toga, A. W. (1999). In vivo evidence for post-adolescent brain maturation in frontal and striatal regions. *Nature Neuroscience, 2,* 859–861.

Spaulding, C. L. (1992). *Motivation in the classroom.* New York: McGraw-Hill.

Spelke, E. S. (1994). Initial knowledge: Six suggestions. *Cognition, 50,* 431–445.

Spelke, E. S. (2000). Core knowledge. *American Psychologist, 55,* 1233–1243.

Spelke, E. S., Breinlinger, K., Macomber, J., & Jacobson, K. (1992). Origins of knowledge. *Psychological Review, 99,* 605–632.

Spelke, E. S., Hirst, W., & Neisser, U. (1976). The skills of divided attention. *Cognition, 4,* 215–230.

Spence, K. W. (1956). *Behavior theory and conditioning.* New Haven, CT: Yale University Press.

Spence, I., Wong, P., Rusan, M., & Rastegar, N. (2006). How color enhances visual memory for natural scenes. *Psychological Science, 17,* 1–6.

Sperling, G. (1960). The information available in brief visual presentations. *Psychological Monographs, 74* (Whole No. 498).

Sperling, G. (1967). Successive approximations to a model for short-term memory. *Acta Psychologia, 27,* 285–292.

Spielberger, C. D. (1966). The effects of anxiety on complex learning in academic achievement. In C. D. Spielberger (Ed.), *Anxiety and behavior.* New York: Academic Press.

Spielberger, C. D., & DeNike, L. D. (1966). Descriptive behaviorism versus cognitive theory in verbal operant conditioning. *Psychological Review, 73,* 306–326.

Spilich, G. J., Vesonder, G. T., Chiesi, H. L., & Voss, J. F. (1979). Text processing of domain-related information for individuals with high and low domain knowledge. *Journal of Verbal Learning and Verbal Behavior, 18,* 275–290.

Spires, H. A. (1990, April). *Learning from a lecture: Effects of comprehension monitoring.* Paper presented at the annual meeting of the American Educational Research Association, Boston.

Spires, H. A., & Donley, J. (1998). Prior knowledge activation: Inducing engagement with informational texts. *Journal of Educational Psychology, 90,* 249–260.

Spires, H. A., Donley, J., & Penrose, A. M. (1990, April). *Prior knowledge activation: Inducing text engagement in reading to learn.* Paper presented at the annual meeting of the American Educational Research Association, Boston.

Spiro, R. J. (1977). Remembering information from text: The "state of schema" approach. In R. C. Anderson, R. J. Spiro, & W. E. Montague (Eds.), *Schooling and the acquisition of knowledge.* Hillsdale, NJ: Erlbaum.

Spiro, R. J. (1980a). Accommodative reconstruction in prose recall. *Journal of Verbal Learning and Verbal Behavior, 19,* 84–95.

Spiro, R. J. (1980b). Constructive processes in prose comprehension and recall. In R. J. Spiro, B. C. Bruce, & W. F. Brewer (Eds.), *Theoretical issues in reading comprehension.* Hillsdale, NJ: Erlbaum.

Spivey, N. N. (1997). *The constructivist metaphor: Reading, writing, and the making of meaning.* San Diego, CA: Academic Press.

Sporer, S. (1991). Deep-deeper-deepest? Encoding strategies and the recognition of human faces. *Journal of Experimental Psychology: Learning, Memory, and Cognition, 17,* 323–333.

Squire, L. R. (1987). *Memory and brain.* Oxford, England: Oxford University Press.

Squire, L. R., & Alvarez, P. (1998). Retrograde amnesia and memory consolidation: A neurobiological perspective. In L. R. Squire & S. M. Kosslyn (Eds.), *Findings and current opinion in cognitive neuroscience* (pp. 75–84). Cambridge, MA: MIT Press.

Stacey, K. (1992). Mathematical problem solving in groups: Are two heads better than one? *Journal of Mathematical Behavior, 11,* 261–275.

Staddon, J. E. R., & Higa, J. J. (1991). Temporal learning. In G. H. Bower (Ed.), *The psychology of learning and motivation: Advances in research and theory* (Vol. 27). San Diego, CA: Academic Press.

Standage, M., Duda, J. L., & Ntoumanis, N. (2003). A model of contextual motivation in physical education: Using constructs from self-determination and achievement goal theories to predict physical activity intentions. *Journal of Educational Psychology, 95,* 97–110.

Standing, L. (1973). Learning 10,000 pictures. *Quarterly Journal of Experimental Psychology, 25,* 207–222.

Stanovich, K. E. (1998). Cognitive neuroscience and educational psychology: What season is it? *Educational Psychology Review, 10,* 419–426.

Stanovich, K. E. (1999). *Who is rational? Studies of individual differences in reasoning.* Mahwah, NJ: Erlbaum.

Starr, E. J., & Lovett, S. B. (2000). The ability to distinguish between comprehension and memory: Failing to succeed. *Journal of Educational Psychology, 92,* 761–771.

Stazyk, E. H., Ashcraft, M. H., & Hamann, M. S. (1982). A network approach to mental multiplication. *Journal of Experimental Psychology: Learning, Memory, and Cognition, 8,* 320–335.

Steele, C. (1997). A threat in the air: How stereotypes shape intellectual identify and performance. *American Psychologist, 52,* 613–629.

Stefanou, C. R., Perencevich, K. C., DiCintio, M., & Turner, J. C. (2004). Supporting autonomy in the classroom: Ways teachers encourage student decision making and ownership. *Educational Psychologist, 39,* 97–110.

Steffensen, M. S., Joag-Dev, C., & Anderson, R. C. (1979). A cross-cultural perspective on reading comprehension. *Reading Research Quarterly, 15,* 10–29.

Stein, B. S. (1978). Depth of processing reexamined: The effects of the precision of encoding and test appropriateness. *Journal of Verbal Learning and Verbal Behavior, 17,* 165–174.

Stein, B. S. (1989). Memory and creativity. In J. A. Glover, R. R. Ronning, & C. R. Reynolds (Eds.), *Handbook of creativity.* New York: Plenum Press.

Stein, B. S., & Bransford, J. D. (1979). Constraints on effective elaboration: Effects of precision and subject generation. *Journal of Verbal Learning and Verbal Behavior, 18,* 769–777.

Stein, B. S., Bransford, J. D., Franks, J. J., Owings, R. A., Vye, N. J., & McGraw, W. (1982). Differences in the precision of self-generated elaborations. *Journal of Experimental Psychology: General, 111,* 399–405.

Steinberg, L. (1996). *Beyond the classroom: Why school reform has failed and what parents need to do.* New York: Touchstone.

Stensvold, M. S., & Wilson, J. T. (1990). The interaction of verbal ability with concept mapping in learning from a chemistry laboratory activity. *Science Education, 74,* 473–480.

Stepans, J. (1991). Developmental patterns in students' understanding of physics concepts. In S. M. Glynn, R. H. Yeany, & B. K. Britton (Eds.), *The psychology of learning science.* Hillsdale, NJ: Erlbaum.

Stephan, W. G., & Stephan, C. W. (2000). An integrated threat theory of prejudice. In S. Oskamp (Ed.), *Reducing prejudice and discrimination* (pp. 23–45). Mahwah, NJ: Erlbaum.

Stephens, C. E., Pear, J. J., Wray, L. D., & Jackson, G. C. (1975). Some effects of reinforcement schedules in teaching picture names to retarded children. *Journal of Applied Behavior Analysis, 8,* 435–447.

Stepich, D. A., & Newby, T. J. (1988). Analogical instruction within the information processing paradigm: Effective means to facilitate learning. *Instructional Science, 17,* 129–144.

Sternberg, R. J. (1996). *Cognitive psychology.* Fort Worth, TX: Harcourt Brace.

Sternberg, R. J. (2003). *Wisdom, intelligence, and creativity synthesized.* Cambridge, England: Cambridge University Press.

Sternberg, R. J., & Davidson, J. E. (1982). Componential analysis and componential theory. *Behavioural and Brain Sciences, 53,* 352–353.

Sternberg, R. J., & Davidson, J. E. (1983). Insight in the gifted. *Educational Psychologist, 18,* 51–57.

Sternberg, R. J., Forsythe, G. B., Hedlund, J., Horvath, J. A., Wagner, R. K., Williams, W. M., Snook, S. A., & Grigorenko, E. L. (2000). *Practical intelligence in everyday life.* Cambridge, England: Cambridge University Press.

Sternberg, R. J., & Frensch, P. A. (1993). Mechanisms of transfer. In D. K. Detterman & R. J. Sternberg (Eds.), *Transfer on trial: Intelligence, cognition, and instruction.* Norwood, NJ: Ablex.

Sternberg, R. J., & Wagner, R. K. (Eds.) (1994). *Mind in context: Interactionist perspectives on human intelligence.* Cambridge, England: Cambridge University Press.

Sternberg, S. (1966). High-speed scanning in human memory. *Science, 153,* 652–654.

Steuer, F. B., Applefield, J. M., & Smith, R. (1971). Televised aggression and the interpersonal aggression of preschool children. *Journal of Experimental Child Psychology, 11,* 442–447.

Stevens, R. J., & Slavin, R. E. (1995). The cooperative elementary school: Effects of students' achievement, attitudes, and social relations. *American Educational Research Journal, 32,* 321–351.

Stevenson, H. C., & Fantuzzo, J. W. (1986). The generality and social validity of a competency-based self-control training intervention for underachieving students. *Journal of Applied Behavior Analysis, 19,* 269–276.

Stevenson, H. W., Chen, C., & Uttal, D. H. (1990). Beliefs and achievement: A study of black, white, and Hispanic children. *Child Development, 61,* 508–523.

Stickgold, R. (2005). Sleep-dependent memory consolidation. *Nature, 437,* 1272–1278.

Stiggins, R. J. (2001). *Student-involved classroom assessment* (3rd ed.). Upper Saddle River, NJ: Merrill/Prentice Hall.

Stiles, J., & Thal, D. (1993). Linguistic and spatial cognitive development following early focal brain injury: Patterns of deficit and recovery. In M. Johnson (Ed.), *Brain development and cognition.* Oxford, England: Blackwell.

Stipek, D. J. (1984). Sex differences in children's attributions for success and failure on math and spelling tests. *Sex Roles, 11,* 969–981.

Stipek, D. J. (1993). *Motivation to learn: From theory to practice* (2nd ed.). Boston: Allyn & Bacon.

Stipek, D. J. (1996). Motivation and instruction. In D. C. Berliner & R. C. Calfee (Eds.), *Handbook of educational psychology.* New York: Macmillan.

Stipek, D. J., & Gralinski, H. (1990, April). *Gender differences in children's achievement-related beliefs and emotional responses to success and failure in math.* Paper presented at the annual meeting of the American Educational Research Association, Boston.

Stipek, D. J., & Kowalski, P. S. (1989). Learned helplessness in task-orienting versus performance-orienting testing conditions. *Journal of Educational Psychology, 81,* 384–391.

Stodolsky, S. S., Salk, S., & Glaessner, B. (1991). Student views about learning math and social studies. *American Educational Research Journal, 28,* 89–116.

Stokes, T. F., & Baer, D. M. (1977). An implicit technology of generalization. *Journal of Applied Behavior Analysis, 10,* 349–367.

Stone, N. J. (2000). Exploring the relationship between calibration and self-regulated learning. *Educational Psychology Review, 12,* 437–475.

Straus, M. A. (2000a). The benefits of never spanking: New and more definitive evidence. In M. A. Straus, *Beating the devil out of them: Corporal punishment by American families and its effects on children.* New Brunswick, NJ: Transaction.

Straus, M. A. (2000b). Corporal punishment by parents: The cradle of violence in the familiy and society. *The Virginia Journal of Social Policy & the Law, 8*(1), 7–60.

Strayer, D. L., & Johnston, W. A. (2001). Driven to distraction: Dual-task studies of simulated driving and conversing on a cellular telephone. *Psychological Science, 12,* 462–466.

Stright, A. D., Neitzel, C., Sears, K. G., & Hoke-Sinex, L. (2001). Instruction begins in the home: Relations between parental instruction and children's self-regulation in the classroom. *Journal of Educational Psychology, 93,* 456–466.

Strike, K. A., & Posner, G. J. (1992). A revisionist theory of conceptual change. In R. A. Duschl & R. J. Hamilton (Eds.), *Philosophy of science, cognitive psychology, and educational theory and practice.* Albany: State University of New York Press.

Strozer, J. R. (1994). *Language acquisition after puberty.* Washington, DC: Georgetown University Press.

Stupnisky, R. H., Perry, R. P., Hall, N. C., & van Winkel, L. M. (2006, April). *A test of Weiner's precursors to causal search in a college classsroom setting.* Paper presented at the annual meeting of the American Educational Research Association, San Francisco.

Sue, S., & Chin, R. (1983). The mental health of Chinese-American children: Stressors and resources. In G. J. Powell (Ed.), *The psychosocial development of minority children.* New York: Brunner/Mazel.

Suina, J. H., & Smolkin, L. B. (1994). From natal culture to school culture to dominant society culture: Supporting transitions for Pueblo Indian students. In P. M. Greenfield & R. R. Cocking (Eds.), *Cross-cultural roots of minority child development.* Hillsdale, NJ: Erlbaum.

Sulin, R. A., & Dooling, D. J. (1974). Intrusions of a thematic idea in retention of prose. *Journal of Experimental Psychology, 103,* 255–262.

Sullivan, J. S. (1989). Planning, implementing, and maintaining an effective in-school suspension program. *Clearing House, 62,* 409–410.

Sullivan, R. C. (1994). Autism: Definitions past and present. *Journal of Vocational Rehabilitation, 4,* 4–9.

Surber, J. R. (2001). Effect of topic label repetition and importance on reading time and recall of text. *Journal of Educational Psychology, 93,* 279–287.

Sussman, D. M. (1981). PSI: Variations on a theme. In S. W. Bijou & R. Ruiz (Eds.), *Behavior modification: Contributions to education.* Hillsdale, NJ: Erlbaum.

Swan, K., Mitrani, M., Guerrero, F., Cheung, M., & Schoener, J. (1990, April). *Perceived locus of control and computer-based instruction.* Paper presented at the annual meeting of the American Educational Research Association, Boston.

Swanson, H. L., Cooney, J. B., & O'Shaughnessy, T. E. (1998). Learning disabilities and memory. In B. Y. L. Wong (Ed.), *Learning about learning disabilities* (2nd ed., pp. 107–162). San Diego, CA: Academic Press.

Swanson, H. L., & Lussier, C. M. (2001). A selective synthesis of the experimental literature on dynamic assessment. *Review of Educational Research, 71,* 321–363.

Swanson, H. L., O'Connor, J. E., & Cooney, J. B. (1990). An information processing analysis of expert and novice teachers' problem solving. *American Educational Research Journal, 27,* 533–556.

Sweller, J. (1994). Cognitive load theory, learning difficulty, and instructional design. *Learning and Instruction, 4,* 295–312.

Sweller, J., & Levine, M. (1982). Effects of goal specificity on means-end analysis and learning. *Journal of Experimental Psychology: Learning, Memory, and Cognition, 8,* 463–474.

Swenson, L. C. (1980). *Theories of learning: Traditional perspectives/contemporary developments.* Belmont, CA: Wadsworth.

Sylva, K., Bruner, J. S., & Genova, P. (1976). The role of play in the problem solving of children 3 to 5 years old. In J. Bruner, A. Jolly, & K. Sylva (Eds.), *Play: Its role in development and evolution.* New York: Basic Books.

Talarico, J. M., LaBar, K. S., & Rubin, D. C. (2004). Emotional intensity predicts autobiographical memory experience. *Memory & Cognition, 32,* 1118–1132.

Talarico, J. M., & Rubin, D. C. (2003). Confidence, not consistency, characterizes flashbulb memories. *Psychological Science, 14,* 455–461.

Talmi, D., Grady, C. L., Goshen-Gottstein, Y., & Moscovitch, M. (2005). Neuroimaging the serial position curve: A test of single-store versus dual-store models. *Psychological Science, 16,* 716–723.

Tamburrini, J. (1982). Some educational implications of Piaget's theory. In S. Modgil and C. Modgil (Eds.), *Jean Piaget: Consensus and controversy.* New York: Praeger.

Tang, J.-C., Kennedy, C. H., Koppekin, A., & Caruso, M. (2002). Functional analysis of sterotypical ear covering in a child with autism. *Journal of Applied Behavior Analysis, 35,* 95–98.

Tarver, S. G. (1992). Direct Instruction. In W. Stainback & S. Stainback (Eds.), *Controversial issues confronting special education.* Boston: Allyn & Bacon.

Taylor, B. A., & Levin, L. (1998). Teaching a student with autism to make verbal initiations: Effects of a tactile prompt. *Journal of Applied Behavior Analysis, 31,* 651–654.

Taylor, B. M. (1982). Text structure and children's comprehension and memory for expository material. *Journal of Educational Psychology, 74,* 323–340.

Taylor, J. C., & Romanczyk, R. G. (1994). Generating hypotheses about the function of student problem behavior by observing teacher behavior. *Journal of Applied Behavior Analysis, 27,* 251–265.

Taylor, M., Esbensen, B. M., & Bennett, R. T. (1994). Children's understanding of knowledge acquisition: The tendency for children to report they have always known what they have just learned. *Child Development, 65,* 1581–1604.

Taylor, M. J., & Kratochwill, T. R. (1978). Modification of preschool children's bathroom behaviors by contingent teacher attention. *Journal of School Psychology, 16,* 64–71.

Taylor, S. M. (1994, April). *Staying in school against the odds: Voices of minority adolescent girls.* Paper presented at the annual meeting of the American Educational Research Association, New Orleans, LA.

Teasley, S. D., & Roschelle, J. (1993). Constructing a joint problem space: The computer as a tool for sharing information. In S. P. Lajoie & S. J. Derry (Eds.), *Computers as cognitive tools* (pp. 229–258). Hillsdale, NJ: Erlbaum.

Tennyson, C. L., Tennyson, R. D., & Rothen, W. (1980). Content structure and instructional control strategies as design variables in concept acquisition. *Journal of Educational Psychology, 72,* 499–505.

Tennyson, R. D., & Cocchiarella, M. J. (1986). An empirically based instructional design theory for teaching concepts. *Review of Educational Research, 56,* 40–71.

Tennyson, R. D., & Park, O. (1980). The teaching of concepts: A review of instructional design literature. *Review of Educational Research, 50,* 55–70.

Tennyson, R. D., & Tennyson, C. L. (1975). Rule acquisition design strategy variables: Degree of instance divergence, sequence, and instance analysis. *Journal of Educational Psychology, 67,* 852–859.

Tennyson, R. D., Youngers, J., & Suebsonthi, P. (1983). Concept learning by children using instructional presentation forms for prototype formation and classification-skill development. *Journal of Educational Psychology, 75,* 280–291.

Tessler, M., & Nelson, K. (1994). Making memories: The influence of joint encoding on later recall by young children. *Consciousness and Cognition, 3,* 307–326.

Thapar, A., & Greene, R. (1993). Evidence against a short-term store account of long-term recency effects. *Memory and Cognition, 21,* 329–337.

Tharp, R. G. (1989). Psychocultural variables and constants: Effects on teaching and learning in schools. *American Psychologist, 44,* 349–359.

Théberge, C. L. (1994, April). *Small-group vs. whole-class discussion: Gaining the floor in science lessons.* Paper presented at the annual meeting of the American Educational Research Association, New Orleans, LA.

Thelen, E., & Smith, L. B. (1998). Dynamic systems theories. In W. Damon (Ed.-in-chief) and R. M. Lerner (Vol. Ed.), *Handbook of child psychology: Vol. 1. Theoretical models of human development.* New York: Wiley.

Thiagarajan, S. (1989). Interactive lectures: Seven more strategies. *Performance and Instruction, 28*(2), 35–37.

Thiede, K. W., Anderson, M. C. M., & Therriault, D. (2003). Accuracy of metacognitive monitoring affects learning of texts. *Journal of Educational Psychology, 95,* 66–73.

Thomas, E. L., & Robinson, H. A. (1972). *Improving reading in every class: A sourcebook for teachers.* Boston: Allyn & Bacon.

Thomas, J. G., Milner, H. R., & Haberlandt, K. F. (2003). Forward and backward recall: Different response time patterns, same retrieval order. *Psychological Science, 14,* 169–174.

Thomas, J. W. (1993a). Expectations and effort: Course demands, students' study practices, and academic achievement. In T. M. Tomlinson (Ed.), *Motivating students to learn: Overcoming barriers to high achievement.* Berkeley, CA: McCutchan.

Thomas, J. W. (1993b). Promoting independent learning in the middle grades: The role of instructional support practice. *Elementary School Journal, 93,* 575–591.

Thomas, S., & Oldfather, P. (1997). Intrinsic motivations, literacy, and assessment practices: "That's my grade. That's me." *Educational Psychologist, 32,* 107–123.

Thompson, A. G., & Thompson, P. W. (1989). Affect and problem solving in an elementary school mathematics classroom. In D. B. McLeod & V. M. Adams (Eds.), *Affect and mathematical problem solving: A new perspective.* New York: Springer-Verlag.

Thompson, R., Emmorey, K., & Gollan, T. H. (2005). "Tip of the fingers" experience by deaf signers: Insights into the organization of a sign-based lexicon. *Psychological Science, 16,* 856–860.

Thompson, R., & McConnell, J. (1955). Classical conditioning in the planarian, *Dugesia dorotocephala. Journal of Comparative and Physiological Psychology, 48,* 65–68.

Thompson, R. A., & Nelson, C. A. (2001). Developmental science and the media: Early brain development. *American Psychologist, 56,* 5–15.

Thompson, S. C. (1999). Illusions of control: How we overestimate our personal influence. *Current Directions in Psychological Science, 8,* 187–190.

Thomson, D. M. (1988). Context and false recognition. In G. M. Davies & D. M. Thomson (Eds.), *Memory in context: Context in memory* (pp. 285–304). Chichester, England: Wiley.

Thorndike, E. L. (1898). Animal intelligence: An experimental study of the associative processes in animals. *Psychological Review Monograph Supplement, 2*(8).

Thorndike, E. L. (1903). *Educational psychology.* New York: Lemcke & Buechner.

Thorndike, E. L. (1911). *Animal intelligence.* New York: Macmillan.

Thorndike, E. L. (1913). *Educational psychology: The psychology of learning* (Vol. 2). New York: Teachers College Press.

Thorndike, E. L. (1924). Mental discipline in high school studies. *Journal of Educational Psychology, 15,* 1–22, 83–98.

Thorndike, E. L. (1932a). *The fundamentals of learning.* New York: Teachers College Press.

Thorndike, E. L. (1932b). Reward and punishment in animal learning. *Comparative Psychology Monograph, 8*(39).

Thorndike, E. L. (1935). *The psychology of wants, interests, and attitudes.* New York: Appleton-Century-Crofts.

Thorndike, E. L., & Woodworth, R. S. (1901). The influence of improvement in one mental function upon the efficiency of other functions. *Psychological Review, 8,* 247–261, 384–395, 553–564.

Thrailkill, N. J., & Ormrod, J. E. (1994, April). *Facilitating lecture recall: Effects of embedded imagery-evoking phrases on memory for proximal and non-proximal material.* Paper presented at the annual meeting of the American Educational Research Association, New Orleans, LA.

Thyne, J. M. (1963). *The psychology of learning and techniques of teaching.* London: University of London Press.

Tiger, J. H., Hanley, G. P., & Hernandez, E. (2006). An evaluation of the value of choice with preschool children. *Journal of Applied Behavior Analysis, 39,* 1–16.

Timberlake, W., & Lucas, G. A. (1989). Behavior systems and learning: From misbehavior to general principles. In S. B. Klein & R. R. Mowrer (Eds.), *Contemporary learning theories: Instrumental conditioning theory and the impact of biological constraints on learning.* Mahwah, NJ: Erlbaum.

Tirosh, D., & Graeber, A. O. (1990). Evoking cognitive conflict to explore preservice teachers' thinking about division. *Journal for Research in Mathematics Education, 21,* 98–108.

Titcomb, A. L., & Reyna, V. F. (1995). Memory interference and misinformation effects. In F. N. Dempster & C. J. Brainerd (Eds.), *Interference and inhibition in cognition.* San Diego, CA: Academic Press.

Tobias, S. (1980). Anxiety and instruction. In I. G. Sarason (Ed.), *Test anxiety: Theory, research, and applications.* Hillsdale, NJ: Erlbaum.

Tobias, S. (1985). Test anxiety: Interference, defective skills, and cognitive capacity. *Educational Psychologist, 20,* 135–142.

Tobias, S. (1994). Interest, prior knowledge, and learning. *Review of Educational Research, 64,* 37–54.

Tobin, K. (1987). The role of wait time in higher cognitive level learning. *Review of Educational Research, 57,* 69–95.

Tobin, K., & Tippins, D. (1993). Constructivism as a reference for teaching and learning. In K. Tobin (Ed.), *The practice of constructivism in science education.* Washington, DC: American Association for the Advancement of Science.

Toglia, M. P. (1996). Recovered memories: Lost and found? In K. Pezdek & W. P. Banks (Eds.), *The recovered memory/false memory debate.* San Diego, CA: Academic Press.

Tollefson, N. (2000). Classroom applications of cognitive theories of motivation. *Educational Psychology Review, 12,* 63–83.

Tolman, E. C. (1932). *Purposive behavior in animals and men.* New York: Century.

Tolman, E. C. (1938). The determiners of behavior at a choice point. *Psychological Review, 45,* 1–41.

Tolman, E. C. (1942). *Drives toward war.* New York: Appleton-Century.

Tolman, E. C. (1959). Principles of purposive behavior. In S. Koch (Ed.), *Psychology: A study of a science* (Vol. 2). New York: McGraw-Hill.

Tolman, E. C., & Honzik, C. H. (1930). Introduction and removal of reward, and maze performance in rats. *University of California Publications in Psychology, 4,* 257–275.

Tolman, E. C., Ritchie, B. F., & Kalish, D. (1946). Studies in spatial learning: I. Orientation and the short-cut. *Journal of Experimental Psychology, 36*, 13–24.

Tomback, R. M., Williams, A. Y., & Wentzel, K. R. (2005, April). *Young adolescents' concerns about the transition to high school.* Poster presented at the annual meeting of the American Educational Research Association, Montreal.

Toplak, M. E., & Stanovich, K. E. (2002). The domain specificity and generality of disjunctive searching for a generalizable critical thinking skill. *Journal of Educational Psychology, 94*, 197–209.

Torgesen, J. K. (1996). A model of memory from an information processing perspective: The special case of phonological memory. In G. R. Lyon & N. A. Krasnegor (Eds.), *Attention, memory, and executive function* (pp. 157–184). Baltimore: Brookes.

Torney-Purta, J. (1994). Dimensions of adolescents' reasoning about political and historical issues: Ontological switches, developmental processes, and situated learning. In M. Carretero & J. F. Voss (Eds.), *Cognitive and instructional processes in history and the social sciences* (pp. 103–122). Mahwah, NJ: Erlbaum.

Torrance, E. P., & Myers, R. E. (1970). *Creative learning and teaching.* New York: Dodd, Mead & Company.

Tourniaire, F., & Pulos, S. (1985). Proportional reasoning: A review of the literature. *Educational Studies in Mathematics, 16*, 181–204.

Trachtenberg, D. (1974). Student tasks in text material. What cognitive skills do they tap? *Peabody Journal of Education, 52*, 54–57.

Trachtenberg, J. T., Chen, B. E., Knott, G. W., Feng, G., Sanes, J. R., Welker, E., & Svoboda, K. (2002). Long-term *in vivo* imaging of experience-dependent synaptic plasticity in adult cortex. *Nature, 420*, 788–794.

Trautwein, U., & Köller, O. (April, 2004). *Time investment doesn't always pay off: The role of self-regulatory strategies in homework execution.* Paper presented at the American Educational Research Association, San Diego, CA.

Trautwein, L., Lüdtke, O., Schnyder, I., & Niggli, A. (2006). Predicting homework effort: Support for a domain-specific, multilevel homework model. *Journal of Educational Psychology, 98*, 438–456.

Trawick-Smith, J. (2003). *Early childhood development: A multicultural perspective* (3rd ed.). Upper Saddle River, NJ: Merrill/Prentice Hall.

Treisman, A. M. (1964). Verbal cues, language and meaning in selective attention. *American Journal of Psychology, 77*, 215–216.

Trenholme, I. A., & Baron, A. (1975). Intermediate and delayed punishment of human behavior by loss of reinforcement. *Learning and Motivation, 6*, 62–79.

Trevarthen, C. (1980). The foundations of intersubjectivity: Development of interpersonal and cooperative understandings in infants. In D. R. Olson (Ed.), *The social foundations of language and thought* (pp. 316–342). New York: Norton.

Trevarthen, C., & Hubley, P. (1978). Secondary intersubjectivity: Confidence, confiding and acts of meaning in the first year. In A. Lock (Ed.), *Action, gesture, and symbol: The emergence of language.* London: Academic Press.

Tryon, G. S. (1980). The measurement and treatment of test anxiety. *Review of Educational Research, 50*, 343–372.

Tschannen-Moran, M., Woolfolk Hoy, A., & Hoy, W. K. (1998). Teacher efficacy: Its meaning and measure. *Review of Educational Research, 68*, 202–248.

Tudge, J. (1990). Vygotsky, the zone of proximal development, and peer collaboration: Implications for classroom practice. In L. C. Moll (Ed.), *Vygotsky and education: Instructional implications and applications of sociohistorical psychology.* New York: Cambridge University Press.

Tudor, R. M. (1995). Isolating the effects of active responding in computer-based instruction. *Journal of Applied Behavior Analysis, 28*, 343–344.

Tulving, E. (1962). Subjective organization in free recall of "unrelated" words. *Psychological Review, 69*, 344–354.

Tulving, E. (1968). Theoretical issues in free recall. In T. R. Dixon & D. L. Horton (Eds.), *Verbal behavior and general behavior theory.* Englewood Cliffs, NJ: Prentice Hall.

Tulving, E. (1975). Ecphoric processes in recall and recognition. In J. Brown (Ed.), *Recall and recognition.* London: Wiley.

Tulving, E. (1983). *Elements of episodic memory.* Oxford, England: Oxford University Press.

Tulving, E. (1991). Concepts of human memory. In L. R. Squire, N. M. Weinberger, G. Lynch, & J. L. McGaugh (Eds.), *Organization and locus of change.* New York: Oxford University Press.

Tulving, E. (1993). What is episodic memory? *Current Directions in Psychological Science, 2*, 67–70.

Tulving, E., & Psotka, J. (1971). Retroactive inhibition in free recall: Inaccessibility of information available in the memory store. *Journal of Experimental Psychology, 87*, 1–8.

Tulving, E., & Thomson, D. M. (1971). Retrieval processes in recognition memory: Effects of associative context. *Journal of Experimental Psychology, 87*, 116–124.

Tunstall, P., & Gipps, C. (1996). Teacher feedback to young children in formative assessment: A typology. *British Educational Research Journal, 22*, 389–404.

Turnbull, C. M. (1961). *The forest people.* New York: Simon & Schuster.

Turner, J. C. (1995). The influence of classroom contexts on young children's motivation for literacy. *Reading Research Quarterly, 30*, 410–441.

Turner, J. C., Meyer, D. K., Cox, K. E., Logan, C., DiCintio, M., & Thomas, C. T. (1998). Creating contexts for involvement in mathematics. *Journal of Educational Psychology, 90*, 730–745.

Turner, J. C., Thorpe, P. K., & Meyer, D. K. (1998). Students' reports of motivation and negative affect: A theoretical and empirical analysis. *Journal of Educational Psychology, 90*, 758–771.

Turner, J. E., Husman, J., & Schallert, D. L. (2002). The importance of students' goals in their emotional experience of academic failure: Investigating the precursors and consequences of shame. *Educational Psychologist, 37*, 79–89.

Turner, L. A., & Johnson, B. (2003). A model of mastery motivation for at-risk preschoolers. *Journal of Educational Psychology, 95*, 495–505.

Turnure, J., Buium, N., & Thurlow, M. (1976). The effectiveness of interrogatives for promoting verbal elaboration productivity in young children. *Child Development, 47*, 851–855.

Turvey, M. T., & Kravetz, S. (1970). Retrieval from iconic memory with shape as the selection criterion. *Perception and Psychophysics, 8*, 171–172.

Tversky, A., & Kahneman, D. (1973). Availability: A heuristic for judging frequency and probability. *Cognitive Psychology, 5*, 207–232.

Tversky, B. (1981). Distortions in memory for maps. *Cognitive Psychology, 13*, 407–433.

Tweed, R. G., & Lehman, D. R. (2002). Learning considered within a cultural context. *American Psychologist, 57*, 89–99.

Tyler, B. (1958). Expectancy for eventual success as a factor in problem solving behavior. *Journal of Educational Psychology, 49*, 166–172.

Tzuriel, D. (2000). Dynamic assessment of young children: Educational and intervention perspectives. *Educational Psychology Review, 12*, 385–435.

Underwood, B. J. (1948). "Spontaneous recovery" of verbal associations. *Journal of Experimental Psychology, 38*, 429–439.

Underwood, B. J. (1954). Studies of distributed practice: XII. Retention following varying degrees of original learning. *Journal of Experimental Psychology, 47*, 294–300.

Underwood, B. J. (1957). Interference and forgetting. *Psychological Review, 64*, 49–60.

Underwood, B. J. (1961). Ten years of massed practice on distributed practice. *Psychological Review, 68*, 229–247.

Underwood, B. J. (1983). *Attributes of memory.* Glenview, IL: Scott, Foresman.

Underwood, B. J., & Erlebacher, A. H. (1965). Studies of coding in verbal behavior. *Psychological Monographs, 79* (Whole No. 606).

Underwood, B. J., Kapelak, S., & Malmi, R. (1976). The spacing effect: Additions to the theoretical and empirical puzzles. *Memory and Cognition, 4*, 391–400.

Underwood, B. J., & Schulz, R. W. (1960). *Meaningfulness and verbal learning.* Philadelphia: J. B. Lippincott.

Urbach, T. P., Windmann, S. S., Payne, D. G., & Kutas, M. (2005). Mismaking memories: Neural precursors of memory illusions in electrical brain activity. *Psychological Science, 16*, 19–24.

Urdan, T. (2004). Predictors of academic self-handicapping and achievement: Examining achievement goals, classroom goal structures, and culture. *Journal of Educational Psychology, 96*, 251–264.

Urdan, T. C., & Maehr, M. L. (1995). Beyond a two-goal theory of motivation and achievement: A case for social goals. *Review of Educational Research, 65,* 213–243.

Urdan, T., & Mestas, M. (2006). The goals behind performance goals. *Journal of Educational Psychology, 98,* 354–365.

Urdan, T. C., & Midgley, C. (2001). Academic self-handicapping: What we know, what more there is to learn. *Educational Psychology Review, 13,* 115–138.

Urdan, T. C., Midgley, C., & Anderman, E. M. (1998). The role of classroom goal structure in students' use of self-handicapping strategies. *American Educational Research Journal, 35,* 101–122.

Urdan, T., Ryan, A. M., Anderman, E. M., & Gheen, M. H. (2002). Goals, goal structures, and avoidance behaviors. In C. Midgley (Ed.), *Goals, goal structures, and patterns of adaptive learning* (pp. 55–83). Mahwah, NJ: Erlbaum.

Valentine, J. C., DuBois, D. L., & Cooper, H. (2004). The relation between self-beliefs and academic achievement: A meta-analytic review. *Educational Psychologist, 39,* 111–133.

Van Camp, C. M., Lerman, D. C., Kelley, M. E., Roane, H. S., Contrucci, S. A., & Vorndran, C. M. (2000). Further analysis of idiosyncratic antecedent influences during the assessment and treatment of problem behavior. *Journal of Applied Behavior Analysis, 33,* 207–221.

van der Broek, P. (1990). Causal inferences and the comprehension of narrative text. In A. C. Graessner & G. H. Bower (Eds.), *Inferences and text comprehension. The psychology of learning and motivation: Advances in research and theory* (Vol. 25). Orlando, FL: Academic Press.

van den Broek, P., Bauer, P. J., & Bourg, T. (Eds.) (1997). *Developmental spans in event comprehension and representation: Bridging fictional and actual events.* Mahwah, NJ: Erlbaum.

van Dijk, T. A., & Kintsch, W. (1983). *Strategies of discourse comprehension.* New York: Academic Press.

Van Dooren, W., De Bock, D., Hessels, A., Janssens, D., & Verschaffel, L. (2005). Not everything is proportional: Effects of age and problem type on propensities for overgeneralization. *Cognition and Instruction, 23,* 57–86.

van Drie, J., van Boxtel, C., & van der Linden, J. (2006). Historical reasoning in a computer-supported collaborative learning environment. In A. M. O'Donnell, C. E. Hmelo-Silver, & G. Erkens (Eds.), *Collaborative learning, reasoning, and technology* (pp. 265–296). Mahwah, NJ: Erlbaum.

Van Houten, R., Nau, P., MacKenzie-Keating, S., Sameoto, D., & Colavecchia, B. (1982). An analysis of some variables influencing the effectiveness of reprimands. *Journal of Applied Behavior Analysis, 15,* 65–83.

van Kraayenoord, C. E., & Paris, S. G. (1997). Children's self-appraisal of their worksamples and academic progress. *Elementary School Journal, 97,* 523–5537.

van Laar, C. (2000). The paradox of low academic achievement but high self-esteem in African American students: An attributional account. *Educational Psychology Review, 12,* 33–61.

Van Meter, P. (2001). Drawing construction as a strategy for learning from text. *Journal of Educational Psychology, 93,* 129–140.

Van Meter, P., Yokoi, L., & Pressley, M. (1994). College students' theory of notetaking derived from their perceptions of notetaking. *Journal of Educational Psychology, 86,* 323–338.

Van Patten, J. R., Chao, C. I., & Reigeluth, C. M. (1986). A review of strategies for sequencing and synthesizing information. *Review of Educational Research, 56,* 437–472.

Van Rossum, E. J., & Schenk, S. M. (1984). The relationship between learning conception, study strategy and learning outcome. *British Journal of Educational Psychology, 54,* 73–83.

VanSledright, B., & Brophy, J. (1992). Storytelling, imagination, and fanciful elaboration in children's historical reconstructions. *American Educational Research Journal, 29,* 837–859.

Vansteenkiste, M., Lens, W., & Deci, E. L. (2006). Intrinsic versus extrinsic goal contents in self-determination theory: Another look at the quality of academic motivation. *Educational Psychologist, 41,* 19–31.

Vansteenkiste, M., Zhou, M., Lens, W., & Soenens, B. (2005). Experiences of autonomy and control among Chinese learners: Vitalizing or immobilizing? *Journal of Educational Psychology, 97,* 468–483.

van Winkel, L. M., Ruthig, J. C., Stupnisky, R. H., Haynes, T. L., & Perry, R. P. (2006, April). *The interaction of perceived control and achievement goals on students' academic strategies and performance.* Paper presented at the annual meeting of the American Educational Research Association, San Francisco.

Vaughan, W. (1988). Formation of equivalence sets in pigeons. *Journal of Experimental Psychology: Animal Behavior Processes, 14,* 36–42.

Vaughn, B. J., & Horner, R. H. (1997). Identifying instructional tasks that occasion problem behaviors and assessing the effects of student versus teacher choice among these tasks. *Journal of Applied Behavior Analysis, 30,* 299–312.

Vecera, S. P., Vogel, E. K., & Woodman, G. F. (2002). Lower region: A new cue for figure-ground assignment. *Journal of Experimental Psychology: General, 131,* 194–205.

Veenman, S. (1984). Perceived problems of beginning teachers. *Review of Educational Research, 54,* 143–178.

Vekiri, I. (2002). What is the value of graphical displays in learning? *Educational Psychology Review, 14,* 261–312.

Verdi, M. P., & Kulhavy, R. W. (2002). Learning with maps and texts: An overview. *Educational Psychology Review, 14,* 27–46.

Verdi, M. P., Kulhavy, R. W., Stock, W. A., Rittschof, K. A., & Johnson, J. T. (1996). Text learning using scientific diagrams. Implications for classroom use. *Contemporary Educational Psychology, 21,* 487–499.

Vermeer, H. J., Boekaerts, M., & Seegers, G. (2000). Motivational and gender differences: Sixth-grade students' mathematical problem-solving behavior. *Journal of Educational Psychology, 92,* 308–315.

Vernon, M. D. (1969). *Human motivation.* Cambridge, England: Cambridge University Press.

Veroff, J., McClelland, L., & Ruhland, D. (1975). Varieties of achievement motivation. In M. T. S. Mednick, S. S. Tangri, & L. W. Hoffman (Eds.), *Women and achievement: Social and motivational analyses.* New York: Halsted.

Viken, R. J., & McFall, R. M. (1994). Paradox lost: Implications of contemporary reinforcement theory for behavior therapy. *Current Directions in Psychological Science, 3,* 121–125.

Vintere, P., Hemmes, N. S., Brown, B. L., & Poulson, C. L. (2004). Gross-motor skill acquisition by preschool dance students under self-instruction procedures. *Journal of Applied Behavior Analysis, 37,* 305–322.

Volet, S. (1999). Learning across cultures: Appropriateness of knowledge transfer. *International Journal of Educational Research, 31,* 625–643.

Vollmer, T. R., & Hackenberg, T. D. (2001). Reinforcement contingencies and social reinforcement: Some reciprocal relations between basic and applied research. *Journal of Applied Behavior Analysis, 34,* 241–253.

Vollmer, T. R., Roane, H. S., Ringdahl, J. E., & Marcus, B. A. (1999). Evaluating treatment challenges with differential reinforcement of alternative behavior. *Journal of Applied Behavior Analysis, 32,* 9–23.

von Glasersfeld, E. (1995). A constructivist approach to teaching. In L. P. Steffe & J. Gale (Eds.), *Constructivism in education* (pp. 3–15). Mahwah, NJ: Erlbaum.

Vosniadou, S. (1991). Conceptual development in astronomy. In S. M. Glynn, R. H. Yeany, & B. K. Britton (Eds.), *The psychology of learning science.* Hillsdale, NJ: Erlbaum.

Vosniadou, S. (1994). Universal and culture-specific properties of children's mental models of the earth. In L. A. Hirschfeld & S. A. Gelman (Eds.), *Mapping the mind: Domain specificity in cognition and culture.* Cambridge, England: Cambridge University Press.

Vosniadou, S., & Brewer, W. F. (1987). Theories of knowledge restructuring in development. *Review of Educational Research, 57,* 51–67.

Voss, J. F. (1987). Learning and transfer in subject-matter learning: A problem-solving model. *International Journal of Educational Research, 11,* 607–622.

Voss, J. F., Greene, T. R., Post, T. A., & Penner, B. D. (1983). Problem-solving skill in the social sciences. In G. H. Bower (Ed.), *The psychology of learning and motivation* (Vol. 17). New York: Academic Press.

Voss, J. F., & Schauble, L. (1992). Is interest educationally interesting? An interest-related model of learning. In K. A. Renninger, S. Hidi, & A. Krapp (Eds.), *The role of interest in learning and development.* Hillsdale, NJ: Erlbaum.

Voss, J. F., Tyler, S. W., & Yengo, L. A. (1983). Individual differences in the solving of socialscience problems. In R. F. Dillon & R. R. Schmeck (Eds.), *Individual differences in cognition.* New York: Academic Press.

Voss, J. F., Wolfe, C. R., Lawrence, J. A., & Engle, R. A. (1991). From representation to decision: An analysis of problem solving in international relations. In R. J. Sternberg & P. A. Frensch (Eds.), *Complex problem solving: Principles and mechanisms.* Hillsdale, NJ: Erlbaum.

Vurpillot, E., & Ball, W. A. (1979). The concept of identity and children's selective attention. In G. A. Hale & M. Lewis (Eds.), *Attention and cognitive development.* New York: Plenum Press.

Vye, N. J., Schwartz, D. L., Bransford, J. D., Barron, B. J., Zech, L., & The Cognition and Technology Group at Vanderbilt (1998). SMART environments that support monitoring, reflection, and revision. In D. J. Hacker, J. Dunlosky, & A. C. Graesser (Eds.), *Metacognition in educational theory and practice* (pp. 305–346). Mahwah, NJ: Erlbaum.

Vygotsky, L. S. (1962). *Thought and language* (E. Haufmann & G. Vakar, Eds. and Trans.). Cambridge, MA: MIT Press.

Vygotsky, L. S. (1978). *Mind in society: The development of higher psychological processes.* Cambridge, MA: Harvard University Press.

Vygotsky, L. S. (1987a). *The collected works of L. S. Vygotsky* (R. W. Rieber & A. S. Carton, Eds.). New York: Plenum Press.

Vygotsky, L. S. (1987b). Thinking and speech. In R. W. Rieber & A. S. Carton (Eds.), *The collected works of L. S. Vygotsky.* New York: Plenum Press.

Vygotsky, L. S. (1997). *Educational psychology.* Boca Raton, FL: St. Lucie Press.

Waddill, P. J., McDaniel, M. A., & Einstein, G. O. (1988). Illustrations as adjuncts to prose: A text-appropriate processing approach. *Journal of Educational Psychology, 80,* 457–464.

Wade, S. E. (1983). A synthesis of the research for improving reading in the social studies. *Review of Educational Research, 53,* 461–497.

Wade, S. E. (1992). How interest affects learning from text. In K. A. Renninger, S. Hidi, & A. Krapp (Eds.), *The role of interest in learning and development.* Hillsdale, NJ: Erlbaum.

Wade-Stein, D., & Kintsch, E. (2004). Summary Street: Interactive computer support for writing. *Cognition and Instruction, 22,* 333–362.

Wagner, J. F. (2006). Transfer in pieces. *Cognition and Instruction, 24,* 1–71.

Wagner, R. K. (1996). From simple structure to complex function: Major trends in the development of theories, models, and measurements of memory. In G. R. Lyon & N. A. Krasnegor (Eds.), *Attention, memory, and executive function* (pp. 139–156). Baltimore: Brookes.

Wahler, R. G., & Fox, J. J. (1981). Setting events in applied behavior analysis: Toward a conceptual and methodological expansion. *Journal of Applied Behavior Analysis, 14,* 327–338.

Wahler, R. G., Vigilante, V. A., & Strand, P. S. (2004). Generalization in a child's oppositional behavior across home and school settings. *Journal of Applied Behavior Analysis, 37,* 43–51.

Walker, E. F. (2002). Adolescent neurodevelopment and psychopathology. *Current Directions in Psychological Science, 11,* 24–28.

Walker, H. M., Mattsen, R. H., & Buckley, N. K. (1971). The functional analysis of behavior within an experimental class setting. In W. C. Becker (Ed.), *An empirical basis for change in education.* Chicago: Science Research Associates.

Walker, J. E., & Shea, T. M. (1995). *Behavior management: A practical approach for educators* (6th ed.). Englewood Cliffs, NJ: Merrill/Prentice Hall.

Wallas, G. (1926). *The art of thought.* New York: Harcourt Brace Jovanovich.

Walls, T. A., & Little, T. D. (2005). Relations among personal agency, motivation, and school adjustment in early adolescence. *Journal of Educational Psychology, 97,* 23–31.

Walters, G. C., & Grusec, J. E. (1977). *Punishment.* San Francisco: W. H. Freeman.

Walters, R. H., & Parke, R. D. (1964). Influence of response consequences to a social model on resistance to deviation. *Journal of Experimental Child Psychology, 1,* 269–280.

Walters, R. H., Parke, R. D., & Cane, V. A. (1965). Timing of punishment and the observation of consequences to others as determinants of response inhibition. *Journal of Experimental Child Psychology, 2,* 10–30.

Walters, R. H., & Thomas, E. L. (1963). Enhancement of punitiveness by visual and audiovisual displays. *Canadian Journal of Psychology, 17,* 244–255.

Walters, R. H., Thomas, E. L., & Acker, W. (1962). Enhancement of punitive behavior by audio-visual displays. *Science, 136,* 872–873.

Walton, G. E., & Bower, T. G. R. (1993). Newborns form "prototypes" in less than 1 minute. *Psychological Science, 4,* 203–205.

Wang, J., & Lin, E. (2005). Comparative studies on U.S. and Chinese mathematics learning and the implications for standards-based mathematics teaching reform. *Educational Researcher, 34*(5), 3–13.

Wang, M. C., & Stiles, B. (1976). An investigation of children's concept of self-responsibility for their school learning. *American Educational Research Journal, 13,* 159–179.

Want, S. C., & Harris, P. L. (2001). Learning from other people's mistakes: Causal understanding in learning to use a tool. *Child Development, 72,* 431–443.

Ward, T. B., Vela, E., & Haas, S. D. (1990). Children and adults learn family-resemblance categories analytically. *Child Development, 61,* 593–605.

Ward, T. J., Jr. (1991, April). The effects of field articulation and interestingness on text processing. In G. Schraw (Chair), *Cognitive processing and text comprehension in specific knowledge domains.* Symposium presented at the annual meeting of the American Educational Research Association, Chicago.

Wartella, E., Caplovitz, A. G. & Lee, J. H. (2004). From Baby Einstein to Leapfrog, from Doom to The Sims, from instant messaging to Internet chat rooms: Public interest in the role of interactive media in children's lives. *Social Policy Report: Giving Child and Youth Development Knowledge Away, 18*(4), 3–19

Wasserman, E. A. (1993). Comparative cognition: Toward a general understanding of cognition in behavior. *Psychological Science, 4,* 156–161.

Waters, H. S. (1982). Memory development in adolescence: Relationships between meta-memory, strategy use, and performance. *Journal of Experimental Child Psychology, 33,* 183–195.

Watkins, M. J., & Watkins, O. C. (1974). Processing of recency items for free-recall. *Journal of Experimental Psychology, 102,* 488–493.

Watson, J. B. (1925). *Behaviorism.* New York: W. W. Norton.

Watson, J. B., & Rayner, R. (1920). Conditioned emotional reactions. *Journal of Experimental Psychology, 3,* 1–14.

Watson, M., & Battistich, V. (2006). Building and sustaining caring communities. In C. M. Evertson & C. S. Weinstein (Eds.), *Handbook of classroom management: Research, practice, and contemporary issues* (pp. 253–279). Mahwah, NJ: Erlbaum.

Watts, G. H., & Anderson, R. C. (1971). Effects of three types of inserted questions on learning from prose. *Journal of Educational Psychology, 62,* 387–394.

Weaver, C. A., III, & Kelemen, W. L. (1997). Judgments of learning at delays: Shifts in response patterns or increased metamemory accuracy? *Psychological Science, 8,* 318–321.

Webb, N. M. (1989). Peer interaction and learning in small groups. *International Journal of Educational Research, 13,* 21–39.

Webb, N. M., & Farivar, S. (1994). Promoting helping behavior in cooperative small groups in middle school mathematics. *American Educational Research Journal, 31,* 369–395.

Webb, N. M., & Farivar, S. (1999). Developing productive group interaction in middle school mathematics. In A. M. O'Donnell & A. King (Eds.), *Cognitive perspectives on peer learning* (pp. 117–149). Mahwah, NJ: Erlbaum.

Webb, N. M., & Mastergeorge, A. M. (2003). The development of students' helping behavior and learning in peer-directed small groups. *Cognition and Instruction, 21,* 361–428.

Webb, N. M., Nemer, K. M., Chizhik, A. W., & Sugrue, B. (1998). Equity issues in collaborative group assessment: Group composition and performance. *American Educational Research Journal, 35,* 607–651.

Webb, N. M., Nemer, K. M., & Zuniga, S. (2002). Short circuits or superconductors? Effects of group composition on high-achieving students' science assessment performance. *American Educational Research Journal, 39,* 943–989.

Webb, N. M., & Palincsar, A. S. (1996). Group processes in the classroom. In D. C. Berliner & R. C. Calfee (Eds.), *Handbook of educational psychology.* New York: Macmillan.

Webber, J., Scheuermann, B., McCall, C., & Coleman, M. (1993). Research on self-monitoring as a behavior management technique in special education classrooms: A descriptive review. *Remedial and Special Education, 14*(2), 38–56.

Wegman, C. (1985). *Psychoanalysis and cognitive psychology.* London: Academic Press.

Weiner, B. (1984). Principles for a theory of student motivation and their application within an attributional framework. In R. Ames & C. Ames (Eds.), *Research on motivation in education: Vol. 1. Student motivation.* Orlando, FL: Academic Press.

Weiner, B. (1986). *An attributional theory of motivation and emotion.* New York: Springer-Verlag.

Weiner, B. (1992). *Human motivation: Metaphors, theories, and research.* Newbury Park, CA: Sage.

Weiner, B. (1994). Ability versus effort revisited: The moral determinants of achievement evaluation and achievement as a moral system. *Educational Psychologist, 29,* 163–172.

Weiner, B. (1995). *Judgments of responsibility: Foundations for a theory of social conduct.* New York: Guilford Press.

Weiner, B. (2000). Intrapersonal and interpersonal theories of motivation from an attributional perspective. *Educational Psychology Review, 12,* 1–14.

Weiner, B. (2004). Attribution theory revisited: Transforming cultural plurality into theoretical unity. In D. M. McNerney & S. Van Etten (Eds.), *Big theories revisited* (pp. 13–29). Greenwich, CT: Information Age.

Weiner, B., Russell, D., & Lerman, D. (1978). Affective consequences of causal ascriptions. In J. Harvey, W. Ickes, & R. Kidd (Eds.), *New directions in attribution research* (Vol. 2). Hillsdale, NJ: Erlbaum.

Weiner, B., Russell, D., & Lerman, D. (1979). The cognition–emotion process in achievement-related contexts. *Journal of Personality and Social Psychology, 37,* 1211–1220.

Weinert, F. E., & Helmke, A. (1995). Learning from wise Mother Nature or Big Brother Instructor: The wrong choice as seen from an educational perspective. *Educational Psychologist, 30,* 135–142.

Weinraub, M., Clemens, L. P., Sockloff, A., Ethridge, T., Gracely, E., & Myers, B. (1984). The development of sex role stereotypes in the third year: Relationships to gender labeling, gender identity, sex-typed toy preference, and family characteristics. *Child Development, 55,* 1493–1503.

Weinstein, C. E. (1978). Elaboration skills as a learning strategy. In H. F. O'Neil, Jr. (Ed.), *Learning strategies.* New York: Academic Press.

Weinstein, C. E., Goetz, E. T., & Alexander, P. A. (Eds.) (1988). *Learning and study strategies: Issues in assessment, instruction, and evaluation.* San Diego, CA: Academic Press.

Weinstein, C. E., Hagen, A. S., & Meyer, D. K. (1991, April). *Work smart . . . not hard: The effects of combining instruction in using strategies, goal using, and executive control on attributions and academic performance.* Paper presented at the annual meeting of the American Educational Research Association, Chicago.

Weinstein, C. E., & Mayer, R. E. (1986). The teaching of learning strategies. In M. C. Wittrock (Ed.), *Handbook of research on teaching* (3rd ed.). New York: Macmillan.

Weinstein, R. S. (1993). Children's knowledge of differential treatment in school: Implications for motivation. In T. M. Tomlinson (Ed.), *Motivating students to learn: Overcoming barriers to high achievement.* Berkeley, CA: McCutchan.

Weinstein, R. S., Madison, S. M., & Kuklinski, M. R. (1995). Raising expectations in schooling: Obstacles and opportunities for change. *American Educational Research Journal, 32,* 121–159.

Weisberg, R. W., DiCamillo, M., & Phillips, D. (1979). Transferring old associations to new situations: A nonautomatic process. *Journal of Verbal Learning and Verbal Behavior, 17,* 219–228.

Weiss, M. R., & Klint, K. A. (1987). "Show and tell" in the gymnasium: An investigation of developmental differences in modeling and verbal rehearsal of motor skills. *Research Quarterly for Exercise and Sport, 58,* 234–241.

Weisz, J. R. (1986). Understanding the developing understanding of control. In M. Perlmutter (Ed.), *Cognitive perspectives on children's social and behavioral development. Minnesota Symposia on Child Psychology* (Vol. 18). Hillsdale, NJ: Erlbaum.

Weisz, J. R., & Cameron, A. M. (1985). Individual differences in the student's sense of control. In C. Ames & R. Ames (Eds.), *Research on motivation in education: Vol. 2. The classroom milieu.* Orlando, FL: Academic Press.

Welch, G. J. (1985). Contingency contracting with a delinquent and his family. *Journal of Behavior Therapy and Experimental Psychiatry, 16,* 253–259.

Welder, A. N., & Graham, S. A. (2001). The influence of shape similarity and shared labels on infants' inductive inferences about nonobvious object properties. *Child Development, 72,* 1653–1673.

Welford, A. T. (1977). Serial reaction-times, continuity of task, single-channel effects and age. In S. Dornic (Ed.), *Attention and performance* (Vol. 6). Hillsdale, NJ: Erlbaum.

Wellman, H. M. (1990). *The child's theory of mind.* Cambridge, MA: MIT Press.

Wellman, H. M., & Gelman, S. A. (1992). Cognitive development: Foundational theories of core domains. In M. R. Rosenzweig & L. W. Porter (Eds.), *Annual review of psychology* (Vol. 43). Palo Alto, CA: Annual Reviews.

Wellman, H. M., & Gelman, S. A. (1998). Knowledge acquisition in functional domains. In W. Damon (Series Ed.), D. Kuhn & R. S. Siegler (Vol. Eds.), *Handbook of child psychology: Vol. 2. Cognition, perception, and language* (5th ed., pp. 523–573). New York: Wiley.

Wellman, H. M., & Hickling, A. K. (1994). The mind's "I": Children's conception of the mind as an active agent. *Child Development, 65,* 1564–1580.

Wells, G. L., & Bradfield, A. L. (1999). Distortions in eyewitnesses' recollections: Can the postidentification-feedback effect be moderated? *Psychological Science, 10,* 138–144.

Wells, G. L., Olson, E. A., & Charman, S. D. (2002). The confidence of eyewitnesses in their identifications from lineups. *Current Directions in Psychological Science, 11,* 151–154.

Wenger, E. (1998). *Communities of practice: Learning, meaning, and identity.* Cambridge, England: Cambridge University Press.

Wentzel, K. R. (1989). Adolescent classroom grades, standards for performance, and academic achievement: An interactionist perspective. *Journal of Educational Psychology, 81,* 131–142.

Wentzel, K. R. (1999). Social-motivational processes and interpersonal relationships: Implications for understanding motivation at school. *Journal of Educational Psychology, 91,* 76–97.

Wentzel, K. R., & Wigfield, A. (1998). Academic and social motivational influences on students' academic performance. *Educational Psychology Review, 10,* 155–175.

Wertheimer, M. (1912). Experimentelle Studien über das Sehen von Bewegung. *Zeitschrift für Psychologie, 61,* 161–265.

Wertheimer, M. (1959). *Productive thinking* (Enl. ed., M. Wertheimer, Ed.). New York: Harper.

Wertsch, J. V. (1984). The zone of proximal development: Some conceptual issues. *Children's learning in the zone of proximal development: New directions for child development* (No. 23). San Francisco: Jossey-Bass.

West, R. F., & Stanovich, K. E. (1991). The incidental acquisition of information from reading. *Psychological Science, 2,* 325–329.

Whimbey, A., & Lochhead, J. (1986). *Problem solving and comprehension* (4th ed.). Hillsdale, NJ: Erlbaum.

White, B. Y., & Frederiksen, J. R. (1998). Inquiry, modeling, and metacognition: Making science accessible to all students. *Cognition and Instruction, 16,* 3–118.

White, B. Y., & Frederiksen, J. (2005). A theoretical framework and approach for fostering metacognitive development. *Educational Psychologist, 40,* 211–223.

White, J. J., & Rumsey, S. (1994). Teaching for understanding in a third-grade geography lesson. In J. Brophy (Ed.), *Advances in research on teaching: Vol. 4. Case studies of teaching and learning in social studies.* Greenwich, CT: JAI Press.

White, R. (1959). Motivation reconsidered: The concept of competence. *Psychological Review, 66,* 297–333.

Whitehead, A. N. (1929). *The aims of education and other essays.* New York: Macmillan.

Whiting, B. B., & Edwards, C. P. (1988). *Children of different worlds.* Cambridge, MA: Harvard University Press.

Whitley, B. E., Jr., & Frieze, I. H. (1985). Children's causal attributions for success and failure in achievement settings: A meta-analysis. *Journal of Educational Psychology, 77,* 608–616.

Whitlock, C. (1966). Note on reading acquisition: An extension of laboratory principles. *Journal of Experimental Child Psychology, 3,* 83–85.

Whitten, S., & Graesser, A. C. (2003). Comprehension of text in problem solving. In

J. E. Davidson & R. J. Sternberg (Eds.), *The psychology of problem solving* (pp. 207–229). Cambridge, England: Cambridge University Press.

Wickelgren, W. A. (1973). The long and the short of memory. *Psychological Bulletin, 80,* 425–438.

Wickelgren, W. A. (1974). *How to solve problems: Elements of a theory of problems and problem solving.* San Francisco: W. H. Freeman.

Wicker, B., Keysers, C., Plailly, J., Royet, J.-P., Gallese, V., & Rizzolatti, G. (2003). Both of us disgusted in my insula: The common neural basis of seeing and feeling disgust. *Neuron, 40,* 655–664.

Wielkiewicz, R. M. (1986). *Behavior management in the schools: Principles and procedures.* New York: Pergamon Press.

Wigfield, A. (1994). Expectancy-value theory of achievement motivation: A developmental perspective. *Educational Psychology Review, 6,* 49–78.

Wigfield, A., & Eccles, J. (1992). The development of achievement task values: A theoretical analysis. *Developmental Review, 12,* 265–310.

Wigfield, A., & Eccles, J. (2000). Expectancy-value theory of achievement motivation. *Contemporary Educational Psychology, 25,* 68–81.

Wigfield, A., & Eccles, J. (2002). The development of competence beliefs, expectancies for success, and achievement values from childhood to adolescence. In A. Wigfield & J. Eccles (Eds.), *Development of achievement motivation* (pp. 91–120). San Diego, CA: Academic Press.

Wigfield, A., Eccles, J. S., Mac Iver, D., Reuman, D., & Midgley, C. (1991). Transitions at early adolescence: Changes in children's domain-specific self-perceptions and general self-esteem across the transition to junior high school. *Developmental Psychology, 27,* 552–565.

Wigfield, A., Eccles, J. S., & Pintrich, P. R. (1996). Development between the ages of 11 and 25. In D. C. Berliner & R. C. Calfee (Eds.), *Handbook of educational psychology.* New York: Macmillan.

Wigfield, A., Eccles, J. S., & Pintrich, P. R. (1996). Development between the ages of 11 and 25. In D. C. Berliner & R. C. Calfee (Eds.), *Handbook of educational psychology.* New York: Macmillan.

Wigfield, A., & Meece, J. L. (1988). Math anxiety in elementary and secondary school students. *Journal of Educational Psychology, 80,* 210–216.

Wigfield, A., Tonks, S., & Eccles, J. S. (2004). Expectancy value theory in cross-cultural perspective. In D. M. McNerney & S. Van Etten (Eds.), *Big theories revisited* (pp. 165–198). Greenwich, CT: Information Age.

Wiggins, J. S. (1996). *The Five-Factor Model of personality: Theoretical dimensions.* New York: Guilford.

Wiley, J., & Bailey, J. (2006). Effects of collaboration and argumentation on learning from Web pages. In A. M. O'Donnell, C. E. Hmelo-Silver, & G. Erkens (Eds.), *Collaborative learning, reasoning, and technology* (pp. 297–321). Mahwah, NJ: Erlbaum.

Wiley, J., & Voss, J. F. (1999). Constructing arguments from multiple sources: Tasks that promote understanding and not just memory for text. *Journal of Educational Psychology, 91,* 301–311.

Wilkins, A. T. (1971). Conjoint frequency, category size, and categorization time. *Journal of Verbal Learning and Verbal Behavior, 10,* 382–385.

Willatts, P. (1990). Development of problem solving strategies in infancy. In D. F. Bjorklund (Ed.), *Children's strategies.* Hillsdale, NJ: Erlbaum.

Williams, S. B. (1938). Resistance to extinction as a function of the number of reinforcements. *Journal of Experimental Psychology, 23,* 506–522.

Williams, D. (1996). *Autism: An inside-out approach.* London: Jessica Kingsley Publishers.

Willingham, D. B. (1998). A neuropsychological theory of motor skill learning. *Psychological Review, 105,* 558–584.

Willingham, D. B. (1999). The neural basis of motor-skill learning. *Current Directions in Psychological Science, 8,* 178–182.

Willingham, D. T. (2004). *Cognition: The thinking animal* (2nd ed.). Upper Saddle River, NJ: Prentice Hall.

Willingham, D. B., & Goedert-Eschmann, K. (1999). The relation between implicit and explicit learning: Evidence for parallel development. *Psychological Science, 10,* 531–534.

Wilson, B. L., & Corbett, H. D. (2001). *Listening to urban kids: School reform and the teachers they want.* Albany: State University of New York Press.

Wilson, J. E. (1988). Implications of learning strategy research and training: What it has to say to the practitioner. In Weinstein, C. E., Goetz, E. T., & Alexander, P. A. (Eds.), *Learning and study strategies: Issues in assessment, instruction, and evaluation.* San Diego, CA: Academic Press.

Wilson, P. S. (1988, April). The relationship of students' definitions and example choices in geometry. In D. Tirosh (Chair), *The role of inconsistent ideas in learning mathematics.* Symposium conducted at the annual meeting of the American Educational Research Association, New Orleans, LA.

Wilson, P. T., & Anderson, R. C. (1986). What they don't know will hurt them: The role of prior knowledge in comprehension. In J. Orasanu (Ed.), *Reading comprehension: From research to practice.* Hillsdale, NJ: Erlbaum.

Windschitl, M. (2002). Framing constructivism in practice as the negotiation of dilemmas: An analysis of the conceptual, pedagogical, cultural, and political challenges facing teachers. *Review of Educational Research, 72,* 131–175.

Wine, J. D. (1980). Cognitive-attentional theory of test anxiety. In I. G. Sarason (Ed.), *Test anxiety: Theory, research, and applications.* Hillsdale, NJ: Erlbaum.

Winer, G. A., & Cottrell, J. E. (1996). Does anything leave the eye when we see? Extramission beliefs of children and adults. *Current Directions in Psychological Science, 5,* 137–142.

Winer, G. A., Cottrell, J. E., Gregg, V., Fournier, J. S., & Bica, L. A. (2002). Fundamentally misunderstanding visual perception: Adults' belief in visual emissions. *American Psychologist, 57,* 417–424.

Wingfield, A., & Byrnes, D. L. (1981). *The psychology of human memory.* New York: Academic Press.

Winik, M. (1994). *Telling.* New York: Random House.

Winkielman, P., & Berridge, K. C. (2004). Unconscious emotion. *Current Directions in Psychological Science, 13,* 120–123.

Winn, W. (1991). Learning from maps and diagrams. *Educational Psychology Review, 3,* 211–247.

Winn, W. (2002). Current trends in educational technology research: The study of learning environments. *Educational Psychology Review, 14,* 331–351.

Winne, P. H. (1995a). Inherent details in self-regulated learning. *Educational Psychologist, 30,* 173–187.

Winne, P. H. (1995b). Self-regulation is ubiquitous but its forms vary with knowledge. *Educational Psychologist, 30,* 223–228.

Winne, P. H., & Hadwin, A. F. (1998). Studying as self-regulated learning. In D. J. Hacker, J. Dunlosky, & A. C. Graesser (Eds.), *Metacognition in educational theory and practice* (pp. 277–304). Mahwah, NJ: Erlbaum.

Winne, P. H., & Jamieson-Noel, D. (2001, April). *How self perceptions of prior knowledge and self-regulated learning interact to affect learning.* Paper presented at the annual meeting of the American Educational Research Association, Seattle, WA.

Winne, P. H., & Marx, R. W. (1989). A cognitive-processing analysis of motivation within classroom tasks. In C. Ames & R. Ames (Eds.), *Research on motivation in education: Vol. 3. Goals and cognitions.* San Diego, CA: Academic Press.

Winne, P. H., & Stockley, D. B. (1998). Computing technologies as sites for developing self-regulated learning. In D. H. Schunk & B. J. Zimmerman (Eds.), *Self-regulated learning: From teaching to self-reflective practice* (pp. 106–136). New York: Guilford Press.

Winograd, E., & Neisser, U. (1992). *Affect and accuracy in recall: Studies of "flashbulb" memories.* Cambridge, England: Cambridge University Press.

Winsler, A., & Naglieri, J. (2003). Overt and covert verbal problem-solving strategies: Developmental trends in use, awareness, and relations with task performance in children aged 5 to 17. *Child Development, 74,* 659–678.

Winston, P. (1973). Learning to identify toy block structures. In R. L. Solso (Ed.), *Contemporary issues in cognitive psychology: The Loyola Symposium.* Washington, DC: V. H. Winston.

Wittenbaum, G. M., & Park, E. S. (2001). The collective preference for shared information. *Current Directions in Psychological Science, 10,* 70–73.

Wittgenstein, L. (1958). *Philosophical investigations* (2nd ed.). Oxford, England: Blackwell.

Wittrock, M. C., & Alesandrini, K. (1990). Generation of summaries and analogies and analytic and holistic abilities. *American Educational Research Journal, 27,* 489–502.

Wixson, K. K. (1984). Level of importance of post-questions and children's learning from text. *American Educational Research Journal, 21,* 419–433.

Wixted, J. T. (2005). A theory about why we forget what we once knew. *Current Directions in Psychological Science, 14,* 6–9.

Wixted, J. T., & Ebbesen, E. B. (1991). On the form of forgetting. *Psychological Science, 2,* 409–415.

Wlodkowski, R. J. (1978). *Motivation and teaching: A practical guide.* Washington, DC: National Education Association.

Wlodkowski, R. J., & Ginsberg, M. B. (1995). *Diversity and motivation: Culturally responsive teaching.* San Francisco: Jossey-Bass.

Wolf, R. M. (1998). National standards: Do we need them? *Educational Researcher, 27*(4), 22–24.

Wolfe, J. B. (1936). Effectiveness of token-rewards for chimps. *Comparative Psychology Monographs, 12*(60).

Woloshyn, V. E., Pressley, M., & Schneider, W. (1992). Elaborative-interrogation and prior-knowledge effects on learning of facts. *Journal of Educational Psychology, 84,* 115–124.

Wolpe, J. (1958). *Psychotherapy by reciprocal inhibition.* Stanford CA: Stanford University Press.

Wolpe, J. (1969). *The practice of behavior therapy.* Oxford, England: Pergamon.

Wolpe, J., & Plaud, J. J. (1997). Pavlov's contributions to behavior therapy: The obvious and the not so obvious. *American Psychologist, 52,* 966–972.

Wolters, C. A. (1998). Self-regulated learning and college students' regulation of motivation. *Journal of Educational Psychology, 90,* 224–235.

Wolters, C. A. (2000). The relation between high school students' motivational regulation and their use of learning strategies, effort, and classroom performance. *Learning and Individual Differences, 3,* 281–299.

Wolters, C. A. (2003a). Regulation of motivation: Evaluating an underemphasized aspect of self-regulated learning. *Educational Psychologist, 38,* 189–205.

Wolters, C. A. (2003b). Understanding procrastination from a self-regulated learning perspective. *Journal of Educational Psychology, 95,* 179–187.

Wolters, C. A. (2004). Advancing achievement goal theory: Using goal structures and goal orientations to predict students' motivation, cognition, and achievement. *Journal of Educational Psychology, 96,* 236–250.

Wolters, C. A., & Rosenthal, H. (2000). The relation between students' motivational beliefs and their use of motivational regulation strategies. *International Journal of Educational Research, 33,* 801–820.

Woltz, D. J. (2003). Implicit cognitive processes as aptitudes for learning. *Educational Psychologist, 38,* 95–104.

Wong, B. Y. L. (1985). Self-questioning instructional research: A review. *Review of Educational Research, 55,* 227–268.

Wood, D., Bruner, J. S., & Ross, G. (1976). The role of tutoring in problem-solving. *Journal of Child Psychology and Psychiatry, 17,* 89–100.

Wood, D., Wood, H., Ainsworth, S., & O'Malley, C. (1995). On becoming a tutor: Toward an ontogenetic model. *Cognition and Instruction, 13,* 565–581.

Wood, E., Motz, M., & Willoughby, T. (1997, April). *Examining students' retrospective memories of strategy development.* Paper presented at the annual meeting of the American Educational Research Association, Chicago.

Wood, P., & Kardash, C. A. M. (2002). Critical elements in the design and analysis of studies of epistemology. In B. K. Hofer & P. R. Pintrich (Eds.), *Personal epistemology: The psychology of beliefs about knowledge and knowing* (pp. 231–260). Mahwah, NJ: Erlbaum.

Woodman, G. F., & Vogel, E. K. (2005). Fractionating working memory: Consolidation and maintenance are independent processes. *Psychological Science, 16,* 106–113.

Woodman, G. F., Vogel, E. K., & Luck, S. J. (2001). Visual search remains efficient when visual working memory is full. *Psychological Science, 12,* 219–224.

Woods, D. W., & Miltenberger, R. G. (1995). Habit reversal: A review of applications and variations. *Journal of Behavior Therapy and Experimental Psychiatry, 26,* 123–131.

Woodworth, R. S. (1918). *Dynamic psychology.* New York: Columbia University Press.

Woolfolk, A. E., & Brooks, D. M. (1985). The influence of teachers' nonverbal behaviors on students' perceptions and performances. *Elementary School Journal, 85,* 513–528.

Wright, R. (1994). *The moral animal: The new science of evolutionary psychology.* New York: Pantheon Books.

Wulbert, M., & Dries, R. (1977). The relative efficacy of methylphenidate (Ritalin) and behavior-modification techniques in the treatment of a hyperactive child. *Journal of Applied Behavior Analysis, 10,* 21–31.

Wynn, K., & Chiang, W. (1998). Limits to infants' knowledge of objects: The case of magical appearance. *Psychological Science, 9,* 448–455.

Yager, S., Johnson, D. W., & Johnson, R. T. (1985). Oral discussion, group to individual transfer, and achievement in cooperative learning groups. *Journal of Educational Psychology, 77,* 60–66.

Yarmey, A. D. (1973). I recognize your face but I can't remember your name: Further evidence on the tip-of-the-tongue phenomenon. *Memory and Cognition, 1,* 287–290.

Yee, D. K., & Eccles, J. S. (1988). Parent perceptions and attributions for children's math achievement. *Sex Roles, 19,* 317–333.

Yell, M. L., Robinson, T. R., & Drasgow, E. (2001). Cognitive behavior modification. In T. J. Zirpoli & K. J. Melloy, *Behavior management: Applications for teachers* (3rd ed., pp. 200–246). Upper Saddle River, NJ: Merrill/ Prentice Hall.

Yerkes, R. M., & Dodson, J. D. (1908). The relation of strength of stimulus to rapidity of habit-formation. *Journal of Comparative Neurology and Psychology, 18,* 459–482.

Yokoi, L. (1997, March). *The developmental context of notetaking: A qualitative examination of notetaking at the secondary level.* Paper presented at the annual meeting of the American Educational Research Association, Chicago.

Younger, B. A. (2003). Parsing objects into categories: Infants' perception and use of correlated attributes. In D. H. Rakison & L. M. Oakes (Eds.), *Early category and concept development: Making sense of the blooming, buzzing confusion* (pp. 77–102). Oxford, England: Oxford University Press.

Zacks, R. T., Hasher, L., & Hock, H. S. (1986). Inevitability and automaticity: A response to Fisk. *American Psychologist, 41,* 216–218.

Zahorik, J. A. (1994, April). *Making things interesting.* Paper presented at the annual meeting of the American Educational Research Association, New Orleans, LA.

Zajonc, R. B. (1980). Feeling and thinking: Preferences need no inferences. *American Psychologist, 35,* 151–175.

Zajonc, R. B. (2000). Feeling and thinking: Closing the debate on the primacy of affect. In J. P. Forgas (Ed.), *Feeling and thinking: The role of affect in social cognition* (pp. 31–58). New York: Cambridge University Press.

Zajonc, R. B. (2001). Mere exposure: A gateway to the subliminal. *Current Directions in Psychological Science, 10,* 224–228.

Zaragoza, M. S., & Mitchell, K. J. (1996). Repeated exposure to suggestion and the creation of false memories. *Psychological Science, 7,* 294–300.

Zaragoza, M. S., Payment, K. E., Ackil, J. K., Drivdahl, S. B., & Beck, M. (2001). Interviewing witnesses: Forced confabulation and confirmatory feedback increase false memories. *Psychological Science, 12,* 473–477.

Zazdeh, L. A., Fu, K. S., Tanak, K., & Shimura, M. (Eds.) (1975). *Fuzzy sets and their applications to cognitive and decision processes.* New York: Academic Press.

Zechmeister, E. B., & Nyberg, S. E. (1982). *Human memory: An introduction to research and theory.* Monterey, CA: Brooks-Cole.

Zeidner, M. (1998). *Test anxiety: The state of the art.* New York: Plenum Press.

Zeitz, C. M. (1994). Expert-novice differences in memory, abstraction, and reasoning in the domain of literature. *Cognition and Instruction, 12,* 277–312.

Zelazo, P. D., Müller, U., Frye, D., & Marcovitch, S. (2003). The development of executive function in early childhood. *Monographs of the Society for Research in Child Development, 68*(3), Serial No. 274.

Zentall, T. R. (2003). Imitation by animals: How do they do it? *Current Directions in Psychological Science, 12,* 91–95.

Zhu, X., & Simon, H. A. (1987). Learning mathematics from examples and by doing. *Cognition and Instruction, 4,* 137–166.

Ziegert, D. I., Kistner, J. A., Castro, R., & Robertson, B. (2001). Longitudinal study of young children's responses to challenging achievement situations. *Child Development, 72,* 609–624.

Ziegler, S. G. (1987). Effects of stimulus cueing on the acquisition of groundstrokes by beginning tennis players. *Journal of Applied Behavior Analysis, 20,* 405–411.

Zigler, E., & Hodapp, R. M. (1986). *Understanding mental retardation.* Cambridge, England: Cambridge University Press.

Zigler, E. F., & Finn-Stevenson, M. (1987). *Children: Development and social issues.* Lexington, MA: Heath.

Zimmerman, B. J. (1981). Social learning theory and cognitive constructivism. In I. E. Sigel, D. M. Brodzinsky, & R. M. Golinkoff (Eds.), *New directions in Piagetian theory and practice.* Hillsdale, NJ: Erlbaum.

Zimmerman, B. J. (1989). Models of self-regulated learning and academic achievement. In B. J. Zimmerman & D. H. Schunk (Eds.), *Self-regulated learning and academic achievement: Theory, research, and practice.* New York: Springer-Verlag.

Zimmerman, B. J. (1994, April). *From modeling to self-efficacy: A social cognitive view of students' development of motivation to self-regulate.* Paper presented at the annual meeting of the American Educational Research Association, New Orleans, LA.

Zimmerman, B. J. (1998). Developing self-fulfilling cycles of academic regulation: An analysis of exemplary instructional models. In D. H. Schunk & B. J. Zimmerman (Eds.), *Self-regulated learning: From teaching to self-reflective practice* (pp. 1–19). New York: Guilford Press.

Zimmerman, B. J. (2004). Sociocultural influence and students' development of academic self-regulation: A social-cognitive perspective. In D. M. McNerney & S. Van Etten (Eds.), *Big theories revisited* (pp. 139–164). Greenwich, CT: Information Age.

Zimmerman, B. J., & Bandura, A. (1994). Impact of self-regulatory influences on writing course attainment. *American Educational Research Journal, 31,* 845–862.

Zimmerman, B. J., Bandura, A., & Martinez-Pons, M. (1992). Self-motivation for academic attainment: The role of self-efficacy beliefs and personal goal setting. *American Educational Research Journal, 29,* 663–676.

Zimmerman, B. J., & Campillo, M. (2003). Motivating self-regulated problem solvers. In J. E. Davidson & R. J. Sternberg (Eds.), *The psychology of problem solving* (pp. 233–262). Cambridge, England: Cambridge University Press.

Zimmerman, B. J., & Kitsantas, A. (1997). Developmental phases in self-regulation: Shifting from process to outcome goals. *Journal of Educational Psychology, 89,* 29–36.

Zimmerman, B. J., & Kitsantas, A. (1999). Acquiring writing revision skill: Shifting from process to outcome self-regulatory goals. *Journal of Educational Psychology, 91,* 241–250.

Zimmerman, B. J., & Kitsantas, A. (2002). Acquiring writing revision and self-regulatory skill through observation and emulation. *Journal of Educational Psychology, 94,* 660–668.

Zimmerman, B. J., & Risemberg, R. (1997). Self-regulatory dimensions of academic learning and motivation. In G. D. Phye (Ed.), *Handbook of academic learning:*

Construction of knowledge. San Diego, CA: Academic Press.

Zimmerman, B. J., & Schunk, D. H. (2003). Albert Bandura: The scholar and his contributions to educational psychology. In B. J. Zimmerman & D. H. Schunk (Eds.), *Educational psychology: A century of contributions* (pp. 431–457). Mahwah, NJ: Erlbaum.

Zimmerman, B. J., & Schunk, D. H. (2004). Self-regulating intellectual processes and outcomes; A social cognitive perspective. In D. Y. Dai & R. J. Sternberg (Eds.), *Motivation, emotion, and cognition: Integrative perspectives on intellectual functioning and development* (pp. 323–349). Mahwah, NJ: Erlbaum.

Zirin, G. (1974). How to make a boring thing more boring. *Child Development, 45,* 232–236.

Zirpoli, T. J., & Melloy, K. J. (2001). *Behavior management: Applications for teachers.* Upper Saddle River, NJ: Merrill/Prentice Hall.

Zola-Morgan, S. M., & Squire, L. R. (1990). The primate hippocampal formation: Evidence for a time-limited role in memory storage. *Science, 250,* 288–290.

Zook, K. B. (1991). Effects of analogical processes on learning and misrepresentation. *Educational Psychology Review, 3,* 41–72.

Zook, K. B., & Di Vesta, F. J. (1991). Instructional analogies and conceptual misrepresentations. *Journal of Educational Psychology, 83,* 246–252.

Zuckerman, G. (1994). A pilot study of a 10-day course in cooperative learning for beginning Russian first graders. *Elementary School Journal, 94,* 405–420.

Zuriff, G. E. (1985). *Behaviorism: A conceptual reconstruction.* New York: Columbia University Press.

Author Index

Subject Index